Advertising

Principles & Practice

Advertising
Principles & Practice

Eighth Edition

Sandra Moriarty
University of Colorado

Nancy Mitchell
University of Nebraska-Lincoln

William Wells
University of Minnesota

Upper Saddle River, New Jersey 07458

Library of Congress Cataloging-in-Publication Data
Moriarty, Sandra E. (Sandra Ernst)
    Advertising : principles and practice / Sandra Moriarty, Nancy Mitchell, William Wells.
—8th ed.
        p. cm.
    Previous editions had William Wells as first author.
    Includes bibliographical references and index.
    ISBN 978-0-13-222415-4
1. Advertising. I Wells, William, II. Mitchell, Nancy, III. Wells.
William, Advertising IV. Title.
    HF5823 .W455 2009
    659.1—dc21   2007036863

AVP/Editor-in-Chief: David Parker
VP/Director of Development: Steve Deitmer
Development Editor: Trish Nealon
AVP/Executive Editor: Melissa Sabella
Project Manager: Melissa Pellerano
Product Development, Editorial: Ashley Santora
Assistant Editor, Media: Denise Vaughn
Marketing Manager: Anne Fahlgren
Marketing Assistant: Susan Osterlitz
Senior Managing Editor: Judy Leale
Associate Managing Editor: Suzanne DeWorken
Permission Project Manager: Charles Morris
Senior Operations Specialist: Arnold Vila
Art Director: Steve Frim
Interior Design: Yellow Dog Designs
Cover Design: Steve Frim
Director Image Resources Center: Melinda Petalli
Manager, Right and Permissions: Zina Arabia
Manager, Visual Research: Beth Brenzel
Manager, Cover Visual Research & Permissions: Karen Sanatar
Photo Researcher: Keri Jean Miksza
Composition: S4Carlisle
Full-Service Project Management: S4Carlisle
Printer/Binder: Quebecor World Dubuque
Typeface: Times

Credits and acknowledgments borrowed from other sources and reproduced, with permission, in this textbook appear on appropriate page within text (or on page 611)

Microsoft® and Windows® are registered trademarks of the Microsoft Corporation in the U.S.A and other countries. Screen shots and icons reprinted with permission from the Microsoft Corporation. This book is not sponsored or endorsed by or affiliated with the Microsoft Corporation.

Pearson Education LTD.   Pearson Education Australia PTY, Limited
Pearson Education Singapore, Pte. Ltd   Pearson Education North Asia Ltd
Pearson Education, Canada, Ltd   Pearson Educación de Mexico, S.A. de C.V.

10 9 8 7 6 5 4 3
ISBN-13: 978-0-13-222415-4
ISBN-10: 0-13-222415-1

This eighth edition of *Advertising: Principles & Practices*

is dedicated . . . to the memory of my mother, Rachel,

whose life journey is my inspiration

Sandra Moriarty

and

in gratitude to my parents who gave me

The Little Engine That Could when I was little.

Nancy Mitchell

BRIEF CONTENTS

PART 1 A PASSION FOR THE BUSINESS

    1 Introduction to Advertising   4

    2 Advertising's Role in Marketing   32

    3 Advertising and Society   64

PART 2 PRINCIPLE: STRATEGY IS CREATIVE, TOO

    4 How Advertising Works   100

    5 The Consumer Audience   128

    6 Strategic Research   162

    7 Strategic Planning   190

PART 3 PRACTICE: WHERE ARE MEDIA HEADING?

    8 Media Basics and Print Media   224

    9 Broadcast Media   254

    10 Internet and Nontraditional Media   284

    11 Media Planning and Buying   312

PART 4 PRINCIPLES: CREATIVITY AND BREAKTHROUGH ADVERTISING

    12 The Creative Side and Message Strategy   350

    13 Copywriting   386

    14 Design and Production   416

PART 5 PRINCIPLES: HOW TO WIN THE BATTLE OF THE BUZZ

    15 Direct-Response Marketing   450

    16 Sales Promotion, Events, and Sponsorships   480

    17 Public Relations   504

    18 Special Advertising Campaigns   532

    19 Evaluation of Effectiveness   560

    Appendix   587

    Glossary   593

    Credits   611

    Notes   615

    Index   625

CONTENTS

Preface xxv

PART 1 A PASSION FOR THE BUSINESS

1. INTRODUCTION TO ADVERTISING   4

IT'S A WINNER: The Truth of the Matter   4

What Is Advertising?   7
Evolution of the Definition of Advertising 7 | Defining the Modern Practice
of Advertising 8 | The Components of Modern Advertising 9 |

Roles and Types of Advertising   11
The Marketing Role 11 | The Communication Role 11 | The Economic
Role 12 | The Societal Role 12 | Types of Advertising 13 |

The Key Players   14
The Advertiser 14 |

A MATTER OF PRACTICE: The Greatest Commercial Ever Made   15

THE INSIDE STORY: Why Do I Love Advertising?   17
The Advertising Agency 17 | The Media 18 | The Suppliers 19 |
Target Audiences 19 |

The Development of Advertising   20
An Advertising Timeline 20 |

A MATTER OF PRINCIPLE: The Sales Approach and Lasker's Reason-Why   23

Current Developments   23
The New Advertising 23 |

PRACTICAL TIPS: Why You Probably Don't Want to Read This   24
Interactivity 24 | Integrated Marketing Communication 25 | Globalization 25 |
What Makes an Ad Effective? 26 | Effectiveness and Award Shows 26 |

IT'S A WRAP: The Truth about the *truth*® Campaign   27

Key Points Summary   27
Key Terms   28
Review Questions   28
Discussion Questions   29
Take-Home Team Projects   29
Yahoo! Hands-On Case   29
Hands-On Case: Dueling Computers   30

2. ADVERTISING'S ROLE IN MARKETING   32

IT'S A WINNER: Puma's Evolution of the Species   32

What Is Marketing?   34
Key Concepts in Marketing 35 |

A MATTER OF PRINCIPLE: It's Pure and It Floats   40

Types of Markets 41 | The Marketing Plan 43 | The Marketing Mix 44 |

A MATTER OF PRACTICE: Creating Concepts   48

The Key Players   48
The Marketer 49 | Suppliers and Vendors 49 | Distributors and Retailers 49 |
Marketing Partners 50 |

How Agencies Work with Their Clients   50
Types of Agencies 53 | How Agency Jobs Are Organized 54 |

THE INSIDE STORY: The Day-to-Day Job of an Account Executive   55
How Agencies Are Paid by Clients 55 |

Current Developments in Marketing   56
Accountability 56 | Integrated (or Holistic) Marketing 57 | Emerging Marketing
Strategies 57 | Global Marketing 58 |

IT'S A WRAP: Puma Leaps Forward   59

Key Points Summary   59

Key Terms   60

Review Questions   61

Discussion Questions   61

Take-Home Team Projects   62

Yahoo! Hands-On Case   62

Hands-On Case: WPP's Owner—a British Knight with Strategic Moves   63

3. ADVERTISING AND SOCIETY   64

IT'S A WINNER: Whirlpool + Habitat for Humanity = Good Business   64

What Is Advertising's Role in Society?   66
Demand Creation Debate 66 | Shape-versus-Mirror Debate 67 |
The Overcommercialization Debate 69 | Other Social Responsibility
Issues 69 |

A MATTER OF PRACTICE: Pizza, Tacos, and Truck Parts: Misuse
and Misdirection of Sex in Advertising   70

A MATTER OF PRINCIPLE: Preston on Puffery   75

Why and How Is Advertising Regulated?   79
Advertising's Legal Environment 79 | Advertising's Regulatory
Environment 83 | Media Review of Advertising 88 | Self-Regulation 88 |

What Guides Ethical Behavior?   91
Personal Ethics 91 |

PRACTICAL TIPS: Brilliant or Offensive Advertising?   92
Professional Ethics 93 | International Standards and Codes 93 |

PRACTICAL TIPS: An Ethics Checklist for Advertisers   94

IT'S A WRAP: Whirlpool Profits by Helping Turn Houses into Homes   94

Key Points Summary   95

Key Terms   95

Review Questions   95

Discussion Questions   96

Take-Home Team Projects   96

Yahoo! Hands-On Case   96
Hands-On Case: Axe Gets Dirty Boys Clean   97

PART 2 PRINCIPLE: STRATEGY IS CREATIVE, TOO

4. HOW ADVERTISING WORKS   100
IT'S A WINNER: Chick-Fil-A Builds Brand with Renegade Cows   100

How Does Advertising Work?   102

How Advertising Works as Communication   103
The Communication Model 103 | Advertising as Communication 104 |
Adding Interaction to Marketing Communication 105 |

The Effects Behind Advertising Effectiveness   106
Traditional Approaches 106 | Sorting Out the Effects 107 |

New Approach: The Facets Model of Effects   108
PRACTICAL TIPS: Marketing Communication Effects   109
See/Hear: The Perception Facet 110 | Feel: The Affective or Emotional
Facet 111 |

A MATTER OF PRINCIPLE: Ice Cubes, Female Breasts, and
Subliminal Advertising   112
Factors Driving the Affective Response 113 | Understand: The Cognitive
Facet 113 |

A MATTER OF PRACTICE: Does Negative Political Advertising Help
or Hinder Citizens?   114
Connect: The Association Facet 116 | Believe: The Persuasion Facet 117 |
Act: The Behavior Facet 119 |

THE INSIDE STORY: The Curiosity-Arousing Function of Antidrug Ads   121

The Power of Brand Communication   122
Interaction and Impact 122 | Strong and Weak Effects 123 |

IT'S A WRAP: Cows Grab Business for Chickens   124

Key Points Summary   124
Key Terms   125
Review Questions   125
Discussion Questions   126
Take-Home Team Projects   126
Yahoo! Hands-On Case   126
Hands-On Case: If It Walks Like the Aflac Duck . . .   127

5. THE CONSUMER AUDIENCE   128
IT'S A WINNER: Dove Redefines Beauty   129

How Does Consumer Behavior Work?   131

Influences on Consumer Decisions   131
Cultural Influences 132 | Social Influences 134 |

A MATTER OF PRINCIPLE: Gay Buying Power   140
Psychological Influences 140 | Behavioral Influences on Consumer
Decisions 146 |

THE INSIDE STORY: The Grand Myth of Early Adoption   147
Trends in Consumer Buying Behavior 148 |

The Consumer Decision Process   149
The Information Approach to Brand Decisions 149 | The Paths to Brand
Decisions 150 | Influences on B2B Decision Making 151 |

Segmenting and Targeting   151
To Segment or Not to Segment? 152 |

A MATTER OF PRACTICE: Using DDB Life Style Data to Segment an Audience 154
Targeting the Right Audience 155 |

What Is Behavioral Targeting?   156
THE INSIDE STORY: Behavioral Targeting: An Emerging Form of Online
Ad Targeting   156
IT'S A WRAP: Love Your Body   157
Key Points Summary   158
Key Terms   158
Review Questions   159
Discussion Questions   159
Take-Home Team Projects   160
Yahoo! Hands-On Case   160
Hands-On Case: Toyota Goes After Tuners   161

6. STRATEGIC RESEARCH   162
IT'S A WINNER: You Do Your Best Thinking in the Shower   162

The Quest for Intelligence and Insight   165
Types of Research 165 |
PRACTICAL TIPS: Web Sites for Advertising Research   167
A MATTER OF PRINCIPLE: Using Research to See If Advertising Makes
Smoking Cool   171
The Uses of Research 171 |

Research Methods Used in Advertising   174
Background Research 174 | Consumer Research 175 | Ways of Contact 175 |
THE INSIDE STORY: The Power of Design Personas   176
A MATTER OF PRACTICE: Online Survey Research   178
Choosing a Research Method 183 |

Research Trends and Challenges   183
Globalization 183 | Media Changes 183 | Embedded Research 184 | Insightful
Analysis 184 |
IT'S A WRAP: Singing in the Shower   185
Key Points Summary   185
Key Terms   186
Review Questions   186
Discussion Questions   186
Take-Home Team Projects   187
Yahoo! Hands-On Case   187
Hands-On Case: What Lies Beneath? Making a Choice   188

7. STRATEGIC PLANNING   190
IT'S A WINNER: Repositioning Kodak for the Digital Age   192

Strategic Planning   192
The Business Plan 193 | The Marketing Plan 195 | The Advertising
or IMC Plan 196 |

A Campaign Plan   197
Situation Analysis 198 | Objectives 199 |

THE INSIDE STORY: A 2-Week Challenge by Special K   200
Targeting 202 | Positioning 202 |

A MATTER OF PRINCIPLE: What Is Diversity and Why Is It Important in
Advertising?   203
Brand Communication Strategy 206 |

A MATTER OF PRACTICE: 7-Up: The Uncola Story   207
Campaign Strategic Approach 208 | Campaign Implementation and
Management 209 |

Account Planning: What Is It?   210
The Research Foundation 212 | Consumer Insight: The Fuel of Big
Ideas 212 | Insight Mining 212 |

PRACTICAL TIPS: How Insights Teams Become Game Changers   213
The Communication Brief 214 |

Planning for IMC   215
Differences in IMC Strategic Planning 215 | Synergy 216 |

IT'S A WRAP: Picture a Winner   217
Key Points Summary   217
Key Terms   218
Review Questions   218
Discussion Questions   218
Take-Home Team Projects   219
Yahoo! Hands-On Case   219
Hands-On Case: Chasing the NASCAR Fan   220

PART 3 PRACTICE: WHERE ARE MEDIA HEADING?

8. MEDIA BASICS AND PRINT MEDIA   224
IT'S A WINNER: Staying Cool with Apple's iPod   224

Media Basics   227
The Changing Media Landscape 227 |

A MATTER OF PRACTICE: The Media Explosion   229
Key Media Players 230 | Key Media Concepts 231 | Media Industry
Trends 232 |

Print Media Characteristics   233

Newspaper Basics   233
Newspaper Ad Sales 235 | Types of Newspaper Advertising 235 | Newspaper
Readership Measurement 236 | Newspaper Industry Trends 237 |

Magazine Basics   237
Types of Magazines 238 | Magazine Advertising 240 | Magazine Readership
Measurement 240 | Magazine Advertising Trends 241 |

Directory Advertising   241

Out-of-Home Advertising   242
Outdoor Advertising 243 |

PRACTICAL TIPS: Outdoor: An Effective Brand Communication Medium   245
On-Premise Signs 246 | Posters 246 | Transit Advertising 248 |

Packaging   248

Using Print and Out-of-Home Advertising   249
   IT'S A WRAP: iPod Dances to a Different Tune   250
Key Points Summary   250
Key Terms   251
Review Questions   251
Discussion Questions   251
Take-Home Team Projects   252
Yahoo! Hands-On Case   252
Hands-On Case: Next Month's Magazine Issue: Credibility   253

9. BROADCAST MEDIA   254
   IT'S A WINNER: Road Warriors Get Smart at Holiday Inn Express   254

Broadcast Media   256

Radio   257
   The Structure of the Radio Industry 257 | The Radio Audience 259 | Radio
   Advertising 260 |

Television   263
   Structure of the Television Industry 263 | Programming and Distribution
   Options 266 | The Television Audience 268 |
   A MATTER OF PRINCIPLE: Trashy Shows Trash Advertisers' Brands   269
   Television Advertising 270 |
   THE INSIDE STORY Selling a Political Party with Humor   274
   Changes and Trends in Broadcast Television 276 |

Other Broadcast Forms   276
   Film and Video 276 |
   A MATTER OF PRACTICE: The Social Harm of Public Service Advertising   278
   Product Placement 278 |

Using Broadcast Advertising Effectively   279
   PRACTICAL TIPS: Broadcast Media Advantages and Limitations   279
   IT'S A WRAP: Holiday Inn Express Stays Smart   280
Key Points Summary   281
Key Terms   281
Review Questions   282
Discussion Questions   282
Take-Home Team Projects   282
Yahoo! Hands-On Case   283
Hands-On Case: Get Sirius with Howard Stern   283

10. INTERNET AND NONTRADITIONAL MEDIA   284
   IT'S A WINNER: eBay® Revolutionizes the Marketplace   284

Interactive Media: Web 2.0 And You   286
   Internet Basics 287 | Internet Tools and Formats 287 | The Internet
   Audience 289 |

The Web as an Advertising Medium   289
   Internet Advertising Formats 290 | E-Mail Advertising 292 | Internet
   Advertising Functions 294 |
   A MATTER OF PRACTICE: Ads in Your Face on MySpace   297
   New Internet Practices 297 |

PRACTICAL TIPS: Using URLs in Advertising—It Makes a Difference   298
Issues in Internet Advertising 300 | Changes and Trends in Internet
Advertising 301 | Advantages and Disadvantages of Internet
Advertising 301 |

Nontraditional Media   302
Guerilla Marketing 302 | Advertainment 302 | Video Games 303 |

THE INSIDE STORY: Nontraditional Media Overview   304
Wi-Fi Communication and Mobile Marketing 305 |

A MATTER OF PRINCIPLE: When Is Too Many Too Much?   307
Nonelectronic New Media 307 |

IT'S A WRAP: eBay Evolves   308

Key Points Summary   308
Key Terms   309
Review Questions   309
Discussion Questions   309
Take-Home Team Projects   310
Yahoo! Hands-On Case   310
Hands-On Case: Second Life Provides Out-of-This-World Opportunities   311

11. MEDIA PLANNING AND BUYING   312

IT'S A WINNER: Game On! Audi's Plan Reaches an Elusive Audience   312

The Media Planning Side of Advertising   314
Key Players 315 | Media Research: Information Sources 315 | The Media
Plan 318 |

Key Media Planning Decisions   318
Target Audience and Media Use 318 |

THE INSIDE STORY: A Week in the Life of a Media Planner   320
The Aperture Concept 320 | Measured Media Objectives 320 | Media Mix
Selection 323 |

A MATTER OF PRINCIPLE: Integrating Advertising and PR Media Planning   324
PRACTICAL TIPS: When to Use Various Media   325

Media Strategy Tools and Techniques   328
Delivering on the Objectives 328 | Delivering on the Targeting
Strategy 329 | Delivering on the Media Mix Strategy 330 | Scheduling
Strategies 331 | Cost Efficiency: CPMs and CPPs 332 | The Media
Budget 333 | IMC Media and Contact Point Planning 334 | Global Media
Strategies 334 |

A Sample Media Plan   334
A MATTER OF PRACTICE: Dentsu's ContactPoint Management Approach   335

Media Buying   339
Media Buying Complexities 339 | Multichannel Buying (and
Selling) 341 | Global Media Buying 342 |

Media Planning Trends   342
Unbundling Media Buying and Planning 342 | Online Media
Buying 343 | New Forms of Media Research 343 |

IT'S A WRAP: Audi's Online Road to Success   344

Key Points Summary   344
Key Terms   345
Review Questions   345

Discussion Questions 345
Take-Home Team Projects 346
Yahoo! Hands-On Case 346
Hands-On Case: P&G Puts the Medium before the Message 347

PART 4 PRINCIPLES: CREATIVITY AND BREAKTHROUGH ADVERTISING

12. **THE CREATIVE SIDE AND MESSAGE STRATEGY** 350
    IT'S A WINNER: A Whole Different Animal 350
    The Two Sides Of Advertising 352
    The Art and Science of Advertising 352 | The Role of Creativity in
    Advertising 354 |
    PRACTICAL TIPS: Ten Creative Tips 355
    Message Planning 356
    The Creative Brief 357 |
    A MATTER OF PRINCIPLE: Do Briefs Change with the Times—and
    with the Agency? 358
    Message Objectives 358 | Targeting 359 | Branding 359 |
    Message Strategies 362
    Creative Strategy Approaches 362 | Strategic Formats and Formulas 364 |
    Matching Messages to Objectives 367 |
    Creative Concepts 370
    Advertising Big Ideas 371 | The ROI of Creativity 371 | The Creative
    Leap 372 | Dialing Up Your Creativity 373 |
    THE INSIDE STORY: Where Do Ideas Come From? Film Murderer Inspires
    Ad Maker! 374
    The Creative Process: How to Get an Idea 375 |
    PRACTICAL TIPS: Exercise Your Creative Muscles 376
    Brainstorming 376 | How to Create Original Ideas 376 | Little Guys and
    Big Ideas 377 |
    Managing Creative Strategy 378
    Extension: An Idea with Legs 378 | Adaptation: Taking an Idea Global 378 |
    A MATTER OF PRACTICE: A Campaign with Legs (and Flippers) 379
    Evaluation: The Go/No-Go Decision 380 | Copy Testing 380 |
    IT'S A WRAP: Fans Rule. Frontier Wins. 380
    Key Points Summary 381
    Key Terms 381
    Review Questions 382
    Discussion Questions 382
    Take-Home Team Projects 383
    Yahoo! Hands-On Case 383
    Hands-On Case: Ask McCann-Erickson about Priceless Creative 384

13. **COPYWRITING** 386
    IT'S A WINNER: Milking Success 386
    Copywriting: The Language Of Advertising 389
    The Copywriter 389 | Advertising Writing Style 390 |

PRACTICAL TIPS: So You Think You Want to Create a Funny Ad?   391

Copywriting For Print   392
How to Write Headlines 392 | How to Write Other Display Copy 395 |
How to Write Body Copy 397 |

A MATTER OF PRINCIPLE: The Principle of Truth   398
Print Media Requirements 398 |

How to Write Radio Copy   400
Tools of Radio Copywriting 401 | The Practice of Radio Copywriting 402 |
Planning the Radio Commercial: Scripts 402 |

How To Write Television Copy   403
Tools of Television Copywriting 404 |

THE INSIDE STORY: The Florida Film Festival: It's a Trip   405
Planning the TV Commercial 406 |

THE INSIDE STORY: The Thinking behind the Doritos "Checkout Girl"   407

Writing for the Web   408
Banners 409 | Web Ads 409 | Other Web Formats 410 |

Copywriting In A Global Environment   410
A MATTER OF PRACTICE: The Ocean Speaks   411
IT'S A WRAP: Got Milk? Got Awards?   412
Key Points Summary   412
Key Terms   413
Review Questions   413
Discussion Questions   413
Take-Home Team Projects   414
Yahoo! Hands-On Case   414
Hands-On Case: Verizon Realizes Opportunity   415

14. DESIGN AND PRODUCTION   416
IT'S A WINNER: Curiously Strong Advertising   416

Visual Communication   419
Visual Impact 419 | Visual Storytelling 420 |

A MATTER OF PRACTICE: If Sex Can't Get Attention, What Can?
or Advertising Gets Religion   421
Brand Image 421 |

Art Direction   422
The Designer's Toolkit 423 | Design Principles 425 | Print Layout 427 |
A MATTER OF PRACTICE: Kitty Slickers and Cat Herders   430

Print Production   431
Print Media Requirements 431 | Print Art Reproduction 432 | Binding and
Finishing 433 |

Broadcast Production   434
Filming and Editing 435 | Producing TV Commercials 437 |

THE INSIDE STORY: Metro Recycling in Stop-Motion Animation   438
The TV Production Process 439 |

A MATTER OF PRINCIPLE: Honda "Cog" Gets It Right,
But Not the First Time   440
Effective Web Design 441 | Action and Interaction 442 |

A MATTER OF PRACTICE: Searching for an Ideal Streaming Technology   443
IT'S A WRAP: Altoids Makes a Mint   444

Key Points Summary	444
Key Terms	445
Review Questions	445
Discussion Questions	445
Take-Home Team Projects	446
Yahoo! Hands-On Case	446
Hands-On Case: The High-Def Future of Advertising	447

PART 5 PRINCIPLES: HOW TO WIN THE BATTLE OF THE BUZZ

15. DIRECT-RESPONSE MARKETING — 450

PRACTICAL TIPS: The Gecko Goes Direct — 450

The Practice of Direct Marketing — 453
Advantages and Disadvantages of Direct Marketing 454 | Direct Marketing and Direct-Response Advertising 454 | The Direct-Marketing Process 455 |

Databases: The Foundation of DM — 458
A Circular Process 459 | Lists 460 | Data-Driven Communication 461 | Customer Relationship Management (CRM) 463 |

The Key Players — 463

The Tools Of Direct Marketing — 465
Direct Mail 465 |

THE INSIDE STORY: Thinking Outside the Mailbox — 467
Catalogs 468 | Telemarketing 469 | Direct-Response Advertising 471 | The Internet and Direct Response 472 |

THE INSIDE STORY: Selling the Colorado Pass Club — 474

Integrated Direct Marketing — 474
Linking the Channels 475 |

Global Considerations in Direct Marketing — 476
IT'S A WRAP: The Gecko Drives Customer Response — 477
Key Points Summary — 477
Key Terms — 477
Review Questions — 478
Discussion Questions — 478
Take-Home Team Projects — 478
Yahoo! Hands-On Case — 478
Hands-On Case: Telemarketers Respond to the National Do-Not-Call Registry — 479

16. SALES PROMOTION, EVENTS, AND SPONSORSHIPS — 480

IT'S A WINNER: Frontier Campaigns for Favorite Animal Votes and Web Hits — 480

The Practice of Sales Promotion — 482
Changes in the Promotion Industry 483 | Reasons for the Growth of Sales Promotion 483 | Categories of Sales Promotion | 484

Consumer Promotions — 484
Types of Consumer Promotions 484 | How to Use Consumer Promotions 486 |

Trade Promotions 488

Types of Trade Promotion 488 | How to Use Trade Promotion 489 |

Crossover Promotions 491

Sponsorships and Event Marketing 491 |

A MATTER OF PRACTICE: Advertising through Sports 492

A MATTER OF PRINCIPLE: The Ad Bowl MVP—The Product 494

Interactive and Internet Promotions 494 | Loyalty Programs 496 |
Partnership Programs 496 |

Promotion Strategy 497

Promotion Objectives 497 | The Issue of Brand Building 497 | Promotion
Integration 498 | Promotion Effectiveness 499 |

IT'S A WRAP: Consumers Vote Frontier the Winner 500

Key Points Summary 500

Key Terms 501

Review Questions 501

Discussion Questions 501

Take-Home Team Projects 502

Yahoo! Hands-On Case 502

Hands-On Case: Upromise Uses Values Marketing to Pay for College 503

17. PUBLIC RELATIONS 504

IT'S A WINNER: GE Goes Green with Ecomagination 504

The Practice of Public Relations 506

Public Opinion 507 | Reputation: Goodwill, Trust, and
Integrity 507 | Comparing Public Relations and Advertising 508 |
Types of Public Relations Programs 509 |

THE INSIDE STORY: A Career in Business Theater 511

A MATTER OF PRINCIPLE: Should Advertising Play a Role in the War
on Terror? 513

Public Relations Planning 513

Research and SWOT Analysis 514 | Targeting 514 | Objectives and
Strategies 515 | The Big Idea 515 | PR's Role in IMC 516 |

Public Relations Tools 517

Advertising 517 | Publicity 520 |

PRACTICAL TIPS: How to Write E-Mail Pitch Letters 522
Publications 522 |

A MATTER OF PRACTICE: The World's Greatest Public Relations Person 523
DVDs, CDs, Podcasts, Books, and Online Video 524 | Speakers and
Photos 524 | Displays and Exhibits 524 | Special Events and
Tours 524 | Online Communication 525 |

Effectiveness and PR Excellence 527

IT'S A WRAP: GE's Green Efforts Mean Good Business 528

Key Points Summary 528

Key Terms 529

Review Questions 529

Discussion Questions 529

Take-Home Team Projects 530

Yahoo! Hands-On Case 530

Hands-On Case: JetBlue's Blues 531

18. SPECIAL ADVERTISING CAMPAIGNS   532

IT'S A WINNER: Think Snow; Think CR-V   532

IMC and Total Communication   535
Driving Consistency through All Messages 535 | Organizing for IMC 535 | Planning an IMC Campaign 536 |

Retail Marketing and Advertising   537
Retail Advertising Planning 537 |

THE INSIDE STORY: Leadership Skills Are Critical   538
Creating the Retail Ad 539 | The Media of Retail Advertising 541 |

Business-to-Business Advertising   541
B2B Buying Behavior 541 | Types of B2B Advertising 542 | Creating B2B Advertising 543 | B2B Advertising Media 544 |

Nonprofit or Social Marketing   544
A MATTER OF PRACTICE: Rebranding a City   545
Fund-Raising 546 | Social Marketing and Public Communication Campaigns 546 | Cause and Mission Marketing 546 |

A MATTER OF PRINCIPLE: It's Your Choice   547

International Advertising and Marketing Communication   548
Stages of Marketing Development 548 | The Global versus Local Debate 548 |

PRACTICAL TIPS: How Advertising Works Cross-Culturally   549
Planning Global Strategies 552 | The IMC Factor in Global Campaign Planning 554 | Putting It All Together 554 |

THE INSIDE STORY: Chasing the Same Dream   555

IT'S A WRAP: Driving Up Honda's Market Share   556

Key Points Summary   556
Key Terms   557
Review Questions   557
Discussion Questions   557
Take-Home Team Projects   558
Yahoo! Hands-On Case   558
Hands-On Case: CareerBuilder.com Means (Monkey) Business   559

19. EVALUATION OF EFFECTIVENESS   560

IT'S A WINNER: Outstanding in the Field   560

Impact: Does It Work?   562
Evaluating Effectiveness 563 | Types and Stages of Evaluation 563 |

THE INSIDE STORY: What Is Great Advertising?   564
Facets: Measuring Responses 565 |

Message Evaluation   565
Copy-Testing Services 565 | Message Development Research 567 |

A MATTER OF PRACTICE: Finding Moments of Truth   568
During Execution: Concurrent Testing 569 | Posttesting: After Execution Research 571 |

Media Evaluation   573
Evaluating Audience Exposure 573 | Advertising ROI and Media Efficiency 574 |

Evaluating Marketing Communication Campaigns   575
  Marcom Tools 576 | Special Advertising Situations 579 | Campaign
  Evaluation 580 | Connecting the Dots 580 |
  IT'S A WRAP: New Holland's Brave New Tractors Conquer the Market   582
Key Points Summary   583
Key Terms   583
Review Questions   583
Discussion Questions   584
Take-Home Team Projects   584
Yahoo! Hands-On Case   584
Hands-On Case: Lovin' It at McDonald's Again   585

Appendix   587

Glossary   593

Credits   611

Notes   615

Index   625

ABOUT THE AUTHORS

Sandra Moriarty, Ph.D., *Professor Emerita, University of Colorado at Boulder*

Sandra Moriarty is cofounder of the Integrated Marketing Communication graduate program at the University of Colorado. Now retired, she has also taught at Michigan State University, University of Kansas, and Kansas State University, where she earned her Ph.D. in education. She specialized in teaching the campaign course and courses on the creative side—both writing and design. She has worked in government public relations, owned an advertising and public relations agency, directed a university publications program, and edited a university alumni magazine. She has been a consultant on integrated marketing communication with agencies such as BBDO and Dentsu, the largest advertising agency in the world, and with their clients in the United States, Europe, and Asia. Professor Moriarty has published widely in scholarly journals on marketing communication and visual communication topics and has authored 11 books on advertising, integrated marketing communication, marketing, visual communication, and typography. A classic book on integrated marketing, *Driving Brand Value,* was written with coauthor Tom Duncan. Most recently she has authored the *Science and Art of Branding* with Giep Franzen, University of Amsterdam. International versions of her books include Spanish, Chinese, Taiwanese, Korean, Japanese, and an English-language version for India. She has spoken to groups and presented seminars in most European countries, as well as Mexico, Japan, Korea, India, New Zealand, and Turkey.

Nancy Mitchell, Ph.D., *Professor, University of Nebraska-Lincoln*

Nancy Mitchell is professor of advertising and chair of the Graduate Committee in the College of Journalism and Mass Communications at the University of Nebraska-Lincoln, where she's taught since 1990. She served as chair of the advertising department for 11 years before heading the graduate program in her college. Prior to her tenure at the University of Nebraska, she taught at West Texas A&M University. She's taught a variety of courses, including advertising principles, design, copywriting, research and strategy, and campaigns and media ethics. She worked as an advertising professional for 15 years before entering academe. She gained experience as a copywriter, designer, editor, fund-raiser, and magazine editor in an array of businesses, including a large department store, a publishing company, an advertising agency, a newspaper, and a Public Broadcasting System affiliate. Her research focuses on creating effective advertising messages to underrepresented groups, ethical issues, and assessment of student learning. Nationally, she served as Advertising Division Head for the Association for Education in Journalism and Mass Communications. She serves on the editorial boards for *Journal of Advertising Education* and *Journalism and Mass Communication Educator.*

William Wells

One of the industry's leading market and research authorities, Bill Wells is a retired Professor of Advertising at the University of Minnesota's School of Journalism and Mass Communication. Formerly Executive Vice President and Director of Marketing Services at DDB Needharn Chicago, he is the only representative of the advertising business elected to the Attitude Research Hall of Fame. He earned a Ph.D. from Stanford University and was formerly Professor of Psychology and Marketing at the University of Chicago. He joined Needham, Harper, Chicago as Director of Corporate Research. Author of the Needham Harper Lifestyle study as well as author of more than 60 books and articles, Dr. Wells also published *Planning for ROI: Effective Advertising Strategy* (Prentice Hall, 1989).

PREFACE

WHAT MAKES ADVERTISING AND MARKETING COMMUNICATION EFFECTIVE?

During a recent Super Bowl, an ad for Anheuser-Busch called "Applause" showed people in an airport spontaneously applauding a group of American troops returning home. Even the audience watching from their living rooms was inclined to join in with applause as part of this graceful display of respect and appreciation. It was touching. Memorable. Beautifully photographed. And the people seemed real, not rehearsed. But was it an effective ad? What was it trying to accomplish?

Advertising can cause you to stop and watch, or even stop and think. It can make you laugh, or squirm in your seat, or bring tears to your eyes. It can inspire you to read about a new product or remember a favorite brand when you're walking down the aisle in a supermarket. Advertising can also leave you free to change the channel or turn a page without being aware of having seen the ad at all.

What is effective advertising? Is it marketing communication that gets talked about? Is it advertising like the Anheuser-Busch commercial that inspires you to applaud? What, exactly, does it mean to say that an advertisement "works"?

Our answer is that advertising—and all other forms of marketing communication—is effective if it creates a desired response in the audience. Advertising *that works* is advertising that affects people; it has impact and it gets results that can be measured.

THE PRINCIPLE: EFFECTIVENESS IS DRIVEN BY AN UNDERSTANDING OF HOW MESSAGES WORK

Advertising is part inspiration and part hard work, but it is also a product of clear and logical thinking. Ultimately marketing communication is evaluated on its ability to generate a desired consumer response that meets a set of carefully crafted objectives. To write objectives, however, you must have some understanding of how these messages work.

This eighth edition of *Advertising: Principles and Practice* has organized the discussion of advertising effects to better explain marketing communication strategy. The Facets Model of Effects presented in this edition is

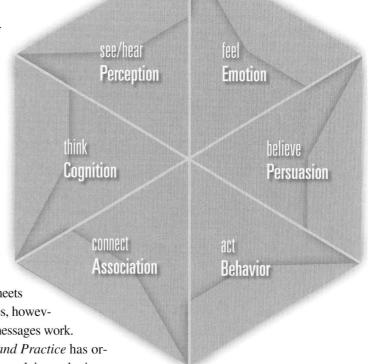

THE FACETS MODEL OF EFFECTS

like a diamond or a crystal whose surfaces represent the different types of effects contained within a marketing communication message. This model and the ideas it represents are used throughout the book to help explain such things as how objectives are decided upon, what strategies deliver what kind of effects, and how an advertisement and other forms of marketing communication are evaluated based on their objectives.

THE PRACTICE: THE EFFECTS BEHIND EFFECTIVENESS

In most cases, you have little idea what the objectives are because that information generally isn't made public—and you sometimes can't tell from the ad itself. Take the "Applause" ad. From what we've told you, what do you think the ad's objectives are? To sell beer? To get viewers to run out and buy the brand? Actually, the ad seems to be a bit removed from a straight sales pitch. Maybe its objective is simply to make people feel good, to see the goodness in a simple patriotic gesture—and, ultimately, to associate that feeling of goodness and warmth with the brand. Does it work? How did you feel when you read over the description of the ad? Even without seeing the commercial, you may have found that the idea touched your emotions.

In this eighth edition of *Advertising: Principles and Practice,* we take you behind the scenes of many award-winning campaigns, such as the Dove "Real Beauty" campaign, to uncover the hard work and explain the objectives, the inspiration, and the creative ideas behind some great advertising campaigns. You will see how the ideas come together; you will live through the decision making; and you will understand the risks the creators of the advertising faced.

The Consumer Audience

CHAPTER 5

campaignforrealbeauty.com *Dove*

New Dove Firming. As tested on real curves.

IT'S A WINNER

Awards:	Company:	Agency:	Campaign:
Grand Effie; Grand Prix, Cannes International Advertising Festival	Unilever	Ogilvy & Mather	"Real Beauty"

Dove Redefines Beauty

In earlier chapters, you read about the *truth*® (anti-smoking) campaign, Puma and Chick-fil-A's brand building, and Whirlpool's relationship with Habitat for Humanity. What made those campaigns effective?

We hope you said their effectiveness was the result of really understanding the consumer. Making connections that resonate with the audience is the hallmark of effective marketing communication. Think about the power of Burger King's "Have It Your Way" campaign and how that line addresses burger buyers' desire to customize what they eat.

Unilever's campaign for Dove, which won a Grand Effie, provides another example of great advertising that recognized a "truth" held by consumers. The "Campaign for Real Beauty" touched a nerve and punctured the cultural obsession with stick-thin bodies and Barbie Doll images. The Dove campaign was risky because it sought to literally redefine beauty in advertising and to acknowledge a change in the way women see themselves. It could have been a bomb, but it was a winner because it spoke to every woman's need to look and feel her best without promising or reinforcing impossible standards of beauty.

The Dove brand has an interesting history. First formulated in the 1940s as a nonirritating skin cleaner for use on burns and wounds, the cleaner was reformulated in the 1950s as the Dove Beauty Bar. The brand grew in the 1990s to include body wash, facial cleanser, and moisturizers, followed by deodorants in 2001 and hair care products in 2003. While these products were successful, Unilever learned from research that consumers thought of it as simple, white, and gentle. The brand lacked energy, and at worst, it represented submissive femininity, according to its ad agency, Ogilvy & Mather.

129

THE PROOF: *ADVERTISING: PRINCIPLES AND PRACTICE* IS EFFECTIVE

It's clear from the headlines in industry publications that advertisers want to know if their ads and other marketing communication efforts work. Advertising costs money—a lot of money in many cases—and advertisers want proof that their advertising and marketing communication is efficient andeffective. That's why we make the claim—and, yes, this is an advertisement—that:

ADVERTISING: PRINCIPLES AND PRACTICE **IS THE BOOK TO READ TO LEARN ABOUT EFFECTIVE ADVERTISING.**

You will learn in this book that all advertising claims need to be supported. We are making a bold claim, but here is how we back it up:

Each chapter opens with an effectiveness award winner. Many of these stories are Effie award-winning campaigns recognized by the New York American Marketing Association as outstanding examples of effectiveness. We also have winners from the Direct Marketing Association's Echo Awards and the Public Relations Society of America's Silver Anvil Awards. At the end of each chapter we loop back to the opening campaign story and show you why it was successful. We match the results to the objectives and provide the data used by professionals to determine whether the advertising worked.

Furthermore, *Advertising: Principles and Practice* is time tested. That's why it has continued as one of the market leaders for a decade and a half. It continues to be in touch with the most current practices in the industry, but it also presents the fundamentals in ways that will give students a competitive edge. That's why students keep this textbook on their shelves as an important reference book as they move through their

Practical Tips

How Advertising Works Cross-Culturally
By Marieke de Mooij, Ph.D., Consultant, Cross Cultural Communication, The Netherlands

In my research, the most important finding for advertisers is that culture influences how we communicate, both in interpersonal communication and in mass communication. The implication of my research is that advertising works differently across cultures, and that thesis is developed in both of my books, *Consumer Behavior and Culture* and *Global Marketing and Advertising*.

I work with the theories of Geert Hofstede, whose dimensional model of national culture is now applied worldwide. I used his country scores to analyze differences in consumer behavior across cultures. Here are some things to think about as you plan or critique cross-national advertising that does—or doesn't—accommodate cultural differences.

* There is no one universal model for information processing. Because people don't process information in the same way, the role of advertising also varies across cultures.
* The dominant information-based theory of advertising processing originated in a U.S.-U.K. context. It is not necessarily valid for other cultures.
* In the collectivistic cultures of the South of Europe, people do not search for information in a conscious way as they do in the North of Europe.
* People who view themselves as well informed to make a buying decision (North Europeans, for example) score high on Hofstede's individualism dimension.
* In a collectivistic country like Spain, frequent social interaction causes an automatic flow of information between people, who, as a result, know things without having to search for information.
* The role of advertising in these collectivistic cultures is not to provide information but to create emotional bonding.

* The idea of the universality of emotions has been discredited in the past decade. Both expression and recognition of emotions vary across cultures. The Chinese, for example, tend to laugh when they feel embarrassed.
* In most of Asia people do not display negative emotions because it disturbs harmony. Generally non-Western subjects categorize Western emotional expressions incorrectly. Examples are disgust, anger, fear, and contempt.
* The more abstract emotions are formulated, the more they are universal. Abstract terms like happiness suggest universality, but what makes people happy varies enormously. As a result, ads for lotteries are very different.
* Personality traits are related to culture, which has implications for connecting personal traits to global brands. I found that people in different countries, for example, attribute different personality traits to successful global brands like Coca-Cola, Nike, and Nivea even though the companies wanted the brand personalities to be consistent.
* Consumers attribute personalities to brands that fit their own cultural values, not the values of the producer.
* Marketing managers' need for cross-cultural consistency is typical of Anglo-Saxon and North-European cultures. In most other countries in the world, people prefer to adapt.

Marieke de Mooij, Ph.D., is a consultant in cross-cultural communications and a visiting professor at various universities in the Netherlands, Finland, Germany, and Spain. She is the author of several books on the influence of culture on marketing and advertising, including *Global Marketing and Advertising*, *Understanding Cultural Paradoxes*, *Consumer Behavior and Culture*, and *Consequences for Global Marketing and Advertising*.

6. Justice
7. Freedom
8. Friendship
9. Knowledge
10. Learning

Dutch scholar Geert Hofstede, an expert on cultural differences, insists that the impact of national culture on business and consumption patterns is huge and should be accommodated in marketing and advertising strategies. Based on a study of 116,000 IBM employees around the world, Hofstede found their cultural differences to be stronger than the legendary IBM corporate culture that he assumed would be a standardizing influence. Hofstede also found that the American values of taking initiative, personal competency, and rugged individualism are not universal values and that some cultures prize collective thinking and group norms rather than independence. The Practical Tips box explains what one researcher has learned about the application of Hofstede's principles to advertising.

A MATTER OF PRACTICE

A Campaign with Legs (and Flippers)
By Shawn Couzens and Gary Ennis, Creative Directors, Grey Advertising

When Frontier has something to sell—whether it's a new city, a Web site, or the frequent flyer program—we let the animals deliver the message in a fun, humorous way. Certain characters are better suited for certain messages than others.

Flip, for example, is the lovable loser who never gets a break. For years, he's been dying to fly to a warm, tropical climate, such as Florida. But instead, he always gets sent to Chicago. This has been a recurring theme in several commercials. So, when Frontier expanded its service to Mexico, this was the perfect opportunity to build upon Flip's storyline. Hence, "Flip to Mexico."

The point is that the campaign has always been episodic, like a situation comedy. With 10-plus TV spots a year, we needed a structure that allowed us to build upon the characters and their storylines.

If our base-brand campaign were a sitcom, then *Flip* to Mexico would be a spin-off. The idea was to blanket the city with the "news" that Flip would quit unless he went to Mexico—and he needed the public's help to get there. We wanted the community to be an active participant in the story. To facilitate this, we launched a series of mock newscasts covering Flip's evolving storyline. We hired "activists" to hold placards and distribute leaflets, and we created an elaborate underground Web site with lots of interactive content. We even involved real Frontier employees, like CEO Jeff Potter, to help blur the line between reality and fiction. Consumers enjoyed the interplay, and they happily rallied for Flip. The

story really captivated the city. It was all over the news. And it deepened the bond between Frontier and the community at a time when other airlines were trying to eat into Frontier's home turf.

But it's no longer about just TV, print, and radio. An idea has to perform across multiple platforms, and new media is a big part of that. Brands will have to find other ways to connect with consumers—like podcasts, interactive Web sites, YouTube Contests, branded entertainment, product placement, long-format digital content, and more. Some brands are creating their own TV shows or Web channels with original programming. The media landscape will continue to change. What won't change is the need for talented writers and art directors who can think outside the parameters of traditional media and make the brand story relevant and entertaining across all these different media and formats.

A campaign is an evolving story, so you can't rest on your awards. When you launch a successful campaign, and everyone likes it, you've set the creative bar pretty high. Everyone's waiting to see what you'll do next. Your job is to keep surprising them, keep raising the bar—because if you don't do it, someone else will.

There's a saying in the industry, "You're only as good as your last ad." It's kind of true. One week, you're being praised for an ad or campaign. But the next week, you have a new creative brief in your hand, and you have to prove yourself all over again.

Even if the campaign theme, slogan, or visual elements are the same across markets, it is usually desirable to adapt the creative execution to the local market, as we explained in the discussion of cultural differences in Chapter 5. Adaptation is especially important if the advertiser wants its products identified with the local market rather than as a foreign import. Advertisements may be produced centrally, in each local market, or by a combination of both. With a standardized campaign, production usually is centralized, and all advertisements are produced simultaneously to reap production cost savings.

An example of a difficult adaptation comes from Apple's series of "Mac vs. PC" ads that show a nerdy PC guy who can't keep up with the activities of a laid-back Mac guy. It uses delicate humor and body language to make subtle points about the advantages of the Mac system. In moving the campaign to Japan, Apple's agency, TBWA/Chiat/Day wrestled with the fact that in Japanese culture, direct-comparison ads are considered rude. The Japanese version was tweaked to make the Apple more of a home computer and the PC a work tool, so the differences were focused more on place than person.[30] The point is that cultural differences often require nuanced and subtle changes to be acceptable beyond the country of their origin.

advertising major. One thing we hear from our young professionals is that they continue to rely on this book as they make their transition to professional life, and you can find it on many of their office shelves, as well.

WHAT MAKES THIS BOOK DIFFERENT FROM OTHER MARKETING COMMUNICATION TEXTBOOKS?

Principles and Practice

The Principle and Practice subheads in the discussion of the effectiveness theme do more than reflect the title of the book, *Advertising: Principles and Practice*. Throughout the book we identify the most important principles that guide effective marketing communication. The Matter of Practice and Matter of Principle features present the ideas of outstanding professionals and professors who help explain the issues and dynamics of this fast-changing industry. On the Practice side, we showcase the work of professionals who are graduates of advertising and marketing programs and who were nominated by their professors to be featured in this book. We also invite them to explain their work in the Inside Story feature.

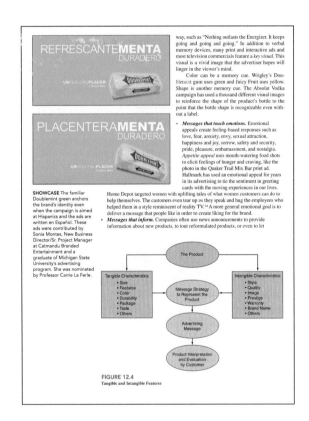

Contributors: VIPs, Stars, Pros, and Profs

The most important change in this eighth edition is the expanded use of contributors from all areas of the advertising industry and the academic community. You can find brief bios of these contributors at the end of this Preface. You'll be amazed at how many people agreed to share their work and ideas with the students who read this edition of *Advertising: Principles and Practice.* The insights and experience of these contributors bring a richness and depth to the study of advertising and marketing communication.

HOW HAS THE BOOK'S ORGANIZATION AND CONTENT CHANGED IN THE EIGHTH EDITION?

In addition to all the changes already mentioned, here are the chapter-by-chapter changes in the Table of Contents:

Table of Contents

This eighth edition is the same length as the seventh in terms of the number of chapters. The order of the chapters also remains the same, but we've done some retitling of chapters to make the focus and logical flow of the book's content more obvious.

Part 1: A Passion for the Business

This set of three chapters includes a part-opening essay by one of our Stars, Wende Zomnir, who explains the seven principles she uses to run Urban Decay and Hard Candy, her unique cosmetics brands.

Chapter 1 Introduction to Advertising: This chapter explains the basic concepts of advertising and marketing communication. It also features an expanded historical discussion used to better explain how these concepts developed as the practice of marketing communication evolved. It ends with an introduction to the concept of effectiveness, which is the theme of this textbook.

Chapter 2 Advertising's Role in Marketing: This chapter describes the basic concepts of marketing. In addition, it discusses the client-agency relationship in terms of the marketer as the advertising agency's client. It also outlines marketing communication jobs and functions on both the agency and the client side.

Chapter 3 Advertising and Society: This chapter has been reorganized. It begins with a discussion of advertising's role in society and exposes students to some of the hot-button issues that sometimes generate criticism. Then it moves to advertising regulation and reviews the legal environment within which marketing communication operates. It concludes with a discussion of ethical practice.

Part 2: Principle: Strategy Is Creative, Too

Pat Fallon and Fred Senn, cofounders of the highly respected Fallon agency, explain their agency's philosophy in seven principles that leverage the power of creativity to move all aspects of the business. In particular, as they explain in their book, *Juicing the Orange*, creative insights are needed to understand, analyze, and plan all areas of effective marketing communication.

Chapter 4 How Advertising Works: This chapter, which is one of the book's unique features, uses the question "How does advertising work?" to explain the logic behind effects and effectiveness. It introduces the book's signature Facets Model of Effects and wraps up with a discussion of the power of advertising. The focus throughout this chapter is on how understanding effects leads to measurable objectives that deliver effective marketing communication.

Chapter 5 The Consumer Audience: Rather than looking at consumer behavior in the abstract, this chapter analyzes consumers as participants in a communication experience that may lead to a consumer decision. It examines various types of influences, as well as the consumer-decision process, and how consumers respond to marketing communication. It concludes with an explanation of how these insights lead to the critical strategic decisions of segmenting and targeting the audience.

Chapter 6 Strategic Research: Based on an understanding of the ways consumers respond to marketing communication, research is presented as the tool used to acquire the information that ferrets out these insights. This chapter presents a discussion of the research methods used in developing marketing communication strategies.

Chapter 7 Strategic Planning: The concept of strategic planning is explained in the context of business, marketing, and marketing communication plans. The focus is on the critical decisions in a campaign plan. The chapter concludes with a discussion of the practice of account planning, which is one of the distinctive features of this textbook.

Part 3: Practice: Where Are Media Heading?

Media is one of the most dynamic and fast-changing areas of marketing communication practice. This part opener includes an essay by media expert and professor Don Jugenheimer in which he identifies five critical trends driving these changes.

Chapter 8 Media Basics and Print Media: This chapter has been retitled slightly to better showcase its content. It begins with an explanation of media basics, those concepts and terms that are common to all areas of media. Then it introduces the basics of print media and concludes with a discussion of out-of-home media.

Chapter 9 Broadcast Media: Broadcast media tend to dominate media budgets, so this chapter is devoted to these important radio, television, and other video media formats, including the increasingly important area of product placement.

Chapter 10 Internet and Nontraditional Media: Without a doubt, the most exciting arena is new media—whether Web-based or nontraditional, by which we mean new media forms that move beyond traditional measured media. These media engage consumers in new forms of brand contact and dialogue. If there's any area where media professionals can flaunt their creativity, it's in the development of new ways to reach people and involve them with a brand.

Chapter 11 Media Planning and Buying: This chapter wraps up the section on media with a more in-depth explanation of how media planning decisions are made. It discusses various media tools used in designing a media mix that will engage consumers and deliver effectively on the marketing communication objectives. The chapter ends with a discussion of the role and responsibilities of a media buyer in implementing a media plan.

Part 4: Principles: Creativity and Breakthrough Advertising

The creative side of advertising involves writing, designing, and producing the marketing communication messages that move consumers to respond. Breaking through the clutter and leaving a positive impression is extremely difficult in the hyperactive marketplace of ideas that we call marketing communication. Professor Sheila Sasser relies on her many years of professional experience to identify the three Ps of advertising creativity.

Chapter 12 The Creative Side and Message Strategy: This chapter is substantially rewritten with more emphasis on the ways marketing communication messages are planned and the most commonly used types of message strategies. But what may be of more interest to students is the expanded discussion of creative thinking and how to get an idea.

Chapter 13 Copywriting: A creative team usually includes a copywriter and an art director. Their mission is to create the words and images that bring a marketing communication strategy to life. This chapter explains how to write copy for different types of media.

Chapter 14 Design and Production: The visual dimension of marketing communication is just as important as the words, so this chapter begins with a discussion of visual communication and then moves to art direction and design principles. Production is also discussed, although that topic has been significantly trimmed in this edition with some of the more technical discussion moved to the book's Web site.

Part 5: Principles: How to Win the Battle of the Buzz

The final section of this textbook reviews a variety of marketing communication functions and tools used in integrated marketing communication programs. Professor Margo Berman shares principles from her book, *How to Win the Battle of the Buzz*, that lead to more integrated and as more powerful marketing communication. The section wraps up with a discussion of the evaluation of effectiveness.

Chapter 15 Direct-Response Marketing: One of the most important marketing communication areas that delivers personal contact with a consumer is direct response. This chapter explains basic practices and types of direct-response advertising, as well as the important role of databases in personalizing communication.

Chapter 16 Sales Promotion, Events, and Sponsorships: The areas discussed in this chapter call for some of the most creative ideas in marketing communication. It begins with a review of consumer and trade promotions and then discusses promotions that cross over with other marketing communication areas to deliver such objectives as loyalty and interactivity.

Chapter 17 Public Relations: It is critical in building a powerful brand that consumers have a positive impression of the brand. This chapter discusses the tools used by PR professionals to manage brand and corporate reputation, as well as crises, public communication campaigns, and marketing public relations. It presents PR approaches to strategic planning, as well as the tools most commonly used in effective programs.

Chapter 18 Special Advertising Campaigns: The title and focus of this chapter has changed slightly. This chapter looks at marketing communication campaigns in terms of specialized situations, such as retail, business-to-business, nonprofit or social marketing, and international. It begins by revisiting the concept of IMC and concludes with a more in-depth analysis of IMC campaign planning.

Chapter 19 Evaluation of Effectiveness: We end with the topic we introduced in Chapter 1—effectiveness. This chapter presents different ways to evaluate the effectiveness of marketing communication during development and implementation and after a campaign has run. It also includes a section on the evaluation of media effectiveness and IMC campaigns.

SUPPLEMENTS FOR INSTRUCTORS AND STUDENTS

CourseSmart

CourseSmart is an exciting new *choice* for students looking to save money. As an alternative to purchasing the print textbook, students can purchase an electronic version of the same content and save up to 50 percent off the suggested list price of the print text. With a CourseSmart e-textbook, students can search the text, make notes online, print out reading assignments that incorporate lecture notes, and bookmark important passages for later review. For more information, or to purchase access to the CourseSmart eTextbook, visit www.coursesmart.com.

Instructor's Manual

Contains chapter overviews and key points, plus detailed chapter outlines, incorporating key terms from the text. Provides support for end-of-chapter material, along with additional class projects and assignments. Also included are "Outside Examples," which offer instructors additional lecture material for each chapter. The examples may include extensions of concepts or company examples briefly mentioned in the chapter or new material that further develops a key concept in the text. "Professors on the Go!" is featured as well, which was created with the busy professor in mind. This helpful feature brings key material up-front in the manual, where instructors who are short on time can take a quick look and find key points and assignments to incorporate into a lecture without having to page through all the material provided for each chapter.

Test Item File

Contains more than 2,800 questions. Each chapter consists of multiple-choice, true/false, essay, and short-answer questions, with page references and difficulty levels provided for each question. *Please note that an entire section is dedicated to application questions.* This resource provides real-life situations that take students beyond basic chapter concepts and vocabulary and asks them to apply their advertising knowledge.

Each chapter of the Test Item File was prepared with the AACSB curricula standards in mind. Where appropriate, the answer line of each question indicates a category within which the question falls.* This AACSB reference helps instructors identify those test questions that support that organization's learning goals.

TestGen

Prentice Hall's TestGen test-generating software is available for this edition as well. This supplement is available from the *IRC Online* only (www.prenhall.com/moriarty). Please note that the TestGen is NOT included on the Instructor's Resource Center on CD.

- PC/Mac compatible and preloaded with all the Test Item File questions
- Manually or randomly view test bank questions and drag and drop to create a test
- Add or modify test bank questions using the built-in Question Editor
- Print up to 25 variations of a single test and deliver the test on a local area network using the built-in QuizMaster feature
- Free customer support available at via e-mail at media.support@pearsoned.com, or call 1-800-6-PROFESSOR between 8 A.M. and 5 P.M. CST.

PowerPoints

When it comes to PowerPoint presentations, Prentice Hall knows one size does not fit all. That's why this eighth edition of *Advertising: Principles and Practice* offers instructors more than one option.

- *PowerPoint BASIC:* This simple presentation includes only basic outlines and key points from each chapter. No animation or forms of rich media are integrated, which makes the total file size manageable and easier to share online or via e-mail. BASIC was also designed for instructors who prefer to customize PowerPoint presentations or want to avoid having to strip out animation, embedded files, or other media-rich features.
- *PowerPoint MEDIA RICH (on CD only):* This media-rich alternative—the best option if you want a complete presentation solution—includes basic outlines and key points from each chapter, plus advertisements and art from the text, discussion questions, Web links, and embedded video snippets from the accompanying video library. Instructors can further customize this presentation using the image library featured on the IRC on CD-ROM.

---

*Please note that not all test questions will indicate an AACSB category.

- *PowerPoints for Classroom Response Systems (CRS):* These Q&A style slides are designed for classrooms using "clickers" or classroom response systems. Instructors who are interested in making CRS a part of their course should contact their Prentice Hall representative for details and a demonstration. CRS is a fun and easy way to make your classroom more interactive.

Aside from these three PowerPoint options, a select number of slides, based on the MEDIA RICH version, are also available as overhead transparencies.

Instructor's Resource Center (IRC)

- *IRC—CD-ROM:* New interface and searchable database make sorting through and locating specific resources easier than ever. Includes all the same supplements hosted at our IRC Online; however, the TestGen is only available online. The CD-ROM also contains many images from the textbook, which you may incorporate into your lectures.
- *IRC—ONLINE:* The Prentice Hall catalog at www.prenhall.com/moriarty is where instructors can access our complete array of teaching materials. Simply go to the Instructor's Resource page for this text and click on the Instructor link to download the Instructor's Manual, Video Guide, Test Item File, TestGen, PowerPoint slides (Basic and CRS versions only), and more. Please note that the PowerPoint MEDIA RICH set is provided only on the IRC on CD-ROM due to its larger file size and embedded video clips.

NOTE: Prentice Hall manually checks *every* password request and verifies each individual's instructor status before issuing a password.

Video

In order to enrich your advertising course, the accompanying video library offers a variety of video segments. Some segments take students on location, profiling well-known companies and their marketing and advertising strategies. Others offer a behind-the-scenes look at a typical day in the life of various advertising employees at different levels in the agency, providing insight into what skills are really needed to succeed in the field. Additionally, a collection of commercial advertisements is included in the video library. These advertisements serve as a great tool to demonstrate to your students what works—and what doesn't—in the field of advertising. You may access the Video Guide on the IRC (online and on CD-ROM).

Companion Web Site

This site serves as a valuable resource for students in preparing for exams. Two student quizzes are offered per chapter. The Concept Check Quiz is administered prior to reviewing the chapter, in order to assess students' initial understanding. The Concept Challenge Quiz is administered after reviewing the chapter to assess students' comprehension. For the eighth edition, additional student resources will be offered on the site, developed by the authors. You can access the Companion Web Site by visiting www.prenhall.com/moriarty.

CONTRIBUTORS: VIPs, STARS, PROFS, AND PROS

We said previously that one of the strengths of this new edition is the quality of the contributions from professionals and professors. Here are the bios of the VIPs, Stars, Pros, and Profs who contributed to the development of this eighth edition.

Advisory Board VIPs

A dedicated group of professionals helped the authors update *Advertising: Principles and Practice* for its eighth edition. They critiqued chapter content in their areas of specialty, contributed their thoughts and their stories, made connections for the authors, and wrote pieces that appear in the Matter of Practice, Matter of Principle, and Practical Tips boxes.

Constance Cannon Frazier

Senior Vice President, AAF Mosaic Center and Education Services, Washington, D.C.

Constance Cannon Frazier joined the American Advertising Federation (AAF) as senior vice president of the AAF Mosaic Center and Education Services. As leader of these vitally important programs, Frazier oversees continuing efforts to promote multiculturalism in the industry and steers the AAF's education programs, which include the Most Promising Minority Students and the AAF Mosaic Awards. As head of the AAF's Education Services, Frazier promotes the organization's 210 college chapters and oversees programs such as the National Student Advertising Competition. She also heads AAF's internship and scholarship programs. In addition to extensive professional experience in advertising, Frazier taught at Howard University where she was the coordinator of the advertising and public relations sequence.

Marty Horn

Senior Vice President and Director of U.S. Strategic Services, DDB, New York

A 30-year veteran of DDB, Horn has unearthed consumer insights and developed communication strategies for major clients such as Anheuser-Busch,

McDonald's, and State Farm. He also is responsible for harnessing the power of DDB's proprietary tools, resources, and consultative services, including the DDB Life Style Study to assist clients throughout the DDB network in energizing, invigorating, and, ultimately growing their brands. Horn has published many articles in scholarly journals; he is a member of the Association for Consumer Research and has twice served on its Board of Directors.

Regina Lewis

Ph.D., Vice President of Consumer Insights, Intercontinental Hotels Group, Atlanta, Georgia

When Dr. Lewis joined this book's Advisory Board, she was Vice President of the Consumer and Brand Insights Group at Dunkin' Brands and contributed many insights into Dunkin' Donuts strategy and planning. Since then she's moved to Intercontinental Hotels, the world's largest hotel group. Before Dunkin' Brands she was a partner in Lewis/Mobilio Research, working with major clients such as Amazon.com and GlaxoSmithKline, among others. She also ran a research program for Women.com network that helped clients use and learn from the organization's multimillion member base. An academic at heart, Lewis started her research career as an assistant professor in the College of Communication at the University of Alabama.

Edward Maibach

MPH, Ph.D., Professor and Director, Center of Excellence in Climate Change Communication Research, The George Mason University, Washington, D.C.

An expert in social marketing communication and research, Dr. Maibach is director of the Center for

Excellence in Climate Change Communication Research. He is a prolific academic author and a highly experienced public health advocate and social change professional who has helped to define the fields of public health communication and social marketing. His edited book, *Designing Health Messages: Approaches from Communication Theory and Public Health Practice*, is widely used by academics and practitioners alike. Previously, Maibach was Worldwide Director of Social Marketing for Porter Novelli, and more recently he was Associate Director of the National Cancer Institute.

Susan Mendelsohn

Ph.D., President, Susan Mendelsohn Consultants, Chicago

Dr. Mendelsohn is president of Susan Mendelsohn Consultants, a Chicago-based company that specializes in brand building and developing creative and integrated communication strategies. Her exceptional account planning experience includes planning in the profit and not-for-profit sectors with clients and brands in more than 60 industries. Mendelsohn is also an adjunct professor of marketing for The School of the Art Institute of Chicago. Prior to starting her consultancy, she was Executive Vice President, Director of Planning for Young & Rubicam and Senior Vice President, Group Planning Director for FCB Worldwide, both in Chicago. She has also worked for Saatchi & Saatchi, Griffin Bacal Inc., and DMB&B.

Ivan L. Preston

Journalism and Mass Communications Professor Emeritus, University of Wisconsin, Madison

Ivan Preston is internationally known for his work on advertising regulation. A faculty member for 31 years, he previously worked in advertising and has spent time in Washington, D.C., as in-house consultant to the Federal Trade Commission. He is also a sought-after consultant and expert witness in law cases on behalf of advertisers and government regulators. Dr. Preston has written two books on deceptive advertising—*The Great American Blow-Up* on puffery and *The Tangled Web They Weave*.

William H. Weintraub

Chief Marketing Officer (retired), Coors Inc., Boulder, Colorado

Weintraub began his career at Procter & Gamble where he spent 15 years managing a range of brands. Over the next 20 years, he was Chief Marketing Officer at Kellogg, then Tropicana, and then Coors. Through his career, he has received a number of awards,

including *BrandWeek's* Marketer of the Year. He now teaches at the University of Colorado and lectures at the Daniels School of Business at Denver University while serving on various boards.

Karl Weiss

President/CEO, Market Perceptions, Inc., Denver, Colorado

Founder and President of Market Perceptions, Inc., Weiss has 18 years experience in marketing research with special expertise on research design and statistical analysis. His background in statistical methods, coupled with experience in marketing research, provides clients with expertise ranging from defining study objectives to design and analysis and online research methods. Weiss's goal in founding Market Perceptions was to build a research firm that allowed clients to become closer to their research and "experience their data" rather than be subjected to it.

Robert Witeck

CEO, Witeck-Combs Communications, Washington, D.C.

Bob Witeck is cofounder with Wesley Combs of Witeck-Combs Communications. A premier marketing communication and public relations consultancy that represents Fortune 500 companies, Witeck-Combs serves the multibillion-dollar GLBT market. Recognized by *American Demographics* magazine as among the top 25 individuals who have made a big difference in consumer niche marketing, Witeck and Combs have appeared in many worldwide media outlets, such as *Fortune, CNBC, CNN, Reuters*, and *Ad Age*, to name a few. Witeck and Combs are coauthors of *Business Inside Out*.

Charles E. Young

Founder and CEO, Ameritest, Albuquerque, New Mexico

Ameritest is an international advertising and brand research company. A graduate of the University of Chicago, Young began his advertising career working as a new product consultant for Leo Burnett and later as a research partner for Euro/Tatham in Chicago. In his 20 years in the business Young has worked extensively in packaged goods, retail, fast-food, entertainment, automotive, telecommunications, and e-commerce categories. He is the inventor of the Ameritest Picture Sorts™ techniques and has published numerous articles in the *Journal of Advertising Research* and other professional journals. He is also author of *The Advertising Research Handbook*. Ameritest is a six-time winner of the David Ogilvy research award, including a Grand Ogilvy award for its work with IBM.

Ad Grad Stars

This eighth edition showcases the contributions of professionals who have graduated from advertising and marketing programs around the country. Most of these pros were nominated by their professors to be featured in this textbook. Their thoughts and experiences are recounted in the Inside Story boxes and their work is noted with the Showcase designation. Their viewpoints and experiences also appear in the Matter of Practice boxes, and some even contributed award-winning work that is featured in the chapter opening stories.

Cheri Anderson

Principal Consultant, SRI Consulting, Menlo Park, California

Before joining SRI Consulting's Values and Lifestyles Program, Cheri Anderson was a strategic planner at DDB Worldwide. She earned her doctorate in mass communication and consumer behavior from the University of Minnesota.

Masura Ariga

Group Account Director, Dentsu Inc., Tokyo

Masura Ariga graduated with a B.A. in Political Science from Waseda University in Tokyo in 1985 and joined Dentsu, one of the largest international marketing communication agencies in the world, upon graduation. In 1992, he was in the first graduating class from the new IMC Master's program at Northwestern University.

Heather Beck

Senior Media Planner, Melamed-Riley Advertising, Cleveland, Ohio

A graduate of the advertising program at Middle Tennessee State, Heather Beck began as a Media Coordinator in 2001 at Stern Advertising before joining Melamed-Riley Advertising.

Jeremy Boland

Art Director and Photographer, Borders Perrin Norrander, Portland, Oregon

A 2003 graduate of the advertising program at the University of Colorado, Jeremy Boland is an award-winning art director at Borders Perrin Norrander.

John Brewer

President & CEO, Billings Chamber of Commerce/CVB, Billings Montana

John Brewer graduated from the University of West Florida in 1992 with a B.A. in Communication Arts. For more than 12 years he has been leading community development organizations like the Billings Chamber of Commerce and the Spokane Regional Convention & Visitors Bureau.

Amanda Correa

Brand Manager, The Richards Group, Dallas, Texas

Amanda Correa graduated in 1999 from the University of North Texas with a B.A. in Journalism and a minor in Marketing. As a brand manager at The Richards Group, she's helped build brands such as Chick-fil-A, Thomasville, NatureSweet Tomatoes, and Kiwi Shoe Polish.

Andy Dao

Copywriter, Leo Burnett, Chicago

Andy Dao graduated from the University of Colorado-Boulder in 2002 with a degree in Advertising. As an art director with Leo Burnett, his work earned him industry recognition as one of the 2005 Young Guns Top 20 Creatives.

Mike Dattolico

Musion Creative, LLC, Gainesville, Florida

Owner of his own design studio, Musion Creative (http://www.musioncreative.com), Michael Dattolico graduated from the University of Florida with degrees in Advertising and English Literature. After studying and working in London, he moved back to Florida to start his own design studio in Gainesville.

Tammie DeGrasse

Account Supervisor, McCann-Erickson, New York

Tammie DeGrasse graduated magna cum laude from Florida State University in the spring of 2000. She then began her career at McCann-Erickson as an assistant account executive, working on two multimillion-dollar accounts (Gateway and Burger King), was promoted to account executive after a little more than a year on the job, and is now an account supervisor.

Kristin Dehnert

Writer/Director, Los Angeles

Kristin Dehnert and her producer Leann Emmert got nationwide attention in 2007 when their commercial, "Checkout Girl," was a finalist in the Doritos Super Bowl competition. Prior to making her leap into writing and directing, Dehnert worked as a location manager and scout on feature films.. A native of Chicago, she is a graduate of the University of Illinois at Urbana-Champaign with a B.A. in Speech Communications.

Sunita Deshpande

Copywriter, Berlin, Cameron, New York

Sunita Deshpande is a graduate of the University of Florida and the Miami Ad School. She also earned a master's degree from Florida International University. Now a copywriter at Berlin, Cameron, Deshpande interned at Mad Dogs and Englishmen, Saatchi & Saatchi, Hallmark Cards, and Time Warner.

Adam Dyer

Account Services, Cactus Marketing Communications, Denver, Colorado

After graduating from the University of Colorado School of Journalism and Mass Communication, Adam Dyer moved to Japan to teach English before landing a job at Cactus Marketing Communications, where he works in Account Services on a variety of social marketing, nonprofit, business-to-business, and consumer accounts.

Leann Emmert

Producer, Los Angeles

Leann Emmert attended the University of Colorado, graduating with a B.A. in International Affairs. Realizing her true passion was film, she began her career as a location scout and has worked on some of the biggest features in Hollywood. Emmert teamed up with Kristin Dehnert to produce a series of commercials that won silver and gold at the International Summit Commercial Awards. When Doritos announced its "Crash the Super Bowl" challenge, Emmert and Dehnert entered "Checkout Girl," which was chosen as a Top 5

finalist out of more than 1,000 submissions and aired during Super Bowl XLI.

Amy Hume

Strategic Media Consultant, Denver, Colorado

Amy Hume graduated from the Advertising program at the University of Colorado. She worked as an associate media director at Starcom Worldwide before becoming media director at Barnhart Communications in Denver and then becoming a media consultant.

Chris Hutchinson

Art Director, Wieden + Kennedy, Portland, Oregon

Chris Hutchinson started as an art director at Bulldog-Drummond in San Diego after graduating from the University of Oregon's advertising program and then moved back to Oregon to work at Wieden + Kennedy.

Melissa Lerner

Business Director, Kinetic Worldwide, New York

Melissa Lerner was formerly an Account Director at WOW, a division of Kinetic Worldwide, until 2007 when she moved to Kinetic as Business Director. WOW handles the out-of-home planning and buying for MindShare clients, including American Express, Unilever, IBM, Sears, Sprint, and Estée Lauder. While at WOW, she received the President's Award and was part of the team that received a Gold Award from OAAA (Outdoor Advertising Agency of America) and Media Plan of the Year.. She earned a B.S. in Business and Economics from Lehigh University.

Ingvi Logason

Principal, HÉR&NÚ, Reykjavik, Iceland

A principal in his own firm, HÉR&NÚ Marketing Communications, Ingvi Logason is a graduate of Western Florida University.

Lara Mann

Copywriter, DraftFCB, Chicago

Lara Mann, a graduate of the University of Florida, works for DraftFCB in Chicago. Prior to this position, she was a copywriter at FHB Advertising in Orlando, Florida.

Harley Manning

Research Director, Customer Experience, Forrester Research, Cambridge, Massachusetts

Harley Manning's work focuses on interactive media, customer experience, and Web site design and development. Manning came to Forrester after 18 years of designing and building interactive services for Dow Jones, AT&T, MCI, Prodigy, and Sears. He received an M.S. in Advertising from the University of Illinois at Urbana-Champaign.

Matt Miller

Art Director, Leo Burnett, Chicago

Matt Miller began working at Leo Burnett in 2004 after graduating from the University of Colorado. An award-winning art director, he has received honors from the One Show, Cannes, Clios, Andy Awards, Kelly Awards, and the Young Guns Top 20 Creatives.

Sonia Montes

Account Executive, New Business Director/Sr. Project Manager at Catmandu Branded Entertainment, Chicago

Sonia Montes graduated from Michigan State University in 2000 with a B.A. in Advertising. While at MSU, she was named one of the 25 Most Promising Minority Students in Communications by *Advertising Age*. She began her career FCB Chicago and has worked on such brands as S.C. Johnson and Kraft. She is a senior account executive at Leo Burnett/Lapiz.

David Rittenhouse

Senior Partner and Planning Director, neo@Ogilvy, New York

David Rittenhouse has worked in the Internet media and marketing space for more than eight years across a variety of technology, telecommunications, and consumer electronics businesses. Prior to joining Ogilvy's digital media specialist group, he worked at MindShare Digital in London. Rittenhouse holds a bachelor's degree in Art History from the University of California, Santa Barbara, and a master's degree in Mass Communication from the University of Colorado at Boulder.

Holly Duncan Rockwood

Director of Corporate Communications, Electronic Art, San Francisco (formerly Senior Director of Field Communications, Old Navy)

A native of San Francisco, Holly Rockwood earned her B.S. in Advertising from the University of Colorado in 1993 and received her M.S. in Integrated Marketing Communications from Northwestern University in 1998. Her career in communications has included tourism, technology, financial services, and retail. She is an occasional special correspondent for the *San Francisco Chronicle*.

Karl Schroeder

Copywriter, Coates Kokes, Portland, Oregon

Karl Schroeder, copywriter at Coates Kokes, is a graduate of the University of Oregon advertising program.

Peter Stasiowski

Art Director, Gargan Communication, Dalton, Massachusetts

A Massachusetts native, Peter Stasiowski graduated from the University of West Florida with a B.A. in Communication Arts and an emphasis in Advertising and Public Relations. He is an art director at Gargan Communication, a marketing and advertising agency.

Aaron Stern

Freelance Copywriter, New York

Aaron Stern grew up in Denver, Colorado, and attended the University of Colorado with an emphasis in Advertising. He began his career in San Francisco, where he worked at leading national advertising agencies such as Goodby, Silverstein and Partners, Black Rocket, and Venables, Bell and Partners. He is now in New York getting his M.F.A. in Writing from New York University, while working as a freelance copywriter.

Mark Thomson

President, Thomson Productions, Inc., Des Moines, Iowa

A graduate of University of West Florida with a degree in general business, Thomson also took advertising and other journalism and communication classes as an unofficial minor. President of his own company, Thomson Productions, he travels throughout the United States, Europe, and Asia producing shows for audiences of 400 to 4,000.

Carson Wagner

Assistant Professor, Ohio University, Athens, Ohio

Carson B. Wagner earned his Ph.D. from the University of Colorado at Boulder in 2002, and his master's from Penn State in 1998. He grew up with and has worked in his father's ad agency, Orrico & Wagner, and served with Bill Clinton's advance team in the 1992 presidential primaries. He is now an Assistant Professor of Advertising at Ohio University, where his research continues to receive honors and grants.

Jennifer Wolfe

Marketing Manager, Vail Resorts, Vail, Colorado

Jennifer Wolfe earned her B.A. in Public Relations from the University of Alabama and her M.A. in Integrated Marketing Communications from the University of Colorado in Boulder. She started her marketing career on the agency side, working with start-ups and small businesses to develop marketing strategy. She also owned her own consultancy before joining Vail Resorts to manage the company's direct marketing and loyalty programs.

Contributors: Profs and Pros

A talented and respected group of professors and professionals contributed their ideas and their work to this eighth edition of *Advertising: Principles and Practice*. You'll find their contributions throughout the chapters in the Part Openers and in the Matter of Practice, Matter of Principle, and Practical Tips boxes.

Edd Applegate

Professor, School of Journalism, Middle Tennessee State University, Murfreesboro

Prof. Applegate has written and/or edited a number of books, including *Personalities and Products: A Historical Perspective on Advertising in America*, *The Ad Men and Women: A Biographical Dictionary of Advertising*, and *Strategic Copywriting: How to Create Effective Advertising*. He also coauthored *Cases in Advertising and Marketing Management: Real Situations for Tomorrow's Managers*. He has contributed some 50 entries and/or chapters to other books and has written more than 20 refereed articles. As a consultant, he has provided marketing and advertising help to business publications and to some 25 organizations.

Bill Barre

Assistant Professor of Advertising, School of Journalism and Mass Communication, Kent State University, Kent, Ohio

Prof. Barre teaches Advertising Copywriting, Account Planning, and Account Management. He recently finished a film about the Uncola campaign, entitled "7-UP: The Uncola Story," (http://www.insight-media.com). Barre became a professor after a 30-year career in advertising during which time he was a creative director and a writer at agencies such as J. Walter Thompson/Chicago and Foote, Cone & Belding/Chicago. Barre's work has won several prestigious awards, including a Clio, Communications Arts' Merit of Excellence, and an Effie. In addition, his work has been featured in *Time* magazine and in several national newspapers and television programs.

Fred Beard

Professor, Gaylord College of Journalism and Mass Communication, University of Oklahoma, Norman

Prof. Beard has published and presented nearly 80 articles and research papers on advertising humor, client-advertising agency relationships, and other topics. He is also the author of the forthcoming book, *Humor in the Advertising Business: Theory, Practice, and Wit* (Rowman & Littlefield Publishers, Inc.).

Margo Berman

Associate Professor, Florida International University, Miami

Prof. Berman teaches advertising and entrepreneurship at Florida International University. An award-winning creative director, she invented tactikPAK®, a patented system of learning, created Mental Peanut Butter® Training, and developed three advertising CDs, plus an inspirational DVD. Another DVD and two 6-CD webinar sets are based on principles from book *Street-Smart Advertising: How to Win the Battle of the Buzz*. Her second book examines the relationship between copywriters and art directors.

Sheri Broyles

Associate Professor, University of North Texas, Denton

Prof. Broyles is head of the advertising sequence at the University of North Texas. Her professional background includes work in advertising, PR, and marketing for a symphony orchestra and as a copywriter and account executive for a Dallas advertising agency. Her research interests focus on different aspects of creativity—from portfolios to those who work in creative departments—and has been published in the *Journal of Consumer Affairs*, *Journal of Consumer Marketing*, *Southwestern Mass Communication Journal*, *Journalism & Mass Communication Educator*, and *Journal of Advertising Education*.

Clarke L. Caywood

Professor and Director of the Graduate Program in Public Relations, Medill Graduate School, Northwestern University, Evanston, Illinois

Prof. Caywood teaches crisis management, communication management, marketing, and public relations. He has published numerous articles and chapters on advertising, marketing, integrated marketing communication, and values in contemporary advertising. Caywood is a leader in the use of databases for media tracking for public relations and marketing. He is editor of the *Handbook of Strategic Public Relations & Integrated Communications*. Caywood was named by *PRWeek* as one of the most influential 100 PR people of the 20th century and one of the top 10 outstanding educators. He also was named Educator of the Year by the Public Relations Society of America.

Linda Conway Correll

Assistant Professor, Southern Illinois University, Carbondale

Creative Director/Copywriter Linda Conway Correll is a veteran of New York, Texas, and New England advertising agencies. She has received more than 50 regional, national, and international awards for her work, including Clio, Addy, Summit, Telly, Creativity, and New York International Festivals Awards. Since 1991, when she entered academe, her students in the United States and India have won more than 150 advertising awards using Creative Aerobics, the ideation system she designed and has presented at professional and academic conferences on four continents. Her book, *Brainstorming Reinvented*, is on library shelves around the world, including the Library of Congress, Washington, D.C.

Shawn M. Couzens

VP, Creative Director, Grey Worldwide, New York

After graduating from Pennsylvania State University, Couzens honed his craft as a copywriter at various Philadelphia agencies before heading to New York's Grey Worldwide. Since then, he has created award-winning campaigns for a variety of clients, including Crown Royal Whisky, Pringles Potato Crisps, and Don Julio Tequila. After winning the Frontier Airlines account in 2003 with the "Talking Animals" campaign, Couzens—along with creative partner Gary Ennis—has created some of the most memorable and effective airline advertising ever. The work has won more than 75 creative awards and distinctions, including New York Festival World Medals, Addys, Clios, Effies, LIAAs, and Mobius Awards.

Marieke de Mooij

Ph.D. Consultant, Cross Cultural Communications, The Netherlands

A pioneer in the intersection of culture and marketing, Prof. Marieke de Mooij is president of her own consultancy, Cross Cultural Communications Company. She is also Associate Professor at the University of Navarre in Spain and has been a visiting professor at various universities in The Netherlands, Finland, and Germany. She has been involved in international advertising education since 1980 both for the International Advertising Association (IAA) and as Managing Director of the BBDO College. De Mooij is the author of several books on the influence of culture on marketing and advertising, including *Global Marketing and Advertising, Understanding Cultural Paradoxes, Consumer Behavior and Culture*, and *Consequences for Global Marketing and Advertising*.

Bonnie Drewniany

Associate Professor, University of South Carolina, Columbia

Prof. Bonnie Drewniany teaches Creative Strategy in Advertising and a seminar course on Super Bowl commercials. She makes frequent presentations on the effectiveness of Super Bowl commercials at academic and professional meetings and conducts an annual Super Bowl ad poll. She is the coauthor of *Creative Strategy in Advertising*.

Lisa Duke

Associate Professor, University of Florida, Gainesville

Prof. Duke's experience as a copywriter/creative supervisor at Long Haymes Carr/Lintas led to industry awards, including Addys, the New York Art Director's Club, the International Film and Television Festival, and *Advertising Age's* best commercials of the year. The American Association of University Women recognized her research on communication's impact on children and young women. She also studies the role of creativity in advertising. Her research has been published in the *Journalism and Mass Communication Quarterly, Journal of Advertising, Psychology and Marketing, Journal of Communication Inquiry*, and *The Annals of the American Academy of Political and Social Science*. Duke also was recognized as Teacher of the Year at University of Florida.

Tom Duncan

Professor Emeritus, IMC Founder and Director, University of Colorado, and Daniels College of Business, University of Denver, Boulder, Colorado

Founder of the Integrated Marketing Communication (IMC) graduate program at the University of Colorado, Prof. Duncan moved to the Daniels College of Business at the University of Denver in 2003, where he directed the first MBA/IMC program in the United States. In 2006 he was a visiting professor at Dartmouth's Tuck School of Business. Before becoming a college professor, Duncan spent 15 years in industry, working on both the agency and client sides. He began at Leo Burnett in account management and research. On the client side he was Manager of Marketing Services for Peter Eckrich & Sons and Vice President of Marketing for Jeno's, Inc.

Gary Ennis

Vice President and Creative Director, Grey Worldwide, New York

His work on brands like Miller Beer, Stroh's beer, Gillette, Pepsi, Coke, Crown Royal, and Frontier Airlines has won Ennis some of the industry's most prestigious awards: Cannes Lions, Clio Gold, Art Directors Club Gold, Andy Awards, Effies, Communications Arts, London International, and The One Show. His work is also in the Clio Hall of Fame. Ennis's work on Frontier Airlines "Talking Animals" campaign, which he won for his agency with his creative partner Shawn Couzens, has won numerous awards. He likes to produce 360° campaigns that merge traditional and alternative media, including audio and video podcasts, blogs, and underground Web sites.

Pat Fallon

Cofounder and Chair, Fallon Worldwide, Minneapolis, Minnesota

Pat Fallon is cofounder and chairman of Fallon Worldwide, a subsidiary of the French-based Publicis Groups, one of the world's largest advertising and media conglomerates. He spends his time nurturing the company's culture, managing and evolving the global vision across four continents, and working on clients' businesses from the frontlines. Fallon's deep knowledge of branding issues, combined with a strong strategic approach to marketing problems of all kinds and his relentless need to achieve, make him particularly valuable to clients' CEOs. He has won virtually every recognition in the business during his career and still spends 80 percent of his time on client work. In 2006, to mark the agency's 25th anniversary, Fallon and Cofounder Fred Senn coauthored *Juicing the Orange: How to Turn Creativity into a Powerful Business Advantage*.

Jami Fullerton

Associate Professor of Advertising, Oklahoma State University, Stillwater

Prior to teaching, Prof. Fullerton worked in the advertising industry in Dallas. She teaches undergraduate advertising and graduate level mass communication courses, including Mass Communication Theory and Research Methods. Named outstanding researcher in her college, Fullerton's research focuses on portrayal of gender in advertising, cross-cultural communication, international and ethnic advertising, and advertising education. She frequently teaches abroad and conducts State Department sponsored research on cross-cultural communication and media globalization. The Association for Women in Communication named her Headliner Award winner for her book *Advertising's War on Terrorism*, which she cowrote with Prof. Alice Kendrick.

Tom Groth

Professor and Head of Advertising, Department of Creative Arts, University of West Florida, Pensacola

Before moving into teaching, Prof. Groth worked on the creative side for BBDO. He's known for his students' performance in the NSAC competition where his teams have won nationals a record four times. He has received six Distinguished Teaching Awards. An active creative consultant, he has won several dozen professional awards, including Addys, Gold and Silver Quills from the International Association of Business Communicators, and a Silver Anvil from the Public Relations Society of America. A professional artist, he also has won dozens of fine art honors, and his work is regularly exhibited in galleries and museums (Art Web site: http://www.absolutearts.com/portfolios/t/tgroth/).

Jean Grow

Associate Professor, Marquette University, Milwaukee, Wisconsin

Prof. Grow's scholarly work focuses on controversial advertising case studies. She has published extensively on Nike women's advertising and DTC advertising of pharmaceuticals. Her current research explores the lack of women in advertising creative departments. In 2006 Grow coauthored a book on creative strategy, *Advertising Strategy: Creative Tactics from the Outside/In*. Prior to joining the academy, she worked in the advertising industry with agencies such as Leo Burnett, DDB Needham, Foote Cone & Belding, and J. Walter Thompson. Grow continues her industry affiliation, providing strategic consulting through her company Grow Creative Resources.

Thomas Harris

Public Relations Consultant and Author, Cofounder of Golin/Harris Communications, Highland Park, Illinois

Thomas Harris is past president of Golin/Harris Communications, one of the largest public relations firms in the world, and before that he was president of Foote Cone & Belding Public Relations and an executive vice president at Edelman Public Relations Worldwide. He is now a management consultant specializing in marketing and public relations and adjunct professor in the IMC program at Northwestern University. A frequent writer and editor on public relations topics, Harris is author of *The Marketer's Guide to Public Relations* and *Value-Added Public Relations*.

Edgar Huang

Associate Professor, New Media Program, Indiana University-Purdue University, Indianapolis

Prof. Huang teaches streaming media technology, video production and editing, advanced Web design, and new media research courses. His articles about rich media enrichment, media convergence, online journalism, documentary photography, digital imaging, and the Internet and national development are seen in *Convergence, Journalism and Communication Monographs, Visual Communication Quarterly, Information Technology for Development*, among others.

Donald Jugenheimer

Professor and Chair of the Department of Advertising, Texas Tech University, Lubbock

Prof. Jugenheimer has worked as both a copywriter and as a media planner and estimator in advertising agencies and has consulted on major advertising campaigns. He is Executive Director of the American Academy of Advertising, which he previously served as President, and was Advertising Division Chair of the Association for Education in Journalism and Mass Communication. He has also been dean, director, department head, and director of graduate studies and research at various major universities. Jugenheimer is the author or coauthor of 14 books about advertising.

Adam Kaplan

Adam Kaplan Creative, Trumbull, Connecticut

Adam Kaplan provides branding and creative solutions through his Connecticut-based agency. A brand-focused creative director with experience as both a copywriter and art director, Kaplan has worked with advertising, direct marketing, and promotion agencies, as well as on the client side with Time Warner. He received a B.F.A. from Syracuse University in Advertising Design.

Alice Kendrick

Professor of Advertising, Southern Methodist University, Dallas, Texas

Prof. Kendrick's research in account planning, advertising content and effects, and advertising education has appeared in *Journal of Advertising Research, Journal of Services Marketing, Journalism & Mass Communication Quarterly*, and *Southwest Mass Communication Review*. Her research and commentary have also been featured and cited in many trade and popular publications. She has received seven teaching awards at the national, regional, and university levels and was awarded the Carl Rosenfeld Education Prize for her research and writing on the effectiveness of promotional products. Kendrick's analysis of public reaction to commercials during broadcast coverage of the Gulf War appears in *Desert Storm and the Mass Media*, and she is coauthor with Prof. Jami Fullerton of *Advertising's War on Terrorism*.

Peggy J. Kreshel

Associate Professor, Department of Advertising, University of Georgia, Athens

Prof. Kreshel's primary teaching and research areas are advertising and society; race, gender, and media; and

feminist media studies. She is an active member of the UGA teaching academy and received the Richard B. Russell Outstanding Undergraduate Teaching Award in 1992.

Hairong Li

Associate Professor, Department of Advertising, Public Relations, and Retailing, Michigan State University, East Lansing

Prof. Li is editor of the *Journal of Interactive Advertising*. His research focuses on emerging issues of marketing communications, especially in interactive marketing and advertising, and his publications have appeared in more than a dozen of academic journals.

Lynda Maddox

Professor of Marketing and Advertising, George Washington University, Washington, D.C.

Prof. Maddox has published in *The Journal of Advertising Research, The Journal of Pharmaceutical Marketing, The Journal of Product and Brand Management, Journalism Quarterly, Business Journal, Current Issues and Research in Advertising*, and *Marketing News*. She has appeared on CNN, CNNfn, *Good Morning America, Fox Morning News*, and *NBC News* and has been quoted in *USA Today, The Christian Science Monitor, Investor's Business Daily, The Washington Post*, and other state and local publications. Maddox also serves as a consultant to many domestic and international clients and is on the board of DigitalBiz Corporation.

Karen Mallia

Assistant Professor, University of South Carolina, Columbia

Prof. Mallia is a former copywriter and creative director now teaching creative strategy, copywriting, and advertising campaigns. Prior to moving to South Carolina, she taught advertising at The City College of New York and at FIT/SUNY. Her New York ad agency career spanned two decades and numerous agencies, from Ogilvy to Scali, McCabe, Sloves to TBWA\Chiat\Day and other smaller shops. Mallia has worked on creative projects ranging from cars to cosmetics, fiberglass to fragrance to financial service. She continues strategic and creative consulting through Mallia Bakaj & Associates.

James M. Maskulka

Associate Professor of Marketing, College of Business, Lehigh University, Bethlehem, Pennsylvania

Prof. Maskulka's teaching interests include global marketing, European marketing, advertising management, and student career advantages derived from study-abroad experiences. His research interests include media performance, marketing communication strategy, and branding strategy. His consulting interests include marketing management, brand management, and marketing communications with an emphasis on effectiveness research.

Cornelia (Connie) Pechmann

Professor of Marketing, University of California, Irvine

Prof. Pechmann's research focuses on the effects of controversial forms of advertising on consumers. She has received $1.5 million in grants to study the effects of pro- and antismoking media messages on adolescents. She has published more than 50 refereed articles, chapters, and proceedings in publications such as *Journal of Consumer Research, Journal of Marketing, Journal of Marketing Research*, and *American Journal of Public Health*. Her work has been cited in the *Wall Street Journal* and other major newspapers. She has served as a consultant to the U.S. Office of National Drug Control Policy's youth antidrug media campaign.

Marilyn Roberts

Associate Professor, College of Journalism and Communications, University of Florida, Gainesville, Florida

Prof. Roberts studies political advertising and communication, as well as international and cross-cultural communication. She has written a number of book chapters on these topics. Her research has focused on political campaigns in the battleground states of Texas, Ohio, and Florida. She served as a media consultant to a U.S. Congressman. Her research has appeared *Political Communication, Journalism Quarterly, Communication Research, Mass Communication Review, Interactive Advertising*, and the *Harvard International Journal of Press and Politics*. Roberts has been an officer of the American Academy of Advertising and the Advertising Division of the Association for Education in Journalism and Mass Communication.

Herbert Jack Rotfeld

Professor of Marketing, Auburn University, Auburn, Alabama

Author of *Adventures in Misplaced Marketing*, Prof. Rotfeld's research has been noted for studies of the conventional wisdom about business theory and practice that assess the validity of perspectives that are frequently repeated without question in textbooks. A scholar of advertising regulation and self-regulation, he was the recipient of the American Academy of Advertising's Outstanding Contribution to Research Award and the Kim Rotzoll Award for Advertising Ethics and Social Responsibility. Rotfeld is currently the editor of *Journal of Consumer Affairs* and was twice honored by the American Academy of Advertising. These publications, as well as his essays in newspapers and magazines and on the Internet, have generated a degree of worldwide fame (or, maybe, "infamy"), and he has been invited to lecture on these topics in the United States and abroad.

Prof. Mike Rothschild

Professor Emeritus, School of Business, University of Wisconsin and Consultant/Researcher, Madison, Wisconsin

Prof. Rothschild's research focuses on social marketing—that is, the use of commercial marketing techniques to change behaviors on public health and safety issues. Currently he is principal investigator on *Road Crew*, a project for the Wisconsin Department of Transportation to reduce alcohol impaired driving. He was Eminent Scholar at the Center for Strategic Dissemination, National Cancer Institute in 2003–2005. In addition, Rothschild has worked on social marketing projects related to reducing obesity, reducing binge drinking on college campuses, increasing produce consumption and exercise, and inhibiting the onset of smoking among teenagers.

Sheila Sasser

Professor of Advertising Creativity, IMC, and Marketing, College of Business, Eastern Michigan, University College of Business, Ypsilanti

Prof. Sasser is an internationally recognized and award-winning pioneer in creativity innovation research in advertising and integrated marketing communications. She is also founder and CEO of Sassco International Ltd., a global knowledge creation research IMC consultancy. Her 20 years of advertising senior management experience include work with Interpublic's Lintas, Campbell-Ewald, BBDO, McCann, Y&R, Wunderman, JWT, Saatchi, and Publicis. She has taught and lectured in the United Kingdom, Europe, and Asia Pacific. Widely published in academic and trade journals, Sasser is also editor of the *Journal of Advertising* Special Issue on Creativity Research.

Fred Senn

Founding Partner, Fallon Worldwide, Minneapolis, Minnesota

Senn began his advertising career by managing advertising for First Bank System. Pat Fallon recruited Senn to the agency side at Martin/Williams Advertising and then asked him to be one of the founding partners of Fallon. His current role is less involved with account management and more involved with talent development as Fallon expands both its scope of services and its geographic reach. In this capacity, Senn is the Chief Learning Officer, runs Fallon University, and guest lectures at the University of Minnesota's Carlson School of Management. He coauthored *Juicing the Orange: How to Turn Creativity into a Powerful Business Advantage* with Fallon.

Mary Ann Stutts

McCoy Professor of Business and Professor of Marketing, Texas State University at San Marcos

Prof. Stutts teaches Promotional Strategy and has co-advised American Advertising Federation National Student Advertising Competition teams at Texas State since 1983. During that time, teams under her guidance won two national AAF/NSAC championships and consistently place among the top four teams at the national competition.

John Sweeney

Head of Advertising and Director of Sport Communication Program, Journalism and Mass Communication, University of North Carolina, Chapel Hill

Well known for his advertising teaching, Prof. Sweeney is also Distinguished Professor in Sports Communication. The winner of 10 teaching awards, he has also taught creativity seminars for companies, including IBM, the Martin Agency, and Aetna Insurance. Sweeney's professional experience includes serving as associate creative director at Draft/FCB in Chicago where, in addition to working on more than 40 national brands, he also handled promotional work for brands associated with the Olympics, the National Basketball Association, and the NCAA.

Bob Thacker

Senior Vice President, Marketing and Advertising, OfficeMax, Naperville, Illinois

Thacker is responsible for the OfficeMax brand and all marketing efforts directed to the company's business and consumer customers. Before that, he was vice president of marketing for Target and senior vice president of creative services for Sears. He also worked as CEO and president of BBDO in Minneapolis. Thacker has been twice selected by *Advertising Age* as one of the Top 100 Marketers in the Nation and was elected to the Retail Hall of Fame in 1992. He was also named a 2007 Media Maven by *Advertising Age*.

Wende Zomnir (aka Ms. Decay)

Executive Creative Director and Founding Partner of Urban Decay and Hard Candy Cosmetics, Costa Mesa, California

Zomnir's chief priority is to keep Urban Decay a step ahead as one of the hippest, most aggressive niche players in the burgeoning cosmetic industry. Originally from Texas, Zomnir was raised for a time in Belgium, where she studied French, did some modeling, ran track, and played basketball. Returning to Texas, she finished high school and then earned an advertising degree at the University of North Texas. Her first advertising job was in Chicago at Leo Burnett on its "youth accounts" (Reebok and Nintendo). A move to Southern California took her Gen X/Y/Z marketing skills to promotional programs for Taco Bell. She also met up with Sandy Lerner and found herself mixing nail polish in her Laguna Beach cottage, which is how Urban Decay started.

Reviewers

Many people have been involved in reviewing the previous edition, as well as manuscript for this revision. In addition to the Advisory Board who reviewed many of the chapters, special thanks go to Katrina Olson, a long-time advertising professional who teaches at the University of Illinois and at Parkland College in Champaign, Illinois, and who contributed detailed critiques of many of the chapters. Thanks also to Tom Duncan, professor emeritus from the University of Colorado and the Daniels School of Business at Denver University, who also critiqued various chapters. University of Nebraska students Stephanie Sparks, Gitte Ostermann, Jenny Boldra, and Katie Shanahan also read chapters and critiqued them from a student perspective.

Other reviewers who helped get the revision started include the following:

William Anderson, *University of Scranton*
Edd Applegate, *Middle Tennessee State University*
Carol Arnone, *Frostburg State University*
Susan Bartel, *Central Methodist University*
Kerry Benson, *University of Kansas*
Courtney Bosworth, *Radford University*
James Cho, *Nevada State College*
Doug Cords, *California State University, Fresno*

Catharine Curran-Kelly, *University of Massachusetts, Dartmouth*
Deborah David, *Fashion Institute of Technology*
Barb Finer, *Suffolk University*
Wayne Gawlik, *Joliet Junior College*
Kathleen Gruben, *Georgia Southern University*
John Henry, *St. Clair County Community College*
Thomas Hodges, *Ohio University*
Susan Houston, *Olivet College*
Paul-Michael Klein, *St. Thomas University*
Renee Lee, *Quinnipiac University*
Ann Little, *High Point University*
Lynda Maddox, *George Washington University*
Al Mattison, *Academy of Art University*
Lee McCain, *Seminole Community College*
Stephen McDonald, *Bentley College*
Laurence Minsky, *Columbia College, Chicago*
David Okeowo, *Alabama State University*
Patricia Orman, *Colorado State University, Pueblo*
Carrie Perry, *California State University, Fullerton*
Gary Rawlings, *Chicago State University*
Dana Saewitz, *Temple University*
Lewis Schlossinger, *Community College of Aurora*
Sloane Signal, *Howard University*
Mukhbir Singh, *Weber State University*
Jan Slater, *University of Illinois*
Lewis Small, *York College of Pennsylvania*
Herb Smith, *Wilmington College*
Bill Troy, *University of New Hampshire*
Melvin Unger, *Berkeley College*
Harold Washburn, *Harvard Extension School*
Ludmilla Wells, *Florida Gulf Coast University*
Anne Zahradnik, *College of Saint Elizabeth*

Finally, we need to recognize the work of the very dedicated team put together by Prentice Hall who made this book happen—David Parker, Melissa Sabella, Anne Fahlgren, Melissa Pellerano, Trish Nealon, Keri Miksza, Emily Zarybnisky, Steve Frim, Suzanne DeWorken, Heather Willison, and Karen Bankston.

Advertising
Principles & Practice

A Passion for the Business

The effectiveness of any business depends on how well its advertising works. It must deliver the intended message, connect with customers, and create impact with creative messages that are attention getting and memorable. *Effectiveness is the science and creativity is the art of advertising.*

Part I of this book provides the "big picture" of professional practice. It also introduces a number of key principles that guide the practice of advertising and marketing. One of those principles is that successful professionals have a passion for their business. Here's how Wende Zomnir, the Executive Creative Director at Urban Decay and Hard Candy Cosmetics, explains her principles of business.

A Passion for the Business

Being the creative force behind a brand like Urban Decay makes me responsible for cranking out great ideas. And in the 10+ years I've been doing this, I've figured out a few things about how to generate creative ideas with which people connect. It begins with a passion for the business. Here are my seven principles about how to run a business creatively:

1. ***Feel a passion for your brand.*** Everyone in product development, design, PR, merchandising, sales, and marketing at Urban Decay loves our makeup and deeply connects to our position as the counterculture icon in the realm of luxury makeup.

2. ***Spot emerging trends.*** Our best ideas don't start from analysts telling us what the trends are. My creative team and I talk about what kinds of colors, visual icons, textures, and patterns we are craving and start from there. Our job at Urban Decay is to lead graphically and with our product design and formulation. Recently we launched a volumizing mascara called Big Fatty and played off the connotations in the name, infusing the formula with hemp oil and wrapping the mascara vial in an Age of Aquarius-inspired print. Shortly after the product's release, a supplier to the cosmetic industry came in to show us a version of our own mascara, giving us a presentation on the coming trends. It's annoying, but when this happens, we know we're doing our job.

Wende Zomnir, Executive Creative Director
Urban Decay & Hard Candy Cosmetics

Part 1

3. ***Cultivate your inner voice.*** You also need to develop a gut instinct for what will work. I felt that skulls were going to be huge because everyone in the office was craving them on T-shirts, shoes, key rings, and so forth. We decided to put them on our seasonal holiday compacts in '05. And the same season that Marc Jacobs launched them, so did we. We had distributors begging us to sell them a version without the skull, but we stood firm and wouldn't change it because we knew it was right. And you know what? The same distributors who balked placed the biggest reorders and complained that we didn't get them stock fast enough.

4. ***Check your ego.*** Listening to that inner voice IS something you can cultivate, but you've got to check your ego at the door in order to do it. That can be hard, because being a creative leader means you've probably generated a lot of great ideas that work. So, you've got confidence in your concepts and your ability to deliver, but you have to be able to admit others have great ideas, too.

5. ***Cherry-pick the best ideas.*** Gut instinct is important, BUT—and this is big—even more crucial is being able to listen to all the ideas and sort out the junk. After you sort through everything, then pick the very best concept, even if it's NOT your idea.

6. ***Little ideas are important, too.*** You've got to rally everyone behind your Big Idea, but realize that all those little ideas that prop up the big one are great, too. That's what makes so many of our products work in the marketplace: a big idea supported by little ideas— and the people who develop them.

7. ***Be flexible.*** My final important creative principle is flexibility. Knowing when to be flexible has resulted in some of the best work we've created here. While working on a body powder for summer that was to be impregnated with water for a cooling sensation on the skin, we ran into production problems. We wanted a powder, and I decided to add flavor instead. That edible body powder became a huge subbrand for us, spawning multiple flavors and generating huge amounts of press and revenue. The cooling powder would have been late, had quality control issues, and probably would have lasted a season. Recently, we've been designing a fragrance for Hard Candy. We created beautiful multihued artwork for the bottle but were having trouble getting the colors to register with each other. So we tried running the design in all black, and the overwhelming response was that it worked better!

Chapter 1

Introduction to Advertising

Chapter 2

Advertising's Role in Marketing

Chapter 3

Advertising and Society

Introduction to Advertising

You don't always die from toba

IT'S A WINNER

Award:	Company:	Agency:	Campaign:
Grand Effie	*American Legacy Foundation®*	*Crispin Porter + Bogusky and Arnold Worldwide*	*The truth® Campaign*

The Truth of the Matter

D o you smoke? Do you have friends who smoke? Have you tried it and given up, or have any of your friends? One reason you and your buddies may not be smokers is the long-running, award-winning *truth*® campaign. With some of the most powerful advertising of all time, the campaign has substantially decreased teen smoking.

Nearly 4 million teens in the United States smoke cigarettes. According to the U.S. Department of Health and Human Services, every day more than 4,000 people ages 12–17 try a cigarette for the first time, and 80 percent of all smokers have their first cigarette before they turn 18.

It probably doesn't come as news to you that cigarettes are harmful to your health. More than 400,000 Americans die annually from tobacco-related diseases, making smoking the number-one cause of preventable death in the nation. The alarming number of young smokers, coupled with the fact that so many people eventually die from tobacco-related illnesses, has provided ample motivation for state attorneys general to do something about the problem.

A massive legal action between attorneys general from 46 states, 5 U.S. territories, and the tobacco industry resulted in the 1998 Master Settlement Agreement. One of the outcomes of the agreement was the creation of the American Legacy Foundation®, with the purpose to build a world where young people reject tobacco and anyone can quit. The *truth*® campaign is a great example of using advertising communication to help change the world.

Chapter Key Points

1. What is advertising, and what are its key components?
2. What are the main roles and most common types of advertising?
3. Who are the key players in advertising?
4. How has advertising evolved, and how have these developments affected current advertising practice?

In a society where marketers spend billions trying to persuade teens to buy products, this campaign tries to get them not to buy something. Its goal is to empower teens to rebel against manipulation. The American Legacy Foundation teamed up with ad agencies Crispin Porter + Bogusky, Miami and Boulder, Colorado, and Arnold Worldwide, Boston, to develop informative documentary-style print ads and commercials that inform youth about the dangers of smoking without preaching to them.

The agencies were able to act upon a crucial consumer insight by recognizing that 12- to 17-year-olds continually strive to exercise some measure of control. The ads take advantage of this insight by featuring young actors talking to teens as peer-to-peer communication. The campaign shows teens the truth about the tactics of the tobacco industry and the truth about addiction, health effects, and social consequences of smoking. The message encourages teens to make informed choices about tobacco by giving them facts. The campaign even enlists teens to participate in a summer grassroots tour around the country in an effort to deliver the antismoking message.

The ads and commercials get right to the point, sometimes in stark ways. One ad features a man standing amid body bags. He's holding a poster that states, "Tobacco kills 1,200 people a day." Another ad shows an overhead view of an office building surrounded by body bags. These ads make the viewer visualize the hard-hitting facts that the *truth*® campaign reveals by presenting sobering messages about the effects of smoking without talking down to the audience.

The campaign appeared on media popular with youth, such as the TV networks MTV, FOX, the WB, fuse, Spike, G4, and BET. Print advertisements for the campaign ran in magazines such as *Vibe, CosmoGIRL!,* and *Transworld Skateboarder.* The commercials even ran during several Super Bowls.

On the original Web site, you could find video games, facts about smoking, links to blogs, and photos from the latest tour. According to the American Legacy Foundation, the site averaged 200,000 unique visitors each month. Other efforts include a grassroots tour that gives teens the opportunity to talk with other teens in peer-to-peer settings around the country. More about this campaign can be found on YouTube (*www.youtube.com/*

This ad from the truth® campaign commands viewers' attention with dramatic images and a compelling message about smoking tobacco.

watch?v=S1C0bBySKUw, for example), as well as on *www.socialmarketing.org/success/cs-floridatruth.html*, and *http://adsoftheworld.com/forum/exhibition/truth_anti_smoking*.

The campaign has won more than 300 awards. We'll explain more about the effectiveness of this campaign in the It's a Wrap section at the end of this chapter.

Sources: "Truth Goes to the Movies," American Legacy Foundation (ALF) news release, February 21, 2007; "New Report Finds State-Sponsored Tobacco Prevention Advertisements Help Reduce Smoking," ALF news release, December 16, 2005; "Nothing Is More Important Than the Truth," ALF news release, July 17, 2006; "Truth Youth Smoking Prevention Campaign Associated with Substantial Decrease in Youth Smoking," ALF news release, February 22, 2005 (all press releases available online at *http://www.americanlegacy.org*).

The *truth*® campaign is an example of an award-winning effort that encourages teens to stop smoking or resist the temptation to try smoking. It has been successful because it addresses teens in a style they can relate to and includes messages that make sense. In this chapter we'll define advertising and describe some of its roles, as well as the types of jobs you might find in the advertising industry. We'll conclude by tracing the development of advertising and its most important concepts.

WHAT IS ADVERTISING?

You're probably well aware of advertising. You've seen it all your life in the many thousands of commercials you've watched on television and the ads you've seen on the Internet, in magazines, on billboards, and in many other places. At this point, it may seem a little silly to ask, "What is advertising?"

A smart observer, however, looks at advertising as something more than a sales message that occupies the space in and around news stories, magazine features, and TV programs. In fact, advertising is a complex form of communication that operates with objectives and strategies leading to various types of impact on consumer thoughts, feelings, and actions.

Advertising is a type of **marketing communication,** which is a broad term that refers to all the communication techniques marketers use to reach their customers and deliver their messages. That includes everything from public relations and sales promotion to direct marketing, events and sponsorships, packaging, and personal selling.

Even though we describe advertising as complex, you can also say that, in a way, advertising is very simple. It's about creating a message and sending it to someone in the hope that he or she will react in a certain way. It's a message delivered, in most cases, by media. If the consumers react as the advertiser intended, then the ad is presumed to be effective. In this book, we're interested in great advertising—advertising that has impact—and the principles and practices that make it effective.

Advertising also is about creativity. As Wende Zomnir explains in her essay that opens Part I, it's about generating big, creative ideas with which people connect—ideas that come from having a passion for the brand and the business.

Advertising is a huge industry that has been around for hundreds of years, so inevitably it has gotten more complex and refined. Let's consider how the definition of advertising has changed as the practice of advertising has evolved.

Evolution of the Definition of Advertising

Some people say advertising is simply a way to sell a product—to announce what products are available, who made them, and where you go to buy them. This mercantile definition, with its emphasis on basic commercial communication, is typical of how advertising started. Let's consider the way advertising has evolved and how its focus has changed over the years.

- *Identification.* Advertising in the form of a sign goes back thousands of years. The earliest forms were simple images on walls and stores that have been found in ancient Babylonia, Egypt, Greece, and Rome. Advertising throughout prehistory, through the

P. T. Barnum was a pioneer in advertising and promotion. His flamboyant circus posters were more than just hype; they also announced important news about the event and its performances.

Dark Ages, and into the medieval period was effective communication if it merely identified a place of business and the type of goods available, such as an image of a loaf of bread for the baker or a shoe for the cobbler. The purpose of this kind of advertising was to identify manufacturers and stores.

• *Information.* Advertising changed during the Renaissance when advances in printing technology led to an increase in literacy. Although printing presses had been around for hundreds of years in China, a big advance came to Europe with the invention of movable type by Johannes Gutenberg in 1455. That invention was important because it mechanized printing and made it possible to create multiple copies with ease and speed. This was also the first step in a progression of technological and social changes that resulted in the development of the mass communication media that advertising uses to reach a widespread mass audience. Gutenberg used his new technology to produce Bibles. Others immediately saw the usefulness of printing for other types of pieces, such as handbills, posters, and newspapers.

The word **advertisement** first appeared around 1655, and by 1660 publishers frequently used the word as a heading in newspapers for commercial information. Early newspaper ads in the colonial United States called attention to commercial information of general public interest. In appearance these ads resembled either handbills or what today we call *classified ads.* They announced land for sale, runaways (slaves and servants), transportation (ships arriving, stagecoach schedules), and goods for sale from local merchants. In most cases this commercial news occupied more space in early newspapers than the news stories. Ad announcements continued to dominate newspapers until the 1800s.

• *Promotion.* Technological and social change speeded up in the late 1700s with the Industrial Revolution. This period had a huge impact on business because it brought the efficiency of machinery to the production and distribution of goods. Manufacturers could produce more than their local markets could consume, and they had access to trains and national roads to move their products around the country. However, people needed to know about these goods, so along with mechanization and the opening of the frontier came new communication media, such as magazines and catalogs.

P. T. Barnum and the manufacturers of patent medicines were among the advertising pioneers who made dramatic changes in the field by moving it from information to *hype*—ad language that is characterized by hyperbole or exaggeration. Barnum was full of promotional ideas that generated great amounts of publicity. His circus posters announcing "A Stupendous Mirror of Departed Empires" and "Pageants and Gorgeous Spectacles" are known to this day for their flamboyant graphics and extravagant headlines.

• *Sales.* As advertising people became more professional, they also became more concerned about the science of advertising—about making ads that worked and defining the standards of effective advertising. In the early 20th century, advertising was referred to by advertising legend Albert Lasker as "*salesmanship in print* driven by a *reason why.*" These two highlighted phrases became the model for stating a *claim* and explaining the *support* behind it. The drive to better understand how advertising works—how people come to know about a product, how they feel and think about a brand, and how they develop loyalty to favorite brands—continues to drive professionals, students, and scholars.

Defining the Modern Practice of Advertising

From this brief review of the evolution of advertising, you can see that definitions of advertising have, at various times, focused on identification, information, promotion, and persuasion. All of those aspects remain important to contemporary advertising.

A modern definition of **advertising** includes other important factors, such as media, audience, and goals. Here is our version:

Advertising is a paid form of persuasive communication that uses mass and interactive media to reach broad audiences in order to connect an identified sponsor with buyers (a target audience) and provide information about products (goods, services, and ideas).

This definition of advertising has five basic factors:

1. Advertising is usually *paid* for by the advertiser, although some forms of advertising, such as public service announcements (PSAs), use donated space and time.
2. Not only is the message paid for, but the *sponsor* is identified.
3. Advertising generally reaches *a broad audience* of potential consumers, either as a mass audience or smaller targeted groups.
4. Most advertising seeks *to inform* consumers and make them aware of the product or company. In many cases, it also tries *to persuade* or influence consumers to do something. Persuasion may involve emotional messages as well as information.
5. The message is conveyed through many different kinds of *mass media,* which are largely *nonpersonal.* In other words, advertising isn't directed to a specific person, although this characteristic is changing with the introduction of the Internet and more *interactive* types of media.

In short, modern advertising is strategic communication that aims to accomplish something—to create *impact,* by which we mean a certain consumer response, such as understanding information or persuading someone to do something. To achieve that consumer response, an advertising strategy is driven by *objectives* (statements of the desired consumer response), and these objectives can be *measured* to determine whether the advertising was effective.

Principle

An effective advertisement is one that can be proven to meet its objectives.

The Components of Modern Advertising

In describing the practice of advertising, we refer to four components: strategy, creative idea, creative execution, and media planning and buying (Figure 1.1). Each demands creative thinking from the advertising professionals who are responsible for development and implementation. We'll refer to these dimensions often, and you will soon appreciate them as important factors driving the practice of effective advertising.

These four areas are also the fundamental concepts professionals use to analyze the effectiveness of their advertising efforts. In other words, in order to predict how well the advertising will work, professionals critique the strategy, the creative idea, the creative execution of their advertising ideas, and the way the message is delivered. Let's look at these four concepts in more detail.

- *Advertising strategy.* The logic and planning behind the advertisement, **strategy** is what gives it direction and focus. The advertiser develops the ad to meet specific objectives, carefully directs it to a certain audience, creates a message to speak to that

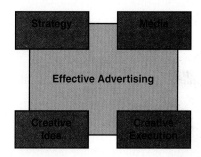

FIGURE 1.1
Four Components of Advertising

SHOWCASE Creativity sometimes comes from an unexpected visual, as in this case of a visual parody on a common package for a soap detergent and a can of soup. Both ads were used to call attention to special promotions by Virgin Megastores. These ads were contributed by Chris Hutchison, a graduate of the advertising program at the University of Oregon and an art director at Wieden + Kennedy in Portland, Oregon.

audience's most important concerns, and runs it in media (print, broadcast, or the Internet, for instance) that will reach this audience most effectively.

- *Creative idea.* The **creative concept** is the ad's central idea that grabs your attention and sticks in your memory. The word *creative* describes a critical aspect that drives the entire field of advertising. Planning the strategy calls for imaginative problem solving: The research efforts need to be creative, and the buying and placing of ads in the media require creative thinking.
- *Creative execution.* Effective ads are also well executed, such as the Virgin Megastore ads demonstrate. That means that the details—the photography, the writing, the acting, the location where the ad is set, the printing, and the way the product is depicted—all reflect the highest production values available to the industry. Advertising often sets the standard or establishes the cutting edge for printing, broadcasting, and Internet design because clients demand the best production their budget allows.
- *Media planning and buying.* Every message has to be delivered somehow. Most advertisers use media that reach a broad audience, such as television, magazines, or the Internet. Deciding how to deliver the message sometimes can be just as creative as coming up with the big idea for the message, a point we'll discuss more in Part III.

Principle
In advertising how you say something and where you say it are just as important as what you say.

Experienced advertisers know that how you say something and where you say it are just as important as what you say. What you say and where you say it come from strategy, whereas how you say it is a product of creativity and execution. Strategy, the creative idea and its execution, and the media used all determine the effectiveness of an advertisement.

ROLES AND TYPES OF ADVERTISING

What does advertising do? Why does it exist? To better understand how advertising works, let's consider the four primary roles advertising plays in business and in society: marketing, communication, economic, and societal.

The Marketing Role

The process a business uses to satisfy consumer needs and wants by providing goods and services is called **marketing.** The marketing department or manager is responsible for selling a company's product, which can be goods (computers, refrigerators, soft drinks), services (restaurant, insurance, real estate), or an idea (support an organization, vote for a candidate). Products are also identified in terms of their **product category.** By category, we mean the classification to which the product is assigned. For example, Levi's is in the jeans category, Harley-Davidson is in the motorcycle category. The particular group of consumers thought to be potential customers for the goods and services constitute the **target market.**

Principle
A product can be services and ideas as well as goods.

    The tools available to marketing managers are the product (design, performance), its price, the place where it is made available (distribution), and its promotion. These are collectively referred to as the **marketing mix** or the **four Ps** (product, price, place/distribution, and promotion), and we will discuss them in more detail in the next chapter. Advertising, of course, is one of the most important promotion tools.

    Marketing professionals are also involved with the development of a **brand,** which is the distinctive identity of a particular product that distinguishes it from its competitors. Colgate, for example, is one brand of toothpaste and Crest is another. They are produced by different companies and compete directly against one another. We'll talk about branding in more detail in Chapter 2.

The Communication Role

Advertising is, first of all, a form of communication. In a sense, it is a message to a consumer about a product. It gets attention, provides information and sometimes a little bit of entertainment, and tries to create some kind of response, such as a sale. The legendary David Ogilvy, founder of the advertising agency that bears his name, Ogilvy & Mather (O&M), explained his view of advertising as conversation:

> I always pretend that I'm sitting beside a woman at a dinner party, and she asks me for advice about which product she should buy. So then I write down what I would say to her. I give her the facts, facts, facts. I try to make it interesting, fascinating, if possible, and personal—I don't write to the crowd. I try to write from one human being to another. . . . And I try not to bore the poor woman to death, and I try to make it as real and personal as possible.[1]

    In reality, however, most advertising is not as personal or as interactive as a conversation because it relies mostly on mass communication, which is indirect and complex. As a form of mass communication, it transmits product information to connect buyers and sellers in the marketplace. In its branding role, it transforms a product by creating an image that goes beyond straightforward facts.

    It is also a form of marketing communication. All of these tools and techniques have different strengths and weaknesses, and they are used to accomplish different objectives. The most important strengths of advertising derive from its ability to reach a large audience, as Table 1.1 illustrates. That's why it is so important in introducing a new product, building awareness, and creating a brand image. It also delivers information that people can use in making product decisions. Advertising is useful for established products where it can remind loyal customers of the satisfying experience they had with the brand. Finally, it is an important way to deliver a persuasive message about a brand and create positive beliefs and feelings about it.

Principle
One of advertising's most important strengths is its ability to reach a large audience.

Table 1.1 The Strengths of Advertising

Strengths	Examples
Can reach a large audience	A commercial in the Super Bowl can reach more than 100 million consumers.
Introduces products and brands	The "1984" commercial for the Apple Macintosh sold out the entire inventory in one day.
Builds awareness of products and brands	The success of the launch of the iPod was due in part to the great silhouette posters that showed people dancing to the music on their iPods.
Creates brand images	The success of the new VW Beetle was largely built on its ability to connect with the antistatus image of the original "lowly" Beetle.
Provides information	The *truth*® campaign informs teens that "Tobacco kills 1,200 people a day."
Reminds and reinforces	Procter & Gamble's Ivory Soap has been advertised continuously since the late 1800s.
Persuades	Nike campaigns, with the "Just do it" personal achievement message, helped increase sales by 300 percent during the 1990s.

The Economic Role

Advertising's economic contributions come from its advantage as a mass-marketing tool. The more people know about a product, the higher the sales—and the higher the level of sales, the cheaper the product. In other words, most economists presume that, because it reaches large groups of potential consumers, advertising brings cost efficiency to marketing and, thus, lower prices to consumers.

Advertising tends to flourish in societies that enjoy some level of economic abundance, in which supply exceeds demand. In these societies, advertising extends beyond a primarily informational role to create a demand for a particular brand. This is done through two techniques: **hard-sell** approaches that use reasons to *persuade* consumers and **soft-sell** approaches that build an *image* for a brand and touch consumers' emotions. An ad trumpeting a special reduced price on a tire or claims about its performance is an example of a hard-sell approach. On the other hand, the long-running Michelin ad campaign that showed a baby sitting inside a tire is a soft-sell; it symbolizes the brand's safety and reliability with an image that touches your emotions.

Two contrasting points of view explain how advertising creates economic impact. In the first, advertising is seen as a vehicle for helping consumers assess value through price cues and other information, such as quality, location, and reputation. Advocates of this school view the role of advertising as a means to objectively provide price/value information, thereby creating more rational economic decisions. By focusing on images and emotional responses, the second approach appeals to consumers making a decision on *nonprice* benefits. This is presumed to be the way images and psychological appeals can be used to influence consumer decisions.[2] This type of advertising is believed to be so persuasive that it decreases the likelihood a consumer will switch to an alternative product, regardless of the price charged.

The Societal Role

Advertising also has a number of social roles. In addition to informing us about new and improved products, it also mirrors fashion and design trends and adds to our aesthetic sense. Advertising has an educational role in that it teaches about new products and their use. It helps us shape an image of ourselves by setting up role models with which we can identify, and it gives us a way to express ourselves in terms of our personalities and sense of style

Retailers sometimes advertise nationally, but much of their advertising is targeted to a specific market, such as this direct-mail piece for T.J. Maxx.

through the things we wear and use. It also presents images capturing the diversity of the world in which we live. There are both negative and positive dimensions to these social roles, which we will discuss in more detail in Chapter 3.

Types of Advertising

Different types of advertising have different roles. Considering all the different advertising situations, we can identify seven major types of advertising.

- *Brand.* The most visible type of advertising is national consumer, or brand, advertising. **Brand advertising,** such as that for the new Volkswagen Beetle, Apple Macintosh, and Polo, focuses on the development of a long-term brand identity and image.
- *Retail or local advertising.* A great deal of advertising focuses on retailers or manufacturers who sell their merchandise in a certain geographical area. In the case of **retail advertising,** the message announces facts about products that are available in local stores. The objectives focus on stimulating store traffic and creating a distinctive image for the retailer. **Local advertising** can refer to a retailer, such as T.J. Maxx, or a manufacturer or distributor who offers products in a fairly restricted geographic area.
- *Direct-response advertising.* **Direct-response advertising** can use any advertising medium, including direct mail, but the message is different from that of national and retail advertising in that it tries to stimulate a sale directly. The consumer can respond by telephone, mail, or over the Internet, and the product is delivered directly to the consumer by mail or some other carrier. The evolution of the Internet as an advertising medium has been particularly important for direct-response advertising.
- *Business-to-business advertising.* **Business-to-business (B2B) advertising** is marketing communication sent from one business to another. It includes messages directed at companies distributing products as well as industrial purchasers and professionals such as lawyers and physicians. B2B is *not* directed at general consumers. Advertisers place most business advertising in professional publications or journals.
- *Institutional advertising.* **Institutional advertising** is also called **corporate advertising.** These messages focus on establishing a corporate identity or winning the public over to the organization's point of view. Many of the tobacco companies are

running ads that focus on the positive things they are now doing, and the ads for America's pharmaceutical companies showcasing leukemia treatment are also adopting that focus.

- *Nonprofit advertising.* Not-for-profit organizations, such as charities, foundations, associations, hospitals, orchestras, museums, and religious institutions use **nonprofit advertising** for customers (hospitals, for example), members (the Sierra Club), and volunteers (Red Cross), as well as for donations and other forms of program participation. The *truth*® campaign for the American Legacy Foundation is an example of nonprofit advertising.
- *Public service advertising.* **Public service advertising** communicates a message on behalf of a good cause, such as stopping drunk driving (as in messages from Mothers Against Drunk Driving) or preventing child abuse. Advertising professionals usually create these advertisements, also called **public service announcements (PSAs),** free of charge, and the media often donate the necessary space and time.

This institutional ad for a pharmaceutical trade association uses a heart-tugging visual and copy to show consumers the value of the organization's activities—producing pharmaceutical drugs that help save lives.

We see, then, that there isn't just one kind of advertising. In fact, advertising is a large and varied industry. But there are some commonalities. All types of advertising demand creative, original messages that are strategically sound and well executed, and all of them are delivered through some form of media. Furthermore, advertisements can be developed as single ads largely unrelated to other ads by the same advertiser or as a **campaign,** which means a set of ads is developed as part of an advertising plan. These related ads are variations on the campaign theme, and they are used in different media at different times for different segments of the audience.

Another commonality is that all the various types of advertising involve a number of people in different roles. Let's close our introduction to advertising with a more in-depth discussion of the key players—and the jobs they do in advertising.

THE KEY PLAYERS

Who is involved in the practice of advertising? As we discuss the organization of the industry, consider that all of these key players also represent job opportunities you might want to consider if you are interested in working in advertising. The players include the advertiser (referred to by the agency as the *client*), the agency, the media, the suppliers, and, of course, the target audience, which is the ultimate focus of all advertising professionals' efforts. The accompanying A Matter of Practice box about the greatest television commercial ever made introduces a number of these key players and illustrates how they all make different contributions to the final advertising.

The Advertiser

Advertising begins with the **advertiser,** the company or organization that uses advertising to send out a message about its business. In the "1984 story," Apple Computer was the advertiser and Steve Jobs, the company's CEO, made the final decision to run the then-controversial commercial. The advertiser is the number-one key player.

Table 1.2 shows the top 10 U.S. advertising categories, followed by the biggest U.S. advertisers by parent company in Table 1.3.[3] As you look at these two tables, notice which categories are increasing and which are decreasing. What do you think is causing those changes?

Principle
All types of advertising demand creative, original messages that are strategically sound and well executed.

A MATTER OF PRACTICE

The Greatest Commercial Ever Made

The advertiser was Apple, the product was its new Macintosh, and the client—the person handling the advertising responsibility and making decisions—was Steve Jobs, Apple's CEO, who wanted a "thunderclap" ad. The agency was California-based Chiat/Day. The medium was the Super Bowl. The "supplier" was legendary British film director Ridley Scott of *Alien* and *Blade Runner* fame. The audience was the 96 million people watching Super Bowl XVIII that winter day in January 1984, and the target audience was all those in the audience who were trying to decide whether to buy a personal computer.

It's a basic principle in advertising: The combination of the right product at the right time in the right place with all the right people involved can create something magical—in this case, Jobs's thunderclap. It also required a cast of 200 and a budget of $900,000 for production and $800,000 for the 60-second time slot. By any measure, it was a big effort.

The storyline was a takeoff on George Orwell's science-fiction novel about the sterile mind-controlled world of *1984*. An audience of mindless, gray-skinned drones (who were actually skinheads from the streets of London) watches a massive screen image of "Big Brother" spouting an ideological diatribe. Then an athletic young woman in bright red shorts runs in, chased by helmeted storm troopers, and throws a sledgehammer at the screen. The destruction of the image is followed by a burst of fresh air blowing over the open-mouthed drones as they "see the light." In the last shot the announcer reads the only words in the commercial as they appear on screen:

> **On January 24th, Apple Computer will introduce Macintosh. And you'll see why 1984 won't be like "1984."**

Was it an easy idea to sell to the client?

First of all, some Apple executives who first saw the commercial were terrified that it wouldn't work because it didn't look like any commercial they had ever seen. After viewing it, several board members put their heads down in their hands. Another said, "Who would like to move on firing Chiat/Day immediately?" Legend has it

that Apple's other founder, Steve Wozniak, took out his checkbook and told Jobs, "I'll pay for half if you pay for the other half." The decision to air the commercial finally came down to Jobs, whose confidence in the Chiat/Day creative team gave him the courage to run the ad.

Was it effective?

On January 24, long lines formed outside computer stores carrying the Macintosh, and the entire inventory sold out in one day. The initial sales goal of 50,000 units was easily surpassed by the 72,000 units sold in the first 100 days. More would have been sold if Apple had been able to keep up with demand.

The 1984 commercial is one of the most talked-about and remembered commercials ever made. Every time someone draws up a list of best commercials, it sits at the top, and it continues to receive accolades more than two decades later. If you haven't seen it, check it out on apple-history.com or *http://s153506479.onlinehome.us/1984.html* and decide for yourself.

Remember, the commercial only ran once—an expensive spot on the year's most-watched television program. The commercial turned the Super Bowl from just another football game into the advertising event of the year. What added to its impact was the hype before and after it ran. People knew about the spot because of press coverage prior to the game, and they were watching for it. Post-coverage of the game was as likely to talk about the 1984 spot as the football score. Advertising became news and watching Super Bowl commercials became an event. That's why *Advertising Age*'s critic Bob Garfield calls it "the greatest TV commercial ever made."

The debate continues about whether the "Big Brother" character was designed to represent IBM. What do you think?

Sources: Kevin Maney, "Apple's '1984' Super Bowl commercial still stands as watershed event," *USA Today*, January 28, 2004, p. 3B; Liane Hansen, host, "Steve Hayden discusses a 1984 Apple ad which aired during the Super Bowl," National Public Radio Weekend Edition, February 1, 2004; Bradley Johnson, "10 Years after '1984': The Commercial and the Product that Changed Advertising," *Advertising Age*, June 1994, p. 1, 12-14; Curt's Media, "The 1984 Apple Commercial: The Making of a Legend," *http://www.isd.net/cmcalone/cine/1984.html.*

Table 1.2   Top Ten U.S. Advertising Categories

Category	Total ad spend in 2006 (millions)	Total ad spend in 2005 (millions)	Percentage change from 2005
Telecommunications	$9,431.1	$8,550.5	10.3%
Auto, nondomestic	8,726.7	8,832.8	−1.2
Local services & amusements	8,687.0	7,879.2	10.3
Financial services	8,681.8	8,508.8	2.0
Miscellaneous retail*	8,322.9	8,258.0	0.8
Auto, domestic	7,615.2	8,625.1	−11.7
Direct response	6,376.1	6,087.0	4.7
Personal care	5,717.2	5,654.1	1.1
Travel & tourism	5,406.4	5,486.1	−1.5
Pharmaceuticals	5,285.4	4,645.8	13.8

Source: TNS Media Intelligence, 2006.

Note: Figures do not include free-standing (newspaper) inserts (FSI) or PSA activity.

*Miscellaneous retail does not include these retail segments: department stores, food stores, home furnishing stores, and appliance stores.

Table 1.3   Top Ten U.S. Advertisers

Company	Total ad spend in 2006 (millions)	Total ad spend in 2005 (millions)	Percentage change from 2005
Procter & Gamble	$3,338.7	$3,230.9	3.3%
General Motors	2,294.8	3,008.0	−23.7
AT&T	2,203.8	1,684.7	30.8
Verizon Communications	1,944.2	1,761.6	10.4
Time Warner	1,824.6	2,073.5	−12.0
Ford Motor Company	1,699.5	1,567.0	8.5
Walt Disney	1,430.4	1,418.3	0.9
DaimlerChrysler	1,421.4	1,591.5	−10.7
Johnson & Johnson	1,302.8	1,623.4	−19.8
News Corp	1,266.8	1,298.5	−2.4

Source: TNS Media Intelligence, 2006.

Note: Figures do not include FSI, house ads, or PSA activity.

The advertiser initiates the advertising effort by identifying a marketing problem advertising can solve. For example, Apple executives knew that the Macintosh easy-to-use computer platform needed to be explained and that information about the launch of the new computer would need to reach a large population of potential computer buyers. Advertising was essential to the success of this new product.

The advertiser also makes the final decisions about the target audience and the size of the advertising budget. This person or organization approves the advertising plan, which contains details outlining the message and media strategies.

Finally, the advertiser hires the advertising agency—in other words, the advertiser becomes the agency's client. As the client, the advertiser is responsible for monitoring the work and paying the bills for the agency's work on its account. That use of the word *account*

THE INSIDE STORY

Why Do I Love Advertising?

Sonia Montes, *New Business Director & Senior Project Manager, Catmandu Branded Entertainment*

I always knew I wanted to be in the ad business. As a child I filmed "commercials" with my parents' video camera. Throughout high school I admired Angela Bower ("Who's the Boss") and thought Amanda Woodward ("Melrose Place") had the best life. In college, I did well in my advertising classes and became heavily involved with the American Advertising Federation (AAF) student chapter. Although by graduation I should have had an inclination of what to expect, I still had a glamorized image of the ad business. No textbook or TV show could have prepared me for what I was about to learn.

"Think Different."

One of the hardest things about being in the advertising business is actually describing to others what I do on a daily basis. Advertising is a dynamic, fast-paced environment, so every day my job is different. There are always new ideas, new creative strategies, and new problems to solve. Analytical, writing, and presentation skills and the ability to reason through problems and think from other people's points of view are necessities. While this is exciting, I always remember that someone else can do it better, which makes me work harder to stay competitive. You need to thrive on stress and challenges to survive advertising.

"Where's the Beef?"

There are no three-hour lunches in the ad business—at least not since I've been in the industry. Most days, I'm lucky if I have a quick lunch at my desk . . . *while* I'm working. Long hours and late nights are practically an industry standard. I try to remind myself that most of my friends experience similar workdays in their business fields.

"It's the Real Thing."

So why do I stay in advertising? Well, I'm lucky. I work in a creative environment with young, passionate, forward-thinking people. It's a challenging field that keeps me on my toes daily. Above all, advertising is fun. I've learned that it's not surprising to be asked to wear a hot pink wig or to see an art director stand on top of a table during client meetings. While my coworkers' hairstyles range from Mohawks to shaved heads, many of us have one thing in common: We are die-hard advertising addicts, constantly blazing our way to a brighter tomorrow with style and good company.

A graduate of the advertising program at Michigan State University, Sonia Montes was nominated by Professor Carrie La Ferle.

is the reason agency people refer to the advertiser as the *account* and the agency person in charge of that advertiser's business as the *account manager.*

Big companies may have hundreds of agencies working for them, although they normally have an **agency-of-record (AOR)** that does most of their business and may even manage the other agencies. Tasks performed by the company's in-house advertising department include the following: select the agencies; coordinate activities with vendors, such as media, production, and photography; make sure the work gets done as scheduled; and determine whether the work has achieved prescribed objectives.

The Advertising Agency

The second player in the advertising world is the **advertising agency** that creates, produces, and distributes the advertising. Advertisers hire independent agencies to plan and implement part or all of their advertising efforts as Chiat/Day did for Apple and Porter + Bogusky and Arnold did for the *truth*® campaign in the opening example.

This working arrangement is known as the *agency–client partnership.* The "1984 story" demonstrates how important it is to cultivate a strong sense of trust between these two partners. An advertiser uses an outside agency because it believes the agency will be more efficient in creating an advertisement or a complete campaign than the advertiser would be on its own. Successful agencies such as Arnold Worldwide typically have strategic and creative expertise, media knowledge, workforce talent, and the ability to negotiate good deals for clients. The advertising professionals working for the agency are experts in their areas of specialization and passionate about advertising as The Inside Story illustrates.

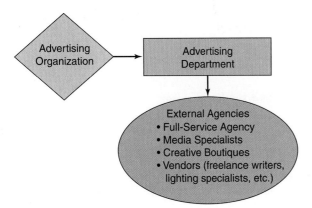

WHEN THE ADVERTISER DOESN'T HAVE AN IN-HOUSE AGENCY

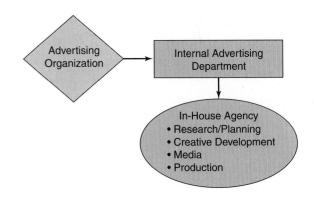

WHEN THE ADVERTISER HAS AN IN-HOUSE AGENCY

FIGURE 1.2
Two Advertising Organization Structures

Not all advertising professionals work in agencies. Large advertisers, either companies or organizations, manage the advertising process either by setting up an advertising department (sometimes called Marketing Services) that oversees the work of agencies or by setting up their own in-house agency, as we see in Figure 1.2.

An **in-house agency** functions similar to a regular agency by producing ads and placing them in the media. Companies that need closer control over their advertising have their own in-house agencies. Large retailers, for example, find that doing their own advertising provides cost savings as well as the ability to meet deadlines. Some fashion companies, such as the Ralph Lauren, also create their own advertising in house to maintain complete control over the brand image and the fashion statement it makes. An in-house agency performs most, and sometimes all, of the functions of an outside advertising agency.

The Media

The third player in the advertising world is the media. The emergence of mass media has been a central factor in the development of advertising because mass media offers a way to reach a widespread audience.

The **media** is composed of the channels of communication that carry the message from the advertiser to the audience. In the case of the Internet, it also carries the response from the audience back to the advertiser. We refer to these media as *vehicles* because they deliver messages, but they are also companies, such as your local newspaper or radio station. Some of these media conglomerates are huge, such as Time Warner and Viacom. Time Warner, for example, is a $40 billion company with some 80,000 employees. It owns America Online, HBO, Time Inc., Turner Broadcasting, Time Warner Cable, Warner Bros. Entertainment, and New Line Cinema. (Note that *media* is plural when it refers to various channels, but singular—*medium*—when it refers to only one form, such as a newspaper.)

Each vehicle (newspaper, radio or TV station, billboard company, etc.) has a department that is responsible for selling ad space or time. Each medium tries to assist advertisers in comparing the effectiveness of various media as they try to make the best choice of media to use. Many media organizations will assist advertisers in the design and production of advertisements. That's particularly true for local advertisers using local media, such as a retailer preparing an advertisement for the local newspaper.

The primary advantage of advertising's use of mass media is that the costs for time in broadcast media, for space in print media, and for time and space in interactive and support media are spread over the tremendous number of people that these media reach. For example, $2 million may sound like a lot of money for one Super Bowl ad, but when you consider that the advertisers are reaching more than 90 million people, the cost is not so

Principle
Mass-media advertising can be cost effective because the costs are spread over the large number of people the ad reaches.

extreme. One of the big advantages of mass-media advertising is that it can reach a lot of people with a single message in a very cost-efficient form.

The Suppliers

The fourth player in the world of advertising is the group of service organizations that assist advertisers, advertising agencies, and the media in creating and placing the ads—the **suppliers,** or **vendors,** who provide specialized services. Members of this group include artists, writers, photographers, directors, producers, printers, as well as self-employed free-lancers and consultants. In the "1984 story," the movie director Ridley Scott was a supplier in that Chiat/Day contracted with him to produce the commercial. The array of suppliers mirrors the variety of tasks required to put together an ad. Other examples include freelance copywriters and graphic artists, photographers, songwriters, printers, market researchers, direct-mail production houses, telemarketers, and public relations consultants.

Why would the other advertising players hire a supplier? There are many reasons. The advertisers may not have expertise in that area, they may be overloaded with work, or they may want a fresh perspective.

Target Audiences

We've been talking about people and roles inside the advertising industry. The fifth and final set of players are the people for whom the advertising is designed. In general, we speak of consumers as people who buy and use products to satisfy their needs and wants. That's a big category. To be more precise we also talk about **target audiences,** a more specific group of people to whom an advertisement is directed and whose responses determine if the advertising is effective.

All advertising strategy starts with identifying the people who are the desired audience for the advertising message. This is called **targeting,** and we'll discuss this concept in more detail in Chapter 5. The character of the target audience has a direct bearing on the overall advertising strategy, especially the creative strategy and the media strategy. The "1984" commercial, for example, targeted people who were in the market for a computer but who weren't computer geeks. In fact, the commercial suggested that the Mac would free regular people from the need to learn the rigid computer systems of competitors, such as IBM.

Purchasers are not always the consumer of the product. In the case of cold cereal, for example, parents may purchase the cereal, but kids consume it and definitely influence the purchase. Kellogg's might actually have two target audiences for a children's cereal and would, therefore, design one ad for the kids' target audience (the influencers) and another for the parents' target audience (the buyers).

Interactive technology has created a new world of targeting, and ads can now be customized to individual consumers to some extent. This customization is growing and will make it even more important to know the target audience and create ads that speak to individual needs. Amazon.com, for example, can greet you when you go to that Web site with a suggestion on a book or CD that might be of interest based on what you have purchased in the past.

THE DEVELOPMENT OF ADVERTISING

Now that we have discussed the roles, types, and players of advertising, let's look at how the principles and practices of advertising developed and then consider where the industry is moving and what trends are currently affecting how it is practiced.

An Advertising Timeline

The advertising industry as it has evolved has been dynamic, as noted in Figure 1.3. In some cases it has *reflected* social trends; in other instances it has *influenced* social trends. This history is far more than names and dates. It's a perspective on how the principles and practices of a multibillion-dollar industry have evolved.[4] The figure divides the evolution of advertising into seven stages, which reflect historical eras and the technological changes that lead to different philosophies and styles of advertising.

- *Stage 1: Age of print.* Ads of these early years look like what we call *classified advertising* today. Their objective was to deliver information. The primary medium of this age was the newspaper, although handbills and posters were also important. Because of the printing press, literacy levels increased, and that encouraged more businesses to advertise.
- *Stage 2: Emergence of consumer society.* By the end of the 19th century advertisers began to give their goods brand names, such as Baker's chocolate and Ivory Soap, and the purpose of advertising during this period was to create demand for these new brands. This period was the beginning of what we now recognize as the advertising industry. The powerhouse agency was Lord & Thomas, which came from the historic

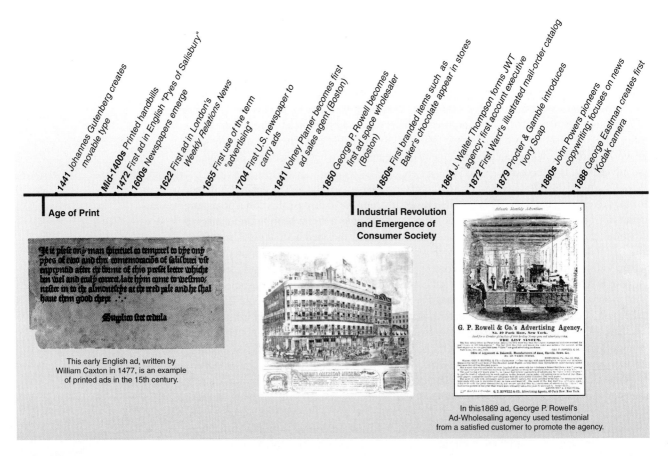

1441 Johannes Gutenberg creates movable type

Mid-1400s Printed handbills

1472 First ad in English "Pyes of Salisbury"

1600s Newspapers emerge

1622 First ad in London's *Weekly Relations News*

1655 First use of the term "advertising"

1704 First U.S. newspaper to carry ads

1841 Volney Palmer becomes first ad sales agent (Boston)

1850 George P. Rowell becomes first ad space wholesaler (Boston)

1850s First branded items such as Baker's chocolate appear in stores

1864 J. Walter Thompson forms JWT agency; first account executive

1872 First Ward's illustrated mail-order catalog

1879 Procter & Gamble introduces Ivory Soap

1880s John Powers pioneers copywriting; focuses on news

1888 George Eastman creates first Kodak camera

Age of Print

Industrial Revolution and Emergence of Consumer Society

This early English ad, written by William Caxton in 1477, is an example of printed ads in the 15th century.

In this 1869 ad, George P. Rowell's Ad-Wholesaling agency used testimonial from a satisfied customer to promote the agency.

FIGURE 1.3
Advertising Timeline

partnership of John E. Kennedy and Albert Lasker. Their mantra—advertising is "salesmanship in print"—became the guiding principle of the industry.

- *Stage 3: Modern advertising era.* In the early 20th century, modern professional advertising adopted scientific research techniques. Advertising experts believed they could improve advertising by blending science and art. Two leaders were Claude Hopkins and John Caples. At the height of Hopkins's career, he was Lord & Thomas's best-known copywriter. Highly analytical, he conducted tests of his copy to refine his advertising methods, an approach explained in his 1923 book, *Scientific Advertising.*

   John Caples, vice president of Batten, Barton, Durstine and Osborn (BBDO), published *Tested Advertising Methods* in 1932. His theories about the pulling power of headlines also were based on extensive tests. Caples was known for changing the style of advertising writing, which had been wordy and full of exaggerations. During the 1930s and 1940s, Daniel Starch, A. C. Nielsen, and George Gallup founded research organizations that are still part of today's advertising industry.

- *Stage 4: Age of agencies.* The agency world and management of advertising developed rapidly after World War I. Consumers were desperate for goods and services, and new products were loading up the marketplace. The J. Walter Thompson (JWT) agency, still flourishing today, led the great boom in advertising during this period. The agency's success was due largely to its innovative copy and the management style of the husband-and-wife team of Stanley and Helen Resor. Stanley developed the concept of *account services;* Helen developed innovative copywriting techniques. The Resors also coined the *brand name* concept as a strategy to associate a unique identity with a particular product as well as the concept of *status appeal* to persuade nonwealthy people to imitate the habits of rich people.

   During and after the Great Depression, Raymond Rubicam emerged as an advertising power and launched his own agency with John Orr Young, a Lord &

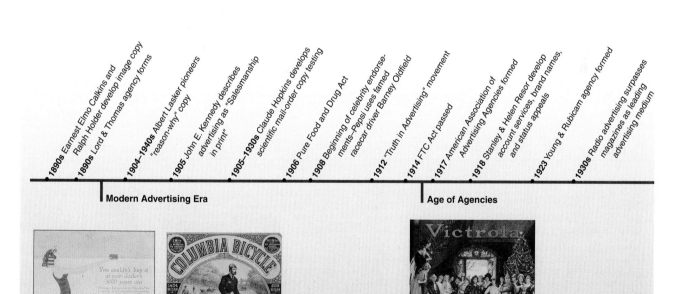

1890s Earnest Elmo Calkins and Ralph Holder develop image copy

1890s Lord & Thomas agency forms

1904–1940s Albert Lasker pioneers "reason-why" copy

1905 John E. Kennedy describes advertising as "Salesmanship in print"

1905–1930s Claude Hopkins develops scientific mail-order copy testing

1906 Pure Food and Drug Act

1908 Beginning of celebrity endorsements—Pepsi uses famed racecar driver Barney Oldfield

1912 "Truth in Advertising" movement

1914 FTC Act passed

1917 American Association of Advertising Agencies formed

1918 Stanley & Helen Resor develop account services, brand names, and status appeals

1923 Young & Rubicam agency formed

1930s Radio advertising surpasses magazines as leading advertising medium

Modern Advertising Era

Age of Agencies

After WW1, "I wanted to be happy" was the call of consumer, and jazz and dancing became popular, as this ad for Victor Talking Machine Co. illustrates.

Thomas copywriter under the name Young and Rubicam. Y&R continues as a leading agency to this day. Their work was known for intriguing headlines and fresh, original approaches to advertising ideas.

• *Stage 5: The creative era.* The creative power of agencies culminated in the 1960s and 1970s in a period marked by the resurgence of art, inspiration, and intuition. Largely in response to the emphasis on research and science, this revolution was inspired by three creative geniuses: Leo Burnett, David Ogilvy, and William Bernbach.

Leo Burnett was the leader of what came to be known as the *Chicago school of advertising.* He believed in finding the "inherent drama" in every product. He also believed in using cultural archetypes to create mythical characters who represented American values, such as the Jolly Green Giant, Tony the Tiger, the Pillsbury Doughboy, and his most famous campaign character, the Marlboro Man.

Ogilvy, founder of the Ogilvy & Mather agency, is a paradox because he represents both the image school of Rubicam and the claim school of Lasker and Hopkins. He created enduring brands with symbols and handled such products as Rolls Royce, Pepperidge Farm, and Guinness.

The Doyle, Dane, and Bernbach (DDB) agency opened in 1949. From the beginning, William Bernbach—with his acute sense of words, design, and creative concepts—was considered to be the most innovative advertising creative person of his time. His advertising touched people by focusing on feelings and emotions. He explained, "There are a lot of great technicians in advertising. However, they forget that advertising is persuasion, and persuasion is not a science, but an art. Advertising is the art of persuasion."[5]

• *Stage 6: The accountability era.* Starting in the 1970s, this period began an industry-wide focus on effectiveness. Clients wanted ads that produced sales, so the emphasis

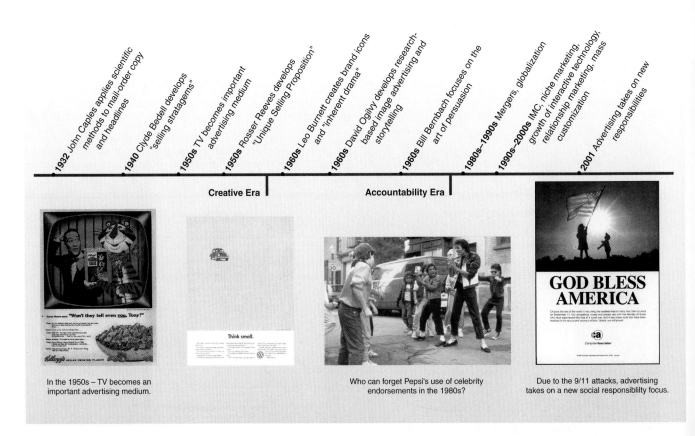

In the 1950s – TV becomes an important advertising medium.

Who can forget Pepsi's use of celebrity endorsements in the 1980s?

Due to the 9/11 attacks, advertising takes on a new social responsibility focus.

FIGURE 1.3 (continued)

A MATTER OF PRINCIPLE

The Sales Approach and Lasker's Reason-Why
By Edd Applegate, *Middle Tennessee State University*

Advertising took a dramatic detour when John E. Kennedy and Albert Lasker formed their historic partnership in 1904 at the powerful Lord & Thomas agency. Lasker was the managerial genius who made the agency a force in the advertising industry. He believed in the principle that ads should sell a product, not just inform.

Because of Lasker's talent, philosophy, and creative staff, the agency was able to make a profit when others were losing money. The agency attracted major clients, including Kimberly-Clark and RCA, and became one of the first agencies to create radio programs for its clients' products.

In 1904 Lasker was pondering the question: What is advertising? Copywriter John E. Kennedy responded with a note that read, "I can tell you what advertising is."

When the two met, Kennedy explained, "Advertising is salesmanship in print."

Thus was born the sales principle of advertising copy. Kennedy's style was simple and straightforward, based on the belief that advertising should present the same arguments a salesperson would use in person. This "reason-why" copy style became the hallmark of Lord & Thomas ads. Referring to his meeting with Kennedy, Lasker said, "The whole complexion of advertising for all America was changed from that day on."

Sources: Merrill DeVoe, *Effective Advertising Copy* (New York: Macmillan, 1956): 21; M. Carole Macklin, ed., "Creativity in Advertising: Lessons from the Legends," Conference of the American Academy of Advertising, St. Louis (1997).

was on research and measurement. To compete, advertising agencies recognized that advertising had to pay its own way and prove its value. After the Internet economy downturn at the start of the 21st century, accountability became even more important, and advertisers demanded proof that their advertising was truly effective.

- *Stage 7: Age of social responsibility.* By the late 1990s, corporations were challenged by shareholders and others in the community not only for reasons of financial accountability, but also on questions of social responsibility and insensitivity to diverse viewpoints. Charges of using sweatshops in low-wage countries and an apparent disregard for the environment concerned critics such as Naomi Klein, who wrote the best-selling book *No Logo*. Companies began to think seriously about how they could be better corporate citizens and not let their drive for profits get in the way of their responsibility to society. This philosophy was the inspiration for Marc Gobe's 2002 book, *Citizen Brands*.

One way to learn more about advertising, its development, and its practices is to become familiar with the literature. The list of books in the Practical Tips box is a good place to start.

CURRENT DEVELOPMENTS

Advertising continues to be a dynamic profession. Long-time concerns—the need for creativity, effectiveness, and social responsibility—continue. What are the current issues and trends, and what's ahead for the advertising industry? Above all, what is "the new advertising"?

The New Advertising

Electronic media, such as the Internet and wireless communication, are changing media landscape and making more intimate, interactive, and personalized forms of communication much more important to advertisers. This "new advertising" challenges the mass

Practical Tips

Why You Probably Don't Want to Read This . . .

By Sheri J. Broyles, *University of North Texas*

This is about the birth of a booklist. If you're just reading this textbook because you have to take a class and really aren't interested in advertising, then stop now. Don't bother reading any further. You would probably hate the adventures of advertising giants David Ogilvy, Mary Wells Lawrence, Jerry Della Femina, Phil Dusenberry, and others, all in their own words.

However, if you're taking this class because you have a passion for the advertising biz, then let me tell you why this booklist may be of interest. A few years ago I was talking to advertising professionals about what we should do as we considered revamping some courses. I heard repeated variations on this refrain: "Advertising graduates today don't seem to know anything about the literature. Don't they ever read books?"

So I decided to put a booklist together for my students. It was a pretty good booklist, but I realized there were probably some great books out there that I had missed. I sent a query to a listserv of advertising professionals as well as those who teach advertising classes, asking them what books they thought anyone going into the advertising industry should read. This extensive list is a result of my own compilation and responses from across the country.

There's a little bit of everything on this list, and you probably won't want to read all these books. But there are some gems for everyone, depending on their area of interest in advertising. For example, if you want to understand the evolution of advertising from before the Creative Revolution to now, then pick up Sivulka's *Soap, Sex and Cigarettes* (specifically Chapters 6 to 9). Perhaps Twitchell's *20 Ads That Shook the World* may give you some insights as well. If you're a "creative," you should really read Sullivan's *Hey, Whipple, Squeeze This.* Or if you want to get a job in creative, then you should be reading Vonk and Kestin's *Pick Me.* If you're interested in account planning, then read Steele's *Truth, Lies and Advertising.* Or maybe you just want a quick, fun read? If so, pick up Freberg's *It Only Hurts When I Laugh* or Garfield's *And Now a Few Words From Me.* Lots of books, lots of choices.

I have one alum working her way through the entire list. Every once in a while, I'll get an e-mail from her: "Just finished _____. Think I'll read _____ next." You'll find many of these books in the library. Or, if you want them to sit impressively on your shelf in your office one day, give the list to mom or dad or others who love you for birthdays and other gift-giving occasions.

Then enjoy the read.

Note: The entire booklist can be found on the Advertising Principles & Practices Web site (*www.prenhall.com/moriarty*).

orientation of older forms of advertising even as it opens up new business opportunities. Some in advertising are fearful: Bob Garfield, a columnist for *Advertising Age,* predicted that advertising was in trouble because its revenue from traditional media was decreasing faster than revenue from the new forms could catch up. In an *Ad Age* survey, 68 percent of readers agreed with this scary assessment of the future of the industry.[6]

The question is: Can the advertising industry keep up with the rate of change? A big debate at the Cannes Lions International Advertising Festival several years ago, for example, centered on whether the innovative BMW Hire campaign counted as advertising. The campaign used short films on the Internet and events, such as a gathering of faithful viewers on a corner in New York City in a live-action scene related to one of the online mini-movies. It was creative; it got attention; it sold cars—but it didn't look like advertising. So is it advertising? Of course, it is. It's just the next step in the evolution of advertising. And advertisers are pushing their agencies to keep up with these changes.

This is where real creativity lies—not just in the development of a big idea for a magazine ad or a television commercial, but in the use of new ways of reaching and communicating with people. The BMW Hire campaign was a novel idea that created **buzz,** which means people talk about the event, the idea, and the brand. So the "new advertising" also is concerned with word-of-mouth and how to get people talking about the brand. Of course, these are not traditional advertising techniques presented in nonpersonal mass media, but they expand the activities that inspire creative ideas from advertising professionals and engage the minds of consumers in new and powerful ways. New advertising, then, is advertising that is more personal and interactive and more likely to employ creative new uses of communication beyond traditional mass media.

Interactivity

The interest in buzz is an indication of another trend that affects advertising, and that is interactivity. Advertising's original definitions assumed a form of one-way communication from an advertiser to a target audience, but that is all changing in the 21st century. People are contacting companies through the Web or by phone, and they are talking to one another in a circle of comments about products and brands. As one expert in interactive telecommunication explained, "We're living through the largest expansion of expressive capability in the history of the human race."[7] Inevitably, that means advertising must change to also become more interactive.

Integrated Marketing Communication

A major trend affecting advertising is integrated marketing communication, which is another factor in expanding the scope of what we refer to as "new advertising." We mentioned earlier that advertising is only one type of marketing communication. The important thing to remember is that all these other areas deliver messages, just as advertising does, and it is important to have them all work together to create a coherent brand message. **Integrated marketing communication (IMC)** is the practice of unifying all marketing communication messages and tools so they send a consistent, persuasive message promoting the brand's goals.[8]

In addition to the profusion of marketing communication tools, the brand's **stakeholders**—all those people who have an interest in the brand—include such groups as employees, vendors and suppliers, distributors, investors, government and regulators, the community, watchdog groups, and the media. Among other reasons, stakeholders are important because they talk to each other and it is important that they have positive and consistent things to say about a brand.

In companies that use IMC, marketers coordinate all these marketing communication messages to create synergy, which means individual messages have more impact working jointly to promote a product than they would working on their own. The goal is to create strategic consistency across all messages a customer receives.[9]

Globalization

This trend toward more consistent communication is complicated by the increasing globalization of marketing programs. In the early 1990s the trade barriers throughout much of Europe came down, making it the largest contiguous market in the world. Eastern Europe, India, Russia, and China also have opened their huge markets to international marketing. As advertisers move into these markets, ad agencies are forming large multinational operations with international research and media-buying capabilities.

The advertising question is whether to practice global or local advertising: Should advertisers standardize ads or advertising strategies across all cultures, or should they adapt their strategies to local markets? How much consistency does a brand and its advertising need to maintain as it moves across borders? Because of the importance of understanding the underlying cultural issues that affect advertising, we devote a section of Chapter 18 to the topic of international advertising.

What Makes an Ad Effective?

Another important trend, one related to the accountability issue, is the emphasis on advertising effectiveness—and this is the central theme of our approach to advertising. Effective ads are ads that work. That is, they deliver the message the advertiser intended and consumers respond as the advertiser hoped they would. Ultimately, advertisers such as Apple want consumers to buy and keep buying their goods and services. To get to that point, ads must first effectively communicate a message that motivates consumers to respond.

What characteristics of effective ads have impact on consumer response? To move consumers to action, they must gain their attention, which was the purpose of the riveting story in the "1984" commercial. In general, an ad or campaign works if it creates a positive impression for a brand, separates the brand from the competition in the minds of customers, and influences people to respond in the desired way. Chapter 4 explains these characteristics of effectiveness in more detail.

Principle
An ad that works—that is effective—is one where the target audience responds as the advertiser intended.

The most important characteristic is that advertising is purposeful: It is created to have some effect, some impact on the people who read or see the message. We refer to this as advertising's **effects,** the idea being that **effective** advertising messages will achieve the advertiser's desired impact and the target audience will respond as the advertiser intended. The desired impact is formally stated as a set of **objectives,** which are statements of the measurable goals or results that the advertising is intended to achieve. The advertising works if it achieves its objectives.

Effectiveness and Award Shows

This chapter opened with the *truth*® campaign, which was identified as award-winning advertising. We are interested in showcasing great advertising, particularly award winners, for their recognized effectiveness. The Effie award, named with a shortened form of the word *effective,* is given by the New York Chapter of the American Marketing Association (AMA) to advertising that has been proven to be effective. That means the campaigns were guided by measurable objectives, and evaluation after the campaign determined that the effort did, in fact, meet or exceed the objectives. Other award shows that focus on effectiveness are the Advertising and Marketing Effectiveness (AME) awards by the New York Festivals company, Canada's Cassie Awards, and the London-based Institute of Practitioners Award (IPA).

It is important to note that even the Effies are broadening out to include the "new advertising" approach we discussed earlier. The award show made headlines in 2006 when it announced that campaigns don't have to use traditional advertising and buy media to be a winner. In fact, events, sponsorships, and package designs could also be Effie winners.[10]

But are all award-winning ads effective ads? Not necessarily. Other award shows judge factors such as creative ideas (for example, the Clios by a private award-show company, the One Show by a New York-based advertising association, and the Cannes Lions Awards by a French award show company), media plans (*Adweek*'s Media Plan of the Year), and art direction (the New York Art Director's Award Show).

Other professional areas also have award shows that reward such things as clever promotional ideas—the Reggies given by the Promotion Marketing Association—and outstanding public relations efforts—the Silver Anvil by the Public Relations Society of America (PRSA). Many other award shows may be mentioned in this book, but this quick introduction should give you some idea of the effort marketing communication professionals make to recognize outstanding work.

The Truth about the *truth*® Campaign

At the beginning of the chapter we noted that the *truth*® campaign has won more than 300 creative awards, which is quite impressive. Remember, though, that winning creative awards doesn't necessarily mean that the campaign was effective. The award-winning innovative approaches and creative accolades mean that the agency gets recognized for its work, but they may fail to address the critical question of effectiveness: Did the campaign work for the client? That's the essential question at the heart of effective advertising. All awards lose their meaning if the message isn't communicated to the consumer.

What is the evidence that the *truth*® campaign worked? After all it did win a Grand Effie award, which uses effectiveness as a criterion for winning.

- *Awareness:* After just eight months on air, 75 percent of U.S. teens could accurately describe one or more of the *truth*® ads. Currently, 57 percent of teens recall seeing the ads.
- *Belief:* More than 70 percent of teens say that seeing the ads makes them feel more negative toward tobacco companies.
- *Persuasion:* More than 90 percent of teens who saw the *truth*® ads say the ads gave them good reasons not to smoke.
- *Behavior:* Dr. Matthew Farrelly and his colleagues conducted a study using a survey of approximately 50,000 students in grades 8, 10, and 12 each spring from 1997 to 2002. They concluded that 22 percent of the overall decline in youth smoking from 2000 to 2002 was directly attributable to the *truth*® campaign. This study indicated that campaign resulted in approximately 300,000 fewer youth smokers.

Dr. Cheryl Healton, president and CEO of the American Legacy Foundation said, "The *truth*® campaign has made a significant impact in reducing youth smoking rates in the United States. The study findings are consistent with previous studies, which demonstrate that effective smoking prevention campaigns are critical to the public health of this nation." The harsh reality of the situation, however, is that despite the success of the *truth*® campaign, the American Legacy Foundation faces a major challenge to keep the campaign alive.

Key Points Summary

1. **Define advertising and identify advertising's key components.** Advertising is persuasive communication that uses mass and interactive media to reach broad audiences in order to connect an identified sponsor with buyers (a target audience) and provide information about products (goods, services, and ideas). The key components of advertising are strategy, creative idea, creative execution, and media planning and buying.

2. **Explain the roles and types of advertising within society and business.** Advertising fulfills a (1) marketing role, (2) communication role, (3) economic role, and (4) societal role. Different types of advertising—brand, retail (or local), direct-response, business-to-business, institutional, nonprofit, and public service—are used to fulfill these roles.

3. **Distinguish among the key players and their responsibilities in creating advertising.** The five key players in the advertising industry are advertisers, advertising agencies, media, suppliers, and target audiences. A firm's advertising can be handled either internally by an in-house agency or externally by an advertising agency.

Companies often have advertising departments to either handle the firm's advertising or oversee the work of an agency. The media are the channels of communication used to deliver a message to and from the target audience.

4. **Trace the evolution of advertising and the current developments that shape the practice of advertising.** The most important periods in the development of advertising are (1) the Age of Print, with its emphasis on delivering commercial information; (2) the Emergence of Consumer Society, in which technology created surplus goods and advertising was used to identify brands and create demand; (3) the Modern Advertising Era, with its emphasis on scientific approaches and testing; (4) the Age of Agencies, during which agency management was emphasized; (5) the Creative Era, a backlash response to the science and management of the earlier years that brought a renewed interest in the art of advertising; (6) the Accountability Era, which was the beginning of the emphasis on effectiveness; and (7) the Age of Social Responsibility, during which advertisers came to realize that being a good corporate citizen was also good for business.

Current trends include (1) expanding the definition of advertising to include interactive forms and media, (2) integrating all the various marketing communication tools and reaching a wider group of stakeholders, and (3) planning and managing marketing communication in a global economy.

Key Terms

advertisement, p. 8
advertiser, p. 14
advertising, p. 9
advertising agency, p. 17
agency of record (AOR), p. 17
brand, p. 11
brand advertising, p. 13
business-to-business (B2B) advertising, p. 13
buzz, p. 25
campaign, p. 14
corporate advertising, p. 13
creative concept, p. 10

direct-response advertising, p. 13
effective, p. 26
effects, p. 26
four Ps, p. 11
hard-sell, p. 12
in-house agency, p. 18
institutional advertising (corporate advertising), p. 13
integrated marketing communication (IMC), p. 25

local advertising, p. 13
marketing, p. 11
marketing communication, p. 7
marketing mix (four Ps), p. 11
media/medium, p. 18
nonprofit advertising, p. 14
objectives, p. 26
product category, p. 11
public service advertising, p. 14

public service announcements (PSAs), p. 14
retail advertising, p. 13
soft-sell, p. 12
stakeholders, p. 25
strategy, p. 9
suppliers, p. 19
target audience, p. 19
targeting, p. 19
target market, p. 11
vendors (suppliers), p. 19

Review Questions

1. What is the modern definition of advertising?
2. What are the four components of advertising, why are they important, and how are they used?
3. Advertising plays four general roles in society. Define and explain each one in the context of the *truth*® and *1984* campaigns featured in this chapter.
4. What are the seven types of advertising, and how do they differ?
5. Who are the five key players in the world of advertising, and what are the responsibilities of each?
6. What challenges are affecting the current practice of advertising? In particular, why is effectiveness important to advertisers?

Discussion Questions

1. "I'll tell you what great advertising means," said advertising major Bill Slater during a heated discussion. "Great advertising is the ability to capture the imagination of the public—the stuff that sticks in the memory, like the Aflac duck—that's what great is." Marketing major Phil Graham disagrees: "Bill, you missed the point. Advertising is a promotional weapon. Greatness in advertising means commanding attention and persuading people to buy something. No frills, no cuteness—great advertising has to sell the public and keep them sold." With whom would you side in this argument? How do you define effective advertising?

2. You belong to an organization that wants to advertise a special event it is sponsoring. You are really concerned that the group not waste its limited budget on advertising that doesn't work. Outline a presentation you would make to the group's board of directors that explains advertising strengths and why advertising is important for this group.

Then explain the concept of advertising effectiveness. In this situation, what would be effective, and what wouldn't be? What kinds of effects would you want the advertising to achieve? How would you know if it works?

3. *Three-Minute Debate:* In class, Mark tells the instructor that all this history of advertising stuff is irrelevant. The instructor asks the class to consider why it is important to understand the historical review of advertising definitions and practices. What would you say either in support of Mark's view or to change his mind? Organize into small teams with pairs of teams taking one side or the other. In class, set up a series of three-minute debates in which each side has 1½ minutes to argue its position. Every team of debaters must present new points not covered in the previous teams' presentations until there are no arguments left to present. Then the class votes as a group on the winning point of view.

Take-Home Team Projects

Form groups of five or six students. Have a spokesperson contact one or two advertising agencies. Question one or more key people about the changes that have taken place in their agencies and the industry during the last five years. (Prepare a list of questions ahead of time.) What kinds of changes do they expect in the next five years? Meet to write a three- to five-page report.

Each person on the team should consult the Web site of any advertising agency. Does the agency make any claim about accountability or effectiveness for the work it produces for its clients? In general what are the agencies saying they do to deliver effective advertising?

Yahoo! Hands-On Case

Read the Yahoo! case in the Appendix before coming to class.

1. In class, discuss the following:
   a. In what ways does this Yahoo! case reflect the expanded definition of advertising?
   b. How does this case illustrate the various roles that advertising campaigns perform?

2. Prepare a new section for this campaign plan that outlines how a campaign like this strengthens and refines the role that advertising plays in Yahoo!'s communication program. In other words, outline for Yahoo! managers why an advertising effort such as this is important to the company. Approach this as a one-page wrap-up for the campaign team's presentation to Yahoo!

HANDS-ON CASE

Dueling Computers

The dorky guy says, "Hi, I'm PC," and the shaggy-haired hip guy replies, "I'm Mac." So begins a charming, awkward relationship between the pair who personify competing computers in Apple's award-winning "Get a Mac" campaign. The purpose of the campaign is to advertise the improved Mac with its Intel chip innards and make Macs as culturally relevant as Apple's phenomenally popular iPod. (Who could forget those silhouetted figures dancing to their own beat?)

Apple hired its longtime agency, TBWA/Chiat/Day, Los Angeles, to work its magic again with the Macs. The agency decided to create a metaphor for the computers with two actors in the commercials. John Hodgman, a former regular on *The Daily Show with Jon Stewart*, stars in the role of the frustrating, complicated PC. You may remember the hero, the Mac guy, Justin Long, from his movie roles in *Dodgeball: A True Underdog Story, Accepted,* and *Live Free or Die Hard.*

The Big Idea for the commercials: create two likable personalities who could talk about product differences. As reported in *Adweek,* Allison Johnson, Apple's vice president of worldwide marketing said, "Apple stands for 'humanizing' technology, and this is a simple, compelling way to talk about product differences. At the same time it was important for us to make it fun and charming."

The gentle banter between the actors reveals a respect for both PC and Mac, while highlighting the superiority of the Apple computer. According to Johnson, one of the most popular spots has been "Virus." In that commercial PC sneezes and says he has a virus that's going around. He then tells Mac that in the previous year there were 114,000 viruses. Mac, more immune to viruses, and says he's OK and hands PC a tissue. Other commercials highlight other Mac advantages, such as its cool "apps" and video-imaging tools.

The presentation of the campaign is simple and effective, like the design of the Mac. Set against an unclut-tered white background with a childlike tune ("Having Trouble Sneezing" by Mark Mothersbaugh), the campaign focuses viewers' attention on the message and its playful tone.

The Mac/PC comparison advertising is accomplishing its goals. It's boosting sales. Apple has seen record sales, and its market share has increased by 42 percent. The New York Marketing Association awarded the campaign its Grand Effie, the top prize for advertising campaigns that communicate great ideas and demonstrate real results in accomplishing their goals.

Although the "Get a Mac" campaign is working for Apple, comparison advertising should be approached carefully. When the campaign first began running, some bloggers did not like the negative advertising technique of bad-mouthing PCs. However, criticism waned as the commercials showed they were not mean-spirited attacks on PC. Viewers can feel affection and even empathize with the PC guy's character. Some critics also argue that when advertisers engage in comparison advertising, they run the risk of giving free advertising to the competition. By showing and talking about the competitor, such advertising runs the risk of helping audiences remember the competition rather than the sponsor of the ad (more about comparison advertising in Chapter 3).

Consider This

1. Do you think Apple's comparison advertising between Mac and PC works? Why or why not?
2. How important do you think each of these elements of the commercial is to the campaign's success: music, actors, dialog, setting, tone?
3. What audience that is Apple trying to reach with these ads?

Sources: Theresa Howard & Jefferson Graham, "Apple Goes Back to its Core in Touting Macs," *USA Today,* October 23, 2006, http://usatoday.com; Joan Voight, "Mac's Friendly Fire," *Adweek* (February 5, 2007, 22-23; New York: AMA. http://www.nyama.org

Advertising's Role in Marketing

IT'S A WINNER

Award:	Company:	Agency:	Campaign:
Puma's marketing communication efforts are widely recognized, although Puma doesn't submit its campaigns to any award shows.	*Puma*	*Puma in-house*	*Puma Suede*

Puma's Evolution of the Species

What do Joe Namath, Pelé, Marcus Allen, Martina Navratilova, Boris Becker, Linford Christie, Serena Williams, Oscar De La Hoya, Vince Carter, the Cameroon football (soccer) team, Jamaican Olympic Federation athletes, the Italian National football team, the Swedish Athletic Association, Red Bull Motorsport teams, and the Puma Volvo Ocean Race team have in common?

They're some of the athletes from across the globe who are or have been associated with Puma products. They are brand builders.

Founded in Germany in 1948, Puma is one of the world's largest providers of athletic footwear, apparel, and accessories. Famous initially as a producer of innovative athletic-training shoes, the brand has evolved through the fusion of sports and fashion. Since its humble beginnings, it's gone global, leaving its paw prints across the world in more than 80 countries. Key to the success is Puma's decision to stick to its core mission of providing the world's best footwear for sports.

What the Puma brand means does not happen by accident but results from key strategic decisions. In this case, the results are based on a commitment to four cornerstone ideas: heritage, sport, technological innovation, and design. According to the Puma Web site (www.puma.com), "the brand is focusing on bringing distinctive designs and a global outlook to each product range by blending influences of sport, lifestyle, and fashion. This fusion is known as 'Sportlifestyle.' Puma views sport as a philosophy on life—one that emphasizes fitness, wellness and simply living an active life. Since sport can be different things to different people, Puma approaches it in a greater-lifestyle context, while not compromising performance."

Chapter Key Points

1. What is marketing, and what are its key concepts?
2. What are the different types of markets, and how do they relate to the marketing process?
3. Who are the key players in marketing?
4. How are agencies organized, and how do they work with their clients?

The Web site also clearly states the direction the company is headed: "Embodied by cutting-edge design, innovative marketing concepts, unique athletes and teams and a management that is dedicated to constant innovation and change, Puma's goal is to become the most desirable Sportlifestyle company."

Communication from Puma adds value to the brand and reflects this approach of blending sports, lifestyle, and fashion. Some of the current efforts can be seen on its Web site. Online shopping, sports, sports fashion, new stuff and a section called "hot spot," with the latest in news and events, demonstrate this emphasis. Tying to the lifestyle focus, the site features a section on urban mobility. You can see what cool designers like Alexander McQueen, Christy Turlington, Philippe Starck, and Yasuhiro Mihara have created. You can even try your hand at designing your own shoes at the Mongolian Shoe BBQ.

Puma communicates how cool its cat brand is in other ways too. One of the recent campaigns features musician and actor Ludacris, who provides a fresh new face for the Puma Suede campaign. In a whimsical TV commercial, Ludacris reaches into a freezer lined with rows of cold, blue suede shoes. He pulls out a pair and "heats" them in the oven where they turn an acceptable, cool Puma red.

In another campaign, "Holiday Heroes," actress Michelle Yeoh, famous for her role in *Crouching Tiger, Hidden Dragon,* welcomed the season. Athletic aesthetics of the martial arts combined with Puma products set against a backdrop of white and crystal visuals to convey that the gear is stylish and sophisticated.

How successfully do you think Puma conveys its brand message? Turn to the It's a Wrap section at the end of the chapter to see.

Sources: Kristina Fields, Puma North America; www.puma.com; James Scully, "Sole Survivor," www.time.com: April 20, 2006.

An advertiser like Puma needs an effective campaign to help its products succeed in the marketplace. However, to succeed, a product must also offer customers value, and much of the value is created by marketing decisions that determine the product's design and ease of use, distribution, and pricing, as well as its marketing communication. Because advertising is just one part of the total marketing effort, it's unlikely that an advertising professional could create effective advertising without a thorough understanding of the client's marketing program. This chapter explains the basic principles of marketing from the perspective of advertising's role in marketing. It also takes a look at the advertising agency, its variations, and its structures, and finally it examines the key role the client-agency relationship plays in executing an integrated marketing communication strategy.

WHAT IS MARKETING?

As with advertising, you are familiar with marketing and have been involved in marketing most of your life. Every time you visit a store, try a product sample, or buy a product, you are engaged in the world of marketing. Even though you are an informal marketing "expert," it may still be useful to formally define marketing.

From a traditional viewpoint, **marketing** is the way a product is designed, tested, produced, branded, packaged, priced, distributed, and promoted. The American Marketing Association (AMA) defines the term with more of a customer focus as "an organizational

What if you could magically get rid of the things you don't like about credit cards?

What if there was a credit card company that put you first?

What if there was a credit card company that talked to you clearly?

That gave you meaningful rewards?

That treated you fairly?

That put you in the driver's seat?

What if there was a credit card company that was committed to not stopping until there were no more "what-ifs"?

DISCOVER
CARD

Find out more at Discovercard.com/*whatif*

function and a set of processes for creating, communicating, and delivering value to customers and for managing customer relationships in ways that benefit the organization and its stakeholders."[1]

Traditionally, the objective of most marketing programs, such as Puma's, has been to sell a product, service, or idea, in the sense that the United Way and the Army are trying to convince people to donate, volunteer, or sign up. The goal has been to match a product's availability—and the company's production capabilities—to the consumer's need, desire, or demand for the product. As Wende Zomnir explained in the Part I opening story, her role as a creative director for the Urban Decay and Hard Candy cosmetic brands is to lead the market with edgy product designs and formulations that appeal to fashion-conscious young women.

This Discover Card ad outlines all the ways the credit card company hopes to serve its customers by putting their interests first. Do you think this is a believable ad? Does it ring true to you? Do you think it works to attract new customers to the Discover Card?

Key Concepts in Marketing

Historically marketers developed a product and then tried to find a market for it. This is referred to as a **product-driven philosophy.** In the great inventive period surrounding the Industrial Revolution, breakthrough products came to market, such as the cotton gin, which was created by Eli Whitney in 1793 and improved over the next 50 years. You may think this boring, but the cotton gin ended the tedious process of removing cotton seeds by hand and made mass production of cotton possible. The sewing machine followed soon after, permitting homemakers and clothing industrialists to mechanize the construction of garments. Thus, the fashion industry was born. The same innovative period saw a flourishing of patent medicines. Lydia Pinkham's Vegetable Compound, for example, made outrageous claims for a tonic with a base of 18 percent alcohol.[2] The pharmaceutical industry continues to be driven primarily by a product-focused philosophy.

The practice of marketing is still evolving. The marketing concept, which turned the marketers' attention to consumer needs and wants, and the concepts of exchange, branding, differentiation, and added value have all nudged marketing closer to a customer-focused philosophy rather than one based on production. These facets have important implications for advertising and for advertising's role in marketing. Let's look briefly at each.

The Marketing Concept: Focus on Consumers   Consider how you or your parents buy an automobile. Are you driving the car you really want or did you find something on the lot that was close and the dealer offered a good price, so you took it? Most of us drive cars that aren't exactly what we want, and that's because the automobile industry isn't geared to provide a built-to-order car. Automakers generally produce a product and hope it will sell. In contrast, Dell has built a successful business on supplying customized computers created to its customers' specifications.

In contemporary marketing, successful marketers try to determine and meet the needs and wants of consumers rather than simply providing a product. Sometimes marketers, particularly those selling to other businesses, will include the customer in the product design and development process in order to better satisfy their needs.

The **marketing concept** is the philosophy that suggests marketing should focus first on identifying the needs and wants of the customer rather than on finding ways to build and sell products that consumers may or may not want. For example, the *consumer-first* approach, also called a *market approach,* is the theme of the Discover Card ad. The opposite approach, the product or corporate-focused approach, is still used, particularly in areas where product innovation is important, such as technology.

A note about terminology: We often use the words *consumer* and *customer* interchangeably, but there are some differences in meaning. **Consumer** is a general term for people who buy and use products and services, which is almost all of us. It's similar to the phrase *general public.* The word **customer,** however, refers to someone who has purchased a specific brand or visited a specific retailer. Customers have a closer link to a brand or a store because they have taken action by buying or visiting. By virtue of that action, these people can be said to have a brand relationship and, if they buy over and over again, may even become loyal to the brand.

Some businesses that have adopted the market-driven perspective include Harley-Davidson, Intel, and United Parcel Services (UPS), all now recognized as leaders in customer-focused marketing. But personalization can have its limits. Consider how you buy a computer from Dell. Online you check the various options and then you specify what you want. You pay for it, and Dell builds it for you and delivers it 10 days later. Dell is having problems, however, because more and more consumers are interested in immediate possession rather than personalization. They can meet that need by going to a store, such as CompUSA, and buying something close to what they want to reduce wait time. This could mean serious trouble for Dell's business model with its emphasis on personalization.[3]

The marketing concept involves two steps: (1) determine through research what the customer needs and wants and (2) develop, manufacture, market, and service goods that fill those needs and wants—that is, create solutions for customers' problems. Advertising planning addresses both of these steps through consumer research and methods that develop insight into consumer decision making. The information gained then feeds back into marketing plans, where it can stimulate new product developments that are better designed to meet customer needs.

In advertising, the difference lies in the focus of the ad. Is the focus on the consumer or on the company? Although a consumer focus is thought to be the strongest approach, there are still times when a product- or company-focused approach is appropriate. United Airlines uses a consumer-focused approach for its Escapes vacation planning service and a product focus for its Mileage Plus frequent flyer program. The product or corporate focus, however, is generally thought to be less effective in driving consumer response.

The marketing concept is at the heart of modern marketing, but some other concepts are also important: exchange, differentiation, added value, and branding. All these concepts affect the planning of advertising messages.

Exchange   Marketing helps to create **exchange**—that is, the act of trading a desired product or service to receive something of value (money) in return. The company makes a product and offers it for sale at a certain price; the customer gives money to the company to buy that product. Money is exchanged for goods or services.

What do we exchange? As we said in Chapter 1, marketers use the word *product* to refer to goods such as cars, refrigerators, and computers, as well as to services (restaurants,

insurance, real estate) and ideas (politics, associations, nonprofit organizations). When we use the word *product,* we are referring to this larger world of things that are provided in exchange for something from the customer. The organization, for example, could be an orchestra that provides the experience of attending a concert in exchange for the price of a ticket. In political advertising, a donation may be given in return for a sense of affiliation with and support for a particular political philosophy.

In addition to economic exchange, marketing also facilitates *communication exchange.* Advertising provides both information and the opportunity for customer-company interaction. Exchange has two meanings in marketing, with the communication meaning being particularly important to advertising and other forms of marketing communication. In other words, people have to know about it before they can buy it or sign up for it or donate to it. Thus marketing is only as effective as the communication practices that make people aware of the product.[4]

Differentiation and Competitive Advantage   Where a brand is different from its competitors and superior in some way, there is **competitive advantage.** This concept is referred to in marketing as **product differentiation.** A product can be differentiated in a variety of ways—in price, design, performance, distribution, and brand image. In the early days of marketing when availability was driven by production capabilities, companies could sell most of what they produced. After the Industrial Revolution, production increased and sales were driven by product claims, sometimes quite extravagant claims. In a market-driven economy, product features and claims, such as quality and cheaper price, helped marketers establish an advantage over the competition.

A classic example of differentiation is Maytag washers, which are sold on quality of design and construction and, hence, reliability. This perception of reliability has been instilled by marketing communication and the use of the famous "lonely repairman." The brand's slogan—"the Dependability People"—also personalizes the product and adds a note of employee responsibility to the image. Note that this differentiation strategy is based on creating an image in the minds of consumers, not on any particular feature of the product itself.

These two ads, both by United Airlines, demonstrate a consumer focus in the United Escapes vacation-planning ad, versus a corporate orientation in the Mileage Plus frequent flyer ad. Do you believe one is more effective than the other? Some argue that corporate-focused advertising is a waste. What do you think?

Added Value　The reason marketing and advertising activities are useful, both to consumers and to marketers, is that they add value to a product. **Added value** means a marketing or advertising activity makes the product more valuable, useful, or appealing to the consumer. A motorcycle is a motorcycle, but a Harley-Davidson Fat Boy is a highly coveted bike because of its brand image.

Beyond advertising, other marketing mix factors add value. For example, the more convenient the product is to buy, the more valuable it is to the customer. Likewise, the lower the price, the more useful features a product has, or the higher its quality, the more a customer may value it. Ensuring the product's utility and convenience is one of the tasks of customer-oriented marketing we discussed previously.

Advertising not only showcases the product's value but also may add value by making the product appear more desirable or more of a status symbol. Providing news and useful information of interest to consumers is another way that advertising adds value, as the United Escapes ad demonstrates.

Basic business practices also add value. Local retailers that compete with big chains such as Wal-Mart, Office Depot, or Home Depot can survive only if they find some way to offer value other than price. For example, a small Oklahoma chain of office supply stores called SPC Office Products holds its own against Staples and Office Depot by having more knowledgeable employees on the floor to answer customer questions than its giant competitors.[5] The additional service adds value for its customers.

Branding　An important contributor to differentiation and added value is **branding,** which is the way marketers create a special meaning for a product. That special meaning, or **brand image,** is the result of communication and the consumer's personal experiences with the product. Harley-Davidson, for example, carried an "outlaw" image from its early association as the bike of choice for the motorcycle gang Hell's Angels. More recently, that meaning has been shaded so that it still has an edgy, slightly dangerous image, but it's now acceptable for everyone from accountants to lawyers and even college professors to be seen riding one.

A brand makes the product distinctive in the marketplace and in its product category, just as your name makes you unique in your community. Mercedes has one of the most valuable brands in the world, with its classy personality and luxury image. This series of ads, however, tries to make Mercedes seem more affordable but yet still maintain its exclusive image.

Branding transforms products. Think about the importance of a brand when you give a gift to a loved one. There's a big difference between giving a watch in a Tiffany box and

Mercedes-Benz of Portland and Wilsonville

RICH UNCLE WON'T DIE?　　C-Class. Under $30K.　

Mercedes-Benz of Portland and Wilsonville

WIN THE LOTTERY LATER.　　C-Class. Under $30K.　

SHOWCASE Mercedes-Benz is an upscale automobile. The tone and humor of the ad copy help make the local dealerships seem like a group of people with a fun personality. These busboards were designed for use inside buses. They were contributed by Karl Schroeder, a copywriter at Coates Kokes in Portland, Oregon, and a graduate of the University of Oregon advertising program.

one in a Wal-Mart bag. The Tiffany box and logo signals a high-quality, status product. Tiffany's brand image also sends messages. A brand can signal status, quality, or good value; sometimes it's a "cool factor." Why is a Coach handbag worth $150 when a nearly identical one without that brand name sells for $15? The reason is the value we place on the Coach brand, along with the brand's meaning as a quality, high-status product.

Branding transforms by creating an emotional connection between consumers and their favorite brands. Marc Gobé, author of *Emotional Branding,*[6] explains in his book how marketing is being transformed from a product-based philosophy to one driven by an understanding of the power of human emotions. Emotional connections intensify the credibility and personality of a brand, leading to a heightened level of trust and thus a viable brand relationship. Think about the brands you seek out. Why do you buy them? How do you feel about these favorite brands? Do you love them? People who love their favorite brands, such as Starbucks, Coke or Pepsi, Levi's, or any other brand, can be fanatics. Kevin Roberts, CEO of Saatchi & Saatchi Worldwide, says in his book *Lovemarks*[7] that a brand touches our emotions because it responds to our basic hopes, fears, and dreams. Is there any brand that speaks to you in that way?

A brand, the distinctive brand name and logo, and the advertising behind it, creates predictability—we're more comfortable buying brands we know. For that reason, a familiar brand is important when we make major purchases such as cars and home appliances, because we have a sense that there is less risk buying them than products whose makers we don't know. Branding is particularly useful to consumers buying fashion items, such as Polo (Ralph Lauren), Rolex, Gucci, Diesel, Oakley, and Doc Martens, where self-identity may also be linked to the brands we buy and wear. These brands are fairly complex psychological messages whose meanings are built up over time through advertising.

The basic principles of branding evolved initially through the marketing innovations of manufacturers such as The Great Atlantic & Pacific Tea Company, which was established in 1861 to sell teas through groups or clubs, rather than stores. It later became the A&P grocery store chain. Another innovation in branding was the development of the Ivory Soap brand by Procter & Gamble. As the Macintosh 1984 commercial in Chapter 1 represents one of the all-time great ads, Ivory represents one of the all-time great marketing stories.

When a brand name or brand mark, such as a distinctive **logo,** is legally protected through registration with the Patent and Trademark Office of the Department of Commerce, it becomes a **trademark.** A trademark is a word, symbol, or design that identifies a product and indicates its source. Nike's "swoosh" is a good example.

These trademarks carry financial significance as well as an identification role, because they contribute to the value of a brand. We use the phrase **brand equity** to refer to the value based on the brand's reputation and meaning that the brand name has acquired over time. It measures the financial value that the brand contributes to the company. Table 2.1 lists the most valuable U.S. brands in terms of brand equity.

Principle
Effective branding transforms a product by creating a special meaning based on an emotional connection.

Table 2.1   Most Valued Global Brands

Brand	Market Value ($ billions)
1. Coca-Cola	$65
2. Microsoft	59
3. IBM	57
4. General Electric	52
5. Nokia	34
6. Toyota	32
7. Intel	31
8. McDonald's	29
9. Disney	29
10. Mercedes-Benz	24

Source: Interbrand Group; quoted in "The 100 Top Brands," *BusinessWeek,* August 6, 2007, p. 59 . Reprinted with permission.

A MATTER OF PRINCIPLE

It's Pure and It Floats

A basic principle of branding is that a brand takes on meaning when it makes a product distinctive within its product category. Procter & Gamble accomplished that by creating identity elements for its brand Ivory before anyone had thought of making a bar of soap a distinctive product. The Ivory brand identity system also called attention to innovative features of the product. Here's the background story about how Ivory came to be one of the first and most successful brands of all time.

Before the Civil War, homemakers made their own soap from lye, fats (cooking grease), and fireplace ashes. It was a soft, jelly-like, yellowish soap that would clean things adequately, but if it fell to the bottom of a pail, it dissolved into mush. In Victorian times, the benchmark for quality soap was the highly expensive castile bar—a pure white soap imported from the Mediterranean and made from the finest olive oil.

William Procter and James Gamble, who were partners in a candle-making operation, discovered a formula that produced a uniform, predictable bar soap, which they provided in wooden boxes to both armies during the Civil War. This introduced the concept of mass production and opened up a huge market when the soldiers returned to their homes with a demand for the bars of soap. But back at home the bars of soap were still yellow and sunk to the bottom.

Procter & Gamble hired a chemist to create a white bar equivalent to the legendary castile bar, which was the first use of scientific-based research and development (R&D) to design a product. In 1878 P&G white soap was invented. It was a modest success until the company began getting requests for the "soap that floats." It turns out that an accident in whipping the ingredients together had added enough air to some of the bars to make them lighter than water. This production accident led to one of the world's greatest statements of a product benefit: "It floats."

Other decisions also helped make it a branding breakthrough. In 1879 one of the P&G family was in

church listening to a scripture about ivory palaces and proposed that the white bar be renamed Ivory Soap. Now the great product had a great name as well as a great product benefit. Rather than asking for soap—soap was soap—and taking a bar from the barrel, customers could now ask for a specific product they liked by name.

But that wasn't the end of P&G's branding innovations. A grandson who was determined to match the quality of the legendary castile soap again turned to a chemist to determine the purity of both castile and Ivory. The research found that the total impurities in Ivory added only to 0.56 percent, which was actually lower than the castile bars. By turning that to a positive, P&G could make the claim that its Ivory is "99 and 44/100 percent pure." Thus was born one of the most famous brand slogans in marketing history.

Sources: Charles Goodrum and Helen Dalrymple, *Advertising in America* (New York: Harry N. Abrams, 1990); Laurie Freeman, "The House That Ivory Built: 150 Years of Procter & Gamble," *Advertising Age*, August 20, 1987, 4–18, 164–220; "P&G History: History of Ivory," http://www.pg.com, June 2004.

Branding is a special case of added value because the value it adds is purely psychological. Nike's image, which focuses on the performance of outstanding athletes, has been constructed primarily through advertising. Customers worldwide who like Nike's products and associate themselves with athletic performance recognize the swoosh logo.

Types of Markets

In addition to the key concepts, let's also consider the types of markets in which advertising professionals and their companies work. The word **market** originally meant the place where the exchange between seller and buyer took place. Today we speak of a market not only as a place (the Rocky Mountain market), but also as a particular type of buyer—for example, the youth market or the motorcycle market. The phrase **share of market** refers to the percentage of the total market in a product category that buys a particular brand.

When marketing strategists speak of markets, they generally refer to groups of people or organizations. As Figure 2.1 shows, the four main types of markets are (1) consumer, (2) business-to-business (industrial), (3) institutional, and (4) channel of distribution. We can further divide each of these markets by size or geography (local, regional, national, or international).

- **Consumer markets. Consumer markets** consist of people who buy products and services for personal or household use. As a student, you are considered a member of the consumer market for companies that sell jeans, athletic shoes, sweatshirts, pizza, music, textbooks, backpacks, computers, education, checking accounts, bicycles, travel and vacations, and a multitude of other products that you buy at drug and grocery stores, which the marketing industry refers to as *package goods.*
- **Business-to-business (industrial, trade) markets. Business-to-business (B2B) markets** consist of companies that buy products or services to use in their own businesses or in making other products. General Electric, for example, buys computers to use in billing and inventory control, steel and wiring to use in the manufacture of its products, and cleaning supplies to use in maintaining its buildings. Ads in this category usually are heavier on factual content than on emotional appeals.
- **Institutional markets. Institutional markets** include a wide variety of nonprofit organizations, such as hospitals, government agencies, and schools, that provide goods and services for the benefit of society. Universities, for example, are in the market for furniture, cleaning supplies, computers, office supplies, groceries, audiovisual material, paper towels, and toilet paper, to name a few. Such ads are similar to business-to-business ads in that they are heavy on copy and light on emotional appeals.

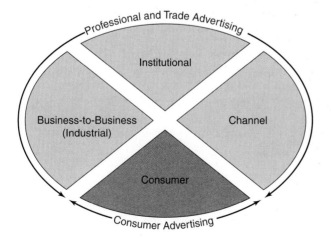

FIGURE 2.1
Four Types of Markets
The consumer market, which is the target of consumer advertising, is
only one of four markets. The other three are reached through
professional and trade advertising.

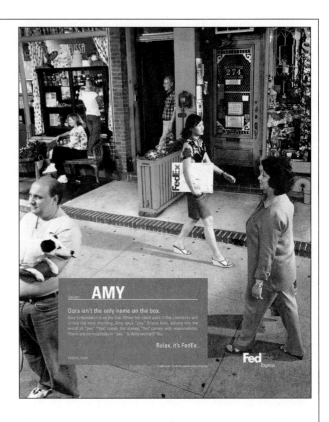

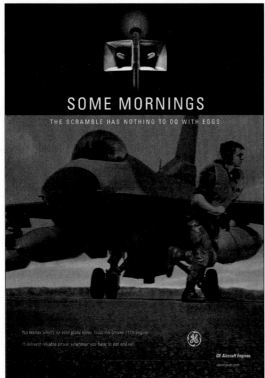

This group of ads demonstrates advertising directed at the four types of markets: consumer (Keds), business-to-business (FedEx), institutional (GE aircraft engines), and channel ("Ka-ching"). What are the similarities and differences in these four types of advertisements?

- *Channel markets.* The **channel market** is made up of members of the distribution chain, which is made up of the businesses we call **resellers,** or **intermediaries.** Resellers are wholesalers, retailers, and distributors who buy finished or semifinished products and resell them for a profit. Microsoft and its retailers are part of the reseller market. Companies that sell such products and services as trucks, cartons, and transportation services (airlines, cruise ships, and rental car agencies) consider resellers their market. **Channel marketing,** the process of targeting a specific campaign to members of the distribution channel, is more important now that manufacturers consider their distributors to be partners in their marketing programs. As giant retailers such as Wal-Mart become more powerful, they can even dictate to manufacturers what products their customers want to buy and how much they are willing to pay for them.

Businesses spend most of their advertising dollars on consumer markets, although business-to-business advertising is becoming almost as important. Firms usually advertise to consumers through mass media such as radio, television, newspapers, general consumer magazines, and direct-response advertising media (that is, direct mail and online). They typically reach the other three markets—industrial, international, and reseller—through trade and professional advertising in specialized media, such as trade journals, professional magazines, and direct mail.

The Marketing Plan

A **marketing plan** is a document that proposes strategies for using marketing elements to achieve marketing objectives. The process of creating a marketing plan—and managing a marketing program—begins with marketing research. The research process leads marketers to make a set of key strategic and tactical decisions that guide deployment of the marketing mix. These steps are listed in this outline and followed by brief explanations. In later chapters on research and planning, we'll explore these topics in more detail.

Steps in the Marketing Process

Step 1. *Research* the consumer market and the competitive marketplace and develop a *situation analysis* or a SWOT analysis (strengths, weaknesses, opportunitites, threats).

Step 2. Set *objectives* for the marketing effort.

Step 3. Assess consumer needs and wants relative to the product; *segment* the market into groups that are likely to respond; *target* specific markets.

Step 4. *Differentiate* and *position* the product relative to the competition.

Step 5. Develop the *marketing mix strategy:* select product design and performance criteria, pricing, distribution, and marketing communication.

Step 6. *Evaluate* the effectiveness of the strategy.

Marketing Research   The marketing process begins with **marketing research** into markets, product categories, consumers, and the competitive situation. Monitoring the external environment is particularly important. For example, when fears about avian flu swept the United States in 2006, chicken companies Tyson Foods and Perdue Chickens were threatened with huge financial losses.[8] Knowing that avian flu was moving from its origins in Asia to Europe helped these managers prepare for the scare.

The objective for planners is to know as much as they can about the marketplace so they can make informed and insightful strategic decisions. Marketing research is focused on gathering information from already existing and published **secondary research** as well as from **primary research,** which is original research undertaken to answer specific questions. Consumer information is extremely critical for most brands.

In addition to collecting information, marketing planners must also make sense of the data they collect. The significance of the research findings becomes clear in the phase of **situation analysis,** which identifies the brand's strengths and weaknesses and corporate and market opportunities and threats. Interpreting marketing information in terms of *strengths, weaknesses, opportunities,* and *threats* (**SWOTs**) helps managers turn data into insights. Thus, the goal of marketing research is both information and insight.

Principle
Marketing research is about more than just the compilation of information; it also produces insights into marketing situations and consumer behavior.

Celestial Seasonings uses its distinctive packages to send messages to consumers about its marketing position. In what way does the package reinforce the brand image?

Key Strategic Decisions   Marketing planners use research to develop strategies for approaching their markets. These strategies in turn give direction to the planning of advertising. Three strategic marketing decisions are key to the planning of effective advertising.

1. *Objectives.* The marketer's first step after the research is done is to set **marketing objectives.** Usually these objectives are business measures, such as increased sales levels, share of market, or broader distribution.
2. *Segmenting and targeting.* The particular group of consumers thought to be potential customers for a marketer's goods or services constitute the **target market.** The assumption is that not everyone in the marketplace wants or needs this product. Identifying those specific groups within the market whose needs and wants intersect with the product and its features is called **segmentation.** In customer-focused programs, marketing planners assess the needs of members of the target market, as along with their propensity to respond, and decide which segments to target as the focus of the marketing strategy.

   A *target audience,* which we introduced in Chapter 1 and will discuss in more detail in Chapter 5, is the audience for a marketing communication message. Marketers talk about target markets; marketing communicators talk about target audiences. They can be the same, but they are often defined differently. To clarify the difference between a target market and a target audience, consider that from a marketing perspective a *target market* for a local newspaper may be the entire community or a single suburb. From the perspective of its staff designing an advertising campaign, however, the newspaper may seek to increase readership among teenagers, and they become the *target audience* for that campaign.
3. *Differentiation and positioning.* Planners also assess the competition and decide where their product's point of **differentiation** lies and then make some decisions about how to present or **position** the product within this competitive environment relative to consumer needs. **Positioning** refers to how consumers view and compare competitive brands or types of products—how they see a brand relative to the other brands in the category. We'll discuss this in detail in Chapter 5.

Setting objectives, targeting, segmenting, differentiating, and positioning are basic marketing strategy decisions and critical factors that drive marketing communication strategies. Although we briefly introduce these key marketing strategic decisions here, we'll discuss them in more detail in later chapters on advertising planning and message strategies. These key strategic decisions are also important because they give direction to the marketing mix decisions.

The Marketing Mix

As Figure 2.2 shows, marketers use the four main elements of the *marketing mix* to achieve their objectives. We referred to these in Chapter 1 as the Four Ps, and we'll describe their rela-

Product	Distribution
• Design and Development • Branding • Packaging • Maintenance	• Distribution Channels • Market Coverage • Storage
Price	Communication
• Price Copy • Psychological Pricing • Price Lining • Value Determination	• Personal Selling • Advertising • Sales Promotion • Direct Marketing • Marketing/Public Relations • Point-of-Sale/Packaging

FIGURE 2.2

Four Components of the Marketing Mix

These four marketing mix elements and their related tools and marketing communication techniques are the basic components of marketing.

tionship to advertising following Figure 2.2. Marketing communication or promotion, which includes advertising, is one of these marketing elements. To a marketing manager communication is just one part of marketing, no more important than product, price, or distribution.

The Product   The product is both the object of the advertising and the reason for marketing. It includes product design and development, product operation and performance, branding, and the physical dimensions of packaging. Marketing begins by asking a set of questions about the product offering. In line with the marketing concept, these questions are most useful when asked from the consumer's perspective: What product attributes and benefits are important? How is the product perceived relative to competitive offerings? How important is service? How long should the product last? Customers view products as "bundles of satisfaction" rather than just physical objects, so what meanings do they attach to the product and its competitors?

Although some brands such as Ivory Soap have been around for a hundred years or more, other brands are new. The marketing manager's challenge is to launch the new brand successfully. Since there is a high failure rate for new products, this is a challenging assignment. For new products, advertising is particularly important because of its ability to reach a wide audience and build brand awareness. Public relations is also useful in new product launches because it contributes news announcements through its publicity function.

Product design, performance, and quality are key factors in determining the success of the product's marketing. Some products such as Puma are known for their design, which becomes a major point of differentiation from competitors. Performance is important for technical products, such as automobiles and software. Computer buyers, for example, will assess performance by asking: Is it easy to use? Does it crash? How big is its memory? Quality is another feature that is often linked to upscale brands, such as Mercedes and Rolex. The idea is that if the product is well engineered and its manufacturer maintains a high standard of quality, then the brand will last and perform at a high level. A 2006 article in *The New York Times* analyzed a widespread concern in Japan that the country's products are losing their edge in quality. Japan is a country obsessed with perfection and quality manufacturing; the concern is that recalls will give an edge to its competitors in China, Taiwan, and South Korea, as well as India.[9]

Distribution   It does little good to manufacture a fantastic product that will meet customers' needs unless you have a mechanism for delivering the product and handling the exchange of payment for the product. What marketers call **distribution** includes the channels used in moving the product from the manufacturer to the buyer.

Puma, for example, is growing because of its unusual approach to distribution. Its channel marketing strategy delivers both to exclusive and mass-market audiences, selling its edgy designs to trendy retailers and then placing its more mainstream products in mall stores. Foot Locker might sell the GV special, a style based on a retro Puma tennis shoe from its glory days 30 years ago; at the same time an independent fashion store might carry a basketball shoe in fabrics like snakeskin or lizard. And in recent years, Puma has expanded its distribution program to include its own stores that greet customers with a unique shopping environment reflecting the personality of the Puma brand.

The two channel factors that affect advertising reflect the distance between manufacturer and customer. **Direct marketing** companies, such as Lands' End and Burpee Seeds, distribute their products directly without the use of a reseller. The more familiar strategy of distributing the product through one or more distributors and retailers is more properly described as *channel marketing*. The products you see in a supermarket or discount store are all marketed indirectly through a complex channel marketing system.

Marketing managers may consider a variety of channels. Coach, the luxury handbag brand, is primarily sold in upscale stores, although it has found a booming business in outlet centers. The question is whether Coach can maintain its upscale image if it is commonly available in discount centers.[10] The Internet has brought another distribution question. "Clicks or bricks" is a phrase used to describe whether a product is sold online (clicks) or in a traditional store (bricks). The music industry, for example, has been suffering from the problem of uncontrolled online distribution of songs through services like Napster. The development of the iTunes model has helped bring some accountability to what music companies viewed as piracy.

Manufacturers often expect retailers in these indirect channels to participate in advertising programs. Through **cooperative (or co-op) advertising** allowances, the producers share with the reseller the cost of placing the advertisement.

A number of strategic distribution decisions develop from the overall marketing strategy and in turn affect advertising strategy.

- *Market coverage strategy.* *Market coverage* refers to the geographic distribution of the product, which is particularly important for the media strategy.
- *Push/pull strategies.* A **pull strategy** directs marketing efforts at the consumer and attempts to pull the product through the channel by intensifying consumer demand. Marketers using this strategy emphasize consumer advertising, along with incentives such as coupons, rebates, free samples, and sweepstakes. Little is expected from resellers other than to stock the product. In contrast, a **push strategy** directs marketing efforts at resellers, and success depends on the ability of these intermediaries to market the product, which they often do with advertising. Advertising may be targeted first at resellers to gain their acceptance, then at consumers through joint manufacturer-reseller advertising. Most marketers use a combination strategy of push and pull. Figure 2.3 summarizes these strategies.

Pricing This component of the marketing mix includes the price at which the product or service is offered for sale and the level of profitability the price establishes. The price a seller sets for a product is based not only on the cost of making and marketing the product but also on the seller's expected profit level. Certain psychological factors also affect the price. Ultimately, the price of a product is based on what the market will bear, the competition, the economic well-being of the consumer, the relative value of the product, and the consumer's ability to gauge the value.

With the exception of price information delivered at the point of sale, advertising is the primary vehicle for telling the consumer about price. The term **price copy,** which is the focus of much retail advertising, designates advertising copy devoted primarily to this type of information. A number of pricing strategies influence advertising strategy.

- **Customary pricing,** or expected pricing, uses a single, well-known price for a long period of time. Movie theaters and manufacturers of candy use this pricing strategy. Advertisers communicate a dramatic or temporary price reduction through terms such as *sale, special,* and *today only.*
- **Psychological pricing** strategies use advertising to manipulate the customer's judgment of value. For example, ads showing prestige pricing—in which a high price is set to make the product seem worthy or valuable—is accompanied by photographs of the

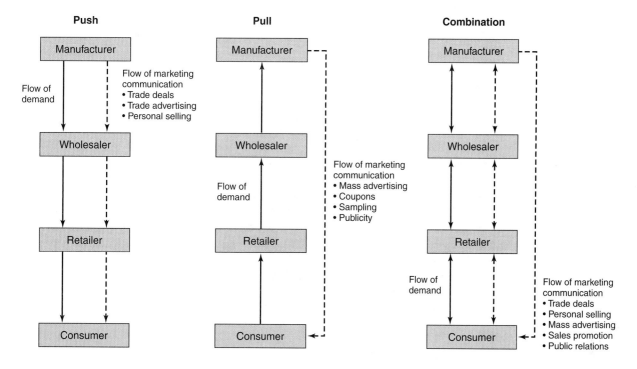

FIGURE 2.3

Push, Pull, and Combination Strategies

Advertising and other communication strategies are a major part of both a pull and push strategy.

"exceptional product" or by copy consisting of logical reasons for this high price. Psychological pricing is often used when a marketer is targeting affluent consumers.

Marketing Communication   What we call marketing communication includes personal selling, advertising, public relations, sales promotion, direct marketing, events and sponsorships, point of sale, and the communication aspects of packaging. We talked about marketing communication in the previous chapter, but note again the variety of forms included in that category.

The same creative spirit that drives Puma's product design also drives its marketing communication, which typically uses nontraditional ways to connect with customers. Retailers praise Puma for its creativity in designing eye-catching in-store merchandising displays. Recognizing the importance of word of mouth, **guerilla marketing** programs promote the brand on the street and on the feet of its devotees. Puma also uses the Internet to spread the word about new products through an online network.

Other clever ideas include promotions at sushi restaurants during the 2003 World Cup, which was held in Japan and South Korea. Puma got a well-known sushi chef to create a special Puma sushi roll that was served in select Japanese restaurants in cities around the world. These restaurants also discretely announced the sponsorship through Puma-branded chopsticks, sake cups, and napkins. At the same time, Puma partnered with the U.K.-based Terence Conran design shop to sell an exclusive version of its World Cup soccer boot and held weekend sushi-making events at the Conran home furnishings store.

One type of communication that we don't discuss in depth in this book is personal sales, but since that area is particularly important to marketing programs, we'll introduce it here. **Personal sales** uses face-to-face contact between the marketer and a prospective customer, rather than contact through media. In contrast to most advertising, whose effects are often delayed, marketers use personal selling to create immediate sales to people who are shopping for some product. Personal sales is also used in business-to-business marketing to reach key decisions makers within a company who can authorize a purchase. The different types of personal selling include sales calls at the place of business by a field representative (field sales), assistance at an outlet by a sales clerk (retail selling), and calls by a representative who goes to consumers' homes (door-to-door selling).

A MATTER OF PRACTICE

Creating Concepts
By Adam Kaplan, *Adam Kaplan Creative*

I had a casual conversation the other day. A woman asked what I did for a living. I replied, "I'm a creative director." She said, "Wow, it must be fun to be creative all day." Therein lies the greatest misnomer in marketing, that creative is actually "creative."

When one thinks about being creative, you might envision a painter expressing his soul through a brush stroke or a musician releasing his inner angst through a deftly played note. Creative, within the marketing world, is not that. Rather, creative is merely the vehicle in which a brand communicates. That said, "marketing-creative" does share an important commonality with "art-creative"—the notion of concept.

Concept is something that I wish more people involved in the marketing discipline understood. Simply put, a marketing concept must support the brand and its needs. It must achieve several key goals: (1) build brand equity; (2) be consistent with brand strategy; (3) be relevant to the target audience; and (4) be memorable enough to cause awareness or, even better, a positive quantifiable market reaction. A good marketing concept is not necessarily supported by the most creative execution (in fact, it rarely is); a good concept is the one that defines the brand's positive attributes to the intended target in a concise manner.

It doesn't matter what creative marketing vehicle a brand decides to take (e.g., television, Internet, radio, print). Without a smart, brand-focused concept, the creative—and, more importantly, the brand—is doomed to fail in that effort.

There are times when a concept is better than the brand itself. This is wonderful marketing. However, an inferior product is a pig no matter how much lipstick you may put on it and will ultimately be exposed for what it is. We, as marketers, cannot let the inferiority of a product get in the way of the task we were hired for—to put the brand in the best possible light. We search for unique sales propositions, category superiority, tangible equity builders, endorsements, or, when all else fails, a promotional hook to spur interest. We try to write taglines that will resonate, design logos that will become icons, and create campaigns that will become part of society's fabric—all in diligent support of the brand. Perhaps that is what is really meant by "creative."

Advertising is often used in conjunction with sales programs. Its role is **lead generation.** What that means is that an advertisement or a direct-mail piece announcing a new product may invite potential prospects to contact the company. Information about these prospects may be given to the sales staff for follow-up contact. This is a common practice in B2B marketing. Sales training programs can be an important type of marketing communication. For example, when Honda decided to target its new Honda Fit to young consumers in the Generation-Y category, a special training program was designed for the 7,500 Honda sales associates. The idea was that this Internet-savvy consumer is also likely to be highly informed about cars in general, and the Honda Fit in particular, and therefore needs a different type of car-buying experience. A trainer explained that, "You need to let the customer drive the process. . . . Let the buyer tell *you* what they want."[11]

Marketing communication is all about Big Ideas—clever creative concepts that catch people's attention and stick in their memory. Creativity is often associated with advertising ideas; however, all the areas of the marketing mix demand creative ideas. The point is that creative thinking is a form of problem solving, and good ideas are needed in product design (Ivory is a good example), as well as distribution, pricing, and all the areas of marketing communication. Furthermore, good marketing concepts, as Kaplan explains in the Matter of Practice box, are ones that are creative and on target in terms of brand strategy.

THE KEY PLAYERS

The marketing industry is a complex network of professionals, all of whom are involved in creating, producing, delivering, and selling something to customers. The four categories of key players include the marketer, suppliers or vendors, distributors and retailers, marketing partners, and agencies, which will be discussed later in the chapter. Consider also that these positions represent jobs, so you can use this information as a career guide should you be interested in working in marketing.

The Marketer

The **marketer,** also referred to as the advertiser or client (from the agency's point of view), is any company or organization behind the brand—that is, the organization, company, or manufacturer producing the product and offering it for sale.

In most companies of any size, the marketing function is handled by a marketing department and represented in the corporate hierarchy by a vice president or director of marketing. The marketing function is usually set up as a department with a number of people managing brands, products and product lines, and marketing services, which includes suppliers such as marketing researchers and marketing communication agencies. Marketing is also a function in nonprofit and governmental organizations, such as hospitals, museums, zoos, orchestras, Junior Achievement, and The United Way.

Some companies may have a **product** or **brand management** organization structure with managers who handle the marketing responsibility. A product or brand manager is the person responsible for all strategic decisions relating to the brand's product design and manufacture as well as the brand's pricing, distribution, and marketing communication. Procter & Gamble was a pioneer in establishing the product/brand management concept.

Suppliers and Vendors

The materials and ingredients used in producing the product are obtained from other companies, referred to as suppliers or vendors. Their work also determines the quality of the final product. The ingredients they provide, as well as the cost of their materials, is a big factor in determining the product's price. This can be very complex. Think about the automotive industry and all the pieces and parts that go into a car. The phrase **supply chain** is used to refer to this complex network of suppliers who produce components and ingredients that are then sold to the manufacturer. Sometimes other companies, acting as *brokers,* are involved in selling the supplies to the manufacturer, while still other companies may be employed to deliver the goods.

In marketing theory, every contribution from the supply chain adds value to the product. In marketing practice these suppliers and vendors are partners in the creation of a successful product. They are also partners in the communication process, and their marketing communication needs to support the brand, particularly in the practice called **ingredient branding,** which means acknowledging a supplier's brand as an important product feature. Think about how important the reputations of the Gore-Tex and Intel brands are to manufacturers who use these ingredients.

Distributors and Retailers

The **distribution chain** or **channel of distribution** refers to the various companies involved in moving a product from its manufacturer to its buyers. These channel members may actually take ownership of the product and participate in the marketing, including advertising. We are particularly concerned because they are target audiences for channel marketing programs.

Wholesalers and retailers, for example, are important parts of the channel, and each is capable of influencing, supporting, and delivering advertising messages. The primary strength of the wholesaler is personal selling. Wholesalers do not advertise often; however, in some instances they may use direct mail, trade papers, or catalogs to reach retailers. The copy tends to be simple and straightforward, and the focus is on product, features, and price. Conversely, retailers are quite good at advertising, especially local advertising. Retailers' main concern is that the advertising be directed to *their* customers as opposed to the customers of the manufacturers.

Sometimes marketers and marketing communicators talk about *the trade.* This general term refers to both the *upstream* players—suppliers and vendors in the supply chain—and the *downstream* players—companies in the distribution chain or channel. The stream metaphor comes from the idea that marketing is a process and certain players are involved before the product is made and others are involved afterward—hence upstream and downstream.

Intel Inside is an example of ingredient branding where a computer manufacturer advertises that it is using Intel chips as a testament to the product's quality. On what brands have you seen this Intel Inside logo exhibited? Do you think ingredient branding like this works?

Marketing Partners

Contemporary marketers look upon their suppliers and distributors, as well as their marketing communication agencies, as partners rather than just hired hands because their support is necessary to build and maintain good customer relationships. As Don Peppers and Martha Roberts, who are experts in marketing relationships, observe, "In many cases, it's left to the channel marketer—a person in corporate marketing who oversees channel relations—to build partner bonds that will keep current customers loyal and bring new ones into the fold."[12]

Marketing relationships also involve cooperative programs and alliances between two companies that work together to create products and promotions. Puma's Nuala yoga collection, for example, is a successful partnership with model Christy Turlington. Other Puma collaborators are designers Philippe Starck and Alexander McQueen. In Puma's partnership with the BMW Mini, Puma sells a black, two-piece driving shoe called the Mini Motion shoe, which is marketed as an accessory to the car. The shoe is similar in design to a Formula 1 racing shoe with a flexible inner slipper and a sturdier outer shoe that provides ankle support and traction. The slipper provides comfort on long trips, or even around the house, and the outer shoe can be worn outdoors and in city traffic where it combats the strain from frequent shifting. As part of the collaborative effort, Mini used functional footwear elements like air mesh for the seats. Puma's logo and its signature "formstripe" are used on the car's exterior.

Affiliate marketing is a particular type of partnership in which one company drives business to another company. Most major online retailers, such as Amazon.com, eBay, and Barnes & Noble, use affiliate marketing in which the Web site generating the business may receive a 5 to 10 percent commission for each paying customer.

HOW AGENCIES WORK WITH THEIR CLIENTS

We've talked about key players in the marketing process and marketing partners, which, of course, include marketing communication agencies. Let's look in more depth at the agency-client relationship.

But first, note that there are *agencies* and then there are *agency networks,* which are large holding companies that include all types of marketing communication agencies, as

Puma and BMW Mini formed a partnership to link a special edition of the Puma shoe with the design of the popular Mini car. Do you think this partnership works? In what way are the two brand images compatible—or not compatible?

well as research firms, Internet and branding consultants, and media-buying companies. Table 2.2 lists the top 10 agency networks worldwide.

Table 2.2 Top 10 Agency Networks

Marketing Organization	Worldwide Revenues ($ millions)
1. Omnicom Group	$11,376.9
2. WPP Group	10,819.6
3. Interpublic Group	6,190.8
4. Publicis Groupe	5,872.0
5. Dentsu	2,950.7
6. Havas	1,841.0
7. Aegis Group	1,825.8
8. Hakuhodo DY Holdings	1,337.0
9. aQuantive	442.2
10. Asatsu-DK	430.0

Source: "Agency Report: World's Top 25 Marketing Organizations," *Advertising Age,* April 30, 2007: S-2.

If you work on the company side, you will probably work in an *advertising department* whose primary responsibility is to act as a liaison between the marketing department and the advertising agency (or agencies). Sometimes this unit is called **marketing services,** and its role is to hire (and fire) agencies and manage the work of all the marketing communication suppliers. Depending on the business, the involvement of this advertising or marketing services department can vary tremendously from company to company. The individual in charge may carry a title such as director of advertising (or marketing services) or advertising manager. Typically, this person has extensive experience in all the facets of advertising. In fact, many have had jobs on the agency side, so they may have worked with advertisers in various capacities and are familiar with their operations.

How do the marketing communication professionals work with their clients? A marketer may have a contractual relationship with one agency, called the *agency-of-record (AOR),* or with many. Usually marketers have different agencies for different types of marketing communication tasks, but sometimes they hire several agencies in the same area because they believe competition will result in better work. Regardless of the arrangement, the agency–client relationship and contract take a lot of nurturing to work effectively. Ideally, the relationship is a partnership with both sides working together on behalf of the brand.

To seek out the best partner(s) for this relationship, a marketer typically invites a **pitch,** which is a formal presentation of an agency's competencies and ideas for the client's advertising, from a group of selected agencies. An example comes from Virgin Airlines, which announced in 2006 it was looking for an agency to handle its new U.S. passenger service. The winning pitch was given by a small two-year-old agency, Anomaly, that didn't just present ad ideas but, in a classic example of "new advertising," also included ideas about the interiors of the planes, the flight attendants' uniforms, and the content of the entertainment system.[13]

Why should a company sign a contract with an advertising agency? Hiring an agency has four main benefits. The agency provides (1) specialized services, (2) objective advice, (3) experienced staffing, and (4) tailored management of all advertising activities and personnel. Ultimately, the primary benefit of hiring an advertising agency is that it can implement the creative vision of the client and help it to reach its advertising goals.

Agencies sometimes have their own style or philosophy of advertising. Note the ads of three different agencies for the three branches of the U.S. military. The differences in approach come from the different goals and strategies of each service, as well as the creative ideas brought to the effort by the agencies that implemented the strategies.

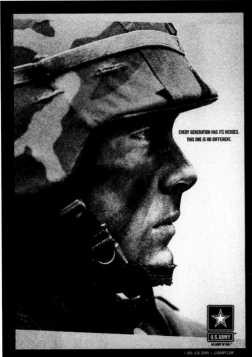

In these three ads for the Navy, Army, and Air Force, can you perceive a difference in approach, style, and strategy? Which do you think would be most effective in recruiting volunteers?

Types of Agencies

We are primarily concerned with advertising agencies in this book, but other areas such as public relations, direct marketing, sales promotion, and the Internet also have agencies that provide specialized services. Since they are all part of an integrated marketing communication approach, we have separate chapters on these functions later in this book.

The biggest agencies are what we call *full-service agencies,* but agencies also can organize their services for their clients in other ways, including specialized agencies and media-buying services. As discussed in Chapter 1, the advertiser can also handle its own advertising internally through an in-house agency.

In advertising, a **full-service agency** includes the four major staff functions—account management, creative services, media planning, and account planning, which may include research. A full-service advertising agency also has its own accounting department, a **traffic department** to handle internal tracking on completion of projects, a department for broadcast and print production (usually organized within the creative department), and a human resources department. The top agencies networks worldwide are listed in Table 2.3, as well as their holding company affiliation.

Table 2.3   Top 10 Consolidated Agency Networks

Agency	Headquarters	06 Revenues (in billions)
1. Dentsu [Dentsu]	Tokyo	$2.49
2. McCann Erickson Worldgroup [Interpublic]	New York	$2.13
3. BBDO Worldwide [Omnicom]	New York	$2.10
4. DDB Worldwide Communications [Omnicom]	New York	$2.08
5. Ogilvy & Mather Worldwide [WPP]	New York	$1.71
6. Young & Rubicam Brands [WPP]	New York	$1.59
7. TBWA Worldwide [Omnicom]	New York	$1.52
8. JWT (WPP) [WPP]	New York	$1.50
9. Publicis Worldwide [Publicis]	Paris	$1.24
10. Leo Burnett [Publicis]	Chicago	$1.19

Source: Agency Report: Top 10 Consolidated Agency Networks," *Advertising Age,* April 30, 2007: S-4.

Many agencies do not follow the traditional full-service agency approach. They either specialize in certain functions (writing copy, producing art, or media buying), audiences (minority, youth), industries (health care, computers, agriculture, business-to-business communication), or markets (minority groups such as Asian, African American, or Hispanic). In addition, some agencies specialize in other marketing communications areas, such as branding, direct marketing, sales promotion, public relations, events and sports marketing, packaging, and point of sale. There are also one-client agencies created to handle the work of one large client as well as in-house agencies and freelancers. Here we will discuss creative boutique and media-buying services.

- *Creative boutiques.* What we call **creative boutiques** are ad agencies, usually small (two or three people to a dozen or more), that concentrate entirely on preparing the creative execution of the idea, or the creative product. A creative boutique has one or more writers or artists on staff, but generally no staff for media, research, or strategic planning. Typically, these agencies can prepare advertising to run in print and broadcast media, as well as out-of-home and alternative media. Creative boutiques usually serve companies but are sometimes retained by full-service agencies when they are overloaded with work.

• *Media-buying services.* Agencies that specialize in the purchase of media for clients are called **media-buying services.** They are in high demand for many reasons, but three reasons stand out. First, media has become more complex as the number of choices grows—think of the proliferation of new cable channels, magazines, and radio stations. Second, the cost of maintaining a competent media department has escalated. Third, media-buying services often buy media at a low cost because they can group several clients' purchases together to get discounts from the media because of the volume of their media buys.

How Agency Jobs Are Organized

In addition to the chief executive officer, if the agency is large enough, it usually has one or more vice presidents, as well as department heads for the different functional areas. We will concentrate on five of those areas: account management, account planning and research, creative development and production, media planning and buying, and internal services.

Account Management The **account management** function acts a liaison between the client and the agency. It ensures that the agency focuses its resources on the client's needs. It develops its own point of view regarding the research and strategy, which the account manager presents to the client. The account manager or supervisor is also responsible for interpreting the client's marketing strategy for the rest of the agency. The president of the Leo Burnett advertising agency described an account management executive as needing "financial acumen, a passion for the creative product, and the ability to build client relationships."[14] The Inside Story focuses on the work of an account executive.

Once the client (or the client and the agency together) establishes the general guidelines for a campaign or advertisement, the account management department supervises the day-to-day development within these guidelines. Account management in a major agency typically has three levels: *management supervisor* who provides leadership on strategic issues and looks for new business opportunities, *account supervisor* who is the key executive working on a client's business and the primary liaison between the client and the agency, and the *account executive* (as well as *assistant account executives*), who is responsible for day-to-day activities and operates like a project manager.[15] Sometimes a fourth level may exist, the *account director,* who is at a higher level on the organizational chart than the account supervisor. A smaller agency will combine some of these levels.

Account Planning and Research Full-service agencies usually have a separate department specifically devoted to planning and sometimes to research as well. Today the emphasis in agency research is on developing an advertising message that focuses on the consumer's perspective and relationship with the brand. An **account planner** gathers all available intelligence on the market and consumers and acts as the voice of the consumer. Account planners are strategic specialists who prepare comprehensive information about consumers' wants, needs, and relationship to the client's brand and recommendations on how the advertising should work to satisfy those elements based on insights they derive from consumer research.

Creative Development and Production The creative members of the agency are the creative directors, creative department managers, copywriters, art directors, and producers. In addition to these positions, the broadcast production department and art studio are two other areas where creative personnel can apply their skills. Generally, the creative department has people who create and people who inspire. A creative group includes people who write (*copywriters*), people who design ideas for print ads or television commercials (*art directors*), and people who convert these ideas into television or radio commercials (*producers*).

THE INSIDE STORY

The Day-to-Day Job of an Account Executive
Tammie DeGrasse, *Account Supervisor, McCann-Erickson, New York*

"So what exactly do you do in advertising?" That is by far the most common question I am asked once someone finds out I'm in Account Management. "Do you create the ads?" "Do you choose the actors?" "Do you decide which magazines to run in?" To be honest, I don't think my own mother has it figured out yet. I've since realized that the best way to define what we, as account people, do in advertising is . . . make it all happen. To use a simple analogy, an account manager is like the supervisor in a car factory's assembly line. We don't physically connect part A to part B, but we do make sure every department fully understands what the car is supposed to look like and how it should run to ensure that it will be created effectively and efficiently, so it can sell.

That's just the big picture; my day-to-day duties aren't so lofty. Now, I could break it down and give you an idea of my typical 9 to 5 day; but to be honest, in advertising there's no such thing as "typical" or "9 to 5." My day entails anything and everything to make sure the job gets done. Whether it's literally running tapes to NBC, viewing casting reels for the next commercial, researching our clients' top competitors, watching focus groups describe what they think makes a good ad (that's always fun), or attending television shoots, my days are anything but typical. Some highlights during my career at McCann include watching a handful of celebrities read our scripts in a recording session and even having myself featured in a national newspaper ad. Hey, anything to get the job done, right?

Nonetheless, it's been amazing so far and a valuable learning experience every step of the way.

For those of you considering entering the advertising industry, deciding which area to concentrate in can be difficult. Every department is so equally appetizing that anyone would have trouble figuring out what the best fit for him or her might be. Being that I possess leadership qualities, enjoy strategizing, and like to get my hands in just about everything, Account Management seemed like my perfect fit. For others it may not be so easy, so I strongly suggest learning more about the specifics of every group. Keep in mind that there are pros and cons to each and only you can decipher on which end of the factory assembly line you would be best to work. That's all for now—have to run . . . client dinner in ten minutes. Best of luck to all of you!"

A graduate of the advertising program at Florida State University, Tammie DeGrasse was nominated by Professor Kartik Pashupati,

Many agencies build a support group around a team of an art director and copywriter who work well together.

Media Planning and Buying   Agencies that don't rely on outside media specialists have a media department that recommends to the client the most efficient means of delivering the message to the target audience. That department has three functions: planning, buying, and research. Because media is so complex, it is not unusual for some individuals to become experts in certain markets or types of media.

Internal Agency Services   The departments that serve the operations within the agency include the traffic department and print production, as well as the more general financial services and human resources (personnel). The traffic department is responsible for internal control and tracking of projects to meet deadlines. The traffic department is the lifeblood of the agency, and its personnel keep track of everything that happens.

How Agencies Are Paid by Clients

Agencies derive their revenues and profits from three main sources: commissions, fees, and retainers. A **commission** is the traditional form of compensation, basing the amount an ad agency charges its client as a percentage of the media cost. For example, if the $85,000 media cost has a 15 percent commission allowance, the agency adds $12,750 to the $85,000 when billing the client. Some clients criticize the standard 15 percent commission as too high and the commission structure as favoring more expensive media. For those accounts still using a commission approach, this rate is rarely 15 percent; it is more likely lower and subject to negotiation between agency and client.

Most advertisers now use a fee system either as the primary compensation tool or in combination with a commission system. The **fee** system is comparable to the system by which advertisers pay their lawyers and accountants. The client and agency agree on an hourly fee or rate. This fee can vary by department, or it may be a flat hourly fee for all work regardless of the salary level of the person doing the work. Charges are also included for out-of-pocket expenses, travel, and other standard items.

An agency also may be put on a monthly or yearly **retainer.** The amount billed per month is based on the projected amount of work and the hourly rate charged. This system is most commonly used by public relations agencies.

The most recent trends in agency compensation are for advertisers to pay agencies on the basis of their performance. One consultant recommends that this arrangement be based on paying the agency either a percentage of the client's sales or a percentage of the client's marketing budget. Procter & Gamble is the pioneer in trying to apply this new system.[16] Another version of this idea is that agencies share in the profits of their client when they create a successful campaign, but that also means they have a greater financial risk in the relationship should the advertising not create the intended impact.[17]

Another innovation in agency compensation is called **value billing,** which means that the agency is paid for its creative and strategic ideas, rather than for executions and media placements. It's always been difficult for agencies to bill for strategic thinking and big ideas, but several agencies led by creative "hotshop" Crispin Porter + Bogusky are experimenting with these new practices. From this discussion it should be clear that the agency-client relationship is healthy to the degree that the client is satisfied with the quality of the advertising produced—both the creative side and the media placement. Equally as important, however, is the success of the financial negotiations that work out the structure of agency compensation. It should be an accurate representation of the value of the agency's work and adequate to cover its expenses. This negotiation is a win-win for both sides depending on the trust and mutual respect clients and agencies have for each other.

CURRENT DEVELOPMENTS IN MARKETING

In Chapter 1, we concluded that advertising is a dynamic industry and subject to challenges and change. The same is true of marketing. Most companies live and die by *innovation*—or the lack thereof—and innovation always brings change. As Jim Stengel, Procter & Gamble's Chief Marketing Officer (CMO), explained, it's not just about doing great TV commercials: "The days of pounding people with images, and shoving them down their eyeballs are over. The consumer is much more in control now."[18] Stengel's four standards underpinning P&G's global marketing strategies include holistic marketing, permission marketing, better measurement, and experimentation.

Experimentation underlies innovation, which is essential if a marketing manager expects to keep up with a changing marketplace. As we noted earlier, creativity is just as important for marketing problem solvers as it is for advertising idea people. Let's consider Stengel's other ideas, as well as some of the other important issues and trends influencing the practice of marketing.

Accountability

Similar to the concern for effectiveness in advertising, accountability is a hot issue in marketing. Marketing managers are being challenged by senior management to prove that their decisions lead to the most effective marketing strategies. In other words, was this the best way to launch a new brand or expand into a new territory?

Accountability is what Stengel was calling for in his quest for better measurement. Marketing managers are under pressure to deliver business results measured in terms of sales increases, the percentage share of the market the brand holds, and corporate return on investment (ROI). The calculation of ROI determines how much money the brand made compared to its expenses. In other words, what did the marketing program cost, and what did it deliver in sales? Do marketing programs pay their own way and deliver an acceptable return on the investment?

Advertising agencies are creating departments to help marketers evaluate the efficiency and effectiveness of their marketing communication budgets. The Interpublic Group, for example, which is a large marketing communication holding company, has created the Marketing Accountability Partnership to determine what the marketer's dollars accomplish or how they can be better used.[19]

Integrated (or Holistic) Marketing

Chapter 1 introduced Integrated Marketing Communication (IMC). A similar approach that applies to marketing is called **Integrated Marketing (IM),** what P&G's Stengel referred to as *holistic marketing.* It is focused on better coordinating all marketing efforts to maximize customer satisfaction. That means the message conveyed by an indifferent customer service employee[20] may have more impact on a customer's positive feelings about a brand than all the millions of dollars spent on the brand's advertising.

Integrated marketing means all areas of the marketing mix, including marketing communication, work closely together to present the brand in a coherent and consistent way.[21] The basic premise is that everything communicates something about the brand—the price delivers a message, the place where you buy the product delivers a message, and the way it handles or performs delivers a message. And, of course, the marketing communication delivers a message. The objective of integrated marketing, then, is to manage all the messages delivered by all aspects of the marketing mix to present a consistent brand strategy.[22]

One area of particular concern is the coordination of the agencies involved in creating the various brand messages. Maurice Levy, CEO of the Publicis Groupe marketing communication holding company, has criticized the way his agencies coordinate their work on behalf of a brand. He contends that the giant company has suffered from a "silo mentality" that hurts clients. He asks, "How do we stop confusing clients with contradictory points of view coming from teams each defending their little piece of turf—to the detriment of the client's interests?"[23]

Emerging Marketing Strategies

Similar to advertising, marketing is struggling to define itself, and several new areas are emerging as marketing activities. These are less inclined to affect the definition of marketing, but they do expand its area of responsibility. Consider the following terms, all of which are trends that affect the way advertising is conducted. Stengel specifically mentioned one of them—permission marketing—as critical to his vision of new marketing.

- *Relationship marketing.* A trend in modern marketing is **relationship marketing,** which considers all the firm's stakeholders, whether employees, distributors, channel members, customers, agencies, investors, government agencies, the media, or community members. Relationship marketing is driven by communication and therefore is best accomplished through an IMC program. **Customer relationship management** (CRM) is a variation originating in sales management that uses databases to drive communication with customers and keep track of their interactions with a company.
- *Permission marketing.* Inviting prospective customers to sign up or self-select into a brand's target market in order to receive marketing communication is referred to as **permission marketing.** This practice has become more feasible with the development of interactive communication technologies, such as the Internet, that allow firms to customize their marketing messages. Advertising can contribute to this practice. Consider, for example, a new product announcement that invites interested consumers to contact the company for additional information.
- *Experience marketing.* This form of marketing uses events and store design, among other means, to engage consumers in a personal and involving way. On a broader level, **experience marketing** means that every encounter with a brand is an experience that determines whether the brand relationship is positive or negative. The idea is to engage consumers in ways that create lasting bonds with a brand.
- *Guerilla marketing.* Guerilla marketing is a really hot area of alternative marketing communication. It creates unexpected personal encounters with a brand, such as

painted messages on streets or costumed brand characters parading across a busy intersection. The idea is to create buzz, or word of mouth, about a brand.

- *Digital marketing.* Using the Internet to conduct e-business, including ordering and selling products, is called **digital marketing.** Amazon.com is the classic case. More conventional marketers, such as automobile manufacturers, are also trying to move their business platforms, or at least parts of them, online.
- *Viral marketing.* This practice is designed to create a groundswell of demand for a product based on messages circulated on the Internet. Through **viral marketing,** consumers create buzz about a product or brand through e-mails and mentions on blogs.
- *Mobile marketing.* The use of wireless communication to reach people on the move with a location-based message is called **mobile marketing.** It is possible, for example, to send text messages or voice mail with news about special sales to people's cell phones or personal digital assistants (PDAs) that use wireless technology (such as Bluetooth) when these customers are in the vicinity of a favorite store or restaurant.
- *Social network marketing.* Commercial information delivered through social networks, such as MySpace.com and Facebook.com, is called **social network marketing.** MySpace.com has surpassed Google and Yahoo as the Web site with the most traffic. Originally designed for teens (MySpace) and college students (Facebook), these sites are a combination personal diary and social club. The networks are easy to join and free, and it is easy to send messages to other members. It's also a trend-making force among young people and a place where movie studios and record labels preview their new works.

Global Marketing

In most countries markets are composed of local, regional, and international brands. A *local brand* is one marketed in a single country. A *regional brand* is one marketed throughout a region (for example, North America or Europe). An *international brand* is available virtually everywhere in the world. Advertising that promotes the same product in several countries is known as *international advertising.* It did not appear in any organized manner until the late twentieth century.

Saturation of the home-country market isn't the sole reason companies venture outside the home market. Research that shows market potential for products in other countries, mergers and acquisitions with foreign businesses, and moving into other markets to preempt development by competitors also prompts international marketing and advertising.

Export marketing and advertising are not the exclusive province of large companies. Bu Jin, an innovative company in Boulder, Colorado, creates and markets martial arts products. With only eight full-time employees, its products fill a high-end international market worldwide. Most of Bu Jin's business is driven by its catalog. Many service providers also market internationally. Airlines and transportation companies that serve foreign markets, such as UPS, are, in effect, exporting a service.

Organizing for International Marketing Once the exporter becomes nationalized in several countries in a regional bloc, the company often establishes a regional management center and transfers day-to-day management responsibilities from the home country to that office. For instance, Coca-Cola has several international regional offices to support its international markets.

A company that has domestic operations and established regional operations in Europe, Latin America, North America, the Pacific, or elsewhere, faces the question of whether to establish a world corporate headquarters. Part of the reason for making such a decision is to give the company a truly global perspective and a corporate philosophy that directs products and advertising toward a worldwide market. Unilever and Shell (both of which have twin world headquarters in the United Kingdom and the Netherlands), IBM, Nestlé, and the advertising holding company Interpublic have changed to a global management structure.

The problem of maintaining control over brand strategy, as branding guru David Aakers explains, is *silos,* or rigid departments that have difficulty coordinating their work with other departments. The silo problem is exacerbated in global marketing, particularly when the company has a policy of decentralizing the organization. Another complication is related departments that don't talk to one another on the local or international level. As Aaker observes, "The challenge of the next 10 years for the global organization is to develop a CMO [chief marketing officer]-led organization that can deal with silos."[24]

International Marketing Management Regardless of the company's form or style of management, the shift from national to international management requires new tools for advertisers, including one language (usually English), one control mechanism (the budget), and one strategic plan (the marketing strategy).

Beyond the considerations in selecting a domestic agency, the choice of an advertising agency for international advertising depends, in part, on whether the brand's messages are standardized across all markets or localized to accommodate cultural differences. If the company wants to take a highly standardized approach in international markets, it is likely to favor an international agency that can handle advertising for the product in both the domestic and international markets. A localized advertising effort, in contrast, favors use of advertising agencies in many countries for planning and implementation. The issue of standardized versus global advertising is discussed in more detail in Chapter 18.

Puma Leaps Forward

IT'S A WRAP

The opening story about Puma touched on a number of key concepts in marketing planning, such as strategic decision making, added value and, most importantly, the concept of branding.

Puma, uses a highly strategic marketing effort to set the brand apart and give it a distinctive personality. Its market communication creates an attitude for the brand, as well as sales.

That philosophy has guided everything from advertising budgets, to product distribution, and promotional partners. Puma, spends significantly less than Nike on its advertising. In spite of the relatively small ad budget, Puma ranks as one of the world's largest providers of athletic footwear, apparel and accessories, distributing its products in more than 80 countries.

Although most of the opening cases in this book highlight specific awards the campaign has won, Puma's choice not to enter award contests underscores the ultimate goal of creating ads that work hard to accomplish the company's marketing and communication objectives rather than focusing on winning awards.

Key Points Summary

1. **What is marketing, and what are its key concepts?**
   Marketing is the way a product is designed and sold, as well as a set of processes for creating customer relationships that benefit the organization and its stakeholders. The *marketing concept* refers to a focus on customers, rather than on products or a company's production capabilities. The

   relationship with the customer is established at the point of *exchange* where money is traded for goods or services. *Competitive advantage* means that the product is *differentiated* and superior in some way to its competitors. At each step in the marketing process *value is added* to the product, including product design, pricing, distribution, marketing communication, and particularly, *branding* which contributes a unique and special meaning to the product. The marketing mix includes the product, its distribution, pricing, and marketing communication.

2. **What are the different types of markets, and how do they relate to the marketing process?** The four main types of markets are *consumer* (people who buy products for their own personal use), *business-to-business* (companies that buy products to use in their business), *institutional* (nonprofit organizations that buy products for to support their operations), and *channel markets* (members of the distribution chain that may take ownership of products as they move them through the channel). The process of creating a marketing plan and managing the marketing process begins with *marketing research* that leads to setting *objectives.* An analysis of *consumer needs and wants* and how they relate to the product leads to *differentiation* and *positioning* strategies. The *marketing mix*—product, pricing, distribution, marketing communication—is designed to deliver on the objectives, and *evaluation* is used to prove the effectiveness of the marketing plan and its execution.

3. **Who are the key players in marketing?** The four important categories of key players in marketing are the marketer, suppliers or vendors, distributors and retailers, and agencies. The *marketer* is the advertiser—the company or organization that produces the product and offers it for sale. *Suppliers and vendors* are companies that provide the materials and ingredients used in running a business and producing a product. The *distribution chain or channel* refers to various companies—distributors, wholesalers, brokers, dealers, and retailers—involved in moving a product from its manufacturer or corporate source to the buyer. *Agencies* are the marketing communication companies that help marketers promote their products.

4. **How are agencies organized, and how do they work with their clients?** The advertising industry is organized into *full-service agencies,* specialized agencies such as *creative boutiques* and *media-buying services,* and *in-house agencies* and *advertising departments* within the marketer's company. In advertising agencies, work is handled by *account managers* who are the liaison with the client; *creative departments* who write and design the advertising; *media planners and buyers* who place the advertisements in the media; *account planners* and *researchers* who conduct research to obtain insights about consumer behavior and preferences; and other internal agency services that help the company operate its business.

Key Terms

account management, p. 54
account planner, p. 54
added value, p. 38
affiliate marketing, p. 50
brand equity, p. 39
brand image, p. 38
branding, p. 38
brand management, p. 49
business-to-business (B2B)
    market, p. 41
channel market, p. 43
channel marketing, p. 43
channel of distribution;
    distribution chain, p. 49
commission, p. 55
competitive advantage, p. 37
consumer, p. 36
consumer market, p. 41
cooperative (co-op)
    advertising, p. 46
creative boutique, p. 53

customary pricing, p. 46
customer, p. 36
customer relationship
    management (CRM), p. 57
differentiation, p. 44
digital marketing, p. 58
direct marketing, p. 46
distribution, p. 45
distribution chain, p. 49
exchange, p. 36
experience marketing, p. 57
fee, p. 56
full-service agency, p. 53
guerilla marketing, p. 47
ingredient branding, p. 49
institutional market, p. 41
Integrated Marketing (IM),
    p. 57
intermediaries, p. 43
lead generation, p. 48
logo, p. 39

market, p. 41
marketer, p. 49
marketing, p. 34
marketing concept, p. 36
marketing objectives, p. 44
marketing plan, p. 43
marketing research, p. 43
marketing services, p. 51
media-buying services, p. 54
mobile marketing, p. 58
permission marketing, p. 57
personal sales, p. 47
pitch, p. 51
position, p. 44
positioning, p. 44
price copy, p. 46
primary research, p. 43
product differentiation, p. 37
product-driven philosophy,
    p. 35

product management, p. 49
psychological pricing, p. 46
pull strategy, p. 46
push strategy, p. 46
relationship marketing, p. 57
resellers, p. 43
retainer, p. 56
secondary research, p. 43
segmentation, p. 44
share of market, p. 41
situation analysis, p. 43
social network marketing,
    p. 58
supply chain, p. 49
SWOTs, p. 43
target market, p. 44
trademark, p. 39
traffic department, p. 53
value billing, p. 56
viral marketing, p. 58

Review Questions

1. What is the definition of marketing, and where does advertising fit within that definition?

2. Explain how advertising relates to the five key concepts that define marketing.

3. In general, outline the structure of the marketing industry and explain where advertising fits and how it relates to the various key players.

4. Outline and explain the key steps in the process of creating a marketing plan.

5. Explain how agency work is organized. In other words, what are the primary functions or professional areas found in an agency?

6. In what ways is marketing changing? What are the main challenges and trends, and how do they affect the definition of marketing?

Discussion Questions

1. Look through the ads in this textbook and find an example of an advertisement that you think demonstrates the marketing concept and another ad that you think does not represent an effective application of the marketing concept. Compare the two and explain why you evaluated them as you did.

2. Coca-Cola is the most recognizable brand in the world. How did the company achieve this distinction? What has the company done in its marketing mix in terms of product, price, distribution, and marketing communications that has created such tremendous brand equity and loyalty? How has advertising aided in building the brand?

3. Imagine you are starting a company to manufacture fudge based on your family's old recipe. Consider the following decisions:

   a. Describe the marketing mix you think would be most effective for this company.

   b. Describe the marketing communication mix you would recommend for this company.

   c. How would you determine the advertising budget for your new fudge company?

   d. What brand image would you recommend for your fudge?

4. *Three-Minute Debate:* This chapter stressed integration of advertising with other components of the marketing mix. A classmate argues that advertising is a small part of the marketing process and relatively unimportant. If you were in marketing management for Kellogg cereals, how would you see advertising supporting the marketing mix? Does advertising add value to each of these functions for Kellogg? Do you think it is a major responsibility for the marketing manager? What would you say either in support of or in opposition to your classmate's view? Organize into small teams with pairs of teams taking one side or the other. In class, set up a series of three-minute debates in which each side has 1½ minutes to argue its position. Every team of debaters must present new points not covered in the previous teams' presentations until there are no arguments left to present. Then the class votes as a group on the winning point of view.

Take-Home Team Projects

1. Interview the manager of a large retail outlet store in your area, such as Target, Kmart, or Wal-Mart. Assess how the retailer uses various elements of the marketing communication mix. Study a few diverse products, such as food items, blue jeans, and small appliances. You might even talk to the automotive service department. Write a one-page report, summarizing how advertising comes into play in this retailer's marketing program.

2. Assess the Web sites of three ad agencies. What differences in offerings do you observe? How sensitive are they to marketing concepts, issues, and trends? Find one that you think is particularly tuned into the marketing needs of its clients. Explain and justify your analysis. (Start with the list of agency networks in Table 2.2. Search for their home pages on a search engine such as Yahoo! or Google.)

Yahoo! Hands-On Case

Review the Yahoo! case in the Appendix.

1. In what ways are the key marketing concepts, as well as the marketing mix elements, important in this campaign? Outline the five key concepts and the four marketing mix elements and explain how this campaign reflects or addresses those elements.

2. You have been asked to strengthen the argument in this plan that this campaign is truly consumer-focused. Explain how the marketing concept applies to Yahoo! and what you would say to strengthen the team's analysis of this campaign's need for a strong customer focus. In other words, why is a customer focus important for this company and this market? Prepare this as a one-page statement supporting the campaign's initial background analysis.

HANDS-ON CASE

WPP's Owner—a British Knight with Strategic Moves

To the uninformed, nothing about Martin Sorrell or his company, the WPP Group, may be quite what it seems. Although he was awarded a knighthood, Sir Martin is anything but a reserved aristocrat. And while WPP is one of the four largest advertising holding companies in the world, the initials actually stand for Wire & Plastic Products, the British company Sorrell used to gobble up some of the world's most famous advertising agencies. The roster of agencies now under the WPP's wings includes industry leaders Ogilvy and Mather, Burson-Marsteller, Hill & Knowlton, Young & Rubicam, J. Walter Thompson, and Grey, to name just a few.

Large conglomerates like WPP made frequent headlines in the 1990s, a period of great consolidation in the advertising industry. Faced with harsh economic and business realities, individual advertising agencies chose to give up independent existence to become parts of large communication companies that offered clients all the tools for an integrated campaign, including advertising, direct marketing, public relations, and sales promotion. In the new millennium, dealing with one (or several) of the four large holding companies, WPP Group (England), Interpublic (United States), Publicis Groupe (France), and Omnicom (United States), is the way the world's biggest advertisers do business.

While each of the conglomerates is led by a charismatic and dynamic individual, none appears to have an edge on Sorrell, who was described in a recent *Fortune* article as "confident, witty, and a tad arrogant, talking rapidly about the future of advertising and the challenges of keeping fractious clients and ad agencies happy." *Fortune* also noted that "in an industry populated by shameless schmoozers, the 59-year-old Sorrell is in a league of his own."

These characteristics have served Sorrell well. Unlike many of his peers, Sorrell has never written a word of copy, nor has he ever penciled a print design or directed a broadcast commercial. Sorrell's talents are organizational and strategic.

How does Martin Sorrell continue to win in the high-stakes agency world? His vision, developed years before most of his rivals caught on, that 21st-century clients would want a complete menu of marketing communication services, all of which work synergistically, is one important reason for his success. Tenacity, energy, focus, and a willingness to do whatever is needed to win are also traits that come to mind. All these are illus-

trated in the story of Sorrell's drive to land South Korean giant Samsung when the company put its advertising up for review in the spring of 2004. Samsung spends almost $400 million each year supporting its brands, which is reason enough for agencies to salivate over the account. The company holds even greater appeal for Sorrell because of his forecast that advertising growth in the 21st century will come disproportionately from Asia.

As a result, Sorrell did whatever he could to attract Samsung's attention. Like any savvy agency head, he assigned his best people to generate creative ideas to pitch to Samsung executives. But unlike most agency heads, he didn't stop there. After discovering that a Samsung-financed museum was having a grand opening in Seoul, South Korea, Sorrell jumped on a plane and ended up being the only agency person there. Samsung executives found themselves receiving e-mails from Sorrell at all times of the day and night. Peter Stringham, marketing director of HSBC, a company that Sorrell landed after several years of trying, commented, "Martin can be quite persistent. He was there from the first meeting to the last. He'd pitched to us a couple of times before and not gotten the account, but he'd had his eye on it for years."

Needless to say, in the fall of 2004, Samsung announced it was awarding its account to WPP. In the new millennium, British knights may not wear armor, carry a crest, or rescue damsels in distress. But Sir Martin Sorrell knows how to triumph in the competitive world of advertising agencies.

Consider This

1. Why do large clients like Samsung wish to work with giant holding companies like WPP instead of with smaller agencies?
2. What qualities help Sorrell to be successful? Why are these qualities so important for his company's success?
3. Explain how Martin Sorrell wins clients and builds positive agency–client relationships. How does he see the agency's role in marketing?

Sources: "Sorrell Cashes in on $30M Incentive Bonus," *Advertising Age,* September 27, 2004; "Advisers Explore Options; Publicis Link Is Possible, as Both Firms Serve P&G," *Wall Street Journal* (Eastern edition), June 29, 2004, B3; Nelson D. Schwartz, "Bigger and Bigger: Martin Sorrell Wants WPP to Be the World's Largest Marketing Machine. With His Most Recent Acquisition, He's Almost There," *Fortune,* November 29, 2004, 146; Erin White, "WPP Group's Tough-Love Artist; Neil French's Role Includes Making Candid Appraisals of Agencies' Global Talent," *Wall Street Journal,* October 20, 2003, B9; Erin White, "WPP Deal Puts Pressure on Havas; Pact to Buy Grey Solidifies Power of Four Big Firms, Leaving French Rival in Cold," *Wall Street Journal* (Eastern edition), September 14, 2004, B14.

Advertising and Society

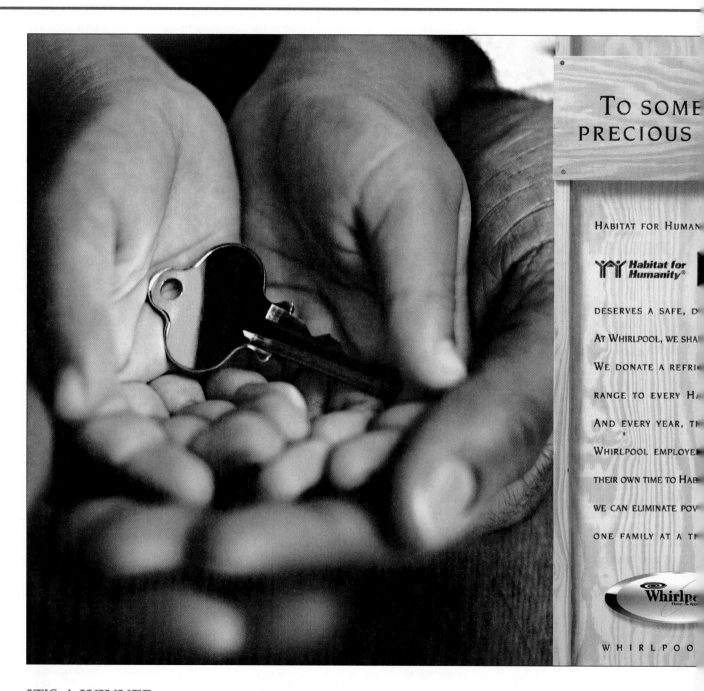

IT'S A WINNER

Awards:	Company:	Agency:	Campaign:
Effie Award	Whirlpool	Publicis New York,	Whirlpool
Cause Marketing		Edelman	REBA/Habitat for
Golden Halo			Humanity
Award			

Whirlpool + Habitat for Humanity = Good Business

Imagine that you're in charge of advertising for Whirlpool's major domestic appliances—stoves, refrigerators, washers, and dryers. Each performs a specific, important household function that makes everyday life a little easier. But consumers tend to think about buying new ones only when the washing machine breaks or they're building or remodeling a house. What would you do to get consumers to think about Whirlpool even when they don't need a new appliance? How would you approach the job of helping Whirlpool stay true to its corporate values while increasing sales and market share?

Whirlpool and its integrated agency partners, know a lot about the consumer audience for major appliances. Whirlpool describes its target audience as "Active Balancers." Those are working women, ages 25 to 54, with children. They must manage their time and chores efficiently. They're outwardly focused and think about their homes, their families, and their careers. The Whirlpool audience is socially aware and involved in—or at least interested in—humanitarian causes.

A consumer insight that proved to be key to this campaign was the discovery that brand loyalty to Whirlpool products is stronger when consumers make an emotional (vs. rational) connection to the brand. The creative strategy recognized that these women believe a "home is more than a place to keep the rain off one's head." Mothers who are sensitive to issues of home and family care about helping others achieve their aspirations of providing help to those in need.

Whirlpool and the agencies realized that communicating Whirlpool's ongoing commitment to Habitat for Humanity and its mission of "building simple, decent, affordable housing in partnership with people in need" would resonate with Active Balancers and help them form an emotional connection to the brand.

Chapter Key Points

1. What kind of power does advertising have in society, and what are its limitations?
2. Why and how is advertising regulated?
3. What guides ethical behavior in advertising?

Jeff Terry, senior manager for the Whirlpool involvement with Habitat for Humanity, said, "The partnership was founded on the simple notion that the home is the heart of the family, and it is people who make a house a home."

To execute the idea, the brand hired Reba McEntire, an idol to this audience, to further the Habitat cause. In addition to sponsoring Reba McEntire/Habitat for Humanity concert tours, the campaign featured the following program elements: television commercials, ads in *Parents Magazine* and *Good Housekeeping*; custom programming on Scripps Network and sponsorships on Country Music TV; a Whirlpool Web site; and a traveling Habitat for Humanity display on an 18-wheeler.

Do you think Whirlpool's plan worked? Read how effective Whirlpool's campaign was at the end of the chapter in the It's a Wrap feature.

Sources: M. Santifort, REBA/Habitat for Humanity, ZenithOptimediaUSA, http://www.zenithoptimedia.com; R. Beech, Habichat: A newsletter for the staff of Habitat for Humanity International, August 12, 2005, http://www.habitat.org; Whirlpool Awards and Achievements, October 2006, http://www.whirlpool.com; "Cause Marketing Forum Recognizes Whirlpool Corporation and its Whirlpool and KitchenAid Brands for Their Nonprofit Partnerships," PR Newswire, May 17, 2006, http://www.newscom.com.

Top 20 Socially and Environmentally Responsible Companies

1. Microsoft
2. Whole Foods Market
3. Kellogg's
4. McDonald's
5. The Home Depot
6. Walt Disney
7. UPS
8. Coca-Cola
9. Starbucks
10. PepsiCo
11. Johnson & Johnson
12. Procter & Gamble
13. Kimberly-Clark
14. Lowe's
15. Target
16. Ford
17. Apple
18. Dell
19. H.J. Heinz
20. Eastman Kodak

Source: Natural Marketing Institute, 2006.

Whirlpool's campaign to align itself with a good cause demonstrates that marketing communication might help make the world a little better. Often when we look at advertising, we focus on what the advertising will do for the advertiser and the consumer. Those are valid concerns. But they're not the only ones that students of advertising should consider. The Whirlpool case shows that advertisers can think beyond the campaign's immediate benefits to consider how their actions might affect a larger sphere—society and the natural environment.

It is important for advertisers to consider what impact their work has on society. This chapter emphasizes the social and cultural impacts of advertising as well as the legal and regulatory responsibilities of advertisers. The chapter concludes with a discussion about how advertisers can apply their ethical decision-making skills.

WHAT IS ADVERTISING'S ROLE IN SOCIETY?

Do you think advertising is inherently good or bad for society? In the first chapter you learned that advertising is persuasive communication that uses mass and interactive media to reach broad audiences in order to connect an identified sponsor with buyers and provide information about products. It is news about products. Most of the time people use advertising for neutral or good purposes, meaning they act in a way that's **social responsibility,** as the accompanying Shell ad demonstrates. The list of the Top 20 Socially and Environmentally Responsible Companies, known as the LOHAS Index™, which was compiled by the Natural Marketing Institute and published in *Brandweek,* illustrates how important a socially responsible reputation is to companies. Microsoft leads the list because of the contributions of the Bill and Melissa Gates foundation. We'll start this chapter with three important debates concerning the role of advertising as an institution in society.

Demand Creation Debate

Some critics charge that advertising causes **demand creation,** which means an external message drives people to feel a need or want—sometimes unnecessarily. Others reject this notion. Does advertising create demand for products people don't need?

Let's start the discussion by considering deodorants. Did you know that no one used deodorants much until about 1919? People didn't realize they had body odor. An ad for a new product, Odorono (great name, and it's still being used, by the way), targeted women because everyone assumed that men were supposed to emit bad odors and women would

SHOWCASE To solve a local crisis in Iceland with its image, Shell used a campaign based on the slogan "Shell—with you all the way." The campaign demonstrated how Shell is involved and "travels" with customers from youth to adulthood, from their work to their home, from the present to the future—shaping the society that people want to build. This ad was contributed by Ingvi Logason, Principal in HER&NU, Reykjavik, Iceland, and a graduate of Western Florida University; his work was nominated by Professor Tom Groth.

be more likely users of the product. The ad in *Ladies' Home Journal* so offended readers that about 200 people canceled their subscription. The ads were effective, however. Sales for the deodorant rose 112 percent.[1] Did advertising make women buy something they didn't even know they needed? Was that a bad thing?

If you think it doesn't happen today, think about Unilever's Axe and Gillette's Tag. Axe pioneered the new category of body spray for men in 2002. Did guys know before 2002 that they needed scented body spray? Is it a good thing advertising convinces people to buy products like deodorants and body sprays? Can such advertising improve consumers' lives? (See Hands-on Case at the end of this chapter.)

Companies often invest much money on research to find out what consumers want before they launch new products. If people do not want the products that are being marketed, they do not buy them. Advertising may convince people to buy a product—even a bad one—once. If they try the product and do not like it, they will probably stop buying it. So to some extent advertising creates demand. At the same time, it is important to remember that audiences may refuse to purchase the product if they don't feel a need for it.

Shape-versus-Mirror Debate

Another important debate about advertising's role in society questions the limits of its influence. At what point does advertising cross the line between reflecting social values and creating them? Critics argue that advertising has repeatedly crossed this line, influencing vulnerable groups, such as children and young teenagers, too strongly. A case in point: Do ultra-thin models in advertising cause young women to have eating disorders, as some have claimed? While it is probable that the images women and girls see influence them in some ways, it's difficult to say that these images directly and solely cause the problems, as many factors in their environment potentially influence their eating choices. But, still, advertising may contribute to the problem.

Can advertising manipulate people's choices? In general, critics of advertising argue that advertising can create social trends and has the power to dictate how people think and act. They believe that even if an individual ad cannot control our behavior, the cumulative effects of nonstop television, radio, print, Internet, and outdoor ads can be overwhelming. On the other hand, advertisers contend that the best they can do is spot trends and then develop advertising messages that connect with them. If people are interested in achieving healthy lifestyles, you will see ads that use health appeals as an advertising strategy. Advertisers believe advertising mirrors values rather than sets them.

One example of using advertising to try to change society and improve the world while still selling products is the RED campaign, instigated by U2 singer Bono in conjunction with major companies like Apple, Gap, and Converse. The purpose of the campaign is to sell RED-branded products to help fight AIDS and HIV in Africa. Does advertising cause people to think about ways to eliminate AIDS and HIV in Africa or does it mirror a societal concern for Africans' welfare?

The RED Campaign demonstrates a collaborative effort by several corporations, including Gap, to fight AIDS in Africa.

Advertising and society's values are probably interactive, so the answer to the debate may simply be that advertising both mirrors and shapes values. Advertising planners spend huge amounts of money and time trying to identify people's motivations before they develop message strategies. They must, then, be searching for something deeper than the impact of a previous ad.

This shape-versus-mirror debate is the most central issue we need to address in considering advertising's role in society. What drives consumers to behave or believe as they do? Is it advertising, or is it other forces? Why do women buy cosmetics, for example? Are they satisfying a deep cultural need for beauty, or were they manipulated by advertising to believe in the hope that cosmetics offer? Women can even purchase a product by philosophy called Hope in a Jar. Or have their families and friends socialized them to believe they look better with cosmetics than without?

The Overcommercialization Debate

Does advertising lead people to be too materialistic? The second half of the 20th century is notable for the rise of a materialistic consumer culture in the Western world. Did advertising create this culture, or does it simply reflect it?

Some argue that advertising heightens expectations and primes the audience to believe that the answer is always a product. If you have a headache, what do you do? You take a pill. What is left unsaid by an advertisement is that you might get rid of the headache just as easily by taking a nap, drinking less alcohol or more water, or taking a walk to relieve stress. Nobody pays for ads to tell you about alternatives. Consumers, however, are not passive sponges who always do what advertisers tell them. As we have said, they have the power to refuse to buy what is being sold.

Another facet of this debate relates to a problem that emerges if the walls blur between advertising and news and entertainment. If advertising becomes intertwined with news, how will audiences know whether the news stories are free from editorial pressure from sponsors who want to control what is said about their brands? As product placement becomes increasingly prevalent, how does that affect entertainment? Does the influence of advertising, for example, change how we watch football games and other sporting events? Does *The Apprentice* become nothing more than an hour-long commercial? Does it bother you that Coke has 2,676 occurrences of product placement in *American Idol,* especially when 16.9 percent of the viewers are under 16?[2]

Other Social Responsibility Issues

The debates about advertising's role in creating demand for products and its ability to shape societal values and make people materialistic are all concerns about how advertising as an institution might affect our culture. It's important to know about these criticisms of advertising and to think about alternative perspectives about what advertising contributes to our daily lives.

To help you understand issues that advertisers face when they can have a direct impact and make a difference to society, we'll discuss six key issues: (1) taste and offensive advertising, (2) stereotyping, (3) body and self-image problems, (4) targeting strategies, (5) problems with advertising claims and other message strategies, and (6) the issues surrounding the marketing of controversial products. If you're interested in these and other related topics, visit the Advertising Educational Foundation Web site for more information: http://www.aef.com/on_campus/asr/mission.

Poor Taste and Offensive Advertising   Although certain ads might be in bad taste in any circumstance, viewer reactions are affected by such factors as sensitivity to the product category, timing (if the message is received in the middle of dinner, for example), and other circumstances, such as whether the person is alone or with others when viewing the message. Some television ads, for example, might not bother adults watching alone but would make them uncomfortable if children were watching.

Also, questionable ads become offensive in the wrong context. Advertisers and media outlets must try to be sensitive to such objections. Recently, outraged advertisers pulled ads from a planned special on Fox that was supposed to feature O. J. Simpson discussing how he would have killed Nicole Brown Simpson had he committed the crime. The program never ran.

A MATTER OF PRACTICE

Pizza, Tacos, and Truck Parts: Misuse and Misdirection of Sex in Advertising
By Herbert Jack Rotfeld, *Professor of Marketing, Auburn University*

An advertisement for a pizza place near a college campus ran an advertisement in the school paper that read, "Put a hot piece between your lips. We're hot and easy, fast and cheesy." In another city, a Mexican restaurant showed a Lycra-clad woman posed with her hands on her hips over the headline, "Tickle my taco."

In each case, the advertiser probably thought it was good advertising, not realizing that the irrelevant use of sex distracts and hinders any communication or persuasion to the target. It should be intuitively obvious that a product is sexually relevant for marketing communications only if people would make a purchase for a sexual reason. While breath mints, clothes, or exercise equipment may be purchased by some people to enhance their self-image of sex appeal, it is doubtful that anyone buys pizza or tacos for anticipation of an orgasmic experience.

A truck supply company owner thought he had client-grabbing pictures on his business calendars with the monthly display of exposed female anatomy, but when many of his customers forgot his company name or "lost" his phone number, he finally realized that the secretaries and office managers who gave the truckers the necessary purchase order forms would never allow such lewd displays on their office walls.

The misplaced marketing problem is more than just simple misdirection and distraction. The people who wrote or produced these ads lost track of what they are trying to say to the target audience. After years of talking to advertisers and watching them produce these less-than-optimal efforts, one realizes that some of the advertising creators believe that publicity from offending people is always beneficial. Instead of communications, attention of any kind, to anything, at any cost, is their goal.

However, advertising is a very limited and limiting form of communication, costly to undertake and difficult to carry out successfully. The marketing question of how best to communicate is a conservative one, but it is also an effort to maximize the likelihood of a favorable consumer response. In the end, there is a communication job to be done.

Too often, advertising writers seem focused on titillating each other with the overuse of lewd imagery, exposed breasts, and other distractions. In the end, the sex does not sell.

Principle
Testing is needed to find the right balance when one group that sees the advertisement finds the message offensive, even though the primary target may think the message is appropriate.

We all have our own ideas about what constitutes good taste. Unfortunately, these ideas vary so much that creating general guidelines for good taste in advertising is difficult. Different things offend different people. In addition, taste changes over time. What was offensive yesterday may not be considered offensive today. The Odorono ad offended people in 1919, but would it today? By today's standards that advertisement seems pretty tame. Today's questions of taste center on the use of sexual innuendo, nudity, vulgarity, and violence. What about the Axe ads for male body sprays? Do you find them offensive or in good taste?

An ad can be offensive to the general public even if the targeted audience accepts it. Advertisers would be wise to conduct research to gauge the standards of taste for the general population as well as the specific target audience. If they fail to do so, advertisers risk alienating potential consumers. Such was the case with Abercrombie and Fitch's sexually explicit ads aimed at young teens that spawned a grassroots campaign to stop the company's marketing tactics. Some might argue that any publicity is good publicity, and offensive advertising calls attention to your product in a memorable way. The Matter of Practice box by Herbert Rotfeld discusses this topic in more detail.

Sex in Advertising   Although the use of sex in advertising is not new, it is becoming more blatant. Advertising that portrays women (or men) as sex objects is considered demeaning and sexist, particularly if sex is not relevant to the product. Ads for cosmetics and lingerie fall into a gray area because sex appeals for these products are usually relevant; the ethical question then is how sexy is too sexy. A TV commercial for Carl's Jr. restaurant chain recently drew criticism for its "overexposure" of hotel heiress Paris Hilton from people who thought her moves were soft-core porn.[3]

Portraying Diverse People Fairly and Accurately   Dumb blondes, sickly older adults, sexy Italians, smart Asians. You're probably familiar with these and other examples of stereotypes. A **stereotype** is a representation of a cultural group that emphasizes a trait or group of traits that may or may not communicate an accurate representation of the group. Sometimes the stereotype is useful (athletes are fit) and aids communication by using easily understood symbolic meanings, but sometimes the stereotype relies on a characteristic that is negative or exaggerated and, in so doing, reduces the group to a caricature. This is the problem with portraying older adults as all being sickly, for instance.

Principle
Stereotyping is negative when it reduces a group of people to a caricature.

The issue of stereotyping also raises the shape-versus-mirror question. For example, stereotyping women as sex objects is a practice that is deeply embedded in our culture. When a woman is portrayed as a sex object in an advertisement, it is reflecting or linking to a cultural value, however negatively some might see that value. Is it an accurate portrayal of women if all the models used in advertising conform to a beauty ideal that is almost impossible to achieve for normal women? Using such strategies also makes advertising a participant in shaping and reinforcing that cultural value.

If we believe that advertising has the ability to shape our values and our view of the world, then it is essential that advertisers become aware of how they portray different groups. Conversely, if we believe that advertising mirrors society, advertisers have a responsibility to ensure that what is portrayed is accurate and representative. Diversity has become an issue as advertisers struggle to target, as well as portray, people outside the white, straight mainstream market. Here are some of the most common problems found in the way advertising portrays people.

- *Gender stereotypes.* Television is a powerful socializing agent and is particularly influential in the area of gender identity. One of the most important lessons it teaches is how people fit into culturally shared gender and racial roles. The way women are cast as characters in commercials and programming can create or reinforce cultural stereotypes.[4]

  Historically, advertising has portrayed gender in distinct and predictable stereotypes. Men are usually shown as strong, independent, and achievement oriented; women are shown as nurturing and empathetic, but softer and more dependent, and they are told that the products being advertised will make their lives less stressful and more manageable. Men are often negatively stereotyped as well. FathersAndHusbands.org formed to promote positive images of men in the media.

  Harmful female stereotypes take a number of forms, from simple housewives to superwomen to sexual objects. Women are sometimes portrayed as indecisive, childlike, frivolous, and only interested in shopping; obsessed with men or their own physical appearance; and submissive to men.

  A study of gender representation in 1,300 prime-time commercials in the late 1990s found that although women make most purchases of goods and services, they are underrepresented as primary characters during most prime-time commercials, except for health and beauty products. Women are cast as younger, supportive counterparts to men, and older women remain the most underrepresented group. Television commercials, in other words, perpetuate traditional stereotypes of women and men.[5]

  However, many advertisers are recognizing the diversity of women's roles. In the 1990s advertisements did a better job of depicting women in roles that were more than one dimensional.[6] They functioned in multiple roles, not just as career women or supermoms.

  A few adventurous companies have even begun to show images suggesting homosexuality in advertising to general audiences through mass media. Such images have appeared fairly extensively in mainstream fashion advertising for brands such as Calvin Klein, Benetton, and Banana Republic. The coming-out episode of ABC's *Ellen* was groundbreaking in more ways than just programming—it was the first time advertisers used prime-time network TV to reach gay and lesbian viewers. Shows like *Queer Eye for the Straight Guy* and *Will and Grace* portray homosexuality through multidimensional characters. Advertisers increasingly try to target the homosexual audience. Viacom's LOGO, a 24-hour gay channel, is supported by a host of national advertisers trying to reach this audience.

• *Body image and self-image.* Closely related to the notion of gender stereotypes is the issue of portraying body images in a way that is socially responsible. Do you think that supermodels project healthy portrayals of women? Advertising has been criticized for glorifying glamorous looks in both men and women. In an interview on National Public Radio, Jean Kilbourne, author of *Can't Buy My Love: How Advertising Changes the Way We Think and Feel,* said that "ads are aimed at the very heart of girls' insecurities" because of the ideal image of beauty that they portray "an absolutely perfect-looking young woman who's incredibly thin."[7]

Playing on consumers' insecurities about their appearance presents advertisers with a classic ethical dilemma because self-image advertising can also be seen as contributing to self-improvement. Sometimes, however, such strategies are questionable because they lead to dangerous practices. Some critics charge that women place their health at risk in order to cultivate an unrealistic or even unhealthy physical appearance. Do you think advertising sends this message? To discover how flagrant or subtle this message is, a group of researchers tested the "thin ideal" on college-age women, the group most vulnerable to this message and to high incidences of eating disorders. They found that students did not perceive any danger in advertisements using excessively thin fashion models as a stereotypical portrayal of beauty. The respondents in the study reacted strongly to other female stereotypes but were far less concerned about images promoting the thin ideal. The authors concluded that although many female stereotypes used in advertising are irritating, offensive, and demeaning, none is potentially more dangerous to health than the thin ideal.[8] Advertising that only features thin models normalizes the thin ideal of beauty. Young women and even men can become obsessed with their weight to the point that they believe they are only beautiful if they are unnaturally thin. The Dove Campaign for Real Beauty that you'll read about in Chapter 5 defies the notion that women need to be thin to be beautiful.

The same problem of stereotyping based on physical appearance exists for men, particularly young men, although the muscular ideal V-shaped body with well-developed chest and arm muscles and wide shoulders tapering down to a narrow waist may not lead to the same health-threatening reactions that young women face, unless men resort to steroids to attain this image. Other stereotyped male images are the rugged western Marlboro man and the clueless buffoon who appears in ads as a bungling dad.

The standard of attractiveness is a sociocultural phenomenon that advertising both mirrors and shapes. Responsible advertisers have, therefore, begun using models of more normal size and weight as a way to reduce the pressure on young people who seem to be the most open to messages about cultural standards of beauty and physical attractiveness.

• *Racial and ethnic stereotypes.* Think about sports teams like the Washington Redskins, Kansas City Chiefs, or Cleveland Indians that reduce Native Americans to a caricature, and you'll know why some critics claim that racial and ethnic groups are stereotyped in advertising. That charge was evident in the Just for Feet ad that showed a black man being hunted down like a wild animal. Similarly, a postcard campaign for the Toyota RAV4 showed a male, African American mouth, exaggerated lips, white pearly teeth, and a gold Toyota Rav4 SUV emblazoned on one of the teeth. The Rev. Jesse Jackson observed that, "All that's missing is a watermelon."

In one study of the prototypical images of African Americans, the researchers found that blacks are portrayed in commercials as staying in the background and having little to say (except in ads designed exclusively for black publications). Men are athletic, tall, dark, handsome, fashionable, outgoing, and not family connected. Women like to shop and are seen as fair-skinned with wavy hair, quiet, petite, and supportive. The most frequently seen image is of a black child or teenager.[9] A study of Asians in television commercials found that they were treated similarly to females in general. In other words, they were underrepresented and given lesser roles.

One myth is that members of minority groups are all the same. The Hispanic/Latino market is a case in point. In 2006, the Hispanic/Latino population in the United States was more than 44.3 million, 14.8 percent of the total.[10] Still, there is a misconception that all Hispanic consumers are alike, when nothing could be farther from the truth: There are major differences in groups whose ancestry is Spanish, Mexican, Cuban, Puerto Rican, or who hail from another Caribbean, Central American, or South American country.

- *Cultural differences in global advertising.* In the global economy advertisers seek worldwide audiences for their products. As they do so, advertisers sometimes make mistakes of overlaying their worldview on that of another culture without thinking about the impact of their advertising. Many oppose the move to a global perspective because of concerns about the homogenization of cultural differences. **Marketing imperialism** or **cultural imperialism.** is a term used to describe what happens when Western culture is imposed on others, particularly the Middle East, Asian, and African cultures. Some Asian and Mid-Eastern countries are critical of what they see as America's materialism and disrespectful behavior toward women and elders. They worry that international advertising and media will encourage their young people to adopt these viewpoints.

  Cultural differences are very real, and we will talk more about them in Chapters 5 and 18. Consider that respect for culture and local customs is so important that insensitivity to local customs can make an ad completely ineffective. Customs can be even stronger than laws. When advertising to children age 12 or older was approved in Germany, for example, local customs were so strong that companies risked customer revolt by advertising. In many countries, naming a competitor in comparative advertising is considered bad form.

- *Age-related stereotypes* Another group that critics say is often subject to stereotyping is senior citizens, a growing segment of the population with increasing amounts of disposable income. Critics object to the use of older people in roles that portray them negatively.

  Barbara Champion, president of Champion & Associates, a research firm specializing in the maturing market, made the following observation: "The needs of maturing consumers, depending on mental and physical acuity as well as life-stage factors, are often different from one another. Whether a consumer is an empty-nester whose children have grown up and left home, a grandparent, a retiree, a widow, or in need of assisted living, for example, will greatly affect how, when, and why goods and services are purchased."[11] Many of the ads for Viagra speak to a specific segment of the population and do so in a tasteful, tactful way.

  In a focus group of women in their 50s, participants had trouble keeping their comments polite when viewing a series of health care ads that showed older women in primarily sedentary activities. One explained that even though she has arthritis, she still wants to see ads show arthritis sufferers working out in a gym, rather than "silver-haired couples walking along the beach with a golden retriever."[12]

- *Advertising to children.* Marketing to youth is one of the most controversial topics in the industry. One reason why advertising to children attracts so much attention is that children are seen as vulnerable. Children do not always know what is good for them and what is not. Concerned adults want to make sure that they protect impressionable minds from exploitation marketers. They want to help children learn to make good choices.

  A current issue that's being addressed relates to selling soft drinks, candy, and food with high fat and sugar content to children. Recognizing that obesity among youth is a major health problem, the Children's Food and Beverage Advertising Initiative recently formed to help 10 major corporations set guidelines to cut down on junk food advertising. The companies, which are responsible for producing almost two-thirds of the food and drink advertising for children under 12, include General Mills, McDonald's, Coca-Cola, PepsiCo, Hershey, and Kellogg.[13]

  Marketing alcohol to black teens is another important issue because of the use of rappers like Ice-T to promote malt liquors and the dozens of pages of alcohol ads that appear in black youth–culture magazines such as *Vibe.* A Georgetown University study contends that the alcohol beverage industry is marketing far more heavily to African American young people than to others in that age group.

You'll read more about the important issue of advertising to children in the regulation section of this chapter.

Message-Related Issues   Most advertisers succeed in creating messages that communicate fairly and accurately. Advertising professionals need to understand what is not considered acceptable so they can avoid unethical and even illegal behavior. Advertising claims are considered to be unethical if they are false, misleading, or deceptive. In the drive to find something to say about a product that will catch attention and motivate the audience to respond, advertisers sometimes stretch the truth. **False advertising**, which is a type of misleading advertising, is simply a message that is untrue. Misleading claims, puffery, comparative advertising, endorsements, and product demonstrations are explained next.

Principle

Advertising claims are unethical if they are false, misleading, or deceptive.

• *Misleading claims.* The target of the heaviest criticism for being misleading is weight-loss advertising, as well as other back-of-the-magazine, self-improvement advertisements for health and fitness products. In a study of 300 weight-loss ads, the Federal Trade Commission (FTC), a regulatory body, found that ads for weight-loss products sometimes make "grossly exaggerated" claims and that dieters need to beware of ads for dietary supplements, meal replacements, patches, creams, wraps, and other products. (The FTC will be described more completely in the regulation section.) The study found that 40 percent of the ads made at least one representation that was almost certainly false, and 55 percent made a claim that was very likely false or at least lacked adequate substantiation.[14]

Misleading claims are not just a problem in the United States. The London-based Barclays credit card was forced (by the U.K.'s Office of Fair Trading, which is equivalent to the FTC in the United States) to withdraw an advertising campaign that promised "0 percent forever." The ad was deemed deceptive because borrowers would enjoy the no-interest offer for only as long as it took for the balance to be cleared. In other words, all new spending on the card would be charged the standard interest rate.[15]

• *Puffery.* Not all exaggerated claims are seen as misleading. **Puffery** is defined as "advertising or other sales representations, which praise the item to be sold with subjective opinions, superlatives, or exaggerations, vaguely and generally, stating no specific facts."[16] Campbell Soup, for example, has used the slogan "M'm!, M'm!, Good!" which is vague and can't really be proven or disproved. It's a classic example of puffery, generally deemed to be of little concern to regulators looking for false or misleading claims because it is so innocuous.

Because obviously exaggerated "puffing" claims are legal, the question of puffery is mainly an ethical one. According to the courts, consumers expect exaggerations and inflated claims in advertising, so reasonable people wouldn't believe that these statements ("puffs") are literal facts. Virtually everyone is familiar with puffery claims for certain products: Sugar Frosted Flakes are "g-r-eat," and send Hallmark cards if you "want to send the very best."

Principle

Puffery may be legal, but if it turns off the target audience, nothing is gained by using such a message strategy.

However, empirical evidence on the effectiveness of puffery is mixed. Some research suggests that the public might expect advertisers to be able to prove the truth of superlative claims, and other research indicates that reasonable people do not believe such claims. Advertisers must decide what claims are and are not socially responsible and when the puffery is unbelievable or over the top.[17] This is particularly important when advertising to children who might not know the difference between fact and opinion.

Should it be legal for advertising messages to make claims based on opinion? Noted advertising scholar Ivan L. Preston does not think all puffs deserve to be protected legally. Find out why he thinks all puffs are not created equal by reading the excerpt in the Matter of Principle feature from a speech he delivered on the topic of puffery in Mexico City in 2006.

• *Comparative advertising.* Although it is perfectly legitimate to use advertising that compares the advertiser's product favorably against a competitor, regulations govern the use of **comparative advertising** that can be challenged as misleading. Advertisers

A MATTER OF **PRINCIPLE**

Preston on Puffery

By Ivan L. Preston, *Professor Emeritus, University of Wisconsin*

I believe some forms of puffery ought to be prohibited. Let me explain by first defining what it is. Puffs are statements that evaluate and present values about a thing rather than facts that state what it is or does. Puffs are offered as the opinions of the source presenting them. In the regulatory context they are almost always called *puffery* or *puffs*, but evaluations or opinions is what they are. Here's a list of six varieties of puffs, listed by strength.

1. *The strongest is best.* That means no competitor equals you. In the United States, Nestle's says it makes the very best chocolate, and Gillette is the best a man can get, and Goodyear has the best tires in the world. Other ways of saying *best* include terms such as *most comfortable, longest lasting, tastiest*—anything that says you're alone at the top of the list.
2. *Best possible.* As in: Nothing cleans stains better than Clorox. This type is also a claim to be at the top, except to claim that nobody is better allows for others to be just as good. It's a clever claim, because research shows that many consumers think it means better than all others.
3. *Better.* You are better than another, or better than many, or just better. The pain reliever Advil says: Advil works better. If it explicitly says better than all others, it goes in Category 1, so this No. 3 is for claims that don't claim explicitly to be better than all others. It's often used when competing mainly against just one other brand.
4. *Good and Specially Good.* The next two categories are both Good, but Specially Good involves strong statements such as *great.* Weber says its barbecue grill is great outdoors. Coty calls its perfume extraordinary. Many products claim to be wonderful or fantastic; Bayer aspirin works wonders. But these claims do not say best or better explicitly.
5. *Good is just plain good.* An insurance company says "You're in good hands with Allstate." Campbell's Soup is "M'm!, M'm!, Good!" Those are weaker claims, lower on the scale.
6. *Subjective claims.* These statements use words that are not explicitly evaluative, but people are likely to take them as valuations. A sports network refers to itself as "Sports Heaven." A candy maker says, "There's a smile in every Hershey Bar."

I hypothesize that evidence from consumers would show that the strongest puffs, especially Number 1, are most likely to lead to consumer perceptions that are false and can produce deception. Those at the bottom, especially Number 6, are least likely to produce such problems. Examples such as the smile in the candy bar, I think are more likely to be seen as fanciful or joking rather than serious.

Puffery in the United States can be factually false and legal. The only puffery I'm talking about prohibiting legally is the false kind. Puffery is an issue only when deception is an issue, and deception is an issue only when there's a claim. Not all ad content is a claim. A lot of it is intended only to get attention so that consumers will stay with the ad and see the part where there is a claim. Other ad content shows sheer enthusiasm, such as appeals to action like "Take a look at this." So remember, no claim, no problem.

---

face the common threat that competitors will misrepresent their products, prices, or some other attributes. While no one expects a competitor to be totally objective, advertisers have regulatory recourse to object to unfair comparisons. The Lanham Act permits awards of damages from an advertiser who "misrepresents the nature, characteristics, qualities, or geographic origin in comparative advertising."

Comparative advertising is a big red flag and advertisers who engage in this practice know that research in support of their competitive claims must be impeccable. Comparative advertising is permitted in the United States, but the ads must compare similar products. Also, companies can't claim that their prices are lower than the competition unless they can prove that the same products are sold at other places for higher prices.

Under the Lanham Act, companies/plaintiffs are required to prove five elements to win a false-advertising lawsuit about an ad making a comparative claim:

1. False statements have been made about either product.
2. The ads actually deceived or had the tendency to deceive a substantial segment of the audience.

3. The deception was "material" or meaningful. In other words, the plaintiff must show that the false ad claim is likely to influence purchasing decisions.
4. Falsely advertised goods are sold in interstate commerce.
5. The suing company has been or likely will be injured as a result of the false statements, either by loss of sales or loss of goodwill.

In addition to the Lanham Act, consumers also may rely on state laws governing unfair competition and false ad claims if the consumer is the victim of a false comparative claim. In California, for example, the Business and Professional Code prohibits "unlawful, unfair, or fraudulent business practices" and "unfair, deceptive, untrue, or misleading" advertising.

An advertisement can harm a brand in other ways. For example, Absolut Vodka pulled an ad after Vail Resorts threatened to sue. The ad showed the distinctive vodka bottle, which has been used for a decade, to put a twist on a visual pun in the shape of a cast for a broken leg. The words "Absolut Vail" were scrawled across it.[18]

The American Association of Advertising Agencies offers 10 guidelines that advertisers should follow to ensure truthful comparative advertising. These are shown in Table 3.1.

- *Endorsements.* A popular advertising strategy is the use of a spokesperson who endorses a brand. That's a perfectly legal strategy, unless the endorser doesn't actually use the product. An **endorsement** or **testimonial** is any advertising message that consumers believe reflects the opinions, beliefs, or experiences of an individual, group, or institution. However, if consumers can reasonably ascertain that a message does not reflect the announcer's opinion, the message isn't an endorsement and may even be misleading.

    Because many consumers rely on endorsements to make buying decisions, the FTC investigates endorsement advertising. Endorsers must be qualified by experience or training to make judgments, and they must actually use the product. If endorsers are comparing competing brands, they must have tried those brands as well. Those who endorse a product improperly may be liable if the FTC determines there is a deception.

Table 3.1 American Association of Advertising Agencies' Ten Guidelines for Comparative Advertising

1. The intent and connotation of the ad should be to inform and never to discredit or unfairly attack competitors, competing products or services.
2. When a competitive product is named, it should be one that exists in the marketplace as significant competition.
3. The competition should be fairly and properly identified but never in a manner or tone of voice that degrades the competitive product or service.
4. The advertising should compare related or similar properties or ingredients of the product, dimension to dimension, feature to feature.
5. The identification should be for honest comparison purposes and not simply to upgrade by association.
6. If a competitive test is conducted, it should be done by an objective testing service.
7. In all cases the test should be supportive of all claims made in the advertising that are based on the test.
8. The advertising should never use partial results or stress insignificant differences to cause the consumer to draw an improper conclusion.
9. The property being compared should be significant in terms of value or usefulness of the product to the consumer.
10. Comparisons delivered through the use of testimonials should not imply that the testimonial is more than one individual's, unless that individual represents a sample of the majority viewpoint.

Source: James B. Astrachan, "When to Name a Competitor," *Adweek* (May 23, 1988): 37. Copyright American Association of Advertising Agencies. Reprinted by permission.

- *Demonstrations.* Product demonstrations in television advertising must not mislead consumers. This mandate is especially difficult for advertisements of food products because such factors as hot studio lights and the length of time needed to shoot the commercial can make the product look unappetizing. Think about the problems of shooting ice cream under hot lights. Because milk looks gray on television, advertisers often substitute a mixture of glue and water. The question is whether the demonstration falsely upgrades the consumers' perception of the advertised brand. The FTC evaluates this kind of deception on a case-by-case basis.

      One technique some advertisers use to sidestep restrictions on demonstrations is to insert disclaimers or "supers," verbal or written words in the ad that indicate exceptions to the advertising claim made. You've probably seen car commercials that start with beauty shots of the product. Suddenly, the message is less clear; for several seconds five different, often lengthy, disclaimers flash on the screen in tiny, eye-straining type, including "See dealers for details and guaranteed claim form" and "Deductibles and restrictions apply."

Product-Related Issues   Marketers need to consider carefully what they choose to produce and advertise. Some key areas of concern include controversial products, unhealthy or dangerous products such as alcohol and tobacco, and prescription drugs.

- *Advertising controversial products.* Advertising reflects the marketing and business ethics of its clients and, because of its visibility, sometimes gets the blame for selling controversial, unsafe, or dangerous products. For example, products that were once considered not suitable to advertise, such as firearms, gambling, hemorrhoid preparations, feminine hygiene products, pantyhose and bras, laxatives, condoms, and remedies for male erectile dysfunctions have become acceptable, although advertising for them may still be offensive to some people.
- *Unhealthy or dangerous products.* Before an agency can create an ad for a client, it must consider the nature of the client company and its mission, marketing objectives, reputation, available resources, competition, and, most importantly, product line. Can the agency and its staff honestly promote the products being advertised? What would you do if you were a copywriter for an agency that has a political client you don't support? Several agencies have resigned from profitable tobacco advertising accounts because of the medical evidence about the harm cigarettes cause. But obviously not every agency has made the same decision. In cases where the agency works on a controversial account, there are still ethical ways to approach the business.

      One way to make ethical decisions is to choose the route that does no one harm. Because there has been so much negative publicity about the health effects of eating a steady diet of heavily processed food, food companies, particularly fast-food producers such as McDonald's and KFC, have reacted to charges of culpability in the nation's obesity problem. McDonald's slimmed down Ronald McDonald, added healthier choices to its menu, and moved away from using cholesterol-causing saturated fats when making French fries. Disney recently announced that it planned to serve healthier food in its theme parks as an effort to improve the diets of children.[19] Wendy's announced it was greatly reducing the amount of trans fats it uses for cooking.[20]

      The point is that marketers are now being forced to consider the social, as well as nutritional, impact of their products. It used to be that consumers were considered responsible for the products they chose to buy, but in a new era of social responsibility, principled marketers are now more sensitive to the negative effects of the products they choose to sell. Responsibility has become a new business principle in some industries that never considered themselves the focus of ethical questions and a corporate concern for industries that have traditionally been under attack.

      One of the most heated advertising issues in recent years has been on restrictions on tobacco advertising. Although Congress passed a law that banned cigarette advertising on television and radio starting in 1971, that did not resolve the issue.

      Proponents of the ban on cigarette advertising argue that since cigarettes have been shown to cause cancer as well as other illnesses, encouraging tobacco use

Principle
The ethical responsibility for selling a controversial or unsafe product lies with the marketing department; however, advertising is often in the spotlight because it is the visible face of marketing.

promotes sickness, injury, or death for the smoker and those inhaling secondhand smoke. They argue that further restricting advertising on those products would result in fewer sales and fewer health problems for America as a whole.

In recognition of the growing public concerns about cigarette marketing, tobacco companies have voluntarily curbed their advertising and pulled ads from magazines with high levels of youth readership and from most outdoor billboards. Most major tobacco companies also run antismoking ads aimed at teenagers. Philip Morris has virtually stopped advertising and shifted its budget to events and other promotions that reach its customers, rather than trying to use advertising to reach new customers.

Opponents of advertising bans counter with the argument that prohibiting truthful, nondeceptive advertising for a legal product is unconstitutional. They feel that censorship is more of a problem than advertising a legal, although unhealthful, product. Opponents of the ban also cite statistics demonstrating that similar bans in other countries have proven unsuccessful in reducing tobacco sales.

In 1996 a governmental agency, the Food and Drug Administration (FDA), established a set of restrictions applicable to tobacco advertisers. Among these were a ban on outdoor ads within 1,000 feet of a school or playground and a rule that limited ads to black-and-white, text only, in magazines with 55 percent readership under the age of 18. The restrictions also stipulated that $150 million be provided to fund antismoking ads targeting children. Following the 1996 action, 46 states have received initial payments from the $206 billion Master Settlement Agreement to be supplied by tobacco companies over a 25-year period. Approximately half the money goes to fund TV and print ads warning children about the dangers of smoking; the other half pays for promotions such as loyalty cards, all-expenses-paid teen summits, and various events.[21] The *truth*® campaign featured in Chapter 1 was supported through these efforts.

Banning tobacco advertising is not unique to the United States. In fact such restrictions are even greater in Europe and Asia. More than 20 countries in Europe have adopted prohibitions or outlawed tobacco advertising.[22] A near-total advertising ban in the United Kingdom took effect in early 2003, and similar restrictions were launched in the European Union two years later.

Television advertising for liquor hasn't been banned; however, there has been a voluntary restriction on such advertising by the companies themselves, and some networks have refused to accept alcohol advertising. However, in 2002 Smirnoff broke the taboo and began running "responsible drinking" ads on *Saturday Night Live* and Comedy Central, and beer advertising is a staple on sports networks and programming.

The biggest issue for the spirits industry is charges of advertising to underage drinkers. In 2003 the FTC became so concerned that it asked several major liquor producers to detail their marketing practices and target audiences and to explain how they had implemented the promises made in the FTC's 1999 report to Congress.[23] About the same time a lawsuit filed in the District of Columbia charged that alcohol marketers are actively engaged in trying to establish brand loyalty among underage consumers.[24]

Liquor executives contend that they follow voluntary advertising guidelines to avoid images and time slots that appeal to kids. That promise has been hard to keep because every major brand is trying to win over young consumers.

The Distilled Spirits Council, a trade organization representing producers and marketers of distilled spirits sold in the United States, offers a model for industry self-regulation. Its Code of Responsible Practices for Beverage Alcohol Advertising and Marketing encourages members to follow the guidelines set forth in the Code when promoting their products. It features specific recommendations regarding responsible placement of advertising and marketing materials aimed at adults and underage audiences.

The beer industry has been the target of strong criticism for several years. Anheuser-Busch pulled its beer advertising from MTV to avoid drawing fire for marketing to underage drinkers and moved its spots to VH-1, a similar network that targets 25- to 49-year-olds. This decision was partly the result of a study by Advertising Age that tracked MTV commercial viewership and found that 50 percent of the viewers were underage.[25] Although it is unlikely that beer advertising will be banned, some companies sensitive to public opinion have initiated proactive programs that educate and discourage underage drinkers.

• ***Prescription drugs.*** In 1997, the FDA loosened its controls on pharmaceutical companies. As a result, the amount of prescription drug advertising has skyrocketed. While these print and TV ads have proven very successful in terms of increased sales, various consumer groups, government agencies, and insurance companies have been quite critical of them. In one study, for example, the National Institute of Health Care Management found that direct-to-consumer prescription advertising has led to an increase in requests for costlier drugs, when the less expensive generic drug would be just as effective.[26]

Also, some doctors claim that they are being pressured to write inappropriate prescriptions because their patients are influenced by the drug ad claims. Other doctors say they appreciate that the advertising has caused consumers to become more active in managing their own health and more informed about their drug options.

Pfizer, the largest drug maker in the United States, and other pharmaceutical companies have agreed to follow a consumer advertising code of conduct that includes a pledge that new drugs won't be advertised until they've been on the market for at least six months. They also agreed to educate doctors before beginning advertising new drugs to consumers.[27]

WHY AND HOW IS ADVERTISING REGULATED?

While it would be ideal if individuals and companies always made socially responsible choices and everyone could agree that those choices resulted in proper actions, sometimes that does not occur and there is a need for regulatory or legal action. The company may decide it is acceptable to advertise certain products, and the government may decide otherwise.

Various systems are in place to monitor the social responsibility of advertising, including laws, government regulations and their regulatory bodies, professional oversight groups, and industry self-regulation. Figure 3.1 identifies the organizations with oversight responsibility for advertising and groups them in terms of five specific categories: government, media, industry, public or community groups, and the competition. Let's examine each of those systems.

Advertising's Legal Environment

Governmental oversight includes two options—law and regulation. Congress makes laws, while courts interpret those laws in specific situations to create case law. Regulatory agencies in the executive branch of the federal government also play a role by developing regulations to enforce laws related to advertising.

In this section, we examine two pivotal areas of case law—trademarks and copyright protection and the First Amendment—as they pertain to advertising.

Trademark and Copyright Protection   A **trademark** is a brand, corporate or store name, or distinctive symbol that identifies the seller's brand and thus differentiates it from the brands of other sellers. A trademark must be registered through the Patent and Trademark Office of the Department of Commerce, which gives the organization exclusive use of the mark, as long as the trademark is maintained as an identification of a specific product. Under the Lanham Trademark Act of 1947, the Patent Office protects unique trademarks from infringement by competitors. Because trademarks are critical communication devices for products and services, they are important in advertising.

Even an audio trademark is protected, as a case in the European Union illustrates. A distinctive audio sound based on the noise of a cock crowing and the way it was represented

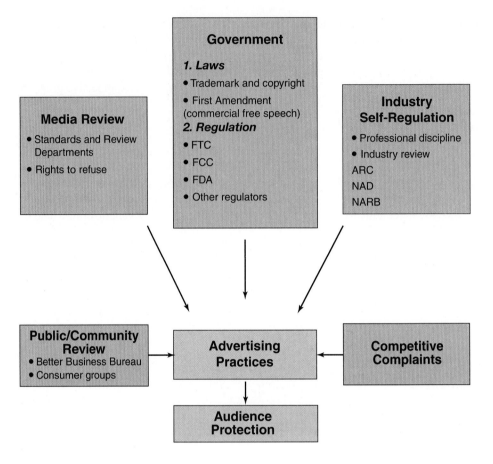

FIGURE 3.1

Advertising Review and Regulation

in Dutch had been registered with the EU's trademark office. When this sound trademark was used by a different company, the first company sued for trademark infringement.[28]

A recent trademark issue is protection for **uniform resource locators (URLs),** which are Internet domain names. Advertisers must remember that URLs have to be registered and protected just like any other trademark. They are issued on a first-come, first-served basis for any domain name not identical to an existing brand name.[29]

A **copyright** gives an organization the exclusive right to use or reproduce original work, such as an advertisement or package design, for a specified period of time. Commonly used designs or symbols, however, cannot be copyrighted. Controls for copyright protection are provided by the Library of Congress. Advertising is a competitive business in which "me-too" or "copycat" ads abound. Copyrighting of coined words, phrases, illustrations, characters, and photographs can offer some protection from other advertisers who borrow too heavily from their competitors.

Copyright infringement can occur when a product is used in an ad without proper permission. For example, the retailer Gap was sued by On Davis, a maker of high-priced metal eyewear, when the eyeglasses were used in a Gap ad without permission. The designer of the glasses explained that he wanted Gap to stop featuring the eyewear because his high-status glasses "aren't compatible in my mind with jeans and sweatshirts." He also claimed the image of his high-end fashion product was hurt by being associated with a mass retailer.[30]

Copycat ads that use the message strategy of another advertiser may also be subject to copyright infringement charges. For example, a commercial for a Sega's NBA videogame was a scene-by-scene copy of Nike's "Frozen Moment" ad from 1996 that featured Michael Jordan. The spot shows fast-paced basketball action and then shifts to slow motion to show riveted fans neglecting things that are going on around them. The ad then returns to normal speed and closes with a Jordan slam dunk. Nike ads have been parodied in the past but the company chose to file suit against Sega because its ad was not a commentary but rather a direct steal of a creative idea.[31]

Advertising and the First Amendment   The most basic federal law that governs advertising is the First Amendment to the U.S. Constitution. The First Amendment states that Congress shall make no law "abridging the freedom of speech, or of the press." How have courts applied the First Amendment to advertising? First Amendment protection extends to **commercial speech,** which is speech that promotes commercial activity. However, that protection is not absolute; it is often restricted, and the Supreme Court generally applies a different standard to commercial speech.

Protection of advertising as commercial speech has varied over the years. In 1980, in conjunction with its ruling on *Central Hudson Gas and Electric v. Public Service Commission of New York,* the Supreme Court established a test that determines to what extent the government can restrict advertising. This decision also stipulated the degree to which advertising is considered commercial speech.

A number of cases have attempted to change the common view of advertising as commercial speech. Most notably, the Supreme Court struck down a Massachusetts law that restricted tobacco advertising. Free speech advocates applauded the decision while critics of tobacco companies lamented. Although no one expects advertising to have the same constitutional protection of free speech that is given to individuals, courts throughout the country are narrowing the gap.

Protection of commercial free speech in the United States is not as widely valued as other forms of free speech, such as that enjoyed by the press and filmmakers. The Supreme Court has cited a "commonsense difference" between commercial speech and other types, such as news; however, that difference is not defined and is hard for advertisers to identify.[32]

In other words, the Supreme Court does permit some restrictions on commercial speech. For example, the court has held that false or misleading commercial speech can be banned. Even truthful commercial speech can be restricted if the government can prove the public good demands such restrictions.[33] The courts have also ruled that such acts as the federal ban on junk faxes is valid and that businesses' right to commercial speech does not include printing their advertisements on other people's fax machines.[34]

Essentially, the Supreme Court has ruled that only truthful commercial speech is protected, not misleading or deceptive statements. Because the nation's courts continue to reinterpret how the First Amendment applies in different cases, advertisers need to keep close track of legal developments. Table 3.2 summarizes First Amendment decisions by the U.S. Supreme Court that affect advertising.

Two recent cases show how varied First Amendment case law can be. The Supreme Court's 1996 decision in *44 Liquormart, Inc. v. Rhode Island* signaled strong protection for companies under the First Amendment. The court struck down two Rhode Island statutes created to support the state's interest in temperance. Both statutes banned the advertisement of alcohol prices. The first statute prohibited advertising alcohol prices in the state except on signs. The second statute prohibited the publication or broadcast of alcohol price ads. The Supreme Court held that Rhode Island's statutes were unlawful because the ban abridged the First Amendment's guarantee of freedom of speech.

In contrast, a sharply divided (5–4) Supreme Court rejected a First Amendment challenge by California fruit growers who objected to part of a federal agricultural marketing agreement that mandated they spend a certain amount of their federal money on generic product advertising and promotion (*Glickman v. Wileman Bros. & Elliott, Inc.*). Does this decision diminish the protection of advertising under the First Amendment? Some legal experts contend that the focus on coerced speech rather than commercial speech suggests otherwise.

Nike has been involved in an important corporate speech case that involves a company's right to defend itself in the court of public opinion.[35] The California Supreme Court ruled that Nike's public statements about its overseas labor practices were subject to claims of false and deceptive advertising. The press releases and ads in question said the company was doing a good job with its overseas labor practices but could do better. Nike's supporters

---

Table 3.2   First Amendment Rulings on Commercial Speech

Valentine v. Christensen (1942)

First Amendment does not protect purely commercial advertising because that type of advertising does not contribute to decision making in a democracy.

Virginia State Board of Pharmacy v. Virginia Citizens Consumer Council (1976)

States cannot prohibit pharmacists from advertising prices of prescription drugs because the free flow of information is indispensable.

Central Hudson Gas & Electric Corporation v. Public Service Commission of New York (1980)

Public Service Commission's prohibition of promotional advertising by utilities is found to be unconstitutional, placing limitations on government regulation of unlawful, nondeceptive advertising.

Posadas de Puerto Rico Associates v. Tourism Company of Puerto Rico (1986)

Puerto Rican law banned advertising of gambling casinos to residents of Puerto Rico.

Cincinnati v. Discovery Network (1993)

Court ruled that the Cincinnati City Council violated the First Amendment's protection of commercial speech when it banned news racks of advertising brochures from city streets for aesthetic and safety reasons, while permitting newspaper vending machines.

Edenfield v. Fane (1993)

Court ruled that Florida's prohibition of telephone solicitation by accountants was unconstitutional.

44 Liquormart, Inc. v. Rhode Island (1996)

Court ruled that two Rhode Island statutes that banned advertising for alcohol prices were unconstitutional.

Glickman v. Wileman Bros. & Elliott, Inc. (1997)

Court ruled that a mandatory generic advertising program, issued in accord with marketing orders of the Agricultural Marketing Act, did not infringe upon the free speech rights of fruit growers.

NYTimes v. Sullivan (1964)

Court ruled that the First Amendment protects criticism of the government that appeared in advertising even though it included some minor factual errors.

Rubin v. Coors Brewing (1995)

Court reaffirmed the regulation of commercial speech in ruling that Coors could publish the alcohol content on its label despite the Federal Alcohol Administration Act prohibition of doing so.

Greater New Orleans Broadcasters Assn. v. U.S. (1999)

Court ruled that federal law prohibits some, but not all, broadcast advertising of lotteries and casino gambling.

---

said the California court's action amounted to applying a gag order, making it impossible for companies to respond to charges and defend themselves. The decision said Nike's defense was no more than another form of advertising and deserved only limited First Amendment protection. Supporters of the court's decision contend that advocacy press releases and ads should be subject to the same standards that govern other types of ads, including prohibitions against misleading and deceptive statements.

The U.S. Supreme Court refused to hear the case, so the California decision stands. Attorneys for the American Advertising Federation said they feared that creative speech of advertising agencies would be silenced in California as corporate speech wasn't deemed fully protected by the First Amendment.[36] Of course, no court decision should be considered permanent. As justices leave the U.S. Supreme Court and state supreme courts and are replaced and as regulatory agencies undergo personnel changes, the interpretation of First Amendment protection for advertisers will likely evolve.

International Laws and Regulations   Earlier in this chapter we mentioned the importance of understanding cultural differences in global advertising. As advertisers, agencies, and media become more and more global, it will be imperative that the players understand local laws in the countries in which they operate. Marketing practices, such as pricing and price advertising, vary in their legal and regulatory restrictions.

Some product categories, such as over-the-counter (OTC) drugs, are particularly difficult because regulations about their marketing and advertising are different in every country. Advertising for certain types of products is banned. Thailand prohibits tobacco ads, as does Hungary. In Hong Kong, outdoor display advertising of tobacco products is banned. Malaysia has banned most forms of tobacco advertising, including print, TV, radio, and billboards. However, these restrictions are fairly ineffective as a result of indirect advertising that features a product other than the primary (controversial) product. Examples of these techniques in Malaysia are quite plentiful. Billboards with the Salem, Benson & Hedges, and Winston names dot the landscape, but they're not advertising cigarettes. They're advertising the companies' travel, clothing, and restaurant businesses.

There also are differences in the legal use of various marketing communication tools. A contest or promotion might be successful in one country and illegal in another. Direct marketing is considered an invasion of privacy in some European countries and is forbidden.

Because of the difficulty in complying with widely varying laws, international advertisers often work with either local agencies or with international agencies that have local affiliates. Then they have someone in the country who knows the local laws and can identify potential legal problems.

Advertising's Regulatory Environment

In addition to the Federal Trade Commission, the Food and Drug Administration and the Federal Communications Commission are dynamic components of the advertising regulatory environment. Let's look in more depth at their missions and the type of advertising practices they regulate.

Federal Trade Commission (FTC)   Established by Congress in 1914 to oversee business, the FTC is the primary agency governing the advertising industry. Its main focus with respect to advertising is to identify and eliminate ads that deceive or mislead the consumer. Some FTC responsibilities are to:

- *Fairness:* Initiate investigations against companies that engage in unfair competition or deceptive practices.
- *Deception:* Regulate acts and practices that deceive businesses or consumers and issue cease-and-desist orders where such practices exist. Cease-and-desist orders require that the practice be stopped within 30 days; an order given to one firm is applicable to all firms in the industry.
- *Violations:* Fine people or companies that violate either (1) a trade regulation rule or (2) a cease-and-desist order given to any other firm in the industry.
- *Consumer participation:* Fund the participation of consumer groups and other interest groups in rule-making proceedings.[37]

Specifically, the FTC oversees false advertising of such items as foods, drugs, cosmetics, and therapeutic devices. In recent years, that oversight has focused on health and weight loss business practices, 900 numbers, telemarketing, and advertising that targets children and the elderly. The FTC hosts the National Do Not Call Registry to help citizens keep from receiving unwanted telemarketing calls. The FTC monitors the ratings system and the advertising practices of the film, music, and electronic games industries. Periodically, it issues progress reports to Congress on youth-oriented entertainment advertising to make sure that ads for products with potentially objectionable content—primarily violent or sexual content—are not seen on media targeted to youth. The FTC's reports to Congress cover advertising on television and Web sites as well as print media.

The existence of a regulatory agency such as the FTC influences advertisers' behavior. Although most cases never reach the FTC, advertisers prefer not to risk long legal battles with the agency. Advertisers are also aware that competitors may complain to the FTC about a questionable advertisement. Such a move can cost the offending organization millions of

Table 3.3 Advertising Legislation

Pure Food and Drug Act (1906)

Forbids the manufacture, sale, or transport of adulterated or fraudulently labeled foods and drugs in interstate commerce. Supplanted by the Food, Drug and Cosmetic Act of 1938; amended by Food Additives Amendment in 1958 and Kefauver-Harris Amendment in 1962.

Federal Trade Commission Act (1914)

Establishes the commission, a body of specialists with broad powers to investigate and to issue cease-and-desist orders to enforce Section 5, which declares that "unfair methods of competition in commerce are unlawful."

Wheeler-Lea Amendment (1938)

Prohibits unfair and deceptive acts and practices regardless of whether competition is injured; places advertising of foods and drugs under FTC jurisdiction.

Lanham Act (1947)

Provides protection for trademarks (slogans and brand names) from competitors and also encompasses false advertising.

Magnuson-Moss Warranty/FTC Improvement Act (1975)

Authorizes the FTC to determine rules concerning consumer warranties and provides for consumer access to means of redress, such as the "class action" suit. Also expands FTC regulatory powers over unfair or deceptive acts or practices and allows it to require restitution for deceptively written warranties costing the consumer more than $5.

FTC Improvement Act (1980)

Provides the House of Representatives and Senate jointly with veto power over FTC regulation rules. Enacted to limit the FTC's powers to regulate "unfairness" issues in designing trade regulation rules on advertising.

The Telemarketing and Consumer Fraud Act and Abuse Protection Act (1994)

Specifies that telemarketers may not call anyone who requests not to be contacted. Resulted in the Telemarketing Sales Rules.

---

dollars. Table 3.3 lists important advertising legislation, most of which shows the growing authority of the FTC to regulate advertising.

The FTC and Children's Advertising   Developing responsible advertising aimed at audiences of children is a critical issue. The FTC and other governmental agencies have gotten involved with the regulation of marketing to children.

After a 1988 study found that the average child viewed more than 20,000 TV commercials per year, a heated debate ensued. One side favored regulation because of children's inability to evaluate advertising messages and make purchasing decisions. The other side opposed regulation, arguing that many self-regulatory mechanisms already existed and the proper place for restricting advertising to children was in the home.

In response, the FTC initiated proceedings to study possible regulations of children's television. Despite the FTC's recommendations, the proceedings did not result in new federal regulations until 1990. In the interim, self-regulation in the advertising industry tried to fill this void.

The National Advertising Division (NAD) of the Council of Better Business Bureaus, Inc., set up a group charged with helping advertisers deal with children's advertising in a manner sensitive to children's special needs. The Children's Advertising Review Unit (CARU), established in 1974, evaluates advertising directed at children under the age of 12.

In 1990 Congress passed the Children's Television Advertising Practice Act, which placed 10.5-minute-per-hour ceilings for commercials in children's weekend television programming and 12-minute-per-hour limits for weekday programs. The act also set rules requiring that commercial breaks be clearly distinguished from programming, barring the use of program characters to promote products.

Advocates for children's television continue to argue that many stations made little effort to comply with the 1990 act and petitioned the Federal Communications Commission to increase the required number of educational programs to be shown daily. In 1996, broadcasters, children's advocates, and the federal government reached an agreement requiring all TV stations to air three hours of children's educational shows a week.

Regulating Deception   Ultimately, advertisers want their customers to trust their products and advertising, so many take precautions to ensure that their messages are not deceptive, misleading, or unreasonable. **Deceptive advertising** is intended to mislead consumers by making claims that are false or by failure to make full disclosure of important facts, or both. The current FTC policy on deception contains three basic elements:

1. *Misleading.* Where there is representation, omission, or practice, there must be a high probability that it will mislead the consumer.
2. *Reasonableness.* The perspective of the "reasonable consumer" is used to judge deception. The FTC tests reasonableness by looking at whether the consumer's interpretation or reaction to an advertisement is reasonable.
3. *Injurious.* The deception must lead to material injury. In other words, the deception must influence consumers' decision making about products and services.[38]

This policy makes deception difficult to prove because the criteria are rather vague and hard to measure. It also creates uncertainty for advertisers who must wait for congressional hearings and court cases to discover what the FTC will permit.

Regulating Substantiation   Claim **substantiation** is an area of particular concern to the FTC in determining whether or not an advertisement is misleading. The advertiser should have a reasonable basis for making a claim about product performance or run the risk of an FTC investigation. Food claims, such as those focused on calories or carbohydrates, must be supported by research about nutrition. Consequently, an advertiser should always have data on file to substantiate any claims it makes in its advertisements. Also, it is best if this research is conducted by an independent research firm. The FTC determines the reasonableness of claims on a case-by-case basis. In general, the FTC considers these factors:

- *Type and specificity of claim made.* For example, Computer Tutor claims you can learn the basics of using a computer by simply going through its three-CD set.
- *Type of product.* FedEx promises a certain delivery time, regardless of weather, mechanical breakdown, and so forth. This product has a great many uncontrollable variables compared to Heinz ketchup, which the company promises will be thick.
- *Possible consequences of the false claims.* A Web site that claims it is secure can cause serious damage to its customers if, in fact, it is not.
- *Degree of reliance on the claims by consumers.* Business-to-business customers depend on the many claims made by their vendors. Therefore, if XPEDX (yes, that's how it's spelled), a manufacturer of boxes and other packages, claims in its ad that it can securely deliver any size product, it had better deliver.
- *The type and accessibility of evidence available for making the claim.* The type of evidence could range from testimonials from satisfied customers to complex product testing in multiple laboratories. It could be made available through an 800 number request or online.

Remedies for Deception and Unfair Advertising   The common sources of complaints concerning deceptive or unfair advertising practices are competitors, the public, and the FTC's own monitors. If a complaint seems justified, the commission can follow several courses of action: consent decrees, cease-and-desist orders, fines, corrective advertising, substantiation of advertising claims, and consumer redress.

- *Consent decrees.* A **consent decree** is the first step in the regulation process after the FTC determines that an ad is deceptive. The FTC simply notifies the advertiser of its finding and asks the advertiser to sign a consent decree agreeing to stop the deceptive practice. Most advertisers do sign the decree to avoid the bad publicity and the possible $10,000-per-day fine for refusing to do so.
  Duracell was forced to modify one of its ads after Energizer complained that the ad inferred that Duracell CopperTop batteries would last three times longer than other

heavy-duty and super-heavy-duty batteries. The ad didn't mention Energizer by name, but Energizer charged the ad was "false and misleading" because consumers would think the comparison was with other alkaline batteries, such as Energizer. In fact, the CopperTop does not last longer than other alkaline batteries. The ad was modified with a disclaimer.[39]

Sometimes the remedy can be more costly than simply modifying an ad. Federal marshals banned two health products—Crave Away and Aide Crème—after the parent company was accused of false advertising. According to the U.S. Attorney's office, the products claims weren't approved by the Food and Drug Administration and hence were "making false and unsubstantiated claims."[40]

- *Cease-and-desist orders.* When the advertiser refuses to sign a consent decree and the FTC determines that the deception is substantial, it issues a cease-and-desist order. The process leading to the issuance of a **cease-and-desist order** is similar to a court trial. An administrative law judge presides. FTC staff attorneys represent the commission, and the accused parties are entitled to representation by their lawyers. If the administrative judge decides in favor of the FTC, the judge issues an order requiring the respondents to cease their unlawful practices. The advertiser can appeal the order to the full five-member commission.

- *Corrective advertising.* The FTC may require **corrective advertising** when consumer research determines that an advertising campaign has perpetuated lasting false beliefs. Under this remedy, the FTC orders the offending person or organization to produce messages for consumers that correct the false impressions the ad made. The purpose of corrective advertising is not to punish an advertiser but to prevent it from continuing to deceive consumers. The FTC may require a firm to run corrective advertising even if the campaign in question has been discontinued.

  A landmark corrective advertising case is *Warner-Lambert v. FTC*. According to the FTC, Warner-Lambert's campaign for Listerine mouthwash, which ran for 50 years, had been deceiving customers, leading them to think that Listerine could prevent or reduce the severity of sore throats and colds. The company was ordered to run a corrective advertising campaign, mostly on television, for 16 months at a cost of $10 million. The case is significant for two reasons. First, the Supreme Court gave the FTC the power to apply remedies to both past and ongoing campaigns to curtail future deceptions. Second, the court rejected the argument that corrective advertising violates the advertiser's First Amendment rights.

  Interestingly, after the Warner-Lambert corrective campaign ran its course, 42 percent of Listerine users continued to believe that the mouthwash was being advertised as a remedy for sore throats and colds, and 57 percent of users rated cold and sore throat effectiveness as a key reason for purchasing the brand.[41] These results raised doubts about the effectiveness of corrective advertising to change impressions and have affected recent court decisions.

  The 1998 decision also prompted the commission (specifically Commissioner Orson Swindle) to publish a statement on the logic of the practice of corrective advertising. In addition to concurring that there is no evidence that corrective advertising works, Commissioner Swindle also noted that the assumption that corrective advertising should run the same length of time as the deceptive ad had run is erroneous.

- *Consumer redress.* The Magnuson-Moss Warranty-FTC Improvement Act of 1975 empowers the FTC to obtain consumer redress when a person or a firm engages in deceptive practices. The commission can order any of the following: cancellation or reformation of contracts, refund of money or return of property, payment of damages, and public notification.

- *Advertising agency legal responsibility.* A more recent solution for deception within the commission and in the federal courts is to make the ad agency liable instead of the advertiser. To quote former FTC chairperson Janet Steiger, "An agency that is involved in advertising and promoting a product is not free from responsibility for the content of the claims, whether they are expressed or implied. You will find the commission staff looking more closely at the extent of advertising involvement."[42]

Table 3.4 Specialized Government Agencies That Affect Advertising

Agency	Effect on Advertising
Federal Trade Commission www.ftc.gov	Regulates credit, labeling, packaging, warranties, and advertising.
Food and Drug Administration www.fda.gov	Regulates packaging, labeling, and manufacturing of food and drug products.
Federal Communications Commission www.fcc.gov	Regulates radio and television stations and networks.
U.S. Postal Service www.usps.com	Controls advertising by monitoring materials sent through the mail.
Bureau of Alcohol, Tobacco, and Firearms www.atf.treas.gov	Division of the U.S. Treasury Department that regulates advertising for alcoholic beverages.
U.S. Patent Office www.uspto.gov	Oversees trademark registration to protect against patent infringement.
Library of Congress www.loc.gov	Provides controls for copyright protection.

Essentially, an agency is liable for deceptive advertising along with the advertiser when the agency is an active participant in the preparation of the ad and knows or has reason to know that it is false or deceptive.

An agency should heed any FTC warnings it receives. Several FTC actions and court cases in the early 1990s show that agencies must be prepared to defend their advertising practices. For example, a federal court found that Wilkinson, the maker of the Ultra Glide shaving system, intended to make misleading claims about Gillette and halted the campaign. The court awarded Gillette damages of nearly $1 million, to be paid by Wilkinson, and another $1 million to be paid by Wilkinson's agency, Friedman Benjamin.

Food and Drug Administration (FDA)   The FDA is the regulatory division of the Department of Health and Human Services that oversees package labeling, ingredient listings, and advertising for food and drugs. It also determines the safety and purity of foods and cosmetics. In particular, the FDA is a watchdog for drug advertising, specifically in the controversial area of direct-to-consumer ads for prescription drugs. Its job is first to determine whether drugs are safe and then to see that these drugs are marketed in a responsible way. Marketing includes promotional materials aimed at doctors as well as consumers.

For pharmaceutical companies, advertising is a commercial free speech issue, and the industry has brought pressure on the FDA to make direct-to-consumer advertising rules for prescription drugs more understandable, simpler, and clearer.[43]

Federal Communications Commission (FCC)   The FCC, formed in 1934 to protect the public interest in broadcast communications, can issue and revoke licenses to radio and television stations. The FCC also has the power to ban messages, including ads, that are deceptive or in poor taste. The agency monitors only advertisements that have been the subject of complaints and works closely with the FTC to eliminate false and deceptive advertising. The FCC takes actions against the media, whereas the FTC is concerned with advertisers and agencies.

Other Regulatory Bodies   In addition to the FTC, the FDA, and the FCC, several other federal agencies regulate advertising. Most other federal agencies that regulate advertising are limited to a certain type of advertising, product, or medium, as we see in Table 3.4. We have already discussed the Patent Office and the Library of Congress and their roles in protecting copyrights and trademarks. Let's now look at other key regulatory agencies.

• **Bureau of Alcohol, Tobacco, and Firearms.** The Bureau of Alcohol, Tobacco, and Firearms (BATF) within the Treasury Department regulates deception in advertising and establishes labeling requirements for the liquor industry. This agency's power comes from its authority to issue and revoke annual operating permits for distillers, wine merchants, and brewers. Because there is a danger that public pressure could result in banning all advertisements for alcoholic beverages, the liquor industry strives to maintain tight controls on its advertising.

- *The U.S. Postal Service.* The Postal Service regulates direct mail and magazine advertising and has control over the areas of obscenity, lotteries, and fraud. Consumers who receive advertisements in the mail that they consider sexually offensive can request that no more mail be delivered from that sender. The postmaster general also has the power to withhold mail that promotes lotteries. Fraud can include a number of questionable activities, such as implausible, get-rich-quick schemes.
- *The States' Attorneys General.* The National Association of Attorneys General seeks to regulate advertising at the state level. Members of this organization have successfully brought suits in their respective states against such advertising giants as Coca-Cola, Kraft, and Campbell Soup. More recently, numerous attorneys general have led the way against the tobacco industry and have supported the advertising restrictions discussed earlier.

Media Review of Advertising

The media attempts to regulate advertising by screening and rejecting ads that violate their standards of truth and good taste. Most networks have a Standards and Practices Department that screens every ad and gives approval before the ad can run. Each individual medium has the discretion to accept or reject a particular ad. For example, *The Reader's Digest* does not accept tobacco and liquor ads, and many magazines and television stations do not show condom ads. In the case of the major television networks, the standards and guidelines designed by the Advertising Review Council (ARC), an industry group, serve as the primary standard.

The First Amendment gives any publisher the right to refuse to publish anything the company does not want to publish, and this sometimes creates battles between media companies and advertisers. For example, some billboard companies in Utah refused to run billboards for a Wasatch Beer company brand named Polygamy Porter. The brand's slogan "Why have just one!" and headlines such as "Take Some Home for the Wives" were deemed offensive to the state's Mormon population. A similar brouhaha arose when the state's Brighton Ski Resort promoted its four-person lifts with a billboard during the Salt Lake City Olympics that read, "Wife. Wife. Wife. Husband." The billboard company that banned the beer ads received letters both for and against its stand, which indicates the difficulty of such decisions.[44]

The FTC pressures magazines and newspapers, in particular, to stop running ads for weight-loss products that it says are misleading. Publishers, however, jealously guard their decision-making rights and resist being pressured by either government agencies or advertisers. But there are some debatable areas where the media have restricted advertising. For example, in 2003 a case was brought before the Superior Court of New Jersey demanding that an injunction be issued to keep CNN from refusing to run ads for the IDT telecommunication company. The IDT commercials claimed that its giant competitors—AT&T, Sprint, Verizon, and WorldCom—charge more because of bad business decisions, and that's why IDT can charge less. IDT says the ban was discriminatory and contrary to the government's policy of encouraging competition.

More recently a political advocacy group, MoveOn, sponsored a contest to find the best commercial opposed to the George Bush presidency and hoped to run it during the Super Bowl. The winning ad, "Child's Play," was a polished, subtle, sobering spot questioning the Bush Administration's rampant deficit spending. After the winner was named, CBS refused to air the ad, claiming it was too controversial, even though it had accepted an ad from the White House.[45] A newspaper editorial that protested what it called the "myopic" CBS decision said it was sad that "outlandish propaganda spots by the White House were accepted but not a respectful, if hard-hitting, political ad."[46]

Self-Regulation

Rather than wait for laws and regulatory actions, responsible advertisers take the initiative and establish individual ethical standards that anticipate and even go beyond possible com-

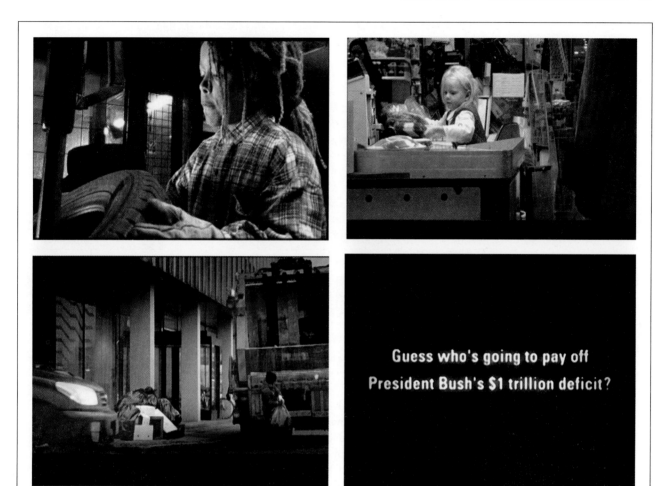

Guess who's going to pay off
President Bush's $1 trillion deficit?

plaints. Such a proactive stance helps the creative process and avoids the kinds of disasters that result from violating the law or offending members of society.

Advertisers practice three types of self-regulation: self-discipline, industry self-regulation, and self-regulation by public and community groups.

Self-Discipline   An organization such as an advertising agency exercises self-discipline when it develops, uses, and enforces norms within its own practices. Virtually all major advertisers and advertising agencies have in-house ad review procedures, including reviews by agency and client attorneys. Typically the attorneys are concerned with how claims are phrased and substantiated. Are the claims verifiable? Is there research and data to prove the truth of the claims? Is there anything in the wording that could be misinterpreted or misleading? Is there anything deceptive in the visual images?

Several U.S. companies (Colgate-Palmolive, General Foods, AT&T) have their own codes of behavior and criteria that determine whether advertisements are acceptable. Companies without such codes tend to have informal criteria that they apply on an ad-by-ad basis. At a minimum, advertisers and agencies should have every element of a proposed ad evaluated by an in-house committee, lawyers, or both.

Industry Self-Regulation   When the development, use, and enforcement of norms comes from the industry, the term used is *industry self-regulation.* In the case of both advertisers and advertising agencies, the most effective attempts at pure self-regulation have come through industry groups, such as the Advertising Review Council (ARC) and the Better Business Bureau. In 1971 several professional advertising associations in conjunction with the Council of Better Business Bureaus established the National Advertising Review Council, which negotiates voluntary withdrawal of national advertising that professionals consider deceptive. The National Advertising Division (NAD) of the Council of Better Business

CBS refused to allow the MoveOn organization to buy advertising time on the Super Bowl for an ad that won its Anti-Bush advertising contest. What do you think—should the media have the right to refuse political statements like these?

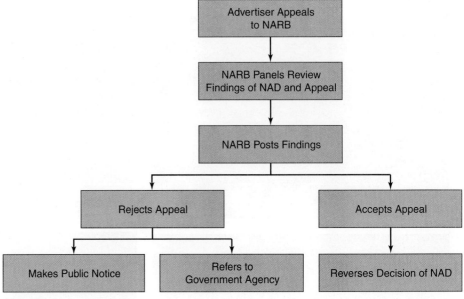

FIGURE 3.2

The NARB Appeal Process

Consumers or groups submitting a complaint to NAD and NARB go through this process. The ultimate power of NAD and NARB is the threat of passing the claim to the FTC. Usually, cases are settled before that point.

Bureaus and the National Advertising Review Board (NARB) are the two operating arms of the National Advertising Review Council. None of these are government agencies.

NAD is a full-time agency made up of people from the field of advertising. It evaluates complaints submitted by consumers, consumer groups, industrial organizations, and advertising firms. NAD also does its own industry monitoring. After NAD receives a complaint, it may ask the advertiser in question to substantiate claims made in the advertisement. If that substantiation is deemed inadequate, NAD representatives ask the advertiser to change or withdraw the offending ad. When a satisfactory resolution cannot be found, NAD refers the case to NARB.

NARB is a 50-member regulatory group that represents national advertisers, advertising agencies, and other professional fields. When the advertiser appeals a case to NARB, it faces a review panel of five people: three advertisers, one agency person, and one public representative. This NARB panel reviews the complaint and the NAD staff findings and holds hearings to let the advertiser present its case. If the case remains unresolved after the process, NARB can (1) publicly identify the advertiser and the facts about the case and (2) refer the complaint to the appropriate government agency, usually the FTC. Although neither NAD nor NARB has any real power other than threatening to invite government intervention, these groups have been effective in controlling cases of deception and misleading advertising. Figure 3.2 summarizes the NARB appeal process.

Self-Regulation by Public and Community Groups   The advertising industry voluntarily involves nonindustry representatives, such as the Better Business Bureau or the media, in the development, application, and enforcement of norms. Local and consumer activist groups represent two ways that self-regulation occurs in this manner.

• *Local groups.* At the local level, self-regulation has been supported by the Better Business Bureau (BBB). The BBB (www.bbb.org) functions much like the national regulatory agencies and also provides local businesses with advice concerning the legal aspects of advertising. Approximately 250 local and national bureaus made up of advertisers, agencies, and media, have screened hundreds of thousands of advertisements for possible violations of truth and accuracy. Although the BBB has no legal power, it receives and investigates complaints and maintains files on violators. It also assists local law enforcement officials in prosecuting violators. The ease with which the BBB can be accessed on the Internet has prompted businesses to be more careful about complying with its standards.

• ***Consumer activist groups.*** Consumer groups of all kinds monitor advertising practices. The Action for Children's Advertising group follows the practices of advertisers who market to children and will file complaints with industry boards or regulatory agencies about advertisements they consider questionable. The consumer group Public Citizen inspired the FDA to require warnings on print ads for certain types of nicotine products. Groups that are focused on media literacy also review the performance of advertisers. For example, the Cultural Environment Movement is a nonprofit coalition of independent organizations and individuals that focuses on fairness, diversity, and justice in media communication.[47]

WHAT GUIDES ETHICAL BEHAVIOR?

By now you are familiar with the social and legal issues facing advertisers. How does this involve you? This section is designed to help you consider your responsibilities and behavior as you think about how to incorporate what you've learned when you encounter ethical dilemmas.

Ethics are the "shoulds" and "oughts" of behavior. Ethics are the "right thing to do." Defining what is right can be challenging. What one person says is right isn't always what others define to be appropriate. Ethics and morals are closely related, but they are not synonymous. **Morals** are frameworks for right actions and are more the domain of religion and philosophy. Examples of moral systems are the Ten Commandments from the Judeo-Christian religious tradition or the Buddhist Eightfold Path. These moral systems provide a framework for behavior. Ethics differ from morals in that ethics are not so much about what is right and wrong, but about making choices from equally compelling options—how should you behave when the answer is unclear? Individuals have the potential to make ethical choices. That is true in advertising as in all other areas of your life.

Doing the right thing is ethical, but it's sometimes hard to know what the right thing is. Sometimes there's no one right answer. An ethical dilemma may arise from equally compelling choices or values. Consider, for example, this situation: You are a graphic designer. You want to use a picture you found on the Internet, and you don't want to copy it unethically. How much do you have to change the digital picture before it becomes your own?

A related dilemma shows how important the issue is. Ad agency Wieden + Kennedy created the Honda Cog commercial that was inspired by a Rube Goldberg device. Setting off one car part generated a chain reaction of car parts that ultimately resulted in the final scene with the announcer saying, "Isn't it nice when things just work?" The commercial took 606 takes to get it right. The commercial won much acclaim for its creative work, but was denied the ultimate Grand Prix at the Cannes Lions Festival that year in part because two filmmakers claimed the commercial based its concept on a half-hour film that had roughly the same idea. How much different did the commercial need to be from the film? Is it possible that both were original concepts?

Determining what constitutes ethical behavior happens on many levels. Individually, advertisers call upon their own moral upbringing. The advertising industry provides codes of ethics and standards of self-regulation. The government helps regulate advertising practices through legal means. The rest of this chapter explores these areas.

Principle

Decisions about ethics are made based on laws, regulations, and professional codes, but more importantly on an internal moral compass that senses when something is right or wrong.

Personal Ethics

Ethical decisions are usually complex and involve navigating a moral maze of conflicting forces—strategy vs. ethics, costs vs. ethics, effectiveness vs. ethics, etc. They demand the ability to do what ethicists call "moral reasoning."[48] In the end, if you are a responsible advertising professional making a decision about a strategy or an execution tactic to be used in an advertisement, you must be aware of industry standards as well as ethical questions that underlie the core issues we have discussed in this chapter.

But more importantly, personal judgment and moral reasoning rest on an intuitive sense of right and wrong, a moral compass that tells you when an idea is misleading, insensitive, too over the top, or too manipulative. And then you need the courage to speak up and tell your colleagues. Do you think that the Benetton advertising described in the accompanying Practical Tips box passes your standards for good advertising?

Practical Tips

Brilliant or Offensive Advertising?

By Fred Beard, Ph.D., *University of Oklahoma*

A photo of a priest kissing a nun. An emaciated AIDS victim at the moment of death, attended by his distraught family. An African guerrilla holding an AK-47 and a human leg bone. A dead soldier's bloody uniform.

So began Italian clothing maker Benetton's selfless, noble, and global advertising effort to encourage brotherhood and condemn indifference to human suffering. Or, depending on whom else you ask, so began a cynical and self-serving effort to take advantage of the world's pain and suffering with a purpose no more noble than selling T-shirts and sweaters, with shock and calculated offense the primary tactics.

When the "United Colors of Benetton" campaign started in 1990, creative director Oliviero Toscani was given free rein. What followed was a steady stream of symbolic, shocking, and often upsetting ads that were only identifiable as Benetton's by a small, green logo. Toscani's 18-year tenure with Benetton ended in 2000, following a firestorm of controversy over the "We, On Death Row" campaign, designed to draw attention to the "plight" of 26 convicted murderers in the United States.

Why would an advertiser purposely want to offend people? Benetton certainly isn't alone. The use of "shockvertising" has grown as advertisers have learned controversy encourages attention and often creates a media buzz far surpassing the reach and frequency of the original media buys. Ethically speaking, though, should advertisers care if they offend people?

The fact is, few people either inside or outside advertising would argue that the presentation of a potentially offensive message is always morally wrong. What questions should we ask to decide for ourselves whether or not an advertising campaign like the "United Colors of Benetton" crosses the line? Here's a start:

- Is it inherently wrong to present words and images that will undoubtedly offend most people if the goal is to draw attention to humanitarian issues and problems?
- Does it make a difference if the goal of widely offensive advertising is solely to sell products?
- Do people have a right not to see ads that offend them? Since some media, such as TV and outdoor, are more intrusive than others, does the medium make a difference?
- What do advertising codes of ethics say about audience offense? Are advertisers professionally and morally obligated to follow them?
- To whom do advertisers owe the most responsibility—their own organizations and stakeholders, society, consumers, other advertising professionals?

This controversial Benetton ad created much media buzz.

Professional Ethics

Professionals in advertising by and large see themselves as ethical people. However, polls indicate that the public tends to see them differently. In a recent Honesty and Ethics Poll conducted by the Gallup organization, advertising practitioners ranked near the bottom, with nurses and doctors at the top. Advertising practitioners ranked ahead of HMO managers and car salesmen. That poll suggests the public is not persuaded that advertising professionals are guided by ethical standards.

Industry standards can provide help with a decision about what is or is not ethically correct. Many professions write **codes of ethics** to help guide practitioners toward ethical behavior. Advertising is no different. Professional ethics are often expressed in a code of standards that identifies how professionals in the industry should respond when faced with ethical questions. The American Association of Advertising Agencies (AAAA) begins its "Standards of Practice" with the line: "We hold that a responsibility of advertising agencies is to be a constructive force in business." The core of the statement, the Creative Code, is reproduced in Figure 3.3.

In the wake of highly public business scandals such as the collapse of Enron, many firms are responding with their own codes of ethics. If this subject interests you, you can look up these codes in a collection compiled by the Center for the Study of Ethics in the Professions at the Illinois Institute of Technology: http://ethics.iit.edu/codes/.

International Standards and Codes

Standards of professional behavior are not found only in the United States or other Western countries. Singapore, for example, has an ad code specifically designed to prevent Western-influenced advertising from impairing Asian family values. Malaysia's requirement that all ads be produced in the country not only keeps that country's advertising aligned with its own standards and cultural values, it also cuts back dramatically on the number of foreign ads seen by its public. Advertisers who violate the ethical code of conduct in Brazil can be fined up to 500,000 U.S. dollars or imprisoned for up to five years. This punishment would certainly prompt an advertiser to be careful.

In the Netherlands, industry members have encouraged the formation of an "ethical office" to oversee all agencies, advertisers, and media. That office is responsible for reviewing advertisements to ensure that they comply with the Dutch Advertising Code and

---

AAAA's Creative Code

We, the members of the American Association of Advertising Agencies, in addition to supporting and obeying the laws and legal regulations pertaining to advertising, undertake to extend and broaden the application of high ethical standards. Specifically, we will not knowingly create advertising that contains:

- False or misleading statements or exaggerations, visual or verbal
- Testimonials that do not reflect the real opinion of the individual(s) involved
- Price claims that are misleading
- Claims insufficiently supported or that distort the true meaning or practicable application of statements made by professional or scientific authority
- Statements, suggestions, or pictures offensive to public decency or minority segments of the population.

We recognize that there are areas that are subject to honestly different interpretations and judgment. Nevertheless, we agree not to recommend to an advertiser, and to discourage the use of, advertising that is in poor or questionable taste or that is deliberately irritating through aural or visual content or presentation.

Comparative advertising shall be governed by the same standards of truthfulness, claim substantiation, tastefulness, etc. as apply to other types of advertising.

FIGURE 3.3
The AAAA's Creative Code

general ethical principles. In Swedish advertising agencies, an executive known as the "responsible editor" is trained and experienced in marketing law; that editor reviews all the advertisements and promotional materials to ensure that they are legally and ethically acceptable.

Developing a strong personal and professional sense of right and wrong is a prerequisite to being able to exercise responsible judgment when you're confronted with an ethical dilemma. The Practical Tips box offers a checklist for advertisers as they consider their ethical decisions and behavior.

Practical Tips

An Ethics Checklist for Advertisers

1. In terms of its social impact, does advertising. . . .
   - violate public standards of good taste?
   - reinforce negative stereotypes?
   - damage people's self-image and create insecurities?
   - promote materialism?
   - create false wants and false hope?
   - contribute to cultural pollution?
   - market dangerous products?
2. In terms of its strategic decisions, does an advertisement. . . . .
   - target vulnerable groups?
   - harm children?
   - appeal to base motivations such as envy and greed?
   - drive demand for unnecessary purchases?
   - prey on people's fears unnecessarily?
   - undercut people's self-image and self-concept?
   - make unsubstantiated claims?
3. In terms of its tactics, does an advertisement. . .
   - use ideas, words, or images that are offensive or insensitive?
   - use inappropriate stereotypes?
   - manipulate people's emotions unnecessarily?
   - make false, deceptive, or misleading claims?
   - use unfair comparisons?
   - create endorsements or demonstrations that exaggerate or lie?
   - use scare or shock tactics?
   - use puffery?

IT'S A WRAP

Whirlpool Profits by Helping Turn Houses into Homes

Does social responsibility pay off for the company? The answer is a resounding yes. Being a good citizen can also be good business. Sales increased dramatically for Whirlpool. Sales increased 12 percent in the same YOY (an acronym that means Year Over Year) period, and Whirlpool also outperformed the industry significantly during this same time period, according to Mick Santifort, research director for ZenithOptimedia USA, one of Publicis's brands. Share grew from 15.8 to 17.2, the first significant share gain for Whirlpool in years, translating to more than $147 million in incremental sales. An advertising tracking study indicated that emotional measures increased significantly beyond the 10 percent goal of increasing Whirlpool's emotional relevance.

What's more, Whirlpool earned much acclaim for its work. Here are a few of its awards. Whirlpool was:

- listed on the 2006/2007 Dow Jones Sustainability World Index (DJSI), an international stock portfolio that evaluates corporate performance using economic, environmental, and social criteria.
- recognized as one of the 100 best corporate citizens by *Business Ethics* in 2006.
- chosen as one of the world's most socially responsible companies by *Global Finance Magazine*.

- selected for the 2005 American Business Ethics Award from the Society of Financial Service Professionals.
- a recipient of a Bronze Effie in 2006 in the category of Corporate Reputation/ Image/Identity.

Key Points Summary

1. **What kind of power does advertising have in society, and what are its limitations?** Can advertising create product demand? Does advertising shape or mirror social values? Does advertising make people too materialistic? These questions are the subject of much debate.

   To some extent advertising does create demand for products; however, the power of advertising to do this is hard to measure. The shape-versus-mirror debate is a central issue in considering advertising's role in society. Critics of advertising tend to believe that it has power to shape social trends and the way people think and act; advertising professionals tend to believe that it mirrors values rather than sets them. In fact, advertising and society's values are probably interactive so the answer may simply be that advertising both mirrors and shapes values. Whether or not advertising causes society to become overcommercialized relates to the criticism that buying products appears to be the solution to every problem. Counterarguments emerge from the position that consumers can make intelligent choices about what they need.

2. **Why and how is advertising regulated?** In a complex society there is usually not one answer to what constitutes "right" behavior. Regulatory agencies help enforce advertising standards. Several governmental bodies help regulate advertising:

   - The FTC is the agency primarily concerned with identifying and eliminating deceptive advertising.

   - The FDA oversees advertising related to food and drugs.
   - The FCC monitors advertising broadcast by radio and television stations.
   - Other regulatory bodies with some advertising oversight include the Bureau of Alcohol, Tobacco, and Firearms, the U.S. Postal Service, the Patent Office, the Library of Congress, and the states' Attorneys General offices.

   In addition to governmental oversight, advertising is also self-regulated. Advertising agencies have in-house ad review procedures and legal staff that monitor the creation of advertising. The industry has a number of bodies that review advertising, such as the Advertising Review Council (ARC), the National Advertising Division (NAD) of the Better Business Bureau, and the National Advertising Review Board (NARB). Other bodies include the various media review boards, competitors who are concerned about unfair advertising that might harm their brands, and public and community groups that represent either local or special interest groups.

3. **What guides ethical behavior in advertising?** Advertisers have a social responsibility to make good ethical choices. At the root of ethical behavior is the individual decision maker's set of moral values. When faced with a dilemma of equally compelling choices, advertisers can consult their personal values, professional codes of ethics, and international standards of ethical behavior to guide their moral decision making.

Key Terms

cease-and-desist order, p. 86
code of ethics, p. 93
commercial speech, p. 81
comparative advertising, p. 74
consent decree, p. 85
copyright, p. 80

corrective advertising, p. 86
cultural imperialism, p. 73
deceptive advertising, p. 85
demand creation, p. 66
endorsement, p. 76
ethics, p. 91

false advertising, p. 74
marketing imperialism, p. 73
morals, p. 91
puffery, p, 74
social responsibility, p. 66
stereotype, p. 71

substantiation, p. 85
testimonial, p. 76
trademark, p. 79
uniform resource locators
   (URLs), p. 80

Review Questions

1. Explain the debate over whether advertising shapes or mirrors society. If you were to take a side in this debate, which side would you choose?

2. What do you consider the most pressing social issues facing advertisers? Explain.

3. Explain how trademarks and copyrights are legally protected, and why the First Amendment is important to advertisers.

4. In addition to the FTC, what other governmental bodies are involved in regulating advertising practices?

5. Explain the three ways in which self-regulation operates in the advertising industry.

6. Define ethics. How do you determine what is ethical? If you are called upon to make a decision about the promotion of an event for one of your clients, where does the ultimate consideration lie?

Discussion Questions

1. The Dimento Game Company has a new basketball video game. To promote it, "Slammer" Aston, an NBA star, is signed to do the commercial. Aston is shown in the commercial with the game controls as he speaks these lines: "This is the most challenging court game you've ever tried. It's all here—zones, man-to-man, pick and roll, even the alley-oop. For me, this is the best game off the court." Is Aston's presentation an endorsement? Should the FTC consider a complaint if Dimento uses this strategy? What would you need to know to determine if you are safe from a challenge of misleading advertising?

2. A pharmaceutical company has repackaged a previously developed drug that addresses the symptoms of a scientifically questionable disorder affecting approximately 5 percent of women. While few women are affected by the "disorder," the company's advertising strategy is comprehensive, including dozens of television, radio, and magazine ads. As a result, millions of women with symptoms similar to those of the disorder have sought prescriptions for the company's drug. In turn, the company has made billions of dollars. What, if any, are the ethical implications of advertising a remedy to a mass audience when the affected group is small? Is the company misrepresenting its drug by conducting a "media blitz"? Why or why not?

3. *Three-Minute Debate:* Zack Wilson is the advertising manager for the campus newspaper. He is looking over a layout for a promotion for a spring break vacation package. The headline says, "Absolutely the Finest Deal Available This Spring—You'll Have the Best Time Ever if You Join Us in Boca." The newspaper has a solid reputation for not running advertising with questionable claims and promises. Should Zack accept or reject this ad? Organize into small teams with pairs of teams taking one side or the other. In class, set up a series of three-minute debates in which each side has 1½ minutes to argue its position. Every team of debaters must present new points not covered in the previous teams' presentations until there are no arguments left to present. Then the class votes as a group on the winning point of view.

Take-Home Team Projects

1. Select three print ads that you feel pose one or more of the ethical issues discussed in this chapter. Ask five people (making sure they vary by gender, age, or background) how they feel about the ads. Conduct a short interview with each of your subjects; it would be helpful to have a list of questions prepared. Write a report on their opinions and response to your questionnaire. Don't be afraid to include your own conclusions about the ads. What differences or similarities do you see across the responses?

2. Check the Web sites of three big-name companies such as:
   • McDonald's (http://www.mcdonalds.com)
   • Avon (http://www.avon.com)
   • Ben & Jerry's (http://www.benjerry.com)
   • Starbucks (http://www.starbucks.com)
   • Body Shop (http://www.thebodyshop.com)
   • Target (http://www.target.com)

Write a two- to four-page report on their efforts to be socially responsible. How is the company's social responsibility position reflected in its advertising?

Yahoo! Hands-On Case

Review the Yahoo! case in the Appendix.

1. Explain the shape-versus-mirror debate in terms of Yahoo!'s advertising efforts. Is the company creating consumer demand or simply trying to meet it? Take a position and argue your point of view in a one-page report.

2. Your team is concerned about the social responsibility issues generated by a campaign to teens and tweens. Develop a one-page analysis of the issues related to advertising to this age group and conclude with a recommendation on how to handle this campaign assignment in a responsible way.

HANDS-ON CASE

Axe Gets Dirty Boys Clean

How dirty is too dirty? Axe's controversial campaign for its shower gel shows how to use sex to get the attention of the 18- to 24-year-old male audience. Unilever and its ad agency, Bartle Bogle Hegarty LLC, tested the limit of what's socially acceptable by creating commercials with scantily clad women doing sexy pole dancing, a plumber who retrieves a variety of sexually related articles from the bathtub drain, and an ice cream vendor who gets ESP (extra sexual perception) when using Axe.

Some people love the Axe approach. Others hate it. The commercials even show up on YouTube.com. Is that part of the strategy? Is it a clever ploy to reach a hard-to-get audience?

Let's start with the problem. How do you convince young guys who like Axe's Body Spray to start using its new Shower Gel? Axe led the way getting young men to use scented body sprays. Launched in 2002 in the United States, Axe deodorant body sprays captured the attention of its audience and soon became the top male deodorant brand in the country.

Expanding its line in men's grooming products with the shower gel represented a great opportunity for Unilever. The advertising objectives aspired to gain mass awareness of new Axe Shower Gel; reinforce the master brand's key personality attributes of "cool," "masculinity," and "up-to-date"; and get guys to perceive the Axe brand as sophisticated, as some users were starting to think of Axe as something for the younger crowd.

Although the core target for Axe is 11- to 24-year-old guys, this campaign focused on the upper end of this range, as guys generally don't buy their own soap until they leave home to go to college or work.

The idea behind the campaign was that Axe Shower Gel would do more than clean guys physically; it would help clean their spirits as well. In other words, guys get clean in some ways and dirty in others.

The campaign's creative work communicates the "dirty message" with strong sexual overtones. The agency chose media to reach and captivate the audience, amplifying the message in situations where guys might be having "dirty thoughts." This emotional approach is one that works particularly well in the broadcast media.

How do you reach these guys? TV commercials led off the campaign running on *Baywatch*, *The Real World*, and *Aqua Teen Hunger Force*, to name a few programs young men watch. Print ads also were placed in *Maxim*, *Playboy*, and the *Sports Illustrated* Swimsuit Issue. Axe also turned up at two of the largest spring break destinations for college guys where they encountered shower gel messages everywhere—on bar posters, hotel shower curtains, floor stickers, and bus wraps.

The "How Dirty Boys Get Clean" campaign helped Axe become the top male shower brand in the United States, and it's won many advertising awards, including an Effie and two Bronze Lions from the Cannes International Advertising Festival. That's one way to clean up.

Consider This

1. How would you evaluate the agency's work? Do you think the sexual message crosses the line of good taste, or is it brilliant advertising?
2. If you were working on this account, what considerations would you have that might guide your decisions about what is acceptable to your audience? To society?
3. Does sex sell? If you think it does, is that a bad thing? Explain.

Sources: "Axe: How Dirty Boys Get Clean," Effie brief, New York American Marketing Association, http://www.nyama.org (accessed October 20, 2006); Theresa Howard, "A Nice-Smelling Man is Good to Find," *USA Today*, July 17, 2005, http://www.usatoday.com.

Principle: Strategy Is Creative, Too

Part I introduced the basics of advertising and marketing practice. Part II focuses on how advertising works and how strategy is shaped by advertising planners.

Chapter 4 answers the big-picture question of "How does advertising work?" Effectiveness factors are spelled out using the Facets Model of Effects. Building on that discussion as a foundation, Chapter 5 introduces the consumer audience and discusses how targeting works. Understanding consumers and the markets requires research skill, which is the topic of Chapter 6. Finally, in Chapter 7 these ideas about how advertising works, how consumers think and behave, and how research is used to understand consumers and markets come together in a strategic plan.

No matter how much advertising and marketing communication change, a basic principle is that applied creativity has the power to move the market. Pat Fallon and Fred Senn, cofounders of the legendary agency, Fallon Worldwide, explain that principle in their book, *Juicing the Orange: How to Turn Creativity into a Powerful Business Advantage.* They have identified seven principles that will help you link creativity and strategic planning to business results.

Seven Principles of Creative Leverage

No matter which new media emerge and which old media fade away, one factor remains crucial: the power of applied creativity to move the market in your favor. These seven principles will help you link creativity and business results.

By Pat Fallon, Cofounder and Chair, and Fred Senn, Cofounder and Partner, Fallon Worldwide

Part

2

1. *Always start from scratch.* Simplify the problem. You know too much. There's a good chance that you know so much that you can't see how the problem could be solved in a fresh way.

2. *Demand a ruthlessly simple definition of the business problem.* Smart people tend to make things too complicated. Be a relentless reductionist. Einstein said, "Make things as simple as possible, but no simpler."

3. *Discover a proprietary emotion.* The key component of any communication program is a powerful consumer insight that leads to a ruthlessly smart strategy executed brilliantly across all platforms. It all starts with the insight, which is the central truth of what you are going to say and how you are going to operate. Once you find an emotional truth, you can make it proprietary through execution.

4. *Focus on the size of the idea, not the size of the budget.* It's our credo that it's better to outsmart than outspend.

5. *Seek out strategic risks.* Understand the benefits of prudent risk. Great big ideas in the early stages are often scary ideas. When Darwin taught us about the survival of the fittest, he didn't mean the strongest. He meant that it's the most nimble—the quickest to adapt to a changing environment—who prosper both in nature and in a capitalist economy.

6. *Collaborate or perish.* This is more than "getting along"; it is about recognizing that the rules of engagement have changed. We live in an era in which victory goes to the best collaborators. This means teams from different disciplines and different corporate cultures will be working together. Teams that are aligned and motivated can make history.

7. *Listen hard to your customers (then listen some more).* Listening is often step Number One on the road to understanding. Listening often yields that precious insight that gives you a competitive advantage; something your competitors have overlooked.

Chapter 4
How Advertising Works

Chapter 5
The Consumer Audience

Chapter 6
Strategic Research

Chapter 7
Strategic Planning

Source: From *Juicing the Orange: How to Turn Creativity into a Powerful Business Advantage,* Harvard Business School Press, 2006.

How Advertising Works

IT'S A WINNER

Awards:	Company:	Agency:	Campaign:
Obie Hall of Fame (Outdoor Advertising Association of America), Silver Effie, Silver Lion at Cannes International Advertising Festival	*Chick-fil-A*	*The Richards Group*	*"Eat Mor Chikin"®*

CHAPTER 4

Chick-fil-A Builds Brand
with Renegade Cows

How do you persuade people to eat chicken sandwiches when everybody else in the world seems to be eating hamburgers? Chick-fil-A faced that very issue when it started its long-running campaign. Chick-fil-A is not your typical quick-service restaurant chain and neither is its advertising. Truett Cathy founded Chick-fil-A with the vision that his chicken-sandwich company would be a leader in the quick-service restaurant industry. Chick-fil-A has become just that, in part by understanding how to put advertising to work to attract consumers' attention and generate a response at the restaurants.

Building the Chick-fil-A brand is a top priority for both Chick-fil-A and its advertising agency, The Richards Group. Agency and client agree that of all the things Chick-fil-A owns, nothing is as important as its brand. Its brand is its future, and great brands have the potential to continue forever.

The Richards Group defines a brand as a promise made to consumers through everything they can observe about a product—its logo, package color, signage, store appearance, and even the employees who sell it. Here's how Chick-fil-A defines its brand: "To choosy people in a hurry, Chick-fil-A is the premium fast-food restaurant brand that consistently serves America's best-loved chicken sandwiches." You'll note that the brand statement identifies a target audience (people in a hurry), a frame of reference (fast-food restaurant), and a point of difference (consistently serves America's best-loved chicken sandwiches).

Once the brand is defined, a campaign can be created to communicate its benefits. You do not have to be a big brand with millions of dollars to have great advertising. The Chick-fil-A "Eat Mor Chikin®" campaign is a great example. Chick-fil-A competes in the fast-food category, one of the largest and most competitive industries. It is outnumbered 15 to 1 in store count and outspent 60 to 1 in media by the likes of McDonald's, Burger King, and Wendy's.

Chapter Key Points

1. Why is communication a key factor in advertising effectiveness?

2. How did the idea of advertising effects develop, and what are the problems in traditional approaches to advertising effects?

3. What is the Facets Model of Advertising Effects, and how does it explain how advertising works?

Faced with these disadvantages in the marketplace, Chick-fil-A and its advertising agency set out to develop a brand campaign that would increase top-of-mind awareness, increase sales, and earn Chick-fil-A a spot in consumers' consideration list of fast-food brands. To do this effectively, the campaign positioned Chick-fil-A chicken sandwiches as the premium alternative to hamburgers.

The company couldn't outspend the competition. It couldn't even afford a national campaign on television, which is where most of its competitors were advertising. So it decided to advertise where its competitors weren't—on billboards. The challenge was how to build a brand using outdoor advertising as the primary medium.

For Chick-fil-A and its agency, overcoming the challenge turned out to be easier than expected. Chick-fil-A's "Eat Mor Chikin®" three-dimensional billboard campaign helped break the fast-food hamburger pattern. The witty use of Holstein cows encouraging the target audience to "Eat Mor Chikin®" instead of beef provided a bold brand personality that broke through industry clutter. Why? The message and execution were simple, the cows were funny, the creative idea was unexpected, and the call to action was powerful.

In this chapter you'll read about dimensions of what we call the Facets Model. This model explains how advertising can generate different types of consumer responses that help persuade people. You will also learn how companies such as Chick-fil-A communicate to consumers different aspects related to brand: identity, position, personality, image, promise, and loyalty.

How well did the cows' campaign work? Turn to the end of the chapter to see the results.

Sources: http://www.chick-fil-a.com; Information courtesy of Mike Buerno, The Richards Group.

How does advertising affect you? What ads can you remember seeing? Do you rush out to buy a new product when you see something advertised that intrigues you?

Do you have favorite ads? Can you remember what brands they were advertising? Did advertising have anything to do with why you like this brand?

These are all important questions to advertising professionals and to students, professors, and critics of advertising. In this chapter we'll try to answer these questions about how advertising and other marketing communication work by looking at the *effects* behind the concept of *effectiveness.*

We are introducing this topic now because understanding how advertising works is a foundation for discussions in the following chapters on consumer behavior, consumer research, and strategic planning. It's our view that you can't make intelligent decisions in those areas unless you have some understanding of how marketing communication works. In this chapter we'll first consider advertising as communication. Then we'll look at various types of consumer responses to messages to identify the key effects, which we organize and present as the Facets Model of Advertising Effects. This chapter, then, lays the groundwork for our explanation of effectiveness.

HOW DOES ADVERTISING WORK?

Would it surprise you to know that a lot of professionals, as well as academics, are really not sure how advertising works—or even if it works well at all. This classic quote attributed to Philadelphia department store baron John Wanamaker in the early 1900s sums up the issue: "I know half my advertising is wasted, but I don't know which half."

Wanamaker is more positive than some advertising experts. The chairman of a British promotions company estimated that only about 1 percent of the average campaign spending actually works because few people are aware of ad messages and of those who are aware, few actually do anything in response.[1]

Research by Syracuse University professor John Philip Jones, who worked for many years at the J. Walter Thompson advertising agency, led him to conclude that only 41 percent of advertising actually works in terms of producing sales.[2]

Of course, not all advertising experts are as pessimistic, and many professionals, including the managers of big global brands, absolutely believe that advertising works both in the short term to create sales and in the long term to build brands. After all, advertising is a $200 billion industry—even larger when you consider all the various related areas of marketing communication.

The problem is that a lot of poorly executed advertising doesn't work as its creators intended. In other words, it doesn't communicate well to its intended audience. Fallon and Senn in the Part II opening vignette emphasize the importance of linking creative idea like advertising communication to business results. So let's begin our discussion of how advertising* works by looking in more depth at its communication role.

HOW ADVERTISING WORKS AS COMMUNICATION

Advertising, and certainly all forms of marketing communication, are first of all a form of communication. In a sense, effective advertising is a message to a consumer about a brand. It gets attention and provides information, sometimes even a bit of entertainment as the Chick-fil-A ads demonstrate. It also seeks to create some kind of response, such as an inquiry, a sale, or a visit to a Web site.

In Chapter 1, we quoted the legendary David Ogilvy explaining how he views advertising as a personal conversation. In reality, however, most traditional advertising is not as personal or as interactive as a conversation because it relies on mass communication. Although other forms of marketing communication, such as personal selling and telemarketing, can deliver the personal contact of a conversation, Ogilvy's comparison ignores the challenge of getting the attention of a largely disinterested audience when using mass communication. So let's look first how *communication* works and then we'll apply that analysis to mass-media advertising.

The Communication Model

Mass communication is a process, as depicted in the communication model in Figure 4.1a, which outlines the important players and steps. The model diagrams how communication works: It begins with a **source** (S), a sender who encodes a message (M), or puts it in words and pictures. The message is presented through **channels of communication** (C), such as a newspaper, radio, or TV. The message is decoded, or interpreted, by the **receiver** (R), who is the reader, viewer, or listener. **Feedback** is obtained by monitoring the response of the receiver to the message. And the entire process is complicated by what we refer to as **noise**, things that interrupt the sending and receiving of the message, such as a bad connection or words with unclear meanings.

Mass communication is generally a one-way process with the message depicted, as in this model, as moving from the source to the receiver. However, **interactive communication**—such as Ogilvy's personal conversation—is two-way communication—a dialogue—and marketing communication is moving in that direction. The difference between one-way and two-way communication is that two-way communication is interactive, and the source and receiver change positions as the message bounces back and forth between them. Figure 4.1b is a model of how a conversation or dialogue works.

---

*Note: It's simpler to just say "advertising," but in this chapter we are referring to advertising as well as the more general area of marketing communication.

A Basic Communication Model

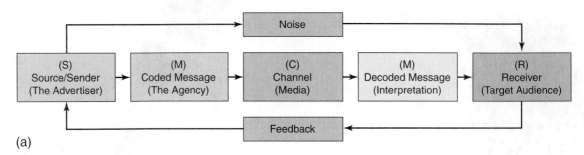

(a)

An Interactive Communication Model

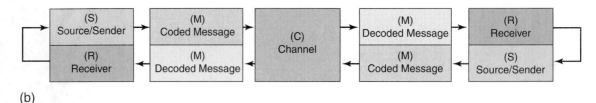

(b)

FIGURE 4.1

Basic Communication Model and An Interactive Communication Model

Mass communication (a) is a one-way process in which the message moves from the source to the receiver. Interactive communication (b) is a conversation or dialogue, and the source and receiver change positions as the message bounces back and forth between them.

Advertising as Communication

To translate the communication model to advertising, consider that the *source* typically is the advertiser assisted by its agency. Together they determine the *objectives* for the message—an advertisement or campaign—in terms of the effects they want the message to have on the *consumer audience (receiver).* If the communication process fails to work and the consumer does not receive the message as intended by the advertiser, then the communication effort is ineffective. The advertising communication model shown in Figure 4.2 describes how this communication process works.

The *message,* of course, is the advertisement or other marketing communication, such as a press release, store sign, brochure, or Web page. The message may be spelled out in the words, but in most advertising the visual elements also carry meaning. In fact, some advertising messages, such as the 1984 commercial for the Macintosh discussed in Chapter 1, are primarily visual.

The *medium* is the vehicle that delivers the message. In advertising, that tends to be newspapers and magazines in print, radio and TV in broadcasting, the Internet, and other forms of out-of-home vehicles, such as outdoor boards and posters. Other media include the phone, fax, specialty items (mugs, T-shirts), in-store signs, brochures, catalogs, shopping bags, inflatables, even sidewalks and toilet doors. The latest entry in the medium of marketing communication is the cell phone, which is fast becoming a major communication technology in people's lives. With instant messaging, podcasting, movie downloads, and photo transmission, the cell phone is the newest "must-have" communication device.[3]

In advertising, as in communication in general, noise hinders the consumer's reception of the message. *External noise* in advertising includes socioeconomic trends that affect the reception of the message. Health trends, for example, often harm the reception of fast-food messages. Problems with the brand's marketing mix (product design, price, distribution, and marketing communication) can also have impact on the consumer's response. Martha Stewart's trial, for example, created negative noise for her company, Martha Stewart Living Omnimedia, and it also had a negative effect on business partner Kmart, which carries Martha Stewart branded products.

External noise can also be related to the advertising media. It can be as simple as bad radio or TV reception. A more likely cause of noise is **clutter,** which is the multitude of mes-

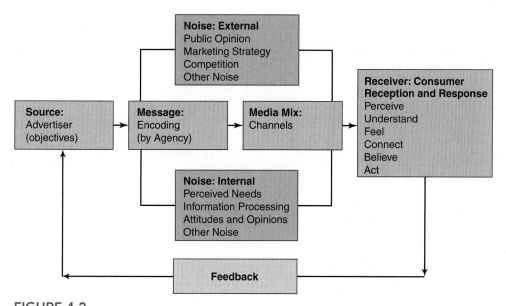

FIGURE 4.2

Advertising Communication Model

The model of advertising communication translates the standard parts of the communication model into an advertising context. It still begins with the advertiser (source) and ends with the consumer or target audience (receiver).

sages all competing to get consumers' attention. More specifically, it is all the ads in a magazine or newspaper, or all the commercials you see on television when watching a program or listening to your favorite radio station. It can even include any of the 3,000 or so commercial messages you see in your daily environment, such as outdoor boards and brand names on T-shirts, as well as in unexpected places, such as painted messages on sidewalks.

The massive number of ads makes it harder and harder for any one ad to get the attention of its intended audience. People use many techniques to avoid clutter and information overload. For the same reason, advertisers use clutter-busting techniques like surprise to break through and get consumer attention. Consumers filter messages they don't want to see by turning the page, switching the channel, hitting the mute button, tossing unopened mail that looks like an ad, and deleting spam without looking at it. Other *avoidance* techniques such as e-mail filters, "no-call" laws, and commercial-skipping digital TV recorders are creating new dilemmas for marketers. Many marketers are experiencing lower response rates to their campaigns as a result of filters and other avoidance techniques.[4]

Internal noise includes personal factors that affect the reception of an advertisement, such as the receiver's needs, purchase history, information-processing abilities, and other personal factors. If you are too tired to listen or your attention is focused elsewhere, then your fatigue or disinterest creates noise that hinders your reception of the message. Distraction from competing brand messages can also be a source of internal noise.

Feedback is the reaction the audience has to a message. It can be obtained through research or through customer-initiated contact with the company. Both of these are important tests of the effectiveness of marketing communication messages.

The last category is the *receiver,* or in advertising terms the consumer, and how the consumer responds to the message. Consumer response is the focus of the rest of this chapter.

Adding Interaction to Marketing Communication

As we said in the previous discussion about advertising as communication based on a one-way model of mass communication, in more interactive marketing communication, these roles switch back and forth (see Figure 4.1). In addition to a purchase, consumers react to a marketing communication message by responding with comments, phone calls, and e-mail inquiries to sales personnel and customer service. If advertisers want to overcome the impersonal nature of mass communication, they need to learn to receive (i.e., *listen to*) as well as send messages to customers.

The Internet has created a new world of interactive communication for marketers who develop Web sites, facilitate chat rooms, and send and receive e-mail messages from consumers. A blog (Web log) enables anyone to have an opinion about a company or brand, communicate it, and listen to the reaction. Activists, as well as company staff and customers, are creating blog sites to reach and interact with people with similar interests.

Two-way communication is one of the objectives of an IMC-focused program because it helps create long-term customer relationships with a brand. Hallmark Loyalty, a spin-off of the Hallmark card company, offers its clients specially designed cards to use in responding to customers who contact them with complaints or payment problems. The cards convey that the company cares and will do what it can to deal with the customer's problem or concern.[5]

Dialogue also creates new ways to listen to customers. In the traditional communication model, customers' responses, or *feedback,* are gathered primarily through research, but in newer approaches to communication, feedback occurs in a real-time environment of ongoing communication. This feedback is achieved by using more interactive forms of marketing communication (personal selling, customer service, online marketing) and monitoring the responses and customer-initiated dialogue that comes through response devices such as toll-free numbers and e-mail addresses.

THE EFFECTS BEHIND ADVERTISING EFFECTIVENESS

Does an ad need to be entertaining to work? (Think about the Chick-fil-A cows and the *1984* commercial.) What about your favorite commercials—do they grip you emotionally? (Think Hallmark and Dove soap.) Do they have a compelling message? (Think the *truth*® campaign featured in Chapter 1.) Just what are the effects that make an advertisement effective?

Principle
The intended consumer response is the message's objective, and the message is effective to the degree that it achieves this desired response.

Good advertising—and marketing communication—is effective when it generates the advertiser's desired response. This intended response is the message's objective, and the message is effective to the degree that it achieves this objective. Thus, a notion of what kinds of effects can be achieved with a marketing communication message is essential to anyone engaged in planning advertising.

Traditional Approaches

When we ask how it works, we are talking about the **impact** an advertisement has on receivers of the message—that is, how they respond to the message. What are the effects that determine whether an advertisement works or not? Over the years, advertising professionals have used several models to outline what they believe is the impact of an advertisement on its audience.

- *AIDA.* The most commonly used explanation of how advertising works is referred to as **AIDA,** which stands for **A**ttention, **I**nterest, **D**esire, and **A**ction. This concept was first expressed around 1900 by an advertising pioneer named St. Elmo Lewis. Because AIDA assumes a predictable set of steps, it also is referred to as a **hierarchy of effects** model. Numerous other hierarchical models have been developed over the years to help advertisers plan their advertising.[6]
- *Think/Feel/Do.* Another relatively simple answer to how advertising works is the **Think/Feel/Do** model developed in the 1970s.[7] Also referred to as the *FCB Model* in honor of the agency where it was developed as a strategic planning tool, the idea is that advertising motivates people to think about the message, feel something about the brand, and then do something, such as try it or buy it. This approach is also basically a set of steps. The problem with these hierarchical, linear models is that advertisers now realize that people don't always respond in such a predictable fashion.
- *Domains.* A different approach that attempted to solve the problem of linear steps is found in Moriarty's Domains Model. It is based on the idea that messages have impact on consumer responses, not in steps, but simultaneously. The three key effects, or domains, identified in this approach are (1) perception, (2) learning, and (3) persuasion.[8] The idea is that a message can engage consumers' perceptions (attention, interest), educate them (think, learn), and persuade them (change attitude and behavior) all at the same time.

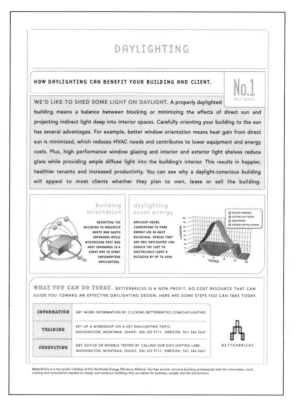

SHOWCASE This campaign, aimed at professionals in the building trades, was designed to be educational in presenting the company's consulting services. Rather than lofty or preachy (like a "Save the planet" ad), the strategy called for the message to be practical and focused on results (good for business), emotional (good for the environment), and rational (make a good business decision). This added up to a win-win-win decision for clients. This ad was contributed by Karl Schroeder, copywriter at Coates Kokes in Portland, Oregon, who is a graduate of the University of Oregon advertising program.

An example is shown in the Better Bricks ad. Even though it is in the business-to-business category, the ad gets the attention of its audience with a dramatic headline—"your client gets burned." It's an educational message, but also persuasive in that it makes the argument that bricks deliver a sustainable, high-performance building.

How do we make sense of all these ideas about how advertising works in order to create a reasonable approach to use in planning and critiquing advertising? How can we organize all these effects so they are useful for setting objectives and, ultimately, evaluating effectiveness?

Sorting Out the Effects

The traditional approaches to defining the effects of advertising pose two problems: (1) the presumption of a set of steps as a predictable pattern of response and (2) missing effects. We touched previously on the problem with the step models. The problem of missing effects is more apparent when we look at research techniques used to evaluate effectiveness. We'll talk more about evaluation in Chapter 19, but because we know evaluation is linked to the setting of "measurable" objectives, then our notion of how advertising works also should consider the key advertising effects researchers attempt to measure.

Consider, for example, that the model of television advertising the Ameritest research company developed to test advertising commercials is based on three factors—attention, brand linkage, and motivation—and two of these—brand linkage and motivation—aren't mentioned in any of the traditional formulas we just discussed.[9] How can a company that specializes in measuring advertising effectiveness be using an approach that is so different from the traditional planning models?

Ogilvy & Mather's corporate Web site refers to its 360° Brand Stewards philosophy. This is the opening page for the agency's presentation of its work for long-time client American Express.

The most important area missing from the traditional models, but not from the Ameritest approach, is brand communication. As an indication of its importance to the professional community, consider that Ogilvy & Mather (O&M), a huge global agency, makes brand communication the foundation of the agency's 360° Brand Stewardship philosophy. On its Web site, the agency says, "We believe our job is to help clients build enduring brands that live as part of consumers' lives and command their loyalty and confidence."[10] To accomplish that aim, O&M describes its role as:

Creating attention-getting messages that make a promise consistent and true to the brand's image and identity. And guiding actions, both big and small, that deliver on that brand promise. To every audience that brand has. At every brand intersection point. At all times.

NEW APPROACH: THE FACETS MODEL OF EFFECTS

Our objective in this chapter is to present a model of advertising effects that does a more complete job of explaining how advertising creates various types of consumer responses. Moving away from a linear model driven by notions of cognitive processing is a seismic change for advertising, but it is necessary to help us better understand how to make advertising—and all marketing communication—more effective.

The simplicity of Think/Feel/Do makes it a good starting point, since all three of these effects are generally recognized as critical consumer responses to advertising. But can we still develop a relatively simple model that includes the missing effects that aren't accommodated in T/F/D?

Several of the linear models begin with terms like *attention, awareness,* and *exposure,* concepts that recognize there is a *perceptual dimension* to advertising impact, as Moriarty's Domains Model suggests. Another missing area is *persuasion,* which explains how beliefs and attitudes are created or changed and conviction is established. Since persuasion relies on both think and feel responses, it doesn't fit at all in the hierarchical models and falls between the cracks if you are trying to use Think/Feel/Do as a model for objectives. Another of the areas missing from most models is *association,* which Preston uses to explain how brand communication works in general, as well as to create brand images. In recognition of its importance to brand communication, this category is also called *brand transformation* or *brand linkage.*

The solution is to build on the effects identified in the Think/Feel/Do approach and add the missing categories. It is interesting that the missing areas we just identified—perception, brand association, and persuasion—are also related to the three areas that the Ameritest research company uses in evaluating effective commercials.

Thus, we arrive at a six-factor model that should be useful both in setting objectives and evaluating the effectiveness of advertising. Our answer to the question of how advertising works is to propose that effective advertising creates six types of consumer responses—(1) see/hear, (2) feel, (3) think/understand, (4) believe, (5) connect, and (6) act/do—all of which work together to create a response to a brand message. These six consumer responses and the categories of effects to which they belong are represented in Figure 4.3.

These six effects are facets—polished surfaces like those of a diamond or crystal—that come together to make up a unique consumer response to an advertising message. The effects are holistic, leading to an impression, or what Preston calls an "integrated perception."[11] An effective message has a diamondlike quality that represents how the message effects work together to create the desired consumer response. The effects can also vary in importance, with some advertising campaigns more focused on one or several of the facets.

FIGURE 4.3
The Facets of Effects Model

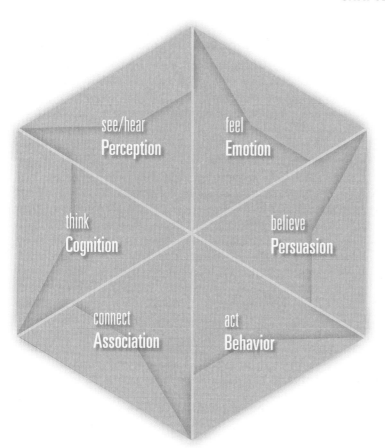

The Practical Tips box summarizes the six facets in terms of the objective of the advertiser and the related consumer responses that can be measured to determine if the objective was met. The third column lists the factors that help drive effectiveness—many of which were in the various lists of effects in the formulas we previously reviewed. Let's now explore these six categories of effects in more detail. We'll start with perception, which is where the consumer response to an advertisement begins.

Practical Tips

Marketing Communication Effects

Here is how to analyze the impact of your advertising in terms of the type of objective you're trying to achieve and how that will be apparent in the way consumers respond to your message. The final column lists factors that can be measured to determine if you achieved the desired type of impact.

Communication Objective	Consumer Response	Drivers
Perception	**See/Hear**	exposure, selection, attention, interest/relevance, awareness, recognition
Emotion/Affective	**Feel**	want/desire, feelings, liking, resonance
Cognition	**Understand**	need, cognitive learning, differentiation, recall
Association	**Connect**	symbolism, conditioned learning, transformation
Persuasion	**Believe**	motivation, influence, involvement, conviction, believability/credibility, preference and intention, loyalty
Behavior	**Act**	trial, buying, contacting, advocating, referral, prevention/avoidance

See/Hear: The Perception Facet

Every day we are bombarded with stimuli—faces, conversations, scents, sounds, advertisements, news announcements—yet we actually notice only a small fraction. Why?

The answer is perception. **Perception** is the process by which we receive information through our five senses and assign meaning to it. If an advertisement is to be effective, first of all, it must get noticed. It has to be seen or heard, even if the perception is minimal and largely below the level of awareness. We "see" ads in magazines even if we page through the publication without stopping to read them; we "see" commercials on TV even as we zip through a recorded program.

Our minds are full of impressions that we have collected without much active thought or concentration. Of course, on occasion we do stop and read an ad or watch a commercial all the way through, so there are various degrees and levels of perception. The Chick-fil-A cow ads were particularly effective at breaking through inattention and building awareness. Breakthrough advertising, then, is advertising that breaks through the perceptual filters and makes an impression on the audience.

Perception Drivers   Consumers select messages to which they pay attention, a process called **selective perception.** Here's how perception works: Some ads for some product categories—personal hygiene products, for example—have a battle getting attention because people don't choose to watch them. However, if the message is selected and attended to, then the consumer may react to it with interest if it is relevant. The result is awareness of the ad or brand, which is filed in memory at least to the point that the consumer recognizes the brand or ad. The key factors driving perception, then, are exposure, selection and attention, interest and relevance, awareness, and recognition. Here is a brief review of these terms and how they relate to advertising impact.

Principle
For an advertisement to be effective, it first has to get noticed or at least register on some minimal level on our senses.

- *Exposure.* The first test of perception is whether a marketing communication message is seen or heard. In advertising, this is called **exposure,** which is an important goal of media planners who try to find the best way to reach consumers with a message.
- *Selection and attention.* The next factor that drives perception is **selective attention,** the process by which a receiver of a message chooses to attend to a message. Amid all the clutter in the media environment, selection is a huge problem. The ability to draw attention that brings visibility to a brand is one of advertising's greatest strengths. Advertisements, particularly television commercials, are often designed to be **intrusive,** which means they intrude on people's perception in order to grab attention.
- *Interest and relevance.* A factor in crossing the selection barrier is **interest,** which means the receiver of the message has become mentally engaged in some way with the ad and the product. Ad messages are designed not only to get attention, but also to hold the audience's interest long enough for the audience to register the point of the ad. That level of interest and attention is sometimes referred to as **stickiness,** particularly for Web sites. One reason people are interested in something is **relevance,** which means the message, such as the accompanying example for the Peace Corps, connects on some personal level.

  The Peace Corps launched a national recruiting campaign with a theme: "Life is calling. How far will you go?" It was designed to address more relevant personal issues for potential volunteers and tell them how the volunteer experience would enrich their lives.
- *Awareness.* When you are aware of something, you know that you have seen it or heard it before. In other words, **awareness** results when an advertisement makes an impression—something registers. New product campaigns, for example, seek to create high levels of brand awareness.
- *Recognition.* Advertisers are interested in two types of memory—**recognition,** which means people remember seeing the ad, and **recall,** which means they remember what the ad said. Recognition is a measure of perception and is used to determine awareness. Recall is a measure of understanding, which we will talk about in a later section on cognitive effects. Recognition relies on simple visuals that lock into memory, such as logos (Nike's Swoosh), as well as colors (IBM's blue), jingles and

sounds (Gershwin's "Rhapsody in Blue" for United Airlines), characters (the Energizer bunny), key visuals (the disbelieving look of the Aflac duck), and slogans (Altoids, "The Curiously Strong Mints"). Memory depends heavily upon repetition to anchor an impression in the mind.

The Subliminal Issue Before we leave the perception category, let's consider the controversial area of subliminal effects. **Subliminal** effects are message cues given below the threshold of perception. In other words, they don't register. You can't perceive them because they are too brief to see or disguised in some way. The idea is that they are designed to get past your perceptual filters by talking directly to your subconscious. People who believe in subliminal advertising presume such messages to be intense enough to influence behavior.

There is confusion between unconscious effects and subconscious effects, and that leads to misunderstanding about the way subliminal messages work—or don't work. We mentioned that it is possible for a message to register at a very low level of awareness, perhaps even when the receiver is relatively unconscious of the message. For example, fast-food restaurants are decorated in hot colors—orange and red—because those colors are thought to stimulate people, nudging them to eat and leave rather than sit around and relax. You may not be aware of such things as color choices and soft music and their effect on you because you don't consciously think about such things. The point is that if you can see it, it's not subliminal—unconscious perception is not the same as a subliminal message that works on the subconscious.

Defenders of advertising contend that there is no real support for subliminal advertising as the Matter of Principle box discusses, because subliminal effects are too weak to drive behavior.

Messages that are relevant speak to a consumer's special interests.

Feel: The Affective or Emotional Facet

Affective responses mirror our feelings about something. Affective describes something that stimulates wants, touches the emotions, creates liking, and elicits feelings.* If you were creating the advertising for a hotel, what would you emphasize—speed of check-in, size of the room, hair dryers, and mints on the pillow? Rather than tangible features like these, Sheraton decided to emphasize the emotional side of traveling and shows people greeting one another. Since it's a global company, the greetings include hugs, bows, and kisses on both cheeks. The company believes that its customers worldwide like to be welcomed, appreciated, and made to feel at home.[12]

Look back at the Facets of Effects Model in Figure 4.3. Notice how *perceive* and *feel* sit side by side at the top of the model. Although this isn't a linear process model, the perceptual process begins with perception if a message registers at all. That also means emotion is a driving factor because it is closely related to perception.

Erik du Plessis, the CEO of a global advertising research firm, makes the argument in his book, *The Advertised Mind,* that attention is driven by emotion.[13] He says our emotional responses to a message determine whether or not we pay attention. The key task of an ad, then, is initially to evoke an emotional response.

---

*Note: *Affective* refers to emotional responses: *effective* refers to how well something works.

A MATTER OF **PRINCIPLE**

Ice Cubes, Female Breasts, and Subliminal Advertising

By Sheri Broyles, *University of North Texas*

For 50 years people have been looking for secret little subliminal messages carefully hidden in advertising we see every day. It began in 1957 in a movie theater experiment when James Vicary subliminally suggested people "eat popcorn" and "drink Coca-Cola" by projecting those words at 1/3,000 of a second on the screen during a movie. News media at the time widely reported his claims that sales of popcorn and soda increased as a result.

Though he later admitted these results were a hoax, it was as if Pandora had let subliminal advertising out of her box. A large majority of people have repeatedly said that they have heard of subliminal advertising (74 to 84 percent), they believe advertisers use this technique (68 to 85 percent), and they think it is effective (68 to 78 percent). Obviously, subliminal advertising continues to be an issue today.

So what is subliminal advertising? By definition, *subliminal* means the stimulus is below your threshold of consciousness. The first thing to know is if you can see something, then it isn't subliminal.

Subliminal also has been misused to mean "suggestive" or "sexual." In the 1970s and 1980s Wilson Bryan Key popularized this view in his books *Subliminal Seduction, Media Sexploitation,* and *The Clam-Plate Orgy.* He

suggested that photographs were embedded (that is, manipulated by airbrushing) with sexual or arousing images in ambiguous portions of the picture. He maintained that products ranging from alcoholic beverages to Ritz Crackers used these sexual embeds. Key's self-proclaimed disciple, August Bullock, makes similar statements in his more recent book *The Secret Sales Pitch.*

There's been a continuing debate over the years about whether subliminal advertising actually exists. However, it's impossible to convince devout believers in subliminal advertising that what they *think* they see isn't there. Even more troubling is their assumption that presence implies effectiveness. Their belief is that because subliminal advertising exists—at least in their minds—it must be effective; otherwise, it wouldn't exist. Perhaps the more important question isn't whether subliminal advertising exists but whether or not it's an effective advertising tool. It should be noted that neither Key nor Bullock offers documentation that subliminal advertising actually works in any of the many examples in their books.

Several studies followed Vicary's theater experiment that explored whether subliminal advertising had an effect on consumers. Many different methodologies were used to test the effectiveness of subliminal stimuli. One 1959 study used early television to test subliminal persuasion. Another used a slide projector to subliminally superimpose a message. Others placed embeds in print ads. Most experiments showed no effect. Those that did either could not be replicated by the researchers or the effect was so weak that it would be canceled out by competing stimuli for the consumer's attention if it were not in a laboratory setting. There is no evidence to suggest that subliminal advertising would persuade real consumers to buy real products.

If subliminal advertising isn't effective, why are we still talking about it 50 years later? While research has repeatedly shown that subliminal advertising doesn't work, the general public hasn't been persuaded, perhaps because they haven't been exposed to the decades of research. Subliminal advertising is like an urban legend or a good conspiracy theory—it's something that people want to believe. However, whether valid or not, it does affect the public's perception of advertising. That, in turn, reduces the credibility of advertisers and their agencies. And that's a concern for everyone in the advertising industry.

PEOPLE HAVE BEEN TRYING TO FIND THE BREASTS IN THESE ICE CUBES SINCE 1957.

The advertising industry is sometimes charged with sneaking seductive little pictures into ads. Supposedly, these pictures can get you to buy a product without your even seeing them. Consider the photograph above. According to some people, there's a pair of female breasts

hidden in the patterns of light refracted by the ice cubes. Well, if you really searched you probably *could* see the breasts. For that matter, you could also see Millard Fillmore, a stuffed pork chop and a 1946 Dodge. The point is that so-called "subliminal advertising" simply

doesn't exist. Overactive imaginations, however, most certainly do. So if anyone claims to see breasts in that drink up there, they aren't in the ice cubes. They're in the eye of the beholder.

ADVERTISING
ANOTHER WORD FOR FREEDOM OF CHOICE.
American Association of Advertising Agencies

A liquor advertising campaign showed ice cubes with shapes in them and deliberately called attention to these "subliminal" messages. Of course, they weren't subliminal because you could see the images. The whole campaign was a spoof on Key's theories.

Sources: Sheri Broyles, "Subliminal Advertising and the Perpetual Popularity of Playing to People's Paranoia," *The Journal of Consumer Affairs*, 40:2 (2006): 392–406; Timothy Moore, "Subliminal Advertising: What You See Is What You Get," *Journal of Marketing, 46* (Spring 1982): 38–47.

This view is supported by recent research in the neurosciences, which advertising professor Ann Marie Barry says "acknowledges the primacy of emotions in processing all communication."[14] She explains further that, "Perception, the process by which we derive meaning from what we see, is an elaborate symphony played first and foremost through the unconscious emotional system."

Factors Driving the Affective Response

Emotional responses are powerful, not only because they drive perception, but also because, as du Plessis explains, they determine whether our unconscious reaction becomes conscious. Furthermore, he suggests that positive emotional responses drive memory as well.[15]

The affective response drivers are wants and desires, feelings, liking, and resonance. Emotion, then, causes us to "feel" something. The "Crash" campaign for the Volkswagen Jetta, for example, used attention-grabbing scenes of car crashes to deliver a safety message. The images were so real they left the audience, as well as the actors, trembling.[16]

- *Wants.* "I want something" implies desire. **Wants** are driven by emotions and based on wishes, longings, and cravings. Impulse buying is a good example. When you are standing in line at a store and see a display of candy bars, you may want one, but that doesn't mean you think about whether or not you need it. It's strictly desire, and desire is driven by emotion. Consider Axe, which pioneered the new category of body spray for men in 2002. Now it boasts an astonishing $150 million in annual sales. Did guys know before 2002 that they would want scented body spray?
- *Feelings.* Our passions and feelings are addressed in a number of ways in advertising, such as humor, love, or fear. Ads that rely on arousing feelings are referred to as using **emotional appeals.** The idea that emotional appeals may have more impact than rational approaches on both attitudes and behavior was supported by a University of Florida study that analyzed 23,000 consumer responses and found that the emotional response is more powerful than cognition in predicting action.[17]
- *Liking.* Two important responses to a message are liking the brand and liking the ad. **Liking** reflects the personality of the brand or the entertainment power of the ad's execution. The assumption is that if you like the ad, then that positive feeling will transfer to the brand. A classic study of advertising testing methods by the Advertising Research Foundation (ARF) found that liking—both the brand and the ad—was the best predictor of consumer behavior.[18]

  On the opposite side of liking is *aversion,* which means people avoid buying a brand because they don't like the ads or what they associate with the brand. We don't like to see condom ads, so they aren't often found in the mass media. Negative political ads demonstrate the flip side of liking. They are an example of an affective strategy that seems to work by putting opponents on the defensive. They may work through the power of suggestion, but most people say they dislike these ads because they sometimes seem unfair or mean-spirited. After the 2006 midterm election, the Annenberg Public Policy Center at the University of Pennsylvania found in its analysis of 115 Republican ads that 91 percent were negative; of the Democrats' 104 ads, 81 percent were negative.[19]
- *Resonate.* Effective advertisements sometimes create **resonance,** or a feeling that the message "rings true." Like relevance, messages that resonate help the consumer identify with the brand on a personal level. Resonance is stronger than liking because it involves an element of self-identification. These sympathetic vibes amplify the emotional impact by engaging a personal connection with a brand.

Principle

A positive response to an ad is important because advertisers hope that liking the ad will increase liking the brand.

Understand: The Cognitive Facet

How many ads you see on television or notice in print contain information that caused you to stop and think about the brand? Can you recall any instance where you learned something new about a product from an ad?

Although perception and its partner, emotion, are the first effects of an advertising message, an advertisement may generate any of the other responses next. For this discussion, we'll talk first about cognitive impact. **Cognition** refers to how consumers search for

A MATTER OF PRACTICE

Does Negative Political Advertising Help or Hinder Citizens?

By Marilyn S. Roberts, Ph.D., *University of Florida*

Negative political advertising is not new. One example of a highly negative campaign dates back to the 1828 presidential election between Andrew Jackson and his opponent, John Quincy Adams.[1] Fast forward to 1952, when the televised political advertising era began and brought new concerns. With the combination of sight, sound, and motion, the merits and criticisms of negative television advertising began debates that continue today.

From a practitioner's perspective, an important question is, "Do negative ads work?"

Almost in unison political media consultants for major U.S. political parties say, "Yes!" One may find that exception is taken by consultants when referring to what they create as "negative" advertising. Instead, many professionals prefer to use the term *contrast advertising* to underscore the differences between their candidate and his/her opponent.

In seminal research over 40 years ago, Patterson and McClure argued that citizens do learn about issues from spot commercials, a finding that flew in the face of convention at the time.[2] The frequency of attack ads in presidential campaigns has risen steadily over the last decades, regardless of party affiliation.[3]

Today scholars hold widely differing opinions as to the beneficial or detrimental role that negative advertising plays in contemporary campaigning and civil society. Kathleen Hall Jamieson attests that there is a strong association between negativity and deception.[4] Her efforts have influenced how journalists report on campaign advertising and led to increased efforts to check the accuracy of advertising content and claims.

John G. Geer offers reasons to rethink opposition to negativity in political campaigns.[5] He compared the quality of nearly 800 positive and negative political ads by applying the following standards:

- The more issues are discussed, the better.
- The more evidence is presented, the better.
- The clearer the differences between candidates, the better.
- The more relevant the appeal is to governing, the better.

Geer's findings suggest that negative information is more issue oriented than positive ads. Attack ads are more likely to be supported by evidence than self-promotional positive ads. Previous research also supported the notion that negative information is more easily recalled than positive information.

Does negativity in campaigns hurt the democratic process? Many observers worry that it does, while others argue the contrary. Whether one views negativity as good, bad, or mixed, politics is about conflict. As interactive political advertising and blogs play a larger role in contemporary campaigns, the questions and concerns about the rise in negativity will not diminish. Citizens, the news media, and candidates and their consultants must monitor and take responsibility for the tone of campaigns.

[1] Kathleen Hall Jamieson. 1996. Packaging the Presidency: A History and Criticism of Presidential Campaign Advertising, Third Edition. New York: Oxford University Press.
[2] Patterson, Thomas E. and Robert McClure. 1976. Unseeing Eye. New York: Putnam.
[3] Geer, John G. 2006. In Defense of Negativity: Attack Ads in Presidential Campaigns. Chicago: University of Chicago Press.
[4] Kathleen Hall Jamieson. 1992. Dirty Politics; Deception, Distraction, and Democracy. New York: Oxford University Press.
[5] Geer, John G. 2006. pp. 47–63.

and respond to information, as well as how they learn and understand something. It's a rational response to a message. Some call this a left-brain approach, based on the left-right brain ways of thinking that evolved from brain hemisphere research. Right brain thinking is presumed to be more emotional and creative. The American Airlines ad uses the left, right brain metaphor to demonstrate the difference between a cognitive and an emotional advertising message.

Factors That Drive a Cognitive Response   With a cognitive response a consumer may need something or need to know something, and the information gathered in response to that need leads to understanding. The information is filed in memory but can be recalled when needed. Advertising and other marketing communication often provide information about products, usually facts about product performance and features, such as size, price, construction, and design. Many consumers seek out and value this kind of information. The Yankelovich research company, for example, found consumers say they want more nutrition information on food labels as well as guidelines on packages.[20] The informative nature of advertising is particularly important for products that are complex (e.g., appliances, cars, insurance, computers, software) or that involve a high price or high risk (e.g., motorboats, vacations, medical procedures).

The key drivers of a consumer's cognitive response are need, learning, comprehension, differentiation, and recall.

- *Need.* Advertisers talk a lot about consumer needs and wants. Generally, **needs** are something you think about, and wants are based on feelings and desires. In other words, when we refer to needs, we are usually talking about the cognitive impact of a message that describes something lacking in consumers' lives. Advertisers address consumer needs through cognitive ads that explain how a product works and what it can do for the user—the benefits it offers to the user. For example, consumers need a virus protection program for their personal computers, but they also may need an explanation of how the program works.

- *Cognitive learning.* Consumers learn about products and brands through two primary routes: cognitive learning and conditioned learning (we'll talk about conditioned learning in the section on association). **Cognitive learning** occurs when a presentation of facts, information, and explanations leads to understanding. Consumers who are trying to find information about a product before they buy it are taking the cognitive learning route. This typically applies to large purchases, such as cars, computers, and major appliances. Learning is also a part of new

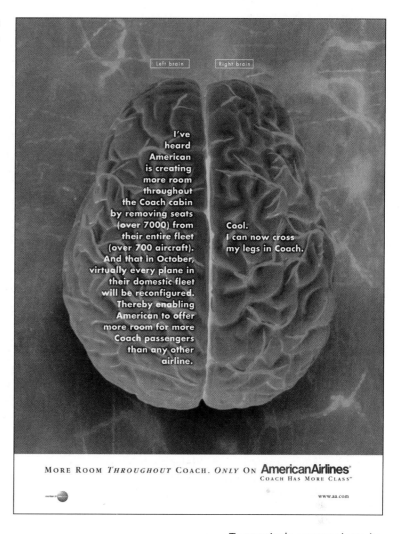

To creatively communicate its new seating in coach, American Airlines used a picture of a brain, with the left brain representing cognitive thinking and the right brain illustrating an affective response.

product introductions—in recent years, we have had to learn to use computers, VCRs, the Internet, TiVo, and the iPod, and that learning process for new technology continues to challenge consumers in emerging nations. **Comprehension** is the process by which people understand, make sense of things, and acquire knowledge.

- *Differentiation.* An indication of cognitive learning is **differentiation,** the consumer's ability to separate one brand from another in a product category. Distinguishing between competing brands is what happens when consumers understand the explanation of a competitive advantage. In a historic but still important study of effective television commercials, researchers concluded that one of the most important effectiveness factors is a brand-differentiating message.[21]

- *Recall.* We mentioned earlier that recognition is a measure of perception and recall is a measure of learning or understanding. When you recall the ad message, you not only remember seeing the ad and hopefully the brand, you also remember the copy points, or the information provided about the brand. In order to recall information presented in the ad, however, you must have concentrated on it and thought about it either as the information was being presented or afterward. Thinking about it—similar to a mental rehearsal of the key points—is a form of information processing that helps anchor ideas in memory and makes recall easier.

Even though this section is on cognitive processing, please note that feeling and thinking work together. Psychologist and advertising professor Esther Thorson and her colleagues have developed the memory model of advertising to explain how commercials are stored in memory as traces that contain bits and pieces of the commercial's message, including the feelings elicited by the message. Recall of any of those elements—especially feelings—can serve as a cue to activate memory of the commercial.[22]

Connect: The Association Facet

What do you think of when you see an ad for Nike, Viagra, or Mountain Dew? The things that come to your mind, such as athletes for Nike, older men for Viagra, and teenage guys having fun for Mountain Dew, are the brands' associations. **Association** is the technique of communicating through symbolism. As such, it is the primary tool used in brand communication. It is the process of learning to make symbolic connections between a brand and desirable characteristics and qualities, as well as people, situations, and lifestyles that cue the brand's image and personality.

You see association at work in advertising in the practice of linking a brand with a positive experience, or a lifestyle, such as Axe with cool young men. The idea is to associate the brand with things that resonate positively with the customer. It's a three-way process: The (1) brand relates to (2) a quality that (3) customers value. Brands take on symbolic meaning through this association process. Professor Ivan Preston in his association model of advertising believes that you can explain how advertising works by understanding how association works.[23]

Factors Driving Association   The goal of association is to use symbolic connections to define the brand and make it distinctive. **Brand linkage** reflects the degree to which the associations presented in the message, as well as the consumer's interest, are connected to the brand. For example, an ad for Bisquick HeartSmart mix shows a pancake in the shape of a heart. In this case, the brand name (Bisquick HeartSmart) is easily associated with the product use (your heart and healthy pancakes). The association drivers we will discuss here are symbolism, conditioned learning, and transformation.

- *Symbolism.* Through association a brand takes on a **symbolic meaning,** which means the brand stands for certain qualities. It represents something, usually something abstract. Bisquick's pancakes shaped like hearts convey the heart-healthy message symbolically. A Rolex watch represents quality, luxury, and status. A visual, such as a Rolex on the arm of a man at the wheel of a yacht, becomes a visual metaphor that depicts the luxury or status qualities for which the brand stands.
- *Conditioned learning.* Although advertisements sometimes use a cognitive strategy, they frequently are designed to elicit noncognitive associations through **conditioned learning**—a group of thoughts and feelings become linked to the brand through repetition of the message. Beer advertising directed at a young male audience, for example, often uses images of sporting events, beach parties, and good-looking young women. People also learn by watching others, which is called **social learning.** We learn fashion by watching how others dress and manners by watching how other people interact. We connect their appearance and manners to certain situations reflected in the ads.
- *Transformation.* The result of the brand association process is transformation. **Transformation,** as explained by former DDB research director Bill Wells[24], means a product takes on meaning when it is transformed from a mere product into something special. It becomes differentiated from other products in the category by virtue of its brand image symbolism and personality cues. Bisquick HeartSmart is more than just flour; it rises above the average product in the category and stands out as something unique and healthy. That transformation in a consumer's mind is a perceptual shift created by the associations cued through advertising messages.

Association Networks   You probably had a number of associations when we asked you to think about Nike. Athletes come to mind, but also shoes, engineering, design, the Swoosh logo, competition, sporting events, maybe even a fun retail experience if you have visited a Nike store. The association process is built on a **network of associations,** called a **knowledge structure.** Solomon in his book on consumer behavior describes these networks as spider webs[25] where one thought cues other thoughts. Your thoughts and feelings about the Nike brand are elements linked in your own individual pattern of associative thinking. Researchers seeking to determine the meaning of a brand will ask people to give their associations with a brand and to re-create these association networks in order to understand how a brand's meaning comes together as an impression in people's minds.

Principle
Advertising creates brand meaning through symbolism and association. These meanings transform a generic product into a specific brand with a distinctive image and personality.

Believe: The Persuasion Facet

When you see ads from the "Got Milk?" campaign with celebrities sporting a milk mustache, what do you think is the objective of the advertising? Is it providing information about milk? Is it trying to connect with you on an emotional level through fear, love, envy, hunger, or some other feeling? Is it trying to get you to run down to the store and load up on milk? The real objective of these ads is to change your attitude toward milk. It aims to convince you that milk isn't just for kids and that attractive, interesting adults drink it, too.

Persuasion is the conscious intent on the part of the source to influence or motivate the receiver of a message to believe or do something. Persuasive communication—creating or changing attitudes and creating conviction—are important goals of most marketing communication. An **attitude** is a state of mind—a tendency, inclination, or mental readiness to react to a situation in a given way. Since advertising rarely delivers immediate action, *surrogate* effects, such as changing an attitude that leads to a behavior, are often the goal of advertising. Attitudes are the most central factors in persuasion.[26]

Attitudes can be positive, negative, or neutral. Both positive and negative attitudes, particularly those embedded in strong emotions, can motivate people to action—or away from action. A negative attitude toward smoking, for example, may keep teenagers from trying cigarettes, and creating that negative attitude was the objective of the *truth*® campaign discussed in Chapter 1.

When people are convinced of something, their attitudes are expressed as **beliefs.** Sometimes attitude strategies attempt to extinguish beliefs—for example, that getting drunk is a badge of masculinity, overeating is acceptable, or racist and sexist comments are funny. Attitude change strategies often use the tools of logic and reasoning, along with arguments and counterarguments, to intensify the feelings on which beliefs are built.

Persuasion, in other words, is an area where cognitive and affective factors are interrelated—persuasion works both through rational arguments and by touching emotions in such a way that they create a compulsion to act. Persuasive strategies can be used to touch both the head and the heart.

Factors Driving Persuasion   There are many dimensions to persuasion, but advertisers identify the following factors to explain how persuasion affects consumers: motivation, influence, involvement, believability and credibility, preference and intention, conviction, and loyalty.

- *Motivation.* A factor in creating a persuasive message is **motivation.** Underlying motivation is the idea that something, such as hunger or a desire to be beautiful or rich, prompts a person to act in a certain way. How strongly does someone feel about acquiring something or about taking a certain kind of action, such as applying to graduate school or signing up for the Peace Corps? This sets up a state of tension, and the product becomes a tool in achieving that goal and thus reducing the tension.
- *Influence.* If you think you need to lose weight or stop smoking, how much of that decision is based on your own motivations and how much of your motivation results from messages from others? Some people, known as **opinion leaders,** may be able to influence other peoples' attitudes and convince them of the "right" decision. The idea is that other people—friends, family, teachers, and experts such as doctors—may affect your decision making. Testimonies—from real people, celebrities (the "Got Milk?" campaign), and experts—are often used to change attitudes. **Bandwagon appeals**—messages that suggest that everyone is doing it—are also used to influence people's decisions. *Word-of-mouth* communication has always been recognized as the most powerful form of persuasion, and that's why strategies that engage influencers are so important.
- *Involvement.* Advertisers distinguish between products, messages, and media on the basis of the level of involvement they require from the buyer.[27] **Involvement** refers to the degree to which you are engaged in attending to an ad and the process you go through in responding to a message and making a product decision. Some products call for a more involving process than others, such as cosmetics rather than toothpaste. **High-involvement** products are **considered purchases** that generate a more intense level of

Principle

Advertising employs both rational arguments and compelling emotions to create persuasive messages.

engagement, such as computers, as well as things you care about a lot like clothes and cosmetics. Examples of **low-involvement** products are aspirin, paper napkins, envelopes, paper clips, milk, and lettuce. The idea is that you think about some products and reflect on the advertising you see for them, but with other products you don't spend much time thinking about them before you buy them. Nor do you pay much attention to their advertising, which you may ignore or file away without much thought.

Some message strategies are more involving than others, such as dramas and humor. Likewise, various types of media are intrinsically more or less involving. Television, for example, is considered to be less involving than print, which demands more concentration from its readers than TV does of its viewers—although a gripping TV drama can be involving because of the power of the story line. Marketing communication tools, such as sales promotions, events, and brand clubs are inherently more involving, particularly the ones that allow customers to have more personal contact with the brand.

- *Conviction.* Effective persuasion results in **conviction,** which means consumers agree with a persuasive message and achieve a state of certainty—a belief—about a brand. A factor in conviction is the power of the **argument,** which uses logic, reasons, and proof to make a point and build conviction. Understanding an argument is a complex cognitive process that demands the audience "follow through" the reasoning to understand the point and reach a conclusion.
- *Preference and intention.* When consumers marry belief with a **preference** for, or an **intention** to try or buy, a product, they are motivated by conviction. Intention can be heightened with reward strategies, such as good deals, sale pricing, and gifts. An example of persuasive work designed to create conviction are the ads for the Orlando, Florida, YMCA. Good intentions are the motivations behind cause marketing and social responsibility. Hewlett-Packard, for example, promotes its computer recycling program to increase preference for HP by its customers. According to the company's vice president of global branding and marketing communications, the PC recycling program attracts consumers to HP products because the company assumes responsibility for recycling its old products. That's a benefit for customers and leads to higher customer satisfaction and, thus, loyalty to the HP brand.[28]
- *Loyalty.* Is there any brand you buy, use, or visit on a regular basis? Do you have a favorite shampoo, restaurant, or beverage? Why is that? What we are referring to when we talk about a "favorite" brand is preference, but also **brand loyalty,** which is both an attitude (respect, preference), an emotion (liking), and an action (repeat purchases). It is a response to brand communication that crosses over between thinking, feeling, and doing—a response that is built on **customer satisfaction.** If you try a product and like it, then you will be more likely to buy it again. If you don't like it, is there a return policy or guarantee that frees you from risk when you buy something for the first time? Providing information about warranties, customer service, and technical support for technology products is an important part of brand loyalty strategies. The idea is to reduce risk and put the customer's mind at ease. Incentives are also used in loyalty programs, such as frequent flyer or frequent buyer programs. In addition, social responsibility and cause marketing programs can build trust, respect, and preference that lead to loyalty.

Believability and Credibility   An important issue in persuasion is **believability,** which refers to the credibility of the arguments in a message. Puffery or unprovable claims, such as the common phrase "9 out of 10 doctors recommend . . ." can strain believability. Related to believability is **credibility,** which is an indication of the trustworthiness of the source. **Source credibility** means the person delivering the message, such as an expert, is respected, trusted, and believable.

Credibility is one of the big advantages of public relations because publicity stories delivered through a supposedly unbiased news medium have higher credibility than advertising, which is seen as self-serving. However, advertising can use a credibility strategy to intensify the believability of its message. Using data to support or prove a claim, for example, gives consumers a **reason to believe** the advertising.

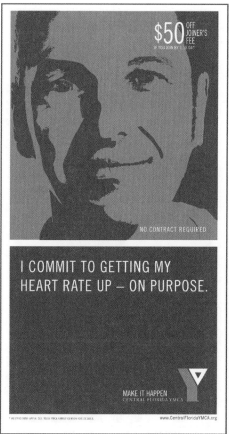

SHOWCASE For a YMCA membership drive in Orlando, Florida, the objective was not just to get new members, but keep them. At the time, the popular perception was that the YMCA was like any other gym. In reality, the YMCA is a family center focused on developing a balanced lifestyle. To resolve these perception issues, the FHB agency developed a campaign highlighting real members' commitments to mind, body, and spirit. With its bold, graphic look, the campaign stood out and was well received. These ads were contributed by Lara Mann, a graduate of the University of Florida, who was nominated by Professor Elaine Wagner.

Act: The Behavior Facet

We introduced loyalty in the previous section on persuasion and noted that it intersects with behavior. Behavior can involve different types of action in addition to trying or buying the product. The goal is to get people to act in various ways—to try or buy the brand, for example, or visit a store, return an inquiry card, call a toll-free number, or click on a Web site. The "I Want You" World War I poster is a classic example of an advertising message that was designed to create action.

We must distinguish, however, between *direct action,* which represents an immediate response (cut out the order form and send it back by return mail), and *indirect action,* which is a delayed response to advertising (recall the message later in the store and select the brand).

Behavioral Response Factors   The behavioral response involving action of some kind is often the most important goal of marketing communication, particularly tools such as sales promotion and direct marketing. Factors that drive a behavioral response include try, buy, contact, advocate, refer, and prevent.

- *Try.* The first step in making a purchase is often to try the product. **Trial** is important for new products and expensive products because it lets a customer use the product without committing initially to a purchase. In other words, the risk is lessened. Sales promotion is particularly good at driving trial through special price deals, sampling,

A highly effective poster designed to create action, this ad was used during World War I to convince young people to join the military. Most modern advertising is more subtle than this, but the motivation to inspire action is still the same.

and incentive programs that motivate behavior, such as a free gift when you go to a dealer to test-drive a new car.

- *Buy.* The objective of most marketing programs is sales. In advertising, sales is sometimes stimulated by the **call to action** at the end of the ad, along with information on where to purchase the product. From a customer perspective, sales means making a purchase. In customer-focused marketing programs, the goal is to motivate people to try or buy a certain brand. But in some marketing programs, such as those for nonprofit organizations, the marketing program may be designed to encourage the audience to sign up, volunteer, or donate. For many managers, however, sales is the gold standard for effective advertising. They feel that, even if they are funny, memorable, or entertaining, ads are failures if they don't help sell the brand. The problem is that it may be difficult to prove that a marketing communication message is the one factor in the marketing mix that delivered the sales. It could be the price, the distribution, the product design and performance, or some combination of the marketing mix elements. Effectiveness programs, such as the London-based Institute of Practitioners Award program (IPA), encourage advertisers to use research to prove that it was, in fact, the advertising that actually drove the sales.

- *Contact.* Trying and buying may be the marketer's dream response, but other actions also can be important measures of an advertisement's behavioral effectiveness. Responding by making contact with the advertiser can be an important sign of effectiveness. Initiating contact is also valuable, particularly in IMC programs designed to maintain brand relationships by creating opportunities for customer-initiated dialog, such as encouraging customers with a complaint, compliment, or suggestion to contact the company.

- *Advocate and refer.* One of the behavioral dimensions of brand loyalty is **advocacy,** or speaking out on a brand's behalf and referring to it when someone asks for a recommendation. Contacting other people is a valuable response, particularly when a satisfied customer brings in more business for the brand by providing testimonials to friends, family, and colleagues on behalf of the brand. In terms of the impact of **referrals,** when a satisfied customer recommends a favorite brand, this form of *word-of-mouth* can be incredibly persuasive, more so than advertising, which is seen as self-serving. Apple computer's success is credited to its passionate customers who, as evangelists for the brand, spread the word among their friends and coworkers.

  This *advocacy level,* which Smith and Cross describe in their book *Customer Bonding,*[29] represents the highest form of a brand relationship. A recommendation to buy a specific brand is the ultimate test of the bond between consumers and their favorite brands. And the opposite—brand aversion—can be disastrous if the dissatisfied customer shares his or her dislike with other people.

- *Prevent.* There are social action situations where advertising messages are designed to deter behaviors, such as limiting car use through clean-air campaigns and antismoking and antidrug campaigns for teens. This is a complicated process that involves counter-arguing by presenting negative messages about an unwanted behavior and creating the proper incentives to stimulate the desired behavior. Because the effects are so complicated, the impact of such campaigns is not always clear. The national Just Say No campaign claims to have had an impact on teenagers' drug use; however, as the Inside Story box explains, sometimes antidrug advertising can boomerang because it calls attention to the unwanted behavior.

THE INSIDE STORY

The Curiosity-Arousing Function of Antidrug Ads

By Carson Wagner, Ph.D., *Assistant Professor, Ohio University*

When I first entered graduate school, perhaps the first (and most important) lesson I learned from my mentor was that the best kind of research reveals "differences that make a difference." The more counterintuitive the research finding, the more value it has in the development of knowledge, and small differences that make big differences are better yet. Ideas for studies like this, he said, usually come from everyday observations and from imagining what the implications would be if our assumptions were turned upside down.

Then one weekend, my father, who is an advertising executive, and I got into a conversation about how it seemed every time a news story aired about illicit drugs, a small epidemic of drug use would ensue. Of course, there's been a lot of research done about the ways media can encourage drug use, but most of that is about popular media such as movies and music. We'd presume that news programs and antidrug ads that are meant to show illicit drugs in a negative light shouldn't lead people toward drugs. But, as almost any student of communication has learned, media don't tell us what to think; they tell us what to think about.

So, I decided to test the idea on antidrug ads—the most counterintuitive possibility—in a small experiment for my master's thesis. I scoured prior research, but I couldn't find anything suggesting that antidrug ads might lead to drug use. Almost all studies showed that drug attitudes became more negative. But, the psychology of curiosity literature suggested something else: If antidrug ads make people think drug use is widespread, they might become curious about experimenting themselves.

The curiosity literature was correct, and oddly enough, I defended my thesis the day after Congress allotted $195 million per year to antidrug ads. The following May, I presented my findings at a conference, and the idea seemed to agitate some of those in the crowd. Then, one day in September, I got a call from a radio show in Los Angeles. They wanted me to be a guest and discuss my study. A bit dumbfounded, I then found several e-mails waiting for me asking to send a copy of the thesis. It turns out the Libertarian party had distributed a press release citing my study to attack the federal government for spending tax money to encourage drug use.

Over the next few weeks, I was a guest on different talk shows, and a number of news and wire stories appeared. One in particular quoted, "You have to watch your source in studies like this, and you have to watch what people will do to rationalize their findings when you know where they are coming from." Of course, Mr. Weiner, spokesman for U.S. Drug Czar Gen. Barry McCaffrey, didn't know. But, Congress called to find out and requested the study be presented in its first review of antidrug ad spending. Since then, a large-scale government-sponsored survey examining the first five years of the campaign uncovered similar relationships between antidrug advertising and drug use, but unfortunately it doesn't seem to have gotten any better reception than mine did.

Nominated by Professor Sandra Moriarty, Wagner received his Ph.D. from the University of Colorado.

Do these ads work? The Just Say No campaign believes they do change the behavior of teens and convince them to avoid drugs. Other researchers believe such ads just make drug taking more attractive. What do you think?

THE POWER OF BRAND COMMUNICATION

The six-factor Facets Model we've been describing is our answer to the question of how advertising works. This model is also useful in analyzing the power and impact of advertising messages through the interaction of these effects.

Interaction and Impact

As we had suggested, these six factors work together to create a coherent brand perception. There are two things to remember about how this model works: (1) the effects are interdependent, and (2) they are not all equal for all marketing communication situations.

In terms of effects interaction, we suggested in the previous discussions that cognitive and emotional responses work together. Consider that memory is a function of both attention (the perception facet) and emotion (the affective facet). As du Plessis explains, "what we pay attention to, we remember." The stronger the emotional hook, the more likely we'll attend to and remember the message. Even informative messages can be made more memorable if they are presented with an emotional story. Furthermore, recent ideas about how advertising memory works suggest that an effective ad helps consumers remember their best moments with a product,[30] so it brings back emotion-laden brand experiences that encompass both feelings and thoughts.

In terms of impact, we recognize that different advertising strategies emphasize different patterns of impact. Sometimes more emphasis in a message strategy needs to be placed on emotion or image building than on reasons and facts. Therefore, a specific strategy for an advertising campaign may be depicted as heavier in one area than another. In such a situation, the actual shape of the Facets Model can change as the pattern of emphasis is adapted to the marketing situation with emotion and association, for example, or cognition or persuasion increasing in size.

Strong and Weak Effects

We introduced this chapter with quotes from professionals and researchers who wonder about the impact of advertising. Now let's consider an ongoing debate among academics and professionals about the power of advertising—and we are concentrating on advertising here, not the other forms of marketing communication This power is analyzed in terms of "strong" and "weak" effects.[31]

Some believe that sales is the only true indication of message effectiveness. The power of advertising, in other words, is determined by its ability to motivate consumers to buy a brand. Others, including the authors of this textbook, believe communication effects include a wide range of consumer responses to a message—responses that may be just as important as sales because they lead to the creation of such things as liking and a long-term brand relationship.

This debate is the source of controversy in the analysis of what advertising effectiveness really represents. The sales-oriented philosophy suggests advertising can move the masses to action. Those who believe in the "Strong Theory" of advertising reason along these lines:

> Advertising increases people's knowledge and changes people's attitudes and, therefore, it is capable of persuading people who had not formerly bought a brand to buy it, at first once and then repeatedly.

In contrast, those who believe in the "Weak Theory" of advertising, like the British promotions person quoted in the beginning of this chapter, believe advertising has only a limited impact on consumers and is best used to reinforce existing brand perceptions rather than change attitudes:

> Consumers are not very interested in advertising. The amount of information communicated is limited. Advertising is not strong enough to convert people whose beliefs are different from those in the ad, overcome their resistance, or change their attitudes. Most advertising is more effective at retaining users rather than converting new ones.

These differences explain why some experts believe that the communication effects, such as emotion, knowledge, and persuasion, are merely "surrogate" effects—communication effects that can be measured more easily than sales but are less important to marketing managers. Others believe these communication effects are important in and of themselves because of what they contribute to brand strength.

Complicating the issue is the recognition that the impact of traditional advertising is seldom immediate. When you see an ad for a new product that catches your attention, such as a new music group or CD, and you concentrate on the message, you may think about the ad later when you find yourself walking by a music store. Thus, your memory is involved in recalling not just the ad and the brand, but the content of the message. But memory is unreliable and the impressions may not be embedded sufficiently in memory to elicit this kind of response at a later date.

In other words, advertising is a victim of **delayed effects**—messages are seen and heard at one time (at home on the TV, in the car on the radio, in the doctor's office in a magazine ad) and may or may not come to mind at a later date when you are in a purchase situation (in a store, in a car looking for a place to eat). Most advertisements are carefully designed to ensure that these memory traces are easy to recall. That's what *sound bites* do in political messages. Ads also use catchy headlines, curiosity, and intriguing visuals to make this recall process as easy as possible and lock the message in memory. But there is always a problem relying on consumer attention, interest, motivation, and memory to bring the message to mind days or weeks later.

We began this chapter with quotes from advertising experts with different views on the effectiveness debate. Considering all that you've learned in this chapter about advertising effectiveness, if you were asked, where would you come down in this debate about the power of advertising?

The important conclusion to the bigger question about how advertising works is that we know that advertising (and other marketing communication), does work when it's carefully planned and executed. It may not work in every situation and every ad may not be equally effective, but if it's done right, then advertising can have impact on consumer responses. That's why the Effie awards, and other award shows that recognize effectiveness, are so valuable.

Long-term research by Syracuse professor John Philip Jones using extensive industry data proves that there is a link between advertising and consumer behavior and that advertising can trigger sales.[32] We know it works; otherwise big savvy companies wouldn't be spending big sums of money on it. The problem has always been in understanding *how it works,* and, in many cases, *how it doesn't work.* The Facets Model takes a big step forward in helping the industry create a logical framework for understanding advertising effects.

Principle

Advertising has delayed effects in that a consumer may see or hear an advertisement but not act on that message until later when in a store.

IT'S A WRAP

Cows Grab Business for Chickens

Chick-fil-A and its advertising agency, The Richards Group, developed one of the most successful integrated brand campaigns in the fast-food industry, one that has been executed across all media over many years.

After the initial rollout as a three-dimensional billboard, the campaign continues to evolve and make its way into every point of contact with the customer. A standup cow became part of the in-store kit, along with banners, table tents, cups, bags, and register toppers. From there, the campaign has added direct mail and ads, promotions, events, TV, radio, the Web, clothing and merchandise. Calendars have been so popular that production numbers have topped 2.4 million. Cow Appreciation Day marked the 10th anniversary of the successful campaign on July 15, 2005. The cows and their quirky antics have become a key symbol of Chick-fil-A's marketing communication.

Chick-fil-A's light-hearted, unconventional campaign has helped increase sales every year. In 1995 when the campaign first began, Chick-fil-A reported just over $500 million in sales. Sales nearly quadrupled in a decade, exceeding $1.975 billion in 2005. Oh yes, the campaign also won scores of awards, including induction into the Obie Hall of Fame (Outdoor Advertising Association of America), a Silver Effie, and a Silver Lion at Cannes International Advertising Festival.

Key Points Summary

1. **Why is communication a key factor in advertising effectiveness?** By analyzing advertising as communication, we have a model for explaining how commercial messages work. Consider that the *source* typically is the advertiser assisted by its agency and the *receiver* is the consumer who responds in some way to the message. The *message* is the advertisement or other marketing communication tool. The *medium* is the vehicle that delivers the message; in

advertising, that tends to be newspapers and magazines in print, radio and TV in broadcasting, the Internet, and other forms of out-of-home vehicles, such as outdoor boards and posters. In integrated marketing communication, the media are varied and include all points of contact where a consumer receives an impression of the brand. *Noise* is both external and internal. *External noise* in advertising includes consumer trends that affect the reception of the message, as well as problems in the brand's marketing mix and clutter in the channel. *Internal noise* includes personal factors that affect the reception of the message. If the communication process fails to work and the consumer does not receive the message as intended by the source, then the communication effort is ineffective.

2. **How did the idea of advertising effects develop, and what are the problems in traditional approaches to advertising effects?** The most common explanation of how advertising works is referred to as AIDA, which stands for Attention, Interest, Desire, and Action. This model in all its subsequent forms is described as a hierarchy of effects because it presumes a set of steps that consumers go through in responding to a message. A different approach—referred to as Think/Feel/Do—recognizes that different marketing communication situations generate different patterns of responses. Two problems are inherent in these traditional approaches: (1) the idea of predictable steps and (2) missing effects, particularly those that govern the way people respond to brands.

3. **What is the Facets Model of Advertising Effects, and how does it explain how advertising works?** The authors believe that marketing communication works in six key ways: it is designed to help consumers (1) see and hear the message (perception), (2) feel something for the brand (emotion or affective response), (3) understand the point of the message (cognitive response), (4) connect positive qualities with the brand (association), (5) believe the message (persuasion), and (6) act in the desired ways (behavior). All of these work together to create a brand perception. An effective message, then, has a diamond-like quality that represents how the message effects work together to create the desired consumer response.

Key Terms

advocacy, p. 121
affective response, p. 111
AIDA, p. 106
argument, p. 118
association, p. 116
attitude, p. 117
awareness, p. 110
bandwagon appeals, p. 117
beliefs, p. 117
believability, p. 118
brand linkage, p. 116
brand loyalty, p. 118
call to action, p. 120
channels of communication, p. 103
clutter, p. 104
cognition, p. 113
cognitive learning, p. 115

comprehension, p. 115
conditioned learning, p. 116
considered purchase, p. 117
conviction, p. 118
credibility, p. 118
customer satisfaction, p. 118
delayed effects, p. 124
differentiation, p. 115
emotional appeals, p. 113
exposure, p. 110
feedback, p. 103
hierarchy of effects, p. 106
high involvement, p. 117
impact, p. 106
intention, p. 118
interactive communication, p. 103
interest, p. 110

intrusive, p. 110
involvement, p. 117
knowledge structure, p. 116
liking, p. 113
low involvement, p. 118
motivation, p. 117
needs, p. 115
network of associations, p. 116
noise, p. 103
opinion leaders, p. 117
perception, p. 110
persuasion, p. 117
preference, p. 118
reason to believe, p. 118
recall, p. 110
receiver, p. 103

recognition, p. 110
referrals, p. 121
relevance, p. 110
resonance, p. 113
selective attention, p. 110
selective perception, p. 110
social learning, p. 116
source, p. 103
source credibility, p. 118
stickiness, p. 110
subliminal, p. 111
symbolic meaning, p. 116
think/feel/do, p. 106
transformation, p. 116
trial, p. 119
wants, p. 113

Review Questions

1. What are the key components of a communication model, and how do they relate to advertising?

2. Why is it important to add interaction to the traditional communication model?

3. What is a hierarchy of effects model? Give an example.

4. What are the six categories of effects identified in the Facets Model? What does each one represent in terms of a consumer's response to an advertising message?

5. What is clutter and why is it a problem?

6. If a friend tells you that subliminal advertising is commonly used by advertisers, how would you respond?

7. Differentiate between wants and needs. How are both of these concepts used in advertising?

8. What does transformation mean, and why is it important as an advertising effect?

Discussion Questions

1. What is breakthrough advertising? What is engaging advertising? Look through this textbook, find an example of each, and explain how they work. Prepare to explain in class why you evaluated the two ads as you did.

2. This chapter identifies six major categories of effects or consumer responses. Find an ad in this book that you think is effective overall and explain how it works, analyzing the way it cultivates responses in these six categories.

3. Uma Proctor is a planner in an agency that handles a liquid detergent brand that competes with Lever's Wisk. Uma is reviewing a history of the Wisk theme, "Ring around the Collar." In its day, it was one of the longest-running themes on television, and Wisk's sales share indicated that it was successful. What is confusing Uma is that the Wisk history includes numerous consumer surveys that show consumers find "ring around the collar" to be a boring, silly, and irritating advertising theme. Can you explain why Wisk is

such a popular brand even though its advertising campaign has been so disliked?

4. *Five-Minute Debate:* You have been asked to participate in a debate in your office about three different views on advertising effects. A copywriter says informing consumers about the product's features is most important in creating effective advertising. An art director argues that creating an emotional bond with consumers is more important. One of the account managers says that the only advertising performance that counts is sales. Organize into small teams with each team taking one of the three sides. In class, set up a series of five-minute debates in which each side has 1½ minutes to argue its position. Every team of debaters must present new points not covered in the previous teams' presentations until there are no arguments left to present. Then the class votes as a group on the winning point of view.

Take-Home Team Projects

1. From current magazines, identify three advertisements that have exceptionally high stopping power (attention), three that have exceptionally high pulling power (interest), and three that have exceptionally high locking power (memory). Which of these advertisements are mainly information and which are mainly emotional and focused on feelings? Which are focused on building a brand or creating associations? Do any of them do a great job of creating action? Rank what you believe are the top three most effective ads in the collection. Why did you choose the top three, and what can you learn from them about effective advertising?

2. An article in the *Financial Times* asks why no auto maker sells the car we really want. In contrast to Dell Computer and its personalization model, the author wonders why we consumers have to put up with what's on the lot rather than getting the one we want. How important is desire to this market? Should auto makers build to order? As a team, do an online search and investigate whether this charge is really true—and how important it is to car buyers. Then develop a one-page position paper that explains what you recommend to your auto client about this issue.

Yahoo! Hands-On Case

Review the Yahoo! case in the Appendix.

1. Explain how advertising works in terms of the Yahoo! campaign. In other words, how does it work as communication? Is the case primarily one-way communication or interactive in its orientation, and is there anything that might be done to strengthen its communication effectiveness?

2. How does this Yahoo! campaign assignment reflect the Facets of Effects Model? In other words, analyze the

Yahoo! marketing communication situation in terms of six effects. Which ones are more important, which are less, and why? Prepare a one-page analysis for the team to consider as they think about creating an advertising campaign that works. Based on this model, what might be done to strengthen the campaign's impact?

HANDS-ON CASE

If It Walks Like the Aflac Duck . . .

You've probably never heard of the American Family Life Assurance Co., nor are you likely to be familiar with its primary service: supplemental workplace medical insurance, a type of insurance that is used by people to help cover the many loopholes and deductibles in their primary insurance coverage. Then again, if you are like 85 percent of U.S. consumers, maybe you *have* heard of the company. In its advertising, it calls itself "Aflac."

The long-running Aflac campaign is the work of Linda Kaplan Thaler, owner of the New York agency that bears her name. Thaler's ads are not known for their subtlety. Among her credits are the Toys "R" Us jingle "I don't want to grow up," and the successful campaign for Clairol Herbal Essences, featuring an "orgasmic" hairwashing experience. The Herbal Essences ads strike some as funny and others as quite possibly offensive, but product sales have skyrocketed to almost $700 million a year.

In many ways Thaler's ads hark back to the 1960s, when it was common to feature "sex, schmaltz, chirpy jingles and 'talking' babies and animals," as the *New York Times*' advertising columnist Stewart Elliott puts it. Industry insiders have been known to snipe at Thaler's work, and few would describe her campaigns as "edgy."

Thaler's Aflac ads, by almost any measure, are her best. Almost all feature a white duck desperately screaming "Aflac!" at people who need supplemental insurance. Unfortunately, the duck's audience never quite seems to hear him. Most of the ads contain a fair amount of slapstick, usually at the expense of the duck, whose exasperated-sounding voice originates with former *Saturday Night Live* cast member Gilbert Gottfried. "He's got the right answer but nobody is listening, and that's a situation that resonates with people," says Kathleen Spencer, director of Aflac's corporate communications. "There's also just something inherently comical about a duck."

The campaign has been enormously successful since its inception in 2000. Since the ads first began running, brand name awareness has increased from 15 percent to 85 percent. The company generates $14.6 billion in sales. Dan Amos, CEO for Aflac, believes that "our name recognition with our advertising campaign and our strong sales force together have combined to truly help our company." *Ad Age* has named the commercial featuring the duck as one of the most-recalled ads in the country.

But what makes the Aflac campaign truly remarkable is how little it has cost the company. The duck has a higher Q score (a measure of a character's familiarity and appeal) than both Ronald McDonald and the Energizer Bunny, but whereas Energizer has spent almost $1 billion over 15 years on advertising, and McDonald's spends almost $700 million every year, Aflac's ad budget was only $75 million in 2006. There is no denying that Thaler's work for Aflac is a triumph of both effectiveness and value.

The duck is not without his problems. Some have suggested making the mascot less visible and audible in coming advertising. Why? It seems that the duck gets all the attention. Everyone knows it as an advertising icon, but some believe customers don't know what it sells. Do you think the duck should have somewhat clipped wings in future campaigns?

Consider This

1. Some viewers don't like the Aflac ads. Can an ad still accomplish its intended purposes if people find it annoying?
2. The Aflac campaign was launched in 2000 and the duck has even been added to the corporate logo. In your opinion, will the campaign stay effective for the foreseeable future?
3. What makes Aflac ads so effective? Is it something more than their entertainment value? If so, what else contributes to their success?

Sources: "Top Spots," *Advertising Age,* January 13, 2003; Stuart Elliott, "Why a Duck? Because It Sells Insurance: Kaplan Thaler Puts Consumers Ahead of Peer Approval," *New York Times,* June 24, 2002, C11; David Haffenreffer, "Aflac Inc.—CEO Dan Amos," *CNN Money Morning,* Transcript #102301cb.129, October 23, 2002; Theresa Howard, "Aflac Duck Gives Wings to Insurer's Name Recognition," *USA Today,* May 17, 2001, 9b; Lisa Sanders, "New CMO Plans to Clip the Aflac Duck's Wings," *Advertising Age,* February 19, 2007, 1, 63.

The Consumer Audience

campaignforrealb

New Dove Firming. As te

IT'S A WINNER

Awards:	Company:	Agency:	Campaign:
Grand Effie; Grand Prix, Cannes International Advertising Festival	Unilever	Ogilvy & Mather	"Real Beauty"

Dove

al curves.

Dove Redefines Beauty

In earlier chapters, you read about the *truth*® (anti-smoking) campaign, Puma and Chick-fil-A's brand building, and Whirlpool's relationship with Habitat for Humanity. What made those campaigns effective? We hope you said their effectiveness was the result of really understanding the consumer. Making connections that resonate with the audience is the hallmark of effective marketing communication. Think about the power of Burger King's "Have It Your Way" campaign and how that line addresses burger buyers' desire to customize what they eat.

Unilever's campaign for Dove, which won a Grand Effie, provides another example of great advertising that recognized a "truth" held by consumers. The "Campaign for Real Beauty" touched a nerve and punctured the cultural obsession with stick-thin bodies and Barbie Doll images. The Dove campaign was risky because it sought to literally redefine beauty in advertising and to acknowledge a change in the way women see themselves. It could have been a bomb, but it was a winner because it spoke to every woman's need to look and feel her best without promising or reinforcing impossible standards of beauty.

The Dove brand has an interesting history. First formulated in the 1940s as a nonirritating skin cleaner for use on burns and wounds, the cleaner was reformulated in the 1950s as the Dove Beauty Bar. The brand grew in the 1990s to include body wash, facial cleanser, and moisturizers, followed by deodorants in 2001 and hair care products in 2003. While these products were successful, Unilever learned from research that consumers thought of it as simple, white, and gentle. The brand lacked energy, and at worst, it represented submissive femininity, according to its ad agency, Ogilvy & Mather.

Chapter Key Points

1. Why is consumer behavior important to advertisers?

2. What cultural, social, psychological, and behavioral influences affect consumer responses to advertising?

3. How does the consumer decision process work?

4. What is the difference between segmenting and targeting?

Seizing an opportunity to enter the beauty products category, Unilever commissioned research that eventually drove the marketing campaign. Some startling statistics from the study included these findings:

- Only 2 percent of the respondents believed themselves to be beautiful.
- Of the respondents, 68 percent indicated they strongly believed that the media and advertising set an unrealistic standard of beauty most women can't achieve.

Based on these findings, Unilever decided to launch a new product, Firming Lotion, to enter the hand and body lotions category. The company decided to begin its campaign by speaking to women about beauty in a new way—not the beauty of emaciated models but that of real women with normal body weight. Showing women of different ages, shapes, and sizes involved some risk. What if Dove became known as a product line for heavy women, to the exclusion of others? In retrospect, of course, the brand has become celebrated for what it's accomplished. Here's how the Dove Campaign for Real Beauty unfolded.

The message of the Dove Campaign for Real Beauty provided a deliberate contrast with that of the competition in beauty and women's magazines like *Glamour*, *Allure*, and *Vogue*. Heavy emphasis was placed on print rather than television because of print media's ability to stop the audience and make them really look at the models in the ad and contemplate the meaning of beauty. Dove even ran an ad during the Super Bowl. The Web site (http://www.campaignforrealbeauty.com) urges a boost in self-esteem by defying stereotypes that define beautiful as perfect—and skinny.

The Real Beauty campaign also used mass media to generate massive publicity. Spending a fifth of a normal personal-care product launch, the Dove advertising was concentrated in the top 10 cities where it would have the most immediate impact. Outdoor and transit advertisements were plastered on billboards and buses to generate public debate.

A similar strategy was used in 2007 to launch Dove's *ProAge* line, which continues the counterintuitive strategy by celebrating older women with their silver hair, wrinkles, and age spots.

Although we live in a culture that worships physical perfection, Dove is trying valiantly to broaden that definition. At the end of the chapter you'll read about the results of the Dove efforts.

Sources: Effie brief supplied by Ogilvy & Mather; "Dove Campaign for Real Beauty case study: Innovative Marketing Strategies in the Beauty Industry," www.datamonitor.com June 2005; Prior, M. Dec. 9, 2005. "Most Innovative Ad Campaign: Dove Campaign for Real Beauty." *Women's Wear Daily.* Vol. 190, Issue 122, pp. 36–39.

The success of great campaigns, such as Dove Real Beauty, hinges on a critical consumer insight that gives direction to the advertising. By recognizing that unnatural standards of beauty can cause self-esteem problems for many women, Dove built an unusual relationship with its customers, particularly women more secure in their self-concept who appreciated that the ads were talking to them.

To better understand that bond, this chapter explores influences on consumers' behavior—in other words, what motivates them as they make purchasing decisions—and then discusses how these factors help define groups of people who might profitably be targeted with marketing communication or advertising messages. By studying these influences on consumer decisions, advertisers can better design effective campaigns through careful targeting of the message.

HOW DOES CONSUMER BEHAVIOR WORK?

Think about something you bought last week. How did the purchase process happen? Was it something you needed or just something you wanted? Did you set out to go to a specific store or just go shopping? Or was it something you saw online or in an ad? Had you been planning the purchase for a while? Did somebody tell you about it, or have you talked to someone about it now that you've made the purchase?

These are the kinds of questions marketers and advertisers ask about their customers. **Consumer behavior** describes how individuals or groups select, purchase, use, or dispose of products as well as the needs and wants that motivate these behaviors. As we proceed through this chapter, keep asking yourself these questions about your own consumer behavior and that of your friends and family.

In the discussion in Chapter 4 of communication processes, we looked at consumers as the audience who respond in some way to a marketing communication message. This chapter provides more insight into how consumers' response to a message affects their decision making—both for products and ideas.

First, let's clarify some terms. **Consumers** are people who buy or use products or adopt ideas that satisfy their needs and wants. **Customers** are specific types of consumers; they are people like Dove's devoted fans who buy that particular brand or patronize a specific store. Brand relationships are created between a brand and the customers who regularly buy a brand or shop at a store. **Prospects** are potential customers who are likely to buy the product or brand.

The question is, to quote a famous line from *Butch Cassidy and The Sundance Kid*, "Who are those guys?" As our opening story stressed, marketing communication planners need to understand what factors turn prospects into customers. Then they need to be able to describe these prospective customers using characteristics that help predict the likelihood that a prospect will respond to a brand message and, ultimately, buy the brand.

There are various ways to profile consumers. One way is to divide them by the type of market they represent—either business or consumer. As we discussed in Chapter 2, these lead to *business-to-business (B2B)* or *business-to-consumer (B2C) marketing strategies*. Another way to categorize consumers is to refer to them either as those who shop for and purchase the product (purchasers or customers), those who actually use the product (users), and influencers—people who help the buyer make a brand choice (children, trendsetters, family, and friends). This distinction is important because purchasers and users can have different needs and wants. In the case of children's cereals, parents (the purchasers) often look for nutritional value and a decent price. In contrast, children (the users) may look for a sweet taste and a package with a prize inside.

Principle
Buyers may not be the users and users may not be the buyers. Buyers and users often have entirely different needs and wants.

INFLUENCES ON CONSUMER DECISIONS

Before we talk about how consumers make a buying decision, let's consider the various factors that influence them: their cultural affinities, their family and friends, their personal needs, and their experiences with a brand. A brand decision, in other words, is rarely as simple as just grabbing something off a shelf.

Figure 5.1 is a general model of consumer behavior. It is also a visual road map for this chapter. We will begin by discussing four types of influences on the way consumers make purchasing decisions. Then we'll use that knowledge to explain how audiences are segmented and targeted for specific types of messages.

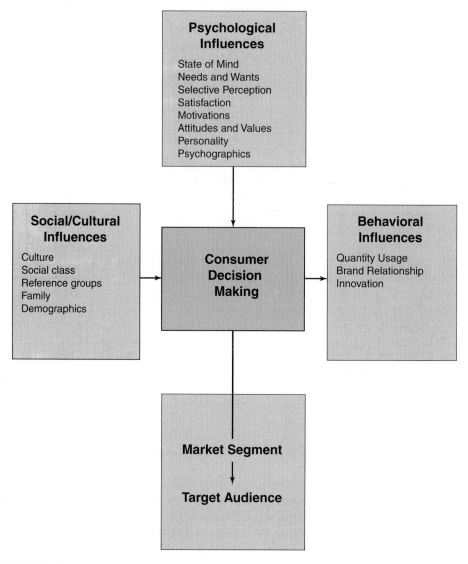

FIGURE 5.1
Influences on Consumer Decision Making

Cultural Influences

Why do you suppose ad critic Bob Garfield called the Dove Real Beauty campaign "an important cultural moment"?[1] His comment suggests that deep-seated cultural values are reflected in advertising, so let's consider the ways in which culture influences consumer decisions.

The culture and the society in which you were raised affect your values and opinions. **Culture** is made up of tangible items (art, literature, buildings, furniture, clothing, and music) and intangible concepts (history, knowledge, laws, morals, customs, and even standards of beauty) that together define a group of people or a way of life. Culture is learned and passed on from one generation to the next.

Norms and Values   The boundaries each culture establishes for "proper" behavior are **norms**, which are simply rules we learn through social interaction that specify or prohibit certain behaviors. The source of norms is our **values**, particularly cultural values, which represent our underlying belief systems. In the United States, we value freedom, independence, and individualism; in other countries, particularly some Asian and Latin countries, people value families and groups more than individualism. An example of ads that appeal to Americans' nostalgia is the 76 campaign aimed at truckers. Of course, there are some

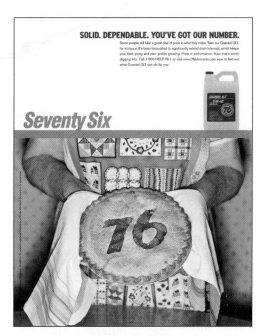

SHOWCASE These ads for 76 motor oil ran in national trade publications for the trucking industry. The creative team wanted to associate the 76 brand with Americana using a nostalgic appeal. The imagery speaks to truck fleet owners who authorize the purchase of commodities such as motor oil. These ads were contributed by Chris Hutchinson, art director at Wieden + Kennedy, who graduated from the advertising program at the University of Oregon.

universals—most people value good health and most women want to look good, as the Dove research discovered.

One example of a difference in cultural values that affects advertising is found in the way Italians approach cleaning compared to Americans. A study by Procter & Gamble found that Italians spend an average of 21 hours on household chores other than cooking, compared with just four hours for Americans. They wash kitchen and bathroom floors at least four times a week; Americans do so just once. The fact this study brought out is that Italians are seriously devoted to keeping a clean house, more so than Americans.[2]

Values are few in number and hard to change. Advertisers strive to understand the underlying **core values** that govern people's attitudes and guide their behavior. An ad's primary appeal aims to match the core values of the brand to core values of the audience. Here are nine basic core values:

1. A sense of belonging
2. Excitement
3. Fun and enjoyment
4. Warm relationships
5. Self-fulfillment
6. Respect from others
7. A sense of accomplishment
8. Security
9. Self-respect

Subcultures Sometimes, a culture can be further broken down into smaller groups called subcultures. **Subcultures** can be defined by geographic regions or by shared human characteristics such as age, values, language, or traditions and ethnic background. The United States encompasses many different subcultures: teenagers, college students, retirees, southerners, Texans, athletes, musicians, and working single mothers, to name a few.

Consider Hispanic culture. American Hispanics—people who speak Spanish as their primary language—predominantly live in Southern California, Texas, Miami, and New

This ad for Tide exhibits the effective targeting of the Hispanic culture. The translation is: "The salsa is something you dance, not what you wear."

York City, although they are represented in small groups in almost every part of the country. Each community is a distinct subculture of the overall Spanish-speaking culture and represents its origins from South America, Cuba, Mexico, Puerto Rico, Spain, Latin America, or beyond. U.S. speakers of *Español* even disagree on the term used to describe their identity—some prefer Hispanic, others Latino.[3]

Corporate Culture   The concept of culture applies to B2B marketing as well as B2C. **Corporate culture** is a term that describes how various companies operate. Some are formal with lots of procedures, rigid work hours, and dress codes. Others are more informal in terms of their operations and communication. The same patterns exist in the way businesses make purchasing decisions: Some rigidly control and monitor purchases; others are loose and easygoing, and purchases may be less controlled or governed more by friendships than rules.

Social Influences

In addition to the culture in which you were raised, you also are a product of your social environment, which determines your social class or group. Reference groups, family, and friends also are important influences on opinions and consumer behavior and affect many of your habits and biases.

Social Class   The position you and your family occupy within your society is **social class**, which is determined by such factors as income, wealth, education, occupation, family prestige, value of home, and neighborhood. In more rigid societies, such as those of India, people have a difficult time moving out of the class into which they were born. In the United States, although people may move into social classes that differ from their families', the country still has a class system consisting of upper, middle, and lower classes. Marketers assume that people in one class buy different goods for different reasons than people in other classes.

Reference Groups   A **reference group** is a group of people you use as a model for behavior in specific situations. Examples are teachers and religious leaders, as well as members of political parties, religious groups, racial or ethnic organizations, clubs based on hobbies, and informal affiliations such as fellow workers or students—your peers. **Brand communities,** such as the Harley Owners Group (HOG) for Harley-Davidson are groups of people devoted to a particular brand. The Internet has had a huge impact by creating new online reference groups, such as virtual communities around interests, hobbies, and brands. For consumers, reference groups have three functions: (1) they provide information, (2) they serve as a means of personal comparison, and (3) they offer guidance.

Ads that feature typical users in fun or pleasant surroundings are using a reference strategy. You also may be attracted to a particular reference group and want to be like the members of that group out of respect or admiration. Advertisers use celebrity endorsements to tap into this appeal. The Dove Real Beauty campaign tried to shatter the myth that the reference group for beauty can only be young, blond, and thin models who represent an unattainable standard for most women. This was a risky strategy, one that follows the Fallon agency's seven principles outlined in the "Juicing the Orange" story in the Part II Introduction. Fallon and Senn observed that great ideas, such as the Dove campaign, "are often scary ideas."

The most important factor in analyzing reference groups is the degree to which this association has an impact on consumer behavior. David Reisman describes individuals in terms of their relationships to other people as *inner-directed* (individualistic) or *outer-directed* (peer group and society). Advertisers are particularly interested in the role of peers in influencing their outer-directed friends' wants and desires. On the other hand, inner-directed people are more likely to try new things first.

Family   The family is the most important reference group for many people because of its formative role and the intensity of its relationships. Other reference groups, such as peers, coworkers, and neighbors, tend to change as we age. According to the U.S. Census definition, a **family** consists of two or more people who are related by blood, marriage, or adoption and live in the same household. A **household** differs from a family in that it consists of all those who occupy a dwelling whether they are related or not. The family is responsible for raising children and establishing a lifestyle for family members. **Lifestyle** reflects family situation, values, and income. It determines the way people spend their time and money and the kinds of activities they value.

For the first time in U.S. history, one-person households in the 21st century outnumber married couples with children.[4] This reflects a growing trend in America over the past 30 years to marry later in life, divorce, or never get married at all. Marketers and their advertisers have been right on top of this familial trend. Banks have created special mortgages, builders are providing homes and apartments to meet the needs of single occupants, and food marketers have introduced "single" portions.

Demographics   All of these social characteristics come together in a concept called **demographics** that we use to describe groups of people. Demographics are the statistical, social, and economic characteristics of a population, including age, gender, education, income, occupation, race, and family size. These characteristics serve as the basis for identifying audiences—knowing these factors helps advertisers in message design and media selection for the target market.

The first place to start analyzing and compiling demographics is the country's census data. In the United States, the Census Bureau compiles a huge collection of demographic information every 10 years—the most recent census was in 2000 and the next one will be in 2010. The Census Bureau also conducts the American Community Survey in between these decades, most recently in 2005. That 2005 data is represented in Table 5.1. These tables represent a moment in time, but, of course, the data is constantly changing. For example the total U.S. population in mid-2005 when these tables were published was 288 million (Table 5.1c); however, the U.S. population moved past 300 million in November 2006. To check on the current population, consult the U.S. Census Bureau web site (http://www.census.gov) where a population clock ticks away in the upper right corner.

- *Age.* The dominant demographic characteristic used by advertising planners is age. People of different ages have different needs and wants. An advertising message must be geared to the target audience's age group and should be delivered through a medium that members of the group use. But age also determines product choice. How old are you? What products did you use 5 or 10 years ago that you don't use now? Look ahead 10 years. What products might you be interested in buying in the future that you don't buy now?

    Consider the age categories in the following list and the breakdowns in Table 5.1a. These are some common categories used by advertising planners. What is the size of

Table 5.1a   2005 U.S. Population Age Breakdowns

Under 10	39,779,464	13.5%
10-19	40,345,077	13.8
20-34	58,088,311	20.1
35-54	85,282,951	29.5
55-64	30,121,807	10.4
65-84	30,949,801	10.4
Over 85	3,810,726	1.3

Source (except where noted otherwise: U.S. Census Bureau, "Current Population Survey, 2005 Annual Social and Economic Supplement," Internet Release Date: October 26, 2006.

Table 5.1b   Home Ownership by Age

Householder by Age	% Owning a Home
Under 35	43.0
35-44	69.3
45-54	76.6
55-64	81.2
65 and over	80.6

Source: U.S. Census Bureau, "Current Population Survey, 2005 Annual Social and Economic Supplement," Internet Release Date: October 26, 2006.

Table 5.1c   2005 U.S. Population and Gender

Total Pop.	288,378,137
Gender:	
Male	141,274,964 (49%)
Female	147,103,173 (51%)

Source: U.S. Census Bureau, "Current Population Survey, 2005 Annual Social and Economic Supplement," Internet Release Date: October 26, 2006.

Table 5.1d   Age of First Marriage

	1980	2005
Male	23.2	27.1
Female	20.8	25.8

Source: U.S. Census Bureau, "Current Population Survey, 2005 Annual Social and Economic Supplement," Internet Release Date: October 26, 2006.

Table 5.1e Children's Living Arrangements

Children under 18	(million)	%
2 married parents	49.3	67.0
1 parent	20.7	28.2
mother	17.2	23.4
father	3.5	4.8
Other	3.5	4.8
Total children	73.5	100

Adapted from Census Bureau Press Release, "Americans Marrying Older, Living Alone More, See Households Shrinking," May 25, 2006, http://www.census.gov.

Table 5.1f Race and Ethnicity in the United States

Race and Ethnicity	% of Population*
White	74.7
Black/African American	12.1
American Indian/Alaskan	.8
Asian	4.3
Native Hawaiian	.1
Hispanic/Latino	14.5

*Percentages add up to more than 100 percent because some respondents check more than one category.

Table 5.1g Educational Attainment

High School Diploma

	2000	2005
Race	%	%
White	88.4	90.0
Black	78.9	81.0
Hispanic	57.0	59.0
All Races	84.1	85.0

Source: U.S. Census Bureau, http://www.census.gov.

your age group? Which groups are the largest, and what types of products would they be most interested in buying? Consider home ownership as a factor of age—notice how the older people are, the more likely they are to own a home (Table 5.1b). Here are some common age-related categories that describe the U.S. population:

Age-Related Population Categories

- Referred to as *The Greatest Generation* by Tom Brokaw in his book by that name, this generation born in the 1910s through the late 1920s fought World War II. A small group, these seniors are in their final years. This group opened up college education to the middle class after the war and lived frugal, yet financially satisfying, lives.
- Known as the *Silent Generation* or *traditionalists*, these people born from the late 1920s to the war years are now active seniors. They were described in a national poll as the generation having the most "positive impact" on the American economy for their role in fueling the post-war boom.[5]
- *Baby boomers*, people born between 1946 and 1964, represent the largest age-related category in the United States. The 76 million consumers are now in the final years of their careers, having made a huge population bulge as they have moved through the life cycle. While they were growing up, boomers' numbers affected first schools, then the job market, and now retirement programs and health care (see the accompanying MetLife ad). This generation has been influenced by significant societal movements and scientific breakthroughs, from the Civil Rights movement to the anti-Vietnam war protests to putting a man on the moon.
- A newly identified subgroup called *Generation Jones* is the younger baby boomers who were born from the mid- to late 1950s through the mid-1960s. The *Jones* reference comes from their continuing need to chase the dream of affluence trying to "keep up with the Joneses."
- *Gen X,* also known as the *baby busters,* is the group whose 45 million members were born between 1965 and 1979. Now adults, they have been described as independent minded and somewhat cynical. They are concerned with their physical health (they grew up during the AIDS outbreak) and financial future (the job market became more difficult just about the time they entered).
- Born between 1980 and 1996, *Generation Y* is also known as *echo boomers* because they are the children of baby boomers. They are important to marketers, because they are next in size to the boomer generation. Also described as the *digital generation* because they grew up with computers and are seen as more technologically savvy, this group is now the youth and young adult market that marketers want most to reach because they are in the formative years of their brand relationships. They are prime targets for technology, travel, cars, homes, and furniture. They also are more interested in altruism than earlier generations.
- The *Millennium Generation* encompasses those children born from the late 1990s into the beginning years of the new century. Marketers have been delighted to find that these kids (and their doting parents) are brand conscious and more willing than their predecessors to wear corporate logos as a badge.[6]

Age also is a key factor in media plans because age usually determines what media you watch, listen to, or read, as Table 5.2 shows. The table breaks down media usage in terms of common age groupings used by advertising planners. The older the age group, the more likely they are to use media daily or several times a week. Study this chart and determine the best medium to use to reach a young adult (18–27) audience. Is that medium the appropriate choice for the other three age groups?

Age is driving a fundamental shift in U.S. marketing strategy. For 50 years, marketers have focused on reaching young people, not only because they are in the formative years of making brand choices, but also because the youth market during that era was huge in terms of numbers. Now with the huge boomer bulge moving into retirement, there is tension between the temptation to focus on young people and the realization that wealth and numbers belong to this active senior market. The accompanying MetLife ad illustrates the new face of senior marketing.

Table 5.2 Media Usage by Age

	Echo Boomers %	Gen X %	Baby Boomers %	Seniors %
Local broadcast news	52	69	83	88
Network broadcast or cable news	51	57	74	88
Local daily newspaper	43	49	66	80
Online news	53	68	70	57
Radio news broadcasts	26	49	64	58
Talk radio	24	35	40	41
Satellite radio	21	23	19	16
National newspaper (*The Wall Street Journal, USA Today, The New York Times*, etc.)	15	23	19	17

Overall usage patterns for each medium vary by age group. This table shows the percentage of persons in each age group who are users of the individual medium. For instance, 88 percent of "mature" audience members watch local broadcast news.

Source: "Seven in 10 U.S. Adults Say They Watch Broadcast News at Least Several Times a Week," The 2006 Harris Poll #20, February 24, 2006, http://www.harrisinteractive.com/harris_poll.

- **Gender.** Another obvious basis for differences in marketing and advertising is gender. The gender breakdown in the 2000 census was 48.9 percent male, 51.1 percent female, and that proportion has stayed the same in 2005 (see Table 5.1c). *Primary* gender differences are physical traits inherent in males or females, such as a woman's ability to bear children. *Secondary* gender traits tend to be associated with one sex more than the other. Wearing perfume and shaving legs are secondary traits associated with women. Many brands are either masculine or feminine. It is unlikely that men would use a brand of cologne called "White Shoulders." Why do you think Dove is a brand for women? The Gillette Company found that the majority of women would not purchase regular Gillette razor blades, so they introduced brands exclusively for women, such as the Daisy disposable razors.

  In addition to the aging of the population, a consultant with the Boston Consulting Group identifies another potential social trend—the first stages of the United States evolving to a matriarchal society.[7] He points to the increasing percentage of women in college—57 percent of undergraduates and 58 percent of graduate students are women—which also may mean eventual changes in income and occupation patterns.

- **Family status.** Age also relates to family status. The 2005 data, compared to 25 years ago, show that people increasingly are older when they marry (Table 5.1d). The number of families also continues to shrink. Although families in 2005 dominated American households at 66 percent, they were fewer in number than in 1980 when they represented 74 percent of all households. In the 2005 census data, 67 percent of children under 18

As baby boomers reach retirement, many companies, such as the insurance giant MetLife, are developing new strategies to reach them.

Table 5.1h   Mean Income by Household Type

Household Type	n	Income
Households	111,090,617	$62,556
Families	74,341,149	72,585
Married Couples	55,224,773	83,887
Nonfamily Households	36,749,468	39,741

Table 5.1i   Salary Levels by Educational Attainment

Educational Level	Male*	Female*
High School Diploma	$31,683	$20,179
Some College	39,601	25,736
Bachelor's or Higher	53,693	36,250
Graduate Degree	71,918	47,319

*In 2005, inflation adjusted dollars

Table 5.1j   The Rich and the Poor in the United States

Income Group	% of Consumer Income
Lowest 20%	3%
Second 20%	9%
Third 20%	15%
Fourth 20%	23%
Fifth 20%	50%

The most affluent 20 percent has 50 percent of the total U.S. consumer income; the bottom three groups combined, which include 60 percent of the population, get by on about one-fourth of the total consumer income.

Source: Peter Francese, "Trend Analysis: U.S. Consumers—Like No Other on the Planet," Advertising Age, January 2, 2006, p. 4.

Principle

Your income is a key demographic factor because you are meaningful to a marketer only if you have the resources needed to buy the product advertised.

lived in two-parent homes, 28 percent lived with one parent, and another 5 percent lived in other types of households, such as with grandparents (Table 5.1e). Another interesting fact is that the United States had an estimated 5.8 million "stay-at-home" parents, which includes 5.6 million moms and 143,000 dads. All of these nuggets of information about families and the way they live provide clues about types of products different people buy and the media they use—diapers and life insurance, for example, as well as single-size or family-size servings.

• *Race and ethnicity.* In the United States, ethnicity is becoming a major criterion for segmenting markets (see Table 5.1f). According to the Census Bureau, the number of African Americans will increase by 15 percent during the next 20 years, Asian Americans by almost 68 percent, and Hispanics by about 64 percent. Meanwhile, the Caucasian population will grow by 13 percent. A census report released in 2007 estimates that the U.S. minority population exceeds one-third of the population. Four states have a "majority-minority" population. In Texas, for example, the combined minority population is now 52 percent. California has the largest Hispanic population of any state with Texas second and Florida third.[8]

Consumer habits within each ethnic segment differ based on factors such as age and income. For immigrants, how long they have lived in the United States also influences their buying preferences. Few cultures are more important to U.S. marketing than the Hispanic culture. It is an important market because it is growing faster proportionately than other ethnic groups. Hispanics are more brand loyal, buy with cash rather than credit, and spend more on their kids and their clothing than other groups. Ethnic groups often bring their brand perceptions with them from their native countries. Colgate outperforms Crest among U.S. Hispanics because Colgate dominates the Mexican market.

Media use differences may also be based on ethnicity. For example, a Nielsen study found that Hispanic viewers are more likely to watch commercials in their entirety than non-Hispanic viewers. Nielsen has found that Hispanic audiences are more influenced by advertising than other U.S. consumers—they are more likely to base their purchasing decisions on advertisements, and they are less cynical about marketing.[9]

• *Education.* According to the 2005 census (Table 5.1g), U.S. males attain higher levels of education than U.S. females, although this is changing, as there are more females in many undergraduate programs than males. Generally white U.S. consumers attain higher levels of education than blacks and Hispanics. For advertisers, education tends to correlate with the type of medium consumers prefer. Consumers with lower education are higher users of television, especially cable. Consumers with higher education prefer print media, the Internet, and selected radio and cable stations. Likewise, education dictates the way copy is written and its level of difficulty. Examine ads in *Fortune* or *Forbes* and you will find different words, art, and products than you will in *People* or tabloid publications. Advertisers don't make value judgments about these statistics. Their objective is to match advertising messages to the characteristics of the target audience.

• *Occupation.* Most people identify themselves by what they do. In the United States there has been a gradual trend from blue-collar occupations (manufacturing, for example) to white-collar occupations (management and information). There have also been shifts within white-collar work from sales to other areas, such as professional, technical, and administrative positions. The number of service-related jobs continues to increase, especially in the health care, education, and legal and business service sectors. Much of this transition is a direct result of computer technologies, which have eliminated many labor-intensive, blue-collar occupations. This shift has affected advertising in a number of ways: Today, advertisements seldom portray blue-collar jobs, for example.

• *Income.* A key demographic indicator for many advertisers is income. You are meaningful to marketers only if you have the resources to buy their products. Study the patterns of income distributions in Tables 5.1h and 5.1i and notice how income varies by household and education.

Affordability correlates strongly with income: If a marketer knows that a consumer needs an annual income of $150,000 to purchase a BMW, it suggests that the setting of the ad should be upscale (country club, executive office tower), and the media used should match (*Fortune, Money, Wall Street Journal, Town & Country*). Income is correlated with other factors such as education, occupation, and gender. Age is also a factor in income. The mature population in the United State controls 70 percent of all the country's wealth and represents 50 percent of all discretionary spending.[10]

Advertisers track trends in income, especially **discretionary income**, which is the amount of money available to a household after paying for taxes and basic necessities, such as food and shelter. Some industries, such as movie theaters, travel, jewelry, and fashion, would be out of business if people didn't have discretionary income. Discretionary income has been found to be a more reliable predictor of spending than income.[11]

Several ominous trends showed up in the 2005 census income data that concern marketers. There is a larger population growth in lower-income households, which means the U.S. income level is decreasing. The income gap also documented both rising poverty and rising affluence—there are both more poor people and more rich people, which signifies a shrinking middle class. The final potential problem is the tendency of fewer men to go to college, since education is related to income. An *Advertising Age* article noted "a disturbing picture of a widening gap between the haves and have-nots" (see Table 5.1j) and "a rising underclass of poorly paid and underinsured people living on the financial edge." It concluded, "That is not a recipe for robust consumer-spending growth."[12] On the other hand, the same article noted several trends that might have a positive impact on the marketplace—the increasing economic power of women, for example, and the development of mass affluence (more people moving into the upper-income level).

- *Geography.* The area in which a target market lives correlates with several demographic characteristics and is important to advertisers. Marketers study the sales patterns of different parts of the country because people residing in different regions need certain products. For example, someone living in the Midwest or the Northeast is more likely to purchase products for removing snow and ice than a Floridian. Differences also exist between urban areas and suburban or rural areas. Swimming pools that sell well in a residential suburban neighborhood would not be in demand in an urban neighborhood filled with apartment buildings.
- *Sexual orientation.* Over the last decade gay and lesbian consumers have become serious target markets. Because some heterosexuals are still offended by the gay lifestyle, advertisers struggle to find the best way to target gay consumers. Companies that advertise in gay media, such as GayDish TV network, *Freshmen,* and *Digital Gay World,* include Sony, Apple, Banana Republic, American Express, Hiram Walker, Miller Brewing, Coors, Subaru, and Visa, to name a few. Some companies that target

For Volvo, the Witeck-Combs agency presented concepts and imagery likely to appeal to gay, lesbian, bisexual, and transgender (GLBT) consumers. After testing, this ad, called "Starting a Family," was found to be the most likely concept to deliver the strategy. Consumers in the GLBT audience said it appealed to them because it was more believable and spoke to their personal interests.

A MATTER OF PRINCIPLE

Gay Buying Power

By Bob Witeck, *CEO, Witeck-Combs Communications*

Understanding buying power is a fundamental way to acknowledge the many valuable day-to-day contributions that gay Americans make as consumers. The question is how much economic clout gay, lesbian, bisexual, and transgender (GLBT) adults wield in today's market.

Buying power is another term for "disposable personal income," which is defined by economists as the total after-tax income available to an individual to spend on personal consumption and saving. Getting this projection right for the gay and lesbian market starts with population estimates.

The *Gay and Lesbian Atlas* found that Census 2000 significantly undercounted same-sex couples and does not include millions of single gay men and lesbians. Among several possible reasons for the undercount is that it is still entirely legal to fire someone just for being gay or lesbian in all but 17 states and the District of Columbia.

Social scientists and market researchers estimate the likely dimensions of the gay and lesbian population to be between 4 percent and 10 percent of American adults. In a nation with nearly 300 million people (at that time), the U.S. Census Bureau in 2004 estimated 220 million are adults over the age of 18. Therefore, the most reliable guesses of the GLBT population may be as low as 9 million or as high as 22 million adults.

In more than 50 online samples conducted over more than five years in the Harris Interactive/Witeck-Combs survey of gay consumers, the percentage of individuals who freely self-identify online as GLBT often has ranged between 6.5 and 7.0 percent. We are comfortable using 6.7 percent as a reasonable benchmark for the GLBT adult population today, which is roughly the median point between the lowest estimate of 4 percent and the highest estimate of 10 percent. With 6.7 percent of adults self-identified, that suggests the adult GLBT population may be as high as 15 million.

We estimate America's GLBT buying power based on several reasonable assumptions. One is that the total disposable personal income for adults in the United States totaled $9.1 trillion in 2005. The GLBT population accounts for 6.7 percent of this total disposable personal income. Thus, the buying power of the GLBT market may be conservatively estimated at $610 billion in 2005.

How do gays and lesbians stack up against the buying power of other population groups? With a population of 38 million in 2005, African Americans were estimated to have $760 billion in buying power. For 42 million Hispanics, their 2005 buying power totals $735 billion. Note that the ethnic groups include all consumers, regardless of age, but the GLBT estimate is focused on adults; if that adjustment were made to ethnic groups, then these three populations are quite similar in buying power,

It is no surprise, therefore, that many Fortune 500 companies are investing more each year to tap this profitable potential and to understand the gay consumer market.

*Source:*This box contains excerpts from Chapter 6 "Gay Buying Power" in Business Inside Out by Bob Witeck and Wesley Combs and published in 2006 by Kaplan Publishing.

gays run the same ad campaign in both straight and gay media. For a company such as furniture retailer IKEA, the risks of not presenting a neutral message are great. If its ads are obviously gay in the choice of words or visuals, they might lose the heterosexual market. Other companies such as Volvo have opted to produce different ads for the gay market. For these companies, the challenge is to create ads that are a respectful portrayal of the gay lifestyle.

Psychological Influences

We have analyzed cultural and social influences on consumer behavior. Now let's look at the internal elements that affect how you respond as an individual. Advertisers are particularly interested in understanding which internal psychological factors motivate people to respond as they do. The psychological factors discussed here include state of mind, needs and wants, motivations, attitudes and values, personality, psychographics, and lifestyles.

Perception and State of Mind   Your state of mind affects the way you perceive information. Your past experiences with a brand, as well as what your friends say about it, can color your feelings and make you more or less receptive to a brand message. Other mental states—such as anger, fatigue, hunger, excitement, or lethargy—can also affect your behavior because they create internal noise that gets in the way of your reception of a message or provide the impetus to drive you to buy something.

Needs and Wants In Chapter 4, we described needs and wants as two different types of responses that lead to different reactions to an advertising message. The basic driving forces that motivate us to do something that reflect basic survival, such as choose a motel (shelter) or restaurant (food) when traveling, are called **needs**. Each person has his or her own set of unique needs; some are innate (biological) and others are acquired. **Innate needs** include the need for water, food, air, shelter, and sex. Because satisfying these needs is necessary to maintaining life, they are also called *primary needs*. In the case of the needs pyramid developed by psychologist Abraham Maslow (see Figure 5.2), these are called physiological and safety needs.

A **want** occurs when we desire or wish for something—we won't die if we don't get it, but it can still provide a strong motivation to try or buy something new. This is particularly true in fashion areas, such as clothing and music. Desire is the driving force behind demand. Schwartz describes the power of what he calls "mass desire" in his little book, *Breakthrough Advertising*. He explains that mass desire is the public spread of a private want; it can't be created by advertising, but advertising can address it and channel it to focus on a particular brand.[13] The trend to more gas-efficient cars has led to a demand for hybrid cars such as the Prius. If there wasn't a mass desire for this type of vehicle, there would be no market for Prius.

Needs we learn in response to our culture and environment are called **acquired needs**. These may include needs for esteem, prestige, affection, power, learning, and, yes, beauty. Because acquired needs are not necessary to your physical survival, they are considered *secondary needs*. Maslow called them *social, egoistic,* and *self-actualization*. The Dove campaign, with its line of personal care products, builds demand for products that address acquired needs. Related to needs are satisfaction and dissonance.

- *Satisfaction.* A feeling of satisfaction is only one possible response to a brand message or brand experience; more troublesome is dissatisfaction or doubt. People can pay attention to a commercial, buy a product, and be disappointed. One of the reasons is that advertising sometimes raises consumers' expectations. If they actually try or buy the product and it doesn't meet their expectations, they may be dissatisfied.
- *Dissonance.* According to the theory of **cognitive dissonance**, we tend to justify or rationalize the discrepancies between what we thought we would receive and what we

Principle
An item we need is something we think is essential or necessary for our lives; an item we want is something we desire.

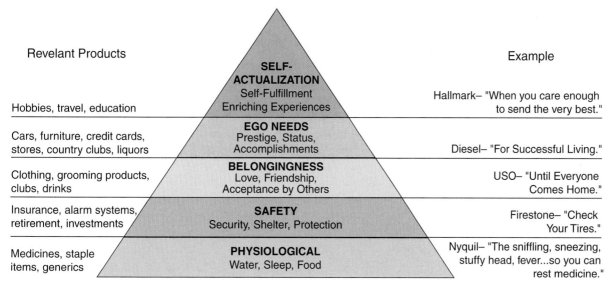

FIGURE 5.2
Maslow's Hierarchy of Needs

The motivation is obvious for a product that helps you avoid catching a cold when you travel. This ad also features the motivation of the product's creator.

actually received. When there is a difference between reality and facts, people engage in a variety of activities to reduce cognitive dissonance. Most notably, we seek out information that supports our decisions—that's why we pay attention to ads for products we have already bought—and ignore and distort information that does not. Advertising can play a central role in reducing dissonance. For example, car makers use testimonials by satisfied customers. A huge category of automotive service called "aftermarketing" is designed to keep customers happy after they buy a car.

Motivations   People are complex, dynamic human beings who are suggestible, changeable, often irrational, and frequently motivated by emotion, greed, or habit. Every person's motivations are individual; however, we are influenced by all the social, cultural, and psychological factors we just discussed, as well as a raft of personal experiences.

A **motive** is an internal force—like the desire to look good—that stimulates you to behave in a particular manner. This driving force is produced by the tension caused by an unfulfilled need. People strive to reduce the tension, as the Airborne ad demonstrates. At any given point you are probably affected by a number of different motives—your motivation to buy a new suit will be much higher if you have several job interviews scheduled next week.

Research into motivation uncovers the "why" questions: Why did you buy that brand and not another? What prompted you to go to that store? Understanding buying motives is crucial to advertisers because the advertising message and the timing of the ad should coincide with consumer's motivations. Unfortunately motivations operate largely at an unconscious level. Some of the reasons may be superficially apparent—you go to a restaurant because you are hungry. But what else governs that choice—is it location, interior decoration, a favorite menu item, or the recommendation of a friend?

Attitudes   Advertisers are interested in attitudes because of their impact on motivations. Because attitudes are learned, we can establish them, change them, reinforce them, or replace them with new ones. However, most attitudes are deeply set, reflect basic values, and tend to be resistant to change—you can hold an attitude for years or even decades. Attitudes also vary in direction and strength; that is, an attitude can be positive or negative, reflecting like or dislike, or it can be neutral. Attitudes are important to advertisers because they influence how consumers evaluate products, institutions, retail stores, and advertising.

Personality   Who is your best friend and how would you describe that person? We typically describe people in terms of their personalities, the distinctive characteristics that make them individual and unlike anyone else we know. These are also the qualities that we find appealing or interesting in that person. In psychological literature, **personality** refers to consistency in behavior in terms of how people react to events and situations and behave in various roles. The idea of personality traits—old-fashioned, lively, efficient, glamorous, rugged, romantic, helpful, snobbish, sophisticated, warm, dependable—has also been adapted to brands with the idea that brand personalities can be created to make them distinctive from their competitors. *The Men's Journal* ad is directed at a certain type of personality, a person who matches or appreciates the magazine's personality.

Psychographics   As demographics wrapped up our discussion of social characteristics, psychographics summarize personal factors. The term **psychographics** refers to lifestyle and psychological characteristics, such as activities, interests, and opinions. The concept combines the psychological factors with other personal consumer characteristics that have a bearing on how a person makes a brand decision. Consumers who have different values, attitudes and beliefs, opinions, interests, motivations, and lifestyles make their product de-

The line "interesting life" refers to both the target audience for *The Men's Journal* as well as to the content of the magazine.

cisions in different ways. Here are some of the major AOI (activities, opinions, interests) components used to construct psychographic profiles of consumers:[14]

- *Activities:* work, hobbies, social events, vacation, entertainment, club membership, community, shopping, sports.
- *Opinions:* self, social issues, politics, business, economics, education, products, future, culture.
- *Interests:* family, home, job, community, recreation, fashion, food, media, achievements.

Sometimes these complex psychographic factors are more relevant in explaining consumer behavior than are the simpler demographics. For example, two families living next door to each other with the same general income, education, and occupational profiles may have radically different buying patterns. One family may be obsessed with recycling, while their neighbors rarely bother to even keep their newspapers separate from their trash. One family is into hiking and other outdoor sports; the other watches sports on television. One is saving money for a European vacation; the other is seriously in debt and can barely cover the monthly bills. The differences lie not in their demographics, but in their psychographics—their interests and lifestyles.

Principle
Often differences in consumer behavior lie in psychographics—consumers' interests and lifestyles—rather than in demographics.

Advertisers use psychographics to depict fairly complex consumer patterns. Libraries of psychographic measures can be purchased from research firms, or a company and its advertising agency can create its own set of psychographic measures to fit its particular product. These psychographic measures can then be used to describe customers (such as heavy users of gourmet coffee), their response to advertising message strategies (taste comparison ads), or their media choices (heavy users of the Internet).

Lifestyles   One type of psychographic analysis looks at lifestyles in terms of patterns of consumption, personal relationships, and leisure activities. *The Men's Journal* ad is a good example of a visual that represents a target audience's lifestyle. The DDB advertising agency has been conducting lifestyle research annually in the United States since 1975. The agency surveys 5,000 men and women on nearly 1,000 questions pertaining to such diverse topics as health, financial outlook, raising kids, shopping, religion, hobbies, leisure activities, household chores, politics, even their desired self-image. The survey also asks people about the products they use (from soup to nuts!) and their media habits. This wealth of information makes it possible to paint a vivid, detailed, multidimensional portrait of nearly any consumer segment that might be of interest to a client—and it also lets the agency spot changes in people's lifestyles over time.

DDB strategy director Marty Horn says that "DDB believes that advertising—and all other forms of marketing communication—is really a personal conversation between the brand being advertised and the consumer, and the better we know the consumer with whom we are conversing, the more engaging, and persuasive our message will be." The agency's Life Style Study is an important source of information that lets this conversation happen. Horn explains, "the DDB Life Style Study helps us get a more 'up close and personal' look at who our clients' customers are than what conventional research alone can provide."

Some of the most common lifestyle patterns are described by such familiar phrases as *yuppies* (young urban professionals) and *yuppie puppies* (their children). These terms are group identifiers, but they also refer to a set of products and the setting within which the products are used. For example, yuppies are characterized as aspiring to an upscale lifestyle, so products associated with this lifestyle might include Cole Haan shoes, Hermes scarves, and BMW cars. Figure 5.3 illustrates the interactions between the person, the product, and the setting in which a product is used.

Some research firms create lifestyle profiles that collectively reflect a whole culture. We'll discuss two of these proprietary tools here: the Yankelovich Monitor's MindBase and the VALS System from SRI Consulting Business Intelligence (SRIC-BI).

- *Yankelovich Monitor's MindBase.* The Yankelovich MONITOR™ has been tracking consumer values and lifestyles since 1971. Its MindBase™ tool uses the MONITOR database to identify groups of people with distinctive attitudes, values, motivations, and lifestyles. Although the database can be used to custom-design segments for individual clients, MindBase has identified eight general consumer groups that span the four generations of matures, baby boomers, Generation X, and echo boomers. The eight MindBase categories are as follows:[15]
  - *"I Am Expressive":* Lives life to the fullest; not afraid to express my personality; active and engaged; "live in the now" attitude; believes that the future is limitless and I can do anything I put my mind to.
  - *"I Am Down to Earth":* Cruising through life at my own pace; seek satisfaction where I can; hope to enhance my life; I like to try new things; I treat myself to novel things.
  - *"I Am Driven":* Ambitious with a drive to succeed; self-possessed and resourceful; determined to show the world I'm on top of my game.
  - *"I Am Sophisticated":* Intelligent, upstanding with an affinity for finer things; high expectations; dedicated to doing a stellar job, but I balance career with enriching experiences.
  - *"I Am at Capacity":* Busy and looking for control and simplification; a demanding and vocal consumer; looking for convenience, respect, and a helping hand; want to devote more of my time to the important things in life.

FIGURE 5.3

Lifestyle Components
Products are linked to lifestyles in the way they reflect the interests of people and the settings in which the products are used.

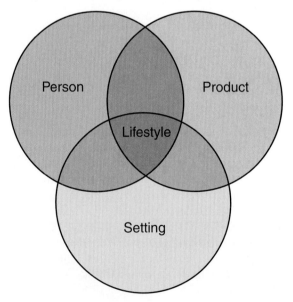

- *"I Measure Twice":* Mature; like to think I'm on a path to fulfillment; live a healthy, active life; dedicated to a secure and rewarding future.
- *"I Am Rock Steady":* Positive attitude; draw energy from home and family; dedicated to an upstanding life; listen to my own instincts for decisions in life and in marketplace.
- *"I Am Devoted":* Traditional; rooted in comforts of home; conventional beliefs; spiritual and content; like things the way they've always been; don't need novelty for novelty's sake or newfangled technology.

VALS™ SRIC-BI, a spinout of SRI International, is known for its VALS system, which categorizes consumers according to psychological traits that correlate to purchase behavior. Originally developed by SRI International, which is a nonprofit research organization in Menlo Park, California, VALS is now owned and operated by SRI Consulting Business Intelligence (SRIC-BI). Advertisers correlate these VALS groups with their clients' products and use this information to design ads and select media.

Figure 5.4 shows the eight VALS groups, as well as their three primary motivations (ideals, achievement, and self-expression) for buying products and services. Thinkers and Believers are motivated by ideals—abstract criteria such as tradition, quality, and integrity.

FIGURE 5.4
The VALS Groups

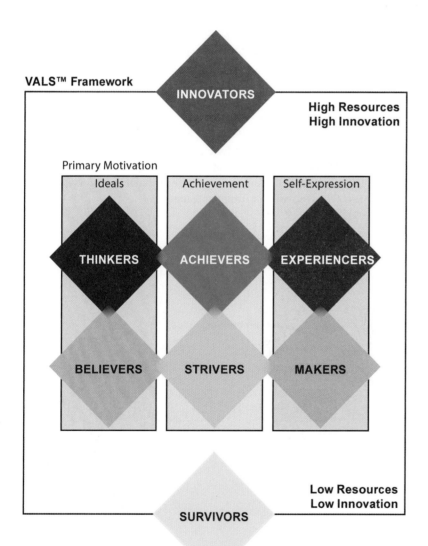

Table 5.3 Consumer Categories Based on Product Usage

Quantity	Brand Relationship	Innovation
Light users	Nonusers	Innovators
Medium users	Ex-users	Early adopters
Heavy users	Regulars	Early majority
	First-timers	Late majority
	Loyal users	Laggards
	Switchers	

Achievers and Strivers are motivated by achievement, seeking approval from a values social group. Experiencers and Makers are motivated by self-expression and make value purchases that enable them to stand out from the crowd or make an impact on the physical world. The VALS groups on the top half of the figure have more resources—a combination of education, income, energy, innovativeness, and self-confidence—than the groups on the bottom half.

The VALS Framework enables advertisers to discover which VALS types buy which products so they can select an appropriate target. VALS also describes the communication styles of each VALS group so the advertiser can design ads using images and copy in a style that will grab the target group's attention. In addition, by using GeoVALS™, the advertiser can place the ad where concentrations of the target live. In addition to the U.S. system, Japan-VALS™ and UK-VALS have also been developed.

Behavioral Influences on Consumer Decisions

Remember in the previous chapter we used the phrase *Think/Feel/Do* to describe a model of how people respond to a message. The behavioral component of that model is a key factor in describing the relationship consumers have with a product category or a brand. That component is almost always used in profiling consumers.

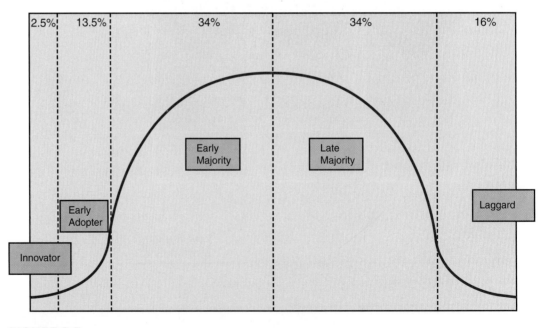

FIGURE 5.5

The Diffusion of Innovation

Source: Adapted from Everett Rogers, *Diffusion of Innovations*, 3rd ed. (New York: The Free Press, 1983).

THE INSIDE STORY

The Grand Myth of Early Adoption
By Cheri L. Anderson, *Principal Consultant, SRI Consulting*

One of the leaders in the area of consumer research is SRI International, which created the well-known VALS segmentation system. Cheri Anderson describes one of the lessons she's learned working with the VALS data.

Our most creative research assignments come from clients who want to preview the future today. These clients want to know what innovative products to put on the shelf in the future and who is most likely to be the early adopters of their innovative products.

At SRI, we use the VALS psychographic segmentation system to identify consumers most likely to be early adopters in the client's category. In addition, VALS is used as a framework to do primary research on the lifestyle and psychological characteristics of early adopters. Our findings show that early adopters:

- Are people involved in unusual activities and whose level of activity will disproportionately affect the behaviors of others.
- Have many weak social contacts.
- Are masters of their own universes.
- Are high media users.
- Have a more complex history of personal and sexual relationships.

Although there are similarities among early adopters, our VALS research found some important differences. Contrary to popular belief, there is no one innovator or early adopter group. Early adopters are in different strata and roles in society and cannot be identified by demographics alone.

Using VALS, we have identified three early adopter groups with different psychological characteristics. The "digerati" early adopters seek novelty, are attracted to risk, and tend to be more fashion conscious. They have a desire for emotional and physical excitement, all the way to the extreme. The "ego-oriented" early adopters desire leadership and enhanced personal productivity. These consumers have a need to feel superior within their peer groups. The "sage-tronic" early adopters are intense information seekers and global in perspective. They have a deep need to know and are expertise focused.

We pursue research on early adopters (and other programs of research) with the objective of using psychographics to understand why consumers do what they do. By understanding what motivates and de-motivates different early adopter groups, we can help our clients identify targets and steer their brands for successful market entry.

Cheri Anderson earned her Ph.D. from the University of Minnesota where she was a student of Bill Wells, who is now an emeritus professor there.

Usage Behavior   A critical behavior predictor called **usage** refers to how much of a product category or brand a customer buys. There are two ways to classify usage: usage rates and brand relationship, as Table 5.3 illustrates. *Usage rate* refers to quantity of purchase: light, medium, or heavy. Heavy users typically buy the most of a product category or a brand's share of the market. An old rule of thumb called the Pareto Rule states that 20 percent of the market typically buys 80 percent of the products. That explains why the heavy user category is so important to marketers and why planners make special efforts to understand this key customer group.

Brand relationship refers to their past, present, or future use of the product: nonusers, ex-users, regulars, first-timers, and users of and switchers from or to competitive products. People who buy the same brand repeatedly display the most brand loyalty. Heavy users and brand loyal buyers are usually a brand's most important customers, and they are the most difficult for competitors to switch away from a brand. **Switchers** are people with low levels of brand loyalty who are willing to leave a brand to try another one.

Innovation and Adoption   Another type of behavior has to do with how willing people are to try something new. Rogers developed the classification system in Figure 5.5, which he called the *Diffusion of Innovation Curve*, to identify these behaviors. This adoption process is identified in terms of personal behavior and how the behavior reflects the speed with which people are willing to try something new, such as *innovators, early*

Principle
In many product categories, 20 percent of the users buy 80 percent of the products.

adopters, early majority, late majority and *laggards*.[16] This system is directly related to the willingness of people to try new products.

The innovator category, which is the group of brave souls willing to try something new, represents only about 2.5 percent of the population. Obviously this group and the early adopters category are important groups for marketers launching new products. The Inside Story relates how the VALS segmentation system can be used to help understand how various types of people can be identified as early adopters.

Risk taking is a personality characteristic, but it combines with behavior in the area of trying a new product. **Perceived risk** is your view of the relationship between what you gain by trying something new and what you have to lose if it doesn't work out. In other words, how important is the consequence of not making a good decision? Price is a huge barrier for high-involvement products; personal status and self-image may be a risk barrier for a fashion product.

Experiences We mentioned in a previous chapter that experience marketing has become an important idea. That's because people are as interested in the experience of doing something as in the acquisition of something. You know the old saying that "getting there is half the fun." The experience of shopping, for some women, is as important, or maybe more important, than what they buy. In a larger sense, our decisions are often based on what our experience has been with the brand—how well it performed, how easy it was to use, how well customer service responded to questions, and so forth.

Trends in Consumer Buying Behavior

The phenomenon of trends and fads is related to lifestyle and psychographic factors as well as the fascination with choice in a consumer culture. We've seen acre homes and fancy bathroom retreats, as well as low-carb diets, healthy food (oat bran, antioxidants), natural products, fitness fads and personal trainers, hybrid cars, carbon trading, simple life (don't buy things), and local products (don't buy things that use a lot of gas in transportation to get to your local store). Even Girl Scout cookies are trying to appeal to people with new formulations that are low in trans fat.[17]

Young people are particularly involved in trends. For example, the way teenagers dress and talk and the products they buy are driven by a continuing search for coolness. **Trend spotters** are professional researchers hired by advertisers to identify trends that may affect consumer behavior. **Cool hunters** are trend spotters who specialize in identifying trendy fads that appeal to young people. They usually work with panels of young people in key trendsetting locations, such as New York, California, urban streets, and Japan. Loic Bizel, for example, hunts Japanese super trendy fads as a consultant for many Western companies and designers. Through his Web site (http://www.fashioninjapan.com), you can get a taste of those cool ideas and fashion in Japan's streets and life, such as studded high tops and spray-on stockings.[18]

Another type of trend spotter is the *brand proselytizer* who works undercover for companies.[19] This person goes where the consumer is and tries to positively influence people about a specific brand by giving them a sales pitch. When people you know tell you how much they like a product, you may not realize that they are working on behalf of the brand—and getting paid for talking to you about it. This practice obviously raises some ethical issues if the brand connection is unknown.

Another trend is the "take charge" mentality of today's consumers. New interactive Web innovations and user-generated content, for example, are reshaping the media landscape and the ways in which we communicate. In recognition of the importance of this trend, *Time* named "you" the 2006 Person of the Year. *Time* wasn't alone in documenting the importance of these trends of consumers not only initiating contact with companies, but also contributing ideas for marketing and advertising. Two major ad industry trade publications, *Advertising Age* and *Adweek,* recognized how consumers are changing media and influencing advertising content. *Ad Age* named "The Consumer" as the 2006 Agency of the Year. In its year-in-review issue, *Adweek* ran a story titled, "World on a String: Consumers Emerged as the New Brand Managers in 2006, Seizing Control of the Media and the Message."[20]

THE CONSUMER DECISION PROCESS

Another important factor in identifying a brand's potential customers is the way consumers go about making product choices. This is largely uncharted territory as researchers have difficulty actually determining what is going in their minds when people decide to buy something.

A complicating factor is the increasing number of choices. Brand variations clutter shelves and media choices seem unlimited. One result, according to Chris Anderson, *Wired* magazine editor and author of *The Long Tail*,[21] is that endless choice is creating unlimited demand—in other words, an entirely new economic model for marketing. He points to the ability of consumers to use the Internet to go deep into a catalog of offerings. We're no longer limited to the CDs on the shelves of stores. Netflix, for example, has found that there is a healthy market for little-known films, which has driven a much bigger catalog of offerings.

Our discussion of the consumer decision process builds on Chapter 4's analysis of how consumers respond to marketing communication messages. In other words, advertisers usually start with a traditional information-processing view of consumer decision making, which basically follows a linear, rational process. However, as we discussed in Chapter 4, other views acknowledge the varied paths that consumers take in making a brand decision, including paths to a decision that are not based on rational thinking. Chicago agency Brandtrust believes the process is "a complex alchemy" set in play by product features, the shopping experience, and consumers' past experiences with shopping in the product category.[22]

The Information Approach to Brand Decisions

The traditional view of consumer decision making, which is similar to the more traditional AIDA-based models of message impact discussed in Chapter 4, suggests that most people follow a decision process with fairly predictable steps: (1) need recognition, (2) information search, (3) evaluation of alternatives, (4) purchase decision, and (5) postpurchase evaluation.

However, as we discussed in Chapter 4, the process consumers go through in making a purchase also can vary between low-involvement and high-involvement purchase decisions (see Figure 5.6). Note that with low-involvement situations, there is little or no information search.

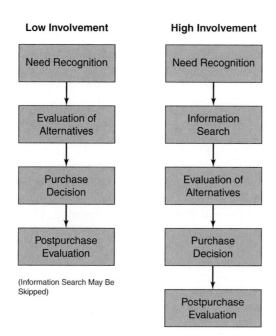

Low Involvement

Need Recognition

Evaluation of Alternatives

Purchase Decision

Postpurchase Evaluation

(Information Search May Be Skipped)

High Involvement

Need Recognition

Information Search

Evaluation of Alternatives

Purchase Decision

Postpurchase Evaluation

FIGURE 5.6
Low- and High-Involvement Decision Processes

- *Need recognition* occurs when the consumer recognizes a need for a product. This need can vary in terms of seriousness or importance. The goal of advertising at this stage is to activate or stimulate this need.
- *Information search* can be casual (reading ads and articles that happen to catch your attention) or formal (searching for information in publications such as *Consumer Reports*). Advertising helps the search process by providing information and making it easy to find and remember. For low-involvement products, particularly products purchased on impulse, this stage may not occupy much time or thought, or it may be skipped altogether. Another way to describe consumer behavior in terms of information needs includes such terms as *searchers* and *impulse buyers*. Searchers are driven by a need to know everything they can about a product before making a purchase, particularly major purchases. In contrast, people who buy on impulse generally do so without much thought based on some immediate desire such as thirst or hunger. Usually there's not much at stake, so the risk of making a bad decision is much lower. It is true, however, that some major purchases, such as cars, can be made on the spur of the moment by people who are not dedicated searchers for information.
- *Evaluation of alternatives* is the stage where consumers compare various products and features and reduce the list of options to a manageable number. They select certain features that are important and use them to judge alternatives. Advertising is important in this evaluation process because it helps sort out products on the basis of tangible and intangible features. Even with low-involvement products, there may be what we call an **evoked set** of brands that are all considered permissible. What are your favorite candy bars? The brands you name makes up your evoked set.
- *Purchase decision* is often a two-part decision. Usually, we select the brand first and then select the outlet from which to buy it. Is this product available at a grocery store, a discount store, a hardware store, a boutique, a department store, or a specialty store? Sometimes we select the outlet first, particularly with impulse purchases. In-store promotions such as packaging, point-of-purchase displays, price reductions, banners and signs, and coupon displays affect these choices.
- *Postpurchase evaluation* is the last step in the rational process and the point where we begin to reconsider and justify our purchase to ourselves. As soon as we purchase a product, particularly a major one, we begin to reevaluate our decision. Is the product what we expected? Is its performance satisfactory? This experience determines whether we will keep the product, return it, or refuse to buy the product again. Even before you open the package or use the product, you may experience doubt or worry about the wisdom of the purchase. We referred to cognitive dissonance before in the discussion of satisfaction. It is also an important factor in the postpurchase evaluation step. Many consumers continue to read information even after the purchase, to justify the decision to themselves. Advertising, such as copy on package inserts, helps reduce the dissonance by pointing out what the key features are, how to best use the product, or how many product users are satisfied. Easy returns are also important for direct marketing for the same reason.

The Paths to Brand Decisions

In Chapter 4 we referred to the Think/Feel/Do model of consumer response to a message. That same model is useful in analyzing the many different ways consumers go about making a brand decision. The idea is that the exact route to a decision depends on the type of product and the buying situation. If you're hungry (feeling first), you grab a candy bar without much information search. If you try a sample product and like it (doing first), then you may buy the product without much evaluation of alternatives. In other words, not all responses begin with thinking about a product, and they don't follow the same route to a decision. Table 5.4 illustrates the many ways a purchase decision can be made.

Given all the different ways consumers go about making a brand choice, you can see why planners need to know how this decision process works for different product categories. Obviously the message would be different for a consumer who is searching for information to buy a car and considering the differences between makes and models in comparison to someone who makes an impulse purchase like buying a candy bar. That's

Table 5.4 Different Paths to a Purchase Decision

Path	Goal	Example	Advertising's Objective
think—feel—do	learning, interest	computer game, CD, DVD	provide information, emotion
think—do—feel	learning, understanding	college, a computer, a vacation	provide information, arguments
feel—think—do	needs	a new suit, a motorcycle	create desire
feel—do—think	wants	cosmetics, fashion	establish a psychological appeal
do—feel—think	impulse	a candy bar, a soft drink	create brand familiarity
do—think—feel	habit	cereal, shampoo	remind of satisfaction

why this information becomes an important part of a consumer profile when identifying prospects to target in a campaign.

Influences on B2B Decision Making

Many of the influences that affect consumer buying also are reflected in business-to-business marketing. However, we know that B2B decision making tends to follow the informational route. Emotion may still be important in certain situations (e.g., the buyer wants to impress the boss), but ultimately these decisions usually are more rational than emotional. We mentioned earlier that corporate cultures operate in distinctive ways and affect the way different companies do business. Some of the consumer factors are relevant in business purchases, but there are also some differences.

- In organizational buying, many individuals are involved in reviewing the options, often with a buying committee making the final decision.
- Although the business buyer may be motivated by both rational and emotional factors, the use of rational and quantitative criteria dominates most decisions.
- The decision is sometimes made based on a set of specifications to potential suppliers who then bid on the contract. Typically in these purchases, the lowest bid wins.
- The decision may span a considerable time and create a lag between the initial contact and final decision. On the other hand, once a decision is made, it may be in place for a long time and sometimes is supported by a contract.
- Quality is hugely important, and repeat purchases are based on how well the product performs.
- Personal selling is also important in B2B marketing, so advertising is used to open the door and generate leads for the sales force.

SEGMENTING AND TARGETING

In order to make advertising interesting, relevant, and attention getting, it needs to be aligned with the audience's interests. Understanding consumers—their desires, interests, and mental state—is the first step in identifying a logical target for a brand message.

Most products don't have unlimited funds to spread their messages in all directions. Instead, efficiency—and effectiveness—demands that marketers (1) segment the market and (2) target the right audience group. **Segmenting** means dividing the market into groups of people who have similar characteristics in certain key product-related areas. **Targeting** means identifying the group that might be the most profitable audience and the most likely to respond to marketing communication. These decisions are central to both the message and media strategies outlined in advertising plans, a topic we'll discuss in Chapter 7.

The idea behind segmenting people is that groups of people to whom advertisers direct their messages are defined by certain key characteristics—usually demographics and psychographics—and these characteristics make them more alike than different. Furthermore, those characteristics also define *how* they are different from others who may not be in the market for the product.

Principle
Segmenting means dividing the market into groups of people who have similar characteristics in common; targeting is identifying the group that is most likely to respond to the brand message.

To Segment or Not to Segment?

The first decision is whether to treat the market as *homogeneous* (that is, as a single, undifferentiated, large unit) or as *heterogeneous* (a market composed of separate, smaller groups known as *segments*). When planners treat the market as homogeneous, they use one marketing strategy that will appeal to as many people as possible. This market strategy is known as an **undifferentiated** or **market aggregation strategy**.

At one point in its history, Coca-Cola viewed the U.S. market as homogeneous and used general appeals—such as "Coke is it!"—for all consumers. But even Coke is sold in different types of places, and people hear about Coke through different types of media. Therefore, customers are grouped almost by definition, based on their contact points with the product. And, of course, there are differences in age—there has to be a big difference between a long-time adult Coke drinker and a teenager. Those differences affect how you address people in advertising and how you reach them in media.

In other words, few examples of homogeneous markets exist. Often, companies take an undifferentiated approach because they lack the resources to target different market segments. For certain types of widely consumed items, such as gasoline, the undifferentiated market approach may make sense because the potential market is large enough to justify possible wasted resources. At one time, the bottled water industry used this approach. Clearly, that has changed as the market for bottled water has evolved and become more competitive based on such factors as price and natural qualities.

Market segmentation is a much more common market approach. It assumes that the best way to sell to the market is to recognize consumer differences and adjust marketing strategies and messages accordingly. In a segmentation strategy, marketers divide the larger heterogeneous market into segments that are homogeneous within these small markets. From these segments, the marketer identifies, evaluates, and selects a **target market**, a group of people with similar needs and characteristics who are most likely to be in the market for the advertiser's product.

By using a segmentation approach, a company can more precisely match the needs and wants of the customer and generate more sales. That's why soft drink manufacturers such as Coke and Pepsi have moved away from the undifferentiated approach and have introduced product variations to appeal to different consumer segments, such as diet, caffeine-free, diet caffeine-free, and flavored versions of their basic products. This approach also allows a company to target advertising messages more precisely based on the interests and attitudes of these consumers.

Types of Segmentation   In general, marketers segment their markets using six broad categories based on the consumer characteristics that have been described in this chapter. The six approaches, illustrated in Figure 5.7, include demographics, life stage, geographics,

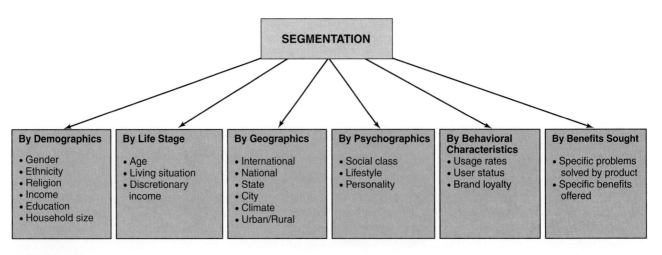

FIGURE 5.7
Market Segmentation Approaches
Market segmentation is based on identifying the factors that best capture the characteristics of people who would be in the market for the product.

psychographics, behavior characteristics, and values and benefits sought (needs-based). Which approach or combination of approaches is best to use varies with the market situation and product category.

- *Demographic segmentation* means dividing the market using such characteristics as gender, ethnicity, and income. Age is often the first characteristic to be used in defining a market segment.
- *Life stage segmentation* is based on the particular stage in consumers' life cycle, which includes such categories as children, young people living at home, college students, singles living on their own, couples, families with children, empty nesters, and senior singles living alone. Age is a characteristic of life stage, as is living situation. Discretionary income tends to vary with life stage.
- *Geographic segmentation* uses location as a defining variable because consumers' needs sometimes vary depending upon where they live—urban, rural, suburban, North, South. The most important variables are world or global, region, nation, state, or city. Factors related to these decisions include climate, population density, and urban/rural character. Geography affects both product distribution and marketing communication.
- *Psychographic segmentation* is primarily based on studies of how people spend their money, their patterns of work and leisure, their interest and opinions, and their views of themselves. This strategy is considered richer than demographic segmentation because it combines psychological information with lifestyle insights. The DDB Blood Center case illustrates this approach.
- *Behavioral segmentation* divides people into groups based on product category and brand usage.
- *Values and benefits-based segmentation* groups people on tangible and intangible factors. *Values segmentation* reflects consumers' underlying value system—spiritual, hedonistic, thrifty, and so forth. *Benefit segmentation* is based consumers' needs or problems. The idea is that people buy products for different benefits they hope to derive. For example, car buyers might be grouped based on whether they are motivated by concerns for safety, gas mileage, durability/dependability, performance and handling, luxury, or enhancement of self-image.

These segmentation approaches are useful in identifying the important characteristics of a group of people in a potential market for a brand message. Notice how data from the DDB Life Style Study was used to identify not only potential blood donors, but, more importantly, the characteristics that made these people different from other people.

Sociodemographic Segments   One common approach to demographic segmentation that has entered mainstream vocabulary comes from referring to people in terms of when they were born. Although these categories are age driven and we discussed them in that section, these market segment terms also refer to lifestyle differences. We've talked about the incredible impact baby boomers have had as a market category, so you can understand their importance as a market segment, but savvy marketers recognize the many differences in lifestyles and attitudes among this huge population. Generations X and Y, as well as the echo boomers, are also important demographic segments, but their sociodemographic characteristics may represent more consistent lifestyle differences.

Seniors are referred to as the *Gray Market* and divided into two categories—young seniors (60–74) and older seniors (75 plus). This is another huge market, especially in the United States, and also a wealthy one. As baby boomers move into their retirement years, this senior market will become even larger relative to the rest of the population.

Other fun terms that have been used to describe demographic and lifestyle segments include the following:

- *Dinkies*: Double income young couples with no kids
- *Guppies*: Gay upwardly mobile professionals
- *Skippies*: School kids with purchasing power
- *Slackers*: A recycled term inspired by the 1991 movie *Slacker*, referring to teenagers and young adults who don't care much or do much

A MATTER OF PRACTICE

Using DDB Life Style Data to Segment an Audience
By Marty Horn, *Senior Vice President and Director of U.S. Strategic Services, DDB*

Several years ago, the Blood Center of Southeastern Wisconsin (now called the Blood Center of Wisconsin) came to DDB with a big problem—a problem you could say was truly a matter of life or death. The Blood Center, which provides blood to local area hospitals, was short 7,000 units of blood due to the declining effectiveness at the time of mobile blood drives. It had to ship in blood (an expensive proposition) from other centers to cover its shortfall.

Consequently, the center was forced to adopt an entirely different recruitment strategy in which donors would now have come to fixed-site locations. As part of the overhaul of its marketing program, the center felt it needed to get a better handle on its donor base and what it was that made them "tick." The marketing director of the Blood Center, who knew about our Life Style Study and its ability to uncover insights into people's lives, asked if we could help.

We included a question in the Life Style Study that asked respondents how often in the past five years they had donated blood. This simple question allowed us to segment the market and identify frequent blood donors—those people who have given blood in the past and would likely come to a fixed-site center in the future.

We then looked at frequent donors' responses to all the Life Style questions, compared them to the rest of the sample, and uncovered some interesting differences. Frequent donors were:

- **Sociable.** They entertain, go to parties, and send greeting cards.
- **Doting parents.** They believe that children are most important in a marriage and that, when making important family decisions, children should be considered first.
- **Hard working.** Many blood donors are in dual-income households; they stay late at work, and their spare time is scarce.

- **Information seekers.** They are well educated and enjoy reading books, and they search for information to help them make better-informed decisions.
  - **Leaders.** Blood donors like to be considered leaders and see themselves as influential in their neighborhoods.

As a result of these and other insights that the Life Style Study revealed about blood donors, the Blood Center made important changes to its marketing and communication programs. For example, donation center hours were expanded to accommodate working people, and the process was streamlined so they could get in and out faster.

In terms of marketing strategy, the recruitment literature was redesigned to be more professional, and the promotional material featured kids who owed their lives to blood transfusions. A direct-mail effort was created around 1,200 "loyal" past donors who were encouraged to participate again and bring a friend or family member.

These strategies achieved the desired results—and then some! The 1,200 loyal donors generated a total of 2,200 donations. The Blood Center went from a deficit of 7,000 units of blood to a surplus of 6,000 units, *a turn-around of 13,000 units.* Instead of having to import blood from other centers to cover its shortfall, the Blood Center could now supply blood to other centers that had not reached their quotas. The Blood Center case illustrates how the DDB Life Style Study can be a powerful tool in getting to better know the customer and identify segments. Furthermore, it demonstrates how a more personal, in-depth knowledge of that customer can be a catalyst to marketplace success.

- *Bling bling generation:* A term coined by rappers and hip hoppers referring to flashy people with a high-rolling lifestyle and costly diamonds and jewelry
- *Ruppies*: Retired urban professionals; older consumers with sophisticated tastes and generally affluent lifestyle

Niche Segments Although advertising has gone global to reach large markets, many advertisers have moved toward tighter and tighter **niche markets**, which are subsegments of a more general market. Individuals in a niche market, such as ecologically minded mothers who won't use disposable diapers, are defined by a distinctive interest or attitude. Instead of marketing to the masses, marketers target narrow segments, such as single women travelers, hockey fans, classical music enthusiasts, or skateboarders. Although large companies may develop niche strategies, niche marketers are companies that pursue market segments of sufficient size to be profitable although not large enough to be of interest to large marketers. Elderhostel, for example, markets to seniors who are interested in educationally oriented travel experiences.

Targeting the Right Audience

A market is first divided to identify segments, and then potentially profitable segments are selected to be the target audience for a marketing communication effort. Through targeting, the organization can design specific communication strategies to match the audience's needs and wants and position the product in the most relevant way to match their interests. Targeting is also the key factor in selecting the right media.

Consider, for example, how Niman Ranch of Bolinas, California, built a luxury brand for its cuts of meat, which is usually considered a commodity. The obvious target would be upscale consumers who value natural food and are willing to pay more for the best. But that's not the route Niman Ranch took. Instead it bypassed consumers and marketed directly to prestigious chefs whose restaurants featured the brand on their menus. By using an innovative targeting strategy, Niman moved from commodity to a cachet brand that has brought huge growth to the little company.[23]

Profiling the Target Audience   The target is first of all described using the variables that separate this prospective consumer group from others who probably are not in the market. The target audience is then profiled using descriptive information based on the demographic and psychographic factors we've discussed in this chapter. For example, what are the consumer's age, income, education, geography, and critical psychographics? What motivates him or her? **Profiles** are descriptions of the target audience that read like a description of someone you know. These are used in personalizing the consumer to develop on-target media and message decisions.

Pretend you're launching a new diaper service. You know that mothers are primary caretakers of infants, and you know that they are not all alike, but what makes one group of mothers different from another set? Some are affluent, while others struggle to get by. Are these the most important factors for the brand, or are there other factors than income to consider? If so, what are those? For example, the latest version of what we used to know as the "soccer mom" (hauling kids to sports activities in a minivan) is the Alpha mom. These people are highly educated, tech-savvy professionals who are likely to have a Blackberry in one hand and a baby in the other. Most importantly, these moms are influencers and trendsetters.[24]

You build a profile by starting with the most important characteristic. In the diaper service example, that would be gender, of course, and then age, let's say women age 18–35. Then you add other factors, such as income, urban versus rural dwellers, education, or whatever factors come up in research as the most important predictive variables. As Figure 5.8 illustrates, each time you add a variable, you narrow the market as you come closer to the ideal target audience. The objective is to get the largest group that still holds together as a group in such a way that you can direct a message that will speak to all or most of the people in that group. Once these predictor variables have been sorted out, it should be possible to build an estimate of the size of this target market.

Principle
Each time you add a variable to a target audience definition, you narrow the size of the target audience.

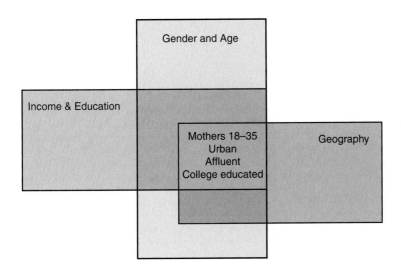

FIGURE 5.8
Narrowing the Target

Gender and Age

Income & Education

Mothers 18–35
Urban
Affluent
College educated

Geography

THE INSIDE STORY

Behavioral Targeting: An Emerging Form of Online Ad Targeting

By David Rittenhouse, *Senior Partner and Planning Director neo@Ogilvy*

It's not a new concept for marketers to observe consumer behavior and use the resulting insights to improve program performance. Advertisers have long led the charge, taking certain types of behavior as indicators of interest, grouping them into segments, and matching ads to them.

Over the past several years, online media have emerged as a preferred channel for this type of behavioral targeting due to the massive amount of data available on Web users' browsing patterns and the dynamic nature of the way ads are delivered. This has opened up new opportunities for online publishers and marketers to potentially better-targeted and cost-efficient advertising and more relevant messages and offers for consumers.

What Is Behavioral Targeting?

Behavioral targeting is not about targeting ads based on media demographics, such as gender, age, or household income. It's not about targeting times of day or geographic locations. Behavioral targeting is about matching ads to interests indicated by recency and frequency of consumer behaviors, collected unobtrusively.

For example, imagine a consumer shopping for a car and researching the purchase online. She visits car-related Web pages and reads reviews, sales listings, and other automotive content. She does this four times in a 30-day time span within a network of Web sites. This type of behavior pegs her as an "auto shopper," a segment comprising type of content plus frequency of recent visits.

A behaviorally targeted ad placement would deliver an impression only after the Web user had met these pre-defined criteria that put her into the "auto shopper" segment. The ads would not necessarily be delivered in automotive content, but in some cases via the least-expensive ad space available.

Proof Points

OgilvyOne was among the first agencies to test behavioral targeting. Our own advertiser case studies have shown behavioral targeting to improve the composition of target audiences, lower the cost of targeted impressions, and increase responsiveness to advertisements.

An early test run in the United Kingdom with a major technology client showed strong increases in audience composition over more traditional types of online ad placements. Since then, we have run behaviorally targeted placements for other clients across other categories, such as financial services and pharmaceutical. These tests confirmed our earlier findings, showing decreased impression and response costs. Other marketplace studies have shown behavioral targeting to increase product sales and brand metrics such as brand awareness and preference.

A Word on Privacy

Internet user privacy has been raised as a potential issue with behavioral targeting. When done properly, no personally identifiable information is collected. Ads are not matched to an individual (name, address, date of birth) but to an interest segment (shopping for a car). Behaviorally targeted ads are paid for and served as part of publisher pages, not pop-ups generated by a piece of spyware, so they are controlled to ensure that the relationship with the reader (and the advertiser's brand) are not damaged.

The Internet Advertising Bureau (IAB) and consumer advocates have come out in favor of behavioral targeting in its present form, so long as consumers are informed and given a choice.

A graduate of the University of Colorado where he received a master's degree, David Rittenhouse was nominated by Professor Sandra Moriarty.

Although behavioral characteristics have always been important, **behavioral targeting** is getting more attention because of new practices in Internet marketing. The Internet makes it possible to deliver ads personalized in terms of a customer's own usage patterns.[25] Amazon, for example, has had success promoting books to people based on their past purchases.

Ethical Issues   In addition to the privacy issue raised in The Inside Story, other ethical issues are involved with segmenting and targeting. These concerns relate to the type of products advertised as well as the messages that are created to reach the audience. Two examples of ethical quandaries surrounding advertising potentially unhealthy products to specific segments are targeting young black men in inner cities with malt beer ads and children with commercials for sugary foods. The issue of stereotypes is related to the messages that are communicated to reach these groups.

One of the biggest issues in targeting is the emphasis in many advertising programs on targeting young consumers. It started back in the 1950s and ever since then, marketers and advertisers have tried to reach the trendsetting youthful audience. The growth in the numbers of older consumers has led to some resentment about the continuing emphasis on young people as a general targeting strategy. It's a particular problem in television programming, most of which is aimed at twenty-somethings. A recent study[26] of 4,220 adults—1,655 of whom were 40 to 59 years old—found that older viewers are less likely than people in other age groups to watch shows or respond to advertising they feel is targeted to a younger audience. Furthermore, they are less likely to buy the advertised brands. The study noted that 78 million boomers are now in "their power years" and advertisers should rethink their emphasis on youth.

Microtargeting   A targeting practice that has emerged from political campaigning is called **microtargeting,** which refers to using vast computer databanks of personal information to identify voters most likely to support one candidate or another. The practice was refined for George Bush's 2004 reelection campaign and used again in the midterm elections by California Governor Arnold Schwarzenegger, as well as other candidates, both Democrat and Republican. From these databanks, political experts can tell what car or cars likely voters will drive, as well as their choices in recreation, leisure time activities, and restaurants. Using this method, Bush's campaign was able to tease out potential supporters in swing states, such as Ohio. Campaign strategists believe "consumer information can reveal voter's politics even better than a party label can."[27] Microtargeting has applications beyond politics. Several marketers have been able to profile prospects by carefully analyzing data on their regular customers to identify these revealing tendencies and characteristics.

IT'S A WRAP

Love Your Body

This chapter identified several key audience traits and behaviors that are relevant to advertisers as they decide how to effectively segment the market and target the audience. Keep in mind that we haven't examined all possible traits and behaviors. Furthermore, those who work on the design and implementation of an advertisement may interpret these traits differently. The point is that the key to effective customer-focused advertising is staying sensitive to consumers and understanding how they think, act, and feel.

The provocative copy in the Dove Campaign for Real Beauty challenges readers to reconsider how they define beauty and to love their bodies, no matter what their age or shape. Although we live in a culture that worships physical perfection, Dove is trying valiantly to broaden that definition. The campaign generated a huge buzz. But did it work to sell the product?

According to Unilever, the campaign resulted in a 24 percent sales increase during the advertising period across the entire Dove brand. Furthermore, after only six months the campaign for the new Firming Lotion generated a share of 2.3 percent in the highly competitive hand and body lotions category.

The brand also fared well globally. When it was launched in the United Kingdom, sales of Dove Firming Lotion reportedly increased by 700 percent in the first seven months after the posters appeared. It generated a substantial press interest, with about 170 editorial pieces written in the first four months after the launch in Great Britain.

The campaign radically changed the Dove brand image with its culturally relevant message. Publicity generated more than 650 million media impressions in the United States, estimated to be worth $21.14 million in free media exposure. According to Ogilvy & Mather, the highlight of the public relations effort was a six-minute segment on The Oprah Winfrey Show, on which Oprah said, "I'm gonna go get me a bar of soap right now."

Moreover, the definition of beauty portrayed in advertising really seems to be changing. When asked about the images in Dove ads, 76 percent said women in the ad are beautiful, and 68 percent said, "It made you think differently about the brand."

Key Points Summary

1. **What is consumer behavior, and why is it important for advertisers to understand?** Consumer behavior describes how individuals or groups select, purchase, use, or dispose of products as well as the needs and wants that motivate these behaviors. Consumers make up the audience for marketing communication. Consumers are people who buy or use products; customers are consumers who buy a particular brand; and prospects are potential customers. There are two types of markets—consumers and business-to-business. The difference is that consumers buy things for their own personal use and businesses buy things to use in manufacturing or the conduct of their business.

2. **What are the cultural, social, psychological, and behavioral influences on consumer responses to advertising?** The social and cultural influences on consumer decision making include society and subcultures, social class, reference groups, age, gender, family status, education, occupation, income, and race. Psychological influences on consumers include perception, learning, motivation, attitudes, personality, psychographics, and lifestyles. In terms of behavior, quantity of usage is an important characteristic of a profitable market. The relationship the consumer has with the brand in terms of use and loyalty is also important. Finally, the innovativeness of

people in the group in terms of their willingness to try something new is another important behavioral factor influencing decision making.

3. **How does the consumer decision process work?** The information-driven decision process involves five stages: need recognition, information search, evaluation of alternatives, purchase decision, and postpurchase evaluation. The paths approach to consumer decision making identifies a multitude of different routes that a consumer may take to reach a purchase decision.

4. **What is the difference between segmenting and targeting?** Segmentation involves dividing a market into groups of people who can be identified as being in the market for the product. Targeting is identifying the group that would be the most responsive to an advertising message about the product. Both segmenting and targeting use social/cultural, psychological, and behavioral characteristics to identify these critical groups of people. Advertisers identify audiences in terms of demographics and psychographics. Demographic profiles of consumers include information on population size, age, gender, education, family situation, occupation, income, and race. Psychographic profiles include information on attitudes, lifestyles, buying behavior, and decision processes.

Key Terms

acquired needs, p. 141
behavioral targeting, p. 156
brand communities, p. 134
cognitive dissonance, p. 141
consumer behavior, p. 131
consumers, p. 131
cool hunters, p. 148
core values, p. 133
corporate culture, p. 134
culture, p. 132
customers, p. 131

demographics, p. 135
discretionary income, p. 139
evoked set, p. 150
family, p. 135
household, p. 135
innate needs, p. 141
lifestyle, p. 135
market segmentation, p. 152
microtargeting, p. 157
motive, p. 142
needs, p. 141

niche market, p. 154
norms, p. 132
perceived risk, p. 148
personality, p. 142
profiles, p. 155
prospects, p. 131
psychographics, p. 142
reference group, p. 134
segmenting, p. 151
social class, p. 134
subculture, p. 133

switcher, p. 147
target market, p. 152
targeting, p. 151
trend spotters, p. 148
undifferentiated (market
    aggregation strategy), p. 152
usage, p. 147
VALS, p. 145
values, p. 132
wants, p. 141

Review Questions

1. In what ways does the culture in which you grew up affect your consumer behavior? Describe and explain one purchase you have made recently that reflects your cultural background.

2. What are reference groups? List the reference groups to which you belong or with which you associate yourself.

3. What are the key behavioral influences on consumer behavior? For example, say you want to go out to eat on Friday. Analyze your decision about where to go in terms of behavioral factors.

4. What are the key steps in the adoption process, and how do they relate to product purchases?

5. Define targeting. How does it differ from segmenting?

6. What are your key demographic and psychographic characteristics? Build a profile of yourself and give an example of how each one might be used in planning an advertising campaign targeted to someone like you.

Discussion Questions

1. You are working as an intern at the Williams Russell agency and the agency has just gotten a new account, a bottled tea named Leafs Alive that uses a healthy antioxidant formulation. The sale of bottled tea, as well as healthy products, is surging. Analyze your market using the following questions:

    a. What consumer trends seem to be driving this product development?

    b. What cultural, social, psychological, and behavioral factors influence this market?

    c. Plot the consumer decision process you think would best describe how people choose a product in this category.

    d. Choose one of the VALS or Yankelovich Monitor's MindBase groups that you think best describes the target market for this product. Explain your rationale.

2. Consider the social factors that influence consumer decisions. Identify two demographic or psychographic factors that you think would be most important to each of these product marketing situations:

    a. Full line of frozen family-style meals (for microwaving) that feature superior nutritional balances

    b. Dairy product company (milk, cheese, ice cream) offering an exclusive packaging design that uses fully degradable containers

    c. A new SUV that is lighter in weight and gets better gas mileage than the average SUV

3. Analyze the decision making involved in choosing your college.

    a. Interview two classmates and determine what were the influences on their decision to attend this school.

    b. How did you—and the people you interviewed—go about making this decision? Is there a general decision-making process that you can outline? Where are the points of agreement and where did you and your classmates differ in approaching this decision?

    c. Draw up a target audience profile for students attending your college. How does this profile differ from another school in your same market area?

4. *Five-Minute Debate*: One of your classmates argues that the information-driven approach to a consumer decision is absolutely the most important route and advertising strategies should focus on that type of situation. Two other classmates disagree strongly: One argues that a feeling-driven approach is much more effective in generating a response, and the other says the only thing that counts is driving action, particularly sales.

    In class, organize into small teams with each team taking one of the three positions. Set up a series of debates with each side having 1½ minutes to argue its position. Every team of debaters must present new points not covered in the previous teams' presentations until there are no arguments left to present. Then the class votes as a group on the winning point of view.

Take-Home Team Projects

1. How do people make decisions to buy soap, soup, potato chips, hand lotion, or aspirin? Choose one of these product categories and assign your team members to different stores (grocery, pharmacy, convenience store, discount store) to do an "aisle check" by standing in the aisle and unobtrusively observing shoppers considering this product. Each person should spend 15 minutes for each observation and do four at different times of the day. Then, as a team, write up a report that describes how people shop for this product. Is it a brand decision? A price decision? Do they study the labels? From what you can observe, what features are important in the selection? Be creative and bring this experience to life for your instructor, who is your hypothetical brand manager. Present your findings in a one-page report.

2. Bottled water is an outgrowth of the health and fitness trend. It has recently moved into second place in the beverage industry behind wine and spirits beating out beer and coffee. The latest twist on bottled water is the "enhanced" category with designer waters that include such things as extra oxygen, vitamins, or caffeine. A few of the emerging brands are Evamor from New Jersey and Trinity Springs from Idaho. Go online and find secondary data about this market. Indicate how you would use this information to design an ad for one of these products.

3. Choose two VALS and two MindBase categories. Find one print advertisement that appears to be targeted to people in each category. Explain why you think the ad addresses that audience. Do you believe that the categories are mutually exclusive? Can consumers (and ads directed to them) be classified in multiple categories? Why or why not?

Yahoo! Hands-On Case

Review the Yahoo! case in the Appendix.

1. From your reading of the case and your knowledge of these age groups, what are the influences that most affect the decisions of teens and tweens regarding their Internet use? Which factors are most important? What consumer decision-making process do they go through in making a decision on an Internet provider?

2. You have been asked by the Yahoo! team to develop profiles for both the primary and secondary target audiences. Since the team has concluded that these are, indeed, different audiences, your profiles should, in addition to describing each group, identify the ways in which they are different. Develop this profile as a personality sketch based on someone you know and give the person a name. Who are these people, and what are they like? Create four sketches—one each for a girl and a boy in both of the target audiences—teens and tweens. Keep this to one page with a paragraph for each of the four types.

HANDS-ON CASE

Toyota Goes After Tuners

Young people with limited incomes often look for a great deal on a new car. One way to save some money is to forgo options and upgrades, like a sunroof or a navigation system. But when Toyota introduced its funky Scion brand, it considered offering a version without something most people assume comes standard: paint. Although they ultimately decided against the idea, at one point Toyota's plan was to sell the brand with just gray primer.

Toyota wasn't really targeting people so cheap they wouldn't spend money on paint. Just the opposite—the car company was going after a group with money to burn, called *tuners*. Tuners are young car buyers who live to customize their cars. The trend really began among young Asian Americans, who typically bought inexpensive Asian import cars and then spent thousands of dollars customizing them. The hobby has spread to other young people, so that today Asian Americans are in the tuner minority. But Japanese brands remain the cars of choice among those dedicated to creating a work of art on wheels. Explaining the idea of a "no paint" option, Jim Farley, Scion general manager, says, "As much as possible, we want to give them [tuners] a blank canvas."

What does a tuner do with a car? He (or she—women make up almost 20 percent of the tuner subculture) might take a basic Honda, add a large and loud exhaust system, paint the intake manifolds, and add ride-lowering springs. Other popular add-ons are technologies that increase vehicle speed, like turbochargers, superchargers, and nitrous kits.

There are some serious bucks involved. The Specialty Equipment Market Association estimates that auto after-market spending (spending on car accessories after the original car purchase) increased from $295 million in 1997 to $2.3 billion in 2002. The average enthusiast spends about $1,800 upgrading the vehicle with fancy wheels, grill guards, and mobile electronics. The motivation? "You build a car for yourself," says one 20-something tuner who one day plans to install an Acura RSX Type-S engine into his Honda Civic. "The satisfaction is in making it your own and knowing that nobody will ever have something that's the same."

The amount of money tuners spend is reason enough to attract the attention of marketers. GM hoped to interest tuners in its Saturn Ion, Chevrolet Cavalier, and Pontiac Sunfire when it launched a "Tuner Tour" of 10 National Hot Rod Association races. GM allowed young car enthusiasts to play games and enter contests for prizes, as it in turn collected names and e-mail addresses. GM's focus on relationship marketing makes sense because tuners don't watch a lot of TV. Both Mitsubishi and Ford believe the best way to reach them is with product placements in movies (Mitsubishi bought air time in the popular film *2 Fast 2 Furious*). But even companies selling products unrelated to cars are interested in the tuner lifestyle. Pepsi has hired tuners to customize some of its promotional vehicles.

In the case of the Scion, Toyota's goal is to make the new car an immediate hit with tuners. Rather than spend a great deal of money on network television, Toyota decided to sponsor a 22-minute movie *On the D.L.* The movie is a comical docudrama that tells the story of a pair of musicians trying to obtain their first driver's licenses. The stars are musicians from youth-oriented bands: Ahmir "?uestlove" Thompson, from the Roots, and DJ King Britt, who played for the Digable Planets. The film premiered at the Tribeca Film Festival, after which segments were shared on peer-to-peer networks such as Kazaa. Toyota hopes that enthusiasts will download the segments and share them with friends.

Consider This

1. Why are tuners so attractive to marketers, even after accounting for their spending power?
2. Evaluate Toyota's strategy of targeting tuners with the Scion campaign. What are the difficulties for a large company in marketing effectively to a youth-oriented subculture? What techniques do you think companies like Toyota are using to try to understand their market?
3. Explain how "tuner" campaigns, such as those by GM and Toyota, work. Analyze these campaigns using the Facets Model of Effects to identify the effects they are designed to achieve. How would you determine if these campaigns are effective?

Sources: Jean Halliday, "Tune In, Trick Out Trend Turns On Carmakers," *Advertising Age,* November 3, 2003; Jean Halliday, "Toyota's Scion Goes to Tribeca Film Fest," *Advertising Age,* April 26, 2004; Gail Kachadourian, "What's Hot with Tuners?" *Automotive News,* November 4, 2002; Frederick Staab, "The Auto Aftermarket Is No Afterthought," *BusinessWeek.com,* October. 31, 2005; Richard Truett, "Scion Considers a No-Paint Option," *Automotive News,* November 3, 2003.

Strategic Research

IT'S A WINNER

Award:	Company:	Agency:	Campaign:
Gold Effie	Holiday Inn Express	Fallon Worldwide, Minneapolis	"Showerhead"

You Do Your Best Thinking
in the Shower

Do you remember this line: "No, but I did stay at a Holiday Inn Express last night"? You may also remember those memorable characters in the long-running "Stay Smart" campaign. One ad featured a guest who piloted a helicopter, leaving the real pilot on the snow-covered mountaintop to the chagrin of his passengers. Another commercial revealed that the rodeo clown who'd just given advice to the bronco rider was really with the children's birthday party in the stands and not the rodeo. The point of the commercials isn't that the travelers aren't actually smarter, but they feel smarter for having made the smart decision to stay at a Holiday Inn Express.

Clever? Yes. "Stay Smart" has won myriad awards, including six Effies for the continued success of the campaign. The accolades for the clever creative are the result of carefully planned and crafted advertising. Let's look at one of the latest efforts for the Holiday Inn Express campaign. As you read through this case briefly, note all the places where the ad agency and client based their decisions on some type of research rather than arbitrary impulses.

Holiday Inn Express knows who its customers are. Mainly, they're about 40 million men, ages 25–54, who travel a lot—three or more nights per month on business. Competing within the limited-service hotel segment, Holiday Inn Express has discovered that its guests don't care about chocolate mints on their pillow. But they do want clean rooms, a good breakfast, and a decent shower.

Guest satisfaction surveys conducted by Holiday Inn Express indicated that guests' experiences with the bathrooms were less than wonderful. Survey respondents said their decision about where to stay hinged on the quality of the bathroom/shower experience. In response, the hotel decided to upgrade guest room bathrooms in all of its 1,400+ North American properties. The centerpiece of the upgrade was a proprietary showerhead that produces a good shower with strong, consistent water pressure.

Chapter Key Points

1. What are the types of strategic research, and how are they used?

2. What are the most common research methods used in advertising?

3. What are the key challenges facing advertising researchers?

More than 7,000 guests at 28 hotels across the United States tested the showerhead and reported that they perceived the new fixtures to be significantly better than the competitors'. Even better is that 26 percent of those tested said their stay was more pleasant because of the new showerhead, an important piece of information for both the client and the agency. It gave them confidence that the message about new showerheads would resonate with the target audience.

Imagine yourself as a creative at Fallon, the agency for Holiday Inn Express. You're faced with the challenge of turning a rather mundane piece of product news about a new showerhead into increased brand preference and higher occupancy rates. What do you need to know to make good decisions about the message or media strategy?

Keeping it simple, Fallon opted to just let the audience know that the new shower had good, consistent water pressure. After all, its surveys showed that's what consumers wanted. The agency knew the message ought to be in keeping with a wacky brand personality rather than some dull product news. From these decisions the big idea emerged. "You do your best thinking in the shower" integrated well with the "Stay Smart" umbrella campaign. For example, the message on the Holiday Inn Express Web site offers a tongue-in-cheek suggestion that using the showerhead "may even trigger a flood of great ideas, leading to unnaturally long showers, missed appointments, missed meals and missed flights. Please use responsibly."

Media decisions built on the insight that business travelers perceive showers as part of their daily routine that they hope goes smoothly, especially when traveling. Fallon decided to connect with the target in their "everyday routine" media. From a combination of qualitative research and Simmons syndicated research, Fallon knew it could reach the audience when they watched cable news, weather, and sports and indulged in shows like *SportsCenter, The Daily Show*, or the History Channel. Although television was given top priority, the campaign also appeared on the Internet as well as newspaper and out-of-home advertising.

Did you spot the research opportunities in this case study? What was the relationship of the research to the creative idea and the media choices? See the results in the It's a Wrap section at the end of the chapter.

Sources: Natasha Gullett, Holiday Inn Express news release, "Holiday Inn Express Franchisees Endorse $20+ million Bathroom Makeover: Proprietary Showerhead, Curved Shower Rods, Upgraded Towels and New Line of Bath Amenities," October 2004 (http://www.hotel-online.com/News/PR2004–4th/Oct04–HIShower.htm); Effie briefs – Holiday Inn Express: Showerhead and Holiday Inn Express: Stay Smart (www.nyama.org)

To understand consumer response to an advertising message and to plan advertising that has a real impact on consumers, marketers such as Holiday Inn need to do research. This effort, which includes market and competitive research, as well as consumer research, becomes the foundation for the advertising plan, which we discuss in Chapter 7. In this chapter we will discuss some key research concepts, beginning with an explanation of the two most basic categories of research—primary and secondary—and the basic categories of research tools—quantitative and qualitative.

THE QUEST FOR INTELLIGENCE AND INSIGHT

"Listen hard to your customers (and then listen some more)" is one of the principles outlined in the "Juicing the Orange" feature in the Part II Introduction for this section. Fallon and Senn then add that listening is the first step in understanding customers.

What does that mean? It means that advertising strategy begins with consumer research, or the tools of listening. This research investigates the topics we discussed in the previous chapter, including attitudes, motivations, perceptions, and behaviors. The research findings then lead to planning decisions based on insight into consumer motivations. But first we must understand the principles and practice of advertising research and how to listen effectively to consumers.

In-house researchers or independent research companies hired from outside the company usually handle a client's market and consumer research. The objective at all stages of the planning process is to answer the question: What do we need to know in order to make an informed decision? Here are the various types of research used in planning advertising and marketing communication, such as the Holiday Inn Express Showerhead campaign.

- **Market research** compiles information about the product, the product category, competitors, and other details of the marketing environment that will affect the development of advertising strategy.
- **Consumer research** identifies people who are in the market for the product in terms of their characteristics, attitudes, interests, and motivations. Ultimately, this information is used to decide who the targeted audience for the advertising should be. In an integrated marketing communication (IMC) plan, the consumer research also acquires information about all the relevant stakeholders and their points of contact with the brand.
- **Advertising research** focuses on all the elements of advertising, including message development research, media planning research, and evaluation, as well as information about competitors' advertising. IMC research is similar, except that it is used to assemble information needed in planning the use of a variety of marketing communication tools. IMC is particularly concerned with the interaction of multiple messages from a variety of sources to present the brand consistently.
- **Strategic research** uncovers critical information that becomes the basis for strategic planning decisions for both marketing and marketing communication. In advertising, this type of research covers all the factors and steps that lead to the creation of message strategies and media plans. Think of strategic research as collecting all relevant background information needed to make a decision on advertising and marketing communication strategy. The importance of the showerhead was a critical finding for the Holiday Inn Express campaign.

In another example, whether you knew it or not, you were engaged in strategic research when you looked for an acceptable college to attend. You conducted market research (what information is available?), strategic research (what factors are most important in making a decision and how do the schools stack up?), and evaluative research (how will I know I made the best decision?). An advertising plan goes through similar stages of development with research as the first step.

Types of Research

New advertising assignments always begin with some kind of informal or formal background research into the marketing situation. This is called *secondary research*, and we'll compare it with primary research, which is original research conducted by the company or brand.

Secondary Research   Background research that uses available published information about a topic is **secondary research.** When advertising people get new accounts or new assignments, they start by reading everything they can find on the product, company,

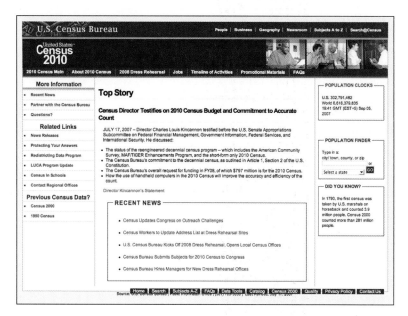

Demographic information, such as that available from the U.S. Census Bureau, is fundamental to advertising planning.

Source: http://www.census.gov/2010census

industry, and competition: sales reports, annual reports, complaint letters, and trade articles about the industry. They are looking for important facts and key insights. This kind of research is called secondary not because it is less important but because it has been collected and published by someone else. Many secondary information sources are available to advertisers doing strategic research.

- *Government organizations.* Governments, through their various departments, provide an astonishing array of statistics that can greatly enhance advertising and marketing decisions. Many of the statistics come from census records on the population's size, geographic distribution, age, income, occupation, education, and ethnicity.

  As we explained in Chapter 5, demographic information of this kind is fundamental to decision making about advertising targets and market segmentation. An advertiser cannot aim its advertising at a target audience without knowing that audience's size and major dimensions. Figure 6.1 lists some government reports that help advertisers make better decisions.

- *Trade associations.* Many industries support trade associations,—professional organizations whose members all work in the same field—that gather and distribute information of interest to association members. For instance, the American Association of Advertising Agencies (AAAA) issues reports that help ad agencies monitor their performance and keep tabs on competitors. The Radio Advertising Bureau publishes *Radio Facts*, an overview of the commercial U.S. radio industry; the Account Planning Group (APG) conducts seminars and training sessions for account planners; and the American Association for Public Opinion Research (AAPOR) serves the professional needs of opinion researchers.

United States

Survey of Current Business: Basic operational statistics on U.S. business. (Bureau of Economic Analysis of the U.S. Department of Commerce)

Requirements of Laws and Regulations Enforced by the U.S. Food and Drug Administration: Laws and regulations affecting food and beverage advertising. (U.S. Department of Health and Human Services, Food and Drug Administration)

Children's Information Processing of Television Advertising: How children react to television commercials. (National Technical Information Services, U.S. Department of Commerce)

Canada

Statistical Profile of Canadian Communities. (Office of the Chief Statistician of Canada)

The Economy in Detail. (Statistics Canada)

Canadian Social Trends. (Statistics Canada)

European Union

Shopping around Europe: European Economic Area. (European Union Eurostat Memo)

Key Data on Relations between the EU and Asian ASEM Countries. (European Union Eurostat Memo)

More Babies Born in the EU. (European Union Eurostat Memo)

FIGURE 6.1
Government Research Reports

Practical Tips

Web Sites for Advertising Research

Here's a sampling of Web sites that may offer useful information if you are doing background research for an advertising assignment:

- BrandEra (*http://www.brandera.com*) offers information by product category.
- MarketPerceptions (*http://marketperceptions.com*) represents a research company that specializes in health care research. The site has information about its focus group capabilities.
- For industry research into technology markets, consult Forrester Research (*http://www.forrester.com*). The independent research company consults on market research into technology industries.

- IndustryClick (*http://www.industryclick.com*) is a collection of business publications categorized by industry. Click on its Research & Tools button.
- Greenbook.org (*http://www.greenbook.org*) is a worldwide directory of marketing research focus group suppliers.
- For demographic information, consult the U.S. Census Bureau (http://www.census.gov), which offers easy access to census data, press releases, a population clock, and clips from the bureau's radio broadcasts.
- Cluetrain (http://www.cluetrain.com) publishes new ways to find and share innovative marketing information and ideas.

- *Secondary research suppliers.* Because of the overwhelming amount of information available through secondary research, specialized suppliers gather and organize that information around specific topic areas for other interested parties. Key secondary research suppliers are FIND/SVP, Off-the-Shelf Publications, Dialog Information Services, Lexis-Nexis, Dow Jones News/Retrieval, and Market Analysis Information Database.
- *Secondary information on the Internet.* For any given company, you're bound to find a Web site where you can learn about the company's history and philosophy of doing business, check out its complete product line, and discover who runs the company. These sites offer credible information for account planners and others involved in market research. Other sources of Internet information are blog sites and chat rooms where you can learn about people's reactions to brands and products. However, it is unlikely that all the needed information will be found on these sites.

A typical advertising campaign might be influenced, directly or indirectly, by information from many sources, including outside research suppliers, as well as agency research.

Primary Research Information that is collected for the first time from original sources is called **primary research.** In this case, companies do their own tracking and monitoring of their customers' behavior, and they also may hire specialized firms to do this research. Toyota, for example, undertook a huge two-year study of ultra-rich consumers in the United States to better market its upscale Lexus brand. A team of nine Lexus employees from various departments were designated the "super-affluent team" and sent on the road to interview wealthy car buyers about why they live where they do, what they do for enjoyment, what brands they buy, and how they feel about car makes and models. The surprising finding was that these consumers don't just buy a car, they buy a fleet of cars because they have multiple homes and offices.[1]

Primary research suppliers (the firms clients hire) specialize in interviewing, observing, recording, and analyzing the behavior of those who purchase or influence the purchase of a particular good or service. The primary research supplier industry is extremely diverse. Companies range from A.C. Nielsen, the huge international tracker of TV viewing habits, which employs more than 45,000 workers in the United States alone, to several thousand entrepreneurs who conduct focus groups and individual interviews, prepare reports, and provide advice on specific advertising and marketing problems for individual clients.

Many advertising agencies subscribe to large-scale surveys conducted by the Simmons Market Research Bureau (SMRB) or by Mediamark Research, Inc. (MRI). These

Some companies either hire outside research firms or they do their own tracking and monitoring of consumer attitudes, opinions, and behavior.

two organizations survey large samples of American consumers (approximately 30,000 for each survey) and ask questions about the consumption, possession, or use of a wide range of products, services, and media. The products and services covered in the MRI survey range from toothbrushes and dental floss to diet colas, camping equipment, and theme parks.

Both SMRB and MRI conduct original research and distribute their findings to their clients. The resulting reports are intended primarily for use in media planning, but because these surveys are so comprehensive, they also can be mined for unique consumer information, which makes them primary sources. Through a computer program called Golddigger, for example, an MRI subscriber can select a consumer target and ask the computer to find all other products and services and all the media that members of the target segment use. This profile provides a vivid and detailed description of the target as a person—just the information creative teams need to help them envision their audiences. To give you an idea of what the media data looks like, check out Figure 6.2 for a sample MRI report of the types of TV programs adults ages 18–34 watch. The report breaks down the 18–34 market into four market segments based on size of household and age of children, if any.

Quantitative and Qualitative Research   Primary research can be both quantitative and qualitative. **Quantitative research** delivers numerical data such as number of users and purchases, their attitudes and knowledge, their exposure to ads, and other market-related information. It also provides information on reactions to advertising and motivation to purchase, sometimes called *purchase intent*. Quantitative methods that investigate the responses of large numbers of people are useful in testing ideas to determine if their market is large enough or if most people really say or behave in a certain way.

Two primary characteristics of quantitative research are (1) large sample sizes, typically from 100 to 1,000 people, and (2) random sampling. The most common quantitative research methods include surveys and studies that track such things as sales and opinions. Quantitative research is usually designed either to accurately count something, such as sales levels, or to predict something, such as attitudes. In order to be predictive, however, this type of research must follow careful scientific procedures.

Qualitative research provides insight into the underlying reasons for how consumers behave and why. Common qualitative research methods include such tools as observation, ethnographic studies, in-depth interviews, and case studies. These exploratory research

Base: Adults	Total U.S. 000	Respondent 18–34 1-Person Household				Respondent 18–34 and Married, no children				Respondent 18–34 and Married, Youngest Child <6				Respondent 18–34 and Married Youngest Child 6+			
		A	B	C	D	A	B	C	D	A	B	C	D	A	B	C	D
		000	% Down	% Across	Index	000	% Down	% Across	Index	000	% Down	% Across	Index	000	% Down	% Across	Index
All Adults	184274	5357	100.0	2.9	100	7559	100.0	4.1	100	18041	100.0	9.8	100	4978	100.0	2.7	100
Program-Types: Average Show																	
Adven/Sci Fi/West-Prime	19969	590	11.0	3.0	102	875	11.6	4.4	107	2303	12.8	11.5	118	694	13.9	3.5	129
Auto Racing-Specials	6590	*226	4.2	3.4	118	*242	3.2	3.7	90	634	3.5	9.6	98	*251	5.0	3.8	141
Awards-Specials	16490	397	7.4	2.4	83	514	6.8	3.1	76	1576	8.7	9.6	98	*451	9.1	2.7	101
Baseball Specials	28019	806	15.0	2.9	99	1128	14.9	4.0	98	2671	14.8	9.5	97	*506	10.2	1.8	67
Basketball-Weekend-College	7377	*222	4.1	3.0	104	*244	3.2	3.3	81	531	2.9	7.2	74	*183	3.7	2.5	92
Basketball Specials-College	17096	529	9.9	3.1	106	694	9.2	4.1	99	1459	8.1	8.5	87	*423	8.5	2.5	92
Basketball Specials-Pro.	32470	1057	19.7	3.3	112	1369	18.1	4.2	103	3128	17.3	9.6	98	886	17.8	2.7	101
Bowling-Weekend	16808	312	5.8	1.9	654	744	9.8	4.4	108	1476	8.2	8.8	90	*386	78	2.3	85
Comedy/Variety	26254	930	17.4	3.5	122	1150	15.2	4.4	107	3257	18.1	12.4	127	999	20.1	3.8	141
Daytime Dramas	7621	*192	3.6	2.5	87	*287	3.8	3.8	92	845	4.7	11.1	113	*343	6.9	4.5	167
Daytime Game Shows	7747	*97	1.8	1.3	43	*194	2.6	2.5	61	734	4.1	9.5	97	*235	4.7	3.0	112
Documen/Information-Prime	22514	532	9.9	2.4	81	504	6.7	2.2	55	1739	9.6	7.7	79	*454	9.1	2.0	75
Early Morning News	12226	280	5.2	2.3	79	*429	5.7	3.5	86	1065	5.9	8.7	89	*330	6.6	2.7	100
Early Morning Talk/Info/News	14681	258	4.8	1.8	60	580	77	4.0	96	1291	7.2	8.8	90	*268	5.4	1.8	68
Early Eve. Netwk News-M-F	25946	596	11.1	2.3	79	836	11.1	3.2	79	1822	10.1	7.0	72	*594	11.9	2.3	85
Early Eve. Netwk News-Wknd	11338	*197	3.7	1.7	60	*208	2.8	1.8	45	795	4.4	7.0	72	*187	3.8	1.6	61
Entertainment Specials	19630	408	76	2.1	71	701	9.3	3.6	87	1719	9.5	8.8	89	*494	9.9	2.5	93
Feature Films-Prime	17232	371	6.9	2.2	74	*538	7.1	3.1	76	1209	6.7	70	72	*475	9.5	2.8	102
Football Bowl Games-Specials	13322	369	6.9	2.8	95	*381	5.0	2.9	70	1512	8.4	11.3	116	*245	4.9	1.8	68
Football Pro.-Specials	44804	1471	27.5	3.3	113	1766	23.4	3.9	96	4555	25.2	10.2	104	1104	22.2	2.5	91
General Drama-Prime	19880	581	10.8	2.9	101	571	76	2.9	70	2095	11.6	10.5	108	*555	11.1	2.8	103
Golf	5161	*102	1.9	2.0	68	*152	2.0	2.9	72	*324	1.8	6.3	64	*15	.3	.3	11
Late Evening Netwk News Wknd	5146	*146	2.7	2.8	98	*114	1.5	2.2	54	*293	1.6	5.7	58	*104	2.1	2.0	75
Late Night Talk/Variety	9590	313	5.8	3.3	112	*297	3.9	3.1	75	1009	5.6	10.5	107	*198	4.0	2.1	76
News-Specials	14508	234	4.4	1.6	55	510	6.7	3.5	86	1297	7.2	8.9	91	*212	4.3	1.5	54
Pageants-Specials	22025	439	8.2	2.0	69	952	12.6	4.3	105	2503	13.9	11.4	116	547	11.0	2.5	92
Police Docudrama	23575	726	13.6	3.1	106	1179	15.6	5.0	122	2309	12.8	9.8	100	731	14.7	3.1	115
Pvt Det/Susp/Myst/Pol.-Prime	28183	673	12.6	2.4	82	763	10.1	2.7	66	1739	9.6	6.2	63	*493	9.9	1.7	65
Situation Comedies-Prime	19097	598	11.2	3.1	108	919	12.2	4.8	117	2737	15.2	14.3	146	688	13.8	3.6	133
Sports Anthologies-Weekend	4847	*218	4.1	4.5	155	*232	3.1	4.8	117	*403	2.2	8.3	85	*108	2.2	2.2	82
Sunday News/Interview	5809	*70	1.3	1.2	41	*116	1.5	2.0	49	*214	1.2	3.7	38	*97	1.9	1.7	62
Syndicated Adult General	10444	*271	5.1	2.6	89	462	6.1	4.4	108	766	4.2	7.3	75	*221	4.4	2.1	78
Tennis	10033	338	6.3	3.4	116	380	5.0	3.8	92	826	4.5	8.2	84	*105	2.1	1.0	39

FIGURE 6.2

MRI Consumer Media Report

Source: Mediamark Research, Inc.

tools are useful for probing and gaining explanations, insight, and understanding into such questions as:

- What type of features do customers want?
- What are the motivations that lead to the purchase of a product?
- What do our customers think about our advertising?
- How do consumers relate to the brand? What are their emotional links to the brand?

Principle

Quantitative research investigates the attitudes, opinions, and behaviors of large numbers of people in order to make conclusions that can be generalized to the total population; qualitative research provides insight into how consumers think and behave.

Qualitative methods are used early in the process of developing an advertising plan or message strategy for generating insights, as well as questions and hypotheses for additional research. They are also good at confirming hunches, ruling out bad approaches and questionable or confusing ideas, and giving direction to the message strategy. Because qualitative research is typically done with small groups, advertisers cannot draw conclusions about or project their findings to the larger population.

Rather than drawing conclusions, qualitative research is used to better understand a market, generalize what the researchers learn, and generate hypotheses that can be tested with quantitative methods.[2] As Sally Reinman, Worldwide Market Planner at Saatchi & Saatchi, wrote for this book, research is more than numbers. She explains:

> Research processes are more varied and exciting than ever before. Examples include asking consumers to draw pictures, create collages, and produce home videos to show how they use a product.
>
> As consumers around the world become better informed and more demanding, advertisers that target different cultures need to find the "commonalities" (or common ground) among consumer groups from these cultures. Research for Toyota's sports-utility vehicle (SUV), the RAV 4, showed that consumers in all the targeted countries had three common desires: They wanted an SUV to have style, safety, and economy.
>
> To find these commonalities, I work with experts to learn the cultural meaning of codes and symbols that people use to communicate. The experts I work with include cultural and cognitive anthropologists, psychologists, interior decorators, and Indian storytellers. Anyone who can help me understand consumers and the consumer decision-making process is fair game.

One of the biggest problems in studying the consumer decision process is that consumers are often unable to articulate the reasons they do what they do. The goal of qualitative research methodologies often is to move beyond the limitations of what consumers can explain in words, which is how most quantitative research is conducted. The Brandtrust agency has found that "consumers don't generally give very reliable answers if you simply ask them, 'Why did you buy this?'"[3] That is because the answer often is found in their emotions rather than their reasons; furthermore, most people aren't so directly tuned in to their own thoughts and thinking process. Another problem with quantitative research is that consumers may try to give answers that they think the researchers are looking for—they want to please the interviewer. These are all reasons why qualitative research has become much more important in advertising and marketing in the last twenty years.

Experimental Research   Tightly controlled scientific studies are sometimes used to puzzle out how people think and respond to messages and incentives. **Experimental research** is designed using formal hypothesis-testing techniques that compare different message treatments and how people react to them. The idea is to control for all factors except the one being tested—if there is a change in the results, then the researcher can conclude that the variable being tested caused the difference. Experimental research is used to test marketing factors as well as advertising appeals and executions in such areas as product features, price, availability, and various creative advertising ideas. The Matter of Principle box explains how researchers have used experimental studies to determine the impact of advertising on behavior.

Sometimes the measurements are electronically recorded using such instruments as MRI or EEG machines or eye-scan tracking devices. Electrodes can be used to monitor heart rate, pulse, and skin temperature to determine if people have a physical response to a message that they may not be able to put in words. Emotional responses, in particular, are hard to verbalize but may be observable using these types of sensors. Hewlett-Packard Company, for example, wired a group of volunteers with electrodes to see how they reacted to photos of people smiling. The study found that there were obvious differences in brain activity in people looking at photos of smiling people, particularly pictures of children smiling.

Brain research is particularly popular in the subfield of *neuro-marketing,* in which planners seek to determine how the brain and emotions react to various stimuli. One study, for example, tries to map how the concept of "cool" (Angelina Jolie and Brad Pitt as op-

A MATTER OF PRINCIPLE

Using Research to See If Advertising Makes Smoking Cool

By Cornelia (Connie) Pechmann, *Professor of Marketing, University of California, Irvine*

Do your professors and instructors talk about the research they conduct? Here's an example of one professor's research about cigarette advertising that has practical implications for the tobacco industry and policy makers. It tests the idea that cigarette advertising can prime (or prepare) teens to think that smoking is cool.

In 1991, I began a program of research on tobacco use prevention through advertising and the mass media. I wondered how often people saw advertisements for products shortly before experiencing the products. It occurred to me that advertising exposure and product experience were perhaps most likely to occur concurrently in the case of cigarette advertising and encounters with smokers. In 1991, cigarette advertising on billboards was ubiquitous and 20 percent of high school seniors smoked daily, so I reasoned that adolescents might see cigarette advertisements and peers smoking concurrently. I also reasoned that encounters with smokers would often be ambiguous.

Looking at the literature, I could find few controlled experiments on cigarette advertising. However, surveys indicated there was a strong association between adolescents' perceptions of smokers and smoking initiation. With the assistance of coauthors, I completed two re-

search projects that documented that cigarette advertisements can prime adolescents' positive beliefs about smokers and thus alter their social encounters with smokers. Specifically, cigarette advertisements serving as primes can favorably bias adolescents' perceptions of peers who smoke and thus increase their intent to smoke. One of our papers on this topic received the Best Paper Award from the *Journal of Consumer Research*. I continue to conduct research in this area.

I am told that my tobacco-related research has been cited by expert witnesses in legal cases such as the federal tobacco case, in legislative hearings, and in U.S. Attorney General meetings. I believe that some academic research should be conducted to inform public policy and that if research is not designed for this purpose, it likely will not have this effect.

Sources: J. A. Bargh, M. Chen, and L. Burrows, "Automaticity of Social Behavior: Direct Effects of Trait Construct and Stereotype Activation on Action," *Journal of Personality & Social Psychology* 71:2 (1996): 230–244; C. Pechmann and S. J. Knight, "An Experimental Investigation of the Joint Effects of Advertising and Peers on Adolescents' Beliefs and Intentions about Cigarette Consumption," *Journal of Consumer Research* 29:1 (2002): 5–19; C. Pechmann and S. Ratneshwar, "The Effects of Antismoking and Cigarette Advertising on Young Adolescents' Perceptions of Peers Who Smoke," *Journal of Consumer Research* 21:2 (1994): 236–251.

posed to office chairs and detergents) stimulates various areas of the brain, an understanding that would help fashion marketers better present their products.[4]

The Uses of Research

Agencies and clients use research to make strategic decisions, as we have just discussed, but advertising agencies rarely *conduct* research. Most research has become so specialized that separate research companies, as well as in-house client research departments, are the most likely research sources. These firms and departments collect and disseminate secondary research data and conduct primary research that ultimately finds its way into advertising. DDB is one of the few large agencies that still does its own in-house research. Its annual Life Style Survey, which we discussed in Chapter 5, is a major source of consumer information.

As markets have become more fragmented and saturated, and as consumers have become more demanding, there has been an increased need for research-based information in advertising planning. Figure 6.3 summarizes the five ways research is used in advertising planning:

1. Market information
2. Consumer insight research
3. Media research
4. Message development research
5. Evaluation research

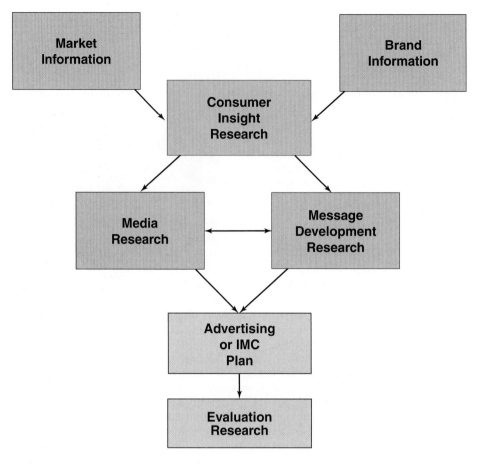

FIGURE 6.3
The Use of Research in Advertising Planning

Market Information   Formal research used by the marketing department for strategic planning is called **marketing research.** It includes surveys, in-depth interviews, observational methods, focus groups (which are like in-depth interviews with a group rather than individuals), and all types of primary and secondary data used to develop a marketing plan and ultimately provide information for an advertising plan. A subset of marketing research, **market research** is research used to gather information about a particular market.

Market information includes everything a planner can uncover about consumer perceptions of the brand, product category, and competitors' brands. Planners sometimes ride with the sales force and listen to sales pitches, tour manufacturing plants to see how a product is made, and work in a store or restaurant to evaluate the employee interaction with customers. In terms of advertising, planners test the brand's and its competitors' advertisements, promotions, retail displays, packaging, and other marketing communication efforts.

Brand information includes an assessment of the brand's role and performance in the marketplace—is it a leader, a follower, a challenger, or a subbrand of a bigger and better known brand? This research also investigates how people perceive brand personalities and images.

Consumer Insight Research   Both the creative team (who create messages) and the media planners (who decide how and when to deliver the messages) need to know as much as they can, in as much depth and detail as possible, about the people they are trying to reach, a goal achieved through **consumer insight research.** Demographic and psychographic information from consumer research is used to describe the target audience, but more importantly researchers try to determine what motivates these people to buy a product or become involved in a brand relationship.

Principle

Both the creative and media teams use research to learn as much as possible, in as much depth as possible, about the people they are trying to reach.

Some research questions try to describe people and their behaviors using the old journalistic technique of asking *who, what, where, when,* and *how.* To get inside their values and motivations, other *why* questions may probe their attitudes using *would, could, should,* and *might.* Associations are investigated by asking people what comes to mind when a word or brand is mentioned. Emotions are elicited by asking consumers what they think people in various photos and situations are feeling.

The objective of consumer insight research is to puzzle out a key consumer insight that will help move the target audience to respond to the message. Identifying consumer insight is the responsibility of the account planner; that role and process will be described in more detail in Chapter 7.

Media Research   Media planning begins with the consumer research and **media research** that helps with the media selection decision. Media planners often work in conjunction with account planners to decide which media formats make the most sense to accomplish the advertising objectives. The goal is to activate consumer engagement with a product or brand.

Next, media researchers gather information about all the possible media and marketing communication tools that might be used in a campaign to deliver a message. Media researchers then match that information to what is known about the target audience. The MRI data shown in Figure 6.2 illustrates the type of information media researchers consult to develop recommendations.

Message Development Research   As planners, account managers, media researchers, and people on the creative team begin the development of an advertisement, they involve themselves in various types of informal and formal **message development research.** They read all the relevant secondary information provided by the client and the planners to become better informed about the brand, the company, the competition, the media, and the product category. Message development often comes from the combination of consumer insight research and media research. The latest trend in strategy is to have experts from the medium—particularly new and alternative forms of media—suggest the best way to create new, exciting messages with novel formats and approaches.

Furthermore, as writers and art directors begin working on a specific creative project, they almost always conduct at least some informal research of their own. They may do their own personal observational research and visit retail stores, talk to salespeople, and watch customers buy. They may visit the information center, browse through reference books, and borrow subject and picture files. They will look at previous advertising, especially that of competitors, to see what others have done, and in their hearts they will become convinced that they can create something better than, and different from, anything that has been done before. This informal, personal research has a powerful influence on what happens later in the advertising process.

Research is used in development of the message strategy. As Jackie Boulter,[5] head of planning at the London-based Abbott Mead Vickers-BBDO agency explained, creative development research is focused on an advertising idea prior to production. It uses qualitative research to predict if the idea will solve the business problem and achieve the advertising's objectives. Sometimes called **concept testing,** it can help evaluate the relative power of various creative ideas. It's a "work-in-progress" type of evaluation.

Evaluation Research   After an advertisement has been developed and produced, it can be evaluated for its effectiveness both before and after it runs as part of a campaign.

Pretesting is research on an execution in its finished stages but before it appears in media. While creative development research looks at the power of the advertising idea, pretesting looks at the way the idea is presented. The idea can be strong, but the target might hate the execution. This type of test elicits a go or no-go decision for a specific advertisement. Sometimes pretesting will also call into doubt the strength of the advertising idea, forcing the creative team to rethink its strategy.

Evaluative research, often referred to as **copy testing,** is done during a campaign and afterward. If it's used during a campaign, the objective is to adjust the ad to make it stronger. Afterward, the research determines the effectiveness of the ad or campaign. We will explore the many different types of evaluation methods in Chapter 19, but let's just mention two common forms here. Memory can be measured using **aided recognition** (or recall). A researcher might page through a magazine (or use some other medium) and ask respondents whether they remember seeing a particular ad. **Unaided recognition** (or recall) means respondents are asked to tell what they remember without being prompted by seeing the magazine (or other medium) to refresh their memories.

Strategic, developmental, and evaluative research share some common tools and processes and we will briefly describe some of these in the following section.

RESEARCH METHODS USED IN ADVERTISING

This section focuses on the types of research used in message development and the research situations where these methods are typically used. The three stages of message development in which research is used are background research, consumer research, and development research.

Background Research

Background research of a variety of types is used to familiarize advertising planners with the market situation. Secondary research includes reading everything that is published or reported on the market, the competition, and consumers. Primary research involves, among other things, personally buying and using the product.

- *The brand experience.* When an agency gets a new client, the first thing the agency team has to do is learn about the brand through brand research. That means learning where the brand has been in the past in terms of the market, its customers, and competitors, as the Holiday Inn Express example illustrated. Also important is the corporate point of view regarding the brand's position within the company's line of products, as well as corporate goals and plans for the brand. Another critical area is the brand's relationships with its customers. Researchers, for example, may go through all the experiences that a typical consumer has in buying and using the product. If you were taking on a pizza restaurant account, for example, you might work in the store and/or visit it as a customer. Brand buying is also a form of commitment to the client: The parking lots of agencies that have automotive accounts are usually full of cars of that make.
- *Competitive analysis.* It's also important to do a competitive analysis. If you handle a soap account, you obviously want to use that brand of soap, but you may also buy the competing brands and do your own personal comparative test just to add your personal experiences to your brand analysis.
- *Advertising audit.* Either formally or informally, most advertising planners will begin an assignment by collecting every possible piece of advertising and other forms of marketing communication by the brand, as well as its competitors and other relevant categories that may have lessons for the brand. This includes a historical collection as well. There's nothing more embarrassing than proposing a great new advertising idea only to find out that it was used a couple of years ago by a competitor.
- *Content analysis.* The advertising audit might include only informal summaries of the slogans, appeals, and images used most often, or they might include more formal and systematic tabulation of competitors' approaches and strategies called a **content analysis.** By disclosing competitors' strategies and tactics, analysis of the content of competitive advertisements provides clues to how competitors are thinking and suggests ways to develop new and more effective campaigns. Planners also try to determine what mental territories or positions competitors claim and which are still available and relevant to the brand.
- *Semiotic analysis.* Another technique used to analyze advertisements is **semiotic analysis,** which is a way to take apart the signs and symbols in a message to uncover layers and types of meanings. The objective is to find deeper meanings in the symbolism that might be particular to different groups of consumers. Its focus is on determining the meanings, even if they are not obvious or highly symbolic, that might relate to consumer motivations.

Principle
There's nothing more embarrassing than proposing a great new advertising idea only to find out that it was used a couple of years ago by a competitor.

For example, the advertising that launched General Motors' OnStar global positioning system (GPS) used a Batman theme. The commercial featured a conversation between Batman and Alfred, his trusted butler, during which most of the features and uses of the OnStar system were explained. By looking at this commercial in terms of its signs and symbols, it is possible to determine if the obvious, as well as hidden, meanings of the message are on strategy. For example, the decision to use a comic book hero as the star created a heroic association for OnStar. However, Batman is not a superhero, but rather more of a common person with a lot of great technology and cool gadgets—remember Jack Nicholson as the Joker and his famous comment: "Where does he get all those wonderful toys?" The "bat beacon" then becomes OnStar for the average person. Batman is also ageless, appealing to young people who read comic books and watch movies today as well as older people who remember Batman from their youth.[6] A highly successful effort, this Batman OnStar campaign won a David Ogilvy Research Award.

- *Customer contact conversations.* We mentioned in the discussion of the communication role of marketing communication that feedback can be obtained from customers as a part of a research program that uses customer service, technical service, and inbound telemarketing calls. You've probably heard the phrase, "This call may be monitored for quality assurance." These recordings are used for training, but they also can be analyzed for marketing intelligence.[7] If customers say they are confused or ask the representative to repeat a phrase, then it could indicate that the sales offer or technical explanation isn't working right. These calls can provide instant feedback about the strength of a brand's offering as well as competitors' offers. Specific questions such as "Where did you hear about this?" are used to monitor brand contact points and media performance.

Consumer Research

Consumer research is used to better understand how users, prospects, and nonusers of a brand think and behave. From this research, segments and targets can be identified, and profiles can be drawn, but rarely do those profiles give insight into the whys of their buys. Why is the consumer in the market for what the brand offers? An example of how this insight is derived comes from Forrester Research and is called "design personas." Harley Manning, research director for customer experience, explains the concept in The Inside Story.

Another way researchers try to uncover the whys of the buys is called *association research.* In association tests, which are used in planning brand strategies, people are asked what they think of when they hear a cue, such as the name of a product category. They respond with all the things that come to mind, and that forms their **network of associations.** Brand perceptions are tested this way to map the structure and logic of these association networks, which lead to message strategies. For example, what do you think of when you think of Taco Bell? Wendy's? Arby's? Each restaurant should bring to mind some things in common (fast food, cheap food), but they also have distinct networks of associations based on type of food (Mexican, hamburgers, roast beef), restaurant design, logo and colors, brand characters, healthfulness, and so forth. Each restaurant, then, has a distinctive profile that can be determined from this network of associations.

Ways of Contact

Consumer research methodologies are often described in terms of the ways researchers contact their respondents. The contact can be in person, by telephone, by mail, through the Internet or cable TV, or by a computer kiosk in a mall or store. In a personal interview the researcher asks questions to the consumer directly. These interviews are often conducted in malls and downtown areas where there are lots of people. With telephone contacts the concept is described or the copy is read and the consumer is asked several questions about the ad via a phone call. Mail contacts are similar, but in this method the test ad is mailed to the consumer along with a set of questions, which the consumer is expected to return promptly. Contacts through the Internet require access to the consumers via e-mail or instructions on how to click through to a research site to view a test ad.

THE INSIDE STORY

The Power of Design Personas

By Harley Manning, *Research Director, Customer Experience, Forrester Research, Cambridge, MA*

In 1999, software inventor Alan Cooper introduced the concept of *personas* in his book, *The Inmates Are Running the Asylum*. Forrester first referenced this idea in a 2001 report on design methodologies. We quickly realized that the concept had captured the imaginations of both designers and their clients. In 2003 we began research for a report focused on best practices for creating and using personas.

What is a persona? It's a model of a customer's goals, needs, attitudes, and behaviors distilled from interviewing and observing real people in a market segment. The result guides designers and their clients by replacing dry data about "the customer" with a vivid profile of a person.

Well-crafted personas are crisp, accurate, and sound like a description of someone you know. As a result, they're easy to both understand and relate to. For example, "Stanley" is a persona used by J. P. Morgan to model its active, savvy investors who won't be satisfied by a simple account summary and instead want advanced portfolio details, such as net liquidating value. Software giant SAP created three personas to inform the design of its call center software, including "Tina Ferraro-Smith," a telesales agent with personal goals, such as putting clients first and going home in a decent mood.

We began our research by contacting a variety of agencies to find out which ones used personas. We followed up with hour-long interviews of creative directors, researchers, and account managers at firms ranging from interactive specialists R/GA to diversified agency ZIBA Design, which creates everything from marketing strategies to physical environments (FedEx Retail Service Centers). We also interviewed the agencies' clients—such as American Express, Ford, Reuters, and Travelocity—to determine why they bought into personas, how they used them, and what results they achieved.

We found that personas are getting very popular, very quickly. Although they started out as a tool for software designers, they're now being used to create marketing campaigns, inform sales training, and play roles in Web sites and call center scripts. We also found that companies that use them correctly report compelling results. This led us to conclude that personas are here to stay and will be increasingly important for all types of design efforts.

A graduate of the University of Illinois, Harley Manning was nominated by the late Kim Rotzell, former dean of the College of Communication.

Evaluation criteria		
Based on direct study of users		**Score**
1. Is the persona based on primary research with target users?		
-2	Based solely on surveys, customer profiles, anecdotal evidence	
-1	Based on interviews of stakeholders with direct user contact (sales reps, service reps)	
1	Based on interviews of target users	
2	Based on interviews and observation of users at the location where they use the product	
2. Can all key elements of the persona be traced back to user research?		
-2	Most elements of the persona can't be traced back to research about the target users	
-1	At least one important element can't be traced back to research about the target users	
1	Every element of the persona can be traced back to research about the target users	
2	As above, plus an interactive version of the persona links to underlying data	
Presented as a real story about a real person		
3. Is the persona formatted as a narrative?		
-2	Formatted as a data set (charts, graphs, tables)	
-1	Formatted as a presentation (bullet points)	
1	Formatted as a narrative (written in paragraphs with illustrative stories woven in)	
2	As above, plus accompanied by a realistic name, photo, age, and quote or vignette	
4. Do stakeholders with direct customer contact recognize the persona?		
-2	Sales and service reps don't recognize the persona as one of their customers.	
-1	Sales and service reps recognize the persona but disagree with one or more of its goals.	
1	Sales and service reps recognize the persona and agree with its goals after additional explanation and discussion.	
2	Sales and service reps immediately recognize the persona and agree with his/her goals.	
Focused on enabling design decisions		
5. Is the persona significantly different from other persona?		
-2	All major goals or behaviors overlap with two or more personas.	
-1	All major goals or behaviors overlap with one other persona.	
1	At least one major, product-related goal or behavior is different from that of all other personas.	
2	The persona represents a unique cluster of needs, goals, and behavior.	
6. Is the persona focused on the current project?		
-2	Does not include relevant user needs, goals, and behavior.	
-1	Focused on demographics and psychographics of the user. Includes some needs, goals, and behavior.	
1	Focused on user needs, goals, and behavior that are relevant to the current project.	
2	As above, plus zeroes in on three to four key goals.	
	Total score	

Scoring per question:		Overall score:	
-2	Little or no value for designers	-12 to -7	Not a persona – start over
-1	Does not qualify as a persona	-6 to 0	Seriously flawed – seek help
1	Qualifies as a persona	1 to 6	Promising, needs improvement
2	Best practice	7 to 12	True persona

FIGURE 6.4

Forrester Personas Coding Sheet

The above is an example of the coding sheet used by Forrester Research to evaluate the strength of the personas they uncover for various types of consumers.

Survey research can be conducted over the phone or in public places such as a supermarket aisle.

In-depth interviews are conducted one-on-one with open-ended questions that permit the interviewee to give thoughtful responses. The informal structure of the questions allows the interviewer to follow up and to ask more detailed questions to dig deeper into attitudes and motivations.

Concurrently, consumers are sent a set of questions about the ad, which they can return electronically. Consumers can also be contacted in malls where they are invited to participate in experimental research projects.

Survey Research   In a survey, questionnaires are used to obtain information about people's attitudes, knowledge, media use, and exposure to particular messages. **Survey research** is a quantitative method that uses structured interviews to ask large numbers of people the same set of questions. The questions can deal with personal characteristics, such as age, income, behavior, or attitudes. The surveys can be conducted in person, by phone, by mail, or online. There are two big questions to consider: how to build a representative sample of people to be interviewed and what method is best to collect the data.

*   ***Sampling.*** The people interviewed can be from an entire group, or **population,** or they can be a representative **sample** of a much larger group, a subset of the population that is representative of the entire population.[8] For survey research to be an accurate reflection of the population of interest, those who participate must be selected at random, where every person who belongs to the population that is being surveyed has an equal likelihood (probability) of being chosen to participate. For a classic example of how nonrandom sampling can create inaccurate results, consider the *Literary Digest* presidential election polling of Landon versus Roosevelt in 1936, which produced the incorrect results of the presidential election, even though it had a sample size of more than 2 million households.

*   ***Collecting data.*** Since survey research first began, the way researchers have gone about collecting data from respondents has seen almost constant change. In the early to mid-1900s, when penetration rates of telephones in American households were relatively low, researchers needed to select and survey respondents at their homes, using door-to-door interviewers.

    As access to telephones increased, calling soon became the survey mode of choice, as it was much less expensive and far less invasive than sending interviewers out to people's homes. All phone numbers were listed in telephone directories, giving researchers the perfect source from which they could draw a random sample. Mail surveys also became popular during this time, as household addresses were readily available and were even less expensive than telephone survey work.

Principle
Careful scientific procedures are used to draw a representative sample of a group in order to accurately reflect the population's behavior and attitudes.

A MATTER OF PRACTICE

Online Survey Research

By Karl Weiss, *President/CEO Market Perceptions Inc., Denver CO*

Instead of door-to-door visits to people's homes, today's data collection method of choice is rapidly becoming the Internet. It allows researchers to gather data quickly and relatively inexpensively, meeting two of the key criteria that they are expected by clients to satisfy.

However, Internet research has its drawbacks, the greatest of which is that, unlike phone books that used to contain everyone's phone number from which a random sample could be drawn, there is no listing of all e-mail addresses for selecting participants for a survey. Instead, online research tends to rely largely on panels of participants—people who have agreed, or opted in, to participate in online surveys, almost always for a financial incentive. Having to rely on opt-in research panels poses the most serious stumbling block to the validity of all online research; because there is no way to know that those people who chose to join a panel are representative of the client's population of interest.

A current solution for improving the representative validity of the data is to **weight** it, meaning the numbers are adjusted to reflect some known demographic characteristic. For example, if you know your population of interest is 60 percent female and 40 percent male, and your survey data comes back 30 percent female and 70 percent male, the data can be statistically "weighted" to reflect the correct male-female ratio. Similarly, it can also be weighted by age, ethnic background, income, and any other characteristics where the researcher knows the true population characteristics.

But this strategy has one very difficult limitation. We cannot assume that two people have anything else in common just because they share a demographic characteristic. That is, we still don't know whether the 30-year-old female who earns $65,000 a year and is willing to complete an online survey has anything in common with the 30-year-old female who also earns $65,000 a year and does not participate in online surveys. We can account for demographics, but we cannot account for potential differences in attitudes and behaviors within the demographic segments; in other words, we cannot account for differences between those who do and do not participate.

While the greatest challenge to successful online research is the quality of the sample, its greatest strength is its flexibility. The online environment allows research participants to complete the survey when and where they want, be it during the day at their work or in the evening at their home. Clearly this is in sharp contrast to the flexibility of a telephone interviewer calling someone at home at 6:30 in the evening. Online research also allows participants to complete the survey in a more anonymous fashion—providing answers through their computer rather than telling an interviewer in person. This is especially important when the subject matter is of a highly personal or sensitive nature.

Furthermore, the online environment allows the researcher to create a true experience for participants by incorporating images, sound, and video to obtain participants' reactions to many different types of stimuli that were not possible with telephone or mail surveys. Researchers can now test print and television advertising and Web site content and even monitor Web browsing behavior, all through online research.

In evaluating online research, the main things to look for are:

- **Panel quality.** How does the research firm obtain participants? What kind of screening process is used to ensure the profiles are accurate and real? Are participants adequately paid to ensure they will provide quality feedback? How often are they allowed to participate in surveys? (If allowed to participate more than every six months, they may be "professional respondents" who participate in survey research as a side income.)
- **Online survey experience.** How does it feel to take a survey using the software? Is it interesting or monotonous? If it is monotonous for you, it probably will be for others as well. When surveys are boring, participants simply try to get through them quickly, often without even reading the questions. An interesting, even entertaining survey environment will help ensure you have participants' attention.
- **Validation.** What does the research firm do to validate the results? Does it call any of the respondents back by phone, after they've completed the online survey, and re-ask some of the questions to see if interviewers get the same answers? Can the firm provide the length of time each respondent spent to complete the entire survey, and even the length of time spent on each page to identify "cheaters," those who just checked off the answers as quickly as possible without reading the questions?
- **Monitoring.** Are you allowed to monitor surveys so you can see the time participants spend answering each question?

Online research has great potential and many advantages over phone and mail surveys, including cost, rapid turnaround, and the ability to present participants with a multimedia experience as part of the survey process. At the same time, researchers are faced with many challenges to ensure that the results of online research are valid, from making sure that the online panel participant who says she is a 34-year-old engineer isn't in reality a 57-year-old unemployed steel mill worker to knowing whether participants actually read the ques-

tions before selecting an answer. As we learn to better monitor, validate, and design online surveys, these challenges will be reduced, but until then, these are major concerns about which users of online research must be cognizant.

Today, the world of data collection is changing again. Landline telephones are on the decline as cell phones become more popular. Unlisted phone numbers are becoming more common. Mail surveys have become largely ineffective, with response rates often in the 1–3 percent range, which fails to meet the criteria necessary for valid random sampling. Researchers have been forced by these changes to find new ways to collect data from respondents. The Internet has opened up new opportunities for collecting data (see the Matter of Practice article), even though some traditionalists in the advertising research community question its "representativeness." Others consider this point erroneous, as they believe consumers recruited online can be organized to be just as representative, if not more so, than traditional mail or phone surveys.[9]

In-depth Interviews   A more qualitative method to ask questions of consumers is the **in-depth interview,** which is conducted one-on-one using **open-ended questions** that require the respondents to generate their own answers. This is the type of research method used by the Lexus "super-affluent team" we discussed earlier. The primary difference between an interview and a survey is the interviewer's use of a more flexible and unstructured questionnaire.[10] Interviews use a discussion guide, which outlines the areas to be covered during the session. These guides tend to be longer than surveys with questions that are usually very broad. Examples include: "What do you like or dislike about this product?" and "What type of television programs do you like to watch?" Interviewers probe by responding to the answer with "Why do you say that?" or "Can you explain in more detail?" Interviews are considered qualitative because they typically use smaller sample sizes than surveys and their results cannot be generalized and are subjected to statistical tests.

Focus Groups   Another qualitative method is a **focus group,** which is a group of 8 to 10 users (or even up to 15 potential users) of a product who are gathered around a table to have a discussion about some topic, such as the brand, product category, or advertising. The objective is to get participants talking in a conversational format so researchers can observe the dialogue and interactions among the group. It's a directed group interview.[11] A moderator supervises the group, providing direction through a set of carefully developed questions that stimulate conversation and elicit the group members' thoughts and feelings in their own words. Other qualitative tools can also be used with groups such as asking participants to create posters, diaries, or poems or complete exercises in day mapping or memory associations (what comes to mind when you think of something, such as a brand, situation, or location).

Focus groups can be used at any step in the planning process, but they are often used early in information gathering to probe for patterns of thought and behavior that are then tested using quantitative research tools, such as surveys. They are also useful in testing advertising ideas or exploring various alternatives in message strategy development. For example, when Kellogg Co. wanted to test the idea of "Corn Flakes as a high-fiber alternative," it conducted nearly a hundred focus groups of people from 40 to 55 years old throughout the United States.

An **expert panel** gathers experts from various fields into a focus group setting. This research tool can stimulate new ways of looking at a brand, product, or customer pattern. A **friendship focus group**[12] takes place in a comfortable setting, usually a private home, where the participants have been recruited by the host. This approach is designed to break down barriers and save time in getting to more in-depth responses. For example, one study of sensitive and insensitive visuals used in advertising directed to black women found that a self-constructed friendship group was easier to assemble and yielded more honest and candid responses than a more traditional focus group where respondents are recruited by a research company.[13]

Focus groups are conducted around a conference table with a researcher as the moderator working from a list of prepared discussion questions. The session is usually held in a room with one-way glass so the other team members from the agency and client can observe the way respondents answer the questions.

The Web is not only a tool for online surveys, but also for online focus groups based on the idea of getting a group of brand loyalists together as a password-protected online community. It started with the Hallmark Idea Exchange, which was launched to explore consumer feelings about humor and sentiment in the post-9/11 world. Online research company Communispace has since created some 225 online communities for marketers, including Kraft Foods, Unilever for its Axe brand, and Charles Schwab.[14]

Observation Research   Like anthropologists, observation researchers study the actual behavior of consumers in settings where they live, work, shop, and play, acting as what Sayre refers to as "professional snoops."[15]

A qualitative form of research, direct **observation research** is closer and more personal than quantitative research. Researchers use video, audio, and disposable cameras to record consumers' behavior at home (with consumer consent), in stores, or wherever people buy and use their products. A marketer may rely on observation in the aisles of grocery, drug, and discount stores to watch people as they make product selections. The observer can watch how people walk the aisle, where they stop, how much effort they make in reading labels, and so forth.

The Consumer Behavior Odyssey was a major observational research project that opened the door for this type of research in marketing. The Odyssey put a team of researchers in a Winnebago on a trip from Los Angeles to Boston. Along the way, the researchers used a variety of observational techniques to watch and record people behaving as consumers.[16]

Ethnographic Research   Related to observation, **ethnographic research** involves the researcher in living the lives of the people being studied. Ethnographers have elevated people watching to a science. In ethnographic research, which combines anthropology and marketing, observers immerse themselves in a culture to study the meanings, language, interaction, and behavior of the people in the group.[17] The idea is that actions speak louder than words and people's behavior tells you more than you can ever get in an interview or focus group. This method is particularly good at deriving a picture of a day in the life of a typical consumer.

Major companies like Harley-Davidson and Coca-Cola now use ethnographic research to get close to their customers. These companies hire marketing professors trained in social science research to observe and interpret customer behavior at rallies and other events. These participant observers then meet with the company's managers, planners, and marketing staff to discuss their impressions.[18]

The case of Eight O'Clock coffee is an example of a videotaped ethnographic study. The brand's agency, New York–based Kaplan Thaler, got 14 families in Pittsburgh and Chicago to use video cameras to record their typical mornings in order to identify the various roles that coffee played in their morning rituals.[19] Today, virtually all major agencies offer their clients the opportunity to conduct ethnographic research. In fact, at Averett, Free & Ginsberg, 9 out of 15 large clients have opted for the service.

Direct observation and ethnographic research have the advantage of revealing what people actually do, as distinguished from what people say they do. It can yield the correct answer when faulty memory, desire to impress the interviewer, or simple inattention to details would cause an interview answer to be wrong. The biggest drawback to direct observation is that it shows what is happening, but not why. Therefore, the results of direct observation often are combined with personal interviews afterward to provide a more complete and more understandable picture of attitudes, motives, and behavior.

Diaries Sometimes consumers are asked to record their activities through the use of diaries. These **diaries** are particularly valuable in media research because they tell media planners exactly what programs and ads the consumers watched. If comment lines are provided, then the activities can also be accompanied by thoughts. Beeper diaries are used as a way to randomize the recording of activities. Consumers participating in the study are instructed to grab the diary and record what they are doing when the beeper goes off. Diaries are designed to catch the consumer in a more realistic, normal life pattern than you can derive from surveys or interviews that rely on consumers to remember accurately their activities. This can also lead to a helpful reconstruction of a typical day in the life of a consumer.

An example comes from Dunkin' Donuts. Regina Lewis, Vice President of Consumer and Brand Insights, explained that she used a young adult diary study to determine when this target audience starts drinking coffee. She recruited 20 people in five cities. From their records, Lewis and her team had hundreds of points of observations. At research centers, the participants were then asked to explain what was going on when they thought about having coffee—what day, what time, why are you thinking about coffee, and so forth. From that research, the team learned that many young adults want "chuggable" coffee, particularly because they want an immediate caffeine hit. As a result, they drink iced coffee because hot coffee is too hot and they can't get their caffeine shot fast enough. Dunkin' responded with "Turbo Ice" coffee with an extra shot of espresso.[20]

Other Qualitative Methods Advertising planners are always probing for reasons, feelings, and motivations behind what people say and do. To arrive at useful consumer insights, they use a variety of interesting and novel research methods. In particular, they use stories and pictures.

Cognitive psychologists have learned that human beings think more in images than in words. Most research continues to use words to ask questions and obtain answers, but recent experiments with visual-based research opens up new avenues of expression that may be better able to uncover people's deep thoughts. Researchers use pictures to uncover mental processes that guide consumer behavior.

Harvard Business School professor Gerald Zaltman believes that the conventional wisdom about consumer research, such as using interviews and focus groups that rely on talking to people and grilling them about their tastes and buying habits, is only good for getting back predictable answers. If you ask people what they think about Coke, you'll learn that it is a "high-energy, thirst-quenching, fun-at-the-beach" kind of drink. But that may not be an adequate description of how people really feel about the soft drink.[21]

Here is a collection of some of the more imaginative ways qualitative researchers are getting insights about people's relationships to the brands they buy.

- ***Fill in the blanks*** is a form of attitude research in which people literally fill in the blanks in a story or balloons in a cartoon. Perceptions can come to the surface in the words participants use to describe the action or situations depicted in the visuals.

Principle
Direct observation and ethnographic research reveal what people actually do, rather than what they say they do, but they also lack the ability to explain why these people do what they do.

L'original

This ad equating Evian sparkling water with a mermaid tries to add a touch of originality to the Evian brand image through a metaphor.

- ***Purpose-driven games*** allow researchers to see how people solve problems and search for information.[22] Games can make the research experience more fun and involving for participants. They also uncover problem-solving strategies that may mirror the participants' approach to information searching or the kinds of problems they deal with in certain product situations.

- ***Theater techniques.*** Games also can be applied in a theater setting where researchers have people use a variety of exercises to understand how people think about their brands, tell stories about products, and convince others to use a brand.

- ***Sculpting and movement techniques.*** Positioning the body as a statue can be a source of insight in brainstorming for creative ideas and new product ideas. Sculpting involves physically putting product users in static positions that reflect how they think about or use a brand. Physical movements, such as dance movements and martial arts, can be added to increase the range of insight.

- ***Story elicitation.*** Consumers are asked to explain the artifacts of their lives, such as the photos displayed in their homes and the objects they treasure. These stories can provide insights into how and why people use or do things.

- ***Artifact creation.*** is a technique that uses such ideas as life collages, day mapping (tracking someone's activities across a day), and the construction of instruction books as ways to elicit stories that discuss brands and their role in daily life. These projects are also useful later in explaining to others—clients, the creative team, or other agencies—the triggers behind consumer insights.[23]

- ***Photo elicitation.*** Similar to artifacts, visuals can be used to elicit consumer thoughts and opinions. Consumers are asked to look at a set of visuals or instructed to visually record something with a camera, such as a shopping trip. Later in reviewing the visuals, they are asked to explain what they were thinking or doing.

- ***Photo sorts.*** In yet another visual technique, consumers are asked to sort through a deck of photos and pick out visuals that represent something to them, such as typical users of the product or situations where it might be used. In identifying typical users, they may be asked to sort the photos into specific piles, such as happy, sad, angry, excited, or innovative people.

- ***Metaphors.*** Some researchers believe that metaphors can enrich the language consumers use to talk about brands. (Remember your grammar: A metaphor compares one thing to another without using the actual words *like* or *as*.) The Evian ad, for example, uses a strong metaphor to define its product. The insight into how people perceive brands through such connections comes from exploring the link between the two concepts. Metaphor games are used in creativity to elicit new and novel ideas, but they can also be used to analyze cognitive patterns in people's thinking.

Harvard professor Zaltman is the creator of ZMET (pronounced ZEE-MET), the Zaltman Metaphor Elicitation Technique, which uses metaphors and visual images to uncover patterns in people's thinking. For a typical session, the respondents bring images that they think relate to the product category or brand being studied. Then they make up stories that describe their feelings about the product or brand.[24] For Coca-Cola in Europe, for example, Zaltman asked volunteers to collect at least a dozen pictures that captured their feelings about Coca-Cola. Then they discussed the images in personal interviews. Finally, the volunteers created a summary image—a digital collage of their most important images and recorded a statement that explained its meaning. The ZMET team found that Coke is not just about feelings of high energy and good times; it also has an element of calm, solitude, and relaxation.[25]

Choosing a Research Method

Determining the appropriate research method to use is an important planning decision. It might help to understand two basic research criteria, validity and reliability, that are derived from what researchers call the "scientific method." **Validity** means that the research actually measures what it says it measures. Any differences that are uncovered by the research, such as different attitudes or purchasing patterns, really reflect differences among individuals, groups, or situations. **Reliability** means that you can run the same test again and get the same answer.

Quantitative researchers, particularly those doing experiments and surveys, are concerned about being faithful to the principles of science. Selecting a sample that truly represents the population, for example, increases the reliability of the research. Poorly worded questions and talking to the wrong people can hurt the validity of surveys, as well as focus groups.

The information you get from surveys of a broad cross section of a population is limited to your ability to develop good clear questions that everyone can understand and answer. This tight control makes it harder to ask questions around the edges of a topic or elicit unexpected or unusual responses. On the other hand, focus groups and in-depth interviews that permit probing are limited by small numbers and possible problems with the representativeness of the sample.

The problem with experiments is twofold: (1) experiments are limited by a small number of people in the experimental group, and (2) they can be conducted under artificial conditions.

In short, the three big objectives of advertising research are: (1) test hypotheses, (2) get information, and (3) get insights. Each method has strengths and weaknesses. Generally, quantitative methods are more useful for gathering data (how many do this or believe that?), and qualitative methods are better at uncovering reasons and motives (why do they do or believe?). For these reasons, most researchers use a variety of research methods—quantitative and qualitative.

RESEARCH TRENDS AND CHALLENGES

Advertising researchers face five key challenges: globalization, new media technology, embedded research, and insightful analysis. Let's examine each challenge briefly.

Globalization

The key issues that global researchers face include how to manage and communicate global brands in widely different localities and how to shift from studying differences to finding similarities around the world. The biggest problem is cross-cultural communication and how to arrive at an intended message without cultural distortions or insensitivities. Researchers are becoming more involved in puzzling out cultural meanings and testing advertising messages for cultural sensitivity in different countries. Legal differences can also affect how research is conducted so global advertisers need an in-depth understanding of government regulations and media availability in various countries used in a campaign.

Media Changes

Changes in media technology can alter the meaning and consequences of almost all of our most familiar research constructs: involvement, brand equity, attitude toward the ad, emotional processing, and cognitive processing, to name a few. Advertising research in the past focused largely on full-page print ads, 30-second television commercials, and more recently, Web sites. As technology changes in the media unfold, the old research measures may become less and less valid.

Because of media fragmentation, researchers and planners develop message strategies that enable media planners to reach consumers most effectively. That includes using multiple product messages in multiple media vehicles to deliver different message effects—Internet for interactivity, print for details, direct mail for personalization, and TV for creating an emotional connection. New media technologies are also opening the door to new ways to conduct permission and relationship marketing.

Embedded Research

In **embedded research,** the research methods are a part of a real purchase and use situation, so that the consumer is a recipient and direct beneficiary of and participant in the information gathering. *Call centers*, both inbound (customer calls to complain or get assistance) and outbound (telemarketing), can also be used as research centers to gain real-time feedback about the brand and its marketing and advertising strategies. In other words, whenever a call is made, for whatever purpose, that contact provides an opportunity to ask a brand-related question.

A non-Internet example of embedded research comes from Nordstrom's Personal Touch Program, which uses a team of *personal shoppers* who are fashion consultants on one level but on another level are trained to gather information from their clients to feed back into the company's business planning and marketing.

The most common Internet approach is to use this medium for product reviews, where customers who want to know more about a product enter the Web site and select from an array of product categories. The opinions of reviewers can be accessed with a click. You see this on the Amazon.com site where reviews of books and music are posted on the page with the product information. Reviews come from other customers, who report their own experience, although some of these reviews may be "planted" by the publisher or author.

Insightful Analysis

Marketers are inundated with information, so getting information is less of a problem than making sense of it. The challenge is not information but rather intelligence. Information overload is a fact in marketing and advertising, and it complicates planning. In analysis, data from one source can take on new meaning when compared with data from other sources. For example, sometimes the research looks at the awareness levels of a campaign

Call center phone feedback is an ongoing research tool used to capture immediate, real-time consumer responses.

theme and concludes that the advertising is working. But when that data is compared with relevance scores, a gap may be seen between what is promised and what the target audience perceives the meaning to be.

The magic in research, then, lies in the interpretation of the findings to uncover unexpected or unrealized insights into consumers, products, and the marketplace situation. That's the gift of people called *account planners,* who we will discuss in the next chapter.

Singing in the Shower

IT'S A WRAP

Research is a key to effective advertising. As you've seen in this Holiday Inn Express case and throughout this chapter, research can and should happen at various points in the campaign. To be effective, you need to know about the product, the target audience, and the competition. You need to know how to reach the target audience with an appropriate message delivered in relevant media. Research can help you figure that out. The final opportunity for research involves evaluating the effectiveness of the campaign by testing whether or not the campaign achieved its objectives.

Not surprisingly, the Holiday Inn Express Showerhead campaign won a Gold Effie in the Travel/Tourism/Destination category and was a 2006 Grand Effie Finalist.

Proof of the campaign's effectiveness is evaluated by looking at the two objectives established before the campaign ran. Follow-up studies showed that the brand image statement "have showers with good water pressure" improved significantly in the minds of the target audience. The second objective, to increase occupancy, was also achieved: Nine months after the campaign launch, occupancy rose a record-breaking 75 percent, up 1.5 points from the previous year. As a bonus, consumer demand resulted in the sale of more than 4,500 showerheads that guests bought for their personal homes. Of course, these serve as a continual reminder of the Holiday Inn Express experience.

Key Points Summary

1. **What are the types of strategic research and how are they used?** Secondary research is background research that gathers already published information, and primary research is original research findings collected for the first time from original sources. Quantitative research is statistical and uses numerical data to investigate how people think and behave; qualitative research is exploratory and uses probing techniques to gain insights and identify questions and hypotheses for further quantitative research. Experimental research tests hypotheses using carefully designed experiments.

Research is used to (1) develop an analysis of the marketing situation; (2) acquire consumer information and insights for making targeting decisions; (3) identify information about available media to match the media to the target audience; and (4) develop message strategies and evaluate their effectiveness.

2. **What are the most common research methods used in advertising?** Survey research is used to amass quantities of responses from consumers about their attitudes and behaviors. In-depth interviews probe the reasons and motivations consumers give to explain their attitudes

and behavior. Focus groups are group interviews that operate like a conversation directed by a researcher. Observation is research that happens in the store or home where researchers watch how consumers behave. Ethnographic research is an anthropological technique that involves the researcher in participating in the day-to-day lives of consumers. Diaries are records of consumers' behavior, particularly their media use. A number of other qualitative methods are used to creatively uncover patterns in the way consumers think and act.

3. **What are the key challenges facing advertising researchers?** Globalization complicates the way research is conducted for global products because it adds a cultural dimension and varied legal restrictions. Media fragmentation and convergence complicate the process of determining media effects. New research techniques are being created as a result of new media technology as well as the Internet, which offers opportunities for virtual interviews. Embedded research is a way to get immediate feedback that comes from the process of buying or using the product. Beyond the accumulation of numbers and information, the search for insight is a driving force in advertising research.

Key Terms

advertising research, p. 165
aided recognition, p. 174
concept testing, p. 173
consumer insight research, p. 172
consumer research, p. 165
content analysis, p. 174
copy testing, p. 173
diaries, p. 181
embedded research, p. 184

ethnographic research, p. 180
experimental research, p. 170
expert panels, p. 179
focus groups, p. 179
friendship focus groups, p. 179
in-depth interviews, p. 179
market research, p. 165
marketing research, p. 172
media research, p. 173

message development research, p. 173
network of associations, p. 175
observation research, p. 180
open-ended questions, p. 179
population, p. 177
pretesting, p. 173
primary research, p. 167
qualitative research, p. 168

quantitative research, p. 168
reliability, p. 183
sample, p. 177
secondary research, p. 165
semiotic analysis, p. 174
strategic research, p. 165
survey research, p. 177
unaided recognition, p. 174
validity, p. 183

Review Questions

1. Explain the difference between primary and secondary research and between quantitative and qualitative research.

2. What are the four uses of research in advertising? Give an example of each one.

3. How many different ways are there to contact people to gain information for use in advertising planning?

4. What is survey research and how is it conducted? How do in-depth interviews differ from surveys?

5. Explain when to use the following research methods: focus group, in-depth interviews, observational research, ethnographic research, and diaries.

6. Explain the difference between validity and reliability and explain how these concepts affect advertising research.

Discussion Questions

1. Suppose you are developing a research program for a new bookstore serving your college or university. What kind of exploratory research would you recommend? Would you propose both qualitative and quantitative studies? Why or why not? What specific steps would you take?

2. The research director for Angelis Advertising always introduces her department's service to new agency clients by comparing research to a road map. What do maps and research have in common? How does the analogy of a map reveal the limitations of research for resolving an advertising problem?

3. Sean McDonnell is the creative director for Chatham-Boothe, an advertising agency that has just signed a contract with Trans-Central Airlines (TCA). TCA has a solid portfolio of consumer research and has offered to let the agency use it. McDonnell needs to decide whether

demographic, psychographic, or attitude/motive studies are best for developing a creative profile of the TCA target audience. If the choice were yours, on which body of research would you base a creative strategy? Explore the strengths and weaknesses of each.

4. A new radio station is moving into your community. Management is not sure how to position the station in this market and has asked you to develop a study to help make this decision.

   a. What key research questions must be asked?

   b. Outline a research program to answer those questions that uses as many of the research methods discussed in this chapter as you can incorporate.

5. *Three-Minute Debate*: You have been hired to develop and conduct a research study for a new upscale restaurant chain coming into your community. Your client wants to know how people in the community see the competition and what

they think of the restaurant's offerings. It uses an unusual concept that focuses on fowl—duck, squab, pheasant, and other elegant meals in the poultry category. A specialty category, this would be somewhat like a seafood restaurant. One of your colleagues says the best way to do this study is with a carefully designed survey and a representative sample. Another colleague says, no, what the client really needs is insight into the market; she believes the best way to help the client with its advertising strategy is to use qualitative research.

In class, organize into any number of small teams with pairs of teams taking one side or the other. Set up a series of three-minute debates with each side having 1½ minutes to argue its position. Every team of debaters must present new points not covered in the previous teams' presentations until there are no arguments left to present. Then the class votes as a group on the winning point of view.

Take-Home Team Projects

1. Your team has been asked to run a focus group to determine consumer attitudes relevant to the launch of the upscale poultry restaurant described in the Three-Minute Debate. Meet to decide on questions and format. Make assignments for note taking, facilitating, and collecting and organizing feedback. Then collect a group of 5–8 friends to be in the focus group. Conduct the focus group to determine what your participants think about the idea. Write a one- to two-page report on both the process and the group's findings.

2. Assume you are working for Gerber Baby Foods. Your assignment is to identify the relevant trends that are forecasted for U.S. birth rates between 2008 and 2012. Identify Internet sources that would provide that information. Gather as much information as you can from these sites and write a one-page report on the trends you find.

Yahoo! Hands-On Case

Review the Yahoo! case in the Appendix.

1. How was research used by the Yahoo! team? What other types of research would you recommend the team consider?

2. You have been asked to develop an online survey for year 2 of this campaign. Create a draft of a one-page survey that

might be used to track the primary target's perception of Yahoo! What would you recommend doing to increase the participation level of your target audience in this research effort?

HANDS-ON CASE

What Lies Beneath? Making a Choice

"If you have a 'buy button' in your brain," the *New York Times* headline asked, "what pushes it?" The *Times* article summarized a recent study in which neurologists monitored the brain activity of participants as they sampled unmarked cups of Coke and Pepsi over several trials and indicated their preference. The scientists observed that participant brain activity was confined to "reward centers" associated with reactions to the pleasurable taste of the beverages. The scientists also observed that the participant preferences were evenly split between Coke and Pepsi.

Then the scientists changed the procedure a bit by clearly marking the samples as Coke or Pepsi. Different regions of the participants' brains were now activated and "overrode" the reward center responses that the researchers had observed earlier. This new pattern of activity seemed to change the participants' sensory experience of the samples, because at the end of the second wave of trials, respondents showed a decided preference for Coke, choosing it 75 percent of the time.

These results are viewed with great interest by scientists and advertisers alike, because they are a clear testament to the power of brands. "At issue," wrote the *Times* reporter, "is whether marketers can exploit advances in brain science to make more effective commercials."

Advertisers have long been fascinated with technologies that promise richer and deeper insights into how people think and feel than do focus groups and surveys, which may fail to capture key aspects of how consumers choose. These traditional methods may fall short not because consumers *won't* tell marketers what they think, but rather because they *can't*.

This intriguing claim is offered by Harvard Business School Professor Gerald Zaltman, who believes that most thinking occurs below our level of consciousness. In Zaltman's view, what we understand as conscious thought represents only about 5 percent of all cognitive processes. The other 95 percent, which is a more important influence on consumer decision making, occurs outside our awareness. In Zaltman's view, "the unconscious mind represents a significant frontier where marketers may establish secure beachheads of competitive advantage. Certainly no firm can claim to understand consumers without colonizing this land of opportunity."

But tapping into the subconscious is not easy. Zaltman believes marketers should consider abandoning traditional research techniques for new methods, including the technologies for measuring brain activity described earlier, along with less-expensive approaches such as metaphor elicitation and response latency techniques.

In metaphor elicitation, such as Zaltman's ZMET technique, consumers are asked to bring a photograph or other symbol of a concept (such as the perfect home) to an in-depth interview. The interviewer's role is to try, in a nondirective way, to help the consumer explore and articulate the meaning of the picture.

In response latency approaches, mental relationships and links are explored by measuring the relative speed of word recognition. Cognitive psychology has demonstrated that people recognize a word faster when the word follows a related concept or idea (for instance, people recognize the term *cream cheese* faster when it appears after *bagel* than when it appears after *Kansas*). Advertising researchers can use this phenomenon to determine whether a brand name or symbol speeds recognition of attributes believed to be associated with the brand. For instance, they might test whether showing people *Honda,* speeds up recognition of the word *reliable.*

Consider This

1. A great deal of current research assumes that people can consciously describe why they do things and what they intend to do in the future. Do you think Zaltman is correct in criticizing this assumption?

2. The *New York Times* article cited in this case also presented views from a strong critic of this kind of research. The critic believes that it is dangerous for companies to learn how to affect consumer subconscious thinking because future campaigns could then be used to affect consumers without their recognition. For the critic, this is a violation of the consumers' free will. What do you think? What limits, if any, should there be on campaigns developed from this new knowledge?

3. How do research methods, such as the "brain science" methods discussed here, help advertising planners gain insights into consumer attitudes and behavior? How would you determine if the research helped create more effective advertising?

Sources: Sandra Blakeslee, "If You Have a 'Buy Button' in Your Brain, What Pushes It?" *New York Times,* October 19, 2004; Gerald Zaltman, *How Customers Think: Essential Insights into the Mind of the Market* (Cambridge, MA: Harvard Business School Press, 2004).

Strategic Planning

IT'S A WINNER

Award:	Company:	Agency:	Campaign:
Gold Effie for Corporate Reputation, Image and Identity; London International Award Winner	*Kodak*	*Ogilvy & Mather*	*The Gallery Campaign*

Repositioning Kodak for the Digital Age

Nothing lasts forever. Not even a Kodak moment—at least not in the film form.

Kodak, the company that could justifiably claim it defined the film category for more than a century, faced an uncertain future in the late 1990s and early this century. Even the success of its classic advertising campaign that cemented the phrase "Kodak moment" into the cultural lexicon couldn't save the company from becoming a dinosaur. After all, who cares about a company whose specialty is making film when the rest of the world is going digital?

Competitors Hewlett-Packard, Sony, Canon, and even cell phones and computers were emerging to challenge Kodak. Digital talk about pixels made Kodak, with its warmhearted appeal urging consumers to capture cherished scenes of weddings, birthdays, family vacations, kids, and cute pets on film, seem old-fashioned. Analyzing the situation, Kodak recognized that it needed to change its brand positioning from a company that made excellent film to one that could compete in the digital world.

While the challenge of helping products succeed in such a changing marketplace might seem daunting, it also presents an exciting opportunity. Helping a client identify what its brand means and communicate that meaning—especially in a changing marketing environment—is part of the function of advertising. To do it well is a great reward.

Chris Wall, senior partner and co-creative director at Ogilvy New York, explained how his agency saw Kodak's precarious situation: "Ironically, Kodak actually invented much of the technology of digital photography. Nearly all digital cameras take advantage of Kodak patents and innovations. It was painful for Kodak because they received no credit for inventing the products that now appeared to be making them obsolete."

Chapter Key Points

1. What is the difference between objectives, strategies, and tactics in strategic planning?
2. How is a campaign plan constructed, and what are its six basic sections?
3. What is account planning and how is it used in advertising?
4. In what ways does an IMC plan differ from an advertising plan?

The natural tendency might be to abandon advertising that has worked in the past in the face of a very different predicament, but that would also mean discarding the equity of the message Kodak had created. Wall warned against such a move, stating, "Brands have enduring power not because of tricks and gimmicks in execution—no matter how good—but because they tap into a human truth. There can be all kinds of reasons why brands fall on hard times, but generally, human truth is still human truth." Wall observed that the "Kodak moment" captured such a truth, one that should endure in spite of technological changes.

Key points from Kodak's situation analysis guided the agency as it created the campaign's strategy:

- Kodak needed to be more direct in adopting a digital point of view.
- Kodak needed to make a big statement.
- Consumers' attitudes toward pictures would probably stay the same. Although people liked the concept of deleting pictures they didn't want—one of the benefits of digital technology—they would realize eventually that what's really important are the pictures they keep, no matter what the technology.

From these observations, Ogilvy's creative team came up with the big idea: Present Kodak as a gallery, a place where all pictures can be kept. As Wall says, the idea was magical yet practical, digital yet emotional.

In this case, the agency solved Kodak's problem by building on, rather than abandoning, the values that Kodak as a brand represented throughout its proud history. It's still about the importance of pictures. The multimedia campaign transformed the brand into contemporary language in the context of current technology.

You can read about the effectiveness of this campaign in It's a Wrap at the end of this chapter.

Sources: Chris Wall, *Communication Arts* August Photography Annual, 2006, http://www.commarts.com/ca/colad/chrW_318.html. Emily Raymond, "Kodak Grabs Top Share in U.S. Market" http://www.digitalcamerainfo.com/content/Kodak-Grabs-Top-Share-in-US-Market.htm. Effie Awards Brief of Effectiveness—Kodak: Brand Transformation, www.nyama.org

Marketing and advertising strategies are chosen from an array of possible alternatives. In most cases, there is no one completely right way to do anything in advertising, but if you understand how advertising works, you may be able to identify the best strategy to accomplish the objectives. This chapter explains the concept of strategic planning as it is used in business, marketing, and advertising/IMC plans. It covers key planning decisions, such as identifying critical problems and opportunities, targeting the right audience, positioning or repositioning the brand against the competition, and making implementation decisions. It will also introduce the concept of account planning and explain its critical role in determining the consumer insights that lead to message and media strategies.

STRATEGIC PLANNING

For marketing communication, **strategic planning** is the process of identifying a problem that can be solved with marketing communication, then determining **objectives** (what you want to accomplish), deciding on **strategies** (how to accomplish the objectives), and implementing the **tactics** (actions that make the plan come to life). This process occurs within a specified time frame.

Even those experienced in advertising sometimes have a hard time telling the difference between an objective and a strategy. Remember, an *objective* is a goal to be accomplished; in advertising, objectives are determined by the effects you want to achieve, as explained in Chapter 4. A *strategy* is the means, the design or plan by which the objective is accomplished—the advertising message and media strategies, for example. In advertising, *tactics* are the way the ads and other marketing communication efforts are executed—how they are designed and what they say.

In the Kodak case, the objective was to reposition the brand from film to photos. The strategy was to focus on Kodak as a gallery, a place and system by which people could keep their favorite photos. The tactic included establishment of an online EasyShare gallery tied in to the brand's new EasyShare digital camera line, printers, accessories, software, and in-store kiosks, ultimately creating a whole EasyShare system.

To sort out the difference between objectives, strategies, and tactics, consider a hypothetical situation: If a marketer's objective is to reinforce brand loyalty for its product, its planners could use any number of strategies. They could set up a frequent buyer club. They could use direct marketing to reach customers individually. They could use advertising to remind customers to repurchase the brand, or they could use sales promotion to encourage buyers to repurchase. A different set of tactics would be needed to implement each strategy. Before we develop the idea of advertising planning, let's review the basics of business and marketing planning, which are also concerned with objectives, strategies, and tactics.

The Business Plan

Strategic planning is a three-tiered process that starts with the business plan and then moves to functional areas of the company such as marketing where a marketing plan is developed that outlines objectives, strategies, and tactics for all areas of the marketing mix. As illustrated in Figure 7.1, both the business plan and the marketing plan provide

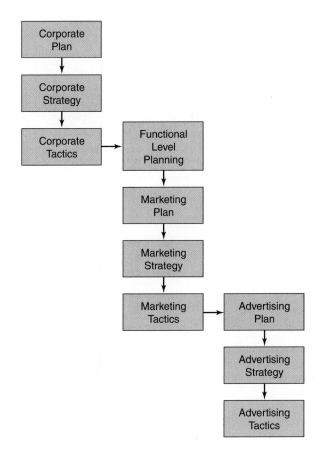

FIGURE 7.1
Strategic Planning from Top to Bottom

Kodak successfully repositioned its brand from film to photos by creating an EasyShare system that includes an EasyShare gallery, digital camera line, printers, accessories, software, and in-store kiosks, all of which make sharing photos easier for the consumer.

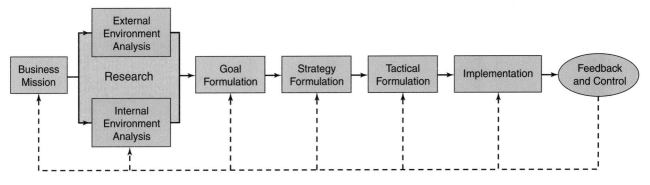

FIGURE 7.2
Steps in the Development of a Business Plan

direction to specific plans for specialist areas, such as advertising and other areas of marketing communication.

A business plan may cover a specific division of the company or a **strategic business unit (SBU)**, which is a line of products or all the offerings under a single brand name. These divisions, or SBUs, share a common set of problems and factors. Figure 7.2 depicts a widely used framework for the strategic planning process in business. The objectives for planning at this level tend to focus on maximizing profit and **return on investment (ROI)**. ROI is a measurement that shows whether, in general, the costs of conducting the business—the investment—are more than matched by the revenue produced in return. The revenue above and beyond the costs is where profit lies.

Note that the business planning process starts with a business **mission statement**, a concise expression of the broad goals and policies of the business unit. The mission statement is unique, focused, and differentiating. Tom's of Maine states its mission clearly on its Web site:

> "Through the years, we have been guided by one simple notion—do what is right, for our customers, employees, communities, and environment. We call this **Natural Care**—a philosophy that guides what we make and all that we do."

The Marketing Plan

A **marketing plan** is developed for a brand or product line and evaluated annually, although sections dealing with long-term goals might operate for a number of years. To a large extent, the marketing plan mirrors the company's business strategic plan and contains many of the same components, although they are focused on a specific brand rather than the larger organization or corporation. Figure 7.3 illustrates the steps involved in creating a marketing plan.

A *market situation analysis* assesses the external and internal environments that affect marketing operations—the company's history, products, and brands, as well as the competitive environment, consumer trends, and other marketplace trends that have some impact on the product category. A set of "what's going on" questions help structure this market analysis.

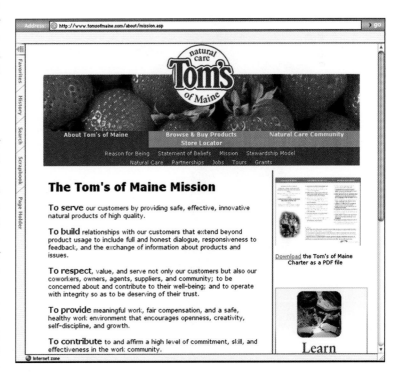

This mission statement for Tom's of Maine helps its managers develop specific business objectives and goals. It also guides all of the company's marketing communication efforts.

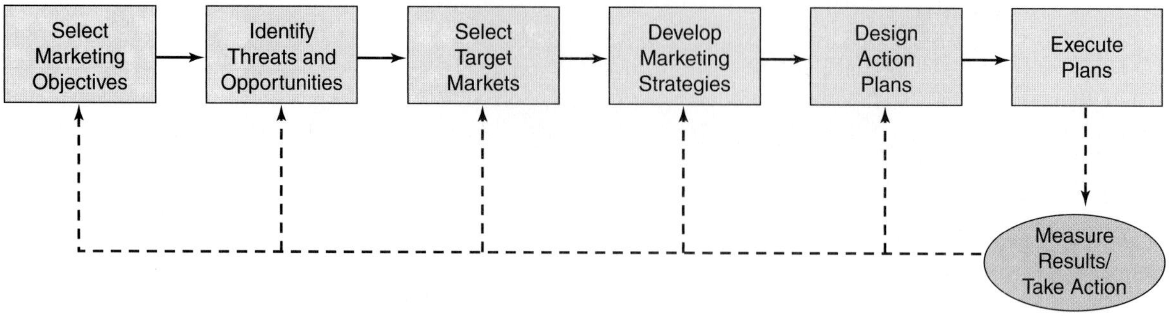

```
┌──────────┐   ┌──────────┐   ┌──────────┐   ┌──────────┐   ┌──────────┐   ┌──────────┐
│  Select  │   │ Identify │   │  Select  │   │ Develop  │   │  Design  │   │ Execute  │
│Marketing │──▶│Threats and│──▶│  Target  │──▶│Marketing │──▶│  Action  │──▶│  Plans   │
│Objectives│   │Opportunities│ │ Markets  │   │Strategies│   │  Plans   │   │          │
└──────────┘   └──────────┘   └──────────┘   └──────────┘   └──────────┘   └──────────┘
```

FIGURE 7.3
Steps in the Development of a Marketing Plan

Answers to these questions help define the marketing problem and, ultimately, the area of message opportunity.

- What is happening with the brand and the category?
- How is it happening?
- Where is it happening?
- When is it happening?
- To whom is it happening?

We could answer those questions for Kodak by summarizing the market situation as a radically different marketplace that was in the process of making Kodak, or at least its film-based consumer business, largely irrelevant.

The objectives at the marketing level tend to be focused on sales levels and **share of market**, measurements referring to the percentage of the category purchases that are made by the brand's customers. Other objectives deal with specific areas of the marketing mix, such as distribution, where an objective might detail how a company will open a new territory.

For advertising managers, the most important part of the marketing plan is the *marketing mix strategy*. This links the overall strategic business plan with specific marketing programs, including advertising and other IMC areas. Whether to use a frequency club, an advertising campaign, or a sales promotion strategy to increase brand loyalty is a marketing communication decision that supports marketing strategies.

I'M COMFORTABLE BEING WRONG SOMETIMES

james j. cramer,
financial guru,
founder of the street.com

be comfortable. uncompromise: start with your feet.

This ad for Rockport shoes is based on the determination that consumers are interested in comfort. This became the focus of the ad and a key product attribute that loyal users appreciate.

The Advertising or IMC Plan

Advertising and marketing communication planning operates with the same concern for objectives, strategies, and tactics that we've outlined for business and marketing plans. The focus, however, is on the communication program supporting a brand. It outlines all the communication activities in terms of the objectives, strategies, tactics, timing, costs, and evaluation.

An example of how all these elements come together in a plan comes from Rockport, a maker of comfortable walking shoes. After doing research on existing customers, the company concluded that Rockport users are actively seeking comfort on every level: physical, emotional, and spiritual. The core Rockport strategy emphasized the need for comfort by challenging the consumer: If you compromise your comfort, you compromise yourself. Rockport's agency invented a rallying cry, "Uncompromise," and launched an integrated marketing communication plan featuring print and TV advertising that used the umbrella theme of "Be comfortable, uncompromise. Start with your feet."

Let's now look at how an advertising or marketing communication plan is developed. The following discussion outlines the basic steps in planning a campaign, as well as the critical strategic decisions planners must make.

A CAMPAIGN PLAN

In addition to or instead of an annual plan, a firm may develop a **campaign plan** that is more tightly focused on solving a particular marketing communication problem in a specified time. Such a plan typically includes a variety of marketing communication (marcom) messages carried in different media and sometimes targeted to different audiences. The following outline traces the steps, and the decisions they represent, in a typical campaign plan.

Typical Campaign Plan Outline

I. Situation Analysis
    • Background research
    • SWOTs: strengths, weaknesses, opportunities, threats
    • Key advertising problem(s) to be solved

II. Key Strategic Campaign Decisions
    • Objectives
    • Target audience (or stakeholder targets in an IMC plan)
    • Brand position: Product features and competitive advantage
    • Campaign strategy: Key strategic approach and marcom tools

III. Media Strategy (or Points of Contact in an IMC Plan)
    • Media objectives
    • Media selection
    • Media planning and buying:
      • Vehicle selection
      • Budget allocation
      • Scheduling

IV. Message Strategy
    • Key consumer insight (brand relationship insight in IMC)
    • Message objectives
    • Selling premise
    • Big idea
    • Message design and executions

V. Other Marcom Tools Used in Support
    • Sales promotion
    • Public relations
    • Direct marketing
    • Personal selling
    • Sponsorships, merchandising, packaging, point-of-purchase
    • Integration strategy (maximize synergy)

VI. Campaign Management
    • Evaluation of effectiveness
    • Campaign budget

The outline is useful as a guide for the planning document, but more importantly, it identifies the key strategic decisions that guide various sections of a campaign plan. They include (1) identifying the key problems and opportunities, (2) stating objectives, (3) targeting the audience, (4) creating or reinforcing a position, (5) identifying the key strategic approach that will deliver the objectives, and (6) using management controls to determine efficiency in budgeting and effectiveness through evaluation. Let's look at these strategic planning decisions in more detail.

Situation Analysis

The first step in developing an advertising plan, just as in a marketing plan, is not planning but *backgrounding*—researching and reviewing the current state of the business that is relevant to the brand and gathering all pertinent information. As discussed in Chapter 6, advertising planning is preceded by market, product/company, and consumer research. After the research is compiled, planners try to make sense of the findings, a process sometimes referred to as a **situation analysis**. Planners collect and analyze information about the company, brand, and competition, along with consumers in general and the brand's customers specifically.

The goal is to identify a problem that can be solved with communication. As Fallon and Senn explained in their "Juicing the Orange" story in the Part II Introduction, you have to start by simplifying the problem. The information collection will probably be huge, but the problem statement should simplify the task.

For example, the DDB agency searches for "Barriers to Purchase,"[1] which are reasons why people do not buy any or enough of a product. These barriers create an opportunity for advertising. The American Dairy Association asked DDB to find out why cheese consumption was declining. A study identified one barrier that was most easily correctable through an advertising message: the absence of simple cheese recipes for home cooks. Ads and the association's Web site (http://www.ilovecheese.com) offer many such recipes.

SWOT Analysis   The primary tool used to make sense of the information gathered and identify a key problem is a **SWOT analysis**, which stands for strengths, weaknesses, opportunities, and threats. The strengths and weaknesses are *internally focused,* and the

The DDB agency found that a barrier to purchasing cheese was the lack of good recipe ideas using cheese products. The American Dairy Association responded by getting more recipes distributed through advertising and its Web site.

opportunities and threats lie in the *external* marketing environment. In strategic planning the idea is to *leverage* the strengths and opportunities and *address* the weaknesses and threats, which is how the key problems and opportunities are identified.[2]

- The *strengths* of a business are its positive traits, conditions, and good situations. For instance, being in a growth industry is a strength. Planners ask how they can leverage this strength in the brand's advertising.
- The *weaknesses* of a business are traits, conditions, and situations that are perceived as negatives. Losing market share is a weakness. If this is an important weakness, then planners ask how they can address it with advertising.
- An *opportunity* is an area in which the company could develop an advantage over its competition. Often, one company's weakness is another company's opportunity. Planners strive to identify these opportunities and leverage them in the brand's advertising.
- A *threat* is a trend or development in the environment that will erode business unless the company takes action. Competition is a common threat. Advertising planners ask themselves how they can address a threat if it is a critical factor affecting the success of the brand.

In the Kodak case, the strength of the brand lies in its ownership of memories recorded photographically as a brand experience labeled a "Kodak Moment." The opportunity existed to transfer the brand identification with all its rich emotion to a new line of digital Kodak products. The threat came from all the competitors that had entered this market with new digital products and from the difficulty in trying to attach the digital position to a company that had been the leader in the film market.

Key Problems and Opportunities   The key word in the title of this section is *analysis,* or making sense of all the data collected and figuring out what the information means for the future success of the brand. Advertising planners must analyze the market situation for communication problems that affect the successful marketing of a product, as well as opportunities the advertising can create or exploit. Analyzing the SWOTs and identifying any problems that can be solved with an advertising message are at the heart of strategic planning. An example of locating a timing opportunity is explained in The Inside Story.

Advertising can solve only message-related problems such as image, attitude, perception, and knowledge or information. It cannot solve problems related to price, availability, or quality, although it can address the perception of these marketing mix factors. For example, a message can speak to the perception that the price is too high, or it can portray a product with limited distribution as exclusive. In other words, advertising can affect the way consumers perceive price, availability, and quality.

Objectives

After planners have examined the external and internal environment and defined the critical areas that need to be addressed, they can develop specific objectives to be accomplished during a specified time period. Remember from Chapter 4 the six categories in the Facets Model of Advertising Effects: perception, emotion, cognition, persuasion, association, and behavior. These main effects also can be used to identify the most common consumer-focused objectives, which are in italics in Figure 7.4.

Although a rule of thumb for advertising is that it should be single-minded, we also know from Chapter 4 that multiple effects are often needed to create the desired impact. Some ads may use an emotional strategy while others are informational, but sometimes the message needs to speak to both the head and the heart. That was particularly true for the Kodak campaign: Customers need to understand the new digital position while still associating the brand with the rich emotions embedded in the "Kodak moment" big idea.

The Logic of Objectives   Given the huge amounts of money spent on advertising, it is important for advertisers to know what to expect from a campaign or ad. The categories of

THE INSIDE STORY

A 2-Week Challenge by Special K
by Amy Hume, *Strategic Media Consultant, Denver CO*

Each year Kellogg's supports its Special K cereal with special marketing efforts during the New Year's resolution season. The idea is to capitalize on consumers' goals to lose weight after the holidays.

A 2-week challenge promises customers will lose up to six pounds in two weeks by replacing two meals a day with Kellogg's Special K and eating a sensible third meal.

As consumers are typically bombarded by TV ads with weight-loss messages around the time of New Year's resolutions, our idea was to reach them in novel targeted locations where they are conscious of their weight and appearance.

The 2-week poster campaign for Special K was specifically designed to reach prospective customers at a moment when they would be most interested in the "lose weight" message. For example, the posters were displayed in locations where women think about their appearance, such as department store dressing rooms, health clubs, doctor's offices, hair or nail salons, and bridal salons. The messages were tailored to each location with such lines as, "The doctor will see (less of you) now."

Reaching consumers at the moment they are in need of a weight-loss solution and delivering a simple diet in the context of their environment was very effective. Business results included an overall increase in the poster markets of 20 percent over nonposter markets.

A graduate of the University of Colorado, Amy Hume was nominated by professor Tom Duncan.

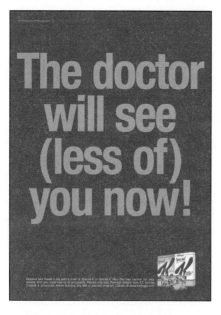

SHOWCASE These Special K posters about weight loss were designed to be posted in locations where people were likely to respond to a message about their weight. These posters were contributed by Amy Hume, a graduate of the University of Colorado.

main effects also can be used as a template for setting advertising objectives, as Table 7.1 shows. Objectives are formal statements of the goals of the advertising or other marketing communication. They outline what the message is designed to achieve and how it will be measured. Note that some objectives are tightly focused on one particular effect, but others, such as brand loyalty, call for a more complex set of effects. To create brand loyalty, for example, an advertising campaign must have both cognitive (rational) and affective (emotional) effects, and it must move people to repeat buying. That's one reason brand loyalty is considered a type of long-term impact developed over time from many experiences that a consumer has with a brand and brand messages.

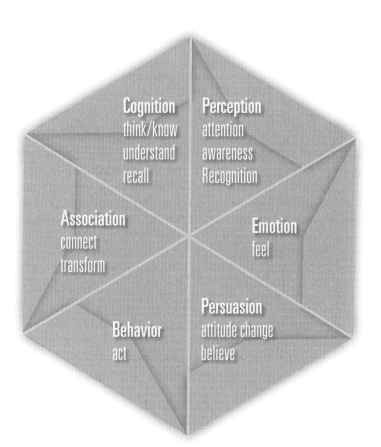

FIGURE 7.4
Effects-Based Advertising
Objectives

Table 7.1 Analyzing Advertising Objectives

Objective	Perception	Cognition	Emotion	Association	Behavior	Persuasion
grab attention and create awareness	•					
establish brand identity	•	•			•	
establish or cue the brand position		•				
establish or cue the brand personality, image				•	•	
create links to associations				•	•	
cue the emotional or psychological appeal			•	•		
stimulate interest	•					
deliver information		•				
aid in understanding features, benefits, differences		•				
explain how to do something		•				
touch emotions			•			
create brand liking			•			
stimulate recognition for the brand	•					
stimulate recall of the brand message		•				
stimulate desire; brand preference, intent to buy						•
create conviction, belief		•				
stimulate change of opinion or attitudes						•
stimulate behavior (buy, call, click, visit, etc.)						•
stimulate repeat purchases						•
stimulate brand loyalty		•	•			•
remind of brand	•	•		•		
create buzz, word of mouth						•
create advocacy and referrals						•

The advertiser's basic assumption is that the campaign works if it creates an impression, influences people to respond, and separates the brand from the competition. Note also that communication objectives may be important, even if they aren't focused directly on a sale. For example, Expedia.com, a travel consulting company, views its advertising as a way to draw attention to itself, create name recognition, and create understanding of the products and services it sells.

Measurable Objectives   We cannot overstate the importance of delineating specific advertising objectives. Every campaign, and the ads in it, must be guided by specific, clear, and measurable objectives. We say *measurable objectives* because that's how the effectiveness of advertising is determined. It is critical that an objective statement be specific, quantified, and **benchmarked**, which means using a comparable effort to predict a logical goal. A measurable objective includes five requirements:

1. a specific effect that can be measured
2. a time frame
3. a baseline (where we are or where we begin)
4. the goal (a realistic estimate of the change the campaign can create; benchmarking is used to justify the projected goal)
5. percentage change (subtract the baseline from the goal; divide the difference by the baseline)

A hypothetical objective, then, would read like this: *The goal of this campaign is to increase the customer awareness of Kodak's digital products from 20 to 25 percent within 12 months.*

Targeting

We ended Chapter 6 with a discussion of targeting and segmenting. These are strategic decisions made possible because of a deep knowledge of consumers. In particular, this research-based knowledge identifies what makes specific groups of consumers different from people in other groups. These characteristics also identify how consumers are similar to others in ways that characterize a specific type of viewpoint or lifestyle. As we discussed in that chapter, segmenting is important to marketing, but marketing communication strategy is based on accurately targeting an audience who will be responsive to a particular type of message, one that meets the advertising objectives.

There is more to targeting than just identifying and profiling a possible audience. Advertising planners also want to know what's going on in people's heads and hearts—what motivates them to attend to a message and respond to it. Getting deeper insight into consumers is the responsibility of the account planning function. We'll return to that role later in this chapter.

We want to emphasize that understanding a target audience demands an appreciation of diversity—the ways people are different from one another—and empathy. Professor Peggy Kreshel explains in the Matter of Principle feature why an appreciation of diversity is essential for everyone who works in advertising.

Positioning

Another reason we revisit targeting here is because understanding the target is the first step in understanding the brand's position within the competitive marketplace. The objective is to establish in the consumer's mind what the product offers and how it compares with the competition. A **position**, then, is a place in consumers' minds where the product or brand stands in comparison to its competitors. A position is usually based on a particular feature or attribute (Holiday Inn Express—showerheads), although it can be psychological, such as heritage (Kodak), or both (Dove). The target decision is the starting point because the brand position is determined by how customers see the brand in the marketplace.

Consider, for example, the case of Haggar clothing, which is a distant competitor to Levi Strauss's Dockers. Haggar has been searching for a strategy that involves figuring out its target market and then its position.[3] Realizing that its previous youth-oriented strategy was going nowhere and a high-fashion position would never fly, the brand's planners finally realized that it serves an average, middle-aged male audience that cares little about

A MATTER OF PRINCIPLE

What Is Diversity and Why Is It Important in Advertising?

By Peggy Kreshel, *Associate Professor, Department of Advertising, University of Georgia*

Diversity is the acknowledgement and inclusion of a wide variety of people with differing characteristics, attributes, beliefs, values, and experiences. In advertising, diversity tends to be discussed primarily in terms of *representations of gender, race, and ethnicity in advertising content*. Ads and the professionals who create them are frequently criticized for lack of inclusiveness and reliance on denigrating stereotypes.

Certainly the profession should be thoughtful, reflective, and vigilant about the images in our ads. However, diversity isn't simply about gender, race, and ethnicity. Consider, for example, primary language, spiritual practices, sexual preference, socioeconomic status, and age. Nor is diversity simply about images. Viewed in all its complexity, diversity affects every aspect of the advertising profession: professional culture, production of content, content itself, the manner in which that content is placed and received, and the ways in which the profession is regulated.

Professional Culture. One of the most visible ways diversity in advertising can be examined is in hiring and promotion practices. A 1978 New York City Commission on Human Rights report[1] concluded that "minority employees continued to be excluded from significant participation in job areas which comprise the heart of the [advertising] business." Nearly thirty years later, the Commission again challenged the industry's record of minority hiring, calling it "an embarrassment for a diverse city."[2] Fifteen agencies responded, submitting goals for minority hiring to the Commission in January 2007.

Production of Content. Who creates the ads we see? The industry's troubled, largely unsuccessful efforts to create a racially and ethnically diverse workplace tell part of the story. Minority-owned advertising agencies provide opportunities for diversity but are frequently viewed as being capable of speaking only to minority audiences. Women comprise the majority of the advertising workforce, yet a 2005 *Adweek* study found only 4 female creative directors in the top 33 advertising agencies.[3] We can only guess at the impact, knowing that creative directors are chiefly responsible for an agency's output.

Content not only reflects those who create it, but also their perceptions of audiences targeted. Advertisers' recent emphasis on 18–34 year olds, a group perceived to be made up of impressionable trendsetters who haven't yet formed brand loyalties, has occurred largely to the exclusion of other demographic groups. This preoccupation in some ways shapes our business (which constructs itself as youthful, rebellious, and cutting edge), media (where reality programming, the "entertainmentization" of news, and technological wizardry

target 18- to 34-year-olds), and culture (reinforcing our celebration of the young, beautiful, and white).

Similarly, marketers define the Hispanic market primarily as "Spanish-speaking." The richness and diversity of the many cultures that comprise that group—from Puerto Rico, to Mexico, to Central and South America—are lost in the desire to construct a homogeneous market large enough to be economically viable.

Media Strategy. Clients and their agencies often try to reach minority audiences using mainstream media. Minority-owned media outlets frequently receive little more than the dollars left over after the bulk of the media budget has been allocated elsewhere; they often struggle for resources to stay afloat.[4] The reluctance to use minority-owned media may be based upon economics but also may be linked to stereotypical notions of minority groups. A now-infamous internal memo by Katz Media Group in 1997 explained why advertisers shouldn't advertise on black-owned radio stations: "When it comes to delivering prospects, not suspects, the urban stations deliver the largest amount of listeners who turn out to be the least likely to purchase."[5]

The problem of relying on stereotypes isn't limited to racial minorities. Gloria Steinem, the founder of the feminist magazine *Ms.*, wrote that the magazine had difficulty convincing advertisers that "feminists spend money." The magazine was forced to close for lack of advertising support, eventually reemerging as a publication not supported by advertising.[6] Similarly, gay publications struggled until advertisers recognized the "gay market" to be lucrative and brand loyal.

Diversity in the 21st Century. As our lives, professional and personal, become increasingly global, diversity will continue to develop and its influence will be experienced in increasingly complex, sometimes tangled ways. In this context, it is essential that advertising professionals adopt broad interpretations of advertising's impact on diversity, and diversity's impact on advertising.

[1]New York City Commission on Human Rights, *Minority Employment and the Advertising Industry in New York City*, June 1978.
[2]Councilman Larry Seabrook quoted in Sanders, Lisa, "NYC to Subpoena Ad Agency Execs in Diversity Probe: Industry's Minority-Hiring Practices Called a City 'Embarrassment,' " *Advertising Age*, March 6, 2006, http://www.AdAge.com.
[3]Bosman, Julie, "Stuck at the Edges of the Ad Game: Women Feel Sidelined in Subtle Ways," *The New York Times*, November 22, 2005, C1.
[4]Creamer, Matthew, "NYC official Slaps Ad Agency Execs for Skipping Diversity Hearing," *Advertising Age*, September 26, 2006, http://www.AdAge.com.
[5]Wilson, Wendy, "Whites Only: How Advertisers Ignore African American Consumers," http://www.journalism.nyu.edu/pubzone/race_class/wilson.htm.
[6]Steinem, Gloria, "Sex, Lies and Advertising," *Ms.*, July/August 1990, 18–28.

the latest fashion trends. Its previous campaign used buff, 20-something male models; this new campaign features ordinary-looking men in their 30s and 40s. This is a major strategic shift for an apparel marketer as most clothing brands are focused on capturing, or at least depicting, young consumers because they believe older audience members still identify with younger images.

Haggar's planners realized that roughly one-third of the population will be over age 50 by 2010, so there is a big opportunity to position the brand for that market. Haggar's agency, Crispin Porter + Bogusky, sent staff members into men's homes to go through their closets and talk to them about their shopping habits. They found out that older men care less about clothing brand names or fashion trends. So the new antifashion campaign focused on quality—unbreakable and unrippable buttons, zippers, and pockets—as well as the humorous situations these men endure in their daily lives.

Principle
The goal of positioning is to establish a product in the consumer's mind based on its features and advantages relative to its competition.

Another starting point for positioning is the product itself and its heritage. As the opening story explained, Kodak has always stood for pictures and over the years has owned the moment of capturing an image with a photo. But Kodak also stands for film, and that was the reason for its problems. Positioning is about locking the brand in the mind based on some quality relevant to consumers. If that point of relevance changes, then the position may need to be adjusted.

To better understand positioning strategy, consider related concepts used to define the competitive situation—product features and attributes, differentiation, and competitive advantage. Then we'll return to how advertising establishes a position in a competitive marketplace.

Product Features and Attributes   An initial step in crafting a position is to identify the **features** of the brand, as well as those of the competition, to determine where the brand has an advantage over its competitors. That means a marketer carefully evaluates the product's tangible features (such as size, color, and ease of use) and other intangible attributes (such as quality, status, value, fashion, and safety) to identify the relevant dimensions of the product that make it different from its competitors.

For example, super-premium dog food maker Eukanuba has launched a new product line that offers breed-specific formulas and targets the line to the pet-specialty shopper. Revamping the brand position began with a massive nutritional effort to identify the needs of various breeds and then develop formulas for such breeds as retrievers, German shepherds, dachshunds, boxers, and Yorkshire terriers. The campaign's Web site (http://www.beautyofthebreeds.com) also features an online beauty contest where people can enter their dogs. The winners were featured in dog magazines in "most beautiful dog" issues.[4]

A technique called **feature analysis** helps structure an assessment of features relative to competitors' products. First, make a chart of the product and competitors' products, listing each product's relevant features, as Table 7.2 illustrates. For example, nutrition, price, and availability are important for pet food. Then evaluate how well the product and the competitors' products perform on those features. What are the brand's strong points or weak points? Next, evaluate how important each feature is to the target audience based on primary research. In other words, how much do consumers care about various features and which ones are most important to them?

Clearly this dog's got a backbone. There it is, right under that amazing strip of hair that won't lay down no matter what the rest of the coat has to say about it. Like a Mohawk on a punk rocker, the ridgeback on the Rhodesian symbolizes the fearlessness of a dog who once hunted lions on the African savannah. We study all the breeds religiously and customize our food to give every dog exactly what it needs. FEED THE BREED.

Eukanuba

Eukanuba's "Feed the Breed" campaign featured photos by a famous animal photographer who created artistic images of the unique features of individual breeds, such as this spine of a Rhodesian Ridgeback.

Competitive Advantage   Using the two factors of importance and performance, **competitive advantage** is found where (1) the product has a strong feature (2) in an area that is important to the target and (3) where the competition is weaker. The product in Table 7.2

Table 7.2   How to Do a Feature Analysis

Feature	Importance to Prospect	Product Performance			
		Yours	X	Y	Z
Price	1	+	−	−	+
Quality	4	−	+	−	+
Style	2	+	−	+	−
Availability	3	−	+	−	−
Durability	5	−	+	+	+

would compete well on both price and style against X, on price against competitor Y, and on style against competitor Z. Competitor X seems the most vulnerable on two features, price and style, that consumers rate as most important decision points.

Differentiation   Most markets involve a high level of competition. How does a company compete in a crowded market? It uses **product differentiation**, a strategy designed to focus attention on product differences that distinguish the company's product from all others in the eyes of consumers. Those perceived differences may be tangible (design, price) or intangible (quality, status). We refer to products that really are the same (examples include milk, unleaded gas, and over-the-counter drugs), as *undifferentiated* or *parity products*. For these products marketers often promote intangible, or psychological, differences.

Branding, the creation of a unique image for a product, is the most obvious way to differentiate one product from another. The popular Swatch watch, for example, differentiates itself as a reasonably priced watch that makes a fashion statement. New Internet-based Mozilla and Craigslist are small companies but big brands. They have created strong brands because they have the support of dedicated users. The customer-brand relationship reflects a leadership position, a brand that has defined or created its category. But it's not just hot Internet companies that have achieved this type of leadership. For example, McIlhenny's Tabasco Sauce, which was launched in 1868, created and still owns the hot sauce category.[5]

Locating the Brand Position   Let's return now to the concept of a position to see how it is created. Positions are difficult to establish and are created over time. Once established, they are difficult to change, as Kodak discovered. Two factors can be used to locate a position for a brand.

- *Psychological factors.* Jack Trout, one of the founders of the position concept, suggests that positioning is easy if something is faster, fancier, safer, or newer, but often brands are designed around nonproduct differences. For psychological positions, consider these examples: Volvo owns the safety position; Coke owns a position of authenticity for colas ("It's the real thing"); Hallmark a quality position ("When you care enough to send the very best"); and Avis an underdog position ("We try harder").
- *Consumer decision factors.* A position is often based on the key factors—usually features or attributes—consumers use to make a decision, such as fashion (high, low) or price (high, low). We've been talking about a position as a point in a consumer's mind, so think of a map—in fact, the way planners compare positions is by using a technique called a **perceptual map** that plots all the competitors on a matrix based on the two most important consumer decision factors. Figure 7.5 illustrates how positions can be mapped for automobiles. Many ad campaigns are designed to establish the brand's position by giving the right set of cues about these decision factors to help place the brand in the consumer's mind.

Repositioning   Another objective for advertising strategy is to reposition a brand, which is the objective of the Kodak story. Positioning experts Al and Laura Reis recommend repositioning when the market changes. Kodak, for example, has always stood for photos, but in this digital age, the brand is being repositioned as a source of digital cameras and imaging equipment. Repositioning, in the view if these researchers, can only work if the new

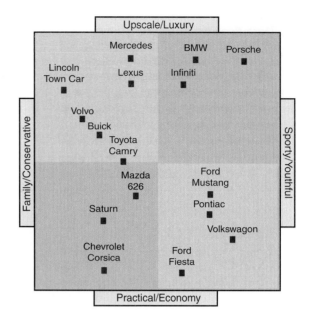

FIGURE 7.5

A Perceptual Map for Automobiles

position is related to the brand's core concept. Ogilvy & Mather hoped to keep the connection alive through an emphasis on pictures. Reis and Reis are wary of this move and believe that the link between the Kodak brand and film is too strong to stretch to digital products. Instead, they recommend using a new brand name for the line of digital products.[6] It will be interesting to see how this repositioning strategy turns out and if Kodak's position is defined more by pictures or film.

For an example of an effective repositioning effort, Reis and Reis point to IBM as a company that repositioned itself from a computer manufacturer to a provider of services. Even though the market for mainframe computers has been declining, they observe that the connection with IBM's brand essence is still there in IBM's new position as a global computer service company.

Advertising shapes the position, but personal experiences anchor it in the target audience's mind. The role of the advertising strategy, then, is to relate the product's position to the target market's life experience and associations. In fact, positioning represents one of advertising's most critical tasks. The challenge to reposition and still retain the brand essence is explained in the Matter of Practice story about a classic example of an effective repositioning campaign.

Brand Communication Strategy

In addition to brand position, let's also consider how consumer response to a message creates a brand perception. Brand managers use many terms to explain how they think branding works, but they all relate in some way to communication. To better understand how a brand can be linked to a perception, we propose an outline of the communication dimensions of branding using the same six effects we presented in the Facets Model.

Consumer's Response	*Advertiser's Objective*
Perceive	Create **brand identity**
Feel	Cue **brand personality**
Think	Cue **brand position**
Associate	Cue **brand image**
Believe	Create **brand promise and brand preference**
Do	Inspire **brand loyalty**

A MATTER OF PRACTICE

7-Up: The Uncola Story

By Bill Barre, *Assistant Professor of Advertising, School of Journalism and Mass Communication, Kent State University*

How do you turn a medicinal product, which is also used as a mixer with whisky, into a soft drink without changing anything about the product or its packaging?

If you said "magic," you'd be correct. But it's not the kind of magic you might think. This is branding magic. It's called positioning. And it created magical results for 7-Up in 1967 when the company repositioned the brand as the Uncola.

Preceding 1967, during the first 37 years that 7-Up was marketed, consumers didn't think of 7-Up as a soft drink, just as we don't think of club soda and tonic water as soft drinks. In 1967, a soft drink was a cola, and a cola was a soft drink.

Four people were in the room when the term "uncola" was first uttered. Three of them are deceased—Orville Roesch, 7-Up's Ad Manager; Bill Ross, Creative Director at JWT; and Bob Taylor, Senior Art Director at JWT. Charlie Martell was the fourth person and just a young writer at JWT at the time of the meeting.

"I remember the meeting to this day," recalls Martell. "We realized that we had to be a lot more specific if we hoped to change people's minds about 7-Up. We had to find a way to pick up that green bottle (7-Up), pick it up mentally in consumers' minds, and move it over to here, where Coke and Pepsi were. And until we did that, anything we did that smacked of soft-drink advertising was going to be rejected by consumers."

The objective was clear, yet getting there proved to be completely perplexing. "They had to find a way to attach the word cola to 7-Up. Nobody had ever done that before. This was before the word *positioning* was even used in advertising and marketing," says John Furr, a management supervisor at JWT at the time.

Martell remembers that the strategy meeting started as it always started for 7-Up. "We got to talking about how to get somebody to move this green bottle from here to there. And I think Orville said something like we had to associate ourselves with the colas. And Bill Ross started talking about, 'Well, how about, maybe, we call ourselves the noncola.' And Orville nodded. Thought that sounded good. And I chimed in with 'Maybe we could call it the uncola.' And everyone nodded and said that was an interesting thought. Didn't blow anybody away at that point. They filed it away in their collective consciousness. Few days later, came back and said, 'Maybe we just got something here.' Uncola—it did everything we had been wanting to do. In one word, it did it all. It positioned 7-Up as a cola, yet not a cola. We said, 'Hey . . . let's make some advertising.'"

Today, the 7-Up Uncola campaign is regarded as perhaps the classic example of brand positioning—and a classic example of how the right brand positioning can lead to marketing magic.

- *Brand identity.* A brand identity must be distinctive. In other words it only represents one particular product within a category, and it must be recognizable and, therefore, memorable. Recognizing the brand means that the consumer knows the brand's identification markers—name, logo, colors, typeface, design, and slogan—and can connect those marks with a past experience or message. All of these can be controlled by the advertiser.
- *Brand personality.* Brand personality—the idea that a brand takes on familiar human characteristics, such as loving (Hallmark, Kodak), competent (IBM), trustworthy (Volvo, Michelin), or sophisticated (Mercedes, Hermes, Rolex)—contributes an affective dimension to the meaning of a brand. Green Giant, for example, built its franchise on the personality of the friendly giant who watches over his valley and makes sure that Green Giant vegetables are fresh, tasty, nutritious, and appealing to kids. Kelley and Jugenheimer explain that it is important to measure the way these personality traits are associated with a brand or a competitor's brand. They observe, "Sometimes it is as important to understand what your brand isn't as much as what it is."[7] There are other methods, such as photo sorts and brand storytelling, but the point is to profile the brand as if it were a person.
- *Brand position.* What does it stand for? Brand strategists sometimes focus on the *soul* or *essence* of the brand. This is related to position, but it goes deeper into the question

of what makes the brand distinctive. As Jack Trout explained, "You have to stand for something," and it has to be something that matters to consumers.[8] Kodak is a classic example of a brand with a soul, one deeply embedded in personal pictures and memories. Hallmark's soul is found in the expression of sentiment. Brand essence is also apparent when a brand dominates or defines its category. Category leadership often comes from being the first brand in the market—and with that comes an ownership position. ESPN, for example, owns sports information, Silk is *the* soy milk drink, Starbucks created the high-end coffeehouse, Google is *the* search engine, and eBay owns the world of online auctions.

• *Brand image.* Understanding brand meaning involves understanding the symbolism and associations that create **brand image**, the mental impression consumers construct for a product. The richness of the brand image determines the quality of the relationship and the strength of the associations and emotional connections that link a customer to a brand. Advertising researchers call this **brand linkage**.

• *Brand promise and brand preference.* A brand is sometimes defined as a promise because it establishes an expectation based on familiarity, consistency, and predictability. And believing the brand promise leads to brand preference and intention to buy. That's what has driven McDonald's to its position as a worldwide leader in the fast-food category. You know what to expect when you walk into a McDonald's anywhere in the world—quality fast food at a reasonable price.

• *Brand loyalty.* A personal experience with a brand can develop into a brand relationship, which is a connection over time that results in customers preferring the brand—thus brand loyalty—and buying it over and over. People have unique relationships with the brands they buy and use regularly, and this is what makes them brand loyal. The company's attitude toward its customers is another factor in loyalty.

To put all this together, a brand perception is created by a number of different fragments of information, feelings, and personal experiences with a brand. You could say that a brand is *an integrated perception*—in other words, all these different aspects of brand communication work together to create brand meaning. In the best of all worlds, these meanings would be consistent from one customer to another, but because of the vagaries of personal experience, different people have different impressions of a brand. The challenge to advertisers is to manage their communication efforts so the fragments fit together to form a coherent impression.

Campaign Strategic Approach

Once the situation has been analyzed and the objectives stated, planners decide *how to achieve* the objectives. That calls for a general statement of strategy. The general strategy that guides a campaign can be described in several ways. For example a strategy can focus on branding, positioning, countering the competition, or creating category dominance. Maybe the strategy is designed to change consumers' perception of the brand's price or price-value relationship. It may also seek to increase what marketers call "share of wallet," or the amount customers spend on the brand, by using such promotions as "buy four and get one free." Other marketing efforts might involve launching a new brand or a brand extension or moving the brand into a new market.

Sometimes a strategy is designed to support some other marketing communication effort. For example, advertising might be used to create excitement about a sales promotion. Of course, marketing communications strategies are designed to create specific types of consumer responses. Using the Facets Model again, consider how the facets can be used to identify various types of strategies and the objectives that define consumer response to the campaign. A perception strategy focuses on building awareness. An emotional strategy hopes to touch people's feelings. Influencing what people think and know about a brand calls for a cognitive strategy, while an association strategy seeks to build a personality for a brand or cue the brand's position by associating it with a certain lifestyle or symbols. A persuasion strategy may change people's beliefs or attitudes, while a behavioral strategy aims to get people to act in a certain way.

An online mini-film commercial for American Express featuring Jerry Seinfeld was designed to entertain and create brand liking. It also generated buzz, which extended its impact through the power of word of mouth.

American Express, for example, sponsored a four-minute humorous online commercial featuring comedian Jerry Seinfeld and an animated Superman that was designed to create *brand liking*. The two sidekicks play the role of neurotic New Yorkers complaining about such earth-shaking topics as the amount of mayonnaise on their tuna sandwiches. They also relate the benefits of using an American Express card. The message is soft sell and embedded in a gag, which makes the commercial feel more like cinema than advertising. Seinfeld jokes that it isn't going to be interrupted with a commercial because it is a commercial.[9]

Campaign Implementation and Management

Once the strategies have been identified, the next step is implementation. The various media and message chapters that follow explore how the campaign direction is implemented through specific decisions in those areas. But before moving to those specific areas, let's first consider two critical details that are included in a campaign plan—budgeting and campaign evaluation.

Budgeting The budget is a critical part of planning an advertising campaign. A $50,000 budget will only stretch so far and probably will not be enough to cover the costs of television advertising in most markets. The budget also determines how many targets and multiple campaign plans a company or brand can support and the length of time the campaign can run.

Determining the total appropriation allocated to advertising is not an easy task. Typically, a dollar amount, say $370,000, is budgeted for advertising during the budget planning process (just before the end of the fiscal year). The big budgeting question at the marketing mix and marketing communication mix level is: How much do we need to spend? Let's examine five common budgeting methods used to answer that question.

- *Historical method.* Historical information is the source for this common budgeting method. A budget may simply be based on last year's budget, with a percentage increase for inflation or some other marketplace factor. This method, although easy to calculate, has little to do with reaching advertising objectives.
- *Objective-task method.* The **objective-task method** looks at the objectives for each activity and determines the cost of accomplishing each objective. For example, what will it cost to make 50 percent of the people in the market aware of this product? This method's advantage is that it develops the budget from the ground up so that objectives are the starting point.

- *Percentage-of-sales method.* The **percentage-of-sales method** compares the total sales with the total advertising (or marketing communication) budget during the previous year or the average of several years to compute a percentage. This technique can also be used across an industry to compare the expenditures of different product categories on advertising. For example, if a company had sales of $5 million last year and an advertising budget of $1 million, then the *ratio* of advertising to sales would be 20 percent. If the marketing manager predicts *sales* of $6 million for next year, then the ad budget would be $1.2 million. How can we calculate the percentage of sales and apply it to a budget? Follow these two steps:

$$\text{Step 1: } \frac{\text{past advertising dollars}}{\text{past sales}} = \% \text{ of sales}$$

$$\text{Step 2: } \% \text{ of sales} \times \text{next year's sales forecast} = \text{new advertising budget}$$

- *Competitive budgets.* This method uses competitors' budgets as benchmarks and relates the amount invested in advertising to the product's share of market. This suggests that the advertiser's share-of-advertising voice—that is, the advertiser's media presence—affects the share of attention the brand will receive, and that, in turn, affects the market share the brand can obtain. Here's a depiction of these relationships:

$$\frac{\text{Share of}}{\text{media voice}} = \frac{\text{Share of}}{\text{consumer mind}} = \frac{\text{Market}}{\text{share}}$$

   Keep in mind that the relationships depicted here are only a guide for budgeting. The actual relationship between *share-of-media voice* (an indication of advertising expenditures) and *share of mind* or share of market depends to a great extent on factors such as the creativity of the message and the amount of clutter in the marketplace.

- *All you can afford.* When a company allocates whatever is left over to advertising, it is using the "all you can afford" budgeting method. It's really not a method, but rather a philosophy about advertising. Companies using this approach, such as high-tech startups driven by product innovation, don't value advertising as a strategic imperative. For example, a company that allocates a large amount of its budget to research and has a superior product may find the amount spent on advertising is less important.

Evaluation: Determining Effectiveness   Evaluation is an important section in an advertising plan because it is the process of determining the effectiveness of the campaign. Evaluation is impossible if the campaign has not established measurable objectives, so this section of the campaign plan specifies how exactly those objectives will be measured. In effect, this section is a research proposal. All of these procedures and techniques for post-campaign evaluation will be discussed in more detail in Chapter 19.

ACCOUNT PLANNING: WHAT IS IT?

When the Eight O'Clock coffee brand wanted to know more about its audience to better target its message, it used videotaped observational research to identify key insights into how people relate to coffee. Rather than a rosy sunrise, the tapes showed that it was a struggle to get moving. "In real life," the strategic planner concluded, "people stumble around, trying to get kids out of bed. Coffee is the fuel that gets them dressed, fed, and out the door." On other tapes, it also showed that coffee was the reward for mom after the kids are out the door. "I have my cup of coffee when the kids leave," one mom observed. "It's my first moment to take a breather. And it gives me energy."[10] Account planning is the tool that analyzes the research to uncover these consumer insights.

   In general, an advertising plan seeks to match the right audience to the right message and present the message in the right medium to reach that audience. These three elements—audience insight, message, and medium—are at the heart of an advertising plan. Note that this planning begins with audience insight, which is always based on some kind of consumer research. As in the Eight O'Clock coffee example, the planner struck gold by finding out that coffee is the fuel that gets adults, particularly moms, through the morning rush—and it's also the reward for surviving that busy routine. From this insight comes clues about how and when to reach the target audience and what to say to her. Here's the planner's mission:

- **Who?** Who are you trying to reach and what insight do you have about how they think, feel, and act? How should they respond to your advertising message?
- **What?** What do you say to them? What directions from the consumer research are useful to the creative team?
- **Where?** How and where will you reach them? What directions from the consumer research are useful to the media team?

The account planning function develops the advertising strategy with other members of the agency and client team and guides its implementation in the creative work and media planning. **Account planning** is the research and analysis process used to gain knowledge of the consumer, understanding that is expressed as a key *consumer insight* about how people relate to a brand or product. An **account planner**, then, is a person in an agency who uses this disciplined system to research a brand and its customer relationships to devise advertising (and other marketing communication) message strategies that are effective in addressing consumer needs and wants. Here's an example from Dunkin' Donuts provided by Regina Lewis, former Vice President of Strategic Insights.[11]

> We heard through Dunkin' Donuts' research that people wanted to try espresso drinks like lattes and cappuccinos, but they were intimidated and thought such fancy coffee drinks were an ordeal to order. Dunkin' Donuts, of course, is known for its coffee and we felt that to be a great coffee player, we had to have an espresso line. It's now the cost of entry in the coffee category. But our brand has always been hot regular coffee for average Joe. We needed to know how to launch espresso and be successful.
>
> We did a lot of studies—looked at secondary data and did positioning focus groups. What we realized was that there was a place in the marketplace for espresso-based drinks for everybody. It doesn't have to be a fancy treat. We learned that a lot of people like the milky steamed beverages, but they were intimidated by whether they would know how to order them. We just use small, medium, and large. We simplified it.
>
> We also developed push-button espresso machines—very fast and easy. We created a world where you can get espresso through the drive-through in less than two minutes.
>
> When we launched our new line, we used the positioning umbrella of the democratization of espresso. We talked about it much more simply and dramatically changed the way our customers view a latte—we eliminated the whole barista thing. We made espresso available for everybody and we also priced our drinks under Starbucks. We launched with a big public relations campaign titled the Espresso Revolution—a shot being fired in New England.

In contrast to account managers who are seen as the voice of the client, account planners are described as the voice of the consumer. As London's Account Planning Group (APG) explains it, "The job is to ensure than an understanding of consumer attitudes and behavior is brought to bear at every stage of communications development via continuous involvement in the process."[12]

Account planners don't design the creative strategy for an ad, as this is usually a team process with the participation of the creative people. Rather, the planner evaluates consumers' relationships with the brand to determine the kind of message to which they might respond. Ultimately, the objective is to help the creative team come up with a better idea—making their discovery process easier and faster. Susan Mendelsohn, a leader in the U.S. account planning industry, explains the account planner's task as the following:[13]

1. Understand the meaning of the brand.
2. Understand the target audience's relationship to the brand.
3. Articulate communication strategies.
4. Prepare creative briefs based on understanding of the consumer and brand.
5. Evaluate the effectiveness of the communication in terms of how the target reacts to it (so that planners can keep learning more about consumers and brand communication).

Principle
The account manager is seen as the voice of the client, and the account planner is seen as the voice of the consumer.

Take off
14 years
in
7 days.*

NEW Crest Whitestrips Premium
is clinically proven to remove up to
14 years of stain build-up in just
7 days – satisfaction guaranteed.**

The Research Foundation

As we said at the beginning of this chapter, understanding begins with consumer research, which is at the core of account planning. Account planners use consumer research—particularly qualitative research—to get inside the targets' heads, hearts, and lives. Some advertisers, such as Johnson & Johnson, insist that consumer researchers and creative teams need to work closely together.[14] That is the role, if not the goal, of most account planners.

As Fallon and Senn outlined in one of their principles in the Part II Introduction, the key to effective advertising is a powerful consumer insight, a central emotional truth about a customer's relationship with a brand. The importance of consumer research leading to this insight is illustrated in the Crest Whitestrips ad.

As discussed in Chapter 6, planners use a wide variety of research tools—from primary research to secondary sources—to do "insight mining." They are particularly interested, however, in applying innovative qualitative research tools that provide methods for deep probing into consumer attitudes and motivations. In a sense they are social anthropologists who are in touch with cultural and social trends and understand how they take on relevance in people's lives. To do that, the account planner is an *integrator* (who brings all the information together) and a *synthesizer* (who expresses what it all means in one startlingly simple statement).

Crest determined from research that consumers want a teeth-whitening product that works fast. This ad equates Whitestrips claim to whiten teeth in seven days to a consumer's desire to eliminate 14 years of staining.

Consumer Insight: The Fuel of Big Ideas

Advertising is sometimes thought to be an idea factory, but account planners look at advertising as an insight factory. As Mendelsohn says, "Behind every famously great idea, there is a perhaps less flashy, but immensely powerful insight." Insights are the fuel that fires the ideas. A great insight always intersects with the interests of the consumer and the features of the brand, as the Practical Tips box explains, by identifying the value that the brand has for the consumer.

Through the process of strategic and critical thinking, the planner interprets the consumer research in terms of a key consumer insight that uncovers the relevance factor—the reason why consumers care about a brand message. Consumer insights reveal the inner nature of consumers' thinking, including such things as mind-sets, moods, motivations, desires, aspirations, and motives that trigger their attitudes and actions.

Insight Mining

Finding the "a-ha" in a stack of research reports, data, and transcripts, which is referred to as **insight mining**, is the greatest challenge for an account planner. The Account Planning Group (APG) association describes this process on its Web site (http://www.apg.org.uk) as "peering into nooks and crannies without losing sight of the big picture in order to identify a key insight that can transform a client's business."

Mendelsohn describes insight mining as "a deep dive" into the meaning of a brand looking for "major truths." She explains that the planner engages in unearthing the relationship (if there is any) that a target audience has with a brand or product and what role that brand plays in their lives. Understanding the brand/consumer relationship is important because account planners are taking on the position of the agency's brand steward. As Abigail Hirschhorn, Chief Strategic Planning Officer at DDB explains, "Our work puts our clients in touch with the souls of their brands."[15]

Practical Tips

How Insights Teams Become Game Changers

By Regina Lewis, Ph.D. *former Vice President of Consumer and Brand Insights Group, Dunkin' Brands*

If you worked for a large company that sells some of the best baked goods and coffee in the country, what would you like to know about your customers in order to create great advertising that appeals to them?

Most large marketers have a group of people dedicated to understanding the customer and customers of the competition. This group may be called an *insights team*, or it may be called a *marketing research* or *planning group*. Regardless, its function is the same—to know what consumers think and feel and how they behave when it comes to the products and services the company sells.

For example, here at Dunkin' Donuts the insights group strives to know everything possible about how and why people consume coffee and baked goods in their day-to-day lives, so we can provide even better products at the best times of the day for those we serve. This group makes our business success possible by making sure the best plans—and advertising—are developed for our customers.

Sometimes this means changing the direction of a strategy or a view of our customers. In order to serve as a "game-changer," therefore, a strategic insights group and its members must have certain characteristics. If you were to serve in this role, consider the following requirements, both personal and organizational.

Key personal characteristics:

- Optimistic and inspirational
- Service oriented, team oriented, and collaborative
- Always willing to take the initiative and act on opportunities
- Able to make presentations that are personal and engaging
- Consistently unafraid and outspoken in sharing consumer truths
- Comfortable with change and creative expression
- Supportive of the belief that any aspect of a business can—and should—be improved

Key organizational characteristics:

- A CEO and other senior leaders who inherently understand the value of strategic insights
- An organizational structure that provides the insights group with objectivity and freedom, that empowers the strategic insights function, and that fosters growth as the business evolves
- Strategic insights team "ownership" of the research budget

If you want to be a member of such a group, you must be committed to the idea that the insights team needs "seats at every table" in the organization. Furthermore, you must believe that ensuring the creation of buzz about customers' thoughts and feelings is critical throughout the organization.

Here's my advice to all insights professionals: Look at the 10 requirements featured here and ask yourselves: Do I have what it takes to be successful in such an effort? How can I make changes—organizationally or personally—to make sure that my insights are listened to and have impact?

The account planning toolkit is made up of questions that lead to useful insights culled from research. Here is a set of questions that can lead to useful insights:

- What is a realistic response objective (perception, knowledge, feelings, attitudes, symbolic meanings, behavior) for this target group?
- What are the causes of their lack of response?
- What are the barriers to the desired response?
- What could motivate them to respond in the desired way?
- What is the role of each element in the communication mix to motivate them or remove a barrier?

An Example Here's an example of how data analysis works: Imagine you are working on a cookie account. Here's your brand share information:

	2006 share (%)	2007 share (%)
Choco Nuts (your brand)	50	40
Sweet 'n Crunchy (your main competitor)	25	30

What's the problem with this situation? Obviously your brand is losing market share to your primary competitor. As a result, one of your goals might be to use a marketing communication mix to drive higher levels of sales. But that goal is so broad that it would be difficult to determine whether communication is sufficient to solve the problem. Let's dig deeper and consider another set of data about household (HH) purchases in a year.

	'06 HH purchases	'07 HH purchases
Choco Nuts	4	3
Sweet 'n Crunchy	2.5	3

What problem can you identify here? It looks like your loyal brand users are reducing their purchases at the same time Sweet 'n Crunchy customers are increasing their purchases. It may even be that some of your customers are switching over to Sweet 'n Crunchy. A strategy based on this information might be to convince people that your brand tastes better and to remind your loyal customers of the reasons they have preferred your brand. Those goals can be accomplished by marketing communication.

When you combine the two pieces of information and think about it, another insight might explain this situation. Perhaps people are simply eating fewer cookies. If that's a problem, then the communication opportunity lies in convincing people to return to eating cookies. That is more of a *category sell* problem (sell cookies) rather than a *competitive sell* (set the brand against the competition). In the Choco Nuts example, it would take more research to know which situation applies here. Here's a summary of these two different strategic approaches.

	Competitive/Brand Sell	**Category Sell**
What?	challenger brand	leader brand
Who?	loyal buyers	medium/light/lapsed buyers
What effect?	compare cookie brands	compare against other snacks
Objective?	increase share of wallet	increase total category sales
Message?	"our cookies are better than theirs"	"cookies are better than candy or salty snacks"

The important dimensions account planners seek to understand in planning brand strategies include relationship, perceptions, promise, and point of differentiation. Most importantly, planners are looking for clues about the brand's *meaning*, which is usually phrased in terms of the brand essence (core, soul), personality, or image, as the Pacific Life ad illustrates.

The Communication Brief

The outcome of strategic research usually reaches agency creative departments in the form of a strategy document called a **communication brief** or **creative brief**, which explains the consumer insight and summarizes the basic strategy decisions. Although the exact form of this document differs from agency to agency and from advertiser to advertiser, the brief is an outline of the message strategy that guides the creative team and helps keep its ideas strategically sound. As the planner's main product, it should be clear, logical, and focused. Here is an outline of a typical communication brief.

Communication Brief Outline

- *Problem.* What's the problem that communication can solve? (establish position, reposition, increase loyalty, get people involved, increase liking, etc.)
- *Target audience.* To whom do we want to speak? (brand loyal, heavy users, infrequent users, competition's users, etc.)
- *Consumer insights.* What motivates the target? What are the "major truths" about the target's relationship to the product category or brand?
- *Brand imperatives.* What are the important features? What's the point of competitive advantage? What's the brand's position relative to the competition? Also, what's the brand essence, personality, and/or image? Ogilvy & Mather says, "What is the unique personality for the brand? People use products, but they have relationships with brands."

Pacific Life has used the image of a leaping whale to reflect its image of a confident insurance company that excels in its market. It's a leadership statement.

- *Communication objectives.* What do we want customers to do in response to our messages? (perception, knowledge, feelings, symbolic meanings, attitudes and conviction, action)
- *The proposition or selling idea.* What is the single thought that the communication will bring to life in a provocative way?
- *Support.* What is the reason to believe the proposition? Ogilvy & Mather explains, "We need to give consumers 'permission to believe'—something that allows them to rationalize, whether to themselves or others, what is in reality an emotionally driven brand decision. The support should be focused on the insight or proposition, the truths that make the brand benefit indisputable."
- *Creative direction.* How can we best stimulate the desired response? How can we best say it?
- *Media imperatives.* Where and when should we say it?

The brief is strategic, but it also should be inspirational. It is designed to ignite the creative team and give a spark to their idea process. A good brief doesn't set up limitations and boundaries but rather serves as a springboard. It is the first step in the creative process. Charlie Robertson, an account planner and brand consultant, likens the brief to a fire starter: "The match is the brief, the ignition is the inspiring dialogue [in the briefing], and the flare is the creative."[16]

Source: This outline was compiled from one contributed by Susan Mendelsohn, as well as from the creative brief outline developed by Ogilvy & Mather and presented on its Web site (http://www.ogilvy.com).

PLANNING FOR IMC

An IMC plan follows the same basic outline as an advertising plan. The difference, however, lies with the scope of the plan and the variety of marketing communication areas involved in the effort. The more tools used, the harder it is to coordinate their efforts and maintain consistency across a variety of messages. The objective in IMC planning is to make the most effective use of all marketing communication functions and to influence or control the impact of other communication elements.

Effective IMC plans lead to profitable long-term brand relationships. The emphasis on brand building is one reason account planning is moving beyond advertising and being used in IMC campaign planning. Jon Steel, author of a book on advertising and account planning, says planning works best as it is integrated into the entire communication mix.[17]

Differences in IMC Strategic Planning

The three main areas where an IMC plan differs from an advertising plan are stakeholders, contact points, and objectives.

- *Stakeholders* The target market in an IMC plan includes more than just consumers. **Stakeholder** refers to any group of people who have a stake in the success of a company or brand. These audiences include all those who might influence the purchase of products and the success of a company's marketing program, as Table 7.3 shows. Employees are particularly important and their support or buy-in for marketing, advertising, and marketing communication programs is managed through an activity called **internal marketing**.

An important thing to remember is that stakeholder groups overlap. Employees, for example, may also be customers, shareholders, and members of the local community, perhaps even elected officials. This fact complicates message strategy and demands that there be a certain core level of consistency in all messages.

- *Contact points.* IMC programs are designed to maximize all the contacts that a consumer and other stakeholders might have with a brand. **Contact points**, also called **touch points**, are all the ways and places where a person can come into contact with a brand, all the points where a message is delivered about the brand. Remember that everything a brand does, and sometimes what it doesn't do, delivers a message.[18]

Table 7.3 Types of Stakeholder Audiences

Corporate Level	Marketing Level	Marketing Communication Level
Employees	Consumers	Target audiences
Investors, financial community (analysts, brokers, and the financial press)	Customers	Target stakeholders
	Stakeholders	Employees
	Market segments	Trade audiences
Government bodies and agencies	Distributors, dealers, retailers, and others in the distribution channel	Local community
Regulatory bodies	Suppliers and vendors, including agencies	Media (general, special interest, trade)
Business partners	Competitors	Consumer activist groups
		General public
		Opinion leaders

- *IMC objectives.* IMC objectives are tied to the effects created by the various forms of marketing communication. All marketing communication tools have strengths and weaknesses. You use public relations, for example, to announce something that is newsworthy, while you use sales promotion to drive immediate action. Therefore, an IMC plan operates with a set of interrelated objectives that specify the strategies for all the different tools. Each area has a set of objectives similar to those outlined in Table 7.1 for advertising; these will be presented in more detail in chapters later in the book. For discussion at this point, Table 7.4 presents the main IMC areas in terms of their primary effects.

Synergy

Given that an IMC plan involves a lot of messages delivered through multiple media at many different contact points, as well as interactive communication, the planner's biggest concern is creating consistent messages. The ultimate difference between an advertising campaign and an IMC campaign is the creation, development, delivery, and evaluation of multiplatform messages. For that reason, IMC planners are looking for ways to intensify

Table 7.4 Marketing Communication Objectives

Marketing Communication Area	Typical Objectives
Public Relations	Announce news; affect attitudes and opinions; maximize credibility and likability; create and improve stakeholder relationships
Consumer Sales Promotion	Stimulate behavior; generate immediate response, intensify needs, wants, and motivations; reward behavior; stimulate involvement and relevance; create pull through the channel
Trade Sales Promotion	Build industry acceptance; push through the channel; motivate cooperation; energize sales force, dealers, distributors
Point-of-Purchase	Increase immediate sales; attract attention at decision point; create interest; stimulate urgency; encourage trial and impulse purchasing
Direct Marketing	Stimulate sales; create personal interest and relevance; provide information; create acceptance, conviction
Sponsorship and Events	Build awareness; create brand experience, participation, interaction, involvement; create excitement
Packaging	Increase sales; attract attention at selection point; deliver product information; create brand reminder
Specialties	Reinforce brand identity; continuous brand reminder; reinforce satisfaction; encourage repeat purchase

the synergy of the messages so that the brand impact is greater than what can be delivered by any one type of message. Synergy is an organizational problem, one that calls for **cross-functional planning.** In other words, everyone involved in delivering messages or responding to consumer messages needs to be involved in planning the campaign so no off-strategy messages undercut the consistency of the effort.

Picture a Winner

Kodak

Advertisers don't create messages by relying on whimsy or a sudden flash of inspiration. They formulate messages to achieve specific objectives that will overcome real problems that are hurting an organization's marketing program. It's a process designed to help advertising planners make intelligent decisions. The strategic decisions that come from researching and analyzing the marketplace include setting objectives, targeting the right audience, uncovering consumer insights, identifying a competitive advantage, creating a brand position, budgeting, and implementing and evaluating the strategy. The results of these decisions lay the foundation for the development of effective advertising messages and media plans.

The Gallery campaign—with its micro Web site, television commercial, film, cinema trailer, print, and outdoor components—connects insights about the audience to the company in a meaningful way. It demonstrates that the innovation that's been one of the hallmarks of the company still flourishes. Wall summarized the lesson: "The point of all this being that brands have enormous power, even old brands, even brands that seem to be spent. And you, as a creative, can play a pivotal role in bringing them back to life."

The Kodak Gallery campaign was the London International Award winner in the interactive category for recreational equipment. The message from the campaign isn't that Kodak is now a digital company, but that it is and always has been a company about pictures, no matter what the technology. The Gallery just gives the company a digital voice.

Kodak also won an Effie for the results the campaign delivered. Launched in mid-2005, the campaign showed a 30 percent increase in the first six weeks in top-of-mind awareness of Kodak as a company that makes digital products and services. During the third quarter of 2005, the sales impact grew from that in the second quarter across a range of key products. Two examples: (1) Kodak's Digital Cameras share grew to 21.3 percent from 19.8 percent, surpassing rivals Sony and Canon, and (2) Kodak's Printer dock/camera bundle share increased 12 percent in August and September versus the previous month, reversing a three-month sales decline.

Key Points Summary

1. **What is the difference between objectives, strategies, and tactics in strategic planning?** Objectives are what you want to accomplish, or goals; strategies are how you will accomplish the objectives, or the design or plan; and tactics are the ways in which you implement the strategies, or the execution.

2. **How is a campaign plan constructed, and what are its six basic sections?** An advertising or IMC plan summarizes the strategic decisions in the following areas: situation analysis (background research, SWOTs, key problem), objectives, targeting, positioning (features, differentiation, competitive advantage), strategic approach

(branding, positioning, category dominance, marketing mix support, consumer response), and campaign management (evaluation, budgeting).

3. **What is account planning, and how is it used in advertising?** Account planning matches the right message to the right audience and identifies the right media to deliver that message. The three key factors are: consumer insight, message strategy direction, and media strategy direction.

4. **In what ways does an IMC plan differ from an advertising plan?** The three additional factors you find discussed in an IMC plan are the stakeholders, the contact points, and a wider set of objectives that identify the interwoven effects of the various marketing communication tools.

Key Terms

account planner, p. 211
account planning, p. 211
benchmark, p. 202
brand image, p. 208
brand linkage, p. 208
campaign plan, p. 197
communication brief, p. 214
competitive advantage, p. 204
contact points, p. 215
creative brief, p. 214

cross-functional planning, p. 217
feature analysis, p. 204
features, p. 204
insight mining, p. 212
internal marketing, p. 215
marketing plan, p. 195
mission statement, p. 195
Natural Care, p. 195

objectives, p. 192
objective-task method, p. 209
percentage-of-sales method, p. 210
perceptual map, p. 205
position, p. 202
product differentiation, p. 205
return on investment, p. 195
share of market, p. 196

situation analysis, p. 198
stakeholder, p. 215
strategic business unit (SBU), p. 195
strategic planning, p. 192
strategies, p. 192
SWOT analysis, p. 198
tactics, p. 193
touch points, p. 215

Review Questions

1. Define objectives, strategies, and tactics, and explain how they differ.

2. What information does an advertising plan derive from the business plan? From the marketing plan?

3. Explain the six basic strategic planning decisions in an advertising plan.

4. What is a situation analysis, and how does it differ from a SWOT analysis?

5. What are the requirements of a measurable objective?

6. Explain how the Facets Model of Advertising Effects can be used to structure a set of advertising objectives.

7. What is a position and how is it established?

8. What is account planning, and what does the account planner bring to an advertising plan?

9. What is the difference between an advertising plan and an IMC plan?

Discussion Questions

1. Think of a product you purchased recently. How was it advertised? Which strategies can you discern in the advertising? Did the advertising help to convince you to purchase the product? Why or why not?

2. The following is a brief excerpt from Luna Pizza's situation analysis for the next fiscal year. Luna is a regional producer of frozen pizza. Its only major competitor is Brutus Bros. Estimate the next year's advertising budgets for Luna under each of the following circumstances:

   a. Luna follows an historical method by spending 40 cents per unit sold in advertising, with a 5 percent increase for inflation.

   b. Luna follows a fixed percentage of projected sales method, using 7 percent.

   c. Luna follows a share-of-voice method. Brutus is expected to use 6 percent of sales for its advertising budget in the next year.

	Actual Last Year	Estimates Next Year
Units sold	120,000	185,000
$ Sales	420,000	580,000
Brutus $ Sales	630,000	830,000

3. You are assigned to the account for a new hybrid automobile. Use the Communication Brief outline and list the research you need to conduct for each step in the strategic decision-making process. What do you need to do to put together a useful brief for the creative team?

4. ***Three-Minute Debate***: You are in a meeting about the strategy for a new automotive client. One of your team members says positioning is an old strategy and no longer useful for modern products. Another person argues strongly that you need to understand the position in the consumer's mind before you can even begin to develop an advertising strategy.

In class, organize into small teams with pairs of teams taking one side or the other. Set up a series of three-minute debates with each side taking 1½ minutes to argue its position. Every team of debaters has to present new points not covered in the previous teams' presentations until there are no arguments left to present. Then the class votes as a group on the winning point of view.

Take-Home Team Projects

1. With a team of classmates, select two print ads, one for a consumer product and one for a business-to-business product. Working from the ads, determine as best you can the target audience, the brand position, and the competitive advantage. What do you believe were the objectives for the two ads? How would you determine if the objectives were achieved?

2. Using resources such as the *Wall Street Journal* online, find an example of a company whose business and advertising strategy match its mission. What evidence leads you to believe its strategy matches its mission? Next, find an

example of a company whose strategy does not seem to match its mission. What leads you to believe its strategy does not match its mission? Support your arguments with points from this chapter.

3. Examine the following web sites: http://www.lexus.com, http://www.infiniti.com, and http://www.mercedes-benz. com. Based on what you find on these sites, compare the positioning strategies for their top-of-the-line SUV models. Analyze the product features, competitive advantage, and points of differentiation.

Yahoo! Hands-On Case

Review the Yahoo! case in the Appendix.

1. This is a case based on the campaign plan developed by the Yahoo! team. Based on what is reported in the case as well as your understanding of this chapter, create an outline of what you think the actual campaign plan looked like. Keep it to one page, but include the key headings as well as brief explanations of the campaign decisions discussed in that section of the plan.

2. You have been asked to spell out the objectives in the Yahoo! case and expand their discussion. In a one-page report, identify the key objectives you believe were driving this campaign. Refer back to the discussion of the Facets Model of Advertising Effects to identify various types of objectives that might be appropriate for this campaign. What did this campaign need to accomplish and to be effective? Include a rationale for each objective.

HANDS-ON CASE

Chasing the NASCAR Fan

What's America's favorite sport, at least in terms of attendance? That's easy, football. How about the second biggest? Would you guess baseball? Basketball?

How about car racing? There are about 35 million NASCAR enthusiasts in the United States, and a large percentage of them are avid fans. That's why lots of companies pony up big bucks to be NASCAR sponsors, including Nextel, which has committed $700 million over the next 10 years as sponsor of the sport's championship cup. More than 100 Fortune 500 companies are NASCAR sponsors; together they spend almost $1 billion.

Small wonder, then, that NASCAR is anxious to keep its sponsors happy. One way to do that is to help sponsors better understand the fans who turn out each weekend to watch the races. But obtaining data on fans is not easy. Companies sometimes learn about lifestyle segments by purchasing readership data from lifestyle-relevant media, but no existing magazine targets the NASCAR audience.

Enter Josh Linkler and his decoder. Make that his e-decoder. Linkler's ePrize company makes an e-decoder that looks nothing like the rings kids used to get out of Cracker Jack boxes. This one looks like a square, bearing the phrase "Race to Win. Grand Prize $10,000 cash." Owners of the e-decoder are instructed to go to a special Web site and hold the device against their screen to see whether they have won NASCAR prizes. Prizes are awarded every day during the NASCAR season. But there is a catch: Fans have to give a small amount of personal information each time they play. Someone who plays regularly can end up giving responses to more than 150 questions, and not all the questions deal with racing.

Some deal with the race fan's hobbies such as camping, and others are meant to find out where fans shop.

In the first two months Linkler's company had distributed more than a million e-decoders, and almost 26,000 fans had gone to the Web site to play. The race promoters are thrilled with the results and plan to put the data to good use. NASCAR marketing spokesperson Keith Karbo gives an example: "If we know that a race fan likes to fish, then one way to reach that fan is to use outdoor media." He adds, "If we have data on that, we can approach fishing-related companies and ask them to become sponsors." Future plans also include targeted e-mails sent to fans on the basis of responses to lifestyle questions.

Consider This

1. Do you see any drawbacks to obtaining fan data this way? How can NASCAR avoid alienating some of its fans, who might be worried about privacy or who might not wish to receive e-mail advertisements?

2. What is attractive about NASCAR sponsorship to companies? How can a decision to sponsor a race team or NASCAR be justified as a part of a company's marketing mix?

3. Evaluate NASCAR's strategy for getting data about its fans. Why might this data be so appealing to sponsors? How can it be used in planning an advertising campaign?

Sources: Jon Fine, "Time Breaks into NASCAR Territory," *Advertising Age,* November 29, 2004; Kris Oser, "Speedway Effort Decodes NASCAR Fans," *Advertising Age,* May 17, 2004; Rich Thomaselli, "Sponsors Sweat New NASCAR Scoring System," *Advertising Age,* February 2, 2004; Rich Thomaselli, "Nextel Antes Up $700 Million to Leverage NASCAR," *Advertising Age,* February 9, 2004.

Practice: Where Are Media Heading?

We talked about strategy and planning in Part II, and now we'll turn to how advertising is actually done—both through creation and delivery of the message. Even though we discuss media planning before creative planning, they are parallel and simultaneous processes that are completely interdependent. The only reason we start with media is because, in many cases, the message has to be designed for the medium in which it runs. In addition, because of the dynamic media environment, more and more the creative challenge has become to pick the perfect place to deliver—or encounter—a brand message. In fact, media planning may be just as creative as message planning.

A crucial point is that the media side of advertising is probably the area with the most change in terms of the media landscape as well as media planning practices. To underscore the importance of this dynamic media environment, Professor Don Jugenheimer, who is the author of many articles and books on media, identifies the five most important trends in the practice of media planning.

The Future of Media in Advertising: Five Trends

Mass media are changing rapidly. Several trends are in operation simultaneously: convergence, interactivity, engagement, commoditization, and cadence.

1. **Convergence** involves the digitization of the media, in which all the mass media save and transmit information through the same digital forms, as well as the integration of the media to work through and with each other. For example, newspapers have Web sites, advertisements can be transmitted by e-mail, and television programs can be downloaded into iPods. Media work together, and audiences can select through which medium they wish to receive their news and entertainment.

   If all the media become similar and if we can record and hold programs and the media content until it is convenient for us, what will happen to the existing media, such as broadcast radio and television newspapers and magazines?

Donald W. Jugenheimer, Professor and Chair Department of Advertising, Texas Tech University

2. *Interactivity* means that audience members can send messages back and forth to the media and to each other. This is a significant change; until recently, most advertising came to us through one-way media, where we only watched or listened or read. Now we can respond, ask questions, and even place orders for products or services. This interactivity can involve more than the Internet; we can gain interactivity on the telephone, through text messaging on cell phones, and while playing video games.

3. *Engagement,* or holding onto the audience through the media using give-and-take messaging, also involves interactivity. If an advertiser can engage audience members, they are more likely to stay "tuned in" to the advertising for a longer period of time and to learn more about the product, service, or idea being advertised—and they are more likely to build a real interest or even intend to purchase. Advertisers, then, want media that provide an opportunity for engagement, which explains the rapid rise in popularity of Internet advertising.

4. *Commoditization* results when many types of products are similar. Customers think that most airlines are pretty much alike, and most banks offer the same services and hours of operation. Pain relievers promise not that they are better than another but that no other brand is stronger. Soft drinks are often flavored alike. Fast-food restaurants offer similar menus. All of this involves commoditization, where products and services are almost interchangeable to customers. The advertising media are similar, too, with broadcast television, cable television, TiVo, and DVD programming all regarded alike by viewers.

5. *Cadence* reflects the pace of today's life. Things move ever faster, attention spans are shorter, and audiences want to spend less time with advertisements. Broadcast viewers are fickle, often watching only portions of programs and switching to new programming whenever commercials appear. The challenge for advertisers is to find media that lend themselves to quick and complete communication while still being selective enough to reach the desired audience.

What happens when we all get all our news, entertainment, and information exchanges through our cell phones or over the Internet? What will be the role of the "older" media? And what is coming next? Few saw the Internet coming, and there are bound to be significant changes in future media as well.

Chapter 8
Media Basics and Print Media

Chapter 9
Broadcast Media

Chapter 10
Internet and Nontraditional Media

Chapter 11
Media Planning and Buying

Media Basics and Print Media

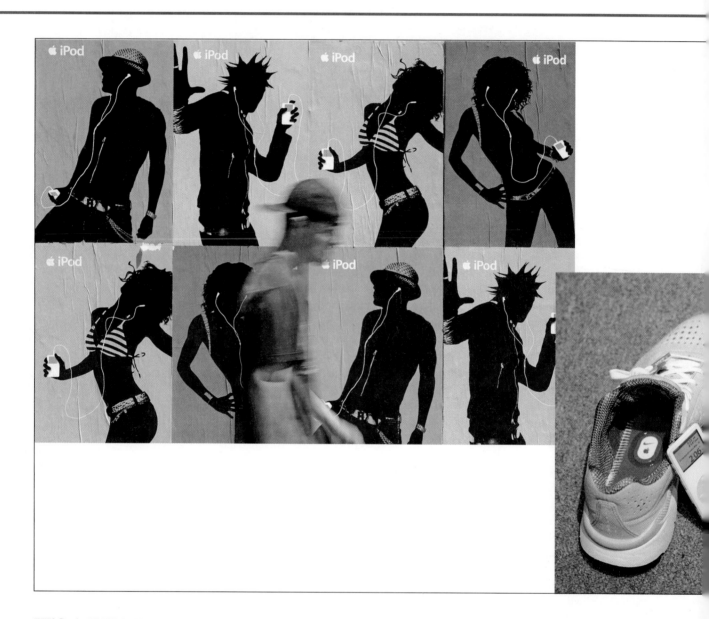

IT'S A WINNER

Award:	Company:	Agency:	Campaign:
Advertising Age's Marketer of the Year Magazine Publishers of America Kelly Award Grand Prize	Apple	TBWA/Chiat/Day	iPod and iTunes

Staying Cool with Apple's iPod

If you don't know what an iPod is by now, you most likely have been living under a rock. When Apple's CEO Steve Jobs announced the new product in 2001, he mentioned the enormity of the target audience. Who doesn't like music? Jobs asked. Who wouldn't like an ultra-portable music player that can hold an entire music library? Apple showed how advertisers can reach a market that includes just about everybody around the world. Apple's story about the launch of iPod and iTunes provides great lessons for reaching audiences effectively.

When Steve Jobs announced the new product, the initial buzz started an effective word-of-mouth campaign among music and computer fans. This public relations effort was phenomenally successful with more than 6,000 iPod and iTunes stories in major publications around the world. Buzz marketing is a great tool for Apple, which has achieved incredible brand loyalty and an army of passionate advocates who spread the word on Apple's behalf.

Apple then launched a combination of iconic print advertising and posters. The ads creatively present the digital player, and its human player, as cool. You may recall the award-winning campaign with its striking silhouetted images of people dancing against brightly colored neon backgrounds. (Don't you wish you'd thought of that campaign?)

The print campaign was followed by an equally interesting television campaign including U2's Bono and Bob Dylan as well as other cool, but unidentifiable, people. The same graphic image that featured iPod's distinctive silhouetted dancers complemented the television ads.

Chapter Key Points

1. Why is the media landscape changing, and how does that affect the key media planning concepts?

2. What key points should advertisers know to make effective decisions about advertising in newspapers and magazines?

3. What factors do advertisers consider in making out-of-home advertising and packaging decisions?

The campaign works. More iPods were sold in 2006 than from 2001 to 2005 combined, and the market for accessories for iPods was estimated at $2 billion, according to iLounge.com. iTunes, which sold more than 2 billion songs in its first four years, is now a huge music retailer, ranking behind only Wal-Mart, Best Buy, and Target.

What does all this prove? First, Jobs was right. Music is a part of everyone's life, and the target market knows no boundaries. The product is something that lots of people want. To get the product accepted, it was essential that Apple communicate to consumers how they would benefit—they could have music their way. What's more, the advertising had to reach people where they could see the messages, whether that be in subways, on television, in print, or on the Internet.

Another important lesson to be learned: Becoming cool is only part of the challenge. Staying cool is a dynamic enterprise, especially when Microsoft threw Zune, its competitor to iPod, into the mix. There's no resting on laurels of award-winning campaigns here.

To follow up the wildly popular silhouette campaign, Apple has made some significant alliances. As you read in Chapter 3, it offered a special red iPod Nano as part of the (Product) RED campaign organized by rock star Bono. A portion of every red iPod Nano sold is donated to the Global Fund to Fight AIDS, Tuberculosis, and Malaria. This cross-brand campaign also involves other companies such as Motorola and Gap.

Another collaborative effort has also yielded a remarkable innovation. What could be more powerful than Apple teaming with Nike to create a product intended to use the iPod's digital power to improve a runner's experience? That's just what happened with the Nike + iPod Sport kit. The two leaders in their respective fields of sports and digital music engineered a solution that links a runner's shoes with computer technology.

A sensor placed in your shoe transmits information wirelessly to the iPod Nano. The iPod provides the music from a playlist of your choosing, adding coaching tips and voice prompts that offer encouragement and a sense of how far you've gone and at what pace. You can even designate a "Power Song" to inspire you if you begin to lose motivation during your run. Once back at your computer, you can track your progress at nikeplus.com and even communicate with an online community of runners.

Related to the Nike + iPod Sport kit, Apple also offers Nike Sports Music section at its iTunes store, and Nike sells apparel and accessories compatible with iPods in addition to specialized shoes.

You as a runner have a better experience because of Apple and Nike, and the companies keep their brands relevant to their customers. Everybody wins.

To read more about iPod's winning efforts, turn to the It's a Wrap section at the end of the chapter.

Sources: Adapted from Jon Swartz, "Apple's New iPod Could Bolster Music Dominance," *USA Today,* January, 1, 2007; Michael Liedtke, "Apple Battles Anti-Piracy," *Boulder Daily Camera,* February 7, 2007, p. A1; Consumer Goods, "2006 Innovation & Technology Awards" http://www.consumergoods.com; Sarah Mahoney, "Nike's iPod Connection Pays," *Marketing Daily,* December 22, 2006; "The 22nd Annual Editors' Choice Awards," *Macworld,* December 11, 2006.

The award-winning iPod campaign used dynamic silhouettes first in posters and then in magazines and on television and billboards to create a cool, memorable image that connected with buyers. This chapter and the three that follow explain the side of the media advertising story you don't see—how the advertising gets placed and why you see the ads you do when you watch, listen, or read. This chapter presents an introduction to the basics of media strategy. Then it focuses on the world of print advertising in all its varied forms from newspaper and magazine ads to packages on the grocery store shelf, outdoor boards, posters, and ads that you look up in phone directories. Subsequent chapters focus on broadcast advertising, the Internet, and alternative forms, sometimes called the new media of advertising. The final chapter in this section discusses media planning and buying, which is the process by which advertising strategies are translated into decisions about the appropriate media to use to best reach specific target audiences.

MEDIA BASICS

People in our contemporary society live in a web of media-delivered news and information, which is supported in most cases by advertising. When we talk about media, we are referring to the way messages are delivered to target audiences and, increasingly, from these audiences. Media is the go-between[1] step in the communication model—the way messages are sent and returned by the source and receiver (Chapter 4).

The media costs in an advertising or marketing communication plan represent the biggest part of a campaign budget. With advertising what you are buying, in addition to the staff costs, are media time and space. In their book on media planning, Kelley and Jugenheimer estimate that media costs account for 80 to 85 percent of the advertising budget.[2] Obviously, designing media activities with a goal of efficiency is critical.

This introduction to advertising media briefly discusses the changing media landscape and the size of the advertising media industry, which was estimated at $960 billion in 2007.[3] Then we turn to the key players, the planning and buying functions, and some of the key concepts used in comparing and analyzing media.

The Changing Media Landscape

Not all that long ago, most American audiences were involved with three TV networks, a newspaper, and one or two magazines. But that media landscape has changed dramatically, as Table 8.1 illustrates. The modern media landscape includes up to 200 television channels in some markets, a huge number of special interest publications, millions of Web sites, and new and novel media forms that weren't even imagined 20 years ago.

Study Table 8.1 and notice the differences in the childhoods of the traditionalists and Generation Y. Where do you fit on this chart? Where do your parents and grandparents fit? If you are in Generation X or Y and you are trying to develop advertising for a senior market, then you must be able to imagine what seniors' lives were like as kids and how that media environment shaped their current attitudes and aspirations. Consider that, in some cases, they grew up before television was easily available, some before the advent of personal and portable music (transistor radios, cassette tapes, Walkmans, CDs), and many before personal computers (the Internet, e-mail) and satellite communication (cell phones, satellite TV, and radio). How do you think these media environments affected their lives and expectations, and how is that different from your life and expectations? The observations in the Matter of Practice feature will help you better grasp the impact of the changing media environment.

Consumer Media Usage   Another area of change is the amount of time people spend with media. In their youthful days the traditionalists' and baby boomers' lives were dominated by work and family activities. In contrast, more recent generations spend more time with media, and those communication channels are more intertwined with their family, work, and leisure time. Related to that trend are two major changes in media use patterns: media-driven lives and media multitasking.

Table 8.1 Evolution of Media Availability among the Generations

	Traditionalists [Born before 1946]	Baby Boomers [Born 1946–1964]	Gen X [Born 1965–1976]	Gen Y [Born 1977–1994]
Newspapers	✓	✓	✓	✓
Magazines	✓	✓	✓	✓
Broadcast Radio	✓	✓	✓	✓
Broadcast TV	•	✓	✓	✓
Transistor Radio	•	✓	✓	✓
8-track Tapes	•	•	✓	✓
Cassette Tapes	•	•	✓	✓
Walkman Radio	•	•	✓	✓
Video Games	•	•	✓	✓
VCRs	•	•	✓	✓
Cable TV	•	•	✓	✓
Personal Computers	•	•	•	✓
Satellite TV	•	•	•	✓
Internet	•	•	•	✓
Cell Phones	•	•	•	✓
Online News	•	•	•	✓
DVD Players	•	•	•	•
Satellite Radio	•	•	•	•
MP3 Players	•	•	•	•
TiVo	•	•	•	•
iPod Video Player	•	•	•	•

Key:

✓ This technology/media format was "always there."

• This technology/media format was invented during this generation's time.

Source: Digital Futurist Consultancy, 2006 (in ASNE report, *Growing Audience: Media Usage: A Generational Perspective*, p. 6, http://www.growingaudience.com)

- *Media-focused lives.* A landmark media research project in 2005, called the Middletown Media Studies[1], study found that the average person spends about nine hours a day with some type of media.[4] The research team from Ball State's Center for Media Design (CMD) used observational and ethnographic research to shadow about 400 people in Muncie and Indianapolis, recording some 5,000 hours of media time. They recorded their participants' activities every 15 seconds and coded their media use in terms of 15 categories, including television, radio, iPods and other music players, cell phones, magazines, newspapers, books, the Internet, instant messaging, and e-mail, among others. A key finding is that about 30 percent of the waking day was spent with media as a sole focus versus 20.8 percent for work. That pattern of media-focused lives also was found in a study released in 2007 by the Census Bureau, which supported the Middletown estimate of nine hours of media per day.[5] This is also the same finding Thacker mentioned in the Matter of Practice box. That's more time than people spend doing anything else, except breathing. It works out to about five months dedicated to media during an average year.
- *Media multitasking.* Another study, the BIGresearch project, is actually an investigation of simultaneous media use. It has tracked the increase in media multitasking over the years. Its 2007 report found that most consumers are using more than one medium at a time:
  - 67.9 percent use other media while watching TV
  - 68.9 percent while reading newspapers

[1]Named after a landmark sociological study conducted between 1924 and 1937 in Muncie, Indiana, by Robert and Helen Lynd. These studies defined Muncie as a protypical "average" community and an ideal location for the study of social trends. Ball State University continues this work through its Center for Middletown Studies.

A MATTER OF PRACTICE

The Media Explosion

By Bob Thacker, *Senior Vice President, Marketing and Advertising, OfficeMax*

Never before has advertising gone through more transformation and evolution than it is today. Today, our profession is at a place in history unlike any other. The media environment is exploding!

In 1985 an important study measured the amount of time that people spend with media. That number was approximately 60 hours per week.

In 2005, the same study was conducted. What's happening now? How much time do people spend today? Sixty hours! It's the same amount of time, which only proves that people have a finite amount of time. Even with cell phones, text messaging, Blackberrys, voicemail, faxes, iPods, TIVO, and all the rest of the devices designed to improve the "quality" of life, we're not gaining quantity of time to spend with them.

So what's different from 1985 to 2005? In 1985 there were approximately four television networks. Cable was in its infancy. Today, there are literally hundreds and hundreds of cable choices.

In '85, there were a few hundred radio stations. Today there are thousands, each with a special niche.

In '85 almost everybody read a daily newspaper. Today newspapers are read mostly by people over 50. Readership is declining daily.

Magazines have grown into specialty publications focused on areas of special interest. Yachting. Cooking. Scrapbooking.

The most important difference is the Web. It was a just a concept in '85. Today the Web is the main link to most information and communication. Hundreds of thousands of Web sites appear each day: blogs, weblogs, and specialty sites. It's endless—and endlessly confusing for traditional advertisers who spend their days trying to cling onto the last vestiges of old media models.

So what does this mean for you as you are about to embark on learning about the rich and rewarding advertising profession? In many ways, you're ahead of the curve! You grew up with the Internet. It's nothing new to you. That gives you a decided advantage.

- 70.7 percent while browsing online
- 56.4 percent while listening to radio (probably lower because a large amount of radio listening occurs while driving)

The Middletown studies[6] also looked at simultaneous media use and found that 30 percent of the time people are using more than one medium. The study also found that women are more likely to use multiple media at the same time than are men and, contrary to popular opinion, levels of media multitasking are higher for ages 40–65 than for those aged 18–39.

Advertising Media Use Traditional advertising media is a huge industry with almost $245 billion in spending. Table 8.2 summarizes the primary categories we refer to as *traditional advertising media*. Although media ad spending slumped during the economic downturn at the beginning of the century, it began to show a turnaround in 2003 with an overall spending increase of 6 percent from the previous year. This pattern continued between 2004 and 2005 but only with an overall increase of 3 percent. Note that the greatest growth was in online newspaper advertising, cable TV, outdoor, and Internet. National newspapers and network television were in decline. Why do you think these various media either showed increases in advertising or declines?

Study Table 8.2. Which are the three biggest media categories in terms of the amount of advertising money they bring in? Which are the smallest? If you look at the column that shows the increase or decrease, what does that say to you about the dynamics of this pattern? Who are the winners and who are the losers?

The Media Plan The challenge advertisers face is how to manage all these media opportunities and yet maximize the efficiency of budgets that are inevitably too small to do everything the advertiser would like to do to reach every potential customer. All this decision making comes together in a **media plan,** which identifies the best media to use to deliver an advertising message efficiently to a targeted audience. The media plan is a subsection within an advertising plan with its own objectives, strategies, and tactics.

Table 8.2 U.S. Media Advertising Expenditures

($ Millions)

	2003	2004	2005	% Change	% of Media
Television	60,746	67,794	67,947	.002	.25
Broadcast TV	41,932	46,267	44,293	−.04	
Cable TV	18,814	21,527	23,654	.10	
Direct Mail	48,370	52,191	55,218	.06	.20
Newspapers	46,155	48,244	49,436	.02	.18
National	7,797	8,083	7,910	−.02	
Retail	21,341	22,012	22,178	.004	
Classified	15,801	16,608	17,312	.04	
Online*	1,216	1,541	2,027	.32	
Radio	19,100	19,581	19,640	.005	.07
Magazines	11,435	12,247	12,847	.05	.05
Directory	13,896	14,002	14,229	.01	.05
Business papers	4,004	4,072	4,170	.02	.02
Out of Home	5,443	5,770	6,232	.08	.02
Internet**	4,434	5,312	5,737	.08	.02
Miscellaneous***	31,990	34,654	35,692	.03	.13
Total All Media	$245,573	$263,867	$271,148	.03	

*Advertising in online newspaper

**Non-newspaper Internet advertising

***Includes weeklies, shoppers, penny savers, and cinema advertising

Source: Adapted from *The Source: Newspapers by the Numbers 2006,* Newspaper Association of America, January 2007, http://www.naa.org/thesource/the_source_newspapers_by_the_numbers.pdf

Key Media Players

In the media industries, there are professionals who both sell and buy advertising. It is important that you understand the difference. First let's look at the professionals who sell space or time in media.

- *Media salespeople* work for a specific vehicle, such as a magazine or local television station, with an objective to build the best possible argument to convince media planners to use the medium they represent. A media salesperson is responsible for assembling packets of information, or **sales kits,** on the medium he or she represents, which usually means compiling profile information about the people who watch, listen, or read the medium, along with the numbers describing audience size and geographical coverage. Currently media conglomerates prevail. In 2007, for example, CBS announced the creation of a coordinated ad-selling division, called CBS RIOT, which stands for radio, Internet, outdoor, and television. The new division will serve primarily local markets and can offer **cross-media** (also called **cross-platform** or **multi-channel**) integrated deals. Disney is reorganizing its ad sales to deliver a similar cross-media ad sales program for its kids' media properties.[7]
- **Media reps** or **brokers** are people (or companies) who sell space (in print) and time (in broadcast) for a variety of media. If an advertising agency wants to buy space in all the major newspapers in the West, for example, the agency's buyer could contract with a media rep firm whose sales rep and brokers handle national sales for all those newspapers. This allows the **media buyer** to place the buy with one order.

On the buying side, media planners, buyers, and researchers work primarily for agencies, although they can also be found working for marketers who handle their own media work in house. Their challenge is to determine the best way to deliver a message, which is called **media planning.** The job functions are as follows:

- **Media researchers** compile audience measurement data, media costs, and availability data for the various media options being considered by the planners.
- *Media planners* develop the strategic decisions outlined in the media plan, such as where to advertise geographically, when to advertise, and which type of media to use to reach specific types of audiences.
- *Media buyers* implement the media plan by contracting for specific amounts of time or space. They spend the media budget according to the plan developed by the media planner. Media buyers are expected to maintain good media supplier relations to facilitate a flow of information within the fast-changing media marketplace. This means there should be close working relationships between planners and buyers, as well as media reps, so media planners can tap this source of media information to better forecast media changes, including price and patterns of coverage.
- *Media buying companies,* mentioned in Chapter 2, are independent companies that specialize in doing media research, planning, and buying. They may be a spin-off from the media department in an advertising agency, but because they are now independent companies, they work for a variety of clients. They consolidate media buying to get maximum discounts from the media for the volume of their buys. They then pass on some of this saving to their clients.

Now let's consider some of the basic concepts that drive the media advertising industry. You will need to be familiar with certain terms to understand the review of basic media forms discussed in this chapter and the chapters that follow.

Key Media Concepts

In most cases a media plan will outline a set of media, called a *media mix*, to be used in achieving the objectives of the advertising plan. This **media mix** is the way various types of media are strategically combined to create a certain kind of impact. For example, the iPod campaign used posters and magazine ads to announce the new product, followed by television advertising that showed how to use the product and billboards that reminded people to look for it in stores. A **media vehicle** is a specific TV program (*60 Minutes, The Simpsons*), newspaper (*The Washington Post, Chicago Tribune, El Nuevo Herald*), magazine (*Woman's Day, GQ*), or radio station or program (NPR's *All Things Considered*, Rush Limbaugh's talk show).

Targets and Audiences   One of the biggest challenges in developing a media plan is matching the advertiser's target audience with the audience of a particular medium. The same terms that are used to describe target audiences (Chapter 5) can be used to describe media audiences. A major study by the Newspaper Association of America (NAA), for example, grouped media audiences into four useful categories by generation: traditionalists, baby boomers, Gen X, and Gen Y (see Table 8.1).[8] The media planners' problem, however, is knowing where to find these people.

The iPod target audience, for example, is a technologically sophisticated young adult. They also need to have enough discretionary income to buy the product. That audience profile led initially to a target of innovators, people who are into cool gadgets and who love music. Now where do you find those people? One place to start was with posters in subways and other urban sites. The campaign also used outdoor boards, print media, and TV commercials in ways that would generate buzz. A key strategy was to get people talking about this new gadget.

Advertisers use a variety of terms to measure print audiences. (Note: We'll discuss broadcast media measurements in the chapter that follows.) The terms are easy to confuse, so let's explain some here before we begin talking about specific print media forms.

- *Impressions.* An **impression** is one person's opportunity to be exposed one time to an ad in a newspaper, magazine, or outdoor location. Impressions can be added up as a measure of the size of the audience

In South Florida, journalistic excellence in *español* means...

El Nuevo Herald is proud to be recognized as the best Spanish-language newspaper in the United States, reaching more than a half million readers over the course of a week.

Your advertisement in any of our award-winning sections is the sure way to be on the spotlight of the nation's third and most affluent Hispanic market with a whopping buying power of $13 billion plus a year!

The fact is, no other daily newspaper has a higher penetration in a Hispanic market nationwide!

For current rates and information call our **Advertising Department at (305) 376-4951.**

El Nuevo Herald is an example of a successful newspaper—a specific advertising vehicle—targeted at an ethnic group, in this case the Spanish-speaking consumer.

either for one medium (one insertion in print) or for a combination of vehicles in a media mix.

- *Circulation.* Impressions are different from **circulation,** because impressions (at least in print) estimate the actual readership, rather than just the circulation, which refers to copies sold.
- *Gross impressions.* Circulation doesn't tell you much about the actual readership of an ad. A magazine may have a circulation of 1 million, but it might be read on average by 2.5 people per issue. This means impressions for that issue would be 2.5 million. If the ad ran in three consecutive issues, then the estimate of total impressions, called **gross impressions,** would be 7.5 million.

Reach and Frequency   What are the measurements used in the decisions to use one vehicle versus another? The reasons behind these choices are based on two critical factors—reach and frequency—that are stated as objectives in a media plan.

The goal of most media plans is to reach as many people in the target audience as often as the budget allows. **Reach** is the percentage of the media audience exposed at least once to the advertiser's message during a specific time frame. When we say that a particular media vehicle, such as the Super Bowl, has a wide reach, we mean that a lot of people are watching the program. When we say it has a narrow reach, such as the *El Nuevo Herald,* we mean that a small percentage of the newspaper audience is reading that publication. The idea for the iPod launch was to reach not just everyone who likes music, but specifically to target technologically sophisticated people who are also opinion leaders (whose thoughts on innovations like the iPod would influence many others).

Equally as important as reach is **frequency,** which refers to the number of times a person is exposed to the advertisement. There's a rule of thumb that you have to hear or see something three times before it makes an impact. That's the reason frequency is so important in many advertising campaigns. Different media have different patterns of frequency. Radio commercials, for example, typically achieve high levels of frequency because they can be repeated over and over to achieve impact. Frequency is more difficult to accomplish with a monthly magazine because its publication—and an ad's appearance in it—is much more infrequent than a radio broadcast.

Principle

The goal of most media plans is to reach as many people in the target audience as often as the budget allows.

Media Industry Trends

Advertising media are in an incredible state of flux, particularly because of the introduction of the computer and the Internet but also because of the way people choose to spend their time for business and leisure activities. The Part III Introduction includes a discussion of change by Professor Don Jugenheimer, with a focus on five trends: convergence, interactivity, engagement, commoditization, and cadence. He explains that the media landscape is reshaping itself dramatically: "Already there are predictions that newspapers are fading away, magazines are merging and becoming fewer in number, and broadcast is predicted to decline." Media are changing so rapidly that it is difficult in a textbook to keep up with the new forms and patterns of use.

One of Jugenheimer's trends is **engagement,** a media buzzword that refers to the captivating quality of media that the audience finds engrossing. Certainly this can apply to television commercials and cinema advertising, but it can also be applied to print and Internet ads on which readers concentrate. Media experts describe engagement as the closeness of fit between the characteristics and interest of viewers and the relevance of the media content.[9] It describes how and why ads capture (or don't capture) the attention of the audiences. This is the way media delivers on that critical "perception" step in the Facets Model.

We conclude this discussion of trends by calling your attention to a trend that is redefining our understanding of media as message delivery systems—brand touch points, a particularly important concept for IMC programs.

We have referred to "traditional media advertising" in several places in recognition of the fact that the definition of media is changing. The term touch points refers to all the various ways a consumer comes in touch with a brand. In addition to traditional media, these points of contact include such experiences as product use, operations (checking in at the airline counter), customer service, and **word-of-mouth.** All of these deliver important message opportunities about a brand and contribute to positive or negative brand impressions. Traditional mass media are becoming less important, not only as the media landscape fragments, but also as other types of experiences are recognized as important points of contact between a brand and consumers. Because of the influence of IMC on media strategy, more effort is being made to analyze the impact of all touch points, including and beyond traditional media.

With this brief introduction to the basics of advertising media, let's turn to a review of print media and the characteristics that make them different from other advertising media forms.

PRINT MEDIA CHARACTERISTICS

Print advertising includes printed promotional messages in newspapers, magazines, brochures, and on other printed surfaces, such as posters and outdoor boards. The last two examples move us into a category called *out-of-home media*. The difficulty with this category is that although the various media types included here have their roots in print, many of these media are also appearing in electronic or digital forms.

In terms of impact, print media generally provide more information, rich imagery, and a longer message life than other forms such as broadcast. It's an information-rich environment so, in terms of our Facets Model of Advertising Effects, print media are often used to generate cognitive responses. If you want someone to read about something new, then a newspaper ad is useful. If you want to explain how something works or give detailed information, then your strategy might call for magazine advertising. If you want to give directions on how to find a store, then you may use an outdoor board or Yellow Pages ad. Some types of print media also deliver rich graphic imagery, such as fashion magazine ads and posters. As a result, print can also be good for brand image advertising. For that same reason, outdoor advertising is used for brand image reminders as well as directions.

Readers find that reading a publication is more flexible than watching or listening to broadcast because they can stop and reread, read sections out of order, or move through the publication at their own speed and on their own time. They can also save it and reread. Because the print message format is less fleeting than broadcast and more concrete, people tend to spend more time with print and absorb its messages more carefully. They can also put it aside and reread at a later time. Print is also highly engaging when targeted toward audiences that have a special interest in the publication's content, such as women and women's magazines. such as *Better Homes & Gardens* and *Family Circle*.

Print has the ability to engage more of the senses than other media because it can be both tactile (different types of paper and other surfaces) and aural (smell). Magazines, for example, have long offered scratch 'n' sniff ads, particularly for perfume, and that's becoming more common in newspapers. Three newspapers announced the availability of aromatic ads in 2007, so the smell of coffee may waft from your morning newspaper.[10]

NEWSPAPER BASICS

Advertisers trying to reach a local market use newspapers, as most newspapers (other than *USA Today* and the *Wall Street Journal*) are identified by the geography of the city or region they serve. Newspapers' primary function is to carry news, which means that advertisers with news to announce, such as a special sale or sale price, may find them a comfortable environment. Studies have consistently found that people consider ads—that is, commercial information—to be news, too, and they read newspapers as much for the ads as they do for the news stories.

A $59 billion industry, newspapers remain an important advertising medium, although newspaper readership has been declining for years, particularly among young people. As Table 8.2 showed, newspapers are third to television in terms of advertising revenue. The

Principle
A basic principle of newspaper publishing is that people read newspapers as much for the ads as they do for the news stories.

two largest U.S. newspapers, *USA Today* and the *Wall Street Journal,* remain healthy, although circulation continues to erode for many local newspapers. In order to balance the budget, Dow Jones, the owner of the *Wall Street Journal,* has sold six newspapers, cut *WSJ* costs, including reducing the page size, and increased its emphasis on its other media and Internet publishing opportunities to lessen its dependence on print ad revenue.[11] The top national advertisers in newspapers are as follows.[12]

	Ad Spend ($mil)	% chg
1. SBC Communications	$804.8	–7.1
2. Verizon	644.3	26.6
3. Federated Dept Stores	474.6	–5.3
4. GM	459.3	68.8

For the most part, newspapers are a local mass medium and their primary advertising revenue comes from local retail advertising and classified advertising. Other sources of revenue include reader subscriptions and single-copy sales at newsstands. Circulation is the primary way newspapers' reach is measured and compared with the reach of other media. *USA Today's* circulation is different from other daily newspapers in that it is targeted to travelers and its primary sales consist of single-copy sales and bulk sales to hotels, rather than subscriptions.[13] The following chart summarizes the key characteristics of newspapers that media planners use in their media strategies.[14]

Newspaper Basics

Types of Circulation

Subscription   Copies delivered to individuals and companies that sign up to receive the publication over a specified time for a certain fee.

Single Copy Sales   Copies sold at newsstands.

3rd Party   Copies bought by hotels, restaurants, and airlines that are distributed to guests.

Frequency of Publication

Dailies   About 1,500 dailies in the United States, usually published in cities and larger towns; combined circulation of more than 53 million with an average of 2.3 readers per copy.

Weeklies   About 6,700 serving towns, suburbs, and smaller cities; also includes "penny saver" papers that specialize in classified advertising.

Sunday Editions   Published by about 30 percent of dailies and a few weeklies, with combined circulation of 55 million and an average of 2.6 readers per copy.

Business or Organization Newspapers   May be published weekly, monthly, quarterly, bimonthly (every other month), or semimonthly (twice a month).

Editions

Morning   Yesterday's events, advance coverage of today's events.

Evening   Today's events (through midday) and advance stories for tomorrow.

All-day   Frequent updates with different editions published during the day.

Special Interest   For example, ethnic (Spanish language, Asian, and African American) and upscale neighborhoods by zip code.

Format and Size

Broadsheet   Standard size generally 22 inches deep and 14 inches wide with eight columns.

Tabloid   Half the size of a **broadsheet** with five or six 2-inch columns

Although newspapers go to a mass audience, they offer *market selectivity* that allows them to target specific consumer groups. Examples of market selectivity are special interest newspapers, ethnic editions, such as *El Nuevo Herald,* special interest sections (business, sports, lifestyle), and advertising inserts delivered only to particular zip codes or zones. Newspapers also exist for special interest groups, religious denominations, political affiliations, labor unions, and professional and fraternal organizations. For example, *Stars & Stripes* is the newspaper read by millions of military personnel. The *Wall Street Journal* and the *Financial Times* are considered specialty newspapers because they concentrate on financial business.

Newspaper Ad Sales

Newspaper advertising is sold based on the size of the space. The charges are published on **rate cards,** which are lists of the charges for advertising space and the discounts given to local advertisers and advertisers who make volume buys. National advertisers are quoted a different, and higher, rate.

Most advertising sales are handled locally by the sales staff of the newspaper; however, brokers are also available to make national buys, which saves an advertiser or its agency from the need to make a multitude of buys to run a national campaign in newspapers. The system is known as *one-order, one-bill*. The Newspaper National Network is a partnership (http://www.nnnlp.com) of a group of newspaper companies that place ads in some 9,000 newspapers. Google has also gotten into this business, allowing advertisers to buy ads in more than 50 daily newspapers through its Web site.[15]

Until the 1980s national advertisers shied away from using newspapers, not only because of the buying problem, but also because each paper had its own peculiar size guidelines for ads, making it difficult to prepare one ad that would fit every newspaper. In the early 1980s, the American Newspaper Publishers Association and the Newspaper Advertising Bureau introduced the **Standard Advertising Unit (SAU)** system to solve this problem. The latest version of the SAU makes it possible for newspapers to offer advertisers a great deal of choice within a standard format. An advertiser can select one of the 56 standard ad sizes and be assured that its ad will work in every newspaper in the country.

Some newspapers discount for frequency or as an incentive to attract certain categories of advertising. To retain current profitable customers, some newspapers offer hybrid rates to regular national advertisers, such as airlines, car rental companies, and hotels, that are lower than the national rate but higher than the local rate. The one-order, one-bill process also avoids some of this price differential.

Another alternative that allows the national advertiser to pay the local rate is cooperative (co-op) advertising with a local retailer. **Co-op advertising** is an arrangement between the advertiser and the retailer whereby the retailer buys the ad and the manufacturer pays half—or a portion depending upon the amount of space the manufacturer's brand occupies.

Types of Newspaper Advertising

Mirroring the circulation patterns, newspaper advertising can be described as national or local (retail), as well as classified and online. Table 8.3 breaks out these categories in terms of sources of ad revenue. Note that the decline in revenues bottomed out in 2001 and 2002 and began to reverse in 2003, although most argue that the industry is still not healthy and numbers in 2006 showed dramatic declines in advertising revenues.[16] Notice also that the revenue increase in 2004 and 2005 is supported, to a large extent, by increasing online advertising revenues. More and more heavy newspaper advertisers, such as automobile dealers, are cutting back on newspaper advertising and moving to the Web.[17]

Table 8.3   Newspaper Advertising by Category

	National		Local/Retail		Classified		Online		Nwspr Total	
	$Mil	% change	$Mil	% change	$Mil	% change	$Mil	% change	$Mil	% change
2000	$7,653	13.7	$21,409	2.4	$19,608	5.1			$48,670	5.1
2001	$7,004	−8.5	$20,679	−3.4	$16,622	−15.2			$44,305	−9.0
2002	$7,210	2.9	$20,994	1.5	$15,898	−4.3			$44,102	−0.5
2003	$7,797	8.1	$21,341	1.7	$15,801	−0.6	$1,216		$46,156	1.9
2004	$8,083	3.7	$22,012	3.1	$16,608	5.1	$1,541	26.7	$48,244	4.5
2005	$7,910	−2.2	$22,187	0.8	$17,312	4.2	$2,027	31.5	$49,435	2.5

Adapted from Value of Newspaper Medium, Newspaper Association of America, 2007.

Three types of advertising are found within the local newspaper: classified, retail/display, and supplements.

- *Classified.* Two types of **classified ads** include advertising by individuals to sell their personal goods and advertising by local businesses. These ads are arranged according to their interest to readers, such as "Help Wanted" and "Real Estate for Sale." Classified ads represent approximately 40 percent of total newspaper advertising revenue.
- *Display.* The dominant form of newspaper advertising is **display advertising.** Display ads can be any size and can be placed anywhere in the newspaper except the editorial page. The *Wall Street Journal* made headlines in late 2006 when it announced it would add a "jewel-box" ad space to the lower right corner of its front page (think an ad the size of a CD case). Display ads can even be found in the classified section. Display advertising is further divided into two subcategories: *local (retail)* and *national (brand).* Advertisers who don't care where their display ads run in the newspaper pay the **run-of-paper (ROP) rate.** If they want more choice over the placement, they can pay the **preferred-position rate,** which lets them select sections in which the ad will appear.
- *Supplements.* Newspaper **supplements** are magazine-style publications inserted into a newspaper, especially in the Sunday edition, that are either syndicated nationally or prepared locally. Syndicated supplements, such as *Parade* and *USA Weekend,* are provided by an independent publisher that sells its publications to newspapers throughout the country. A **free-standing insert (FSI)** is the set of advertisements, such as the grocery ads, that are inserted into the newspaper. These preprinted advertisements range in size from a single page to more than 30 pages and may be in black and white or full color. This material is printed elsewhere and then delivered to the newspaper. Newspapers charge the advertiser a fee for inserting the supplement into the newspaper. FSI advertising is growing in popularity with retail advertisers for three reasons: (1) it allows greater control over the reproduction quality of the advertisement; (2) it commands more attention that just another ad in the paper; and (3) advertisers can place free-standing inserts in certain newspapers that are delivered to certain neighborhoods, or even certain people.

Newspaper Readership Measurement

By all demographic standards, the newspaper is a solid mass-market medium, connecting with 78 percent of the U.S. population at least once a week, according to the Newspaper Association of America.[18] The Newspaper National Network reports that newspapers are read daily by 78 million people or 52 percent of American adults.[19] Nearly half of all adults receive home delivery of a Sunday or weekday newspaper; delivery levels are highest in medium-sized cities and lowest in rural locations and larger metropolitan areas. Historically, newspaper reading tends to be highest among older people and people with a higher educational and income level. It is lowest among people in their late teens and early twenties and among lower education and income groups. Newspaper readership tends to be selective, with a greater percentage reading specific sections rather than the whole paper. Business and organizational newspapers, such as *Ad Age,* have particularly high readership levels.

Newspapers measure their audiences to attract advertisers who want to reach their readers. This type of information facilitates the media planner's ability to match a certain newspaper's readership with the target audience. Newspapers obtain objective measures of newspaper circulation and readership by subscribing to one or both of the following auditing companies:

- *The Auditing Bureau of Circulations (ABC).* The ABC is an independent auditing group that represents advertisers, agencies, and publishers. This group verifies statements about newspaper circulation statistics and provides a detailed analysis of the newspaper by state, town, and county. ABC members include only paid-circulation newspapers and magazines. Newspapers that do not belong to an auditing organization such as the ABC must provide prospective advertisers with either a publisher's statement or Post Office Statement.

- **Simmons-Scarborough.** Simmons-Scarborough Syndicated Research Associates provides a syndicated study that annually measures readership profiles in approximately 70 of the nation's largest cities. The study covers readership of a single issue and the estimated unduplicated readers for a series of issues. Simmons-Scarborough is the only consistent measurement of audiences in individual markets.

Newspaper Industry Trends

The biggest problem newspapers face is declining readership, particularly among young people. Although newspapers still make money, their reps are having a harder time selling advertisers, particularly national advertisers, on the medium.

The increased costs of newspaper production have resulted in a general consolidation in the newspaper industry. This consolidation has helped the industry implement new technologies and delivery mechanisms. Some technological advances include online circulation information systems, electronic libraries, and database publishing.

The emergence of the Internet as a mechanism for delivering a newspaper, or part of a newspaper, has had a tremendous impact on the newspaper industry. Virtually every major newspaper and many medium-sized newspapers are now online and its becoming a growth area for the newspaper industry. Data from the Nielsen audience research company has found that newspaper Web site visitors are online more often than other Internet users (72.6 percent versus 57.8 percent for overall Internet users). Furthermore 88 percent of newspaper Web site visitors are online five or more times a week.[20] In addition to conventional Internet sites, stories are now being distributed through Web-enabled phones, pagers, e-mail, and Palm Pilots. Busy executives are now able to download stories from the *Wall Street Journal* and the *New York Times* via a cell phone any time and anywhere. Likewise these online publications are becoming more important as advertising vehicles. The Newspaper Association of America reports double digit growth in online advertising for 13 straight quarters since NAA began keeping track in 2004.[21]

MAGAZINE BASICS

We know that 92 percent of all American adults read at least one magazine per month and the average reader spends 44 minutes reading each issue.[22] Furthermore, 80 percent of these readers consider magazine advertising "helpful as a buying guide." In general, media planners know that people tend to pay more attention to magazine advertising than to television advertising because they are concentrating more on the medium and the ads are relevant to their interests. Readers also spend more time reading a magazine than they do reading a newspaper, so there is a better opportunity to provide in-depth information.

Quality of reproduction is one of the biggest strengths of magazines and therefore magazine advertising. It allows the advertiser's products and brand image to be presented in a format superior to the quality of newspapers.

A $36.6 billion industry, the more than 6,000 magazines appeal to every possible interest. Only a few of them—*Time, Newsweek, Reader's Digest,* for example—reach a general audience. Most magazines today aim at niche markets with a focus on every hobby, every sport, every age group, every business category, and every profession. These special-interest publications, however, are not necessarily small. The number-one magazine in terms of circulation is *AARP The Magazine* with a circulation of 23 million, followed by *Reader's Digest* at 10 million. These circulation leaders are not necessarily pulling in the highest advertising revenue—*Reader's Digest* is number 8 and the AARP magazine is number 42 in terms of ad revenue.

Historically, over half of all new magazines fail. Despite the high risks associated with the magazine business, new publications continue to emerge, especially those that target business markets and growing market segments such as computer users, skateboarders, and scrapbookers. Women's magazines continue to be healthy, as well. But the greatest growth area is in online magazines, called **zines,** and the online versions of traditional printed magazines. For the Oscars, for example, *People* magazine (http://www.people.com), *Vanity Fair*

Table 8.4   Top 20 Magazine Advertising Leaders
(ranked by total U.S. advertising and circulation gross revenue in 2005)

Rank			Gross Ad Revenue	
'05	'04	*Magazine*	*$Mil*	*% change*
1	1	People	$1,374.2	8.1
2	5	Better Homes & Gardens	971.5	9.4
3	3	Time	944.6	–6.0
4	2	Sports Illustrated	925.7	–9.8
5	4	TV Guide	726.1	–20.9
6	7	Parade	626.0	1.6
7	6	Newsweek	622.0	–4.8
8	8	Reader's Digest	586.9	5.5
9	9	Good Housekeeping	586.5	7.8
10	11	Woman's Day	502.7	11.2
11	10	Cosmopolitan	472.8	3.5
12	13	InStyle	455.4	8.5
13	15	Family Circle	434.6	9.9
14	14	USA Weekend	431.4	3.6
15	22	Us Weekly	417.4	28.5
16	19	Ladies' Home Journal	412.9	12.3
17	12	BusinessWeek	396.5	–7.8
18	20	Vogue	392.8	8.5
19	16	Forbes	381.6	–0.2
20	23	The New York Times Magazine	373.8	21.1

Source: Maureen Morrison, "Leading Magazines Gain 5.2% to $36.6 Billion," *Advertising Age,* October 23, 2006, S-13.

Principle
If you want to start a successful magazine, create a special-interest publication aimed at a narrow or niche audience.

(http://www.vanityfair.com), *Entertainment Weekly* (http://www.ew.com), and other magazines dedicated sections of their Web sites to this event, piggybacking on the immense viewership—second only to the Super Bowl—the Oscars capture.

In terms of advertising revenue and ad pages, *People* is the leader, followed by *Better Homes & Gardens.* Table 8.4 ranks these publications in order of their advertising revenues. As you study this table, consider which ones are increasing in their advertising revenues and which are decreasing. Find the top two leaders and decliners and explain what you think is happening to these publications.

Types of Magazines

The focus of audience interest is the number one factor in classifying magazines. There are two main categories of audiences for magazines: consumer and business. **Consumer magazines,** directed at consumers who buy products for personal consumption, are distributed through the mail, newsstands, and stores. Examples are *Reader's Digest, Lear's, Time,* and *People.* As you see from Table 8.5, the top U.S. advertisers reflect different patterns of spending between consumer magazines and Sunday publications.[23]

Business magazines target business readers; they include the following types of publications:

- *Trade papers* aimed at retailers, wholesalers, and other distributors; *Chain Store Age* is an example.
- *Industrial magazines* aimed at manufacturers; an example is *Concrete Construction.*
- *Professional magazines* aimed at physicians, lawyers, and other professionals; *National Law Review* targets lawyers, and *MediaWeek* targets advertising media planners and buyers.
- *Farm magazines* aimed at those working in agriculture; *Farm Journal* and *Feed and Grain* are examples.

Table 8.5   Top Advertisers in U.S. Magazines

Consumer and Local Magazines	Ad Spend ($mil)	% chg	Sunday Magazines	Ad Spend ($mil)	% chg
1. Procter & Gamble	$619.8	4.3	1. Dell	$83.6	6.6
2. GM	478.2	4.5	2. Bose Corp.	65.0	12.7
3. Altria Group	419.8	11.8	3. Bradford Exchange	59.4	9.6
4. Ford	370.6	31.1	4. Nat. Consumer Mktng	42.4	–31.6

Business magazines are also classified as vertical or horizontal publications. A **vertical publication** presents stories and information about an entire industry. *Women's Wear Daily,* for example, discusses the production, marketing, and distribution of women's fashions. A **horizontal publication** deals with a business function that cuts across industries, such as *Direct Marketing.*

The following factors also explain how magazines are classified.

Advertisers look at the audience, geographic coverage, demographics, and editorial diversity of magazines as criteria for using them in a media plan.

- *Geography.* Many magazines have a national audience, but some cater to certain sections or regions of the country or have regional editions. The area covered may be as small as a city (*Los Angeles Magazine* and *Boston Magazine*) or as large as several contiguous states (the southwestern edition of *Southern Living Magazine*). Geographic editions help encourage local retail support by listing the names of local distributors in the advertisements. Most national magazines also offer a zone edition that carries different ads and perhaps different stories, depending on the region of the country.
- *Demographics.* Demographic editions group subscribers according to age, income, occupation, and other classifications. Some magazines for example, publish a special "ZIP" edition for upper-income homes sent to subscribers who live in specific zip codes and who typically share common demographic traits, primarily based on income. *Newsweek* offers a college edition, and *Time* sends special editions to students, business executives, doctors, and business managers.
- *Editorial content.* Each magazine emphasizes a certain type of editorial content. The most widely used categories are general editorial (*Reader's Digest*), women's (*Family Circle*), shelter (*House Beautiful*), business (*Forbes*), and special interest (*Ski*).
- *Physical characteristics.* Media planners and buyers need to know the physical characteristics of a magazine because ads containing various elements of words and pictures require a different amount of space. The most common magazine page sizes are 8½ × 11 inches and 6 × 9 inches. Ads running in *Reader's Digest,* which is a 6 × 9 format, allow for fewer visuals and little copy.
- *Ownership.* Some magazines are owned by publishing companies (*Glamour, Gourmet, Vanity Fair,* and *The New Yorker* are owned by Condé Nast), and some are published by organizations such as AARP. Some magazines are published by consumer companies, such as Kraft's *Food & Family,* that sell ads and carry stories and ads for many of their own products.
- *Distribution and circulation.* Magazine revenues come from advertising, subscriptions, and single-copy sales. According to the Magazine Publishers Association (MPA),[24] advertising in general contributes 55 percent of magazine revenue and circulation is 45 percent (subscriptions 32 percent, single-copy sales 13 percent).

Traditional delivery is through newsstand purchases or home delivery via the U.S. Postal Service. Nontraditional delivery methods include hanging bagged copies on doorknobs, inserting magazines in newspapers (such as *Parade* magazine), delivering through professionals' offices (doctors and dentists), direct delivery (company magazines or those found on airplanes), and electronic delivery, which is being used by organizational publications, such as university alumni magazines. Nontraditional delivery is referred to as **controlled circulation,** meaning that the magazine is distributed free to specific audiences.

Magazine Advertising

Media planners and buyers analyze a magazine's circulation so they can assess circulation potential and determine whether the audiences that best match a campaign's target will be reached. In deciding in which magazines to place ads, advertisers need to consider factors such as format and technology.

Format   Although the format may vary from magazine to magazine, all magazines share some format characteristics. For example, the inside and back cover pages are the most costly for advertisers because they have the highest level of exposure compared to all the other pages in a magazine. The inside back cover is also a premium position.

Normally, the largest unit of ad space that magazines sell is the **double-page spread,** in which two ad pages face each other. A double-page ad must jump the **gutter,** the white space running between the inside edges of the pages, meaning that no headline words can run through the gutter and that all body text is on one side or the other. A page without outside margins, in which the color extends to the edge of the page, is called a **bleed page.** Magazines sometimes offer more than two connected pages (four is the most common number) that fold in on themselves. This kind of ad is called a **gatefold.** The use of multiple pages that provide photo essays is an extension of the gatefold concept.

Another popular format for advertisers is a special advertising page or section that looks like regular editorial pages but is identified by the word "advertisement" at the top. The content is usually an article about a company, product, or brand that is written by the advertiser. The idea is to mimic the editorial look in order to acquire the credibility of the publication's articles. Multiple-page photo essay ads are more common in magazines such as *Fortune* and *BusinessWeek;* these magazines may present, for example, a 20-page ad for businesses in a foreign country. Finally, a single page or double page can be broken into a variety of units called *fractional page space* (for example, vertical half-page, horizontal half-page, half-page double spread, and checkerboard in which ads are located on double-page upper left, lower right, on both pages).

Technology   New technologies have enabled magazines to distinguish themselves from one another. For example, *selective binding* and *ink-jet imaging* allow publishers to personalize issues for individual subscribers. Selective binding combines information on subscribers kept in a database with a computer program to produce magazines that include special sections for subscribers based on their demographic profiles. Ink-jet imaging allows a magazine such as *U.S. News & World Report* to personalize its renewal form so that each issue contains a renewal card already filled out with the subscriber's name, address, and so on. Personalized messages can be printed directly on ads or on inserts ("Mr. Jones—check our new mutual fund today").

Satellite transmission, along with computerized editing technology, allows magazines to print regional editions with regional advertising. This technology also permits publishers to close pages (stop accepting new material) just hours before press time (instead of days or weeks as in the past) so that advertisers can drop up-to-the-minute information in their ads. Sophisticated database management lets publishers combine the information available from subscriber lists with other public and private lists to create complete consumer profiles for advertisers.

Magazine Readership Measurement

Several companies attempt to verify the paid circulation of magazines, along with demographic and psychographic characteristics of specific readers. Magazine rates are based on the **guaranteed circulation** that a publisher promises to provide. Magazine circulation is the number of copies of an issue sold, not the readership of the publication. A single copy of a magazine might be read by one person or by several people, depending on its content.

Time magazine turned the industry upside down by announcing that in 2007 it will trim its rate base by almost 20 percent to 3.25 million from 4 million. More importantly, it will also offer advertisers a figure for its *total audience*, which it estimates at 19.5 million. Because of *Time's* leadership role, this move is expected to start a trend among magazines to better report the real readership as total audience, rather than just guaranteed circulation.[25]

As with newspapers, the ABC is responsible for verifying circulation numbers. The ABC audits subscriptions as well as newsstand sales and also checks the number of delinquent subscribers and rates of renewal. *MediaMark,* which provides a service called MRI, is the industry leader in readership measurement. MRI measures readership for many popular national and regional magazines (along with other media). Reports are issued to subscribers twice a year and cover readership by demographics, psychographics, and product use. The *Simmons Market Research Bureau* (SMRB) provides psychographic data on who reads which magazines and which products these readers buy and consume. Other research companies such as Starch, Gallup, and Robinson provide information about magazine audience size and behavior.

One problem with these measurement services is the limited scope of their services. MRI, for example, only measures about 210 magazines. That leaves media buyers in the dark regarding who is actually seeing their ads in those other magazines. Without the services of an objective (outside) measurement company, advertisers must rely on the data from the magazines themselves, which may be biased.

One interesting change in magazine measurement is the move, which is supported by the Magazine Publishers Association (MPA), to quantify the "experience" of reading the magazine, rather than just the circulation of the title. A major study to pilot-test this concept was conducted by the MPA, the Northwestern University Media Management Center, and the American Society for Magazine Editors (ASME). The study identified a set of 39 types of experiences that people report having with their magazines. More importantly, the study found that the more engaged people were in the magazine experience, the more impact the advertising had.[26]

Magazine Advertising Trends

Magazine editors are under constant pressure to include product placements in their editorial content. That means marketers would pay the magazine for running an article that features a product, usually just seen in a visual, as part of the story. The Magazine Editors Association is against this, but members have conceded that it will probably happen.

As with newspapers, emerging technology—particularly online technology—is changing the magazine industry. For example, AmericanProfile.com is a virtual magazine distributed weekly on the Internet. Circulation experts question whether Internet subscription sales will be large enough to supplement more traditional methods.

Magazines and newspapers have existed for several years in their current format because they provide interesting writing in a portable form. The Web is most certainly not that yet, which begs the question: Will people really want their newspapers and magazines online after the novelty has worn off?[27]

The question is not the inherent superiority of the Internet over traditional print. The question is which works better as part of an intelligently developed media strategy for a particular target audience. And that leads us to the diverse category we'll discuss later in this chapter—out-of-home advertising.

DIRECTORY ADVERTISING

Newspapers and magazines are important print media types, but directory advertising is another form that is particularly effective at driving specific types of consumer responses. Directories are books like the Yellow Pages that list the names of people or companies, their phone numbers, and their addresses. In addition to this information, many directories publish advertising from marketers who want to reach the people who use the directory.

One of the biggest advantages of advertising in directories is that if people have taken the initiative to look for a business or service, then the listing is reaching an audience already in the market for something. Directory advertising doesn't have to create a need because it is the number one shopping medium. That's why directory advertising's biggest advantage is *directional advertising:* It tells people where to go to get the product or service they want. If you are going to move across town and you want to rent a truck, you will consult the local phone book. Directory advertising is the main medium that prospects consult once they have decided to buy something they need or want. The key difference between directional advertising and brand-image advertising is this: Directory advertising reaches prospects, people who already know they have a need for the product or service, and brand-image advertising seeks to create a need and attractive personality for a brand. Almost 90 percent of those who consult the Yellow Pages follow up with some kind of action.

The most common directories are those that a community's local phone service produces. The listings and ads in the Yellow Pages are a major advertising vehicle, particularly for local retailers. The **Yellow Pages,** which lists all local and regional businesses that have a telephone number, was a $16 billion industry in 2006. National advertisers such as Pizza Hut also use them extensively. In fact, the Yellow Pages is Pizza Hut's second largest media expenditure after TV. The industry's core advertisers are service providers (restaurants, travel agents, beauty parlors, and florists, for example). For some small businesses, the Yellow Pages is the only medium of advertising, because it's where customers find out about them and it's affordable. In addition to the phone number listing, retailers can buy display space and run a larger ad.

Because AT&T never copyrighted the name "Yellow Pages," any publisher can use it. As recently as 1995, local phone companies controlled around 96 percent of yellow page directory advertising space; that share has dropped to around 86 percent, and phone companies continue to lose share to competing directories in many markets. In fact, there are so many competing directories in some areas that publishers advertise their directories to build customer loyalty.

Because a directory ad is the last step in the search for a product or service by a committed consumer, the ads don't have the intrusiveness problem, but there is a clutter problem. Finding that breakthrough concept or a dramatic graphic image is the key to creating impact. Other decisions are driven by the budget and competition, such as decisions about ad size, use of color, and listings in several sections of the directory.

In addition to the Yellow Pages, an estimated 7,500 directories cover all types of professional areas and interest groups. For example, the *Standard Directory of Advertisers and Advertising Agencies* (known as the Red Book) not only lists advertisers and agencies; it also accepts advertising targeted at those who use the directory. *The Creative Black Book,* another directory used by advertising professionals, also takes ads for photographers, illustrators, typographers, and art suppliers. Most of the directories have been transformed into an electronic version accessible through the Internet.

OUT-OF-HOME ADVERTISING

Out-of-home (OOH) advertising includes everything from billboards to hot-air balloons. That means ads on public spaces, including buses, posters on walls, telephone and shopping kiosks, painted and wrapped cars and semi-trucks, taxi signs and mobile billboards, transit shelters and rail platforms, airport and bus terminal displays, hotel and shopping mall displays, in-store merchandising signs, grocery store carts, shopping bags, public restroom walls, skywriting, in-store clocks, and aisle displays. And don't forget blimps and airplanes towing messages over your favorite stadium. There's not much that's standard about these formats, although many use some form of print to convey the message.

Principle
The principle behind directory advertising is that it is directional—it tells people who already are in the target market where to go to get the product or service they want.

Out-of-home advertising, such as this on-premise sign from Las Vegas, is a highly creative medium, as well as the second fastest growing medium after the Internet.

Total spending on out-of-home media is hard to estimate because of the industry's diversity but is estimated at more than $6.3 billion. This category ranks second only to the Internet as the fastest growing marketing communication industry.[28] The following chart lists the top U.S. outdoor advertisers:[29]

	Ad Spend ($mil)	% chg
1. Time Warner	$70.9	91.2
2. Anheuser-Busch	58.8	–0.5
3. GM	48.3	49.2
4. Verizon	41.4	46.7

Source: Ad Age 2006 Fact Book: 11.

Why is it such a growth area? Out-of-home advertising's defining characteristic is that it is situational: It can target specific people with specific messages at a time when they are most interested. A sign at the telephone kiosk reminds you to call for reservations at your favorite restaurant; a sign on the rail platform suggests that you enjoy a candy bar while riding the train; and a bus card reminds you to listen to the news on a particular radio station. As mass media has decreased in impact, *place-based forms,* such as outdoor, have become more attractive to many advertisers.

Outdoor Advertising

One of the growth areas in the out-of-home category is **outdoor advertising,** which refers to billboards along streets and highways, as well as posters in other public locations. By the end of 2005, outdoor advertising increased 8 percent from the previous year.[30] Of the $5.8 billion spent on outdoor, billboard ads accounted for approximately 60 percent, while street furniture, such as signs on benches, and transit ads brought in the rest.

An advertiser uses outdoor boards for two primary reasons. First, for national advertisers, this medium can provide reminders to the target audience, as the McDonald's board illustrates. A second use for billboards is directional; it acts as primary medium when the board is in close proximity to the product. The travel and tourism industries are major users of billboards directing travelers to hotels, restaurants, resorts, gas stations, and other services.

Wire dancers on an oversized billboard brought the Microsoft logo to life for the launch of the new Vista operating system.

Size and Format   In terms of size and format, there are two kinds of billboards: printed poster panels and painted bulletins. **Printed posters** are a type of billboard created by designers (provided by the advertiser or agency), printed, and shipped to an outdoor advertising company. They are then prepasted and applied in sections to the poster panel's face on location, much like applying wallpaper. They come in two sizes based on the number of sheets of paper used to make the image—8 sheet (5 × 11 feet) and 30 sheet (12 × 25 feet).

The other kind of billboard is the **painted bulletin.** Painted bulletins differ from posters in that they are normally created on site and are not as restricted as billboards in size or shape, although their standard size is 14 x 48 feet. They can be painted on the sides of buildings, on roofs, and even natural structures, such as the side of a mountain.

Designers can add **extensions** to painted billboards to expand the scale and break away from the limits of the long rectangle. These embellishments are sometimes called **cutouts** because they present an irregular shape.

More recently an outdoor advertising innovation for billboards, electronic posters, and kiosks is the use of *digital displays* using wireless technology, which can be quickly changed to reflect an advertising situation (rainy weather) or the presence of a target audience member. Google has filed for a patent for the new technology.[31] Mini USA invited some of its owners to join a pilot test of a new program called Motorby. The drivers provide some basic information and agree to participate. They are given special key fobs that trigger Mini billboards to deliver personal messages.[33]

Practical Tips

Outdoor: An Effective Brand Communication Medium

By James Maskulka, *Associate Professor of Marketing, Lehigh University*

In a recent campaign, the outdoor industry proclaimed, "Outdoor is not a medium. It's a large." In the contemporary view of outdoor, it is not just complementary but an integral part of a multiplatform advertising campaign and a viable alternative for establishing a brand's image, in addition to building brand awareness. Here are some tips on how to plan for and use outdoor for maximum effectiveness.

1. *Frequency of Exposure.* The successful execution of a transformational advertising strategy to build brand image requires frequent exposure over an extended time period—a primary benefit of outdoor.

2. *Brand Image Touch-Up.* "Great brands may live forever," according to famous adman Leo Burnett, but even great brands may need image updating. This is the area where outdoor may have its greatest relevance to branding. Shifting a brand's image in response to changing consumer lifestyles guarantees that the brand remains relevant. The dynamic imagery of outdoor is an important tool in brand touch-ups.

3. *The Power of the Visual.* Certain brand advertisers, such as those handling fashion and food, use visually driven creative as the brand's *raison d'etre.* The campaigns must have consistent production values from market to market, a benefit offered by national outdoor campaigns.

4. *A Friend in the Neighborhood.* Rather than building a brand on attributes and differentiation, brands with strong philosophies and attitudes build on relationships with consumers. Outdoor delivers consistent exposure of brand personality cues to targeted customers who relate to the brand.

5. *Brand Image Build-Up.* The 30-day posting period is long enough so that these exposures can be seen as repositories of long-term brand image leading to favorable consumer attitude accumulation. It's like making a deposit in a bank and watching your wealth grow.

6. *Speaking the Language of Consumers.* Brands increasingly serve as a form of consumer communication shorthand. The compact information of outdoor advertising matches consumers' limited processing time. To illustrate, a billboard combined with a vinyl-wrapped car and reinforced by a transit ad or a taxi poster reaches the time-starved consumer with much less investment in personal processing time.

7. *Clarity of Focus.* Usually the shorter the outdoor ad copy, the more effective the message. The outdoor message imposes a creative and disciplined band communication lexicon that ensures ongoing reinforcement of the brand message.

8. *A Gigantic Canvas.* Successful outdoor advertisers see billboards as "a gigantic canvas" on which the brand advertiser can create "mega art" that links the brand with relevant icons and symbols. Some of the most important slogans and images in advertising have been captured on billboards.

Source: Adapted from "Outdoor Advertising: The Brand Communication Medium," an Outdoor Advertising Association of America (OAAA) special report, November 1999. The original can be found at http://www.oaa.org.
Herbert Graf, "Outdoor as the Segue Between Mass & Class," *Brandweek,* July 20, 1999, 19.

Because of the very short time consumers are normally exposed to a traditional billboard message, typically, three to five seconds, the message must be short and the visual must have stopping power. No more than 8 to 10 words is the norm. An example of an unusual billboard with immense attention-getting power is the Microsoft Vista billboard with wire dancers that appeared in New York. A similar spectacular featured two live players on wires playing a game of (vertical) soccer in the Adidas "Football Challenge" outdoor board that captivated audiences in Japan.

Buying Outdoor Space The outdoor advertising industry uses a system based on **showings,** which refers to a standard unit for space sales based on the opportunity a person has to see a particular outdoor board. This is typically based on a traffic count—that is, the number of vehicles passing a particular location during a specified period of time. If an advertiser purchases a 100 showing, the basic standard unit is the number of poster boards in each market that will expose the message to 100 percent of the market population every day. If three posters in a community of 100,000 people achieve a daily exposure to 75,000 people, the result is a 75 showing. Conversely, in a small town with a population of 1,200

For advertisers, outdoor boards provide brand reminders and deliver simple brand-image messages.

and one main street, two boards may produce a 100 showing. From that it should be clear that the number of boards required for a 100 showing varies from city to city.

Advertisers can purchase any number of units (75, 50, or 25 showings daily are common quantities). Boards are usually rented for 30-day periods, with longer periods possible. Painted bulletins are bought on an individual basis, usually for one, two, or three years.

On-Premise Signs

Retail signs that identify stores have been with us throughout recorded history and are today the most ubiquitous form of advertising. Signs are found on small independent businesses, restaurants and chains like Starbucks, hospitals, movie theaters, and other public facilities like zoos and large regional shopping centers. In this complex environment an effective sign may be relatively simple, like McDonald's giant M or more complex, like those found on the strip in Las Vegas with their large illuminated and animated visual extravaganzas. Signs that are mounted on a store or its property are described as directional as well as informational. The Signage Foundation describes them as "The Speech of the Street." Without signs consumers would find it difficult to locate the shops they patronize and businesses would become largely invisible to their prospective customers. For some businesses, a sign, along with an ad in the local phone directory, may be the most important forms of advertising. For businesses that serve travelers, such as fast-food restaurants, gasoline stations, and motels, the sign is their primary way to attract business.[34]

Posters

Posters are used on kiosks, bulletin boards, and the sides of buildings and vehicles. In London, daily hand-lettered posters are used to announce newspaper headlines, and the walls of the subway or Tube stations are lined with posters advertising all kinds of products, but particularly theater shows. The iPod was launched in London with walls of posters

SHOWCASE These three posters for the Court TV television program were created by Aaron Stern when he was an award-winning copywriter at Venables Bell & Partners in San Francisco. A graduate of the University of Colorado, Aaron is now in New York working on an MFA in Creative Writing at NYU.

that Tube riders encountered coming up or down the escalators. The walls were papered with the distinctive silhouetted images against their neon backgrounds. The repetition of the images created a strong billboarding effect.

More enduring posters than the hand-lettered London newspaper sign are printed by lithography, which is a high-quality, color printing process. Lithography created the "golden age" of the poster beginning in the late 1880s when posters were the work of serious artists. These posters are now considered art and valued as collector items, as are movie posters, both historic and contemporary. Obviously the impact of a poster is derived primarily from its striking design. In most cases there are few words, although posters designed for places where people wait, such as transit stops and kiosks, may carry longer messages, as well as take-along materials such as tear-off coupons. The impact of a poster is also determined by its location.

Special structures called **kiosks** are designed for public posting of notices and advertising posters. Kiosks are typically located in places where people walk, such as a many-sided structure in a mall or near a public walkway, or where people wait. The location has a lot to do with the design of the message. Some out-of-home media serve the same function as the kiosk, such as the ad-carrying bus shelter.

Transit Advertising

Transit advertising is mainly an urban advertising form that places ads on vehicles such as buses and taxis that circulate through the community as moving billboards. Some of these use striking graphics, such as the designs on the sides of the Mayflower moving trucks. Transit advertising also includes the posters seen in bus shelters and train, airport, and subway stations. Most of these posters must be designed for quick impressions, although people who are waiting on subway platforms or bus shelters often study these posters, so here they can present a more involved or complicated message than a billboard can.

There are two types of transit advertising: interior and exterior. *Interior transit advertising* is seen by people riding inside buses, subway cars, and taxis. *Exterior transit advertising* is mounted on the sides, rear, and tops of these vehicles, so pedestrians and people in nearby cars see it. Transit advertising is reminder advertising; it is a frequency medium that lets advertisers get their names in front of a local audience who drive a regular route at critical times such as rush hour.

Transit messages can be targeted to specific audiences if the vehicles follow a regular route. Buses assigned to a university route will expose a higher proportion of college students, while buses that go to and from a shopping mall will expose a higher population of shoppers.

PACKAGING

In today's marketing environment, a package is both a container and a communication vehicle, and it works both in home and out of home. In particular, it is the last ad a customer sees before making the decision to buy a product, and once on the shelf at home or in the office, it is a constant brand reminder. That's the reason we include it in this chapter. An article in *Advertising Age* explained the importance of the package as a communication medium: "Even if you can't afford a big advertising budget, you've got a fighting chance if your product projects a compelling image from the shelf."[35]

Principle
A package is the last ad a customer sees before making a decision on which brand to buy.

Pepperidge Farm, with its consistent design and distinctive brand image, dominates the cookie shelf because of the power of its repeated design across all the brand's variations.

Impact on the shelf is the goal of packaging strategy. In an attempt to win over undecided consumers at the point of purchase, many manufacturers focus on creating innovative, eye-catching packages. Although the industry has never developed a standard for measuring impressions from a shelf, advertisers are aware of the billboarding effect of a massed set of packages, a practice that Pepperidge Farm uses to good effect.

When the package works in unison with consumer advertising, it not only catches attention and presents a familiar brand image, it can communicate critical information and tie back to a current campaign. The package serves as a critical reminder of the product's important benefits at the moment the consumer is choosing among several competing brands. Sometimes, the package itself is the focus of the advertising, particular if there is a new size or innovation, such as Coca-Cola's introduction of a plastic bottle in its classic curved shape. In sum, packaging is a constant communicator, an effective device for carrying advertising messages, and a strong brand reminder.

Packages can also deliver customer benefits. For example, recipes for Quaker Oats famous Oatmeal Cookies, Nestlé Tollhouse Cookies, Chex Party Mix, and Campbell's Green Bean Bake all started as promotional recipes on the product's packaging and turned into long-time favorites in homemakers' recipe boxes. There is even a Web site for these classic recipes (http://www.backofthebox.com), which features more than 1,500 recipes featured on packaging.

USING PRINT AND OUT-OF-HOME ADVERTISING

This review of print and out-of-home advertising should be helpful in explaining when and why various types of media are included in a media mix. To summarize these key decisions, consider using newspaper advertising for messages that include an announcement of something new. Newspapers are also good for targeting local markets. Magazines are great for targeting people with special interests. They also have great production values and are good for messages that either focus on brand image or need space for a more complete explanation. Outdoor targets audiences on the move and provides directional information. Outdoor messages are also good for brand reminders. Directory ads catch people when they are shopping. Table 8.6 summarizes the advantages and limitations of these various media.

Table 8.6   Print Media Advantages and Limitations

Advantages

Newspaper Advertising	*Limitations*
Good for news announcements	Short life span
Good market coverage	Clutter
Good for comparison shopping	Limited reach for certain groups
Positive consumer attitudes	Poor production values
Good to reach educated and affluent consumers	
Flexibility—geographic; scheduling	

Magazine Advertising	
High production values	Long lead times—limited flexibility
Targets consumers' interests—specialized audiences	Lack of immediacy
Receptive audience	High cost
Long life span	Sometimes limited distribution
Format encourages creativity	
Good for brand messages	
Good for complex or in-depth messages	

Directory Advertising	
Directional: Consumers go to directories for shopping information	Lack of flexibility—can be a long time before a change can be made
Inexpensive	Competitive clutter and look-alike ads
Good ROI of 1:15—every dollar spent of an ad produces $145 in revenue	Low production quality
Flexible in size, colors, formats	
Long life	

Outdoor Advertising, Including Transit	
Good situational medium	Traffic moves quickly
Directional	Can't handle complex messages—designs must be simple
Brand reminder medium	May be easy to miss (depending on location)
High-impact—larger than life	Some criticize outdoor ads "polluting" the landscape
Least expensive	Transit lacks the size advantage of other outdoor media
Long life	

Packaging	
Stimulates point-of-purchase decision making	Cluttered environment
Last ad a consumer sees	Shelf space may be limited
In-home is brand reminder on shelf	Can get inconvenient placement—such as bottom shelf
Billboarding effect can dominate shelf	Limited space needs simple message
Reinforces brand advertising	
Delivers product information	

IT'S A WRAP

iPod Dances to a Different Tune

We started this chapter with a story about the evolution of a successful brand and its approach to media advertising. Apple's iPod teaches that great campaigns start with an innovative product that people want—and media, such as dramatic posters, that catch their attention. What's Apple selling, anyway? The product is the universal freedom to enjoy music—anywhere—including on the streets and in subway stations. The Silhouette campaign resonated with audiences who could see themselves in the black figures with the trademark white earpieces enjoying their music.

Equally important was Apple's choice of media for the campaign. People could interact with the messages in everyday places, everywhere. TWBA/Chiat/Day, Apple's agency for iPod, argued that the campaign's media, like music, should be ubiquitous and creative.

Efforts to keep the brand vibrant by creating collaborations have paid big dividends. Spurred by sales of its Nike + iPod and Converse lines, Nike reported a 10 percent increase in sales for its second quarter to $3.8 billion compared to $3.5 billion for the same period the previous year, according to MediaPost's *Marketing Daily*. According to nikeplus.com, runners logged more than 4 million miles in the first five months since its introduction. The Nike + iPod Sport kit won Consumer Goods' 2006 Innovation & Technology Award for Most Innovative Product. Macworld awarded it with a 2006 Editors' Choice Award as one of the 29 favorite hardware, software, and online products.

Apple's advertising for its iPod and companion iTunes has been rewarded many times over. Among many examples, it won two Gold Effies in 2005. Apple's iPod led mobile media players with 62 percent of the market share in late 2006.

Key Points Summary

1. **Why is the media landscape changing, and how does that affect the key media planning concepts?** More media are available to today's audience and consumers are spending a lot more time with media than in the past. Advertisers are using more new media, such as the Internet, and are less inclined to use traditional media. A media mix is the way various types of media are strategically combined in an advertising plan. A media plan, which is prepared by a media planner, is a document that identifies the media to be used to deliver an advertising message to a targeted audience. Media buying is the identification of specific vehicles and the negotiation of costs and details to advertise in them. Reach is the percentage of the media audience exposed at least once to the advertiser's message during a specific time frame, and frequency is the number of times a person is exposed to the advertisement.

2. **What are the key points that advertisers should know to make effective decisions about advertising in newspapers and magazines?** Newspapers are great for announcements of news. They also provide local market coverage with some geographic flexibility, plus an interaction with national news and the ability to reach shoppers who see the paper as a credible source.

   Magazines reach special interest audiences who have a high level of receptivity to the message. People read them slowly, and they have long life and great image reproduction. They have long lead times, a low level of immediacy, and limited flexibility, and they generally do not reach a broad mass market.

3. **What factors do advertisers consider in making out-of-home advertising and packaging decisions?** Out-of-home advertising includes everything from billboards to hot-air balloons. A common out-of-home medium is outdoor advertising, which refers to billboards along streets and highways as well as posters. Outdoor is a high-impact and directional medium; it's also effective for brand reminders and relatively inexpensive with a long life. Other forms of out-of-home advertising include on-premise signs, posters, and transit advertising.

Packaging is the last ad a consumer sees before making a purchase decision. A strong shelf facing can create a bill-boarding effect to convey a strong brand presence. On the shelf at home a package is a brand reminder.

Key Terms

bleed page, p. 240
broadsheet, p. 234
circulation, p. 232
classified ads, p. 236
consumer magazines, p. 238
controlled circulation, p. 240
co-op advertising, p. 235
cross-media (cross-platform or multi-channel), p. 230
cutouts, p. 244
display advertising, p. 236
double-page spread, p. 240
engagement, p. 232
extensions, p. 244

free-standing insert (FSI), p. 236
frequency, p. 232
gatefold, p. 240
gross impressions, p. 232
guaranteed circulation, p. 241
gutter, p. 240
horizontal publication, p. 239
impression, p. 231
kiosks, p. 247
media buyer, p. 230
media mix, p. 231
media plan, p. 229
media planning, p. 230

media reps (brokers), p. 230
media researchers, p. 231
media vehicle, p. 231
multichannel, p. 230
outdoor advertising, p. 243
out-of-home (OOH) advertising, p. 242
painted bulletins (outdoor), p. 244
preferred-position rate, p. 236
printed posters (outdoor), p. 244
rate card, p. 235
reach, p. 232

run-of-paper (ROP) rate, p. 236
sales kits, p. 230
showings, p. 245
standard advertising unit (SAU), p. 235
supplements, p. 236
tabloid, p. 234
touch point, p. 232
vertical publication, p. 239
word-of-mouth, p. 233
Yellow Pages, p. 242
zines, p. 237

Review Questions

1. What is the difference between media planning and buying?
2. Explain the roles of media salespeople, media planners, media buyers, and media researchers.
3. What is the difference between reach and frequency?
4. Explain how newspapers vary based on frequency of publication, format and size, and circulation.
5. Explain how newspaper readership is determined and measured.
6. How is magazine readership measured?
7. Explain how advertising impact is measured for outdoor advertising?
8. What is the greatest advantage of outdoor advertising? Directory advertising? Packaging?

Discussion Questions

1. You are the media planner for an agency handling a small chain of upscale furniture outlets in a top-50 market that concentrates most of its advertising in the Sunday supplement of the local newspaper. The client also schedules display ads in the daily editions for special sales. Six months ago a new, high-style metropolitan magazine approached you about advertising for your client. You deferred a decision by saying you'd see what reader acceptance would be. Now the magazine has shown some steady increases (its circulation is now about one-quarter of the newspapers'). If you were to include magazine on the ad schedule, you'd have to reduce the newspaper media somewhat. What would be your recommendation to the furniture store owner?

2. Since his freshman year in college, Phil Dawson, an advertising major, has waited tables at Alfredo's, a small

family-operated restaurant featuring excellent Italian food and an intimate atmosphere. A Yellow Pages representative approaches the owner to run a display ad in addition to its listing. The owner asks Phil for advice on whether such an ad would help, and if so, what the ad should look like. What should Phil recommend?

3. ***Three-Minute Debate:*** Petra Wilcox, a display ad salesperson for *The Daily Globe,* thought she had heard all the possible excuses for not buying newspaper space until she called on the manager of a compact-disc store that sold new and used discs. "I heard about newspaper reader studies that prove how wrong the audience is for me. Readership is too adult—mostly above 50 years of age," he said. "And besides, readers of newspapers are families with higher incomes—the wrong market for our used disc business," he continued. How should Wilcox try to counter the manager's views?

In class, organize into small teams, with each team developing a position team members feel is most compelling on the advantages of newspaper advertising. Set up a series of three-minute debates with each side having 1½ minutes to argue its position. Every team of debaters has to present new points not covered in the previous teams' presentations until there are no arguments left to present. Then the class votes as a group on the winning point of view.

Take-Home Team Projects

1. Your team has been asked to advise on where advertising should be placed for a new restaurant in town that specializes in low-fat and low-carb healthy food. Have different members contact as many media as possible in your community. Consider newspaper, magazines, outdoor, and directory advertising business. What do you need to know about the appropriateness of these media for this restaurant? Ask as many questions as you need to develop your recommendations. Compare the types of information and services available. Was the customer service helpful? Is this the right media choice for your company? Analyze the results in a brief report; begin by stating your advertising goals, then state what you might or might not accomplish by advertising in each print medium.

2. Collect Web site versions of three online newspapers. Write a one- or two-page report on how these vehicles could better position themselves as advertising media. What are their strengths and how should they position themselves in a competitive media marketplace?

Yahoo! Hands-On Case

Review the Yahoo! case in the Appendix.

1. Explain the concepts of reach and frequency. How were these critical media objectives used in the Yahoo! plan? Do you believe the reach and frequency objectives are realistic? Why or why not?

2. The print media use in the Yahoo! plan was primarily for magazines. Are there any other print media opportunities the team might consider? Brainstorm on other possible uses of print and prepare a one-page report for the team that includes some other ideas.

HANDS-ON CASE

Next Month's Magazine Issue: Credibility

Most newspapers and magazines maintain a boundary that cannot be crossed between the news or feature stories created by the publication's writers, sometimes called the *editorial matter,* and the advertising. The separation of these two is so strict it has been called "the church-state rule." Publications work hard to convince readers (though not always successfully) that advertising revenue does not drive story selection, the flavor or scope of news coverage, or critical reviews and recommendations. That independence has long been viewed as a lynchpin for the credibility of a publication's articles.

Some savvy TV viewers realize that no such independence exists for many TV shows, where product placements are more and more common. Think about the product placements for Coca-Cola on American Idol as just one example.

This type of entanglement between advertisers and television networks is nothing new. In the early days of TV, almost every program was sponsored by a single key advertiser that paid for all production costs associated with the show and frequently had a strong say in the development of scripts.

Unlike TV networks, newspapers and magazines have fought to maintain the independence of their product from the influence of advertising, but that independence may be weakening. Consider these examples:

* *Country Living Magazine* runs an eight-page insert advertisement for Expo Design Center. On the facing page, before the insert begins, is a story describing how the "help and careful planning" of Expo have helped to turn "a dreary kitchen" into "an efficient workspace."
* *Rolling Stone* places movie star Angelina Jolie on its cover. Jeep takes advantage by buying a cover foldout ad featuring the actress (as Lara Croft) in a Jeep.
* *Playboy* runs ads for Tommy Hilfiger featuring Playmates modeling the designer's clothes.

Each of these cases raises some concerns about whether the practices in question follow guidelines of the American Society of Magazine Editors (ASME) for separating ads from content. Jann Wenner, publisher of *Rolling Stone,* apologized for his magazine's ad and promised *Rolling Stone* would not do it again. But advertiser Jeep saw nothing wrong. Jeff Bell, a Jeep vice president of marketing, denied the ad implied that the company had any influence over *Rolling Stone* or its Jolie interview. "Did we tell them, 'No, please ask her if she likes Jeep'? It's an interview. She's going to say what she wants to say."

Jeep is not alone in wanting to leverage its ad dollars, and many advertisers are pressuring print vehicles, especially magazines, to be more accommodating. In a competitive marketplace in which advertisers can place ads in a wide variety of media, magazines may have a hard time saying no. And, some may ask, why should they? Perhaps the best answer comes from Mark Whitaker, ASME president and *Newsweek* editor. In an interview with the *Wall Street Journal,* Whitaker offered this rationale for why magazines should avoid offering advertisers "branded entertainment and product placement" opportunities:

> One of the great things about magazines is the very personal relationship that readers have with them. That's one of the things that advertisers should want. On the other hand, to my mind, that relationship depends in part on magazines having independence and credibility with their readers, as being produced by editors for readers primarily. I think that the problem with product placement is that it runs the risk of undermining that special relationship.

Consider This

1. Evaluate Whitaker's rationale for the "wall" between editorial content and advertising in magazines. Do you agree with his argument? Consider the issue from the perspective of each of these groups: consumers, magazine publishers, and advertisers.
2. What are advertisers trying to get from the blending of product promotion and magazine content? What long-term effects are likely to result from this blending?
3. Is there some other way besides pressuring magazines to blur content and advertising that advertisers can achieve the same goals? What other print tools might be used?

Sources: Brian Steinberg, "Blurring the Line? Magazines Face New Pressure as Marketers Seek to Blend Advertising with Content," *Wall Street Journal* (Eastern edition), August 9, 2004, B1; Brian Steinberg, "Taking a Stand as Lines Blur between Editorials and Ads," *Wall Street Journal* (Eastern edition), August 18, 2004, 1; Brian Steinberg and Emily Nelson, "Unit of WPP Will Own Stake in ABC Shows," *Wall Street Journal* (Eastern edition), December 1, 2003, B1; Suzanne Vranica, "Advertising: Hollywood Goes Madison Avenue; Television Shows Have Met the Sponsor: It Is Them," *Wall Street Journal* (Eastern edition), December 15, 2003, B5.

Broadcast Media

IT'S A WINNER

Award:	Company:	Agency:	Campaign:
Six Effies, including several gold	Holiday Inn Express	Fallon	"Stay Smart"

CHAPTER 9

Road Warriors Get Smart
at Holiday Inn Express

The concept for the commercials is simple: Take ordinary people; put them in an absurd situation where they can accomplish some extraordinary feat. Then add a memorable tag line, "No, but I did stay in a Holiday Inn Express last night." What have you got? A campaign of fun-spirited commercials that captivate the audience so much it has become part of our pop culture.

Chapter 6 discussed the strategic research Holiday Inn Express conducted to extend its award-winning Stay Smart campaign. This chapter explores how the choice of using TV commercials helped Holiday Inn Express create a distinctive brand and win six Effies.

In 1997 Holiday Inn decided to compete with Marriott and Hampton Inn by offering a new limited-service hotel, Holiday Inn Express. These new properties are called a *subbrand* or *line extension* of Holiday Inn. Unlike Holiday Inn, which appeals to an older clientele and families who want lots of amenities, Holiday Inn Express offers basic comfort for business travelers who don't need all the frills.

The challenge for Holiday Inn Express's agency, Fallon Worldwide, was to create a brand in a well-established category and find a way to distinguish the subbrand from Holiday Inn. Facing this challenge with less than half the budget of its fiercest competitor, Fallon knew it had to outsmart rather than outspend.

The campaign focuses on what Fallon calls the "real road warriors": independent business travelers who usually spend their own dime or a small per diem. Using ethnographic research, the agency traveled with the road warriors and listened to what they said. Fallon learned that these travelers get more than a good night's rest at the limited service hotel. They get an emotional reward because they spent their money wisely, opting only for essential services. No mints on the pillow necessary for this group. Fallon realized that it could create a message about smartness, not just economy.

Chapter Key Points

1. How does radio work as an advertising medium?
2. How does television work as an advertising medium?
3. How do advertisers use movies, as well as film and video, as advertising media?
4. What is product placement, and how is it used by advertisers?

According to Pat Fallon and Fred Senn, co-founders of Fallon Worldwide, the big idea for this campaign came to a veteran copywriter as he stood on a street corner in Minneapolis: Show a person who stepped up in some kind of emergency to save the day as a result of having stayed at Holiday Inn Express. The client loved the sense of humor in a category that previously had only portrayed their hotel properties and amenities. By focusing on the wacky "smart" people, Holiday Inn Express was able to create its brand in a tremendously popular and memorable way.

TV was the primary medium for this campaign. Fallon believed commercials would best showcase the provocative and fun message and generate water cooler buzz and free press mentions, also known as earned media. As Fallon put it, "Our goal as an organization is to understand culture so well that we can use its idioms and nuances to transcend blatant selling messages." It worked. The message, conveyed primarily by buying television time, connected with the target audience and became part of pop culture.

The limited Holiday Inn Express national TV budget forced Fallon media planners to create a smart, precise media buy. The ethnographic research showed that target travelers planned their week's work on Sundays or Mondays. Fallon thought if the commercials ran only on those days, they could reach these travelers at home. Adopting a media strategy of buying a larger presence in a few places rather than a smaller presence in more places, Fallon bought spots on the cable stations watched by the road warriors: ESPN, CNN, and the Weather Channel.

See how well this campaign has worked by turning to the It's a Wrap section at the end of the chapter.

Sources: Adapted from Pat Fallon and Fred Senn, *Juicing the Orange: How to Turn Creativity into a Powerful Business Advantage* (Boston: Harvard Business School Press, 2006): 57–72; "Holiday Inn Express Announces Hotel in Northern California," Nov. 27, 2006, http://www.hotelinteractive.com.

In this chapter, we explore the uses, structure, audiences, and the advantages and disadvantages of radio and television as advertising media. We will also review film and video formats that use advertising, as well as the use of product placement in film and television.

BROADCAST MEDIA

When we speak of **broadcast media**, we are discussing media forms that transmit sounds or images electronically. These include radio, television and other video forms, movie advertising and product placements, and now cell phones. Print is a static medium bought by amount of space, such as column inch; in contrast, broadcast media are dynamic and bought by amount of time (seconds, minutes). Broadcast media messages are also fleeting, which means they may affect the viewer's emotions for a few seconds and then disappear, in contrast to print messages that linger and can be revisited and reread. In broadcast media, impressions estimate *viewers* for television and *listeners* for radio.

Broadcast media messages differ from print advertising messages in large part because broadcast engages both sight and sound; in particular, television adds audio as well as motion to a visual experience. Cell phones add text messages to the audio and visual dimensions of television. What that means, in terms of our Facets Model of Effects, is that broadcast is more entertaining, using both drama and emotion to attract attention and en-

Broadcast advertising can be engaging because of the power of music in radio or drama on television.

gage the feelings of the audience. Radio is primarily a music-driven medium, but advertisements can also engage the imagination to create stories in the mind. Likewise, television has movie-like qualities that bring stories to life and create powerful brand imagery. TV can make believers of people who see something demonstrated. Both radio and television use music for emotional effects and to intensify memory of the message through the repetition of tunes.

RADIO

Even with the all-pervasiveness of television, there are more than 10,000 commercial radio stations in the United States, and most of them, except for the new Internet stations, serve a local market. In recent years the radio industry's growth has been flat, with a 5 percent increase in ad revenues for national advertising reported in 2007 and a decrease in local ad sales of 1 percent.[1] That's worrisome to the industry as some 75 percent of advertising revenue comes from the local market.

The Structure of the Radio Industry

Figure 9.1 shows the basic structure of radio. Traditional radio stations are found on the AM/FM dial and primarily serve local markets. Other options for radio listeners include public radio, cable and satellite radio, low-powered stations, and web radio.

Stations with a broadcast range of approximately 2.5 miles are considered local stations. Regional stations may cover an entire state or several states. The most powerful stations are called **clear channel** stations and can deliver signals for long distances.

Radio stations are delivered by two different ranges of **signals**, or radio wave frequencies: AM or FM. The strength of an AM signal depends on the transmitting power the FCC grants the station, but AM signals tend to be stronger, sometimes reaching as far away as 600 miles. An FM station typically sends a signal that travels 50 miles. The tonal quality of an FM signal is superior to that of AM, which is why music stations prefer FM and talk radio and stations that broadcast sporting events are often found on AM. For an advertiser, knowing the advantages and disadvantages of AM and FM radio, as well as determining the technical quality needed for the transmission of the radio commercial, assists in better targeting.

Public radio is very much like its television counterpart and must abide by the same rules and regulations. Local public radio stations are usually affiliates of National Public Radio (NPR) and carry much of the same programming, although they have to buy or subscribe to the NPR services. For that reason, some local public radio stations might carry a

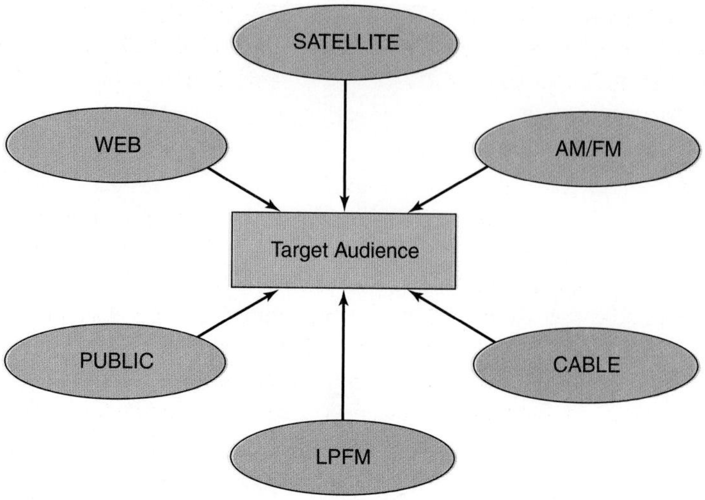

FIGURE 9.1

The Structure of the Radio Industry

full range of NPR programming, while others that are less well funded may only carry a partial list of NPR programs.

These stations are considered noncommercial in that they rely on listener support for most of their funding. In recent years, however, they have slowly expanded their corporate sponsorship messages. Although public television is losing market share to the many new cable competitors, public radio is growing relative to its competitors. Audience size of public radio increased by nearly 60 percent during the 1990s. Likewise, corporate underwriting (or sponsorship) has increased along with the audience size because public radio is one of the few media that can deliver an audience of well-educated, affluent consumers.

The radio industry in the United States includes several other broadcast forms:

* *Cable radio.* Launched in 1990, **cable radio** technology uses cable television receivers to deliver static-free music via wires plugged into cable subscribers' stereos. The thinking behind cable radio is that cable television needs new revenue and consumers are fed up with commercials on radio. The service typically is commercial-free and costs $7 to $12 per month. An example of cable radio is Digital Music Express, which offers CD-quality sound around the clock in 30 music formats from rock to classical.
* *Satellite radio.* The newest radio technology is **satellite radio**. It can deliver your favorite radio stations, regardless of where you are in the continental United States. Sirius and XM satellite radio introduced their systems in 2002 and proposed merger in 2007. For a monthly fee, the system allows you to access some 100 stations. A few car manufacturers offered three-band radios (AM/FM/SAT) in their high-end models. The retailers Circuit City, the WIZ, and others are marketing satellite-compatible car radios.
* *LPFM.* If you're a college student, you probably have a **low-power FM (LPFM)** station on your campus. These nonprofit, noncommercial stations serve a small market, with a reach of three to five miles. Although the FCC has not allowed these stations to carry advertising, many have positioned themselves in case this ruling is changed. Advertising would provide revenue to the stations and local advertisers would enjoy a new, affordable outlet. Often, these stations provide unusual programming unavailable through other radio venues.
* *Web radio.* Web radio provides **webcasting**, which is audio streaming through a Web site. Webcasting station operators from giant Clear Channel Communications to smaller station groups such as Buckley Broadcasting and Emmis Communications all provide radio programming through the Internet. Web radio offers thousands of stations as well as highly diverse radio shows that play mostly to small select

audiences. Moreover, Web-based radio could offer advertisers spots that run only in certain parts of a city, something impossible with broadcast radio. Such localization would open up new opportunities for smaller advertisers and help them handle their budgets more efficiently.

The Radio Audience

Some 233 million people listen to the radio at any point in time.[2] A $20 billion industry, radio is tightly targeted based on special interests (religion, Spanish language, talk shows) and musical tastes. In other words, radio is a highly segmented advertising medium. About 85 percent of the radio stations are focused on music. Program formats offered in a typical market are based on music styles and special interests, including hard rock, gospel, country and western, top-40 hits, soft rock, golden oldies, and nonmusic programs such as talk radio and advice, from car repair to finances to dating. Virtually every household in the United States (99 percent) has at least one radio and most have many sets.

Principle
Media planners use radio for tight targeting of narrow, highly segmented markets.

Listener Segments   Radio listeners can be separated into four segments: station fans, radio fans, music fans, and news fans.

- *Station fans* make up the largest segment of radio listeners. They have a clear preference for one or two stations and spend up to eight hours or more each day listening to their favorites. Most station fans are women between the ages of 25 and 44.
- *Radio fans* represent a third of the listeners. They may listen to four or five different stations per week, and they show no preference for one particular station. Most are under 35 years of age, although many women aged 55 and older are radio fans.
- *Music fans* are most likely to be men between the ages of 25 and 45, although many older adults also fit into the profile.
- *News fans* are a smaller percentage of radio listeners who choose their stations based on a need for news and information. They have one or two favorite stations, listen in short segments, and are almost exclusively aged 35 or older.

Experts contend that much of the future success of radio comes from its ability to reach kids and teens. Recent research has provided some findings that bode well for radio. One study, for example, found that radio listeners are far less likely to change the dial during ads than are television viewers. An unexpected 92 percent listen through the four- and six-minute commercial pods. The percent is even higher for in-car listeners. The study also found a high level of loyalty among listeners for their favorite station.[3]

Dayparts   Advertisers considering radio are most concerned with the number of people listening to a particular station at a given time. Radio audiences are grouped by the time of day when they are most likely to be listening, and the assumption is that different groups listen at different times of the day. The typical radio programming day is divided into five segments called **dayparts** as follows:

Morning Drive Time: 6–10 a.m.

Mid-Day: 10 a.m.–3 p.m.

Evening Drive Time: 3–7 p.m.

Evening: 7 p.m.–midnight

Late Night: midnight–6 a.m.

The 6–10 a.m. segment, or **morning drive time**, is the period when the most listeners are tuned in to radio. This drive-time audience is getting ready for work or commuting to work, and radio is the best medium to reach them.

Measuring the Radio Audience   The radio industry and independent research firms provide several measures for advertisers, including **coverage**, which is similar to circulation for print media. The most basic measure is the station's coverage. This is simply the number of homes in a geographic area that can pick up the station clearly, whether those homes are actually tuned in or not. A better measure is station or program **ratings**, which measures

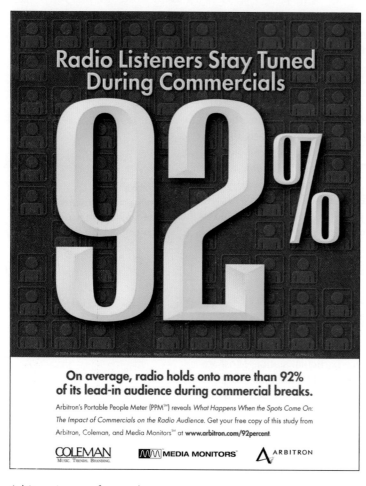

Arbitron is one of several major audience-rating services in the advertising industry. It estimates the size of radio audiences for more than 250 U.S. markets.

Principle

Radio advertising has the power to engage the imagination and communicate on a more personal level than other forms of media.

the percent of homes actually tuned in to the particular station. Factors such as competing programs, types of programs, and time of day or night influence the circulation figure.

• *Arbitron.* Several major audience-rating services operate in the advertising industry. One, the Arbitron Ratings Company, estimates the size of radio audience for more than 250 markets in the United States. Arbitron uses a seven-day, self-administered diary that the person returns to Arbitron at the end of the week. Editors check that each diary has entries for every day and that the postmark shows the diary wasn't mailed before the week was over. The 2007 study that discovered that listeners usually listen to the advertising pods was conducted using a new Arbitron technology called Portable People Meters. This is an audience measurement technology that detects codes embedded in the audio programming.[4]

• *RADAR.* A second audience-rating service is Radio's All-Dimension Audience Research (RADAR). This company, owned by Arbitron, deals with both local and network radio. For RADAR, Statistical Research calls 12,000 respondents for seven consecutive days and asks about network radio listening done the day before. The company contacts respondents before beginning data collection, asking them to pay close attention to their listening habits.

Radio Advertising

The radio listening experience is unlike any of the other media, creating both challenges and opportunities for radio advertisers. It can be a more intimate experience, because we tend to listen to it alone, particularly for people wearing headphones. Media planners use radio to deliver a high level of frequency because radio commercials, particularly **jingles**, which are commercials set to music, lend themselves to repetition.

Radio can also engage the imagination more than other media because it relies on the listener's mind to fill in the visual element. That means radio dramas and ads can involve the audience on a more personal level. Many radio ads use drama, especially **public service announcements (PSAs),** which are spots created by agencies that donate their time and services on behalf of some good cause. PSAs run for free on radio and TV stations. Check out the Ad Council Web site (http://www.adcouncil.org) for a collection of these types of spots.

Radio can be effective at creating humorous mini-dramas that capture listeners' attention. It can also be used in a local market to reach people who aren't reading the newspaper, which is why local newspapers frequently advertise on radio, as the following script for the (Portland, Oregon) *Register-Guard* newspaper classifieds illustrates.

Radio advertising is available on national networks and in local markets. Its revenue is divided into three categories: network, spot, and local. Network revenues are by far the smallest category, accounting for approximately 5 percent of total radio revenues. Local advertising revenues account for 75 percent, and national spot advertising makes up the remainder.[5] We will now examine network, syndicate, and spot radio advertising.

• *Network radio advertising.* Radio advertising can be bought from national networks that distribute programming and advertising to their affiliates. **Network radio** is a group of local affiliates connected to one or more national networks through telephone wires and satellites. There are five major radio networks: Westwood One, CBS, ABC,

Register-Guard **Classifieds Radio Script**

ANNCR:	If you want an easy, fast and convenient way to buy, sell, job hunt or hire, nothing works better than the *Register-Guard* Classifieds. Well, actually, there is maybe one easier way:
SFX:	Knocking. Door opens.
NEW GUY:	Hello, I'm your new neighbor. I brought you an apple pie.
WOMAN:	Well, come in! I'll give you a tour of the house!
NEW GUY:	Oh lovely! Say, hardwood floors!
WOMAN:	Upstairs and downstairs. 3 bedrooms, two baths. Care to take it off my hands?
NEW GUY:	What?
WOMAN:	Buy it. It's for sale.
NEW GUY:	But I just bought the house next door.
WOMAN:	Do you have an out-of-state mother-in-law?
NEW GUY:	Good point. I'll take it— Oooh, a gazebo!
ANNCR:	Yes, they could walk right up to your doorstep, ready to buy, but, really, how many rich, apple-pie toting neighbors can you expect in a month? Three, tops, right? Yes, better to stick with the premiere marketplace of Western Oregon. With more listings and readers than all the competition combined, nothing connects buyers with sellers better than the *Register-Guard* Classifieds, with fresh listings in print and online every day.
SFX:	Knock, knock. Door opens.
NEW GUY:	Sorry, deal's off. The other neighbors have a pool!
WOMAN:	Darn it! Those Johnsons!
ANNCR:	The *Register-Guard*. Get more out of it. Move those homes and make some money! Call 342-twelve-twelve today!

SHOWCASE Karl Schroeder, copywriter at Coates Kokes, Portland, Oregon, and a graduate of the University of Oregon advertising program, contributed this script. He explained that the strategy development began with research to compare the *Register-Guard*'s perception of itself with consumers' perceptions. One insight the agency discovered is that people will say they don't read the newspaper and then admit they read certain sections, such as the TV section. The campaign's objectives were to make the newspaper more approachable by using humor and to remind the one-section readers that the paper also had a useful classifieds section.

Unistar, and Clear Channel. The largest network by far is Clear Channel, with more than 1,200 stations. Satellite transmission has produced important technological improvements that also make it easier to distribute advertising to these stations. Many advertisers view network radio as a viable national advertising medium, especially for food and beverages, automobiles, and over-the-counter drugs. The growth of network radio has contributed to an increase in syndicated radio, creating more advertising opportunities for companies eager to reach new markets. In fact, syndication and network radio have practically become interchangeable terms.

- *Spot radio advertising.* In **spot radio advertising** an advertiser places an advertisement with an individual station rather than through a network. Although networks broadcast blocks of prerecorded national advertisements, they also allow local affiliates open time to sell spot advertisements locally. (Note: national media plans sometimes buy spots at the local level rather than through the network, so it is possible to have a national spot buy.) Thanks to the flexibility it offers the advertiser, spot radio advertising makes up nearly 80 percent of all radio advertising. With so

Lids can be CDs. Used to promote new music offerings, the "enhanced" multimedia CDs can sample songs and provide video clips and other content viewable on computers. In case you're wondering, the straw fits through the hole in the middle of the disk.

many stations available, spot messages can be tailored for particular audiences. In large cities such as New York, Chicago, and Los Angeles, 40 or more radio stations are available. Local stations also offer flexibility through their willingness to run unusual ads, allow last-minute changes, and negotiate rates. Buying spot radio and coping with its nonstandardized rate structures can be very cumbersome, however.

- **Syndicated radio advertising.** Program **syndication** has benefited network radio because it offers advertisers a variety of high-quality, specialized, and usually original programs. Both networks and private firms offer syndication. A local talk show may become popular enough to be "taken into syndication." Here we're not talking about reruns of *Seinfeld*, which is the kind of programming that makes up syndicated television, but original radio programming playing on a large number of affiliated stations, such as the Paul Harvey show, which is broadcast on some 1,200 stations. Advertisers value syndicated programming because of the high level of loyalty of its audience.

Using Radio Effectively   We have seen that radio is highly targeted and inexpensive. Although radio may not be a primary medium for most businesses, it does have excellent reminder and reinforcement capability and is great about building frequency through repetition, particularly if the message can be delivered through a jingle. It's a great tool for targeting audiences through specialized programming, such as talk shows and musical interests. It also sparks the imagination because of its ability to stimulate mental imagery through the *theater of the mind*, which uses humor, drama, music, and sound effects to tell a story. Radio advertising messages tend to have a higher level of acceptance than television because radio listeners are more loyal to their favorite programs and stations.

The president of the Radio Advertising Bureau (RAB) explained that radio has a dynamic consumer engagement that can be measured using audience metrics of reach, relevance, and receptivity. He cites the moving PSAs from the Ad Council's Generous Nation campaign as an example. You can listen to this campaign, which was created in response to the Katrina disaster, on the group's Web site (http://www.adcouncil.org). You'll find the Generous Nation campaign under the "Community" category.

To maximize the impact of a radio spot, timing is critical and depends on understanding the target audience's aperture (when they are most likely to be responsive). Restaurants run spots before meals; auto dealerships run spots on Friday and Saturday, when people are free to visit showrooms; and jewelry stores run spots before Christmas, Valentine's Day, and Mother's Day. For Pizza Hut and similar franchises, radio buys at the local level supplement national television and cable. Radio acts as a reminder, with 30-second spots concentrated from 11 a.m. to noon and 4 to 7 p.m. The messages focus on the location of local Pizza Hut restaurants and any special promotions. Radio is also flexible and allows for easy changes to schedules. For example, a local hardware store can quickly implement a snow-shovel promotion the morning after a snowstorm.

One problem for radio is that it plays in the background for many of our activities. Although the radio is on, the multitasking listener may not really be listening to or concentrating on the message. Listeners tend to tune in and tune out as something catches their attention, which is why effective radio advertising is designed to "break through" the surrounding clutter, which is a problem particularly on AM stations. Recent research found that radio ad clutter is lower than television, which averages 12–14 minutes per hour of commercials versus 10 minutes on radio.[6] Also, the lack of visuals can be a problem for products that need to be demonstrated.

Trends in Radio/Audio Advertising Exciting new opportunities for audio advertising are showing up in novel new formats. For example, mini-CDs are now being embedded in the lids of soft drink cups at movie theaters and theme parks. In an entirely different area of audio surprises, supermarket shoppers may be caught off guard when they walk down an aisle and a voice addresses them from the shelf. Narrowly targeted laser-like sound beams can pinpoint individual shoppers with prerecorded messages, encouraging them to try or buy some product. The audio messages also can be combined with plasma screens carrying electronic visual messages. The most exciting innovation, however, is **podcasting**, which means audio broadcasts—and their advertising—can be heard by people using an iPod or other portable media players who subscribe to the service.

TELEVISION

Television has become a mainstay of American society, with 278 million sets in use. Some 98 percent of American households have one or more television sets with 2.4 televisions in 114 million homes in the United States. Sixty percent of households have three or more TVs.[7] Television is pervasive—it's in almost every home and some homes have televisions in almost every room. In 51 percent of U.S. households, the TV is on "most" of the time.[8] The television audience, however, is highly fragmented, tuning in to a hundred or more different channels in the United States. In spite of that, Nielsen Media Research found that in 2006 the average U.S. household watched a record eight hours of television a day.[9]

The heavy use of television by children is of concern to parents and early childhood experts. Recent studies found that U.S. children spend an average of nearly four hours a day watching television, DVDs, and videos. Furthermore, 77 percent of sixth graders had a TV in their bedroom in 1999. The reason this is important is that children who have a TV in the bedroom spend on average 1 1/2 more hours watching television than those without a TV. Nielsen Media Research shows in 2006 that kids ages 2–11 watched 8.54 hours of kids' programming a week and 5.68 hours of general programming. Overall they watched television for 17.3 hours a week in 2006, an increase from 17.1 in the previous year.[10] Advertisers are happy to hear that kids haven't abandoned TV programming for games and the Web, but these numbers are still worrisome for critics of children's programming and advertising.

Television advertising is embedded in programming, so most of the attention in media buying, as well as in the measurement of television advertising's effectiveness, is focused on the performance of various shows and how they engage their audiences. Some programs are media stars and reach huge audiences—the Super Bowl is a good example with its 93 million viewers in 2007. Others reach small but select audiences, such as *The News Hour with Jim Lehrer* on PBS.

It's become popular to measure the size of the final viewing audience for well-loved programs such as *M*A*S*H* and *Friends* as a gauge of a program's popularity. Table 9.1 offers program comparisons and an indication of how the size of viewing audiences has changed over the years. Three of five homes tuned in to the final episode of *M*A*S*H*, for example, which set the record for the largest audience in the history of television. As the television audience has fragmented, audiences that size are increasingly difficult to attract. Note also that, with the exception of the *Frasier* final episode, which was overshadowed by its NBC sibling, *Friends,* the price of a 30-second ad has increased even as the size of the audience has decreased.

To better understand how television works, let's first consider its structure and programming options. Then we'll look at the television as an advertising medium and the way it connects with its audience, as well as its advantages and disadvantages.

Principle
Television advertising is tied to television programming and its effectiveness is determined by the popularity of the television program.

Structure of the Television Industry

The key types of television delivery systems include wired and unwired networks, local stations, public stations, and cable or subscription. Specialty, syndicated, interactive television,

Table 9.1   Final Episodes

Show	Date Aired	Viewers (in millions)	Av Price/30 sec ad
M*A*S*H CBS	February 1983	105.4	$450,000 ($846,000*)
Cheers NBC	May 1993	80.4	$650,000 ($843,000*)
Seinfeld NBC	May 1998	76.2	$1.5 million ($1.72 million*)
Friends NBC	May 2004	50.0	$2 million
Frasier NBC	May 2004	25.4	$1.2 million

*Adjusted for inflation

Source: Suzanne Vanica, "'Friends' Costly Farewell," *Wall Street Journal*, April 27, 2004, B1; "'Frasier' Finale Calls Off 'Bets,'" May 16, 2004, http://www.csifiles.com; Broadcasting and Cable, May 10, 2004, http://www.broadcastingcable.com.

and TiVo offer different types of programming and ways to manipulate the programming. Figure 9.2 shows these options.

Network Television   A **broadcast network** exists whenever two or more stations are able to broadcast the same program that originates from a single source. The FCC (Federal Communications Commission) defines a *network* as a program service with 15 or more hours of **prime-time** programming per week between the hours of 8 and 11 p.m. Currently, there are four national, over-the-air television networks in the United States: the American Broadcasting Company (ABC), the Columbia Broadcasting System (CBS), the National Broadcasting Company (NBC), and Fox Broadcasting. The big three networks' hold on the viewing audience dropped from 75 percent in 1987 to 36 percent in 2006. When Fox is included, networks still only capture 45 percent of the audience. Independent stations have 11, while PBS stations claim 2 percent. Other on-air networks that are emerging include CW, which was created from the merger of WB and UPN in 2006, and PAX.

The ABC, CBS, and NBC networks own 15 regional stations. The remaining 600 regional stations are privately owned **affiliates** that have a contractual relationship with the broadcasting company (each network has about 150 affiliates). Costs of the network and station operations are paid for from local and national advertising carried on these channels. CW is an example of a cable-delivered network with operational costs supported in part by advertising and in part by subscriptions.

The major networks originate their own programs and provide the programming to local affiliates that in return provide the audience. The affiliate station signs a contract with the national network agreeing to carry network-originated programming during a certain

FIGURE 9.2

The Structure of the Television Industry

Advances in technology have expanded the number of television options advertisers can use to deliver their messages to audiences, as well as threats from TiVo and other operations.

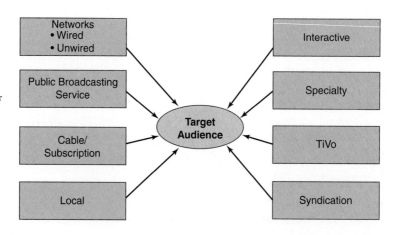

part of its schedule. The network sells some commercial time to national advertisers and leaves some open for the affiliates to fill with local advertising. Affiliates pay their respective networks 30 percent of the fees they charge local advertisers. In turn, affiliates receive a percentage of the advertising revenue (12 to 25 percent) paid to the national network. This advertising is the primary source of affiliate revenues.

In over-the-air network scheduling, the national advertiser contracts with a national network to show commercials on a number of affiliated stations. Sometimes an advertiser purchases only a portion of the network coverage, known as a *regional leg*. This type of purchase is common with sports programming in which different games are shown simultaneously in different parts of the country.

The problem facing network TV is that its audience—at least the audience for the big networks like NBC, CBS, and ABC—continues to erode as other viewing opportunities make inroads on their audiences. It's particularly a problem for reaching young men who are turning to cable, computers, and video games for their entertainment. Bob Garfield, ad critic for *Advertising Age*, noted a decade-long erosion of the young male audience, which he called a "tectonic shift."[11] Others speculate that these young male viewers, who are a critical target audience for a number of product categories such as MTV, Pepsi, Coke, and Sony Playstation, are now playing video games or surfing the Internet.[12] Although young people devote an average four hours to media consumption, the consumption patterns are switching away from television.

Cable and Subscription Television   The initial purpose of **cable television** was to improve reception in certain areas of the country, particularly mountainous regions and large cities. However, cable systems have grown rapidly because they provide highly targeted special-interest programming options. Cable is the most familiar example of **subscription television**, which means that people sign up for service and pay a monthly fee. Currently, two out of three homes subscribe to cable through traditional cable delivery systems. Research has also determined that subscription levels increase with household income.

Cable is stealing ad revenue from network TV. For example, network television increased its ad dollars by 2.5 percent from 1998 to 2003, but cable increased 82 percent during the same five-year period, and that trend continues today. Clearly cable is a significant threat to the financial health of the networks. One reason is that cable stations have developed programs that get high viewership, such as *The Sopranos* on HBO. Viewing time for cable also has increased. The average American watches cable or satellite for nearly as many hours as network TV. In fact, the Cabletelevision Advertising bureau found that ad-supported cable has taken over the lead from the Big Four broadcast networks.[13]

Through its long run, which ended in 2007, the highly successful Sopranos series brought new power and visibility to cable station HBO.

Some cable stations develop and air their own programs in addition to programs initiated by other stations. Pay programming and on-demand programming, available to subscribers for an additional monthly fee, offers movies, specials, and sports under such plans as Home Box Office, Showtime, and The Movie Channel. Pay networks do not currently sell advertising time.

Another form of subscription television is **satellite television**. Launched in 1994, DirectTV offers the equipment, including the satellite dish, to access some 125 national and local channels. Satellite television is particularly useful for people who live in rural areas without local service.

About 8 percent of cable programming comes from independent cable networks and from independent **superstations**. These networks include Cable News Network (CNN), the Disney Channel, the Entertainment and Sports Programming Network (ESPN), and a group of independent superstations whose programs are carried by satellite to cable operators (for example, WTBS-Atlanta, WGN-Chicago, and WWOR-New York).

The two categories of cable scheduling are network and local. **Network cable** scheduling runs commercials across the entire subscriber group simultaneously. With **local cable** scheduling, advertisers can show their commercials to highly restricted geographic audiences through **interconnects**, a special cable technology that allows local or regional advertisers to run their commercials in small geographic areas through the interconnection of a number of cable systems. Interconnections offer small advertisers an affordable way to reach certain local television audiences.

Local Television   Most local television stations are affiliated with a network, as explained previously, and carry both network programming and their own programs. **Independent stations** are local stations not affiliated with networks. Costs for local advertising vary, depending on the size of the market and the demand for the programs carried. For example, a major station in Houston may charge local advertisers $2,000 for a 30-second spot during network prime time. This same time slot may cost $50 in a smaller town. The local television market is substantially more varied than the national market. Most advertisers for the local market are local retailers, primarily department stores or discount stores, financial institutions, automobile dealers, restaurants, and supermarkets. Advertisers buy time on a station-by-station basis.

National advertisers sometimes buy local advertising on a city-by-city basis, using **spot buys**. They do this to align the buy with their product distribution, to "heavy-up" a national schedule to meet competitive activities, or to launch a new product in selected cities.

Public Television   Although many people still consider **public television** to be commercial-free, in 1984 the FCC liberalized its rules. It allowed the approximately 350 Public Broadcasting System (PBS) stations some leeway in airing commercial messages, called **program sponsorships**. The FCC says these messages should not ask for a purchase or make price or quality comparisons. PBS is an attractive medium for advertisers because it reaches affluent, well-educated households. As the PBS Kids ad demonstrates, it also attracts households with children. In addition, PBS still has a refined image, and PBS advertisers are viewed as good corporate citizens because of their support for noncommercial TV.

Current FCC guidelines allow ads to appear on public television only during the local 2.5-minute program breaks. Each station maintains its own acceptability guidelines. Some PBS stations accept the same ads that appear on paid programming. However, most PBS spots are created specifically for public stations. Some PBS stations will not accept any commercial corporate advertising, but they do accept noncommercial ads that are "value neutral"—in other words, ads that make no attempt to sell a product or service.

Programming and Distribution Options

Different types of programming options and distribution formats other than traditional networks are available to stations and advertisers. Distribution options include low-power TV, pay-per-view, and program syndication. These all reduce or eliminate advertising opportunities.

- *Low-power.* The FCC has licensed **low-power television (LPTV)** to provide programming outlets to minorities and communities that are underserved by full-power stations. LPTV stations have signals that cover a radius of 15 miles. (Full-power stations reach viewers in a 70-mile radius.) Homes pull in LPTV signals

Television programs advertise in other media in order to build their audiences, such as this ad for the PBS KIDS GO! program Fetch!

through special antennas and LPTV carries advertising for local retailers and businesses. Hotels and restaurants use multipoint distribution systems (MDS) to provide guests with movies and other entertainment. Although specialty systems like these can carry ads, they are a minor delivery system.

- *Pay-per-view.* Delivered by satellite, **pay-per-view television** is usually used for major sporting and music events. Commercial customers, such as restaurants and bars, and home viewers subscribe to live delivery of the events without commercials.
- *Program syndication.* Independent TV and cable stations are fueling the syndication boom. One of the biggest growth areas in the media industry, syndicated programs are television programs purchased by local stations to fill time in open hours. **Off-network syndication** includes reruns of network shows, like *M*A*S*H, The Bob Newhart Show, Star Trek,* and *ER. Seinfeld* went into syndication in 1998. Each episode was sold for $6 million, meaning that the 160 episodes generated nearly $1 billion, $50 million of which went directly to Jerry Seinfeld as producer. *Everybody Loves Raymond* went into syndication in the summer of 2001 and also has been a huge success. Sometimes current network shows such as *Law and Order* and *CSI* are purchased from the networks by syndication distributors, such as Starcom Worldwide or Viacom, and moved into syndication even as the shows' owners continue to produce new episodes. This process is called **first-run syndication**.

New Technology and Innovative Television   New technology is having an impact on programming options, as well as on distribution patterns and systems. Innovations, such as interactive TV and high-definition TV, expand advertising opportunities.

- *Interactive television.* An interactive TV set is basically a television with computer capabilities. With some systems it is possible to do everything you can do online, except that the monitor is either the TV screen or a picture-in-picture configuration that lets you watch one or more television programs while surfing the Internet. **Interactive television** development appears to be taking off, thanks to **broadband**. Simply defined, broadband has more capacity to send data and images into a home or business through a cable television wire than the much smaller capacity of a traditional telephone wire or television antenna system. The iTV Institute in the United Kingdom reports that 34 million households worldwide and 20 million in the United States subscribed to iTV service in 2006. [14]
- *High-definition TV (HDTV).* Like interactive TV, **high-definition TV (HDTV)** has been slow to build demand, although that seems to be changing. HDTV is a type of TV set that delivers movie quality, high-resolution images. Of course, the station or network has to broadcast the program in an HDTV format. It's been a struggle getting enough programming to build demand on the consumer side. As stations upgrade their equipment, however, they are moving to HDTV, and the availability of programming is now making it more desirable for consumers who are buying new TV sets. Advertisers are happy to know that this population is expected to increase dramatically from 48 million in 2006 to 151 million in 2011 worldwide. [15] Viewers will be forced to change to the HDTV format, however, as the last day of analog transmission in the United States is February 17, 2009.

Digital Video Recorders (DVRs)   Another new technology that is having a profound effect on television programming and the way people watch television are **digital video recorders (DVRs)**. Introduced by Replay TV and TiVo in 1999, DVR systems allow users to record favorite TV shows and watch them whenever they like. Users get a digital recording "box" and subscribe to a service that distributes programming. The revolutionary technology makes it possible to record the programming without the hassles of videotape, letting users pause, do instant replays, and begin watching programs even before the recording has finished. It's known as **time-shifting**. More than 15 million U.S. households had DVR technology by 2007, roughly 12 to 20 percent of all U.S. households.

Here's the rub for advertisers: DVR viewers need not fast-forward through commercials if their service gives them the option to program out commercials as the shows are

With TiVo, you'll never have to watch bad TV again. Unless, of course, you really like watching bad TV.

Hey, it's your time. Spend it watching whatever you want to. You tell TiVo what shows you like, and TiVo takes care of it. Records 'em all, no questions asked (or judgments rendered), so you can watch 'em later, like after you finish dinner.

TiVo DVRs are like VCRs, but with a hard disk and without the hassles of videotape. It hooks up to cable, satellite or antenna and digitally records up to 60 hours of your favorite stuff. And it's very easy. Just buy the box ($399), subscribe to the TiVo service, and call it a night—whatever kind of night you like. Still say you can live without it? Ask any TiVo subscriber.

Order now to get Free Shipping and a 30-Day Money-Back Guarantee at www.tivo.com/MH07 or call 1-877-BUY-TIVO (289-8486) Code: MH07.

Season Pass™	Control Live TV	WishList	Series2 DVR
Choose your favorite shows and the TiVo service will automatically record every episode, whenever it airs.	With TiVo you can pause, rewind, and stereo live TV.	Got a favorite actor? Special hobby? The TiVo service will find and record programs based on your interests.	Now, up to 80 hours recording time.

DVR technology poses a challenge for advertisers since it enables consumers to bypass commercials.

recorded. TiVo is a substantial threat to marketers because it allows consumers to skip commercials completely. Advertisers and television executives are alarmed over the increasing popularity of the technology. It calls into question audience measurement numbers: If 20 percent of the audience is recording *24* on Monday night only to watch it Saturday morning commercial-free, then is the Monday night measurement accurate?

It also raises the issue of how advertisers should respond. Should they seek legislation to block such technology? After all, ads are what keep television (relatively) free, at least on network TV. Or should they seek new ways to send messages? Coca-Cola, for example, has created ads that appear on screen when a DVR user pauses a program for a few minutes.

A Nielsen study released in 2007, however, found that viewers are not zipping through commercials as much as advertisers feared. The study found that DVR owners watch 40 percent of the commercials they encounter either because they like the ads or they simply can't be bothered to fast-forward.[16] To further understand this pattern, TiVo has also announced that it is considering a service that will provide second-by-second data about which programs the company's subscribers are watching and which commercials they are skipping.[17] The proposal faces some privacy questions, but the data would be a pot of gold for advertisers who are constantly searching for information about the effectiveness of their commercials to catch and hold viewers' attention.

The Television Audience

A great number of advertisers consider television their primary medium. Can television deliver a target audience to advertisers effectively? The Matter of Principle box reviews this question in terms of the objectionable content of some programs.

What do we really know about how audiences watch television? Is it a background distraction? Do we switch from channel to channel without watching any single show? Or do we carefully and intelligently select what we watch on television? Television viewers are often irritated by what they see, particularly the advertising, and are not reluctant to switch channels, zip through commercials, or avoid them altogether using TiVo. The Super Bowl is one of the few programs where viewers actually watch in order to see the commercials. In 2007, A. C. Nielsen found that the average drop in viewing between the game and the commercials was less that 1 percent. CBS says that the typical drop during a normal program is approximately 5 percent.[18]

Clutter is part of the problem advertisers face and the audience has become very good at avoidance, unless the ads are intrusive or highly engaging as the Boost Mobile commercials for ring tones demonstrate. Check out the company's Web site for information related to the "Where you at?" campaign (http://www.boostmobile.com).

Measuring the Television Audience   Similarly to print media, television audiences are measured in terms of exposure and impressions. For television programs, the exposure is estimated in terms of number of viewers. The 2007 Super Bowl featuring the Chicago Bears and Indianapolis Colts, for example, was the second most viewed Bowl game ever, with some 93 million viewers—compared to the 1996 Dallas vs. Pittsburgh game with its 97 million viewers. The 2007 event was actually the third most watched program in broadcast history; the record holder remains the *M*A*S*H* final episode in 1983.

Exposure is television's equivalent to circulation. Exposure measures households with sets turned on, a population referred to as **households using television (HUT)**. But a

A MATTER OF PRINCIPLE

Trashy Shows Trash Advertisers' Brands

Critics sometimes complain about the trashiness of many television programs—sex and exposed body parts, profanity, violence, sexism, racism, infidelity, and other sins. It's particularly a problem for children's shows and prime-time shows that children are likely to see.

The industry has heard these complaints and responded by developing a rating system similar to movie ratings. Frustrated parents contend, however, that it conceals more than it informs. At least the movie industry ratings are supported by reviews that tell more of the story behind the ratings. Likewise, the industry's V-chip, which relies on this same rating system, is of questionable help to parents who want to block the viewing of trashy programs by their kids.

But the problem is more than just kids' viewing adult programs. A Duke professor believes that television violence is used deliberately by advertisers to target TV's most valuable demographic—male viewers ages 18–34 who are the top consumers of violent shows. Since they are prone to switch to video games, television fights back with increasingly violent content. Research shows that TV violence desensitizes viewers to violence and increased aggression, and the younger the viewers are, the greater the impact.

How do advertisers respond to these charges? Many of them are concerned about alienating their target audiences by advertising on programs that are not family friendly. And they are also worried about aligning their brands with programs seen as trashy.

Is there a list of the "dirty dozen" TV shows that savvy media buyers know to avoid? *Media Life* magazine queried its readers in 2006 in an online survey, and here are the results. See if you agree that these are the dirty dozen of television programming:

1. "Jerry Springer"
2. Fox's "Cops"
3. FX's "Nip/Tuck"
4. (tie) Fox's "America's Most Wanted"
5. Fox's "Family Guy"
6. (tie) "WWE"
7. Syndicated court shows
8. NBC's "Law & Order: Special Victims Unit"
9. (tie) ABC's "Desperate Housewives"
10. Fox's "The War at Home"
11. "Sex and the City" (syndicated)
12. Any MyNetwork show

Sources: James T. Hamilton, "Does TV Make Kids Killers?" Duke Policy News, May 19, 1998, http://www.pubpol.duke.edu; Frederica Mathewes-Green, "While TV Moguls Dither, Parents' Guides Deliver," Hoover Institution Policy Review, March/April 1997, http://www.hoover.org; Diego Vasquez, "No-no List: The Dirty Dozen TV Shows," Media Life, February 12, 2007, http://www.medialifemagazine.com.

HUT figure doesn't tell you if anyone is watching the program. Remember from Chapter 8 that we defined an **impression** as one person's opportunity to be exposed one time to an ad. Like print, the impressions from television—the number of viewers watching a program—might be greater than the number of households reached since there may be more than one viewer watching and the commercial may be repeated several times in a program or during a time period. We add all these impressions up and call them **gross impressions**.

- *Ratings.* These gross impression figures become very large and difficult to work with, which is why the television industry, similar to radio, uses ratings (percentage of exposure), which is an easier measurement to work with because it converts the raw figure to a percentage of the households. When you read about a television show having a rating of 20.0 that means that 20 percent, or one fifth of all the households with televisions, were tuned in to that program. Note: one rating point equals 1 percent of the national's estimated 1,114,000 TV homes; that's why planners describe this program as having 20 **rating points**, or percentage points. A 20 rating is actually a huge figure, since the fragmentation of cable has diversified television watching and made it very difficult to get 20 percent of the households tuned to any one program.
- *Share.* A better estimate of impressions might be found in a program's **share of audience**, which refers to the percent of viewers based on the number of sets turned on. The share figure is always larger than the rating, since the base is smaller. For example the 2007 Super Bowl got a rating of 43 (43 percent of all households with television), but its share was 64, which means 64 percent of all televisions turned on were tuned to the Super Bowl.[19]

SHOWCASE These four commercials in the "Where you at?" campaign were contributed by Sunita Deshpande, copywriter at Berlin Cameron in New York. The commercials for Boost Mobile announced the new service of CallTones—something you hear instead of a ring. They used Nick Cannon as the sought-after star demonstrated his use of the cell phone ring tones to deliver different messages to different callers.

Several independent rating firms periodically sample a portion of the television viewing audience, assess the size and characteristics of the audiences watching specific shows, and then make these data available, for a fee, to advertisers and ad agencies, which use them in their media planning.

Currently, A. C. Nielsen dominates this industry and provides the most commonly used measure of national and local television audiences. The calculation is based upon audience data from about 5,000 measurement instruments, called **people meters**, which record what television shows are being watched, the number of households that are watching, and which family members are viewing. The recording is done automatically; household members indicate their presence by pressing a button. These are placed in randomly selected households in the 210 television markets in the United States. The company also uses viewer diaries mailed out during the **sweeps** period, which are quarterly periods when more extensive audience data and demographics are gathered. About 1 million diaries are returned each year.

Nielsen continues to add people meters in its top markets to track local viewing patterns. Currently, people meters only determine audience demographics on a national basis. On a local basis, meters are used only to determine what show is being watched, and not the specific demographics of who is watching it. Demographic data come from the diaries. The new locally based meter system will also allow Nielsen to identify the age, race, and sex of viewers on a nightly basis, which is a significant improvement over the old measuring system; it will make the viewing audience measurements more reliable at the local level.[20]

Television Advertising

Television is used for advertising because it works like the movies—it tells stories, engages the emotions, creates fantasies, and can have great visual impact. Because it's an action medium, it is also good for demonstrating how things work. It brings brand images to life and adds personality to a brand. An example of the dramatic, emotional power of television comes from one of the greatest commercials of all time. Called "Iron Eyes Cody," the Ad

Council PSA was created as part of an environmental campaign. It shows a Native American paddling a canoe through a river ruined by trash.

Forms of Television Advertising   The actual form of a television commercial depends on whether a network, local, or cable schedule is used, as we see in Figure 9.3. Networks allow sponsorships, participations, and spot announcements through their affiliates. In turn, local affiliates allow local sponsorships, spot announcements, and national spots. Cable systems allow system (national) spots and local spots. Finally, interactive television allows (national) spots and local spots.

To read about this "Keep America Beautiful" campaign, go to http://www. adcouncil.org and choose "Historic Campaigns" from the list on the left; then scan down to the "Pollution: Keep America Beautiful" heading.

- *Sponsorships.* In program **sponsorships**, the advertiser assumes the total financial responsibility for producing the program and providing the accompanying commercials. *The Hallmark Hall of Fame* is an example of a sponsored program. Sponsorship can have a powerful effect on the viewing public, especially because the advertiser can control the content and quality of the program as well as the placement and length of commercials. However, the costs of producing and sponsoring a 30- or 60-minute program make this option too expensive for most advertisers. Several advertisers can produce a program jointly as an alternative to single sponsorship. This plan is quite common with sporting events, where each sponsor receives a 15-minute segment.
- *Participations.* Sponsorships represent less than 10 percent of network advertising. The rest is sold as **participations**, where advertisers pay for 10, 15, 20, 30, or 60 seconds of commercial time during one or more programs. The advertiser can buy any time that is available. This approach, which is the most common one used in network advertising today, provides a great deal more flexibility in market coverage, target audiences, scheduling, and budgeting. Participations do not create the same high impact as sponsorships, however. Finally, the "time avails" (available time slots) for the most popular programs are often bought up by the largest advertisers, leaving fewer good time slots for small advertisers.

    The price of a commercial is based on the rating of the surrounding program (note the rating is for the program, not the commercial). The price is also based on the

Principle
If you are going to use television, design a message that takes advantage of its visual and emotional impact.

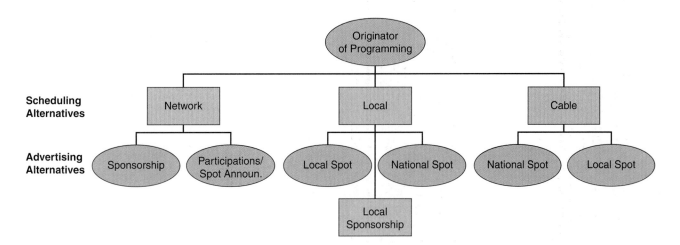

FIGURE 9.3

The Television Advertisers' Media Choices
DVR technology poses a challenge for advertisers since it enables consumers to bypass commercials.

daypart during which the commercial is shown. The following table shows the Television Standard Dayparts. The most expensive time block is prime time.

Standard Television Dayparts

Early morning	M–F 7–9 a.m.
Daytime	M–F 9 a.m.–4:30 p.m.
Early fringe	M–F 4:30–7:30 p.m.
Prime access	M–F 7:30–8 p.m.
Prime time	M–S 8–11 p.m.
	Su 7–11 p.m.
Late news	M–Su 11–11:30 p.m.
Late night	M–Su 11:30 p.m.–1 a.m.
Saturday morning	Sa 8 a.m.–1 p.m.
Weekend afternoon	Sa–Su 1 p.m.–7 p.m.

Note: All times are Eastern Standard Time (EST).

• *Spot announcements.* The third form a television commercial can take is the **spot announcement**. Spot announcements are commercials that appear in the breaks between programs, which local affiliates sell to advertisers who want to show their ads locally. Commercials are sold on a station-by-station basis to local, regional, and national advertisers. However, local buyers dominate spot television. PSAs are also distributed to stations for local play based upon the station's time availability.

Rating Commercials   We mentioned earlier that most rating systems are designed to evaluate audience for the television programs. That has always been a problem for advertisers who wonder if there is carryover from viewing the program to viewing the commercials that appear within them. To address those concerns, Nielsen has plans to develop a ratings system for TV commercials. This will provide a new level of accountability for advertisers because they will know who and how many are actually watching their commercials, rather than just the programs in which the ads appear.[21]

Another proposal is to start a new rating system that will compete with Nielsen, whose critics feel its set-top boxes are outmoded. A group of media companies and advertisers is working with the erinMedia research company to develop a new system that will also consider the impact of DVRs and other technologies that help viewers skip commercials. The erinMedia technology will track all television behavior, not just a representative panel, and ads as well as programs. The technology will also make it possible to direct ads to particular cable subscribers based on their interests and behavior.[22]

Using Television Advertising Effectively   The television networks have been suffering as their audiences have splintered. Some marketers even suggest the days of traditional television advertising are over. The Chief Marketing Officer (CMO) for Philips Electronics, for example, tells us, "The traditional 30-second commercial is in serious danger." More than that, he contends that "advertising is becoming increasingly irrelevant," because of the new media environment and the changing patterns of consumer media use.[23]

In spite of this dismal assessment, television advertising is still cost effective, not because it is cheap, which it is not, but because of its mass appeal and wide reach. It remains the most cost-effective way to deliver a mass media message to a large audience. For an advertiser attempting to reach a largely undifferentiated market, a 30-second spot on a top-rated show may cost a penny or less for each person reached. Furthermore, television also has a buzz factor with viewers talking with friends about their favorite programs.

Television advertising also makes a strong visual and emotional impact. The interaction of sight, sound, color, motion, and drama creates a stronger emotional response than most other forms of advertising media. In Chapter 8 we mentioned the new buzzword *engagement*, which certainly applies to TV. Television is particularly good at creating messages that can be highly engrossing. Even with TiVo, people still sit through advertisements and use online search engines to seek out advertising that is relevant to them.[24] Television

Principle

Network television is an expensive medium, but because of its traditionally high reach to a mass audience, it is considered cost efficient.

The Ad Council and the American Legacy Foundation have created two new spots for the antismoking youth campaign discussed in Chapter 1. These new commercials focus on the dangers of secondhand smoke. Using a twist on the idea of "passing gas," the humorous commercials are based on the fact that cigarette smoke contains toxic gases and, therefore, smokers should be sensitive about exposing nonsmokers. In the commercials, family and friends ask them to step outside to "pass gas."

is also good for delivering messages that require need action and movement, such as demonstrations and dramas, as The Inside Story illustrates.

Television has some drawbacks, as well. The commercial breaks between programs can be difficult time slots for advertisers because there is a great deal of clutter from competing commercials, station breaks, and public service announcements. Commercial breaks also tend to be the time when viewers take a break from their television sets. Research has found that the best position is at the beginning and the end of the commercial break—the spots in the middle have only a quarter of the impact.[25]

The downside of large reach to a mass audience is **wasted reach**—communication directed at an audience that may not fit the advertiser's target market. Cable television is much more targeted than network and spot television, so it has less waste. Disinterest is another problem because people are often inclined to **zip** (fast forward) or **zap** (change channels) commercials if they don't have TiVo.

Another big drawback is that television advertising is expensive relative to other media, both for time and production costs. A 30-second, prime-time spot averages about $185,000, and most advertisers would want to run a commercial multiple times. That average, however, doesn't mean much as costs vary considerably for a highly rated prime-time

THE INSIDE STORY

Selling a Political Party with Humor

By Ingvi Logason, *Principal HÉR&NÚ, Reykjavik, Iceland*

Advertising for political parties is one of the most challenging assignments in the advertising business. The competition is far more fierce and ruthless than in any consumer category, and the media is saturated with political ads, making it hard to stand out. That's true in the U.S. political arena, but it's also true in elections in other countries as well.

Framsokn, one of three largest political parties in Iceland, found itself in a downward spiral in popularity for the parliament election in the 2000s. According to research, the party's image was old, "heavy," negatively conservative, rural, and out of sync with what the true party was. Even though it had been in a successful government for 12 years, opinion polls showed that the party registered an all-time low in opinion polls. The party was also in the forefront of various unpopular issues supported by the government such as environmental problems and the invasion in Iraq.

The objective as defined by the ad agency HÉR&NÚ Marketing Communications was to correct the image problem, inspire voters with vote of confidence in the party, aim for 17 percent of voters support (an increase from 10 percent), and get more seats in parliament.

What do you do to completely turn around voters' image of a political party?

You use humor with a serious selling point. You do "product advertising" for a political race. And you use engaging television ads.

The agency's mission was to break the mold of political advertising with a new fresh approach to politics—political ads don't have to be boring, serious, and "gloomy." Its fully integrated, multilayered campaign took more of a consumer advertising approach. All advertisement had to pass the "what's in it for me" test and have a strong selling point.

One of the strategic decisions was to focus on TV advertising as the cornerstone of the campaign because of its ability to reach a broad target audience, as well as its ability to deliver the image message and resonate in a gently humorous way with the concerns of voters. TV counted for 65 percent of media budget.

Not only was the party a winner, the campaign was rewarded with a gold Effie for turning around the party's image. It was the best political campaign that year—and possibly ever in Iceland.

The commercial opens with a middle-aged man walking into a TV area. He turns on the TV and as he searches for his glasses, his son grabs the TV remote, takes a seat in the chair, and changes to a loud rock station. With surprise and irritation the older man realizes he's lost his place in front of the TV. The commercial ends with an announcer voiceover saying, "Make it easier for people to buy their own house. . . . Vote for Framsokn."

Ingvi Logason is a principal in HÉR&NÚ Marketing Communications and a graduate of Western Florida University. Logason's work was nominated by Professor Tom Groth.

Table 9.2   Time Is Money: The Top Shows by Ad Rates

2006	$/:30
American Idol	$600,000
Desperate Housewives	$394,000
24	$364,000
CSI	$347,000
Grey's Anatomy	$344,000
Survivor	$296,000
2004	**$/:30**
Friends	$473,500
Will & Grace	$414,500
2001	**$/:30**
ER	$425,400
Friends	$353,600
1998	**$/:30**
Seinfeld	$575,000
ER	$560,000
1992	**$/:30**
Murphy Brown	$310,000
Roseanne	$290,000
1987	**$/:30**
Cosby Show	$369,500
Cheers	$307,000
1980	**$/:30**
M*A*S*H	$150,000
Dallas	$145,000

Sources: Claire Atkinson, "'Desperate Housewives' Keeps Sunday Rates Competitive," *Advertising Age,* September 21, 2006, http://www.adage.com; 2006-2007 Prime Time TV Season 30 Sec Ad Rates, http://www.frankwbaker.com; Joe Mandese, "The Buying and Selling," *Advertising Age,* Spring 1995, 20; "Top 10 Shows by Ad Rates," *Advertising Age,* September 15, 1997, S2.

show versus a lower rated program. Table 9.2 shows TV ad rates during relatively current shows, such as *American Idol* and *Desperate Housewives*. You can also see that these prices have quadrupled since the 1980s.

Production costs are higher than ads in other media, as well. They include filming the commercial (several thousand to several hundred thousand dollars) and paying the talent—writers, directors, and actors. For celebrities, the price tag can be millions of dollars. The cost of producing an average commercial can range from about a quarter to half of the cost of the time. That could add approximately $50,000 to $100,000 in production costs for an $185,000 ad buy.

Another problem is clutter, and its stepchildren, intrusiveness and irritation. In the past, the National Association of Broadcasters (NAB) restricted the allowable commercial time per hour to approximately six minutes, but the Justice Department overturned this restriction and the number of commercials has increased. As the number of commercials increases, the visibility and persuasiveness of television advertising diminishes. As clutter has increased, advertisements are becoming more intrusive to grab attention from a disinterested and irritated audience. The high irritation level is what has led viewers to mute and zap commercials and use DVRs that make it possible to eliminate the advertising altogether.

Principle
As the number of commercial messages increase, the visibility and persuasiveness of television advertising diminishes.

Changes and Trends in Broadcast Television

New forms of television advertising are increasing with sponsorships, product placements, and advertiser-controlled programming. Wieden & Kennedy, the agency for Nike, is actively developing itself into an entertainment company with the goal to make its client a content provider on television, rather than just an advertiser or sponsor. Similarly in London, the MindShare media unit of advertising conglomerate WPP is developing shows for its clients. With clutter and the rising cost of network TV, media and advertising planners are finding that they need to offer clients a different way of marketing brands.[26]

Second, the telecommunication industry and the cable industry are battling over who will control digital TV technology. Digitization (the transfer of analog pictures, text, and video into a series of ones and zeros) will allow information to flow into households just as electricity does today. As a result, tomorrow's viewers may see only what they want to see. Switching channels will be a thing of the past because TVs will be programmed to send only programs preselected by the viewer. The question is then which medium (telephone or cable) is better able to deliver this new technology.

That question leads us to convergence and blurring of media, the point Jugenheimer was making in his Part III Introduction. Similar to the changes in print media, video images are also being digitized and moved to the Internet. The MTV music channel, for example, which reaches a largely teen audience, is moving to a multidevice, multiplatform, multichannel world. To keep its new formats appealing to teens, MTV has hired a 16-year-old to help program its new ventures.[27] And amateurs displaying their videos on YouTube have created a whole new—and challenging—world of video for advertisers to consider.

Advertising executives are also being challenged by new delivery systems—including streaming video on the Web and on cell phones. An Advertising.com study in 2006 found that 66 percent of Web users said they view streaming content at least once a week and 94 percent said they preferred seeing ads rather than paying a fee.[28] Advertising executives were most surprised by the meteoric growth of video outlets, such as YouTube (viewer generated video) and Second Life (virtual reality Web sites), as well as the popularity of content mash-ups created, again, by viewers.[29]

Watching TV shows on the Web is another example of a trend we've talked about in previous chapters—the blurring of media forms. Disney, for example, offers an ad-supported broadband player that lets viewers watch prime-time shows on the Internet. The ad space sold out immediately. Among others, ABC.com is launching "America's Funniest Home Videos" online, and ESPN is launching programs on the Verizon Wireless network.[30]

The implications of these changes for the media planner are significant. Most notably, the advantage of traditional network television to deliver a message to a mass audience is quickly disappearing. Instead, television is becoming an increasingly fragmented medium, which means that reaching a mass audience will be increasingly difficult.

OTHER BROADCAST FORMS

Radio and television dominate broadcast, but there are other forms that also carry advertising and marketing communication messages. We'll discuss film and video here, as well as product placements.

Film and Video

Movie theaters, particularly the large chain theaters, sell time at the beginning of their film showings for commercials, called **trailers**. Most of these trailers are previews advertising upcoming films, but some are national commercials for brands or ads for local businesses. These ads can be targeted to a certain extent by the nature of the film and the rating, such as G or PG. Some films, such as *The Calendar Girls*, draw an audience that is heavily female, while action films, such as the *Matrix* series, draw more males.

Movie trailers are one of the fastest growing types of advertising because of advances in digital technology. According to the Cinema Advertising Council, in-theater advertising is a $500 million industry.[31] The cost of the trailer is based on the number of theaters showing the spot and their estimated monthly attendance. Generally the cost of a trailer in a first-run theater is about the same as the cost of a 30-second television spot in prime time.

The reason trailers are valued by advertisers is that they play to a captive audience with their attention on the screen, not reading or talking to other people. The attention level is higher for these ads than for most any other form of commercials. But the captive audience dimension is also the biggest disadvantage of movie advertising because people who have paid $6 to $10 for a ticket resent the intrusion. They feel they paid for the ticket so they shouldn't have to pay with their time and attention to watch commercials.

Public service ads (PSAs) are usually placed through television channels that donate time for the spots, but in a recent move 41 state attorneys general have called on motion picture studios to insert anti-smoking PSAs from the *truth*® campaign, which we profiled in Chapter 1, before movies that depict smoking. The group sent a letter along with three of the ads to key entertainment industry leaders.[32]

The question is: How effective is advertising at changing behaviors that are seen as socially undesirable? Auburn Professor Herb Rotfeld challenges the use of such messages in the Matter of Practice box. He argues that "just as advertising people like to claim power in moving products, they also claim an equally great ability to move the public mind in 'selling' various social goals." He questions that assumption:

The Cinema Advertising Council (CAC) is an organization devoted to advertising in movies. This ad was placed in *Advertising Age* to reach media buyers and remind them of the power of cinema advertising to target particular groups of moviegoers.

> Just because advertising sometimes can help generate consumer interest in specific brand names does not also mean that every advertised effort will get people to make significant changes in their behavior. There are numerous pragmatic differences between selling brand name products or services and convincing people to change the way they live their lives.

What do you think? Is public service advertising worth the effort or a waste of time and money?

DVD and video distributors are also placing ads before their movies and on the cases. The targeting strategy is the same as that for theater ads where the ad is matched to the movie audience. Unlike the theaters, rental videos tend to carry more brand advertising than movie previews. Even some billboards are now equipped to run mini-movies and ads electronically. The job search company Monster.com has been successful with trailers that replay as electronic signboard messages in public spaces—another example of media convergence with video appearing as out-of-home media.

Promotional video networks run programs and commercials, such as the channels you see in grocery stores, doctor's offices, and truck stops that distribute commercials by video or satellites. The Kmart in-store channel, for example, is sent by satellite to 2,300 stores.[33] Finally, videos and DVDs are used for product literature, as well as in public relations for news releases to the media.

More recently marketers, such as General Electric and Pepsi, are experimenting with short video clips—both live-action and animated—that can be watched free on the video-on-demand service available to Time Warner cable customers. The shorts can also be seen on the GE Web site (http://www.ge.com/imaginationtheater), as well as on sites like myspace.com, video.google.com, and YouTube.com.[34]

A MATTER OF PRACTICE

The Social Harm of Public Service Advertising
By Herbert Jack Rotfeld, *Professor of Marketing, Auburn University*

Government and public agencies concerned about date rape, drunk driving, road rage, unsafe sexual practices, underage cigarette smoking, illegal drug use, and even littering all expect advertising to reduce the incidence of these not-infrequent socially undesirable activities. Yet no one asks whether mass media advertising *can* persuade anyone to change their "problem" behaviors. The power of advertising is presumed and people behind most public service advertising campaigns see advertising itself as the solution.

The Advertising Council, which is dedicated to using the great resources of the advertising industry to serve the public interest, is the largest producer of public service mass communications campaigns in the United States. Free public service work from anyone is admirable, and the Advertising Council's dedication to public service is a wonderful credit to business groups supporting it. But many Advertising Council campaigns finish their efforts with few people ever knowing they existed, running their entire span with few target consumers ever seeing the commercials. Since the Advertising Council and other groups depend on time or space donated by the media for public service announcements (PSAs), they take the placements they can get for free. No one is in a position to make certain the free media placements reach the intended audience.

There are examples of successful communications efforts that are locally targeted and carefully planned and that appeal to the values of a closely defined audience. Over the long term, some campaigns can change the public agenda, increasing public awareness and changing general perceptions of issues previously ignored. But in most cases, advertising can't do anything to help solve the problem. Instead, for a variety of reasons, the people involved with public health issues acquire a misplaced trust in the power of advertising to change the world.

Advertising is not magic.

Maybe, sometimes, in some ways, it can do some good with some people, but that weak collection of "maybes" is not a valid basis for all the faith it gets from people wanting to serve social goals. And for the deep-seated problems behind many social ills, mass media advertising is a very weak or near-useless tool.

Yet despite these intrinsic limitations and inherent problems that make it a wasted effort, many people feel that they are doing "something" by advertising. Since this advertising effort misdirects resources as well as attention, this trust in advertising that is not a real solution becomes part of the problem.

Product Placement

What company was featured in the movie *Castaway*, starring Tom Hanks? In that story, as you may remember, Hanks plays a Federal Express employee who winds up on a deserted island and, ultimately after his rescue, delivers the package. Some movie critics joked that the whole movie is really a FedEx commercial. In fact, it's a good example of the practice known as **product placement**, which means a company pays to have verbal or visual brand exposure in a movie or television program.

Product placement is becoming popular because it isn't as intrusive as conventional advertising, and audiences can't zap the ads, as they can for television advertising using the remote control or a DVR like TiVo. At the same time, it makes the product a star.[35] Sometimes the product placement is subtle as when a particular brand of aspirin is shown in a medicine chest or a character drinks a particular brand of beverage. In other cases, like FedEx, the brand is front and center. That happened with the prominent role of a BMW Z28, which became a star in the James Bond movie *The World Is Not Enough*. The movie placement, in fact, was the car's launch vehicle.

Television programs have also gotten into the product placement game. An example is the use of well-known stores and products in the Fab Five makeover series, *A Queer Eye for the Straight Guy*. Both the Coca-Cola brand and the Ford Motor brand have been embedded into the successful talent show *American Idol*. And the Target bulls-eye is frequently seen as part of the action sets and props on *Survivor*.

The greatest advantage of product placement is that it demonstrates product use in a natural setting ("natural" depending upon the movie) by people who are celebrities. It's unexpected and catches the audience when their resistance to advertising messages may be dialed down. It's also good for engaging the affections of other stakeholders, such as employees and dealers, particularly if the placement is supported with its own campaign.

The biggest problem is that the placement may not be noticed. There is so much going on in most movies that you need to call attention to the product in order for its appearance to register. A more serious problem occurs when there is not a match between the product and the movie or its audience. Another concern is that advertisers have no idea whether the movie will be a success or failure as they negotiate a contract for the placement. If the movie is a dud, what does that do to the brand's image?

USING BROADCAST ADVERTISING EFFECTIVELY

Now that we have reviewed television and radio media, as well as movie advertising and product placement, we can summarize how to use broadcast media effectively. The Practical Tips box summarizes advantages and limitations of these media and provides guidelines for broadcast media decisions.

Practical Tips

Broadcast Media Advantages and Limitations

Advantages	*Limitations*
Radio Advertising	
• Pervasiveness; in most every home and car	• Listener inattentiveness; may just be on in the background
• Reaches specialized target audiences	• Lack of visuals
• Reaches them at critical apertures (morning and evening drive time)	• Clutter
• Affordability	• Scheduling and buying difficulties in local buys
• Offers high frequency; music can be repeated more easily than other forms of advertising	• Lack of control: talk show content is unpredictable and may be critical
• Flexible, easy to change	
• Good for local tie-ins and promos	
• Mental imagery can be highly engaging	
• High level of acceptance; not considered irritating	
• Audience less likely to switch channels when ads come on	

Advantages (continued)

Limitations (continued)

Television Advertising

- Pervasiveness; in most every home
- High level of viewing
- Reaches a mass national audience although can be targeted by programs
- High impact: Has audio, video, motion, music, color, high drama
- Cost efficient

- Clutter—cable offers a large number of channels
- High production costs
- Wasted reach
- Inflexibility; can't easily make last-minute changes
- Intrusiveness—some audience resistance to advertising leads to zipping and zapping

Movie Advertising

- Captive audience
- No need for intrusiveness because audience can't do multi-tasking
- High impact

- Audience resistance is high; hates being a captive audience
- Expensive; Needs high value production

Product Placement

- Not as intrusive
- If product fits the story line, can be a naturalistic demonstration or testimony
- Association with celebrities
- Association with glitzy movie, hopefully a well-liked film

- Can get lost in the story
- Potential for poor match between product and movie storyline
- Movie may turn out to be a dud

IT'S A WRAP

Holiday Inn Express Stays Smart

Fallon's hunches and hard work paid off. The insights into the target audience proved accurate. The net result was bottom-line business results for Holiday Inn Express, which has doubled the number of properties since the campaign broke in 1999.

Jenifer Zeigler, senior vice president of global brand management for Inter Continental Hotels and Resorts (Holiday Inn Express's parent corporation) was named as one of its "Marketers of the Next Generation" for her leadership of the brand by *Brandweek* in 2004. She said, "We have a rock solid operational model, and our franchisees are doing a great job of consistently delivering on the brand promise. But make no mistake about it. The level of familiarity and momentum we enjoy is due to the Stay Smart campaign."

Evidence of brand momentum was revealed in a study that showed that Holiday Inn Express was better than competitors as "good value for the money," "a good hotel for business travelers," and "growing more popular."

For these achievements and the staying power of the campaign, Holiday Inn Express has earned six Effies, including several golds, and the reputation as the limited-service category leader. It's been honored with awards by *Entrepreneur*, *Business Travel News*, and the Travel Industry Association. American Brands Council named Holiday Inn Express one of America's Greatest Brands.

Although the extra exposure from the buzz about the commercials is difficult to measure, the client surely gets high returns on its campaign investment when Al Gore utters the famous tagline and it shows up elsewhere on ESPN, the *Chicago Tribune*, the *Washington Post*, David Letterman, and NPR.

Key Points Summary

1. **How does radio work as an advertising medium?** The traditional radio stations are found on AM and FM and primarily serve local markets. AM and FM are only the beginning of the radio listener's options, which also include public radio, cable and satellite radio, low-powered stations, and Web radio. Radio dramas engage the imagination, but radio is primarily a music-driven medium, which serves audiences defined by their musical tastes. Listeners can have a very intimate relationship with radio and can be quite loyal to their favorite stations, but radio also serves as background.

2. **How does television work as an advertising medium?** The key types of television delivery systems are wired and unwired network, local stations, public stations, cable, and subscription. Specialty, syndicated, interactive television and DVRs offer ways to manipulate the programming. Television is useful as an advertising medium because it works like a movie with story, action, emotions, and visual impact. TV audiences are fragmented, often irritated by advertising, and prone to avoidance.

Audiences are measured in terms of ratings and share. TV's greatest advantage is that it is pervasive and cost efficient when reaching a large number of viewers. Because of the special interest aspect of cable programming, it is good at reaching more narrowly targeted audiences.

3. **How do advertisers use movies, as well as film and video, as advertising media?** Movie theaters sell time for advertisements before their films. Advertising is also carried on videocassettes and DVDs, as well as in lobbies and other public spaces. Video-generated commercials can also be seen in supermarkets, transit stations, and waiting rooms for professional services such as doctors.

4. **What is product placement, and how is it used by advertisers?** Product placement, which shows a product embedded in a movie or TV program, is popular because it isn't as intrusive as conventional advertising. To use it strategically the product must fit into the storyline and play a role. The main problem is that the product may be overlooked.

Key Terms

affiliates, p. 264
broadband, p. 267
broadcast media, p. 256
broadcast network, p. 264
cable radio, p. 258
cable television, p. 265
clear channel, p. 257
coverage, p. 259
dayparts, p. 259
digital video recorder (DVR), p. 267
exposure, p. 268
first-run syndication, p. 267
gross impressions, p. 269
high-definition TV (HDTV), p. 267
households using TV (HUT), p. 268

impressions, p. 269
independent station, p. 266
interactive television, p. 267
interconnects, p. 266
jingles, p. 260
local cable, p. 266
low-power FM (LPFM), p. 258
low-power television (LPTV), p. 266
morning drive time, p. 259
network cable, p. 266
network radio, p. 260
off-network syndication, p. 267
participations, p. 271

pay-per-view television, p. 267
people meters, p. 270
podcasting, p. 263
prime time, p. 264
product placement, p. 278
program sponsorships, p. 266
public radio, p. 257
public service announcements (PSAs), p. 260
public television, p. 266
rating points, p. 269
ratings, p. 259
satellite radio, p. 258
satellite television, p. 265
share of audience, p. 269

signals, p. 257
sponsorship, p. 271
spot announcement, p. 272
spot buy, p. 266
spot radio advertising, p. 261
subscription television, p. 265
superstations, p. 266
sweeps, p. 270
syndication, p. 262
time-shifting, p. 267
trailer, p. 276
wasted reach, p. 273
webcasting, p. 258
zap, p. 273
zip, p. 273

Review Questions

1. How can radio be used most effectively, and what are the advantages and limitations of advertising on radio?

2. How can television be used most effectively, and what are the advantages and limitations of advertising on television?

3. What are trailers and how are they used as an advertising form? How can movie advertising be used most effectively, and what are its advantages and limitations?

4. What is product placement, and why has it become popular as an advertising medium? How can product placement be used most effectively, and what are its advantages and limitations?

Discussion Questions

1. Message clutter affects both radio and television advertising. Advertisers fear that audiences react to long commercial groupings by using the remote control for the television set or the tuner on the radio to steer to a different channel. Some have proposed that advertisers should absorb higher time costs to reduce the frequency and length of commercial interruptions. Others argue that broadcasting should reduce the number of commercials sold and also reduce program advertising even if it means less profit for broadcasters. Which of these remedies would be better?

2. You are the media planner for a cosmetics company introducing a new line of makeup for teenage girls. Your research indicates that television advertising might be an effective medium for creating awareness about your new product line. In exploring this idea, how do you design a television advertising strategy that will reach your target market successfully? What stations do you choose? Why? What programs and times do you choose? Why? Do you consider syndicated television? Why or why not?

3. *Three-Minute Debate:* You are a major agency media director who has just finished a presentation to a prospective client in convenience food marketing. During the Q and A period, a client representative says: "We know that network television viewers' loyalty is nothing like it was 10 or even 5 years ago because so many people now turn to cable, VCRs, and the Web. There are smaller audiences per program each year, yet television time costs continue to rise. Do you still believe we should consider commercial television as a primary medium for our company's advertising?" How would you answer?

   In class, organize into small teams with each team developing what team members consider the best response to that question. Set up a series of debates with each team taking 1½ minutes to argue its position. Every team of debaters has to present new points not covered in the previous teams' presentations until there are no arguments left to present. Then the class votes as a group on the winning point of view.

Take-Home Team Projects

1. Each student should make a chart for three radio stations. List the type of station (easy listening, top 40, classical, and so on), the products commonly advertised, and the probable target markets for these products. Note the time of the day these products are advertised.

   Now put all of the products in a hat for teams of three to draw. Each team is now responsible for choosing the radio stations for its product. Each team needs to allocate a budget of $2,500 among the five stations for a week's worth of programming. Assume 30 seconds of air time costs $250. Have the teams present their work, and as a class compare the different patterns of radio use.

2. Study the list of "Trashy Shows" in the Matter of Principle box on p. 269. Pick one of these shows, and develop a chart depicting the following profile.

   a. Describe who you think is in the audience for this program. (You can research this online to get a better feel for this audience.)

   b. In a second column, identify the five most frequent advertisers on the show.

   c. Write a one-page report that analyzes the show's content, your audience profile, and the products advertised, and identify why those advertisers chose this show.

   d. Develop a second one-page analysis that identifies products that definitely would not be appropriate for this show and explain why.

Yahoo! Hands-On Case

Review the Yahoo! case in the Appendix.

1. Review the advantages and disadvantages of using radio, television, and outdoor media in terms of the Yahoo! case strategy. Which ones do you think might receive more or less emphasis in the plan? Explain your thinking.

2. The broadcast part of the media plan is focused on eight TV programs and radio ads in the six concert markets. If you could increase the broadcast media budget by 30 percent, how would you adjust this plan? In other words, what additional broadcast media opportunities would you consider? Justify your recommendations.

HANDS-ON CASE

Get Sirius with Howard Stern

There has been no shortage of excitement for communication company Sirius during its short history. Sirius is trying to change the way people listen to radio by convincing them to pay a monthly fee (around $13) for almost 200 channels of radio, much of it commercial free. But Sirius is not alone in the satellite radio business, and the first two years of competition have largely favored competitor XM Satellite Radio Holdings Inc., which claimed 2.5 million subscribers to Sirius's 600,000 in 2004. In 2003 Sirius almost went under before finding investors willing to help the company pay off its substantial debt. And from 2000 to 2004, shares of Sirius stock fell from a high of $66.50 to under $5.

Sirius is hardly out of the picture, however. It has inked partnerships with DaimlerChrysler and Ford to offer satellite radio as an option for new car models. In 2004 the company announced it would pay close to $200 million for the rights to carry NFL football telecasts. Possibly its biggest move came in January 2006 when radio personality Howard Stern left Viacom radio airwaves to join Sirius.

The signing was an audacious gamble for Sirius. The original "shock jock," Howard Stern describes himself somewhat tongue in cheek as the "King of Media." His daily radio audience at Viacom of close to 8 million loyal listeners attracted enough advertising to bring that corporation between $80 million and 90 million in ad revenue annually. Sirius knew the bidding would be high, and the deal with Stern was expected to be expensive.

Sirius executives said that for the deal to be profitable, Stern must bring 1 million new subscribers to the network. Could such a large number of people, who currently listen to the show for nothing on inexpensive radios, be convinced to pay a monthly fee and buy equipment that can cost a couple hundred dollars? It appears that the answer is yes.

Stern's presence on the satellite radio network helped Sirius end 2006 with more than 6 million subscribers, about 3.5 million more than the company had when he started in 2004. The swell of listeners earned Stern a $82.9 million stock bonus in January 2007. This bonus adds to the five-year $500 million contract Stern agreed to in October 2004.

Even if Stern did attract listeners to Sirius, the deal was not without risk. Both Sirius and its main competitor, XM, have posted significant financial losses in the process of spending big on talent and sports programming to attract new subscribers. In February 2007, the two satellite radio competitors announced that they would merge.

Consider This

1. Stern is one of the highest paid and highest profile entertainers in radio. What are the implications of his signing for Sirius and for satellite radio in general? Has the signing meant that satellite radio has entered a new phase in its development?

2. Even though Stern brought new subscribers to Sirius, can you think of other ways that the deal might still be risky for Sirius? For Stern?

3. Cable television changed the face of television broadcasting. In your opinion, does satellite radio offer the same possibility for the radio industry? How would you determine its effectiveness?

Sources: Krysten Crawford, "Howard Stern: I May Be Out Soon," CNN *Money*, November 11, 2004; "Howard Stern Gets $82.9 Million Stock Bonus," *USA Today*, January 9, 2007, http://www.usatoday.com; Emmanuel Legrand, "The World According to Karmazin," *Billboard*, November 10, 2004; Jube Shiver, "With Howard Stern, Sirius Hopes to Make Waves," *Los Angeles Times*, October 10, 2004.

Internet and Nontraditional Media

IT'S A WINNER

Award:	Company:	Agency:	Campaign:
Grand Prize Winner, London International Awards	*eBay*	*BBDO New York*	*"it"*

eBay® Revolutionizes the Marketplace

Pierre Omidyar, founder of eBay®, started a marketing revolution in 1995 when he sold a broken laser pointer via the Internet for $13.83. eBay pioneered online commerce by providing a communication link between individuals and small companies about the sale of goods and services.

Now millions of people are brought together locally, nationally, and internationally to transact their business each day. From Auckland, New Zealand, to Zanesville, Ohio, individuals advertise what they have, hoping that someone, somewhere, will want that old, but barely used, set of golf clubs that's been taking up space in the garage.

Collectors search the site for a missing piece of the china pattern, Pez dispenser, or Star Trek memorabilia. A few of the more unusual eBay sales: a single cornflake fetched a £1.20 for a Coventry University student, Disney sold a retired monorail for $20,000, and the original Hollywood sign sold for $450,400. Who would have thought?

It started as an online flea market or garage sale—a way to clean out attics, basements, closets, and, yes, garages. But eBay is more than just a dot-com auction. The powerhouse Web merchant has become the world's largest online marketplace—a worldwide bazaar of individual buyers and sellers—and a new way to do business. There are no shops, no booths, no displays, just a computer and Internet connection.

In contrast to the early dot-com entrepreneurs who threw money at big-budget advertising media such as the Super Bowl, eBay didn't start advertising until 2002. The company built its business from the ground up through word of mouth and the passion of its users.

Chapter Key Points

1. How does the Internet work, and what are the roles it plays in marketing communication?

2. How does Internet advertising work?

3. How does e-mail advertising work?

4. In what ways are the different forms of interactive and alternative new media changing how advertising works?

Its first campaign used a campy rewrite of the Sinatra standard, "My Way," rephrased as "Do It eBay." The campaign featured a balding Sinatra look-alike belting out the eBay version as he dances through various scenes and croons funny lines about mainstream retails. The objective was to reposition eBay from an online flea market to a broad-based Web marketplace. The campaign also reminded users of its entertainment value—the game, the search, the discovery, the adventure.

Staying true to its customer-focused values, eBay's advertising agency, Goodby, Silverstein & Partners, presented the advertising concept first as storyboards to the auction faithful for their review and critique. The eBay participants were pleased to be consulted and supportive of the campaign idea. BBDO New York has the account now and continues eBay's winning ways with the "it" campaign, which prompts consumers to get "it" on eBay.

To think it all started with a broken laser pointer. Don't you wonder what that laser pointer would fetch today? Turn to It's a Wrap at the end of the chapter to learn more about how eBay has evolved and achieved its incredible success.

Sources: Eric Auchard, Reuters, "eBay Takes Web Ads to Next Level," *USA Today,* June 11, 2006; Bloomberg News, "eBay Will Buy StubHub for $310 Million," *New York Times,* January 11, 2007; Keith Bradsher, "For eBay, It's about Political Connections in China," *New York Times,* December 22, 2006; eBay.com; Ed Finkel, "eBay's Old-School Business Wisdom," *Kellogg World,* Summer 2004, http://www.Kellogg.Northwestern.edu; Catharine Taylor, "The eBay Way: Brand It Now," *Brandweek,* October 20, 2003, PM20.

eBay is one example of a well-known company that conducts its business totally online, taking advantage of the Internet's ability to create personal interaction between buyers and sellers. In this chapter we will discuss a number of interactive media, including the Internet and e-mail. We'll also talk about nontraditional new media—formats that open up novel ways to deliver advertising messages and connect with consumers.

INTERACTIVE MEDIA: WEB 2.0 AND YOU

It's a Web world for most of us. Because new technology is exploding, media planners are racing to try to understand the implications of this rapidly changing media landscape for advertising and marketing communication. eBay is important because it represents a new way of doing business as well as a new way of thinking about buying, selling, and advertising. Google, MySpace, Facebook, Wikipedia, Craigslist, YouTube, and Second Life, like eBay, are all sites that provide tools permitting users to customize messages and interact. The Part III Introduction by Don Jugenheimer highlighted these changes, particularly in terms of interactivity.

The creation of social networking and entertainment sites builds on the interactive power of the Internet with astounding effects, a trend referred to as *Web 2.0,* which calls attention to the shift in control of media from publishers to consumers. As we noted in Chapter 5, users of the Internet are not only contributing and interacting, they are taking control of the content on new media forms. User-generated content is having a huge impact on both traditional media industries and on advertising. As the authors of *Citizen Marketers* say, "Corporate decision makers are losing even the illusion of control."[1]

Another trend noted by Jugenheimer in the Part III Introduction is the convergence and blurring of media forms, a shift that is challenging media planners. The Internet is the ultimate convergence medium because it bridges print and broadcast media and blurs the distinction between them. Newspapers, magazines, and other print forms can be delivered online, and their messages still look like print. Video is moving online and even on to cell phones. We've talked about convergence in previous chapters, but the Internet is driving this trend by creating an increasingly wired and connected world. And the changes are happening in a blur.[2]

Big media companies are also acquiring Internet properties that extend their online offerings and offer the opportunity for cross-media promotions. Rupert Murdoch's News Corporation, for example, purchased MySpace, the teen social network. Disney is putting its ABC television shows on iTunes and using video streaming to move them to the Web.[3]

Working with our Facets Model of Effects, the Internet by definition is a connected medium so users are linked to a network of brand information as well as brand buzz. These new media forms encourage more involvement by users and sharing of experiences, both of which lead to more persuasive impact for Web-delivered messages.

Before we talk about Web advertising, let's first review the basics of the Internet.

Internet Basics

Based on data collected in the 2000 census, the U.S. Census Bureau reported that more than 50 percent of households owned a computer and 42 percent went on the Internet at least once a day. By 2004 the number of households with computers reached 60 percent.[4] Although computer access continues to increase, the Internet is still a long way from the penetration levels of traditional print and broadcast media. The computer has, however, revolutionized the way we communicate—and advertise—in this wired and wireless world.

Technically, the **Internet** is a linked system of international computer networks. The **World Wide Web** is the information interface that allows people to access the Internet through an easy-to-use graphical format. However, most people use these terms interchangeably.

Internet Tools and Formats

You may be familiar with many of these terms, but let's review how the Web is shaping up for advertisers. Sometimes called a **home page**, a company's **Web site** is the online face it presents to the public. The Web site is a communication tool that blurs the distinction between marketing communication forms, such as advertising, direct marketing, and public relations. In some cases it looks like an online corporate brochure, or it may function as an online catalog. The Web site can also be an information resource with a searchable library of stories and data about products, product categories, and related topics.

In some cases, the Web site is the business. Amazon.com's Web site contains complete information about the product offerings, such as book reviews, as well as a way to place an order, pay for it, and contact customer service if there is a problem. The Web site operates like a direct mail catalog, but interactivity makes it even more useful than the print alternative. Customers can make inquiries and the company can use its databases to personalize customer communication. Here are some basic Internet terms and tools:

- *URLs and domain names.* A Web site has an address called a **URL** (Uniform Resource Locator), which is its **domain name**, a global address that identifies a specific location in cyberspace on the Web where a document or Web site lives.
- *Portals.* A **portal** is a site that provides doors, or **links**, to other Web sites. Yahoo!, for example, is a directory, or online guide to the Web. It started as a group of favorite Web sites compiled by a couple of Stanford University students, who began categorizing the sites as the list grew into the giant library now known as Yahoo! It is considered the top Internet brand and is among the most trafficked Web sites in the United States. Yahoo! has some 122 million visitors a month, closely followed by Time Warner Network (119 million), MSN-Microsoft (115 million), and Google (86 million).[5]
- *Search engines.* Google is the biggest **search engine** used to find information and access other sites. You don't have to know a specific Web site address; instead, you can type in a **keyword** and the search engine will seek out all the sites that provide information on the topic. Most search engines also carry advertising, so they can be considered advertising media. Examples of more specific search sites are SeenOn.com, an online shopping guide that lets TV fans find and purchase many of

Yahoo! is among the largest Web sites in the United States in terms of number of visitors.

the products they see on TV, and iLike.com, which was set up by musicians to help consumers find music they like. Craigslist provides local community-based information—who can repair a radio, where to find supplies for stained glass repairs, how to locate job opportunities. This noncommercial list doesn't accept advertising, but brands sometimes can be found there or searched for on the site.

- **Chat rooms.** Groups of people with a special interest can contact one another and exchange their opinions and experiences through **chat rooms**, which are sites located online, sometimes as part of an organization's Web site, but sometimes completely independent of any company. For example, numerous chat rooms are organized around various computer systems (Linux, Apple, ThinkPad, Sega) and topics (1:1 marketing, guerilla marketing, virtual marketing). The communication is so fast that announcements, rumors, and criticisms can circulate worldwide within a matter of minutes. Chat rooms also are good information sources about customer experiences as well as competitors' offerings.

- **Blogs.** You may even have a **blog**, a diary-like Web page created by individuals to talk about things that interest them. Blogs are produced by some 100 million digital essayists worldwide. A survey by the Pew Research Center found that most bloggers are under age 30 and use their blogs for creative expression. Some are interested in making money, and others are into politics.[6] These personal publishing sites also contain links to related sites the bloggers consider relevant. Corporations also use blogs in addition to their traditional Web sites. Corporate blogs are a way to keep employees and other stakeholders informed, but employees may also be encouraged to have personal blogs. Microsoft has several hundred staffers blogging on personal sites. Sales staffs have found that blogs are changing the sales process by making more experiences with a product available to prospects and keeping customers current with fast-changing technological trends.

- *Vlogs.* Video blogs or **vlogs** are visual essays available online. They are similar to podcasts available through iTunes and other such outlets, except that videos, rather than songs or audio, are downloaded to a computer or cell phone. When Apple launched its video iPod in 2006, it opened the door for advertising commercials to be presented online. Vlog advertising is predicted to reach $1 billion in 2008.[7] A popular vlog is the satirical news show, *Rocketboom.com*, which was founded in 2004 and three years later had some 1.6 million downloads per week.
- *Netcasting.* The emergence of vlogs follows development of new technology that makes it possible to broadcast TV and radio online, a practice called **netcasting.** Blip.tv offers new Web TV series and helps the producers find sponsors and advertisers. The decision by ABC to put previously run episodes of its hit shows online and CBS's experiments with "March Madness on Demand" video streams for the college basketball championships are pushing this technological revolution. MTV is working with Google to move its video content to the Web, and Disney has released some of its movies for use on a video iPod.

TV producers are even starting to produce shows designed for the tiny 2.5-inch cell phone screen. In a new twist on convergence, a start-up wireless carrier contributed a political parody show it created, the animated *Lil' Bush*, to Comedy Central. This is the first time a U.S. TV network broadcast a show that was initially produced for cell phones. Netcasting also appeals to advertisers searching for new ways to reach audiences who no longer are sitting in front of televisions.[8] A study in late 2006 found advertisers predicting a 42 percent increase in their online advertising budgets, shifting significant broadcast and cable TV budgets to the Web.[9] Already by 2007, the online video advertising marketplace had grown to $161 million, and it is estimated to grow to $5 billion by 2011.[10]

The Internet Audience

From its early days as a tool for government agencies and academics to share information, the Internet has exploded as a standard communication medium for businesses and consumers. Traditional media companies are concerned that the Internet will cut into their audience base. For example, a Harris Poll in 2007 found that users say they watch less TV because of the time they spend on the online entertainment sites.[11]

Similar to magazines and cable channels, Internet use has expanded over the years to encompass sites devoted to just about any age or interest group. A recent article, for example, celebrated a new site, BoomerGirl.com, that reaches women over 50 with news, blogs, and "tips on health, fashion, family, finances, and fitness."[12] It's not the only site for this population: Boomerwomenspeak.com and eons.com focus on concerns of both male and female boomers.

The most sought-after audience on the Web, however, continues to be young people, particularly young males who are hard to reach with traditional media. Teens spend more time online than any other age group.

THE WEB AS AN ADVERTISING MEDIUM

Internet advertising, although still the new baby on the advertising block, is a growing industry. After a slowdown that began in the late 1990s and continued into the early 2000s (see Figure 10.1), advertising on Web sites has pulled in double-digit percentage gains, in contrast to traditional media that have seen ad spending growth in the 2 to 5 percent range. Advertising analysts say this reflects the "ongoing shift in advertising dollars from traditional media into nontraditional media, most notably the Internet."[13] Web media buying company ZenithOptimedia predicted that Internet ad spending would grow 29 percent between 2006 and 2007. The research company eMarketer predicts that online advertising will grow to $25 billion in 2010 from $15.9 billion in 2007.[14]

More than 90 percent of Internet advertising is found on a small group of large, established news media sites that operate as electronic publishers, such as nytimes.com,

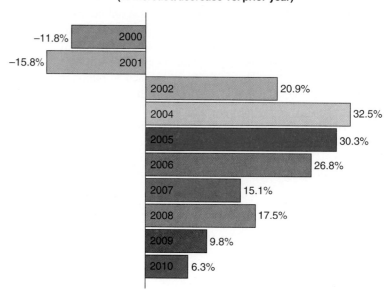

U.S. Online Advertising Spending Growth, 2000–2010
(% increase/decrease vs. prior year)

FIGURE 10.1

The Boom, Bust, and Rebuilding of Online Advertising

NOTE: eMarketer benchmarks its U.S. online advertising spending projections against the Interactive Advertising Bureau (IAB)/PricewaterhouseCoopers (PWC) data, for which the last full year measured was 2005.

Source: eMarketer, June 2007

Sources: "At 26.8% Growth, Online Ad Spending Slows, But Is Still Strong," eMarketer, September 28, 2006, http://www.emarketer.com.

WSJ.com and ESPN.com, as well as on major search engines and service providers, such as Google and Yahoo!. The media organizations have established reputations, and they know how to sell advertising, so they have been pioneers in the development of Internet advertising.

Advertisers and their media buyers get access to Internet sites through providers such as DoubleClick, an Internet advertising service that places more than 60 billion online ads per month. DoubleClick provides reports on the placement and performance of these ads to both publishers and advertisers.

Online advertising serves three primary purposes. First, it provides a brand reminder message to people who are visiting a Web site. Second, it works like an ad in traditional media and delivers an informational or persuasive message. The third purpose, however, is most critical: It provides a way to entice people to visit the advertiser's site by clicking on a banner or button to the Web site. This is called *driving traffic* to the Web site.

Some people may find an advertiser's Web site after doing a search using a search engine; others may come across the Web site address in some other communication, such as an ad or brochure. But another way is to encounter on a related site an ad with enough impact to entice the visitor to leave the original site and move to this new one. Internet strategists are keenly aware of the difficulty of driving people to Web sites. The auction giant eBay, which has resisted advertising on its site, is now experimenting with text ads on some of its Web sites outside the United States. The company is also developing "click-to-call" technology that will allow customers to call advertisers directly using phone connections through eBay's Skype Internet phone service.[15]

Internet Advertising Formats

What kinds of Internet advertising are available today? The industry is moving so quickly that by the time you read this passage, other categories may replace or supplement those we discuss here. Essentially, Internet advertising can be delivered as a traditional ad, just like those you see in a magazine, or it can be presented in a number of formats via new forms of web advertising, such as banner ads and other interactive formats.

Banner Ads   IBM introduced banner ads in 1994. **Banner ads** are small ads on other Web pages on which people can click to move to the advertised Web site, such as the one featured here for Zippo lighters. Banner ads are easy to create and are usually placed on a Web site featuring complementary products or related topics. In her research on banner ads, Professor Lynda Maddox reports:

> We also looked at banner ads and their effect on brand recall, attitude toward the brand, and purchase consideration. We found that banner ads work and that "click-through" should not be the only measure of success because it may underestimate the effect of the banner. When the objective is building brand or product awareness and shaping attitudes, however, click-through appears to be an irrelevant metric.

While banner ads were very popular when they first appeared and continue to dominate online advertising, the overall **click-through** rate, which takes the viewer to the advertiser's Web site, has dropped to less than 1 percent. The most successful banner ads achieve 7 percent click-through. The difference lies in the creativity and attention-getting power of the banner ad. The more they are tailored to the interest of Web site viewers, the more likely they are to have a high click-through rate. The problem is that as viewers have gotten more sophisticated and are less attracted to advertising they haven't requested. For a collection of funny banners, check the Web site http://www.valleyofthegeeks.com.

The design of Internet advertising is constantly changing as the industry advances. Here are some other common formats:

- *Skyscrapers.* The extra-long, skinny ads running down the right or left side of a Web site are called **skyscraper**s. The financial site CBSMarketWatch.com, for instance, regularly runs this kind of ad. Response rates for skyscrapers, which began to be used aggressively by more companies in 2000, can be 10 times higher than for traditional banner ads.
- **Pop-ups** and **pop-behinds.** Pop-up ads burst open on the computer screen either in front of or behind the opening page of the Web site. Companies like Volvo and GlaxoSmith-Kline (for its Oxy acne medicine) use these forms to present games and product information. However, they are seen as intrusive and annoying, so some Internet advertisers have moved away from this format.

This series of banners for the Zippo lighter develops a message as the banners unfold. The message takes off on the blackouts urban areas sometimes experience in the summer when electrical use is high.

- *Minisites.* **Minisites** allow advertisers to market their products without sending people away from the site they're visiting. The General Motors minisite appears on the Shell Oil site, and the consumer can access and enlarge it later. This type of advertising gets a higher click rate; the portal About.com estimates that 5 percent of the people who see the sites click on them.
- *Superstitials,* unveiled by online marketer Unicast in 1999, are thought of as "the Internet's commercial," designed to work like TV ads. When you go from one page on a Web site to another, a 20-second animation appears in a window. These ads now run on more than 350 Web sites.
- *Widgets.* These tiny computer programs allow people to create and insert professional-looking content into their personal Web sites. They include news notes, calculators, weather feeds, stock tickers, clocks, book or music covers, or other Web gadgets that can be framed by a brand name promotional offer. It's a way to get a nonintrusive ad on the desktop, Web site, or blog. Widgets also refers to mini-applications that pull content from some other place on the Web and add it to your site. In addition to getting onto MySpace pages, they also can monitor contacts when someone clicks on the feature. The founder of Widgetbox.com classifies them as (1) self-expression (photos, clips, games); (2) revenue generators on blogs (eBay categories, favorite DVDs or CDs from Amazon.com); and (3) site-enhancement devices (news updates, discussion forums).[16]

Animation   Originally banner ads were jazzed up using relatively simple animation techniques to make elements move. New technologies—including plug-ins, Java script, Flash, and media streaming—provide even more active components. A recent study by Greg Interactive, New York, and ASI Interactive Research found that the click-through rate nearly doubles when motion and an interactive element is added to a banner ad.

As advertisers have searched for more effective ways to connect with their audiences, some Web sites have used animation to become more entertaining with games and contests, interviews with celebrities, even musical performances. For example, check out the OwnyourC.com Web site. It is part of an antismoking campaign that uses fun and flashy graphics, as well as an irreverent tone, to get the attention of 12- to 18-year-olds.

E-Mail Advertising

One of the attractive features of e-mail advertising is that it is so inexpensive. All it takes is a list of e-mail addresses, a computer, and an Internet connection. Today's improved data-

SHOWCASE An antismoking campaign targeted to teens uses a flashy Web site called *OwnyourC* (the C stands for choices). Adam Dyer, who works for Cactus Marketing Communication, contributed this Web site on behalf of the State Tobacco Education and Prevention Partnership of the Colorado Department of Public Health and Environment.

bases allow marketers to target prospects with unsolicited e-mail. In fact, the response rate for an unsolicited e-mail campaign is many times higher than for a banner ad campaign. Unfortunately for e-mail advertisers, people generally do not welcome unsolicited e-mail. **Permission marketing** attempts to address this problem by asking potential consumers for their permission to send them e-mail.

Opt In and Opt Out   Two solutions to the spam problem usually incorporate one of two permission marketing strategies for consumers to control their inclusion on e-mail lists. **Opt in** means that all bulk e-mailers have to get your permission before sending an e-mail. Legitimate e-mail advertising businesses use this permission form, which is tougher for spammers to abuse and more sensitive to consumer rage when they do. **Opt out** means that e-mailers can send the first e-mail but must give recipients the means to refuse any further e-mails from that business.

Viral Marketing   An e-mail practice designed to deliver a groundswell of opinion or marketplace demand for a product is called **viral marketing.** This advertising is sent from consumer to consumer over the Internet. It uses e-mail to circulate a message among family and friends. It's an opt-in medium that directs recipients to seek out videos or click on an e-mail link.

Remember "The Diet Coke/Mentos Experiment" that resulted in a geyser and exploded again and again on the Internet? That viral advertising was watched by millions, and guess what? Other viewers concocted their own versions and uploaded them on YouTube. Mentos mint sales rose 15 percent. Was that entertainment, or was that advertising?

YouTube has become the engine that drives viral marketing and generates a storm of e-mails. For a viral campaign, which often is a spoof or an irreverent approach to brand marketing that speaks to the under-25 set, experts say that reaching 1 million YouTube viewers is the "magic number." That's the level that generates buzz and delivers significant impressions to create a market response.[17]

Spam   Blasting millions of unsolicited e-mail messages to e-mailboxes for everything from loans to computer cartridges to pornographic sites is called **spamming.** Consumers who are irritated by the avalanche of solicitations that clutter their inboxes may think of **spam** as "junk e-mail," but providers prefer to call it *bulk e-mail*. They see bulk e-mail as an exciting new business opportunity and a legitimate commercial activity.

Critics would like to see the government close down these operations. There are technological problems to controlling these practices, however, and spammers have proven creative in finding ways to get through filters installed by service providers and host corporations, such as companies and universities. It's become a worldwide problem as spammers from outside the United States have helped to double the volume of unwanted e-mail between 2006 and 2007. As spammers become more sophisticated, critics contend these operations have gotten out of control.

There is a register of spammers known as *Rokso,* or Register of Known Spam Operations. It's a kind of "most wanted" list maintained by Internet hosts and service providers like AOL, whose computers strain to handle the huge bulk of e-mails[18] and are quick to kick off known spammers. An antispam Web site called spamhaus.org is also available, and Congress is getting into the debate with various proposals for regulating spam. But the spammers have ways to get around these technologies. For one thing they use huge networks of computers that belong to users who have unknowingly downloaded rogue programs that spin off spam e-mails. The use of messages embedded in images is another way spammers have gotten around filters.

Does spam bring in revenue? Spammers solicit business from sources like AOL's profiles where people indicate their interests and activities. A spammer might send out 100,000 e-mails and get only two to five clients, which seems like a totally unacceptable number of responses. But a spammer who charges $300 to send out 100,000 messages or $900 for a million might make $14,000 to $15,000 on those few responses. That's not a bad return when you consider the cost of getting into the business—a computer and an Internet connection.

Principle
Opt-in and opt-out strategies make mass e-mail campaigns more acceptable because customers give permission to marketers to contact them.

Internet Advertising Functions

Marketers and advertisers are most interested in the **e-business** or **e-commerce** function of the Internet, which refers to all the hardware, software, and computer know-how that provides a platform for businesses that use the Internet to sell products and manage their business operations, along with their advertising, customer service, personal sales, internal communication to employees, and external communication to outside stakeholders. The most familiar form of e-business involves companies that sell products online, such as eBay and Amazon.com. In addition to the e-commerce role, other Internet functions that are important to advertisers include the information, entertainment, social, and dialogue roles.

The Information Role   The most important advertising-related role that the Internet plays is to provide information. The Internet has developed into a giant online library for consumers. Beyond shopping on e-business sites, people of all ages use the Internet to search for information, including product information as well as news and references.

- *Online publishing.* Most traditional media also have Web sites that adapt the information from their more mainline format. Travel sites, such as the one shown here for the magazine *Budget Travel*, are particularly popular. Although the Internet has grown increasingly important, for many people it is still a supplement to traditional news media. A study found that although many go online for news, most still also go to newspapers and television for in-depth news.[19] Other publications exist solely online. **Zines**, for example, are magazines or newsletters that are only available over the Internet.

- *Online encyclopedias.* Wikipedia, the online encyclopedia, is another huge source of information. It publishes contributions from anyone who wants to write and edit entries in a collaborative system of information collection. Millions of people go to the site to answer questions on any topic. The site is so popular that it has spun off a number of other specialized sites that are advertising supported, such as wikiHow, which is a how-to guide (how to cook a brisket, how to fix a garage door opener) built on the same principles as Wikipedia. ShopWiki offers product reviews, Wikitravel provides tourism information, and Wikia is a portal for some 1,500 really esoteric subsites that wouldn't make it on Wikipedia, such as the Star-Wars focused Wookieepedia.[20]

The Entertainment Role   Many users connect to the Web for entertainment, such as poker and other games, playing the stock market, fashion, music, and videos. Some are fun, and some are personally challenging, but they all engage their users either as escape or relaxation.

Sites that appeal to the coveted demographic of young men, who are so difficult to reach with traditional media, include Heavy.com, which attracts viewers to its mix of racy, humorous video programming (animation, music, video games, home movies of weird characters, chicks in bikinis, and pop culture parodies) and keeps their attention with wisecrack commercials. Virgin Mobile uses Heavy.com to reach viewers in their late teens and 20s.[21] TMZ.com is another entertainment site that publishes celebrity news and rumors in real time—Tom and Katie spotted with their baby, Paris Hilton having a Big Mac, Britney going bald.

This ad claims that Budget Travel is the fastest and easiest way to find the best travel deals. The Web site is a partnership between Arthur Frommer's *Budget Travel* magazine and the MSNBC channel.

Source: © 2004 Newsweek Inc. and MSNBC.com. Photo © Martin Barraud/ Getty Images. All rights reserved. Reprinted with permission.

The gorilla of Web entertainment, however, is YouTube.com, which is a site that carries consumer-generated film and video clips—teenage video diaries, stupid pet tricks, ad parodies, ideas for TV shows, and actual shows downloaded from TV. Launched in December 2005, the video-sharing service plays more than 100 million clips per day with some 65,000 clips uploaded daily.[22] It was acquired by Google for $1.65 billion a year after it was launched.

Sometimes popular TV commercials are uploaded by viewers to their YouTube pages to be shared with the whole YouTube world as a form of *viral video*. Mock ads cobbled together from clips and amateur video also are of interest to ad agencies because they are, in some cases, highly creative. Some ad agencies, such as Arnold Worldwide, are designing commercials that fit into the YouTube style, such as the "Stupid Things" campaign for Vonage, the nation's largest Internet phone provider, that mimics the daredevil stunts seen on the MTV series *Jackass*.[23]

But the mock ads can also be troublesome, such as a fake Volkswagen commercial that shows a man detonating a car bomb in his VW in front of a busy café. The interactive creative director at Crispin Porter + Bogusky, Volkswagen's agency, said, "You have absolutely no control over stuff like that. . . . it's like brand terrorism on the Internet."[24] Film studios are even threatening lawsuits over the copyrighted material that shows up online.

Major broadcasters are also joining the YouTube world. BBC was the first global media company to sign a deal with YouTube to provide news and entertainment clips from its broadcasting. These clips also carry advertising.[25] Other broadcasters, however, are challenging YouTube and its owner Google for broadcasting their shows, which are protected by copyrights. The media giant Viacom, for example, sued Google in 2007 for videos uploaded by YouTube members, such as *The Daily Show with Jon Stewart*.

Another innovation in Internet entertainment is Second Life, which operates like a parallel universe video game in which users create a fantasy digital version of themselves, called **avatars**, who inhabit a 3-D world. The population of the virtual-reality public space on Second Life is more than 4.5 million, and its residents do both normal things, such as chatting with friends and playing sports, and extraordinary feats, such as riding a rocket to the moon. One real-world feature, however, is that Second Life has its own currency, and you still have to pay for stuff. And that's opened up a number of business opportunities for marketers.

Marketers are now getting into the game. Nissan, for example, created a gigantic driving course for its Sentra car, so Second Lifers can drive the digital cars, which are available from a gigantic vending machine. Along the route are billboards and other promotional spots encouraging people to visit Nissan Island, which is "leased" from the site's operating company. Sony BMG Music, Wells Fargo, and Adidas/Reebok lease other "islands."[26]

The Social Role A new category of Web sites that focus on **social networking** allow users to express themselves, interact with friends, and publish their own content on the Internet. MySpace, which targets young people and musicians, and Facebook, which is a real-time online journal for college students, are sites that allow users to share personal information with friends. Like the old mall and arcade hangouts, these are places where teens spend hours talking to friends about their joys, crushes, and disappointments.

With more than 200 million members in 2007, MySpace attracts more than one-third of the entire social networking audience in the United States. The smaller, but still phenomenally popular Facebook has created a community of 24 million members—college buddies who share photos, favorite music, and personal stories. Originally started in 2003 by musicians for sharing their tunes, MySpace has been so successful since it began that it is second only to Yahoo! in the number of pages it displays each day—a number in excess of 1 billion. In one California study, 81 percent of the students said they were MySpace members.[27]

Originally an advertising-free site, MySpace began to sell banner ads and sponsored pages, particularly when Rupert Murdoch's News Corporation bought the site in 2006 for $649 million. A new concept permits businesses to have MySpace pages with their own brand profiles just like any other member. The marketers hope to make friends with their young visitors. These advertisers use video clips, quizzes, downloadable gifts like ring

These frames from a Second Life site show how virtual words can be constructed online.

tones and icons, and, of course, links to their own Web sites. For example, eBay has a special "Student Superstore" page on Facebook called Half.com, a discount e-commerce site.

Politicians, who have been active users of Web sites, are also creating MySpace and Facebook profiles with cool and funny things about themselves. It is all about connecting with this young population to attract votes, volunteers, and donations.

The reason these social networking sites are so attractive to marketers is that they engage the power of relationships. Because of these relationships, network members are more likely to respond to messages on the sites, including ads, if they are effective at becoming part of the social context. Marketers are interested because these relationships also are influential in consumer decision making. Hairong Li, who wrote the Matter of Practice box, explains that "consumption often involves the construction of narratives of self and collective identify and that the meanings of possession and consumption practices are often construed in terms of personal relationships with other people. Sharing experience with others is integral to how we construct a coherent yet often fragmented sense of self in a networked society."

The Dialogue Role   In addition to providing information and associating themselves with entertainment and social networking, advertisers are turning to the Internet because it opens up the possibility of two-way communication. Thus, we recognize two basic objectives that drive advertisers' use of the Internet: (1) creating a dialogue with customers and (2) creating a dialogue among and between customers and potential customers.

The first objective relates to the interactivity dimension of the Internet. Remember from Chapter 4 that two-way communication is the most persuasive type of communication available to marketers. With interactive media, it is possible for a consumer to use the medium to contact the company and get a personal answer. The point is that the closer the medium is to a dialogue or the more a user can generate or manipulate the content, the more it can properly be described as interactive communication and the farther it moves from traditional advertiser-controlled advertising.

Principle

The more interactive a medium and the closer it is to a dialogue, the more personal and persuasive the communication experience.

A MATTER OF PRACTICE

Ads in Your Face on MySpace

By Hairong Li, *Associate Professor, Department of Advertising, Michigan State University*

Do you have a page on Facebook or My-Space? Does it carry advertising?

Blogs, wikis, podcasts, social networking, and video sharing Web sites have become the hottest territories in the online advertising space. In these social media, users not only create content to share but also interact with each other. For example, in MySpace you may have a hundred or even thousands of friends of all kinds with whom you can share opinions and product information—instantly. These characteristics—personal content, user engagement, social relationships, and group dynamics—differentiate social media from conventional mass media.

Social media are all about relationships. Think about your friends in Facebook or MySpace. Some of them are people you first met in person and then continued that relationship online, and some are people with whom you are acquainted only online. Whether you've ever met them in person, some online acquaintances are close friends, some are merely random friends, and the rest are probably in between.

Your relationships with these friends will affect how you respond to ads in social media. For example, a close friend of yours may post a comment about a new product she just bought and how she likes it. Wouldn't that make you think about the product after reading her comment?

As with any new medium, consumer-generated media have quickly caught the attention of advertisers. In-novative advertisers have started to experiment with new forms of advertising in social media, including publishing product profiles on social networking Web sites, sponsoring podcasts, distributing video clips, and hiring bloggers. A new technique is recruiting individuals to serve as viral marketing agents to take advantage of the social relationships these people have with their network of friends.

You may have already seen some movie trailers and album posters on the pages of your friends. These trailers and posters actually represent one of the newest forms of advertising—user-generated ads. By user-generated ads, we mean the content of commercial nature that is created or posted on the pages of users in social media that promotes a product, service, or cause.

New services have emerged to promote advertising in social media. For example, an Italian-based provider of social media services, data.net, partnered with Google's AdSense to launch a program that offers bloggers and social networkers a way to earn cash from their content. Users are invited to sign up for the program so that they can place ads on their blogs, profiles, and next to photos and videos. They can earn cash from Google ads that appear on their own pages and from messages that appear on the pages of friends they have invited. This move is likely to accelerate online viral marketing.

What will you do in front of so many opportunities for users, advertisers, and social media service providers?

The second objective relates to the power of word-of-mouth communication. Advertising planners have developed a growing respect for media that generate **buzz** or **word of mouth.** The idea is to get people talking about a brand because of the recognition that the most important factor in consumer decision making is often the opinions of others, such as family and friends. An annual study of media use by the BIGresearch firm that polled 15,000 consumers found that the most influential form of media is word of mouth (WoM). The finding was supported by other research that has found word of mouth to be the most important influence on consumer decision making—considerably more important than traditional media.[28]

Ty Montague, Chief Creative Officer at JWT, points to his agency's work for JetBlue as a brand built almost entirely on word of mouth. He explains that the airline's advertising "is designed to provide as many ways as possible for fans of the brand to spread the word themselves, from stuff like a high-tech booth where they can literally create their own testimonials, which get run on TV, to things as simple and high touch as prepaid postcards in seatback pockets that they can use to share their experiences."[29]

New Internet Practices

Of course, the Internet itself is a new advertising form, but it is also a catalyst for new thinking about how advertising should be handled. We'll talk about five practices that are creating

Practical Tips

Using URLs in Advertising—It Makes a Difference

By Lynda Maddox, *Professor of Marketing and Advertising, George Washington University*

Does it make any difference to consumers if advertisers use a Web address (URL) in their advertising? I've been looking into that question since this practice first started showing up in the mid-1990s.

My colleagues and I have found a number of practices that can increase advertising effectiveness:

- Using a Web address positively affects consumers' perceptions of the advertiser, and this effect happens before they ever click on a link or visit the Web site.
- Web addresses are noticed by both those who use the Internet and those who have never used it.
- The mere existence of a URL in many cases enhances the advertiser's image.
- Advertisers with Web addresses are considered to be more customer-oriented, more responsive to consumers' needs, more informative, more "high-tech," more sophisticated, and likely to stay in business longer.
- When Internet usage in the United States was growing, many consumers who were not currently using the Internet reported that they would log on within the next month to visit an advertised Web site.

We first found these effects in the United States but later found they're observable in a developing country such as China.

- Consistent with the previous U.S. study, our research revealed that the mere inclusion of a URL in advertising enhanced the image of the advertiser.
- Compared to those without URLs in their ads, advertisers with URLs were perceived more positively by Chinese consumers.
- Nearly half of the Chinese respondents expect advertisers currently without a URL to include one in their ads, and 62 percent think advertisers *should* include URLs in their advertising.

In short, advertisers in both the United States and in developing countries should consider all benefits and effects of Web advertising. They should not just consider the click-through rates but should also seek to measure awareness and effectiveness from the time the URL appears.

My research in the United States has been conducted with Darshan Mehta of Digital Biz Corporation and Dr. Hugh Daubek of Purdue University. The China studies were with Dr. Wen Gong of Howard University.

---

opportunities in this new Web world—offline advertising, search marketing, brand experiences, webisodes, and the global Web world.

Offline Advertising for Web Sites   One of the most difficult problems facing Internet marketers is driving traffic to their sites. One way to do this is to use **offline advertising,** which appears in conventional media to drive traffic to a Web site. Print is particularly useful because it offers the opportunity to present the URL in a format that makes it possible for the reader to note the address. It's harder to present that information in broadcast media where the message is here and gone. Whatever the medium, including URLs in traditional ads does matter to consumers, as the Practical Tips box explains.

Search Marketing   Related to the consumer search function is the marketer's ability to position its brand messages adjoining the topics that are compiled in response to a keyword by search engines.[30] This is called **search marketing.** With a credit card and a few minutes, a small business owner can set up a link between his or her brand and a keyword, such as *chocolate éclairs* or *faux painting*. It's the ultimate in brand relationship building.

Since consumers initiate the search, the adjoining ads are not perceived to be as intrusive as other forms of advertising. People do hundreds of millions of searches a day, and businesses spend some $8.3 billion to have their ads displayed next to the results produced by these keyword searches.

A benefit of online consumer searches is that they leave a trail of clues about products, features, and advertising approaches. This behavior can be mined for insights that lead to new products.

Search engines such as Google and Microsoft's adCenter auction off positions that let advertisers' ads be seen next to specific search results. This has brought a fountain of money to Google over the years. These related ads are priced based on the number of consumer clicks on the ad, with rates averaging around 50 cents per click. Companies spent $5.1 billion on search-related ads in 2006, which was up 31 percent from the previous year.[31]

Search optimization is the practice of maximizing the link between topics and brand-related Web sites. Weblinx is an Internet advertising company that specializes in search engine optimization, guaranteeing that customers will visit a client's site (http://www. weblinx.biz). The Practical Tips box suggests some techniques to use to make your Web site more visible. An important first step for marketers in creating a viable Web site is getting it registered with popular search engines so that it shows up early on the list provided by the search engine. A list of strategies to optimize the visibility of your Web site is featured on this book's Web site (http://www.prenhall.com/moriarty/), along with some links to sites that explain this topic in more detail.

Brand Experiences on the Web   Many consumers consider pop-ups, banner ads, and superstitials annoying and therefore ineffective. As a result, many companies instead are making their Web sites more engaging and entertaining. Web sites for Nike and the Gap are excellent examples of this practice. The Nike site features engaging subsites within the main site, each dedicated to a different sport. For example, NikeBasketball outlines Nike's 30 years of marketing basketball shoes, and NikeGoddess provides content and shopping targeted to women.

Burger King has developed an interactive Web site that lets visitors make a human being in a chicken suit dance, jump, watch TV, or do push-ups. The crazy chicken that responds to viewers' commands is featured on the site, http://www.subservientchicken.com, and appeals to the zany side of Web surfers. It also experiments with a dimension of virtual interactivity, as the chicken seems to interact with its viewers through what appears to be a Web-cam window.[32] The chicken also relies on viral marketing for its visibility, recognizing that the young Web surfer audience is likely to share the site with friends. Originally, only 20 people who were friends and coworkers of the staff at Burger King's agency, Crispin Porter + Bogusky knew about the site. Since then the site has received 15 to 20 million hits, and visitors spend an average of six minutes playing with the chicken.

Webisodes   Similar to television programs with recurring episodes in a developing story, **webisodes** have created a new form of Web advertising. Fallon Worldwide created the original experiment in this new format for its client BMW. Known as the "BMW films," the series consisted of high-action minimovies by well-known action movie directors (John Woo, Guy Ritchie, and Ang Lee), all of which featured various BMW models in starring roles. Randall Rothenberg, an advertising critic, wrote that the highly entertaining films reinvented advertising.[33]

The Global Web of Advertising   The Web is an international marketing and advertising medium, and that's a real strength for global marketers. But it also faces access, legal, linguistic, currency, and technological barriers. First, not everyone around the globe has the access or ability to use the Internet via computer, but the number of Internet users is growing exponentially. The Internet audience is growing faster internationally than it is in the United States, particularly in developing countries such as China and India.

Second, advertising and sales promotion laws differ from country to country. Differences in privacy laws between Europe and the United States are expected to force American companies to change the way they collect and share the consumer information they monitor and retrieve from customers' Web behavior.

Language is another factor. Although English is the dominant language on the Internet, some advertisers who want to provide different Web sites for different countries have trouble ensuring consistency across all sites. Another issue is exchange rates. Companies must decide whether to offer prices in their own currency or in the local currency. For example, one Canadian shopper reported that books on a Canadian Web site were cheaper than the same books on Amazon.com. In addition, some companies make different offers available in different countries.

Marketers must also keep in mind the technological differences among the worldwide Internet audiences. Users in some countries have to pay per-minute charges and therefore want to get on and off quickly, which precludes sophisticated graphics that take a long time to load. In other countries, users have access to fast lines and may expect more sophisticated Internet programming.

Issues in Internet Advertising

Two issues online advertisers continue to study are measuring Internet advertising and privacy concerns.

Measurement   The advantages of the Internet as a potential advertising vehicle are tremendous, with rapid, near instantaneous feedback and results chief among them. Rather than wait weeks or months to measure the success of an advertising campaign, marketers can instead run tests online, measure meaningful results within days, and quickly invest in the best performers with minimal switching costs. One problem, however, is a lack of standards to measure Internet effectiveness. At the heart of the problem is the question of what exactly is to be measured—readers, viewers, visitors? And how do such metrics equate to the reach of other media?

Consider **hits** (the number of times a particular site is visited), viewers (the number of viewers to a site), unique visitors (the number of different viewers during a particular time period), and page views (the number of times viewers view a page). These measures track a consumer through a Web site, but they offer no insights as to motivation, nor do they tell us whether a visitor paid any attention to the surrounding ads.

The primary method currently used to measure consumer response to Internet advertising is click-through (the number of people who click on a banner ad). Many Internet advertisers consider this measure insufficient, and a host of private research providers have emerged to expand on that measure. For example, Denver-based Match Logic identifies for its clients what viewers do next after *not* clicking on a banner ad.

Having the ability to quantitatively measure audiences is particularly important to media buyers, who need to show what the click-through, page view, or total traffic means to their clients. It would also be meaningful for advertisers or media buyers to obtain similar information from comparable sites so that they could see if they were getting a fair deal. This information about audience measurement is good for companies who want to structure their advertising rates based on the actual activity on their Web sites. Accurate audience measurement also helps advertisers determine the effectiveness of their ads.

Some of the biggest changes, however, are happening in the area of measurement as the Internet becomes more like mainstream television. Media planners and buyers hope to be able to use the same daypart data, as well as reach and frequency tools, to evaluate the effectiveness of online advertising. Planners believe Web site clicks will eventually be audited the same way viewership and readership are for traditional media.

Principle

Companies that keep track of their customers' online behavior are better able to personalize their advertising messages.

Internet Targeting and Privacy   In addition to providing information, e-businesses also capture information and use it to direct their marketing communication efforts to make messages more personal and relevant to consumers. This is true for Internet advertising as well as e-mail advertising.

Every time you order something from Amazon.com, for example, the company keeps track and starts building a profile of your interests. When you go to Amazon the next time, the site will probably open with an announcement about some new book or CD that might interest you. If you have given Amazon permission, it will also send these announcements to you by e-mail. In other words, companies that collect data about the behavior of their customers can better target them with advertising messages and personalize special promotional offers.

But there are other tracking mechanisms that you may not be aware of, such as **cookies**, which are little electronic bugs that can be placed on your computer by a Web server to track your movements online. They don't do anything bad, like a virus does, but they do report back to their owners what sites you visited and from that can build an online profile about you and your interests. On the good side, cookies let companies store information about your registration, as well as your preferences, so you don't have to retype everything every time you go to that site.

Are cookies a bad practice or good? Critics say they are an invasion of privacy, but marketers say they are just a way to gather marketing information without the tedious survey process. In fact, many people recognize the trade-off: If they provide a company with information, they will get more personalized service in return. For more information about how you can get your Internet service provider to remove cookies, check out the Web site, http://www.webwasher.com.

Many people have issues with the collection of personal information. Their concern is with how the information is used and whether its use violates their privacy. AOL, for example, assembles a huge database of customer information, some of which it sells to other direct marketers. It admits this practice in its privacy policy, which is published on its Web site. It also buys information about its subscribers from other outside database suppliers, which it can use to better target its customers interests. And that's the primary reason companies collect this type of information: It lets them better target their advertising messages.

Some companies try to maintain a responsible position by posting their **privacy policy** on their Web sites, which details, among other things, how or whether the site is collecting data on its visitors and how that data is used. Sometimes this information is easy to find, sometimes it is buried on the site and difficult to access, and in some instances the Web site doesn't have any published privacy statement at all. A number of consumer activists follow this privacy issue; if you want to learn more about their activities, check the watchdog site Junkbusters (http://www.junkbusters.com). The government also has an Electronic Privacy Information Center (http://www.epic.org), which monitors information-collecting practices and privacy issues.

Changes and Trends in Internet Advertising

One of the biggest problems Internet advertisers face is the varying levels of users' technological sophistication. Some use high-speed connections that deliver data rapidly. Many people, however, are still using slow dial-up modems that make online access and transmission tedious. **Bandwidth** refers to the amount of digital information that can be sent through a phone line or fiber optic line. As the technology has improved, and many users now have appropriate software, a high-speed modem, and a broadband line (such as DSL or cable), it is becoming easier to download the images of rich media.

The convergence of video and the Internet is also creating some technological challenges as users scramble to upgrade for the latest innovation. Newer interactive ads that deliver multimedia effects using sound, still images, and full-motion video are referred to as **rich media**. We've discussed **streaming video,** which fuels the social networking sites, but not all computers have been upgraded to receive these formats. Internet designers continue to search for easier and more reliable ways to present video on the Web.

Advantages and Disadvantages of Internet Advertising

Internet advertising is growing in popularity because it offers some distinct advantages over other media, in addition to the explosion in its use by consumers. Most notably, it is relatively inexpensive. Advertisers see it as a relatively low-cost alternative to mainstream advertising media. It is also a form that reaches people who aren't watching much television or reading newspapers. The key benefit of Internet advertising is that it is relatively easy to track and effective at reaching a highly targeted audience.

Also, advertisers can customize and personalize their messages over the Internet. Thanks to database marketing, an advertiser can input key demographic and behavioral variables, making the consumer feel like the ad is just for him or her. Check out http://www.classmates.com for an example. Ads appearing on a particular page are for products that would appeal to a particular age group. Someone who graduated from high school in 1960 would see banner ads for investments that facilitate retirement as opposed to someone graduating in 2000, who might see career ads.

For the B2B advertiser, Internet advertising can provide excellent sales leads or actual sales. Users of a typical B2B site, for example, can access the product catalogs, read the product specifications in-depth, request a call from a salesperson, and make a purchase online.

The Internet can level the playing field for small and medium-sized companies that compete against larger organizations. The cost of creating a Web site, a set of ads, and a database is affordable for virtually every marketer.

Undoubtedly, the most serious drawback is the inability of strategic and creative experts to consistently produce effective ads and to measure their effectiveness. Consider, too, that clutter is just as much a problem with the Internet as it is in other media. In fact, because multiple ads may appear on the same screen—many moving or popping up—the clutter may be even worse.

NONTRADITIONAL MEDIA

As we said, mainstream media of all types are hurting, particularly network television, which is under assault from cable, DVRs, the social networking sites, and now video games. Advertisers are searching for new ways to reach their targeted audiences. These new media forms are called either *new media*, a phrase that has been used to refer to new electronic forms or *alternative media*, which refers to nontraditional or unexpected communication tools and events. This section will discuss the trends in both these areas.

Principle
The media person's search for new ways to deliver messages is just as creative as the creative person's search for new advertising ideas.

The search for new media—that is, new ways to reach target audiences—is particularly important for advertisers trying to reach the elusive youth market, since teens are often the first to experiment with new media forms. In some ways, this search for new ways to deliver messages is just as creative as the message concepts developed on the creative side of advertising. That's why one of the principles of this book is that the media side can be just as creative as the creative side of advertising. It's also the point of The Inside Story, which describes the activities of a young advertising professional who works for a company that specializes in alternative and out-of-home media.

Guerilla Marketing

Guerilla marketing is the use of unconventional and low-budget brand experiences and encounters designed to grab attention. The idea is to use creative ways to reach people where they live, work, and walk to create a personal connection and a high level of impact. If it works, the encounter gets talked about by word of mouth—buzz. For example, a Danish firm has designed eerily lifelike holograms that project images in public spaces. Wireless carrier Vodaphone used these holographic ads featuring Portuguese soccer players dribbling balls for the opening of one of its concept stores in Portugal.

More about matching wits than matching budgets, guerilla marketing has limited reach. For example, Sony Ericsson Mobile Communications Ltd. hired actors to create buzz about a new mobile phone that is also a digital camera. The actors pretended to be tourists who wanted their picture taken, thus allowing consumers to try the product. As a typical guerilla marketing campaign, it only reached those who encountered the actors.

Sometimes, however, a guerilla marketing campaign will generate publicity that extends the impact—and sometimes the publicity isn't positive. In 2007 the Cartoon Network, a Turner Broadcasting network, used a campaign in nine cities featuring blinking electronic signs that displayed a boxy-looking cartoon character, some with protruding wires, to promote its *Aqua Teen Hunger Force* show. In Boston a wave of panic brought out bomb squads, and officials shut down highways and bridges. The unconventional promotion eventually led to the resignation of the Cartoon Network head, as well as the arrest of the men who placed the devices around the city. Turner Broadcasting paid $2 million to compensate the city for the emergency response costs.

Advertainment

In an attempt to stand out among the media clutter, several companies have begun integrating brands into the thematic heart of television shows, known as **advertainment** or **branded entertainment**. This is more than just product placement, because the program is built around the brand. Similar to the presence of FedEx in *Castaway*, these shows use the product as a prop or central feature of the program. Further examples include plans by Mattel and Columbia Pictures to make films based on Hot Wheels and ABC's decision to

In the continual search for new ways to reach audiences, innovative media placements are being explored in the form of ads on conveyer belts at airports, the sides of vehicles, and stenciled messages in the sand on beaches.

base a program on Geico's popular cavemen characters. Branded entertainment blurs the line between advertising and entertainment and more aggressively promotes a product than product placement. Described as *situational* or *contextual ads*, they are embedded in specific programs, which makes it harder for viewers to dismiss immediately the content as ads because the product is a character in the program.

Video Games

As we've noted before, marketers and media planners have been frustrated trying to reach young people with traditional ads on mainstream media. That has led to an increased focus on Internet advertising, but also on unusual media that are clearly the province of young people, such as video games. Now a global $16 billion industry, the video game business is developing as a major new medium for advertisers to target 12- to 34-year-old males, although girls are getting into the act as well. More than 220 million computer and video games are sold in the country every year.

The current hardware giants are Sony's PlayStation 3, Nintendo's Wii, and Microsoft's Xbox 360. The top online computer game, with more than 8 million subscribers who pay about $15 a month to play, is World of Warcraft.

Opportunities will be mined both by creating online games as well as placing products within games. For example, games feature product placements for Puma athletic shoes, Nokia mobile phones, and Skittles candies, among others. Volkswagen of America bought a placement on Sony Computer Entertainment's Gran Turismo 3 car-racing game.

THE INSIDE STORY

Nontraditional Media Overview

By Melissa Lerner, *Business Director, Kinetic Worldwide, New York, NY*

As our society becomes increasingly mobile, nontraditional media helps advertisers make an impact on audiences at different times and locations throughout their day. Innovative media not only reach people while they are on the go, but also allow advertisers to intercept particular consumers via highly targeted messaging.

Nontraditional media include emerging media and digital enhancements, place-based, branded environments, and guerilla executions. These media provide an entrée for new advertisers and expand current advertiser portfolio. They are nothing for advertisers to fear!

These new formats are often used in conjunction with out-of-home (OOH) media. New technologies allow for consumer interaction in the outdoor environment. For example, at my agency WOW, a division of

Kinetic Worldwide, which specializes in outdoor and nontraditional media, we sometimes combine traditional outdoor boards with digital/interactive technology to boost the impact and brand perception.

There is nothing better than working on a nontraditional media concept that comes to fruition and generates exciting PR and buzz within a marketplace. Creative thinking is necessary to brainstorm and plan "never been done before" campaigns. Clients are demanding more unique plans and ideas than ever before because impact and engagement help them to become trendsetters in their respective industries. The following chart illustrates the variety of different vehicles and opportunities we use at WOW to relay messages to consumers through alternative and OOH media.

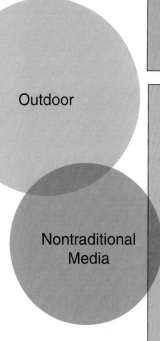

Outdoor
8-Sheets
30-Sheets
Bulletins
Premiere Panels
Scaffolds
Spectaculars
Wallscapes
Street Furniture
Bus Benches/Shelters
Phone Kiosks
Mall Displays
Newsstands/Racks
Sidewalk Displays
Urban Panels
Transit
Airport Media
Bus Media
Commuter Rail Media
Mobile Billboards
Subway Media
Truck-Side Media
Taxi

Outdoor

Nontraditional Media

Place/Affinity Based
Place-Based Broadcast:
Airport TV
In-Store TV/Radio
Mall TV
Physician/Pharmacy TV
Theatre Radio

Affinity-Based:
Bar/Restaurant Media
Cinema
C-Store Media
College Media
Day Care Center Media
Gas/Service Station Media
Golf Media
Health Club Media
In-Flight Media
In-Office Building Media
In-School Media
In-Stadium Media
In-Store Media
Leisure Media
Physician Media
Ski Media
VIP Airline Lounge Media
Wild Posters

Alternative/Guerrilla
Alternative:
Aerial Media
Custom Media
Event Sponsorships
Experiential Media
Interactive Kiosks
Naming Rights
Projection Media
Sampling
Specialty Media
Sports Sponsorship
Travel Affinity Sponsorships
New Technology

Guerrilla Media:
Coffee Cups/Sleeves
Graffiti Murals
Mobile Media (i.e. AdVans)
Pizza Boxes
Street Teams
Umbrellas
Deli Bags

FIGURE 10.2
WOW Alternative Media Chart

The advertisement may be a simple product placement or make the product the star. Burger King's weird "King" mascot shows up in Microsoft Xbox games sold in its stores. Sony is launching its own 3-D game that was built by players who participated in the game's development through social marketing sites. Home is a networked 3-D game for PlayStation 3. Similar to Second Life, it opens the door to a world that features video games for the players' avatars to play, as well as virtual arcades, movies, music, and other Sony-branded media.

As video games develop as an advertising medium, planners and buyers are asking for standardized independent data that proves their effectiveness. Nielsen Media Research is developing a system that will track how many gamers see the ads in the console-based video games. The new service will probably use a device like the set-top boxes used to monitor TV viewing, supplemented by follow-up phone surveys.

Wi-Fi Communication and Mobile Marketing

Cell phone technology has exploded as a popular form of **wireless (Wi-Fi)** or mobile communication that links the common phone to a computer and to the Internet. Telecommunication experts believe we've just scratched the surface of the possibilities. Some places, like the Scandinavian countries, Japan, and Korea, are highly advanced in wireless communication, and consumers there are far more accustomed to using smart phones, videophones, and instant messaging than are Americans.

Cell phones have also introduced new product lines such as graphic faceplates and specialty ring tones. The fact that there is a market for these products demonstrates that young people use their phones as fashion accessories and to make personal style statements. Young people also consider their phones to be part of their entertainment en-

These painted stairs at the Denver Pavilions, an entertainment complex in downtown Denver, advertise membership in the nearby Colorado Athletic Club. Called a "captive ad," it is unavoidable for people walking up or down the stairs.

vironment, and that opens up promotional opportunities similar to those being used by more conventional advertising media that are exploring the edge of advertainment.

As we mentioned in the discussion of mobile marketing, videos are becoming popular on cell phones, and these can be far more engaging than anything on conventional television. For example, CBS has created a cell phone version of "America's Next Top Model" where viewers can play with animated versions of the show, pick dresses, and experiment with the stars' makeup. To make these experiments work, carriers are searching for ways to gain ad support for the programs. Reuters, for example, has begun offering ad-supported free mobile newscasts.[34]

When Toyota launched its Yaris, the media plan focused on sponsoring a series of "mobisodes" tied to the Fox TV show *Prison Break*. The two-minute episodes, which were designed specifically for mobile phones and carried a Yaris commercial at the beginning of the video, were downloaded 255,000 times in the first four weeks of the campaign.[35]

Mobile marketing is developing as a specialized promotion industry as marketers develop innovative ways to grab consumers by the ears as they pass through the streets. The Mobile Marketing Association defines *mobile marketing* as the use of wireless media, primarily cellular phones and PDAs, to deliver content and encourage direct response within a cross-media communication program. Mobile marketing includes instant messaging, video messages and downloads, and banner ads on mobile Web sites.[36]

If a cell phone user, for example, registers with a favorite store, then that store can contact the user when he or she is in the neighborhood. These calls can announce special deals or invite the customer in for a taste test or some other type of promotion. Experts predict that advertisers will double what they spend for mobile marketing, reaching some $2.9 billion in 2011.[37] New specialized agencies, such as Third Screen Media, are designing small-screen advertisements for these new media.

Another company has created a free application that lets viewers download news and watch TV programs as they are broadcast. The ad-supported service is free because it carries small banner ads across the top or bottom of the screen.

Text and Instant Messaging   Young people are more adept at exploring connection opportunities with new communication systems than are older people. Teens, particularly girls,

use their cell phones to chat with their friends using **text messaging (TM)**, which allows them to keyboard brief messages into a cell phone. Bluetooth and other technologies allow easy networking between devices, such as PDAs, laptops, and phones. **Instant messaging (IM),** which occurs when two people chat from their computers, is more of a dialogue than text messaging.

An international phenomenon, emerging markets are rushing to this new communication tool. In China, for example, the largest cell phone operator with more than 360 million accounts experienced a 48 percent increase in text messages during the 2007 Chinese New Year when people traditionally greet friends and family.[38]

Younger teen girls use text messaging daily to reach their friends, far more than do adults. As teens have mastered the skill of talking with their thumbs, they also have developed an abbreviated code that lets them communicate rapidly. An example comes from a headline on a story about instant messaging: "Wot R They Up 2?"

Bluetooth is a technology that appeals more to business people, and it also brings opportunities for commercial interaction between companies and their customers. One unexpected use is called "bluejacking," which refers to anonymous messages sent to users in crowded settings such as bars and trains. But messages can also be sent to customers in these settings if they have opted in through permission marketing.

The **short code** is used by marketers as an easy technique for consumers to reach them. These text messages are delivered by four- to six-digit company cell phone addresses—466453 for Google, for example—to connect consumers to news updates on sporting teams or special promotions such as coupons for freebies at nearby fast-food chains. Weather 33606 is the short code for Google's current weather and forecasts. Google can also send movie listings, sports scores, stock prices, and phone numbers to cell phone users.[39]

The problem is that many teens hate IM/TM advertising because they see it as invasive. Although IM/TM advertising—primarily in the form of product notices—is big in Japan, it's still seen as an invasion of privacy in the United States. As in other forms of advertising, the way to be less intrusive is to be more relevant and offer opt-in options. Teens may permit advertising if it offers them information they want, such as news about music, games, sports, cosmetics, and fashion. In Japan, a bar code can be sent for a free sample or some other promotion. Like a free coupon, it can be redeemed when a cashier scans the code.

Click-and-dial systems use wireless phones to access Web sites. For example, if it is your mother's birthday, a reminder note may come through on your phone, and you can respond by clicking a button that connects you to your favorite florist to place an order. These are interesting and innovative uses of wireless communication, but the industry is so new that we haven't begun to explore all the possibilities this technology offers for advertising and permission marketing.

Hybrid Technologies Convergence is a big word in the traditional media industries where the differences between television, print, and the Internet media seem to be blurring. The potential of interactive media is that they may combine the advantages of broadcast (high-impact visuals), print (the ability to inform), and the Internet (personalization and interactivity). Convergence is also creating opportunities in the wireless environment where companies like Nokia are offering cell phones that also work as cameras, gaming devices, and MP3 players. Apple's launch of the iPhone, with its cell phone, iPod, and video iPod capability, is a prime example of how these media are merging.

Podcasts, or audio shows from the Web that can be downloaded to an MP3 player, are also opening up new ways for advertisers to reach the ears of customers. Apple has helped by integrating podcast capability into its popular iTunes jukebox Web site. Walt Disney was one of the first companies to explore the potential of podcasts for promotions when it used a series of podcasts for Disneyland's 50th anniversary celebration.

A MATTER OF PRINCIPLE

When Is Too Many Too Much?

By Tom Duncan, *IMC Founder and Director Emeritus, University of Colorado* and
Daniels School of Business at the University of Denver

The questions advertisers have to ask themselves when approving a plan that involves nontraditional media is whether they are using this tool effectively and with respect for consumers. Are advertisers trying to find every possible contact point they can identify or are they creating logical associations that consumers will appreciate?

The fact is that we are inundated with commercial messages from advertising of all sorts in all kinds of unexpected places that we routinely encounter. Message clutter is overwhelming every aspect of our daily lives.

Think about something as noncommercial as attending a symphony. You may find a new car in the lobby as well as promotional signs for any number of products—not to mention the symphony itself, which is promoting concerts and season subscriptions. Of course, there are ads in the program, but there may also be ads in the bathrooms and around the snack counter you visit at intermission. And when you leave, you'll probably see more posters in windows adjoining the concert hall. You might even find a flyer tucked under the windshield wiper on your car.

There is a difference between "buying eyeballs" and delivering messages in a context that will intersect with a target audience's interests.

Wilson Sporting Goods, for example, sponsors Tennis Camps by furnishing practice balls and making racquets available that participants can try for free. Even though the camp may be surrounded by Wilson, the message is relevant and the brand experiences are positive.

The point is that the less relevant the messages, the more irritating they become.

Why is this a problem?

The tipping point in impact is when the percentage of irrelevant messages is so high that people respond by tuning out ALL commercial messages—the relevant along with the irrelevant.

One reason TiVo became popular is because viewers can time-shift programs and zip through commercials. In what ways will consumers create defense mechanisms to protect themselves from nontraditional media that assault them in unwanted ways in inappropriate times.

How many messages can we surround them with before they rebel?

It's a new technology and research has found that as of 2007 only about 6 percent, or 9 million U.S. adults, have downloaded podcasts to their computers and mobile phones, but the growth potential is obvious. The study also found that more than 75 percent of those downloading podcasts were young males.[40]

Nonelectronic New Media

Ads have been appearing in unexpected places, such as the back of toilet stall doors, for some time. Anywhere the eye can see—eggs and apples, subway turnstiles, pizza boxes and Chinese food cartons, airline seatbacks and motion sickness bags, and paper liners in doctor's examination rooms, to name a few—is likely to be a place for an ad. A flip-flop company is etching brand logos into the soles of its sandals so wearers can leave imprints in the sand. NASCAR is a great example of logos covering every inch of space on its race cars, and major league soccer teams are selling ad space on their players' jerseys.

Target is even displaying its distinctive bull's-eye logo on the roofs of its stores where they can be seen by people in planes. Another high-flying idea comes from NASA, which has considered printing emblems and logos alongside NASA's on space shuttles and the space station. McDonald's, for example, can put its golden arches on the kitchen "galley," in return for promoting space exploration to kids in its restaurants. And a group of students at MIT have launched a Web site, YourNameIntoSpace.org, that will sell space on satellites where marketers can place their logos, slogans, and images.

The Yankelovich market research firm estimates that city residents see about 5,000 ad messages a day, compared with some 2,000 three decades ago.[41] Is there a problem with all these spaces in our lives being filled with commercial messages? Professor Tom Duncan speculates on the impact of the growth of nontraditional media in the Matter of Principle box.

IT'S A WRAP

eBay Evolves

This entire chapter on interactive and alternative new media is about changes in the media industry, so there's no need to wrap up this chapter by trying to figure out what's next. The changes are coming so fast that it's impossible to predict what new media forms are on the horizon. It is important to realize, however, that some of the most creative ideas in advertising are seen in the areas of interactive and alternative new media. The Internet has revolutionized the media industry just as eBay is revolutionizing retailing.

eBay has come a long way from selling that first broken laser pointer. It is now recognized as the premier online auction site. Benefiting from consumers' seemingly insatiable appetite for a good deal, eBay has proven that it offers a successful business model. eBay celebrated its 10th year in business by amassing a cool $4.55 billion in revenue.

In the 10-plus years it's been in business, eBay continues to evolve. One recent development involves growing its business by moving into the lucrative ticket industry that generates $10 billion in annual sales with the acquisition of StubHub, an online ticket reseller.

Another advancement involves Web ads. Similar to the strategies used on Google and Yahoo!, eBay allows affiliates to run contextual ads for its auctions in exchange for a portion of the eBay sales. For example, a sports Web site might feature links to sports equipment or memorabilia from eBay.

In yet another development involving its global ties, eBay closed its Web site in China and joined forces with a Chinese e-commerce company after it realized that it lacked important political influence and knowledge about the Chinese market.

Most likely eBay's management will guide the company through other changes in the future. What is most remarkable about the story, though, is that this business that computer programmer Pierre Omidyar started in 1995 recognized the importance of selling person to person. This insight has helped spawn a revolution that demonstrates the power of the consumer in shaping the way we advertise and market today.

Key Points Summary

1. **How does the Internet work, and what are the roles it plays in marketing communication?** Most Internet advertising is found on established news media sites that operate as electronic publishers, such as nytimes.com, WSJ.com, and ESPN.com, as well as on major search engines and service providers, such as Google and Yahoo!. Advertisers place ads on the Internet through providers, such as DoubleClick, an Internet advertising service.

2. **How does e-mail advertising work?** E-mail advertising is a way to send an advertising message to a list of e-mail addresses. Unsolicited e-mail, called *spam*, and is generally disliked; permission marketing asks potential customers to opt-in and put themselves on the list.

3. **In what ways are the different forms of interactive and alternative new media changing the way advertising works?** Because of the problems faced by traditional media, there is a continual search for new and novel ways to reach consumers. That's particularly true for the youth market. Video games, webisodes, instant messaging, and guerilla marketing are being used to create new forms of communication. The new media also open up opportunities for new types of personal brand experiences.

Key Terms

advertainment, p. 302
avatars, p. 295
bandwidth, p. 301
banner ads, p. 291
blogs, p. 288
branded entertainment, p. 302
buzz, p. 297
chat rooms, p. 288
click-through, p. 291
cookies, p. 300
domain name, p. 287
e-business, p. 294
e-commerce, p. 294
guerilla marketing, p. 302

hits, p. 300
home page, p. 287
instant messaging (IM), p. 306
Internet, p. 287
keywords, p. 287
link, p. 287
minisites, p. 292
mobile marketing, p. 305
netcasting, p. 289
offline advertising, p. 298
opt in, p. 293
opt out, p. 293
permission marketing, p. 293

podcasts, p. 306
pop-up, pop-behind, p. 291
portal, p. 287
privacy policy, p. 301
rich media, p. 301
search engines, p. 287
search marketing, p. 298
search optimization, p. 299
short code, p. 306
skyscrapers, p. 291
social networking, p. 295
spam, spamming, p. 293
streaming video, p. 301

superstitials, p. 292
text messaging (TM), p. 306
URL, p. 287
viral marketing, p. 293
vlogs, p. 289
webisodes, p. 299
Web site, p. 287
Wi-Fi, p. 305
wireless communication,
   p. 305
word of mouth, p. 297
World Wide Web, p. 287
zines, p. 294

Review Questions

1. What is a Web site, and how does it differ from other forms of advertising?

2. Describe search engines, chat rooms, and blogs, and explain how they can be used in a company's advertising program.

3. Define and describe a banner ad. Some experts say the effectiveness of banner ads is declining. Is that an accurate assessment? Why or why not?

4. Explain the concept of offline advertising. What is its primary objective?

5. How is the Internet audience measured?

6. What are the advantages and disadvantages of Internet advertising? Of e-mail advertising?

7. What are some of the new forms of alternative media with which advertisers are experimenting? Explain how they work and what advantages they provide.

Discussion Questions

1. One interesting way to combine the assets of print and broadcast is to use the visuals from a print ad or a television commercial in an Internet ad. Why would an advertiser consider this creative strategy? What limitations would you mention? In what situations would you recommend doing this?

2. This chapter briefly discussed the concept of rich media. Visit various sites related to Internet marketing and find out what is being said about this new form. Start with the Interactive Advertising Bureau (IAB), which you can find at http://www.iab.com and DoubleClick at http://www.doubleclick.com. Then find several other sites that have discussions on this topic. Put together a report entitled "Rich Media and Its Advertising Implications" for your instructor.

3. *Three-Minute Debate*: You are a sales rep working for a college newspaper that has an online version. How would

you attract advertising? One of your colleagues says there is no market for online advertising for the paper, but you think the paper is missing an opportunity. Consider the following questions: What companies would you recommend to contact? How can Internet sites like your online newspaper entice companies to advertise on them? What competitive advantage, if any, would Web advertising for your paper provide?

   In class, organize into small teams with each team developing an argument on the advantages or disadvantages of Internet advertising. Set up a series of debates with each team taking 1½ minutes to argue its position. Every team of debaters has to present new points not covered in the previous presentations until there are no arguments left to present. Then the class votes as a group on the winning point of view.

Take-Home Team Projects

1. Examine the various ads found on major corporate sites, such as http://www.nike.com, http://www.IBM.com, and http://www.sears.com. Which ads did you find most appealing? Engaging? Motivating? Which ones do you think could easily be used as television commercials? As radio commercials? Write a one- to two-page report on your assessment.

2. You are the media planner for a cosmetics company introducing a new line of makeup for teenage girls. Your research indicates that the Internet might be an effective medium for creating awareness about your new product line. How do you design an Internet advertising strategy that will reach your target market successfully? What Web sites would you choose? Why? What advertising forms would you use on these sites and why? What other media would you recommend using as part of this campaign and why?

3. Your small agency works for a local retailer (pick one from your community) that wants to create buzz and get people talking about it. The retailer has very little money to use on advertising. Your agency team agrees that guerilla marketing would be a solution. Brainstorm among yourselves and come up with a list of at least five ideas for guerilla marketing that would get people talking about the store. Write the ideas as a proposal to the store owner and prepare a presentation to share your ideas with the class.

Yahoo! Hands-On Case

Review the Yahoo! case in the Appendix.

1. Explain why the Internet received the focus it did in the Yahoo! case. Tie the justification to what the case tells you about the target audience.

2. The Yahoo! case made extensive use of the Internet. You have been asked to develop a plan to make more intensive use of alternative media. Brainstorm as a team and develop more ideas on how to reach this target with the Yahoo! message. Explain and justify your recommendations.

HANDS-ON CASE

Second Life Provides Out-of-This-World Opportunities

Imagine a world where you can be anybody you want to be, meet the friends you like, and do whatever you want. These parallel universes exist—sort of. You can join Second Life, a virtual community. Participants in this virtual world create alter-egos, called *avatars*, of their own choosing and enter the world to meet friends, work, and play. They can buy islands, build houses, and be entertained. They can even fly from place to place—no airplane needed.

Created in 1999 as an online entertainment, Second Life attracts about 30,000 visitors daily. This activity has caught the attention of real-world businesses. Coca-Cola, American Apparel, Pontiac, Coldwell Banker, Sony BMG, Adidas, and Reebok are some of the companies that have plunked down real cash to occupy real estate in the virtual community.

Even universities are venturing into this fake world. Ohio University opened doors to its virtual campus where sophisticated graphics replicate the feel of being there. It erected several buildings on its virtual campus, including a student center and arts complex, to entice current and potential students to explore and learn in a different way.

It costs real money to be in Second Life. People exchange American cash for Second Life's Linden dollars to pay for their purchases. For example, Ohio University reportedly built its campus for a few thousand dollars and paid for some software development time to create the buildings. Relatively speaking, though, the costs for an online presence are considerably less than a full-blown marketing campaign in the real world.

Underlying the investment is a desire on the part of the venues' owners to reach an important community—those influencers, bloggers, and early adopters they hope to reach in the real world. Coldwell Banker reportedly has attracted 60,000 visitors who have averaged about 10 minutes each in its brand-based location learning about real and fake property for sale. The real estate firm has even had avatars visit the site asking about employment opportunities.

Pontiac has had some success with its presence in Second Life, too. By creating a store and racetrack and giving away land to other car-related venues, Pontiac has attracted a community. It's earned the highest "dwell"

quotient in Second Life, which is based on the number of visitors to its location and the length of the visit over a period of time.

Latino marketers and agencies are venturing into Second Life, knowing that Latinos are more likely to play online games than those in the general market. Vidal Partnership, the biggest independent U.S. Hispanic marketing agency, developed El Dorado on one of its six islands in Second Life. It features sculptures by leading artists and a four-screen movie theater that screens films. It's got a café under construction that will invite visitors to enjoy various aspects of Latino culture.

In another effort to attract tech-savvy Latino consumers, Sprint Nextel sponsors a virtual arena, which is a replica of its Sprint Center in Kansas City. It will showcase entertainment, including Latin artists in concert. In an *Ad Age* report, Sprint Nextel's director of digital marketing Ted Moon said, "We were looking for an opportunity to amplify our Hispanic marketing efforts in an innovative way. It's not about just slapping our logo somewhere."

The Internet is a frontier that still has not been fully explored. Presumably, some vendors in the virtual world will do better than others, just as they do in the real world. Industry experts are skeptical about what the marketing value is for participants in Second Life or other virtual worlds. In some ways that misses the point. According to a report in *Ad Age*, Coke's director of global interactive marketing Michael Donnelly said, "At the end of the day, it's all about us learning to be better marketers in new environments. In this case, it's a virtual environment."

Consider This

1. What characteristics would entice you to participate in a virtual world?
2. What other innovations can you think of that involve the Internet? What impact has the Internet had on advertising?
3. What kinds of businesses would do well to advertise in virtual worlds like Second Life? Which ones might have trouble? Why?

Sources: Linda L. Briggs, "Ohio University Opens Virtual Doors," *Campus Technology*, February 21, 2007, http://www.campustechnology.com; Brooke Capps, "How to Succeed in Second Life," *Advertising Age*, May 28, 2007, 6; Richard Siklos, "A Virtual World but Real Money," *New York Times*, October 19, 2006, http://www.nytimes.com; Laura Martinez Ruiz-Velasco, "Latino Marketers and Agencies Set Out to Explore Virtual Work," *Advertising Age*, May 7, 2007, 36.

ATTENTION:

If you have any information regarding the location of a 2006 Audi A3 with VIN WAUZZZ8P65A045963, please contact Audi of America at audiusa.com/A3 or call 1-866-OK-RECOVER.

IT'S A WINNER

Award:	Company:	Agency:	Campaign:
Cannes Silver Lion for media; Bronze Lion for interactive	Audi	McKinney + Silver	"The Art of the Heist" Campaign

Game On! Audi's Plan Reaches an Elusive Audience

Audi wanted to launch its new luxury A3 hatchback but knew it faced some tough obstacles on the road to success. BMW and Mercedes had already failed in their efforts to introduce similar models. Plus Audi also knew that Americans associated hatchbacks with cheap economy cars—not exactly the ideal image for an upscale model. Another potential pothole: Audi had a marketing budget about one-third of that of an average luxury car launch. What brilliant media idea could make this launch a winner?

The first step might be finding out more about the target audience. Audi identified those who would be specifically attracted to the A3 as highly affluent ($150,000+ incomes), 24- to 30-year-old males who are generally hard to reach with and skeptical of traditional advertising. Typically, new luxury automobiles are launched with the help of slick television campaigns costing millions of dollars. The media team at Audi's advertising agency, McKinney + Silver, realized that a limited budget, along with the target's attitudes, prohibited such a plan. So the media planners needed a new approach.

With the campaign objective of creating buzz and excitement for the new A3 that would translate into sales while not tarnishing the luxury brand, the ad agency took a risk. To generate buzz among the target audience, it created an elaborate Web-based alternate reality game, The Art of the Heist (http://www. mckinney-silver.com/A3_H3ist/).

McKinney + Silver strategized that the audience would be immersed in the game and then spread the word about the game, and even more importantly, the car.

So it created a game, a project that cost Audi about $5 million to create supported by a total media budget of between $10 million and $20 million. Spanning a three-month period, the complicated serialized mystery about a stolen A3 started with a security camera video of men breaking in and stealing a new A3 from New York dealership. It was "leaked" on the Internet.

Chapter Key Points

1. What is media aperture, and why is it important?
2. How do media planners calculate media objectives?
3. What are the key media strategy decisions?
4. What are the responsibilities of media buyers?

The adver-game used a variety of media to drive traffic and create buzz. The media mix took advantage of the media team's strategic insight about how this target audience uses media. Knowing they had a relatively limited budget, the media planners incorporated a variety of media into the game itself. The use of television, radio, newspaper, consumer magazines, point of purchase, live events, out-of-home, interactive/online and public relations were used to involve the hardcore gamers intent on solving the mystery of the stolen car.

Media planners chose vehicles designed specifically to reach the affluent young male target audience. A billboard in New York's Times Square, small classified ads in the *New Yorker* and *USA Today*, VH1 television interviews, various Web sites (including Monster.com and Yahoo!), blogs, podcasts, e-mails, and wild postings (displaying eye-level impressions such as posters in highly visible outdoor locations) were some of the media tactics that provided clues and information for those trying to solve the mystery of the stolen A3.

This unconventional use of media engaged the audience in the 24-hour-a-day alternate reality. The media selections blurred the line between fact and fiction so much that the audience didn't just watch the game, they participated in it. In fact, some of the actors hired to play parts on the Web sites were so realistic that mainstream press sought actors' expert advice on matters related to their fictional businesses.

To find out whether *The Art of the Heist* achieved its media objectives, turn to the It's a Wrap feature at the end of the chapter.

Sources: McKinney http://www.mckinney-silver.com; Cannes Lions International Advertising Festival http://www.canneslions.com; David Kiley, "A New Kind of Car Chase," *BusinessWeek*, May 16, 2005; Neal Leavitt, "Audi's Art of the Heist Captured Leads," July 26, 2005, http://www.imediaconnection.com; "Yes, We Cannes," June 23, 2006, http://news.juicytemples.net.

As Audi and the media planners at McKinney + Silver know, media planning is a problem-solving process. The problem: How can media choices help meet the marketing and advertising objectives? The ultimate goal is to reach the target audience with the right message in the best possible way at the best possible time in the most efficient way possible. In this chapter, we review how a media plan is developed—how media planners set objectives and develop media strategies. We then explore the media-buying function and explain how media buyers execute the plan.

THE MEDIA PLANNING SIDE OF ADVERTISING

As Jugenheimer spelled out in the Part III Introduction, an upheaval in traditional media approaches has challenged agencies and media-buying shops. Most traditional media (newspapers, TV, radio, and magazines) are being challenged as carriers of ad messages by the new world of online and alternative media. Furthermore, convergence, as Jugenheimer explained, is even changing the basic form of these media as well as the interplay between and among them.

In 2007, an ad tracking firm reported that the 50 biggest U.S. advertisers had cut their spending on traditional media such as TV and print by 1.5 percent even though the total U.S. ad spending grew 4.1 percent. In 2007 General Motors made headlines when it cut 23.6 percent from its traditional advertising—ostensibly to shift more of its money to new media that are not measured by traditional ad tracking sources.[1] In other words, by 2007 it was clear that a big shift in advertising budgets was under way.[2]

Because of the complexity that has developed with the fragmentation of the media landscape and the explosion of new media, media planning and buying have become highly creative activities, leading to exciting new approaches such as Audi's Heist adver-game. In other words, the development of a media plan is as much a creative challenge as is developing the creative idea for the message strategy. One of the international companies that gives advertising awards identified the most creative media agency as Omnicom's OMD agency, followed by Starcom MediaVest and MindShare. These awards were announced in 2007 by the London-based *Gunn Report*.[3]

Although we talk about advertising media, media are used in all the other areas of marketing communication. Public relations, for example, places stories and corporate and advocacy ads in print and broadcast media; it also uses the Internet, other print forms such as brochures, and activities such as special events. Sales promotion also relies on ads in various media to deliver the announcement about a promotional offer. These marketing communication areas are also considerations in a media plan developed as part of an IMC campaign. Most of this chapter focuses on traditional advertising media; however, we will occasionally introduce IMC concepts and strategies that also relate to media planning.

Key Players

Traditionally, the advertising agency has been responsible for developing the media plan, which is usually devised jointly by the agency's media department, the account and creative teams, and the marketer's brand management group. More recently, media buying companies have moved into the planning stage as well, bringing the expertise of their media researchers and negotiators to the media plan. Some major agencies have spun off the media function as a separate company; then they contract with that company for their media planning and buying services. Others have kept the planning in house but contract with an outside media-buying service. Once the media plan is developed, a media-buying unit or team, either internal in the ad agency or external in a separate media company, executes it.

Given the industry trends, the hot new media-buying shops being launched have specialties in new media. For example, the long-established Ogilvy agency launched neo@Ogilvy as a digital-media specialist to help advertisers figure out how to allocate their ad budgets in the vast array of new media, such as online video, social networking sites, and search advertising. The Inside Story by David Rittenhouse in Chapter 5 explains how agencies such as neo@Ogilvy approach online behavioral targeting.

Media Research: Information Sources

Some people believe that media decisions are the hub in the advertising wheel, the central point where all campaign elements—that is, the spokes of the wheel—are joined. Not only are media decisions central to advertising planning, media research is central to media planning. That realization stems from the sheer volume of data and information that media planners must gather, sort, and analyze before media planning can begin. Figure 11.1 illustrates the wide range of media information sources and the critical role media research plays in the overall advertising planning process.

- *Client information.* The client is a good source for various types of information media planners use in their work, such as demographic profiles of current customers (both light and heavy users), previous promotions and their performance, product sales and distribution patterns, and, most importantly, the budget of how much can be spent on media. Geographical differences in category and brand sales often affect how the media budget is allocated for each region. *Sales geography* is critical information for national brands. With consumer goods and services especially, rates of consumption can differ greatly from one region to another.
- *Market research.* Independently gathered information about markets and product categories is a valuable tool for media planners. Mediamark Research, Inc. (MRI), Scarborough (local markets), and Mendelsohn (affluent markets) are groups that provide this service. This information is usually organized by product category (detergents, cereals, snacks) and cross-tabulated by audience groups and their consumption patterns. Accessible online, this wealth of information can be searched

FIGURE 11.1

The Central Role of Media Research

Media planners look for data from sources, including creative, marketing, and media sources. All this information is used in both media planning and buying.

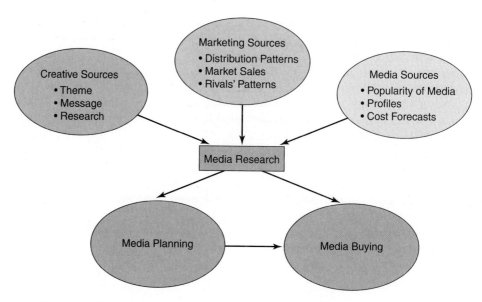

and compared across thousands of categories, brands, and audience groups. Although the reports may seem intimidating, they are not that difficult to use. Figure 11.2 is a page from an MRI report showing how to read MRI data. Media planners use MRI data to check which groups, based on demographics and lifestyles, are high and low in category use, as well as where they live and what media they use.

- *Competitive advertising.* In crowded product categories such as household products, food, and durable goods, companies must keep aware of competitors' advertising activity. In such situations media planners make scheduling decisions based on the amount of competitive traffic. The objective is to find media where the advertiser's voice is not drowned out by competitors' voices. This concept, called **share of voice,** is a measure of the percentage of total advertising spending by one brand in a product category. For example, if the total spent on airline advertising last year was $200 million, and $50 million of that was spent by United Airlines, UA's share of voice would be 25 percent ($50 \div 200 = 25\%$). Most agencies recommend that a brand's share of voice be at least as high as its share of market. For a new brand, obviously its share of voice needs to be more than its share of market if it wants to grow.

- *Media usage profiles.* The various media and their respective media vehicles provide information about the size and makeup of their audiences. Although media-supplied information is useful, keep in mind that this is an "inside job"—that is, the information is assembled to make the best possible case for advertising in that particular medium and media vehicle. For that reason, outside research sources, such as media rep companies and the Nielsen reports, also are used. As discussed in previous chapters, Nielsen Media Research audits national and local television, and Arbitron measures radio. Other services, such as the Auditing Bureau of Circulations (ABC), Simmons, and Mediamark Research, Inc. (MRI) monitor print audiences, and Media Metrix measures Internet audiences. All of these provide extensive information on viewers, listeners, and readers in terms of the size of the audience and their profiles.

- *Media coverage area.* One type of media-related information about markets is the broadcast coverage area for television. Called a **designated marketing area (DMA),** the coverage area is referred to by the name of the largest city in the area. This is a national market analysis system, and every county in the United States has been assigned to a DMA. The assignment of a county to a DMA is determined by which city provides the majority of the county households' (HHs') TV programming. Most DMAs include counties within a 50- to 60-mile radius of a major city center. Even though this system is based on TV broadcast signals, it is universally used in doing individual market planning.

- *Consumer information.* We mentioned some of the consumer research sources in Chapter 5 that are used in developing segmentation and targeting strategies. They are also useful in planning media strategies. For example, media planners use such

How to Read an MRI CrossTab

The CrossTab format is a standard research display format that allows multiple variables of related data to be grouped together. Below is a screen capture of an MEMRI[2] CrossTab, complete with explanations of key numbers. Please note that all the numbers are based on the 2004 Spring MRI study, and that the projected numbers (000) are expressed in thousands.

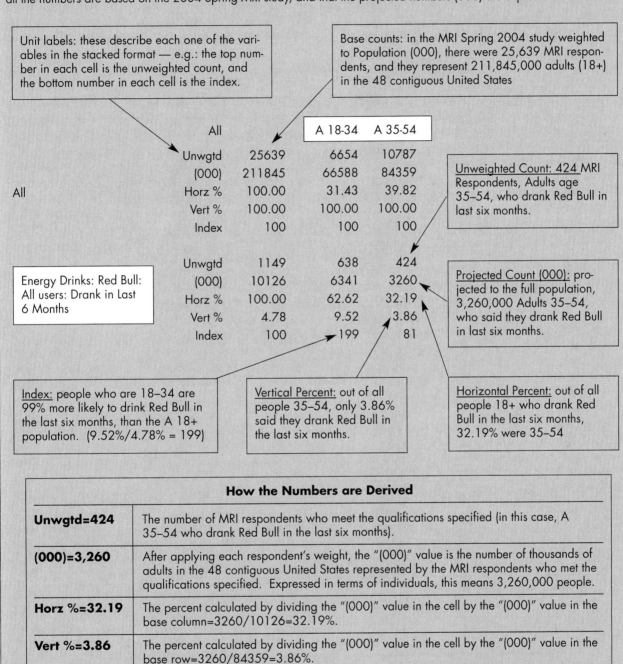

Unit labels: these describe each one of the variables in the stacked format — e.g.: the top number in each cell is the unweighted count, and the bottom number in each cell is the index.

Base counts: in the MRI Spring 2004 study weighted to Population (000), there were 25,639 MRI respondents, and they represent 211,845,000 adults (18+) in the 48 contiguous United States

	All	A 18-34	A 35-54
Unwgtd	25639	6654	10787
(000)	211845	66588	84359
Horz %	100.00	31.43	39.82
Vert %	100.00	100.00	100.00
Index	100	100	100
Unwgtd	1149	638	424
(000)	10126	6341	3260
Horz %	100.00	62.62	32.19
Vert %	4.78	9.52	3.86
Index	100	199	81

Unweighted Count: 424 MRI Respondents, Adults age 35–54, who drank Red Bull in last six months.

Energy Drinks: Red Bull: All users: Drank in Last 6 Months

Projected Count (000): projected to the full population, 3,260,000 Adults 35–54, who said they drank Red Bull in last six months.

Index: people who are 18–34 are 99% more likely to drink Red Bull in the last six months, than the A 18+ population. (9.52%/4.78% = 199)

Vertical Percent: out of all people 35–54, only 3.86% said they drank Red Bull in the last six months.

Horizontal Percent: out of all people 18+ who drank Red Bull in the last six months, 32.19% were 35–54

How the Numbers are Derived

Unwgtd=424	The number of MRI respondents who meet the qualifications specified (in this case, A 35–54 who drank Red Bull in the last six months).
(000)=3,260	After applying each respondent's weight, the "(000)" value is the number of thousands of adults in the 48 contiguous United States represented by the MRI respondents who met the qualifications specified. Expressed in terms of individuals, this means 3,260,000 people.
Horz %=32.19	The percent calculated by dividing the "(000)" value in the cell by the "(000)" value in the base column=3260/10126=32.19%.
Vert %=3.86	The percent calculated by dividing the "(000)" value in the cell by the "(000)" value in the base row=3260/84359=3.86%.
Index=199	The percent calculated by dividing either the horz % in the cell by the horz % in the base row (62.62/31.43) or by dividing the vert % in the cell by the vert % in the base column (9.52/4.78). Either calculation generates the same result, because, when the horz % numbers and vert % numbers are expressed in terms of "(000)", the relationship is identical.

FIGURE 11.2

How to Read MRI CrossTabs

The MRI market research service provides information on 4,090 product categories and services, 6,000 brands, and category advertising expenditures, as well as customer lifestyle characteristics and buying style psychographics.

Source: Courtesy of Mediamark Research Inc.

services as the Claritas PRIZM system, Nielsen's ClusterPlus system, and supermarket scanner data to locate the target audience within media markets.

The Media Plan

The **media plan** is a written document that summarizes the objectives and strategies pertinent to the placement of a company's brand messages. The goal of a media plan is to find the most effective and efficient ways to deliver messages to a targeted audience. In a traditional media plan, the emphasis is on **measured media**, which is evaluated using such metrics as CPMs (cost per thousand, discussed later in this chapter) and other performance data derived from industry and media audits.

When IMC planners develop a media plan, they often refer to *contact points*, or *touch points*, which include all the diverse ways people—customers as well as other stakeholders—come in contact with a brand and have a brand experience. These include exposure to traditional mass media as well as word of mouth, place-based media, in-store brand exposures, and all the new, interactive media. To see where media planning and buying fit into the overall advertising process, refer to Figure 11.3, which outlines the primary components of a media plan.

KEY MEDIA PLANNING DECISIONS

The media-planning field also has undergone a metamorphosis because of the fragmentation of mainstream media—think of all the new cable television channels—as well as the proliferation of new media. But it's more than just choosing from a longer list of media options. Traditional measured media are chosen based on such metrics as GRPs and CPMs, which are explained later in this chapter, but the new media lack similar metrics and are characterized more by such considerations as the quality of the brand experience, involvement, and personal impact. Old-line advertising media planners are intent on buying reach and frequency, but the problem is that many of their clients are looking for engaging experiences and brand-building relationships. Thus, the framework for making media-planning decisions is changing along with the list of media options.

The basic decisions that guide the media plan continue to be targeting, setting media objectives, and designing a media mix. Before we review those specific activities, consider The Inside Story and how it characterizes the life of a media planner.

Target Audience and Media Use

As we have discussed in earlier chapters on planning, a key strategic decision is identifying a target audience. In media planning the idea is to match the advertiser's target with the audience of a particular medium. In other words, does the group of people who read this magazine, watch this television program, or see these posters include a high proportion of the advertiser's ideal target audience? If so, then that medium may be a good choice for the campaign, depending upon other strategic factors, such as timing and cost.

Media planners, for example, are unlikely to run ads for women's products on the Super Bowl, which is skewed 56 percent male; instead, they buy time on the Oscars, which has a much higher female viewership. However, Revlon used the Super Bowl to announce a new hair-coloring product because it still attracts more women in sheer numbers than the Oscars.[4] These are the kinds of decisions that make media planning both fun and challenging.

As you can imagine, every media vehicle's audience is different and therefore varies regarding what percent of its audience is in the brand's target audience. For example, Mercury Marine, which makes outboard boat motors, targets households (HHs) that own one or more boats. It prefers to advertise in magazines where it can feature beautiful illustrations of its products as well as room to explain the many benefits of its motors. Should it advertise in *Time* or *Boating* magazine? *Time* magazine reaches 4 million HHs, of which 280,000 HHs have boats; in comparison, *Boating* has only 200,000 HH subscribers. If you said *Time*, sorry, you're not being very cost efficient. This is because even though *Time* reaches 80,000 more boat-owning households, it also reaches 3.7 million HHs that don't own boats. Mercury would have to pay to reach all readers, even those not in its target audience. By advertising in *Boating*, it can pretty well assume that subscribers either own a boat or at least are interested in boating.

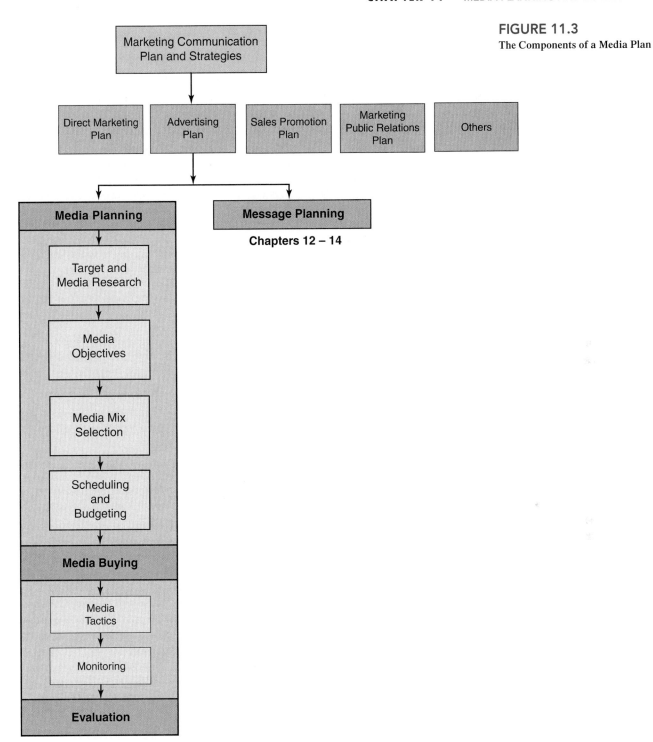

FIGURE 11.3
The Components of a Media Plan

In addition to information compiled by the team's media researchers, consumer insight research also is used to identify and analyze the target audience's media use patterns. For the Audi A3 launch, the McKinley + Silver media team knew it needed an in-depth understanding of its target audience to develop a media plan that would work for this difficult-to-reach group. For example, the media planners knew that young males typically don't read or watch traditional media. They don't read the papers the same way their parents do. They're busy and skeptical about commercial messages. The McKinley + Silver team came up with a profile of the target, which they described as "intelligent, independent, and innovative" and heavy users of new media. This target audience for this product category is made up of opinion leaders who influence their peers. They are not as interested in buying an entry-level car as they are in getting "what's next."

THE INSIDE STORY

A Week in the Life of a Media Planner
By Heather Beck, *Senior Media Planner, Melamed Riley Advertising, Cleveland, Ohio*

People often ask me what exactly it is that I do all day at work. There are twelve media planners in my office, and each of us would have a different answer to that question.

Monday morning there is a conference call involving everyone who works on an account. The client shares information such as sales numbers from the past week, as well as budget changes or which markets are going to run a test campaign. The agency shares results from market research and the status of current projects. The next couple hours of the day are spent requesting and researching information from media sources for new projects.

It's lunch time now! Once or twice a week, media reps either bring in a deli tray for the office, or they take us out for a lunch meeting to pitch their product. It is the job of the media planner to analyze all the options and determine what is best for the client, so we don't let a nice lunch or fancy gift basket sway our judgment. After lunch, I return phone calls and reply to e-mails. I spend the rest of the day gathering and organizing any information I have received and analyzing the data.

The rest of the week is similar. Tuesday morning conference calls are split up so that groups can talk specifics about their projects with their counterparts on the client side. This is the time to share detailed feedback. What works best in one market might not work well in another, so these results are essential in tailoring the media plans. Wednesday mornings are when the agency has informal status meetings within the departments to see how we can help each other as a team. With no scheduled meetings or conference calls on Thursday, this is a good time to check in with clients. Then the day is spent finalizing projects. Fridays are when all the agency players on an account put their projects together and determine the best way to present the results to clients. Another typical Friday task is to place the planned media buys for the following week or month.

This is a generalized example of a typical week in the life of a media planner. Some days you might work until midnight, and other days you'll take long lunch breaks. It might seem like the same thing day to day, but the actual projects vary enough to keep it interesting and challenging. If you need a break from a monotonous project, you can always catch up on the latest issues of *Media Week* or *Ad Age*.

A graduate of the advertising program at Middle Tennessee State, Heather L. Beck is a media planner at Melamed Riley Advertising in Cleveland, Ohio.

The Aperture Concept

For many product categories, prospective customers have one or more ideal times or places at which they are most receptive to receiving and paying attention to a brand message. This ideal time/place is called an **aperture**. Movies and restaurants advertise on Thursdays and Fridays, knowing these are the days when potential customers are planning for the coming weekend. Ads for sporting goods, beer, and soft drinks pop up at athletic venues because sports fans are thinking about those products as they watch the game.

Regardless of whether a company spends a few hundred dollars on one medium or millions of dollars on a variety of media, the goal is still the same: to reach the right people at the right time with the right message. A series of Nick@Nite "spoof" ads illustrate the use of inappropriate media.

Principle
Advertising is most effective when it reaches the right people at the right time and place with the right message.

Measured Media Objectives

In the vast majority of planning situations, media planners are given a media budget. Traditionally, the creative strategy is developed before the media strategy. In other words, media planners are not only restricted in what they can spend, but also may be told what types of media work best with the message strategy. The media planner's job from that point has been to come up with the best media mix maximizing reach and frequency to generate the greatest impact for the money spent.

Although creative decisions are sometimes made before media planning, this is changing. With the increasing variety of media options available, smart clients and agencies are having up-front cross-functional planning meetings that include creatives, media planners, and account executives. The point is that the media and message strategies are interdependent and decisions in one area affect decisions in the other.

Nick@Nite is where viewers and advertisers go for family-friendly, funny and familiar favorites. No wonder we're #1 with women and adults (18-49 and 18-34).

These ads ran in advertising trade publications to promote the family-friendly nature of the Nick@Nite channel. The ads illustrate how a media buy may be inappropriate for a product because it places the brand in an absolutely wrong environment.

Marketing communication objectives, as you will recall, describe what a company wants target audiences to think, feel, and most importantly, do. **Media objectives** describe what a company wants to accomplish regarding the delivery of its brand messages and their impact on the target audience. As we mentioned in Chapter 8, the two basic media objectives are reach and frequency. Let's consider how planners create strategies that deliver on those objectives.

The Reach Objective   The percent of different people exposed to the message is referred to as **reach**—how many different members of the target audience can be exposed to the message in a particular time frame. Different, or **unduplicated**, **audiences** are those who have at least one chance to be exposed to a message. Most advertisers realize that a campaign's success is due in part to its ability to reach as many of the targeted audience as possible. Consequently, many planners feel that reach is the most important objective and that's the place to start in figuring out a media plan.[5]

Using demographic and lifestyle data, planners can focus on a **targeted reach,** which identifies specific types of households (e.g., empty nesters, homes with two+ children under 18, single parent households, HHs with incomes over $100,000) or individuals (males 25–49, people who rent). This enables planners to better match media profiles with the characteristics of the campaign's target audience.

The Frequency Objective   As we explained in Chapter 8, **frequency** refers to the repetition of exposure. Although the reach estimate is based on only a single exposure, frequency estimates the number of times the exposure is expected to happen. Because frequency is an *average,* it can be misleading. The range of frequency is often large: Some people see the message once, while others may see it 10 times. Average frequency, then, can give the planner a distorted idea of the plan's performance because all those people reached vary in the number of times they have the opportunity to be exposed to a message.

Principle
Reach is the first place to start in setting objectives for a media plan.

Suppose a media mix includes four magazines and each magazine carries one ad a week for four weeks. The total number of message insertions would be 16 (4 magazines × 1 insertion a week × 4 weeks = 16 total insertions). It is possible that a small percentage of the target audience could be exposed to all 16 insertions. It is also possible that some of the target would not have the opportunity to be exposed to any of the insertions. In this case the frequency ranges from 0 to 16. Thus, F = 8, but you can see how misleading this average frequency number is.

For this reason planners often use a **frequency distribution** model that shows the percentage of audience reached at each level of repetition (exposed once, twice, and so on). Media planners use a *frequency quintile distribution analysis* that divides an audience into five groups, each containing 20 percent of the audience. Employing media-usage modeling, it is then possible to estimate the average frequency for each quintile as shown in the following table. For example, this table shows that the bottom 20 percent has an average frequency of 1, while the top 20 percent has an average frequency of 10. In this hypothetical distribution, let's say the average frequency is 6.

Quintile	Frequency (average number of exposure opportunities)
Top 20% of universe	10
20%	7
20%	5
20%	3
Bottom 20%	1

If the media planner feels it is necessary that 80 percent of those reached should have an average frequency of 8, then a more intensive media plan would be needed to raise the bulk of the target audience higher into the distribution. In other words, to shift the average from 6 to 8, more of the audience would need to be in the top two quintiles.

Effective Frequency Reach alone is not a sufficient measure of the strength of an advertising schedule. Because of the proliferation of information and clutter, there should be a threshold, or minimum frequency level. A standard rule of thumb is that it takes three to ten exposures to have an effect on an audience. Obviously this frequency range is extremely wide. The "right" frequency number is determined by several factors, including level of brand awareness, content of the message, and sophistication of the target audience. This concept essentially combines the reach and frequency elements into one factor known as **effective frequency.** The idea is that you add frequency to reach until you get to the level where people respond.

Kelley and Jugenheimer explain that media planners also can translate effective frequency into effective reach, which means that a desired percent of the audience is reached more than three times and therefore will respond in the intended way.[6] Some planners call this *effective reach* because it is making the reach level more effective; however, it does this by increasing frequency. In his book on media planning, Surmanek uses the term *effective reach* and defines it as the number of individuals (or homes) reached by a media schedule at a given level of frequency.[7] The focus on frequency is the reason why we call it *effective frequency* in this book, but you should understand that both phrases refer to the same concept.

Given this discussion of the relationship between reach and frequency, it should be clear that usable media objectives would include both of those dimensions. Examples of media objectives are:

1. Reach 60 percent of target audience with a frequency of 4 within each 4-week period in which the advertising runs.
2. Reach a maximum percent of target audience a minimum of 5 times within the first 6 months of advertising.
3. Reach 30 percent of the target audiences where they have an opportunity to interact with the brand and users of the brand.
4. Reach category thought leaders and influencers in a way that will motivate them to initiate measurable word of mouth (WOM) and other positive brand messages.

The first of these objectives is the most common. It recognizes that you can seldom ever reach 100 percent of your target audience. It also acknowledges that a certain level of frequency will be necessary for the brand messages to been seen/heard/read. The second objective would be for a product where the message is more complex; through research (and judgment) it has been decided that prospects need to be exposed to the message at least five times to be effective. In this case frequency is more important than reach. Put another way, it is more important to reach a small portion of the audience five or more times and have them respond than it is to reach a major portion fewer that five times and have little or no response.

Objectives 3 and 4 deal directly with impact. To achieve these objectives, media buyers will have to find media vehicle and contact points such as events and sponsorships where interaction with the brand and its users is possible as opposed to using more passive media such as traditional mass media. Note that number 4 is not measurable as stated.

Media Efficiency and Waste   The goal of media planning is to maximum efficiency. Kelley and Jugenheimer define media efficiency in terms of waste—excessive overlap or too much frequency. They explain, "Too much media overlap is inefficient. . . . Too much frequency is also inefficient. . . . Too many nonprospects seeing your advertising is inefficient, too."[8]

Although this discussion has been focused on measured media and their objectives, it's useful to note that the other IMC disciplines are also concerned about proving their efficiency. It is interesting to note that public relations is trying to establish metrics comparable to those used in evaluating advertising media. The Matter of Principle box explains how important it is to integrate media planning in these other areas with advertising media planning. The author also explains the concept of earned media, in contrast to purchased (and measured) media.

Media Mix Selection

We mentioned earlier that you can rarely reach your total target audience with just one medium. Most brands use a variety of targeted media vehicles, called a **media mix,** to reach current and potential customers. ESPN, for example, uses a variety of media to advertise its programming, including TV, magazines, radio, and the Internet, as well as original programming on its own ESPN channel.

There are a number of reasons for using a media mix. The first is to reach people not reached by the first or most important medium. Using a number of media vehicles distributes the message more widely because different media tend to have different audience profiles. Some people even reject certain media: Television advertising, for example, is considered intrusive and Internet advertising is irritating to some people.[9] Other reasons for spreading the plan across different media include adding exposure in less expensive media and using a medium that has some attractive characteristics that enhance the creative message.[10]

Even within a traditional approach, new options complicate the media plan. General Motors, although traditionally a big user of television commercials, has been reducing its spending on network TV and moving more budget to cable channels. It is even experimenting with the video-on-demand services offered by cable operators. Betsy Lazar, GM's executive director of advertising and media operations, still feels that cars need to be seen on a big screen. Of course, GM also uses direct marketing, Web sites, online video, events, branded entertainment, and Internet advertising.[11]

Still, the reason for choosing a particular medium or a set of media depends upon the objectives. What media will best deliver what effects—and can you reinforce and extend those effects with a mix of media? Believability is an example. Print and television are considered more trustworthy, so they might be used by a media planner for a campaign that seeks to establish credibility for a product. Different media also have different strengths in terms of reach and frequency. For example, media planners often use television to build reach and radio to build frequency. The Practical Tips box summarizes the reasons media planners choose various media.

A MATTER OF PRINCIPLE

Integrating Advertising and PR Media Planning

By Clarke Caywood, *Professor and Director of the Graduate Program in Public Relations, Medill Graduate School, Northwestern University*

Ask any advertising director in a company or agency what profitable target media they have chosen for message delivery for their new corporate or product/service brand strategy. They will probably give a list of traditional mass media advertising vehicles.

Then ask any PR director in the same company or company PR agency what their targeted media will be for the same program. If will often be a list of news and feature story outlets.

In an integrated approach to media planning, the communication leaders should be targeting the same media to reach similar readers, viewers, and listeners. If not, the C-Suite—chief executive officer (CEO), chief financial officer (CFO), and chief marketing officer (CMO)—in the client company would want to know why not.

These newer models of media planning seem to be aligned with the growth of the large holding companies that contain advertising, direct database marketing, e-commerce, public relations, and, now, media buying agencies where coordination and cross-functional planning are essential.

In the IMC program at Medill, we define integrated media planning as "coordinated research, planning, securing and evaluation of all purchased and earned media." **Earned media** is used by marketing and PR practitioners to differentiate paid media about a product, service, or company (advertising, promotions, direct mail, Web ads, etc.) from positive or negative broadcast, print, and Internet media articles and simple mentions about the product, service, or company. The term *earned* is used to avoid the term *free*, which accurately suggests

the company does not pay the media for the placement, but it does not address the fact that the publication of such stories requires hours of effort or years of experience by PR professionals to persuade journalists to cover the product, service, or company for the benefit of their readers or viewers.

Just as selecting media for advertising has become a science and management art, the field of selection and analysis of earned media (including print, broadcast, and blogs) for public relations is now more of a science. Today the existence of far richer database systems assist media managers who want to know which reporters, quoted experts, trade books, new publications, broadcasts, bloggers, and more are the most "profitable" targets for public relations messages. In other words, when we refer to *media planning*, we mean coordinating and jointly planning the earned media of public relations along with advertising and other purchased media.

Using the new built-in media metric systems, PR directors can calculate return on investment on advertising versus PR. With PR, they can read and judge a range of positive, neutral, or negative messages, as well as share-of-mind measures of media impact, advertising equivalency estimates, and other effectiveness indicators (see http://www.biz360.com).

Now, when the chief marketing officer and other C-Suite officers ask the integrated agency directors of advertising, public relations, or IMC if the media are fully planned to reach targeted audiences, they can answer affirmatively.

Multiplying Media Strengths Media choices are sometimes based on using one medium to deliver an audience to another medium or marketing communication tool. For example, mass media have frequently been used to promote special events and sales promotions. The emergence of the Internet has intensified what you might call a two-step media platform. Print and broadcast, which are basically informative and awareness building media forms, are often used to drive traffic to the Internet, which is a more interactive and experiential medium. The Frontier "Web" ad is an example of this use.

Media selection is driven by cost efficiency as well as message considerations. Among the most important tools media planners use in designing a media mix is a calculation of a media schedule's gross rating points (GRPs) and targeted rating points (TRPs).

GRPs and TRPs **Gross rating points,** or **GRPs,** indicate the weight, or efficency, of a media plan. To find a plan's GRPs, you multiply each media vehicle's rating by the number of ads inserted into this media vehicle during the designated time period and add up the total of all the vehicles.

Practical Tips

When to Use Various Media

Use newspapers if . . .

- You are a local business.
- You want extensive local market coverage.
- You sell a product that has a news element.
- You are creating a news element through a sale or some other event.
- You want to reach an upscale, well-educated audience.
- You have a moderate budget.
- You need to explain how something works, but it doesn't need to be demonstrated.
- The quality of the image is not a factor.

Use magazines if . . .

- You have a target audience defined by some special interest.
- You have a product that needs to be shown accurately and beautifully.
- A high-quality image is important.
- You need to explain how something works, but it doesn't need to be demonstrated.
- You have a moderate to large budget.

Use out-of-home if . . .

- You are a local business and want to sell to a local market.
- You are a regional or national business that wants to remind or reinforce.
- You need a directional message.
- You need a situational, place-based message.
- Your product requires little information.
- You have a small to medium budget.

Use directories if . . .

- You are a local business or can serve local customers.
- You want to create action.
- You need to provide basic inquiry and purchase information.
- You need to provide directional information.
- You have a small to moderate budget.

Use radio if . . .

- You are a local business and want to reach a local market.
- You want to build frequency.
- You have a reminder message.
- You know the timing when your audience is considering the purchase.
- Your audience's interests align with certain types of music or talk shows.
- You have a personal message that benefits from the power of the human voice.
- You have a message that works well in a musical form or one that is strong in mental imagery.
- You have a relatively small budget.

Use national television if . . .

- You need to reach a wide mass audience.
- You have a product that needs both sight and sound.
- Your message calls for action or drama.
- You want to create an emotional response.

- You need product demonstration—how to use, how it works.
- You need to create or reinforce brand personality.
- Your audience's interests align with a certain type of program (particularly on cable TV).
- You want to prove something so people in your audience can see it with their own eyes.
- You want the halo effect of a big TV ad to impress other stakeholders, such as dealers and franchisees.
- You have a large budget.

Use local or spot television if . . .

- Your product is not distributed nationally.
- You want to "heavy up" in certain cities or regions where sales are higher.
- You have a moderate budget.

Use movie ads if . . .

- You are advertising a national brand.
- You want your brand to be associated with a movie's story and stars.
- The people in the audience match your brand's target audience.
- Your commercial has enough visual impact and quality production that it will look good next to the movie previews.
- You have a moderate to high budget.

Use product placement if . . .

- You want your brand to be associated with a movie or program's story and stars.
- The people in the audience match your brand's target audience.
- There is a natural fit between the product and the movie's storyline.
- There is an opportunity in the storyline for the brand to be a star.
- The placement will appeal to the brand's stakeholders.
- You have the budget for a campaign to support the placement.

Use the Internet if . . .

- Your target audience is difficult to reach with traditional media.
- You want to create buzz.
- You want your target audience to engage in dialogue with others.
- You want to provide information.
- You want to collect customer information.
- You want to engage your audience in an online activity, such as a game.
- You want to reach people on their own time.

Use alternative media if . . .

- Your target audience is difficult to reach with traditional media.
- You want to create buzz.
- You want to engage your target audience in brand experiences.
- Reach is not a big objective.

Check out the web.

Get double miles, free DIRECTV® service and our guaranteed
lowest fares when you book on our new web site*.

frontierairlines.com

*Book online by 6/15/06 and receive free DIRECTV and double miles in our
EarlyReturns® Mileage Program. Travel must be complete by 12/31/06.

This ad demonstrates the use
of a creative print ad to drive
traffic to a Web site.

Once the media vehicles that produce the GRPs are identified, computer programs can be used to break down the GRPs into reach and frequency numbers. These R&F models are based on consumer media use research and produce data showing to what extent audiences/viewers/readers overlap.

To illustrate how GRPs are determined and the difference in R&F from one media plan to another (using the same budget), look at the two media mixes that follow. Both are for a simple TV media plan for a pizza brand using a set budget. As you will remember from Chapter 8, a **rating point** is one percent of a defined media universe (country, region, DMA, or some other target audience description) of households unless otherwise specified. *Insertions* means the number of ads placed in each media vehicle/program within a given period of time (generally four weeks). For example, in Table 11.1, if the plan delivered a household rating of 6 with 8 insertions, the program Survivor would achieve an estimated 48 GRPs.

Using the same budget, the two different media mixes produce different GRP totals. A good media planner will look at several different selections of programs that reach the target audience, figure the GRPs for each, and then break this calculation into reach and frequency estimates for each plan. Because ratings are in percentages, the GRPs in both the plans in these tables indicate they reach more than 100 percent. Of course, this is impossible, just as it's impossible to eat 156 percent of a pie. This is why these numbers are called *gross* rating points; they include exposure duplication. Nevertheless, knowing the GRPs of different plans is helpful in choosing which plan delivers more for the money budgeted.

How would computer models calculate reach and frequency numbers based on these GRPs? In plan A, the media mix model would estimate something close to the following: R = 35, F = 6.9. (Even though reach is a percent, industry practice is to not use the percent sign for reach numbers.) For plan B, the estimated R&F would be R = 55, F = 3.2.

Table 11.1A   Calculating GRPs—Plan A R=35; F=6.9

Program	HH Rating	Insertions	GRPs
Survivor	6	8	48
Lost	7	8	56
American Idol	9	8	72
24	4	8	32
	Total		208

Table 11.1B   Calculating GRPs—Plan B R=55; F=3.2

Program	HH Rating	Insertions	GRPs
Survivor	6	8	48
Desperate Housewives	7	8	56
Boston Legal	5	8	40
Monday Night Football	4	8	32
	Total		176

How do you decide which is best? If a brand has a tightly targeted audience and wants to use repetition to create a strong brand presence, then Plan A might be a wise choice. If, however, a brand has a fairly simple message where frequency is less important, a planner would probably choose Plan B because it has significantly higher reach. The reason for the higher reach with Plan B, even though the GRPs are less, is that Plan B has a much more diverse set of programs that attract a more diverse audience than Plan A. But because Plan B has a higher reach, it also has a lower frequency.

It is important to remember that GRPs are a combination of R × F. When R increases, F decreases, and vice versa, within the constraints of the budget. Once experienced planners are given budgets, they generally have a good feel for how many GRPs those budgets will buy. The planning challenge is to decide whether to find a media mix with more reach or more frequency. And of course, this depends on the level of brand development, the competitive situation, and the message.

The two media plans shown previously are based on HH rating points. For products that have a mass-market appeal, HHs are often used in targeting. However, for more specialized products, such as tennis racquets, sports cars, and all-natural food products, target audiences can be more narrowly defined. For example, let's say that those consuming the most natural food products are female, ages 25–49, with a college degree; in addition, we know that they participate in at least one outdoor sport. This would be the target audience for most brands in this category. Therefore, when developing a media plan for a natural food brand, a media planner would be interested not in a media vehicle's total audience, but on the percentage of the audience that can be defined as being in the campaign's target audience.

Since the total audience obviously includes waste coverage, the estimate of **targeted rating points (TRPs)** adjusts the calculation so it more accurately reflects the percentage of the target audience watching the program. Because the waste coverage is eliminated, the TRPs are lower than the total audience GRPs. Targeted rating points are, like R&F, determined by media usage research data, which is available from syndicated research services like MRI and from the major media vehicles themselves.

To illustrate the difference between HH GRPs and TRPs, we'll use media plan A, shown previously. As shown in the following chart, the first column is HH rating points, while the new second column shows target rating points, or the percent of homes reached that include a female, age 25–49, with a college degree and an affinity for at least one outdoor sport. The insertions remain the same, but the TRPs are greatly reduced, as you can see when you multiply targeted ratings by insertions.

When the 80 TRPs are compared to the 208 HH GRPs, you can see that 128 GRPs (208 − 80 = 128) were of little or no value to a natural food brand. These 128 GRPs demonstrate what we earlier referred to as *media waste*. The less waste, the more efficient the media plan.

Another reason to tightly describe a target audience, especially in terms of lifestyle, is to take advantage of the many media vehicles—magazines, TV programs and channels, and special events—that connect with various types of lifestyles. Examples of media that offer special interest topics are *Runners World,* which features topics of interest to runners; *This Old House*, the TV program that describes home improvement and remodeling; *Self* magazine, which focuses on health and fitness; and *Budget Travel* for those looking for interesting but economical trips and vacations.

Principle

Reach and frequency are interrelated: When reach increases, frequency decreases, and vice versa, within the constraints of the advertising budget.

Table 11.2   Calculating TRPs—Plan A

Program	HH Rating	Targeted Rating	Insertions TRPs	Total TRPs
Survivor	6	3	8	24
Lost	7	3	8	24
American Idol	9	1	8	8
24	4	3	8	24
			Total	80

Cross-Media Integration Media selection also considers message needs. Here is where media planning and message planning intersect. Brand reminders, for example, are often found in television commercials and on out-of-home media. More complex information-laden messages are more likely to be found in magazines, direct mail, or publicity releases. If you want to stimulate immediate action, you might use daily newspapers, radio, or sales promotion.

The challenge is to create *cross-media integration*, which means the various media work together to create coherent brand communication. Planners seek to create a synergistic effect between the messages delivered in different media. This is also called **image transfer** and refers to the way radio, in particular, reinforces and recreates the message in a listener's mind that was originally delivered by other media, particularly TV.

We've been discussing the basic decisions made in media planning. Let's now consider the tools and techniques that deliver these planning decisions.

This photo illustrates the use of transit advertising—in this case a panel on the top of a taxi—to advertise the *Wall Street Journal*. The media plan would give direction to the decisions about the size of the sign and the duration of its appearance.

MEDIA STRATEGY TOOLS AND TECHNIQUES

Strategic thinking in media involves a set of decision factors and tools that help identify the best way to deliver the advertising message. **Media strategy** is the way media planners determine the most cost-effective media mix to reach the target audience and satisfy the media objectives.

The strategic challenge is to come up with ideas about how best to accomplish the objectives. If the objectives state a reach of 80 percent and a 4-week frequency of 4, then how can you best do that? These strategies generally include decisions that focus on who (target audience), what (the media used), when (time frame), how long (duration), and how big (size). In this section on media strategy, we'll discuss these strategies in terms of the target audience, the media mix, and scheduling.

Delivering on the Objectives

In terms of a media strategy, some plans might emphasize reach while others emphasize frequency, but it's also possible to work for a balance of both. A high-reach strategy, for example, might be used to deliver a reminder message for a well-known mass-marketed brand or to launch a new product, particularly if it is a fairly easy to understand product extension of an existing brand.

Low-frequency strategies are used with well-known brands and simple messages. Some argue that advertising for established brands need only be seen once in the immediate prepurchase period to have an effect.[12] If you are advertising a two-liter Coke for 89 cents, you don't need to repeat it a lot, but if you are trying to explain how TiVo works, then you may need much more frequency. High-frequency strategies may be used because more complex messages may need more repetition or because you want to build excitement about a new product or an upcoming event. Frequency is also used to counter competitive offers and to build the brand's share of voice in a highly cluttered category.

Delivering on the Targeting Strategy

The media plan implements the targeting strategy by finding ways to reach the target audience in the most efficient ways possible. Consider all the different types of audiences that can be reached just with magazines. Now add the varieties of cable channels, network programs, newspapers, Web sites, radio, and out-of-home and alternative media. You can see how important it is to effectively match a medium's audience to the target audience.

For the new Audi A3, the media planners had a fairly specific profile—one that suggested the target audience would be difficult to reach with conventional media. They don't sit around and watch a lot of television. They do talk a lot to one another, so anything that can get them to talk about the new Audi would help make the brand hard to ignore. The breadth of the target, as defined in the advertising plan, determines whether the media planner will be using a broad mass media approach or a tightly targeted and highly focused approach, as in the Audi case. The tighter the focus, the easier it is to find appropriate media to deliver a relevant and focused message.

Principle
The tighter the focus on a target market, the easier it is to find appropriate media to deliver a relevant message.

Assessing the media for target audience opportunities is a major challenge for media planners. The evening news on television, for example, reaches a broad mass-market audience; if your target is women ages 25–49, then you have to consider the targeted reach of that news program. Obviously both men and women watch news, so if you find that a news program has a HH rating of 6, then you know that your audience would probably be half or less of that, especially since you are targeting a specific age group. Maybe the evening news isn't a good option to reach this target because there would be so much waste in the viewing audience.

Media Use   That's why planners consult research services like MRI to find programs that reach a large proportion of the target audience. In most cases, no one program or publication will reach the target perfectly. Finding connections like this based on matching consumer insights and media information is one of the creative aspects of the media planner's role. Additional target information used by media planners includes consumer media use, geography, and the target's consumption patterns.

The consumer research used in targeting and segmenting almost always asks for information about what media people use, as well as what other activities engage their time. Media planners realize that young people are moving away from traditional media and spending more time with video games and the Internet, including blogs and social networking sites such as Facebook and MySpace.com. Media planners also know that business publications have high readership among professionals in the market.

Geographical Strategies   Another factor planners use in analyzing the target audience is geography. Are potential customers found all over the country, therefore calling for a national campaign, and does the client have the budget to afford such an extensive media plan? In most cases, the media plan will identify special regions or DMAs to be emphasized with a **heavy-up** schedule, which means proportionately more of the budget is spent in those areas. The company's sales coverage area (i.e., geography) is a major factor used to make this decision. There's no sense advertising in areas where the product isn't available. Most national or regional marketers divide their market geographically. The amount of sales produced in each geographic market will vary, and marketers try to match advertising investment with the amount of forecasted sales or the sales potential.

To determine which geographical areas have the highest (and lowest) rate of consumption for a particular product category, marketers compute a **category development index (CDI)** for each market in which they are interested. Then they calculate a **brand development index (BDI)** that estimates the strength of the brand in the various geographical areas. If General Mills were to bring out a new line of grits, for example, it wouldn't advertise nationally as most grits are consumed in the South.

A CDI is calculated for product categories. It is an index number showing the relative consumption rate of a product in a particular DMA or region as compared to the total universe (national or regional). A BDI is an index of the consumption rate of a brand in a particular market. The CDI tells you where the category is strong and weak, and the BDI tells you where your brand is strong and weak. CDI data can be found in industry and government sources and BDI information is available through such services as Simmons and Scarborough, as well as company data.

There are different strategies for dealing with these levels, and they have implications for the media mix and schedule. Planners typically don't make heavy allocations in weak sales areas unless strong marketing signals indicate significant growth potential. Conversely, strong sales markets may not receive proportional increases in advertising unless clear evidence suggests that company sales can go much higher with greater advertising investment.

Principle

The CDI tells you where the category is strong and weak, and the BDI tells you where your brand is strong and weak.

Delivering on the Media Mix Strategy

In our earlier discussion of media mix strategy, we looked at the efficiency of various media plans. Executing a media mix may involve other factors as well as the estimates of reach, frequency, and rating points. One factor may be knowledge of media use. Tools involve techniques for calculating the weight of a media schedule and optimizing the schedule using computer models.

An example of the importance of understanding media dynamics comes from Procter & Gamble, the world's biggest marketer. The following table shows how P&G's media mix has evolved over time based on an analysis of changing media patterns. Note how P&G has allocated its budget across four of its largest media categories over a three-year period.[13] If you study the table, you will see that print and the Internet are increasing as TV spending declines. What does that tell you about the importance of the Internet to P&G's customer base?

	TV	National Mags	Other Print	Internet
2006	69.3 %	25.4%	2.8%	1.4%
2005	71.3	24.2	1.8	1.0
2004	74.2	21.0	2.1	0.5

Media Weighting   Media planners often use decision criterion called **weighting** to help them decide how much to budget in each DMA or region and for each target audience when there is more than one. For example, if a media planner is advertising disposable contact lenses, there might be two target segments to consider: consumers and the eye doctors who make the recommendations. Do you recall the discussion of push and pull strategies from Chapter 2? If the strategy is to encourage the consumer to ask the doctor about the product, the planner might recommend putting more emphasis on consumer publications to execute a **pull strategy** rather than focusing on professional journals for eye doctors, which would represent a **push strategy**. A weighting strategy might be to put 60 percent of the budget on consumers and 40 percent on doctors. In the case of DMAs, weak markets may be given more than their share of media weight in hopes of strengthening the brands in these markets, a practice known as *investment spending*. On the other hand, if competition is extremely heavy in a brand's strong markets, the strategy may be to give them more than their proportional share of media dollars to defend against competitors. Weighting strategies are also used in terms of seasonality, geography, audience segments, and the level of brand development by DMA.

Size, Length, and Position   In addition to selecting the media mix, a media planner works with the creative team to determine the appropriate size and length the message will run in each medium. This question of scope and scale applies to all media—even transit advertising, as the Yellow Cab ad shown previously illustrates. The size or length chosen should relate to the advertising objectives. If the objective is to educate the target audience through a great deal of technical information, a full-page ad or a 60-second spot might be necessary. However, a 10-second spot might be sufficient to create name recognition. Research on where to place an ad on a page or in a pod of TV spots has found that in magazines, for example, the back cover and inside front cover and first few pages have higher readership. Also, placement of ads adjacent to compatible stories in print or within related broadcast programs often has an enhancing effect.

Media Optimization Modeling   Media mix modeling is a computer technique that enables marketers to determine the relative impact of a media mix on product sales and optimize the efficiency of the media mix.[14] The development of this **optimization** software began in the packaged goods sector as a result of the supermarket scanner systems that enabled advertisers to run local promotions and immediately measure the impact on sales. One optimization model came about through the partnering of McCann-Erickson Worldwide and Media Plan, a developer of media planning software and systems. They created a media allocation software system code named MediaFX. The system can create an unlimited number of media combinations and then simulate the sales produced by each. The media planner can then make intelligent decisions, given factors such as budget, timing, and so forth. The objective, of course, is to develop the most efficient plan possible that will deliver the most impact.

Scheduling Strategies

If advertising budgets were unlimited, most companies would advertise every day. Not even the largest advertisers are in this position, so media planners manipulate schedules in various ways to create the strongest possible impact given the budget. Three scheduling strategies involve timing, duration of exposure, and continuity of exposure.

- *Timing strategies: When to advertise?* Timing decisions relate to factors such as seasonality, holidays, days of the week, and time of day. These decisions are driven by how often the product is bought and whether it is used more in some months than in others. Timing also encompasses the consumer's best aperture and competitors' advertising schedules. Another consideration is **lead time,** or the amount of time allowed before the beginning of the sales period to reach people when they are just beginning to think about seasonal buying. Back-to-school advertising is an example. Advertising typically starts in July or early August for a school calendar that begins in late August or September. Lead time also refers to the production time needed to get the advertisement into the medium. There is a long lead time for magazines, but it is shorter for local media, such as newspapers and radio.
- *Duration: How long?* For how many weeks or months of the year should the advertising run? If there is a need to cover most of the weeks, advertising will be spread rather thin. If the amount of time to cover is limited, advertising can be concentrated more heavily. Message scheduling is driven by use cycles. For products that are consumed year-round, such as fast food and movies, advertising is spread throughout the year. In general, if you cannot cover the whole year, you should *heavy up* the schedule in higher-purchase periods. For example, movie marketers do most of their newspaper advertising on the weekends, when most people go to movies.

   Another question is how much is enough. At what point does the message make its point? If the advertising period is too short or there are too few repetitions, then the message may have little or no impact. If the period is too long, then ads may suffer from **wearout**, which means the audience gets tired of them and stops paying attention.
- *Continuity: How often?* **Continuity** refers to the way the advertising is spread over the length of a campaign. A **continuous strategy** spreads the advertising evenly over the campaign period. Budgets that cannot afford to do continuous scheduling have two other methods to consider: pulsing and flighting, as shown in Figure 11.4.

   A **flighting strategy** is the most severe type of continuity adjustment. It is characterized by alternating periods of intense advertising activity and periods of no advertising, called a *hiatus.* This on-and-off schedule allows for a longer campaign without making the advertising schedule too light. The hope in using nonadvertising periods is that the consumers will remember the brand and its advertising for some time after the ads have stopped. Figure 11.5 illustrates this awareness change. The jagged line represents the rise and fall of consumer awareness of the brand. If the flighting strategy works, there will be a *carryover effect* of past advertising, which means consumers will remember the product across the gap until the next advertising period begins. The critical decision involves analyzing the *decay* level, the rate at which memory of the advertising is forgotten.[15]

FIGURE 11.4

The Continuity Strategies of
Pulsing and Flighting

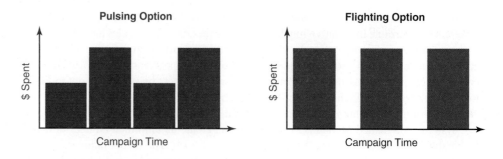

FIGURE 11.5

Consumer Awareness Levels in a
Flighting Strategy

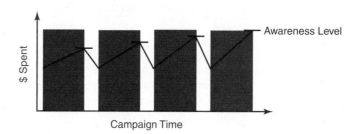

A **pulsing strategy** is a combination of continuous and flighting strategies. Pulsing is used to intensify advertising before a buying aperture and then to reduce advertising to lower levels until the aperture reopens. The pulse pattern has peaks and valleys, also called *bursts.* Fast-food companies such as McDonald's and Burger King often use pulsing patterns as they increase media weight during special promotional periods. Although the competition for daily customers suggests continuous advertising, they will greatly intensify activity to accommodate special events such as new menu items, merchandise premiums, and contests. Pulsed schedules cover most of the year, but still provide periodic intensity.

After a media schedule has been worked out in terms of what media will run when and for how long, these decisions are plotted on a **media flow chart**. Across the top is the calendar for the period of the campaign and down the side is the list of media to be used in this campaign. Bars are then drawn across the calendar that identify the exact timing of the use of various media. When the chart is complete, strategies such as pulsing and flighting are easy to observe. You can also see where reminder advertising in less expensive media (in-store signs) may fill in between bursts and pulsing in more expensive media such as television.

Cost Efficiency: CPMs and CPPs

Advertisers don't make decisions about the media mix solely in terms of targeting, geography, and schedule considerations. Sometimes the decision comes down to cold, hard cash. The advertiser wants prospects, not just readers, viewers, or listeners; therefore, they compare the cost of each proposed media vehicle with the specific vehicle's ability to deliver the target audience. The cheapest vehicle may not deliver the highest percent of the target audience, so the selection process is a balancing act.

The process of measuring a target audience's size against the cost of reaching that audience is based on calculations of efficiency as measured by two commonly used metrics—**cost per thousand (CPM)** and **cost per point (CPP)**.

• *Cost per thousand.* This is the cost to expose 1,000 audience members to an ad message. CPM is best used when comparing the cost of vehicles within the same medium (comparing one magazine with another or one television program with another). This is because different media have different levels of impact. To be more precise and determine the efficiency of a potential media buy, planners often look at the **targeted cost per thousand (TCPM)**.

To calculate a CPM, you need only two figures: the cost of an ad and the estimated audience reached by the vehicle. Multiply the cost of the ad by 1,000 and divide that number by the size of the broadcast audience or in the case of a print ad, by the circulation. You multiply the cost of the ad by 1,000 to calculate a "cost per thousand."

In the case of print, CPMs are based on circulation, or number of readers. *Time* magazine has a circulation of 4 million but claims a readership of 19.5 million. The difference between circulation and readership is due to what is called **pass-along readership**. In the case of *Time*, this means each issue is read by about 5 people. As you would suspect, media vehicles prefer that agencies use readership as this produces a much lower CPM. In the following example, CPM is calculated based on *Time* readership and the price of a one-page, 4-color ad, $240,000.

$$CPM = \frac{\text{Cost of ad} \times 1,000}{\text{Readership}}$$

$$CPM = \frac{\$240,000 \times 1,000}{19,500,000} = \$12.31 \text{ CPM}$$

To figure the TCPM, you first determine how many of *Time*'s readers are in your target audience. For the sake of discussion, we'll say that only 5 million of *Time*'s readers fall into our target audience profile. As you can see from the following calculation, the TCPM greatly increases. This is because you still have to pay to reach all the readers, even though only about one-fourth of them are of value to you.

$$TCPM = \frac{\text{Cost of ad} \times 1,000}{\text{Readers in target audience}}$$

$$TCPM = \frac{\$240,000 \times 1,000}{5,000,000} = \$48.00 \text{ TCPM}$$

Now we'll look at how to determine CPP and TCPP, which are used for comparing broadcast media programs. Divide the cost of running one commercial by the rating of the program in which the commercial will appear. If a 30-second spot on *Lost* costs $320,000, and it has a rating of 8, then the cost per rating point would be $40,000.

$$CPP = \frac{\$320,000}{8 \text{ rating}} = \$40,000 \text{ CPP}$$

To figure the TCPP, you determine what percent of the audience is your target. In the case of *Lost,* we will estimate that half of the audience is our target. Thus, the overall rating of 8 is reduced to 4 (50% × 8 = 4 rating). Now we divide the one-time cost of $320,000 by 4 and find the TCPP is $80,000. We can do this calculation for several different programs to identify those with lower costs.

$$TCPP = \frac{\$320,000}{4 \text{ target rating}} = \$80,000 \text{ TCPP}$$

The Media Budget

The media planner begins and ends a media plan with the budget. An initial assessment of the amount of money available (small budget, large budget) determines what kinds of media can be used. A small budget campaign, for example, may not be able to afford television, which is the most costly of all media. A small budget may also dictate that the campaign be local or limited to a few areas rather than aiming for a national audience. Small budgets are a creative challenge for media planners.

At the end of the planning process, after the media mix has been determined, the media planner will prepare a *pie chart* showing *media allocations*, which means allocating the budget among the various media chosen. The pie chart shows the amount being spent on each medium as a proportion of the total media budget. For example, the pie chart on the right shows how Procter & Gamble, the world's largest marketer, split its media budget in 2006 in terms of its four main media categories.[16]

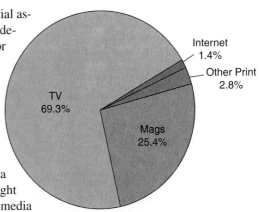

Procter & Gamble Media Budget

IMC Media and ContactPoint Planning

As we have noted previously, when most people think about media, they think about traditional mass media and advertising. When IMC planners think about media, they think about message delivery systems. Media planning in an IMC campaign focuses on every important contact point, the touch point where a consumer has an opportunity to connect with a brand and respond in some way to a brand message. A list of contact points a planner might consider would be endless, but a sample list is available online on this book's Web site (www.prenhall.com/moriarty).

Tokyo-based Dentsu, which is the world's largest individual agency, has a strong IMC orientation, which shows up in the way Dentsu planners create IMC media plans. Dentsu's ContactPoint Management is a section in its IMC Version 2.0 model that identifies a wide diversity of contact points, including but not limited to such separate communication functions as public relations, sponsorship, direct-response marketing, events, word of mouth (WOM), in-store (signage, POP, personnel), sales promotion, traditional advertising media (broadcast, print, OOH), sports, entertainment, interactive (Web, podcasting), mobile media, and new OOH media. This approach to IMC media planning is explained in the Matter of Practice box.

Global Media Strategies

Advertising practitioners can debate global theories of advertising, but one fact is inescapable: Global media do not currently exist. Television can transmit the Olympics around the globe, but no one network controls this global transmission. An advertiser seeking global exposure, therefore, must deal with different networks and different vehicles in different countries.

Satellite transmission now places advertising into many homes, but its availability is not universal because of the *footprint* (coverage area of the satellite), technical limitations, and regulations of transmission by various governments. Satellites beam signals to more than one country in Europe, the Asian subcontinent, North America, and the Pacific, but they are regional, not global, in coverage. Despite its regional limitation, satellite transmission is still an enormous factor in the changing face of international advertising. Star TV, with an audience spanning 38 countries, including Egypt, India, Japan, Indonesia, and Russia's Asian provinces, reaches a market of some 2.7 billion people. It is closely followed by CNN and ESPN. Sky Channel, a U.K.-based network, offers satellite service to most of Europe, giving advertisers the opportunity to deliver a unified message across the continent.

The North American, European, Asian, and Latin American markets are becoming saturated with cable TV companies offering an increasing number of international networks. Such broadcasters include the hugely successful Latin American networks of Univision and Televisa, whose broadcasts can be seen in nearly every Spanish-speaking market, including the United States. One of Univision's most popular programs, *Sabado Giganta*, is seen by tens of millions of viewers in 16 countries.

After this review of media planning, let's stop for a moment and look at how a media plan comes together. The following section is built around a media plan constructed for hospital-based Women's Health Services. After this discussion, we'll turn our attention to media buying and explain how a plan is executed.

A SAMPLE MEDIA PLAN

Media plans do not have a universal form, but there is a common (and logical) pattern to the decision stages. To illustrate one style of presentation in a real-life setting, we use an actual media plan for a Women's Health Services program based in hospitals. This media plan example is contributed by Amy Hume, who was Media Director at the Denver-based Barnhart Communications at the time she prepared this plan. Let's briefly explore each major section in this plan.

- *Objectives.* Media objectives are designed to deliver on the campaign's overall communication objectives. The primary communication objective for this Women's Health Services campaign was to build awareness. The media-related objectives that

A MATTER OF PRACTICE

Dentsu's ContactPoint Management Approach

The objective of Dentsu's ContactPoint planning is to select the most effective contact points to achieve the communication goals and implement optimum integrated communication programs that eliminate waste. ContactPoint Management focuses on two strategies that are critical in delivering effective integrated communication:

1. Identify the Value ContactPoints—the emotion-driving points at which or during which consumers come in contact with a brand.
2. Move away from the traditional B→C model (business targets a consumer with a message) to a more interactive B→C→C model (business to consumers who talk to other consumers). This approach uses mass media to stimulate inter-consumer communications, or word of mouth, which delivers messages more persuasively.

Media selection recognizes that (1) contact points that work well must differ depending on the communication goal and (2) contact point effectiveness will differ from product category to product category and from target to target.

An example of how Dentsu manages a full set of brand contact points comes from an automotive campaign where two target audiences have been identified as Fathers (male, 50s) and Daughters (female, 20s). The communication objective is to position the new subcompact car model as "fun driving for grown men" and "a small cute model for young women."

The various contact points considered are evaluated and ranked using a proprietary contact point planning system called VALCON (Value ContactPoint Tracer). Dentsu planners also have access to hundreds of media-related databases with vast volumes of contact point information to consult in this process. The final decisions about media usage are based on the roles and effects of the various media.

For the new subcompact, contact points were evaluated based on three objectives: their ability to launch a new product (recognition, build awareness), arouse interest (evaluation), and make the target feel like buying (intention, attitude). Here are the results:

	Father	Both		Daughter
Awareness	1. newspaper 2. OOH ads	3. direct mail	4.	1. train poster 2. TV ad 3. magazine ad
Interest	1. car on display at event	3. car on streets 4. TV ad 2. catalog 5. nwspr insert	1. 2. 5. 8.	3. automaker's Web site 4. cars owned by friends
Intention	3. car magazine story	2. catalog 1. car on display 6. test drive	1. 2. 3.	4. TV ad

As you can see, the plan calls for contact points that reach both audiences (TV ads, catalogs, street media newspaper inserts, and direct mail). Newspaper ads, OOH ads, the car on display at the dealers' showroom, and car magazine stories were added or emphasized for the Father audience. For the Daughter audience, magazine ads, a Web site, transit ads, radio ads, family WOM, and TV ads were added. Here is how this complex media plan is diagrammed in terms of its effects.

	Recognition	Evaluation	Attitude
Father	Newspaper & OOH ads, car display at dealer		Car magazine stories
Both	TV ads, catalogs, street media, newspaper inserts, direct mail	TV ads, friends WOM	Catalog, car display at dealer, test drive
Daughter	magazine and transit ads, Web site	radio ads, family WOM	TV ads

Sources: "Dentsu Launches Next-Generation Communication Planning System IMC ver.2.0™" Dentsu Press Release, April 13, 2006; "Integrated Communication by Use of ContactPoint Management®," PowerPoint Presentation, Tokyo, November 2006.

Women's Health Services Media Plan

Launching in Fall 2008, in hospitals throughout the central United States, the Women's Health Services Program combines the health care services that women may be exposed to throughout their lives, all under one roof. It brings together services beyond just gynecology, including oncology, dermatology, cardiology, and more. It aids women by providing one central point of contact—a concierge—to coordinate their appointments.

Communication Objectives
- Establish awareness of a new Women's Health Services Program opening in select local hospitals throughout the Heartland of the United States.
- Generate buzz and word of mouth.
- Drive requests for information via Web and phone.

Strategic Plan Development
Although "all women" were the target, we knew that the best opportunity started with wealthy, more educated women who would act as influencers in the market. As a result, we focused demographically on:
   Working Women ages 30–54 with household income (HHI) of $75,000+, with or without kids.
   It was important for us to gain further insight into their behaviors and attitudes relating to health care, communication, and everyday routines. Via both syndicated research and primary research, we uncovered many insights that helped direct the plan:

Activities/Behaviors
- They work out—at home, in club, or outdoors.
  - They exercise to manage their weight, be more relaxed, and reduce health problems.
  - While most women are not passionate about working out, many say it is an essential part of their lives.
- They travel to/from work an average of 7.5 miles—either in car or public transportation (depending on the market).
- They go to a coffee shop usually once a day—both independents and chains.
- They use the Internet for e-mail and to research just about anything—particularly health-related issues; two-thirds of online health site users are female.
- Women make 75 percent of health care decisions, spend two-thirds of health care dollars, and account for two-thirds of hospital procedures.

Attitudes
- Women's most influential source of information or advice is their circle of friends.
  - Women rely on advice and opinions of those individuals around them who have proven themselves in the past.
  - They respond to anecdotes/storytelling and connect to an engaging narrative relating lives and experiences of other women.
  - Through our primary research we found that many women have phone conversations with female relatives once/day.
  - Conversation serves many purposes in women's lives: recharging, validation, and learning.
- Women focus on the emotional—happiness, peace of mind, fulfillment, self-confidence—vs. more traditional, material, outward manifestations of success.
- When choosing health care they are looking for:
  - "Someone who knows me," "Ability to help with issues," "Treat me as an individual."
  - Communications on a personal level.
  - An easier, less-stressful way to find a physician who's interested in their overall health.

Media Objectives and Budget
Due to the absence of substantive competitive reach and frequency benchmarks by competition or like programs, we based weight-level objectives on history and experience:
  - During launch, generate 85 reach with 4.0 frequency per month.
  - For follow-up months, 65 reach with 3.0 frequency as budget allows.

FIGURE 11.6
Women's Health Services Media Plan

Key Strategies

With this background and research, we were able to establish our key strategies:

- Overall, we determined that we would be most effective by using a combination of traditional and nontraditional vehicles that intersect with women in relevant, yet respectful places and in nontraditional ways.
- We knew that it was important to seek contacts that increase relevance and tie into her perception of healthy living—nutrition, fitness, and relaxation—and into her passion—family and hobbies.
- Also, we needed to recommend contacts that would help provide impact and thus increased receptivity of the message—those that would signal "for me" (personal, part of my world), be trustworthy, and provide opportunity for narrative/storytelling.
- Finally, it was important to get out of the traditional health care mold and get her to react.

Who (Target)

Active Female Health Managers
- Working women, married, ages 30–54, with or without kids.
- More likely to ask their doctor to send them to a preferred specialist or hospital.
- Indirectly, their knowledge, experience, and passion for updated health information make them a valuable resource—they have a large sphere of influence.

Where (Geography)

While the program itself was launching in 10 cities, we decided to focus initially on the more efficiently priced, mid-sized metro areas in the Central United States—Minneapolis, Denver, Kansas City, and St. Louis.

When (Timing/Seasonality)

- Launch September 2008 to coincide with multicity opening; also coincides with time of "renewal" with the back-to-school mentality.
- Provide additional support in January as people are making resolutions, mostly in the area of health.
- Follow up with an effort in May tied into Women's Health Month.

SAMPLE MEDIA PLAN FOR WOMEN'S HEALTH SERVICES

	2005						2006						BUDGET
	JULY	AUGUST	SEPTEMBER	OCTOBER	NOVEMBER	DECEMBER	JANUARY	FEBRUARY	MARCH	APRIL	MAY	JUNE	
Magazines													$ 720,000
Radio													$ 600,000
Out of Home													$ 300,000
Place-Based													
Health Clubs													$ 180,000
Coffee Sleeves													$ 90,000
Produce Section													$ 45,000
Mall boards													$ 45,000
Online													
Media													$ 300,000
Website													tbd
Events													$ 200,000
GRAND TOTAL													**$ 2,480,000**

What (Vehicle Selection)

Magazines: Be where they're searching for health care information—62 percent of women ranked magazines as their #1 source of information for healthy eating habits, fitness, and overall well-being. They provide the opportunity for long-form messaging. Recommend use of local magazines as well as regional editions of national magazines to provide reach.

Radio: Close to 50 percent of active health managers listen to the radio every day, and 50 percent always listen when they're in their car. They rely on radio to keep them informed, but they tend to change the station when commercials come on. Thus, we need to use radio in a nontraditional manner. Recommended using one or two top-reaching stations per market and establish relationships with key DJs. Bring them to the Center's preopening to experience the staff and atmosphere and expose them to the services so that they will then talk about the Center during their shows. This will allow women to hear from a trusted source via a good reach medium, while not immediately turning the dial.

(continued)

FIGURE 11.6

Women's Health Services Media Plan—continued

Out-of-Home Media: Use traditional billboards and transit advertising to intersect women during their daily routine. Helps create a surround-sound approach.

Place-Based Media: Based on their daily routines and behaviors, we recommended placements in Health Clubs, Coffee Shops, Grocery Stores, and Mall/Retail Centers. The messages would need to be specially tailored to these environments.

Online: Determine key sites within each city and talk with top-rated health sites nationally to gain a presence, particularly contextually via articles. Research blogs and chat rooms to determine other electronic avenues for contact.

Web: Develop a Web site that will provide resources and links for women, including the opportunity for community such as blogging, chat rooms, and message boards, as well as a feedback and research tool.

Events/Seminars: Invite women in each community to a grand opening celebration with two or three key speakers. Follow up with quarterly seminars that encourage women to spread the word—"bring your sister or your mom." Develop a membership program that will provide an opportunity for Brand Ambassadors, creating a women's health care "community."

How Much: Weighting and Budget

We analyzed competitive advertising pressure of other hospitals and health centers in these markets as well as prominent women's programs like Brigham & Women's in Boston, Oregon Health & Science University Center for Women's Health, and the Iris Cantor Women's Health Center in New York City. We determined that there was little consistent mass media pressure in any market by these entities, so we used history and experience to determine the relative importance of the various media.

We were working with a Year One budget of $3.0 million to cover all markets. The Pie Chart explains how that budget was allocated across our various media tools.

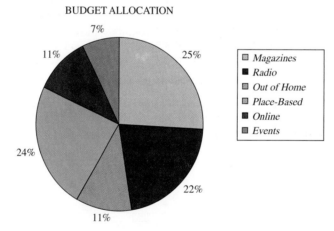

BUDGET ALLOCATION

☐	*Magazines*
■	*Radio*
☐	*Out of Home*
☐	*Place-Based*
■	*Online*
☐	*Events*

A graduate of the University of Colorado, Amy Hume was nominated by Professor Tom Duncan.

FIGURE 11.6
Women's Health Services Media Plan—continued

would deliver this awareness involved two tasks: generating buzz among the target audience and creating enough interest that the campaign would cause the target to search for information using the Web site and phone number provided in the campaign materials.

- ***Strategic plan development: Consumer insights.*** The key to this media plan is understanding the consumer market for Women's Health Services. Background research from the campaign's situation analysis is used to describe the women in this market in terms of their activities and behaviors, as well as their attitudes and feelings.
- ***Key media strategies.*** Identifying the appropriate media involved locating those apertures where messages about the Women's Health Services would be most welcome. That involves understanding the patterns in the target audiences' lives and the intersection of their activities with media opportunities. Another important aspect

of media strategy is spelling out the media mix, which includes the various media to be used and strategies that drive how they support and reinforce one another. For the Women's Health Services program, the key decision was to use both traditional media and nontraditional vehicles that are specific to their lives and personal activities. The key strategic decisions in this media plan can be summarized as: who, where, when, how much, and what.

MEDIA BUYING

The media plan is a recommendation that the client must approve before any further steps are taken. In fact, planning is only the first stage in advertising media operations. Once the plan directions are set, media buyers convert objectives and strategies into tactical decisions. They select specific media vehicles and negotiate and contract for the time and space in media. In this section we explain how the media buyer makes the media plan come to life. A media buyer has distinct responsibilities as outlined in Figure 11.7.

Media Buying Complexities

Buying is a complicated process. The American Association of Advertising Agencies (AAAA) lists no fewer than 21 elements of a media buy. The most important one, however, is matching the media vehicle to the strategic needs of the message and the brand. A crisis erupted in 2007 when Don Imus got in trouble for his outrageous comments about the Rutgers womens' basketball team, comments that eventually got him fired from his MSNBC talk radio show. Advertising professor Bobbi Kay Hooper wonders why the mainstream advertisers (Staples, General Motors, Procter & Gamble, and others) who were so upset by his rant decided to advertise on his program in the first place. She observes that they must have known that the odds were that he would say something that they and their customers would find offensive.[17] It was a risky media buy, to say the least.

In this section, we examine the most important buyer activities: providing information to media planners, selecting the media vehicles, negotiating costs, monitoring the media choices, evaluating the media choices after the campaign, and handling billing and payment.

- *Providing inside information.* Media buyers are important information sources for media planners. They are close enough to day-to-day changes in media popularity and pricing to be an important source of inside current information. For example, a

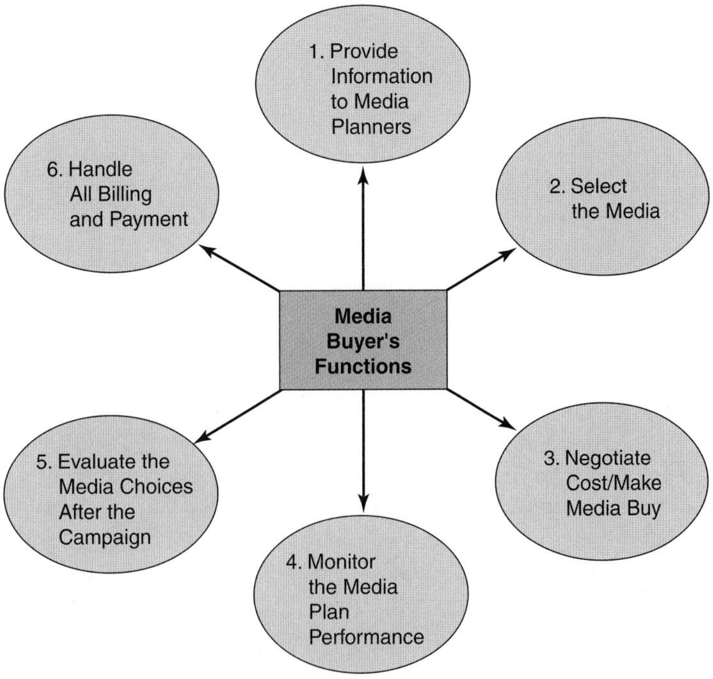

Principle
Media buyers should be consulted early in planning as they are a good source of information on changes in media.

FIGURE 11.7
The Functions of a Media Buyer

GOT THAT DAILY VEGETABLE THING DOWN YET?

Take a shortcut on the road to better eating. Each 12-ounce bottle of V8® has more than a full serving of vegetables and good things like potassium and the antioxidant vitamins A & C. Now, if they could just bottle that daily exercise thing.

Physical characteristics of a magazine can affect its ability to deliver the desired message. For example, this V8 ad, which appeared in *Readers' Digest*, uses simple visuals and minimal copy to accommodate the smaller page size. *Readers' Digest* may not be the best choice for a complex ad.

newspaper buyer discovers that a key newspaper's delivery staff is going on strike, or a magazine buyer's source reveals that the new editor of a publication is going to change the editorial focus dramatically. All of these things can influence the strategy and tactics of current and future advertising plans.

- *Selecting media vehicles.* The key function of media buying is choosing the best media vehicles that fit the target audience's aperture. The media planner determines the media mix, but the buyer is responsible for choosing the specific media vehicles. Armed with the media plan directives, the buyer seeks answers to a number of difficult questions: Does the vehicle have the right audience profile? Will the program's current popularity increase, stabilize, or decline? How well does the magazine's editorial format fit the brand and the message strategy (see the V8 ad example)? The answers to those questions bear directly on the campaign's success.

- *Negotiation.* Just as a person buying a car often negotiates for the best price, so does a media buyer negotiate for the best prices. The key questions are whether the desired vehicles are available and whether a satisfactory schedule and rates can be negotiated. Aside from finding the aperture of target audiences, nothing is more crucial in media buying than securing the lowest possible price for placements.

Every medium has a published rate card, but media buyers negotiate special prices with discounts for volume buys. The buyer must understand the trade-off between price received and audience objectives. For example, a media buyer might be able to get a lower price for 30 commercials on ESPN, but part of the deal is that half the spots are scheduled with programs that don't reach the primary target audience. So the price may not be a good deal in the long run. Here are some other negotiation considerations:

- *Preferred positions.* Media buyers must bargain for **preferred positions,** the locations in magazines and other print media that offer readership advantages. Imagine the value a food advertiser would gain from having its message located in a special recipe section that the homemaker can detach from the magazines for permanent use. How many additional exposures might that ad get? Because they are so visible, preferred positions often carry a premium surcharge, usually 10 to 15 percent above standard space rates.

- *Extra support offers.* With the current trend toward using other forms of marketing communication in addition to advertising, buyers often demand additional promotional support. These activities, sometimes called **value-added media services**, can take any number of forms, including contests, special events, merchandising space at stores, displays, and trade-directed newsletters. The "extra" depends on what facilities each media vehicle has and how hard the buyer can bargain.

- *Billing and payment.* Bills from the various media come in continuously. Ultimately, it is the responsibility of the advertiser to make these payments. However, the agency is contractually obligated to pay the invoice on behalf of the client. Keeping track of the invoices and paying the bills are the responsibility of the media buyer in conjunction with the accounting department.

- *Monitoring the media buy.* A media buyer's responsibility to a campaign does not end with the signing of space and time contracts. The media buyer is responsible for tracking the performance of the media plan as it is implemented and afterward as part of the campaign evaluation. Buys are made in advance, based on forecasted audience levels. What happens if unforeseen events affect scheduling? What if newspapers go on strike, magazines fold, or a television show is canceled? Buyers must fix these problems. Underperformance and schedule problems are facts of life. Poorly performing vehicles must be replaced, or costs must be modified. Buyers also check the publication issues to verify whether advertisements have been placed correctly. Buyers also make every attempt to get current audience research to ensure that schedules are performing according to forecast. Media buyers are even found out "riding the boards," which means they check the location of the outdoor boards to verify that the client is receiving the outdoor exposure specified in the plan.

- *Make goods.* Temporary snags in scheduling and in the reproduction of the advertising message are sometimes unavoidable. Buyers must be alert for missed positions or errors in handling the message presentation and ensure that the advertiser is compensated appropriately when they occur. A policy of compensating for such errors is called "making good on the contract," known as **make goods**. Here are some examples.

  - **Program preemptions.** Special programs or news events sometimes interrupt regular programming and the scheduled commercials. In the case of long-term interruptions, such as war coverage, buyers may have difficulty finding suitable replacements before the schedule ends.

  - *Missed closings.* Magazines and newspapers have clearly set production deadlines, called **closings**, for each issue. Sometimes the advertising materials do not arrive in time. If the publication is responsible, it will make good. If the fault lies with the client or the agency, the publication makes no restitution.

  - *Technical problems.* Technical difficulties are responsible for numerous goofs, glitches, and foul-ups that haunt the advertiser's schedule. **Bleed throughs** (the printing on the back side of the page is visible and conflicts with the client's ad on the front side) and **out-of-register** colors (full-color printing is made from four-color plates, which sometimes are not perfectly aligned) for newspapers, torn billboard posters, broken film, and tapes out of alignment are typical problems.

- *Postcampaign evaluation.* Once a campaign is completed, the planner's duty is to compare the plan's expectations and forecasts with what actually happened. Did the plan actually achieve GRP, reach, frequency, and CPM objectives? Did the newspaper and magazine placements run in the positions expected? Such analysis is instrumental in providing guidance for future media plans.

Multichannel Buying (and Selling)

We mentioned earlier that media planners are constructing multichannel media platforms when they outline a media mix. They know that their audiences are involved with multiple forms of media; therefore their media plans also have to be multichannel. ESPN, for example, promotes its programming using a **multichannel** plan that includes TV, magazines, radio, and the Internet, as well as original programming on its own channels. The idea is to match the media use of the target audience in all its complexity.

On the other side of that coin is the *cross-media buy*, which is made easier by media companies that sell combinations of media vehicles in a single buy. This approach makes it easier to buy media across all these platforms with a single deal rather than six phone calls. Giant media groups, such as Viacom and Disney, are packaging "deals" based on the interests of the target audience. ESPN, for example, serves the sports market and can provide media integration that includes TV, magazines, radio, and the Internet. The media conglomerate Disney created a one-stop buying opportunity for advertisers targeting kids. To create this opportunity, Disney reorganized its ad sales staff to create one sales force for its various properties that reach children—two cable networks Disney Channel and Toon Disney, kids' programming on ABC, Radio Disney, Disney.com, and Disney Adventures magazine.[18]

These multichannel deals are also a result of media convergence. Rupert Murdoch's giant News Corporation, for example, has a new network called Mobizzo that offers Fox television content on cell phones. News Corp. also owns the social networking site MySpace and is developing video sections on that site to rival YouTube. As content moves across these various forms of new media, so also does advertising.

Global Media Buying

The definition of global media buying varies widely, but everyone agrees that few marketers are doing it yet. However, many are thinking about it, especially computer and other information technology companies that are being pursued by media such as CNN. Today, the growth area is media buys across a single region. But as media become more global, some marketers are beginning to make the leap across regions. About 60 percent of ad buys on CNN International are regional, and 40 percent are global.

In Europe, the rise of buying "centrals" came about with the emergence of the European Union and the continuing globalization of trade and advertising. Buying centrals are media organizations that buy across several European countries. Their growth also began with the development of commercial broadcasting and the expansion of media choices. These firms have flourished in an environment of flexible and negotiated rates, low inflation, and a fragmented advertising market. The buying centrals have nearly three-fourths of the media market in France, nine-tenths in Spain, and about two-fifths in Britain, Holland, Italy, and Scandinavia.

The important thing, however, is to be able to consider cultural implications in media use. For that reason media planning and buying companies are also specializing or buying companies that know specific cultures, such as the Hispanic market in the United States and the Chinese market in Asia. Zenithoptimedia, for example, is a London-based media-buying company that has created ZO Multicultural, a multicultural unit that initially will help clients trying to reach Hispanics in the United States.

MEDIA PLANNING TRENDS

Advertising experts have been proclaiming the demise of mass media advertising for a number of years. Bob Garfield, the *Advertising Age* columnist, for example, got industry-wide attention in 2005 with his feature, "The Chaos Scenario," in which he speculated about the media landscape in coming years when over-the-air network TV is gone and everyone accesses their news, entertainment, and advertising any way they wish: TV, phone, camera, laptop, game console, or MP3 player. Contrary viewpoints pointed to the continuing profitability of TV advertising in 2006 and 2007 and charged that Garfield was overestimating the impact of new online media.[19]

The truth is that the media landscape is dynamic and changing so fast that it's hard to keep track of how the media business is practiced. All of these changes create new ways of operation and new opportunities for innovative media planners and buyers.

Unbundling Media Buying and Planning

We've mentioned before the growth of media-buying services, such as the media megashop Starcom MediaVest, as separate companies that specialize in media buying. This is a shift in the way the media industry is organized, a change referred to as **unbundling media services.** This happens when an agency transforms its media department into a separate profit center, apart from the agency. This then allows the media group to work for clients who may be competitors to some of those handled by the agency. Because these companies control the money, they have become a powerful force in the advertising industry, leading to a tug of war over control of planning. Faced with competition from these independent media companies, many large agencies have set up or bought their own buying services to compete with the independents and go after outside business.

Some of these media companies are now offering **consolidated services,** which means bringing the planning and buying functions back together. To take advantage of this consolidation argument, some media companies are also adding special planning teams for other related areas such as events, product placement, Internet, and guerilla marketing programs. WPP's MindShare created an agency-within-the-agency called the Wow Factory to develop ideas for nontraditional media.[20] For a major presentation to Coca-Cola, Starcom MediaVest pulled a team together that represented basic media planning and buying, research, consumer insights, programming, product placement, entertainment marketing, and integration solutions.[21] At this point, these big media companies begin to look more like traditional agencies.

Online Media Buying

A scarier threat to agencies than media-buying services comes from Google and eBay, which, although not ad agencies, are making inroads into media buying and selling. Google is using its Web site to sell ads primarily to small advertisers and publishers who find its automated advertising network, Google AdWords, to be a cost-effective way to connect with one another. eBay sells ads through its Media Marketplace. Agencies are trying to figure out if Google and eBay are friends or enemies and what their move in to online media buying will do to the revenue stream. Google, however, is betting that its expertise in search advertising, which matches ads to user interests, will give it an advantage over traditional ad media services.[22]

Buying media through the Internet has changed the way media buyers do business. For example, GMTradeExchange.com, the business-to-business Web site GM set up for its vendors to buy and sell their goods and services also includes a section on media buying. A comparable system to GM's has been set up by more than 50 consumer-goods companies, including Procter & Gamble, Coca-Cola, and Unilever. The Internet technology allows them to buy billions of dollars in advertising on the Internet. Zimmerman, an advertising agency owned by Omnicom, provides online buying for a number of media—print, radio, direct mail, and in-store ads, as well as the Internet.

New Forms of Media Research

As we mentioned earlier, one challenge media planners face is the lack of reliable audience research and measurement metrics for the new media. The traditional "measured" media with their CPMs were at least somewhat predictable in level of impact. But the metrics for online media—hits and clicks—don't really tell us much about impact. Comparing TRPs and clicks is like comparing apples and oranges.

Search advertising on the Internet is also complicating things because, if it's successful, it steals viewers away from the original site. Does ESPN benefit when viewers leave its site to click on the banner ad for Pontiac, "the official performance machines of the NCAA"? As one critic observed, search advertising may make sense as a form of direct marketing, but it is a nightmare for content publishers who sell advertising on their pages.[23] In such a situation, how do you evaluate efficiency of the publisher's site? Of the search advertising? If one is a winner, doesn't that automatically mean the other is a loser?

The problem is deeper than the metrics as the advertising industry continues to challenge the validity of even the traditional media monitoring systems, such as the Nielsen ratings. According to *Advertising Age*, "as the industry confronts change, it is increasingly clear that the tools and key metrics used as the basis for hundreds of billions of dollars spent on media, especially TV and print, may no longer be adequate to the task."[24] Calls for reform, which include better metrics on all media, are needed to reflect the different ways consumers are using media as well as new forms such as TiVo and interactive TV.

Some experts are calling for innovative media monitoring systems that measure outcomes and results instead of simply delivery. In other words, media measures should recognize advertising response functions, along with as program delivery.[25]

Another problem is that media research is based on each medium as a silo—separate studies for separate media. Most of the research services are unable to tell you much about the effectiveness of combined media; the impact such as seeing the same message on television and then reading about it in a newspaper story or ad is difficult to evaluate. One British company, Knowledge Networks/Statistical Research (KN/SR), is developing a tool for measuring a multimedia, consumer-centric approach to media that also offers uniform measurements across media.[26]

IT'S A
WRAP

Audi's Online Road to Success

THE ART
OF THE H3IST
AN AUDI PROJECT

The media planners for Audi's *The Art of the Heist* campaign took some risks. They speculated that the young, affluent male audience would engage in the mystery, alternative reality game, generate buzz about the new A3 model, and then influence others in the category to buy the luxury hatchback.

It worked. It reached the campaign objective of creating buzz. More than a half-million people participated in the game on an ongoing basis. The Heist generated more than 45 million PR impressions, including stories that ran in *BusinessWeek* and the *Wall Street Journal*.

While some bloggers saw the game as a "lame publicity stunt," most participants didn't seem to care. The thrill of the game captivated them. The game led to more than 10,000 leads for dealers and about 4,000 test drives. As predicted, the buzz led to sales that were 15.9 percent over "aggressive goals." By inviting people to participate in the mystery, Audi was able to successfully introduce a new luxury model at a third the cost of the average luxury car launch and strengthen favorable impressions of the brand.

In the process, the unorthodox campaign won a Silver Effie Award in the media category and a Bronze Lion in the interactive category at the world-renowned Cannes Lions Festival. Could this be the wave of the future in advertising?

Key Points Summary

1. **What is media aperture, and why is it important?** Aperture is a media concept that says advertising should be delivered and is most effective when people are receptive to the product information.

2. **How do media planners calculate media objectives?** Media planners consider three critical elements in setting specific media objectives: the degree of exposure (number of impressions), the number of different people exposed to the message (reach), and the amount of repetition needed to reach those people and make an impression on them (frequency).

3. **What are the key media strategy decisions?** Media strategies are designed to find media opportunities that will deliver on the media objectives and reach the appropriate target audience. The key strategies include targeting strategies, geographical strategies, media mix selection, scheduling strategies, cost efficiency decisions, and budgeting decisions.

4. **What are the responsibilities of media buyers?** Media buyers have inside information about the media industries that they feed back into the planning. Their responsibilities as buyers include selecting media vehicles, negotiating rates, handling the billing and payment, and monitoring the effectiveness of the media buy.

Key Terms

aperture, p. 320

bleed throughs, p. 341

brand development index (BDI), p. 329

category development index (CDI), p. 329

closings, p. 341

consolidated services, p. 342

continuity, p. 331

continuous strategy, p. 331

cost per point (CPP), p. 332

cost per thousand (CPM), p. 332

designated marketing area (DMA), p. 316

earned media, p. 324

effective frequency, p. 322

flighting strategy, p. 331

frequency, p. 321

frequency distribution, p. 322

gross rating points (GRPs), p. 324

heavy-up, p. 329

image transfer, p. 328

lead time, p. 331

make goods, p. 341

measured media, p. 318

media flow chart, p. 332

media mix, p. 323

media objectives, p. 321

media plan, p. 318

media strategy, p. 328

multichannel, p. 341

optimization, p. 331

out-of-register, p. 341

pass-along readership, p. 333

preferred positions, p. 340

program preemptions, p. 341

pull strategy, p. 330

pulsing strategy, p. 332

push strategy, p. 330

rating point, p. 326

reach, p. 321

share of voice, p. 316

targeted cost per thousand (TCPM), p. 332

targeted rating points (TRPs), p. 327

targeted reach, p. 321

unbundling media services, p. 342

unduplicated audiences, p. 321

value-added media services, p. 340

wearout, p. 331

weighting, p. 330

Review Questions

1. Explain the differences between media planning and media buying.

2. What is aperture, and how is it used in media planning?

3. How are gross impressions and gross rating points calculated?

4. What are some of the strategic considerations that determine the level of reach? Frequency?

5. Give some examples of strategic decisions that deliver the reach and frequency objectives.

6. How do consumer media use, geography, and consumption patterns affect a media plan?

7. What is the difference between a continuous, flighting, and pulsing schedule?

Discussion Questions

1. You have just begun a new job as a media planner for a new automobile model from General Motors. The planning sequence will begin in four months, and your media director asks you what data and information you need from the media research department. What sources should you request? How will you use each of these sources in the planning function?

2. The marketing management of McDonald's restaurants has asked you to analyze the aperture opportunity for its breakfast entrees. What kind of analysis would you present to management? What recommendations could you make

that would expand the restaurant's nontraditional, as well as traditional, media opportunities.

3. Your client is a major distributor of movies. Its early media plan for magazines has been settled, and you are in negotiation when you learn that a top publishing company is about to launch a new magazine dedicated to movie fans and video collectors. Although the editorial direction is perfect, there is no valid way to predict how the magazine will be accepted by the public. Worse, there won't be solid research on readership for at least a year. The sales representative offers a low charter page rate if the advertiser

agrees to appear in each of the first year's 12 issues. To use it you will have to remove one of the established magazines from your list. Is the risk worthwhile? Should you bother the client with this information, considering that the plan is already set? The new magazine will also be available online. Should you take advantage of this opportunity? Make some recommendations to your client and explain your reasoning.

4. *Three-Minute Debate*: You have been hired as a media consultant for the Women's Health Services campaign outlined in this chapter as a sample media plan. You and

another member of your team disagree on whether the plan should be more focused on reach or frequency.

In your class, organize into small teams with each team taking the reach or frequency position. Set up a series of three-minute debates with each side having 1½ minutes to argue its position. Every team of debaters has to present new points not covered in the previous teams' presentations until there are no arguments left to present. Then the class votes as a group on the winning point of view.

Take-Home Team Projects

1. In performing an aperture analysis, consider the following products: video games (Nintendo, for instance), men's cologne (such as Axe), computer software (such as PhotoShop), and athletic shoes for aerobics (Reebok, for example). Pick two of these products, analyze their marketing situation, and give your intuitive answers to the following questions:

   a. How does aperture work for each of these products?

   b. Which media should be used to maximize and leverage the prospect's media aperture?

   c. Explain how the timing and duration of the advertising can improve the aperture opportunity.

2. Go to either http://www.google.com/adsense/ or http://searchmarketing.yahoo.com. Indicate how you would use the information provided by this site in developing your media plan for a new reality TV show. Focus on the Internet as a primary medium. Write a one- to two-page report.

Yahoo! Hands-On Case

Review the Yahoo! case in the Appendix.

1. What were the primary target audience insights that led to the development of the Yahoo! media plan? How were the media decisions matched to the target's lifestyle? How are the differences between the primary and secondary targets supported in the media plan?

2. The Yahoo! plan focused on 30 key markets. Your team wants to reconsider that decision. Write a one-page

proposal that outlines the rationale for using a more national campaign. How would such a decision affect the various choices in this media plan? In other words, in what ways would this plan be different if it were a truly national campaign?

HANDS-ON CASE

P&G Puts the Medium before the Message

To borrow and slightly modify an old ad slogan, when Proctor & Gamble speaks, people listen. At least, people in the advertising business do, because P&G is one of the biggest spenders on advertising and promotions in the world. You know the brands: Crest toothpaste, Tide detergent, Charmin toilet paper, Pringles potato chips, and dozens of others.

In early 2004, P&G was speaking. The company was saying that it intended to revolutionize the process by which advertising is developed. Its new approach, called *communications planning*, puts the medium before the message. The idea is to strategically select media first, then to develop creative messages that best take advantage of each channel. This approach is, of course, a reversal of the tried-and-true method of developing what you want to say before you decide where to say it.

To make P&G's idea a bit less abstract, imagine creating a campaign for a P&G brand the old way. The agency creatives working for Charmin, P&G's toilet tissue brand, would start with the message strategy; for example, they might decide that the Big Idea for a campaign should convey the softness and comfort of the tissue. After coming up with the creative strategy, they would then consider the best way to communicate it. Charmin's agency creatives might decide, for example, that consumers should see a demonstration of the brand's softness (Charmin's old commercials featured store manager "Mr. Whipple," who was constantly trying to stop consumers from impulsively squeezing rolls of Charmin). The creatives' decision to illustrate the Big Idea via a demonstration would strongly increase the likelihood that television will be an important medium for the campaign, as TV is effective for product demonstrations.

This message-then-medium approach seems logical, so why has P&G abandoned it? The answer can be found in changes occurring in the media world. For years large advertisers have been questioning the wisdom of spending massive amounts of money on network TV as viewership dwindles and media choices have expanded.

How might our example of the Charmin campaign develop under a communication-planning approach? The initial work is done by media specialists, who might conclude that television is a poor choice for reaching Charmin's desired audience, perhaps because of its expense or because some other medium better reaches the target audience. The specialists would then select media and other promotional channels that more efficiently and effectively reach the target. Once these choices were made, the campaign would be sent to the creatives, who would be asked to develop creative strategies best suited to the chosen media. The whole idea is to choose effective media before creating effective messages.

In 2004 the company announced it was choosing two media agencies, Starcom MediaVest (a subsidiary of the Publicis Groupe) and the Aegis Group and its subsidiary Carat, to direct more than $3.5 billion in media buys. Starcom and Aegis would help P&G decide how to allocate spending across various media, including both television and less traditional media.

At least three major campaigns launched by P&G in 2005 showed evidence of this shift in media strategy. Always and Tampax feminine products, Pampers' "Feel and Learn" campaign, and "Tide To Go" reflected the new approach to communication planning, combining Web marketing, public relations, and word of mouth to connect content with contact.

Has P&G revolutionized the way advertising is done? Perhaps it's still too early to know the effect of P&G's communication-planning approach on the advertising industry. One thing's for sure, though. The new approach has caught the attention of many. P&G was named *Media*'s 2005 Media Client of the Year, the first such award.

Consider This

1. Evaluate the marketplace realities that seem to be driving communication planning. Is P&G's approach a sensible response to those realities? Why or why not?
2. How will major players in the advertising world, including media companies, agencies, and advertisers, likely be affected if the communication-planning approach becomes dominant?
3. Explain how the communication-planning approach will affect traditional media planning and buying. How would you determine if this is an effective approach?

Sources: Jonah Bloom, "P&G's Public Commitment to Planning Marks a Watershed," *Advertising Age*, August 2, 2004; John Consoli, "Post Mortem: Big Six Got Their Way," *MediaWeek*, June 21, 2004, 4; Jack Feuer, "Who Will Follow P&G into Communications Planning?" *Adweek*, April 12, 2004; Jack Feuer, "Team Spirit Marks SMG's McCann," *Adweek*, August 9, 2004; Joe Mandese, "Media Client of the Year: Procter & Gamble," MediaPost Publications, January 2006, http://mediapost.com; Suzanne Vranica, "Publicis and Aegis Win Big with P&G," *Wall Street Journal* (Eastern Edition), July 15, 2004, B6; Paul Woolmington, "Unbundled Bundling," *Adweek*, July 26, 2004.

Principles: Creativity and Breakthrough Advertising

The new century brought unprecedented competition for the attention of customers. It also created a huge challenge for advertising creatives who had to create advertising messages that would not get lost in the media explosion. The problem is that the more commercials that appear, the less effective they are. Overwhelmed consumers often respond by avoiding advertisements.

The creatives' challenge is to create clutter-busting ads. The ads accomplish this by using creativity to get attention and by delivering messages that people want to watch, hear, and read. As clutter continues to increase, the creative stakes get higher.

How do agencies organize, motivate, and inspire their creative people to produce breakthrough advertising? To help you understand the environment and the mission of creative departments in advertising, Professor Sheila Sasser explains what her research has found out about how creativity works—the place, the people, and the processes they use to come up with breakthrough ideas.

The 3 Ps of Advertising Creativity: Place, Person, and Process

Advertising agencies represent the perfect "think tank" to inspire creativity research, given client creative mandates, culture, communication, integration, economics, mergers, and resource acquisitions. Ad agencies are hubs of creativity, buzzing with deadlines, excitement, new media, and new creative ideas.

Yet, there is a gap in research on advertising creativity; progress has not been adequate, especially considering the importance it plays in advertising practice. Advertising agencies spend a great deal of time and energy competing for creative awards, and many creative ad campaigns define our popular artistic culture.

Sheila Sasser, Professor of Advertising, IMC, and Marketing, Eastern Michigan University College of Business

The key themes and research streams for creativity, innovation, and integration may be grouped under the following three Ps:

1. *Place: Environmental models* focus on areas of the agency office or workspace setting that have an impact on creativity and the creative process. This includes controllable and uncontrollable variables present in the ad agency based on image, structure, culture, integration, communication, and other factors. Creative boutique agencies have playful offices to stimulate their creative team's ideas. Colorful, artistic, and evocative creative department spaces exist even within the most conservative agency.

2. *Person: Individual models* provide research insight into what makes individuals creative or what makes them tick. These insights focus on how creative people think and behave in different patterns to prompt their creative juices. Personality and motivation, also known as the *passion to create*, occupy key roles driving interactive effects to stimulate individual creativity. Everyone has some level of internal creativity.

3. *Process or output models* focus on the creative product or outcome, the actual campaign. Most researchers search for a true definition of creativity in this area, yet there is great confusion and a reluctance to say what is creative. Most people have their own definition of creativity, which is very subjective. Originality, appropriateness, and artistry affect creativity, as does the impact of audience experience. There are many opportunities to better understand creativity, integration, and innovation and how they may be defined and analyzed in advertising agencies.

Why advertising and creativity? Ad agencies are natural research incubators since the product is a creative advertising campaign developed within a service-driven setting. Advertising creatives must be innovative and use ideational thinking and processes in spite of many constraints and political pressures from clients. Many advertisers openly claim they actively seek out new advertising agencies to achieve stronger or better creative work.

The three Ps of creativity are alive and well in advertising agencies as they evolve with new media options, individual diversity, exciting new brands, and intense deadlines.

Chapter 12
The Creative Side and Message Strategy

Chapter 13
Copywriting

Chapter 14
Design and Production

Sources: Adapted from Sheila L. Sasser, *Creativity, Innovation, and Integration in the Global Advertising Agency Channel Relationships: Creativity in the Real World* (Ann Arbor, MI: Proquest UMI Publishing, 2006); Sheila Sasser and Scott Koslow, "3 Ps of Creativity CD," Research in Advertising Pre-Conference, American Academy of Advertising Proceedings, March 30, 2006, Reno, Nevada, pp. 1–4.

The Creative Side
and Message Strategy

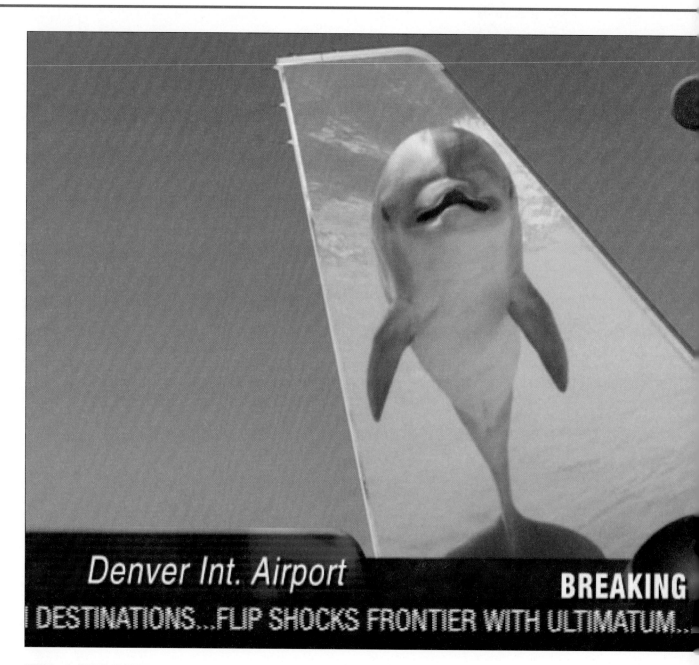

IT'S A WINNER

Awards:	Company:	Agency:	Campaign:
Silver Clio, Silver Effie, Gold Mobius ("Best of Show" Nomination)	Frontier Airlines	Grey Worldwide	"Send Flip to Mexico"

A Whole Different Animal

When low-cost carrier Frontier Airlines started up in 1994, it took off with animals emblazoned on the tails of its planes. Frontier's distinctive aircraft tails, all 60 of which depict a variety of wildlife images, have made Frontier's brand name synonymous with the airline's western heritage.

The animals on the tails of each plane are "so compelling that people line up at the airport with their noses pressed against the glass just to catch a glimpse of the plane," according to Diane Willmann, Frontier's director of advertising.

In 2003, Grey Worldwide brought the tail animals to life. The humorous ad campaign broke away from the buttoned-up approach used by most airlines and built an emotional connection between the brand and its customers. More importantly, the talking animals also helped Frontier accomplish its corporate goals.

A recent assignment asked the creative team to advertise Frontier's service to Mexico in a fun and attention-getting way. If you're Shawn Couzens and Gary Ennis, Grey's creative directors, you come up with a wild, wacky idea that's right on strategy. You create a campaign that lets one of Frontier's animals do your talking for you.

The outspoken spokesanimals have been carrying on debates on the tarmac since Couzens and Ennis launched the "whole different animal" campaign in 2003. But for this Mexico campaign they focused on Flip the Bottle-Nose Dolphin who becomes the star. He gripes that he only gets sent to cold Chicago and never to sunny, warm Mexico, which, of course, is a Frontier route. The other animals have always needled Flip about his route problems. Larry the Lynx, who sounds like he's seen too many Don Rickles routines, tells him in one spot to "chill out," saying, "Your blowhole is leaking."

Chapter Key Points

1. How do we explain the function and most important parts of a creative brief?

2. What are some key creative strategy approaches?

3. Can creative thinking be defined, and how does it lead to a Big Idea?

4. What characteristics do creative people have in common, and what is their typical creative process?

Couzens and Ennis used their creative wizardry to cast a spell on the Denver market. They conceptualized the commercials not as stand-alone spots but as 30-second episodes in an ongoing storyline. The campaign featured ads with Flip, fake news spots on Flip's demand that he be allowed to fly to Mexico, staged protests, podcasts, blogs, Flip's anthem on iTunes, and a Flip-mobile that was conspicuous around Denver to generate awareness. Fans caught the spirit and started demonstrating on Flip's behalf. The four-week campaign culminated in an ad that played during the Super Bowl announcing that Flip was finally going to Mexico.

Magic happened: Frontier became the top story on the evening news. Just after the Super Bowl, one newscaster announced that people in Denver were not rooting for the Steelers or Seahawks, but rather for the Dolphin—Flip the Dolphin to be precise. The results? Turn to the It's a Wrap section at the end of the chapter to see how Flip won the hearts of Frontier fans.

Sources: Shawn M. Couzens, Garry Ennis interview, February 21, 2007; http://youtube.com/watch?v=l-NC8UtLJCA (Frontier Airlines Documentary: How Flip Got to Mexico); http://www.frontierairlines.com; http://www.fliptomexico.com/visitor/ (all sites accessed February 25, 2007).

Effective advertising is both an art in its creative dimension and a science in its strategic dimension. This chapter explores how the two dimensions come together as creative strategy—the logic behind the message. We also examine how the strategy works with creative ideas to deliver on the message objectives. This includes a discussion of a planning tool called a *creative brief*, which provides direction for the execution of the Big Idea and for the evaluation of the creative strategy. We end with a discussion of the characteristics of creative people and the process of creative thinking, with the aim of showing how you can be a more creative thinker.

THE TWO SIDES OF ADVERTISING

Great advertising is both seen and enjoyed. That means it is successful because the right media delivers the right message to the right target audience. In Part III we concentrated on the media side of advertising, and in Part IV—the next three chapters—we'll concentrate on the creative side. It's important to keep in mind, however, that these are like two hands clapping: Both media and message need to work together to create effective advertising.

You saw the media side of the diagram in Figure 11.3 in Chapter 11. Now we'll complete the diagram, adding the creative activities that work in parallel with the media strategy.

The Art and Science of Advertising

Effective advertising is not only focused on media and messages, it's also a product of both logic and creativity. As Sasser explained in the Part IV Introduction, creative people "must be innovative and use ideational thinking and processes in spite of many constraints and political pressures from clients." The message plan, for example, is a rational analysis of a problem and what's needed to solve that problem. The advertisement itself translates the logic of the planning decisions into a creative idea that is original, attention getting, and memorable, such as the idea of talking animals as "spokes characters" for Frontier airlines. Planning a strategy is a form of problem solving and creative thinking, the mental tool used in figuring things out.

In their book *Creative Strategy in Advertising*, Jewler and Drewniany say that an ad "needs to contain a persuasive message that convinces people to take action." To be creative,

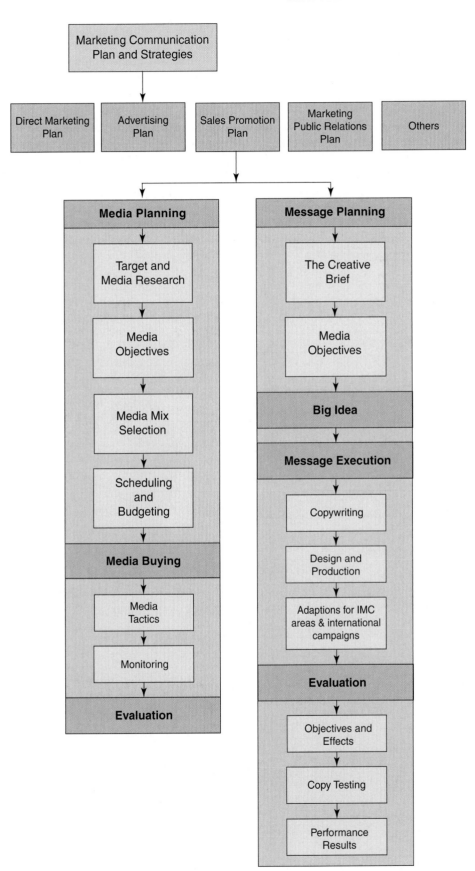

FIGURE 12.1
Media and Message Strategy
Work in Parallel

Principle

Effective advertising is a product of both science (persuasion) and art (creativity).

however, they suggest that an ad "must make a relevant connection with its audience and present a selling idea in an unexpected way."[1] This description of creative advertising supports the principle that advertising is both a science—in the way a message is designed to be persuasive—and an art—in presenting an original and unexpected idea.

The Role of Creativity in Advertising

All agencies have copywriters and art directors who are responsible for developing the creative concept and crafting the execution of the advertising idea. They often work in teams, are sometimes hired and fired as a team, and may work together successfully for several years. Broadcast producers can also be part of the team for television commercials. The creative director manages the creative process and plays an important role in focusing the strategy of ads and making sure the creative concept is strategically on target. Because advertising creativity is a product of teamwork, copywriters and art directors work together to generate concept, word, and picture ideas. Their writing or design specialties come into play in the execution of the idea.

FIGURE 12.2
The Creative Personality

■ ■ ■

Leonardo DaVinci, Albert Einstein, and Georgia O'Keefe excelled in different fields, but all three qualify as creative geniuses.

How Creative Are You?

Do you ever wonder whether you are creative? Does creativity have anything to do with your personality? Your personality is your own distinctive and consistent pattern of how you think, feel, and act. You may not be a creative genius but still you may have creative abilities that can be nurtured and developed. A current view of creativity suggests that the area of personality most related to creativity is how open you are to new experiences. According to researchers McCrae and Costa, how open you are to new experiences can be measured by survey questions that ask if you agree or disagree with the following statements:

1. "I enjoy working on 'mind-twister'-type puzzles."

2. "Once I find the right way to do something, I stick to it."

3. "As a child I rarely enjoyed games of make-believe."

4. "I enjoy concentrating on a fantasy or daydream and exploring all its possibilities, letting it grow and develop."

Source: Information and self-test provided by Sheri J. Broyles, University of North Texas. Also based on R. R. McCrae and P. T. Costa Jr., "Openness to Experience" in *Perspectives in Personality*, Vol. 1, ed. R. Hogan and W. H. Jones (Greenwich, CT: JAI Press, 1985): 145-172.

Creative ideas, such as the award-winning Frontier Different Kind of Animal campaign, aren't limited to advertising. Highly creative people range from Henry Ford, the father of the Model T, to Steven Jobs, the cofounder of Apple Computer, to Lucille Ball of *I Love Lucy* fame. They are idea people, creative problem solvers, and highly original thinkers. Creative people are found in business, science, engineering, advertising, and many other fields. But in advertising, creativity is both a job description and a goal. Figure 12.2 is a mini-test to evaluate your own creative potential.

Creativity is a special form of problem solving, and everyone is born with some talent in that area. Media planners, market researchers, copywriters, and art directors are all searching for new ideas. Ty Montague, Chief Creative Officer and Co-President at JWT New York, made this point in a speech at the Effie Awards presentation. He said that even though the word "creative" is attached to his job, that doesn't mean its use is limited to the creative side. Montague noted that "every client I have ever worked with desperately wants every facet of the development of a product and its marketing to be infused with as much creativity as possible."[2]

Montague points to Apple CEO Steve Jobs who, in his opinion, is "the current world heavyweight champion in the marketing world and who makes sure that the entire Apple brand stands for creativity." In other words, when Apple launched iPod, "the creativity begins with the way the product looks, works, and feels." And everything else is a creative challenge—packaging, distribution, PR, the events, the business model—it's all creative. "Creativity was baked into the iPod way before the agency got involved."

Realizing that creativity drives most every decision made in advertising, this chapter begins with a review of creative message strategy and concludes with an analysis of Big Ideas and explanations of how creative thinking works and how you can be a more creative

Practical Tips

Ten Creative Tips

By Tom Groth, *University of West Florida*

Tigers talk, Rice Krispies talk, and ducks pitch insurance. It's almost magic.

Who thinks of this stuff? Creatives! Art directors, copywriters, and of course, creative directors—innovative, artsy, eccentric, nonconformist, and soooo cool. How do they come up with fresh ideas seemingly out of thin air? In an ever-changing world, creativity is the fundamental skill for success.

Too bad there isn't a pull-down menu on your computer for creativity. Until then, try these 10 creative tips. Soon your classmates might be asking, "How did you come up with that?"

Creative Tip 1

Live big. Prepare. Be smart. Work hard. Don't be lazy. Laugh.

Often an ad is dull and boring simply because its creator is dull and boring. The only thing that you can put into an ad is yourself. Nothing more.
- Dig into life. Immerse yourself in art, music, pop culture, books, advertising, the Internet, your client, your product, and most of all, your prospect.
- Breakthrough creative is not in the research or on the Internet—it is within you.

Creative Tip 2

The right answer is the wrong answer.

Too often we are looking for "the correct answer," the safe answer, the answer the teacher or client expects. The expected solution is not a solution. It is often a rut, a cliché. Think dull, boring, been-there-done-that.

Education = apple
$5 \times 5 = 25$
Sky = blue
Insurance = a duck!

"I never thought of it that way!"
- Creativity forgets the way things are supposed to be!

Creative Tip 3

What do you want to say?

Discover the core message about your brand before you ever pick up a pencil. Have a clear strategy.
- You cannot communicate a message if you don't know what the message is.

Creative Tip 4

Warning! Do not use a computer to create.

A computer immediately thrusts you into your left brain.

Which font?
Which point size?
Which program?
Where do I get a picture of a giraffe smiling?

• Always carry a notepad. Ideas may come in the shower, in the middle of the night, on a date, or at a stoplight. Oh, that breakthrough concept can vanish in a heartbeat. Get it down fast.

Creative Tip 5

Use the power of play.

You remember how to play, don't you?
　　Try free play. Recess. No rules, no coach—shut down your adult, left brain, and all the tired baggage that comes with it. Start with lots and lots and lots of thumbnails. All ideas are valid now. Don't evaluate yet. Wait. Pick your winner another day.

Creative Tip 6

Play the *what if* game.

What if . . . a pink bunny sold batteries?
Pretend . . . a green giant raised peas!
Suppose . . . a clown with red hair pitched burgers.
Imagine . . .

• Give yourself permission to suspend reality! Look beyond the facts to what might be. Imagine the possibilities!

Creative Tip 7

Don't play scared.

Fear says, "There already exists one answer and you'd better find it."
　　Creativity says, "The world is not done. There are more pages possible!"
• Fear kills creativity. Fear of ridicule. Fear of being a fool. Fear of being fired. Fear it won't be perfect.
• Perfection kills ideas. Take a risk. Be brave. Be braver.

Creative Tip 8

Think of it as. . .

• Use associations. This is how your brain works and how great ads work too.
　A pet is a . . . *date magnet.*
　A crayon is a . . . *power tool.*
　Cough syrup is . . . *silent night.*
• Just link two previously unrelated ideas. This breaks the boredom barrier and dramatizes your brand's benefit!

Creative Tip 9

Set-up & punch line.

Set-Up: Two antennas meet on a roof, fall in love, and get married.
Punch line: The ceremony wasn't much, but the reception was brilliant.
• Bad joke; but a review of any awards annual will reveal this approach is the basis of many killer ads! Here's how it works.

　Step 1　The *set-up* creates a question through curiosity.
　　　　　(It shows or says something that disrupts expectation.)

　Step 2　The *punch line* answers the question and reveals the core brand message.
• Set-Up: *By the end of this sentence you'll be thinking of a turkey with a green beak.*

Creative Tip 10

Have fun!

People like to work with people who have a sense of humor. People buy brands from ads they like. A sense of humor wins accounts, makes friends, sells brands, and turns good creative into great creative.

Thomas Groth is a professor of advertising in the Department of Communication Arts at the University of West Florida, Pensacola, and head of its advertising program since 1988.

MESSAGE PLANNING

The art and science of advertising come together in the phrase *creative strategy*. An advertising idea must be both *creative* (original, different, novel, unexpected) and *strategic* (right for the product and target; meets the advertising objectives). It's not just about coming up with a novel idea that no one has thought of before, but rather advertising creativity is about coming up with an idea that solves a communication problem in an original way.

　　The Road Crew social marketing campaign is an example of creative problem solving for a good cause. We'll be using the Road Crew campaign throughout this chapter to illustrate different aspects of message strategy. The problem was to get young men in Wisconsin small towns who drink and drive to use a ride service. The objective was to reduce the incidence of alcohol-related car crashes by 5 percent. The breakthrough creative concept was to use the idea of a road crew for a group of young partiers who needed a ride on their big night out.

People who create advertisements also make a distinction between creative strategy and creative executions. **Creative strategy**, or **message strategy**, is *what* the advertisement says—**execution** is *how* it is said. This chapter focuses on creative strategy, and the two chapters that follow explore the writing, design, and production of advertising executions.

The Creative Brief

The creative strategy and the key execution details are spelled out in a document called a **creative brief** (or *creative platform*, *worksheet*, or *blueprint*). The brief is the document prepared by the account planner to summarize the basic marketing and advertising strategy. It gives direction to creative team members as they search for a creative concept. The following outline summarizes the key points in a typical brief:

- *Problem* that can be solved by communication
- *Target audience* and key *insights* into their attitudes and behavior
- *Brand position* and other branding decisions, such as *personality* and *image*
- *Communication objectives* that specify the desired response to the message by the target audience
- *Proposition* or *selling idea* that will motivate the target to respond
- *Media considerations* about where and when the message should be delivered
- *Creative direction* that provides suggestions on how to stimulate the desired consumer response. These aren't creative ideas but may touch on such execution or stylistic direction as the ad's **tone of voice**.

Different agencies use different formats, but most combine these basic advertising strategy decisions. The briefs typically are in outline form, to be filled in by account planners and given to the creative team. The point is that advertising planning—even planning for the creative side—involves a structured, logical approach to analysis, which may leave out the intuitive, emotional message effects, as the Matter of Principle box illustrates. The Crispin Porter + Bogusky agency, for example, designs its advertising by looking for what it calls "tension points." Its brief asks planners to consider: "What is the psychological, social, categorical, or cultural tension associated with this idea?"

The Road Crew campaign planning began with a creative brief. The ultimate goal was to encourage guys who like to party and visit bars to rely on a limousine ride service rather than trying to drive home themselves. Here is the creative brief that shows the thinking behind the campaign:

- *Why are we advertising at all?* To create awareness for an evening alternative ride service.
- *What is the advertising trying to do?* Make the new ride service appealing to men in order to reduce the number of alcohol-related crashes.
- *What are their current attitudes and perceptions?* "My car is here right now. Why wait? There are few options available anyway. I want to keep the fun going all night long."
- *What is the main promise we need to communicate?* It's more fun when you don't have to worry about driving.
- *What is the key moment to which we tie this advertising?* "Bam! The fun stops when I need to think about getting to the next bar or getting home."
- *What tone of voice should we use?* The brand character is rugged, cool, and genuine. We need to be a "straight shooter" buddy on the barstool next to the target. They do not want to be preached to or told what to do. We need to communicate in a language to which they can relate. (Words like "program" may cause our audience to "tune out.")

A MATTER OF PRINCIPLE

Do Briefs Change with the Times—and with the Agency?

By Lisa Duke, *Associate Professor, University of Florida*

Creative brief formats are often treated as proprietary by many influential agencies that position their version as a point of differentiation among agencies pitching new business. But how different are creative briefs from agency to agency? And how are changes in the industry reflected in the briefing documents of major advertising agencies?

In a content analysis of 162 creative briefs from top U.S. agencies, I worked with a team of researchers that included John Sutherland and Ziad Ghanimi from the University of Florida and Avery Abernethy from Auburn University. We found that information in briefs is substantially the same across agencies.

However, some information traditionally thought to be important did not appear as often as expected. The most frequently occurring types of information were a *general description of the target audience*, designation of the *main selling point*, *support points for the main message*, and *mandatories*. Less frequently appearing items (those that appeared in less than half the sample) included *marketing and communication objectives*, *marketing situation/background*, *marketing strategy*, and specific information, including *psychographics*, about the target group.

Because so few products offer true points of difference, Cooper has compared the importance of today's ESP (emotional selling proposition) with the USP (unique selling proposition) that has been the holy grail of adver-

tising message makers. Also, because larger agencies are more likely to employ account planners, we were curious to find out if "soft" content, such as consumer insights, emotional touch points, and creative inspiration, is as prevalent in briefs as more factual, informational content.

The results provided little evidence that major agencies' briefs are employing account planning terminology and concepts, such as *consumer and/or market insights*. Less than one-third of the briefs contained headings related to this type of information. Further, qualitative input such as *emotional response that the brand evokes, creative inspiration,* and *emotional state objectives* (how the consumer should feel) also occurred infrequently.

In other words, many agencies are still using a traditional information-processing approach to planning advertising. Unfortunately, that focus may be driven by the logical nature of these briefs. As agencies struggle to keep up with changes in objectives that specify interaction, engagement, and brand relationships, they will probably need to broaden the scope of their creative briefs.

Sources: Adapted from Lisa Duke, John Sutherland, Avery Abernethy, and Ziad Ghanimi, "How Brief? A Content Analysis of Creative Briefs from 153 Top US Agencies," 2007 American Academy of Advertising Conference, Burlington, Vermont; Alan Cooper, How to Plan Advertising, London/New York: Continuum, 2007.

Message Objectives

In planning creative strategies, what do you want the message to accomplish? What message objectives would you specify for the Road Crew campaign in order to meet the goal of reducing alcohol-related crashes by 5 percent?

Some experts say advertising's role is to create awareness or announce something; others say it is to inform or persuade.[3] Hard-nosed businesspeople say the only real objective is to create sales. In some cases, the objective is to build or change demand for a brand. In Chapters 4 and 7, we introduced the concept of the Facets Model of Effects (review Figure 4.3). Here is a review of some common advertising objectives that relate to the most critical facets of effectiveness:

- See/hear—create attention, awareness, interest, recognition
- Feel—touch emotions and create feelings
- Think/learn—deliver information, aid understanding, create recall
- Believe—change attitudes, create conviction and preference
- Connect—establish brand identity and associations, transform a product into a brand with distinctive personality and image
- Act—stimulate trial, purchase, repurchase, or some other form of action

Of course, these effects are also driven by the demands of the marketing situation, target audience insights, and the needs of the brand. We mentioned that the primary goal of the Road Crew campaign was to reduce the number of alcohol-related crashes. Other objectives involved creating awareness of the ride service program and positive attitudes toward it, as well as establishing a cost-efficient level of rides in the first year of operations, which involved fund-raising, the solicitation of volunteers, and other community support. The heart of the problem uncovered by the Road Crew research, however, was a gap between *awareness* (don't drink & drive), *attitudes* (risky, scary, potentially dangerous), and *behavior* (get someone else to drive). The campaign was designed to address this gap and encourage the target audience's behavior to change in accordance with their attitudes and awareness.

Targeting

The target decision is particularly important in planning a message strategy. For example, we mentioned in the media chapters that advertisers have a difficult time reaching young men. New cable TV programs, as well as Web and cell phone opportunities, are developing to deliver this critical demographic, but what should the message say in these new media formats? It may sound like a cliché, but video-on-demand channel RipeTV has a simple formula for success that carries over to the advertising—lots of scantily clad women and frisky entertainment involving sports, music, and gross comedy.[4]

The target audience for the Wisconsin Road Crew campaign was identified as 21- to 34-year-old single men with a high school education and employed in blue-collar jobs. They were the primary target for the ride service because research found that this group is responsible for the most alcohol-related crashes, they kill more people than any other age group, and they themselves are most likely to die in an alcohol-related crash.

What moves this group? Research found that many of these guys tended to worry about driving home drunk as the end of the evening approached and this worry took the edge off an otherwise delightful end of the evening. So the ride service made their evening more fun because it reduced their worry.

Branding

The demands of the brand are also important considerations. Brand positions and brand images are created through message strategies and brought to life through advertising executions. Finding the right position is difficult enough, but figuring out how to communicate that position in an attention-getting message that still conveys the idea with some level of consistency across multiple executions and various media is even more difficult. Frontier's Flip campaign, which is part of the long-running A Whole Different Animal campaign, was carefully planned to deliver the brand personality.

Advertising and other forms of marketing communication are critical to creating what brand guru Kevin Keller calls *brand salience*[5]—that is, the brand is visible and has a presence in the marketplace, consumers are aware of it, and the brand is important to its target market. For example, Hewlett-Packard, a leader in the computer industry, has always been a follower in brand image behind the more creative Apple. To drop its stodgy image and imbue the brand with a sense of cool, a Web site (http://www.fingerskilz.tv) uses what appears to be fingers doing soccer tricks on a desk with a wadded-up paper ball. Later revealed to be an HP "viral" ad, the site attracted more than 180,000 visitors and lit up discussions on blogs and chat rooms.[6]

Burger King takes on market leader McDonald's by being cool because of the power of its icon with an attitude—the Burger King king. Sometimes called creepy, the King has made BK hipper and kept it on "the cutting edge of pop culture."[7] The mute BK King is only one of a group of brand icons that lend personality, emotion, and stories to their brands. The Geico Gecko is another one of these brand-savvy characters that are making the earnest Mr. Clean, Pillsbury Doughboy, and Jolly Green Giant look like dinosaurs. The difference is that these new-age characters are self-aware and even a little self-mocking, and they speak to the ad resistance of today's consumers with irony and inner conflict.[8]

Advertising agency Grey NYC created a playful brand personality for Frontier Airlines with its campaign to send Flip the dolphin to a warm climate.

GREYnyc

Fade in on several Frontier planes chilling out on the tarmac at Denver Int. Airport.

SFX: Airport noise. Planes landing and taking off...

Larry:
So Flip, you get that Florida gig?

Cut to a close up of Flip. He talks...

Flip:
Nope. Chicago again. We got a zillion flights to Florida and where do they send me? The Windy City! I'm a dolphin. Dolphins belong in Florida.

They continue to banter.

Larry:
Chill out—your blowhole's leaking.

PAUSE.

LARRY:
So who is going to Florida?

Cut to a 3rd plane taxing past them. It's Grizwald, rattling off a list.

Grizwald wiggles his ass as he says "thong."

Griz:
Sunscreen, check. Beachball, check. Thong, check.

In 2003, years before "Flip to Mexico," the above commercial hit the airwaves. Since then, Flip's storyline continued to grow as he was consistently denied travel to warm, tropical climates. In Nov. '05, when Frontier increased service to Mexico, Flip thought he'd finally get his chance. But instead, they gave the routes to a new character—Hector the Mexican Otter. Flip had finally had enough . . . and the "Flip to Mexico" campaign was born.

GREYnyc

Flip is obviously annoyed.

Dolphin:
Did he say thong? Please tell me he didn't say thong.

Larry is equally disgusted.

Larry:
That'll clear the beach.

Cut to graphic map treatment over clouds...

Super onto the frame.

MUSICAL STING UNDER...

SFX: Whoosh!

SUPER:
Over 90 nonstops daily from DIA.

Cut to tagline and logo

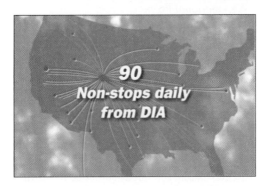

SFX: Whoosh!

SUPER:
A Whole Different Animal.

FRONTIER

MESSAGE STRATEGIES

Once you have an objective or set of objectives to guide the advertising message, how do you go about translating those goals into strategies? Remember, there is no one right way to do advertising—in most cases there are a number of ways to achieve a communication objective. Planners search for the best creative strategy—the approach that makes the most sense to use given the brand's marketing situation and the target audience's needs and interests. Also, how do you talk about the various strategic approaches you might consider? In other words, how do you put strategy into words?

Creative Strategy Approaches

First let's review some simple ways to express a strategic approach—head or heart and hard or soft sell. Then we'll look at some more complex models that get a little deeper into the complexities of message strategy.

Head and Heart   Two basic approaches are sometimes referred to as *head or heart strategies*. In the Facets Model the cognitive objectives generally speak to the head, and the affective objectives on the right are more likely to speak to the heart. For example, in the strategy statement for Volkswagen's long-running "Drivers Wanted" campaign, the agency identified both rational and emotional dimensions to the VW brand:

> *VW's rational brand essence:*
> *"The only brand offering the benefits and 'feeling' of German engineering within reach."*

> *VW's emotional brand essence:*
> • Exciting
> • Different driving feeling
> • Different way of living
> • More feeling, fun, alive, connected

Another way to refer to head and heart strategies are hard- and soft-sell approaches. A **hard sell** is an informational message that is designed to touch the mind and create a response based on logic. The assumption is that the target audience wants information and will make a rational product decision. A **soft sell** uses emotional appeals or images to create a response based on attitudes, moods, and feelings. The assumption with soft-sell strategies is that the target audience has little interest in an information search and will respond more favorably to a message that touches their emotions or presents an attractive brand image. A soft-sell strategy can be used for hard products. NAPA auto parts ran an emotional ad that showed a dog sitting at a railroad crossing, forcing a truck to brake hard to avoid hitting him as a train bears down on the scene. The slogan puts the heart-stopping visual story into perspective: "NAPA because there are no unimportant parts."

Systems of Strategies   Head or heart, hard sell or soft sell—these terms all refer to some basic ideas about message strategy. But these are simple concepts, and advertising creative strategy is more complex. We'll look at two of approaches that address other aspects of advertising strategy—Frazer's Six Creative Strategies and Taylor's Strategy Wheel.

University of Washington Professor Charles Frazer proposed a set of six creative strategies that address various types of advertising situations.[9] Although not comprehensive, these terms are useful to identify some common approaches to advertising strategy. The strategies are described as follows:

Table 12.1 Frazer's Six Creative Strategies

Strategy	Description	Uses
Preemptive	Uses a common attribute or benefit, but brand gets there first—forces competition into me-too positions.	Used for categories with little differentiation or new product categories.
Unique Selling Proposition	Uses a distinct difference in attributes that creates a meaningful consumer benefit.	Used for categories with high levels of technological improvement and innovations.
Brand Image	Uses a claim of superiority or distinction based on extrinsic factors such as psychological differences in the minds of consumers.	Used with homogeneous, low-tech goods with little differentiation.
Positioning	Establishes a place in the consumer's mind relative to the competition.	Used by new entries or small brands that want to challenge the market leader.
Resonance	Uses situations, lifestyles, and emotions with which the target audience can identify.	Used in highly competitive, undifferentiated product categories.
Affective/ Anomalous	Uses an emotional, sometimes even ambiguous message, to break through indifference.	Used where competitors are playing it straight and informative.

Principle
To stand out from the competition, do something different.

Professor Ron Taylor of the University of Tennessee developed a model that divides strategies into the Transmission view, which is similar to the more rational "head" strategies, and the Ritual view, which is similar to the more feeling-based "heart" strategies. He then divides each into three segments: Rational, Acute Need, and Routine on the Transmission side; and Ego, Social, and Sensory on the Ritual side. Then he identifies the appropriate message objective for each segment relative to typical product categories. Figure 12.3 depicts his model.

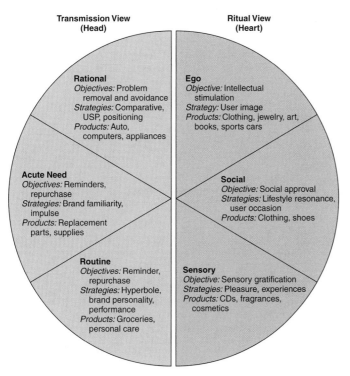

FIGURE 12.3
Taylor's Six-Segment Strategy Wheel
The wheel divides message strategy into two general views—the Transmission view and the Ritual view. These are roughly equivalent to our "head" and "heart" strategies.

Source: Adapted from Ronald Taylor, "A Six-Segment Message Strategy Wheel," *Journal of Advertising Research,* November-December 1997, 7–17.

This ad for the Panasonic Toughbook dramatizes the problems that might assault a computer while it is being used.

Strategic Formats and Formulas

Even though advertising is a search for a new and novel way to express some basic truth, there are also some tried and true approaches that have worked over the years. We'll talk about these options from a literary viewpoint and from a sales viewpoint, and end this discussion with a list of common formulas used to package a storyline.

Lectures and Dramas Most advertising messages use a combination of two basic literary techniques to reach the head or the heart of the consumer: lectures and dramas.[10] A lecture is a serious instruction given verbally. The speaker presents evidence (broadly speaking) and uses a technique such as an argument to persuade the audience. The advantages of lectures are many: they are relatively inexpensive to produce and are compact and efficient. A lecture can deliver a dozen selling points in seconds, get right to the point, and make the point explicitly. In advertising we use the phrase *talking head* to refer to an announcer who delivers a lecture about a product. This can also be a celebrity spokesperson or an authority figure, such as a doctor or scientist.

Drama, however, relies on the viewer to make inferences. Through dramas, advertisers tell stories about their products; the characters speak to each other, not to the audience. Like fairy tales, movies, novels, parables, and myths, advertising dramas are essentially stories about how the world works. They can be funny as well as serious. Viewers learn from these commercial dramas by inferring lessons from them and by applying those lessons to their everyday lives, as the Panasonic ad demonstrates. The Leo Burnett agency built a creative philosophy around "Inherent Drama," which describes the storyline built into the agency's archetypal brand characters, such as the Marlboro Man, Charlie the Tuna, the Jolly Green Giant, and Tony the Tiger.

Selling Strategies Advertising has developed a number of strategic approaches that speak to the head with a sales message. A **selling premise** states the logic behind the sales offer. A premise is a proposition on which an argument is based or a conclusion is drawn. This type of message strategy is usually a rational approach, an appeal to the head.

The psychological appeal of the product to the consumer is also used to describe a message strategy that appeals to the heart. An **appeal** connects with some emotion that makes the product particularly attractive or interesting, such as security, esteem, fear, sex, and sensory pleasure. Although emotion is at the base of most appeals, in some situations, appeals can also be logical, such as saving money for retirement. Appeals generally pinpoint the anticipated response of the audience to the product and the message. For example, if the price is emphasized in the ad, then the appeal is value, economy, or savings. If the product saves time or effort, then the appeal is convenience. Advertisers use a status appeal to establish something as a high-quality, expensive product. Appetite appeal using mouth-watering visuals is used in food advertising, such as the Quaker trail mix bar ad.

A basic selling premise, however, is designed to sell a product based on tested principles, or selling premises, that, as Edd Applegate reminds us in his advertising writing book, *Strategic Copywriting*, have been shown to work time after time.[11] To have a practical effect on customers, managers must identify the product's **features** (also called **attributes**), in terms of those that are most important to the target audience. Another type of selling premise is a **claim**, which is a product-focused strategy that is based on a prediction about how the product will perform. Health claims on food products like oatmeal, for example, suggest that the food will be good for you.

A rational, prospect-centered selling premise identifies a reason that might appeal to potential customers and motivate them to respond. Here is a summary of these rational customer-focused selling premises.

Quaker Chewy Trail Mix Bars
Lots of flavors, each packing a whole mouthful of wholesome.

The appetite appeal of the trail mix bar is dramatized by an extremely close-up visual that shows all the nuts and raisins larger than life.

- *Benefit.* The **benefit** emphasizes what the product can do for the user by translating the product feature or attribute into something that benefits the consumer. For example, a GM electric car ad focuses on the product feature (the car doesn't use gas) and translates it into a benefit: lack of noise (no pistons, valves, exhaust).
- *Promise.* A **promise** is a benefit statement that looks to the future and predicts that something good will happen if you use the product. For example, Dial soap has promised for decades that if you use Dial, you will feel more confident.
- *Reason why.* This type of benefit statement emphasizes the **reason why** you should buy something, although the reason sometimes is implied or assumed. The word "because" is the key to a reason-why statement. For example, an Amtrak ad tells you that train travel is more comfortable than flying because Amtrak is a more civilized, less dehumanizing way to travel.
- *Unique selling proposition (USP).* A **USP** is a benefit statement that is both unique to the product and important to the user. The USP is a promise that consumers will get this unique benefit by using this product only. For example, an ad for a camera states, "This camera is the only one that lets you zoom in and out automatically to follow the action."

Most selling premises demand facts, proof, or explanations to support the sales message. Proof statements that give the rationale, reasoning, and research behind the claim are used to substantiate it. The proof or substantiation needed to make a claim believable is called **support**. In some cases this calls for research findings. With claims, and particularly with comparisons, the proof is subject to challenge by the competitor as well as industry review boards. A judge, for example, blocked commercials for DirectTV that claimed its high-definition service was better than the service provided by Time Warner Cable.[12]

Message Formulas   In addition to the basic categories of selling premises, some common message formats or **formulas** emphasize different types of effects. The planner uses these terms as a way to give direction to the creative team and to shape the executions. Here are some common formats:

- *Straightforward.* A **straightforward** factual or informational message conveys information without any gimmicks, emotions, or special effects. For example, in an ad for www.women.com, the Web site advertises that "It's where today's educated, affluent women are finding in-depth coverage on issues they care about" and that more than 2 million women visit each month.

The Kellogg's Smart Start ad uses 28 cereal bowls to demonstrate the amount that Special K and Smart Start equal in weight loss. Jerry Seinfeld appeared in a four-minute humorous online commercial with an animated Superman where the two sidekicks discover the benefits of using an American Express card. Buick used a teaser on the Regal's Web site to build curiosity about the new car model.

- *Demonstration.* A **demonstration** focuses on how to use the product or what it can do for you. For example, an ad for Kellogg's Special K and Smart Start uses cereal bowls to demonstrate how a daily regimen of healthy cereal would help a dieter lose six pounds.
- *Comparison.* A **comparison** contrasts two or more products to show the superiority of the advertiser's brand. The comparison can be direct, with competitors mentioned, or indirect, with just a reference to "other leading brands." In comparison, as in demonstration, seeing is believing, so conviction is the objective. When people see two products being compared, they are more likely to believe that one is better than the other.
- *Problem solution/problem avoidance.* In a **problem solution** format, also known as **product-as-hero**, the message begins with a problem and then showcases the product as the solution. A variation is the **problem avoidance** message format, in which the product helps avoid a problem.
- *Humor.* Advertisers use **humor** as a creative strategy (using a comedian such as Jerry Seinfeld as the star, for example) because it grabs attention and they hope people will transfer the warm feelings of being entertained to the product.
- *Slice of life.* The **slice-of-life** format is an elaborate version of a problem solution staged in the form of a drama in which "typical people" talk about a common problem and resolve it.
- *Spokesperson.* In the **spokesperson** (**spokes character**, **brand icon**) or **endorser** format, the ad uses celebrities we like (Tiger Woods), created characters (the Aflac

duck, the Geico Caveman), experts we respect (the Maytag repairman, doctors), or someone "just like us" whose advice we might seek out to speak on behalf of the product to build credibility.

- *Teasers.* **Teasers** are mystery ads that don't identify the product or don't deliver enough information to make sense, but they are designed to arouse curiosity. These are often used to launch a new product. The ads run for a while without the product identification and then when curiosity is sufficiently aroused, usually at the point when the product is officially launched, a concluding ad runs with the product identification.

Matching Messages to Objectives

We have talked about message planning, including objectives, and then we moved to a discussion of various types of message strategies. Now, let's try to bring those two together. What types of messages deliver which objectives? When you analyze the message situation, you should be asking yourself what type of strategy is most likely to achieve the objectives? What approach can best overcome a weakness or solve a problem? If it's a credibility problem, for example, you might want to think about a testimonial, a demonstration of proof, a reason why, or even a press release with the built-in believability of a news story.

- *Messages that get attention.* To be effective, an advertisement needs to get exposure through the media buy and get attention through the message. Getting consumers' attention requires stopping power. Creative advertising breaks through the old patterns of seeing and saying things—the unexpectedness of the new idea (the Geico Caveman) creates stopping power. Ads that stop the scanning and break through the clutter can also be high in personal relevance. Intrusiveness is particularly important in cluttered markets. Many clutter-busting ads are intrusive and use loud, bold effects to attract viewer attention—they work by shouting. Others use engaging, captivating ideas, curiosity, or mesmerizing visuals.

> **Principle**
> To get attention, an ad has must have stopping power, which comes from originality, relevance, or intrusiveness—an idea that is novel or surprising.

- *Messages that create interest.* Getting attention reflects the stopping power of an advertisement; keeping attention reflects the ad's pulling power. An interesting thought keeps readers' or viewers' attention and pulls them through to the end of the message. One way to intensify interest is through curiosity, such as using a teaser campaign where the message unfolds over time. Ads that open with questions or dubious or ambiguous statements are designed to create curiosity.
- *Messages that resonate.* Ads that amplify the emotional impact of a message by engaging a personal connection with a brand are said to resonate with the target audience. The women's campaign for Nike, for example, does a good job of speaking to women in a way that addresses their concerns about personal achievement, rather than the competitive theme of the more traditional men's campaign. If a woman identifies with this message, then it is said to resonate for her.
- *Messages that create believability.* Advertising sometimes uses a credibility strategy to intensify the believability of a message. Using data to support or prove a claim is critical. The use of brand characters such as Colonel Sanders for KFC, who was a real person and the creator of the famous chicken recipe ("11 herbs and spices"), is designed to give consumers *a reason to believe* in a brand by cementing conviction.
- *Messages that are remembered.* Not only does advertising have to *stop* (get attention) and *pull* (create interest), it also has to *stick* (in memory), which is another important part of the perceptual process. Repetition is used both in media and message strategy to ensure memorability. Jingles are valuable memorability devices because the music allows the advertiser to repeat a phrase or product name without boring the audience. Esther Thorson says asking the consumer to make a moral or value judgment also anchors the copy point in memory, such as relating the point to a good cause.[13]

> **Principle**
> Not only does advertising have to *stop* (get attention) and *pull* (create interest), it also has to *stick* (in memory).

Clever phrases are useful not only because they catch attention, but also because they can be repeated to intensify memorability. Advertisements use **slogans** for brands and campaigns, such as "Get Met. It Pays" (MetLife) or Nike's slogan, "Just Do It." **Taglines** are used at the end of an ad to summarize the point of the ad's message in a highly memorable

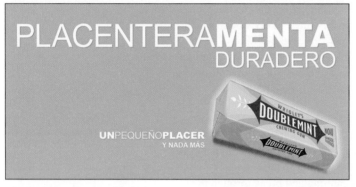

SHOWCASE The familiar Doublemint green anchors the brand's identity even when the campaign is aimed at Hispanics and the ads are written en Español. These ads were contributed by Sonia Montes, New Business Director/Sr. Project Manager at Catmandu Branded Entertainment and a graduate of Michigan State University's advertising program. She was nominated by Professor Carrie La Ferle.

way, such as "Nothing outlasts the Energizer. It keeps going and going and going." In addition to verbal memory devices, many print and interactive ads and most television commercials feature a *key visual*. This visual is a vivid image that the advertiser hopes will linger in the viewer's mind.

Color can be a memory cue. Wrigley's Doublemint gum uses green and Juicy Fruit uses yellow. Shape is another memory cue. The Absolut Vodka campaign has used a thousand different visual images to reinforce the shape of the product's bottle to the point that the bottle shape is recognizable even without a label.

- *Messages that touch emotions.* Emotional appeals create feeling-based responses such as love, fear, anxiety, envy, sexual attraction, happiness and joy, sorrow, safety and security, pride, pleasure, embarrassment, and nostalgia. *Appetite appeal* uses mouth-watering food shots to elicit feelings of hunger and craving, like the photo in the Quaker Trail Mix Bar print ad. Hallmark has used an emotional appeal for years in its advertising to tie the sentiment in greeting cards with the moving experiences in our lives.

Home Depot targeted women with uplifting tales of what women customers can do to help themselves. The customers even tear up as they speak and hug the employees who helped them in a style reminiscent of reality TV.[14] A more general emotional goal is to deliver a message that people like in order to create liking for the brand.

- *Messages that inform.* Companies often use news announcements to provide information about new products, to tout reformulated products, or even to let

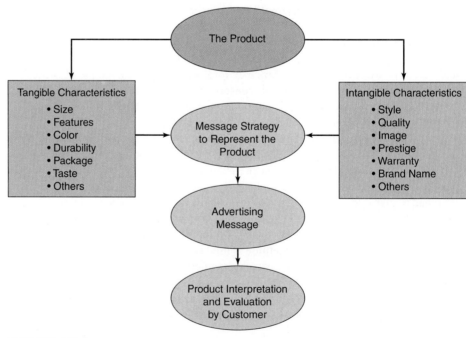

FIGURE 12.4

Tangible and Intangible Features

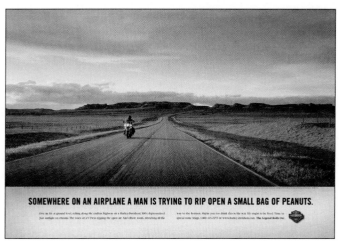

SOMEWHERE ON AN AIRPLANE A MAN IS TRYING TO RIP OPEN A SMALL BAG OF PEANUTS.

The Sunkist ad compares its oranges to candy but in the comparison it identifies tangible product characteristics. The Harley-Davidson ad uses intangibles—it associates the Harley brand image with the personality of people who ride on the edge of life.

consumers know about new uses for old products. The news angle, which is usually delivered by publicity stories, is information-focused. Sometimes this means a long-copy approach in print or an infomercial in television. Informative ads that focus on features and attributes seek to create understanding about a product's advantages. Attributes can be both tangible and intangible (see Figure 12.4). The ads for Sunkist oranges and Harley-Davidson focus on tangible and intangible features. Comparison ads are used to show a product's point of difference,

- *Messages that teach.* People learn through instruction so some advertisements are designed to teach, such as demonstrations that show how something works or how to solve a problem. Educational messages are sometimes designed to explain something, such as why it is important to brush your teeth or get involved in local politics. Learning also is strengthened through repetition, as in the famous Pavlovian experiment where the dog learned to associate food with the sound of a bell. That's why repetition is such an important media objective.

- *Messages that persuade.* Persuasive advertising is designed to affect attitudes and create belief. Strategies that are particularly good are *testimonials* and messages that generate word of mouth about the product. Endorsements by celebrities (the Seinfeld commercial) or experts (the HP "Machine Shop" ad) are used to intensify conviction. Selling premises that focus on how the product will benefit the consumer, state a reason why, or explain a unique selling proposition (USPs) are persuasive particularly as they provide proof or support. Torture tests, comparisons, and before-and-after demonstrations also are used to prove the truth of a claim. Conviction is often built on strong, rational arguments that use such techniques as test results, before-and-after visuals, testimonials by users and experts, and demonstrations to prove something.

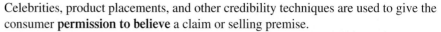

Principle
When advertising gives consumers permission to believe in a product, it establishes the platform for conviction.

Celebrities, product placements, and other credibility techniques are used to give the consumer **permission to believe** a claim or selling premise.

• *Messages that create brand associations.* The transformative power of branding, where the brand takes on a distinctive character and meaning, is one of advertising's most important functions. **Image advertising** is used to create a representation of a brand, an image in a consumer's mind. Advertising's role is to provide the cues that make these meanings and experiences come together in a coherent brand image. The Sunkist ad associated oranges with candy to convey the message of sweetness.

An association message strategy delivers information and feelings symbolically by connecting a brand with a certain type of person or lifestyle. This link is often created through visuals. A consumer gets a feeling about the product—who uses it and how and where they use it— through these symbolic cues. Some advertising strategies want you to identify with the user of the product or see yourself in that situation. Fashion and cosmetic products invite you to project yourself into the ad and make a fashion statement when you wear or use the product.

The idea that some moments, such as eating cupcakes and cookies, require a glass of milk is the creative concept behind the award-winning "Got Milk?" campaign. The creative concept is expressed both in words and pictures in this ad.

• *Messages that drive action.* Even harder to accomplish than conviction is a change in behavior. It often happens that people believe one thing and do another. The Road Crew campaign was designed to overcome a gap between attitudes and behavior. Sometimes an advertising message can drive people to act by offering something free or at a discounted sales price. Sales promotion, for example, works in tandem with advertising to stimulate immediate action using sampling, coupons, and free gifts as incentives for action.

Most ads end with a signature of some kind that serves to identify the company or brand, but it also serves as a **call to action** and gives direction to the consumer about how to respond, such as a toll-free phone number, Web site URL, or e-mail address.

Advertising can drive people to a Web site or to a toll-free number to call a company. Similar to the Road Crew campaign, another form of action is to discourage or extinguish actions such as smoking, drug use, or driving drunk.

Ultimately, advertisers want loyal customers who purchase and repurchase the product as a matter of habit or preference. **Reminder** advertising, as well as distributing coupons or introducing a continuity program (such as a frequent flyer program) is designed to keep the brand name in front of customers to encourage their repeat business. The "Got Milk?" campaign is driven by a question that reminds people to buy milk.

CREATIVE CONCEPTS

Advertising is an idea business. But what do we mean by an idea? An **idea** is a thought or a concept in the mind. It's formed by mentally combining pieces and fragments of thoughts into something that conveys a nugget of meaning. It's a form of construction—a mental creation. Advertising creatives sometimes use the term **concepting** to refer to the process of coming up with a new idea, such as "Got Milk?" There's even a book called *Concepting* that explains how concept branding leads to ideas that mean something to consumers and create identification with the brand.[15]

As advertising legend James Webb Young, a founder of the Young & Rubicam agency, explained in his classic book on creative thinking, an idea is a new or unexpected combination of thoughts. Young claims that "the ability to make new combinations is heightened by an ability to see relationships."[16] An idea, then, is *a thought that comes from placing two previously unrelated concepts together* as the Harley "Steak for Your Ears" ad demonstrates.

This Harley-Davidson ad equates the taste of a steak with the throaty roar of a Harley engine.

Advertising Big Ideas

In advertising, this idea becomes a point of focus for communicating the message strategy—a theme or central concept—what we call a **Big Idea**, or **creative concept**. The Marlboro Man with its connotation of Western independence and self-reliance is a Big Idea that has been worth millions, maybe billions of dollars in brand equity over the years.

The name of the Road Crew project was the defining element of that campaign's Big Idea. It was supported with a slogan—"Beats driving"—that conveyed the benefit of the program in the language of the target audience. The logo was in the style of the Harley-Davidson logo. The Road Crew planners realized that a Big Idea that reflects the lifestyle of the target audience in appealing language and tone can motivate behavior and change attitudes.

The ROI of Creativity

A Big Idea is more than just a new thought because in advertising it also has to accomplish something—it has a functional dimension. According to the DDB agency, an effective ad is *relevant*, *original*, and has *impact*—which is referred to as **ROI**. That formula sounds like the way a businessperson would talk metaphorically about creativity in terms of "return on investment."[17] According to this DDB philosophy, ideas have to be **relevant** and mean something to the target audience. **Original** means one of a kind—an advertising idea is creative when it is novel, fresh, unexpected, and unusual. Because it is novel, it is surprising and gets your attention. To be effective, the idea also must have **impact**, which means it makes an impression on the audience.

But how do you know if your idea is creative? Any idea can seem creative to you if you have never thought of it before, but the essence of a creative idea is that *no one else has thought of it either*. Thus, the first rule is to avoid doing what everyone else is doing. In an industry that prides itself on creativity, **copycat advertising**—that is, using an idea that

The Road Crew creators wanted to create a design in the spirit of the Harley image, realizing that members of the target audience were all Harley fans.

someone else has originated—is a concern. Advertising expert John Eighmy estimates that about 50 percent of the advertising in the United States falls into this category.[18]

The importance of originality may be obvious, but why is relevance important to an advertising Big Idea? Consider the award-winning California Milk Board campaign "Got Milk?" The consumer insight is that people drink milk with certain foods such as cookies. If milk is unavailable to drink with those foods, people are—to say the least—frustrated. Thus, associating these products with milk is a highly relevant idea.

Likewise, why is impact important? We know that many advertisements just wash over the audience. An idea with impact, however, breaks through the clutter, gets attention, and sticks in memory. A *breakthrough ad* has stopping power and that comes from an intriguing idea—a Big Idea that is important and relevant to consumers.

The Creative Leap

We all use different ways of thinking in different situations. For example, the term **divergent thinking** is used to describe a style of thinking that explores possibilities rather than using rational thinking to arrive at the "right" or logical conclusion. The heart of creative thinking, divergent thinking uses exploration (playfulness) to search for alternatives. Another term for divergent thinking is **right-brain thinking**, which is intuitive, holistic, artistic, and emotionally expressive thinking in contrast to **left-brain thinking**, which is logical, linear (inductive or deductive), and orderly. How can you become a more creative thinker—someone who uses the right brain for divergent explorations?

Michelin's dependability and durability surround and protect a car's precious cargo.

First, think about the problem as something that involves a mind shift. Instead of seeing the obvious, a creative idea looks at a problem in a different way, from a different angle. That's called *thinking outside the box*. It doesn't matter how dull the product might appear to be, there is always an opportunity to move it beyond its category limitations through a creative Big Idea.

An example of out-of-the-box thinking is Michelin's tire advertising, which is driven by the strategic idea that the tire is durable and dependable—language that would make a pretty boring ad. The creative idea, however, comes to life in the long-running campaign that shows a baby sitting in a tire. The visual is reinforced by the slogan, "Because so much is riding on your tires." The creative concept "leaps" from the idea of a durable tire to the idea of protecting your family, particularly precious members like tiny children, by surrounding them with the dependability of a Michelin tire.

Second, put the strategy language behind you—Michelin's "durable and dependable." Finding the brilliant creative concept entails what advertising giant Otto Kleppner called *the creative leap*[19]—a process of jumping from the rather boring business language in a strategy statement to an original idea. This new idea transforms the strategy into something unexpected, original, and interesting. Since the creative leap means moving from the safety of a predictable strategy statement to an unusual idea that hasn't been tried before, this leap is often referred to as *creative risk*. If it hasn't been tried before, it's a gamble.

All creative ideas in advertising involve this element of risk. Alex Bogusky, Chief Creative Officer (CCO) at Crispin Porter + Bogusky, one of the country's hottest creative agencies, says he welcomes over-the-top work (think the Subservient Chicken and the Burger King king) because it gets talked about. "I don't mind spectacular failure or spectacular criticism," he says, because those ideas make headlines, which means everybody's talking about them. "There's so much advertising that nobody knows even exists," he adds. "That's the stuff that I worry about making."[20]

Karl Schroeder, copywriter at the Coates Kokes agency, explains how he moved from doughnuts to black magic for the advertising he created for a client, Voodoo Doughnuts, a boutique doughnut shop in Portland, Oregon. The idea of black magic fit right in with the

SHOWCASE The idea behind these two posters for Voodoo Doughnuts is that the one who holds the doughnut has the power—be it human or arachnid.
These posters were contributed by Karl Schroeder, copywriter at Coates Kokes and graduate of the advertising program at the University of Oregon. He was nominated by Professor Charles Frazer.

store's name, as well as its late-night hours, unusual doughnut flavors, and the fact that the owners call their vats "cauldrons." The new idea is that magical powers are found in the hands of whoever holds the doughnut.

The Inside Story explains how one advertising creative person came up with an idea, and you will notice many of these techniques at work. In particular, however, the author insists that our own personal experiences are a great source for creative ideas.

Dialing Up Your Creativity

How creative are you? You probably know people who are just naturally zany, who come up with crazy, off-the-wall ideas. As Sasser reminded us in the Part IV Introduction, "everyone has some level of internal creativity." Creative advertising people may be weird and unconventional, but they can't be eccentric. They still must be focused on creating effective advertising that's on strategy.

Coming up with a great idea that is also on strategy is an emotional high. According to Derek Clark, a copywriter at Detroit's Campbell-Ewald agency, "Creative advertising at the national level has to be one of the biggest emotional roller coasters in the business world. When it's bad, you feel like fleeing the country. When it's good, there's nothing better. I love it."

Principle
Getting a great advertising idea that is also on strategy is an emotional high.

THE INSIDE STORY

Where Do Ideas Come From? Film Murderer Inspires Ad Maker!
By Ingvi Logason, *Principal, HÉR&NÚ, Reykjavik, Iceland*

All creative people will tell you there are many ways to come up with ideas. Whole libraries have been written about the origin of ideas—and some of those books are actually quite good—but no matter how they come about, in my world, all ideas are inspired by what we have experienced in one form or another.

That was the case for one of our TV ads for SORPA (the capital area recycling center). The project was to encourage people who were recycling to minimize the volume of their waste, which increased the correct sorting of recyclable items. The initiative for the idea came from the unlikeliest of sources.

After working on this project—a series of TV ads—for a few days and drafting several ideas, the idea behind this ad came to me while channel surfing and stumbling on a specific scene in a film I had seen before—*Fargo*.

In the film a murderer is trying to dispose of his murder victim with little success by putting the body part by part in a tree shredder. Even though it is obviously a bloody scene and has no correlation with recycling and the only link to the ad is the shredder—it still lit my lightbulb.

From that scene we created what came to be a humorous ad that was one in a series that helped SORPA reach its highest likability ever measured—91 percent of the population said they were positive toward the brand, which again led to an increase in waste brought in for recycling.

The initiative for my ideas can almost always be traced to things I have done, experienced, seen, heard, or read. Regularly I have gone through creative phases that directly correlate with my personal life.

In a creative world it is important to try new things and live life like a discoverer. There are discoveries to be made all around us. They can be made through a book you read, in your vacation, in the stories you hear, in the jokes people tell you, or simply when slouching on your sofa. Truly read, see, and listen to life. Incorporated with the right idea-generating techniques, this openness will make you much more creative.

The Ad: "SPEAKERS"

We open in a quiet somewhat conservative neighborhood where a young death metal fan comes home. He locks the many locks on his room door, not to be disturbed as he gets ready to play the latest release from one of his favorite heavy metal bands. He inserts the CD in the player, presses play, turns the volume up to the maximum, and starts head-banging—only to find out there is no music. He looks around, surprised, to the now-empty corners of the room once occupied by stereo speakers. Simultaneously, we start hearing in increasing strength a sawing/churning noise from outside. We see the terrified look on the rocker as he realizes what is happening. The point of view switches to the outside where we see the father of the boy in a happy-frantic-tired-of-the-noise kind of way rip apart the speakers and put them in a tree shredder where they are turned to pulp.

Voice-over: Remember; minimize the volume of your waste before you bring it in for recycling. SORPA

Source: Contributed by Ingvi Logason, who owns his own advertising agency in Iceland. A graduate of the University of West Florida, his work was nominated by Professor Tom Groth.

Research by the Center for Studies in Creativity in Buffalo, New York, has found that most people can sharpen their skills and develop their creative potential. First, let's explore the characteristics of a creative person. Research indicates that creative people tend to be independent, assertive, self-sufficient, persistent, and self-disciplined, with a high tolerance for ambiguity. They are also risk takers with powerful egos that are internally driven. They don't care much about group standards and opinions and typically have inborn skepticism and strong curiosity. Here are a few of the key characteristics of creative people who do well in advertising:

- *Problem solving.* Creative problem solvers are alert, watchful, and observant and reach conclusions through intuition rather than through logic. They also tend to have a mental playfulness that allows them to make novel associations.
- *The ability to visualize.* Most of the information we accumulate comes through sight, so the ability to manipulate visual images is crucial for good copywriters as well as designers. They can see products, people, and scenes in the mind's eye, and they can visualize a mental picture of the finished ad while it is still in the talking, or idea, stage.
- *Openness to new experiences.* As we said earlier, one characteristic that identifies creative people is that they are open to new experiences. Over the course of a lifetime, openness to experience may give you many more adventures from which to draw. Those experiences would, in turn, give a novelist more characters to write about, a painter more scenes to paint, and the creative team more angles from which to tackle an advertising problem.[21]
- *Conceptual thinking.* It's easy to see how people who are open to experience might develop innovative advertisements and commercials because they are more imaginative.[22] Such imagination led to a famous Nike commercial in which Michael Jordan and Larry Bird play an outlandish game of horse—bouncing the ball off buildings, billboards, and places that are impossible to reach.

As important as creative thinking is for advertising professionals, strategic thinking is just as important. In taking a peek into the minds of those who hire new creative people, researchers found repeated verbatim comments from creative directors concerning the importance of strategic Big Ideas. "Emphasize concept," said one creative director. "Teach them to think first and execute later."[23]

Principle
Emphasize concepts. Worry about executions later.

The Creative Process: How to Get an Idea

Only in cartoons do lightbulbs appear above our heads from out of nowhere when a good idea strikes. In reality, most people who are good at thinking up new ideas will tell you it is hard work. They read, study, analyze, test and retest, sweat, curse, and worry. Sometimes they give up. The unusual, unexpected, novel idea rarely comes easily—and that's as true in science and medicine as it is in advertising.

But most experts on creativity realize that there are steps to the process of thinking up a new idea. One approach called *creative aerobics* is a thought-starter process that works well in advertising because it uses both the head and the heart.

The creative process usually is portrayed as a series of steps. English sociologist Graham Wallas was the first to outline the creative process, but others followed, including Alex Osborn, one of the founders of the BBDO agency and the Creative Education Foundation.[24] Let's summarize these approaches in the following steps:

Step 1: Immersion. Read, research, and learn everything you can about the problem.

Step 2: Ideation. Look at the problem from every angle; develop ideas; generate as many alternatives as possible.

Step 3: Brainfag. Don't give up if—and when—you hit a blank wall.

Step 4: Incubation. Try to put your conscious mind to rest to let your subconscious take over.

Step 5: Illumination. Embrace that unexpected moment when the idea comes, often when your mind is relaxed and you're doing something else.

Step 6: Evaluation. Does it work? Is it on strategy?

Practical Tips

Exercise Your Creative Muscles

By Linda Conway Correll, Assistant Professor, Southern Illinois University

Developed by Linda Conway Correll, Creative Aerobics is a four-step, idea-generating process, which is explained here in terms of finding a creative idea for a hypothetical client—oranges:[25]

1. *Facts.* The first exercise is left brain and asks you to come up with a list of facts about a product (an orange has seeds, is juicy, has vitamin C).
2. *New names.* In the second exercise you create new "names" for the product (Florida, a vitamin supplement, a kiss of sunshine).
3. *Similarities.* The third exercise looks for similarities between dissimilar objects. (What are the similarities between the new names and the product? For instance, Florida sunshine and oranges both suggest warmth, freshness, sunshine, the fountain of youth.)

4. *New definitions.* The fourth exercise, a cousin of the pun, creates new definitions for product-related nouns. Peel (face peel, peel out), seed (seed money, bird seed), navel/naval (naval academy, contemplating one's navel), pulp (pulp fiction), C/see/si/sea (C the light). Headlines derived from those definitions might be: "Seed money" (the money to purchase oranges), "Contemplating one's navel" (looking at oranges), "Peel out" (when your grocer is out of oranges), "Navel intelligence" (information about an orange), "Pulp fiction" (a story about an orange), "C the light" (the orange is a low-calorie source of vitamin C). These new definitions stimulate the flowering of a new Big Idea.

Brainstorming

As part of the creative process, some agencies use a thinking technique known as **brainstorming** where a group of 6 to 10 people work together to come up with ideas. One person's idea stimulates someone else's, and the combined power of the group associations stimulates far more ideas than any one person could think of alone. The group becomes an idea factory.

That's how the Road Crew concept was developed. This Big Idea evolved out of many brainstorming sessions with the project leadership team, as well as with people in the communities where the team was working with local leaders to build coalitions to sponsor the effort. A list of names for the project was compiled and guys in bars who fit the target audience profile voted on the winner, which turned out to be Road Crew. The slogan "Beats driving" was developed using the same process.

The term *brainstorming* was coined by Alex Osborn, founder of the advertising agency BBDO and explained in his book *Applied Imagination*. The secret to brainstorming is to remain positive and defer judgment. Negative thinking during a brainstorming session can destroy the informal atmosphere necessary to achieve a novel idea.

To stimulate group creativity against a deadline, some agencies have special processes or locations for brainstorming sessions with no distractions and interruptions, such as cell phones and access to e-mail, and walls that can be covered with sheets of paper on which to write ideas. Some agencies rent a suite in a hotel and send the creative team there to get away and immerse themselves in the problem. When the GSDM agency was defending its prized Southwest Airlines account, president Roy Spence ordered a 28-day "war room/death march" that had staffers working around the clock, wearing Rambo-style camouflage, and piling all their trash inside the building to keep any outsiders from rummaging around for clues to their pitch.

The following list builds on our previous discussion of creative thinking. It can also be used as an outline for a brainstorming session.

How to Create Original Ideas

To create an original and unexpected idea, use the following techniques:
- ***What if?*** To twist the commonplace, ask a crazy "*what if*" question. For example, what if wild animals could talk? That question is the origin of the Frontier Talking Animals campaign.

- *An unexpected association.* In **free association** you think of a word and then describe everything that comes into your mind when you imagine that word. If you follow a chain of associations, you may come to an idea that sets up an unexpected juxtaposition with the original word or concept. An ad for Compaq used a visual of a chained butterfly to illustrate the lack of freedom in competitors' computer workstations.
- *Dramatize the obvious.* Sometimes the most creative idea is also the most obvious. That's true for the Voodoo Doughnuts campaign. The idea of magical power residing in a doughnut is new, but the black magic idea comes directly from the name of the product.
- *Catchy phrasing.* Isuzu used "The 205 Horsepower Primal Scream" for its Rodeo headline.
- *An unexpected twist.* An ad for Amazon.com used the headline, "460 books for Marxists. Including 33 on Groucho." A road crew usually refers to highway construction workers or the behind-the-scenes people on a concert tour, but for the Road Crew campaign, the phrase was twisted to refer to limo drivers who give rides to people who have had too much to drink.
- *A play on words.* Under the headline "Happy Camper," an ad for cheese showed a picture of a packed sports utility vehicle with a huge wedge of cheese lashed to the rooftop.
- *Analogy and metaphor.* Used to see new patterns or relationships, **metaphors** and **analogies** by definition set up juxtapositions. Harley-Davidson compared the legendary sound of its motorcycles to the taste of a thick, juicy steak.
- *Familiar and strange.* Put the familiar in an unexpected situation: UPS showed a tiny model of its familiar brown truck moving through a computer cord.
- *A twisted cliché.* They may have been great ideas the first time they were used, but phrases such as "the road to success" or "the fast track" become trite when overused. But they can regain their power if twisted into a new context. The "Happy Camper" line was twisted by relating cheese to an SUV.
- *Twist the obvious.* Avoid the predictable, such as a picture of a Cadillac on Wall Street or in front of a mansion. Use instead an SUV on Wall Street ("fast tracker") or a basketball hoop in front of a mansion ("slam dunk").

To prevent unoriginal ideas, avoid or work around the following:
- *The look-alike.* Avoid copycat advertising that uses somebody else's great idea. Hundreds of ads for escape products (resorts, travel, liquor, foods) have used the headline "Paradise Found." It's a play on "paradise lost" but still overused.
- *The tasteless.* In an attempt to be cute, a Subaru ad used the headline, "Put it where the sun don't shine." An attempted twist on a cliché, but it doesn't work.

Little Guys and Big Ideas

There's a tendency to think that only big organizations and big agencies have the brain-power to come up with Big Ideas. But that's not true. Small agencies, particularly boutique creative agencies, are very good at brainstorming and generating ideas that might not fly in a big organization averse to experimentation and risky new ideas.

Another way a small advertiser can find great ideas is to use a source like Zimmerman Advertising, based in Fort Lauderdale, Florida, that sells stock advertising online. Zimmerman's automated system called Pick-n-Click is an automated ad creation system started with ad ideas for automotive advertisers. It has 150,000 components, such as voice-overs, video footage, and text options.[26]

Another approach comes from Denver-based Thought Equity, which recycles unused advertisements. A professional licensing firm, Thought Equity operates an online footage library and handles rights and clearances for ads that never ran contributed by more than 300 agencies. Local advertisers can get great ads on the cheap with great production they could never afford. All they have to do is add their own identification at the end of the ad and make sure the content fits their business.

Another new source of creative ideas is **user-generated** "citizen ads" contributed through contests and new media such as YouTube. Dove invited its fans to submit a 30-second TV ad for new Dove Cream Oil Body Wash. The winning ad by a Sherman Oaks, California, woman was shown on the 2007 Academy Awards. The contest was announced in print advertising, and the rules and winning entry were available online at http://www.dovecreamoil.com. The Web site also offered contestants art and photos they could use, or contestants could upload their own images.

The 2007 Super Bowl featured advertising contests for Doritos and Chevrolet. The Doritos contestants produced their own ads, but the Chevy winning ad idea was produced by Chevy's agency for the big game. The winning idea came from a freshman at the University of Wisconsin-Milwaukee. The fact that consumers and students can come up with ideas that good is a little scary for ad agencies.[27] These ads can be viewed at http://promotions.yahoo.com/doritos/ and http://www.cbs.com/chevy.

On the political scene, a YouTube ad that was a parody of Apple's 1984 spot, featured in Chapter 1, portrayed Hillary Clinton as "Big Sister" whose talking head image was shattered by a young woman runner with iPod buds in her ears. The ad, which drew more than 2 million hits in its first days, closed with a line that said 2008 would be different because of Barack Obama. The perpetrator was unmasked as a Web wizard who worked for a company that maintained Obama's Web site.[28] The point is that these citizen ads are now easy to create and post online, and there is nothing candidates, corporations, and other organizations can do to dampen this surge of consumer-generated creativity.

MANAGING CREATIVE STRATEGY

We've talked about creative strategy and how it is developed, along with the types of effects advertising creates and the message strategies that deliver on these objectives. Let's now look at management issues that affect the formulation of creative strategies: extension, adaptation, and evaluation.

Extension: An Idea with Legs

One characteristic of a Big Idea is that it gives *legs* to a campaign. By that we mean that the idea is strong enough to serve as an umbrella concept for a variety of executions in different media talking to different audiences. It can be endlessly extended.

The Geico Caveman, for example, was created as a series of television ads in 2005. As a measure of its extendability, the idea has since been translated into an interactive video and a Web site (http://www.cavemans-crib.com) where the storyline of the commercials is translated into a tour of the urbane Caveman's home. With a click, viewers can change songs on his iPod, wander through the rooms, turn the pages on his books and magazines, and even rearrange word jumble magnets on his refrigerator. The interactive video has been a viral marketing success with more than 400,000 views on YouTube.[29] The idea has even been turned into an ABC television program.

Extendability is a strength of the Frontier talking animals campaign as well. The logic and structure of the concept is explained by the campaign's creators in the Matter of Practice box.

Adaptation: Taking an Idea Global

Global campaigns, like domestic campaigns, require ideas that address the advertising objectives and reflect the product's positioning. The opportunity for standardizing the campaign across multiple markets exists only if the objectives and strategic position are essentially the same. Otherwise, a creative strategy may call for a little tweaking of the message for a local market or even major revision if there is a great deal of cultural and market differences.

In the case where the core targeting and positioning strategies remain the same in different markets, it might be possible for the central creative idea to be universal across markets. Although the implementation of this idea may vary from market to market, the creative concept is sound across all types of consumers.

A MATTER OF PRACTICE

A Campaign with Legs (and Flippers)
By Shawn Couzens and Gary Ennis, *Creative Directors, Grey Advertising*

When Frontier has something to sell—whether it's a new city, a Web site, or the frequent flyer program—we let the animals deliver the message in a fun, humorous way. Certain characters are better suited for certain messages than others.

Flip, for example, is the lovable loser who never gets a break. For years, he's been dying to fly to a warm, tropical climate, such as Florida. But instead, he always gets sent to Chicago. This has been a recurring theme in several commercials. So, when Frontier expanded its service to Mexico, this was the perfect opportunity to build upon Flip's storyline. Hence, "Flip to Mexico."

The point is that the campaign has always been episodic, like a situation comedy. With 10-plus TV spots a year, we needed a structure that allowed us to build upon the characters and their storylines.

If our base-brand campaign were a sitcom, then *Flip to Mexico* would be a spin-off. The idea was to blanket the city with the "news" that Flip would quit unless he went to Mexico—and he needed the public's help to get there. We wanted the community to be an active participant in the story. To facilitate this, we launched a series of mock newscasts covering Flip's evolving storyline. We hired "activists" to hold placards and distribute leaflets, and we created an elaborate underground Web site with lots of interactive content. We even involved real Frontier employees, like CEO Jeff Potter, to help blur the line between reality and fiction. Consumers enjoyed the interplay, and they happily rallied for Flip. The story really captivated the city. It was all over the news. And it deepened the bond between Frontier and the community at a time when other airlines were trying to eat into Frontier's home turf.

But it's no longer about just TV, print, and radio. An idea has to perform across multiple platforms, and new media is a big part of that. Brands will have to find other ways to connect with consumers—like podcasts, interactive Web sites, YouTube Contests, branded entertainment, product placement, long-format digital content, and more. Some brands are creating their own TV shows or Web channels with original programming. The media landscape will continue to change. What won't change is the need for talented writers and art directors who can think outside the parameters of traditional media and make the brand story relevant and entertaining across all these different media and formats.

A campaign is an evolving story, so you can't rest on your awards. When you launch a successful campaign, and everyone likes it, you've set the creative bar pretty high. Everyone's waiting to see what you'll do next. Your job is to keep surprising them, keep raising the bar—because if you don't do it, someone else will.

There's a saying in the industry, "You're only as good as your last ad." It's kind of true. One week, you're being praised for an ad or campaign. But the next week, you have a new creative brief in your hand, and you have to prove yourself all over again.

Even if the campaign theme, slogan, or visual elements are the same across markets, it is usually desirable to adapt the creative execution to the local market, as we explained in the discussion of cultural differences in Chapter 5. Adaptation is especially important if the advertiser wants its products identified with the local market rather than as a foreign import. Advertisements may be produced centrally, in each local market, or by a combination of both. With a standardized campaign, production usually is centralized, and all advertisements are produced simultaneously to reap production cost savings.

An example of a difficult adaptation comes from Apple's series of "Mac vs. PC" ads that show a nerdy PC guy who can't keep up with the activities of a laid-back Mac guy. It uses delicate humor and body language to make subtle points about the advantages of the Mac system. In moving the campaign to Japan, Apple's agency, TBWA/Chiat/Day wrestled with the fact that in Japanese culture, direct-comparison ads are considered rude. The Japanese version was tweaked to make the Apple more of a home computer and the PC a work tool, so the differences were focused more on place than person.[30] The point is that cultural differences often require nuanced and subtle changes to be acceptable beyond the country of their origin.

Evaluation: The Go/No-Go Decision

How do you decide if the creative idea is strong enough to justify the expense of creating a campaign based on it? Whether local or global, an important part of managing creative work is evaluation, which happens at several stages in the creative process. Chapter 19 focuses on evaluation, but we'll introduce some basics here to help you understand this important final step in the creative process.

The first question is: Is it on strategy? No matter how much the creative people, client, or account executive may like an idea, if it doesn't communicate the right message or the right product personality to the right audience at the right time, then it is not effective. That's the science of advertising.

Structural Analysis   The Leo Burnett agency has an approach for analyzing the logic of the creative strategy as it is being developed. The Burnett creatives use it to keep the message strategy and creative concept working together, along with the head and heart appeals. This method, called **structural analysis**, relies on these three steps:

1. Evaluate the *power of the narrative* or story line (heart).
2. Evaluate the *strength of the product claim* (head).
3. Consider *how well the two are integrated*—that is, how the story line brings the claim to life.

Burnett creative teams check to see whether the narrative level is so high that it overpowers the claim or whether the claim is strong but there is no memorable story. Ideally, these two elements will be so seamless that it is hard to tell whether the impact occurs because of the power of the story or the strength of the claim. Such an analysis keeps the rational and emotional sides of an advertisement working together.

Copy Testing

A formal method to evaluate the effectiveness of an ad, either in a draft form or after it has been executed, is called **copy testing**. Remember: To evaluate the results of the advertising, the objectives need to be measurable—which means they can be evaluated to determine the effectiveness of the creative strategy. Copy testing uses a variety of tools to measure and predict the impact of the advertisement. Chapter 19 explains these tools in more detail.

Although evaluation is based on research, at some point there is a personal go/no-go decision, either by the creative team or the client. The president and CEO of PepsiCo explains, "You must have a clear vision and have the nerve to pull the trigger." BBDO's president Phil Dusenberry says, "On Pepsi, the kill rate is high." He explains, "For every spot we go to the client with, we've probably killed nine other spots."[31]

A particular problem that Big Ideas face is that the message is sometimes so creative that the ad is remembered but not the product. That's called **vampire creativity**, and it is one reason some advertisers shy away from really novel or entertaining strategies. That's also why it is important to copy-test the effectiveness of the ad's creative features while still in the idea stage.

IT'S A WRAP

Fans Rule. Frontier Wins.

Who says airline advertising has to be stuffy? That's certainly not the message from Frontier Airlines or Grey Worldwide. The campaign to send Flip to Mexico engaged the audience in goofy fun and made Frontier Denver's favorite airline.

Frontier's Flip campaign also is a good example of both the art and science of advertising. At the same time the message strategy resulted in a hard-nosed, business-building effort, the creative idea also captivated consumers. The advertising works not only because it delivers on the brand promise, but also because customers like the airline more because of the campaign and are engaged enough with the Frontier brand to follow the stories of its cast of characters.

In addition to being chosen Denver's Favorite Airline, the Flip campaign saw the following business results: Bookings rose 56 percent. The results were similar to a study of the power of the campaign when it was launched. That study determined that unaided awareness rose within a year from 40 percent to 78 percent following the introduction of the animals. That means that about 8 of 10 people mentioned Frontier without being prompted when listing airlines. That's about double the number who mentioned it before the campaign ran.

In fewer than four years, Frontier's advertising has been recognized with more than 80 awards. Frontier was nominated for "Best of Show" at the International Mobius Awards for two years in a row. Frontier was awarded a Silver Clio for the prestigious "Content & Contact" Category. And it won a Silver Effie as well.

Key Points Summary

1. **How do we explain the function and most important parts of a creative brief?** From the advertising strategy comes the problem statement, the objectives, the target market, and the positioning strategy. The message strategy decisions include the appropriate type of creative strategy, the selling premise, and suggestions about the ad's execution, such as tone of voice.

2. **What are some key creative strategy approaches?** Creative strategies are often expressed as appeals to the head, the heart, or both. More complex systems of strategies have been proposed by Frazer and Taylor. Creative strategy formats include lectures and dramas and selling strategies. Different formulas have evolved that deliver these strategies and guide the development of executions.

3. **Can creative thinking be defined, and how does it lead to a Big Idea?** To be creative an ad must make a relevant connection with its audience and present a selling idea in an unexpected way. There is both a science (the way a message is persuasive, convincing, and relevant) and an art (the way a message is an unexpected idea). A Big Idea is a creative concept that makes the message attention getting and memorable.

4. **What characteristics do creative people have in common, and what is their typical creative process?** Creative people tend to be independent, assertive, self-sufficient, persistent, and self-disciplined, with a high tolerance for ambiguity. They are also risk takers with powerful egos that are internally driven. They don't care much about group standards and opinions and typically have inborn skepticism and strong curiosity. They are good problem solvers with an ability to visualize and do conceptual thinking. They are open to new experiences. A typical creative process involves immersing yourself in background research; developing alternatives through ideation; getting past brainfog, where you hit the wall and can't come up with anything; and embracing illumination of the great idea.

Key Terms

analogies, p. 377
appeal, p. 364
attributes, p. 364
benefit, p. 365
Big Idea (or creative concept), p. 371
brainfag, p. 375
brainstorming, p. 376
brand icon, p. 366
call to action, p. 370
claim, p. 365

comparison, p. 366
concepting, p. 370
copycat advertising, p. 371
copy testing, p. 380
creative brief, p. 357
creative concept, p. 371
creative (or message) strategy, p. 357
demonstration, p. 366
divergent thinking, p. 372
endorser, p. 366

execution, p. 357
features (or attributes), p. 364
free association, p. 377
formulas, p. 365
hard sell, p. 362
humor, p. 366
idea, p. 370
ideation, p. 375
illumination, p. 375
image advertising, p. 370
immersion, p. 375

impact, p. 371
incubation, p. 375
left-brain thinking, p. 372
message strategy, p. 357
metaphors, p. 377
original, p. 371
permission to believe, p. 370
problem avoidance, p. 366
problem solution, p. 366
product-as-hero, p. 366
promise, p. 365

reason why, p. 365
relevant, p. 371
reminder, p. 370
right-brain thinking, p. 372
ROI, p. 371
selling premise, p. 364

slice of life, p. 366
slogans, p. 367
soft sell, p. 362
spokes character, p. 366
spokesperson, p. 366
straightforward, p. 365

structural analysis, p. 380
support, p. 365
taglines, p. 367
teaser, p. 367
tone of voice, p. 357

unique selling proposition
    (USP), p. 365
user-generated ads, p. 377
vampire creativity, p. 380

Review Questions

1. This chapter argues that effective advertising is both a science and an art. Explain what that means.

2. How do various strategic approaches deliver on the objectives identified in the Facets Model of Effects?

3. What is an appeal? How do advertisements touch people's emotions? Describe two techniques.

4. Explain the four types of selling premises.

5. What is a Big Idea, and what are its characteristics?

6. When a creative director says your idea needs to make a "creative leap," what does that mean?

7. Describe the five steps in the creative process.

8. Explain how brainstorming is used in advertising.

9. Give an example of a technique you might use as a thought starter to stimulate a creative idea.

10. List five characteristics of creative people. How do you rate yourself on those factors?

11. Explain structural analysis and copy testing and how they are used in evaluating the creative strategy.

Discussion Questions

1. Find the ad in this book that you think is the most creative.
   - What is its Big Idea? How and why does it work?
   - Analyze the ad in terms of the ROI formula for evaluating effective creative advertising.
   - Re-create the creative brief that would summarize the ad's message strategy.

2. Divide the class into groups of 6 to 10 people and discuss this problem: *Your community wants to encourage people to get out of their cars and use alternative forms of transportation.* Brainstorm for 15 minutes as a group, accumulating every possible idea. How many ideas are generated? Here's how to run this brainstorming group:
   - Appoint one member to be the *recorder* who lists all the ideas as they are mentioned.
   - Appoint another member to be the *moderator* and suggest techniques described in this chapter as idea starters.
   - Identify a *cheerleader* to keep the discussion positive and find gentle ways to discourage critical or negative comments.
   - Work for 15 minutes throwing out as many different creative concepts as your team can come up with, regardless of how crazy or dumb they might initially sound.
   - Go back through the list as a group and put an asterisk next to the 5–10 ideas that seem to have the most promise.

   When all the groups reconvene in class, each recorder should list the group's best ideas on the blackboard. As a class, pick out the three ideas that seem to have the most potential. Analyze the experience of participating in a brainstorming group and compare the experiences of the different teams.

3. *Three-Minute Debate:* Here's the topic: Is entertainment a useful objective for an advertising campaign? This is an issue that advertising experts debate because, although entertainment may get and keep attention, some experts believe the focus should be on selling products not entertaining consumers. Build a case for your side—either pro or con on the effectiveness of entertaining ads.

   In class, organize into small teams with pairs of teams taking one side or the other. Set up a series of three-minute debates with each side having 1½ minutes to argue its position. Every team of debaters has to present new points not covered in the previous teams' presentations until there are no arguments left to present. Then the class votes as a group on the most compelling argument.

Take-Home Team Projects

1. As a team of two or three, find at least two newspaper or magazine advertisements that your team believes are bland and unexciting. Rewrite them, first to demonstrate a hard-sell approach and then to demonstrate a soft-sell approach. Explain how your rewrites have improved the original ad. Also explain the how the hard-sell and soft-sell appeals work. Which do you believe is the most effective for each ad? If you were a team of professionals working on these accounts, how would you go about evaluating the effectiveness of these two ads? In other words, how would you test your intuitive judgment of which one works best?

2. Your team of three or four people is working for your local campus newspaper as the promotion staff. Consult the brandera.com Web site. Find an idea that your team thinks is creative and useful in promoting your newspaper and building a strong brand for it. Summarize the discussion and relate it to things you have learned in this chapter about how creative strategies are developed and what such a strategy could accomplish.

Yahoo! Hands-On Case

Review the Yahoo! case in the Appendix.

1. What is the Big Idea behind the Yahoo! campaign? The idea is briefly explained in the case study. Write a more complete explanation in a one-page report that also explains how the creative concept would be "tweaked" for each of the two audiences. In other words, there must be some differences between tweens and teens or they wouldn't have been identified as separate target audiences. How are they different and how would the Big Idea be adapted to each group?

2. Your creative team of three or four people has been asked to come up with the next campaign for Yahoo! to reach this target market. Do you continue with this creative concept, evolve it in a new direction, or dump it and create something new? In a one-page report, explain (1) how you would go about making this decision, and (2) given what you know from this case explanation, what your team would recommend, just using your intuitive judgment. Explain your thinking.

HANDS-ON CASE

Ask McCann-Erickson about Priceless Creative

The McCann-Erickson advertising agency was hungry for fresh talent when it hired a young copywriter named Joyce King Thomas. It was the mid-1990s, and McCann was in a creative slump. Its biggest and most famous client, Coca-Cola, had fired the agency after decades of collaboration on some of the greatest ads in history. McCann's creative director Nina DiSesa had liked King Thomas's work at another agency and thought she could help lead a creative revival at McCann.

McCann got its chance when credit card giant MasterCard became a client in 1997. MasterCard wanted something fresh that could help it regain lost ground against top competitor Visa. "Visa was the aspirational, globe-trotting card, and MasterCard was the everyday, hardware-store card. We needed to take the ordinariness of the card and glorify it," recalled executive creative director Jonathan Cranin. Eric Einhorn, McCann's head of strategic planning, put it this way: "We considered it a travesty that you could use your MasterCard wherever you could use your Visa—and in more places around the world. But Visa was it and MasterCard was just another card."

King Thomas, Einhorn, and Cranin thought they should avoid a benefits focus and shoot for ads that would strike an emotional chord. The ideas did not come easily, but after days of brainstorming, false starts, and lots of crumpled paper, Cranin came up with "There are some things money can't buy. For everything else, there's MasterCard." That was good, everyone agreed, but how to present it? King Thomas suggested a "shopping list" approach. She described a father and son attending a baseball game. As the two enjoy food and souvenirs together, an announcer checks off the dollar costs (Two tickets: $28; two hot dogs, two popcorns, and two sodas: $18; one autographed baseball: $45) leading up to the emotional close: "Real conversation with 11-year-old son: Priceless."

The group members believed they had a winner but were taking no chances. When they presented their ideas to MasterCard, the ads were encased in books covered in blue velvet. Most of the pitch was done by King Thomas, who backed up the creative with clips taken of the enthusiastic focus groups that had watched the ads. "It was cho-reographed beautifully," recalls a McCann executive. "Joyce took us through the work, and she had such passion for it." The client's reaction? "Without naming names, there were a few tears at the presentation," says Cranin.

Thus, a hit was born. The long-running MasterCard campaign has led to large gains in both consumer awareness and card usage. The ads are cultural icons, inspiring parodies on *Saturday Night Live* and the HBO program *Arliss*. The campaign is a global sensation too. Audiences in more than 105 countries have seen the advertising, which has appeared in 48 languages. Since the inception of this campaign, the number of MasterCard's new credit cards has increased twice as fast as Visa's rate. As for King Thomas? She succeeded DiSesa and is now chief creative officer in McCann Erickson's flagship office in New York City, overseeing about 150 people.

The McCann story holds some important lessons for agencies: Fancy reputation? Good. Impressive roster of past clients? Noteworthy. The best creative talent in the business? Priceless.

Consider This

1. Campaigns that seek an emotional connection are difficult to pull off. As Joyce King Thomas noted, "One thing we were worried about was that people would think we were telling them they would have to spend money to have a close relationship. But that hasn't come up." King Thomas worried from the start that the campaign might be deemed manipulative or sappy by the consumer. "This kind of work can easily slip into bad Hallmark advertising." What in McCann's work has helped MasterCard to avoid this problem?

2. When the HBO program *Arliss* used the "Priceless" tagline in one episode, MasterCard sued for trademark and copyright infringement. Would you have advised MasterCard to protect its slogan this way? Why or why not?

3. What makes the MasterCard "Priceless" theme a winning creative idea? How would you determine if it is truly effective?

Sources: Hank Kim, "Mastercard Moments." *Adweek*, April 12, 1999; Mallorre Dill, "Creative Briefs," *Adweek*, July 17, 2000; Eugenia Levenson, "Six Teams That Changed the World," *Fortune*, May 31, 2006, http://www.cnnmoney.com; Kathleen Sampey, "King Thomas Takes Over Creative at McCann Flagship," *Adweek*, October 25, 2004; Todd Wasserman, "Credit Cards," *Adweek*, April 26, 2004.

Copywriting

IT'S A WINNER

Awards:	Company:	Agency:	Campaign:
Advertising Age Top 100 Advertising Campaigns, along with awards from the Effies, Clios, Addys, and the One Show	*California Milk Processor Board and Milk Processor Education program (MilkPEP)*	*Goodby, Silverstein & Partners*	*Got Milk?*

Milking Success

You're probably familiar with the milk mustache ads. They feature celebrities, movie and television stars, musicians, fictional characters, sports stars, and supermodels who endorse milk while sporting prominent milk mustaches. Well-loved people, celebrities, and characters show up in "Got Milk?" ads, including the Olsen twins, Serena and Venus Williams, Beyoncé, Spike Lee, Carrie Underwood, Batman, Superman, David Beckham, and football stars Peyton, Eli, and Archie Manning, among many others. Check them out at the campaign's Web site: http://www.milknewsroom.com/ads.htm. This case will show you how this simple Big Idea became an American icon.

The campaign was created in 1993 in California to turn around a 15-year decline in milk consumption. Commenting on the challenge, Jeff Manning, the executive director of the California Milk Processor Board, said, "What could you say about milk? It was white and came in gallons. People felt they knew all there was to know about it, so it was hard to find a strategic platform."

Manning hired San Francisco ad agency Goodby, Silverstein & Partners, and the Goodby team turned a consumer insight into a campaign that has had long-running success, first on a regional level and then nationally.

The campaign that ran prior to "Got Milk?" proclaimed, "Milk Does a Body Good." Research told Manning that more than 90 percent of people knew that milk was good for them—yet milk consumption declined. People thought of milk as wholesome but boring, especially when compared to the appeal of popular, sugary soft drinks associated with youthful rebellion and individuality (think Pepsi Generation). Manning and the Goodby team made the decision to abandon the nutrition theme and try to make drinking milk cool to people of all ages.

Chapter Key Points

1. What basic style of writing is used for advertising copy?
2. Which copy elements are essential to a print ad?
3. How can we characterize the message and tools of radio advertising?
4. What is the best way to summarize the major elements of television commercials?
5. How is Web advertising written?

Qualitative research indicated that people loved drinking milk with peanut butter sandwiches, Oreos, and other sweet, gooey snacks. The creative team realized that people felt deprived if they had the peanut butter or cookies, but no milk. The creative team used a deprivation strategy—what would happen if you didn't have milk to go with your favorite foods? The ads reminded drinkers of the disappointment they felt when they were missing milk. The core concept was executed with simple copy, a tagline that asked, "Got milk?"

The original vision of the campaign aimed to change the way people viewed dairy products. The fresh thinking of the Got Milk? campaign allows the product to be associated with endorsements from a variety of people who demonstrate that drinking milk is cool.

You may or may not remember the first commercial that was created, but it became one of the most popular ads of the 1990s. It featured a nutty history expert who couldn't come up with "Aaron Burr," the winning answer that he obviously knew when asked a question on a radio trivia quiz. Why not? He had peanut butter stuck to the roof of his mouth. Too bad he didn't have milk, which would have saved the day and earned him $10,000. Viewers loved the spot.

A more recent ad partnered with another organization to deliver a message that benefited both. Diane Heavin, cofounder of the fitness chain Curves, stars in the ad. Pairing the health benefits of drinking milk with a relatively small business helps the milk processors, dairy farmers, and the business. Curves benefits from the national exposure. And the milk folks benefit from being associated with a well-liked fitness group that targets women, a key audience for the campaign. Everybody wins.

The clever line "Got milk?" is a federally registered trademark that has been licensed since 1995. The campaign is also ubiquitous because it has remarkable extendibility (what we called "legs" in the previous chapter). That means the core idea has been used in many advertisements with many people and situations over a long period of time. Licensed products that use the famous line also extend the campaign to baby bottles, Barbie dolls, and kitchenware. Grocers sell bananas with stickers that ask consumers if they might need milk to go with their cereal and bananas.

To see what kind of success this long-running campaign has achieved, go to the It's a Wrap section at the end of the chapter.

Sources: Douglas B. Holt, "Got Milk?" http://www.aef.com/on_campus/classroom/case_histories/3000; http://www.gotmilk.com; http://www.milkdelivers.org/gotmilk; Pamela Accetta Smith, "Campaign Weighs In" http://www.dairyfield.com (all sites accessed March 1, 2007).

Words and pictures work together to produce a creative concept. However, the idea behind a creative concept in advertising is usually expressed in some attention-getting and memorable phrase, such as "Got milk?" Finding these "magic words" is the responsibility of copywriters who search for the right way to warm up a mood or soften consumer resistance. This chapter describes the role of the copywriter and explains the practice of copywriting in print, broadcast, and Internet advertising.

COPYWRITING: THE LANGUAGE OF ADVERTISING

The creative element is the most visible—and, in some respects, the most important—dimension of advertising. As Sasser explained in the Part IV Introduction, "Many advertisers openly claim they actively seek out new advertising agencies to achieve stronger or better creative work."

Some creative concepts are primarily visual, but intriguing ideas can also be expressed through language. A long-running campaign for the NYNEX Yellow Pages illustrates a word-oriented creative concept. The campaign used visual plays on words to illustrate some of the headings in its directory. Each pun makes sense when the visual is married with the heading from the directory. One commercial in the series included three train engineers with overalls, caps, and bandannas sitting in rocking chairs in a parlor and having tea to illustrate the "Civil Engineering" category; a picture of a bull sleeping on its back illustrates the category "Bulldozing."

The NYNEX ads feature puns based on Yellow Pages category headings. This ad, which is directed to media buyers, uses that same creative technique with a visual pun on the heading.

Although advertising is highly visual, words are crucial in four types of advertisements.

1. If the message is complicated, words can be more specific than visuals and can be read over and over until the meaning is clear.
2. If the ad is for a high-involvement product, meaning the consumer spends a lot of time considering it, then the more information the better. That means using words.
3. Information that needs definition and explanation, like how a new wireless phone works, is best delivered through words.
4. If a message tries to convey abstract qualities, such as justice and quality, words tend to communicate these concepts more easily than pictures.

Words are powerful tools in advertising, and the person who understands their beauty and power, as well as how best to use them in situations like these, is the copywriter.

The Copywriter

The person who shapes and sculpts the words in an advertisement is called a **copywriter**. *Copy* is the text of an ad or the words people say in a commercial. In most agencies, copywriters work in teams with art directors who design the way the ad will look. A successful advertising copywriter is a savvy marketer and a literary master, sometimes described as a "killer poet." Copywriters love words and search for the clever twist, the pun, the powerful description, the punch, the nuance. They use words that whip and batter, plead, sob, cajole, and impress. They are experts on words, or rather, students of them, as the YMCA ad demonstrates. They know the meanings, derivations, moods, and feelings of words and the reverberations and vibrations they create in a reader's mind.

Many copywriters have a background in English or literature. In addition to having an ear for the perfect phrase, they listen to the way people talk and identify the tone of voice that best fits the target audience and advertising need. Versatility is a common trait of copywriters. They can move from toilet paper to Mack trucks and shift their writing style to match the product and the language of their target audience. Like poets, copywriters spend hours, even days, crafting a paragraph. After many revisions, others read the copy and critique it. It then goes back to the writer, who continues to fine-tune it. Copywriters must have thick skins as there is always someone else reading their work, critiquing it, and asking for changes.

SHOWCASE Part of a membership drive campaign, this ad demonstrates how a copywriter plays with language to deliver a selling point with style. Lara Mann, a graduate of the University of Florida advertising program, contributed this ad. She was a copywriter at FHB Advertising in Orlando and now works as a copywriter at DraftFCB in Chicago. She was nominated by Professor Elaine Wagner.

Principle

Effective copy is succinct, single-minded, and tightly focused.

Advertising Writing Style

Advertising has to win its audience, no small task given that it usually competes in a cluttered environment. For that reason, the copy should be as simple as possible. It is succinct and single-minded, meaning that it has a clear focus and usually tries to convey only one selling point. Advertising writing is tight. Every word counts because both space and time are expensive. Ineffective words and phrases—such as *interesting, very, in order to, buy now and save, introducing, nothing less than*—waste precious space.

Copywriters try to write the way the target audience thinks and talks. That often means using direct address. For example, an ad for Trojan condoms makes a pointed argument on a touchy subject for its young, single-person target audience. Combining headline with body copy, it reads as a dialogue:

I didn't use one because I didn't have one with me.
Get real.
If you don't have a parachute, don't jump, genius.

Copywriters revise copy seemingly a hundred times to make it as concise as possible. The tighter the copy, the easier it is to understand and the greater its impact. Simple ads avoid being gimmicky or coming off as too cute; they don't try too hard or reach too far to make a point. The following list summarizes some characteristics of effective copy.

Writing Effective Copy

- **Be succinct.** Use short, familiar words, short sentences, and short paragraphs.
- **Be single-minded.** Focus on one main point.
- **Be specific.** Don't waste time on generalities. The more specific the message, the more attention getting and memorable it is.
- **Get personal.** Directly address your audience whenever possible as "you" rather than "we" or "they."
- **Keep a single focus.** Deliver a simple message instead of one that makes too many points. Focus on a single idea and support it.
- **Be conversational.** Use the language of everyday conversation. The copy should sound like two friends talking to each other, so don't shy away from incomplete sentences, thought fragments, and contractions.
- **Be original.** To keep your copy forceful and persuasive, avoid stock advertising phrases, strings of superlatives and brag-and-boast statements, and clichés.
- **Use variety.** To add visual appeal in both print and TV ads, avoid long blocks of copy in print ads. Instead, break the copy into short paragraphs with subheads. In TV commercials, break up television monologues with visual changes, such as shots of the product, sound effects, and dialogue. The writer puts these breaks in the script while the art director designs what they will look like.
- **Use imaginative description.** Use evocative or figurative language to build a picture in the consumer's mind.

In sharp contrast, the pompous overblown phrasing of many corporate statements doesn't belong in ads. We call it **your-name-here copy** because almost any company can use those words and tack a signature on the end. For example, a broadband company named Covad started off an ad like this:

Opportunity. Potential. These are terms usually associated with companies that have a lot to prove and little to show for it. But on rare occasion, opportunity can be used to describe a company that has already laid the groundwork, made the investments, and is well down the road to strong growth.

It's all just platitudes and clichés—and any company could use this copy. It isn't attention getting and it doesn't contribute to a distinctive and memorable brand image. That's

Practical Tips

So You Think You Want to Create a Funny Ad?

By Fred Beard, Professor, Gaylord *College of Journalism and Mass Communication, University of Oklahoma*

These parting words of British actor Sir Donald Wolfit should give anyone thinking of creating a funny ad second thoughts: "Dying is easy, comedy is hard." Writing a funny, effective ad is especially hard when you consider that the ad must make people laugh at the same time it accomplishes an advertising objective—an increase in attention, recall, favorable attitudes, or an actual purchase. If you're still not deterred, keep in mind that funny ads work best when the following circumstances apply:

1. *Your goal is to attract attention.* Decades of research and the beliefs of advertising creative professionals match up perfectly on this one.
2. *Your goal is to generate awareness and recall of a simple message (think Aflac).* Most advertising creatives agree that humor works best to encourage recall of fairly simple messages, not complex ones.
3. *Your humor is related.* Did you ever laugh at an ad and forget what it was advertising? Creatives will tell you humor is a waste of money if it isn't related to a product's name, uses, benefits, or users.
4. *Your goal is to get the audience to like your brand.* Research shows people often transfer their liking of funny ads to the brand.

5. *You expect the audience to initially disagree with your arguments.* An ad's humor can distract people from arguments they disagree with, encouraging them to lower their perceptual defenses, accept the message, and be persuaded by it.
6. *Your target audience is men, especially young ones.* Creative professionals say younger male audiences respond best to humor, and research confirms men favor more aggressive humor.
7. *Your audience has a low Need for Cognition (NFC) or a high Need for Humor (NFH).* People with a low NFC don't enjoy thinking about things—they prefer emotional appeals like humor. People with a high NFH seek out humor. If your audience is low NFC and high NFH, you can't miss.
8. *You have good reasons for using the broadcast media.* By far, the majority of creatives believe humor works best in radio and TV ads.
9. *You're advertising a low-involvement/low-risk product or service.* Academic researchers and creative professionals agree funny ads seem to work best for routine purchases people don't worry about too much.
10. *Your humor is definitely funny.* Research shows if an ad's humor fails, not only will there be no positive outcomes, it could even produce negative responses.

always a risk with company-centered copy, which doesn't say anything that relates to the customer's needs, wants, and interests.

Tone of Voice   To develop the right tone of voice, copywriters write to the target audience. If the copywriter knows someone who fits the audience profile, then he or she may write to that person as if they were in a conversation. If the writer doesn't know someone, one trick is to go through a photo file, select a picture of the person who fits the description, and write to that "audience member."

Molson Beer won awards for a commercial it created, called "The Rant," which mirrors the attitude of many Canadians. The commercial starts softly with an average Joe character disassociating himself from Canadian stereotypes. As he talks, he builds up intensity and at the end, he's in a full-blown rant ending with the line: *"My name is Joe, and I am Canadian."* The commercial was so successful it was played at events all around the country.

Humor is a particular type of writing that copywriters use to create entertaining, funny ads. The idea is that, if the humor works, the funny copy will lend a positive aura to a brand. It's particularly important to master funny writing if you are trying to reach an audience that's put off by conventional advertising, such as young males. The Practical Tips box provides some suggestions on how to use humor in advertising copy.

Grammar   Copywriters also are attuned to the niceties of grammar, syntax, and spelling, although sometimes they will play with a word or phrase to create an effect, even if it's grammatically incorrect. The Apple Computer campaign for the Macintosh that used the slogan "Think different" rather than "Think differently" caused a bit of an uproar in Apple's school market. That's why copywriters think carefully about playing loose with the language even if it sounds right.[1]

Adese   Formulaic advertising copy is one problem that is so infamous comedians parody it. This type of formula writing, called **adese**, violates all the guidelines for writing effective copy that we described in the Practical Tips box. It is full of clichés, superlatives, stock phrases, and vague generalities. For example, consider this copy:

> *Now we offer the quality that you've been waiting for—at a price you can afford. So buy now and save.*

Can you hear yourself saying things like this to a friend?

Another type of adese is **brag-and-boast copy**, which is "we" copy written from the company's point of view with a pompous tone, similar to the Covad ad. Consider a print ad by Buick. The ad starts with the stock opening, "Introducing Buick on the move." The body copy includes superlatives and generalities such as, "Nothing less than the expression of a new philosophy," "It strikes a new balance between luxury and performance—a balance which has been put to the test," and "Manufactured with a degree of precision that is in itself a breakthrough." Because people are so conditioned to screen out advertising, messages that use this predictable style are easy to ignore. This discussion of advertising style has been general, so now let's look at how copy is written for print and broadcast media.

COPYWRITING FOR PRINT

A print advertisement is created in two pieces: a copy sheet and a layout. Even though they work together to create a creative concept, we'll discuss copy in this chapter and layout in the next chapter.

The two categories of copy that print advertising uses are display copy and body copy (or text). **Display copy** includes all elements that readers see in their initial scanning. These elements—headlines, subheads, call-outs, taglines, and slogans—usually are set in larger type sizes than body copy and are designed to get attention and to stop the viewer's scanning. **Body copy** includes the elements that are designed to be read and absorbed, such as the text of the ad message and captions. Table 13.1 summarizes the primary copy elements that are in the copywriter's toolkit.

How to Write Headlines

The **headline** is a key element in print advertising. It conveys the main message so that people get the point of the ad. It's important for another reason. The headline works with the visual to get attention and communicate the creative concept. This clutter-busting Big Idea breaks through the competitive messages. It comes across best through a picture and words working together, as the DuPont ad illustrates. The headline carries the theme ("To Do List for the Planet") and the underline ("Find food that helps prevent osteoporosis") makes a direct connection with the visual. People who are scanning may read nothing more, so advertisers want to at least register a point with the consumer. The point has to be clear from the headline or the combination of headline and visual. Researchers estimate that only 20 percent of those who read the headline go on to read the body copy.

Headlines need to be catchy phrases, but they also have to convey an idea and attract the right target audience. Tobler has won Effie awards for a number of years for its clever headlines and visuals advertising its chocolates. For Tobler's Chocolate Orange, the creative concept showed the chocolate ball being smacked against something hard and splitting into orange-like slices. The headline was "Whack and Unwrap." The next year the headline was "Smashing Good Taste," which speaks to the candy's British origins and to the quirky

Principle
Good headlines interrupt readers' scanning and get their attention.

Table 13.1   The Copywriter's Toolkit

No one ad uses all of the copy elements; however, they are all used in different ads for different purposes. Here are the most common tools in the copywriter's toolkit:

Headline: A phrase or a sentence that serves as the opening to the ad. It's usually identified by larger type or a prominent position and its purpose is to catch attention. In the Corporate Angel Network ad, for example, the headline is "Cancer Patients Fly Free."

Overlines and **underlines**: These are phrases or sentences that either lead into the headline or follow up on the thought in the headline. They are usually set in smaller type than the headline. The purpose of the overline is to set the stage, and the purpose of the underline is to elaborate on the idea in the headline and serve as a transition to the body copy.

Body copy: The text of the ad. It's usually smaller-sized type and written in paragraphs or multiple lines. Its purpose is to explain the idea or selling point.

Subheads: Used in longer copy blocks, subheads begin a new section of the copy. They are usually bold type or larger than the body copy. Their purpose is to make the logic clear to the reader. They are useful for people who scan copy and they help them get a sense of what the copy says. The Corporate Angel Network ad uses subheads.

Call-outs: These are sentences that float around the visual, usually with a line or arrow pointing to some specific element in the visual that they name and explain. For example, Johnson & Johnson once ran an ad that used call-outs as the main pieces of the body copy. The head read: "How to bathe a mommy." Positioned around a picture of a woman are short paragraphs with arrows pointing to various parts of her body. These "call outs" describe the good things the lotion does for feet, hands, makeup removal, moisture absorption, and skin softening.

Captions: A sentence or short piece of copy that explains what you are looking at in a photo or illustration. Captions aren't used very often in advertising because the visuals are assumed to be self-explanatory; however, readership studies have shown that, after the headline, captions have high readership.

Taglines: A short phrase that wraps up the key idea or creative concept that usually appears at the end of the body copy. It often refers back to the headline or opening phrase in a commercial. For example, see the line, "Need a lift? Just give us a call. We'll do the rest," in the Corporate Angel Network ad.

Slogans: A distinctive catch phrase that serves as a motto for a campaign, brand, or company. It is used across a variety of marketing communication messages and over an extended period of time. For example, see "The Miracles of Science" line that serves as a corporate motto for the DuPont company.

Call to action: This is a line at the end of an ad that encourages people to respond and gives information on how to respond. Both ads—Corporate Angel Network and DuPont—have response information: either an address, a toll-free phone number, an e-mail address, or Web address.

Cancer Patients Fly Free

So near, yet so far.

Critical treatment centers, often thousands of miles away, are frequently a cancer patient's best chance for survival. But costly airfare, stressful delays, and unnecessary exposure to crowds are the last thing these patients need.

We give cancer patients a lift.

We are Corporate Angel Network, the nationwide public charity with only one mission—to arrange passage for cancer patients to treatment centers using the empty seats on corporate jets.

Our five employees and 60 highly involved and compassionate volunteers work directly with patients and families to coordinate their travel needs with the regularly scheduled flight plans of our Corporate Angels—500 major corporations, including 56 of the top 100 in the *Fortune 500*, who generously make empty seats on their aircraft available to our patients.

To date, they've flown more than 15,000 flights with Corporate Angel Network patients onboard.

Need a lift?
Just give us a call. We'll do the rest.

Corporate Angel Network, Inc.
Westchester County Airport
One Loop Road, White Plains, NY 10604
Phone (914) 328-1313   Fax (914) 328-3938
Patient Toll Free — (866) 328-1313
Info@CorpAngelNetwork.org   www.CorpAngelNetwork.org

combination of chocolate and orange flavors. The headline and visual also tell consumers how to "open" the orange into slices—by whacking it.

Agencies copy-test headlines to make sure they can be understood at a glance and that they communicate exactly the right idea. Split-run tests (two versions of the same ad) in direct mail have shown that changing the wording of the headline while keeping all other elements constant can double, triple, or quadruple consumer response. That is why the experts, such as ad legend David Ogilvy, state that the headline is the most important element in the advertisement.[2] Because headlines are so important, some general principles guide their development and explain the particular functions they serve:

• A good headline will attract only those who are prospects—there is no sense in attracting people who are not in the market. An old advertising axiom is, "Use a rifle, not a shotgun." In other words, use the headline to tightly target the right audience.
• The headline must work in combination with the visual to stop and grab the reader's attention. An advertisement by Range Rover shows a photo of the car parked at the edge of a rock ledge in Monument Valley with the headline, "Lots of people use their Range Rovers just to run down to the corner."
• The headline must also identify the product and brand and start the sale. The selling premise should be evident in the headline.
• The headline should lead readers into the body copy. For readers to move to the body copy, they have to stop scanning and start concentrating. This change in mind-set is the reason why only 20 percent of scanners become readers.

Headlines can be grouped into two general categories: **direct-** and **indirect-action**. Direct-action headlines are straightforward and informative, such as "The Power to Stop Pain." It links the brand to the benefit. Direct-action headlines are highly targeted, but they may fail to lead the reader into the message if they are not captivating enough. Indirect-action headlines are not as selective and may not provide as much information, but may be better at drawing the reader into the message and building a brand image.

Types of Direct Action Headlines

• *Assertion.* An assertion is a headline that states a claim or a promise that will motivate someone to try the product.
• *Command.* A command headline politely tells the reader to do something.
• *How-To Heads.* People are rewarded for investigating a product when the message tells them how to use it or how to solve a problem.
• *News Announcements.* News headlines are used with new-product introductions, but also with changes, reformulations, new styles, and new uses. The news value is thought to get attention and motivate people to try the product.

Types of Indirect Action Headlines

• *Puzzles.* Used strictly for their curiosity and provocative power. Puzzling statements, ambiguity, and questions require the reader to examine the body copy to get the answer or explanation. The intention is to pull readers into the body copy.
• *Associations.* These headlines use image and lifestyle to get attention and build interest.

The "Help, I Think I Need a Tourniquet" headline draws us into the Motorola Talk About™ ad. Headlines like this one, which also plays on the sounds of words, are provocative and compel people to read on to find out the point of the message. Sometimes these indirect headlines are called "blind headlines" because they give so little information. A **blind headline** is a gamble. If it is not informative or intriguing enough, the reader may move on without absorbing any product name information, but if it works as an attention getter, it can be very effective.

This ad for Motorola Talk About™ two-way radio ran in *Backpack* magazine and caught the attention of readers by using a creative headline to demonstrate the problem with bad radio reception.

How to Write Other Display Copy

Next to the headline, **captions** have the second highest readership. In addition to their pulling power, captions serve an information function. Visuals do not always say the same thing to every person; for that reason, most visuals can benefit from explanation. In addition to headlines, copywriters also craft the **subheads** that continue to help lure the reader into the body copy. Subheads are considered display copy in that they are usually larger and set in different type (bold or italic) than the body copy. Subheads are sectional headlines and are also used to break up a mass of "gray" type (or type that tends to blur together when one glances at it) in a large block of copy.

Taglines are short catchy phrases and particularly memorable phrases used at the end of an ad to complete or wrap up the creative idea. An ad from the Nike women's campaign used the headline "You are a nurturer and a provider. You are beautiful and exotic" set in an elegant script. The tagline on the next page used a rough, hand-drawn, graffiti-like image that said, "You are not falling for any of this."

Slogans, which are repeated from ad to ad as part of a campaign or a long-term brand identity effort, also may be used as taglines. To be successful, these phrases have to be catchy and memorable, although many corporate slogans fall back into marketing language or clichés and come across as leaden ("Total quality through excellence," "Excellence through total quality," or "Where quality counts").[3] The best ones have a close link to the brand name ("With a name like Smucker's, it has to be good," "America runs on Dunkin"). Consider the distinctiveness and memorability of the following slogans.

TEST YOURSELF: IDENTIFY THE COMPANY

Match the company with its slogan:

1. Together we can prevail
2. Imagination at work
3. Communication without boundaries
4. A mind is a terrible thing to waste
5. Our challenge is life
6. Know How
7. A business of caring
8. Melts in your mouth, not in your hands
9. Always surprising
10. Inspire the next
11. When you care enough to send the very best
12. Where patients come first
13. Can you hear me now?
14. For successful living
15. Inspiration comes standard
16. When it absolutely, positively has to be there overnight

a. Merck
b. Bristol-Myers Squibb
c. Hallmark
d. Swatch
e. Avaya
f. Hitachi
g. Verizon
h. Cigna
i. FedEx
j. Diesel
k. Canon
l. Chrysler
m. M&Ms
n. United Negro College Fund
o. Aventis
p. GE

Answers to Companies: 1:b Bristol-Myers Squibb; 2:p GE; 3:e Avaya; 4:n United Negro College Fund*; 5:o Aventis; 6:k Canon; 7:h Cigna; 8:m M&Ms*; 9:d Swatch; 10:f Hitachi; 11:c Hallmark*; 12:a Merck; 13:g Verizon*; 14:j Diesel; 15:l Chrysler; 16:i FedEx*

Study the slogans in the matching activity. Which ones did you get and which ones stumped you? Note that six of the companies are identified with an asterisk in the answers. Those six have been recognized by *Advertising Week* as winners and were celebrated during the magazine's Walk of Fame (http://advertising.yahoo.com/advertisingweek_07/). In your view, why were they selected for this honor, and what makes them different (from a copy standpoint rather than media buy) from the others on the list?

America's favorite slogan for the 2006 *Adweek* Walk of Fame was the "Don't Mess with Texas" antilitter slogan. Created in 1986 by Austin-based GSD&M for the Texas Department of Transportation, the award-winning social-marketing campaign built around this slogan features billboards, print ads, radio and TV spots, and a host of celebrities (Willie Nelson, Stevie Ray Vaughan, Matthew McConaughey, George Foreman, and LeAnn Rimes, among others) who take turns with the tough-talking slogan that captures the spirit and pride of Texans. One billboard, for example, warns, "Keep Your Butts in the Car." The dontmesswithtexas.org Web site, where you can see all these ads, including the commercials, has been featured by *Adweek* as a "Cool Site."

Copywriters use a number of literary techniques to enhance the memorability of subheads, slogans, and taglines. These are other techniques copywriters use to create catchy slogans:

- *Direct address.* "Have it your way"; "Think small."
- *A startling or unexpected phrase.* Twists a common phrase to make it unexpected, as in the NYNEX campaign: "If it's out there, it's in here."
- *Rhyme, rhythm, alliteration.* Uses repetition of sounds, as in the *Wall Street Journal*'s slogan, "The daily diary of the American Dream."

- *Parallel construction.* Uses repetition of the structure of a sentence or phrase, as in Morton Salt's "When it rains, it pours."
- *Cue for the product.* Folgers' "Good to the last drop"; John Deere's "Nothing runs like a Deere"; Wheaties' "Breakfast of Champions"; "Beef. It's What's for Dinner."
- *Music.* "In the valley of the Jolly, ho-ho-ho, Green Giant."
- *Combination (rhyme, rhythm, parallel).* "It's your land, lend a hand," which is the slogan for Take Pride in America.

How to Write Body Copy

The body copy is the text of the ad, and its primary role is to maintain the interest of the reader. It develops the sales message, states the argument, summarizes the proof, and provides explanation. It is the persuasive heart of the message. You excite consumer interest with the display elements, but you win them over with the argument presented in the body copy, assuming the ad uses body copy.

Consider the way the copy is written for this classic ad that comes from the award-winning Nike women's campaign. Analyze the argument the copywriter is making and how the logic flows to a convincing conclusion. The Matter of Principle box explains the logic and message strategy behind the Nike's women's campaign. The Play ad is a more recent version of this sentiment.

> *A magazine is not a mirror. Have you ever seen anyone in a magazine who seemed even vaguely like you looking back? (If you have, turn the page.) Most magazines are made to sell us a fantasy of what we're supposed to be. They reflect what society deems to be a standard, however unrealistic or unattainable that standard is. That doesn't mean you should cancel your subscription. It means you need to remember that it's just ink on paper. And that whatever standards you set for yourself, for how much you want to weigh, for how hard you work out, or how many times you make it to the gym, should be your standards. Not someone else's.*

There are as many different kinds of writing styles as there are product personalities, but there are also some standard approaches:

- *Straightforward.* Factual copy usually written in the words of an anonymous or unacknowledged source.
- *Narrative.* Tells a story in first person or third person.
- *Dialogue.* Lets the reader "listen in" on a conversation.
- *Explanation.* Explains how something works.
- *Translation.* Technical information, such as that written for the high-tech and medical industries, which must be defined and translated into understandable language.

Two paragraphs get special attention in body copy: the **lead** paragraph and the **closing**. The lead, the first paragraph of the body copy, is another point where people test the message to see whether they want to read it. Notice in the copy from the Nike women's campaign how the first lines work to catch the attention of the target audience: "A magazine is not a mirror."

Closing paragraphs in body copy serve several functions. Usually, the last paragraph refers back to the creative concept and wraps up the Big Idea. Direct action messages usually end with a **call to action** with instructions on how to respond. A Schwinn bicycle ad that is headlined "Read poetry. Make

This "play" ad from the Nike women's campaign ad reflects this campaign's strategy of talking to women about sports in a way that reflects their attitudes and feelings.

A MATTER OF PRINCIPLE

The Principle of Truth

By Jean Grow, *Associate Professor, Marquette University*

"It wasn't advertising. It was truth. We weren't selling a damn thing. Just the truth. And behind the truth, of course, the message was brought to you by Nike."

—Janet Champ, *Nike*

The creatives who produced early Nike women's advertising (1990–1997) were an amazing trio of women (Janet Champ, copywriter, and Charlotte Moore and Rachel Manganiello, art directors). Their work was grounded in the principle of truth, fueled by creativity, and sustained by nothing less than moxie.

"Nike in 1990 was not the Nike of today," Manganiello said. There was always this "political stuff about big men's sports. And, you know, (it was like we were) just kind of siphoning off money for women. So, in some ways we couldn't be as direct as we sometimes wanted to be." However, being direct and being truthful are not always the same thing. And truth for the Nike women's brand, and for themselves, was what these women aspired to.

Living the principle of truth, and trusting their gut, is what defined their work ethic and ultimately the women's brand. Moore explained, "I would posit that market research has killed a lot of advertising that was based on effective human dialogue, because it negates faith in intuition. Guts. Living with your eyes open."

To launch the women's brand within the confines of the male parent brand was no easy assignment. The creative team members began with their "gut" and with their "eyes open." They created campaign after campaign that moved the needle, but each time the approval process was a test of their principles, with meetings that were more than tinged with gender bias.

"We were almost always the only women in the room, and they killed the stuff because it scared them," said Champ. "But we always came back. And they let us do what we wanted, as long as we didn't 'sully' the men's brand . . . and as long as women's products kept flying off the shelves, they were happy."

As time went on, their instincts and principles earned them respect. According to Champ, "We told them, pretty much, that we believed in it and they had to run it and trust us, and they sighed, once again. They were soooooo tired of hearing me say that. And they ran it and they were SHOCKED at what a nerve it touched."

In trusting their guts—in telling the truth—they created award-winning campaigns and exceeded marketing expectations. "As creative people," Moore said, "we had found our home and our voice, and we'd found the most fertile ground for the brand."

In the end, truth and the willingness to "trust your gut" are what make great brands and create fertile ground for others. When you consider the terrifically truthful Dove campaign, I suggest we owe a debt of gratitude to the women of early Nike women's advertising, who stood for truth nearly 20 years ago.

---

peace with all except the motor car," demonstrates a powerful and unexpected ending, one that is targeted to its youthful audience:

> *Schwinns are red, Schwinns are blue.*
> *Schwinns are light and agile too.*
> *Cars suck. The end.*

Print Media Requirements

The media in the print category—from newspapers and magazines to outdoor boards and product literature—all use the same copy elements, such as headlines and body copy. However, the way these elements are used varies with the objectives for using the medium.

Newspaper advertising is one of the few types of advertising that is not considered intrusive because people consult the paper as much to see what is on sale as to find out what is happening in City Hall. For this reason, the copy in newspaper advertisements does not have to work as hard as other kinds of advertising to catch the attention of its audience. Because the editorial environment of a newspaper generally is serious, newspaper ads don't have to compete as entertainment, as television ads do. As a result, most newspaper advertising copy is straightforward and informative. The writing is brief, usually just identifying the merchandise and giving critical information about styles, sizes, and prices.

SHOWCASE These posters for the Coffee Rush group of small, drive-through coffee shops, told newcomers that Coffee Rush sold more than just "a cup of joe." The copy, which had to be simple to be read by people in a car, was designed to tease people into tasting these fun drinks. These posters were contributed by Karl Schroeder, a graduate of the University of Oregon and a copywriter at Coates Kokes in Portland, Oregon. He was nominated by Professor Charles Frazer, University of Oregon.

Magazines offer better quality ad production, which is important for brand image and high-fashion advertising. On the other hand, consumers may clip and file advertising that ties in with the magazine's special interest as reference information. This type of magazine ad can be more informative and carry longer copy than do newspaper ads. Copywriters also take care to craft clever phrasing for the headlines and the body copy, which, as in the Nike women's campaign, may read more like poetry.

Directories that provide contact information, such as phone numbers and addresses, often carry display advertising. In writing a directory ad, copywriters advise using a headline that focuses on the service or store personality unless the store's name is a descriptive phrase such as "Overnight Auto Service" or "The Computer Exchange." Complicated explanations don't work well in the Yellow Pages either, because there is little space for such explanations. Putting information that is subject to change in an ad can become a problem because the directory is published only once a year.

Posters and outdoor boards are primarily visual, although the words generally try to catch consumers' attention and lock in an idea, registering a message. An effective poster is built around a creative concept that marries the words with the visual. For the Coffee Rush chain, Karl Schroeder created a series of posters to change consumers' perceptions that the shop was merely a drive-through for fast, cheap coffee. Schroeder's team did this by promoting a line of cold drinks with captivating names such as Mango Guava and Wild Berry.

One of the most famous billboard campaigns ever was for a little shaving cream company named Burma Shave. The campaign used a series of roadside signs with catchy little poems, which is a most unlikely format for a highway sign. Some 600 poems were featured in this campaign, which ran for nearly 40 years, from 1925 to 1963, until the national interstate system made the signs obsolete.[4] The product was always a hero:

If you think
she likes
your bristles
walk bare-footed
through some thistles
Burma Shave

My job is
keeping faces clean
And nobody knows
de stubble
I've seen
Burma Shave

More recently, the city of Albuquerque used the Burma Shave format to encourage drivers to reduce their speeds through a construction zone. Today, a construction zone is about the only place where traffic moves slowly enough to use a billboard with rhyming copy.

Through this maze of machines and rubble
Driving fast can cause you trouble
Take care and be alert
So no one on this road gets hurt.

The most important characteristic of copywriting for outdoor advertising is brevity. Usually, a single line serves as both a headline and product identification. Often the phrase is a play on words. A series of black-and-white billboards in the Galveston-Houston area, recruiting priests for the Roman Catholic diocese, features a Roman collar with witty wording such as, "Yes, you will combat evil. No, you don't get to wear a cape." Others are more thoughtful, "Help wanted. Inquire within yourself." Some experts suggest that billboard copywriters use no more than six to seven words. The copy must catch attention and be memorable. For example, a billboard for Orkin pest control showed a package wrapped up with the word Orkin on the tag. The headline read, "A little something for your ant."

Sometimes called **collateral materials** because they are used in support of an advertising campaign, product literature—brochures, pamphlets, flyers, and other materials— provide details about a product, company, or event. They can be as varied as hang tags in new cars or bumper stickers. Taco Bell's little messages on its tiny taco sauce packages are an example of clever writing in an unexpected place with messages like: "Save a bun, eat a taco," "Warning! You're about to make a taco very happy," and "My other taco is a chalupa."

Typically, product literature is a heavy copy format, or at least a format that provides room for explanatory details along with visuals; the body copy may dominate the piece. For a pamphlet with folds, a writer must also consider how the message is conveyed as the piece is unfolded. These pieces can range from a simple three-panel flyer to a glitzy multipage, full-color brochure.

HOW TO WRITE RADIO COPY

Ads that are broadcast on either radio or television are usually 15, 30, or 60 seconds in length, although 10- and 15-second spots may be used for brand reminders or station identification. This short length means the commercials must be simple enough for consumers to grasp, yet intriguing enough to prevent viewers from switching the station. That's why creativity is important to create clutter-busting ads that break through the surrounding noise and catch the listener's attention.

Because radio is a transitory medium, the ability of the listener to remember facts (such as the name of the advertiser, addresses, and phone numbers) is difficult. That's why copywriters repeat the key points of brand name and identification information, such as a phone number or Web address. Radio is pervasive in that it surrounds many of our activities, but it is seldom the listener's center of attention and is usually in the background. Radio urges the copywriter to reach into the depths of imagination to create a clutter-busting idea that grabs the listener's attention.

Radio's special advantage, referred to as **theater of the mind**, is that in a narrative format the story is visualized in the listener's imagination. Radio copywriters imagine they are writing a musical play that will be performed before an audience whose eyes are closed. The copywriter has all the theatrical tools of voices, sound effects, and music, but no visuals. How the characters look and where the scene is set come from their listener's imagination.

As an example of theater of the mind, consider a now-classic commercial written by humorist Stan Freberg for the Radio Advertising Bureau. The spot opens with an announcer explaining that Lake Michigan will be drained and filled with hot chocolate and a 700-foot mountain of whipped cream. The Royal Canadian Air Force will fly overhead and drop a ten-ton maraschino cherry, all to the applause of 25,000 screaming extras. The point is that things that can't be created in real life can be created by radio in the imagination of listeners.

The Radio Advertising Bureau has used the slogan "I saw it on the radio" to illustrate the power of radio's ability to evoke rich images in the listener's mind. Research indicates that the use of imagery in radio advertising leads to high levels of attention and more positive general attitudes toward the ad and its claims.[5] Even though we're talking about imagery, it is produced by the copywriter's masterful use of the tools of audio—voice, music, and sound effects.

Tools of Radio Copywriting

Print copywriters use a variety of tools—headlines, body copy, slogans, and so forth—to write their copy. In radio advertising, the tools are the audio elements the copywriter uses to craft a commercial, which are voice, music, and sound effects.

Voice The most important element in radio advertising is voices, which are heard in jingles, spoken dialogue, and announcements. Most commercials use an announcer either as the central voice or at the closing to wrap up the product identification. The voices the copywriter specifies help listeners "see" the characters in the commercial. The copywriter understands that we imagine people and what they are like based on their voices. Dialogue uses character voices to convey an image of the speaker: a child, an old man, an executive, a Little League baseball player, or an opera singer. Copywriters specify voices for commercials based on the evocative qualities they contribute to the message. Radio announcer Ken Nordine's voice was once described as sounding like warm chocolate; Ray Charles was described as having a charcoal voice.

Radio advertising relies on conversational style and vernacular language. A good radio copywriter also has an ear for the distinctive patterns of speech for the target audience. Spoken language is different from written language. We talk in short sentences, often in sentence fragments and run-ons. We seldom use complex sentences in speech. We use contractions that would drive an English teacher crazy. Slang can be hard to handle and sound phony, but copy that picks up the nuances of people's speech sounds natural. In radio advertising, speaking style should match the speech of the target audience. Each group has its own way of speaking, its own phrasing. Teenagers don't talk like 8-year-olds or 50-year-olds.

Principle
Radio copywriters try to match the conversational style of the target audience.

Music Similar to movie scriptwriters, radio copywriters have a sense of the imagery of music and the role it plays in creating dramatic effects. Music can be used behind the dialogue to create mood and establish the setting. Any mood, from that of a circus to that of a candlelit dinner, can be conveyed through music. Advertisers can have a piece of music composed for a commercial or can borrow it from a previously recorded song. Numerous music libraries sell stock music that is not copyrighted.

The primary use of music is in support of **jingles**, which is a commercial in song. Radio copywriters understand the interplay of catchy phrases and "hummable" music to create little songs that stick in our minds. Anything consumers can sing along with helps them remember and get involved with the message.

One of the most famous jingles of all time was a song "I'd like to teach the world to sing" produced for Coca-Cola in 1969 by its agency, McCann-Erickson. The jingle became a television commercial, but it also was an instant hit worldwide. It was recorded as a pop song without the Coke reference and sold millions of copies. Called "Hilltop," the TV commercial shows young people singing "I'd like to buy the world a Coke" on a hilltop in Italy. Surveys continue to identify it as one of the best commercials of all time, and the sheet music continues to sell more than 30 years after the song was first written. Here are the lyrics to this famous song that is still run by Coke on special occasions:

> *I'd like to buy the world a home and furnish it with love,*
> *Grow apple trees and honey bees, and snow white turtle doves.*
> *I'd like to teach the world to sing in perfect harmony,*
> *I'd like to buy the world a Coke and keep it company.*
> [Repeat the last two lines, and in the background]:
> *It's the real thing, Coke is what the world wants today.*

Jingle houses are companies that specialize in writing and producing commercial music, catchy songs about a product that carry the theme and product identification. A custom-made jingle created for a single advertiser can cost $10,000 or more. In contrast, many jingle houses create "syndicated" jingles made up of a piece of music that can be applied to different lyrics and sold to several different local advertisers in different markets around the country for as little as $1,000 or $2,000.

Sound Effects   The sound of seagulls, automobile horns honking, and the cheers of fans at a stadium all create images in our minds to cue the setting and drive the action. The Freberg commercial shows how **sound effects (sfx)** are used in a radio script, along with the importance of these effects in making a commercial attention-getting and memorable. Sound effects can be original, but more often they are taken from *sound-effect libraries* available on CDs or online.

The Practice of Radio Copywriting

The following guidelines for writing effective radio commercials address the distinctive characteristics of radio advertising:

- *Keep it personal.* Radio advertising has an advantage over print—the ability to use the human voice. The copy for radio ads should use conversational language—as if someone is "talking with" the consumer rather than "selling to" the consumer.
- *Speak to listeners' interests.* Radio allows for specialized programming to target markets. Listeners mostly tune in to hear music, but talk radio is popular, too. There are shows on health, pets, finance, politics—whatever interests people. Copywriters should design commercials to speak to that audience interest and use the appropriate tone of voice. If the station plays heavy metal music, then the style and tone of the commercial might be raucous and spirited.
- *Wake up the inattentive.* Most people who are listening to the radio are doing something else at the same time, such as jogging, driving, or fixing breakfast. Radio spots must be designed to break through the inattention and capture attention in the first three seconds with sound effects, music, questions, commands, or something unexpected.
- *Make it memorable.* To help the listener remember what you are selling, commercial copy should mention the name of the product emphatically and repeat it. An average of three mentions in a 30-second commercial and five mentions in a 60-second commercial may not be too frequent, as long as the repetition is not done in a forced and/or annoying manner. Copywriters use taglines and other key phrases to lock the product in consumers' memories.
- *Include call to action.* The last thing listeners hear is what they tend to remember, so copywriters make sure the product is it. In radio that's particularly important since there is no way to show a picture of the product or the label. Those last words communicate the Big Idea in a way that serves as a call to action and reminds listeners of the brand name at the close of the commercial. "Got Milk?" is not only a highly memorable slogan, it's also a strong call to action.
- *Create image transfer.* Radio advertisements are sometimes designed to link to a television commercial. Called **image transfer**, the visuals from the TV version are re-created in a listener's mind by the use of key phrases and ideas from the TV commercial.

Planning the Radio Commercial: Scripts

Copywriters working on a radio commercial use a standard **radio script** format to write the copy to certain time blocks—all the words, dialogue, lyrics, sound effects, instructions, and descriptions. The instructions and descriptions are to help the producer tape the commercial so that it sounds exactly as the copywriter imagined. The script format usually has the source of the audio written down the left side, and the content—words an announcer reads, dialogue, and description of the sound effects and music—on the right. The instructions and descriptions, anything that isn't spoken, are in capital letters.

An example comes from Karl Schroeder, a copywriter in Portland, Oregon, who got the assignment to write radio ads that would sell listeners on using newspaper classified ads. By way of background, Schroeder explained that the *Register-Guard*, Oregon's second largest newspaper, wanted to boost classified ad sales. He explained that his creative team at the Coates Kokes agency started with consumer research. "One insight we discovered was that a lot of people just get the paper for a section or two, not the whole thing. Taking what we learned and applying it to Classifieds, it made sense to make the paper more approachable by using humor in the advertising. Maybe they'll buy the paper more often if it seems less stuffy. We thought it also made sense to remind those one-section users that the paper has a useful Classifieds section. In addition, we wanted to reinforce the message that the Classifieds will reach more people in Lane County than any other selling tool." So that was the strategy behind using radio ads to sell newspaper ads.

HOW TO WRITE TELEVISION COPY

Television copywriters understand that it is the moving image—the action—that makes television so much more engaging than print. The challenge for the writer is to fuse the images with the words to present not only a creative concept, but also a story, as the Frontier commercials discussed in the previous chapter do so well.

One of the strengths of television is its ability to reinforce verbal messages with visuals or reinforce visuals with verbal messages. As Ogilvy's Peter Hochstein explains,

> The idea behind a television commercial is unique in advertising. The TV commercial consists of pictures that move to impart facts or evoke emotion, and selling words that are not read but heard. The perfect combination of sight and sound can be an extremely potent selling tool.[6]

Viewers watching a program they enjoy often are absorbed to a degree only slightly less than that experienced by people watching a movie in a darkened theater. Storytelling is one way that copywriters can present action in a television commercial more powerfully than in other media. Television's ability to touch our emotions and to show us things—to demonstrate how they look and work—make television advertising highly persuasive. Effective television commercials can achieve this level of audience absorption if they are written to maximize the dramatic aspects of moving images and storytelling.

These are just a few of the techniques used in television advertising. Here are more.

Principle
In great television commercials, words and pictures work together seamlessly to deliver the creative concept through sight, sound, and motion.

Technique	Message Design
• *Action:* When you watch television, you are watching a walking, talking, moving world that gives the illusion of being three-dimensional.	• Good television advertising uses the effect of action and motion to attract attention and sustain interest. Torture tests, steps, and procedures are all actions that are easier to present on TV than in print.
• *Demonstration:* Seeing is believing. Believability and credibility—the essence of persuasion—are high because we believe what we see with our own eyes.	• If you have a strong sales message that lends itself to demonstration, such as how-to messages, television is the ideal medium for that message.
• *Storytelling:* Most of the programming on television is narrative, so commercials use storytelling to take advantage of the medium's strengths.	• TV is our society's master storyteller because of its ability to present a plot and the action that leads to a conclusion in which the product plays a major role. TV can dramatize the situation in which a product is used and the type of people using it.

• *Emotion:* The ability to touch the feelings of the viewer makes television commercials entertaining, diverting, amusing, and absorbing. Real-life situations with all their humor, anger, fear, pride, jealousy, and love come alive on the screen. Humor, in particular, works well on television.

• Emotional appeals are found in natural situations with which everyone can identify. Hallmark has produced some tear-jerking commercials about the times of our lives that we remember by the cards we receive and save. Kodak and Polaroid have used a similar strategy for precious moments that are remembered in photographs.

Tools of Television Copywriting

Television copywriters have two primary toolkits: audio and visual. Both words and pictures are designed to create exactly the right impact. Because of the number of video and audio elements, as well as the many ways they can be combined, a television commercial is one of the most complex of all advertising forms.

Video When we watch a commercial, we are more aware of what we're seeing than anything else. Copywriters keep in mind that visuals and motion, the silent speech of film, should convey as much of the message—the Big Idea—as possible. Likewise, emotion, which is the effect created by storytelling, is expressed convincingly in facial expressions, gestures, and other body language. Because television is theatrical, many of the copywriter's tools, such as characters, costumes, sets and locations, props, lighting, optical and computerized special effects, and on-screen graphics, are similar to those you would use in a play, television show, or movie.

The creative team working on a television commercial thinks in terms of how the narrative splits into scenes. Underlying the internal logic of a commercial is a key visual or **key frame** that summarizes the idea behind the commercial. The Inside Story describes a campaign that used television spots and key frames from the commercials as images on posters. The TV tagline, "Where Will It Take You?" appears on the posters to express the thought that the Film Festival will take you to some exotic locations.

Audio As in radio, the three audio elements are music, voices, and sound effects, but they are used differently in television commercials because they are connected to a visual image. The copywriter, for example, may have an announcer speak directly to the viewer or engage in a dialogue with another person, who may or may not be on camera. The copywriter writes the words they will say and blocks out on paper how this "talk" happens. A common manipulation of the camera–announcer relationship is the **voice-over**, in which an announcer who is not visible describes some kind of action on the screen. Sometimes a voice is heard **off camera**, which means you can't see the speaker and the voice is coming from the side, behind, or above.

A commercial for Geico Insurance won a John Caples International Award for its engaging use of a voice. The copywriter was responsible for both the words and the way they were delivered. In a spot titled "Collect Call," which was set in a hospital waiting room, a man places a collect call to his parents:

To save on the costs of the call, he states as his name:

"Bob Wehadababyit'saboy."

The message is delivered, but the call is refused by his parents who didn't understand the message. The next scene shows him trying to cram even more information into his name:

"Bob Wehadababyit'saboyeightpoundssevenouncesMom'sfine."

The voice-over at the end advises the audience that they don't have to cheat the phone company to save money. A 15-minute call to Geico can save them up to 15 percent on their insurance.

Music is also important in most commercials. Sometimes it is just used as background; other times the song is the focus of the commercial. In recognition of the role of music in advertising, Universal Music released a CD in 2001 called "As Seen on TV: Songs from

THE INSIDE STORY

The Florida Film Festival: It's a Trip
By Lara Mann, *Copywriter, DraftFCB, Chicago*

Each spring in Central Florida, the Florida Film Festival screens the best independent films of the year. These are generally innovative, offbeat films—not your typical Hollywood formula.

My former agency, Fry Hammond Barr Advertising in Orlando, was charged with generating buzz for the event and increasing attendance. The team included myself as copywriter, Sean Brunson as art director, Tim Fisher as creative director, John Deeb as photographer, and Brad Fuller as director.

To encourage average moviegoers to expand their horizons, we placed attendees in dramatically unexpected surroundings. The contrast between watcher and environment illustrated the excitement in leaving one's comfort zone. It's not just watching a movie—it's traveling unexplored territory.

We decided to advertise with TV commercials because they best replicated the movie-watching experience. When it comes to creating dramatic tension in advertising, nothing beats a television commercial. (At least, for now!)

We used posters as a supporting medium because they inexpensively provided visual impact in a prime location for our target: movie theaters where the festival films would eventually be screened. Taking the "travel" concept even further, we created giant travel posters that advertised states of mind as actual travel destinations.

The campaign worked. It generated buzz, increased attendance, and won a slew of awards at the Orlando ADDY awards, including Best of Show.

An advertising graduate of the University of Florida, Lara Mann was nominated by Professor Elaine Wagner.

Commercials," a collection of tunes that have become popular—or resurrected—thanks to their use in TV commercials. Included among the 20 songs are "Mr. Roboto" by Styx, "Right Here, Right Now" by Fatboy Slim, "Lust for Life" by Iggy Pop, and "Got to Give It Up" by Marvin Gaye. All of these songs have been used effectively in a television commercial. Clash's "London Calling" song became the theme for a highly successful sales event for Jaguar.

Other TV Tools The creative tools examined next are the setting, casting, costumes, props, and lighting—all of which the copywriter must describe in the script. The setting, or **set**, is where the action takes place. It can be something in the studio, from a simple tabletop to a constructed set that represents a storefront or the inside of a home. Commercials shot outside the studio are said to be filmed **on location**, which means the entire crew and cast are transported somewhere away from the studio.

For many commercials, the most important element is the people, who are called **talent**. Finding the right person for each role is called **casting**. People can be cast as:

- *Announcers* (either onstage or offstage), presenters, introducers
- *Spokespersons* (or "spokesthings," such as the Geico Gecko)
- *Character types* (old woman, baby, skin diver, police officer)
- *Celebrities*, such as Tiger Woods who is the world's current most-valued endorser

Costumes and makeup can be an important part of the story depending upon the characterizations in the commercial. Of course, historical stories need period costumes, but modern scenes may also require special clothing such as ski outfits, swimsuits, or cowboy boots. Makeup may be important if you need to change a character from young to old. The copywriter must specify all these details in the script. The director usually manipulates the lighting, but the copywriter might specify special lighting effects in the script. For example, you might read "Intense bright light as though reflected from snow," or "Light flickering on people's faces as if reflecting from a television screen."

Copywriters might also have to specify the commercial's **pace**—how fast or slowly the action progresses. Some messages are best developed at a languid pace; others work better when presented at an upbeat, fast pace.

Planning the TV Commercial

Copywriters must plan how long the commercial will be, what shots will appear in each scene, what the key visual will be, and where and how to shoot the commercial. Other key decisions the copywriter must consider in planning a commercial are the length, number of scenes, and key frames. The common lengths of commercials are 10, 15, 20, 30, and 60 seconds. The 10-, 15-, and 20-second lengths are used for reminders and product or station identification. The 60-second spot, which is common in radio, has almost disappeared in television because of the increasing cost of air time. The most common length for a TV commercial is 30 seconds.

A commercial is planned in **scenes**—segments of action that occur in a single location. A scene may include several shots from different angles. A 30-second commercial usually is planned with four to six scenes, but a fast-paced commercial may have many more. Because television is a visual medium, the message is often developed from a key visual that conveys the heart of the concept. A key frame is that visual that sticks in the mind and becomes the image viewers remember when they think about the commercial.

Copywriters need to answer many questions when planning a television spot. How much product information should there be in the commercial? Should the action be fast or slow? Is it wise to defy tradition and create unusual, even controversial ads as Axe does? How intrusive should the ad be? Every producer and director will respond to these questions differently, depending on personal preferences and the advertising objectives. Nevertheless, these general principles as outlined by Drewniany and Jewler in their creative strategy book and earlier editions of their book are relevant for most effective television commercials:[7]

- *What's the big idea* you need to get across? In 30 seconds you barely have time to do much more than that. Alternative concepts are also tested as key visuals in developing the idea for the commercial. For each idea, a card with the key visual drawn on it is given to a respondent, along with a paragraph that describes the concept and how it will be played out in the commercial.
- *What's the benefit* of that big idea, and who does it benefit? Connect the big idea back to the target audience.
- *How can you turn that benefit into a visual element?* This visual is what sticks in people's minds.
- *How can you gain the interest* of viewers at the beginning? The first three seconds are critical.

- *How can you focus on a key visual*, a scene that encapsulates your entire selling message into one neat package?
- *Is the commercial single-minded?* Tell one important story per commercial. Tell it clearly, tell it memorably, and involve your viewer.
- *Is the product identified and shown* in close-up at the end?

Scripts, Storyboards, and Photoboards Commercials are planned with two documents—a **television script** prepared by the copywriter and a storyboard drawn by the art director. Similar to a radio script, a TV script is the written version of the commercial's plan. It contains all the words, dialogue, lyrics (if important to the ad message), instructions, and descriptions of the details we've been discussing—sets, costumes, lighting, and so forth. For television commercials that use dialogue, the script is written in two columns, with the audio on the right and the video on the left.

The key to the structure of a television script is the relationship between the audio and the video. Note how the video includes descriptions of key frames, characters, actions, and camera movements in the commercial. The dialogue is typed regular but the instructions and labels are typed in all-capital letters. Sometimes the script is in a two-column format with the video instructions on the left and the audio in the right column, although this script uses a simpler format.

The Doritos "Checkout Girl" is an example of a television script. This commercial was one of the finalists in a competition by Frito-Lay that invited viewers to submit commercials to be run on the Super Bowl. This commercial was written and directed by Kristin Dehnert and produced by Leann Emmert. The Inside Story describes how the team developed the Checkout Girl strategy. A version of the script follows.

A **storyboard**, which is a visual plan or layout of the commercial, shows the number of scenes, composition of the shots, and progression of the action. The script information usually appears below the key images. A **photoboard** uses photographic stills instead of art to illustrate the progression of images. (See Flip commercial in Chapter 12.)

THE INSIDE STORY

The Thinking behind the Doritos "Checkout Girl"

By Kristin Dehnert and Leann Emmert

Our strategy was simple—to come up with a commercial specific to Doritos that makes people laugh. In writing the spot, writer/director Kristin found inspiration in the multitude of interesting and silly names for the different flavored chips, such as *Blazin' Buffalo & Ranch* and *Salsa Verde*. She also found humor in the idea of the mundane life of a checkout person being rocked by an exciting product. This humor and branding was then folded into the idea of the spot, which was a flirtatious interaction between two unsuspecting Doritos lovers at a grocery store.

Placing the spot at a grocery store gave us several advantages. We were operating on a shoestring budget (out of our pockets), so we had plenty of Doritos products available to us. We made sure that any product seen on camera was either Doritos, or fell under the umbrella of the parent companies Frito-Lay or Pepsi. Also, grocery stores are visually interesting and colorful, giving our spot a higher production value.

Our strategy with casting was to stick with the humor of the spot. We held a casting session, and out of the 25 or so actors that came to read for the spot of the

Checkout Girl, Stephanie Lesh-Farrell nailed it. We cast our friend George Reddick as the Male Customer, knowing that his great look and subtle humor would play well off the explosive energy of our checkout girl. Along with the talented cast and hilarious script, we put together a skilled production crew to bring the spot to life.

During filming and later during postproduction, we labored over every moment and frame, always referring back to the original goal: Make it funny and showcase the product. With this strategic combination of humor, branding, and we can't leave out all the stars aligning, "Checkout Girl" was selected to air during the 2007 Super Bowl, which is the biggest advertising touchdown possible.

Kristin Dehnert graduated from the University of Illinois, and Leann Emmert graduated from the University of Colorado.

Doritos: Checkout Girl

:30 seconds

Video	Audio
INTERIOR GROCERY STORE AT CHECKOUT REGISTER	
A REGULAR GUY CUSTOMER at the checkout register buys bags and bags of Doritos. The odd, offbeat CHECKOUT GIRL asks in a monotone voice:	CHECKOUT GIRL: Paper or plastic?
	GUY: Paper's fine.
Action starts mellow, then builds.	
She scans the first bag of Doritos	CHECKOUT GIRL: I like these.
She scans another bag.	CHECKOUT GIRL (CONT'D): Oh, Nacho cheese. (chest bang) Old school.
He smiles, thinks she's kinda nuts. She scans another—	CHECKOUT GIRL (CONT'D): Fiery Habanero. (passionately yells) Yeah! Those are hot!
She composes herself. He's weirdly turned on now. She scans another—	CHECKOUT GIRL (CONT'D): Oh, Salsa Verrrrrde. Arrgh! (tiger sound)
Flirting, he growls back to her—	GUY: Arrrrrrrrrr.
Now she's super frisky! Scans another!!!!—	
CUT TO:	CHECKOUT GIRL: Blazin' Buffalo and Ranch!!
EXPLODING DORITOS TAG!	Giddy up!
CUT BACK TO:	
INTERIOR GROCERY STORE AT CHECKOUT REGISTER	
Sound of MICROPHONE FEEDBACK as the Checkout Girl grabs the microphone at the register. She looks like she's been through the ringer—	SFX: MICROPHONE FEEDBACK
	CHECKOUT GIRL: I'm gonna need a clean up on register six.
	SFX: She chomps into a Doritos chip—
	CRUNCH.

WRITING FOR THE WEB

The Web is more interactive than any other mass medium. Not only do viewers initiate the contact, they can send e-mail on many Web sites. This makes Web advertising more like two-way communication, and that's a major point of difference from other advertising forms. As a result, the Web copywriter is challenged to attract people to the site and to manage a dialogue-based communication experience. Web advertisers have to listen and respond as well as target messages to audiences. That's a major shift in how Web marketing communicators think about advertising.

In this complicated, fast-changing medium, there aren't a lot of rules. For banners and other formats that look like advertising and seek to attract someone to a company's Web site, verbosity is a killer. In that situation, no one wants to read a lot of type online. However, the Web is an information medium and users come to it, in some cases, for extensive reference information—formats that look a lot like catalogs, or even encyclopedias. The dontmesswithtexas.org Web site, for example, invites visitors into the campaign with advertising materials, testimonials, letters, special events, and involvement programs. The language reflects the tough-talking slogan. For example, one section asks, "Who wants to live in a pig sty? . . . Why swim in an ashtray?"

The challenge for Web advertisers is to understand the user's situation and design messages that fit the user's needs. That means Web copywriters have to be able to write everything from catchy phrases for banners to copy that works like traditional advertisements, brochures, or catalogs. A basic principle, however, is that good writing is good writing, whether it be for traditional advertising media or for the Web.

Principle
To write great copy for the Web, copywriters must think of it as an interactive medium and open up opportunities for interaction with the consumer.

Banners

The most common form of online advertising are small banner ads containing text, images, and perhaps animation. Banners in this extremely small format have to be creative to stand out amidst the clutter on a typical Web page and, similar to outdoor advertising, they have to grab the surfer's attention with few words. Effective banners must arouse the interest of the viewer, who is often browsing through other information on the computer screen. The key to stopping surfers is vivid graphics and clever phrases. In general, the copywriter has these strategies for grabbing the surfer.[8]

The copywriter must think about:

1. *Offering a deal* that promises a discount or a freebie as a prize.
2. *Using an involvement device* such as a challenge or contest.
3. *Changing the offer frequently,* perhaps even daily. One of the reasons people surf the Internet is to find out what's happening now. Good ads exploit "nowness" and "newsiness."
4. *Keeping the writing succinct* because most surfers have short attention spans and get bored easily.
5. *Focusing surfers' attention* by asking provocative questions or offering knowledge they can use.
6. *Using the advertisement* to solicit information and opinions from users as part of your research. Reward surfers for sharing their opinions with you by offering them three free days of a daily horoscope or something else they might find fun or captivating.

Sometimes banners provide brand reminder information only, like a billboard, but they usually also invite viewers to "click" on the banner to link to an ad or the advertiser's home page. The effectiveness of such efforts is monitored by the number of click-throughs. Their creators make banners entertaining by using multimedia effects such as animation and sound, interactivity, emotional appeals, color, and provocative headlines. One mistake copywriters sometimes make, however, is to forget to include the company name or brand in the banner or ad. Surfers should be able to tell immediately what product or brand the banner is advertising. Effective banner ads satisfy the need for entertainment, information, and context (a link to a product), and often use promotional incentives, such as prizes or gifts, to motivate visitors to click through to the sponsor's Web site[9] to drive action.

Web Ads

Similar to traditional advertising, Web ads are designed to create awareness and interest in a product and build a brand image. In terms of creating interest, good copywriting works well in any medium, including the Internet. The "Ocean Speaks" ads in the Matter of Practice box illustrate how the same writing style can transfer from print to the Internet to maintain a brand personality. In contrast Burton Snowboards (http://www.burton.com/company) uses copy that speaks in the voice of the product's user but also builds an association with a distinctive brand personality:

We stand sideways.
We sleep on floors in cramped resort hotel rooms.
We get up early and go to sleep late.
We've been mocked.
We've been turned away from resorts that won't have us.
We are relentless.
We dream it, we make it, we break it, we fix it.
We create.
We destroy.
We wreck ourselves day in and day out and yet we stomp that one trick or find
that one line that keeps us coming back.
We progress.

It closes with the following corporate copy:

Burton Snowboards is a rider driven company solely dedicated to creating the
best snowboarding equipment on the planet.

Other Web Formats

Many marketers are experimenting with new forms of Web advertising such as games, pop-up windows, daughter windows, and side frames. For example, one Procter & Gamble site supports the Scope "Send-a-Kiss" campaign, where visitors can send an electronic kiss to the special people in their lives. The site is customized for special holidays such as Valentine's Day and Mother's Day. P&G has found that of those who visit the site, 20 percent actually send e-mail kisses to Mom on Mother's Day.

Ultimately, these marketers want Web ads that are totally interactive. An Internet approach that uses broadcast media as a model may be the answer. They want to make Internet advertising better than television advertising—all the visual impact of traditional broadcast with the additional value of interactivity. The creative team comes up with the ideas for such Web formats, and it's up to the copywriter to put the idea in words and explain how the user's experience with this Web site will work.

COPYWRITING IN A GLOBAL ENVIRONMENT

Language affects the creation of the advertising. English is more economical than many other languages. This creates a major problem when the space for copy is laid out for English and one-third more space is needed for French or Spanish. However, English does not have the subtlety of other languages such as Greek, Chinese, or French. Those languages have many different words for situations and emotions that do not translate precisely into English. Standardizing the copy content by translating the appeal into the language of the foreign market is fraught with possible communication blunders. It is rare to find a copywriter who is fluent in both the domestic and foreign language and familiar with the culture of the foreign market.

Headlines in any language often rely on a play on words, themes that are relevant to one country, or slang. Because these verbal techniques don't cross borders well, copywriters must remove them from the advertising unless the meaning or intent can be re-created in other languages. For this reason, international campaigns are not literally translated. Instead, a copywriter usually rewrites them in the second language. An ad for a Rome laundry shows how a poor translation can send the wrong message: "Ladies, leave your clothes here and spend the afternoon having a good time."

Although computer words and advertising terms are almost universally of English derivation, some languages simply do not have words equivalent to other English expressions. Since 1539 the French have had legislation to keep their language "pure" and now have a

A MATTER OF PRACTICE

The Ocean Speaks

The scuba diving industry wanted to revive interest in the sport of scuba, both with current divers and potential newcomers. The objective of this striking campaign was to build a relationship with diving and move people from print to the company's Web site.

Art director Chris Hutchinson explains, "We created a campaign in the literal voice of the ocean. The Ocean irreverently compares itself to the dull world up above and invites people to come down for a visit. Instead of using traditional beauty shots of scuba diving, we commissioned surreal organic underwater scenes. The ads were recently featured in Archive. The creative idea is that the ocean not only has a personality, it speaks in the body copy."

First read the copy from these ads, then consider how that style of writing has been transferred to the Web site.

> **Dear Hollywood,**
> *You're blowing this whole shark thing out of proportion.*
> *Not every shark becomes a ravenous lunatic at the scent of a paper cut.*
> *Most of them would rather eat fish than divers anyway. The neoprene gets stuck in their teeth.*
> *—the Ocean*

> **Excuse me Mr. Jobs.**
> *This whole iMac thing—distinctly shell-like.*
> *I think you ripped those colors from me too.*
> *Let's give credit where credit is due, huh?*
> *—the Ocean*

The ocean also speaks on the Web site (http://time2dive.com). Once on the home page, visitors identify themselves as either new divers or experienced divers. Each page has its own message from the ocean at the top, followed by a sign-up sheet. This is from the new diver page:

> **About this weekend.**
> *I have 15,000 unidentified species down here all waiting to be classified.*
> *But if you have to help somebody move or something, I'll understand.*
> *—the Ocean*

And this is from the old timers' page:

> **Haven't seen you in a while. So what's up?**
> *It's come to my attention that you haven't been diving in what, 6 months?*
> *Did I do something wrong? Was it that rip tide when you were body surfing? Lighten up.*
> *—the Ocean*

Source: Ads contributed by Chris Hutchinson, art director for Weiden + Kennedy, Portland, Oregon, and previously with Bulldog Drummond, San Diego, where he designed these ads. A graduate of the University of Oregon, he and his work were nominated for this feature by Professor Charles Frazer.

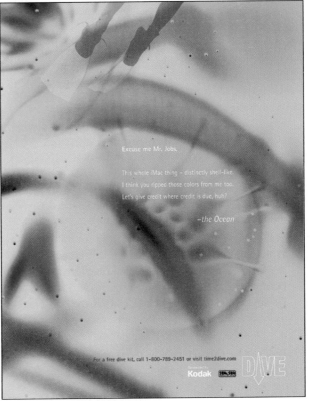

government agency to prevent words, especially English words, from corrupting the French language. The words *marketing* and *weekend*, unacceptable to the French government agency, are translated literally as "study the market" (or "pertaining to trade") and "end of the week," respectively.

Experience suggests that the most reasonable solution to the language problem is to use bilingual copywriters who understand the full meaning of the English text and can capture the essence of the message in the second language. It takes a brave and trusting international creative director to approve copy he or she doesn't understand but is assured is right. A **back translation** of the ad copy from the foreign language into the domestic one is always a good idea, but it seldom conveys a complete cultural interpretation.

IT'S A WRAP

Got Milk? Got Awards?

got milk?

Good creative ideas like the Got Milk? advertising campaign work, not just because they are funny or touch the emotions, but because they stick in the memory and move people to respond.

You can imagine that a campaign that's become part of the American culture has probably won lots of awards. That's true for the Got Milk? campaign. The Aaron Burr commercial won Best in Show at the 1994 Clio Awards. The campaign was named in *Ad Age*'s Top 100 Advertising Campaigns.

The National "Got Milk?" Milk Mustache campaign has also been highly honored with prestigious awards, including Clios, Addys, One Show, and Effies. All the honors are rewarding, but did the campaign accomplish its objective to reverse the 15-year downward slide of the consumption of milk? After the first year of the campaign, California's milk sales rose to 755 million gallons from the previous year's 740 million gallons. Drinking milk is cool. So is the advertising.

Key Points Summary

1. **What basic style of writing is used for advertising copy?** Words and pictures work together to shape a creative concept; however, it is the clever phrases and "magic words" crafted by copywriters that make ideas understandable and memorable. Copywriters who have an ear for language match the tone of the writing to the target audience. Good copy is succinct and single-minded. Copy that is less effective uses adese to imitate the stereotyped style of advertising.

2. **Which copy elements are essential to a print ad?** The key elements of a print ad are the headlines and body copy. Headlines target the prospect, draw the reader's attention, identify the product, start the sale, and lure the reader into the body copy. Body copy provides persuasive details, such as support for claims, as well as proof and reasons why.

3. **How can we characterize the message and tools of radio advertising?** Radio commercials are personal and play to consumers' interests. However, radio is primarily a background medium. Special techniques, such as repetition, are used to enhance retention. The three audio tools are voice, music, and sound effects.

4. **What is the best way to summarize the major elements of television commercials?** The elements of TV commercials are audio and video tools. Television commercials can be characterized as using action, emotion, and demonstration to create messages that are intriguing as well as intrusive.

5. **How is Web advertising written?** Web advertising is interactive and involving. Online advertising has primarily focused on banners, although advertisers are using new forms that look more like magazine or television ads. Banners and other forms of Web advertising have to stand out amid the clutter on a typical Web page and arouse the viewer's interest.

Key Terms

adese, p. 392
back translation, p. 412
blind headline, p. 394
body copy, p. 392
brag-and-boast copy, p. 392
call to action, p. 397
captions, p. 395
casting, p. 406
closing paragraph, p. 397
collateral materials, p. 400

copywriter, p. 389
direct-action headline, p. 394
display copy, p. 392
headline, p. 392
image transfer, p. 402
indirect-action headline,
   p. 394
jingle, p. 401
key frame, p. 404

lead paragraph, p. 397
off camera, p. 404
on location, p. 406
pace, p. 406
photoboard, p. 407
radio script, p. 402
scene, p. 406
set, p. 405
slogans, p. 395

sound effects (sfx), p. 402
storyboard, p. 407
subheads, p. 395
taglines, p. 395
talent, p. 406
television script, p. 407
theater of the mind, p. 400
voice-over, p. 404
your-name-here copy, p. 390

Review Questions

1. What is adese, and why is it a problem in advertising copy?
2. Describe the various copy elements of a print ad.
3. What is the difference between direct and indirect action headlines? Find an example of each and explain how it works.
4. What qualities make a good tagline or slogan?
5. What is the primary role of body copy, and how does it accomplish that?
6. Explain the message characteristics of radio advertising. What does "theater of the mind" mean to a radio copywriter? What are the primary tools used by the radio copywriter?
7. What are the major characteristics of TV ads? Describe the tools of television commercial copywriting.
8. Discuss how Web advertising is written.

Discussion Questions

1. Creative directors say the copy and art must work together to create a concept. Consider all the ads in this chapter and the preceding chapter and identify one that you believe best demonstrates that principle? Explain what the words contribute and how they work with the visual.
2. One principle of print copywriting is that the headline catches the reader's eye, but the body copy wins the reader's heart and mind. Find an ad that demonstrates that principle and explain how it works.
3. A principle of TV message design is that television is primarily a visual medium. However, very few television commercials are designed without a vocal element (actors or announcers). Even the many commercials that visually demonstrate products in action use an offscreen voice to provide information. Why is there a need to use a voice in a television commercial?
4. *Three-Minute Debate:* Professor Strong has set up a debate between the advertising sales director of the campus

newspaper and the manager of the campus radio station, which is a commercial operation. During the discussion the newspaper representative says that most radio commercials sound like newspaper ads, but are harder to follow. The radio manager responds by claiming that radio creativity works with "the theater of the mind" and is more engaging than newspaper ads.

In class, organize into small teams with pairs of teams taking one side or the other. Set up a series of three-minute debates with each side having 1½ minutes to explain what these media selling points mean. In other words, make the case for either newspaper or radio advertising in a local market. Every team of debaters must present new points not covered in the previous teams' presentations until there are no arguments left to present. Then the class votes as a group on the winning point of view.

Take-Home Team Projects

1. What do we mean by *tone of voice*, and why is it important in advertising? Find a magazine ad that your team thinks has an appropriate tone of voice for its targeted audience (the readers of that particular magazine) and one that doesn't. Write a one-page report that explains your analyses of these two ads.

2. Select a product that is advertised exclusively through print using a long-copy format. Examples might be business-to-business and industrial products, over-the-counter drugs, and some car and appliance ads. Now write a 30-second radio and a 30-second TV spot for that product. Present your work to the class, along with an analysis of how the message design changed—and stayed the same—when you moved from print to radio and then to TV.

3. Critique the following (choose one):

   a. Jingles are a popular creative form in radio advertising. Even so, there may be as many jingles that you don't want to hear again as there are ones that you do. As a team, identify one jingle that your group really dislikes and another one that you like. Write an analysis in a one-page report of why these jingles either work or don't work effectively for you.

   b. As a team, surf the Web and find one banner ad that you think works to drive click-throughs and one that doesn't. Print them out and write an analysis in a one-page report that compares the two banner ads and explains why you think one is effective and the other is not.

4. In Chapter 6, your team was asked to develop a research plan for a new upscale restaurant chain that focuses on fowl—duck, squab, pheasant, and other elegant meals in the poultry category. Now your creative team is being asked to develop the creative package for the restaurant chain. A specialty category, this would be somewhat like a seafood restaurant. You have been asked to develop the creative package to use in launching these new restaurants in their new markets. Develop the following:

   • The restaurant's name
   • A slogan for the restaurant chain
   • A list of five enticing menu items
   • A paragraph of copy that can be used in print to describe the restaurant
   • The copy for a 30-second commercial to be used in radio

Yahoo! Hands-On Case

Review the Yahoo! case in the Appendix.

1. The case briefly explains the copy tone. Write a more complete explanation using the rationale presented in this section along with other information in this case. Describe in more detail the tone of voice—such things as attitude, word choice, phrasing, and emotion—for both print and television. Give examples of how this voice would sound. How and why would it appeal to the two audiences?

2. Write a new print ad for the next year of this campaign. Then transform it into a radio ad and a Web ad. In other words, draft the copy that might be used to extend the copy into the next year. Prepare a one-page report that explains your thinking behind the writing in these three ads.

HANDS-ON CASE

Verizon Realizes Opportunity

As discussed throughout this chapter, the copywriter's job is to find a memorable way to express the creative concept. All of a copywriter's talent will do no good if the audience cannot relate to the "magic words." This plays out in a number of ways. It's possible that copywriters might lack an appropriate consumer insight or unintentionally insult or ignore a potential customer. The bottom line is this: Copywriters bear the responsibility for understanding their audience.

Verizon is one company that has earned high marks for its approach to attracting a multicultural audience by listening to those with whom they intend to communicate. In fact, Verizon did such an outstanding job that the American Advertising Federation named Verizon and Burrell Communications the 2006 Mosaic Award winners as Advertiser/Agency of the Year for the Realize campaign.

Chicago-based Burrell, a leader in understanding and motivating consumer behavior in the African American and young adult Yurban® (a term coined by Burrell meaning young and urban) markets, helped Verizon create a first-of-its-kind integrated, multicultural grassroots marketing campaign. The campaign attempts to reach young entrepreneurial types and those who have a passion for community service. To achieve that goal, the multimedia marketing efforts feature real people with similar interests who are using Verizon broadband services.

The campaign showcases real people from the neighborhoods where the advertising runs, focusing on how they are making a difference with the help of Verizon's services. According to BlackNews.com, Jerri DeVard, Verizon's senior vice president of brand management and marketing communications, said, "This grassroots effort is the result of marketing insights that reveal large percentages of working African Americans and other minorities in the country are investing—often as a 'side business'—in their entrepreneurial dreams."

People who are featured in the campaign include a photographer who used Verizon to send his photos around the world, a translator who helps clients around the world using Verizon Online DSL, and a barber with a passion for helping young boxers in an after-school pro-

gram who uses Verizon to download videos of boxing greats to share with his kids.

The concept is executed using traditional and nontraditional media. Posters, mobile billboards, wraps for hair salon magazines, radio and bus shelter ads, and the Verizon Incubator, where a real entrepreneur worked for 21 days in a Philadelphia storefront, communicate the message.

The recognition that marketers need to be able to communicate with diverse audiences is not new. According to DiversityInc, PepsiCo was one of the first companies to lead efforts to reach diverse audiences in the late 1940s. To gain an advantage in the cola war between Coke and Pepsi, Pepsi President Walter S. Mack hired a team of black salesmen to become part of the community and to help attract black consumers. These marketing efforts resulted in print advertising that featured black Americans as consumers and tried to counter negative black stereotypes.

Today diversity has expanded to include many multicultural efforts, including Verizon's award-winning Realize campaign.

Consider This

1. Why is it important for copywriters to understand diversity issues?
2. How can advertisers do a better job reaching diverse audiences?
3. How important is it that copywriters come from the same background as the audiences for which they write? In other words, should advertising intended for a particular ethnic audience be written by someone of similar heritage? Does this hold true for age, gender, or class characteristics as well? If you are a copywriter or account manager for a campaign targeted to a different cultural group than one with which you are familiar, how can you cross this barrier to be able to better assess the effectiveness of the copy?

Sources: "Verizon Takes Real Customer Stories to the Streets in Grassroots Multi-Media Multicultural Campaign," http://www.BlackNews.com (accessed July 1, 2007); "Budding Entrepreneur to Live 21 Days in Storefront 'Incubator,'" http://www.BlackNews.com (accessed July 1, 2007); Yogi Cole, "Multicultural Marketing? How PepsiCo Got It Started," http://www.diversityinc.com (accessed July 1, 2007); American Advertising Federation, http://www.aaf.org.

Design and Production

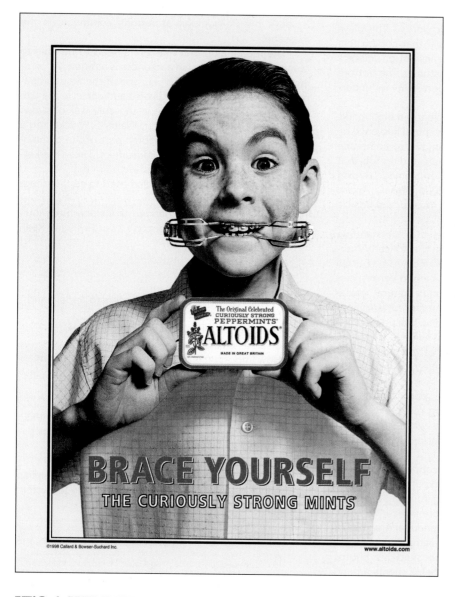

IT'S A WINNER

Award:	Company:	Agency:	Campaign:
Two Kelly Awards, including the 2006 Grand Prize, two One Show prizes, three Clios, the New York Festival Grand Prix	*Kraft Foods (now Wm. Wrigley Jr. Co.)*	*Leo Burnett (now Publicis & Hal Riney)*	*"Curiously Strong Mints"*

Curiously Strong Advertising

Here's your assignment: Figure out how to visualize extreme taste. You know, the hot, burn-your-tongue-then-suck-on-an-ice-cube kind of hot.

Since 1995, Leo Burnett copywriters and art directors working on Altoids have struggled to bring to life the intense flavor of this "extreme mint." Their challenge is to depict visually the impact of this flavor—what it's like to suck on this miniature atom bomb—and dramatize the brand slogan, "Curiously Strong Mints."

Nearly 200 years old, the Altoid mint was created in England to relieve intestinal discomfort and was eventually repositioned as a mint to fight bad breath. But it was largely unknown in the United States until Kraft Food purchased it in 1995 and turned its advertising over to the Leo Burnett agency.

Its brand personality comes through in its packaging. Altoids sports a distinctive old-world looking red-and-white metal tin with the slogan "The Original Celebrated Curiously Strong Peppermints," printed in an old-fashion typeface. By the late 1920s ads began plugging the "curiously strong" mint-flavored lozenges. The Burnett creatives adapted that phrase as a wry slogan for an advertising campaign: "The Curiously Strong Mint."

The name itself reflects the brand's old British ancestry. The Latin word *alt* meaning "to change" and the Greek word *oids* meaning "taking the form of" are combined to form the product name.

The campaign tone features a type of amusing, rather British self-deprecation, as if the brand doesn't take itself seriously. That

Chapter Key Points

1. What is the role of visual communication in advertising?

2. How can we define *layout* and *composition*, and what's the difference between the two?

3. How are art and color reproduced in print advertising?

4. Which steps in planning and producing broadcast commercials are most critical?

5. What are the basic techniques of Web design?

approach struck a nerve with the largely cynical, sometimes sarcastic Generation X and Y males who have been the brand's most loyal fans.

But let's get back to the problem of visualizing the taste. Altoids' hard-to-forget ads have featured a muscle builder with the line "Nice Altoids," a 1950s teenager with oversized braces and the headline "Brace Yourself," and a stern-looking nurse carrying the little red-and-white Altoids tin with the headline, "Now This Won't Hurt a Bit." Another ad proclaimed, "No Wonder the British Have Stiff Upper Lips." Some of these ads are available to view on the Altoids Web site (http://www.altoids.com).

More recently, a Burnett copywriter and art director team—Andy Dao and Matt Miller—won a Gold Pencil from the One Show for an Altoids Cinnamon ad that showed a firewalker tiptoeing across a patch of the little white mints. This Altoids Cinnamon ad builds on a truth about the product. The cinnamon candies are curiously hot. Just stepping on them would be an experience. You see the ad. You laugh. You associate the message with a product attribute. Just maybe you remember the brand when you're in the checkout line.

As you probably know, the Altoids brand has expanded to include new flavors, from cinnamon and wintergreen to ginger and sours (in a round tin), as well as gum and strips. And there's a new line of Chocolate-Dipped Mints with a reworked slogan, "Curiously Chocolate." No longer do we think of Altoids for its medicinal qualities.

And the campaign that started in print media—magazine ads, posters, outdoor boards—has now moved to television commercials with some equally wacky spots. Some of these can be viewed on YouTube (http://www.youtube.com).

Altoids has been a winner for Kraft, so much so that it sold the brand to Wm. Wrigley Jr. Co. for the minty fresh sum of $1.46 billion.

The success of the campaign is based on more than its humor. Altoids ads have a distinctive look. Most of the ads feature a headline that is only a few words long in all capital letters and a drop shadow outline. Many of the ads are laid out on a plain, mint green background with a double rule border—a great retro look. Most of the visuals feature a single person with the headline. The last thing you see in the ad is "The Curiously Strong Mints."

To see how well the advertising has performed for this intense, extreme mint, read about its effectiveness at the end of the chapter in the It's a Wrap section.

Sources: Jeremy Mullman and Stephanie Thompson, "Loss of Creatively Lauded Altoids a Psychological, if not Financial, Blow to Shop," *Advertising Age,* January 8, 2007, 8; Abra Sauer, "Altoids—Cool," brandchannel.com, January 13, 2003, http://www.brandchannelcom/features_profile.asp?pr_id=106; http://www.kraft.com/100/innovations/altoids.html; Magazine Publishers of America, "Leo Burnett Campaign for Altoids Named the Best Magazine Campaign of 2006," press release, June 14, 2006, http://www.magazine.org/Press_Room/MPA_Press_Releases/17264.cfm; http://www.altoids.com; "A Curiously Strong Invasion—Altoids Mints," Adams Outdoor Advertising, September 26, 2002, http://www.adamsoutdoor.com/html/randcs/case_studies.htm; Beth Cox, "A Curiously Quirky Ad Campaign," EmailLabs, August 16, 2002.

The visual consistency and wry humor in the Altoids campaign go far beyond the ability of words to describe things. The quirky images communicate ideas about the brand personality, as well as the feelings and sense of humor of the brand's target market. This chapter is about the visuals used in advertising—how they are designed and what they contribute to the meaning of the ad. First we review some basic ideas about visual impact, both in print and broadcast, and the role of the art director. Then we consider print art production and television production and end with a discussion of the design of Internet advertising.

VISUAL COMMUNICATION

Look at the opening ads for Altoids. Think about what makes them visually remarkable. Do they grab your attention? How do the visuals build brand personality? Are they interesting? Do you remember them? How does all this work together?

In effective advertising, both print and television, it's not just the words that need to communicate the message—it's the visuals, too. The visuals normally work with the words to present the creative concept, as the Altoids campaign illustrates. However, visuals do some things better than words, such as get attention and demonstrate something. How would you demonstrate the smallness of a computer chip or a new miniature hard drive? IBM did it through a visual analogy—its hard disk drive is as small as an egg or a newborn chick.

Even radio can evoke mental pictures through suggestive or descriptive language and sound effects. The effective use of visuals in advertising can be related to a number of the effects we have outlined in our Facets Model of Effects.

IBM used a chick and an egg to demonstrate the smallness of its hard disk drive, which is about the size of a large coin.

1. **Grab attention.** Generally visuals are better at getting and keeping attention than words.
2. **Stick in memory.** Visuals persist in the mind because people generally remember messages as visual fragments, or key images that are filed easily in their minds.
3. **Cement belief.** Seeing is believing, as the IBM chick ad demonstrates. Visuals that demonstrate add credibility to a message.
4. **Tell interesting stories.** Visual storytelling is engaging and maintains interest.
5. **Communicate quickly.** Pictures tell stories faster than words, as the Altoids ads demonstrate. A picture communicates instantly, while consumers have to decipher verbal/written communication word by word, sentence by sentence, line by line.
6. **Anchor associations.** To distinguish undifferentiated products with low inherent interest, advertisers often link the product with visual associations representing lifestyles and types of users, as the Hemingway and Bogart campaigns for Thomasville Furniture demonstrate later in this chapter.

Visual Impact

In most advertising, the power to get attention primarily lies with the visual. The excitement and drama in a television commercial is created through moving images. But it is an intriguing idea that grabs attention and remains in memory. An example is found in the "Welcome" doormat poster used with a twist by Columbia Sportswear.

In general, print designers have found that a picture in a print ad captures more than twice as many readers as a headline does. Furthermore, the bigger the illustration, the more the advertisement grabs consumers' attention. Ads with pictures also tend to pull more readers into the body copy; initial attention is more likely to turn to interest with a strong visual. People not only notice ad visuals, they remember ads with pictures more than those composed mostly of type. Both the believability factor and the interest-building impact of a visual story are reasons why visuals are anchored so well in memory.

A Big Idea is intriguing and captures attention. An example of a simple story told totally through the visuals is the Best of Show award for a One Show competition that showcased a British campaign for Volkswagen. It featured a gently humorous 30-second commercial built around the low price of the VW Polo. Fallon's Bob Barrie, who was president of The One Club, an association for people in the creative side of advertising, explained that it was possibly the quietest, most understated TV spot entered in the show. The idea was simple: A woman sits at her kitchen table. Her scanning of the newspaper—and her hiccups—stop abruptly as she discovers an ad for the VW Polo with its "surprisingly ordinary" price.[1]

Big Ideas that capture attention can be puzzling, shocking, or funny, as the Matter of Practice box discusses. A Vonage campaign for its Web-based phone service uses videos of

Principle

The visual's primary function in an advertisement is to get attention.

SHOWCASE This poster for Columbia Sportswear twists the welcome concept and welcomes you to come out rather than in. The ad, which won a One Show Merit Award, was contributed by Jeremy Boland, art director and photographer at Borders Perrin Norrander in Portland, Oregon, and a graduate of the University of Colorado. He was nominated by Professor Brett Robbs.

people doing silly things to illustrate its message: "That people do really stupid things. Like pay too much for home phone service." The commercials show a man cutting down a tree that falls on his car and a man on a treadmill who loses his footing and falls off. The stunts seem to defy credibility but, in fact, they are actual footage from the reality TV show *America's Funniest Home Videos.*[2] Attention, interest, memorability, believability—these factors help explain the visual impact of advertising messages.

Visual Storytelling

Visual storytelling is important, even for abstract concepts such as "empowered," "inspired," and "inventive," which are the focus of commercials in the PBS "Be More Inspired" campaign. In the "Be more empowered" commercial, a goldfish makes its escape from its little round bowl in an apartment and jumps from a puddle to a bottle to a river where it works its way upstream accompanying giant salmon who are leaping up waterfalls in their annual migration.

In another commercial titled "Be more inspired," a composer agonizes over the right notes and eventually hits a point of total frustration. As he looks out the window, he sees a group of birds sitting on a set of five power and telephone wires that are conveniently aligned to look like music staff. From the bird's positions he crafts a line of music that becomes the theme for his composition. PBS uses these clever little visual stories to present itself as a creative force that inspires people to use their imaginations.

The idea is that the visual sets up a narrative. In television, for example, the commercial begins and ends with visual elements that establish the scene and the conclusion. An example of a simple, but powerful, visual story comes from a YMCA commercial. It begins

A MATTER OF PRACTICE

If Sex Can't Get Attention, What Can? or Advertising Gets Religion

By Karen L. Mallia, *Assistant Professor, University of South Carolina*

Sex has long been a classic tool for getting attention—both as an underlying appeal, and through use of sexual imagery in ads. But more and more researchers are finding that young consumers are oversaturated with sexual imagery and have become either bored or disinterested in it.

If sex doesn't sell, what does? Religion appears to be the answer—at least right now.

I'm seeing more and more advertisers tapping religious symbols, icons, and imagery. My research suggests that not only is the use of religious imagery on the rise, but the way it's used is becoming more dramatic and controversial. England's Advertising Standards Authority actually received more complaints about the use of religious imagery in 2004 and 2005 than any other topic, while complaints about "acceptability" (taste and decency) declined.

Why religion? Shock works—as a combination of norm violation and surprise. And religion is the last taboo. It's the one area creative people haven't heavily mined for inspiration, because few clients are willing to risk offending people.

Using religious symbolism also dovetails with another concurrent trend: the decreasing emphasis on words, and increased reliance on nonverbal communication in advertising. Religious concepts function as mnemonics. Our brains put together a larger "picture" from visual shorthand. In the same way logos and other devices trigger our association with a brand, religious concepts and symbols create a much bigger memory than what the content would at first glance imply.

What kind of images are advertisers using? Icons like Christian crosses and Jewish stars, visual representations of Biblical stories, God, Jesus, the devil, angels, nuns, Eastern and Western monks, priests, and rabbis. Some imagery classified as religious could be considered an art reference, such as the host of parodies that have employed DaVinci's "Last Supper." Indeed that was the line taken by fashion house Girbaud in its successful defense against a ban of its Last Supper ad in France.

Let's just look at the change in tenor with one example. Priests. In 1975, Xerox Corporation's "Brother Dominick" spot starred a sweet, earnest monk invoking a "miracle" in duplicating 500 illuminated manuscripts. Fast-forward to 1991, when Benetton shocked the world with a priest and nun kissing (see Chapter 3, p. 92). In the mid-1990s, the "Got Milk?" campaign featured a priest getting violent with a vending machine. In 2005, Stella Artois' "Skating Priests" spot swept award shows with a riveting homage to filmmaker Krzysztof Kieslowski with surreal, almost sinister, humor. It's over before you realize that a group of priests would rather see their fellow priest drown than lose a beer. The same year, a Lincoln Mark IV spot was pulled prior to its Super Bowl airing due to accusations of glorifying pedophile Catholic priests.

In 2006, Pirelli Tire launched a worldwide campaign with a 10-minute Web film, "The Call," starring John Malkovich as a priest called upon to exorcise a car and Naomi Campbell as the devil. The tone brings a new level of darkness to advertising featuring priests.

Are we seeing the tip of a trend or a passing fad? We'll see.

---

with the sound of a lawnmower coming through an open window, then moves to a shot looking out the window as a teenager walks away from the lawnmower, which has just cut a huge letter Y in the yard.

Brand Image

We've talked in previous chapters about the important role advertising plays in the creation of a brand image. Much of that contribution comes from the visual elements—the symbolic images associated with the brand and the elements that define the brand, such as the trademark and logo.

A **logo**, which is the imprint used for immediate identification of a brand or company, is an interesting design project because it uses typography, illustration, and layout to create a distinctive and memorable image that identifies the brand. Think of the cursive type used for Coca-Cola, the block letters used for IBM, and the apple with a bite out of it (in both rainbow stripes and white) for Apple computers.

YOUR KIDS TRYING TO TELL YOU SOMETHING?

SHOWCASE This commercial for the YMCA tells a simple story of a teenager using a lawnmower to make a statement about his intention to go to the Y. It was contributed by Lara Mann, copywriter at Foote Cone Belding in Chicago. She graduated from the University of Florida and was nominated by Professor Elaine Wagner.

The Altoids success story is primarily a result of the consistent graphic presentation of the brand. The visual consistency is not only apparent in the design of the ads, it also reflects the history of the brand as a quirky old British lozenge. Shown here is one of the Altoids ads that used visual association to create curiosity but also to reflect the meaning of the slogan.

There's always a tension in advertising between doing something over the top that's creative and attention getting and being responsible to the brand image, the strategy, and society. The acceptability of a wacky image in an ad depends, in part, on its targeting, but it also depends on judgment and intuition. Our ethics discussions in this book often focus on the appropriateness of an image. For example, an ad for Vaseline Intensive Care Lotion shows a conference room with a speaker and a group of businesspeople—both men and women—paying careful attention to the presentation. In the foreground is a happy woman in a business suit with her back to the speaker and her colleagues. Her legs are up on the table and she's caressing them. Unfortunately she's also a black woman. The headline reads: "Nothing keeps you from handling your business." So does Vaseline Intensive Care want us to know that if women use their product, they become totally clueless in a business meeting? The point is that what appears to the creative team to be a dynamite visual may, on reflection, send a number of contrary messages.

ART DIRECTION

The person most responsible for creating visual impact, as well as the brand identification elements, is the art director. The art director is in charge of the visual look of the advertisement, both in print and TV, and how it communicates mood, product qualities, and psychological appeals. The art director and copywriter team usually work together to come up with the Big Idea, but the art director is responsible for bringing the visual side of the idea to life. As Sasser explained in the Part IV Introduction, this team is driven by a "passion to create."

Specifically, art directors make decisions about whether to use art or photography in print and film or animation in television and what type of artistic style to use. They are highly trained in graphic design, including art, photography, typography, the use of color, and computer design software. Although art directors generally design the ad, they rarely create the finished art. If they need an illustration, they hire an artist. Newspaper and Web advertising visuals are often **clip art** or **click art**, images from collections of copyright-free art that anyone who buys the clip-art service can use.

In addition to advertising, art directors may also be involved in designing a brand or corporate logo, as well as merchandising materials, store or corporate office interiors, and other aspects of a brand's visual presentation, such as shopping bags, delivery trucks, and uniforms.

The Designer's Toolkit

One of the most difficult problems that art directors—and those who work on the creative side of advertising—face is to transform a creative concept into words and pictures. During the brainstorming process, both copywriters and art directors are engaged in **visualization**, which means they are imagining what the finished ad might look like. The art director, however, is responsible for translating the advertising big idea into a visual story. To do this, the art director relies upon a toolkit that consists of illustrations or animation, photos or film shots, color, type, design principles, layout (print), and composition (photography, video, or film), among other visual elements.

This ad offers a visual pun, playing on the product name and the slang "nice 'toids." Pairing the unexpected—the hunk's pectoid muscles and the product—helps create a memorable association.

Illustrations and Photos   When art directors use the word "art," they usually mean photographs and illustrations, each of which serves different purposes in ads. For instance, photography has an authenticity that makes it powerful. Most people feel that pictures don't lie (even though they can be altered). For credibility, then, photography is a good medium.

A photograph is more realistic and an illustration (or animation in television) is more fanciful. Photos convey a "seeing is believing" credibility. Illustrations, by definition, eliminate many of the details you see in a photograph, which can make it easier to understand their meaning since what remains are the "highlights" of the image. This ease of perception can simplify the visual message as it can focus attention on key details of the image. Illustrations also use artistic techniques to intensify meanings and moods, making illustrations ideal for fantasy (think about comic books and animated films).

The decision to use a photograph or an illustration is usually determined by the advertising strategy and its need for either realism or fanciful images. Photographs, of course, can also evoke fanciful images. For example, the billboard art for British beer brand John West is given a dramatic touch by making the rings on top of the can look like rings of rippling water cast from a fishing bobber.

Color   In addition to photos and illustrations, another important visual element that art directors manipulate is color, which they use to attract attention, provide realism, establish moods, and build brand identity. Art directors know that print ads with color, particularly those in newspapers, get more attention than ads without color. Most ads—print, broadcast, and Internet—are in full color, especially when art directors use photographs.

Black and white also lend a dignity and sophistication to the visual, even if it's a boot as the Dunham ad demonstrates. A historical effect can be created by shooting in black and white, or using a sepia tone can make the images look like old prints that have been weathered by time.

In print, designers also use **spot color**, in which a second color in addition to black (a black-and-white photo or illustration with an accent color) is used to highlight important

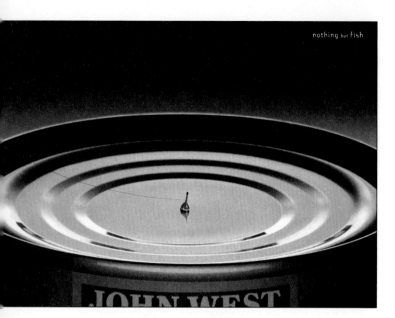

A simple photograph of the top of a can takes on new meaning when the can's rings are associated with the rings in water from a fishing bobber. The 4Runner ad for Toyota uses illustration to capture a fantasy image of American wilderness.

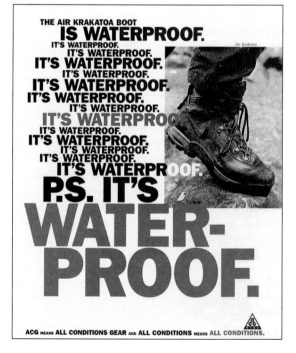

The layout for the Dunham boot ad shown here speaks in a quiet voice about the beauty of nature. Even though it's a boot ad, it projects an elegance that reflects an appreciation for nature and serene outdoor scene (footprints in the snow). The ACG "Air Krakatoa" ad with an asymmetrical layout uses spot color effectively as an accent to identify the product and the brand. Note how the layout "shouts," in contrast to the soft tone of the Dunham boot ad.

elements. The use of spot color is highly attention getting, particularly in newspaper ads. The ACG ad uses red spot color to accent the product and brand name.

When realism is important to convey in an ad, full-color photographs may be essential. Some products and ad illustrations just don't look right in black and white—pizza, flower gardens, and nail polish, for instance. Color also can help an ad convey a mood.

Warm colors, such as red, yellow, and orange, convey happiness. Pastels are soft and often bring a friendly tone to a print ad. Earth tones are natural and no-nonsense. Cool colors, such as blue and green, are aloof, calm, serene, reflective, and intellectual. Yellow and red have the most attention-getting power. Red may symbolize alarm and danger as well as warmth. Black communicates high drama and can express power and elegance. Note that these color associations are culturally determined and uses like these are common in Western countries, but may not be effective in other cultures. White, for example, is the color of death in many Asian countries.

Typography Not only do art directors carefully choose colors, they also specify the ad's **typography**—the appearance of the ad's printed matter. In most cases, good typesetting does not call attention to itself because its primary role is functional—to convey the words of the message. Type or lettering, however, also has an aesthetic role, and the type selection can, in a subtle or not so subtle way, contribute to the impact and mood of the message, as the ACG boot ad demonstrated. The Petersen magazine group ad is an example of the use of typography as art. In this case, the heavy, bold, hand-drawn type has an attitude that reflects the readers of the Petersen's RAW Sport Group, which includes such publications as *Dirt Rider, Mountain Biker, MX Racer, BMX Rider, Inline,* and *sNoBoard.*

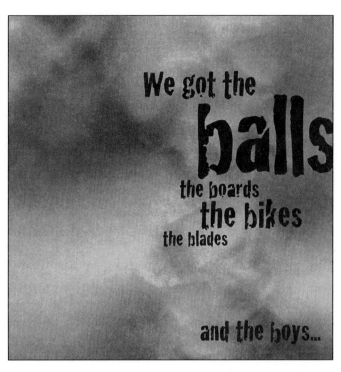

This is the cover for a four-page ad for Peterson publications inserted into advertising trade publications to dramatize that the group's magazines can deliver a youthful male audience. The message is in the words, but it's also in the style of the type.

Ad designers choose from among thousands of typefaces to find the right one for the ad's message. Designers are familiar with type classifications, but it is also important for managers and other people on the creative team to have some working knowledge of typography to understand what designers are talking about and to critique the typography and make suggestions. Figure 14.1 summarizes many of the decisions an art director makes in designing the type, such as:

- The specific typeface, or **font**
- The way capitalization is **handled,** such as all caps or lowercase
- Typeface variations that come from manipulating the shape of the letterform
- The edges of the type block and its column width
- The size in which the type is set (vertical height)
- **Legibility,** or how easy it is to perceive the letters

Design Principles

The arrangement of the pieces in a print ad or video shot is governed by basic principles of design. The design has both functional and aesthetic needs—the functional side makes the visual message easy to perceive; the aesthetic side makes it attractive and pleasing to the eye.

These design principles guide the eye by creating a visual path that helps the viewer scan the elements. For example, dominant elements that are colorful or high in contrast (big versus small, light versus dark), catch attention first. How all the elements come together is a function of the unity and balance of the design. Direction or movement is the way the elements are positioned to lead the eye through the arrangement. Simplicity is also a design principle, one that is in opposition to visual clutter. In general, the fewer the elements, the stronger the impact, an idea expressed in the phrase "less is more." Another saying is KISS, which stands for "Keep It Simple Stupid." The Frontier Moose ad is a powerful image because of its use of a simple horizontal photo across a two-page spread.

Let's look at how these design principles are used in print layout and in the composition of a shot in video and film.

a)

A Font

14 pt
ABCDEFGHIJKLMNOPQRSTUV
abcdefghijklmnopqrstuvwxyz
1234567890

Serif (top) and Sans Serif (bottom)

ABCDEFGHIJKLMNOPQRSTUVWXYZ ABCD
ABCDEFGHIJKLMNOPQRSTUVWXYZ ABCD

All caps (top), lower case (middle), and u&lc (bottom)

THIS IS TIMES ROMAN IN ALL CAPS.
this is times roman in lower case.
This is Times Roman in Upper and Lower Case.

Typeface variations

This is set in a light typeface.
This is set in a normal weight.
This is set in a boldface.
This is set in italic.
This is set in an expanded typeface.
This is set in a condensed typeface.

Type has an aesthetic role in an ad. Art directors choose a serif or sans serif font, as well as a font's size and style, to support the tone of the advertising message.

b)

This is justified text. This is justified text. This is justified text. This is justified text. This is justified text. This is justified text. This is justified text. This is justified text. This is justified text. This is jus-tified text.

This is centered text. This is
centered text.

This is left aligned text. This is
left aligned text.

This is right aligned text. This
is right aligned text.

Where the type sits on the ad and how it relates to the margin has an effect on the ad's overall look.

c)

6 Point
ABCDEFGHIJKLMNOPQRSTUVWXYZABCDEFGHIJKLMNOPQRSTUVWXYZABCDEFGHIJKLMNOPQRSTUVWXYZABCDEFG
abcdefghijklmnopqrstuvwxyzabcdefghijklmnopqrstuvwxyzabcdefghijklmnopqrstuvwxyzabcdefghijklmnopqrstuvwxyz 1234567890

12 Point
ABCDEFGHIJKLMNOPQRSTUVWXYZABCDEFGHIJKLMNOPQ
abcdefghijklmnopqrstuvwxyzabcdefghijklmnopqrstuvwx 1234567890

18 Point
ABCDEFGHIJKLMNOPQRSTUVWXYZAB
abcdefghijklmnopqrstuvwxyzabc 1234567890

Here is a set of different sizes for the Times Roman typeface.

d)

THIS IS CAPITAL LETTERS.

This is reverse type letters.

This is ornamental type letters.

This is type surprinted over something highly patterned.

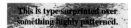

Research has shown that some typography presentations, such as those shown here—all cap letters, reverse type, overly ornamental type, and surprinted type—hinder the reading process.

FIGURE 14.1
The Art of Typefaces

With over 300 non-stops daily, crossing the country has never been easier.

FRONTIER. A whole different animal.

Sometimes the most powerful images are the simplest in structure—just a wide horizontal landscape with a swimming caribou leaving a trail in the water and a plane flying above him. Notice how the antlers point to the Frontier plane with a caribou on its tail. The whole composition is designed to pull your eye to the right and then up.

Print Layout

For print advertising, once art directors have chosen the images and typographic elements, they manipulate all the visual elements on paper to produce a layout. A **layout** is a plan that imposes order and at the same time creates an arrangement that is aesthetically pleasing.

Different layouts can convey entirely different feelings about a product. For example, look at the two ads for work boots. The ACG "Air Krakatoa" boot ad screams "waterproof!" signaling the boots' ability to stand up to the most serious weather conditions. In contrast, the ad for the Dunham boot looks like a work of fine art. The difference between the two campaigns clearly lies with the visual impact that comes from the layouts as well as the imagery.

Types of Layouts   Here are some common types of ad layouts the art director might use:

- *Picture window.* A common layout format is one with a single, dominant visual that occupies about 60 to 70 percent of the ad's space. Underneath it is a headline and copy block. The logo or signature signs off the message at the bottom. The Altoids ads in the opener are of this style.
- *All art.* The art fills the frame of the ad and the copy is embedded in the picture. The Frontier Moose ad is an example.

This ad for Schwinn bicycles uses a plumbing drain motif to convey the industrial-strength features of the bike. It is a nonlinear design in that it doesn't matter where you start and what you read next. The text is carried in call-outs that point to different visual elements in the layout.

- *Panel or grid.* This layout uses a number of visuals of matched or proportional sizes. If there are multiple panels all of the same size, the layout can look like a window pane or comic strip panel. The Dunham boot ad uses two side-by-side panels.
- *Dominant type or all copy.* Occasionally, you will see layouts that emphasize the type rather than the art, or even an all-copy advertisement in which the headline is treated as type art, such as the ACG ad. A copy-dominant ad may have art, but it is either embedded in the copy or placed in a subordinate position, such as at the bottom of the layout.
- *Circus.* This layout combines lots of elements—art, type, color—to deliberately create a busy, jumbled image. This is typical of some discount store ads or ads for local retailers, such as tire companies.
- *Nonlinear.* This contemporary style of layout can be read starting at any point in the image. In other words, the direction of viewing is not ordered, as in the "What a Ride" ad for Schwinn. This style of ad layout works for young people who are more accustomed to nonlinear forms.
- *Grunge.* This style shows what is presumed to be a Generation X–inspired lack of concern for the formalities of art, design, type styles, and legibility. The Peterson magazine ad is in this style.

Layout Stages   The stages in the normal development of a print ad may vary from agency to agency or from client to client. Figure 14.2 shows the six-stage development of an Orly nail polish ad that agency Wiley & Associates created. This ad went through **thumbnail sketches**, which are quick, miniature preliminary sketches; **rough layouts**, which show where design elements go; **semicomps** and **comprehensives**, which are drawn to size and used for presentation either inside or to the client; and **mechanicals**, which assemble the elements in their final position for reproduction. The final product is a high-resolution computer file used for actual production of the ad.

Composition   We've been talking about layout, which is a term used to describe how print ads are arranged. **Composition** refers to the way the elements in a picture are arranged (think a still-life painting) or framed through a camera lens (think a landscape photo or movie scene). (Note: The term *composition* is also used to refer to the process of typesetting.) Photographers and **videographer**s (people who shoot a scene using a video camera) handle composition in two ways: (1) they may be able to place or arrange the elements in front of their cameras and (2) they may have to compose the image by manipulating their own point of view if the elements can't be moved. In other words, they move around to find the most aesthetic way to frame an image that isn't movable, such as a scene

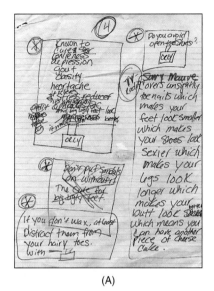

(A)

(B)

(C)

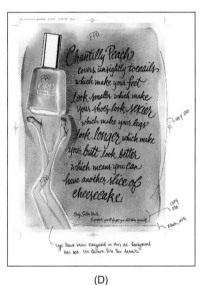

(D)

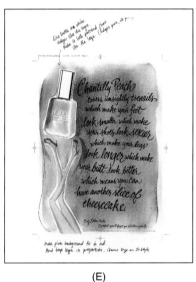

(E)

(F)

FIGURE 14.2

Orly "Chantilly Peach" Creative Process

(A) **Thumbnail Sketches** These ideas for Orly were developed by the Wiley creative team late at night over Diet Coke and Chinese chicken salad. (B) **Rough Layout** Transitioning to legs and painted toenails, the layout begins to give some glamour and personality to the product. (C) **Semicomps** Type, color, and tagline are still not finalized, but layout is more complete. (D) **Comprehensives** Tagline approved. Illustrator has added more glitz to the layout. (E) **Mechanicals** Quark file before retouching. Client still made small changes at this stage, but had approved the ad's layout and copy. (F) Final High-Resolution Film The film house had to retouch, creating separate files for the legs and background image so that the proportion of the leg illustration would be correct.

or landscape, as well as to catch different lighting situations, such as bright sun and shade or shadow.

Similar to the way layouts are developed by using sketches, video images are also drawn and presented as **storyboards**, which are sketches of the scenes and key shots in a commercial. The art director imagines the characters and setting as well as how the characters act and move in the scene. The art director sketches in a few key frames the visual idea for a scene and how it is to be shot and how one scene links to the scenes that follow. In addition, the storyboard sketches also reflect the position and movement of the cameras recording the scene, a description of which is spelled out both in the script and on the storyboard.

A MATTER OF PRACTICE

Kitty Slickers and Cat Herders

EDS, a company that essentially invented the information technology (IT) industry back in the 1960s, found itself with an unhip Old Economy image as the New Economy exploded in the late 1990s. Although a leader in such New Economy areas as Web hosting, digital supply chain management, and networking, EDS got no respect from its would-be high-tech partners.

The assignment given to the Minneapolis-based Fallon agency was to change those perceptions and infuse energy and pride into the EDS workforce. Fallon's strategy was to leverage EDS's proven experience and rock-solid infrastructure, which enabled it to tackle enormous IT problems. The strategy came together in the positioning statement: "EDS thrives on defeating complexity."

How do you depict an organization defeating complexity? A catch phrase popular in the Silicon Valley culture—"It's like herding cats"—was the perfect metaphor for how EDS wrangles technology and manages complexity. And that's what the Fallon creative team did—it filmed a team of rugged cowboys herding thousands of housecats.

Even though cats can be trained to do a number of things, including swimming a stream and sitting on a horse's saddle, the magic in the EDS Herding Cats commercial was found in the computer manipulation of the digitized images that created a herd from a small number of real cats.

The commercial, which was designed to run on the Super Bowl, won an Effie and every online poll ranking Super Bowl commercials that year. And it did so by erasing the company's rigid and unapproachable image and supplanting it with a down-to-earth, tongue-in-cheek image that appealed to the cynical dot-com industry.

In addition to being the favorite Super Bowl commercial, the Cat Herders spot started EDS's telephones ringing and its Web site overflowed with visitors. The company estimated 2 million hits on its Web sites the next day, 10 times the normal volume. In terms of Fallon's objectives, one of which was to create brand awareness and buzz in the industry, EDS estimated that its $8 million investment in the ad and its supporting campaign netted an additional $12 million in PR. The campaign was also designed to generate sales and new business inquiries, and EDS reported that its sales were up 20 percent and its new business leads grew by 40 percent.

One final goal of the campaign was to energize the workforce. "Cat Herders" gave EDS employees an inspiring image of themselves as wranglers in an epic undertaking whose message is: "No job is too tough." The company's employee turnover rate dropped, and thousands of employees sent letters to the president thanking him for the inspiring symbol of the cat herder.

Sources: Adapted from the EDS Effie brief provided by EDS and Fallon; "Super Ad Has EDS Purring," *Washington Technology* 14:24, March 20, 2000, 46; Becky Ebenkamp, "Creative: On Location: Kitty Slickers," *Adweek*, January 17, 2000, 24–26.

Working within the framework of the creative strategy, art directors create the look of the TV commercial. The look of the award-winning "Cat Herders" commercial that the Fallon agency created for Electronic Data Systems (EDS) was a parody of the American West, much like a John Ford movie, with horses, craggy-faced cowboys who acted as cat wranglers, and stampeding animals (the cats).

PRINT PRODUCTION

Art directors need to understand print media requirements and production because these aspects affect both the look of the ad and its costs.

Print Media Requirements

Different media put different demands on the design and production of advertising. Newspapers and directories, for example, are printed at high speed on an inexpensive, rough-surfaced, spongy paper called **newsprint** that quickly absorbs ink on contact. Newsprint is not a great surface for reproducing fine details, especially color photographs and delicate typefaces. Most newspapers offer color to advertisers, but because of the limitations of the printing process, the color may not be perfectly **in register** (aligned exactly with the image). For that reason, ads such as the Oklahoma City ads are specifically designed for high-contrast black-and-white printing. These work well for both newspaper and directory ads.

Magazines have traditionally led the way in graphic print production because their paper is better than newsprint. Excellent photographic and color reproduction is the big difference between newspapers and magazines. Magazine advertisements are also turning to more creative, attention-getting devices such as pop-up visuals, scent strips, and computer chips that play melodies when the pages are opened. An Altoids ad that launched Altoids chewing gum, for example, ran in magazines with a novel print production technique. It showed a box of Altoids chewing gum on one page, and a singed logo burnt onto the cartoon on the opposite page.

The key to an effective poster or outdoor board is a dominant visual with minimal copy. Because billboards must make a quick and lasting impression from far away, their layout should be compact with a simple visual path. The Outdoor Advertising Association of America (OAAA) recommends these tips for designers.

- *Graphics.* Make the illustration an eye-stopper.
- *Size.* Images in billboards are huge—a 25-foot-long pencil or a 43-foot pointing finger. The product or the brand label can be hundreds of times larger than life.
- *Colors.* Use bold, bright colors. The greatest impact is created by maximum contrast between two colors such as dark colors against white or yellow.[3]
- *Figure/ground.* Make the relationship between foreground and background as obvious as possible. A picture of a soft drink against a jungle background is hard to perceive when viewed from a moving vehicle at a distance. The background should never compete with the subject.
- *Typography.* Use simple, clean, uncluttered type that is easy to read at a distance by an audience in motion. The industry's legibility research recommends avoiding all-capital letters, fanciful ornamental letters, and script and cursive fonts.
- *Product identification.* Focus attention on the product by reproducing the label or package at a huge size.
- *Extensions.* Extend the frame of the billboard to expand the scale and break away from the limits of the long rectangle.
- *Shape.* For visual impact, create the illusion of three-dimensional effects by playing with horizons, vanishing lines, and dimensional boxes. Inflatables create a better 3-D

High-contrast graphics are the key to good reproduction in a newspaper. The art in these ads simulates an old wood engraving.

effect than most billboards can, even with superior graphics. Made of a heavyweight, stitched nylon, inflatables can be freestanding, or they can be added to outdoor boards as an extension.

• *Motion.* Add motors to boards to make pieces and parts move. Disk-like wheels and glittery things that flicker in the wind create the appearance of motion, color change, and images that squeeze, wave, or pour. Use revolving panels, called *kinetic boards*, for messages that change.

Print Art Reproduction

In general there are two types of printed images: line art and halftone. A drawing or illustration is called **line art** because the image is solid lines on a white page, as in the Oklahoma City ads. Photographs, which are referred to as **continuous tone** or **halftone**, are much more complicated to reproduce because they have a range of gray tones between the black and white, as shown in Figure 14.3.

Printers create the illusion of shades of gray in converting photos to halftones by shooting the original photograph through a fine **screen** converting the image to a pattern of dots that gives the illusion of shades of gray—dark areas are large dots that fill the screen and light areas are tiny dots surrounded by white space. The quality of the image depends on how fine the screen is: Newspapers use a coarse screen, usually 65 lines per inch (called a 65-line screen), while magazines use fine screens, which may be from 120 up to 200 or 300 lines per inch.

Screens are also used to create **tint blocks**, which can either be shades of gray in black-and-white printing or shades of color. A block of color can be printed solid or it can be screened black to create a shade. These shades are expressed as a range of percentages, from 100 percent (solid) down to 10 percent (very faint). Figure 14.4 gives examples of screens in color.

FIGURE 14.3

Line Art and Halftone Art

An example of a figure reproduced as line art (left) and as a halftone (right).

10%   **100%**

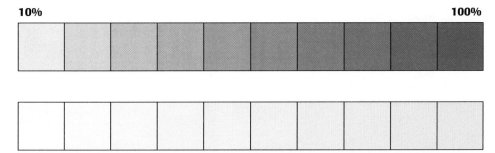

Color Reproduction   It would be impossible to set up a printing press with a separate ink roller for every hue and value in a color photo. How, then, are these colors reproduced?

Full-color images are reproduced using four distinctive shades of ink called **process colors**, in order to produce **four-color printing**. These colors are *magenta* (a shade of pinkish purple), *cyan* (a shade of bright blue), *yellow*, and *black*. Printing inks are transparent, so when one ink overlaps another, a third color is created and that's how the full range of colors is created. For example, red and blue create purple, yellow and blue create green, yellow and red create orange. The black is used for type and, in four-color printing, adds depth to the shadows and dark tones in an image. The process printers use to reduce the original color image to four halftone negatives is called **color separation**. Figure 14.5 illustrates the process of color separation.

Digitization   If an ad is going to run in a number of publications, there has to be some way to distribute a reproducible form of the ad to all of them. The duplicate material for offset printing is a slick proof of the original mechanical. More recently **digitization** of images is used to distribute reproducible images. This is also how computers now handle the color reproduction process. These digitized images can then be transmitted electronically to printers or clients, across a city for local editions of newspapers, or by satellites for regional editions of magazines and newspapers such as *USA Today*. Agencies also use this method for transmitting ad proofs within the agency network and to clients.

Digitization makes it possible to create some spectacular effects in out-of-home advertising. Some outdoor boards have become digital screens complete with changing and moving images. A new technique in transit advertising comes from Atlanta where the city's buses are wrapping their sides with something called "glow skin." The ads use electroluminescent lighting to make the ads glow at night and appear to jump off the sides of the buses.[4]

Binding and Finishing

Art directors can enhance their ads and other printed materials by using a number of special printing effects. For example, USRobotics, a maker of minicomputers, once used a small brochure the actual size of a Palm Pilot to demonstrate its minicomputer's size. The shot of the Palm Pilot was glued to a photo of a hand. As the ad unfolded it became a complete product brochure that visually demonstrated the actual size of the minicomputer. Other mechanical techniques include:

* *Die cutting.* A sharp-edged stamp, or die, used to cut out unusual shapes. A common **die-cut** shape you're familiar with is the tab on a file folder.
* *Embossing or debossing.* The application of pressure to create a raised surface (**embossing**) or depressed image (**debossing**) in paper.
* *Foil stamping.* The application of a thin metallic coating (silver, gold) molded to the surface of the image.
* *Tip-ins.* Separate preprinted ads provided by the advertiser to be glued into a publication as the publication is being assembled or bound. Perfume manufacturers, for example, tip in samples that are either scratch-and-sniff or scented strips that release a fragrance when pulled apart.

Another example of a nifty production trick is illustrated in the ad for Specialized Bikes using a "see-through" technique. The graphic elements are separated and printed on the front

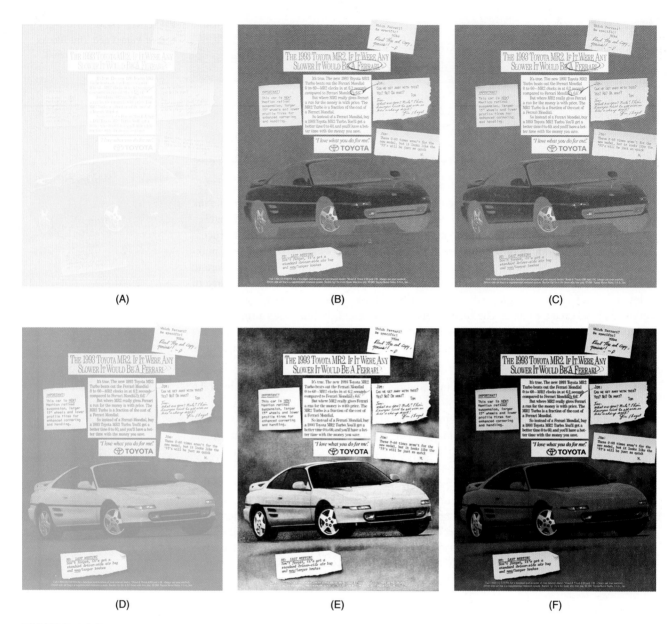

FIGURE 14.5

The Color Separation Process

These six photos illustrate the process of creating four-color separations: (A) yellow plate, (B) magenta plate, (C) yellow and magenta combined plate, (D) cyan plate. (Note: After cyan is added, there would also be combined plates showing it added first to yellow, then to magenta, then to the combined yellow and magenta. These steps were left out to simplify the presentation.) (E) black plate, (F) finished ad with all four process colors combined.

and back of a page. When you look at the ad you see people in the foreground going about their business but in the background a faint image shows a daredevil bike rider jumping from one building to another or riding on a handrail going down the middle of a set of steps.

BROADCAST PRODUCTION

Where does an art director start when putting together a commercial? Obviously the first consideration is the nature of the image. The art director can arrange for filming on a constructed set or in a real location or choose to use **stock footage**—previously recorded images, either video, still slides, or moving film. Typical stock footage files are shots from a satellite, historical scenes such as World War II battles, or a car crash.

Other graphic elements such as words, product logos, and still photos are digitized or computer-generated right on the screen. A **crawl** is computer-generated letters that appear

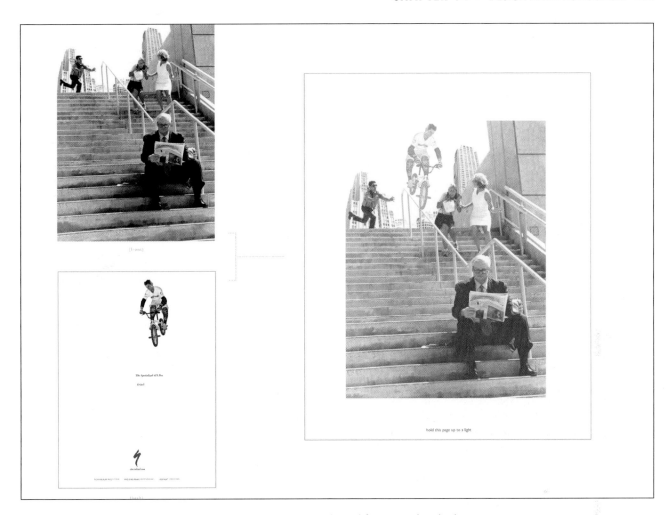

SHOWCASE Contributed by Aaron Stern, who worked on this ad for Specialized Bikes when he was at Venables Bell & Partners in San Francisco, the ad shows a creative use of the "see-through" capability of print. A graduate of the University of Colorado, Stern is now in New York working on an MFA in Creative Writing at NYU. He was nominated by Professor Brett Robbs.

to be moving across the bottom of the screen. All of these are designed or specified by the art director. A Thomasville Bogart commercial opens with letterboxed, black-and-white film shot as if viewers were watching a 1940s style party in a movie with a Bogart look-alike actor. It then moves to full screen in color and ends with shots of the furniture that complement a contemporary home.

Sophisticated computer graphics systems, such as those used to create the Star Wars special effects, have pioneered the making of artistic film and video advertising on comput-ers. Computer graphic artists brag that they can do anything with an image. They can look at any object from any angle or even from the inside out. One of the most creative video techniques is called **morphing**, in which one object gradually changes into another. Pho-tographs of real objects can change into art or animation and then return to life. Computer graphics specialists use tools such as the Paint Box software to create, multiply (that's how 50 cats can be made to look like hundreds), and manipulate video images.

Filming and Editing

Most local retail commercials are simple and inexpensive, and they are typically shot and taped at the local station. The sales representative for the station may work with the adver-tiser to write the script, and the station's director handles the taping of the commercial.

Creating a national TV commercial is more complex and requires a number of people with specialized skills. The ad agency crew usually includes the copywriter, art director,

The classy image of movie star Humphrey Bogart and his Hollywood lifestyle was used to create a 1940s visual statement for this commercial that announces Thomasville Furniture's Bogart Collection.

and producer. The producer oversees the production on behalf of the agency and client and is responsible for the budget, among other things. The director, who is the person responsible for filming the commercial, is usually someone from outside the agency. This person takes the art director's storyboard and makes it come to life on film.

The producer and director make up the core of the production team. The commercial's effectiveness depends on their shared vision of the final commercial and the director's ability to bring it to life as the art director imagined it. In the case of the Cat Herders commercial, the director was chosen by the agency because of his skill at coaxing naturally humorous performances from nonprofessional actors. In this commercial he worked with real wranglers on their semi-scripted testimonials about their work with kitties. The following list summarizes the responsibilities of broadcast production personnel.

Who Does What in Broadcast Production?

Copywriter	Writes the script, whether it contains dialogue, narrative, lyrics, announcements, descriptions, or no words at all.
Art Director	In TV, develops the storyboard and establishes the look of the commercial, whether realistic, stylized, or fanciful.
Producer *(can be an agency staff member)*	Takes charge of the production, handles the bidding and all production arrangements, finds the specialists, arranges for casting talent, and makes sure the expenses and bids come in under budget.
Director	Has responsibility for the actual filming or taping, including how long the scene runs, who does what, how lines are spoken, and how characters played; in TV determines how the camera is set up and records the flow of action.

Composer	Writes original music and sometimes the lyrics as well.
Arranger	Orchestrates music for the various instruments and voices to make it fit a scene or copy line. The copywriter usually writes the lyrics or at least gives some idea of what the words should say.
Editor	Puts everything together toward the end of the filming or taping process; evaluates how to assemble scenes and which audio elements work best with the dialogue and footage.

Producing TV Commercials

There are a number of ways to produce a message for a television commercial. It can be filmed live or prerecorded using film or videotape. It can also be shot frame-by-frame using animation techniques. Let's look at these production choices.

Typically the film is shot on 35 mm film or videotape and then digitized, after which the editor transfers the image to videotape for dissemination, a process called **film-to-tape transfer**. Art directors work closely with editors who assemble the shots and cut the film to create the right pacing and sequence of images as outlined in the storyboard.

Obviously the Big Idea for the Cat Herders ad created some real production challenges. In the spot, the Fallon art director decided that the metaphor of herding cats meant that the cats had to swim across a river, but is it possible? Here's how it was done: The trainers taught a few cats that weren't adverse to water to swim by starting them out in one-quarter inch of water in a child's swimming pool and then gradually adding water to the pool until it was deep enough for the cats to swim. The "river" was actually a small pool warmed by a portable heater—art director Hanson described it as "a little kitty Jacuzzi." Multiple copies of the swimming kitties were made and manipulated using computer graphics until an entire herd had been created. And that's how this famous scene came about—a creation of Hanson's unlikely vision of a herd of cats swimming a river.

Animation   The technique of **animation** traditionally meant drawing images on film and then recording the images one frame at a time. Cartoon figures, for example, were sketched and then resketched for the next frame with a slight change to indicate a small progression in the movement of an arm or leg a facial expression. Animation is traditionally shot at 16 drawings per second. Low-budget animation uses fewer drawings, so the motion looks jerky. The introduction of computers has accelerated the process and eliminated a lot of the tedious hand work.

Animation effects can also be used to combine created characters such as the little green Geico gecko with live action figures, or even with other animated characters. The famous Aflac duck was created as a collaboration between Warner Brothers and the Aflac agency, the Kaplan Thaler Group in New York. More advanced techniques, similar to those used in movies like *Lord of the Rings* and *Matrix Reloaded* create lifelike images and movement. A technique called "mental ray" was used in a Levi Strauss ad featuring 600 stampeding buffalo. Mental ray is so good it not only created lifelike images but even added realistic hair on the animals.[5]

Stop Motion   A particular type of animation is **stop motion**, a technique used to film inanimate objects like the Pillsbury Doughboy, which is a puppet. The little character is moved a bit at a time and filmed frame-by-frame. The Inside Story tells about how one art director settled on that technique for a commercial that changed residential recycling behavior in his community.

The same technique is used in **claymation**, which involves creating characters from clay and then photographing them one frame at a time. Both have been popular with art directors who create advertising where fantasy effects are desired, although new computer effects also are simplifying these techniques.

Music and Action   Specifying the music is usually done as part of the copywriting; however, matching the music to the action is an art director or producer's responsibility. In some cases, as in high-production song-and-dance numbers, the music is the commercial. Other times, it is used to get attention, set a mood, and lock the commercial into memory.

Principle
Visual storytelling in television commercials is constructed through the careful design of individual shots and the sequencing of moving images.

THE INSIDE STORY

Metro Recycling in Stop-Motion Animation

By Karl Schroeder, *Copywriter, Coates Kokes*

When I concept a TV campaign, I'll often think live-action first.

If I even consider animation, it's probably computer graphics or illustrations. I really hadn't considered stop motion before. It was perfect for this assignment and arguably the only solution for this concept. What was nice about it, when you consider that the spots needed to appeal to EVERYONE who recycles in the area, was that it got us away from casting racially ambiguous, hard-to-pin-an-age-on talent.

Everything was shot in a studio and composited in the computer. Both spots have three layers. All of the foreground elements, from the glass bottles to the yellow bins, are the actual objects. The animator used rods and arms to painstakingly move each item frame by frame.

Furthermore, each frame was shot twice. Normally you'd only need to shoot each frame once. But because we were shooting in front of a green screen and because we were using glass bottles (which reflect), we had to shoot each frame twice, one in front of the green screen and the second in front of a "natural background."

So now with two sets of images (as if all this weren't enough work), next up was to clip out the bottles that had the alien green reflection (from the green screen) and drop in the bottles that sported the natural reflections from the other shots, again frame by frame. The next layer is more straightforward, featuring the house and yard. The third layer has the sky and clouds (which move if you look closely). Since the plastic bag spot didn't have glass, it was a little simpler but otherwise followed the same process.

Lastly, we didn't want the logo, tag, and info to be tacked on at the end against a black background. Instead, we integrated the information by animating it against a tight shot of our yellow bin. The effect is much less jarring and better unites the "business" with the rest of the spot.

After it was all said and done, we had two spots that not only solved some issues, but were unlike any other on air.

This story was contributed by Karl Schroeder, copywriter at Coates Kokes in Portland, Oregon. Nominated by Professor Charles Frazer, Schroeder is a graduate of the University of Oregon advertising program.

For example, a recent JanSport commercial for its Live Wire Euphonic Pack, a backpack with built-in earphones and volume controls, cries out for a musical demonstration. The unlikely song picked for the spot, which targets the MTV crowd, was "Do-re-mi" from the 1959 *Sound of Music* musical. You might wonder why the creative team at the DDB Seattle agency would choose such a piece. Actually the rendition is not from the early recording but rather an ethereal, techno-pop version. The stick-in-the-head lyrics match the action on screen in a contemporary version of the classic story boy meets girl, boy loses girl, boy finds girl.[6]

The TV Production Process

For the bigger national commercials, the steps in the production process fall into three categories: preproduction, the shoot, and postproduction. Figure 14.6 shows the steps in the TV production process.

Preproduction   The producer and staff first develop a set of **production notes**, describing in detail every aspect of the production. These notes are important for finding talent and locations, building sets, and getting bids and estimates from specialists. In the Cat Herders commercial, finding the talent was critical. Some 50 felines and their trainers were involved in the filming. Surprisingly, different cats have different skills—some were able to appear to be asleep or motionless on cue, while others excel as runners or specialize in water scenes.

Once the bids for production have been approved, the creative team and the producer, director, and other key players hold a preproduction meeting to outline every step of the production process and anticipate every problem that may arise. Then the work begins. The talent agency begins casting the roles, while the production team finds a location and arranges site use with owners, police, and other officials. If sets are needed, they have to be built. Finding the props is a test of ingenuity, and the prop person may wind up visiting hardware stores, secondhand stores, and maybe even the local dump. Costumes must be made, located, or bought.

The Shoot   The film crew includes a number of technicians, all of whom report to the director. For both film and video recording, the camera operators are the key technicians. Other technicians include the **gaffer,** who is the chief electrician, and the **grip**, who moves props and sets and lays tracks for the dolly on which the camera is mounted. You've probably seen those positions in the credits at the end of movies. The script clerk checks the dialogue and other script details and times the scenes. A set is a busy crowded place that it appears, at times, to be total confusion and chaos.

The audio director records the audio either at the time of the shoot or, in the case of more high-end productions, separately in a sound studio. If the sound is being recorded at the time of shooting, a **mixer**, who operates the recording equipment, and a mic or boom person, who sets up the microphones, handle the recording on the set. In the studio it is usually recorded after the film is shot so the audio is synchronized with the footage. Directors often wait to see exactly how the action appears before they write and record the audio track. However, if the art director has decided to set the commercial to music, then the music on the audio track may be recorded before the shoot, as in the "Do-re-mi" audio track, and the filming done to the music.

The director shoots the commercial scene by scene, but not necessarily in the order set down in the script. Each scene is shot, called a **take**, and after all the scenes in the storyboard are shot they are then assembled through editing. If the director films the commercial on videotape, it is played back immediately to determine what needs correcting. Film has to be processed before the director can review it. These processed scenes are called **dailies. Rushes** are rough versions of the commercial assembled from cuts of the raw film

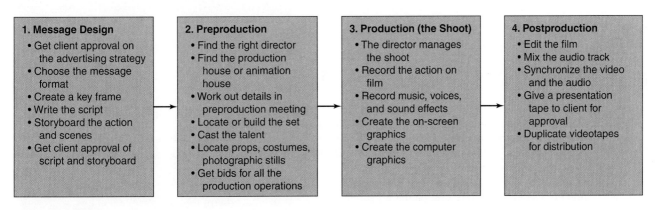

FIGURE 14.6

TV Production Process

In general, there are four steps in the production of a television commercial.

A MATTER OF PRINCIPLE

Honda "Cog" Gets It Right, But Not the First Time

It's tempting to think it was created through computer animation, but the Honda "Cog" commercial was filmed in real time without any special effects. It took 606 takes for the whole thing to work.

The lengthy process begins with a rolling transmission bearing, and moves through valves, brake pedals, tires, the hood, windshield wipers, and so forth. Every step of the process was carefully choreographed so that the part would do what it had to do exactly as planned. If there were any mistakes—and there were 605—then the filming started all over again from the beginning.

The commercial ends with the car driving away and Garrison Keillor, the star of the *Prairie Home Companion* radio show, asking "Isn't it nice when things just work?" The director and all the other people involved in the commercial were asking the same thing when it finally did work on the 606th take.

Because it was filmed using a British model that isn't sold in the United States and also because the cost of running a two-minute commercial would be prohibitive, the commercial was not shown in the United States, other than on news and feature shows and videos of award show winners. One of the most talked-about spots ever made, the publicity given to the commercial was probably even more valuable than an advertising buy.

The Cog commercial won a Grand Clio (a creative award show), as well as a Gold Lion at the Cannes Advertising Festival. Altogether, it picked up no fewer than 20 awards from various U.K. and international organizations. The spot can be seen at http://www.ebaumsworld.com.

Source: Stuart Elliott, "Is That Honda Commercial Real?" *The New York Times Direct,* June 10, 2003 (NYTDirect@nytimes.com); "Honda's Cog Does It Again, Taking the Grand Clio," *AdForum Alert,* May 19, 2004 (info@adforum.net).

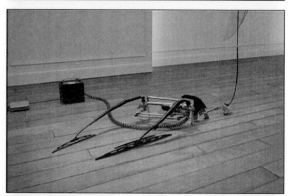

A two-minute commercial made in Britain for Honda by Wieden + Kennedy/London had viewers shaking their heads in disbelief and asking if it was for real. The spot shows all the many parts of a car, each set up in a domino fashion, that fall together piece by piece creating a kinetic sculpture that ultimately turns into a new Honda that drives away at the end.

footage. The director and the agency creative team view them immediately after the shoot to make sure everything's been filmed as planned. In some rare cases, an entire commercial is shot as one continuous action rather than individual shots edited together in postproduction. Probably the most interesting use of this approach is "Cog," an award-winning commercial for the Honda Accord. The principle in filming this kind of commercial is to get it right, even if you have to do it over and over.

Postproduction   For film and video, much of the work happens after the shoot in **postproduction**—when the commercial begins to emerge from the hands and mind of the editor. The objective of editing is to assemble the various pieces of film into a sequence that follows the storyboard. Editors manipulate the audio and video images, creating realistic 3-D images and combining real-life and computer-generated images. The postproduction process is hugely important in video because so many digital effects are being added to the raw film. In the Cat Herders commercial, Fallon could not film the cats and horses at the same time because of National Humane Society regulations. The director had to film the horses, background, and kitties separately. An editor fused the scenes together during postproduction, editing seamlessly to create the illusion of an elaborate cat drive.

Another goal of **video editing** is to manipulate time, which is a common technique used in commercial storytelling. Condensing time might show a man leaving work, then a cut of the man showering, then a cut of the man at a bar. The editor may extend time. Say a train is approaching a stalled car on the tracks. By cutting to various angles it may seem that the train is taking forever to reach the car—a suspense tactic. To jumble time, an editor might cut from the present to a flashback of a remembered past event or flash forward to an imagined scene in the future. All of these effects are specified by the art director in the storyboard.

The result of the editor's initial work is a **rough cut**, a preliminary edited version of the story that is created when the editor chooses the best shots and assembles them to create a scene. The editor then joins the scenes together. After the revision and reediting are completed, the editor makes an **interlock**, which means the audio and film are assembled together. The final version with the sound and film mixed together is called an **answer print**. The answer print is the final version printed onto a piece of film. For the commercial to air on hundreds of stations around the country, the agency makes duplicate copies—a process called **dubbing**. The dubbed copies are called **release prints**.

EFFECTIVE WEB DESIGN

Web design includes creating ads that run on the Web as well as the Web site itself. Banner ads are designed more like outdoor boards than conventional print ads because their small space puts intense requirements on the designer to make the ad communicate quickly and succinctly, and yet attract attention and curiosity to elicit a click-through response. You can check out banner ads online at http://www.banneradmuseum.com.

Designers know that Web pages, particularly the first screen, should follow the same layout rules as posters: The graphics should be eye-catching without demanding too much downloading time; type should be simple, using one or two typefaces and avoiding ALL CAPs and letter spacing that distorts the words. Because there is often a lot to read, organizing the information is critical. In terms of legibility, black type on a high-contrast background usually is best; all the design elements—type and graphics—should be big enough to see on the smallest screen.

Sometimes the illustrations and photos are obtained from clip-art services, or rather click art, such as that provided by http://www.eyewire.com or http://www.1stoppictures. net. Actually, any image can be scanned and manipulated to create a Web image, which is causing a copyright problem for artists. Because of the magic of digitizing, Web pages can combine elements and design styles from many different media: print, still photography, film, animation, sound, and games.

The combination of interactive navigation, live streaming video, online radio, and 360-degree camera angles creates Web pages that may be more complex than anything you see on TV, which is why ease of use is a factor in Web site design. The following discussion describes research on the best and worst site design practices conducted by Forrester Research, a company that specializes in monitoring the effectiveness of Internet advertising. The information was contributed by Harley Manning, Principal Analyst at Forrester Research and a graduate of the advertising program at the University of Illinois. Over the years, as he explains,

> Forrester has graded the quality of user experience on hundreds of Web sites with a technique called "heuristic evaluation." Today, variations on this methodology are used by virtually every interactive design agency and testing lab to judge the effectiveness of sites. It's also used in-house by many companies, including Ford and Johnson & Johnson. To identify some of the best and worst examples of Web design at the time, we used it to grade five sites in each of four industries: automotive, media, retail, and travel. When we published the results we kicked up quite a storm because we named names.

Here are two key results from Forrester's research into the best and worst of site design as explained by Manning.

- The retail category came out best overall, with the highest low score (JCPenney) as well as the highest high score (Lands' End). This finding was consistent with the results from the 375 sites we had graded previously, using versions 2 and 3 of our methodology.
- The automotive sites we graded laid firm claim to the cellar, with both the lowest low score (Toyota) and the lowest high score (Mini USA). This, too, was consistent with our earlier studies, in which the automotive manufacturer category ranked last among industry categories.

So what explains the relatively poor showing of automotive sites versus retail sites? Here's how Manning analyzed the results:

> One reason is that online retailers' business success ties directly to the quality of customer experience on their sites: When customers can't find a product or complete the check-out process, it shows up immediately in lost sales. This feedback loop drives retail site designers to quickly find and fix problems like inadequate product information, confusing menus, and poor reliability. In contrast, managers of automotive sites struggle to even measure business results, like dealer leads that actually result in a sale. And when Web traffic logs show car shoppers wandering around their sites, it's hard to tell whether the prospects are fascinated or just lost.

Web designers use a completely different toolbox than other types of art directors. Animation effects, as well as sophisticated navigation paths, are designed using software programs such as Flash, Director, Blender, Squeak, and nonlinear editing tools such as Premier, FinalCut, and AfterEffects, among others. It's such a rapidly changing design world that it's difficult to keep track of the most recent innovations in Web design software, although the use of streaming video has certainly made Web sites more like television. The Matter of Practice box explains how this tool is best used.

An example of a good Web site design is crewcuts.com, which was designated as the Best Web Site by the Internet Professional Publisher's Association. It's hard to convey here why the site is effective because of the animation, so check out http://www.crewcuts.com. One source for tips on Web site design is http://www.eMarketers.com. For more examples of excellence in Web site design and reviews of the top Web sites, check out:

http://www.netroadmap.com	http://www.clioawards.com
http://www.imarvel.com	http://www.oneclub.com
http://www.topsiteslinks.com	http://www.ippa.org

Action and Interaction

Web advertisers are continuing to find ways to bring dramatic action to the small screen to make the imagery more engaging. For example, Ford used a banner on the Yahoo! home page with the familiar Ford oval and a bunch of little black birds on a wire. Then three of

A MATTER OF PRACTICE

Searching for an Ideal Streaming Technology

By Edgar Huang, Associate Professor New Media Program, *Indiana University-Purdue University, Indianapolis*

As of the end of 2006, 78 percent of the U.S. active home online population connects via broadband according to data released by http://www.netratings.com/. A previous study found that the consumption of streaming videos is positively correlated to whether the consumer has a broadband connection.

Therefore, for multimedia specialists and rich media content providers in different businesses, especially mass media companies, advertisers, and small businesses, knowing how to do their streaming job right to better serve their audiences has become increasingly important.

In August 2006, my research partner, Clifford Marsiglio, and I published online a study *Searching for an Ideal Streaming Technology*, in which we examined and compared five streaming technologies, Adobe Flash Video, Apple QuickTime, Microsoft Windows Media, Real RealOne, and VX30 Zentu Encoder in the context of on-demand video (see http://www.iupui.edu/~nmstream).

We encoded the same videos with these streaming technologies and Web-authored the streaming videos with the best solutions provided by each of these companies. While encoding, we measured the time needed for encoding a video in each technology and the file size of each encoded video. We searched each company's Web site to find out how much it would cost to set up on-demand streaming with each of those technologies.

We posted the videos online in a survey and recruited professionals around the nation to take the survey and give feedback on the streaming videos in terms of compatibility (can play without downloading any software or plug-in), image quality, and streaming quality (frequency and length of buffering). In other words, the result of the study represents these expert users' opinions, not the authors'. Our survey also automatically detected each respondent's computer's operating system, browser used, Internet connection speed, and other factors.

After the data were collected, we ranked each technology for each factor mentioned previously and then assigned an average score to each technology based on the itemized ranking scores.

http://www.vx30.com, a Java-based streaming technology, rose to the top, followed by Flash, Windows Media, Real, and QuickTime. The study concludes,

Our study shows that VX30 has the best overall performance while Flash outperforms other streaming technologies in terms of user accessibility, perceived image quality, initial buffering delay and rebuffering.

If a streaming video producer does not care about Flash's long encoding time and large file sizes, and if a company or organization can afford the cost to set up and maintain streaming, Flash is probably today's best streaming technology.

If a company or organization is looking for a streaming technology that has little learning curve, encodes and Web-authors streaming videos fast, generates decent image quality and streaming quality and small video file sizes, and is inexpensive, VX30 is the top choice.

---

the birds flew down to the middle of the page and started pecking at what looked like birdseed, uncovering an image of the new Explorer. The link read: "Click to uncover the next territory." Those who did click probably expected a pop-up image, but instead the page shook, the birds scattered, and a big red Ford Explorer drove up to the front of the screen, replacing most of the content. It was a surprising, highly involving, and effective announcement of the vehicle.

Because users can create their own paths through the Web site, designers have to make sure that their sites have clear **navigation**. Users should be able to move through the site easily, find the information they want, and respond. Navigation problems can really turn off viewers. Eyetracking research (studies that use a camera to follow eye movement when looking at a page or screen) has found that if the navigation is cluttered or unclear, viewers will give up and move on to some other site.[7] Ideally, users who visit a site regularly should be able to customize the site to fit their own interests and navigation patterns.

Online video has also expanded the avenues for action on the small screen on minicomputers, personal digital assistants, and cell phones. Web video is becoming a new business opportunity for businesses that want to use videos to display their products. The secret is to plan these videos specifically for a small screen and not just try to use regular television or film images because the screen is just a fraction of the size of a television and a lot of the detail in an image can get lost.[8]

If a site is well designed, people may want to interact with the organization sponsoring the site. For example, Texture/Media, a Boulder, Colorado, Web design firm, created a seven-episode series over five months that detailed the journey of two men attempting to climb the Meru Sharksfin summit in India, for client Marmot Mountain Works. Called ClimbMeru.com, it chronicled the team's training and trip and hosted contest giveaways that helped gather information about Marmot's customers. Texture/Media's objective with its award-winning Web sites is to make the consumer a participant in its brand stories.

IT'S A WRAP

Altoids Makes a Mint

ALTOIDS®

The Altoids campaign has a strong consistent look strengthened by the continuing presence of the distinctive Altoids tin. Repetition of the look is the key to brand recognition. This campaign is recognizable because it builds on the principle that the more times viewers see an ad with a consistent format, the more likely they are to remember the product.

According to an *Ad Age* report, "the 'Curiously Strong' campaign is arguably one of the most awarded and successful campaigns in the last 12 years..." In 2006 alone, it garnered two Kelly Awards for magazine advertising. On the creative side it has won two One Show creative prizes and three Clios. It won an international effectiveness award when it won the New York Festival's Grand Prix.

There have been a long string of Kelly Awards in previous years. The Magazine Publishers of America (MPA) bestowed its $100,000 Grand Prize Kelly Award for outstanding magazine advertising for Altoids "Burn Through" campaign that launched Altoids gum.

The low-cost, edgy campaign has also been a business builder. The brand had virtually no presence in 1995 when Kraft bought it, but by 2000 it dominated the extreme mint market with a 25 percent share. In the 12 markets where the campaign was focused, Altoids enjoyed a 60 percent increase in overall volume of sales. Altoids' share in those 12 markets grew by 500 percent compared to markets without advertising.

That is what makes this campaign a winner—the memorability and extendability of a hot idea.

Key Points Summary

1. **What is the role of visual communication in advertising?** Visual communication is important in advertising because it creates impact—it grabs attention, maintains interest, creates believability, and sticks in memory. It also tells stories and creates brand images.

2. **How can we define layout and composition, and what's the difference between the two?** A layout is an arrangement of all the ad's elements. It gives the reader a visual order to the information in the ad; at the same time, it is aesthetically pleasing and makes a visual statement for the brand. Principles that designers use in print advertising include direction, dominance, unity, white space, contrast, balance, and proportion. Composition is the way the

elements in a picture are arranged, either through placement or by manipulating the photographer's viewpoint.

3. **How are art and color reproduced in print advertising?** Illustrations are treated as line art and photographs are reproduced through the halftone process by using screens to break down the image into a dot pattern. Full-color photos are converted to four halftone images, each one printed with a different process color—magenta, cyan, yellow, and black—through the process of color separation.

4. **Which steps in planning and producing broadcast commercials are most critical?** Commercials are planned using scripts and storyboards. TV commercials are shot

live, shot on film or videotape, or created "by hand" using animation, claymation, or stop action. There are four stages to the production of TV commercials—message design (scripts and storyboards), preproduction, the shoot, and postproduction.

5. **What are the basic techniques of Web design?** Web advertising can include ads and banners, but the entire Web site can also be seen as an advertisement. Art on Web pages can be illustrations or photographs, still images as well as moving ones, and may involve unexpected effects such as 360-degree images. When designers plan a Web page, they need to consider navigation—how people will move through the site. They also need to consider how to incorporate elements that allow for interaction between the consumer and the company that operates the site.

Key Terms

animation, p. 437
answer print, p. 441
claymation, p. 437
clip art (or click art), p. 423
color separation, p. 433
composition, p. 428
comprehensives, p. 428
continuous tone (or halftone), p. 432
crawl, p. 434
dailies, p. 439
debossing, p. 433
die cut, p. 433
digitization, p. 433

dubbing, p. 441
embossing, p. 433
film-to-tape transfer, p. 437
foil stamping, p. 433
font, p. 425
four-color printing, p. 433
gaffer, p. 439
grip, p. 439
halftone, p. 432
handled, p. 425
in register, p. 431
interlock, p. 441
layout, p. 427
legibility, p. 425

line art, p. 432
logo, p. 421
mechanicals, p. 428
mixer, p. 439
morphing, p. 435
navigation, p. 443
newsprint, p. 431
postproduction, p. 441
process colors, p. 433
production notes, p. 439
release prints, p. 441
rough cut, p. 441
rough layouts, p. 428
rushes, p. 439

screen, p. 432
semicomps, p. 428
spot color, p. 423
stock footage, p. 434
stop motion, p. 437
storyboard, p. 429
take, p. 439
thumbnail sketches, p. 428
tint blocks, p. 432
tip-ins, p. 433
typography, p. 425
video editing, p. 441
videographer, p. 428
visualization, p. 423

Review Questions

1. Explain why visual impact is so important in advertising.
2. What are the responsibilities of an art director?
3. Compare the use of black and white, spot color, and full color in terms of visual impact.
4. Explain the aesthetic role of typography. Find an ad that illustrates how type can add meaning to the message.
5. List the design principles and explain each one.
6. What's the difference between line art and halftones?
7. What does the phrase *four-color printing* mean? What are the four process colors? What does the phrase *color separation* mean, and how does that work?

8. Explain the following video terms:
   - stock footage
   - crawl
   - morphing
   - animation
   - stop motion
   - claymation
9. Explain the three steps in the video production process.
10. Draw up a list of guidelines to use in designing a Web site.

Discussion Questions

1. One of the challenges for creative ad designers is to demonstrate a product whose main feature cannot be seen by the consumer. Suppose you are an art director on an account that sells shower and bath mats with a patented system that ensures that the mat will not slide (the mat's underside is covered with tiny suction cups that gently grip the tub's surface). Brainstorm some ways to demonstrate this feature in a television commercial. Find a way that will satisfy the demands of originality, relevance, and impact.

2. One approach to design says that a visual image in an ad should reflect the image of the brand. Find a print ad that you think speaks effectively for the personality of the brand. Now compare the print ad with the brand's Web site. Does the same design style continue on the site? Does the

site present the brand personality in the same way as the print ad?

3. *Three-Minute-Debate:* Your team is assigned to a new client, which is a new hand lotion for men, one that is designed to help men whose hands take a beating in their jobs. One of your colleagues, a photographer, believes the only way to visualize the product and its use in an ad is through photography. Another colleague, an artist, argues that there are times when art is a much better way to illustrate a product than photography and that this production is a good example. Analyze the differences between using an illustration and using a photograph. What

are their roles, and how do they create different types of effects? Are there certain product categories where you would want to use an illustration or a photograph? Which would work best for this new product?

In class, organize into small teams with each team developing a case for using photography or artwork. Set up a series of three-minute debates with each team having 1½ minutes to argue its position. Every team of debaters has to present new points not covered in the previous teams' presentations until there are no arguments left to present. Then the class votes as a group on the winning point of view.

Take-Home Team Projects

1. As a team choose one of the following design critique problems:

   a. **Print:** What principles govern the design of a magazine ad? As a team, collect two sample ads, one you consider a good example of effective design and one that you think is not effective. Critique the two ads and explain your evaluation based on what you know about how design principles work in advertising layouts. Make suggestions for how the less effective ad could be improved.

   b. **Television:** As a team, find a television commercial that you thought was creative and entertaining. Then find one that you think is much less creative and entertaining. Analyze how the two commercials work to catch and hold your attention. How do the visuals work? What might be done to make the second commercial more attention getting? You can also use online sources to find commercials at http://www.adcritic.com and at http://www.badads.org.

2. Select a product that is advertised exclusively through print. Examples of such products are business-to-business and industrial products, school supplies, many over-the-counter drugs, and some food items. Your objective is to develop a

30-second television spot for this product. Divide the class into groups of four to six. Each team should develop a creative brief (see Chapter 12) to summarize the ad's strategy. In your small groups, brainstorm about ways to develop a creative idea for the commercial. Then write a script and develop a storyboard to present your idea for this product. In the script include all the key decisions a producer and director would make. Present your work to the class.

3. You have been asked to design a Web page for a local business or organization (choose one from your local community). Go to http://www.1stoppictures.net and choose a visual to illustrate the Web site by trying to match the personality of the organization to a visual image. Then identify the primary categories of information that need to be included on the page. Develop a flowchart or map that shows how a typical user would navigate through the site. What other image could you find on 1stoppictures.net that might be used on inside pages to provide some visual interest to this business's online image? Now consider interactivity: How could this site be used to increase interactivity between this company and its customers? Create a plan for this site that includes the visual elements and a navigation flowchart.

Yahoo! Hands-On Case

Review the Yahoo! case in the Appendix.

1. Develop a design memo that explains the look of the "Dave" campaign. If you were the art director on this campaign, how would you describe its design features? What does Dave look like? What does he wear? Describe his environment.

2. Your team has been asked to expand and critique the explanation of the Web site developed for this campaign. What do you like about it? What would you change or further develop? Prepare a one-page report that explains your thinking behind your critique of this Web site design.

HANDS-ON CASE

The High-Def Future of Advertising

You could call October 29, 1998, an historic day, for on that date John Glenn, the then 77-year-old former astronaut and senator, returned to space aboard the shuttle *Discovery*. He became the oldest person to ever go into orbit. In perhaps somewhat less dramatic fashion, history was made another way that day, because network coverage of Glenn's mission included the first five TV commercials ever broadcast in high-definition (HDTV). HDTV is a special kind of digital format, one that provides movie theater-quality pictures and stereo-quality audio.

Historic, yes, but the special quality of these five Proctor & Gamble commercials probably went unnoticed by most viewers, since in 1998 HDTVs were still very rare in the United States. In fact, even as late as 2005, despite intense efforts by broadcasters and television manufacturers, HDTV sets could be found in only about 10 million homes. By the end of 2006, however, U.S. homes with HDTV increased to about 27.7 million, more than half of the number of HDTV homes worldwide. As HDTVs become more affordable and the amount of programming broadcast in the format rises, the number of homes worldwide equipped with HDTV sets is expected to increase dramatically, reaching about 151 million by 2011.

The advertising world is taking notice, too. During the 2004 Super Bowl only one advertiser chose to run an ad in high-definition, whereas more than half of the advertisers did so for the 2006 game. Why? As *Advertising Age* put it:

> Imagine watching the Super Bowl this year in high-definition on your new big-screen plasma TV. Watch the quarterback's eyes dart from side to side as he calls a play in Dolby surround sound. Watch nervous defensive ends drip sweat as they wait for the call. Cut to commercial, and suddenly the screen shrinks from a wide screen to a small squared-off box with a flat and dull-looking product inside it. Now imagine you're the brand manager of that product. Imagine picking up the phone and calling your advertising agency to query, "I paid $2.4 million for that?"

What challenges face an advertiser told by its agency to film a commercial in HD? As you might expect, cost is an issue, since ads filmed in the format can cost 10 to 15 percent more than analog commercials. However, benefits may be worth the extra cost.

One industry survey, sponsored by the iNDemand Network, found that 62 percent of respondents say they enjoy watching commercials in HD, 51 percent believe they pay more attention to HD commercials, and 69 percent think advertisers that show commercials in HD are "more cutting edge."

TVPredictions.com also reports some interesting findings from a study conducted by Nielsen: "HDTV owners were able to remember 15 percent more of Super Bowl commercials after the game than those who did not own HD sets; HDTV owners were 168 percent more likely to watch the game in a group of six or more people; and HDTV owners were 27 percent more likely to find the ads in the 2007 Super Bowl at least as entertaining as last year's game." HD seems to be redefining how we watch television advertising.

Consider This

1. Evaluate the arguments for and against creating high-definition ads. Under what conditions would you counsel an advertiser to spend the extra money on this new format?

2. Can you think of some advertisers who might be attracted to the high-quality picture and sound of HDTV even though they have traditionally avoided television?

3. Explain how production considerations, such as the use of HDTV, might influence the planning and design of a television commercial. How would you determine if using HDTV is effective?

Sources: Beth Snyder Bulik and Kirs Oser, "High Time for Ads to Move to High-Def," *Advertising Age*, December 13, 2004; Kate Fitzgerald, "Visuals Only Get Better," *Advertising Age*, February 24, 2003; Bradley Johnson, "TV-Set Brands Carefully Enter Digital Future," *Advertising Age*, November 9, 1998; Laura Petrecca, "More Super Bowl Marketers Shoot High-Def Ads," *USA Today*, January 12, 2006, http://www.usatoday.com; Jennie L. Phipps, "Digital Debate: Video vs. Film, *Advertising Age*, June 18, 2001; Phillip Swann, "HDTV: The Price Is Right: But the Consumer Electronics Industry Must Do a Better Job of Letting People Know," September 29, 2004, http://www.tvpredictions.com; Phillip Swann, "HDTV Owners More Likely to Recall Super Bowl Ads," February 9, 2007, http://www.tvpredictions.com.

Principles: How to Win the Battle of the Buzz

Hundreds of different communication activities deliver brand messages both formally through planned marketing communication programs and informally through other activities. This section provides a framework for you to understand how all these programs and tools can work together to send target audiences consistent, persuasive messages that get people talking about a brand.

In this section we will introduce a collection of key marketing communication tools whose activities need to be coordinated with advertising as part of an integrated communication plan. To help you understand how a coordinated program can make you street-smart and deliver winning brand communication, consider the 12 principles identified by Professor Margo Berman.

12 Steps to Street-Smart Advertising: How to Win the Battle of the Buzz

The following principles and techniques are described in the book, DVD, and webinar series of the same name: *Street-Smart Advertising*.

1. Define and develop your own USP (Unique Selling Proposition). Understand specifically what you offer that's different from your competitors. Consider how your audience sees your company. Then, develop an on-target message that delivers what you want them to think.

2. Focus on developing on-strategy, on-target promotions that drive home your USP. Create campaigns with legs for consistent branding in any medium.

3. Brainstorm for ideas to use alternative media. Remember innovative places where you've seen messages. Think about where else you can reach your audience. Concentrate on how you can interrupt them through media intersection and media-specific advertising.

Margo Berman, Associate Professor,
Florida International University

Part 5

4. Create sticky slogan solutions. Be inspired by 16 powerful techniques like reason why, vernacular, and interrogative to invent distinctive, unforgettable branding.

5. Discover the power of type. Understand typography's unique personality. Notice how fonts can be formal, casual, whimsical, or serious. Recognize how replacing the font can change the tone and effect the overall impression of your promotion.

6. Write killer copy using techniques like an ABA structure and other writing techniques such as weaving, connectors, parallel construction, contractions, and alliteration. Build an arsenal of writing ammunition, so you're armed to do battle in the marketplace.

7. Uncover the inside secret to great design. Learn a library of layouts that you can use in a flash. Then, keep a pocketful of templates handy. Note when to use a circus or a rebus, a frame or a split design. See how to create a unique look for instant recognition.

8. Delve into the psychology of colors. Explore color meanings around the world. Find out what colors work best for which companies and why. Identify the colors that raise your heart rate and increase your appetite, as well as the ones that have a tranquil effect.

9. Consider what you can do online. Offer valuable, but free information to generate a loyal base of followers who opt in to receive your message. Give them reasons to come back, become more involved, and learn more about your services or products.

10. Introduce interactive promotions to engage and entertain your audience, while encouraging participation. Explore various interactive campaigns and think about how to arouse your audience's imagination. Establish interactive marketing that focuses on fun.

11. Always develop new self-promotions for your firm, whether you're a freelancer or global ad agency. Continuously investigate new media and emerging technology. Stay ahead so you're always on the cutting edge. Attend conferences, webinars, and teleclasses to see what's happening in your field. Have all your materials reflect new trends.

12. Look to see how your marketing can be more innovative. Ask yourself these kinds of questions: Should you develop contests? Add interactivity on your Web site? Integrate more online promotions? Offer more free information? Remember to focus on this question: What can you do to increase relevance and value for your audience?

Chapter 15
Direct-Response Marketing

Chapter 16
Sales Promotion, Events, and Sponsorships

Chapter 17
Public Relations

Chapter 18
Special Advertising Campaigns

Chapter 19
Evaluation of Effectiveness

Direct-Response Marketing

IT'S A WINNER

Award:	Organization:	Agency:	Campaign:
Effie, Echo	*GEICO*	*The Martin Agency, Richmond, Virginia*	*"The Gecko"*

The Gecko Goes Direct

Odds are that you know this little fellow. Maybe you were one of the half-million people who voted to make the GEICO Gecko the one of two favorite advertising icons. The Gecko's biography will show you what a far-reaching impact he's had on the car insurance business and how direct marketing can successfully employ spokes-creatures to replace a sales force.

GEICO is the leading direct-response auto insurer in a low-involvement category dominated by major brands, such as Allstate and State Farm. Its biggest marketing challenge is to generate inquiries for rate quotes and to motivate people to call or go online to find out how they can save money, which is reflected in its long-standing brand promise, "15 minutes could save you 15 percent or more on car insurance."

The birth of The Gecko (that's his whole name) occurred in 1999 as ad honchos at The Martin Agency labored over what to do with an account they had for GEICO, an acronym for the not-so-catchy-sounding Government Employees Insurance Company. One member of the creative team noted that customers often mispronounced "GEICO" as "Gecko," and someone drew a doodle of the little guy.

Interestingly, Ted Ward, GEICO's vice president for marketing, didn't immediately fall in love with the idea of The Gecko. Ward said, "I quickly became much more fond of him as we sold more policies. I'm a big fan of anything that makes our phone ring or Web site click. He really has helped us brandwise."

Chapter Key Points

1. How do we define direct marketing and its process?
2. How are databases used in direct marketing?
3. Who are the key players in direct marketing?
4. What are some steps in evaluating the tools and media available to direct-response programs?

The Gecko tells fundamental truths about the human condition in goofy ways. The oddball humor caught on with the audience.

"He's cute, he's green, he works hard, he's got a great attitude, and he could save people a lot of money on their car insurance," said Steve Bassett, creative director of the Martin Agency.

Spokespersons, or rather a spokes-creature in this case, can do much to turn customers' attention to the client's product. According to William Weir of *The Hartford Courant*, Gecko is a new breed of brand character. He's upfront with audiences that his job is to sell GEICO insurance. His personality communicates with the skeptical audience who's hyper-aware of marketing.

It's not just that GEICO's icon is endearing that makes the campaign work. GEICO uses The Gecko strategically to accomplish the work that its rival auto insurers do by hiring an army of sales middlemen.

The volume of direct mail and commercials GEICO uses is astounding, and it makes sense to maximize efforts to get more sales, given the current profitability of the auto insurance industry. As accident rates—and claims—have decreased, auto insurers are trying to grab a bigger share of the market. Seth Stevenson, contributor to *Slate*, said, "The quickest way to do that is by ramping up your television ads."

You may have noticed that GEICO doesn't just stick with The Gecko in all its commercials. The reason has much to do with the size of the market, which includes just about anyone who drives a car. Realizing that one creative approach will not appeal to everyone, GEICO uses a diverse approach to reach a wide audience. That means The Gecko appeals to some, while the indignant cavemen capture others' attention, and customer testimonials with celebrities like Little Richard reach even others. The concept is simple: different strokes for different folks. The different creative approaches are GEICO-ized by using a common humorous tone.

If it's true that imitation is the sincerest form of flattery, you can see the effect GEICO's advertising has had on the industry. Watch competitors' advertising. Competitors like State Farm and Allstate, which have advertised for years with gentle, homespun messages promoting family and security, are now including more humor, high action, and other attention-getting techniques to make you remember their brand when it comes time to buy auto insurance.

Just how successful are The Gecko's efforts to sell insurance? Turn to It's a Wrap at the end of the chapter to find out.

Sources: GEICO.com; Theresa Howard, "Gecko Scores Well in USA Today Ad Track," *USA Today*, July 16, 2006; Seth Stevenson, "The Best Ad on Television," Slate.com, July 25, 2005, http://www.slate.com; Suzanne Vranica, "GEICO's Gecko Shook Up Insurance Ads," *Wall Street Journal*, January 2, 2007, B1; William Weir, "Character Counts: Brand Icons Get Story Lines, Emotions," *The Hartford Courant*, November 2, 2006, http://www.aef.com/industry/news/data/2006/6093.

A big change is taking place in marketing and advertising as marketers are moving to more direct and interactive forms of communication with their customers and prospects. In the past, marketing communication was a monologue as advertisers talked to anonymous consumers through the mass media. Now communication is becoming a dialogue. Using computers and the Internet, mail, video, and telephone, advertisers can talk directly with, rather than at, customers. This advertising dialogue is achieved through direct marketing. In this chapter we'll discuss the practice and process of direct marketing, the key players, the tools of direct marketing, and the principles of integrating direct marketing into the total brand communication effort.

THE PRACTICE OF DIRECT MARKETING

Advertisers use direct marketing in every consumer and business-to-business category. IBM, Xerox, and other manufacturers selling office products use direct marketing, as do almost all banks and insurance companies. Airlines, hotels, and cruise lines use it. Packaged-goods marketers such as General Foods, Colgate, and Bristol Myers; household product marketers such as Black and Decker; and automotive companies use it. Direct marketing shows up in membership drives, fund-raising, and solicitation for donations by nonprofit organizations such as the Sierra Club and Audubon Society and by political associations.

The Direct Marketing Association (DMA) is the professional association for this industry, although DMA describes the field as *a business strategy* rather than an industry. We'll define **direct-response marketing (DM)** as a multichannel system of marketing that uses a variety of media to connect sellers and customers who deal with each other directly rather than through an intermediary, such as a wholesaler or retailer. Using an interactive communication model, the contact is designed to elicit an immediate response, usually a sale.

As noted in Figure 15.1, DM includes a strong focus on marketing research to guide strategy and database development to better target customers and prospects and invite them to interact with a company. Direct marketers use a variety of media, including catalogs, direct mail, telephone, the Internet, mass-media advertising, and new forms of media such as cell phones, podcasts, and Blackberries (personal digital assistants, or PDAs). The important thing about direct marketing is that it opens up the door for interactivity. As Berman explained in the Part V Introduction, direct marketers need to "explore various interactive campaigns and think about how to arouse your audience's imagination . . . with interactive marketing that focuses on fun."

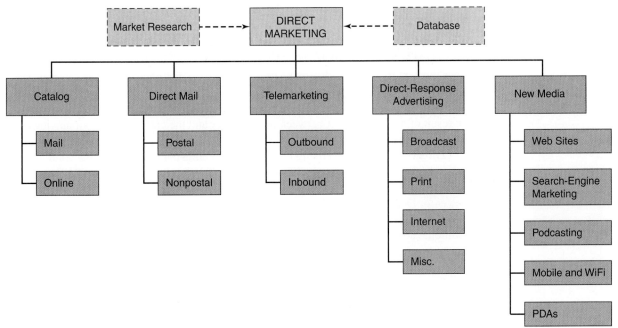

FIGURE 15.1

The Direct-Marketing Industry

The direct-marketing industry focuses on research and database building. Its main tools are catalogs, direct mail, telemarketing, direct-response advertising, the Internet, and new media.

Direct marketing is an exciting, dynamic field that is becoming more dominant in marketing communication because many, if not most, marketers are moving to interactive forms of customer communication. The DMA says direct marketing generates sales of more than $1.93 trillion and generates 10.3 percent of the U.S. gross domestic product (GDP).[1]

Advantages and Disadvantages of Direct Marketing

Advantages of direct marketing over indirect marketing, such as advertising, can be summarized in one word—accountability. DMA describes this strength as the ability to track, measure, and optimize marketing communication.[2] The advantages include the following:

- Direct-marketing messages can be personalized, which makes them much more persuasive than nonpersonalized (mass-media) messages.
- Direct-marketing results are measurable so the return on investment (ROI) is easily known.
- Direct-marketing technology allows for the collection of relevant information about the customer, contributing to the development of a useful database and selective reach, which reduces waste.
- Products have added value, through the convenient purchase process and reliable/quick delivery mechanisms of direct marketing. Purchase is not restricted to a location.
- The marketer controls the product (rather than the wholesaler or retailer) until delivery.
- Advertising carrying direct-marketing components is more effective.
- Direct marketing affords flexibility both in form and timing.

Like all tools, direct marketing has some weaknesses. Most notably, consumers are still reluctant to purchase a product they cannot touch and feel. Another weakness is the annoyances associated with direct marketing, such as too many catalogs, junk mail, online pop-ups, ad clutter, spam e-mail, and unwelcome phone calls. There are serious problems with customer privacy and data sharing as well as concerns about identity theft. Finally, in the tension between creating a long-term brand image and driving immediate sales, direct marketing tends to be more attuned to the latter. But that doesn't mean brand building is impossible with direct marketing. In particular, direct marketers, such as L.L. Bean, Amazon.com, Nature Conservancy, and Dell Computer, have built strong brands primarily through direct marketing.[3]

Direct Marketing and Direct-Response Advertising

Since this text focuses on advertising, it is necessary to distinguish between direct marketing and direct-response advertising. Direct marketing includes the whole marketing process, as diagrammed in Figure 15.2. It is a way of doing business that produces sales as the result of a direct contact between the marketer and the customer without any intermediaries, such as retailers, wholesalers, or other members of the distribution chain.

Direct-response advertising is a type of marketing communication that combines the characteristics of advertising and sales promotion—attention-getting visuals, interesting copy, an offer, and relevant timing. Most importantly, it provides a way for the reader, viewer, or listener to respond directly and contact the advertiser. The contact element can be a toll-free phone number, an order coupon, a Web site or e-mail address. In contrast to traditional advertising, which generally offers a long-term implicit promise, direct advertising provides the opportunity for immediate action. Therefore, the ROI can be measured much more accurately than the return on image advertising.

Some advertisers see direct response as less effective than brand or image advertising because it doesn't reach as many people or, if it does, the cost of reaching each individual is very high. Proponents justify the costs by noting that the objective is action rather than recall or attitude change. Today the high-cost argument is being reconsidered. Although it costs a lot per impression, direct-response advertising, particularly direct mail, is well targeted. It reaches a prime audience—people who are likely, for reasons related to their demographics or lifestyles, to be interested in the product.

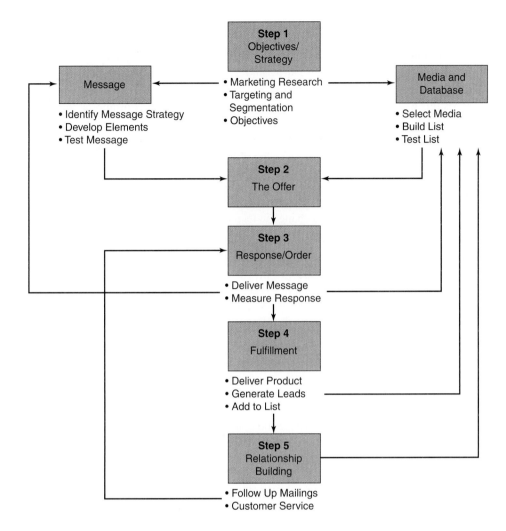

FIGURE 15.2

The Direct-Marketing Process
The direct-marketing process has five main steps. The direct marketer's challenge is to manage these steps and build a relationship with the consumer.

The Direct-Marketing Process

As outlined in Figure 15.2, there are five basic steps in direct marketing: (1) the establishment of objectives and strategic decisions (research helps advertisers target, segment, prospect, and set objectives); (2) the communication of an offer (the message) by the seller through the appropriate medium; (3) response, or customer orders; (4) fulfillment, or filling orders and handling exchanges and returns; and (5) maintenance of the company's database and customer service.

Objectives and Strategies   As in all planning processes, we begin by delineating the specific objectives to achieve. Direct marketing can be used to achieve six basic objectives:

1. ***Provide product information.*** Typically direct-marketing pieces provide space for detailed information about a product or service. The Crane & Company "Banknote" brochure is an example.
2. ***Create sales.*** The most typical DM objective is to create sales by convincing customers to order products, make payments, or take some other action, such as visiting a dealer, returning a response card, or visiting a Web site.
3. ***Retain and strengthen customer relationships.*** Because it costs so much to acquire new customers, smart companies work hard not only to retain their current customers but to strengthen their relationships with them so these customers will buy more and speak well of the brand to others.
4. ***Develop leads.*** With *considered purchases* (e.g., cars, insurance, automobiles), prospects need to think about them for a while before making a purchase decision. DM can be used to identify those who may be interested in the product so follow-up phone calls, personal sales calls, or other forms of contact can be made to help

influence purchases. This practice is called **lead generation**. For example, a Volvo dealer rents a database of consumers who meet the criteria for being potential Volvo owners and sends out a direct-mail piece that offers $50 to anyone taking a test drive on a specific set of dates. The assumption is that those who respond are interested not only in the $50 but also in learning more about the Volvo. Generating leads this way is called **prospecting,** which refers to a technique of mining information in a database to identify prospective buyers.

5. *Generate traffic.* As with lead generation, some DM efforts are aimed at motivating customers to visit a store, attend an event, or in some other way interact with a brand.

6. *Test offers.* Because DM is a closed-loop marketing process that is measurable, it is an excellent way to test most aspects of a marketing plan such as pricing, packaging, or promotional offers. Once the results of a test are known, the company can better predict the effects of making a change in its marketing plan.

Direct marketers make these basic objectives more specific by spelling out such factors as timing, amount of increase, and more information about consumers' specific behavior, such as where they see the product or in what kind of action they might engage. For example, a local Volvo dealership might expect its direct-marketing program to increase showroom traffic by 60 percent in the next 90 days.

Targeting   One of the most important decisions made in DM is selecting those who are to receive the offer. For those DM messages conveyed via catalog, phone calls, and mail, the CPM is very high. Therefore, if the DM effort is to have a positive ROI, it is critical that the target prospects have a higher-than-average interest in the product.

The best customer prospects of direct marketers are current customers. If someone has bought from a company several times before, they are much more likely to buy again from that company than someone who has never bought from that company. In other words, current customers have already been sold on the brand, so it is much easier (i.e., less costly) to motivate them to buy again.

Direct marketers have identified three criteria that help them predict who is most likely to repurchase: **recency, frequency, and monetary (RFM)**. The more recently customers bought from a company, the more likely they are to buy again. The more frequently customers bought from a company, the more likely they are to buy again. And finally, the more money customers have spent buying from a company, the more likely they are to buy again. Computer models are used to do ongoing analyses of customers' buying behaviors and to produce lists, using these criteria, of who the company can best afford to send more catalogs, e-mails, and promotional letters. This is called **optimization**.

For acquiring new customers, a targeting strategy is to *profile current customers* and then look for potential customers who have similar profiles from databases of customer information. For example, if Wendy's finds that a high percentage of its customers in a college town are graduate students, then it should try to find mailing lists of graduate students so it can mail promotional coupons as this target audience has a higher probability of responding than the average person.

The Offer   All direct marketing contains an **offer**, typically consisting of a description of the product, terms of sale, and payment, delivery, and warranty information. In its offer, a successful DM campaign must communicate benefits to buyers by answering the enduring question: "What's in it for me?" Also, many DM offers include an incentive for responding quickly, as marketers know that the longer people think about responding, the less likely they will respond.

An effective DM offer, as with all marketing offers, clearly calls on the buyer to take some action. All the variables that are intended to satisfy the needs of the consumer are considered part of the offer. These variables include the price, the cost of shipping and handling, optional features, future obligations, availability of credit, extra incentives, time and quality limits, and guarantees or warranties. The offer is supported by a message strategy, a media strategy, and the database.

Message and Media Strategy   Because DM messages can be individually targeted, the more personalized the message the better. For example, when a customer orders a book

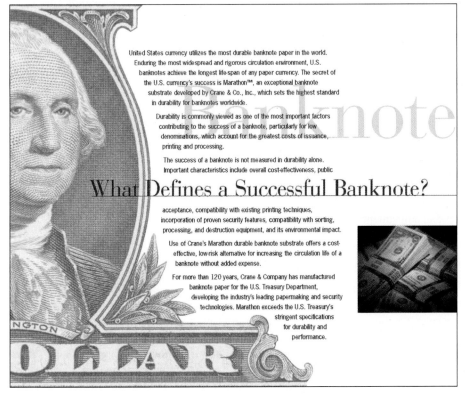

SHOWCASE This beautifully designed brochure was created by Peter Stasiowski when he was art director at Gargan Communications in Dalton, Massachusetts. It promotes the durability of Crane & Company's banknote paper. You're looking at the cover (which wraps front to back) and an inside page. Crane is the primary provider of banknote paper to the U.S. Mint. The impact of the piece comes from the unity of creative concept, the product itself, the selling premise, and the visual elements. Stasiowski is a graduate of the advertising program at the University of West Florida, and his work was nominated by Professor Tom Groth.

from Amazon.com, the company's system immediately suggests similar books. When one of the airlines sends out promotional offers to its frequent flyers, these messages often show the number of miles traveled in the last year and the number of rewards earned year to date. This is obviously a personalized message and definitely attracts more attention.

General guidelines apply to message development in direct marketing. First, the message is often longer and contains more explanation and detail because as stated before, if this message doesn't motivate the receiver to respond it some way, the message is wasted. Messages must contain clear comparisons or characteristics such as price, style, and convenience to be persuasive. Second, copy tends to be written in a personal, one-to-one conversational style. Third, the message should reflect whether the offer is a one-step offer or two-step offer. Because a **one-step offer** asks for a direct sale response, it must include a mechanism for responding to the offer. A **two-step offer** is designed to gather leads, answer consumer questions, set up appointments, and drive customers to a Web site or retail store.

The Response/Order   Generating a response is the third step in the direct marketing process (see Figure 15.2). To maximize the response/order rate, the DM message must make it as easy as possible for customers to respond. One way to do this is to offer a variety of ways in which to respond—online, mail, phone, and fax. Also, if phone is one channel, then the more hours the phone lines are open, the better. When customers respond online, it is important that the company immediately acknowledge the response, thanking the customer for the order and advising when the product will arrive. The types of customer service offered, such as toll-free telephone numbers for product support, free limited-time trials, and acceptance of several different credit cards, are important techniques for overcoming customer resistance to responding. To create urgency, the direct-marketing message may also include a promotional device such as a gift or limited-time-only price deal.

Fulfillment and Customer Maintenance   The next step in the direct-marketing process is called **fulfillment**, which is responding to customers' responses by getting the product to the customers who ordered it. Fulfillment includes all the back-end activities to process the transaction, including delivering the product, receiving payment, and providing customers with tracking numbers so they can trace the delivery of their orders. The most critical aspect of successful direct marketing, however, is maintaining a customer relationship. Direct marketers use a database to track customer interactions and transactions, the final step in Figure 15.2.

Measurement and Evaluation   Direct marketing is not a "shot-in-the-dark" approach. DM professionals continually evaluate and accurately measure the effectiveness of various offers in a single campaign. By employing such measurement tools as tracking printed codes on mail-in responses that identify different offers and using different telephone numbers for each commercial (by time slot, station, or length), the DM professional can clearly identify those offers that yield the best results and modify the campaign to take advantage of them. Because of this constant evaluation, there is an emphasis in DM to learn what is most effective and employ that information in succeeding efforts. Such accurate measurements and adjustments are largely responsible for DM's success.

Principle

Because direct-marketing messages are constantly being measured, it is easier to learn what works and modify succeeding campaigns based on results than with advertising.

DATABASES: THE FOUNDATION OF DM

Direct marketers use **databases** to keep track of customers and identify prospective customers. They are also a segmentation tool to communicate relevant offers to customers and prospects. A database is at the heart of direct marketing.

For example, consider how Carnival Cruise Lines uses databases to manage its customer relationships. Information is gathered at check-in when customers get their Sail & Sign card, which serves as money on the cruise (it also allows Carnival to track its customers' purchases and activities). New customers receive a standard card but returning passengers get a gold card that triggers "Welcome back" messages from staff. Frequent cruisers get a platinum card and automatic membership in the Concierge Club with perks such as priority embarking and debarking, dining times, and spa reservations. This data is then used to target follow-up e-mail and direct-mail offers.[4]

Don Peppers and Martha Rogers are authors of a set of books that focus on one-to-one marketing, which they define as a strategy that delivers customer-focused objectives by treating different customers differently. Through the use of databases, they describe the *learning relationship* that results from customer dialogue. Here is how this data-driven relationship works as described by Peppers and Rogers:[5]

> If you're my customer and I get you to talk to me, I remember what you tell me, and I get smarter and smarter about you. I know something about you competitors don't know. So I can do things for you my competitors can't do, because they don't know you as well as I do. Before long, you can get something from me you can't get anywhere else, for any price. At the very least you'd have to start all over somewhere else, but starting over is more costly than staying with us.

An example of using a database to identify good customers and treat them differently comes from a direct-response campaign designed by Wisconsin-based Carlson Marketing that segmented customers by usage. By analyzing its database, a large multinational packaged goods company was able to send a premium quality direct-mail piece with a unique shape to the top 15 percent of the company's 200 million customers. The middle-tier customers—55 percent of the customer base— received a more modest flat mail piece and the bottom group received cost-effective e-mails.[6]

A Circular Process

A database is important at both the beginning of the direct-marketing process where it is a critical source of information and at the end of the process where it captures and updates information for the next interaction. It's a circular process—if you look at relationship-driven communication programs as the ultimate goal of direct-response marketing, then the information gathered through customer interaction feeds back into the process and becomes an input for the next round of communication efforts.

Database marketing is possible because of innovations in computer technology that have helped companies keep up with their customers. People move, have children, marry, divorce, remarry, change jobs, age, and retire and change their purchase behavior through all of these changes. The purpose of the database is to produce up-to-date information on customers and prospects as well as their interactions with the company. According to the DMA, a marketing database has these primary objectives:[7]

Principle
A reliable database of customer and prospect contact information lies at the heart of effective direct marketing.

- To record names of customers, expires (names no longer valid), and prospects
- To provide a vehicle for storing and analyzing responses
- To provide a vehicle for storing and analyzing purchasing performance
- To provide a vehicle for continuing direct communication with customers

The database management process is illustrated in Figure 15.3. It begins with an initial information collection point. This could be the completion of a warranty card, entering a contest or sweepstake, opting in on a Web site, or filling out a card at a trade show, to name a few. The second stage is to enter the data into the computer to merge it with other information already in the file or added at the same time. Stage three allows the marketer to assess the data and determine the relevant level of detail. In stage four, the direct marketer can create clusters of characteristics and behaviors representing valuable consumer segments or

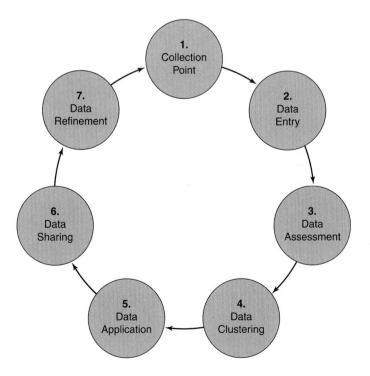

FIGURE 15.3
The Database Marketing Process
Using database marketing, advertisers can continually improve the effectiveness of their campaigns.

target markets (audiences). Stage five applies the database to the specific marketing problems or strategies. An example might be sending coupons to a particular customer segment. In stage six, the direct marketer makes decisions about data sharing and partnerships. A manufacturer may decide his retail outlets could use the data. Finally, the database goes through a refinement process that includes corrections, updates, additions, and deletions.

If either expertise or resources are lacking, a company can hire database management firms whose sole purpose is to collect, analyze, categorize, and market an enormous variety of detail about customers. Companies such as National Decision Systems and Donnelly Marketing Information Systems are only a few of the firms that provide these **relational databases**—that is, their databases contain information useful in profiling and segmenting as well as contact information. Donnelly, for example, developed Hispanic Portraits, a database of households that segments the U.S. Hispanic population into 18 cluster groups.

Lists

Customer and prospect lists that contain contact information (addresses, phone numbers, e-mail addresses) are used by all areas of direct marketing. Direct-mail **lists** that match market segments identified in the advertising plan can be purchased or rented from list brokers who maintain and sell thousands of lists tied to demographic, psychographic, and geographic breakdowns. They have further classified their data on such characteristics as hobbies, affiliations, and personal influence, such as the Response Alliance database of decision makers. Geography is a common classification; American households can be broken down to their postal carrier routes. For instance, one company has identified 160 zip codes it calls "Black Enterprise" clusters, inhabited by "upscale, white-collar, black families" in major urban fringe areas.

New lists can be created by merging and purging. If you want to target older women in New England who play tennis, most major firms would be able to put together a list for you by combining lists, called **merging**, and deleting the repeated names, called **purging**. For example, you may want to develop a list of people who are in the market for fine furniture in your city. You could buy a list of new home buyers and combine that with a list of people who live in a desirable census tract. These two lists together—a compiled list—would let you find people who have bought new homes in upscale neighborhoods. There are three types of lists: house lists, response lists, and compiled lists.

- *House list.* A **house list** of the marketer's own customers or members is its most important target market and probably its most valuable list. Stores offer credit plans,

This is a postcard mailed to B2B direct marketers offering lists classified into 47 different types of buying characteristics. It separates prospects in terms of 47 "buying influence selectors" that include such factors as job function, industry, and decision-making patterns.

service plans, special sale announcements, and contests that require customers to sign up to maintain this link. Some stores, such as Radio Shack, fill in customers' names and addresses at the cash register, and those customers join the list.

- *Response list.* A **response list** is made up of people or households who respond to some type of direct-response offer. The more similar the product to which they responded is to the advertiser's product, the more valuable the list as these people should be more similar to company's current customers. For example, if you sell pet food, you might like a list of people who have responded to a magazine ad for a pet identification collar. Two important criteria are obvious from such a list—these people very likely have a pet, and they are open to buying from a catalog, mail offer, or Web site.
- *Compiled list.* A **compiled list** is a list of some specific category, such as sports car owners, new home buyers, graduating seniors, new mothers, association members, or subscribers to a magazine, book club, or record club. Luxury car manufacturers are always interested in lists of people who own luxury cars, because these people obviously like and can afford such cars.

The growth in the number of databases has also seen an increase in consumer resistance to what appears to some to be a barrage of "junk mail" in print, spam e-mail, and unwanted phone calls. Here are some of the ways consumers can reduce the amount of direct mail or spam they receive:[8]

- If you enter a contest or order an item by mail, you may wind up on a mailing list. To protect your contact information, check the "opt-out" box and write "No mailing lists" beside your contact information.
- Use the "contact us" link on retailers' Web sites to ask to be taken off mailing lists.
- Check the "privacy" link at the bottom of a company's home page for directions on removing your name from its mailing lists.
- The Mail Preference Service of DMA permits you to register for $5 to get off mailing lists (http://www.dmaconsumers.org/cgi/offmailing).
- To get off credit card solicitation lists, call 888-5-OPT-OUT. A recorded message will ask for your contact information, but that's just confirmation. This service already has your contact information; providing it by phone confirms your identity so your request can be processed.
- GreenDimes (http://www.greendimes.com) is a service that charges $36 a year to contact direct mailers on its customers' behalf.
- Another service, StopTheJunkMail.com, lets you select from its database of retailers to send letters asking that your name be removed from their list. The annual fee for this service is $19.95.
- To register for the federal do-not-call list, go to donotcall.gov and sign up. That will cut down on unwanted phone calls from marketers.
- To reduce the amount of spam you receive, register at e-MPS, which is DMA's e-mail Preference Service (http://dmaconsumers.org/consumers/optoutform_emps.shtml).

You might note that in most cases, if you have a relationship with a company—which means you've ordered something within the past 12 months—you won't be deleted from those lists. Blanket requests to end unsolicited calls or mail may not apply to charities and politicians because of First Amendment issues. Nonprofit organizations do a lot of solicitations by mail.

Data-Driven Communication

Gathering information about customers and prospects is also the beginning of a new round of interaction. Using the insights captured from previous interactions to create **data-driven communication**, companies are better able to target, respond to, and interact with their customers. Keeping track of interactions lets the company respond with some sense of their customers' interests and a history of their relationship with the company. Ultimately, the knowledge in the database is the tool used to build and maintain customer relationships through recognition and rewards.

Principle
Data-driven communication lets the brand speak with a sense of the history of the customer relationship because it tracks the customer's interactions with the brand.

The Melissa Data Web site explains the services offered by this company in database collection and maintenance.

Today, computers and database software programs are getting smarter. Services such as Prodigy and Melissa Data (see the Web site download) provide users with online buying services, remember purchases, and, over time, can build a purchase profile of each user. This kind of information is valuable to marketers, resellers, and their agencies. It's also of concern to consumer activists and consumers who worry about privacy.

Nintendo uses the 2 million names in its database when it introduces more powerful versions of its video game system. The names and addresses are gathered from a list of subscribers to its magazine, *Nintendo Power*. The company believes that many of its current customers will want to trade up systems, and this direct communication makes it possible for Nintendo to speak directly to its most important target market about new systems as they become available. Nintendo began its database in 1988 and credits database marketing with helping it maintain its huge share of the $6 billion to $7 billion video game market.

Data Mining　The practice of sifting through and sorting information captured in a company's database to target customers and maintain a relationship with them is called **data mining**.[9] Such information includes comprehensive profiles based on demographics, lifestyle, and behavior, as well as basic contact information.

How is data mining used? Marketers collect information about their customers to better target customers who might really be interested in their offers. This is called *behavioral targeting*, to which we referred in Chapter 5. Instead of sending mass e-mails (spam) to everyone on a list, marketers can send information to people who are really interested in their product or service.

Data mining is also used to spot trends and patterns—frequent flyers may also be buyers of international phone cards, for example. It also can be used to profile prospects based on key characteristics of current customers, a practice called prospecting. If a grocery store that uses a loyalty card to track its customers' purchases notices that the young families in its customer pool live in certain neighborhoods, then it can target family-oriented advertising promotions to those particular neighborhoods rather than spraying them across its entire geographical market.

Issues: Privacy   In Chapter 10 we mentioned the privacy issues that challenge some of the practices of Web marketers, such as cookies that track your online visits. Loyalty cards are used by airlines and retail stores to track the behavior of customers and reward them for certain types of purchases. Sophisticated software can record every move you make online and then combine it with other data about you collected by stores where you shop and organizations to which you belong. If you have signed up for any of the free online services offered by Yahoo!, then you are probably being tracked by the company. Google, however, has resisted using its records for behavioral targeting because it values the trust of its customers.

Companies like Florida-based Catalina Marketing combine loyalty and sales data from more than 20,000 stores and use it to profile shoppers and identify prospects. Although Catalina doesn't identify specific customers, the records do have identification tags that let merchants attach the profiles back to their customers when they subscribe to Catalina's database.[10]

That's why cookies and cards worry privacy advocates. Privacy is a huge concern for all direct marketers, not just those engaged in e-commerce. And companies are increasing the amount of data they collect on their customers—sometimes with their permission and knowledge, but often without customers even being aware of the practice.[11]

Privacy is particularly an issue with data mining. Here's the problem: You can't do this kind of narrow targeting without collecting personal information. At what point is efficiency of targeting compromised by invasion of privacy?

Customer Relationship Management (CRM)

One of the most powerful tools to emerge from database marketing, **customer relationship management (CRM)** is a result of the improved management of information contained in customer databases. CRM identifies and analyzes patterns in customer behavior to maximize the profitability of each relationship. It has been described as integrating and aligning "the people, processes, and technologies of all the business functions that touch the customer—marketing, sales, and customer service."[12] In Figure 15.2, customer relationship management is step 5, but notice that it begins at step 3, the response/order.

Behind CRM is sophisticated database software that establishes links between transactions and the corresponding customers' characteristics. Armed with this knowledge, the company can pursue strategies to improve services that are important to their most profitable customers, attract new customers with similar characteristics, reward best customers, and identify and eliminate those customer relationships that drain company resources.

There are many examples of the successful use of CRM to improve customer relationships and services. Consider the true story of someone who flies nearly 2 million miles annually on American Airlines. While he was preparing to fly from San Diego to New York on a recent trip, the plane developed mechanical problems on the ground. Before this person even started to inquire, an American Airlines' Special Services person came aboard, escorted him off the plane, handed him a ticket for another flight to New York, and sent him on his way. These positive experiences are based on the ultimate principle of CRM: Identify a company's most profitable customers and give them something that makes them feel prized and privileged so they continue to be a customer but also so they become advocates for the company.

THE KEY PLAYERS

There are four main players in direct-response marketing: (1) advertisers who use direct response to sell products or services; (2) agencies that specialize in direct-response advertising; (3) the media that deliver messages by phone, mail, or the Web; and (4) consumers who are the recipients of the information and sometimes the initiator of the contact.

The Advertisers　More than 12,000 firms are engaged in direct-response marketing. Their primary business is selling products and services by mail or telephone. This number does not include the many retail stores that use direct marketing as a supplemental marketing communication program. Traditionally, the types of companies that have made the greatest use of direct marketing have been book and record clubs, publishers, insurance companies, sellers of collectibles, manufacturers of packaged foods, and gardening firms.

Dell has built a huge direct marketing business selling computers directly to consumers rather than through dealers, as its competitors do. This is also true for Geico. Why don't Compaq, Hewlett-Packard, and IBM copy the Dell model and sell computers directly? For one thing, their retail dealers, who deliver big sales to these companies, would retaliate if these companies started experimenting with direct sales. Furthermore, it takes a lot of effort and infrastructure to set up a direct-marketing business. Rather than an army of sales reps, Dell employs an army of people in fulfillment who take the order, match the product to customer specifications, handle the money, and arrange for shipping.

The Agencies　The four types of firms in direct-response advertising include advertising agencies, independent direct-marketing agencies, service firms, and fulfillment houses:

- *Advertising agencies.* Major agencies whose main business is mass-media advertising either have a department that specializes in direct response or own a separate direct-response company. Even if there isn't a special division or department, the staff of the agency may still be involved in producing direct-marketing pieces.
- *Direct-marketing agencies.* The independent, full-service, direct-marketing agencies specialize in direct response, and many of them are quite large. The largest direct-marketing agencies include firms that specialize in direct response and others that are affiliated with major agencies.
- *Service firms.* Service firms specialize in supplying printing, mailing, list brokering, and data management, as the Melissa Data Web site illustrates.
- *Fulfillment houses.* The fulfillment house is a type of service firm that is vital to the success of many direct-marketing strategies. This is a business responsible for making sure consumers receive whatever they request in a timely manner, be it a catalog, additional information, or the product itself.

The Media Companies　Direct-marketing media include mail, phone, Web sites, and e-mail. In other words, all those outlets can be used to make an offer with a prospect. One of the most active direct-mail marketers is the U.S. Postal Service. There are also thousands of telemarketing and Web marketing firms that handle contact with consumers.

This brochure was created by the U.S. Postal Service to explain the benefits of direct-mail advertising. The attention-getting cover poses an interesting thought that is explained inside.

The Customers   Although people might dislike the intrusiveness of direct-response advertising, many appreciate the convenience. It is a method of purchasing goods in a society that is finding itself with more disposable income but with less time to spend it. A new generation of consumers armed with push-button phones and a billfold full of credit cards likes to shop and bank from home. This push-button shopper is joined by an even larger group of mouse-clicking shoppers. It takes some daring to order a product you can't see, touch, feel, or try out. These consumers are confident and willing to take a chance but don't like to be disappointed.

THE TOOLS OF DIRECT MARKETING

Direct marketing employs five primary tools to achieve its objectives: (1) direct mail, (2) catalogs, (3) telemarketing, (4) direct-response advertising, and (5) Web-based e-marketing.

Direct Mail

Direct mail is the granddaddy of direct response and still commands big marketing dollars. Of those organizations that use direct marketing, direct mail is the most popular method, with more than 75 percent compared to the next largest category, which is 64 percent for e-mail.[13]

Anyone with a mailing address has received direct mail. Experts estimate the average person will spend about eight months of his or her lifetime dealing with advertising mail.[14] The U.S. Postal Service estimates it delivers more that 90 billion pieces of unsolicited mail each year.[15]

A direct-mail piece is a print advertising message for a product or service that is delivered by mail. It may be as simple as a single-page letter or as complex as a three-dimensional package consisting of a letter, a brochure, a sample, a premium, and an order card with a return envelope. With the advances in digital printing, it is now possible to personalize not only the address and salutation on the letter but also other parts of the information as well as the offer. Called **variable data campaigns**, these marketing messages can be highly targeted, even unique to the recipient. Kodak's NexPress is specifically designed for this application.

One advantage of direct mail is that it has a tactile quality missing in most other forms of marketing communication. An insurance company once sent out a mailing that contained one leather glove. A message accompanying the glove invited recipients to call the insurance agency if they would like to have the matching glove and hear a little more about the company's insurance policies.

Most direct mail is sent using a third-class bulk mail permit, which requires a minimum of 200 identical pieces. Third class is cheaper than first class, but it takes longer for delivery. Estimates of nondelivery of third-class mail run as high as 8 percent. The response rate for direct mail can vary from 0.1 to 50 percent, but it's typically in the 2–3 percent range. The primary variables are the offer and target audience. Offers mailed to current customers generally have a higher response rate than those sent to noncustomers.

Because of the high level of nonresponse, direct mail is also a fairly costly tool in terms of CPM. It can be cost-efficient, however, because it is much easier to calculate the actual payout rate—at what point do the returns of the investment begin to exceed the costs? That's why it is considered so much more accountable than other forms of advertising. As summarized in Table 15.1, direct mail has a number of advantages and disadvantages.

Direct-Mail Message Design   How the direct-mail piece looks is as important as what it says. The functions of a direct-mail message are similar to the steps in the sales process. The message must move the reader through the entire process, from generating interest to creating conviction and inducing a sale. It's all done with a complex package of printed pieces. Progressive direct marketers, supported by research findings, have discovered that the appearance of a direct-response ad—the character and personality communicated by the graphics—can enhance or destroy the credibility of the product information.

General Motors uses a sophisticated customer database to create personalized messages during times when specific groups of its customers are most likely to be in the market for a new car. It targets 3.5 million of its 5 million cardholders with unique offers on specific models presented dramatically with full-color impact and targeted features. The highly targeted

Table 15.1   Advantages and Disadvantages of Direct Mail

Advantages	Description
Tells a story	The medium offers a variety of formats and provides enough space to tell a complete sales story.
Engages attention	Because direct mail has little competition when it is received, it can engage the reader's attention.
Personalizes the message	Because of the use of databases, it is now possible to personalize direct mail across a number of consumer characteristics, such as name, product usage, purchase history, and income.
Builds in feedback	Direct mail is particularly conducive to marketing research and can be modified until the message design matches the needs of the desired target audience.
Reaches the unreachable	Direct mail allows the marketer to reach audiences who are inaccessible by other media.

Disadvantages	Description
Negative perceptions	The main drawback of using direct mail is the widespread perception that it is junk mail. According to a Harris-Equifax Consumer Privacy Survey, about 46 percent of the public see direct-mail offers as a nuisance, and 90 percent consider them an invasion of privacy.
Cost	Direct mail has a higher cost per thousand than mass media. A great deal of this high cost is a result of postage. (However, it reaches a more qualified prospect with less waste.) Another cost factor is the maintenance of the database.
Mailing list	To deliver an acceptable response rate, the quality of the mailing list is critical. It must be maintained and updated constantly.
Response rate	Because of the changing nature of mailing lists, as well as the difficulty of keeping relevant data in the database, the response rate can be as low as 2 or 3 percent. Even with that low response, however, database marketers can still make money.
Vulnerability	Direct-mail delivery is vulnerable to natural disasters as well as catastrophes such as the 9/11 terrorist attacks.

mailings doubled the response rate for GM's mailings, but more importantly, they drove a 34 percent faster response rate, 48 percent increase in repeat orders, 25 percent greater average value on each order, and a 32 percent increase in overall revenue.[16]

The following guide can be helpful for putting together direct-mail pieces.

Creating Effective Direct Mail

- Get the attention of the targeted prospect as the envelope comes from the mailbox.
- Create a need for the product, show what it looks like, and demonstrate how it is used.
- Answer questions, as a good salesperson does, and reassure the buyer.
- Provide critical information about product use.
- Inspire confidence, minimize risk, and establish that the company is reputable.
- Make the sale by explaining how to buy, how to order, where to call, and how to pay for the purchase.
- Use an incentive to encourage a fast response.

Most direct-mail pieces follow a fairly conventional format. The packaging usually consists of an outer envelope, a letter, a brochure, supplemental flyers or folders, and a reply card with a return envelope. These can be one-page flyers, multipanel folders, multipage brochures, or spectacular **broadsheets** that fold out like maps big enough to cover the top of a table. The most critical decision made by the target is whether to read the mailing or throw it away, and that decision is based on the outer envelope. The envelope should state the offer on the outside and spark curiosity through a creative idea. More recently the format has changed to accommodate CDs, which substitute for a brochure. AOL has mailed millions of these over the years. CD mailers are cheaper to produce and mail.

Creativity is important, particularly for the envelope. A mailing for Krispy Kreme got attention with its coupon mailer in the shape of a box of doughnuts. Attached to the mailer was an offer to buy a box of a dozen and get another dozen free. Instead of the usual 2–3 percent response rate, Krispy Kreme got an 11 percent response.[17] Other ideas about using direct mail creatively are offered in The Inside Story.

THE INSIDE STORY

Thinking outside the Mailbox

By Michael Dattolico, *Musion Creative, LLC*

Direct mail is probably one of the trickiest ways to get your message out there. Not only are you competing with a wide array of other pieces that clutter the consumer's mailbox, but direct mail is one of the few media that a client can actually just throw away. Then your message is lost forever.

You can choose from dozens of strategies to make your direct-mail piece attention getting and to elicit a response. Some companies try unique die-cuts or interactive designs, some companies try a fruitful coupon or incorporate a wide range of starbursts and colors. Although some of these techniques might achieve the desired result, they leave a smaller client's budget gushing.

The most creative way to get people's attention with direct mail is to go back to the basics. A synergetic message and visual can go a long way toward achieving your result. Here's an example of an effective direct-mail campaign.

The client, Texins Activity Centers, is a deluxe fitness center located on a Texas Instruments campus in Dallas, Texas. It focuses a majority of its marketing on specific programs and services offered, but it also wanted to blanket a large group of nonmembers who may be aware of the fitness facility but are not currently using it. Since the benefits of the center are diverse and the pricing options for TI employees are largely discounted from other clubs, research showed that TI employees who did not join do not currently go to fitness centers at all. As a result, the major objective was not to get them to switch fitness centers but to encourage the target market to start using a fitness center. In effect, Texins is a brand leader for our target market, so we focus on encouraging activity and changing the targets' health and wellness habits, instead of trying to pull them away from outside competitors. This "next step" toward health was the first part of our strategy.

The other portion of our strategy focuses on a national trend. Although America tries to be the front runner in most statistics, holding the highest national average obesity level in the world is not one we covet. Statistics show the national weight gain is due to an increase in fast-food consumption, reliance on "easy" weight loss and exercise fads as a sole means of fitness, and—in the case of the younger market—an increase in indoor activities combined with an extinction of outdoor activities. We chose to focus on these three truths (after eliminating a plethora of weaker ideas) to fortify our campaign.

The problem is not that Americans don't know their activity level is unhealthy, it's that they don't act to change it. Instead of just presenting the information, we developed a strong visual and clear headline that would stand out in a pile of direct mail and encourage the market to read it, agree with it, and read the information on the back of the piece.

Recognizing that consumers are overloaded with health information, the back of the piece keeps to the point by conveying a clear, powerful fact. It then ties this fact to a particular service or program that Texins offers, followed by a broad statement that there's more where that came from.

The issue of obesity in America is complex and far-reaching. This campaign breaks that down to a smaller, more concise objective for consumers. It doesn't talk down to them by offering a "miracle" solution for weight loss or laying on guilt for their current lack of concern with wellness. It states the truth and offers a solution. Those are the basics of good marketing.

Owner of his own design studio, Musion Creative, LLC (http://www.musioncreative.com), Michael Dattolico graduated from the advertising program at the University of Florida and a creative advertising program in England at University College Falmouth.

Don't believe everything you see on TV.

Take fitness advice from professionals not infomercials.

TEXINS ACTIVITY CENTERS
Take the next step to a healthier you.

Your children are not at play.

TEXINS ACTIVITY CENTERS
Take the next step to a healthier you.

Excessive eating can be hazardous to you health.

TEXINS ACTIVITY CENTERS
Take the next step to a healthier you.

Historically, the letter has been the most difficult element in a direct-mail package. Over the years many techniques have proven effective in getting consumers to read a direct-mail letter. Dean Rieck, an internationally respected direct-response copywriter, designer, and consultant, offers these hints for writing an effective letter.[18]

1. *Attention.* To grab attention or generate curiosity, use pictures and headlines that tout the product's benefits.
2. *Personalize.* Use a personalized salutation. If the individual's name is not available, the salutation should at least be personalized to the topic, such as, "Dear Cat Lover."
3. *Lead in.* Begin the letter with a brief yet compelling or surprising statement—"Dear Friend: I could really kick myself!"
4. *The offer.* Make the offer as early in the body of the letter as possible.
5. *The letter.* Use testimonials or evidence that clearly describe benefits to the customer.
6. *The closing.* End by repeating the offer and stating additional incentives or guarantees and a clear call to action.

Issue: Trees, Water, and Waste   Critics of direct mail cite its environmental impact. Production of direct mail uses an estimated 100 million trees and 28 billion gallons of water annually.[19] And untold millions of dollars are spent for disposal and recycling. In Colorado alone, recycling experts estimate that junk mail accounts for more than 340 million pounds of trash annually.[20]

Is there a need for a more aggressive ban on direct mail? Consider local mailings. What would be the impact of such a ban on your local pizza restaurant, video store, or hair salon, which might rely on direct-mail offers? How do such businesses announce their presence in the market? Does the waste and irritation factor of "junk mail" justify a ban on this form of advertising? On the other side of the debate, might banning direct mail infringe on advertisers' right to commercial free speech? What's fair, what's right, and what's a responsible advertiser to do?

Catalogs

A **catalog** is a multipage direct-mail publication that shows a variety of merchandise. The big books are those produced by such retail giants as Lands' End and L.L. Bean. One of the biggest catalog marketers, L.L. Bean mails some 250 million catalogs a year.[21]

Even though some have issued warnings about how the Internet would kill off catalogs, in fact they are increasing in number. As an L.L. Bean executive explained, "It is the best way for us to get lasting impressions in front of our customers."[22] The reason is that most people hang onto catalogs for weeks, giving them a longevity that beats all other media except, perhaps, for magazines.

However, as technology has improved, catalog marketers are refining their databases and culling consumers who receive catalogs but don't order from them. In spite of the fact that catalog marketers are cutting back on the waste in their mailings, there are still a lot of catalogs in mailboxes. Overall catalog mailings have increased from 16 billion in 2002 to more that 20 billion in 2006. That's a lot of trees. Some of the merchandise is inexpensive, such as the Hanover line, which usually offers items for $10 or less. In contrast, marketers such as Dell offer more expensive products such as computers costing hundreds of dollars.

Catalogs are the chief beneficiaries of the social changes that have made armchair shopping so popular. However, the catalog marketer must make sure the ordering process is easy and risk free. Catalogs have become so popular that direct-response consumers receive mailings offering them lists of catalogs available for a fee. People pay for these catalogs the way they pay for magazines, and an increasing number of catalogs can be purchased at newsstands.

Some catalog retailers have their own stores, such as Williams-Sonoma and Tiffany's. Banana Republic, which began as a catalog marketer and then moved into retailing, is now launching its first catalog since 1988. Many large retailers are now multichannel, using catalogs, Web sites, and stores. Others, such as Hanover House and FBS, offer their merchandise only through catalogs or other retailers. Some marketers, such as L.L. Bean, have also seen their catalog mailings driving business to their Web sites. Bean expects that its online

Table 15.2   Advantages and Disadvantages of Catalogs

Advantages	Description
Targeted	Can be directed at specific market segments.
Engages attention	Employs high-quality design and photography (see Alsto's cover).
Complete information	Extensive product information and comparisons are provided.
Convenience	Offer a variety of purchase options.

Disadvantages	Description
Negative perceptions	Catalogs are viewed as junk mail by many recipients.
Costs	The cost per thousand of catalogs is higher than mass media.
Response rate	The response is relatively low at 3 to 4 percent.
Mailing list	Databases must be constantly maintained.

sales will soon overtake its catalog business, but it will still send out catalogs as a way to recruit e-commerce.[23] In addition to driving traffic to stores or online, catalogs also serve as reference tools as well as inspiration and motivation to buy.

The real growth in this field is in the area of specialty catalogs. There are catalogs for every hobby and for more general interests. You can find catalogs specifically for purses, rings, cheese and hams, stained-glass supplies, garden benches, and computer accessories, to name just a few. Balducci's fruit and vegetable store in Greenwich Village, New York, produces a catalog promising overnight delivery of precooked gourmet meals.

The environmental issues that bedevil catalogs and other direct mail have been a challenge for marketers that consider themselves socially responsible. Victoria's Secret, for example, was criticized for using catalog paper made with pulp from a Canadian forest that is a wildlife center. The company eventually responded by shifting its catalog production to paper that is either recycled or comes certified by the Forest Stewardship Council.[24]

The advantages and disadvantages of advertising via catalogs are listed in Table 15.2.

A number of advertisers are using video catalogs because these provide more information about their products. Buick developed an electronic catalog on CD. The message is interactive and features animated illustrations. It presents graphic descriptions and detailed text on the Buick line, including complete specifications. You can even custom-design your dream car. The electronic catalog has also been marketed to readers of computer magazines.

Telemarketing

At one time, before telemarketing calls were so pervasive they were greatly limited by government-supported do-not-call lists, more direct-marketing dollars were spent on **telemarketing** phone calls than on any other DM medium. That's because telemarketing is almost as persuasive as personal sales, but a lot less expensive. A personal sales call may cost anywhere from $50 to $1,000 after factoring in time and transportation. In comparison, a telephone call ranges from $2 to $15 per call. That is still expensive if you compare the cost of a telephone campaign to the CPM of an advertisement placed in any one of the mass media ($10–$50 per thousand); however, the returns are much higher than those generated by mass advertising because they are personalized and interactive. The caller can respond to buyers' objections.

A typical telemarketing campaign usually involves hiring a telemarketing company to make a certain number of calls using a prepared script. These callers work in **call centers**, which are rooms with large banks of phones and computers. Most calls are made from databases of prospects who were previously qualified on some factor, such as an interest in a related product or a particular profile of demographics and psychographics. Occasionally a **cold call** is used, which means the call center staff are calling unqualified numbers, sometimes just randomly selected, but this practice has a much lower response rate.

Call centers are large rooms with multiple stations for staff who make the calls (outbound) or answer calls from people placing orders (inbound).

Types of Telemarketing There are two types of telemarketing: inbound and outbound. An **inbound** or incoming telemarketing call is initiated by a customer. The consumer can be responding to an ad, catalog, e-mail, or fax. L.L. Bean's telephone representatives are trained to handle inbound calls in such a helpful manner that the company often features their friendly approach in its catalogs. Calls originating from the firm are outgoing or **outbound**. These calls typically generate the most consumer resistance because they are uninvited, intrusive, and unexpected.

Telemarketing Message Design The key point to remember about telemarketing solicitations is that the message has to be simple enough to be delivered over the telephone. If the product requires a demonstration or a complicated explanation, then the message might be better delivered by direct mail. The message also must be compelling. People resent intrusive telephone calls, so there must be a strong initial benefit or reason-why statement to convince prospects to continue listening. The message also must be short; most people won't stay on the telephone longer than two to three minutes for a sales call.

Issues: Intrusion, Fraud, Privacy Telemarketing has its drawbacks. Perhaps the most universally despised telemarketing tool is **predictive dialing**. Predictive dialing technology makes it possible for telemarketing companies to call anyone—even those with unlisted numbers. Special computerized dialing programs use random dialing. This explains why, from time to time, when you answer your phone you simply hear an empty line; the predictive dialer has called your number before a call agent is free. Many people consider these calls a nuisance, and they can even be alarming, because burglars have been known to call a house to see if anyone's home before they attempt a break-in.

Telemarketing's reputation also has been tarnished by fraudulent behavior, such as promising a product or service in exchange for an advance payment, convincing consumers they need some kind of financial or credit protection that they don't really need, or enticing consumers to buy something by promising them prizes that are later discovered to be worthless. In response to these telemarketing abuses, the Federal Trade Commission enacted the Telemarketing Sales Rule (TSR) in 1995 to protect consumers. The TSR prohibits telemarketers from calling before 8 a.m. or after 9 p.m., imposes strict informational disclosure requirements, prohibits misrepresentative or misleading statements, and provides for specific payment collection procedures. More recently, FTC regulations have required telemarketing firms to identify themselves on caller ID.

The most serious restriction on telemarketing is from state and national "do-not-call" lists. The national Do Not Call Registry had 31.6 million signups even before it took effect in 2003 and grew to more than 149 million by 2007. Telemarketing companies responded by challenging the legality of these lists in court based on what they believe to be an illegal restriction on commercial free speech. In late 2004, however, the U.S. Supreme Court let stand a lower-court ruling that the industry's free speech rights were not violated by the do-not-call list. The do-not-call lists do not restrict companies from calling their own customers and allow nonprofits to continue calling and market research firms to continue conducting phone surveys. Telemarketers subscribe to the database and check the list at least monthly for numbers they need to delete. The subscription cost is $62 for each area code with a $17,000 maximum for a national list. The no-call list registration expires after five years, so consumers are finding that they may have to reregister.[25]

Phone companies also offer their customers a service called "Privacy Manager" that screens out sales calls. For customers who have Caller ID, numbers that register as "unavailable" or "unknown" are intercepted by a recorded message that asks callers to identify themselves. If the caller does so, the call rings through.

Direct-Response Advertising

The common thread that runs through all types of direct-response advertising is that of action. The move to action is what makes direct-response advertising effective. Syracuse University Professor John Philip Jones points to direct advertising as more effective than general advertising and says advertisers have a lot to learn from direct marketers.[26]

DraftFCB, for example, is a direct-marketing firm that specializes in determining returns on the direct-response ads it runs using special toll-free numbers and Web addresses that can track ad response.[27] Draft's unique approach to advertising was considered by Wal-Mart in 2006 in an attempt to turn around its weak store sales. The idea was to trade its mass-market strategy for one that used more targeted advertising for specific groups of consumers, such as suburbanites and ethnic groups.[28] This approach was dumped when questions arose about the ethics of a Wal-Mart marketing executive. The issue of moving Wal-Mart toward more targeted advertising remains on the table, however, as the giant retailer struggles to maintain its market position.

Print Media   Ads in the mass media are less directly targeted than are direct-mail and catalog, but they can still provide the opportunity for a direct response. Ads in newspapers and magazines can carry a coupon, an order form, an address, or a toll-free or 900 telephone number. The response may be either to purchase something or to ask for more information. In many cases the desired response is an inquiry that becomes a sales lead for field representatives.

In their book *MaxiMarketing,* direct-marketing experts Stan Rapp and Tom Collins discuss the power of double-duty advertising that combines brand-reinforcement messages with a direct-response campaign by using a premium, a sample, or a coupon.[29] American Express used this double-duty concept when it launched *Your Company,* a quarterly mailed to more than 1 million American Express corporate card members who own small businesses. Four sponsors launched *Your Company:* IBM, United Parcel Service, CIGNA Small Business Insurance, and American Express Small Business Services. Such efforts combine the editorial direction of a magazine with direct advertising's ability to target a narrow audience based on demographics and lifestyle. Magazines have been trying to do this with demographic editions and selective bindings as well.

In magazines, response cards may be either **bind-ins** or **blow-ins**. Both are free-standing cards that are physically separate from the ad they support. Bind-in cards are stapled or glued right into the binding of the magazine adjoining the ad. They have to be torn out to be used. Blow-in cards are attached to the magazine after it is printed by special machinery that puffs open the pages. These cards are loose and may fall out in distribution, so they are less reliable.

Broadcast Media   Television is a good medium for direct marketers who are advertising a broadly targeted product. A direct-response commercial on radio or TV can provide the necessary information (usually a simple, easy-to-remember toll-free phone number or Web address) for the consumer to request information or even make a purchase. Direct-response advertising on television used to be the province of the late-night TV with pitches for Vegematics and screwdrivers guaranteed to last a lifetime.

Radio's big advantage is its targeted audience. For example, teenagers are easy to reach through radio. Also, radio has had some success selling products such as cellular phones and paging systems specifically to a mobile audience. Radio is often used to supplement other forms of direct response. For example, publishers use radio to alert people that a sweepstakes mailing is beginning and to encourage participation.

Cable television lends itself to direct response because the medium is more tightly targeted to particular interests. QVC and the Home Shopping Network reach more than 70 million households and service their calls with huge phone banks. As more national marketers such as Geico move into the medium, the direct-response commercial is becoming more general in appeal, selling clothes and entertainment as well as insurance and financial services.

Direct-response TV also makes good use of the infomercial format. The Salton-Maxim Juiceman infomercial took the company from $18 million to $52 million in sales overnight and made a marketing superstar of George Foreman. Infomercials blur the lines

A leading direct-response auto insurer, Geico uses its Gecko character as a spokesperson to sell its products.

Television shopping networks handle sales orders by using hundreds of customer service agents.

between retail and direct response. The Salton commercial made Juiceman the brand to buy, whether direct from television or from a local department store or mass merchant. Infomercials have been around since the emergence of the cable industry and have become a multibillion-dollar industry. An infomercial is typically 30 or 60 minutes long and tends to be played during non-prime-time periods.

Today, the infomercial is viewed as a viable medium because: (1) consumers now have confidence in infomercials and the products they sell; (2) with the involvement of upscale advertisers, the quality of infomercial production and supportive research has improved; (3) consumers can be better segmented and infomercials are coordinated with respect to these audiences; and (4) infomercials can easily be introduced into foreign markets. Advertisers are more likely to use the infomercial format if their product needs to be demonstrated, is not readily available through retail outlets, and has a relatively high profit margin.

The Internet and Direct Response

Direct marketers saw the Internet's potential early. Actually, direct marketing—particularly catalog marketing—is the model for e-commerce. The Internet provides the same components found in direct mail and telemarketing. Amazon.com is the leader of the pack, but other companies that sell merchandise direct include Columbia House Online (http://www.columbiahouse.com), eBags (http://www.eBags.com), and CDNow (http://www.cdnow.com). The Web is moving marketers much closer to one-to-one marketing.

Another feature of Internet direct marketing is greater sampling opportunities. Online music stores now have hundreds of thousands of music clips for shoppers to listen to before making a purchase. Eddie Bauer lets site visitors "try on" clothes in a virtual dressing room. It also sends them e-mail messages offering special prices on items based on their past purchasing patterns.

The technology of the Internet has produced dramatic changes in the direct-mail industry. At a most basic level, the Internet has facilitated the ease in producing and distributing traditional direct mail. Take USA Direct, which introduced the USAMailNow Web site in early 2001. This company identified the most frustrating and time-consuming processes of direct-mail campaigns and constructed a Web site that handles these processes for companies. USAMailNow's streamlined process allows a company of any size to point and click its way through a series of choices to make predesigned mailer templates priced and sorted by industry, mailing lists, and various mail media (postcards, letters, flyers, or newsletters), which customers can customize with their logo and other proprietary images or copy.

On a more sophisticated level, the Internet has begun to reconcile an ongoing conflict within the direct-mail industry: the debate over sending small personalized mailings or big mass mailings. With their long letters, ornate brochures, free gift enclosures, and other attention-grabbing devices, personalized mailings are thought to grab consumers' attention. However, this attention comes at a high per-unit price, so personalized mailings have a limited scope. In contrast, cheaper mass media (postcards, short form letters, flyers, and newsletters) are particularly well suited to boost a company's reach and frequency. Unfortunately, they lack much of the allure of their more personalized cousins. How has the Internet helped reconcile this debate? Today, the use of extensive database information and innovative e-mail technology, combined with creative marketing strategies, has brought the benefits of highly personalized, inexpensive messages to far-reaching mass campaigns.

The use of e-mail as a marketing tool has not been restricted to the usual e-commerce companies. Well-known corporate brands such as BMW are using this tool. In one campaign, it invited existing and prospective customers to view a collection of Web movies about new BMW models. Another campaign notified BMW owners of a new section at BMW.com reserved strictly for their use. Called the "Owner's Circle," the section allows owners to obtain special services and set up profiles that track maintenance items specific to their cars. Shortly after the mailing, enrollment in the Owner's Circle doubled, and participation in BMW's financial services program tripled.[30]

Issue: Spam   Although e-mail marketing has enjoyed increased success, the practice has received intense criticism for generating too much unwanted e-mail, otherwise known as **spam**. The FTC has determined that 90 percent of all spam involving business and investment opportunities contains false or misleading information. The problem also exists with nearly half of the messages advertising health products and travel and leisure. This is why Congress passed the CAN-SPAM Act in 2003. The problem is so big that some industry experts estimate that more than half of all e-mail messages are spam. Amazon has filed lawsuits in U.S. and Canadian courts to stop e-mail spammers it says have been fraudulently using its identity to send out spam, a practice known as spoofing. One of the largest e-mail marketers, OptInRealBig, has been sued by the state of New York for allegedly sending misleading and fraudulent e-mail solicitations. Microsoft also sued the company for bombarding its Explorer service with spam.

Permission Marketing   The negative impact of spam on consumers is a huge problem for legitimate e-mail marketers who have responded to the criticism in two ways. For one, companies now search their rich databases for customers' buying habits or recent purchases. They then send these customers e-mail that offer deals on related products and connect their offers to their customers' previous interactions with the company. More recently, direct marketers have used a second approach called *permission marketing* to reduce criticism about spam. Permission marketing gives customers an opportunity to *opt in* to a notification service from a company. The e-mail will ask if the recipient wants further e-mails and wants to be on the mailing list. When opting in, customers are often asked to complete a questionnaire about their purchasing habits or other information, which is used to personalize the service.

Permission marketing also gives customers an opportunity to *opt out* of the service when they no longer need a company's product or services. They can sometimes even *opt down* by reducing how frequently they receive messages. These options give customers control over the amount and type of e-mail messages they receive, and companies reduce wasted resources on marketing to uninterested individuals. The concept at the heart of permission marketing is that every customer who opts in to a campaign is a qualified lead.[31]

The highly competitive ski industry offers ideal direct-marketing opportunities. For example, consider how Vail Resorts attracts and keeps its customers. As Jennifer Wolfe,

THE INSIDE STORY

Selling the Colorado Pass Club

By Jennifer Wolfe, *Marketing Manager, Vail Resorts*

Here's the problem: How do you drive up business for a ski area? I work for Vail Resorts and that's one of my biggest challenges.

Although the destination market is important, so are season passes. Season pass sales, which focus on locals, are a significant contributor to the bottom line. They are also very competitive as our resorts are pitted against other Colorado resorts to secure the widest base of passholders.

Our company is in a unique position to attract skiers and snowboarders with five mountains: Vail, Beaver Creek, Breckenridge, Keystone, and Arapahoe Basin. Our largest competitor in Colorado offers Copper Mountain, Winter Park, and Steamboat Springs.

One of our strengths is our robust customer databases, which contain both customer transactions and traditional marketing information. The combination of the two permits very strong segmentation for e-mail and direct-mail efforts. We also track revenue generated from those efforts so that we can assess their ROIs and strengthen the next campaign.

Vail also has more than 70,000 e-mail addresses for our Colorado Pass™. In accordance with the "canned spam" laws, everyone on the list has opted in and asked for e-mail promotions and information. This is a perfectly qualified database of customers—they own our product and raised their hands for more information.

As we headed into the selling season for 2007–2008 season passes, the marketing department was charged with ensuring that (1) our loyal passholders stayed loyal and renewed, (2) previous passholders returned, and (3) individuals with competitor passes converted to the Colorado Pass™.

What could we do to take advantage of that passholder database?

The Colorado Pass Club is a good example of permission marketing. Marketers can also gain valuable insight into their customers' habits and interests using such a loyalty card.

The concept of the Colorado Pass Club (CPC) was introduced as the 2006–2007 ski season wound down. The objectives for the CPC were to distance the Colorado Pass from competitive passes by offering elevated benefits. In particular, we wanted to create a sense of community among Colorado Pass™ holders.

Our CPC program included biweekly e-mails full of promotions, offers, and discounts exclusively for passholders. Promotions ranged from dining and event tickets to deeply discounted lodging, ski tune-ups, and discounts on gear. We also gave away tickets to a hockey game, the Harlem Globetrotters, roller derby, and music events. Called "Random Acts of Passholder Kindness," these offers were diverse enough to create a strong response and a lot of interest.

Many of our efforts were also supported by radio spots and a special CPC Web site that recapped the contents of our biweekly e-mails. Slowly these e-mails started creating buzz in the passholder community, and soon they were being forwarded to friends and family.

Two months into the campaign, CPC e-mails generated more than $60,000 in trackable revenue—everything from lodging purchases to pass renewals. Our spring season pass sales far exceeded our pass sales from the prior year, giving the company a strong leading edge as we headed into the primary selling season in the fall.

Jennifer Wolfe received her B.A. in Public Relations from the University of Alabama and her M.A. in Integrated Marketing Communications from the University of Colorado-Boulder. She was nominated by Professor Sandra Moriarty.

Vail Resorts' marketing manager, explains, "Although the ski industry in Colorado has experienced the four most profitable seasons in history, in terms of skier visitation, a ski resort's growth is largely dependent on either attracting skiers away from other resorts or generating more revenue per skier visit." The Inside Story explains how Vail used direct marketing to create long-term relationships with its customers.

INTEGRATED DIRECT MARKETING

Historically, direct marketing is the first area of marketing communication that adopted an integrated marketing approach. In fact, it would be appropriate to rename direct marketing integrated direct marketing. As technology has provided more and better ways to interact with customers, the challenge to direct marketers has been to integrate direct mail, catalogs, telemarketing, Web sites, e-mail, text messaging, and instant messaging with other marketing communication, such as advertising.

One reason integration plays so well in the direct-response market is because of its emphasis on the customer and its measurability. The coordination problem is a challenge due to the deluge of data bombarding direct marketers from many different channels. The only way to manage the information is to focus it around customer needs and interests. By using databases, companies can become more sensitive to customer wants and needs and less likely to bother them with unwanted commercial messages.

Integrated direct marketing (IDM), also known as **integrated relationship marketing**, can be defined as a systematic way to get close to your best current and potential customers. Sharon Henderson, CEO of a direct-marketing agency, explains that "in the last couple of years the big marketers are saying 'we want integrated relationship marketing' and that means integrating at every customer touch point." For her agency, that means developing total business solution programs.[32]

Linking the Channels

Instead of treating each medium separately, as advertising agencies tend to do, IDM companies seek to achieve precise, synchronized use of the right media at the right time, with a measurable return on dollars spent. Here's an example: Say you do a direct-mail campaign, which generates a 2 percent average response. If you include a toll-free 800 number in your mailing as an alternative to the standard mail-in reply—with well-trained, knowledgeable people handling those incoming calls with a carefully thought-out script—you can achieve a 3 to 4 percent response rate. If you follow up your mailing with a phone call within 24 to 72 hours after your prospect receives the mailing, you can generate a response two to eight times as high as the base rate of 2 percent. So, by adding your 800 number, you bring the response rate from 2 percent to 3 or 4 percent. By following up with phone calls, you bring your total response rate as high as 5 to 18 percent.

The principle behind integration is that not all people respond the same way to direct-response advertising. One person may carefully fill out the order form. Someone else may immediately call the 800 number. Most people, if an ad grabs them, tend to put it in the pending pile. That pile grows and grows, and then goes into the garbage at the end of the month. But, if a phone call follows the direct-mail piece, the marketer may get the wavering consumer off the fence. Hewlett-Packard, AT&T, Citibank, and IBM have all used integrated direct marketing to improve their direct-marketing response rates.

Safeway Stores have become interested in integrated direct marketing. Essentially, Safeway has signed up manufacturers such as the Quaker Oats Co. and Stouffer Food Corp. (owned by Nestlé) for a database marketing program that provides trade dollars in exchange for quality customer data. The program exemplifies the convergence of two trends: Grocers looking for manufacturers to supplement their own shrunken marketing budgets and manufacturers eager to allocate new field marketing support dollars are working more closely as partners. A number of manufacturers whose products are carried in the store fund Safeway's quarterly mailings in exchange for in-store support and sales data.

A common failure in IDM is that direct-marketing messages and advertising messages often do not reinforce each other as well as they should because the two functions—advertising and direct marketing, which often are handled by different agencies— don't talk to one another. This will change, however, as clients demand more coordination of their marketing communication programs. Capital One's award-winning "What's in Your Wallet?" campaign achieved an incredible level of consumer awareness—around 98 percent (up from 40 percent before the campaign started)—by marrying a direct-mail effort to the well-known television advertising.[33]

The point is that direct marketing can add impact to an IMC campaign and increase its efficiency. Being part of a campaign also increases the level of the response to the direct marketing. For example, Xerox moved from sending individualized mass mailings to an integrated B2B campaign. The campaign began with a personalized mailer that invited the prospects to confirm receipt of the mailer online. At the Web site, they completed a short survey, which became part of a database. Once they registered at the site, they were then invited in an e-mail to a personalized portal that offered relevant information based on the prospect's industry. The integrated approach moved Xerox's campaign results from 1 percent to between 6 and 15 percent. A Xerox manager explained, "A random direct-mail piece that's not connected to another channel won't mean anything if it's not part of a larger story."[34]

Creating Loyalty One of the greatest advantages of direct marketing is its ability to do one-to-one marketing. When effective, that translates into customer loyalty. Perhaps the most ambitious attempt to create consumer loyalty is through a concept called **lifetime customer value (LCV)**. LCV is an estimate of how much purchase volume companies can expect to get over time from various target markets. To put it formally, LCV is the financial contribution through sales volume of an individual customer or customer segment over a length of time. The calculation is based on known consumption habits plus future consumption expectations. The estimate of the contribution is defined as return on investment, or revenue gains as a function of marketing costs. In simpler terms, by knowing your consumers' past behavior, you can decide how much you want to spend to get them to purchase and then repurchase your product, and you can track your investment by measuring the response.

Consumer resistance to direct marketing must be considered in efforts to build loyalty. Changing attitudes about direct marketing has not been easy because consumers resent companies that know too much about them. If the company can demonstrate that it is acting in the customer's best interest rather than just trolling for dollars, it might gain and maintain consumers' loyalty. Saks Fifth Avenue, for example, identified the customers who account for half of all sales and offered the group exclusive benefits through a program called Saks First. The benefits include fashion newsletters and a first crack at all sales.

GLOBAL CONSIDERATIONS IN DIRECT MARKETING

The direct-marketing industry is growing fast in many Far Eastern and European countries—in some places, even faster than in the United States. The global trend is fueled by the same technological forces driving the growth of direct marketing in this country: the increasing use of computer databases, credit cards, toll-free phone numbers, and the Internet, along with the search for more convenient ways to shop. The growth may be even greater in business-to-business marketing than in consumer marketing.

Direct marketing is particularly important in countries that have tight restrictions on advertising and other forms of marketing communication. However, there are restrictions on direct marketing as well. The privacy issues are even more intense in some countries than in the United States. In some countries, lists are not available, or they may be of poor quality. Databases can be more freely transferred between European countries than they can between the United States and European countries.

There are outright bans on direct marketing in some countries, although these restrictions seem to be loosening up. China lifted its national ban on direct sales, such as Amway and Avon, in late 2005. The ban had been in place since 1998 because of a series of scandals and frauds.[35]

Governmental regulation of the postal service may also place limitations on the use of direct mail. For example, language and characters are a problem, particularly for American companies that may not understand that the letter *e* isn't the same as *é, è, ê,* or *ë* in an address. Computers and typesetting systems have to accommodate these differences. The format of the address has to be exactly correct in some countries, such as Germany, where the Deutsche Post has strict rules about correct address formats. In Hungary the street name is in the third line of the address, whereas it is on the second line along with the postal code in Germany. Presorted mail in a wrong format may result in charges to the end user that significantly raise the cost of the mailing.

Cross-border campaigns can be particularly complex as planners try to accommodate differing regulations, standards, and cultural meanings in different countries. Consumer law varies across different regions, so what is acceptable in terms of claims and promotions in one country may not be acceptable elsewhere. The critical issue is the appropriateness of the creative message. Does the concept have the same meaning in different cultures? Does the visual mean the same? Can the words be translated and maintain the same meaning? Translating text can cause problems because some languages occupy more space than others.

The Gecko Drives Customer Response

IT'S A WRAP

In this chapter we identified many benefits of using direct response. It can reach a large, diverse audience efficiently to generate customers for auto insurance. Geico's aggressive effort to blanket the nation with an array of campaigns, including The Gecko, the cavemen, and the customer/celebrity testimonials, demonstrates how effective direct-response advertising can sell a product to a wide-ranging audience.

According to a 2007 report in the *Wall Street Journal*, Allstate, State Farm, and Progressive still led Geico in the private passenger auto insurance as of 2005, the last date for which figures were available. However, Geico is closing in as its share of premiums increased to 6.25 percent that year from 4.61 percent in 2001.

Geico spent approximately $403 million on advertising in 2005, and its budget increased another 20 percent in the first nine months of 2006. Evidence that this approach works comes from Warren Buffett, chairman of Berkshire Hathaway, the company that owns Geico. Noting the success of past efforts, he said he planned to increase ad spending by another 20 percent in 2007. In lieu of a sales force, direct advertising does the job.

Key Points Summary

1. **Define direct marketing and explain the direct-marketing process.** Direct marketing always involves a one-on-one relationship with the prospect. It is personal and interactive and uses various media to effect a measurable response. The process involves setting objectives and strategies, targeting, deciding on the offer, developing a message and media strategy, facilitating the response or order, filling the order, and evaluating the direct-marketing effort.

2. **Explain how databases are used in direct marketing.** Direct-marketing advertising has benefited from the development and maintenance of a database of customer names, addresses, telephone numbers, and demographic and psychographic characteristics. Advertisers use this information to target their campaigns to consumers who, based on demographics, are likely to buy their products.

3. **Name the players in direct marketing.** The four players in direct marketing are the advertisers, the agencies, the media that deliver the message, and the consumers.

4. **List the various media and tools that direct-response programs can use.** Direct-response media include direct mail, catalogs, telemarketing, print media, broadcast media, and the Internet.

Key Terms

bind-ins, p. 471
blow-ins, p. 471
broadsheets, p. 466
call centers, p. 469
catalog, p. 468
cold call, p. 469
compiled list, p. 461
customer relationship
   management (CRM),
   p. 463
databases, p. 458
data-driven communication,
   p. 461

data mining, p. 462
direct mail, p. 465
direct-response advertising,
   p. 454
direct-response marketing
   (DM), p. 453
fulfillment, p. 458
house list, p. 460
inbound telemarketing, p. 470
integrated direct marketing
   (IDM) (or integrated
   relationship marketing),
   p. 475

lead generation, p. 456
lifetime customer value
   (LCV), p. 476
lists, p. 460
merging, p. 460
offer, p. 456
one-step offer, p. 457
optimization, p. 456
outbound telemarketing,
   p. 470
predictive dialing, p. 470
prospecting, p. 456

purging, p. 460
recency, frequency, and
   monetary (RFM), p. 456
relational databases, p. 460
response list, p. 461
spam, p. 473
telemarketing, p. 469
two-step offer, p. 457
variable data campaigns,
   p. 465

Review Questions

1. What are the advantages and disadvantages of direct marketing?
2. What are the five steps in the direct-marketing process?
3. If you are using data mining to develop a prospecting program for a client, what would you be trying to accomplish?
4. What is a database, and how do direct marketers use it?
5. What is the objective of data-driven communication?
6. Explain CRM and how it relates to database marketing.
7. What is spam, and how does it relate to permission marketing?
8. How is integrated direct marketing used in an IMC program?
9. What is a loyalty program, and how does LCV enter into the planning for such a program?

Discussion Questions

1. Most people hate telemarketing. Say you work for the local campus environmental organization. How could you conduct a campus and community telemarketing effort that would not generate resistance? Apply your ideas to developing a telemarketing program to promote campus fund-raising for a good cause, such as a campus Habitat for Humanity project. Your primary targets are students, faculty, and staff.

2. Kali Johnson, a recent college graduate, is interviewing with a large garden product firm that relies on television for its direct-response advertising. "Your portfolio looks very good. I'm sure you can write," the interviewer says, "but let me ask you what is it about our copy that makes it more important than copy written for Ford, Pepsi, or Pampers?" What can she say that will help convince the interviewer she understands the special demands of direct-response writing?

3. One of the smaller, privately owned bookstores on campus is considering a direct-response service to cut down on its severe in-store traffic problems at the beginning of each semester. What ideas do you have for setting up some type of direct-response program to take the pressure off store traffic?

4. The success of infomercials helps validate direct marketing as a revenue generator. What characteristics of a product must you consider when determining whether to use an infomercial?

5. *Three-Minute Debate:* How does the recent fervor surrounding personal privacy affect direct marketing—specifically, telemarketing and e-mail advertising? You are designing a direct-marketing campaign for a local business that employs telemarketing and e-mail advertising, but your client is reluctant because of privacy concerns.

   In class, organize into small teams with pairs of teams either arguing the direct marketing position or the privacy position. Set up a series of three-minute debates with each side having 1½ minutes to argue its position. Every team of debaters has to present new points not covered in the previous teams' presentations until there are no arguments left to present. Then the class votes as a group on the winning point of view.

Take-Home Team Projects

1. Divide the class into groups. Each group should select a consumer product that normally is not sold through direct marketing, but could be. Create a direct-marketing campaign for this product. Be sure to specify your objectives and indicate the parts of the offer as well as the medium used. Develop a mock-up of some of the campaign's pieces that illustrates your ideas about message design.

2. Amazon.com is one of the most well-known direct marketers on the Internet. Browse the company's Web site and, as a team, identify what direct marketing strategies the company employs. Which do you think are the most successful? Why? What are the least effective? Why?

Yahoo! Hands-On Case

Review the Yahoo! case in the Appendix.

1. What is the chief advantage of direct marketing? Is that advantage useful to a Web company like Yahoo! that is trying to reach an audience of teens and tweens? Explain your thinking on why or why not the Yahoo! project should include a direct-marketing component, Which of the various forms of direct marketing seem most appropriate for this client and why?

2. You work for a direct-marketing firm, and you have been asked to develop a direct-marketing plan for Yahoo! for these two audience groups for the following year. Brainstorm as a group and develop at least three ideas that could be proposed to Yahoo! In a one-page report, outline your three ideas and provide a rationale why each one should be considered.

HANDS-ON CASE

Telemarketers Respond to the National Do-Not-Call Registry

It's a good bet that most consumers would rank telemarketing near the bottom of their list of favorite ad appeals. When Congress created the National Do-Not-Call Registry in 2003, which made it illegal for companies to call people who choose to opt out of telemarketing calls, there was broad public support.

Telemarketing grew phenomenally in the years leading up to the creation of the registry. In 2002 alone, telemarketers spent $80 billion and placed 16 million calls. This effort yielded $274 billion in sales, up from just $10 billion in 1980. But telemarketing's success may have helped to create its own downfall. Andy Orr, a newspaper circulation consultant, suggests that Congress stepped in after consumers had had enough. "After the 1980s everyone got on the [telemarketing] bandwagon and consumers began to feel assaulted. Then, computerized dialing machines came on the scene and became a nuisance. To protect themselves, people began paying for caller ID, they demanded that companies develop internal do-not-call lists, and they lobbied for legislation to create statewide registries."

The Registry has proven immensely popular. As of early 2007, more than 139 million phone numbers, including cell phone numbers, have been listed as Americans opt out of telemarketing calls. Each call made to someone registered on the list can be punishable with a fine of up to $11,000.

The registry has affected telemarketers in different ways. For some organizations the new law has had little impact; groups such as charities and political organizations are exempted. Companies that used telemarketing as a small component of their marketing mixes have shifted their spending elsewhere without much effect. But a few companies have been unable to replace telemarketing as a tool for building business. AT&T, MCI, Scholastic, and Gannett all publicly blamed financial losses in 2004 on their inability to market via the phone.

Several companies have taken a fresh look at what might be considered an even more intrusive strategy for building customers—door-to-door sales efforts. Cable company Comcast found that by going door to door in 2004, it was able to win back 40,000 customers from its competitors. Newspapers have used door to door to build circulation and have tried to turn a problem into an opportunity. The Do-Not-Call Registry, says National Association of Newspapers vice president John Murray, "is forcing people to do what they should have done long ago: balance multiple sales sources."

Other companies have found ways to telemarket legally by taking advantage of gaps in the law. Companies can still legally phone individuals with whom they have an "existing relationship," which in practice means the consumer has bought a service and/or product or has contacted the company within the previous 18 months. Individuals in the registry can also give up their immunity if they subsequently agree to let marketers contact them. A company called CoolSavings, based in Chicago, takes advantage of this registry "loophole" by gathering information from visitors to third-party Web sites who indicate they would be receptive to offers. CoolSavings makes money by then selling the contact information to companies that can now safely call the newly "unregistered" individuals.

Figuring that a carrot always beats a stick when it comes to relationship building, Coca-Cola, the Weather Channel, and Proctor & Gamble are all hoping they can convince cell phone users to call them. P&G supports its Herbal Essences brand by offering young cell phone users branded content, including downloadable music and pictures. Callers can also use the Herbal Essences mobile Web site to play games and send messages. The bill for all of this activity is paid by the cell phone user who is charged by his or her carrier. Sometimes it really is better when they call you.

Consider This

1. Analyze why telemarketing is simultaneously an effective way to market and yet is widely disliked by many consumers.
2. Could the telemarketing industry have prevented the Do-Not-Call Registry? Or was it inevitable that legislators would step in?
3. Can you think of products or services about which many people would not mind being contacted either by phone or in person by a salesperson?

Sources: Yuki Noguchi, "New Ad Frontier: Cell Phones. Marketers Bet Consumers Will Ask for Text Messages," *MSNBC News,* November 7, 2003, http://msnbc.msn.com/id/3403665/; Jim Edwards, "A Year After Do Not Call, Some Hangups Remain," *Brandweek,* October 4, 2004, 9; Federal Trade Commission press release, "The Truth about Cell Phones and the Do Not Call Registry," February 6, 2007, http://www.fcc.gov; Anne Lallonde, "Telemarketing's Aftermath: Circulation Executives Seek and Find New Ways to Make the Sale," Newspaper Association of America, January 23, 2004, http://www.naa.org; "Justices Uphold 'Do Not Call' Registry," *New York Times,* October 5, 2004, C2; Jane Spencer, "Ignore That Knocking: Door-to-Door Sales Make a Comeback," *Wall Street Journal,* April 30, 2003, D1; Brian Steinberg, Suzanne Vranica, and Yochi Dreazen, "'Do Not Call' Registry Is Pushing Telemarketers to Plan New Pitches," *Wall Street Journal,* July 2, 2003, A1.

Sales Promotion, Events, and Sponsorships

IT'S A WINNER

Award:	Company:	Agency:	Promotion:
Nominated for National Emmy	Frontier Airlines	Grey Worldwide	"Denver's Favorite Animal"

Frontier Campaigns for Favorite Animal Votes and Web Hits

How do you follow up a successful campaign like Frontier Airline's Flip to Mexico (see Chapter 12's opening story)? Frontier handed Shawn Couzens and Gary Ennis, creative directors from Grey Worldwide in New York City, their next challenge: Drive consumers to the Web site. Airlines prefer passengers to book on the Web because the company saves money, and capturing e-mails builds the airline's database.

Sometimes to reach the marketing and campaign objectives, advertisers need to be willing to take risks to be rewarded. How far could Couzens and Ennis push Frontier?

Couzens explained, "We would never do something 'out there' just to do it. It has to line up with the strategy and reflect who we are. A brand is a lot like a person. It has a distinct personality, a unique identity, and a belief system. And just like a person, if we misrepresent the brand, then people won't trust it. So, whenever we embark on an assignment, we ask, 'Is this consistent with our brand personality? Does this deliver on our brand promise?' And if the idea doesn't fit who Frontier is or what people expect from us, then we dump it."

The Grey team created an online contest that let citizens vote for their favorite animal. Seven of the animals campaigned via the Frontier Web site in a satire of real political campaigns. Would people pick Grizwald the Bear, Flip the Dolphin, Hector the Otter, Jack (who else?) the Rabbit, Larry the Lynx, the Penguins, or Sal the Cougar?

Couzens described how the contest fit the brand: "Fortunately, our brand personality is easygoing, friendly, and fun. We're 'a whole different animal,' so we can do things that demonstrate how different and unique we are—and that comes through not just in the ads but in the brand experience as a whole."

Chapter Key Points

1. Which principles drive the use of sales promotion, and what are some current trends?

2. How are various consumer promotions used?

3. What are the types and purposes of trade promotions?

4. How do other types of promotions—sponsorships and events, interactive promotions, loyalty programs, and comarketing programs—work?

5. How are promotions used strategically in marketing in terms of brand building, new product launches, integration, and effectiveness?

Fans could go to Frontier's home page to get to the contest, then click on a squeaky door to enter the virtual Campaign Headquarters. Once there, visitors could interact with various aspects of the campaign: They could listen to a debate between trash-talking contestants, order posters of their favorite animal, watch commercials on a TV set, order real press kits with T-shirts, listen to each contestant's platform, join a YouTube group, or participate in an online forum.

Here's a sample of the animals' political platforms. Griz the Bear wants to give voters free all-you-can-eat buffets, back massages, and free flights for every man, woman, and child, none of which, unsurprisingly, are endorsed by Frontier. Jack runs on an environmental platform. He promises lower health-care costs, a statewide cap on fuel costs, and reductions in greenhouse emissions. Hector apparently chooses to run on his good looks: He is cute and cuddly and can make squishy sounds with his cheeks. The commercials even let the candidates engage in a bit of political backbiting.

Built-in fun on the site captured visitors' attention with a clock that actually told time, a spinning fan and a coffee cup that spilled when you clicked on it.

The results? Turn to the It's a Wrap section at the end of the chapter to see who won the hearts of Frontier fans.

Source: Shawn M. Couzens, Garry Ennis interview, February 21, 2007; http://www.frontierairlines.portline.com/HQ_restore.html; http://www.thewhitehouseproject.org (all sites accessed February 25, 2007).

Frontier Airlines' Favorite Animal Contest is an example of an award-winning promotion that captivated viewers and involved them personally in building loyalty to the airline and generating traffic to its Web site. This chapter is about the fun, creative, and exciting ideas that the sales promotion industry uses to spur action and build strong brand relationships. This chapter explains the difference between consumer and trade promotions as well as other programs, such as loyalty programs, tie-ins, and sponsorships, which cross the line between advertising and promotion. First let's discuss the concept and basic principles of sales promotion.

THE PRACTICE OF SALES PROMOTION

When a marketer increases the value of its product or brand by offering an extra incentive to purchase it, the marketer is creating a sales promotion, which is the subject of this chapter. In most cases the objective of sales promotion is to encourage action. Promotion (we will use the word *promotion* to refer to sales promotion) can also help build brand identity and awareness, as the Frontier Airlines case illustrates. Sales promotion is a type of marketing communication similar to, but not synonymous with, advertising. While advertising is designed to build long-term brand awareness, sales promotion is primarily focused on creating action.

The American Marketing Association (AMA) offers this definition of **sales promotion**: "The media and non-media marketing pressure applied for a predetermined, limited period of time at the level of consumer, retailer, or wholesaler in order to stimulate trial, increase consumer demand, or improve product availability."[1]

Let's examine this definition. First, it acknowledges that consumers are an important target for promotions, but so are other stakeholders, such as the company's sales representatives and members of the trade (wholesalers, retailers). Second, the definition recognizes that sales promotion is a set of techniques that prompts members of three target audiences—consumers, sales representatives, and the trade (distributors, retailers, dealers)—to take action, preferably immediate action. Simply put, sales promotion offers an extra incentive to act, usually in the form of a price reduction, but it also entails additional amounts of the product, cash, prizes and gifts, premiums, special events, and so on. One example of an incentive is a $1 million offer by Netflix to consumers who could offer ideas for improving its movie recommendation software.[2] It may also be just a fun brand experience, as Frontier Airlines' Favorite Animal Contest illustrates.

Although an action response is the goal of most sales promotions, some programs such as the Frontier Airlines campaign are designed to build awareness first, but always with action as the ultimate goal. Consumers get to choose the animal they like best to represent Frontier, but in the long run the airline wants consumers to book flights online. What better way to get them to the site than generating Web traffic via an entertaining contest?

Principle
Sales promotion is primarily designed to motivate people to act by offering incentives.

Changes in the Promotion Industry

Until the 1980s, advertising was the dominant player in the marketing communication arena. But during the 1980s more marketers found themselves driving immediate bottom-line response through the use of sales promotion. As a result, in the 1980s and particularly in the 1990s the budget share switched from 60 percent advertising and 40 percent sales promotion to the reverse: 40 percent advertising and 60 percent sales promotion. That trend reversed again in the late 1990s as the dot-com companies spent huge sums on advertising to establish their brands. Even though the promotion industry continued to grow, with spending increasing 8.1 percent, that growth rate was slower than that of advertising, which saw spending increase by 9.8 percent in the early 2000s.[3] The industry has continued to grow in the 2000s, however, with a total sales promotion expenditure of more than $44 billion reported in 2007.[4]

A *Promo* magazine 2007 Industry Trends report found "two/thirds of all firms now plan promotions as part of their overall marketing strategy" and marketing budgets are pretty evenly split among consumer promotions, advertising and trade promotions.[5] Over the years, advertising and sales promotion have been battling for their share of the marketing communication budget, but sales promotion, including both consumer and trade promotions, now accounts for more than half of the budget.

Global incentive programs are also experiencing explosive growth. Kurt Hosna, international product manager for Maritz Incentives, indicates that the number of clients seeking global incentive programs has increased dramatically in the last five years. Some of the reasons for this growth include the interest of multinational corporations in aligning all units with corporate goals, increasing bottom-line efficiency, and taking advantage of the rise of the Internet.[6] Online promotions spending, for example, grew from $6.7 billion in 2006 to $8.7 billion (estimated) in 2007 and an estimated $11.1 billion in 2008 according to *Promo* magazine's 2007 Industry Report. That's an annual growth averaging around 27 percent and it far surpasses all the other categories of promotional spending.[7]

Reasons for the Growth of Sales Promotion

The most common reasons that companies are spending more money on sales promotion stem from the pressure for short-term profits and the need for accountability for marketing communication efforts. Sales promotions are relatively easy to evaluate in terms of their impact on sales.

In terms of accountability, most U.S. companies focus on immediate profits, a drive that sales promotion satisfies. Product managers are under pressure to generate quarterly sales increases. Because the benefits of advertising are often more apparent in the long term, companies invest more money in sales promotion when they want quick results. Advertisers also cite economic reasons for the shift. Traditional media costs have escalated to the point where alternative types of media must be considered. As the networks raised their advertising prices, their share of prime-time television viewers has dropped dramatically. The proliferation of media and competition for audiences' attention also factor in the need for accountability. Advertisers, therefore, are exploring marketing communication forms that cost less and produce immediate, tangible results. Sales promotion can deliver these results.

Another reason for sales promotion's accountability is that it is relatively easy and quick to determine whether a sales promotion strategy has accomplished its objectives because there is usually an immediate response of some kind.

From the consumers' perspective, sales promotion reduces the risk associated with a purchase by giving them something of *added value* such as a coupon, rebate, or discounted price. Promotions typically offer the consumer added value, or "more for less," as a Southwest Airlines promotion illustrates. Developed in conjunction with Alamo, this promotion promised those who fly Southwest and rent vehicles from Alamo that they could earn double Rapid Rewards credit toward a free flight—for a limited time, of course.

Principle
Sales promotion reduces the risk of trying a new product by giving something of added value to motivate action.

Other reasons for the move to sales promotion match changes in the marketplace, such as these:

- *Consumer behavior.* Shoppers today are better educated, more selective, and less loyal to brand names than in the past, which means they are more likely to switch brands.
- *Pricing.* Consumers have come to expect constant short-term price reductions such as coupons, sales, and price promotions.
- *Market share.* In most industries, the battle is for market share rather than general product growth. Sales promotion encourages people to switch products, increasing market share.
- *Parity products.* Sales promotion is often the most effective strategy for increasing sales of a parity product when the products in the category are largely undifferentiated. When products are similar, promotions become the tie-breaker in the consumer's decision making.
- *The power of the retailer.* Dominant retailers, such as Safeway, Wal-Mart, Toys "R" Us, and Home Depot, demand a variety of promotional incentives before allowing products into their stores.

Categories of Sales Promotion

The most common sales promotion strategies target the three audiences of promotions: consumer, trade, and sales force. The first two—customer sales and trade support—have direct implications for advertising and are the focus of this chapter. In the third category, sales force promotions include two general sets of promotional activities directed at the firm's salespeople to motivate them to increase their sales levels. The first set of activities includes programs that better prepare salespeople to do their jobs, such as sales manuals, training programs, sales presentations, and supportive materials (training films, slides, videos, and visual aids). The second set of activities deals with promotional efforts or incentives that motivate salespeople to work harder, such as contests.

In the rest of this chapter we examine consumer promotions, then trade promotions. Another section covers crossover promotions that blur the lines between promotions, advertising, and public relations. Finally, we discuss overarching issues that relate to promotional strategy.

CONSUMER PROMOTIONS

Although trade promotion claims the greatest percent of the promotion budget, we'll start with consumer promotions because these are familiar to most people. Consumer sales promotions are directed at the ultimate user of the good or service. They are intended to provide an incentive so that when consumers go into a store they will look for a particular brand. The primary strengths of consumer sales promotions are their variety and flexibility.

Types of Consumer Promotions

A product manager can use and combine many promotion techniques to meet almost any objective. Sales promotion works for all kinds of businesses. Here's a summary of the most common types of consumer promotions.

- *Price deals.* A popular sales promotion technique is a **price deal**, a temporary price reduction or a sale price, as in the Macy's and Zappos.com ads. The four common price deals include:
    1. A *cents-off deal* is a reduction in the normal price charged for a good or service (for example, "was $1,000, now $500," or "50 percent off") announced at the point of sale or through mass or direct advertising.
    2. *Price-pack deals* provide the consumer with something extra through the package itself—a prize in a cereal box, for instance.
    3. *Bonus packs* contain additional amounts of the product free when consumers purchase the standard size at the regular price. For example, Purina Dog Food may offer 25 percent more dog food in the bag.
    4. *Banded packs* are more units of a product sold at a lower price than if they were bought at the regular single-unit price. Sometimes the products are physically packaged together, such as bar soap and six-packs of soft drinks.
- *Coupons.* There are two general types of **coupons** that provide a discount on the price of a product—retailer and manufacturer. Retailer-sponsored coupons can be redeemed only at the specified retail outlet. Manufacturer-sponsored coupons can be redeemed at any outlet distributing the product. They are distributed directly (direct mail, door-to-door), through media (newspaper and magazine ads, free-standing inserts), in or on the package itself, or through the retailer (co-op advertising). Manufacturers pay retailers a fee for handling their coupons.
- *Refunds and rebates.* A **refund** or **rebate** is a marketer's offer to return a certain amount of money to the consumer who purchases the product. Sometimes the refund is a check for a certain amount of money, but other times it may be a coupon to encourage repeat use.
- *Sampling.* Allowing the consumer to try the product or service is called **sampling**. Advertisers can distribute samples to

This ad includes not only a price discount, but also several other deals to encourage store visits.

Zappos.com seeks to persuade customers to buy more by giving free shipping.

consumers in numerous ways. Sampling tables, particularly for food products, can be set up in stores. Small samples of products can show up with newspapers and on house doorknobs, in doctors' and dentists' offices, and, most commonly, through the mail. Advertisers can design ads with coupons for free samples, place samples in special packages, or distribute samples at special in-store displays. Product samples influence consumers more than other types of in-store promotions, according to one survey.[8]

- *Contests and sweepstakes.* Contest and sweepstakes promotions create excitement by promising "something for nothing" and offering impressive prizes. **Contests** require participants to compete for a prize or prizes based on some sort of skill or ability. **Sweepstakes** require only that participants submit their names to be included in a drawing or other chance selection. In keeping with a society that is in love with cell phones, sweepstakes are now offered via mobile marketing. Redbook and Procter & Gamble's Max Factor brand have both sponsored such promotions.[9] A **game** is a type of sweepstake. It differs from a one-shot drawing type of sweepstake because the time frame is longer, so it establishes continuity by requiring customers to return several times to acquire additional pieces (such as bingo-type games) or to improve their chances of winning.

   There are legal as well as ethical issues with contests, sweepstakes, and games. McDonald's, for example, got burned in 2000 when its Who Wants to Be a Millionaire? and Monopoly games turned into scams. One of the employees of the company hired to run the games distributed winning game pieces to a network of accomplices. McDonald's didn't return to game promotions until 2003 after it had developed strict security procedures.[10]

   The games that award prizes are different from those on the Internet that try to build interest in the product by amusing the visitor, such as Frontier's Web site featured in the chapter-opening case.

- *Premiums.* A **premium** is a tangible reward for a particular act, usually purchasing a product or visiting the point of purchase. Premiums are a type of incentive that work by adding value to the product. Examples of premiums are the toy in Cracker Jacks, glassware in a box of detergent, and a radio given for taking a real estate tour. Premiums are either free or low in price. The two general types of premiums are direct and mail. Direct premiums award the incentive immediately, at the time of purchase. The four variations of direct premiums are (1) store premiums, given to customers at the retail site; (2) in-pack premiums, inserted in the package at the factory; (3) on-pack premiums, placed on the outside of the package at the factory; and (4) container premiums, in which the package is the premium. Mail premiums require the customer to take some action before receiving the premium. A **self-liquidator** premium usually requires that a payment be mailed in along with some proof of purchase before the customer receives the premium. The payment is sufficient to cover the cost of the premium. Another type of mail premium requires the customer to save coupons or special labels attached to the product that can be redeemed for merchandise.

- *Specialties.* **Specialty advertising** presents the brand's name on something that is given away as a reminder, such as calendars, pens and pencils, T-shirts, mouse pads, tote bags, and water bottles. The ideal specialty is an item kept out in the open where other people can see it, such as a coffee mug.

How to Use Consumer Promotions

To demonstrate the strategy behind the use of these tools in a new product launch, let's suppose we are introducing a new corn chip named Corn Crunchies. Promotion is particularly useful to launch the corn chip because it has a number of tools designed to encourage trial, but it can also be used later in the brand's life to maintain or increase its share of market and to remind and reward loyal customers.

Awareness   Our first challenge is to create awareness of this brand, which is the real strength of advertising and, you may remember from Chapter 5, the first step in consumer decision making. However, sometimes awareness can be increased when advertising is combined with an appropriate promotion to call attention to the brand name to get people to try the product. Awareness-building promotion ideas for this new corn chip might include colorful point-of-purchase displays, sponsorship of a Corn Crunchies team, or a special event that will attract people in the target market.

Trial Creating awareness will only take the product so far, however. Consumers must also perceive Corn Crunchies as offering some clear benefit compared to the competition. Sales promotion does this by arranging for experiences, such as special events where people can try the product or see it demonstrated. Trial is one of the most important objectives of promotion, but it is essential to get the right people, the targeted audience, involved with the product. Sales promotion has other tools that lead to trial, such as sampling. An effective way to get people to try Corn Crunchies is to give away free samples at events, in stores, or through direct mail to the home. Sampling is an effective strategy for introducing a new or modified product or for dislodging an entrenched market leader by enticing potential users to try the product. As a general rule of thumb, retailers and manufacturers maintain that sampling can boost sales volume as much as 10 times when used with a product demonstration and 10 percent to 15 percent thereafter. Sampling is generally most effective when reinforced on the spot with product coupons. Most consumers like sampling because they do not lose money if they do not like the product. To be successful, the product sampled must virtually sell itself with a simple trial experience.

Another way sales promotion can motivate people to try a new product like Corn Crunchies is to offer a price deal—you try this product and we will give it to you cheaper than the usual price. These price deals are usually offered through coupons, refunds, rebates, or premiums. Refunds and rebates are effective because they encourage consumers to purchase a product before a deadline. In addition, refunds stimulate sales without the high cost and waste associated with coupons.

Coupons mainly encourage trial, induce brand switching, and reward repeat business. The main advantage of the manufacturer's coupon, such as those that run in consumer magazines, is that it allows the advertiser to lower prices without relying on cooperation from the retailer to distribute them. Announcements for cents-off deals include the package itself and signs near the product or elsewhere in the store. Advertising for these deals include sales, flyers, newspaper ads, and broadcast ads.

Maintain or Increase Market Share In addition to encouraging trial of a new product, another purpose of price deals is to convince prospective users to switch from an established competing brand, such as Cheetos in the Corn Crunchies case. Later, after the Corn Crunchies brand is established, a price deal can be used to reward loyal users and encourage their repeat business. Price deals are particularly effective in those situations where price is an important factor in brand choice or if consumers are not brand loyal.

To maintain a brand's presence or increase its market share after it is launched, marketers use promotional tools such as coupons, premiums, special events, and contests and sweepstakes. The Blue Bunny brochure was used as a Sunday newspaper supplement. It features the entire Indulge line of low-carb and low-fat products, as well as coupons to encourage trial.

In addition to serving as a reward for buying a product, premiums can enhance an advertising campaign or a brand's image. Characters like the Campbell Soup Kids, Tony the Tiger, Cap'n Crunch, and Ronald McDonald are used on premiums, such as soup or cereal bowls, to reinforce the consumer's association of the brand with the character. Cereal manufacturers are among the biggest users of in-pack premiums as reminder devices.

Brand Reminder In addition to new product launches, promotions are also used in the reminder stage. This means that you change advertising copy to remind customers about the positive experience they had with the product and use sales promotion to reinforce their loyalty with coupons, rebates, and other rewards. After the initial purchase you want the customer to remember the brand and repeat the purchase, so specialty items, such as a Corn Crunchies snack bowl, can serve as a brand reminder. Specialty advertising serves as a reminder to the consumer to consider the product. Specialties also build relationships, such as items given away as new year or thank-you gifts (the calendar hanging in the kitchen). Advertisers use specialty items to thank customers for patronage, to reinforce established products or services, and to generate sales leads.

The Blue Bunny brochure uses strong appetite appeal in its visuals to emphasize the good taste of its low-carb and low-fat products.

TRADE PROMOTIONS

Consumer awareness and desire mean nothing unless Corn Crunchies is available where the consumer thinks it should be. Somehow the trade must be convinced that the product will move off the shelves. Marketers know they must engage the trade in the program if their consumer promotions are to be effective. In such programs, *trade* refers to all the people involved in the distribution channel, including buyers, brokers, distributors, wholesalers, dealers, franchisees, and retailers.

Principle
Consumer promotion is of little use if the product isn't available where the consumer can find it.

Typically companies spend more than half of their total promotion budget on promotions directed at the trade. The 2006 *Promo* magazine report found that companies directed 27.5 percent to the trade or channel market and 27.9 percent to the consumer market, which is to say that although consumer promotion is highly visible, trade promotion is equally important as a marketing communication strategy.[11] Let's look at the types of trade promotion.

Types of Trade Promotion

Trade advertising directed at wholesalers and retailers provides trade members with information about the new product and its selling points. In addition, trade promotion techniques, especially price discounts, point-of-purchase displays, and advertising allowances, motivate retailers to provide shelf space for products and consumer promotions. Resellers, the intermediaries in the distribution channel, employ millions of people, including nearly

15.3 million in retail and 5.9 million in wholesale trading, who distribute the products manufacturers make.[12] The Corn Crunchies manufacturer in our fictional example will be more encouraged that the product is acceptable if resellers are willing to carry and help promote it. Many promotional devices designed to motivate resellers to engage in certain sales activities are available to the manufacturer. Here are the most common types of trade promotion tools.

- *Point-of-purchase displays.* A manufacturer-designed display distributed to retailers who use it to call their customers' attention to product promotions is known as a **point-of-purchase (POP) display**. Another popular POP form is the merchandising display, which retailers use to showcase their products and create a personality for their stores. Although POP forms vary by industry, they can include special racks, display cartons, banners, signs, price cards, and mechanical product dispensers, among other tools.
- *Retailer (dealer) kits.* Materials that support retailers' selling efforts or that help representatives make sales calls on prospective retailing customers are often designed as sales kits. The kits contain supporting information, such as detailed product specifications, how-to display information, and ad slicks—print ads that are ready to be sent to the local print media as soon as the retailer or dealer adds identification, location, promotion price, or other information.
- *Trade incentives and deals.* Similar to consumer price deals, a manufacturer may reward a reseller financially for purchase of a certain level of a product or support of a promotion. These promotional efforts can take the form of special displays, extra purchases, superior store locations, or greater local promotion. In return, retailers can receive special allowances, such as discounts, free goods, gifts, or cash from the manufacturer. The most common types of **trade deals** are buying allowances for increasing purchases and advertising allowances, which include deals on cooperative advertising and display allowances, or deals for agreeing to use promotional displays.
- *Contests.* As in the case of consumer sales promotion, advertisers can develop contests and sweepstakes to motivate resellers. Contests are far more common than sweepstakes, mainly because resellers find it easy to tie contest prizes to the sale of the sponsor's product. A sales quota is set, for example, and the retailer or person who exceeds the quota by the largest percentage wins the contest.
- *Trade shows and exhibits.* The **trade show** is where companies within the same industries gather to present and sell their merchandise and to demonstrate their products. Exhibits are the spaces that are designed to showcase the product.

How to Use Trade Promotion

The ultimate gauge of a successful trade promotion is whether sales increase. Trade promotions are primarily designed to get the cooperation of people in the distribution channel and to encourage their promotion of the product to consumers. Sales promotion brings resellers to that point of conviction. There are two primary roles for a trade promotion:

1. *Trade support.* To stimulate in-store merchandising or other trade support (for example, feature pricing, superior store location, or shelf space).
2. *Excitement.* To create a high level of excitement about the product among those responsible for its sale.

In addition, trade promotion is also used to accomplish other marketing objectives, such as manipulating levels of inventory held by wholesalers and retailers and expanding product distribution to new areas of the country or new classes of trade.

Demand: Push-and-Pull Strategies   As noted previously, manufacturers hope to see their trade partners push a product. To understand the role of trade promotion, consider how sales promotion is used in push-and-pull strategies (see Figure 2.3). Consumer and trade promotions interact through complementing push-and-pull strategies. If people really want to try Corn Crunchies based on what they have heard in advertising and publicity stories, they will ask their local retailers for it, which is called a *pull strategy*; that is, by asking for it, they will pull the product through the distribution channel. Sometimes the advertising and publicity are focused on a sales promotion, which can be used to intensify demand for the product. By conducting a contest in conjunction with sampling, for example, we can increase the pull of a promotion at the same time we get people to try the new product.

However, you might use a *push strategy* to push the product through the channel by convincing (motivating or rewarding) members of the distribution network to carry Corn Crunchies. For example, we want grocery stores not only to carry them, but also to allocate good shelf space in the crowded chip aisle. Here are the most common types of incentives and trade deals used with retailers as part of a push strategy.

- **Bonuses.** A monetary bonus, also called *push money* or *spiffs*, is paid to a salesperson based on units the salesperson sells over a period of time. For example, an air conditioner manufacturer might give salespeople a $50 bonus for the sale of one model and $75 for a fancier model, within a certain time frame. At the end of the sales period, each salesperson sends in evidence of total sales to the manufacturer and receives a check for the bonus amount.
- **Dealer loaders.** These are premiums, comparable to a consumer premium, that a manufacturer gives to a retailer for buying a certain amount of a product. A buying loader rewards retailers for buying the product. Budweiser offered store managers a free trip to the Super Bowl if they sold a certain amount of beer in a specified period of time. Display loaders reward retailers by giving them the display after the promotion is over. For example, Dr. Pepper built a store display for the July 4th holiday that included a gas grill, picnic table, basket, and other items. The store manager was awarded these items after the promotion ended.
- **Buying allowances.** A manufacturer pays a reseller a set amount of money or offers a discount for purchasing a certain amount of the product during a specified time period.
- **Advertising allowances.** The manufacturer pays the wholesaler or retailer a certain amount of money to advertise the manufacturer's product. This allowance can be a flat dollar amount, or it can be a percentage of gross purchases during a specified time period.
- **Cooperative advertising.** In a contractual arrangement between the manufacturer and the resellers, the manufacturer agrees to pay a part or all of the retailers' advertising expenses.
- **Display allowance.** A direct payment of cash or goods is given to the retailer if the retailer agrees to set up the point-of-sale display.

Attention Some trade promotions are designed to get the attention of both trade members and their customers. POP displays, for example, are designed to get the attention of shoppers when they are in the store and to stimulate impulse purchases. They are used by retailers, but provided by manufacturers. As we have moved to a self-service retail environment in which fewer and fewer customers expect help from sales clerks, the role of POP continues to increase. The Point-of-Purchase Advertising International Association (POPAI) released a study that examined the effect of various POP forms on sales. Topping the POP list were displays communicating a tie-in with entertainment, sports, or charities.[13]

In addition to getting attention in crowded aisles and promoting impulse purchases, marketers are designing POP efforts to complement other promotional campaigns. As part of getting attention, retailers appreciate POP ideas that build store ambience.[14] Club Med designed a floor display for travel agents that featured a beach chair with a surfboard on one side and a pair of skis on the other to show that Club Med has both snow and sun destinations. Advertisers must design POP displays that appeal to both end users and the trade. Retailers will use a POP only if they are convinced that it will generate greater sales.

Advertisers use POP displays to call attention to a product and increase sales.

Motivation   Most trade promotions are designed to motivate in some way trade members to cooperate with the manufacturer's promotion. Incentives such as contests and trade deals are used. If conducted properly with a highly motivating incentive or prize, contests can spur short-term sales and improve the relationship between the manufacturer and the reseller. They encourage a higher quantity of purchases and create enthusiasm among trade members who are involved with the promotion. Trade incentive programs are used to stimulate frequency and quantity of purchase and encourage cooperation with a promotion.

Information   Trade shows display products and provide an opportunity to sample and demonstrate products, particularly for trade buyers, the people who buy for stores. The food industry has thousands of trade shows for various product categories, and the manufacturer of Corn Crunchies would want to sponsor an exhibit featuring the new corn chip at the appropriate food shows. Trade shows permit companies to gather information about their competition. In an environment where all the companies are attempting to give a clear picture of their products to potential customers, competitors can easily compare quality, features, prices, and technology.

CROSSOVER PROMOTIONS

So far we have looked at consumer sales promotions and trade promotions. But marketers have more promotion techniques at their disposal. In this section, we focus on sponsorships, event marketing, interactive and Internet promotions, loyalty programs, and comarketing or partnership promotions. Many of these promotion techniques, such as sponsorships and event marketing, cross over to other areas of marketing and blur the lines between promotions, advertising, and public relations.

Sponsorships and Event Marketing

Sponsorships occur when companies support an event, say a sporting event, concert, or charity either financially or by donating supplies and services. **Event marketing** means building a product's marketing program around a sponsored event, such as the Olympics or a golf tournament. Sponsorships and event marketing include sports sponsorships (events, athletes, teams); entertainment tours and attractions; festivals, fairs, and other annual events; cause marketing (associating with an event that supports a social cause); and support for the arts (orchestras, museums, etc.). Sponsorships typically cost a lot of money. Sponsors for major golf tournaments, for example, are expected to invest between $6 million and $8 million.[15] The Matter of Practice box discusses the explosion of sports-related promotions.

Companies undertake sponsorships to build brand associations and increase the perceived value of the brand in the consumer's mind. The important thing is that the event must project the right image for the brand. That's particularly important in troubled economic times when companies with budget problems find it hard to justify spending money on glitzy events. Companies that use sponsorships focus their efforts on supporting causes and events that matter most to employees and customers.[16]

Procter & Gamble discovered that using its Prilosec OTC heartburn medication to sponsor bunco tournaments was a natural fit. About 70 percent of frequent heartburn sufferers are women, which matches the audience that likes to play the old party-time dice game.[17]

Hundreds of companies sponsor NASCAR cars both to reach the sport's expanding fan base and to link their brand to a winning car and driver. Sponsors shell out in excess of $650 million to get NASCAR's top 35 cars in the Nextel Cup Series to put their logos on the car. The investment pays. Marketing analyst Joyce Julius & Associates estimates that in 2005 Dale Earnhardt Jr. earned the equivalent of $149 million in televised exposure time for his sponsor Budweiser, quite a bargain considering Anheuser-Busch is believed to have spent only $15 million on the sponsorship.[18]

Just think about sponsorships associated with football bowl games and other sporting events. The first bowl to have a sponsor, the Sunkist Fiesta Bowl, led the way in 1986, followed by the Tostitos Fiesta Bowl, the Outback Bowl, the Meinecke Car Care Bowl and others. The Peach Bowl was replaced by the Chick-fil-A Bowl.[19] A twist on the sports

A MATTER OF PRACTICE

Advertising through Sports

By John Sweeney, *Professor, Head of Advertising and Director of Sports Communication Program, University of North Carolina*

There has been remarkable growth in the relationship between sports and advertising. *Sports Business Journal* estimates that advertising in sports totaled more than $27 billion in 2001. The entire sports industry approaches $200 billion and includes advertising, tickets, licensing, equipment, media, sponsorships, travel, and equipment. The games we watch and play have become very big business.

The first reason for the enormous growth in sports advertising comes from the fracturing of media in general. We have gone from a nation of three national television networks to hundreds of cable channels, DVDs, VODs, and webcasts—and that's just one medium. Marketers are now following the passions of target audiences and making associations with them as a way to break through the enormous media clutter. This leads directly to the enormous passion people feel for sports.

The second reason for the rise of sports is the way both leagues and sponsors have organized to make sports an effective tool for marketing. Leagues now operate as singular brands in the marketplace. The National Football League organizes itself to sell exclusive national media rights and sponsorships and distribute licensed merchandise. This seems simple enough until you realize that it requires 32 fiercely competitive teams to move in a disciplined manner for the good of marketing. It is politically demanding, but the rewards are breathtaking. The NFL makes $2 billion a year in media rights and sells more than $3 billion in licensed goods.

Sponsors have also organized to leverage their association with major leagues and events. In a fractured media world, companies present their sponsorship across dozens of media platforms. Visa uses its Olympic sponsorship throughout the world in television, print, interactive, outdoor, and numerous other ways involving the more than 19,000 banks that work under the card name. The Olympics is a perfect event for a global strategy.

Even seemingly small sports events can hold tremendous value for advertisers. Volvo sponsors the Volvo Ocean race, a grueling sailing competition where boats race for over nine months covering 39,000 miles. This race claims 15,000 published articles in 11 territories reaching 686 million unique readers. The event reaches more than 1 billion radio listeners and a cumulative television audience of 2 billion. There are more than 3 million unique visitors to the Web site where Volvo ran a promotional sweepstakes, and the carmaker was able to recruit customers for test drives at the 12 ports around the world. An estimated 500,000 people came to each port to see the boats. It is clear that there is a lot more to running a sponsorship than placing an ad.

The new world of sports marketing continues to grow in both popularity and cost. As sports become a standard strategy for advertisers, they face the same demands for accountability as other marketing methods. The modern sports sponsorship must prove its effectiveness just like the traditional print campaign or television commercial. In that way, it has joined the big time of marketing with both enormous money and equal pressure to succeed.

---

sponsorship concept comes from convenience store chain 7-Eleven, which made a deal with the Chicago White Sox: The baseball club's games now start at 7:11.[20]

The importance of sponsorships is growing worldwide. Mengniu Milk, a Mongolian milk company, is raising its profile by backing the NBA in China. Beyond exposure, these events give corporations the opportunity to build their image and reputation by associating with an activity that audiences enjoy.[21]

Event Marketing   The term *event marketing* describes the marketing practice of linking a brand to an event, such as the Jose Cuervo beach volleyball tournament. Marketers use related promotional events, such as a tour or the appearance of the product or its spokesperson at a mall or sporting event, to gain the attention and participation of people in the target audience who attend the event. The event showcases the brand, often with sampling, coupons, and other incentives. Business-to-business promotions also use events to reach trade audiences, which can include the sales staff, distributors, retailers, and franchisees. These stakeholders are invited to participate in the event as a reward for their support.

Vail Resorts introduced the Colorado Pass Club by capturing the attention of its target audience with a successful event with the Colorado Rockies, designed to celebrate Passholder Appreciation Day.

To be successful, the event must match the brand to the target market's lifestyle. For example, the launch of the Colorado Pass Club by Vail Resorts, featured in Chapter 15, included a number of effective sales promotions that matched the brand to the target market's lifestyle. But the most successful idea was the final CPC event for the season, which was a large-scale promotional effort with the Colorado Rockies. The Passholder Appreciation Day included a picnic that was a huge success, with more than 600 people attending. The event also included several in-game ski promotions and stadium graphics. As Jennifer Wolfe, Vail Resorts' marketing manger, explained, "We gave away 300 pairs of tickets to the Rockies vs. Braves game to new 2007–2008 passholders and then offered half-price tickets to the rest of the passholders. The 300 pairs of tickets were gone in 3 minutes and created some server problems because of the load. We had over 1,200 passholders attend the game, which made for a prominent showing as they waved their CPC rally towels in the stands."

Read about what research shows is a good Super Bowl commercial in the Matter of Principle box.

Ambush marketing is the term given to promotional stunts used at events, such as the Olympics and the soccer and rugby World Cups, by companies that are not official sponsors. Ambush marketing typically occurs when "one big brand is trying to dilute the presence of a rival that is sponsoring an event, thus diminishing the return on the official sponsor's investment."[22] In 2006, Dutch fans were forced to take off the orange lederhosen given to them by Dutch brewery Bavaria to wear at the Argentina World Cup match. American firm Anheuser-Busch, maker of Budweiser beer, was one of 15 companies that was an official sponsor of the World Cup; Bavaria was not. FIFA, organizer of the event, said ambush marketing was not permitted. The idea of fans removing their pants in itself was potentially amusing, and the ambush tactic detracted from the official sponsor Anheuser-Busch.[23]

Other Promotional Support Advertisers use blimps, balloons, and inflatables—even skywriting planes—to capture attention and create an aura of excitement at events. Everybody has probably heard of the Goodyear blimp, but other companies sponsor dirigibles as well. MetLife, which uses characters from the popular Peanuts comic strip in its advertising, has two blimps, Snoopy I and Snoopy II, that connect with the corporate campaign to provide brand reminder messages. Inflatables, giant models of products, characters, and packages are used at all kinds of events, including grand openings, sporting events, parades, trade shows, beaches, malls, and other places where they can make an impression for a new product rollout. A giant inflatable, such as Spider-Man on a building, demands attention and provides an entertaining and highly memorable product presentation. Its effectiveness comes from its huge size and three-dimensional shape.

A MATTER OF PRINCIPLE

The Ad Bowl MVP—The Product

By Bonnie Drewniany, *Associate Professor, University of South Carolina*

Super Bowl Sunday is the one day of the year when consumers welcome advertisers into their homes. The reason? The commercials promise to be as entertaining as the game. Although there are numerous measures of an ad's success, the *USA Today* Super Bowl Ad Meter has caught the attention of advertisers because, like the big game, it reaches the masses. In their quest to land on top of the Ad Meter, advertisers go to extremes to entertain viewers. Considering the cost of a Super Bowl commercial—$2.6 million to air a 30-second spot in 2007—the stakes are high. It's no wonder why advertisers hope to find the magic formula to come out on top.

A tongue-in-cheek ad for FedEx features the top 10 items needed to win the Super Bowl ratings game. In the 2005 Super Bowl commercial, Burt Reynolds (1. Celebrity) meets a bear (2. Animal) and the two start to dance (3. Dancing animal). A cute boy (4. Cute kid) exclaims, "That bear can dance!" and the bear accidentally kicks Reynolds in the crotch (5. Groin kick). The bear apologizes (6. Talking animal), and two gorgeous cheerleaders (7. Attractive females) say in unison, "Hey, that bear can talk!" Reynolds gives a quick message about FedEx (8. Product message. Optional) and the commercial closes with a riff from a popular song (9. Pop song) and a quip from the bear (10. Bonus ending).

Did FedEx crack the code? Hardly. The commercial came in 16th place in the 2005 *USA Today* Ad Meter. Although previous winners of the Ad Meter did feature celebrities, dancing animals, cute kids, and so on, these weren't the reasons for their success. In fact, many of the lowest rated ads have used the very same tactics.

What is the secret to coming out at top? To get the answer, I reviewed every top-rated commercial since the *USA Today* Ad Meter began in 1989. To my surprise, I found only one consistent element. Every number one commercial put the brand front and center. Whether it's Budweiser's 2007 King Crab commercial, in which fiddler crabs worship a Budweiser ice chest that looks like a giant crab, or Pepsi's 1997 commercial, where bears line dance to "P-E-P-S-I" (set to the tune of "Y-M-C-A"), or McDonald's 1993 commercial, in which Larry Bird plays one-on-one against Michael Jordan to win a Big Mac, or the 1989 commercial in which Dana Carvey and Jon Lovitz, then of *Saturday Night Live*, go to the Super Bowl and learn that American Express card is welcomed while the "other" card isn't, every top-rated commercial incorporated the brand from the beginning to the end.

I went into this exercise thinking that many of the winning commercials would entertain me but leave me wondering what brand was being advertised. To my delight, this didn't happen. It's refreshing to know that product message isn't optional. Maybe $2.6 million is a bargain after all.

Interactive and Internet Promotions

Frontier Airlines' Favorite Animal Contest used the Internet effectively to increase Web traffic with the goal of increasing the online purchase of flights. Advertisers can use the Internet for sales promotion programs in a number of ways, including sampling, sweepstakes and contests, price deals, and coupons. Internet promotion is one of the hot areas of sales promotions. Brand marketers indicated that Internet/digital marketing was one of their highest spending priorities (31.8 percent) in 2005 in the sales promotion industry.[24] Many advertising campaigns include a campaign-dedicated Web site, such as the "microsite" designed as a tie-in. New Holland Tractors created a microsite to demonstrate the advantages of New Holland over John Deere. That Effie award-winning effort is described in the opening case for Chapter 19.

Sampling has been a mainstay of interactive promotions on the Internet. Some companies sample their products on their Web page. Recently, Dove® enticed customers with free samples of its new Dove® Body Nourishers and Dove® Ultimate Clear deodorant; however, most farm out the efforts to online companies that specialize in handling sample offers and fulfillment. Some of these online sampling companies are: freesampleclub.com, startsampling.com, freesamples.com, and sampleville.com. In addition, freebie portals such as amazingfreebies.com, nojunkfree.com, and the freesite.com have endless offers for

To help promote the opening of the movie Spider-Man, *inflatables like this one were placed along buildings in major cities throughout the world.*

gratis goodies. Sampling over the Internet is not cheap for companies. Although traditional store sampling costs 17 cents per sample and event sampling runs about 25 cents per sample, online sampling costs 75 to 90 cents.[25] The reason for the high cost is the money it takes to set up and run the Web site and to ship samples.

Sweepstakes and contests are effective promotional tools for driving people to marketers' Internet sites. America Online has conducted numerous promotions to drive users to its advertisers' sites. One recent promotion gave visitors a chance to win a $1 million drawing and one of the dozens of daily prizes, including merchandise emblazoned with the online service's logo. The results from Internet sweepstakes can be huge. Steven Krein, president and chief executive of Webstakes, an online sweepstakes company, says, "Sweepstakes, combined with the Internet's direct marketing tools, equals sweepstakes on steroids. You're not just filling in information on a card. There's so much more interaction, that's why the results can be astronomical."[26]

Some sites offer price promotions only to online purchasers. The promotions might be discounted prices, rebates, or free offers such as frequent flier miles. *Promo* magazine has found that consumers are more receptive to rebates online than offline.[27] Incentive programs offered by online marketers FreeRide Media (http://www.freeride.com), Intellipost (http://www.bonusmail.com), MotivationNet (http://www.mypoints.com), and Netcentives (http://www.clickrewards.com) offer discounts to customers who enroll with them before buying from other merchants.

Coupons can be delivered via the Internet. Several sites have been designed for this. Catalina's ValuPage Web site (http://www.valupage.com) allows users to print coupons they can use at 7,000 supermarkets. The coupon is printed with a barcode and is used with the shopper's store card. If Corn Crunchies were to offer coupons this way, the site could link the shopper's Internet information with store card information, which the Corn Crunchies brand manager could use in determining the effectiveness of the coupon strategy.

Loyalty Programs

Another type of program that crosses the line between advertising and promotion is frequency, or loyalty, programs. A **loyalty program**, also called a **continuity** or **frequency** program (such as airline frequent flyer programs), is a promotion to increase customer retention. Marketers typically design loyalty programs to keep and reward customers for their continued patronage, which is why they are called *continuity programs*. Typically, the higher the purchase level, the greater the benefits.

Today loyalty programs are synonymous with the word *frequent*. The frequent flyer club, first created by United and American Airlines in 1981, is the model for a modern continuity program. These programs offer a variety of rewards, including seat upgrades, free tickets, and premiums based on the number of frequent flyer miles accumulated. Although the frequent flyer programs were originally established to create customer loyalty, they have turned into a rewards program. For example, people can earn miles through credit card purchases.[28] Continuity programs work in competitive markets in which the consumer has difficulty perceiving real differences between brands. TGI Friday's, for example, has used a "Frequent Fridays" program with several million members. The key to creating a successful loyalty program is offering memorable incentives that consumers want.

Marketers like membership programs because they also generate information for customer databases. The enrollment application at TGI Friday's, for example, captures name, address, telephone number, birth date, and average visit frequency. The database can also record the restaurant locations, date, time, purchase amount, and items ordered on each visit. Marketers can then use this information to more specifically target customers with promotions and advertising materials.

Partnership Programs

Another promotion tool that crosses the lines is the partnership program. **Comarketing** involves manufacturers developing marketing communication programs with their main retail accounts, instead of for them. If done right, these partnerships strengthen relationships between manufacturers and retailers. Comarketing programs are usually based on the lifestyles and purchasing habits of consumers who live in the area of a particular retailer. The partnership means that the advertising and sales promotions build equity for both the manufacturer and the retailer. For example, Procter & Gamble and Wal-Mart might develop a spring cleaning promotion directed at Wal-Mart shoppers that features P&G cleaning products sold at reduced prices or with premium incentives.

Cobranding   When two companies come together to offer a product, the effort is called **co-branding**. An example of co-branding is when American Airlines puts its logo on a Citibank Visa card and awards AAdvantage points to Citibank Visa card users. Both companies are equally present in the product's design and promotion, and both get to build on the other company's brand equity.

The PGA licenses the use of its logo to other advertisers who want to associate themselves with the PGA Tour event and pros.

Licensing   With **licensing**, legally protected brand identity items, such as logos, symbols, and brand characters, must be licensed—that is, a legal contract gives another company the right to use the brand identity element. In brand licensing, a company with an established brand "rents" that brand to other companies, allowing them to use its logo on their products and in their advertising and promotional events. Fashion marketers such as Gucci, Yves St. Laurent, and Pierre Cardin have licensed their brand names and logos for use on everything from fashion accessories to sunglasses, ties, linens, and luggage, and they do this because it makes them money and extends their brand visibility. The PGA Tour is a golf brand that has become recognizable through an elaborate, integrated marketing campaign. Charles Schwab, the financial investment house, has used the PGA Tour logo as a part of its advertising. This lets the company associate its brand with a golf event that has a lot of interest and positive associations for the target audiences.

Tie-Ins   Another type of cooperative marketing program is a **tie-in**, which is an effective strategy for marketers using associations between complementary brands to make one plus one equal three. For example, Doritos may develop a tie-in promotion with Pace salsa in which bottles of salsa are displayed next to the Doritos section in the chip aisle (and vice versa). The intent is to spur impulse sales. Ads are also designed to tie the two products together, and the sponsoring companies share the cost of the advertising.

The biggest tie-in deals are arranged around movies and other entertainment events. The movie *Spider-Man 3* was accompanied by a Burger King marketing program that let customers play a scratch-and-win game.[29] McDonald's Corp. and Dreamworks Animation teamed to offer a global effort that tied to the opening of *Shrek the Third*. This multimedia promotion, offered in eight languages, includes Shrek-related Happy Meals, collectible glasses, and a Web site for kids.[30]

Some products tie in with worthy causes. A number of companies support breast cancer awareness and research, including KitchenAid, Yoplait, and Sun Chips. In 2005 pink products totaled $35 million of the Komen Foundation's $200 million in revenue for breast cancer education and research.[31] In the long run, sponsors and their charities mutually benefit.

Tie-ins succeed because brands can leverage similar strengths to achieve a bigger impact in the marketplace. Typically, marketers align themselves with partners that provide numerous complementary elements, including common target audiences, purchase cycle patterns, distribution channels, retailer penetration, and demographics to drive their products and promotions through retail channels and into the minds of consumers.

PROMOTION STRATEGY

As we explained in Chapter 2, promotions are just one element of the marketing communication mix available to marketers. Here we discuss the strategy behind the use of promotions, as well as how advertising and promotions complement each other, particularly in building brands.

Promotion Objectives

Our earlier discussion of the use of promotion identified a number of reasons for using promotions, and these can easily be translated into objectives. Many of the reasons focused on the use of promotions in a new product launch and how that can deliver trial. Promotions can offer consumers an immediate inducement to try or buy a product, often simply by making the product more valuable. Sales promotion can make consumers who know nothing about the brand develop awareness and trial and persuade them to buy again once they've tried it. It can push the product through the distribution channel by generating positive brand experiences among resellers and buyers in many places along the channel and purchase continuum.

In addition to helping to introduce a new product and create brand awareness, promotions can build a brand over time by reinforcing advertising images and messages. Promotions can create an affinity between brands and buyers and provide new channels for reaching audience segments. They can create brand involvement and positive experiences that people associate with the brands.

Promotions are not effective in achieving all marketing objectives. For example, promotions alone cannot create an image for a brand. They cannot do much to change negative attitudes toward a product, overcome product problems, or reposition a brand. Brand building, however, is an interesting challenge to promotion, so let's look at it in more depth.

The Issue of Brand Building

For years a heated debate has focused on sales promotion and brand building. Advertisers claim the strength of advertising is creating and maintaining brand image, and sales promotion's price deals actually negate all their hard work by diverting the emphasis from the brand to the price. The result, sales promotion critics complain, is a brand-insensitive consumer. Consider McDonald's, which has long based its image on everyday value, one of the four pillars of McDonald's marketing mantra: Quality, Service, Cleanliness, and Value (QSC&V).

This coupon encourages customers to increase their consumption of the brand. It rewards regular customers at the same time it builds brand relationships and increases their purchase of the line of products.

Advertisers contend that price promotions like a 99-cent Big Mac damage more than the company's bottom line because the price promotion undercuts the value pillar. In other words, if value is central to McDonald's pricing, then it wouldn't need to offer special sale prices.[32]

Procter & Gamble's division manager of advertising and sales promotion explains it this way: "Too many marketers no longer adhere to the fundamental premise of brand building, which is that [brand] franchises aren't built by cutting price but rather by offering superior quality at a reasonable price and clearly communicating that value to consumers. The price-cutting patterns begun in the early 1970s continue today, fostering a short-term orientation that has caused long-term brand building to suffer."[33] Critics point to a general decline in consumer brand loyalty as just one negative result of price-based promotions.

The problem is that brand building is a long and time-consuming process of establishing the brand's core values. Promotion, whether a sale price, premium, coupon, or some other incentive, is inherently short term, so the promotion can undermine the brand's established values if not handled carefully. Critics of General Motors, for example, claim that the auto giant undermines its brand value when it offers substantial incentives to buy vehicles.[34] The fear is that discounts may send a message that the vehicles Detroit builds are not worth buying unless they are on sale.[35]

Sales promotion experts argue that their practices can help to build brand image. They refer to many cereal brands, rental car companies, airlines, and hotels that have used a variety of well-planned sales promotion strategies (like loyalty programs, for example) to enhance their brand images. Second, they acknowledge that continuous promotion—particularly continuous price promotion—does not work well with brand building, except for discount marketers, whose image is built on the notion of sale prices, although even Wal-Mart is rethinking its "always low prices" positioning strategy.

According to one industry expert, the solution to the debate is to make advertising more accountable and promotion more brand-focused. He explained, "In isolation, neither traditional advertising nor promotion can deliver the level of long-term image and profitable volume-building that's now required."[36] In other words, the advertising and promotion need to work more closely together and, in particular, short-term campaigns shouldn't be at odds with one another. More integration is needed in the planning of marketing communication programs.

Promotion Integration

Advertising and promotion both contribute to the effectiveness of a marketing communication plan, primarily because they do different things and have different objectives. In an effective plan, the two work together, along with other marketing communication tools, to accomplish the overall marketing communication objectives.

The major differences between advertising and sales promotion concern their methods of appeal and the value they add to the sale of the product or service. Advertising is primarily used to create a brand image and high levels of brand awareness over time; promotions are primarily used to create immediate action. To accomplish this immediate goal, sales promotion may rely heavily on rational appeals, such as price deals. In contrast, advertising often relies on emotional appeals to promote the product's image. In other words, advertising tends to add intangible value—brand personality and image—to the good or service. Promotions add tangible value to the good or service and contribute greatly to the profitability of the brand.   Here is a summary of the differences between these two marketing tools in terms of their primary orientations:

Advertising	Sales Promotion
• Creates a brand image over time	• Creates immediate action
• Relies on emotional appeals	• Added value strategies rely on rational appeals; impulse appeals use emotion
• Adds intangible value to product or service through image	• Adds tangible value to product or service
• Contributes moderately to short-term profitability	• Contributes greatly to short-term profitability

Some objectives advertising and promotion share include increasing the number of customers and increasing the use of the product by current customers. Both objectives attempt to change audience perceptions about the product or service, and both attempt to make people do something. Of course, advertisers accomplish these tasks in different ways. In most cases, advertising is needed to support promotions. Price deals, for example, are advertised as a way to build traffic in a store. Contests, sweepstakes, and special events won't work if no one knows about them.

In terms of the integration of promotion with other marketing communication activities, a *Promo* magazine survey indicated that more than two-thirds (69 percent) of the agency executives said their clients ask for greater integration of their marketing communications. Only 16 percent say clients weren't looking for higher levels of integration.[37] In other words, most of them were planning promotion as part of an integrated marketing communication program.

Promotion Effectiveness

Since promotions are so focused on action, it makes sense that sales volume is the primary measure of their effectiveness. After all, they are called *sales promotions*. Response rate—consumers calling the company, sending back a card—is also important to sales promotion. So are redemption rates, which are the rates at which people redeem coupons, refunds, and rebates, which are used to evaluate the effectiveness of these promotional programs. All of these will be discussed in more detail in Chapter 19.

An important dimension of sales promotion effectiveness is **payout planning**. The goal of creating a payout plan is to produce promotions that increases sales and profits. Needless to say, a promotion should not cost the company money in the long run.

An example of poor payout planning comes from Maytag and an ill-fated U.K. promotion. It was a simple offer: Customers in Great Britain and Ireland were offered two free airline tickets to the United States or Continental Europe when they purchased at least $150 worth of Hoover products. Hoover planned to use the commissions it made from land arrangements, such as hotel reservations and car rentals, to help pay for the airline tickets. How did the promotion turn into a catastrophe? Unfortunately, the commissions were less than anticipated, and the ticket demand was far greater. Maytag's travel agents began attaching unreasonable demands to the free tickets, expensive extras, inconvenient airports, and undesirable departure dates to discourage acceptance of the offer. All these strategies turned happy winners into complaining customers. In the aftermath, Hoover fired three top executives and set up a $30 million fund to pay for the airline tickets.

The trade press is full of stories about poorly designed or performing promotions. Such failures hurt companies' reputations, waste money, and sometimes even hurt consumers. For example, in 2001, Burger King had to recall 400,000 toy boats given away with kids' meals after reports that children had been stuck with metal pins that came off the boats too easily. That recall came a week after McDonald's recalled a Happy Meal "Scooter Bug" toy. In 1999 the fast-food industry reeled from the deaths of two infants who suffocated from containers used in a Pokémon promotion. About 25 million of those toys were recalled. As you've read in this chapter, promotions can successfully deliver sales to a company, but they must be well planned and executed if they are to enhance the brand's reputation.

IT'S A WRAP

Consumers Vote Frontier the Winner

Like the Flip to Mexico campaign (described in the opening case in Chapter 12), the Favorite Animal Contest proved to be a winner. Fans engaged in the democratic process in the mock election, posting more than 4,000 entries on the Forum and logging over a million votes. Recognizing that all the candidates were male, more than 1,000 fans signed a petition to draft the only female animal, Foxy the Fox, into the race. Even The White House Project, an organization that supports women in politics, got into the act, creating its own "Draft Foxy" commercial and posting a story online urging people to vote for Foxy as Denver's favorite animal.

In case you were wondering, the Penguins were announced the winners of the Favorite Animal Contest in a 60-second commercial that ran during last half hour of the Academy Awards. Maybe they had a little bump in popularity from *Happy Feet*, a movie about penguins that won an Academy Award for Best Animated Feature Film that same night.

Frontier won big, too. Web traffic was up almost 50 percent over the same period in the previous year, and qualified e-mail addresses increased more than 400 percent. The airline even sold more than 1,200 press kits online, proving that the characters were more popular than ever.

In fewer than four years, Frontier's advertising has been recognized with more than 80 awards. Frontier was nominated for Best of Show at the International Mobius Awards for two years in a row. It was awarded a Silver Clio for the prestigious Content & Contact category and a Silver Effie as well. Denver's Favorite Animal Campaign received a nomination for a National Emmy for Outstanding Achievement in Advanced Media Technology.

Key Points Summary

1. **Which principles drive the use of sales promotion, and what are some current trends?** Sales promotion offers an "extra incentive" to take action. It gives the product or service additional value and motivates people to respond. Sales promotion is growing rapidly for many reasons. It offers the manager short-term bottom-line results; it's accountable; sales promotion is less expensive than advertising; it speaks to the current needs of the consumer to receive more value from products; and it responds to marketplace changes.

2. **How are various consumer promotions used?** Sales promotions directed at consumers include price deals, coupons, contests and sweepstakes, refunds, premiums, specialty advertising, continuity programs, and sampling. Their purpose is to pull the product through the distribution channel.

3. **What are the types and purposes of trade promotions?** Sales promotions directed at the trade

include point-of-purchase displays, retailer merchandising kits, trade shows, and price deals such as discounts, bonuses, and advertising allowances. These are used to push the product through the channel.

4. **How do other types of promotions—sponsorships and events, interactive promotions, loyalty programs, and comarketing programs—work?** Sponsorship is used to increase the perceived value of a brand by associating it with a cause or celebrity. Internet promotions can be used to drive people to a sponsor's Web page. Licensing "rents" an established brand to other companies to use on their products. Loyalty programs are designed to increase customer retention. Comarketing programs are designed to build stronger relationships between manufacturers and retailers.

5. **How are promotions used strategically in marketing in terms of brand building, new product launches, integration, and effectiveness?** Promotion offers an

incentive to action and stimulates trial, which is important in launching a new product. In brand building it can reinforce advertising images and messages and encourage or remind consumers to buy the brand again. It can be used to push or pull a product through the distribution channel by

creating positive brand experiences. Interactive promotions are more involving. Sales promotion is used with advertising to provide immediate behavioral action. It is effective when the return on the investment more than covers the cost of the promotion.

Key Terms

ambush marketing, p. 493

co-branding, p. 496

comarketing, p. 496

contests, p. 486

coupons, p. 485

event marketing, p. 491

game, p. 486

licensing, p. 496

loyalty (continuity, frequency)
  program, p. 496

payout planning, p. 499

point-of-purchase (POP)
  display, p. 489

premium, p. 486

price deal, p. 485

rebate, p. 485

refund, p. 485

sales promotion, p. 482

sampling, p. 485

self-liquidator, p. 486

specialty advertising, p. 486

sponsorship, p. 491

sweepstakes, p. 486

tie-ins, p. 496

trade deal, p. 489

trade show, p. 489

Review Questions

1. Define sales promotion and explain how it contributes to an integrated marketing program.

2. Explain the three types of sales promotion and how they differ.

3. What are the primary objectives that consumer promotions can deliver?

4. What are the key objectives of trade promotions?

5. List the primary tools of consumer and trade promotions. How can the Internet be used as a sales promotion tool?

6. How do push and pull marketing strategies relate to sales promotion to consumers? To trade audiences?

Discussion Questions

1. Tom Jackson's marketing professor is covering some promotion methods, explaining that in selecting the consumer sales promotion, planners must know the brand situation and objectives before techniques are chosen. Some techniques tend to increase product use, and others are used to get new consumers to try the product. "Which methods belong with which objective and why?" the professor asks. How should Tom answer this question?

2. Janice Wilcox is a brand manager for a new line of eye cosmetics. She is about to present her planning strategy to division management. Janice knows her company has been successful in using sales promotion plans lately, but she has strong misgivings about following the company trend. "This new line must create a consumer brand franchise, and promotion isn't the best way to do that," she thinks to

herself. How is sales promotion weak in building and maintaining a brand? Should Janice propose no promotion, or is there a reasonable compromise for her to consider?

3. *Three-Minute Debate:* You have just been named product manager for a new FDA-approved pharmaceutical, a diet pill, that helps reduce hunger. Should you use a push or pull strategy to introduce this new product? Organize into small teams with each team taking one side or the other. In class, set up a series of three-minute debates, with each side having 1½ minutes to argue its position. Every team of debaters has to present new points not covered in the previous teams' presentations until there are no arguments left to present. Then the class votes as a group on the winning point of view.

Take-Home Team Projects

1. Select a print ad for a national marketer. Redesign the ad, including the use of a consumer sales promotion. Show both the before version and the after version to five people in your group. Assess whether the second version increases their intention to buy.

2. Check the Web site for Camp Jeep® (http://www.jeep.com, then type the "campjeep" keyword). Explain how the event works to build and reinforce customer relationships. Each person in the group should find another company that uses a special event to create a relationship-building program, explain that program, and compare it to Camp Jeep®. Compare your findings with others in your group. Which do you believe is the most effective special event and why?

Yahoo! Hands-On Case

Review the Yahoo! case in the Appendix.

1. How does the new promotional Web site, "Dave's Site," help accomplish the goals of the Yahoo! campaign? What are the incentives for the Switchers and Choosers? Do you think they will be effective?

2. Analyze the promotional aspects of the Yahoo! campaign. Your boss likes this plan so much that she's asked you to create additional promotional materials for this campaign. What other types of promotions might you suggest in your plan? Why would you include these? Write a one-page report describing your plan.

HANDS-ON CASE

Upromise Uses Values Marketing to Pay for College

Most consumers are familiar with loyalty programs from airlines, hotel chains, and car-rental companies. Airlines call them frequent flyer miles; people who choose a particular airline each time they fly can accumulate them to redeem for a free flight or an upgrade. The program rewards regular travelers and encourages flyers to remain loyal to an airline for a reason besides low fares.

Many people probably believe it would be great if loyalty programs like these existed for the places where most consumers spend the bulk of their money—for example, grocery stores and gas stations. In fact, such a program does exist. Upromise, a college-savings loyalty network, was started in 2001 by Michael Bronner and George Bell. The idea is simple: When consumers shop at participating stores, a portion of the receipts is set aside for a college-savings plan in the consumer's name. There is no cost for the shopper, other than the time necessary to sign up for the program.

One obvious benefit of participation is the opportunity for people to make painless, regular contributions to their children's college savings. The National Center for Education Statistics estimates that in order to have tuition and board for a child attending a private college in 2010, parents would have needed to save $800 a month starting in 1998. At those prices, most parents want any help they can get. Of course many people do not spend enough on groceries and gas to generate even $100 a month, but Upromise allows families to pool contributions. That means grandparents and other relatives can use their grocery purchases to help as well. What if you've just graduated from college? Upromise allows recent grads to enroll in the program to pay off their student loans.

Helping people to pay a big expense is an important benefit of the Upromise program, but some see much more. "As a marketer, I am giving money and I'm expecting the customers to say 'I'm going to do more business with them because I like their values,'" says Rick Barlow, chairman-CEO of Frequency Marketing. "It's a brilliant and a powerful idea because it combines an aspirational and an altruistic goal." Bronner puts it this way, "I see the evolution from value marketing to values marketing."

There are benefits for participating Upromise sponsors as well. Companies can track participant purchases because people in the program have to use either a major credit card (such as Citibank cards) or a grocery chain card. A small brand can build customer loyalty and encourage consumers to switch by offering a larger credit than its competitors.

Upromise has proven successful. The company has signed partnerships with major brands, including Exxon-Mobil, AOL, Citibank, and Publix supermarkets. Marketing costs are low since program sponsors do the bulk of the advertising. And consumers are signing up in droves. The program currently has 7.5 million participants who can allocate all or a portion of their rebates from the popular rewards program to a 529 college savings plan or toward a federal or private student loan with Sallie Mae, which acquired Upromise in 2006.

Consider This

1. What are the risks for brands that become Upromise sponsors? What are the risks for those that don't?
2. Although the program seems like a "win-win" for consumers and marketers, some critics have pointed out that most people will not be able to save for a college education exclusively by participating in Upromise. In addition, some suggest that people are spending in an unhealthy way in order to maximize their credits. How should Upromise respond to these criticisms?
3. How does the use of a sales promotion, such as the Upromise program, benefit a brand? How would you recommend evaluating the effectiveness of the promotion?

Sources: Cara Beardi, "Been There, Done That," *Advertising Age,* July 23, 2001; Dale Buss, "Giving Credit Where It's Due," *Brandweek,* July 26, 2004; Anne Marie Chaker, "How Shopping Can Pay for College; Rewards Programs Offering Tuition Benefits Emerge as a Popular Savings Tool," *Wall Street Journal,* September 23, 2004, D2; Jane J. Kim, "Sallie Mae to Expand Financial-Aid Perks," *Wall Street Journal,* February 16, 2007, http://www.wsj.com; Kaja Whitehouse, "Shopping Rebates Promise to Ease College Tuition Costs," *Wall Street Journal,* June 12, 2002, D2.

Public Relations

IT'S A WINNER

Award:	Corporation:	Agency:	Campaign:
Silver Effie	General Electric	BBDO New York	"Ecomagination"

GE Goes Green with Ecomagination

More than a century ago, in 1890 to be exact, inventor Thomas Alva Edison founded the Edison General Electric Company, which has evolved into the corporate behemoth we now know as General Electric. He said, "I never perfected an invention that I did not think about in terms of service it might give others."

The core of Edison's statement reflects a genuine concern for users of his products. Public relations is used to generate goodwill for an organization, which is what Edison practiced instinctively, as public relations as an industry did not develop until the early 1900s.

Much has changed since Edison's time when the company focused on his innovative incandescent electric lamp and the new electric industry. GE has evolved into an enormous multinational conglomerate with 2006 revenues of $163.4 billion.

At the same time, much has stayed the same. No matter how big a corporation gets, it needs to communicate with its **publics**, those groups of people with which a company or organization interacts, to build goodwill.

Just as Edison was concerned about the people who would use his inventions, current GE Chairman Jeff Immelt said, "GE is making a new commitment to our customers around the world to define the cutting edge in cleaner power and environmental technology. We have taken a long look around, and this is what we see: diminishing domestic oil and natural gas reserves; our continued dependence on foreign sources of energy; increasingly scarce resources like water in an ever more populated world; and signs of global climate change." In short, Immelt announced a corporate strategy to go green, a departure from attitudes held by many corporations that view environmentalism as a hindrance to business.

Chapter Key Points

1. What is public relations, and what are different types of public relations programs?
2. What key decisions do public relations practitioners make when they create plans?
3. What are the most common types of public relations tools?
4. Why is measuring the results of public relations efforts important, and how should that be done?

GE's commitment to this strategy it calls Ecomagination is considerable. The corporation pledged an investment in research and development of green technologies of $1.5 billion by 2010, an increase from $750 million in 2004.

GE's efforts could have an impact on the environment. GE believes that energy savings could power more than a million homes for more than a year if every U.S. household replaced one 100-watt incandescent light bulb with a GE compact fluorescent bulb. GE's Evolution Series train locomotives harness the energy of 16 cylinders of horsepower with only 12 cylinders, using less fuel more efficiently. If all conventional coal plants in the United States used GE's coal gasification technology, carbon dioxide emissions could be cut by nearly 320 million tons.

Fundamentally, this integrated marketing campaign aims to convince customers, prospects, shareholders, employees, and the media that the green strategy makes sense for the corporation and the people it serves.

Campaign tactics include online and broadcast TV commercials, such as one that featured an elephant dancing in the rainforest, and newspaper and magazine ads. Other efforts include events, employee engagement, and an informative and entertaining microsite that explains ecomagination with interactive online games like Washer Derby and Harness the Wind and calculators that let consumers figure out energy savings and the effects of green products on the environment.

Other companies are jumping on the green marketing bandwagon, hoping those efforts also boost their sales. Wal-Mart, Toyota, and Starbucks are involved in environmental-related projects aimed at using renewable materials, reducing emissions, and improving drinking water around the world.

Is green marketing good PR? The results of GE's highly acclaimed campaign are detailed in the It's a Wrap feature at the end of this chapter.

Sources: Bob Garfield, "Spot Highlighting GE's Shift to Eco-friendly Is Quite a Catch," *Advertising Age*, March 5, 2007, 43; Theresa Howard, "Being Eco-friendly Can Pay Economically," *USA Today*, August 14, 2005, http://www.usatoday.com; John Teresko, "Technology Leader of the Year Connecting Profits and Preservation," *IndustryWeek*, December 1, 2005, http://www.industryweek.com; GE Ecomagination http://ge.ecomagination.com/site/index.html; "GE Glows Green for Ecomagination Campaign," *DM News*, July 15, 2005, http://www.dmnews.com.

Reminiscent of Edison's claim that he did not invent products without thinking about the people who used them, GE's promotional strategy reflects a concern for the environment and ultimately the stakeholders the corporation serves. This chapter considers the role of public relations in an organization and how goodwill can be used effectively in a marketing communication program. It discusses many aspects of public relations, including the types of PR programs, planning, and tools and, of course, gauging their effectiveness.

THE PRACTICE OF PUBLIC RELATIONS

Public relations is used to generate goodwill for an organization. That mission is as broad in scope as the definition suggests: "**Public relations** is the management function that establishes and maintains mutually beneficial relationships between an organization and the publics on which its success or failure depends."[1]

Public relations focuses on all the relationships an organization has with its various publics. By publics, we mean all the groups of people with which a company or organization interacts: employees, members, customers, local communities, shareholders, other institutions, and society at large. Another term for this is **stakeholders**, which refers more specifically to people who have a stake, financial or otherwise, in a company or organization. In the General Electric case, the Ecomagination campaign reaches multiple publics.

Public relations is practiced by a wide range of organizations: companies, governments, trade and professional associations, nonprofit organizations, the travel and tourism industry, educational systems, labor unions, politicians, organized sports, and the media. Most organizations have in-house public relations departments that handle the firms' public relations work, although many also hire outside public relations agencies. Although public relations has a distinguished tradition, people often mistake it for **publicity**, which refers to getting news media coverage. Publicity, however, is focused on the news media and their audiences, which is just one aspect of public relations.

On one level, public relations is a tactical function in that PR staff produce a variety of communication tools to achieve corporate image objectives. On a higher level, it is a management function that monitors public opinion and advises senior corporate managers on how to achieve positive relationships with various audiences (publics) to effectively manage the organization's image and reputation. Its publics may be external (customers, the news media, the investment community, the general public, government bodies) and internal (shareholders, employees). Sir Martin Sorrell, CEO of WPP Group, one of the largest advertising and marketing services groups in the world, believes that "public relations and public affairs are probably higher up on the CEO's agenda than advertising, market research, or other forms of specialist communication." As Sorrell notes, public relations practitioners have "access to the CEO's office," which can give them more influence on corporate policies.[2]

Public Opinion

Public relations programs are built on an understanding of public opinion on issues critical to the organization, such the company's impact on the environment and its local community or workers' rights and how a company deals with its employees. **Public opinion**, the term describing what a group of people thinks, "expresses beliefs, based not necessarily on facts but on perceptions or evaluations of events, persons, institutions, or products."[3]

The public relations strategist researches the answers to two primary questions about public opinion to design effective public relations programs. First, which publics are most important to the organization, now and in the future? Second, what do these publics think? Public opinion is sometimes confused with mass opinion. Public opinion differs from mass opinion in that public opinion examines specific subgroups rather than a more general mass audience.[4] Particular emphasis falls on understanding the role for each of the publics of **opinion leaders**, important people who influence the opinions of others.

Reputation: Goodwill, Trust, and Integrity

Public **goodwill** is the greatest asset any organization can have. A well-informed public with a positive attitude toward an organization is critical to the organization's survival—and that is why creating goodwill is the primary goal of most public relations programs. A public relations program that is tuned to creating goodwill operates as the conscience of the organization. Creating goodwill demands that both public relations professionals and the clients they represent act with integrity. Howard Rubenstein, an elder statesman in public relations, advises clients and colleagues that deliberately deceiving is "a career limiting move." He has a paperweight in his office in his 50-year-old agency to remind him that "If you tell the truth, you don't have to remember anything."[5]

To underscore the importance of acting ethically as a prerequisite for creating goodwill, public relations organizations have created codes of ethics, which encourage ethical behavior of industry members. The Public Relations Society of America's Code of Professional Standards for the Practice of Public Relations spells out core values of conduct, such as truth, accuracy, fairness, and responsibility to the public. It also includes specific provisions regarding the free flow of information, fair competition, disclosure of information, protection of confidential and private information, and avoidance of conflicts of interest.[6] Other industry organizations, such as The International Association of Business Communicators (IABC) and the Council of Public Relations Firms, offer similar codes.

It is critical that public relations professionals act ethically. It is equally important that the clients they represent act with integrity. The trust on which goodwill is based comes from corporate integrity. In these post-Enron days many companies have dedicated more resources and efforts to creating an integrity platform for the company. Some companies have even created a chief integrity officer (CIO) position or made that assignment an important part of the PR office's mission.[7] One communications expert with experience with multinational corporations and the U.S. State Department contends that corporate reputation and corporate responsibility are inseparable.[8]

A reputation for integrity involves more than image. Image is a perception based on messages delivered by advertising and other marketing communication tools. Reputation, however, is based on an organization's actual behavior. Image mirrors what a company says about itself, but reputation reflects what other people say about the company.[9]

Comparing Public Relations and Advertising

Designing ads, preparing written messages, and buying time or space are the key concerns of advertisers. Their objective is to create the consumer awareness and motivation that deliver sales. The goal of public relations specialists is communicating with various stakeholders, managing the organization's image and reputation, creating positive public attitudes, and building strong relationships between the organization and its constituents. Ultimately, the difference between advertising and public relations is that public relations takes a longer, broader view of the importance of image and reputation as a corporate competitive asset and addresses more target audiences. Public relations and advertising also differ in how they use the media, the level of control they have over message delivery, and their perceived credibility. Daniel Edelman, founder and chairman of Daniel J. Edelman, Inc., a major public relations firm, describes this as the "golden age of public relations," in part because of the many ways PR engages with its publics who are active participants in the communication process.[10] Here are some specific differences between public relations and advertising:

- *Media use.* In contrast to buying advertising time and space, public relations people seek to persuade media gatekeepers to carry stories about their company. **Gatekeepers** include writers, producers, editors, talk-show coordinators, and newscasters. This aspect of public relations is called *publicity* and carries no direct media costs. Even when public relations uses paid-for media like advertising, the message focuses on the organization, with little or no attempt to sell a brand or product line.
- *Control.* In the case of news stories, the public relations strategist is at the mercy of the media gatekeeper. There is no guarantee that all or even part of a story will appear. PR writers write the story, send it to the media, and cross their fingers that this story will appear. In fact, there is the real risk that a story may be rewritten or reorganized by an editor so that it no longer means what the strategist intended. In contrast, advertising runs exactly as the client who paid for it has approved. And it runs as scheduled.
- *Credibility.* The public tends to trust the media more than they do advertisers. This consumer tendency to confer legitimacy on information simply because it appears in the news is called the **implied third-party endorsement** factor. Thomas Harris, in his book *Value-Added Public Relations*, observes that today's sophisticated and skeptical consumers know when they are being informed and when they are being "sold to." He explains, "PR closes the marketing credibility gap because it is the one marketing communication tool devoted to providing information, not salesmanship."[11]

In a recent study researchers found that that a media placement has about the same effectiveness as advertising. Contrary to the oft-repeated assumption that editorial coverage would generate more value than equivalent advertising, they did not find that PR scored higher on most of the measures: brand recognition, message believability, overall interest, or consumer preference.[12]

Another way to build credibility is through good acts. Bill Gates' philanthropic efforts boosted public opinion of Microsoft and generated goodwill in the process. Gates is seen as genuinely caring, and he adds credibility to his corporation.[13]

Principle
Public relations is the conscience of the company, with the objective of creating trust and maintaining the organization's integrity.

Types of Public Relations Programs

The word *relations* in *public relations* refers to relationships with various stakeholders. In fact, the main subspecialties in the field—public affairs, media relations, employee relations, and financial relations—call attention to important relationships with such groups as the general public, media, employees, and financial community. Figure 17.1 outlines the various publics, or stakeholders, for a multinational company. The term **relationship marketing** introduces a point of view in marketing planning that resembles that of public relations.[14]

The key publics addressed by relationship programs in public relations are the media, employees, shareholders and others in the financial community, government, and general public.

- *Media relations.* The area that focuses on developing media contacts—knowing who in the media might be interested in the organization's story—is called **media relations**. When you say *public relations*, most people immediately think about publicity, which indicates the importance of this media function. The organization initiates publicity and provides pertinent information to the media. A successful relationship between a public relations person and editors and producers is built on a PR person's reputation for honesty, accuracy, and professionalism. Once this reputation is tarnished or lost, the public relations person cannot function effectively as a liaison between a company and the media.
- *Employee relations.* Programs that communicate information to employees are called **employee relations**. This function may belong to public relations, although it may also be the responsibility of human resources. A related program is called **internal marketing**, which are communication efforts aimed at informing employees about marketing programs and encouraging their support.

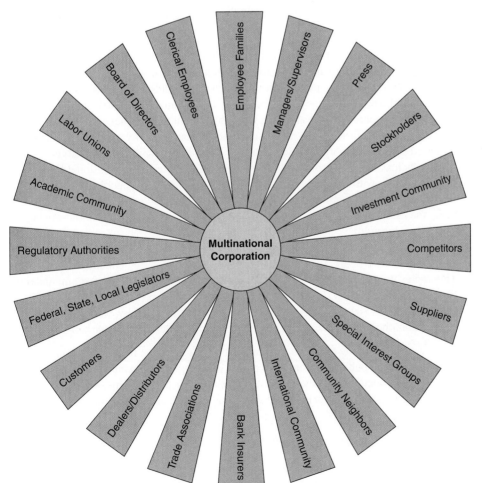

FIGURE 17.1

Twenty Key Publics
Of the twenty key publics of a typical multinational corporation, relationship management programs focus on the media, employees, the financial community, government, and the general public.

Source: Fraser P. Seitel, *The Practice of Public Relations,* 10th ed. (Upper Saddle River, NJ: Prentice Hall, 2007): 9.

TEST YOURSELF: WOULD I LIKE TO WORK IN PUBLIC RELATIONS OR PUBLIC AFFAIRS?

Here's a short list of required skills for public relations managers or public affairs specialists:

1. Knowledge of how public relations and public affairs support business goals
2. A knack for discerning which opponents to take seriously
3. The ability to integrate all communications functions
4. An understanding of how to control key messages
5. The ability to have influence without being too partisan
6. A talent for synthesizing, filtering, and validating information
7. An aptitude for information technology
8. A global perspective

Source: Doug Pinkham, "What It Takes to Work in Public Affairs and Public Relations," *Public Relations Quarterly,* Spring 2004, 15.

- *Financial relations.* All the communication efforts aimed at the financial community, such as press releases sent to business publications, meetings with investors and analysts, and the annual report, which the federal government requires of publicly held companies, are referred to as **financial relations**.
- *Public affairs.* Corporate communication programs with government and with the public on issues related to government and regulation are called **public affairs**. For example, a company building a new plant may need to gain the approval of government health and public safety regulators. Public affairs also includes **lobbying**, when the company provides information to legislators to get their support and vote on a particular bill. It also includes communication efforts with consumer or activist groups who seek to influence government policies. **Issue management** is another term for this function. In addition to government relations, public affairs programs also monitor public opinion about issues central to the organization's interest and develop programs to communicate to and with the public about these issues.
- *Fund-raising.* **Fund-raising** is the practice of raising money by collecting donations. It is used by nonprofit organizations, such as museums, hospitals, and emergency groups such as the Red Cross and directed to potential donors. Professional fund-raisers know how to make the initial contacts that inspire other people to participate, how to use other marketing communication tools such as advertising, and how to make the best use of special events and public recognition. Sometimes fund-raising is called **development**.
- *Cause marketing.* When companies associate themselves with a good cause by providing assistance and financial support, the practice is called **cause marketing**. This topic, along with the related areas of nonprofit marketing, public communication campaigns, social marketing, and mission marketing, will be discussed in more detail in Chapter 18. Whirlpool's association with Habitat for Humanity, which was described in the opening case of Chapter 3, is an example of cause marketing.

Other areas of public relations, such as corporate reputation management, crisis management, marketing public relations, and public communication campaigns are distinctive because of their focus rather than their target audience. See The Inside Story by Mark Thomson for an example of an unusual career that relates to public relations.

Corporate Reputation Management   The area that focuses on an organization's image and reputation is called **corporate relations**. The overriding goal of **reputation management** in a corporate relations program is to strengthen the trust that stakeholders have in an organization. Public relations expert Fraser Seitel offers advice about the importance of managing corporate image in *The Practice of Public Relations:*

THE INSIDE STORY

A Career in Business Theater

By Mark Thomson, *President of Thomson Productions, Inc., Des Moines, Iowa*

One of the most remarkable aspects of a career in advertising is that it can lead to something completely unexpected. Here's my story of how I ended up in *business theater.*

Classes, club activities, the American Advertising Federation (AAF) student competition, independent study—along the way with these projects and campus activities, a door opened to a career in advertising and I began to discover what I loved to do.

I had always enjoyed producing slide shows, so one of my projects in an independent study was to do a multi-image sales presentation (multiple slide projectors synced to a sound track) for a corporation's exhibit at a robotics trade show in Chicago. I arrived in Chicago with a truck full of slide projectors and "scenic" set pieces, only to find out that my set was too big for the exhibit space. I had to saw the set in half to fit the space. You can't beat real-world education, as painful as it may be!

After school I did other things—my first job was as a sales trainee, then an account coordinator at an advertising agency. But I got a yearning to produce slide shows again. Joining a small agency, I was allowed to start a "nontraditional" agency service of wide-screen, multi-image, multimedia shows. I discovered there was a market for what I really loved to do.

The slide shows led to bigger productions, and I struck out on my own. Today the Thomson Productions firm produces *business theater* for Fortune 500 companies and national associations all over the world.

The term *business theater* loosely means using live, Broadway-style productions to unveil new corporate products, motivate and recognize salespeople at national meetings, or kick off big conventions with spectacular "opening ceremonies."

My company hires choreographers, dancers, singers, orchestras, celebrities, and motivational speakers. Depending on the client's objectives, the productions can also include a variety of media such as video, computer graphics, lasers, pyrotechnics, megaprojections (walls, sides of buildings), illusions, lighting, interactive technologies, and all kinds of unique staging and special effects.

If I knew back in college what I know now, it would be this: Follow your dream. Find out what you really love to do and start doing it. If you follow your dream, everything else usually falls into place.

A graduate of the University of West Florida, Mark Thomson was nominated by Professor Tom Groth.

Most organizations today understand that corporate image is a fragile commodity, and to improve that image they must operate with the 'implicit trust' of the public. That means that for a corporation in the 21st century, winning favorable public opinion isn't an option—it's a necessity, essential for continued long-term success.[15]

Since corporate reputation is a perception, it is earned through deeds, not created by advertising. Starbucks and Wal-Mart offer examples of corporations working hard to create positive perceptions.

Starbucks is battling misperceptions from being known as a corporate giant with a media- and consumer-focused PR initiative called "Voices behind the Bean." The program shows that people at every level of the supply chain make Starbucks what it is. The program took journalists to Costa Rica to visit farmers and exporters. The story is also being shown to the consumer audience as well.[16]

Wal-Mart, one of the world's biggest companies with more than $300 billion in annual sales, also faces the challenge of maintaining a positive image. Edelman, a public relations firm, is working to promote Wal-Mart as a positive social force. One such effort: Wal-Mart donated $15 million to Hurricane Katrina relief funds. Other efforts include orchestrating a 49-state rollout with dignitaries and publicity events to announce Wal-Mart's plan to sell an array of generic drugs at $4 per prescription. It also organized a grassroots group called Working Families for Wal-Mart that allowed the retailer's defenders to strike back at critics.[17] Reputation management is critically important to companies that want to earn goodwill from their constituencies.

Crisis Management   There is no greater test for an organization than how it deals with a crisis. The key to **crisis management** is to anticipate the possibility of a disaster and plan

Principle
Reputation is earned based on what you do, not what you say about yourself.

how to deal with the bad news and all the affected publics. The massacre of students at Virginia Tech University, poisoned dog food, and spinach that makes people sick are all examples of crises that public relations professionals would handle.

Jack Welch, former chairman and CEO of General Electric, wrote about crisis management—or lack thereof—before and after Hurricane Katrina. Although the United States had never before experienced this magnitude of death and destruction from a hurricane, Welch points out that this catastrophe is a case study of the five stages people experience during severe crises in companies large and small all over the world. The stages are: denial, containment, shame-mongering, blood on the floor, and fixing the crisis.

Although New Orleans is not a company, it is an organization, and Welch contends that the model applies to this natural disaster's impact on the city. In the denial stage people tend to think the problem is not that bad ("The storm is an over-hyped Weather Channel event"). The containment stage suggests that leaders try to make the problem disappear by giving it to someone else to solve (the city, state, and federal government passed the buck about who should provide the help). Parties with a stake in the problem defend themselves, assigning blame and claiming credit in the third stage, shame-mongering (Democrats took the crisis to a political level, claiming that this was a test of presidential leadership and a reflection of race and poverty in America; Republicans were slow to respond to the criticisms). In just about every crisis, Welch says, a high-profile person pays with his or her job, sometimes taking others down as a result (FEMA Director Michael Brown lost his job). The fifth and final stage entails resolving the crisis in some way as life goes on (as the water recedes, Superdome is repaired, and people return home, at least some of them).[18]

An effective crisis plan can help to both avoid crises and ease the damage if one occurs. A plan outlines who contacts the various stakeholders who might be affected (employees, customers, suppliers, civic and community leaders, government agencies), who speaks to the news media, and who sets up and runs an on-site disaster-management center. Companies also should conduct unannounced crisis training during which staff must drop everything and deal with a simulated crisis as it unfolds. One example of crisis preparation is KFC's contingency plan to educate consumers and reassure them that it's safe to eat chicken should fears of a bird flu pandemic rise.[19]

Marketing Public Relations One area where advertising and public relations overlap is **marketing public relations** (MPR). Tom Harris, author of *The Marketer's Guide to Public Relations*, says MPR is the fastest-growing area of public relations. He defines MPR as the process of planning and delivering programs that encourage sales and contribute to customer satisfaction by providing communication that addresses the needs and wants of consumers.

MPR is different from a more general public relations approach in its consumer and sales focus. However, the need to establish a credibility platform is similar in both; that's what PR brings to marketing and is PR's greatest strength in an integrated marketing communication program. In other words, MPR supports marketing's product and sales focus by increasing brand credibility and the company's credibility with consumers.

Public Communication Campaigns Used as a way to change public opinion, **public communication campaigns** also discourage socially harmful behaviors, such as driving in areas with high levels of air-pollution. Sometimes they are engaged in counter marketing as they try to argue against other advertising messages. For example, the Florida *truth*® campaign by the Porter Novelli agency was designed to counter big tobacco companies' advertising that appeals to teenagers. The strategy was to get young people to rebel against the tobacco industry. An extension of that campaign by Crispin Porter + Bogusky featured teens in one award-winning commercial piling body bags outside Phillip Morris's New York headquarters (see Chapter 1). The campaign produced the largest single-year decline in teen smoking in nearly 20 years.

Other work in the area of public communication is offered by Professor Edward Maibach of George Washington University and his coauthors Lorien Abroms and Mark Marosits. Their academic work recognizes the importance of communication and marketing as tools to promote public health. They propose a theoretical framework that identifies the attributes of people (as individuals, as social networks, and as communities or populations) and places (or environments) that influence people's health behaviors and health. They show

A MATTER OF PRINCIPLE

Should Advertising Play a Role in the War on Terror?

By Alice Kendrick, *Professor, Southern Methodist University, and*
Jami Fullerton, *Associate Professor, Oklahoma State University*

In late 2002, after the 9/11 attacks and at a time when polls showed that America's image was declining abroad, the U.S. State Department launched its first integrated marketing campaign targeted to the Muslim world.

The controversial "Shared Values Initiative" featured five 2-minute testimonial "mini-documentaries" about American Muslims living comfortable and prosperous lives in the United States. There were also newspaper advertisements, a Web site, a radio version of the television spots, and a four-color magazine called *Muslim Life in America*.

The campaign, which was designed to run for five weeks during the season of Ramadan, was created by former advertising executive Charlotte Beers. Secretary of State Colin Powell called Beers out of retirement to leverage America's marketing and communication expertise in the name of improving the country's image around the world.

Beers had been the mastermind of many successful campaigns for corporate clients such as Sears, Jaguar, and Mars. Together with agency McCann-Erickson, Beers began by analyzing data from around the world about the relative importance of cultural values. The Roper organization survey data showed that while the U.S. people and Muslims in various countries assigned different levels of importance to such values as individuality and modesty, they were in agreement about the importance of faith, family, and learning. Thus, the Shared Values strategy was developed, with an initial focus on how Muslims in America could freely live and practice their faith.

The television spots ran in Kuwait, Malaysia, Pakistan, and Indonesia and on the Pan-Arab satellite, which resulted in additional exposure among people in several other countries. State Department documents indicated that up to 288 million people were exposed to the messages; in Indonesia, where McCann Erickson commissioned a post-campaign survey, recall of the television commercials and their main message was quite high, reaching levels up to 67 percent.

Because not all of the Middle East and Asian countries targeted by the media plan agreed to run the pro-American commercials, many journalists and politicians labeled the campaign a failure. The campaign also was criticized because many believed that advertising was not an appropriate way for the U.S. government to conduct public diplomacy. Newspapers wrote about the campaign, "You can't sell Uncle Sam like you sell Uncle Ben's (rice)."

Those interested in seeing this first-of-a-kind campaign and reading more about how similar public diplomacy advertising efforts might be used—and evaluated—in the future can find more information at http://www.svibook.com.

Alice Kendrick and Jami Fullerton coauthored *Advertising's War on Terrorism: The Story of the U.S. State Department's Shared Values Initiative* (Marquette Books, 2006).

how communication can be used both to help people make healthy lifestyle choices *and* to create environments, such as schools, workplaces, and neighborhoods, in which it's easy to make good on those choices. For example, communication campaigns such as the *truth*® campaign can be used in efforts to convince teens not to smoke. They can also be used to convince state officials to ban smoking in public venues and to increase the tobacco tax, both of which are known to decrease rates of smoking. Public health agencies are increasingly realizing that developing effective communication and marketing skills is essential for those who want to help people make healthy decisions and create health-promoting environments.[20]

You can read about another public communication campaign, an attempt to change public opinion about the War in Iraq, in the Matter of Principle box.

PUBLIC RELATIONS PLANNING

Planning for a public relations campaign is similar to planning an advertising campaign. The plan should complement the marketing and advertising strategies so the organization communicates with one clear voice to its various publics. The plan also identifies the various key publics and the public relations activities that PR people use to address the interests of its various publics. In addition to identifying key targets, public relations plans also specify the objectives that give direction to the PR program or campaign. Assessing the effectiveness of the campaign in achieving its objectives is important, just as it is for advertising campaigns.

Research and SWOT Analysis

Research is used by an organization, as well as outside PR agencies, throughout the planning and implementation of a PR plan. It's also used afterward to determine if the effort was successful and if the organization is spending its money wisely on the public relations efforts.

The PR effort may also begin with a more formal type of background research, called a **communication audit**, to assess the internal and external PR environment that affects the organization's audiences, objectives, competitors, and past results. An annual audit or a campaign-specific audit can be used to ensure that a program is on track and performing as intended. Often **benchmarking** is used to identify baselines from previous audits or audits of other related companies and industries so there is a point of comparison.[21] A **gap analysis**, which measures the differences in perceptions and attitudes between groups or between the organization and its publics, may be part of the analysis.[22]

Practitioners categorize publics so they can develop effective public relations plans to address issues. They consider **latent publics** as those who are unaware of their connection to an organization regarding some particular problem. **Aware publics** are those who recognize the connections between the problem and themselves and others but who do not communicate about it. **Active publics** are those who communicate and organize to do something about the issue or situation.[23] For the Ecomagination campaign, General Electric wants to reach aware publics and let them know about GE's green marketing. It also wants to transform latent and aware publics into active publics who will help solve environmental problems by using GE's products.

Since public opinion is so central to public relations programs, companies often use ongoing research to monitor opinions and attitudes. The Porter Novelli agency annually tracks American institutions' credibility and consumers' concerns about such topics as health, nutrition, and their lifestyles. The agency suggests that such information is useful in identifying people's orientation to health messages. It's also helpful in targeting various types of publics based on their general attitudes toward key issues, such as antismoking. The survey has consistently found that the credibility of institutions such as government, the media, and corporations is declining.

As in marketing or advertising planning, a PR plan begins with background research leading to a situation analysis, or SWOT analysis, that evaluates a company's strengths, weaknesses, opportunities, and threats. This analysis reflects a general understanding of the difficulty of changing people's attitudes about issues such as corporations and their role in protecting the environment. Understanding the nature of the problem makes it easier to determine the appropriate communication objectives and the target stakeholder audiences, or publics, who will be addressed by the PR efforts. In public relations planning, the situation analysis can include such topics as changes in public opinion, industry and consumer trends, economic trends, governmental regulations and oversight programs, and corporate strategies that affect a company's relationships with stakeholders.

Targeting

As in advertising and other marketing communication areas, it is important to understand the target audience before designing the campaign. Research is conducted to identify the appropriate publics to which to address the public relations message.

The CIGNA insurance company, for example, realized that consumers have little empathy for insurance companies and view the industry as one that takes your money, gives back reluctantly, and raises premiums when its costs go up. In order to launch its Power of Caring campaign, which was a philanthropic sponsorship program that featured well-known personalities and their charitable causes, such as Alex's Lemonade Stand. CIGNA conducts primary research to identify the "conscientious consumer" and having this information keeps CIGNA from inadvertently putting out a campaign that its target audience might find irritating or self-serving.

Objectives and Strategies

A variety of objectives guides a PR plan, and the company can use myriad strategies to carry out the plan. Public relations objectives are designed by PR planners to make changes in the public's knowledge, attitudes, and behaviors related to a company, brand, or organization. Usually, these objectives focus on creating credibility, delivering information, and building positive images, trust, and corporate goodwill.

A company may also seek to change behavior, as the Ecomagination campaign attempted to do, but that is a difficult task. Before changing behavior, a communication effort may need to change people's beliefs, attitudes, and feelings. In many PR efforts, these communication effects are easier to accomplish and measure than behavior change. Typical public relations objectives include:

CIGNA provided a grant to support Alex's Lemonade Stand, a nonprofit dedicated to childhood cancer as part of its Power of Caring initiative.

Principle
Before changing behavior, a communication program may need to change beliefs, attitudes, and feelings.

- Creating a corporate brand
- Shaping or redefining a corporate reputation
- Positioning or repositioning a company or brand
- Moving a brand to a new market or a global market
- Launching a new product or brand
- Disseminating news about a brand, company, or organization
- Providing product or brand information
- Changing stakeholder attitudes, opinions, or behaviors about a brand or company
- Creating stronger brand relationships with key stakeholders, such as employees, shareholders and the financial community, government, members (for associations), and the media
- Creating high levels of customer (member) satisfaction
- Creating excitement in the marketplace
- Creating buzz (word of mouth)
- Involving people with the brand, company, or organization through events and other participatory activities
- Associating brands and companies with good causes

Change Agent Strategies Changing the attitudes that drive behavior is central to public relations programs. **Change agent** programs can be internal strategies focused on employees (sometimes called internal marketing) or external and focused on other publics, such as customers and other stakeholders. Regardless of the reason for change, "communication with principal stakeholders ranks high in the hierarchy of factors that predict success. Communication is second only to the main stakeholders' participation in the process."[24]

Involvement Strategies Public relations uses participation to intensify stakeholder involvement with a company or brand. Involvement can create interest and a feeling of excitement, but more importantly it can drive loyalty.[25] Getting people to participate in an action plan is one way to drive behavior change. For example, Pizza Hut's Book It effort is an incentive program used by 50,000 schools to offer free pizzas to reward students for reading. Involvement strategies need to be carefully conceived, however, as Pizza Hut's effort has been criticized for promoting unhealthy eating habits.[26]

The Big Idea

Creative ideas are just as important in public relations as in advertising. And for the same reason—to get attention. The Clark County Desert Conservation Program in Nevada wanted to promote desert environments and threats to their ecology. Mojave Max, a desert tortoise that is at least 50 years old became the group's mascot and announces the arrival of spring,

Mojave Max is a desert tortoise used as a mascot for a desert conservation program in Nevada.

just like Punxsutawney Phil does in the East. Who would have thought you could make a media star of a tortoise? The 15-pound Max has become the poster reptile for desert ecology and attracts the attention of children as well as adults.

PR stunts designed to get publicity are also part of the promotional arsenal. Janet Jackson's big exposure during the 2004 Super Bowl is an example of a stunt that got lots of visibility for the performer. Critics say the overexposure was in poor taste, but other PR experts say it was an example of a stunt that will be talked about for years. Jackson also gathered twice the number of U.S. press mentions as the Super Bowl commercials did that year.[27]

Sometimes PR stunts generate negative publicity, such as the attempt by a guerrilla marketing campaign to promote "Aqua Teen Hunger Force" for Turner Broadcasting System's Cartoon Network and its "Adult Swim" block of programs. In an attempt to generate attention for the show, promoters placed electronic light boards under bridges that showed cartoon characters giving passing motorists the finger. It generated more than attention, causing a bomb scare that shut down bridges and terrified Bostonians. The two promoters were charged with using a hoax device to create panic and disorderly conduct.[28] TBS's chairman and CEO issued an apology immediately. TBS agreed to pay $2 million in compensation for the emergency response efforts, and the head of the Cartoon Network was forced to resign from a position he held for 13 years.[29] Some argue that this stunt was a marketing campaign gone bad, while others thought it much ado about nothing. Was this effective public relations? Is any publicity good publicity?

PR's Role in IMC

In integrated programs, advertising and public relations aim at selected targets with different but complementary messages. As one researcher observed, "In IMC, company assets

A publicity stunt aimed at generating attention for the cartoon series Aqua Teen Hunger Force resulted in a bomb scare in Boston.

and product assets are managed at the same time."[30] In many companies, advertising and public relations are separate, uncoordinated functions. People working in public relations are often trained as journalists, with little background in marketing, and they focus on corporate image rather than product sales. These different orientations can sometimes create inconsistencies in a company's communication efforts.

Public relations uses a variety of marketing communication tools just as advertising does. Advertising is particularly useful in corporate image and reputation programs. Direct marketing is sometimes useful in sending out corporate books and DVDs. The Internet is important because the corporate Web site is one of the primary ways to disseminate information about an organization. PR activities, such as publicity and special mailings of DVDs, can help drive traffic to the corporate Web site. Sales promotion is used in support of PR activities, such as special events. In some cases, it's hard to know whether an event is a sales promotion or public relations effort. But it's not just the use of these tools that makes PR a viable IMC function, it's also the fact that PR can contribute some valuable effects, such as credibility.

A study conducted by *Advertising Age* and the Council of Public Relations Firms asked marketers in what roles they considered public relations effective. They responded that raising awareness was most effective (83 percent), followed by providing credibility (67 percent), reaching influencers (63 percent), educating consumers (61 percent), prompting trial (28 percent), persuading skeptics (22 percent), and driving sales (22 percent).[31] They also indicated that the most important contribution to marketing programs is in providing media contacts (67 percent). About half cited creative ideas (48 percent) and strategic support (45 percent). Less than a third of the respondents (only 29 percent) mentioned industry/competitor insight as an important contribution from PR firms to marketing programs. Some see this as an important development: "As media fragments and consumers gain more control of their time and media habits, PR and advertising need to merge or at least find common ground."[32] Messages aimed at reaching mass audiences in the shifting media environment are less effective, and new opportunities are emerging for public relations, publicity, and product placements to be integral parts of integrated marketing communication programs.

PUBLIC RELATIONS TOOLS

The public relations practitioner has many tools, which we can divide into two categories: controlled media and uncontrolled media. **Controlled media** include house ads, public service announcements, corporate (institutional) advertising, in-house publications, and visual presentations. The sponsoring organizations pay for these media. In turn, the sponsor maintains total control over how and when the message is delivered. **Uncontrolled media** include press releases, press conferences, and media tours. The most recent new media are electronic, which might be categorized as **semicontrolled**. Corporations and businesses control their own Web sites, for example, but other Web sites (particularly those that are set up by critics and disgruntled ex-employees) and chat rooms about the company are not controlled.

Likewise, companies set special events and sponsorships in place, but participation by the press and other important publics is not under the control of the sponsoring company. Word of mouth, or buzz, is important to PR programs because of the persuasive power of personal conversation. PR programs, particularly employee communication programs, may be designed to influence what people say about the company, but ultimately the comments are outside the company's control. Table 17.1 summarizes these tools.

Advertising

Public relations programs sometimes employ advertising as a way to create corporate visibility or strengthen relationships with its various stakeholder audiences. The primary uses of advertising are house ads, public service announcements, and corporate advertising.

House Ads   A company (or a medium, such as a newspaper, magazine, or broadcast station) may prepare a **house ad**, which is an ad for use in its own publication or programming. Consequently, no money changes hands. For instance, a local television station may run a house ad announcing its new fall programming within its evening news program; likewise, a company may run an ad advocating a point of view or promoting a special employee

Table 17.1   Public Relations Tools

Controlled Media	*Uncontrolled Media*
(company controls the use and placement)	*(media control the use and placement)*
• House ads	• News release (print, audio, video, e-mail, faxes)
• Public service ads	• Features (pitch letters)
• Corporate, institutional, advocacy advertising	• Fillers, historical pieces, profiles
• Publications: brochures, flyers, magazines, newsletters	• The press conference and media advisory (media kits, fact sheets, background info)
• Annual reports	• Media tours
• Speakers	• Bylined articles, op-ed pieces, letters to the editor
• Photographs	
• Films, videos, CD-ROMs	• Talk and interview shows
• Displays, exhibits	• Public service announcements
• Staged events	
• Books	

Semicontrolled Media

(some aspects are controlled or initiated by the company, but other aspects aren't)
- Electronic communication (Web sites, chat rooms)
- Special events and sponsorships
- Word of mouth (buzz)
- Weblogs (blogs)

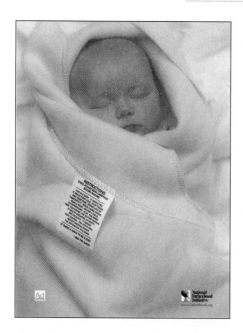

The Advertising Council has sponsored a number of public communication campaigns in support of good causes. The participating agencies donate their time and talent and media donate the time and space to run the PSAs. This one is for new dads and encourages them to learn more about parenting.

benefit program within its corporate magazine. These house ads are often managed by the public relations department.

Public Service Announcements   The ads for charitable and civic organizations that run free of charge on television or radio or in print media are **public service announcements (PSAs)**. The United Way, American Heart Association, and local arts councils all rely on PSAs. These ads are prepared just like other print ads or commercials, and in most instances ad agencies donate their expertise and media donate time and space to run the ads.

The Advertising Council represents a PR effort for the entire advertising industry and has produced most of the PSAs you see on television and in print, such as the "Friends Don't Let Friends Drive Drunk" campaign, the United Negro College Fund ("A Mind is a Terrible Thing to Waste"), the Keep America Beautiful antilitter campaign, and the more recent "I am an American" campaign that was developed following the tragedies of September 11, 2001. The classic Smokey the Bear campaign ("Only you can prevent forest fires") is one of its longest and best-recognized efforts.

Getting donated time and space is not easy. The PSA directors at various media receive a barrage of public service campaigns every week on different issues, and they must choose which ones to run. There is no guarantee which markets will see the campaign elements, and there is no guarantee that the same people will see the print and TV versions of a campaign. Some PSA campaigns do not get any airtime or print placements.

The art director for this **pro bono** Handgun Control campaign (*pro bono* means all services, time, and space are donated) explained the objective was keeping guns out of the hands of children. Note the dramatic visuals and the way the words work to reinforce the impact of the visual.

SHOWCASE The pro bono Handgun Control campaign was designed as a wakeup call following the Columbine High School shootings. Chris Hutchinson, art director at Wieden + Kennedy, explained that "Children killing children with guns is a very real issue and we wanted to communicate the horror of this. The visuals are meant to shock, juxtaposing toys with gun violence." Nominated by Professor Charles Frazer, Hutchinson graduated from the advertising program at the University of Oregon.

Studies of PSA effectiveness help guide nonprofit organizations. For instance, a look at PSAs to combat drunk driving, particularly among the college population, found that the usual anti-drunk-driving messages are not as relevant to this audience as they might be. They do not address the students' greatest fear: being pulled over and charged with a DUI. The study also found that a localized PSA, one that mentions or uses a local community angle, is more meaningful to the college-age group.[33]

Corporate Advertising With **corporate advertising**, a company focuses on its **corporate image** or viewpoint. There is less emphasis on selling a particular product unless it is tied in to a good cause. For that reason, the ad or other campaign materials may originate in the public relations department rather than the advertising department.

An example of corporate advertising that is tied to a socially redeeming program is the Target Guest Card. To increase use of the card, the Martin/Williams agency of Minneapolis had to find a compelling reason for people to shop at Target and use the card. Target's typical customer is female, aged 25 to 54, and her most important concern is her family. The agency team proposed a Take Charge of Education campaign, a simple fund-raising program for local schools tied to use of the Target Guest Card. One percent of the value of the purchases made with the card would go to a qualifying K–12 school of the cardholder's choice. The fund-raising program for schools showcased Target's commitment to education, an area of great importance to Target customers. The Target Take Charge of Education campaign included a number of other public initiatives such as Arts in Education Grants, Good Neighbor Volunteers, and an environmental club for kids called EarthSavers®, all of which reflect a strong public affairs orientation. So far Target has given more than $200 million to schools.[34]

Corporate identity advertising is another type of advertising that firms use to enhance or maintain their reputation among specific audiences or to establish a level of awareness of the company's name and the nature of its business. Johnson & Johnson targeted its "Healthy Start" institutional campaign at pregnant women to position itself as a concerned company. Companies that have changed their names, such as Nissan (formerly Datsun), have also used corporate identity advertising. To polish its corporate image, the CIGNA insurance company has attempted to brand an intangible—a caring business philosophy. Edward A. Faruolo, CIGNA marketing communications vice president, stated: "If we could build our brand around the concept of caring, we could not only obtain a highly coveted position in the marketplace, but also earn the trust and loyalty of our customers and our employees."[35]

Sometimes companies deliver point-of-view messages called **advocacy advertising**. General Electric's Ecomagination campaign, for example, shows that the company wants to be a caretaker of the environment and is creating products in line with that philosophy. Another example comes from Procter & Gamble. Recognizing that many animals are injured or killed by the 24 million gallons of oil that pollute North American waters each year, its campaign for Dawn liquid dishwashing detergent challenges people to be part of the solution. Dawn's Make a Difference campaign aims to inspire 1 million people to get involved.[36] The detergent, known for its grease-cutting ability, makes a natural connection with this advocacy effort.

Publicity

Moving away from controlled messages, consider the various tools and techniques used by media relations specialists to get publicity in the news media on behalf of a company or brand. Human footwear maker Teva created sandals for an Asian elephant with foot problems. The result was an article and photo that ran as news items.[37] PR expert Tom Harris calls this type of media coverage "an endorsement that money can't buy."[38]

Media relations is often seen as the most important core competency for PR professionals.[39] Media relations specialists know media that would be interested in stories about their companies. They also develop personal contact with reporters and editors who write regularly on topics related to their organization's industry.[40] As Carole Howard, author of a media relations book, explains, "Good media contacts proliferate once they are established."[41] In addition to personal contact, the primary tool used in media relations is the news release, along with press conferences and media tours.

News Releases   The **news release** is the primary medium used to deliver public relations messages to the various external media. Although the company distributing the news release controls its original form and content, the media decide what to present and how to present it. What the public finally sees, then, is not necessarily what the originating company had in mind, and so this form of publicity is uncontrolled by the originating company.

The decision to use any part of a news release is based on an editor's judgment of its news value. News value is based on such considerations as timeliness (something just happened or is about to happen), proximity (a local angle), impact (importance or significance), or human interest. Figure 17.2 illustrates how product categories rank in terms of news value to editors.

News releases must be written differently for each medium, accommodating space and time limitations. Traditional journalism form is followed, which means the 5W format is standard—in other words, the release should lead with answers to questions of who, what, why, when, where, and how. The more carefully the news release is planned and written, the better the chance it has of being accepted and published as written. Note the tight and simple writing style in the news release from global public relations and communications firm Weber Shandwick.

The news release can be delivered in a number of ways—in person, by local delivery service, by mail, by fax, or by e-mail. Sometimes a company is hired that specializes in dis-

FIGURE 17.2

Media Assessment of News Values

This figure shows how product categories rank in terms of news value to editors.

Source: Adapted from Thomas L. Harris, *The Marketer's Guide to Public Relations* (New York: Wiley, 1993), 58.

High News Value	Low News Value
Computers Cars Entertainment A	Beer Soft Drinks Athletic Shoes C
B Soup Cereal Aspirin	D Cigarettes Car Mufflers Cookies

A	High news value
B	Less interesting than A, but still considered to have a high news value
C	Low news value
D	Lower interest value than C

For immediate release
Contact:
Cassie Cataline | 703.852.5709
ccataline@kettler.com
OR
Erica Chlada | 410.558.2100
echlada@webershandwick.com

KETTLER PURCHASES PENTAGON CITY LAND FOR $220 MILLION
Ten-Phase, 3,200-unit Transit Oriented Development

McLean, VA. May 14, 2007— Kettler, one of the Washington area's leading diversified real estate development and property management companies, announced today that it has purchased 19.6 acres in Pentagon City from affiliates of Vornado Realty Trust for approximately $220.4 million. Kettler closed on the initial 11 acres today for $104.3 million, and plans to purchase the remaining acreage over the next year.

"This purchase gives us a long-term stake in one of Washington's most dynamic urban neighborhoods, and it deepens our established commitment to Arlington County and Pentagon City," said Robert C. Kettler, founder and chairman of Kettler.

For more than seven years, Kettler (formerly KSI) has been the ground lessee of the 19.6 acres for a ten-phase apartment development of 3,850 units. With today's purchase the firm takes title to the land under its existing and future buildings on the tract, which lies east and west of the Pentagon City Fashion Centre. To date, the firm has built 1,050 high rise apartments on the first three of the ten phases, including The Metropolitan at Pentagon Row, The Metropolitan at Pentagon City and The Gramercy at Metropolitan Park.

According to Kettler President, Richard W. Hausler, "The Pentagon tract is unique for its size and location on two major Metro lines with rail access to every part of the D.C. area." Over coming years, he said, "We look forward to working with Arlington County in completing this extraordinary transit oriented development."

Established Kettler developments on the Pentagon land include The Metropolitan at Pentagon City, which delivered 325 units in 2002 and The Metropolitan at Pentagon Row, which delivered 326 units in 2005. The latest Kettler undertaking in Pentagon City is The Gramercy at Metropolitan Park, a 399-unit apartment building which is nearing completion and set to open this summer. The Gramercy features architecture and interiors by renowned New York architect, Robert A.M. Stern. Future phases of Pentagon development include an additional 2,183 units -- and Stern also penned the master plan for these upcoming phases.

"Robert A.M. Stern brings a new dimension in urban design to this market," stated Kettler.

About Kettler

Based in Northern Virginia and celebrating its 30th anniversary in 2007, Kettler is a leading developer of award-winning, mixed-use residential and commercial properties across the Washington Metropolitan area. In 2007, Kettler was named one of the area's largest private companies by the Washington Business Journal and is one of the nation's top 15 multifamily developers. Kettler has developed more than five million square feet of commercial space and more than 50,000 homes. The company also owns and manages 9,000 apartments in 40 locations. Current projects include urban and transit-oriented developments, multifamily housing, commercial and mixed-use developments and resort communities.

###

The format of this piece from Weber Shandwick shows a typical news release format. It includes contact information at the top and a headline that summarizes the point of the news release.

tribution, such as the U.S. Newswire. Originally these companies sent news releases by mail or delivery services, but today news releases are now more likely to be distributed electronically through satellite and Web-based networks. PR Newswire, U.S. Newswire, and BusinessWire are services that provide targeted distribution to special interest media outlets or handle mass distribution of news releases, photos, graphics, video, audio, and other materials. If your organization decides to use e-mail, here is a set of guidelines for delivery:[42]

- Use one reporter's name and address per "to" line.
- Keep subject line header simple.
- Boldface "FOR IMMMEDIATE RELEASE" on the first line above the date.
- Catch attention with a good headline.
- Limit length (shorter than print's 500 word limit).
- Use the 5W format.
- Do not include attachments.
- Link to a URL where other background information and photos are posted.
- Remember readability and use short paragraphs, bullets, numbers, and lists to keep it scannable.
- Put contact information below the text.
- Close with conventional end signs such as "30" or ######.

Practical Tips

How to Write E-Mail Pitch Letters

1. Never list all recipients in the "To" line. No one wants to see all the reporters who received the pitch, since these story ideas are supposed to be made available to the medium on an exclusive basis—in other words, no other medium will be offered that story.
2. Avoid attachments. They take time to open and read, and busy reporters often dismiss them. They can also carry viruses.
3. Keep your pitches less than a page in length. The first paragraph should capture the who, what, and why of the story.
4. Help reporters do their jobs. Some reporters won't rewrite a news release because they want to write the story their own way. For those reporters, provide them with a great story idea, including visuals and other resources, and with contacts, so they can round out the story.
5. Make it personal. Use their first names and mention the publication name.
6. Keep subject-line headers to fewer than four or five words. The header should be clear and to the point; don't waste the space running the term "press release" itself.
7. Never follow up an e-mail pitch by asking, "Did you get it?" Instead, call within an hour (things move quickly in the online world) to ask reporters if they need more information.

Source: "Seven Tips for Getting Your E-Mail Pitches Read," direct mailing from Ragan Communications, September 2000.

Video news releases (VNRs) contain video footage for a television newscast. They are effective because they show target audiences the message in two different video environments: first as part of a news report and then reused later in an advertisement. Of course, there is no guarantee that a VNR will be used. One study found that VNRs aired in the Miami market were used because they had high visual quality and simple stories.[43]

Pitch Letters   Ideas for **feature stories**, which are human interest stories rather than hard news announcements, have to be "sold" to editors. This is done using a **pitch letter** that outlines the subject in an engaging way and sells a story idea. Companies use this form to feature interesting research breakthroughs, employees, or corporate causes. Not only is the distribution of press releases moving online, so are the letters pitching editors with story ideas. Ragan Communications, publisher of *Interactive Public Relations*, lists some tips for getting reporters and editors to read e-mail pitch letters. (See the Practical Tips box.)

Press Conferences   A **press conference**—an event at which a company spokesperson makes a statement to media representatives—is one of the riskiest public relations activities because the media may not see the company's announcement as being real news. Companies often worry about whether the press will show up for a press conference. Will they ask the right questions, or will they ask questions the company cannot or does not want to answer? Read about Apple, a company that can count on the press showing up for its announcements in the A Matter of Practice box.

To encourage reporters to cover press conferences, companies may issue a **media kit**, usually a folder that provides all the important background information to members of the press, either before or when they arrive at the press conference. The risk in offering media kits (also called press kits) is that they give reporters all the necessary information so that the press conference itself becomes unnecessary.

Media Tours   A **media tour** is a press conference on wheels. The traveling spokesperson makes announcements and speeches, holds press conferences to explain a promotional effort, and offers interviews.

Publications

Organizations may provide employees and other publics with pamphlets, booklets, annual reports, books, bulletins, newsletters, inserts and enclosures, and position papers.

The Securities and Exchange Commission (SEC) requires that each publicly held company publish an **annual report**. A company's annual report is targeted to investors and may be the single most important document the company distributes. Millions of dollars

A MATTER OF PRACTICE

The World's Greatest Public Relations Person

By Thomas Harris, *Public Relations Consultant and Author, Cofounder of Golin/Harris Communications*

Steve Jobs has done it again.

While everybody else was showing off their new stuff at the giant Consumer Electronics Show in Las Vegas in January, Apple CEO Steve Jobs deliberately counter-scheduled the annual MacWorld Expo for his big new product announcement in San Francisco.

The media left Las Vegas and every other tech company in the universe to see what the man behind the iMac and the iPod had up his sleeve this time.

The result, as reported by Michael Malone of ABC-News.com in the *Wall Street Journal*:

Unless you were one of the poor reporters who had to yo-yo between Las Vegas and San Francisco, you may not have noticed a hidden message in all the hoopla over the new Apple iPhone, a message that not only does Apple not inhabit the same universe as the rest of the consumer electronics world, but that its announcement would trump anything coming out of Vegas.

And boy, did it!

Malone wrote, "The blogosphere lit up the moment Steve Jobs took the stage. CNN, as is usual with Apple, turned its news coverage into a day-long iPhone flack." *USA Today* reported that Steve's "bet paid off like a gushing Vegas jackpot."

Harvard Business School professor David Yoffie told the paper: "The avalanche of headlines and TV news stories about the iPhone already have generated $400 million in free publicity. No other company has received that kind of attention for a product launch. It's unprecedented."

Reporters dutifully reported Steve's declaration that "Every once in a while a revolutionary product comes along that changes everything." Headline writers reiterated his claim that the iPhone "would reinvent wireless communications" and "leapfrog" past the current generation of smart phones.

As the world now knows, the ultra-thin iPhone allows users to play music, surf the Internet, send e-mail, and, oh, yes, make phone calls.

USA Today pointed out that Microsoft, Intel, Oracle, and Adobe all stage splashy events to unveil products but "only Apple succeeds in turning these kinds of events into headlines."

Charles Wolf, an analyst for Needham & Co., says, "Most CEOs come on stage with an endless round of platitudes. Steve leaves all the crap out of his presentation and focuses on what's important."

So why does Apple need to spend millions on advertising when it has the media doing its marketing for free? If you saw the Academy Awards, you know why.

Nobody does advertising better. The iPhone teaser commercial featured TV and movie clips of Lucille Ball, Humphrey Bogart, Robert DeNiro, Jackie Gleason, Marilyn Monroe, Steve McQueen. Robert Redford, John Travolta, and Betty Rubble of "The Flintstones" saying "Hello" on old-fashioned phones. The spot ran three times and trounced all the other commercials on the Oscars—and the Super Bowl, for that matter.

By the time the iPhone went on sale six months later, it had been the subject of 11,000 print articles and had generated 69 million hits on Google for what bloggers were calling the "Jesus phone." Did the hype work? People started lining up at the Apple store on New York's Fifth Avenue for at least three days to get their hands on an iPhone on iDay, June 29, 2007.

On the opening weekend, Apple sold a half million iPhones. Analysts predicted that 3 million sets would be sold by the end of 2007.

Source: Thomas L. Harris, ViewsLetter, April 2007, 3.

are spent on the editing and design of annual reports. These reports are especially important to stockholders and potential investors.

Some companies publish material, often called **collateral material**, to support their marketing public relations efforts. For example, Corning Fiberglass Insulation offers a free booklet on home insulation do's and don'ts as an integral part of its promotion effort. The booklet is highlighted in its advertising campaign. Much of this information is available on the Web as well.

Corporate publication, marketing, and sales promotion departments and their agencies also produce training materials and sales kits to support particular campaigns. Target's Co-ordinators Kit, for instance, was produced by Target for school representatives to help run the Take Charge of Education campaign. Target also used a number of different brochures, such as a series included in a School Fund-raising Made Simple kit designed to train and support school representatives involved in the campaign.

DVDs, CDs, Podcasts, Books, and Online Video

DVDs and podcasts have become major public relations tools for many companies. Corporate books have also become popular with the advent of simplified electronic publication.[44] Costing $1,000 to $2,000 per minute to make, videos are not inexpensive. However, they are an ideal tool for distributing in-depth information about a company or program. Because they are easier to duplicate, DVDs are reducing this cost. Some companies have taken stock of the YouTube phenomenon and are using online video to reduce costs and draw attention to messages on corporate Web sites. Monsanto, for example, posted video clips of testimonials from farmers using Monsanto products on its site, hoping to attract customers, employees, and policy makers.[45]

Speakers and Photos

Many companies have a **speakers' bureau** of articulate people who will talk about topics at the public's request. Organizations as varied as Apple Computer, Harvard University, and the Children's Hospital in Houston, Texas, all have speakers' bureaus for presentations to local groups and classes.

Some publics, particularly the news media, may want pictures of people, products, places, and events. That's why PR departments maintain files of photographs that are accurate, up to date, and well composed. The permissions for ads in this book were provided because they present the advertisers in a positive light. Companies seldom give permission to use ads that authors intend to criticize.

Displays and Exhibits

Displays and exhibits, along with special events and tours, may be important parts of both sales promotion and public relations programs. Displays include signage and booths, racks, and holders for promotional literature. A model of a new condominium complex, complete with a literature rack offering brochures about its development, is an example of a display. Exhibits tend to be larger than displays; they may have moving parts, sound, or video and usually are staffed by a company representative. Booth exhibits are important at trade shows, where some companies may take orders for much of their annual sales.

Special Events and Tours

Some companies stage events to celebrate milestones, such as key anniversaries. These are high-visibility activities designed to get maximum publicity. Special events can be the public relations manager's responsibility as well as a sales promotion activity. They include open houses and even birthday celebrations. For example, when Barnum's Animal Crackers turned 100, Nabisco invited people to decide what new critters should join the circus of 17 animals in the traditional box. The use of fancier staged events has seen the most growth. Corporate sponsorship of various sporting events has evolved into a favorite public relations tactic.

Events can also be important in internal communication. Learning objectives and employee buy-in for a new campaign are often accomplished through meetings, seminars, and workshops sponsored by a company, typically in conjunction with training materials and other publications. To facilitate internal marketing, **town hall forums** are sometimes used.[46] This is an opportunity for management to make a presentation on some major project, initiative, or issue and invite employees to discuss it.

In addition to media tours, tours of all kinds are used in public relations programs, such as plant tours and trips by delegates and representatives. The Spokane Regional Convention and Visitors Bureau and the International Trade Alliance in Spokane, Washington, teamed up to travel to Calgary, Alberta, to promote the Spokane as an area for trade and tourism. Thirty-seven Spokane business leaders, travel suppliers, and trade professionals embarked on the four-day mission to Calgary. The group chartered a 50-passenger motor coach, which doubled as a traveling billboard. "Team Spokane," as they were known, attended industry trade shows and a consumer travel show. John Brewer, former president and general manager of the Spokane Regional Convention and Visitors Bureau, deemed the effort a phenomenal success. Another example is the tour for *truth*®, the largest national youth smoking prevention campaign for teens; these tours annually reach some 750,000 teens with information about cigarette smoking and its harmful effects.[47]

Named The Spokane Stampede, the mission allowed Spokane County hospitality suppliers to network and conduct business with media, travel agents, meeting and tour group planners, and potential leisure travelers in Calgary, Alberta. This visit was a step toward developing stronger ties between Canada and the Spokane Region for economic development and community relations.

Online Communication

PR practitioner and author Fraser Seitel says, "It is irrefutable that the Internet has changed communications forever with its immediacy and pervasiveness. But on the other hand, the Internet hasn't replaced human relationships as the essence of societal communications. The Internet and communicating via the computer is but another tool in the public relations arsenal."[48] E-mail, **intranets** (which connect people within an organization), **extranets** (which connect people in one business with its business partners), Internet advertising and promotions, and Web sites have opened up avenues for public relations activities.

External Communication   As a recent workshop conference on the Web's usefulness in public relations notes, "The World Wide Web can be considered the first public relations mass medium in that it allows managed communication directly between organizations and audiences without the gatekeeping function of other mass media."[49] General Electric features a section on its Web site about its Ecomagination campaign (http://ge.ecomagination. com/). The site offers information about what GE is doing and about how visitors to the site can make a difference by making their homes "greener" and energy-efficient.

Corporate Web sites have become an important part of corporate communications. These sites can present information about the company and open up avenues for stakeholders to contact the company. Web site newsrooms distribute a company's press releases to the media and other interested stakeholders. One study noted that the Web's interactive dimension is particularly important: "If you built a highly interactive and informative Web site, then you can capitalize on building brand and corporate image through longer and more intense exposures than any other type of campaign." The study also found that interactivity—being able to contact the company—is more important than the actual information.[50]

In addition to Web sites, the Internet has become the favorite tool of media relations professionals as well as journalists. E-mail is now used more frequently to contact reporters than phone, fax, or personal visits, and reporters indicate that corporate Web sites are their most important source of financial information.[51] Furthermore, most press releases are now distributed online either by sending them directly to reporters or to such services as PR Newswire, which then handles mass distribution online to appropriate publications.

Internal Communication   E-mail is a great way for people in separate sites to communicate. You can get a fast reply if people on the other end are checking their mail regularly. It is also an inexpensive form of internal communication. Internal company e-mail may have its public relations downside, however. It can be used in court. Some of the most damaging evidence the federal government presented against Microsoft in its antitrust suit came from e-mail messages exchanged within the company.

Internal company networks do have great benefits. Intranets and corporate portals (an extensive collection of databases and links that are important to people working in a company) encourage communication among employees in general and permit them to share data, such as customer records and client information. Some companies urge employees to set up personal home pages as part of the company portal, which allows them to customize the material they receive and set up their own links to crucial corporate information such as competitor news, product information, and case histories.

Web Challenges   The Internet presents at least as many challenges to public relations professionals as it does opportunities. Search engine optimization is a major issue for online experts who continually try to improve the process of key word searching that leads interested Web users to their sites.[52]

Although the Internet makes it possible to present the company's image and story without going through the editing of a gatekeeper, it is much harder to control what is said about the company on the Internet. According to Parry Aftab, a lawyer specializing in computer-related issues, "It used to be that you could control the information because you'd have one spokesman who represented the company. Now where you have thousands of employees who have access to an e-mail site, you have thousands of spokesmen."[53] All employees have "an inside view" of their company, whether sanctioned by the PR department or not.

Gossip and rumors can spread around the world within hours. Angry customers and disgruntled former employees know this and have used the Internet to voice their complaints. A number of these people have set up Web sites, such as the Official Internet AntiNike Web site, alt.destroy.microsft, I Hate McDonald's, Toys R Us Sucks, GTE Sucks, Why America Online Sucks, Packard Bell Is Evil, and BallySucks. As a defense against this negative press, some companies are registering domain names that might cause them trouble. For example, JP Morgan Chase bank owns IHateChase.com, ChaseStinks.com, and ChaseSucks.com, but not chasebanksucks.com, which is an active Web site critical of the company.[54]

Some companies monitor the Internet to see what is being said about them so they can respond to protect their reputations. Thousands of companies have hired eWatch, a firm that provides Web monitoring services, to collect such information.

The Bottom Line: Getting Attention in a New-Media World   As you've seen throughout this chapter, businesses and organizations have many ways to reach their publics. It's critical to find a way to break through the media clutter for public relations as well as advertising messages. Some tips from an article[55] about how small businesses can communicate their messages effectively include:

- *Wrap your story around a bigger idea.* Find a broader context or news hook for your product or service and show how your company fits into it.
- *Keep it short and personal.* When reaching out to journalists, a few quick sentences via e-mail, free from industry jargon, explaining who you are and what your business is usually will suffice. Try to keep the first e-mail readable without having to scroll down. Also, referring to past works by journalists shows you understand their area of coverage.
- *Pay attention to Web basics.* Building a Web site and getting good rankings on search engines such as Yahoo! and Google can help customers find businesses, especially new ones. Consider blogging as a way to tell your story and interact with the public. Using sites such as technorati.com can help turn up other like-minded bloggers. Podcasting and online video-sharing sites such as YouTube.com can help tell your story, but do it creatively, avoiding purely commercial pitches.
- *Host events.* These don't have to be expensive, but small themed events with food and drink for customers can be a good draw, particularly on streets crowded with multiple merchants.
- *Seek out brand ambassadors.* Find customers willing to talk up your product to others, and encourage their word-of-mouth marketing with discounts or first looks at new products and sales.
- *Publish a newsletter.* It sounds old-fashioned, but with so much information coming to people online these days, a mailed paper newsletter to customers can seem more personal than mass e-mails and help your business stand out.

EFFECTIVENESS AND PR EXCELLENCE

An important part of professional practice in public relations, as well as advertising, is evaluation. The Institute for Public Relations has developed a set of measurement standards to help evaluate the effectiveness of public relations. As in advertising, public relations evaluation is based on setting measurable objectives from the beginning of planning. Objectives that specify the impact the program seeks to have on the various publics can be evaluated by the PR manager if they contain benchmarks and target levels.

However, measuring the impact of public relations efforts has been difficult. It's hard to know what effect clips (or news stories about the company or organization) have on the bottom line, for example. Catalogs from retailers that feature over-the-top gifts have some value, even if the items are never sold, because publicity has its own value. The theory is that even consumers who don't purchase the swanky gifts like a $1.8 million Virgin Galactic Charter to Space, available through Neiman Marcus, still want to be associated with such luxury.[56] It is also difficult to separate the effects of public relations from advertising or direct mail. In an effort to solve this problem, Procter & Gamble has developed an analytic tool to quantify the sales impact of public relations.[57] In the end, public relations activities need to be evaluated against specific objectives established in the public relations plan.

Figure 17.3 illustrates that various public relations tactics are controlled, semicontrolled, or uncontrolled messages. They all play a role in a communication campaign plan. The model identifies perception, emotion, cognition, persuasion, association, and behavior as categories of effects that might need to be measured in an evaluation program.

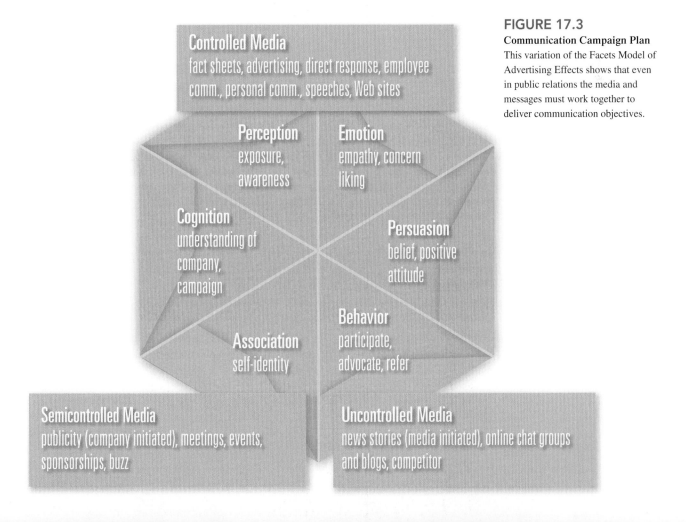

FIGURE 17.3

Communication Campaign Plan
This variation of the Facets Model of Advertising Effects shows that even in public relations the media and messages must work together to deliver communication objectives.

Public relations practitioners track the impact of a campaign in terms of output (how many news releases lead to stories or mentions in news stories) and outcome (attitude or behavior change). PR firms and companies can hire companies such as BurellesLuce that specialize in monitoring media coverage. Such tracking and the evaluation of attitude and behavior change is done to prove the effectiveness of the PR program, so that they learn from their efforts and fine-tune future campaigns. To get a comprehensive picture of PR's impact, practitioners evaluate process (what goes out) and outcome (media use, effect on the target audience).

IT'S A WRAP

GE's Green Efforts Mean Good Business

Ad critic Bob Garfield explained in his *Ad Age* column that advertising has a remarkable quality seldom asked of it—that is, the power to persuade and to change people's minds and feelings on a large scale. He reviewed the GE Ecomagination campaign two years after its implementation, asking whether GE's efforts were genuine or a hollow marketing ploy.

He concluded:

The campaign legitimately reflects the corporate vision to develop cleaner technologies for industrial customers in energy, transportation and so on—45 products (up from 17 at launch) that will generate $13 billion in 2007 revenue.

The campaign won a 2006 Silver Effie in the category of Corporate Reputation/Image/Identity. *Industry Week* named GE its Technology Leader of the Year for connecting corporate profits with the cause for global and national preservation.

The campaign seems to be a hit with consumers as well. *USA Today's* Ad Track polled readers. Of those familiar with the dancing elephant commercial, 49 percent said they like it "a lot," which more than doubles the Ad Track average of 21 percent.

GE spokesperson Jonathan Klein said the corporation's online commercials are popular too: "More than 50 percent of users who visited our online TV ads have sent links to a friend." That's effective Public Relations, getting the consumers to help spread the company's goodwill. Ultimately, the efforts do just what Edison did; they connect the corporation with the people they serve.

Key Points Summary

1. **What is public relations, and what are different types of public relations programs?** Public relations is a management function that communicates to and with various publics to manage an organization's image and reputation. In addition to the key areas of government, media, employee, and investor relations, PR programs also include corporate relations and reputation management, crisis management, marketing public relations (MPR), and public communications campaigns.

2. **What key decisions do public relations practitioners make when they create plans?** Planning for a public relations campaign begins with a SWOT, or situation analysis, that is used as background to identify the target audience and develop objectives and strategies. Research is needed when planning a PR program and evaluating its effectiveness.

3. **What are the most common types of public relations tools?** Uncontrolled media tools include the news story

that results from a news release or news conference. Controlled media are tools that the company uses to originate and control content. Some examples of these are house ads, corporate advertising, and public service ads. Semicontrolled tools are controlled in that the company is able to initiate use of the tool, but uncontrolled in that the content is contributed by others. A few examples include electronic communication (Web sites and chat rooms), word of mouth (buzz), and blogs.

4. **Why is measuring the results of public relations efforts important, and how should that be done?** Public relations evaluation usually focuses on outputs and outcomes and may include relationship management and excellence. The evaluation effort is made to determine how well a PR program meets its objectives.

Key Terms

active publics, p. 514
advocacy advertising, p. 520
annual report, p. 522
aware publics, p. 514
benchmarking, p. 514
cause marketing, p. 510
change agent, p. 515
collateral materials, p. 524
communication audit, p. 514
controlled media, p. 517
corporate advertising, p. 519
corporate identity advertising, p. 519
corporate image, p. 519
corporate relations, p. 510
crisis management, p. 511

employee relations, p. 509
extranets, p. 525
feature stories, p. 522
financial relations, p. 510
fund-raising (or development), p. 510
gap analysis, p. 514
gatekeepers, p. 508
goodwill, p. 507
house ad, p. 517
implied third-party endorsement, p. 508
internal marketing, p. 509
intranets, p. 525
issue management, p. 510
latent publics, p. 514

lobbying, p. 510
marketing public relations (MPR), p. 512
media kit, p. 522
media relations, p. 509
media tour, p. 522
news release, p. 520
opinion leaders, p. 507
pitch letter, p. 522
press conference, p. 522
pro bono, p. 518
public affairs, p. 510
public communication campaigns, p. 512
public opinion, p. 507

public relations, p. 506
publics, p. 505
public service announcement (PSA), p. 518
publicity, p. 507
relationship marketing, p. 509
reputation management, p. 510
semicontrolled media, p. 517
speakers' bureau, p. 524
stakeholders, p. 507
town hall forums, p. 524
uncontrolled media, p. 517
video news releases (VNRs), p. 522

Review Questions

1. Explain why public opinion is important to the success of public relations.
2. Compare and contrast the practice of advertising and the practice of public relations.
3. What is marketing public relations, and how does it differ from other forms of public relations, such as corporate relations?

4. In analyzing PR tools, compare the use of controlled and uncontrolled media. Explain the difference between the two categories.
5. What are the primary tools of publicity?
6. In evaluating the effectiveness of public relations, explain the difference between output and outcome evaluations.

Discussion Questions

1. Why is public opinion so important to the success of public relations? In how many different ways does it affect the success of a program like GE's Ecomagination?
2. What is reputation management, and how does it intersect with advertising programs? Find a corporate reputation campaign and analyze its effectiveness.
3. *Three-Minute Debate:* Think about a publicity stunt that backfired, such as the Aqua Teen Hunger Force bomb scare in Boston. Is all publicity good publicity? Or was this just a

bad idea that hurt the client? Organize into small teams, with each team taking one side or the other. In class, set up a series of three-minute debates with each side having 1½ minutes to argue its position. Every team of debaters has to present new points not covered in the previous teams' presentations until there are no arguments left to present. Then the class votes as a group on the winning point of view.

Take-Home Team Projects

1. Divide the class into groups of three or four people. Each group should adopt a local cause that operates on a low budget and needs public relations help. As a team, develop a public relations plan for that nonprofit organization.

2. Consult the two teen-targeted antismoking Web sites listed here and compare them in terms of their appeal to a teen audience. Which one do you think is the most interesting to this age group? Compile the best ideas from both and write a report to your instructor on why the ideas are good and what else a Web site can do to reach a teen market.

- http://www.thetruth.com
- http://www.generationfree.com

Yahoo! Hands-On Case

Review the Yahoo! case in the Appendix.

1. The Yahoo! case describes promotions and public relations in one section. Which activities are promotions, and which are public relations? What additional public relations efforts would you suggest, and why do you think they would be effective?

2. Review the types of public relations programs, and identify what type was employed in this case. What key decisions do you think guided the Yahoo! team as it created the public relations portion of the campaign? How could it judge the effectiveness of the public relations efforts?

HANDS-ON CASE

JetBlue's Blues

Founded in 1998 as an air carrier known for value, service, and style, JetBlue has won highest marks in airline customer satisfaction in research conducted by J.D. Power and Associates in both 2005 and 2006. JetBlue prides itself on award-winning service and free TV, ample legroom for passengers, and low fares. That's all well and good, but what happens when its reputation for great service is threatened?

That's exactly what happened when a 2007 Valentine's Day ice storm froze the company's operations in the Eastern United States. It was bad. While most airlines canceled their flights and sent passengers home, JetBlue tried to weather the storm, maintain its schedules, and serve its passengers. That didn't happen.

Planes filled with passengers left the terminal to wait for the weather to clear on the taxiways. Other planes took their spots at the gate, making it impossible for the nearly departed planes to return to the gate. Then the equipment used to move planes became frozen. You get the messy picture.

Passengers were stranded in the New York airport for as long as 11 hours without access to food or proper toilet facilities, and they weren't happy. Stories ran in newspapers across the country about passenger reactions to the debacle. Honeymooners described the Valentine's Day ordeal as "horrific." Photos showed people camped out in New York's John F. Kennedy Airport. But the problems didn't end on Valentine's Day. JetBlue canceled nearly 1,100 flights from February 14 (Wednesday) through the following Monday, affecting an estimated 130,000 customers, many of whom were livid about their experience.

Enter founder and chief executive of JetBlue, David Neeleman. His reaction was swift and decisive. He apologized for the monumental communications meltdown, admitting that the company didn't have a plan. Quickly he responded with a JetBlue Customer Bill of Rights, a comprehensive customer promise and compensation program. In an effort to restore JetBlue's reputation for excellent customer service, Neeleman promised customers travel credits for excessive waits on his airplanes.

Neeleman, the public face of the airlines, gave television interviews and talked with journalists. One newspaper article quotes Neeleman: "What we did was wrong, and we didn't have a plan." He appeared on the CBS talk show, *Late Show with David Letterman*, and told the host, "We're going to learn from this experience like nothing that's ever happened to us before." He also issued an apology via YouTube.

Bad things happen. Ice storms shut down airports. Was Neeleman's apology a sufficient public relations effort to restore JetBlue's reputation? A story posted on *PR Tactics and The Strategist Online* suggests that PR pros had mixed reactions to JetBlue's damage control. Some professionals were effusive in their praise of the handling of the situation, and they lauded the immediacy of the airline's efforts to face its problem publicly. Others said the initial communication failed to inform passengers what was going on and called the response to the affected passengers "totally inadequate." One PR consultant suggested that JetBlue should have taken immediate action for those passengers, offering them something like $1,000 for each hour they were stranded or a lifetime pass on the airline, along with announcements of management restructuring and new policies on passenger rights.

The people who matter most when it comes to the public relations efforts, though, are its customers. What do they think? Was it sufficient to keep them loyal to JetBlue? One indication that the public is forgiving: JetBlue was awarded again the highest honors in airline customer satisfaction among low-cost airlines from J.D. Powers just four months after the crisis that followed the ice storm.

Incidentally, Neeleman is no longer the CEO of JetBlue, although he will serve as nonexecutive Chairman of the Board, according to a May 2007 JetBlue press release.

Consider This

1. How do you think JetBlue did in handling this crisis? Should it have done anything differently?
2. If you were the CEO of a company, what types of communication planning might you undertake that would anticipate crises?
3. Other airlines were affected by the storm as well. Why do you suppose JetBlue was the focus of so much negative media attention? Could the CEO do anything to deflect this negative publicity?

Sources: Associated Press, "Grumps on a Plane," *Lincoln Journal Star,* February 16, 2007; Associated Press, "JetBlue Introduces Customer Bill of Rights," *Lincoln Journal Star,* February 21, 2007; Jeff Bailey, "JetBlue's C.E.O. Is 'Mortified' After Fliers Are Stranded," *New York Times,* February 19, 2007, http://www.nytimes.com; Chris Cobb, "PR Pros Evaluate JetBlue's Crisis Response," *PR Tactics and The Strategist Online,* February 27, 2007, http://www.prsa.org; JetBlue press releases, May 10, 2007, and June 19, 2007, http://www.jetblue.com; Dan Reed, "JetBlue Tries to Make Up With Fliers," *USA Today,* February 20, 2007, http://www.usatoday.com.

Special Advertising Campaigns

IT'S A WINNER

Award:	Company:	Agency:	Campaign:
Effie (Iceland)	*Honda*	*HÉR&NÚ, Reyk-javík*	*"4×4xbus/car/cart"*

Think Snow; Think CR-V

Think Iceland. Think snow. Think four-wheel drive. When the Honda dealership in Iceland became a client of my agency in 2004, its challenge to us was to increase its market share. So we thought SUV.

By way of background, the Iceland Honda dealership carried a small line and only offered cars in 4 of 12 consumer categories, but still had been doing fairly well.

We began with a detailed analysis of the market to see what position the brand held and where we could take it. The analysis showed that what needed to be addressed to increase the brand's market share was a specific segment where the sales potential was extraordinary—the small SUV segment. So we relaunched a slightly upgraded Honda CR-V.

Icelandic climate, road conditions, and mentality have always inflated the need for four-wheel-drive vehicles. Close to half the vehicles sold in Iceland are four-wheel-drive, but the majority were fullsize SUVs or pickups.

Most ads for the SUV segment focused on off-road capabilities and mountain activities. Our research showed that the people buying SUVs were not necessarily involved in those activities. Rather, we found that what people wanted from those cars was mostly space, both for people and stuff (groceries, luggage, kids, sporting equipment) and minimum off-road capabilities. They wanted the ability to drive on dirt and gravel roads and the benefit of not being stuck in town (or at home) on heavy snow days.

Our research also showed that the Honda brand was seen as high quality, well built, and reliable—but also expensive and dull. The pricing issue was a thing of the past as today's Hondas are competitively priced. Another negative was Honda's low awareness: It was 11th in top-of-mind scores. However, purchase intent studies showed that 20 percent of people intending to buy a new SUV strongly considered a Honda.

Chapter Key Points

1. What is retail advertising all about, and what makes it distinctive?
2. How does B2B advertising work?
3. What are the basic goals and operations of nonprofit and social marketing?
4. Which strategic decisions are behind international advertising and IMC?

We designed a strategy to combat the negatives and exploit the positives. We set ambitious objectives. In one year we intended to increase strong purchase intent for Honda SUV to 25 percent (an increase of 25 percent) and move the top-of-mind scores to seventh place (up four places). This should support the sales objective of increasing sales by 70 percent.

We came up with a Big Idea that would be executed in two stages to take full advantage of the brand's strength while erasing its image problem. First, reposition the CR-V as a competitively priced SUV without tarnishing the quality image. Second, build on the positive attributes of the car and tie them to the actual lifestyle of the target group.

We built a campaign positioning the CR-V as "an inner-city SUV with space and maneuverability for your daily activities." At the same time, competitors were promoting their small SUVs as sport SUVs or off-roaders.

Our Big Idea was to use the worldwide symbol for four-wheel-drive cars—"4×4"—and tie that symbol in with the target group's true lifestyle. Their real use was mostly for daily chores—grocery shopping, driving children to school, and so on with a light mixture of rural activities.

All our headlines played off words for things on wheels that could be used to make your life easier in daily chores, but they were also words that gave indication of large storage and carrying capability. Headlines such as "4×4×Grocery-cart", "4×4×School-bus," "4×4×Golf-cart," "4×4×Baby-carriage (4×4×Stroller)," "4×4×Ski-bus," "4×4×Toy-car" were the building blocks for universal themes in all promotional materials for Honda CR-V. When tested, these headlines showed that the target group experienced our exact aim: "a four-wheel-driven car with enough space to handle my every day." Different target groups identified with different headlines.

To tackle the brand's image problems, we invented branding phrases such as "Honda good price" and "Honda reliability" to indicate that the car was a good buy/low price but still retained the image of Honda reliability and quality.

To correct the pricey image, we used a simple layout with yellow background color to indicate inexpensive but not cheap, since psychologically yellow equals inexpensive. We emphasized the headline and had the price in large fonts, again to indicate a good buy. We pulled out quotes and awards that the car had won to support the believability of the headline and strengthen the quality image.

The result was that sales and market share increased and the campaign was awarded a gold Effie in Iceland for outstanding cooperation between advertiser and advertising agency. We'll tell you more about how the effectiveness of this campaign was evaluated in the It's a Wrap discussion at the end of the chapter.

By Ingvi Logason, Principal, HÉR & NÚ Advertising, Reykjavik, Iceland

The Honda case is about an award-winning integrated campaign that illustrates how international marketers make decisions about their local advertising. It combines two of the subjects we cover in this chapter, integration and international advertising. Other topics in this chapter are retail, B2B, and nonprofit marketing communication. All these specialized areas use many of the basic advertising principles and generally strive to coordinate their messages; however, there are some distinct differences that we will call to your attention in this chapter.

IMC AND TOTAL COMMUNICATION

We have referred to integrated marketing communication (IMC) throughout this book, but let's begin this chapter by explaining some of the principles that guide the practice of IMC, particularly an IMC campaign. A campaign is a complex set of interlocking, coordinated activities. In IMC a campaign plan outlines the objectives and strategies for a series of different but related marketing communication efforts that appear in different media, use different marketing communication tools, and convey different but complementary brand-consistent messages to a variety of stakeholders. Consistency comes from the creative theme and the consistent presentation of the brand position and personality.

Driving Consistency through All Messages

IMC is the practice of strategically coordinating all marketing communication (marcom) tools and brand messages to communicate in a consistent way to and with all stakeholder audiences. As explained throughout this book, each marketing communication function has its special strengths, just as each cooking spice has its unique flavor. When several spices are combined, the objective is to create a single delicious taste. The same is true for a campaign. When the various marcom functions and media are combined, they should create a focused impact for a brand. As various ingredients in the campaign are added and taken away, changes in brand tracking results can show the effects and help identify what combinations of marketing communication functions and media work best for a brand.

Because everything a brand does sends a message, IMC planners strive to manage a total communication program to deliver a consistent brand presence. Consider the Honda CR-V campaign and its execution. The 4×4 message was used in every form of media from TV to Internet banners and events. It was a simple message using a preemptive strategy that let CR-V build dominance in the category. It was also an easy theme to present consistently. Every time consumers saw or experienced the CR-V, they did so through the 4×4 theme.

The media emphasis previously had been on print only (newspaper and magazines). Logason explained, "We shifted the emphasis to a 360-degree integrated approach where we focused on media with large reach at the expense of high frequency." Newspaper still served as the main carrier with heavy support from TV, Internet, radio, and magazines. The HÉR&NÚ team also extended the media buy into other marcom areas. The showroom, for example, delivered an experiential message in the way it displayed the 4×4 theme, and props helped consumers follow the theme from their initial point of interest to their point of trial. As Logason explained, "We even had a special area where you could try/see how a baby carriage or golf cart would fit in the trunk."

Other experiential media included sponsorship of big sporting and cultural events that tied in with the car owners' lifestyles. For example, the CR-V sponsored golf tournaments in which participants could win a new car. The entire golf course was dressed with 4×4 decorations. CR-V also sponsored live skiing tournaments, children's shows, and other events.

Organizing for IMC

An IMC campaign is even more complex than a traditional advertising plan because it uses more marcom tools and addresses more audiences. Coordinating all these messages is an organizational problem best solved through **cross-functional management**, which means a team of people from all the relevant parts of a company that interact with customers, other stakeholders, and with outside agencies plan marketing communication, monitor its impact, and track consumer response.

Table 18.1 Typical Objectives for Various IMC Tools

Advertising: reach wide audience through mass media; acquire new customers; establish brand image and personality; define brand position; identify points of differentiation and competitive advantage; counter competition; deliver reminders.

PR: announce news; affect attitudes and opinions; maximize credibility and believability; generate likeability; create and improve stakeholder relationships; stimulate buzz.

Consumer Sales Promotion: stimulate behavior; generate immediate response; intensify needs, wants, and motivations; reward behavior; stimulate improvement and relevance; create pull through the channel; encourage repeat purchase.

Trade Sales Promotion: build industry acceptance; push through the channel; motivate cooperation; energize sales force, dealers, and distributors.

Point of Purchase: increase immediate sales; attract attention at decision point; create interest; stimulate urgency; encourage trial and impulse purchasing.

Direct Marketing: stimulate sales; create personal interest and relevance; provide information; create acceptance and conviction; encourage repeat purchase; maintain relationship.

Sponsorship and Events: build awareness; create brand experience; create opportunity for participation, interaction, and involvement; create excitement; stimulate buzz.

Packaging: increase sales; attract attention at selection point; deliver product information; create brand reminder at point of purchase.

Specialties: reinforce brand identity; provide continuous brand reminder; reinforce satisfaction; encourage repeat purchase.

Guerilla Marketing: intercept prospects where they work, live, and visit; create curiosity and excitement; provide opportunity for involvement; stimulate buzz.

Customer Service: answer questions; solve customer problems; record complaints and compliments; turn bad customer experiences to positive experiences; listen to consumer perceptions and record feedback; notify appropriate departments of complaints and compliments; test market communication strategies and copy points.

Planning an IMC Campaign

The decision about which marcom tools to use is based on an analysis of their strengths and weaknesses and how they can best be employed to meet the campaign's objectives. As we explained in Chapter 7, certain tools are better at delivering specific objectives. Table 18.1 provides a more extensive outline of the tools and their objectives.

The end result of integration is message **synergy**, which means that when all the pieces work together, the whole is greater than the sum of its parts. Integration also brings coherence between what a company says and what it does. In *Driving Brand Value*, the authors describe the "Integration Triangle," which identifies three key aspects that must work together to create integration—what the company or brand says about itself *(say)*, how the company or brand performs *(do)*, and what other people say about it *(confirm)*. Figure 18.1 shows these relationships.

FIGURE 18.1

The Integration Triangle
The Say, Do, Confirm model explains how planned marketing communication messages are either reinforced or undercut by unplanned messages (what others say) and messages delivered by the product or service (how well the brand and company perform its business). A brand is integrated when there are no gaps between the say, do, and confirm messages.

Source: Adapted from Tom Duncan and Sandra Moriarty, *Driving Brand Value* (New York: McGraw-Hill, 1997): 91.

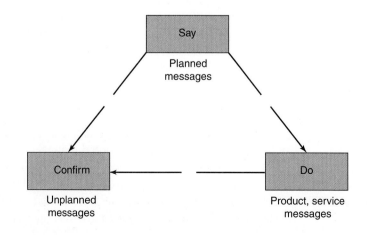

In most cases the drive for brand consistency is a strategic need, but at other times it reflects cost-efficiency. IMC messages can be more effective because of their repetition, and this reinforcement, along with synergy, creates more cost-efficient campaigns. Research has shown that using multiple tools and channels in a consistent way is more profitable and builds longer lasting customer relationships than just relying on one tool, such as advertising.[1] Now let's consider the practice of retail marketing.

RETAIL MARKETING AND ADVERTISING

The face of retailing is changing as malls convert to open-air markets, eBay operates an international flea market, and the Internet becomes a primary information source for buyers. *Clicks and bricks* are changing places as store-based retailers (*bricks*) set up Web sites and e-marketers (*clicks*) set up stores. NikeTown stores sell sports as entertainment and ESPN takes the X Games to malls. The more the retail world changes, the more need there is for information and promotion.

A significant part of the United States economy, big stores such as Wal-Mart, Target, Kohl's, Sears, and JCPenney account for more than 10 percent of all U.S. consumer goods spending. In some estimates, retail advertising accounts for nearly half of all the money spent on advertising.

Retail advertising has two missions: (1) selling the brand of the retail store and (2) selling individual branded items the store carries. Best Buy, for example, uses marketing communication to promote itself as these ads demonstrate, but it also sells a variety of electronics brands—everything from Adobe to Yamaha with hundreds of brands in between. Increasingly, retail food and drug chains are giving more space and promotional support to their own **store brands**, also called **private label** or **house brands**.

The three basic types of retail stores are those that are *independently owned* such as a barber shop, those that are part of a *franchise* such as KFC and Hertz, and those that are owned by a major *corporation* such as Starbucks and Macy's. Retailers such as Sears, OfficeMax, Home Depot, and Best Buy advertise nationally and locally. Local advertising is targeted at consumers who live within a geographical market, what we called a DMA in Chapter 11. The Inside Story explains the job of one communication director at Old Navy, a major retail chain.

For franchises, local owners may pay a percent of sales to headquarters to help pay for national advertising. These stores also are generally required to use a certain percent of their sales to do local advertising. When there are several different franchises in a local market (auto dealers, for example), they may form a co-op advertising committee, pool their money, and run local advertising.

Retail Advertising Planning

As mentioned previously, retailers sell not only a range of product brands, but also they sell themselves as destinations for buying a selection of products. A positive, distinctive image is a valuable asset and especially important for upscale retailers like Saks Fifth Avenue. Retailers who want to build a brand image, particularly an upscale one, must clearly and consistently communicate that image to consumers through advertising, other forms of marketing communication, pricing strategies, location, and the physical appearance of the store.

Retail Objectives   Customers base their decisions about where to shop on the quality of the shopping experience, as well as on such retail decision factors as choice, selection, and service. These, in turn, affect retail marcom objectives.

The primary objective is to build **store traffic**, which advertising does by featuring reduced prices on popular items and promoting an appealing store image and shopping experience. Other objectives focus on retail benefits, such as unusual or varied selection of merchandise, friendly and knowledgeable clerks, or prestige brands.

In addition to traffic, most retailers use advertising to help attract new customers, build store loyalty, increase the amount of the average sale, maintain inventory balance by

THE INSIDE STORY

Leadership Skills Are Critical

By Holly Duncan Rockwood, *Former Senior Director of Field Communications, Old Navy*

A day in my life looks different from one day to the next . . . no two are ever the same! Sometimes I come to work to discover there has been an issue in one of our stores, and I need to engage in some fast crisis communications. Other days I might write a speech for an executive, lead my team in a creative brainstorm, or spend time planning a meeting for leaders in our stores' organization.

I travel to our stores at least once a month. We have 40,000 employees who work in more than 900 Old Navy stores in North America. We employ a diverse population of employees from New York to New Orleans, Portland to Puerto Rico, Wichita to Winnipeg. Yet the common thread among all our employees is that they share a love for the brand, which makes it incredibly rewarding for my team to create employee engagement through effective communications.

Old Navy is a fun brand. Customers experience this fun through promotions, marketing, and advertising campaigns. It's also fun for employees of the brand, and we strive to make it a great place to work.

Several years ago two former employees got married to each other and came back to Old Navy to take their wedding pictures under the "item of the week" sign display in our store! Not many brands around the country can create an emotional connection with employees and customers like Old Navy.

My education at the University of Colorado taught me a lot of practical skills for work, but outside the classroom I learned that I had to teach myself my own leadership style.

I'm fortunate to have had a lot of mentors and role models during my career. Some I have aspired to model their leadership behaviors—and others I have been determined not to follow their example!

I treat every experience as a learning opportunity. I enjoy meeting new people, I read a ton, I'm passionate about international travel, I continue to take classes on a variety of subjects—in short, I learn every chance I get.

But it all comes down to this: Every leader is unique; no one can tell you what kind of leader you should be. This is something that is learned through experience. Only you can determine your personal brand of leadership.

Holly Duncan Rockwood earned her B.S. in Advertising from the University of Colorado and an M.S. in Integrated Marketing Communication from Northwestern University.

A positive, distinctive image is a valuable asset and especially important for upscale retailers like Saks Fifth Avenue.

moving out overstocks and outdated merchandise, and counter seasonal lows (see Figure 18.2). Another characteristic of retail advertising is an inherent sense of urgency—"weekend special," "prices good this Saturday only," or "while supplies last." To motivate consumers to switch from a competitor or build loyalty, retail stores also use frequent buyer programs and special services such as banking, pharmacies, and even coffee shops.

Many retailers use any reason they can find to have a sale (President's Day, back-to-school, tax time, overstocks). Stores also search for themes to use in their advertising, such as an exotic place (Madras India was the theme of a special JCPenney sale) or period (see the '70s sale by Virgin Megastore).

Retail Targeting   In targeting consumers, a retailer's first strategic concern is geography: Where do my customers live? How far will they drive to come to my store? In large DMAs individual retailers who only have one or two stores try to find media that just reaches those within their stores' shopping area (generally a two- to five-mile radius).

The next concern is consumer taste, which may also reflect geography. National retailers try to develop offers that appeal to consumers in different parts of the country, as well as in different neighborhoods. H.E.B. Supermarkets operates its stores in both central and south Texas. In San Antonio, the stores located in Mexican-American neighborhoods have a very different merchandise assortment, as well as different advertising than do its stores in other locations.

Cooperative Advertising   One way local retailers can compensate for their smaller advertising budgets and limited expertise is to take advantage of **cooperative (co-op) advertising** (Chapters 2, 8 and 16), in which the national brand reimburses the retailer for part or all of the advertising expenses. Also called **ad allowances** or **promotional allowances**, these co-op funds have become so common that most retailers won't even consider taking on a new brand, especially one in a heavily advertised category, without receiving some support. Large drug and discount chains periodically produce special advertising supplements. Their suppliers are offered an opportunity to buy space in these supplements. The result is that much or all of retail advertising is paid for by the brands carried in the advertising.

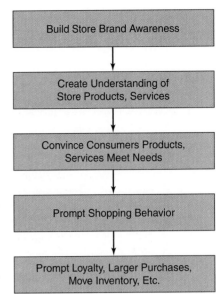

FIGURE 18.2
Retail Advertising Objectives
To build and maintain store traffic, a retail ad strives to meet these objectives.

Principle
The first strategic consideration in retail advertising is geography.

Creating the Retail Ad

Prior to actually writing copy or drawing a layout, creative advertising experts Jeweler and Drewniany suggest that advertisers answer this question: Why would you shop in your store? Possible answers to this question can provide direction for the creative process. They suggest these typical reasons:[2]

- Store's personnel
- Store's location
- Store's pricing policy
- Store's products
- Store's history
- Store's stand on social responsibility issues

Price, for example, can be a factor in establishing a store's image and a reason for shopping. Most discount stores signal their type of merchandise with large, bold prices. Other retailers emphasize price by offering coupons in their print advertising. Featuring prices doesn't necessarily apply only to ads that give the store a bargain or a discount image, however. Price can help the consumer comparison-shop without visiting the store. Discounters like Target and Wal-Mart also use a **price-value strategy** that suggests they offer the best quality you can get for that price level.

Because the main object of retail ads is to attract customers, store location (or telephone number, if advertising is a service) is essential. For merchandise that is infrequently purchased, such as cars, furniture, wallpaper, and hearing aids, the ad should include a map or mention a geographic reference point (for example, three blocks north of the state capitol building) in addition to the regular street address.

Most retail advertising is created and produced by one or a combination of the following: in-house staff, local media, ad agencies, and/or freelancers. The larger the retail operation, the more likely it is to have an in-house advertising staff because few outside agencies are prepared to handle the large number of day-to-day copy changes and the fast deadlines that are typical of major retail advertising.

In the case of national chains and franchises, the national headquarters provides ad formats, TV commercials, and radio spots, all of which can be localized. All local media also are willing to create and produce ads for retailers as a way to get them to use their media. With the exception of television stations, most provide this service free.

Local retailers will sometimes use local agencies to create a campaign they can run over time. If successful, as the Virgin story illustrates, the creative idea may become a national campaign. Generally outside agency work is the most costly way to produce retail ads on a regular and frequent schedule so agencies are used instead to create image ads or campaigns.

Small and medium-sized retailers often save money by using stock artwork in their ads. All daily newspapers subscribe to click art services that provide a wide range of photographs and line art drawings (some for free, others for a fee). Larger retailers or upscale specialty retailers, such as Tiffany's, generally have their art designed by a staff or agency designer to give all their ads a similar look and a distinct image. Some manufacturers also provide a **dealer tag**, which is time left at the end of a radio or television spot or space left at the bottom of print materials, where the local store is mentioned. Retail chains make their

SHOWCASE For Virgin Megastore's "Forever '70s" sale, Chris Hutchinson came up with the idea of a character who was stuck in the '70s—his music, his style, his lingo, his attitude. Where to find this cool cat? The perfect person turned out to be the art director himself who worked out a great outfit—a huge Afro, tight bellbottoms, and an orange leather jacket that his father wore in the real 1970s. The photographer shot on the run to get a semi-documentary look. The client loved the print so the art director directed himself in a set of TV spots, as well. The sale was a huge success nationwide. At the time Hutchinson worked for Bulldog Drummond in San Diego, but he has since moved to Portland, Oregon, where he works at Weiden + Kennedy.

broadcast production more efficient by using a **donut** format in which the opening and closing sections are the same, while the middle changes to focus on different merchandise or local stores.

The Media of Retail Advertising

At the national level, retail chains use a variety of traditional and nontraditional media—newspapers, magazines, television, outdoor, the Internet—for their image or institutional advertising. Manufacturers also provide window banners, free-standing displays, and special direct-mail pieces, such as four-color supplements for the local paper that carry the store's name and address. Other media used by retailers include banners, posters, **shelf talkers** (signs attached to a shelf that let the consumer take away some piece of information or a coupon) and other merchandising materials, such as end-of-aisle displays and shopping cart ads. New interactive electronic kiosks with touch-screen computers, CD-ROM databases, full graphics, and product photos are moving into the aisles in many stores, where they provide more information about more products than the store can ever stock on its shelves.

Unlike national advertisers, local retailers generally prefer reach over frequency since the majority of their advertising is for special promotions. Because retailers can choose from many local media, they are careful to use media that minimize waste. That's why direct mail is now the second-largest advertising medium used by retailers, next to newspapers.

Newspapers have always made up the bulk of retailer advertising because the local newspaper fits the retailer's desire for geographic coverage and immediacy. Retailers can gain some measure of audience selectivity by advertising in specific sections of the paper, such as sports (for sporting goods stores) and financial pages (for banks and loan companies), and in **zone editions** (certain versions of the paper that go to certain counties and suburbs). Free-distribution newspapers called **shoppers** are also popular advertising vehicles for retailers, as are **preprints**, also called **free-standing inserts (FSIs)**, which are placed inside newspapers.

Nearly all major markets now have at least one local independent station and a public television station. Radio is used by local retailers because it has a relatively low cost, a high degree of geographic and audience selectivity, and flexibility in scheduling. Many of the top-50 markets in the United States have at least one local magazine offering retailers high-quality, four-color ads to reach upscale consumers. Some national magazines have regional or metropolitan editions that also enable local retailers to buy exposure within their trading area only.

The Internet is making a huge difference in business operations as some retailers are selling as much online as they do from their stores—a successful clicks and bricks strategy. In addition to online business, retailers have found interesting ways to use the Web for marketing communication. Some fashion retailers, for example, employ their own bloggers who review the store's lines.[3]

BUSINESS-TO-BUSINESS ADVERTISING

Advertising directed at people in business who buy or specify products for business use is called **business-to-business (B2B) advertising**. Business marketing is the marketing of goods and services to other businesses. Although personal selling is the most common method of communicating with business buyers, business advertising is used to create corporate brand awareness, enhance the company's reputation, support salespeople and other channel members, and generate new business leads.

B2B Buying Behavior

Businesses buy goods and services for two basic reasons: (1) they need ingredients for the products they manufacture, and (2) they need goods (such as computers, desks, and chairs) and services (legal, accounting, maintenance) for their business operations. Business marketing differs from consumer marketing in terms of who buys a product, what the buying motive is, and how the buying decision is made. Buying decisions are

DUMP THEM, YOU BREAK THE LAW. RECYCLE IMPROPERLY, YOU BREAK THE LAW. MEANWHILE, MORE TIRES JUST CAME IN.

Whether your company produces waste, tries to recycle it or depends on a steady supply of raw materials, your business is bound to be affected by environmental controls.

There are thousands of regulations, both in the U.S. and overseas, designed to protect the environment. These environmental standards are in a constant state of flux, and can have far-reaching risk implications for all kinds of businesses.

Fortunately, AIG specializes in designing the kind of custom coverages you need to cope successfully with changing conditions. In fact, AIG is the only worldwide insurance and financial organization that helps manage your business risks with a broad range of customized services. Services like environmental remediation coverage, hedging and market-making in commodities and stop-loss protection. And we've got the top financial ratings to back us up. So we'll be there to help keep your business rolling along.

WORLD LEADERS IN INSURANCE AND FINANCIAL SERVICES
American International Group, Inc., Dept. A, 70 Pine Street, New York, NY 10270

Government regulations affect many businesses. AIG advertising assures business purchasers that the company offers customized coverage to help clients deal with government regulations. The decision factors for business customers tend to be price, service, quality, and assurance of supply. This AIG ad offers its insurance and financial services as safeguards against regulatory problems.

Principle

B2B buyers are driven by rational, pragmatic considerations, and those concerns must be addressed by B2B advertising.

often made by committees on behalf of the people who use the products, and the actual purchase is negotiated by a specialist in that category called a **buyer**. Department stores, for example, have a team of buyers who select the merchandise for their different departments.

As you can see in the AIG advertisement, purchasing objectives in B2B marketing center on rational, pragmatic considerations such as price, service, quality of the good or service, and assurance of supply. For that reason, B2B advertising tends to use rational strategies and focus on reasons and benefits.

Types of B2B Advertising

Businesses are grouped according to the **North American Industry Classification System (NAICS)**, which was formerly known as *The Standard Industrial Classification (SIC) system* (see http://www.census.gov/epcd/www/naics. html). This system allows a business advertiser to determine its customers' business category and then obtain media lists that include the publications this group uses. As we see in Figure 18.3, the primary B2B industries are classified as industrial, government, trade, professional, and agricultural.

- *Industrial advertising.* Original equipment manufacturers (OEMs), such as International Harvester and General Motors, purchase industrial goods or services that either become a part of the final product or aid business operations. **Industrial advertising** is directed at OEMs. For example, when General Motors purchases tires from Goodyear, information needs focus on whether the purchase will contribute to positively to the car. When Goodyear purchases packaging materials to ship the tires it manufactures, information needs focus on prompt, predictable delivery.
- *Government advertising.* The largest purchasers of industrial goods in the United States are federal, state, and local governments. These government units purchase virtually every kind of goods, from $15 hammers to multimillion-dollar missiles. Such goods may be advertised in *Commerce Business Daily* or *Defense News*. These purchases are usually made by bids and contracts, and the decision is made on price and specifications.
- *Trade/channel advertising.* **Trade advertising** is used to persuade distribution channel members, such as distributors, wholesalers, dealers, and retailers to stock the manufacturer's products. *Chain Store Age, Florist's Review*, and *Pizza and Pasta* are examples of trade publications, and there are thousands more covering every possible product category. Resellers want information on the profit margins they can expect to receive, the product's major selling points, and the producer's plans for consumer advertising and other promotional support.
- *Professional advertising.* Advertising directed at a group of mostly white-collar workers such as lawyers, accountants, technology consultants, doctors, teachers, funeral directors, and advertising and marketing specialists is known as **professional advertising**. Advertisers interested in attracting professionals advertise in publications such as the *Music Educators' Journal* and *Advertising Age*.
- *Agricultural advertising.* Agricultural advertising promotes a variety of products and services, such as animal health products, seeds, farm machinery and equipment, crop dusting, and fertilizer. Large and small farmers alike want to know how industrial products can assist them in the production of agricultural commodities. They turn to such publications as *California Farmer* and *Trees and Turf* for such assistance.

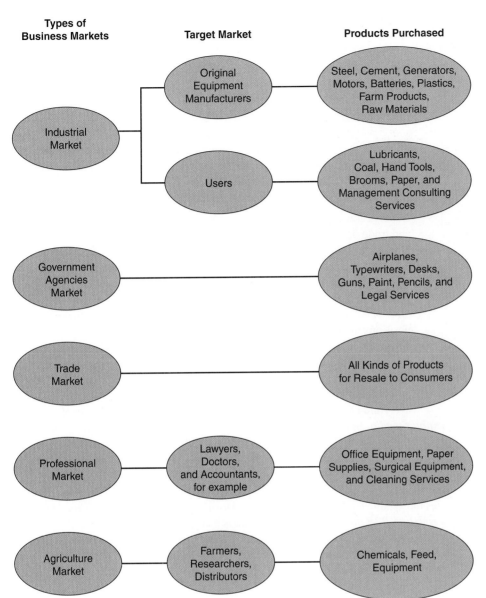

Types of Business Markets

Target Market

Products Purchased

FIGURE 18.3
Types of Business Markets
The overall B2B market has five distinct markets, each of which purchases its products and services differently.

Creating B2B Advertising

In terms of objectives, B2B advertising is used to create and maintain brand awareness and to support the personal selling function. As a result, B2B advertising objectives center on creating company awareness, increasing overall selling efficiency, and generating leads (see Figure 18.4). When buyers are aware of a company's reputation, products, and record in the industry, salespeople are more effective. Also advertising in trade magazines and general business publications is a much less expensive way to reach influencers than personal sales calls. In other words, advertising is used to presell while a sales force is used to close sales.

As in consumer advertising, the best B2B ads are relevant and understandable and strike an emotional chord in the prospective client. Business-to-business advertisers follow these guidelines to create effective ads:

- Make sure the ad selects the strongest benefit and presents it prominently and persuasively.
- Dramatize the most important benefit, either by showing the product in action or by visualizing a problem and offering your product or service as a solution.

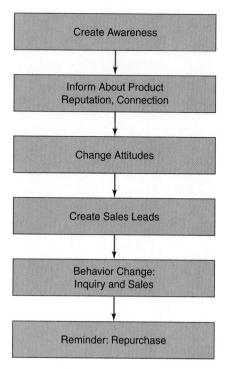

FIGURE 18.4

Business-to-Business Objectives
B2B advertising has six main objectives.

- Make sure the visual is relevant to the key message. It should help readers understand how your product or service works or instantly show that you understand the problem.
- Make the offer as clear as possible. What exactly do you want the reader to do as a result of seeing your ad?
- Provide contact information. It should be easy for the potential customer to follow through with a response.

B2B Advertising Media

Although some business advertisers use traditional consumer media, most rely on general business or trade publications, Web sites, industrial directories, direct marketing, or some combination of these media.

- *General business and trade publications.* As we saw in Chapter 8, business and trade publications are classified as either horizontal or vertical. **Horizontal publications** are directed to people who hold similar jobs in different companies across different industries. For example, *Purchasing* is a specialized business publication targeted to people across industries who are purchasing agents. In contrast, **vertical publications**, such as *Iron Age and Steel* or *Advertising Age*, are targeted toward people who hold different positions in a particular industry.
- *Directory advertising.* Every state has an industrial directory, and there are also a number of private ones. One of the most popular industrial directories is the New York-based *Thomas Register*. The 19-volume *Register* contains 50,000 product headings and listings from 123,000 industrial companies selling everything from heavy machine tools to copper tubing to orchestra pits.
- *Consumer media.* Sometimes businesses advertise in consumer magazines, such as *Golf, Time,* or *Newsweek,* in the hope of building widespread brand recognition, such as the "Intel Inside" campaign. There also has been some growth in business television programming, which provides a good message vehicle for certain B2B companies. For example, Financial Network News (FNN) produces its own business shows and carries the syndicated business shows *This Morning's Business* and *First Business.*
- *The web and B2B advertisers.* The Internet is a key medium for B2B advertisers. Company Web sites allow business clients to view product lists, place orders, check prices and availability, and replace inventories automatically. The Internet is also a primary research tool used by B2B marketers to check out competitors and to find areas of new business and suppliers. One of the most popular B2B sites on the Internet is the FedEx site, which allows clients to track packages, obtain price information, and learn about FedEx software and services. It receives 1.7 million tracking requests a month, 40 percent of which probably would have been called in to the company's 800 number if the Web site were not available. Because handling each call costs approximately $1, its Web site saves FedEx more than $8 million a year.
- *B2B direct marketing.* Direct mail has the capacity to sell a B2B brand, provide sales leads, and lay the groundwork for subsequent sales calls. Business advertisers use print and online catalogs and product literature to reach their target markets, which support the selling function by providing technical data about the product and supplementary information concerning price, availability, delivery, and warranties. Direct marketing is widely used because most target audiences are smaller than the audiences for many consumer brands; therefore, B2B marketers can target their messages (because they know names and addresses) and greatly minimize media waste.

NONPROFIT OR SOCIAL MARKETING

Effective marketing and advertising techniques are not only important for businesses, but also for nonprofit organizations involved in community issues, public policy, and good causes. Nonprofit marketing is used by organizations such as hospitals, government agencies, zoos, museums, orchestras, religious organizations, charities, and universities and schools to "sell" their services, programs, and ideas, as the Matter of Practice box illustrates.

A MATTER OF PRACTICE

Rebranding a City

By John Brewer, *President and CEO, Chamber of Commerce, Billings, Montana*

Reinvent, reinvent, reinvent! Our marketplace, national trends, and future projections change constantly, as do the relevance and expectations of a Chamber of Commerce and its members.

In 2005 I became the new CEO. We had a new staff and an enthusiastic board seeking new directions for the Chamber. We found that the Chamber needed a new image, a new position in the community, a new set of core functions, a new strategic plan, a new staff with passion to move Billings forward, and a reenergized membership.

Even a nonprofit organization has a business life cycle; one that has not maintained relevancy can suck the breath out of the organization. The Chamber needed to examine all facets of its operations and dramatically reinvent itself to better serve the community and its members.

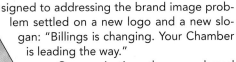

One of our first steps was to ask our membership how we could position our efforts to assist them more effectively and why they felt membership was declining. We did this through Web-based surveys as well as dozens of one-on-one meetings and a four-part focus group called "Java with John," an opportunity for community members to share their thoughts in small group settings with the President/CEO. We also examined industry best practices by identifying 17 Chambers across the country similar to ours and then developing a matrix of their best practices to help in our goal setting.

One major theme was consistent and resulted in changing our mission and vision. That theme was that the *Chamber should serve the entire community* and, if we did a good job at that, our membership would benefit.

What that meant was that we needed to rebrand the Chamber to be more relevant to the community and to our membership. Three task forces were organized to move the Chamber in that direction. The group as-

signed to addressing the brand image problem settled on a new logo and a new slogan: "Billings is changing. Your Chamber is leading the way."

Communicating the new brand and all of its elements and its meaning became our number one challenge. A complete corporate rebranding requires all print, electronic, and other forms of communication to present the new brand face on its launch date. Prior to the launch, we wanted to build interest and excitement through teaser pieces (direct mail, newsletter, and media releases). By the August 17 launch date, the interior and exterior signage had to be replaced, as well as the e-news, the newsletter, and the stationary package. The launch event itself was widely broadcast and open to the public.

The new logo, through unique graphic positioning of the words, reads: "It's in Billings." Though very simple and fun in design, the logo speaks volumes as to why we choose to call Billings home. It also reflects the abundance of reasons people visit here, relocate a business, or move their families to Billings. Our new brand image, as reflected in this design, shouts out change, energy, and excitement.

The campaign was (and continues to be) a great success both anecdotally as well as through a few key measurements established prior to the campaign—an increase in the member retention rate, in our membership dues base, in committee participation, and in positive media coverage. In less than two years, the Billings Chamber has an all-time high number of members.

We discovered that in an ever-changing and competitive marketplace, change was necessary. And the community response supported our efforts.

A graduate of the University of West Florida, Brewer was nominated by Professor Tom Groth.

Many people make the mistake of thinking that competition only exists between for-profit companies. Nothing could be farther from the truth. Nonprofits often have to compete as hard, if not more so, than for-profit companies because they know consumers and businesses have just so much money and time to donate to nonprofit organizations. It is also a myth to think that nonprofits are not businesses. The Red Cross and the Salvation Army, for example, have hundreds of full-time paid staff and multimillion-dollar annual budgets.

Nonprofit organizations have a number of goals, such as *membership* (AARP, chamber of commerce), *donations* (Red Cross, United Way, American Cancer Society), *participation* (Habitat for Humanity), *sales* (museum gift shops), *recruitment* (the military, universities), *attitude change* (political parties), *advocacy* (Weyerhauser for forest management), and *visits or attendance* (state tourism programs, art museums). These goals also can be described in terms of specific types of campaigns.

Fund-Raising

One activity that almost all nonprofits do is **fund-raising**, sometimes called **development**, often under the guidance of a *development officer* who is a professional specializing in fund-raising. Groups such as Save the Children and the Nature Conservancy use sophisticated segmentation and message strategies to target audiences and raise funds.

Universities and other organizations such as museums and hospitals use **capital campaigns** designed to raise a specified amount of money in a set time frame to finance new buildings, equipment purchases, and other programs. These campaigns operate with a carefully designed strategy that involves sophisticated motivation strategies based on segmentation, targeting, goal setting, and leadership identification. Events, direct marketing, and campaign literature are important tactical tools.

Social Marketing and Public Communication Campaigns

The use of marketing programs and marketing communication tools to create awareness of a social need is called **social marketing**. It is also used to motivate consumers and businesses to act in certain ways, such as give money, volunteer time, or adopt certain policies. The antismoking and antidrug campaigns are examples of social marketing.

Social marketing is also called public communication. **Public communication campaigns** are undertaken by nonprofit organizations as a conscious effort to influence the thoughts or actions of the public. The biggest and longest-running program is the Advertising Council, which is a network of advertising agencies, media, and suppliers that donate their services to create ads and campaigns on behalf of socially important causes—crime prevention, child abuse, mental illness, and the environment. The "Smoky the Bear" fire prevention effort is one of the longest-running and best-known Ad Council campaigns.

Another well-known public communication campaign is "Just Say No" by the Partnership for a Drug Free America and the Ad Council. It has used advertising and public relations to fight teen drug use. The *truth*® campaign we featured in Chapter 1 is a national antismoking campaign aimed at teens that seeks to demonize smoking and the tobacco industry. Other campaigns from various state health departments have taken different approaches. For example, The Own Your C campaign, which is featured in the Matter of Principle box, is an example of one state's integrated public communication campaign plan that attempts to appeal to teens in a more positive way.

Cause and Mission Marketing

Concern for social issues is increasingly important for for-profit companies as they want to be seen as good corporate citizens. To help achieve this objective, many companies use some of their marketing communication dollars to explain how they are being socially responsible. A **societal marketing** philosophy describes the operations of companies whose corporate mission reflects their desire to do good—the business philosophies of Ben & Jerry's, Tom's of Maine, and the Body Shop, for example. Their commitment is expressed in the way they design, produce, and market their products.

In addition to a societal marketing business philosophy, corporate public relations activities are sometimes designed to create a positive company image by emphasizing a company's concern for social issues and the steps it takes to make a positive contribution to society.

Adopting a good cause and helping in its fund-raising and other community-oriented efforts is called **cause marketing**. Sometimes called "sales promotion with a PR spin," cause marketing is described as doing good things and getting credit for it.[4] For example, Wal-Mart was an early responder to the Katrina disaster with truckloads of water as well as special placement help for its employees who were affected. Target has donated a huge amount of money to its local communities as part of its community caring effort. Carol Cone, president of the Cone agency, calls these efforts *passion branding* because they link brands to causes for which people feel passion.[5] Allstate Insurance has a distracted-driver

A MATTER OF PRINCIPLE

It's Your Choice

Colorado's Tobacco Education & Prevention Partnership (STEPP) wanted to speak to teens about smoking in a style they would find appealing and interesting. That agency hired Denver-based Cactus Marketing Communication in 2006 to create its antismoking campaign.

The objective of the campaign was to help teens realize that their choices define who they are and who they will become. Using the slogan, "Own your C" (Own your Choices), the campaign was designed to give them the information they needed to make informed choices about smoking.

The campaign started with a variety of marketing research efforts that included secondary research, focus groups, surveys, a youth online forum, and ethnography studies. The research led to a number of insights, including the finding that teens are surrounded by negative messages and respond more to messages that reflect their optimism. They are "aspirational" and want to see messages that reflect this idealized image of themselves. Future is important, but it is also immediate—just a few years down the road. They understand their decision may affect their futures, but they also act impulsively. They are social, influenced by their peers, and live with a self-induced pressure to belong.

Most of all, the research found that teens want to be in control of their lives—hence the decision to use "choice" as a strategy. Choice is universal, relevant, emotionally appealing, and empowering. It is summarized in this position statement:

> "Your C is your choice. Every choice you make defines you. Own your C."

An integrated campaign, it used a multilayer approach that combined traditional and new media. The most important element was the www.ownyourC.com interactive Web site. It includes discussion boards, tools to download (art, music, ring tones). The concept is a virtual town called C-Ville with a "Park" area featuring decision-making aids, a "Downtown" area with the C Campaign elements, and a "Drive-in" area featuring information and the cessation program. The site is also used to communicate about contests, events, and new content. Other campaign tools include:

- Irreverent television ads that parody government-sponsored PSA campaigns, classic horror movies, and superheroes
- Banner ads for online advertising
- The C-ride tour (a small, customized truck that made appearances statewide at youth-oriented events)
- Mobile marketing (cell phone wallpapers, ring tones, and text messages)
- Promotional items (stickers, T-shirts, and hats designed by artists)
- Quit kits
- A cessation tool that combined a Web site with text messaging in a quit support program
- Posters supporting the cessation Web site and program

The director of teen programming at STEPP said the success of the program lies in its ability to create a community. She explained, "We've created an evolving educational campaign with multiple touch points designed to engage, entertain, and inform teens that the casual choice to use tobacco today can lead to being an addicted adult tomorrow."

Source: "Own your C" STEPP's 2006 Youth Tobacco Prevention and Cessation Campaign Overview, produced by Cactus Marketing Communication, Denver, Colorado, 2007.

campaign called the "dedicated investor" that warns against text messaging while driving, an offense referred to as DWT (driving while texting).[6]

If a commitment reflects a company's core business strategy, as in Tom's of Maine and Ben & Jerry's environmental commitment, Dove's "real women" campaign, and Avon's support of breast cancer research, it is called **mission marketing**. Mission marketing links a company's mission and core values to a cause that connects with the company's and its customers' interests. It is more of a commitment than cause marketing because it reflects a long-term brand building perspective and the mission becomes the focal point for integrating all the company's marketing communication.[7] It also unites the entire organization and its stakeholders, particularly its employees, through their commitment to the effort.

Principle
Cause marketing and mission marketing are driven by the passion employees and other stakeholders, as well as customers, feel for a good cause.

INTERNATIONAL ADVERTISING AND MARKETING COMMUNICATION

The globalization of marketing communication is driven by the development of international media, globalization of brands, and the spread of market-based economies in countries and regions such as China, South America, India, and Eastern Europe. Also, the expanded use of English as an international language is helping spread Western ideas of marketing to the rest of the world. The Web has had a huge impact bringing the ability to market internationally to even the smallest of companies.

Stages of Marketing Development

Virtually every product category can be divided into local, national, regional (trading bloc), and international markets and brands. Typically this involves a process that begins when a national company expands to a few foreign markets by **exporting** its products. Then at stage two it begins to internationalize its operations by selling to a group of markets in a region (Europe or Asia, for example) and eventually moves to a global perspective, the third stage, with brands sold throughout the world.

A characteristic of globalized companies is that the **country of origin** label often doesn't apply. Nokia and Motorola, even though they are not U.S. companies, are both familiar brands to U.S. consumers. Country of origin can also be a problem as McDonald's found out when its restaurants were targeted because it represents America in a time when the country's political actions are being criticized worldwide. McDonald's has been boycotted in the Philippines and Argentina, as well as in many Arab countries—not for anything it does but simply because of its image as an iconic American brand. Efforts by McDonald's local franchisees have included trying to present a local face by using its employees in traditional dress standing outside the store and by making contributions to local charities.[8]

The Global versus Local Debate

There is an old axiom, "All business is local." An extension of this saying is: "Think globally, act locally." Although advertising campaigns can be created for a global market, it must be relevant to a transaction that is completed at or near home or in the office.

A classic article by Harvard Business School professor Theodore Levitt ignited a debate over how to conduct global marketing. Levitt argued that companies should operate as if there were only one global market. He suggested that differences among nations and cultures were not diminishing and people throughout the world are motivated by the same desires and wants.[9] Other scholars argued that Levitt misinterpreted the importance of cultural differences and cited the success of such brands as Coca-Cola, PepsiCo, and McDonald's in developing products and marketing for the various cultures they serve.[10]

In support of Levitt's thinking, some researchers propose sets of what they call *universal values* that cross cultures. They include such values as:

1. Protecting the family
2. Honesty
3. Health and fitness
4. Self-esteem
5. Self-reliance

Practical Tips

How Advertising Works Cross-Culturally

By Marieke de Mooij, *Ph.D., Consultant, Cross Cultural Communication, The Netherlands*

In my research, the most important finding for advertisers is that culture influences how we communicate, both in interpersonal communication and in mass communication. The implication of my research is that advertising works differently across cultures, and that thesis is developed in both of my books, *Consumer Behavior and Culture* and *Global Marketing and Advertising*.

I work with the theories of Geert Hofstede, whose dimensional model of national culture is now applied worldwide. I used his country scores to analyze differences in consumer behavior across cultures. Here are some things to think about as you plan or critique cross-national advertising that does—or doesn't—accommodate cultural differences.

- There is no one universal model for information processing. Because people don't process information in the same way, the role of advertising also varies across cultures.
- The dominant information-based theory of advertising processing originated in a U.S.-U.K. context. It is not necessarily valid for other cultures.
- In the collectivistic cultures of the South of Europe, people do not search for information in a conscious way as they do in the North of Europe.
- People who view themselves as well informed to make a buying decision (North Europeans, for example) score high on Hofstede's individualism dimension.
- In a collectivistic country like Spain, frequent social interaction causes an automatic flow of information between people, who, as a result, know things without having to search for information.
- The role of advertising in these collectivistic cultures is not to provide information but to create emotional bonding.

- The idea of the universality of emotions has been discredited in the past decade. Both expression and recognition of emotions vary across cultures. The Chinese, for example, tend to laugh when they feel embarrassed.
- In most of Asia people do not display negative emotions because it disturbs harmony. Generally non-Western subjects categorize Western emotional expressions incorrectly. Examples are disgust, anger, fear, and contempt.
- The more abstract emotions are formulated, the more they are universal. Abstract terms like happiness suggest universality, but what makes people happy varies enormously. As a result, ads for lotteries are very different.
- Personality traits are related to culture, which has implications for connecting personal traits to global brands. I found that people in different countries, for example, attribute different personality traits to successful global brands like Coca-Cola, Nike, and Nivea even though the companies wanted the brand personalities to be consistent.
- Consumers attribute personalities to brands that fit their own cultural values, not the values of the producer.
- Marketing managers' need for cross-cultural consistency is typical of Anglo-Saxon and North-European cultures. In most other countries in the world, people prefer to adapt.

Marieke de Mooij, Ph.D., is a consultant in cross-cultural communications and a visiting professor at various universities in the Netherlands, Finland, Germany, and Spain. She is the author of several books on the influence of culture on marketing and advertising, including *Global Marketing and Advertising, Understanding Cultural Paradoxes, Consumer Behavior and Culture,* and *Consequences for Global Marketing and Advertising.*

6. Justice
7. Freedom
8. Friendship
9. Knowledge
10. Learning

Dutch scholar Geert Hofstede, an expert on cultural differences, insists that the impact of national culture on business and consumption patterns is huge and should be accommodated in marketing and advertising strategies. Based on a study of 116,000 IBM employees around the world, Hofstede found their cultural differences to be stronger than the legendary IBM corporate culture that he assumed would be a standardizing influence. Hofstede also found that the American values of taking initiative, personal competency, and rugged individualism are not universal values and that some cultures prize collective thinking and group norms rather than independence. The Practical Tips box explains what one researcher has learned about the application of Hofstede's principles to advertising.

The outgrowth of the local-versus-global debate has been three schools of thought on advertising across national borders:

- *Standardization.* The **standardization** school of thought contends that differences between countries are a matter of degree, so advertisers must instead focus on the similarities of consumers and a consistent brand presentation.
- *Localization (adaptation).* The **localization** or **adaptation** school of thought argues that advertisers must consider differences among countries, including local culture, stage of economic and industrial development, stage of life cycle, media availability, research availability, and legal restrictions.
- *Combination.* This school of thought reasons that a combination of standardization and localization may produce the most effective advertising. Some elements of brand identity and strategy, for example, may be standardized, but advertising executions may need to be adapted to the local culture.

The reality of global advertising suggests that a combination approach is best. The challenge for advertisers is to balance variations nationally or regionally with a basic global brand plan that maintains brand consistency. The adaptability continuum shown in Figure 18.5 elaborates on these three perspectives.

As we have said, most companies use the combination approach or lean toward localization. Honda, for example, uses a decentralized advertising strategy for its CR-V. The auto manufacturer has a global brand guideline that all agencies must follow; however, these guidelines apply mostly to use of the logo. There is a global Web site with a standard look and format. The advertising strategy varies with the market. In Iceland, as Ingvi Logason explained, "We created a completely unique strategy based on our local research and knowledge." The following list summarizes the benefits of standardization and local strategies:

When to Use a Standardization Advertising Strategy

- Standardization will lead to savings through economies of scale (advertising production, planning, control).
- Standardization ensures that advertising messages of a product are complementary and reinforcing.
- The company maintains control over the image projected by advertising for the brand.
- Global media create opportunities for global marketing.
- Converging buyer wants and needs mean that buyers everywhere will increasingly want the same products.
- There is little or no competition in many foreign markets.
- Graphic and visual advertising approaches can be used to overcome cultural differences.

When to Use a Localized Advertising Strategy

- A better fit with local markets means the advertiser is less likely to overlook local variations that affect buyer behavior.
- As a general rule, the fewer the people who have to approve decisions, the faster they can be made.
- Getting local managers and employees involved and motivated is much easier if those people have a say in the advertising decisions.
- Any cost reductions resulting from globalization often are offset by mistargeted ads.
- The chance of cultural blunders decreases.
- Strategically sound advertising is more likely to be successful.

Principle

Globalization is a fact, so marketers strive for a consistent brand strategy that still allows them to honor cultural differences when those differences are relevant to the brand's marketing strategy.

FIGURE 18.5

The Adaptability Continuum
Most global companies fall in the middle and right side of the continuum in their global strategies.

| Totally Standardized Strategy and Execution | Standardized Strategy, Translated Execution | Standardized Strategy, Modified Execution | Totally Localized Strategy and Execution |

Cultural Meanings   The expression of advertising messages may vary in different cultural settings because of cultural meaning. The major distinction is between **high-context cultures**, in which the meaning of a message can be best understood when contained within contextual cues, and **low-context cultures** in which the message can be understood as it stands.[11] In other words, in Japanese a word can have multiple meanings. Listeners or readers will not understand the exact meaning of a word unless they clearly understand the context in which the word is used. In contrast, English is a low-context language—most of its words have clearly defined meanings that are not highly dependent on the words surrounding them. Figure 18.6 lists cultures from the highest to lowest context, with Japanese being the highest-context culture. This model helps explain the difficulties of advertising in other languages.

Advertising messages constructed by writers from high-context cultures might be difficult to understand in low-context cultures because they may offer too much detail to make the point clearly. In contrast, messages authored by writers from low-context cultures may be difficult to understand in high-context cultures because they omit essential contextual detail.

Central Control versus Local Adaptation   As noted previously, some advertisers develop tightly controlled global campaigns with minimum adaptation for local markets. Others develop local campaigns in every major market. Most companies are somewhere in the middle. How are global campaigns created? International advertising campaigns have two basic starting points: (1) success in one country and (2) a centrally conceived strategy. Planning approaches also include variations on the central campaign and bottom-up creativity.

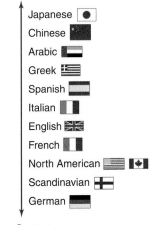

FIGURE 18.6
High- to Low-Context Cultures
The language of advertising messages is not as easy to craft in high-context cultures as in low-context cultures, where the meaning of a sentence is not so dependent on surrounding sentences.

- *Local initiative.* A successful advertising campaign, conceived for national application, is modified for use in other countries. Wrigley, Marlboro, IBM, Waterman, Seiko, Philips, Ford, and many other companies have taken successful campaigns from one country and transplanted them around the world, a practice called *search and reapply.* When a local campaign is found to be successful, that campaign is taken to one or two countries that are similar to see how well the campaign works in these areas. If it is successful, use of the campaign is expanded and can eventually become the brand's primary international campaign. What is interesting about this strategy is that it provides additional motivation for local agencies. While all local agencies want to do a good job to keep their local business, it is a major ego boost—not to mention the additional financial awards—when a local campaign is taken beyond its original country's borders.

    The Honda CR-V is an example. As Logason explains, "Because of the effectiveness of the campaign—both the insights behind the strategy and the idea of ownership of the 4×4 concept, which was so successful in Iceland—the campaign caught the eye of the global office, and it has been distributed and showcased globally to dealers in other markets as an example of strong, clever positioning."

- *Centrally conceived campaigns.* The second approach, a centrally conceived campaign, was pioneered by Coca-Cola and is now used increasingly in global strategies. Microsoft uses a centralized strategy for its Xbox video game system; since it was a new brand, a consistent marketing strategy was deemed to be essential. Although the centralization concept is simple, its application can be difficult. A work team, task force, or action group (the names vary) assembles from around the world to present, debate, modify, if necessary, and agree on a basic strategy as the foundation for the campaign. Cost is a huge factor. If the same photography and artwork can be used universally, this can save thousands of dollars over each local variation.

- *Variations on central campaigns.* Variations on the centrally conceived campaign also exist. For example, BBDO's many local agencies were used to adapt the creative ideas for all the markets served by DaimlerChrysler (now Chrysler after the company split). The office that develops the approved campaign would be designated the **lead agency** and would develop all the necessary elements of the campaign and prepare a standards manual for use in other countries. Because photography, artwork, television production, and color printing are costly, developing these items in one location and

The Honda CR-V campaign in Iceland was successful because it gave the CR-V ownership of the 4×4 position by equating the CR-V with some kind of carrier. In this ad, the connection was made to a golf cart and the Post-Its were used as call-outs to further explain the features of the car.

then overlaying new copy or re-recording the voice track in the local language saves money. However, since some countries, such as Malaysia, require that all ads be locally produced, this approach gives direction to the message but still allows for local requirements to be met.

• **Bottom-up creativity.** Sometimes a competition may be used to find the best new idea. For example, to extend McDonald's I'm lovin' it campaign, McDonald's global chief marketing officer held a contest among McDonald's ad agencies all over the world. One winner, which became part of the international pool of ads, came from China, which is developing a lively creative advertising industry that produces edgy, breakthrough ads for young people. McDonald's strategy was not just to do the creative work in the United States but rather to "Let the best ideas win."[12]

Planning Global Strategies

Assuming that the ad campaign has been approved centrally, with a local application approach its execution must be adapted to suit the local market, and that may involve modifying basic strategy decisions, such as objectives, targeting, and perhaps even positioning.

Global Objectives   The problem of managing brand consistency is largely responsible for limiting most global marketing objectives to awareness and recall, two effective yet easily attainable marketing communication measures, although more specific objectives may be needed in individual markets. For example, a brand may be well known in one market, so its primary objective, then, is reminder. At the same time it may be newly launched in another country, so the objectives there are awareness building and trial.

Targeting Issues   International marketers need to answer three basic targeting questions: (1) What countries? (2) What level of market development? (3) Which cultural cohort groups?

Where to Advertise   This is generally the easiest to answer as it is driven by where the brand is distributed.

Market Development Level   Countries, especially developing countries, vary greatly in market infrastructure, literacy levels, economic level, and level of media development. Some countries' standard of living is such that luxury brands, for example, would not find a large enough segment of the population to cover the cost of setting up distribution and supporting the brand with advertising and a sales force.

Cultural Cohorts   A cultural cohort is a segment of customers from multiple countries sharing common characteristics that translate into common wants and needs. New mothers are an example. Regardless of their nationality, new mothers want their babies to be happy and healthy. Teenagers are another cohort—teens in Tokyo and New York City may have more in common than a teen and his father.

Positioning the Global Brand   Research must be conducted to identify the problems and opportunities facing the product in each of the international markets to be entered, as the Charmin commercial illustrates. Particularly important is a good understanding of consumer buying motives in each market. This is almost impossible to develop without locally based consumer research. If analysis reveals that consumers' buying behavior and the competitive environment are the same across international markets, it may be possible to use a standardized positioning throughout.

Setting the Budget   All the budgeting techniques discussed in Chapter 7 apply in foreign markets. When preparing a single advertising plan for multiple markets, many companies use an objective-task budgeting approach that entails a separate budget for each foreign market. (Remember that this approach looks at the objectives for each activity and determines the cost of accomplishing each objective.) This technique adds some flexibility to localize campaigns as needed. However, local practices also may affect the budget decision. Most notably, the exchange rate from country to country may affect not only the amount of money spent in a particular market, but also the timing of the expenditures. The cost of television time in Tokyo is approximately twice what it is on U.S. networks, and, rather than being sold during an up-front market every spring, Japanese TV time is wholesaled several times during the year.

Executing the International Campaign   The execution of a global campaign is usually more complex than a national plan. The creative may need to be reshot with local models and settings as well as language translation. Language is always a problem for a campaign that is dependent on words rather than visuals as the primary meaning carrier. A team of language experts may be needed to adjust the terms and carry over the meanings in the different languages. The Pepsi slogan, "Come Alive," for example, was translated in Taiwan as, "Pepsi will bring your ancestors back from the dead." KFC's "Finger licking good" slogan, translated into Chinese as "Eat your fingers off."

Product names can even be a problem. In Canada, Mercedes-Benz found that its GST model name is also the familiar initials of a tax commonly referred to in English as the "gouge and screw tax."

Government approval of television commercials can be difficult to secure in some countries. As advertisers move into international and global advertising, they also face many of the same ethical issues that advertisers deal with in the United States, such as the representation of women and advertising to children, but they may also have to deal with questions about the Americanization or westernization of local cultures.[13] An example comes from a Nike ad used in China that showed LeBron James teaching moves to martial arts masters. Chinese officials banned it because they consider it insulting to national dignity.

But it's not just government bans that can trouble ad strategies. Social responsibility is taken seriously in some countries and, with the Internet and e-mail, consumer concerns can create a huge issue. For example, an ad by fashion house Dolce & Gabbana showed a bare-chested man pinning a glamorous woman to the ground while his buddies looked on. Consumers in Spain, Italy, and the United States complained that it trivialized violence against women, and the many e-mail complaints led the company to drop the ad.[14]

International Media Buying   In terms of the media buy, media is different in every country—not only different, but also developing and evolving. As a result, it is absolutely essential that a local agency be used to handle the media buy. In the early 1990s in China, for example, there was hardly an advertising industry or advertising media opportunities. By 2007 media spending in the country reached $14 billion, and China is widely recognized as the world's "most fragmented market." Television has 95 percent penetration with more than 2,200 channels. Internet use in China grew 23 percent from 2006 to 2007, reaching 137 million registered users. That's only 10.5 percent of China's population, so you can see the incredible growth opportunities for this medium.[15]

Adjustments may need to be made for seasonality. For example, a campaign in the Southern Hemisphere, especially for consumer goods, requires major changes from a Northern Hemisphere campaign. In the Southern Hemisphere, summer, Christmas, and back-to-school campaigns are all compressed from November through January. Holidays also differ based on local history and religion. Christmas, for example, is celebrated in Christian lands and Ramadan in Muslim countries.

Positioning is one of the key strategic elements that brands usually try to keep consistent from country to country. Charmin, for example, continues to emphasize softness through the device of a cuddly bear, even in Mexico where this commercial ran. Note that it is largely a nonverbal execution, which is easier to use for global campaigns than those with a lot of words.

Everything takes longer internationally—count on it. The New York business day overlaps for only three hours with the business day in London, for two hours with most of Europe, and for one hour with Greece and not at all with Japan, Hong Kong, the Middle East, or Australia. For these reasons e-mail that permits electronic transfer and telecopy transmission is a popular mode for international communication. E-mail and fax numbers have become as universal as telephone numbers on stationery and business cards in international companies. Time is an enemy in other ways. France and Spain virtually close down in August for vacation.

Organizing for International Campaigns   Agencies must develop an organizational structure to manage global brand messages. The organizational structure depends heavily on whether the client company is following a standardization or localization strategy. Some agencies exercise tight control, while others allow more local autonomy. All these approaches fall into three groups: tight central international control, centralized resources with moderate control, or a match of the client's organization—if the client is highly centralized, then the agency account structure will be highly centralized.

The IMC Factor in Global Campaign Planning

Integrated marketing communication means that all the messages a consumer receives about a brand work together to create a coherent brand impression. To do that on a global level requires both horizontal and vertical coordination. The vertical effort represents the coordination of the key planning decisions, such as targeting, positioning, objectives, strategies, and tactics across all the various tools used in the communication program. The horizontal level requires coordination across all the countries and regions involved in the plan.

Because of this complexity, it takes a dedicated manager to ensure that all the various marketing communication activities are staying consistent to the brand and campaign strategy. The Inside Story explains how an account director at Dentsu, the world's largest single agency, approaches integration on behalf of his clients.

Because of the complexity, IMC planners use planning grids to plot strategic coordination of messages across countries and across marcom programs. The table below illustrates how such a grid might be constructed. The messages are plotted indicating how they may vary locally for different cultures, as well as what brand elements are used, such as position or personality, to maintain consistency. Some companies sell not just one brand but a portfolio of subbrands or brand extensions, and the challenge is to maintain brand consistency across these different product lines. There may also be differences in the message strategy for different stakeholder groups.

Marcom Tool	Country A	Country B	Country C	Country D
Advertising	Brand Messages:			
Direct Response	• Country specific			
Public Relations	• Consistency elements			
Etc.				

Putting It All Together

This chapter started with IMC and then reviewed a number of specialized marketing areas. Let's bring some of these various areas together—integration, B2B, and international—with an example of a global B2B company that is working through a rebranding effort to drive consistency through all its operations.

Based in Buffalo, New York, Moog, Inc., is a $1 billion industrial technology company that serves customers who need precisely engineered motion control products—think Formula 1 race cars and flight simulators. With 23 global subsidiaries all doing their own thing, the driving goal was to develop consistent, integrated communication programs to truly become "one company, one brand."[16]

THE INSIDE STORY

Chasing the Same Dream

By Masaru Ariga, *Group Account Director, Dentsu Inc.*

Masaru Ariga is a group account director of Dentsu Inc., one of the largest international marketing communication agencies in the world. He is responsible for several well-known Japanese companies conducting communication activities mostly in the domestic market, the second largest advertising market after the United States. Before assuming this role, Ariga was a planning director in charge of international clients and actively engaged in pan-Asian campaigns, traveling extensively throughout the region.

Without doubt, markets are getting similar to one another. But I feel there exist fundamental differences in the business of communication.

The societal implications of advertising itself are significantly different between Japan and the United States. The meaning of advertising generally goes beyond just a means of selling in Japan. People "enjoy" advertising. Good advertising becomes the talk of the town and often invigorates corporate reputations, providing a ripple effect on employee satisfaction and recruitment of talented people. Bad advertising does exactly the opposite.

It is understandable, therefore, that Japanese advertisers tend to think of advertising more holistically than their American counterparts. Consumers and society do remember the messages a company sends. Successful companies, therefore, need to have a long-term and holistic view of communication activities.

In Japan, the client-agency relationship also tends to be considered longer term. In fact, a food company I handle has been Dentsu's client for more than a century—since the agency was founded in 1901. While short-term accountability should not be undermined, the fact that agency and advertiser are solidly intertwined, sharing common value and history, is definitely a plus for

building a strong, cohesive brand. After all, a brand develops in consumers' minds over a long period of time.

Advertisers rely on agencies for a wider range of communication issues in Japan than in the United States—advertising agencies are called in for much of what an American company would have called in consulting firms or specialized agencies. In the case of a hotel/transportation conglomerate I am responsible for, Dentsu's work includes creating the mission statement, internal marketing, hotel naming and logo or mark design, and even industrial design of a new commuter train and signage for the stations. Those tasks are in addition to conventional marketing communication such as mass media advertising, PR, sales promotion, events, and the Internet. I make sure that my team provides holistic solutions to business issues of clients in a cohesive way.

I believe that the power of integrated communication is still undervalued. When communication activities are truly integrated based upon a solid mission and direction, a company can obtain a strong, durable competitive edge.

After all, true IMC requires organizational integration by which people in a variety of fields creatively chase the same dream. But it is extremely difficult for different people to have the same dream. Hand in hand with the top management, I feel an agency can play a critical role to "coordinate" disoriented messages and guide the organization to move forward in the same direction.

Ariga graduated with a B.A. in Political Science from Waseda University in Tokyo in 1985 and joined Dentsu upon graduation. In 1992, he was in the first graduating class from the new IMC Master's program at Northwestern University. His graduate education was sponsored by Dentsu.

The project involved an analysis of brand scope to determine "What business are we in?" That was supported by an effort to better organize the firm's brand portfolio with guidelines for both existing brands and new ones. A global brand position strategy was crafted with input from customers in 10 markets around the world. A brand-training program was offered, since employees play a particularly important role in delivering a positive B2B experience. The brand planners also designed a set of brand metrics to use in the firm's regular IT reporting systems.

All this came together in a new integrated communication program. The redesigned brand identity was launched via trade shows, print communication, a brand extranet for key stakeholders, a customer Web site, direct marketing, and other forms of electronic communication. Captured in a brand plan, Moog was able to design a new brand strategy to guide the company for the long term.

IT'S A WRAP

Driving Up Honda's Market Share

The results of the Honda CR-V campaign we discussed in the beginning of this chapter were phenomenal. You remember its mission was to increase the sales of an international auto brand, the Honda CR-V, in Iceland. It also was designed as an integrated campaign.

Logason believes that the campaign was successful because it effectively used the tools of marketing communication. He explained, "Building a great campaign can be like building a sentence: You don't need new words to be effective; it's how you organize the current ones that define its comprehension."

So what were the results? In a market where competitive SUVs were being heavily subsidized, the Honda dealership sold all cars with minimal discounts (3 to 5 percent off list price is standard in Iceland), which demonstrated the brand's strength. Interest among intended new buyers measured 27 percent (2 percentage points above the campaign's aim of 25 percent), top-of-mind scores placed the brand at 6 (1 higher than the goal). This led to a sales increase of 99 percent, along with a 25 percent reduction in advertising spending per car sold.

After trailing the market leader by more than half, the CR-V became the second best-selling car in Iceland and by far the most sold SUV. Furthermore, Honda became the second best-selling brand—up from sixth when HÉR&NÚ took over. Today Honda in Iceland has by far the highest market share of all Honda dealerships in Europe.

As Ingvi Logason, the owner of the agency, explained, "All in all it was a textbook campaign of strategic planning where creative insight derived from research, visualized for the target group in a simple yet meaningful way that built a bridge between a brand and buyer. Putting to use methods that great instructors had put down on paper before us and organizing it through our creative thinking gave us a new effective sentence using old words."

Key Points Summary

1. **What is retail advertising all about, and what makes it distinctive?** Retailers are merchants who sell directly to consumers. Most retail businesses are locally owned and advertise at the local level. However, retail advertising at the national and international levels is becoming more common. Co-op advertising with manufacturers and service providers is common. Retail advertising directed at a local audience typically focuses on attracting customers through price and promotion information. It may also focus on store image, product quality, and style. The main medium used for retail advertising is newspapers. However, retailers also use shoppers, preprinted inserts, magazines, television, radio, and the Web. Apart from traditional store retailing, some businesses engage in nonstore retailing, including use of the Web.

2. **How does B2B advertising work?** Business-to-business advertising is used to influence demand and is directed at people in the business arena who buy or specify products for business use. Its objectives include creating company awareness, increasing selling efficiency, and supporting channel members. Compared to the consumer market, the market for business goods is limited; decision making tends to be shared by a group of people and purchasing decisions center on price, services, product quality, and assurance of supply. B2B media consist of general business and trade publications, directories, direct mail, catalogs, data sheets, the Web, and consumer media.

3. **What are the basic goals and operations of nonprofit and social marketing?** Nonprofits use all the tools of marketing communication to achieve their goals, which tend to focus on fund-raising and recruitment. Social marketing uses marketing programs and marketing communication tools for the good of society. It can be a corporate strategy or a strategy used by a nonprofit organization. Cause marketing and mission marketing are tools used to align companies with socially responsible business practices.

4. **Which strategic decisions are behind international advertising and IMC?** Marketing begins with a local

brand, expands to a regional brand, and, finally, goes global. Advertising follows the same path. The biggest strategic decision involves how much of the marketing communication strategy is globalized or localized. Ultimately, such campaigns should be centrally controlled and centrally conceived. There should also be local

applications and approval. In international as in all IMC campaigns, the challenge is to create brand consistency in all messages and customer experiences with the brand. Getting everyone involved in these message delivery systems to coordinate their programs calls for cross-functional management.

Key Terms

ad allowances (promotional allowances), p. 539
business-to-business (B2B) advertising, p. 541
buyer, p. 542
capital campaigns, p. 546
cause marketing, p. 546
cooperative (co-op) advertising, p. 539
country of origin, p. 548
cross-functional management, p. 535
dealer tag, p. 540

donut, p. 541
exporting, p. 548
free-standing inserts, p. 541
fund-raising (development), p. 546
high-context culture, p. 551
horizontal publications, p. 544
industrial advertising, p. 542
lead agency, p. 551
localization (adaptation), p. 550
low-context culture, p. 551

mission marketing, p. 548
North American Industry Classification System (NAICS), p. 542
preprints (free-standing inserts (FSIs), p. 541
price-value strategy, p. 539
professional advertising, p. 542
promotional allowance, p. 539
public communication campaigns, p. 546

shelf talkers, p. 541
shoppers, p. 541
social marketing, p. 546
societal marketing, p. 546
standardization, p. 550
store brands (private label or house brands), p. 537
store traffic, p. 537
synergy, p. 536
trade advertising, p. 542
vertical publications, p. 544
zone editions, p. 541

Review Questions

1. How do retail advertising objectives differ from business-to-business objectives?
2. What are the types of B2B advertising, and how do these differ from more general consumer advertising?
3. Explain how both for-profit companies and nonprofit organizations can use social marketing.
4. What is a public communication campaign, and how does it differ from product advertising? Give an example.

5. Explain cause marketing and mission marketing. How do they differ?
6. How does culture relate to the decision to globalize or localize a campaign?
7. Explain how a global IMC program is more complex than an IMC program operated nationally.

Discussion Questions

1. Choose a restaurant in your community. What types of people does it target? Would you recommend that its advertising focus on price or image? What is (or should be) its image? Which media should it use?
2. You work for a large sporting goods chain that would like to focus all of its local philanthropic activities in one area. You believe the company could benefit from a mission marketing program. Develop a proposal for the marketing VP that explains mission marketing and presents an example of a mission marketing project that might work for the company.
3. Dean Bennett has gotten a new assignment for an upscale pen made in Switzerland under the brand name of Pinnacle. Its primary advantage is that it has an extremely long-

lasting cartridge, one that is guaranteed to last for at least five years. The pen is available in a variety of forms, including roller ball and felt tip, and a variety of widths, from fine to wide stroke. Use the adaptability continuum to analyze the globalization or localization options for launching this pen first in Europe and then globally, including North America and Asia. What would your recommendation be on standardizing the advertising?
4. Define the difference between a high-context and a low-context culture. If you are an international student, analyze your own culture and compare it with the United States. In class illustrate the difference by finding two ads in this textbook that you think effectively demonstrate these two message strategies. Explain how they work.

5. *Three-Minute Debate:* Tom and Wendy Butler have just purchased a sandwich shop and intend to turn it into a gourmet sandwich shop that features different types of sandwiches from different countries. They found a good lease in a neighborhood shopping center, but the costs of franchising, leasing, and other charges have left them very little for advertising. With limited funds, Tom and Wendy are arguing about which local media make the most sense if they only have funds for one medium—a Yellow Pages display ad, a series of advertisements in the area's weekly shopper, or advertising in the local college newspaper (the campus is six blocks from the store). Which of these media will best help Tom and Wendy build awareness for their new shop?

In class, organize into small teams with each team arguing on behalf of one of the three media options. Set up a series of three-minute debates with each side having 1½ minutes to argue its position. Every team of debaters has to present new points not covered in the previous teams' presentations until there are no arguments left to present. Then the class votes as a group on the winning point of view.

Take-Home Team Projects

1. To demonstrate the problems of language in advertising, divide the class into teams of five or six. Each team should choose a print advertisement it believes would have universal appeal. Take the headline to a language professor or someone who is proficient in a language other than English and ask them to translate it. Next, take that translation to another professor or native language speaker of the same language and ask for a "back translation" into English. Compare and report on how well the concept translated. Did the headline retain is original meaning in the translation and back translation? If not, what caused the problem?

2. Compare the speed, convenience, and content of the following three business-to-business sites: http://www.americanexpress.com, http://www.dell.com, and http://www.officedepot.com. Write a one- or two-page report on your analysis of these sites. What would your team recommend to improve their usefulness to consumers?

Yahoo! Hands-On Case

Review the Yahoo! case in the Appendix.

1. This chapter elaborated on the concept of integrated marketing communication. Explain how consistency is created in IMC campaigns and why it is important to a brand. Now consider the Dave campaign for Yahoo! In what ways did the team maximize consistency in the brand presentation? Were there any aspects of the campaign that might potentially get off message or off brand strategy? Can you make any suggestions on how to further strengthen consistency in this campaign?

2. Yahoo! is an international marketer, so it makes sense that this campaign might eventually go global. Analyze the targeting strategy in terms of cultural cohorts, and decide if it makes sense to use this same campaign in different countries. Write a one-page report analyzing the global/local (standardization versus adaptation) decision. Conclude with your recommendation, and explain your thinking.

HANDS-ON CASE

CareerBuilder.com Means (Monkey) Business

Effective campaigns exhibit a message synergy that results from the integration of all aspects of a company's marketing efforts—what it says about itself, how the company performs, and what other people say about it. Such is the case with the synergy created by CareerBuilder's popular campaign created to reach two audiences, potential employees and employers.

CareerBuilder teamed with agency Cramer-Krasselt to connect with its audience through a creative strategy that used humor in the workplace—chimps to be exact. The campaign, which made its TV debut during the 2005 Super Bowl, showed what it's like to work with a bunch of monkeys, face a moment of truth, and realize that a new job search might be the ticket to happiness.

"Humor is a great way to grab a viewer's attention," said Peter Krivkovich, Cramer-Krasselt president and CEO, "but an ad can't just be funny for funny's sake. There needs to be a strategic insight behind it and, at the end of the day, it needs to move the needle for your client's brand. This campaign did that overwhelmingly."

Extending the strategy of targeting people who feel frustrated about their jobs, Cramer-Krasselt created "Monk-e-Mail" on its Web site and launched it 12 days before the Super Bowl in January 2006. Site visitors could send customized e-messages to friends, using the voices of now famous monkeys, who more-or-less lip-synch personalized messages. The viral campaign created an enormous buzz among the target audience, who spread the word without CareerBuilder having to spend any media dollars. It featured the most effective advertising of all—word of mouth from friend to friend.

Peter Krivkovich said, "This campaign has tapped into the collective consciousness of working Americans. Anyone who has ever had a job understands the humor of sending or receiving a Monk-e-Mail. It has allowed millions of people to blow off steam and make their daily grind more endurable, and perhaps reflect on the fact that they too at times work with a bunch of monkeys—a good reason to start thinking about a job change."

How did CareerBuilder and its agency Cramer-Krasselt evaluate the effectiveness of the monkeys? You probably guessed—millions responded to CareerBuilder's monkey ads by going to the Web site. CareerBuilder.com claims at least 23 million unique visitors (up from 16 million unique visitors before the Super Bowl ads started running in 2005) and lists more than 1.5 million jobs. But what's the evidence that the *campaign* worked?

The CareerBuilder.com 2006 Super Bowl commercials were so successful in getting the message to job seekers and employers that the site saw enormous growth. CareerBuilder's traffic increased 70 percent to 1.4 million people after the Super Bowl, according to *Advertising Age*.

Richard Castellini, CareerBuilder's vice president of consumer marketing summarized the success of the Monk-e-Mail portion of the campaign: "In an era challenged by consumers opting out of marketing messages at a record pace, we need to introduce more innovative and creative communications programs to engage our audience in meaningful ways." He explained, "Monk-e-Mail is a critical component of our success, having engaged nearly 10 million unique visitors for approximately six minutes each."

Advertising doesn't necessarily need to be award winning to be effective. However, this campaign won big. It won an Effie. It was listed among the most popular ads on *USA Today's* Super Bowl Ad Meter poll, named funniest television commercial of the year (TBS online poll), and won *Adweek's* BUZZ Awards Best Internet Campaign and Best Overall Campaign of the Year. Not bad for a bunch of goofy monkeys.

Despite this success, Cramer-Krasselt resigned the account in February 2007, following reports that the CareerBuilder had put the account up for review, which means that it was searching for another agency. *MarketWatch* reported that CareerBuilder, which is jointly owned by *USA Today* parent Gannett Co., *Chicago Tribune* parent Tribune Co., and McClatchy, was unhappy that the commercials did not rank higher in the *USA Today* annual poll of Super Bowl commercials.

Consider This

1. Explain how the Integration Triangle, described earlier in this chapter, applies to the CareerBuilder.com campaign. How does the campaign create message synergy?
2. Do you think that the CareerBuilder.com campaign is B2B advertising or consumer advertising, or both? Explain.

Sources: Katherine Hunt, "CareerBuilder's Ad Agency Resigns Account: Report," *MarketWatch*, February 24, 2007, http://www.marketwatch.com; Michael McCarthy, "CareerBuilder Ads Find Humor in the Workplace," *USA Today*, May 15, 2005, http://www.usatoday.com; "Cramer-Krasselt Ads Voted Most Popular, Funniest of the Year," http://www.lexdon.com; Kris Oser, "How CareerBuilder.com Used the Web to Lead into its Super Bowl Ad Buy," *Advertising Age*, February 8, 2006; "CareerBuilder.com's Monk-e-Mail Takes Top Prize at BUZZ Awards," http://www.prnewswire.com.

Evaluation of Effectiveness

Everything about our 18 to 55 hp Boomer™ tractors is designed to make work easier. Like innovative SuperSteer.™ Turf-protecting Sensitrak™ 4WD. And advanced ergonomics. Visit a New Holland dealer or newholland.com

NOT ALL THE HOTTEST NEW TECHNOL IS DESIGNED TO FIT IN YOUR POCKET.

IT'S A WINNER

Award:	Client:	Agency:	Title:
Gold Effie in Agri-cultural/Indus-trial/Building Category	New Holland Trac-tors	Colle+McVoy, Minneapolis	"Brave New Trac-tors"

Outstanding in the Field

Before this campaign, when you asked farmers to name a tractor, they were likely to answer John Deere, Kubota, or Case—not New Holland. New Holland, a century-old hay tools company, faced the challenge of reinventing and reintroducing itself as a tractor brand.

In a fiercely competitive industry, New Holland set two objectives: (1) strengthen the New Holland name as a tractor brand and increase New Holland market share by 5 percent and (2) increase dealer satisfaction with New Holland brand image by 10 percent. It was a tall order considering New Holland's sliding market share in a shrinking market, not to mention its limited media budget. Competitors were spending 6 to 10 times what New Holland spent on media buys.

New Holland's agency, Colle+McVoy, discovered some key consumer insights. Unlike consumers who preferred market leader John Deere as a symbol of success, those who favored New Holland felt choosing a nontraditional brand was empowering. Independent New Holland consumers had the confidence to select a better solution, even when making a major tractor purchase.

The big idea for the campaign was the opportunity to position New Holland as the tractor brand of the future. Doing so effectively repositioned John Deere as yesterday's tractor—a tractor for traditional, conformist purchasers.

To communicate the big idea, Colle+McVoy knew it needed to depart radically from traditional advertising for the category. From a creative standpoint, the modern and unconventional look matched the message. The agency took the tractor out of its natural habitat, showing it against desert sand dunes or artic tundra. The clean and compelling visuals forced viewers to look at the tractors and not to be distracted by crops in the background. Not only were the machines heroes of the ads, they became futuristic.

Chapter Key Points

1. How well do you understand why and how advertising evaluation is conducted?

2. Can you list and explain the stages of message evaluation?

3. What are the key areas of media evaluation?

4. How are campaigns and IMC programs evaluated?

Traditional media drove consumers to the microsite (whyblueisbetter.com) and New Holland Web site, where prospective consumers could learn exactly what features made New Holland the tractor of the future, the tractor of choice.

Colle+McVoy tested these ideas with representative members of its audience. It set the following objectives for copy testing the proposed campaign:

- Understand overall impact of product communications on brand equity and brand associations.
- Solicit overall takeaway and reactions to the ads.
- Investigate effectiveness of copy, headlines, and visuals.
- Specifically understand how communications conveyed the brand direction—modern, innovative, and dynamic.

The agency then conducted a series of one-on-one interviews with 12 participants, who were current New Holland owners or owners of competitor equipment, to respond to the proposed campaign. Thinking that this particular group of respondents would reflect what other prospective buyers might think, respondents represented core marketing demographics (acreage, geography, livestock). Results of the copy test showed that the ads provoked brand reassessment in nonusers, while strengthening the brand pride of owners, confirming the direction that the agency proposed for the new campaign. The message strategy seemed to be on target.

A good company with a challenging situation, specific objectives, insightful consumer research, a Big Idea, and strategic media choices combined to help New Holland establish itself as a tractor brand. Did it work? Check the It's a Wrap feature at the end of this chapter to see the results for the Brave New Tractors campaign.

Source: Effie brief provided by New Holland and Phil Johnson at Colle+McVoy.

Throughout this book you've read about the effectiveness of advertising. We've emphasized that effective campaigns do more than win awards for creativity. They work hard to achieve the campaign's communication and marketing goals, as does the New Holland Brave New Tractors campaign. As you will see in this chapter, there are many ways to evaluate the effectiveness of various aspects of an advertising and marketing communication program. Specifically, four categories of work get evaluated in advertising and marketing communication programs—the message execution, the media, the campaign, and the other marketing communication areas and their synergistic effect as part of an IMC program. This chapter discusses the basic concept of the evaluation of effectiveness and then examines those four areas. The New Holland tractor campaign illustrates some of the thinking behind this Effie award winner and provides insight into the evaluation process.

IMPACT: DOES IT WORK?

When advertising works—when marketing communication is effective—it has impact and generates a response of some kind from its target audience. The critical phrase—"as intended"—means there are multiple objectives, as well as multiple ways to evaluate effectiveness.

Many executives feel advertising works only if it produces sales. Syracuse University Professor John Philip Jones, who has written many books and articles on the topic, estimates that of the $500 billion spent annually on advertising, only 41 percent produces sales—less than half.[1] Jones contends that "advertising must generate an immediate jolt to sales before it can be expected to produce any further effect."[2] Simon Broadbent, another leading figure in effectiveness research, disagrees with Jones's short-term sales focus and suggests instead that advertising should emphasize long-term brand building.[3]

Determining effectiveness based on sales can be difficult because of the impact of other marketing mix factors. For example, an article in *Business 2.0* reported that an ad for the Six Flags amusement park was a smash success in viewer surveys. However, because attendance at the company's 31 theme parks fell after the campaign instead of increasing, it must be deemed ineffective. But sales isn't the only reason brands advertise: One of the major objectives of advertising is to create higher levels of brand awareness. Perhaps the Six Flags awareness level increased, but the reason people didn't come to the parks has to do more with the lack of new attractions. Does that mean the advertising is ineffective?[4]

It's our view that advertisers intend for their messages to accomplish a variety of goals, such as build a brand personality, recruit volunteers or donations, or entice people to visit a Web site, which is why the other 60 percent of ads studied by Jones may be effective in their own way. That's why this book uses the Facets Model of Effects to broaden the way we evaluate message effectiveness.

An example of the importance of dimensions other than sales comes from a well-known campaign by Chrysler that used the automaker's CEO Dr. Dieter Zetsche as a star. Criticism of Dr. Z's persona led the company to discontinue the campaign, but the Millward Brown Research company found different, but very positive, results for the campaign: 76 percent of consumers who intended to buy a car found the ads memorable, and 73 percent understood Chrysler combined the best of American and German engineering. Furthermore, the ads produced 43 percent higher brand recall and 63 percent higher message recall than other Chrysler ads.[5] In short, the campaign delivered strong communication effects, leading us to wonder if perhaps the sales problem had more to do with the car than the advertising.

Evaluating Effectiveness

Some evaluation is informal and based on the judgment of an experienced manager. There is always a need for the intuitive analysis of experienced professionals. The Inside Story illustrates how personal judgment guides the initial evaluation of professionals as they seek to predict the potential effectiveness of an ad idea.

In addition to intuition and judgment, measurement that tracks consumer response is also needed and can be built into a campaign plan as structured feedback, such as response cards and calls. Often, however, the evaluation effort involves a more formal research project, which also needs to be part of the campaign planning.

Personal insights into what makes an ad great are important, but why do we also need formal evaluation? The first reason is that the stakes in making an advertising misstep are high. By the time an average 30-second commercial is ready for national television, it has cost about $200,000 in production costs. If it is run nationally, its sponsor can invest several million dollars in airtime. The second reason is advertising optimization, or reducing risk by testing, analyzing, tracking brand performance, and making changes where possible to increase the effectiveness of the advertising. The third reason is to learn what works and what doesn't—in other words, to identify best practices so a brand's advertising continues to improve.

Types and Stages of Evaluation

Evaluation is done through testing, monitoring, and measurement. Testing is used to predict results, monitoring tracks performance, and measurement evaluates results. In other words, for major campaigns a sample of the ads is typically tested before they run as a way to predict effectiveness. Ideally, the results of preliminary evaluative research should be available before large sums of money are invested in finished work or in media buys.

THE INSIDE STORY

What Is Great Advertising?

By Amanda Correa, *Brand Manager, The Richards Group*

All of the advertising concepts for a new campaign have just been presented. The room is quiet, and the spotlight turns to you, "What are your thoughts about the work?"

Whether you're just out of school or someone who's been in advertising or marketing for several years, everyone in the room will be listening to what you have to say. How well you respond to this question will determine the level of influence you have in the decisions being made.

What's the formula for getting people to listen to your opinion? Two things: Your response must be well informed, and it must be clearly articulated. Combine those two elements, and you have the power to persuade people to consider your way of thinking.

To become well informed, turn to the experts—people who live and breathe advertising. Borrow their brainpower to expand your knowledge about the characteristics of great advertising.

Of the books and articles I've read, I've developed the opinion that there are five common qualities that all great ads share.

1. *Great advertising is single-minded.* When consumers are bombarded with several messages, there's not enough time to take it all in—they forget what the advertiser is telling them. But if they hear only one message, then the probability is greater that they'll remember what the advertiser has to say.
2. *Great advertising is simple.* When experts say great advertising is simple, they mean it is uncomplicated. But it is never simple-minded. Simple-minded means that an idea lacks depth.
3. *Great advertising is memorable.* Advertisers can use a variety of techniques to make an ad memorable. A

few of those approaches include originality, provocativeness, intelligence, entertainment, or revealing product or consumer insights.

One thing worth noting is that a memorable ad in and of itself is not enough. The consumer must remember the product or brand. There are plenty of ads that are memorable, but consumers don't remember who or what they were advertising. Advertising cannot be great if people don't remember the brand or the product.

4. *Great advertising is likable.* Stan Richards, founder of The Richards Group, says, "The more people like what you say and how you say it, the more they like you. And the more they like you, the more likely they are to want to do business with you." Enough said.
5. *Great advertising is often a Big Idea.* A Big Idea is something that's "campaign-able." It also means that the campaign is capable of longevity—it can stand the test of time.

As you broaden your knowledge about great advertising, take what you learn and apply it by studying the ads you see every day. Continually give thought to ads. Dissect them and then be able to tell your story about them.

When you become so comfortable with your thoughts that you can say on the fly, "I have an opinion. Here's what it is. And here's why I think that," then you will have an opinion that people seek.

A graduate of North Texas State University, Amanda Correa was nominated by Professor Sheri Broyles.

As a campaign unfolds, the performance is tracked to see whether any elements need to be changed. Sales may fall, or they may not increase as rapidly as expected. Is the advertising at fault? The results, the actual effects, are measured after the ad or campaign runs. Diagnostic research also is used in all three stages to deconstruct an ad to spot message problems. Four types of research are used in evaluation:

1. **Developmental research** through pretesting estimates the likelihood that an ad idea will work or that one idea is better than another.
2. **Concurrent research** using tracking studies and test marketing monitors the way the campaign is unfolding and how the messages and media are working.
3. **Posttesting research** evaluates impact after the campaign is over or after the ad ran. Postcampaign research encompasses benchmark or baseline studies to gauge movement. These can be research company norms, or they can be based on previous campaigns by this brand.
4. **Diagnostic research** deconstructs an ad to see what elements are working or not working. Researchers who evaluate commercials use frame-by-frame or moment-by-moment analysis to identify strengths and weaknesses in an ad.

Facets: Measuring Responses

Most advertisers would be happy if evaluation could simply tell them how much the advertising contributed to their sales effort. That's difficult for a number of reasons. Factors other than advertising affect sales (e.g., pricing, distribution, product performance, competition), and that makes it hard to isolate advertising to determine its impact. Furthermore, advertising effects tend to be delayed, so it's difficult to link the advertising seen at one time to a purchase made days or weeks later. Exceptions are direct-response advertising and ads carrying promotional offers good for only a limited time.

Usually advertising is measured in terms of its communication effects—the mental responses to a message, which become *surrogate measures* for sales impact. Such factors as awareness of the advertising, purchase intention, preference, and liking all suggest that the advertising message can make a positive contribution to an eventual purchase decision. According to research professionals at Ipsos-ASI, one of the largest U.S. providers of advertising pretesting, "Ads work best when they engage viewers' interest, when consumers enjoy watching them, when they are relevant, and when they tell their story in a unique and interesting way."[6] Those are some of the dimensions of effectiveness, but others also are important, as we know from our discussion of how advertising works in Chapter 4.

On the other hand, some ads don't work, and it is just as important to understand why that happens. Some confuse the audience or fail to get attention or connect with consumers. In some cases, the ad can even boomerang, an effect mentioned in a feature on antidrug ads in Chapter 4. The same problem was noted with antismoking ads when the American Legacy Foundation announced that a study of smoking prevention ads by the tobacco industry actually increased the likelihood that teens would try smoking.[7]

Good evaluation objectives are based on a model of human response to an advertisement that identifies key effects. We developed the Facets Model of Advertising Effects in Chapter 4 as a guide for both setting objectives and evaluating effectiveness. Table 19.1 groups the key factors of effectiveness and then matches them to the types of research questions advertisers can use to determine effectiveness.

Principle
Good evaluation plans, as well as effective professional work, are guided by a model of how people respond to advertising.

MESSAGE EVALUATION

Copy-testing is a general term that describes various kinds of research used at different stages in the advertising development process—before, during, and after an ad or campaign has run. Before we talk about specific types of studies, consider first the various copy-testing services and the factors they feel are important to evaluate.

Copy-Testing Services

Copy-testing companies have different specialties that focus on different effectiveness dimensions. The most successful of these companies have conducted enough tests that they have developed **norms** for common product categories. In other words, after they pretest an ad, they can compare its score with scores from comparable ads. Norms allow the advertiser to tell whether a particular advertisement is above or below the average for the brand or its product category. Without norms the advertiser would not know whether a score of 23, for example, is good or bad.

Most of these companies have also developed diagnostic methods that identify strong and weak points of the ad. Here is a list of some of the more prominent companies and the types of tests they provide:

- *Ameritest:* brand linkage, attention, motivation, communication, flow of attention and emotion through the commercial
- *ARS:* persuasion, brand/ad recall, communication
- *Diagnostic Research:* brand recall, main idea, attribute statements (importance, uniqueness, believability)
- *Ipsos-ASI:* recall, attention, brand linkage, persuasion (brand switch, purchase probability), communication

Table 19.1   Effectiveness Research Questions

Effect	*Research Questions*
Perception	
Awareness/Noticed	Which ads do you remember seeing?
	Which ads were noted?
Attention	What caught your attention?
	Did the ad stand out among the other ads and content around it?
	What stood out in the ad?
Recognition (Aided)	Have you seen this ad/this campaign?
	Sort elements into piles of remember/don't remember.
Relevance	How important is the product message to you? Does it speak to your interests and aspirations?
Emotion	What emotions did the ad stimulate?
	How did it make you feel?
Liking/Disliking	Do you like this brand? This story? The characters (and other ad elements)?
	What did you like or dislike about the brand? The ad?
Desire	Do you want this product or brand?
Cognition	
Interest	Did you read/watch most of it? How much?
	Did it engage your interest or curiosity?
	Where did your interest shift away from the ad?
Comprehension/ Confusion	What thoughts came to you? Do you understand how it works? Is there anything in the ad you don't understand? Do the claims/product attributes/benefits make sense?
	Do you have a need for this brand or can it fulfill a need for you?
Recall (Unaided)	What happened in the commercial? What is the main message? What is the point of the ad?
Brand Recall/ Linkage	What brand is being advertised in this ad?
	[In open-ended responses, was the brand named?]
Differentiation	What's the difference between Brand X and Y?
Persuasion	
Attitude	Do you have a favorable or unfavorable opinion of the brand? The ad?
	How excellent or weak is the brand? The ad?
	Do you respect it?
Preference	In Category X (or product set), which brand would you choose? (Usually a pre- or posttest question)
	What brand do you prefer?
Intention	Do you want to try or buy this product/brand?
	Would you put it on your shopping list?
Argument/Counter Argument)	What are your reasons for buying it? Or for not buying it—or its competing brand/s? How does it compare to competitors' brands?
	Did you argue back to the ad?
Believability/ Conviction	Do you believe the reasons, claims, or proof statements?
	Are you convinced the message is true? The brand is best?
Trust	Do you have confidence in the brand?
Association	When you think of this brand, what (products, qualities, attributes, people, lifestyles, etc.) do you connect with it?
	Do you link this brand to positive experiences?
Personality/Image	What is the personality of the brand? Of whom does it remind you? Do you like this person/brand personality?
	What is the brand image? What does it symbolize or stand for?
Self-Identification	Can you see yourself or your friends using this brand?
	Do you connect personally with the brand image?

- *Mapes & Ross:* brand preference change, ad/brand recall, idea communication, key message delivery, like/dislike, believability, comprehension, desire to take action, attribute communication
- *Millward Brown:* branding, enjoyment, involvement, understanding, ad flow, brand integration, feelings to ad, main stand-out idea, likes/dislikes, impressions, persuasion, new news, believability, relevance
- *RoperASW:* overall reaction, strengths and weaknesses, understanding, clutter-busting, attention, main message, relevance, appeal, persuasiveness, motivate trial, purchase intent

Now let's consider how the services of such companies and the research they conduct can be used at various points in the development and evaluation of a marketing communication effort.

Message Development Research

Deciding what facts to convey in advertisements is never easy. Research is needed to develop and test alternative message strategies. Planners conduct research with members of the target audience to develop the message strategy and test the relative effectiveness of various selling premises—hard sell or soft sell, informational or emotional, and so forth. Insights into consumer motivations and purchasing decisions help solve the often-difficult puzzle of selecting the most relevant information and motivating promise as well as the emotional appeal that best engages the audience.

Concept Testing   Advertising and other marketing communication messages usually incorporate a Big Idea, a creative concept that is attention getting and memorable. Research in **concept testing** compares the effectiveness of various message strategies and their creative ideas. This testing often relies on a *key concept card*, which is an artist's drawing of the visual idea with a sentence underneath that captures the essence of the idea. A researcher may use a pack of three, five, or more idea cards or rough layouts to elicit consumer responses in a mall or through discussions in a focus group.

An example of effective concept testing that was used in a campaign's development is Volvo's GLBT campaign, which was the first campaign of its kind to receive an Advertising Research Foundation (ARF) David Ogilvy award. Witeck-Combs Communications in collaboration with Prime Access, Inc. developed a set of concepts and rough ad executions representing a range of GLBT-specific imagery and copy. Ford and Volvo managers selected their top three choices from the group of proposed ad ideas. The messages were tested to assess the constructs of branding, communication, and persuasion, including the concept of consumer connection, or whether the ad makes consumers feel closer to the brand. These constructs were measured in four ways—cognitive, behavior, emotional, and aspirational dimensions.

Pretesting   Another type of evaluative research, called **pretesting**, helps marketers make final go/no-go decisions about finished or nearly finished ads. Pretesting differs from concept testing or message strategy research, which reveals the strengths and weaknesses of different versions of a concept or approach as marketers develop them. Pretesting assesses the strength of the finished message and predicts how well it will perform.

In terms of print advertisements, the ideas to be tested are often full mockups of the ad. In television, advertisers can test the commercials as storyboard ideas or **photoboards** (still photos arranged as a storyboard), but more often commercials are in the form of **animatics** (drawings or still photos shot on videotape synchronized with a rough version of the audio track). Advertisers can show these versions of the commercial to individuals, to focus groups, or in a theater testing situation. They follow the viewing of the advertisement with a survey, a more open-ended interview, or a set of questions for a group discussion.

Diagnostics   Many advertisers and agencies are moving away from copy-testing methods that rely on single scores to evaluate an ad and turning to methods that are more focused on diagnosing strengths and weaknesses. The reason is that they believe an advertisement is too complex to be reduced to one factor and one simple score. Instead they are using research methods designed to diagnose strengths and weaknesses of their advertising ideas to

A MATTER OF PRACTICE

Finding Moments of Truth
By Charles E. Young, *President, Ameritest*

The most powerful search engine of all is the human eye, which googles advertising film, television commercials, and Web videos, continuously deciding on an unconscious level whether the visual information streaming toward it is important enough to let into consciousness. Because our conscious minds have limited bandwidth or workspace, much of the imagery that advertisers are trying to communicate to consumers is ignored or deleted by our preconscious eye-brain filters as so much visual spam.

The Ameritest Picture Sorts® is a set of nonverbal research tools that have been developed for the Internet to survey the right-brained scanning and sorting processes involved in visual communication. These tools make use of the power of still photographs to capture an instant of time and store our fleeting emotions.

By sorting a randomized deck of pictures taken from the ad itself—which is like the visual vocabulary of the film—the ad researcher can reconstruct consumers' moment-by-moment attention and emotional response to an ad they just saw. Three different sorting exercises enable the advertiser to perform the equivalent of putting on 3-D glasses to see advertising through the eyes of its target audience.

The *Flow of Attention*®, the first of three measurement dimensions, is like a visual spell-checker that the researcher can use to analyze whether or not a piece of advertising film or Web video has been put together well according to principles of proper film syntax or good visual grammar. The flow of attention graph reveals the hidden structure of audience attention to moving pictures, which, like music, follows a rhythmic beat of cognitive processing. The beat, or focal points of attention, is where the most important information in an ad, like the brand identity, is conveyed.

From the emotional hook at the beginning, to the turning points in a story, to the surprise ending of a funny commercial, engaging the emotions of consumers is essential to motivating them. The *Flow of Emotion*® graph measures not only the volume of emotions pumping through ad film but also reveals which of four archetypal dramatic structures is being used in the creative design. Knowing this structure tells the advertiser when the timing is exactly right to first introduce the brand in the ad, which might be at the beginning, or somewhere in the middle, or not until the end of a commercial.

The *Flow of Meaning*® shows the researcher where key communication points or brand values are being cued visually. Meaning is created when thought and emotion come together, in a few memorable and emotionally charged moments in a commercial when memories are being created. Because there are three distinct memory systems in the mind, branding moments come in three flavors: (1) images that convey concepts or rational ideas go into our Knowledge, or semantic, memory system; (2) images that evoke emotions go into our Emotion, or episodic, memory system; and (3) images that rehearse or mirror the behavior the advertiser is trying to influence go into our Action, or procedural, memory system (where memories of how you ride a bike or play a violin are stored). Taken together, this learn-feel-do imaging process is how the long-term work of advertising is performed, building a brand's image.

This diagram demonstrates the flow of attention across a commercial for Unilever's Thermasilk. The selected still frames represent those places in the commercial where the attention is high (above the red line) or low (below the red line). Note the highest attention points, which are indicated with the red arrows. In this commercial, that tight shot of the executive's face is the "moment of truth," the most highly attended to frame in this execution.

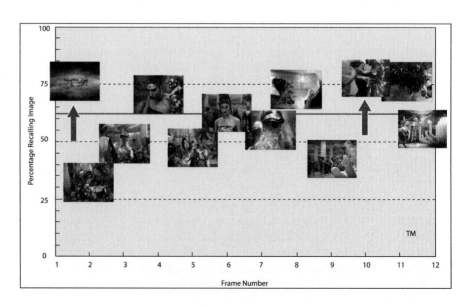

improve the work while it is still in development or to learn more from the ad to improve subsequent advertisements.

In theater tests for TV commercials, for example, respondents may have a black-box device and can press a button to record different types of responses—indicating what they liked or didn't like or how long they paid attention by letting up on the button when their attention shifts.

Moment-by-moment tests of commercials, as described in the Matter of Practice box, provide an analysis of the impact of the internal logic of the commercial. The procedure includes showing a **clutter reel**, a group of commercials that includes the test commercial, competitors' commercials, and other ads, and conducting interviews afterward. The Ameritest company, whose work is described in the box, also uses a **picture sort** to diagnose the viewer's attention to and emotional engagement with different elements in the commercial. The viewers receive a deck of key frames from the commercial and sort them into images they remember seeing and ones they don't remember. Then they sort them into five categories from strong positive to strong negative. Advertisers tabulate the sets to depict a flow of impact for both attention and emotion. In particular, they want to analyze key moments in the commercial such as the solution to a problem or the introduction of the brand and analyze them in terms of viewers' attention and emotion.[8]

During Execution: Concurrent Testing

Concurrent testing takes place while the advertising is running. There are three primary techniques: coincidental surveys, attitude tests, and tracking studies. The first two assess communication responses; tracking studies evaluate actual behavior.

The **coincidental survey** technique is most often used with broadcast media. Random calls are made to individuals in the target market. By discovering what stations or shows people are tuned to, the researcher can determine whether the target audience has seen/heard the ad and, if so, what information or meaning the audience members now have of the brand. This technique can be useful in identifying basic problems. For example, several years ago Pepsi discovered that the use of Madonna as a spokesperson was a terrible mistake.

In Chapter 4 we discussed the relationship between an attitude—a favorable or unfavorable disposition toward a person, brand, idea, or situation—and consumer behavior. This relationship is the basis of *attitude tests*. Researchers survey individuals who were exposed to the ad, asking questions about the spokesperson, the tone of the ad, its wording, and so forth. Results that show strong negative attitude scores may prompt the advertiser to pull an ad immediately. A favorable attitude indicates that people are more likely to purchase a brand than if they have an unfavorable attitude.

Tracking Studies   Studies that periodically (generally every three or six months) measure top-of-mind brand awareness (first brand mentioned) are called **tracking studies**. These studies can also measure unaided and aided awareness of an ad and trial and repeat purchases. They sometimes ask the same questions of competing brands.

Tracking studies show how a marketer's brand is performing over time, especially after changes are made in the marketing communication. Because several different measures are taken, findings can indicate if there is an attention-getting problem, a recall problem (saw message but can't remember what it said), a trial problem (remembered the advertising but not moved to try the brand), or a repeat problem (tried the brand but have not repurchased for some reason).

Brand tracking is an approach that tracks the performance of the brand rather than or in addition to the advertising. The assumption is that with fragmented media and an abundance of high-quality but similar products, it is more important to track the brand because it reflects the quality of the customer's brand relationship. Instead of focusing on attributes and claims about a product, this research identifies how customers are involved with the brand and whether they are more favorably disposed toward it than toward other brands. As Peppers and Rogers point out, you also need a centralized customer database that allows you to track customer activity across channels.[9]

This analysis as depicted in Figure 19.1 is also based on the factors identified in the Facets Model of Effects.

FIGURE 19.1
Tracking Brand Response

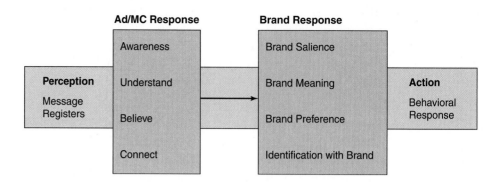

Brand tracking studies generally use sets of brand-related questions, but Bain & Company, a highly respected consulting firm, is promoting the use of a single-question test to track attitudes to a brand. Called *net promoter*, it tracks the response to a simple question: "How likely is it that you would recommend us to a friend or colleague?"[10] Another single measure is **brand penetration**, which is the number of customers who purchase the brand relative to the total population in the market.[11]

Although these single measures are useful as a broad indication of brand effectiveness, the other questions found in brand tracking studies, such as those about awareness and credibility, for example, are particularly important in an IMC program because they provide diagnostic information about areas of marketing communication that might need to be changed or refined.

Because spending information enters the analysis, much of the focus of tracking studies is on the target market, the selection of media vehicles, the schedule, the marketing communication mix, and the media mix. Account planners use several methods to collect tracking data, such as attitude tests, wave analysis, consumer diaries, and pantry checks.

- *Wave analysis.* **Wave analysis** looks at a series of interviews during a campaign. The tracking begins with a set of questions asked of a random sample of consumers on a predetermined date. After the person is qualified as hearing or seeing the ad, the researcher asks a series of follow-up questions. The answers serve as a benchmark and allow adjustments in the message content, media choice, and timing. Perhaps two months later, the researcher makes another series of random calls and asks the same questions. The second wave is compared with the first until management is satisfied with the ad's market penetration and impact.
- *Consumer diaries.* Sometimes advertisers ask a group of representative consumers to keep a diary during a campaign. The consumers record activities such as brands purchased, brands used for various activities, brand switches, media usage, exposure to competitive promotions, and use of coupons. The advertiser can then review these **consumer diaries** and determine factors such as whether the message is reaching the right target audience and whether the audience is responding to the message as intended. One common unfavorable finding from consumer diaries is that no attitude or behavioral change occurred because of exposure to the campaign.
- *Pantry checks.* The **pantry check** provides much of the same information as the diary method but requires little from the consumer. A researcher goes to homes in the target market and asks what brands or products they have purchased or used recently. In one variation of this procedure, the researcher counts the products or brands currently stocked by the consumer. The consumer may also be asked to keep empty packages, which the researcher then collects and tallies.

Test Markets A **test market** might serve to evaluate product variations, as well as elements of a campaign or a media mix. These are generally conducted in two or more markets with the same number of similar markets chosen to act as controls. In the control markets the researcher can either (a) run no advertising or (b) continue to run the old ad. The new advertising (or product variation) is used in the test cities. Before, during, and after running the advertising, marketers compare sales results in the test cities. Some cities, such as Buffalo, Indianapolis, and San Antonio, are considered excellent test markets because their demographic and socioeconomic profiles are representative of either the United States or a particular target market. Furthermore, they are relatively isolated as media markets so the advertising impact is less likely to be affected by what is happening in other markets.

The possibilities for isolating variables in test markets are almost limitless. Researchers can increase the frequency of advertising or try a different media schedule, for example. They can see whether an ad emphasizing brand convenience will stimulate sales to two-career families. They can try an ad that plays up the brand's fiber or vitamin content or compare the effectiveness of a two-for-one promotion versus a cents-off coupon.

Posttesting: After Execution Research

Evaluative research occurs after an ad has run to determine if it met its objectives. The most common evaluative research techniques account planners and advertising researchers use include memory tests, persuasion tests, direct response counts, frame-by-frame tests, in-market tests such as test markets, and brand tracking. The idea is that advertising—and other types of marketing communication messages—vary in the way they affect people, so the measurements also must be different.

Breakthrough: Attention   Most advertising is evaluated in terms of its ability to get and keep attention. This is a simple concept but difficult to measure. Similar to pretesting, some researchers use instantaneous tracking in a theater setting where viewers with a keypad indicate what they watch and don't watch—or rather what interests them and doesn't interest them. The Ameritest methodology asks respondents who have just watched a collection of ads to indicate which ones interested them.[12] Another firm's method asks viewers to rate how enjoyable the ad is, which confounds the attention score with a liking response. Other methodologies use noted scores for print ads or ask viewers to recognize the concept of a commercial and attach it to a brand.

Engagement Tests   Interest in a commercial is determined by concentration and excitement. **Eye-tracking** research is a mechanical technique that traces **saccadic eye movement**, the path the eye takes in scanning an ad. Since scanning involves a lot of stops and starts and revisits, this complex map of how a visual is scanned identifies what first caught the viewer's attention—the visual point of entry—and where it moved to next. It also records those elements that eye kept revisiting either to focus on because it was an appealing visual or because it needed more study. It also shows what elements didn't get noticed at all. The e-Motion system from the New Jersey-based firm PreTesting identifies eye fixations but also the amount of vibrations in the retina. The vibration is very minute, but it does indicate a level of excitement—the more the retina vibrates, the more interested the viewer.[13]

Memory Tests   Memory tests are based on the assumption that an advertisement leaves a mental residue with the person who has been exposed to it—in other words, the audience has learned something. One way to measure an advertisement's effectiveness, then, is to contact consumers who saw the ad and find out what they remember. Memory tests fall into two major groups: recognition tests and recall tests.

One way to measure memory is to show the advertisement to people and ask them whether they remember having seen it before. This kind of test is called a **recognition test**. In a **recall test**, respondents who have read the magazine are asked to report what they remember from the ad about the brand. In aided recall tests, the interviewer may go through a deck of cards containing brand names. If the respondent says, "Yes, I remember seeing an advertisement for that brand," the interviewer asks the interviewees to describe everything they can remember about the ad. Obviously recall is a more rigorous test than a recognition test.

Similarly, a TV commercial is run on network television within a regular prime-time program. The next evening, interviewers make thousands of random phone calls until they have contacted about 200 people who were watching the program at the exact time the commercial appeared. The interviewer then asks a series of questions, such as the following:

- Do you remember seeing a commercial for any charcoal briquettes?
- (If no) Do you remember seeing a commercial for Kingsford Charcoal briquettes? (Memory prompt)
- (If yes to either of the above) What did the commercial say about the product? What did the commercial show? What did the commercial look like? What ideas were brought out?

The first type of question is called **unaided recall** because the particular brand is not mentioned. The second question is an example of **aided recall**, in which the specific brand name is mentioned. The answers to the third set of questions are written down verbatim. The test requires that the respondent link a specific brand name, or at least a specific product category, to a specific commercial. If the commercial fails to establish a tight connection between the brand name and the selling message, the commercial will not get a high recall score.

Emotion Tests   Advertising is just beginning to move into this new area of research. There are several ways to get at the emotional response. Ameritest uses photo sorts with still frames from commercials to identify the positive and negative moments that touch people's emotions.[14] Other researchers are wiring up viewers of television ads to monitor brain activity using a functional magnetic resonance imaging (fMRI) machine. The fMRI images identified ads from the 2007 Super Bowl that produced anxiety, fear, anger, and insecurity, as well as positive feelings.[15]

Likability Tests   A study by the Advertising Research Foundation (ARF) compared a variety of different copy-testing methods to see if any of them were better able to predict sales impact. Surprisingly, it wasn't awareness, recall, communication, or persuasion measures that won out but rather *likability tests*. Likability, however, is not easy to measure because it's difficult to know if the consumer likes the ad, the brand, or some other factor, such as the person giving the test. A number of the copy-testing companies offer a likability score, but they suggest it needs to be interpreted relative to other consumer responses. Questions that try to evaluate likability investigate such things as: personally relevant, important to me, stimulates interest or curiosity, creates warm feelings, enjoyable, entertaining, and fun.

Persuasion Tests   Another evaluative research technique is a **persuasion test**, or attitude change test. The basic format is to ask consumers how likely they are to buy a specific brand. Next they are exposed to an advertisement for that brand, usually as part of a collection of brands. After exposure, researchers again ask them what they intend to purchase. The researcher analyzes the results to determine whether *intention to buy* has increased as a result of exposure to the advertisement. This test is sometimes referred to as an **intend-to-buy** or **motivation test**. The validity of a persuasion test depends in part on whether participants in the experiment represent a good sample of the prospects the advertiser is trying to reach. A dog food advertiser, for example, would not be interested in responses from people who do not own dogs.

Inquiry Tests   A form of action response, **inquiry tests** measure the number of responses to an advertisement. The response can be a call to a toll-free number, an e-mail or Web site visit, a coupon return, a visit to a dealer, an entry in a contest, or a call to a salesperson. Inquiry tests are the primary measurement tool for direct-response communication, but they also are used to evaluate advertisements and sales promotions when the inquiry is built into the message design. Inquiry tests also are used to evaluate the effectiveness of alternative advertisements using a spit-run technique in magazines, where there are two versions of the magazine printed, one with ad A and the other with ad B. The ad (or direct-mail piece) that pulls the most responses is deemed to be the most effective.

Scanner Research   Many retail outlets, especially drug, discount, and food stores, use electronic scanners to tally up purchases and collect consumer buying information. When you shop at your local Safeway, for example, each product you buy has an electronic bar code that conveys the brand name, the product code, and its price. If you are a member of Safeway's frequent buyer program and have a membership card that entitles you to special promotional offers, the store can track your purchases.

Scanner research is also used to see what type of sales spikes are created when certain ads and promotions are used in a given market. Both the chain and the manufacturers of the brands are interested in this data. The regional Safeway system may decide to establish a consumer panel so it can track sales among various consumer groups. In **scanner research**, you would be asked to join a panel, which might contain hundreds of other customers. You would complete a fairly extensive questionnaire and be assigned an ID number. You might receive a premium or a discount on purchases for your participation. Each time you make a purchase, you also submit your ID number. Therefore, if Safeway runs a two-page newspaper ad, it can track actual sales to determine to what extent the ad worked. Various manufacturers who sell products to Safeway can do the same kind of testing. The panel questionnaire also contains a list of media that each member reported using, so media performance can also be evaluated.

Scanner research reads the information from a shopper's identification card and records that along with product information. Many retail outlets use electronic scanners to track sales among various consumer groups.

Single-Source Research Using scanner data and the cooperation of local cable networks, researchers are closer to showing a causal relationship between advertising/promotion and sales because of **single-source research**. Single-source research companies, such as A. C. Nielsen, arrange to have test commercials (and sometimes test newspaper ads) delivered to a select group of households (HHs) within a market, comparing it to a control group of HHs. Purchase behavior of each group of HHs is collected by scanners in local stores. Because advertising is the only manipulated variable, the method permits a fairly clear reading of cause and effect. Data collected in this way are known as *single-source data* because advertising and brand purchasing data come from the same HH source.

Syracuse University Professor John Philip Jones, who spent many years at J. Walter Thompson, has used single-source data from JWT combined with Nielsen TV viewing data to prove that advertising can cause an immediate impact on sales. His research has found that the strongest campaigns can triple sales, while the weakest campaigns can actually cause sales to fall by more than 50 percent.[16]

Although fairly expensive, single-source research can produce dependable results. Advertisements are received under natural conditions in the home, and the resulting purchases are actual purchases made by consumers. One drawback, besides cost, is the three to six months required to set up and run this test. Critics also say that single-source research is better for short-term immediate sales effects and doesn't capture very well other brand-building effects.

MEDIA EVALUATION

Advertising has little chance to be effective if no one sees it. Analyzing the effectiveness of the media plan is another important part of evaluation. Did the plan actually achieve reach and frequency objectives? Did the newspaper and magazine placements run in the positions expected and produce the intended GRP and CPM levels? In other words, did the advertisers get what they paid for?

Evaluating Audience Exposure

For major campaigns, agencies do post-buy analyses, which involve checking the media plan against the performance of each media vehicle. The critical question is whether the reach and frequency objectives were obtained.

Verifying the audience measurement estimates is a challenge. Media planners are working sometimes with millions of dollars, and they can't afford to get it wrong. We discussed

This outdoor board from the United Kingdom attracted attention because of its interesting visual but also because of its challenging idea. Research based on traffic counts find it difficult to account for the impact of messages like these.

how various media channels measure their audiences. For print, services such as the Auditing Bureau of Circulations (ABC), Simmons-Scarborough (SMRB), and Mediamark (MRI) provide data. Likewise for broadcast, Arbitron, RADAR, and A. C. Nielsen provide audience monitoring. Initially media planners use these estimates to develop a media plan, and media buyers use them later to verify the accumulated impact of the media buy after the campaign has run.

Media planning oversight is usually handled in-house by the media buyer, but it can also be contracted by the advertiser to independent companies who specialize in conducting media audits of the agency's media planning and buying operations. Nissan and Procter & Gamble are examples of companies that have hired outside media-auditing firms to confirm the execution of their media plans.

As the job gets more complex, media planners are being asked to prove the wisdom of their recommendations in an area where the data they use are sometimes suspect or unreliable, particularly if there are problems with the media measurement companies' formulas and reporting systems. Nielsen, for example, has been subject to much criticism for its television ratings.

In order to better understand the problems in media evaluation, let's look at two specific areas where media performance is hard to estimate—outdoor and the Internet. As you would expect, accurately measuring the mobile audience for outdoor advertising is challenging. Traffic counts can be gathered, but the problem is that traffic does not equal exposure. Just because a car drives by a board doesn't mean that the driver and/or passengers see it, particularly since some outdoor boards are more attention getting than others, as the "road rage" board illustrates.

Similarly, the measures of effectiveness used to evaluate offline campaigns don't seem to transfer well to the online world. Is the Web site visitor or banner ad viewer similar to print or broadcast audiences? The industry hasn't been able to establish online equivalencies for GRPs and CPMs. Similarly, the industry is still trying to define what makes an effective Internet ad and to develop a system that accurately measures online advertising effectiveness. At the heart of the problem is the question of what exactly is to be measured and how that equates to other media—readers, viewers, visitors, hits, click-throughs, or minutes spent with a site? Alternative media, such as those used in guerilla marketing campaigns, are even harder to measure and media planners lack the ability to equate exposure numbers from these new sources to the performance of traditional measured media.

Advertising ROI and Media Efficiency

Advertisers continue to improve how they measure *advertising ROI* (return on investment, which means the costs of creating and running the advertisement versus the revenue it generates). Another way to look at it is the cost-to-sales ratio.

Since the dollar impact for advertising—and public relations, especially—are difficult to measure, ROI is hard to calculate. The campaigns must be carefully designed not only to increase sales, but also to ensure that advertisers can isolate the impact of the message and verify that the advertising caused the increase in sales. ROI is easier to calculate for direct marketing (because there are fewer variables between the message and the sales) and for sales promotion (because there is an immediate response, which is easier to link to the message).

One question related to ROI is how much spending is too much? How do you determine whether you are overadvertising or underadvertising? That's one of the key reasons to use test marketing. If a campaign is launched in several different, but matched, cities at different levels of media activity, a comparison of the campaign results (sales or other kinds of trackable responses) can determine the appropriate level and type of media spending.

Wearout   The point where the advertising, because it has been seen multiple times, no longer stimulates much of a response is called **wearout**. This is also the point where recall stabilizes or declines and irritation levels increase because people are tired of hearing or seeing the same ad.

Wearout is a combination of creative impact and media buying. The more intrusive or the less interesting the creative technique, the higher the level of irritation. It's like a joke: You may pay attention the first couple of times you hear it, but then it gets "old." Other types of advertising are less prone to wearout. Good jingles, for example, can be repeated almost endlessly. The more people like to hum along, the less likely there will be a wearout problem.

The issue is how long and how much is needed to create the necessary impact. John Philip Jones, who has done extensive research into effectiveness issues, argues that research supports higher continuity. He recommends spreading the budget out and adding weeks to the media schedule as much as possible.[17] Another way to evaluate such decisions is through media optimization models.

Media Optimization   One of the biggest challenges in media planning is media efficiency—getting the most for the money invested. You may remember from Chapter 11 that media planners operate with computer models of **media optimization**—or the optimum media performance—that they use in making decisions about media selection, scheduling, and weights (amount of budget). Models are always theoretical, so one result of postevaluation is that the actual performance of a plan can be compared with the results projected by the media planner's model. The goal of media optimization is to optimize the budget—to get the most impact possible with the least expenditure of money. That is the critical finding derived from the comparison of performance with projections. In addition to meeting the reach and frequency objectives, was the media plan efficient?

EVALUATING MARKETING COMMUNICATION CAMPAIGNS

Evaluation is the final and, in some respects, most important step in an advertising campaign because it determines whether the campaign effort was effective. A campaign evaluation will assess the campaign's performance in terms of its message and media objectives. It employs either internal performance data or results from an outside research organization that monitors brand performance, such as Gallup-Robinson, Decision Analyst Inc., and Millward Brown.

Even though this book focuses on advertising, we recognize that advertising is just one part of the market communication mix. An IMC campaign employs various marcom tools, such as sales promotion, public relations, direct marketing, events and sponsorships, personal sales, packaging, point of purchase (PoP), and specialties. You'll find that most of these areas have their own metrics by which performance is measured. Even though an IMC

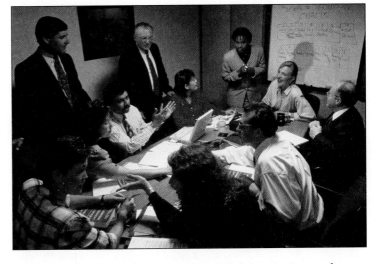

Evaluation doesn't just happen at the end of a campaign or after the ad is run. It has to be planned into the campaign from the very beginning as this planning meeting illustrates.

campaign is evaluated in terms of its overall impact on a brand, the pieces of the mix may also be evaluated to determine the effectiveness of their performance.

Marcom Tools

As Table 19.2 illustrates, marketers can use the Facets Model of Effects to identify the objectives commonly associated with the various marketing communication areas as well as the types of measures used to evaluate performance. The idea is that certain marketing communication functions, such as public relations and sales promotion, do some things better than other areas. Therefore, in an integrated plan, we would use the best tool to accomplish the desired effect. In Table 19.2, the main effects are located in column one, with a collection of surrogate measures identified in the second column (this list is not inclusive, it's just a sample). The last column lists the communication tool or tools that may be most appropriate for achieving the objective.

An examination of Table 19.2 shows that advertising is particularly effective in accomplishing several objectives, such as creating exposure, awareness, and brand image. It is also good at providing brand reminders to the customer and encouraging repurchase. However, other marketing communication tools, such as sales promotion, are better at getting people to respond with an immediate purchase, and public relations is particularly strong at building credibility. Let's look briefly at these other marketing communication areas in terms of their evaluation.

Direct Response   The objective of direct-response communication is to drive a transaction or generate some other type of immediate behavioral response, such as a donation or visit to a dealer. What makes this marketing communication tool so attractive to marketers is that response is so easily measurable. Some advertisements request direct response via a toll-free number, a mail-in coupon, a Web site or e-mail address, or an offer embedded in the body copy. Instead of depending on consumers' memory or ads' persuasion or some other indirect indication of effectiveness, the advertiser simply counts the number of viewers or readers who request more information or buy the product. (See the American Airlines Ad.)

Principle

Advertising is particularly effective in accomplishing such objectives as creating exposure, awareness, and brand image and delivering brand reminders.

Table 19.2   Message Effectiveness Factors

Key Message Effects	Surrogate Measures	Communication Tools
Perception	Exposure	Adv Media; PR, PoP
	Attention	Adv; Sales Promo, Packaging; PoP
	Interest	Adv; SP; PR, Direct; PoP
	Relevance	Adv; PR; Direct; PoP
	Recognition	Adv; PR, Pkging; PoP, Specialties
Cognitive	Understanding	Adv; PR; Sales; Direct
	Recall	Adv; SP; PR, PoP, Specialties
		Adv; PR; Pkging
Affective	Emotions & Liking	Adv; Sales Promo, Pkging; PoP
	Appeals	Adv; PR; Sales; Events/Spnsrshps
	Resonate	Adv; PR; Events/Spnsrshps
Persuasion	Attitudes	Adv; PR; Direct
	Preference/Intention	Adv; PR; Sales; Sales Promo
	Credibility	PR
	Conviction	PR; Sales; Direct
	Motivation	Adv; PR; Sales; Sales Promo
Brand Assoc.	Brand Image	Adv; PR, Events/ Spnsrshps
Action	Trial	SP; Sales; Direct, PoP
	Purchase	SP; Sales; Direct
	Repeat Purchase	Adv; SP; Sales; Direct, Specialties

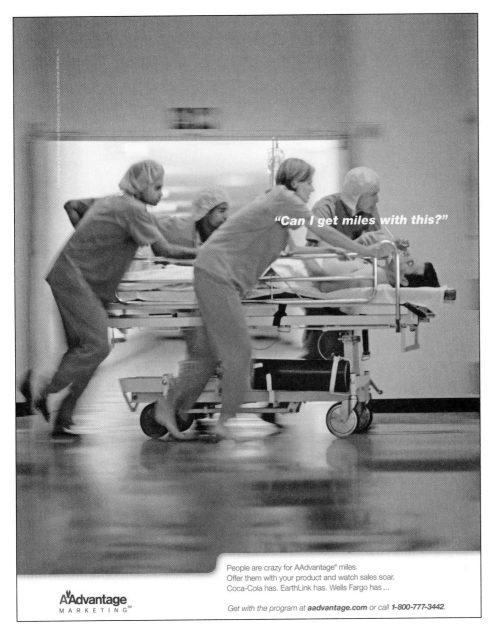

"Can I get miles with this?"

People are crazy for AAdvantage® miles.
Offer them with your product and watch sales soar.
Coca-Cola has. EarthLink has. Wells Fargo has ...

AAdvantage
M A R K E T I N G℠

Get with the program at **aadvantage.com** or call **1-800-777-3442**.

This print ad includes contact information that allows advertiser American Airlines to count the responses to the ad as part of its evaluation program.

In some ways, direct response mechanisms are the easiest marketing communication tool to evaluate both in terms of message effectiveness and in terms of ROI efficiency—the sales-to-cost ratio. The efficiency of a direct-response offer is measured in terms of response per thousand (RPM). To calculate the RPM, use the following formula:

$$\frac{\text{Total responses}}{\text{Total mailed}} \times 1,000 = \text{RPM}$$

This calculation lets you compare the response rate of alternative mailings. For example if one mailing of 15,000 pulled 750 responses, then the RPM was 50 per 1,000. If a different mailing of 12,000 pulled 800 responses, then the RPM was 66 per 1,000, making it a more effective offer.

Sales Promotion Sales promotion programs for packaged goods and other products that use distribution channels need to evaluate both the impact of consumer (or end user) direct promotions and promotions targeted at retailers and other channel members. You will recall the discussions of promotional allowances offered to retailers who agree to feature a brand in their ads or provide special in-store display and price discounts. These are measured by proof of performance such as copies of store ads and pictures of in-store displays. One responsibility of the sales force is to do store checks to verify that stores are doing what they promised.

As for consumer promotions, the following evaluation measures are the most popular:

Measure	% used
Sales	46
Response Rates	20
Awareness	10
Other Mix	9
Redemption Rates	4

Promotions that contain a response device, such as coupons, have a built-in evaluation measure.

The efficiency of a sales promotion offer can be evaluated in terms of its financial returns more easily than advertising. We compare the costs of a promotion, called a **payout analysis**, to the forecasted sales generated by the promotion. A **break-even analysis** seeks to determine the point at which the total cost of a promotion exceeds the total revenues generated, identifying the point where the promotion is not wise to do. Figure 19.2 depicts this analysis.

Public Relations   The evaluation of public relations examines the success of getting a message out to a target audience in terms of *output* (materials produced and distributed) and *outcomes* (acceptance and impact of the materials). Outcomes can be measured in terms of changes in public opinion and relationship tracking. The output evaluation is conducted by asking such questions as: How many placements (news releases that ran in the media) did we get? How many times did our spokesperson appear on talk shows? How much airplay did our public service announcements receive? The results are presented in terms of counts of minutes, mentions, or inches.

FIGURE 19.2

A Sales Promotion Break-even Analysis

At the break-even point, where 30,000 premiums are delivered at a cost of $45,000, the sales revenues exactly cover, but do not exceed, total costs. Below and to the left of the break-even point (in the portion of the diagram marked off by dashed lines), the promotion operates at a loss. Above and to the right of the break-even point, as more premiums are sold and sales revenues climb, the promotion makes a profit.

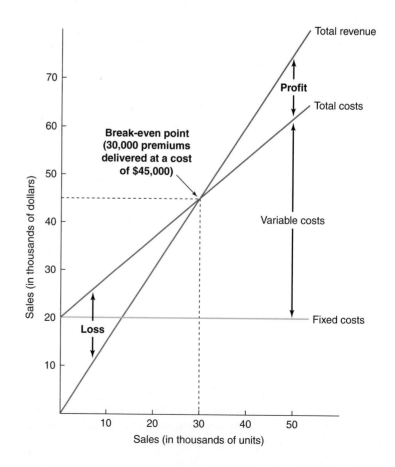

Content analysis also helps determine the favorability of the coverage, share of voice, and issue and competitor coverage. Ongoing public opinion tracking studies include such questions as: Has there been a change in audience knowledge, attitudes, or behavior (e.g., pretesting versus posttesting)? Can we associate behavior change (for example, product trial, repeat purchase, voting, or joining) with the public relations effort?

The following table summarizes the most common measures of output and outcomes in public relations:

Output Objectives Achieved

- **Production.** Number of PR messages, such as news releases or brochures, generated.
- **Distribution.** Number of media outlets (TV stations, newspapers) receiving PR products.
- **Coverage.** Number and size of clips, column inches, or minutes of time or space.
- **Impressions.** Media placements multiplied by circulation or broadcast reach.
- **Advertising value.** Equivalent ad costs for time or space.
- **Content analysis.** Positive or valence (whether the story or mention seems to be more positive or negative), key messages (the idea in the story), sources, and prominence.

Outcome Objectives Achieved

- **Awareness.** Aided and unaided recall.
- **Attitudes.** Perceptions, preferences, and intent to buy.
- **Behavior.** Did target do what you wanted them to do?

The search for methods to tie public relations activities to bottom-line business measures, such as ROI (return on investment), is like the quest for the Holy Grail. PR practitioners would like to demonstrate ROI because it would provide even more support for the importance of PR effects. Unfortunately, research methods and analytical techniques that provide this support are elusive. A surrogate ROI measure can be based on shareholder value, which can be seen as a company or brand's reputation capital. For example, research conducted on companies with the most effective employee communication programs has determined that they provide a much higher total return to shareholders.

Web Site Evaluation   Evaluating the communication effects of Web site advertising is still a new game. Some performance indicators are traffic volume, such as **page views** or the simple number of visitors to a site.

Banner advertising and other online ads are evaluated using **click-through rates**, and the one thing the industry has learned is that this form of advertising is decreasing in effectiveness. One problem is that people who have little or no interest in the product may click on the banner by accident or curiosity. Since this type of advertising is sold by **pay-per-click (PPC)**, the advertiser has to pay regardless of the reason for the click. Pop-up banners can get more attention, but they are also seen as more irritating.

Instead of click-through rates, some advertising use a **cost-per-lead** metric that records how well the click-through generates prospects, an attempt to get at ROI. The most important metric for Internet advertising, however, is **conversion rate**, which is the percentage of visitors to a site who complete a desired action, such as playing a game, signing up for a newsletter, or buying something. Of course, online sales is itself an important measure of a Web site's effectiveness.

The more sophisticated conversion rate services not only measure how well the site generates action but also how customers navigated the site. This information is obtained by tracking where they come from, what search terms they used, how they move around within the Web site, and where they go when they leave. It gives a more comprehensive picture of the path visitors and customers use in navigating a site.

Special Advertising Situations

The various types of advertising identified in Chapter 18 are evaluated using many of the tools discussed previously; however, they each have their own particular objectives that affect how they are evaluated.

The primary objective of *retail advertising* is to generate store traffic. The results of traffic-building promotions and advertising are simple counts of transactions as well as the change in sales volume of brands receiving promotional support. Participation counts can be used to estimate the pull of special events. Loyalty is evidenced through participation in frequency buyer programs and measured in terms of registration, store visits, and average purchases per visit.

In *B2B marketing*, a common form of evaluation is a count of sales leads based on response devices such as calls, e-mails, and cards returned to the advertiser. Another common B2B objective is *conversion*, similar to the conversion rate in the online discussion; this refers to the number of leads that turn into customers who make a purchase. Conversion rates, which are percentages of the leads, are also calculated for most marketing communication tools used in support of B2B programs.

International marcom is difficult to evaluate because of market differences (e.g., language, laws, cultural norms) and the acceptability of various research tools. There may also be incompatibilities among various measurement systems and data analysis techniques that make it difficult to compare the data from one market with similar data from another market. An international evaluation program for advertising should focus, at least initially, on pretesting because unfamiliarity with different cultures, languages, and consumer behaviors can result in major miscalculations. Pretesting helps the advertiser correct major problems before miscommunication. To evaluate the global/local question, the best approach is to test two ads that are both based on the global advertising strategy: a locally produced version of the advertising and an original ad produced locally.

Campaign Evaluation

While it is ideal to know how each marketing communication function has performed, the reality in most campaigns is that a variety of functions and media are used to reach and motivate customers to respond. Time is a factor as well. We mentioned in the beginning of this chapter that there is a debate about advertising's ability to impact short-term sales results as well as long-term branding. University of Southern California Professor Gerard Tellis reminds us that advertising not only has *instantaneous* effects (consumer responds immediately) but also *carryover* effects (delayed impact).[18] Any evaluation of campaign effectiveness needs to also be able to track both types of effects over time.

The Synergy Problem If the campaign planning is well integrated, which means each specialty area cooperates with all the others in message design, delivery, and timing, then there should be a synergistic effect. This means that the overall results are greater than the sum of the individual functional areas if used separately.

The problem with evaluating campaigns—particularly IMC campaigns—is estimating the impact of synergy. Intuitively we know that multichannel communication with messages that reinforce and build on one another will have more impact than single messages from single sources; however, that can be difficult to prove.

A number of studies have attempted to evaluate IMC impact by comparing campaigns that use two or three tools to see what is gained when more message sources are added to the mix. For example, a study by the Radio Ad Effectiveness Lab reported that recall of advertising is enhanced when a mix of radio and Internet ads are used rather than just Web site advertising alone.[19] Such studies are beginning to tease out the effects of synergy, but they are a long way from evaluating the effects of a total communication program.

The most common way of measuring a campaign's total impact is the brand tracking approach mentioned previously. As various ingredients in the campaign are added and taken away, changes in tracking study results can show the effects and help identify what combinations of marketing communication functions and media work best for a brand. In other words, has the brand become stronger on critical dimensions of the image, such as personality and positioning cues, because of the campaign?

Connecting the Dots

The challenge in campaign evaluation is to pull everything together and look at the big picture of campaign performance rather than the individual pieces and parts. One of the first

places to start is defining the objectives—all the various effects—and then adequately and realistically measure the campaign's performance against those objectives. Here's an example that demonstrates how evaluation methods can be matched to the original campaign objectives.

Effie award winner UPS wanted to reposition itself by broadening its package delivery image.[20] Although UPS owned ground delivery, it lost out to Federal Express in the overnight and international package market. UPS knew from its customer research that to break out of the "brown and ground" perception, the company had to overcome the inertia of shipping managers who use UPS for ground packages and FedEx for overnight and international. The company also had to shift the perception of senior executives from a company that handles packages to a strategic partner in systems planning. From these insights came three sets of objectives that focused on breaking through awareness, breaking the inertia trance, and breaking the relevance trance. Here's how the campaign performed on those objectives. Notice the mix of perception, image, and behavioral measures.

Objective 1: Breaking Through

- Awareness of the Brown campaign outpaced *all* past UPS advertising measured in the 10-plus-year history of its brand-tracking study.
- Among those aware of the campaign, correct brand linkage to UPS was 95–98 percent across all audiences (compared to a historical average of 20–40 percent for past UPS advertising).
- "What can BROWN do for you?" has taken hold in popular culture. For instance, the tagline was mentioned in both *Saturday Night Live* and *Trading Spaces* shows.

Objective 2: Breaking the Inertia Trance

- With shipping decision makers, the brand showed steady and significant gains in key measures like, "Helps my operation run more smoothly," "Dynamic and energetic," and "Offers a broad range of services."
- International shipping profitability increased 150 percent, and overnight volume spiked by 9.1 percent after the campaign ran. The targets' total package volume increased by 4.39 percent.
- From the start of the campaign in March to the year-end, annual ground shipping revenue grew by $300 million.
- The campaign was a hit in terms of response with a 10.5 percent response rate and an ROI of 1:3.5. In other words, every dollar spent on the campaign generated $3.5 dollars in revenue.

Objective 3: Breaking the Relevance Trance

- For the first time in the 10-plus-year history of the brand tracking study, UPS leads FedEx in all image measures among senior-level decision makers. All significant brand image measures continued upward.
- Among senior decision makers, the biggest gains were in key measures like, "For people like me," "Acts as a strategic partner to my company," "Helps in distribution and supply chain operations," and "Provides global competitive advantage."
- At the start of the campaign, annual nonpackage (supply chain) revenue was approximately $1.4 billion. By the end of the year, nonpackage revenue had almost doubled to $2.7 billion.

Bringing It All Together   Beyond connecting the objectives to the measurements, advertisers continue to search for methods that will bring all the metrics together and efficiently and effectively evaluate—and predict—communication effectiveness. A small Florida agency, Zimmerman Advertising, promises to deliver long-term brand building as well as short-term sales. The president explains, "The biggest problem marketers face today is connecting advertising to retails sales." To help determine the impact of its ads on sales, Zimmerman measures ad response immediately using a toll-free number and proprietary software that tracks sales to specific ads.[21]

The giant media research company, Nielsen, has undertaken a project to find the links in its various marketing metrics. In particular, the company wants to connect its Nielsen Media Research TV ratings, with its A. C. Nielsen retail scanner and consumer panel data. Then it wants to mix in data from its Nielsen/NetRatings for online advertising and Nielsen Buzzmetrics online-buzz measurement system.[22] This is just one example of how important it is to connect the dots to draw an accurate picture of consumer response to marketing communication.

Many pieces are still missing in the evaluation of advertising, not to mention more complex IMC programs. Research think tanks are struggling to find better ways to measure consumers' emotional connections to brands and brands' relationships with their customers[23] and how those connections and relationships are affected by various types of marketing communication messages.

Ultimately, the goal is to arrive at holistic, cross-functional metrics that are relevant for integrated communication, a task undertaken by Dell Computers and its agency DDB. Given Dell's direct-marketing business model, the company had extensive call and order data in its database. DDB helped organize the collection of detailed marcom information, which made it possible to begin linking orders to specific marcom activities. This new marcom ROI tracking system made it possible for Dell to recognize a 3 percent gain in the efficiency of its marketing communication. As the metrics system became more sophisticated, it also began to move from a reporting and metrics evaluation engine to a strategic tool providing deeper insights into consumer behavior.[24]

IT'S A WRAP

New Holland's Brave New Tractors Conquer the Market

I n this chapter you've read about many different ways of testing advertising effectiveness. In addition to copy testing completed prior to the campaign's launch, Colle+McVoy conducted evaluative research after the campaign ran to determine whether it met its objectives.

The first objective, to strengthen New Holland as a tractor brand and increase New Holland market share by 5 percent, was exceeded. At a time when industry sales of tractors having less than 40 horsepower were down slightly, New Holland sales increased by 17 percent. New Holland's market share for this category grew 21 percent. In the high horsepower tractor category, New Holland rose 36 percent, while sales in the industry for similar tractors fell 11 percent. New Holland's market share grew an astounding 85 percent in this area.

The second objective, to increase dealer satisfaction with New Holland brand image by 10 percent, was also exceeded. Its image with dealers improved 37 percent over a two-year period.

In sum, New Holland reversed years of sliding market share and posted a 9 percent increase in overall tractor sales in a down market. In addition, dealer satisfaction scores rose 37 percent and online initiatives that drive purchase intentions attracted more than 68,000 to New Holland Web sites, resulting in the most successful marketing program to date for the company.

All this was enough to convince Effie judges to give New Holland and Colle+McVoy an Effie for a highly effective campaign.

Key Points Summary

1. **How well do you understand why and how advertising evaluation is conducted?** Advertising evaluation is used to test, monitor, measure, and diagnose advertising messages. The factors tested are the key effects outlined in a model of advertising effectiveness.

2. **Can you list and explain the stages of message evaluation?** Message evaluation is conducted before (pretesting), during (tracking), and after (posttesting) an ad or campaign has run. Diagnostic evaluation can be conducted at all three stages.

3. **What are the key areas of media evaluation?** Media evaluation begins by verifying the media exposure in terms of the achievement of the reach and frequency objectives, as well as the audience measurement reports of the media used. Media ROI evaluations considers such as questions as how much is enough, particularly in terms of advertising wearout.

4. **How are campaigns and IMC programs evaluated?** A campaign's performance is assessed in terms of how well it meets its message and media objectives. IMC plans also assess the performance of the various marketing communication tools, as well as the synergistic effect of the elements working together.

Key Terms

aided recall test, p. 572	cost-per-lead, p. 579	page views, p. 579	saccadic eye movement, p. 571
animatics, p. 567	eye-tracking, p. 571	pantry checks, p. 570	
brand penetration, p. 570	inquiry tests, p. 572	payout analysis, p. 578	scanner research, p. 573
break-even analysis, p. 578	intention-to-buy (or motivation) test, p. 572	pay-per-click (PPC), p. 579	single-source research, p. 573
click-through rates, p. 579		persuasion test, p. 572	test market, p. 570
clutter reel, p. 569	media optimization, p. 575	photoboards, p. 567	tracking studies, p. 569
coincidental survey, p. 569	moment-by-moment tests, p. 569	picture sort, p. 569	unaided recall test, p. 572
concept testing, p. 567		pretesting, p. 567	wave analysis, p. 570
consumer diaries, p. 570	motivation test, p. 572	recall test, p. 571	wearout, p. 575
conversion rate, p. 579	norms, p. 565	recognition test, p. 571	

Review Questions

1. Why do advertisers conduct evaluation of their advertising and marketing communication programs?

2. This chapter suggests that evaluation is most useful when based on a model of advertising response. Why is that so?

3. Why are diagnostic research methods becoming more important to advertisers?

4. What is a tracking study and how is it used? A test market?

5. What is single-source research, and how does scanner data relate to it?

6. What is media efficiency, and how does that relate to ROI?

7. Why is an IMC campaign difficult to evaluate?

Discussion Questions

1. Many creative people feel that formal copy-testing research doesn't do justice to their ideas. In particular, they feel that research results are designed to reward cognitive approaches and don't do a good job of evaluation for brand image ads and emotional ads. From what you have read in this chapter about copy testing, why do they feel that way? Do you believe that is a legitimate criticism of copy testing?

2. Most clients want a quick and easy answer to the question of whether the ad works. Advertising professionals, however, tend to believe that a one-score approach to copy testing is not appropriate. Why do they feel that way? If you were helping an agency prepare for a presentation on its copy-testing results, what would you suggest the agency say to explain away the idea that you can evaluate an ad with a single test?

3. *Three-Minute Debate:* You are hiring a research consulting company to help a client evaluate the effectiveness of its advertisements. One of the consultants recommends using focus groups to evaluate their effectiveness. Another consultant suggests that focus groups aren't very effective for posttesting and recommends other measures. Which viewpoint do you believe is most insightful?

   In class, organize into small teams with pairs of teams taking one side or the other. Set up a series of three-minute debates with each side having 1½ minutes to argue its position. Every team of debaters has to present new points not covered in the previous teams' presentations until there are no arguments left to present. Then the class votes as a group on the winning point of view.

Take-Home Team Projects

1. Put together a portfolio of ten ads for a set of product categories targeted to a college audience. Set up a focus group with participants recruited from among your friends and ask them to look at the ads. In a test of unaided awareness, ask them to list the ads they remember. Identify the top performing ad and the bottom ad in this awareness test. Now ask the focus group participants to analyze the headline, the visual, and the brand identification of each ad. How do the two ads compare in terms of their ability to get attention and lock the brand in memory?

2. As a team, explore the Web sites for two copy-testing companies such as Ameritest (http://www.Ameritest.net), IPSOS-ASI (http://www.ipsos.com), Diagnostic Research (http://www.diagnostic.com), or the ARS Group (http://www.ars-group.com), and compare the services they offer. If your team were looking for a company to pretest a campaign for a cosmetic product, which one would you prefer? Why?

Yahoo! Hands-On Case

Review the Yahoo! case in the Appendix.

1. The Yahoo! case doesn't explain much about the testing and evaluative research the team conducted, other than the initial research used in planning. Review the discussion in this chapter of message development and concurrent evaluation measures. Explain where and how these various research methods could be used to make the go/no-go decision for this Yahoo! campaign.

2. The last section of a campaign plan often includes a proposal for an evaluation plan that will determine the effectiveness of the campaign after it has run. You have been asked to add that section to this plan. In a one-page report, prepare a posttesting proposal to include in this Yahoo! plan that will explain how you believe the effectiveness of this plan could be determined.

HANDS-ON CASE

Lovin' It at McDonald's Again

In 2003 McDonald's, one of the biggest advertisers in the world, decided to consolidate its media-buying operations, which are responsible for placing nearly $1 billion in advertising each year.

Cost savings were not the reason for the change. "We don't believe we were getting our money's worth out of our media," claimed company official Larry Light. "We're not trying to see how much we can cut in our advertising. We're looking to be the most powerful voice in advertising, to be more effective."

McDonald's also launched a global campaign featuring the tagline "I'm lovin' it." *Ad Age* critic Bob Garfield was unimpressed, writing, "If 50 Cent were kidnapped by the New Christy Minstrels, and forced to record a video soundtrack commissioned by Mentos, you'd have the introduction to the new McDonald's campaign. Alert the media: The clown is dead, and the Pepsi Generation is on Ecstasy." But McDonald's had the last laugh, as its stores have seen double-digit sales growth, far outpacing the competition. Along the way, it's won some Effies, including a Silver Effie in the Global category for its efforts to reconnect customers to its brand.

McDonald's, like other large advertisers, is interested in creating effective ads. But what is the metric of effectiveness? Every client, of course, wants to see sales increase, but is that a fair standard for an agency's work? Agencies have long pointed out that great advertising cannot make a substandard brand succeed. In point of fact, McDonald's instituted a number of other changes at the same time it refocused its advertising, including adding new healthier product lines, like salads and fruit and yogurt. The company also changed its promotional relationship with Disney and focused hard on improving the consumer experience at its restaurants. How does one separate the effects of the ads from the other changes?

Most people probably believe effective ads are the ones they like and talk about, and there is logic to that. After all, if consumers like an ad, they should be willing to watch it over and over, reducing wearout. Perhaps they will also think about the brand more positively; marketing research suggests that a consumer's attitude toward an ad influences his or her attitude toward the brand. In real life it doesn't always seem to work out that way, though. One of the most popular campaigns of the late 1990s was one for Taco Bell that featured a talking Chihuahua. But when sales at franchises grew stagnant, Taco Bell fired the agency that developed the campaign and replaced it with an agency that got rid of the dog and focused more on the product.

BBDO's efforts for KFC had the same result. BBDO's ads, featuring *Seinfeld* alum Jason Alexander, were well received by consumers and were among the most highly recalled of 2002. But KFC's same-store sales over the time period were actually negative, and the agency was fired. Poor advertising? Perhaps, but other explanations are possible. Branding consultant Michael Markowitz points out that "The fundamental product offering— fried chicken—has been countertrend for years. Fried chicken is not a first-tier choice for people any longer." He adds, "No matter how clever the ads are, it can't mask or disguise the fundamental weaknesses in business." Besides, if a company fails to achieve its sales targets, "shoot the agency seems to be the rule," observes Ron Paul, a food-service consultant. "It doesn't mean that it's their fault, but it's an easy place to point the finger."

Paul's point probably suggests that the key to McDonald's success is both improved advertising and an improved product. That seems like a sound way for any advertiser to be effective.

Consider This

1. Most clients seem interested in sales increases as a benchmark for judging the quality of their agency's work. From a client perspective, why does this make sense?

2. From an agency perspective, defend the idea that increased product sales is not always an appropriate benchmark. If short-term sales gains are not the metric of success, what metrics would you propose agencies use for their work?

3. What would you propose for a more comprehensive evaluation program for the McDonald's campaign? Using the Facets Model of Effects as an outline, how would you determine the effectiveness of the campaign?

Sources: Richard Gibson, "McDonald's Hopes to Increase Effectiveness of Its Advertising," *Wall Street Journal* (Eastern edition), December 3, 2003, 1; Emma Hall, "Spotlight," *Advertising Age*, April 12, 2004; Kathryn Kranhold, "Omnicom Group to Measure How Ads Do," *Wall Street Journal* (Eastern edition), October 21, 1999, B16; Kate MacArthur, "Rivals Not Lovin' McD's Comeback," *Advertising Age*, July 26, 2004; Brian Steinberg and Suzanne Vranica, "KFC Seeks a Crisp Take on Its Ads; Fried-Chicken Chain Aims to Revive Sluggish Sales with a Fresh Campaign," *Wall Street Journal* (Eastern edition), August 1, 2003, B6; http://www.effie.org (accessed July 7, 2007).

Positioning Yahoo! to Youth 13–17

The following case was written by Dr. Mary Ann Stutts, Professor of Marketing at Texas State University-San Marcos. She is co-advisor, along with Jody Gibson, Instructor in Mass Communications, of the **i5** Advertising student team that won the American Advertising Federation National Student Advertising Competition in 2005. The competition is the oldest and largest advertising competition in the United States. For the past 34 years, students, professors, and practitioners have looked to the NSAC to provide real-world experience to the best and brightest students hoping to pursue careers in advertising and marketing.*

WHAT'S GOING ON OUT THERE

Since Yahoo!'s inception in 1994, this Web portal has provided useful information and valuable services to millions of users each day. Yahoo! is the top Internet brand globally, reaching the largest audience worldwide. Two important market segments for Yahoo! to reach are teens (13–17) and "tweens" (8–12), primarily because of their numbers (i.e., approximately 42 million in 2003), their influence on household spending, and their potential to be brand-loyal consumers in the future. Yahoo! is the top Internet provider for teens in all areas except for instant messaging and search functions. AOL is number one in instant messaging, and Google is the most popular search engine.

OVERALL INDUSTRY TRENDS

Paid search and pay-per-click are forecast to be the fastest growing forms of online advertising, increasing from $2.6 billion in 2005 to $5.5 billion in 2009. With the growing popularity of broadband DSL and Internet-friendly mobile phones, users access massive amounts of Internet content at a fast, convenient pace. A new DSL subscriber signs up every second, totaling 96 million subscribers in 2004. However, this led to an influx of unpopular Web content, including porn, hate sites, and spam, that wastes users' time and leads them to fear for their security or their children's security on the Internet.

*Recruiters from the advertising industry attend the district and national competitions to hire students who participate in the American Advertising Federation NSAC. Approximately 150 universities are involved in the NSAC. We thank Yahoo!, the winning **i5** Advertising team from Texas State University-San Marcos, and the American Advertising Federation for providing material for this case. Special thanks go to Murray Gaylord and Gladys Norte at Yahoo! and Connie Frazier at AAF for their help.

TRENDS AMONG "CONNECTED YOUTH"

Instant Messaging (IM). Teens send 9 billion IMs a month, four times the amount of postal mail. Seventy-two percent exchange IMs at least once a month, and 75 percent of teens who IM exchange messages with one to four people at the same time.

Blogs. More than 2 million teens ages 13–19 write or respond to blogs.

Cell Phones. Approximately 50 percent of 10- to 18-year-olds own a cell phone. Teens and tweens are most interested in multifunction cell phones; for example, 71 percent want wireless phones that convert to MP3 players, and 70 percent are interested in cell phones that double as a digital camera and/or TV. Ring tones and downloadable games are a $3 billion business.

Games. Forty-three percent of all gamers play online games, and 40 percent of teen gamers are female.

Web Sites. Fifty percent of teens have a personal Web site.

Multitasking. Teens watch TV, listen to music, eat, and do homework while online. They spend an average of 45.5 hours a week watching TV, using computers, and engaging in other electronic activities, such as downloading music and instant messaging. They typically have four screens open on their computers at once.

PRIMARY RESEARCH

To learn more about these teens and tweens, **i5** Advertising conducted secondary and primary research. Examples of secondary research included, but were not limited to, *Getting Wiser to Teens, The Pew Study, Hoovers, Taylor Group,* and *MRI Teen Mark.* Primary research consisted of surveys, focus groups, personal interviews, attendance at the "What Teens Want" research conference in Beverly Hills, CA, and sponsorship of a high school advertising competition to let teens design an ad for Yahoo!

TARGET MARKET

The primary target market for Yahoo! is 13- to 17-year-olds, called "Switchers." The secondary market is 8- to 12-year-olds, called "Choosers." The rationale for including this secondary market is that these children are already exposed to computers by the time they're eight years old, and teens influence what tweens think is cool. To build brand loyalty, Yahoo! must target these young consumers before they have decided on a provider for instant messaging, search engines, and the many other services offered by Yahoo!

The following findings from secondary and primary research were important in developing the IMC campaign directed at:

Primary Target Market (Switchers): Eighty-five percent of teens have access to a computer at home with the Internet. They primarily use the Internet for instant messaging, to check e-mail, and to play games. The primary barrier to using Yahoo! Messenger is "because all my friends are on AOL's AIM." Fifty percent of teens use Yahoo! from their mobile phones, and 58 percent listen to music through Yahoo!'s Launch.

With regard to lifestyle, the pursuit of "cool" is crucial to most teens. Communicating is most important to girls, while guys are more into entertainment. Independence, experimentation, aspiration, induplication (individuality and affiliation), and having fun are key descriptors. They are "hip to hype." According to *Getting Wiser to Teens,* favorite things for teen girls are: silver jewelry, taking photos, partying, having a boyfriend, low-rise jeans, rap music, hip hop, healthy eating, coloring their hair, and MP3 players. For boys, it's going to the movies, having a girlfriend, downloading music, partying, T-shirts with graphics, silver jewelry, rap music, MP3 players, extreme sports, and college basketball. Teens strongly value relationships with family and friends.

Secondary Target Market (Choosers): Eighty-nine percent of tweens have access to a computer at home with the Internet. These "teen wannabes" are most interested in music, movies, video games, computers, online chat, fashion, sports, and hanging out. The four main motivators that drive their choices are power, freedom, fun, and belonging. This generation only knows instant gratification and is very demanding. Tweens, along with teens, are the most diverse U.S. market segment. One in three belongs to a minority group.

CREATIVE STRATEGY

Given that teens are adept at sorting through marketing messages, it is important to position Yahoo! as a brand that is in sync with the target audience. Yahoo! has strong brand recognition among teens, but they do not use all the services that Yahoo! offers, especially instant messaging and search. Therefore, the following positioning statement was developed:

Positioning Statement: Yahoo! provides teens with free, fun, customizable online services that enable them to interact with friends, music, video, shopping and games from one convenient portal.

The Big Idea: A relatable character, "Dave," serves as a link between intangible services and the target audience. In essence, Dave acts like an older brother, telling teens and tweens about Yahoo! services while personifying the brand through his silly antics.

Copy Tone: Simple, conversational copy with a humorous overtone that is careful to "tell them, not sell them."

Executions: Both print and television use Dave in a humorous snippet of his life in which he talks to Switchers and Choosers about a particular Yahoo! service (instant messenger, search, launch, or mobile) and directs them to the Web site. In television ads the target market is also entertained with a funny, but random/unrelated, video clip.

Rationale: According to the book *Getting Wiser to Teens,* rules for advertising to teens include: be honest, use humor that makes them laugh, be clear, tell them something important about the product, and don't try too hard to be cool. By creating a memorable character who is always being silly in unexpected and random ways, the possibilities are endless. Dave can continue to enlighten the target audience with new features, developments, and improvements of Yahoo! services. He'll become a household name who continues to entertain, thus creating a bond with the audience that it will not want to let go. In fact, Dave was used in a viral ad, without mention of Yahoo!, to create underground buzz prior to the kickoff of the actual campaign. The ad ran only on the Internet and received more than 7,000 hits in just two months as teens and tweens forwarded the ad to their friends just because it was "cool."

PROMOTIONS AND PUBLIC RELATIONS ($1,432,177)

Promotions begin with a new promotional Web site, "Dave's Site," focusing on Yahoo! Messenger. With Messenger download, Switchers and Choosers automatically gain access to other Yahoo services free of charge. The Web site is a link off the current Yahoo! home page and contains Dave's "Hot Dates" calendar, along with links and information about all marketing, promotions, and partnerships vital to the "Dave" campaign. An interactive image of Dave appears on the calendar, and viewers can click on him to hear comments that convey his personality. There are four major "Dave" promotions throughout the campaign: "Dave Needs More Friends," "Dave Jams Out Concert," "Where on the Web Is Dave in His Hummer," and "Dave's Stash of Funniest Clips and Music."

"Dave Needs More Friends" encourages teens, via e-mail blasts and postcards to register, sign on, and round up their friends to do the same. Promotional giveaways are provided while supplies last, and the number of new users added to their lists determines the prize each participant receives.

For **"Dave Jams Out Concert"** Yahoo! teams up with partners SBC, Cingular, and Sony to host the biggest concert event of the summer, donating $1 of every ticket sold to the National Center for Missing and Exploited Children. The concerts are featured in six major cities simultaneously in one night. Teens vote for the bands they want to appear. Sony provides on-site televisions, along with game kiosks for PlayStation. SBC streamlines all six concerts to appear on Yahoo! Entertainment and Launch. Cingular kiosks allow concertgoers to check out its latest "cool tools," and participants can download ring tones, games, or graphics. Yahoo! kiosks allow participants to check out the newest Yahoo! mobile services such as Yahoo! Messenger, Mobile Alerts, and Yahoo! Photos. Concertgoers are encouraged to take pictures with their cell phones and upload them on site to "Dave's Photos" online account. Reactrix is on hand to demonstrate the interactive abilities of a Yahoo! ad.

"Where on the Web Is Dave in His Hummer" offers participants a chance to win one of 30 H2 Hummer stretch limo rides for winners and their friends. The promotion sends the current Yahoo! user on a scavenger hunt through the Web, with Dave giving clues. The target must use Yahoo! Search to find Dave in the Hummer or on cosponsored sites.

"Dave's Stash of Funniest Clips and Music" supports the creative concept by encouraging the target to share its original video clips, pictures, and music. Contestants submit their entries via Yahoo! Messenger, Yahoo! Mobile, Yahoo! Launch, and Yahoo! Mail, which increases the time the target spends on Yahoo!

MEDIA

The media objectives are to reach 90 percent of the Switchers and Choosers with an average monthly frequency of 3.5 for Switchers and 2.9 for Choosers. Co-op savings and value-added were obtained where possible in media buys. Thirty markets were chosen based on cross-referencing the following criteria: U.S. teen population, unwired markets on the forefront of wireless technology, top competitor markets, and top broad- and narrow-band markets.

Nontraditional Media ($2,117,890)

Because teens and tweens are wary of traditional advertising, nontraditional media is heavily used to deliver the message. The following nontraditional media are suggested: Reactrix, stencils, cinema advertising, tear-away posters, wildcards, and product placement.

Reactrix is a high-involvement technology that displays the advertiser's message when the target market interacts with what at first appears to be a stable object like an ad on the floor inside a cinema. Once the subject touches or walks on the ad, it moves and changes, tweaking the interest of the target market. Another creative idea for cinemas is for Yahoo! to run a preview spot reminding viewers to turn off cell phones but prompt them to answer trivia questions by text-messaging using Yahoo! and encourage them to enter to win prizes on Dave's promotional site.

It is suggested that Yahoo! employ a guerilla marketing company to stencil sidewalks, manhole covers, lamp posts, and walls in 30 markets near places the target market visits. Stencils have the effect of being underground, which appeals to teens and tweens. Tear-away vinyl posters of Dave are placed on walls near schools; Switchers and Choosers can take these posters home for their rooms. Wildcards, with a picture of Dave, will be placed in popular retail stores where Switchers and Choosers shop, such as Abercrombie and Fitch, American Eagle, Best Buy, and Urban Outfitters, encouraging recipients to "Visit Yahoo! and Save." Because teens and tweens spend so much time online, **i5** suggests that Yahoo! be part of that online life with averaging, viral ads, and skyscraper and split-screen Web ads. A final consideration is product placement in an upcoming movie or TV show that is popular with the target.

Traditional Media ($4,775,467)

Though not as appropriate as nontraditional media for teens and tweens, traditional media outlets provide national reach and help create buzz for Yahoo! Suggested shows on network and cable television include the following: *The Simpson's, That '70s Show, The OC, American Idol, Nickelodeon, Toon Disney, Comedy Central*, and *MTV.* TV flight dates correspond to Dave's new clips releases, the winning clip from Dave's Clips promotion, and ads prior to Dave's concert. Radio ads air two weeks prior to the Dave Jams Out Concert in the six concert markets. Finally, full-page ads are placed in four magazines: *CosmoGIRL, AmiPro, ESPN the magazine,* and *Seventeen.*

BUDGET ($10,000,000)

Yahoo's 2005 budget to reach 13- to 17-year-olds, shown in Figure 1, is $10 million, including media, creative, promotions, public relations, and production.

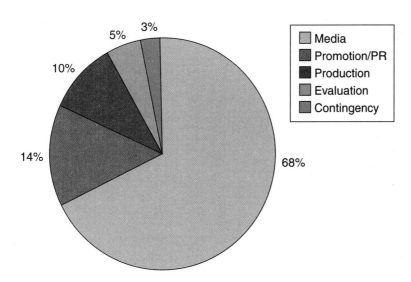

Here's Where the Money Went

- Media
- Promotion/PR
- Production
- Evaluation
- Contingency

FIGURE 1
Campaign Budget Allocation

The Texas State University-San Marcos, **i5** Advertising student team members: Rebecca Barbour, Lorayne Bond, Ashley Brinkman, Lacey Edgar, Karie Gilliland, Cindy Grove, Abby Hagemeier, Yuri Han, Matt Kuhles, John Livingston, Caroline Mendez, Albert Nance, Janet Okoro, Melissa Pursley, Mike Rohal, Mark Tidwell, Brian Weber, Jennifer Whitaker, and Heather Young. Faculty advisors: Jody Gibson and Mary Ann Stutts

Please note: While Yahoo! is delighted that it is the subject of this case, it regrets that it does not have the resources to field calls concerning the case. Please do not contact the company headquarters for additional information, research, or interviews. Some current information is available on the company's Web site: http://www.yahoo.com.

The Yahoo case study plans book and video featuring the work of the winning Texas State team are available through the American Advertising Federation at the AAF Web site: http://www.aaf.org/nsac/.

GLOSSARY

A

Account management *(p. 54)* People and processes at an ad agency that facilitate the relationship between the agency and the client.

Account planner *(pp. 54, 211)* The person responsible for the strategy and its implementation in the creative work.

Account planning *(p. 211)* A process of using research to gain information about the brand in its marketplace, the consumer's perspective, or both, and to use that research to contribute directly to advertising development.

Acquired needs *(p. 141)* A driving force learned from culture, society, and the environment.

Active publics *(p. 514)* Those people who communicate and organize to do something about an issue or situation.

Ad allowances *(p. 539)* In cooperative advertising, funds are provided by manufacturers to retailers who feature the manufacturers' products in the retailers' local advertising.

Adaptation *(p. 550)* See Localization.

Added value *(p. 38)* A marketing activity, such as advertising, makes a product more appealing or useful.

Adese *(p. 392)* Formula writing that uses clichés, generalities, stock phrases, and superlatives.

Advertainment *(p. 302)* A form of persuasive advertising in which the commercials look like TV shows or short films, and provide entertainment as opposed to high levels of information.

Advertisement *(p. 8)* A notice about a product (good, service, or idea) that is designed to get the attention of a target audience.

Advertiser *(p. 14)* A person or organization that initiates the advertising process.

Advertising *(p. 9)* Paid nonpersonal communication from an identified sponsor using mass media to persuade or influence an audience.

Advertising agency *(p. 17)* An organization that provides a variety of professional services to its client who is the advertiser of a product.

Advertising department *(p. 13)* A department within the company that acts as a facilitator between outside vendors and internal advertising management.

Advertising plan *(pp. 13, 184)* A plan that proposes strategies for targeting the audience, presenting the advertising message, and implementing media.

Advertising research *(p. 165)* The process of gathering information about consumers and the marketplace in order to make sound strategic planning decisions.

Advocacy *(p. 121)* A type of advertising that communicates a viewpoint.

Advocacy advertising *(p. 520)* A type of corporate advertising that involves creating advertisements and purchasing space to deliver a specific, targeted message.

Affective response *(p. 111)* A response caused by or expressing feelings and emotions.

Affiliate *(p. 264)* A station that contracts with a national network to carry network-originated programming during part of its schedule.

Affiliate marketing *(p. 50)* A program in which one company drives business to another partner company.

Agency-of-record *(p. 17)* An advertising agency that manages the business between a company and the agencies it has contracts with.

AIDA *(p. 106)* A hierarchy of effects identified as Attention, Interest, Desire, and Action.

Aided recognition recall *(pp. 174, 572)* When one can remember an idea after seeing a cue.

All capitals *(p. 392)* Type set in all capital letters.

Ambush marketing *(p. 493)* In event marketing, a competitor advertises in such a way that it steals visibility from the designated sponsor.

Analogies *(p. 377)* A statement that finds some point of similarity between two things that are otherwise dissimilar.

Analysis *(p. 174)* Making sense of all the data collected and figuring out what the information means for the future success of the brand or product.

Animatics *(p. 567)* Drawings or still photos shot on videotape synchronized with a rough version of an audio track.

Animation *(p. 437)* A film or video technique in which objects or drawings are filmed one frame at a time.

Annual report *(p. 522)* A financial document legally required of all publicly held companies.

Answer print *(p. 441)* The finished version of the commercial, with the audio and video recorded together.

Aperture *(p. 320)* The ideal moment for exposing consumers to an advertising message.

Appeal *(p. 364)* An advertising approach that connects with some need, want, or emotion that makes the product message attractive, attention getting, or interesting.

Argument *(p. 118)* A cognitive strategy that uses logic, reasons, and proof to build convictions.

Art director *(p. 357)* The person who is primarily responsible for the visual image of the advertisement.

Association *(p. 116)* The process used to link a product with a positive experience, personality, or lifestyle.

Attention *(p. 105)* Concentrating the mind on a thought or idea.

Attitude *(p. 117)* A learned predisposition that we hold toward an object, person, or idea.

Attributes *(p. 364)* A distinctive feature of a product.

Audiometer *(p. 257)* A measuring instrument attached to a TV set that records which channel a TV is tuned to.

Avatars *(p. 295)* A representation, character, or personality constructed by a computer user to serve or represent that person.

Average frequency *(p. 299)* The average number of times an audience has an opportunity to be exposed to a media vehicle or vehicles in a specified time span.

Aware publics *(p. 514)* Those people who recognize the connection between a problem and themselves or others but do not communicate about it.

Awareness *(p. 110)* The degree to which a message has made an impression on the viewer or reader.

B

Back translation *(p. 412)* The practice of translating ad copy into a second language and then translating that version back into the original language to check the accuracy of the translation.

Bandwagon appeals *(p. 117)* The idea that people respond to popular causes and ideas and want to join up or adopt a trendy viewpoint.

Bandwidth *(p. 301)* In electronic communication, this is what governs the amount of digital information or data that can be sent from one place to another in a given time.

Banner ad *(p. 291)* Small, often rectangular-shaped graphic that appears at the top of a Web page.

Banners *(p. 291)* See "banner ad."

Behavioral targeting *(p. 156)* The practice of identifying groups of people who might be in the market for a product based on their actions—particularly the patterns of their online behavior.

Beliefs *(p. 117)* A term related to a person's cognitive processing—how they arrive at a position, viewpoint, or decision based on their knowledge, attitudes, and opinions.

Believability *(p. 118)* The extent to which a marketing communication message is accepted as true.

Benchmarking *(pp. 202, 514)* Comparing a result against some other known result from a comparable effort.

Benefits *(p. 365)* Statements about what the product can do for the user.

Big Idea *(p. 371)* A creative idea that expresses an original advertising thought.

Bind-ins *(p. 471)* Cards bound into the binding.

Bleed *(p. 240)* A full-page ad with no outside margins—the color extends to the edge of the page.

Bleed throughs *(p. 341)* In printed communication, the image on one side of a sheet of paper can be seen on the other usually because the ink has thoroughly saturated the paper.

Blind headline *(p. 394)* An indirect headline that gives little information.

Blog *(p. 288)* A personal diary-like Web page.

Blow-ins *(p. 471)* Cards blown in loose between the pages of a publication.

Body copy *(p. 392)* The text of the message.

Brag-and-boast copy *(p. 392)* Self important copy that focuses on the company rather than the consumer.

Brainfag *(p. 375)* In creative thinking, this is the point where concentration ceases to produce ideas because of mental fatigue and the mind closes down.

Brainstorming *(p. 376)* A creative thinking technique using free association in a group environment to stimulate inspiration.

Brand *(p. 11)* A name, term, design, or symbol that identifies the goods, services, institution, or idea sold by a marketer.

Brand advertising *(p. 13)* An advertising strategy that focuses on creating an image or perception of a brand.

Brand communities *(p. 134)* Groups of people devoted to a particular brand, such as the Harley Owners Group (HOG) for Harley-Davidson.

Brand development index (BDI) *(p. 329)* A numerical technique used to indicate a brand's sales within a particular market relative to all other markets where the brand is sold.

Brand equity *(p. 39)* The value associated with a brand; the reputation that the brand name or symbol connotes.

Brand icon *(p. 366)* A character used to represent the brand.

Brand image *(pp. 38, 208)* A special meaning or mental representation created for a product by giving it a distinctive name and identity.

Brand linkage *(pp. 116, 208)* The extent to which an advertising message is connected to the brand and locked into the memory of people who see the message.

Brand loyalty *(p. 118)* The degree of attachment that a customer has to a particular brand as expressed by repeat sales.

Brand management *(p. 49)* An organizational structure that places a manager or management team in charge of a brand's total marketing efforts.

Brand mark *(p. 35)* The part of the brand that cannot be spoken, also known as the logo.

Brand name *(p. 35)* The part of the brand that can be spoken, such as words, letters, or numbers.

Brand penetration *(p. 570)* The number of customers who purchase a certain brand compared against the total market population.

Branded entertainment *(p. 302)* Programs, such as the Hallmark Hall of Fame, that are sponsored by a particular brand.

Branding *(p. 38)* The process of creating a unique identity for a product.

Brand loyalty *(p. 118)*

Break-even analysis (payout planning) *(p. 578)* A type of payout plan that seeks to determine the point at which the total cost of the promotion exceeds the total revenues, identifying the point where the effort cannot break even.

Brief *(p. 198)* A strategy document that explains the consumer insight and summarizes the message and media strategy.

Broadband *(p. 267)* A bandwidth that has more capacity to send data and images into a home or business through a cable television wire than the much smaller capacity of a traditional telephone wire or television antenna system.

Broadcast media *(p. 256)* Media, such as radium television, and interactive media, which transmit sounds or images electronically.

Broadcast network *(p. 264)* A national group of affiliated stations through which programming and advertising are distributed.

Broadsheet *(pp. 234, 466)* A newspaper with a page size eight columns wide and 22 inches deep.

Brokers *(p. 230)* People or companies who sell space (in print) or time (in broadcast) for a variety of media.

Business marketing *(p. 510)* The marketing of goods and services to organizations.

Business strategic plan *(p. 182)* A business plan that deals with the broadest decisions of the organization.

Business-to-business (B2B) market *(p. 41)* Organizations that are buy products for use in conducting their business.

Business-to-business (B2B) advertising *(pp. 13, 541)* Targets other businesses.

Buyer *(p. 542)* A specialist who negotiates an actual purchase in a certain category.

Buzz *(pp. 25, 297)* Gossip created by people over a popular interest in something.

C

Cable radio *(p. 258)* A technology that uses cable television receivers to deliver static-free music via wires plugged into cable subscribers' audio systems.

Cable television *(p. 265)* A form of subscription television in which the signals are carried to households by a cable.

Call centers *(p. 469)* Facilities with banks of phones and representatives who call prospects (outbound) or answer customer calls (inbound).

Call to action *(pp. 120, 370, 397)* A concluding line that tells people how to buy the product.

Call-out *(p. 361)* A block of text separate from the main display copy and headline where the idea is presented.

Campaign *(p. 14)* A comprehensive advertising plan for a series of different but related ads that appear in different media across a specified time period.

Campaign plan *(p. 197)* A comprehensive outline of all activities for a series of related advertisements and other marketing communication efforts.

Capital campaigns *(p. 546)* Fund-raising method used to raise a certain amount of money in a set period of time to finance new buildings, equipment, and so on.

Captions *(p. 395)* Text which explains what is happening in a corresponding photo or illustration.

Carryover effect *(p. 307)* A measure of residual effect (awareness or recall) of the advertising message some time after the advertising period has ended.

Casting *(p. 406)* Finding the right person for the role.

Catalog *(p. 468)* A multipage direct-mail publication that shows a variety of merchandise.

Category development index (CDI) *(p. 329)* A numerical technique that indicates the relative consumption rate in a particular market for a particular product category.

Cause marketing *(pp. 510, 546)* Sponsoring a good cause in the hope that the association will result in positive public opinion about the company.

Cease-and-desist order *(p. 86)* An FTC remedy for false or deceptive advertising that requires an advertiser to stop its unlawful practices.

Change agent program *(p. 515)* A program designed to intervene in corporate culture and change stakeholder behaviors.

Channel market *(p. 43)* The members of a distribution chain, including resellers or intermediaries.

Channel marketing *(p. 43)* Advertising and promotion efforts directed at members of the distribution channel.

Channel of communication *(p. 103)* The media through which an advertisement is presented.

Channel of distribution *(p. 49)* People and organizations involved in moving products from producers to consumers.

Chat room *(p. 288)* A web site that allows users to share information.

Circulation *(p. 232)* The number of copies sold.

Claim *(p. 365)* A statement about the product's performance.

Classified advertising *(p. 236)* Commercial messages arranged in the newspaper according to the interests of readers.

Claymation *(p. 437)* A stop-motion animation technique in which figures sculpted from clay are filmed one frame at a time.

Clear channel *(p. 257)* Powerful radio stations that can deliver signals for long distances beyond their local market.

Click art *(p. 423)* See Clip art.

Click-through *(pp. 291, 579)* The act of clicking on a button on a Web site that takes the viewer to a different Web site.

Clip art *(p. 423)* Generic, copyright-free art that can be used by anyone who buys the book or service.

Close *(p. 364)* The last paragraph of the body copy that often refers back to the creative concept and wraps up the Big Idea.

Closing *(pp. 341, 397)* Represents the last date to send an ad to production.

Clutter *(p. 104)* The excessive number of messages delivered to a target audience.

Clutter reel *(p. 569)* A reel of commercials used in ad testing on which one ad is the one being tested and the others are included to simulate the clutter of a typical advertising break in a program.

Co-branding *(p. 496)* A product offered by two companies with both companies' brands present.

Code-of-ethics *(p. 93)* The rules and standards for a system of socially responsible professional practice.

Cognition *(p. 113)* How consumers respond to information, learn, and understand.

Cognitive dissonance *(p. 141)* A tendency to justify the discrepancy between what you receive and what you expected to receive.

Cognitive learning *(p. 115)* When advertisers want people to know something new after watching or hearing a message.

Coincidental survey *(p. 569)* Random phone calls made to viewers to determine what shows they are watching at that time.

Cold calling *(p. 469)* Sales calls made to individuals and businesses who haven't been informed in advance of the call.

Collateral materials *(pp. 400, 524)* Brochures and other forms of product literature used in support of an advertising, public relations, or sales promotion effort.

Color separation *(p. 433)* The process of splitting a color image into four images recorded on negatives; each negative represents one of the four process colors.

Co-marketing *(p. 496)* Programs through which manufacturers partner with retailers in joint promotions.

Commercial speech *(p. 81)* Our legal right to say what we want to promote commercial activity, as defined by the First Amendment.

Commission *(p. 55)* The amount an ad agency charges to the client, often a percentage of media cost.

Communication audit *(p. 514)* A type of background research that assesses the internal and external PR environment that affects the organization's audience, objectives, competitors, and past results.

Communication brief *(p. 214)* A strategy document that explains the consumer insight and summarizes the message and media strategy.

Comparative advertising *(p. 74)* A message strategy that explicitly or implicitly compares the features of two or more brands.

Comparison *(p. 366)* An advertising strategy that compares two or more brands.

Competitive advantage *(pp. 37, 204)* Features or benefits of a product that let it out perform its competitors.

Compiled list *(p. 461)* In database marketing, a list that is created by merging several lists and purging duplicate entries.

Composition *(p. 428)* The art of arranging the way the elements in a photograph are positioned.

Comprehension *(p. 115)* The process by which people understand, make sense of things, and acquire knowledge.

Comprehensives *(p. 428)* A layout that looks as much like the final printed ad as possible.

Concept testing *(pp. 173, 567)* When a simple statement of an idea is tried out on people who are representative of the target audience in order to get their reactions to the Big Idea.

Concepting *(p. 370)* Creating a big idea.

Conditional learning *(p. 116)* Learning through association by connecting a stimulus to a reward through repeated exposure to a stimulus that eventually leads to the reward.

Consent decree *(p. 85)* A formal FTC agreement with an advertiser that obligates the advertiser to stop its deceptive practices.

Considered purchase *(p. 117)* Buying something after gathering and evaluating information.

Consolidated services *(p. 342)* Company action of bringing planning and buying functions together.

Consumer behavior *(p. 131)* The process of an individual or group selecting, purchasing, using, or disposing of products, services, ideas, or experiences to satisfy needs and desires.

Consumer diaries *(p. 570)* A record kept of brands purchased, what they are used for, if consumers switched from one brand to another, and consumer response to coupons and other offers.

Consumer insight research *(p. 172)* Research that seeks to determines the underlying motivations that drive consumer attitudes and behaviors.

Consumer magazine *(p. 238)* A publication oriented to a general (non-business) audience.

Consumer market *(p. 41)* Selling products to a general (non-business) audience.

Consumer rate *(p. 579)*

Consumer research *(p. 165)* A type of market research that identifies people who are in the market for a product.

Consumer *(pp. 36, 131)* The buyer or user of goods, services, and ideas.

Contact points *(p. 215)* The media, as well as other places and ways, where a consumer engages in a brand experience.

Content analysis *(p. 174)* Research that analyzes articles, news stories and other printed materials for themes and positive or negative mentions of a brand or company.

Contest *(p. 486)* A form of promotion that requires participants to compete for a prize or prizes based on some sort of skill or ability.

Continuity *(pp. 331, 496)* Even, continuous advertising over the time span of the advertising campaign.

Continuous strategy *(p. 331)* A media strategy that spreads the advertising evenly over a period.

Continuous tone *(p. 432)* Photographs are images that have a range of tones from white to black and all the shades of gray in between.

Controlled circulation *(p. 240)* Publications that are distributed, usually free, to selected individuals.

Controlled media *(p. 517)* Media that the direct marketer either owns or has delivered through carefully controlled criteria by a contracted company.

Conversion rate *(p. 579)* In sales, changing a prospect into a customer.

Conviction *(p. 118)* A particularly strong belief that has been anchored firmly in one's attitudes.

Cookies *(p. 300)* Web "bugs" that can be placed on your computer by a Web server to track your online movements.

Cool hunters *(p. 148)* People who specialize in spotting trends.

Co-op advertising *(pp. 46, 235)* Also called cooperative advertising; an arrangement between a retailer and manufacturer in which the manufacturer reimburses the retailer for all or part of the retailer's advertising costs.

Cooperative advertising *(p. 539)* See Coop advertising.

Copycat advertising *(p. 371)* Using some other brand's creative idea.

Copyright *(p. 80)* The owner or creator of certain types of original works have the sole right to reproduce and distribute the work.

Copy-testing *(pp. 173, 380)* Evaluating the effectiveness of an ad, either in a draft form or after it has been used.

Copywriter *(p. 389)* The person who writes the text for an ad.

Core values *(p. 133)* Underlying values that govern a person's (or a brand's) attitudes and behavior.

Corporate advertising *(pp. 13, 519)* A type of advertising used by firms to build awareness of a company, its products, and the nature of its business.

Corporate culture *(p. 134)* The values and attitudes that shape the behavior of an organization and its employees.

Corporate identity advertising *(p. 519)* Promotional method aimed at enhancing or maintaining a company's reputation in the marketplace.

Corporate image *(p. 519)* A perception of a company that its stakeholders create in their minds from messages and experiences with the company.

Corporate relations *(p. 510)* Relations between a corporation and the public involving an organization's image and reputation.

Corrective advertising *(p. 86)* An FTC directive that requires an advertiser to run truthful ads to counter deceptive ads.

Cost per point *(p. 332)* A method of comparing alternative media vehicles on the basis of what it costs to deliver 1,000 readers, viewers, or listeners; the cost of an advertising unit (30-second TV or radio spot, for example) per 1,000 impressions.

Cost per thousand (CPM) *(p. 332)* The cost of exposing each 1,000 members of the target audience to the advertising message.

Cost per lead *(p. 579)* Record of how well a click-through generates prospects.

Country of origin *(p. 548)* Indication of the country that globalized companies consider their base of operation.

Coupons *(p. 485)* Legal certificates offered by manufacturers and retailers that grant specified savings on selected products when presented for redemption at the point-of-purchase.

Coverage *(p. 259)* The degree to which a particular advertising medium delivers audiences within a specific geographical area.

C-prints *(p. 403)* High quality proofs used in printing.

Crawl *(p. 434)* Computer-generated letters that move across the bottom of the screen.

Creative boutique *(p. 53)* An advertising agency that specializes in the creative side of advertising.

Creative brief *(pp. 214, 357)* The document that outlines the key strategy decisions and details the key execution elements.

Creative concept *(pp. 10, 371)* A Big Idea that is original, supports the ad strategy, and dramatizes the selling point.

Creative director *(p. 331)* The person responsible for managing the work of the creative team.

Creative platform *(p. 345)* A document that outlines the message strategy decisions for an individual ad.

Creative strategy *(p. 357)* The determination of the right message for a particular target audience, a message approach that delivers the advertising objectives.

Credibility *(p. 118)* The believability or reliability of a source of information.

Crisis management *(p. 511)* Management of people and events during times of great danger or trouble.

Cross-functional management *(p. 535)* A practice that uses teams to coordinate activities that involve different areas in and outside a company.

Cross-functional planning *(p. 217)* A type of planning that involves people from different parts of an organization, particularly all those departments whose work in some way has impact on the customer.

Cross-media *(p. 230)* See Multichannel.

Cross-platform *(p. 230)* See Multichannel.

Cultural and social influences *(p. 128)* The forces other people exert on your behavior.

Cultural imperialism *(p. 73)* Imposing a foreign culture on a local culture; usually referred to as the impact of Western culture, products, and lifestyles on a more traditional culture.

Culture *(p. 132)* The complex whole of tangible items, intangible concepts, and social behaviors that define a group of people or a way of life.

Culture-orientation model *(p. 521)* A strategy that emphasizes the cultural differences between people.

Customary pricing *(p. 46)* Using a single, well-known price for a long period of time.

Customer *(pp. 36, 131)* Current or prospective purchaser of a product.

Customer relationship management (CRM) *(pp. 57, 463)* A database process that identifies and analyzes patterns in customer behavior to maximize the profitability of each relationship.

Customer satisfaction *(p. 118)* The degree to which there is a match between the customer's expectations about a product and the product's actual performance.

Cut *(p. 407)* An abrupt transition from one shot to another.

Cutouts *(p. 244)* Irregularly shaped extensions added to the top, bottom, or sides of standard outdoor boards.

D

Dailies *(p. 439)* Processed scenes on film that a director reviews to determine what needs correcting.

Data mining *(p. 462)* Shifting through and sorting a company's computer database records to target customers and maintain relationships with them.

Data sheets *(p. 515)* Advertising that provides detailed technical information.

Database marketing *(p. 428)* A tool and industry that utilizes databases to predict trends and monitor consumers in order to more effectively implement direct-marketing strategies.

Databases *(p. 458)* Lists of consumers with information that helps target and segment those who are highly likely to be in the market for a certain product.

Data-driven communication *(p. 461)* Communication strategy used in direct marketing that is based on customer information and previous interactions with the brand.

Daypart *(p. 259)* The way the broadcast schedule is divided into time segments during a day.

Dealer tag *(p. 540)* Time left at the end of a manufacturer's TV or radio commercial to insert local retail store information.

Debossing *(p. 433)* A depressed image created on paper by applying heat and pressure.

Deceptive advertising *(p. 85)* Advertising that misleads consumers by making claims that are false or by failure to fully disclose important information.

Delayed effects *(p. 124)* An advertisement's impact occurs at a later time (than its time of delivery).

Demand creation *(p. 66)* An external message creates a want or need.

Demographics *(p. 135)* Human traits such as age, income, race, and gender.

Demography *(p. 131)* The study of social and economic factors that influence how individual consumers behave.

Demonstration *(p. 366)* An advertising strategy that shows how the product works.

Designated marketing area (DMA) *(p. 316)* Households in each major U.S. metropolitan area, or TV or radio broadcast coverage area.

Development *(pp. 510, 546)* Department of a company focused on fund-raising.

Diaries *(p. 181)* In advertising research, consumers record their consumption activities, including media use.

Die cut *(p. 433)* A sharp-edged stamp used to cut irregular shapes.

Differentiation *(pp. 44, 115)* An advertising strategy that calls to the consumer's attention the features that make a product unique or better than the competition.

Digital marketing *(p. 58)* Using new media and electronic media, particularly the Internet, to reach customers and make a sale.

Digital video recorder *(p. 267)* Technology that allows people to record TV programs and play them back when they want.

Digitization *(p. 433)* Converting art into computer-readable images.

Direct mail *(p. 465)* A type of direct marketing that sends the offer to a prospective customer by mail.

Direct marketing (DM) *(pp. 46, 453)* A type of marketing that uses media to contact a prospect directly and elicit a response without the intervention of a retailer or personal sales.

Direct-action headline *(p. 394)* A headline that is straightforward and informative and leads to some kind of action.

Directional advertising *(p. 233)* Tells people where to go to find goods and services.

Direct-response advertising *(pp. 13, 454)* A type of marketing communication that achieves an action-oriented objective as a result of the advertising message.

Direct-response counts *(p. 545)* Evaluative tests that count the number of viewers or readers who request more information or who purchase the product.

Discretionary income *(p. 139)* The money available for spending after taxes and necessities are covered.

Display advertising *(p. 236)* Sponsored messages that can be of any size and location within the newspaper, except the editorial page.

Display copy *(p. 392)* Type set in larger sizes that is used to attract the reader's attention.

Distribution *(p. 45)* In marketing, the channel of distribution describes the route a product takes moving from its manufacturer to the customer.

Distribution chain or channel *(p. 49)* The companies involved in moving a product from the manufacturer to the customer.

Divergent thinking *(p. 372)* In creative thinking, people trying to come up with a creative idea are advised to move away from logical thinking (inductive, deductive) and look for unexpected ideas by making mental jumps and creative leaps.

Domain name *(p. 287)* Sometimes referred to as a Web address, the domain name is the part of the address that identifies the host server on which a Web site resides.

Donut format *(p. 541)* A format for a radio commercial where the manufacturer records the beginning and end and the local retailer drops in the middle.

Double-page spread *(p. 240)* An advertisement that crosses two facing pages in a magazine.

Dubbing *(p. 441)* The process of making duplicate copies of a videotape.

E

Earned media, *(p. 324)* A term used in public relations, it refers to the media impressions delivered through publicity rather than through advertising media buys.

E-business *(p. 294)* The practice of conducting business online.

E-commerce *(p. 294)* Selling goods and services through electronic means, usually over the Internet.

Effective *(p. 26)* Marketing communication is deemed to be effective when it accomplishes its objectives.

Effective frequency *(p. 322)* A planning concept that determines a range (minimum and maximum) of repeat exposures for a message.

Effects *(p. 26)* The type of impact delivered by an advertisement or other marketing communication.

Embedded research *(p. 184)* Research that is measured through real purchase and use situations which benefits the consumer, manufacturer, and retailer.

Embossing *(p. 433)* The application of pressure to create a raised surface image on paper.

Emotional appeals *(p. 113)* Message strategies that seek to arouse our feelings.

Employee relations *(p. 509)* Relations between the company and its workers.

Endorsement or testimonial *(p. 76)* Any advertising message that consumers reasonably believe reflects the opinions, beliefs, or experiences of an individual, group, or institution.

Endorser *(p. 366)* A person who testifies on behalf of the product (goods, service, or idea).

Engagement *(p. 232)* Advertisement that gets and holds the attention of its audience.

Ethics *(p. 91)* A set of moral principles that guide our actions.

Ethnographic research *(p. 180)* A form of anthropological research that studies the way people live their lives.

Evaluative research *(p. 157)* Research that determines how well the ad or campaign achieved its goals.

Event marketing *(p. 491)* Creating a promotion program around a sponsored event.

Evoked set *(p. 150)* A set of brands that come to mind when a product category is mentioned.

Exchange *(p. 36)* The process whereby two or more parties transfer something of value to one another.

Execution *(p. 357)* The different variations used to represent the message of a campaign.

Experience marketing *(p. 57)* Marketing programs that seek to build positive interactions between customers and products.

Experimental research *(p. 170)* Scientific research in which an investigator controls most of the key variables in order to study the impact of manipulating one or more—changing the product's price or the type of appeal in an ad, for example.

Expert panel *(p. 179)* A type of research that involves obtaining the opinions from a group of people who are recognized as experts in the area being studied.

Exporting *(p. 548)* Selling items to a foreign country.

Exposure *(pp. 110, 268)* The opportunity for a reader, viewer, or listener to see or hear an advertisement.

Extensions *(p. 244)* Embellishments to painted billboards that expand the scale and break away from the standard rectangle limitations.

Exterior transit advertising *(p. 231)* Advertising posters that are mounted on the sides, rear, and tops of vehicles.

Extranets *(p. 525)* Networked systems of electronic communication that allow employees to be in contact with each other in one business with its business partners.

Eye-tracking *(p. 571)* A mechanical technique that tracks the eye's response while reading an advertisement to determine interest.

F

False advertising *(p. 74)* Advertising that is misleading or simply untrue.

Family *(p. 135)* Two or more people who are related by blood, marriage, or adoption and live in the same household.

Feature *(pp. 204, 364)* A product attribute or characteristic.

Feature analysis *(p. 204)* A comparison of your product's features against those of competing products.

Feature story *(p. 522)* In the media, these are human-interest stories, in contrast to hard news.

Federal Communications Commission (FCC) *(p. 70)* A U.S. government agency that regulates broadcast media and can eliminate ads that are deceptive or offensive.

Federal Trade Commission (FTC) *(p. 66)* A U.S. government agency responsible for regulating several advertising issues including banning deceptive or misleading advertising.

Fee *(p. 56)* An hourly amount charged to the client by the agency.

Feedback *(p. 103)* Response to a message by a receiver that is conveyed back to the source.

Film-to-tape transfer *(p. 437)* A procedure by which film is shot, processed, and then transferred to videotape.

Financial relations *(p. 510)* Communications with the financial community.

First-run syndication *(p. 267)* Network shows that move into syndication even though new episodes are continuing to be produced.

Flexography *(p. 403)* A printing process that uses a flexible rubber printing plate in order to print on unusual shaped objects.

Flighting strategy *(p. 331)* An advertising scheduling pattern characterized by a period of intensified activity called a flight, followed by a period of no advertising called a hiatus.

Focus groups *(p. 179)* A group interview led by a moderator.

Foil stamping *(p. 433)* The application of a thin metallic coating (silver, gold) molded to the surface of the image with heat and pressure.

Font *(p. 425)* The basic set of letters in a particular typeface.

Food and Drug Administration (FDA) *(p. 70)* A regulatory division of the Department of Health and Human Services that oversees package labeling and ingredient listings for food and drugs.

Formulas *(p. 365)* Different ways of shaping the creation of an advertisement; may be straightforward, demonstration, comparison, problem solution, humor, spokesperson, or teaser.

Four Ps *(p. 11)* The marketing mix, which includes the product (design and performance), price (value), place (distribution), and promotion (marketing communication).

Four-color printing *(p. 433)* A printing process that replicates the full color of a photograph although it only uses four colors of ink.

Free association *(p. 377)* Getting a new idea by creating a juxtaposition between two seemingly unrelated thoughts—usually done by describing everything that comes into your mind when you are given a word to think about.

Free-standing insert advertisement (FSI) *(pp. 236, 541)* Preprinted advertisement placed loosely in the newspaper.

Frequency *(p. 321)* The number of times an audience has an opportunity to be exposed to a media vehicle or vehicles in a specified time span.

Frequency *(p. 232)* The number of radio waves produced by a transmitter in one second.

Frequency distribution *(p. 322)* A media planning term describing exactly how many times each person is exposed to a message by percentage of the population (reach).

Frequency program *(p. 496)* A loyalty program that rewards customers for repeat purchases.

Friendship focus groups *(p. 179)* Group interviews with people who know one another and have been recruited by the person who hosts the session, which is usually held in that *person*'s home.

Fulfillment *(p. 458)* The back-end operations of direct marketing, which include receiving the order, assembling the merchandise, shipping, and handling returns and exchanges.

Full-service agency *(p. 53)* An agency that provides clients with the primary planning and advertising services.

Fund-raising *(pp. 510, 546)*

G

Gaffer *(p. 439)* Chief electrician on a film shoot.

Game *(p. 486)* A type of promotional sweepstakes that encourages customers to return to a business several times in order to increase the chances of winning.

Gap analysis *(p. 514)* A research technique that measures the differences in perceptions and attitudes between groups or between them and the organization.

Gatefold *(p. 240)* Four or more connected pages that fold in on themselves.

Gatekeepers *(p. 508)* Individuals who have direct relations with the public such as writers, producers, editors, talk-show coordinators, and newscasters.

Global brand *(p. 519)* One that is marketed with the same name, design, and creative strategy in most or all of the major regional market blocs.

Globalization *(p. 23)* The deepening relationships and broadening interdependence among people from different countries.

Goodwill *(p. 507)* A positive attitude about a company among the general public.

Grip *(p. 439)* Individual who moves the props and sets on a film shoot.

Gross impressions *(pp. 232, 269)* The sum of the audiences of all the media vehicles used within a designated time span.

Gross rating points (GRPs) *(p. 324)* The sum of the total exposure potential of a series of media vehicles expressed as a percentage of the audience population.

Guaranteed circulation *(p. 241)* Publications such as magazines guarantee to their advertisers that a certain number of copies will be sold or distributed to subscribers.

Guerrilla marketing *(pp. 47, 302)* A form of unconventional marketing, such as chalk messages on a sidewalk, that is often associated with staged events.

Gutter *(p. 240)* The white space, or inside margins, where two facing magazine pages join.

H

Halftone *(p. 432)* (Continuous tone): Image with a continuous range of shades from light to dark.

Handled *(p. 425)* The way a feature, such as capitalization, is portrayed.

Hard sell *(pp. 12, 362)* A rational, informational message that emphasizes a strong argument and calls for action.

Headline *(p. 392)* The title of an ad; it is display copy set in large type to get the reader's attention.

Heavy-up strategy *(p. 329)* In media planning, a schedule can be designed that spends proportionately more of the budget in certain key ways, such as season or geography.

Hierarchy-of-effects *(p. 106)* A set of consumer responses that moves from the least serious, involved, or complex up through the most serious, involved, or complex.

High-context culture *(p. 551)* The meaning of a message is dependent on context cues.

High definition *(p. 267)*

High-definition TV (HDTV) *(p. 267)* A type of television set that delivers movie quality, high-resolution images.

High involvement *(p. 117)* Perceiving a product or information as important and personally relevant.

High-involvement decision process *(p. 116)* A decision process that relates to higher-risk products purchased infrequently.

High-resolution film *(p. 429)*

Hit *(p. 300)* The number of times a Web site is visited.

Home page *(p. 287)* The opening page on a Web site.

Horizontal publications *(pp. 239, 544)* Publications directed at people who hold similar jobs.

House ad *(p. 519)* An ad by an organization that is used in its own publication or programming.

House brand *(p. 537)* See Store brands.

House list *(p. 460)* A compilation of a company's past customers or members.

Household *(p. 135)* All those people who occupy one living unit, whether they are related or not.

Households using television (HUT) *(p. 268)* A measure of households using TV.

Humor *(p. 366)* An advertising message strategy that tries to be funny to attract an audience, build a positive brand connection, and lock the product in memory.

I

Idea *(p. 370)* A thought or product of thinking.

Ideation *(p. 375)* The process of creating an idea.

Illumination *(p. 375)* The point when a new idea strikes.

Image *(p. 478)* The use of intangible attributes to create a specific perception.

Image advertising *(p. 370)* A type of advertising that creates a unique brand meaning.

Image transfer *(pp. 328, 402)* When the presentation in one medium stimulates the listener or viewer to think about the presentation of the product in another medium.

IMC research *(p. 157)* Research used to plan and evaluate the performance and synergy of all marketing communication tools.

Immersion *(p. 375)* Gathering information and concentrating your focus on a problem.

Impact *(pp. 106, 371)* The effect of the message on the audience.

Implied third-party endorsement *(p. 508)* When the media endorse a product and the public finds it credible.

Impression *(pp. 231, 269)* In media planning, one person's opportunity to be exposed to an advertising message.

In register *(p. 431)* When the four colors used in full-color printing are perfectly aligned with the image.

Inbound telemarketing *(p. 470)* Incoming calls initiated by the customer.

Incubation *(p. 375)* A step in the ideation process, when you turn your attention elsewhere and let your subconscious play with a problem.

Independent stations *(p. 266)* Local stations unaffiliated with a national network.

In-depth interview *(p. 179)* One-on-one interview using open-ended questions.

Indirect advertising *(p. 71)* Advertising that features one product instead of the primary (controversial) product.

Indirect marketing *(p. 44)* Distributing a product through a channel structure that includes one or more resellers.

Indirect-action headlines *(p. 394)* Headlines that aim to capture attention although they might not provide much information.

Industrial advertising *(p. 542)* Advertising directed at suppliers or original equipment manufacturers (OEMs).

Ingredient branding *(p. 49)* Acknowledging a supplier's brand as an important product feature.

In-house agency *(p. 18)* An agency within an advertiser's organization that performs all the tasks an outside agency would provide for the advertiser.

Innate needs *(p. 141)* Primary needs connected with survival.

Inquiry tests *(p. 592)* Evaluation that measures the number of responses to a message.

Insight mining *(p. 212)* Finding some nugget of truth in a stack of research findings that lead to a key understanding of how consumers feel, think, or behave.

Instant messaging *(p. 306)* Exchanging text-based messages in real time via an Internet communications service.

Institutional advertising *(p. 13)* A type of corporate advertising that focus on establishing a corporate identity or viewpoint.

Institutional market *(p. 41)* Usually a non-profit organization, such as hospitals, government agencies, or schools, that buy products to use in delivering their services.

Institutional retail advertising *(p. 507)* Advertising that focuses on the image of the store rather than selling merchandise.

Integrated direct marketing *(p. 475)* A method of achieving precise, synchronized use of the right mediums at the right time, with a measurable return on dollars spent. Also known as integrated relationship marketing.

Integrated marketing *(p. 57)* The process of meeting customers' needs through the coordination of the marketing mix and the other business functions.

Integrated marketing communication (IMC) *(p. 25)* The practice of unifying all marketing communication efforts so they send a consistent, persuasive message to target audiences.

Intend-to-buy (motivation) test *(p. 572)* An evaluation determining if people are more likely to buy a product once they are exposed to an advertisement for it.

Intention *(p. 118)* A preference that motivates consumers to want to try or buy a brand.

Interactive communication *(p. 103)* Personal conversations between two people.

Interactive Television *(p. 267)* A television with computer capabilities.

Interconnects *(p. 266)* A special cable technology that allows local advertisers to run their commercials in small geographic areas through the interconnection of a number of cable systems.

Interest *(p. 110)* Activities that engage the consumer.

Interior transit advertising *(p. 231)* Advertising posters that are mounted inside vehicles such as buses, subway cars, and taxis.

Interlock *(p. 441)* A version of the commercial with the audio and video timed together, although the two are recorded separately.

Intermediaries *(p. 43)* Companies that buy finished or semi-finished items and resell them for a profit.

Internal marketing *(pp. 215, 509)* Providing information about marketing activity and promoting it internally to employees.

International advertising *(p. 52)* Advertising designed to promote the same product in a number of countries.

International brand *(pp. 52, 519)* A brand or product that is available in most parts of the world.

Internet *(p. 287)* A linked system of international computer networks.

Intranets *(p. 525)* Networked systems of electronic communication that allow employees to be in touch with one another from various locations.

Intrusive *(p. 110)* Marketing communication messages that intrude on people's perception in order to grab attention.

Involvement *(p. 117)* The intensity of the consumer's interest in a product.

Issue management *(p. 510)* The practice of advising companies and senior management on how public opinion is coalescing around certain issues.

J

Jingles *(pp. 260, 401)* Commercials set to music.

Justified type *(p. 392)* A form of typeset copy in which the ends of the lines in a column of type are forced to align by adding space between words in the line.

K

Key frame *(p. 404)* An image from a commercial that sticks in the mind and becomes the visual that viewers remember when they think about the commercial.

Keyword *(p. 287)* A word or phrase typed into a search engine to finds Web sites relevant to a certain topic.

Kiosks *(p. 247)* Multisided bulletin board structures designed for public posting of messages.

Knowledge structure *(p. 116)* See Network of associations.

L

Latent publics *(p. 514)* Those people who are unaware of their connection to an organization regarding a problem.

Layout *(p. 427)* A drawing that shows where all the elements in the ad are to be positioned.

Lead agency *(p. 551)* In international marketing, the agency that develops the campaign.

Lead generation *(pp. 48, 456)* The identification of prospective customers.

Lead paragraph *(p. 397)* The first line or paragraph of the body copy that is used to stimulate the reader's interest.

Lead time *(p. 331)* Production time; also time preceeding a sesonal event.

Left-brain thinking *(p. 372)* Logical, linear, and orderly thought; inductive or deductive.

Legibility *(p. 425)* How easy or difficult a type is to read.

Letterpress *(p. 402)* A printing process that prints from a raised surface.

Licensing *(p. 496)* The practice whereby a company with an established brand "rents" it to another company.

Lifestyle *(p. 135)* The pattern of living that reflects how people allocate their time, energy, and money.

Lifestyle analysis *(p. 141)* Examining the ways people allocate their time, energy, and money.

Lifetime customer value (LCV) *(p. 476)* An estimate of the revenue coming from a particular customer (or type of customer) over the lifetime of the relationship.

Likability tests *(p. 541)* Evaluation of positive responses to an ad.

Liking *(p. 113)* Positive feelings about the brand that are aroused by the ad.

Line art *(p. 432)* Art in which all elements are solid, with no intermediate shades or tones.

Links *(p. 287)* A path used to connect to a Web site.

Lists *(p. 460)* Databases of prospects' and customers' contact information.

Loaders *(p. 462)* Trade promotions that encourage retailers to stock up on a product.

Lobbying *(p. 510)* A form of public affairs involving corporations, activist groups, and consumer groups who provide information to legislators in order to get their support and to get them to vote a certain way on a particular bill.

Local advertising *(pp. 13, 505)* Advertising targeted to consumers who live within the local shopping area of a store.

Local brand *(p. 52)* A brand that is marketed in one specific country.

Local cable *(p. 266)* Cable scheduling that allows advertisers to show their commercials to highly restricted geographic audiences through interconnects.

Localization (Adaption) *(p. 550)* A strategy in international advertising that adapts the message to local cultures.

Logo *(pp. 39, 421)* A distinctive brand mark that is legally protected.

Low-context cultures *(p. 551)* The meaning of a message is obvious without needing a sense of the cultural context.

Low-involvement *(p. 118)* Perceiving a product or information as unimportant.

Low-involvement decision process *(p. 116)* A decision process that relates to products purchased frequently with low risk.

Low-power FM *(p. 258)* Nonprofit, non-commercial stations that serve a small are market, such as a college campus.

Low-power television *(p. 266)* Local stations that serve a limited market because their signals only cover a radius of 15 miles.

Low-power television *(p. 266)*

Loyalty program *(p. 496)* A program designed to increase customer retention by rewarding customers for their patronage.

M

Make goods *(p. 341)* Compensation that media give to advertisers in the form of additional message units. These are commonly used in situations involving production errors by the medium and preemption of the advertiser's programming.

Market *(p. 41)* An area of the country or a group of buyers.

Market aggregation strategy *(p. 147)* An undifferentiated segmentation strategy that treats consumers as homogenous.

Market orientation model *(p. 521)* A strategy in international marketing that emphasizes the differences in cultures.

Market research *(pp. 165, 172)* A type of marketing research that investigates the product and category, as well as consumers who are or might be customers for the product.

Market segmentation *(p. 152)* The process of dividing a market into distinct groups of buyers who might require separate products or marketing mixes.

Market selectivity *(p. 214)* When the medium targets specific consumer groups.

Marketer *(p. 49)* The company or organization behind the product.

Marketing *(pp. 10, 34)* Business activities that direct the exchange of goods and services between producers and consumers.

Marketing communication mix *(p. 42)* A combination of marketing communication activities, such as personal selling, advertising, sales promotion, marketing public relations, and packaging, to produce a coordinated message strategy.

Marketing communications *(p. 7)* The element in the marketing mix that communicates the key marketing messages to target audiences.

Marketing concept *(p. 36)* An idea that suggests that marketing should focus first on the needs and wants of the customer, rather than finding ways to sell products that may or may not meet customers' needs.

Marketing imperialism *(p. 73)* Marketing practices that result in imposing foreign cultural values on a local culture with different vlaues and traditions.

Marketing mix *(p. 11)* A blend of four main activities: designing, pricing, distributing, and communicating about the product.

Marketing objectives *(p. 44)* The business objectives that give direction to a marketing plan usually stated as sales or share of market.

Marketing plan *(pp. 43, 195)* A written document that proposes strategies for using the elements of the marketing mix to achieve objectives.

Marketing public relations (MPR) *(p. 512)* A type of public relations that supports marketing's product and sales focus by increasing the brand's and company's credibility with consumers.

Marketing research *(pp. 43, 172)* Research that investigates all elements of the marketing mix.

Marketing services *(p. 51)* This includes a variety of suppliers hired by marketers, such as researchers and various types of marketing communication agencies.

Measured media *(p. 318)* Media used in advertising that are evaluated by auditing companies that track performance data, such as circulation, readership, and viewership.

Mechanicals *(p. 428)* A finished pasteup with every element perfectly positioned that is photographed to make printing plates for offset printing.

Media *(pp. 18, 211)* The channels of communication that carry the ad message to target audiences.

Media buyers *(p. 230)* Specialists who implement the media plan by contracting with various media for placement of an advertisement.

Media flow chart *(p. 332)* A planning document that shows how the media plan well run in terms of the scheduling of the various media used.

Media kit *(p. 522)* Also called a press kit, a packet or folder that contains all the important information for members of the press.

Media mix *(pp. 231, 323)* Selecting the best combination of media vehicles, nontraditional media, and marketing communication tools to reach the targeted stakeholder audiences.

Media objective *(p. 321)* A goal or task a media plan should accomplish.

Media optimization *(p. 575)* The best use of various communication methods to promote the company.

Media plan *(pp. 229, 318)* A decision process leading to the use of advertising time and space to assist in the achievement of marketing objectives.

Media planning *(p. 230)* The way advertisers identify and select media options based on research into the audience profiles of various media.

Media relations *(p. 509)* Relationships with media contacts.

Media reps *(p. 230)* Media salespeople who sell media time and space for a variety of media outlets.

Media research *(p. 173)* The process of gathering information about all the possible media and marketing communication tools available to be used in a marketing communication plan.

Media researchers *(p. 231)* The specialists who gather information about media audiences and performance.

Media salespersons *(p. 213)* People who work for a specific medium and call on media planners and buyers in agencies to sell space or time in that medium.

Media strategy *(p. 328)* The decisions media planners make to deliver the most effective media mix that will reach the target audience and satisfy the media objectives.

Media tour *(p. 522)* A traveling press conference in which the company's spokesperson travels to different cities and meets with the local media.

Media vehicle *(p. 231)* A single program, magazine, or radio station.

Media-buying services *(p. 54)* Service providers that specialize in the purchase of media for their clients.

Medium *(p. 101)* A single form of communication (television, billboards, online media).

Merging *(p. 460)* The process of combining two or more lists of data.

Message *(p. 99)* The words, pictures, and ideas that create meaning in an advertisement.

Message development research *(p. 173)* Research findings gathered by planners to help decide message strategy.

Message strategy *(p. 357)* The determination of the right message for a particular target audience that delivers the advertising objectives.

Metaphors *(p. 377)* A figure of speech in which a term or phrase from one object is associated with something entirely different to create an implicit comparison.

Microtargeting *(p. 157)* The practice of using vast databases of personal information to predict attitudes and behavior of selected groups.

Minisites *(p. 292)* Smaller Web sites that exist on a marketing partner's site permitting viewers to click on the minisite for additional information without leaving the original Web site.

Mission marketing *(p. 548)* Linking the mission of the company to a good cause and committing support to it for the long term.

Mission statement *(p. 195)* A business platform that articulates the organization's philosophy, as well as its goals and values.

Mixer *(p. 439)* The individual who operates the recording equipment during a film shoot.

Mobile marketing *(pp. 58, 305)* The use of wireless communication to reach people on the move with a location-based message.

Moment-by-moment tests *(p. 569)* A research method that evaluates viewers' response to a commercial frame by frame.

Morals *(p. 91)* The framework for separating right from wrong and identifying good behavior.

Morning drive time *(p. 259)* On radio the day part that reaches people when they are commuting to work.

Morphing *(p. 435)* A video technique in which one object gradually changes into another.

Motivation (motive) *(pp. 117, 142)* An unobservable inner force that stimulates and compels a behavioral response.

Motivation test *(p. 572)* Research that evaluates consumers' intention to act.

Multichannel *(pp. 230, 341)* An advertising plan that uses several different forms of media, such as TV, print, radio, and online.

N

Natural Care *(p. 195)* A philosophy to do what is right for customers, employees, communities, and the environment.

Navigation *(p. 443)* The action of a user moving through a Web site.

Needs *(p. 115)* Basic forces that motivate you to do or to want something.

Negative space *(p. 395)* In a layout, the white (unprinted) space surrounding the ad's elements.

Netcasting *(p. 289)* Using video on personal sites (vlogs) or corporate sites particularly broadcasting TV or radio online.

Network *(p. 250)* When two or more stations are able to broadcast the same program that originates from a single source.

Network cable *(p. 266)* Cable scheduling that runs commercials across an entire subscriber group simultaneously.

Network of associations *(pp. 116, 175)* The linked set of brand perceptions that represent a person's unique way of creating meaning.

Network radio *(p. 260)* A group of local affiliates providing simultaneous programming via connection to one or more of the national networks through AT&T telephone wires.

News release *(p. 520)* Primary medium used to deliver public relations messages to the media.

Newsprint *(p. 431)* An inexpensive paper with a rough surface, used for printing newspapers.

Niche markets *(p. 154)* Subsegments of the general market which have distinctive traits that may provide a special combination of benefits.

Noise *(p. 103)* Anything that interferes with or distorts the advertising message's delivery to the target audience.

Nonprofit *(p. 18)* Noncommercial organizations.

Nonprofit advertising *(p. 14)* Advertising programs used by nonprofit organizations, such as charities, associations, and hospitals.

Nonpromotional product advertising *(p. 507)* A form of advertising that talks about merchandise that is new, exclusive, and of superior quality and design.

Nontraditional delivery *(p. 223)* Delivery of magazines to readers through such methods as door hangers or newspapers.

Norms *(pp. 132, 565)* Simple rules that each culture establishes to guide behavior.

North American Industry Classification System (NAICS) *(p. 542)* The federal system of grouping businesses based on the major product or service provided.

O

Objective *(pp. 26, 192)* The goal or task an individual or business wants to accomplish.

Objective-task method *(p. 209)* Budgeting approach based on costs of reaching an objective.

Observation research *(p. 180)* Qualitative research method that takes researchers into natural settings where they record people's behavior.

Off camera *(p. 404)* In television, a voice is coming from an unseen speaker.

Offer *(p. 456)* A direct marketing tool that provides potential customers with an item's information, description, terms of sale, and often an incentive for quick action in buying.

Offline advertising *(p. 298)* Advertising in traditional media that is designed to drive consumers to an advertiser's Web site.

Off-network syndication *(p. 267)* Reruns off network shows.

Offset printing *(p. 402)* A printing process that prints an image from a smooth surface chemically treated printing plate.

On location *(p. 406)* Commercials shot outside the studio.

One-order, one-bill *(p. 218)* When media companies buy newspaper advertising space for national advertisers and handle the rate negotiation and billing.

One-step offer *(p. 457)* A message that asks for a direct sales response and has a mechanism for responding to the offer.

Open-ended questions *(p. 179)* A qualitative research method that asks respondents to generate their own answers.

Opinion leaders *(pp. 117, 507)* Important people who influence others.

Opt in (Opt out) *(p. 293)* In e-mail advertising (and direct mail) consumers agree to be included or not included in the list.

Optimization *(pp. 331, 456)* Computer modeling that helps media planners determine the relative impact and efficiency of various media mixes.

Original *(p. 371)* Unique and the first of it kind.

Outbound telemarketing *(p. 470)* Telemarketing sales calls initiated by the company.

Outdoor advertising *(p. 243)* Advertising on billboards along streets and highways.

Out-of-home advertising *(p. 242)* All advertising that is displayed outside the home, from billboards, to blimps, to in-store aisle displays.

Out-of-register *(p. 341)* When the four colors used in full-color printing are not perfectly aligned with the image.

Overlines *(p. 361)* Text used to set the stage and lead into the headline of copy.

P

Pace *(p. 406)* How fast or slowly the action progresses in a commercial.

Package goods *(p. 41)* Products sold for personal or household use.

Page views *(p. 579)* The number of times a Web site is visited.

Painted bulletin *(p. 244)* A type of advertisement that is normally created on-site and is not restricted to billboards as the attachment.

Pantry checks *(p. 570)* A research checks home-owners' pantries to determine their purchases.

Participations *(p. 271)* An arrangement in which a television advertiser buys commercial time from a network.

Pass-along readership *(p. 333)* The view that a magazine, although only bought by one consumer, may actually be read by several; difference between circulation and readership.

Pay-per-click *(p. 579)* Online advertising where a company is charged every time a potential customer visits (clicks) on their Web site.

Pay-per-view television *(p. 267)* Specialty television programming delivered by satellite for a fee.

Payout analysis *(p. 578)* A comparison of the cost of a promotion against the forecasted sales generated by the promotion.

Payout plan *(pp. 499, 578)* A way to evaluate the effectiveness of a sales promotion in terms of its financial returns by comparing the costs of the promotion to the forecasted sales of the promotion.

People meters *(p. 270)* Boxes on a TV set that record viewing behaviors.

Perceived risk *(p. 148)* The relationship between what you gain by making a certain decision and what you have to lose.

Percentage-of-sales method *(p. 210)* A budgeting technique based in the relationship between the cost of advertising and total sales.

Perception *(p. 110)* The process by which we receive information through our five senses and acknowledge and assign meaning to this information.

Perceptual map *(p. 205)* An analytical technique that plots the mental positions held by consumers of a set of competitors on a matrix.

Permission marketing *(pp. 57, 293)* A method of direct marketing in which the consumer controls the process, agrees to receive communication from the company, and consciously signs up.

Permission to believe *(p. 370)* Credibility building techniques that increase consumers' conviction in making decisions.

Personal selling *(p. 47)* Face-to-face contact between the marketer and a prospective customer that intends to create and repeat sales.

Personality *(p. 142)* The consistent attitudes and behaviors that make us an individual.

Persuasion *(p. 117)* Trying to establish, reinforce, or change an attitude, touch an emotion, or anchor a conviction firmly in the potential customer's belief structure.

Persuasion test *(p. 572)* A test that evaluates the effectiveness of an advertisement by measuring whether the ad affects consumers' intentions to buy a brand.

Photoboards *(pp. 407, 567)* A mockup of a television commercial that uses still photos for the frames.

Photostats *(p. 403)* Photoprint proofs that are cheap to produce.

Pica *(p. 392)* A unit used to measure width and depth of columns; there are 12 points in a pica and 6 picas in an inch.

Picture sort *(p. 569)* Viewers receive a deck of photos and sort them into categories as requested by the researcher.

Pitch *(p. 51)* A formal presentation by an agency to a marketer that showcases the agency' competencies, previous work, and ideas for the potential client's advertising.

Pitch letter *(p. 522)* A letter to a media outlet that outlines a possible story idea that the PR person would like to provide.

Podcasting *(p. 263)* The practice of using audio shows broadcast from the Web to be downloaded to an MP3 player.

Podcasts *(p. 306)* Audio shows broadcast from the Web that an be downloaded to an MP3 player.

Point *(p. 392)* A unit used to measure the height of type; there are 72 points in an inch.

Point of differentiation *(p. 338)* The way a product is unique from its competitors.

Point-of-purchase (POP) display *(p. 489)* A display designed by the manufacturer and distributed to retailers to promote a particular brand or line of products.

Pool-outs *(p. 522)* Variations on a core campaign theme.

Population *(p. 177)* An entire group of people from which a sample is drawn.

Pop-ups and pop-behinds *(p. 291)* Types of ads that burst open on the computer screen either in front of or behind the opening page of a Web site.

Portal *(p. 287)* A Web site that provides doors or links to other Web sites.

Position *(pp. 44, 202)* A brand location in the consumer's mind relative to competing brands based on the relative strengths of the brand and its competitors.

Positioning *(p. 44)* The way in which consumers perceive a product in the marketplace.

Poster (panels printed posters) *(pp. 228, 244)* A type of advertisement that is created by designers, printed, and shipped to an outdoor advertising company who prepastes and applies it in sections to the poster panel's face on location.

Postproduction *(p. 441)* In TV production, assembling and editing the film after the film has been shot.

Predictive dialing *(p. 470)* Technology that allows telemarketing companies to call anyone by using a trial and error dialing program.

Preference *(p. 118)* Favorable positive impression of a product that leads to an intention to try or buy it.

Preferred-position rate *(p. 236)* Charges by media for space or time that are in high demand because they have a special appeal to the target audience.

Preferred positions *(p. 340)* Sections or pages of print media that are in high demand by advertisers because they have a special appeal to the target audience.

Premium *(p. 486)* A tangible reward received for performing a particular act, such as purchasing a product or visiting the point-of-purchase.

Preprints *(p. 541)* Advertising circulars furnished by a retailer for distribution as a freestanding insert in newspapers.

Press conference *(p. 522)* A public gathering of media people for the purpose of establishing a company's position or making a statement.

Pretesting *(pp. 173, 567)* Evaluative research of finished or nearly finished ads that leads to a go/no-go decision.

Price *(p. 44)* An amount a seller sets for a product that is based not only on the cost of making and marketing the product, but also on the seller's expected profit level.

Price copy *(p. 46)* A term used to designate advertising copy devoted to information about the price and the associated conditions of a particular product.

Price deal *(p. 485)* A temporary reduction in the price of a product.

Price-value strategy *(p. 539)* Promotional method suggesting customers buying a certain product will get the best quality possible at a particular price.

Primary research *(pp. 43, 167)* Information that is collected from original sources.

Primary research suppliers *(p. 159)* Research firms that specialize in interviewing, observing, recording, and analyzing the behavior of those who purchase or influence the purchase of a particular good or service.

Prime time *(p. 264)* Programming on TV that runs between the hours of 8 p.m. and 11 p.m.

Print production *(p. 51)* A department that takes a layout, type, and artwork and turns it into a reproducible format.

Printed poster *(p. 244)* A type of billboard that uses printed formats in standardized sizes that are pasted to the board's surface.

Privacy policy *(p. 301)* A statement on a company's Web site that explains what user data it collects and how it uses the data.

Private label brands *(p. 537)* See Store brands.

Pro bono *(p. 518)* Situation in which all services, time, and space are donated.

Problem avoidance *(p. 366)* A message strategy that positions the brand as a way to avoid a problem.

Problem solution format *(p. 366)* A message strategy that sets up a problem that the use of the product can solve.

Process colors *(p. 433)* Four basic inks—magenta, cyan, yellow, and black—that are mixed to produce a full range of colors found in four-color printing.

Product category *(p. 11)* Classification to which a product belongs.

Product differentiation *(pp. 37, 205)* A competitive marketing strategy that tries to create a competitive difference through real or perceived product attributes.

Product management *(p. 49)* An organizational structure that places a brand manager or management team in charge of a brand's total marketing effort.

Product placement *(p. 278)* The use of a brand name product in a television show, movie, or event.

Product reviews *(p. 184)* A record of opinions by people who have purchased a particular item.

Product-as-hero *(p. 366)* A form of the problem-solution message strategy.

Product-driven philosophy *(p. 35)* A marketing approach that starts with the development of a product, rather than with consumer needs.

Production notes *(p. 439)* A document that describes in detail of every aspect of a commercial's production.

Professional advertising *(p. 542)* Advertising that is targeted at professionals.

Profile *(p. 155)* A composite description of a target audience using personality and lifestyle characteristics.

Program preemptions *(p. 341)* Interruptions in local or network programming caused by special events.

Program sponsorships *(p. 266)* Commercial announcements used in public broadcasting to underwrite programming costs.

Promise *(p. 365)* Found in a benefit statement, it is something that will happen if you use the product.

Promotional allowances *(p. 539)* Retail advertising that is focused on price or a special sale.

Prospecting *(p. 463)* In database marketing, this is the process of identifying prospects based on how well they match certain user characteristics.

Prospects *(p. 131)* Potential customers who are likely to buy the product or brand.

Psychographics *(p. 142)* All psychological variables that combine to share our inner selves and help explain consumer behavior.

Psychological pricing *(p. 46)* A strategy that tries to manipulate the customer's purchasing judgment.

Public affairs *(p. 510)* Relations between a corporation, the public, and government involving public issues relating to government and regulation.

Public communication campaigns *(pp. 512, 546)* Social issue campaigns undertaken by nonprofit organizations as a conscious effort to influence the thoughts or actions of the public.

Public opinion *(p. 507)* People's beliefs, based on their conceptions or evaluations of something, rather than on fact.

Public radio *(p. 257)* A network of radio stations that use public broadcasting material usually provided by National Public Radio (NPR).

Public relations *(p. 506)* A management function enabling organizations to achieve effective relationships with various publics in order to manage the image and reputation of the organization.

Public service advertising (PSA) *(p. 14)* A type of public relations advertising (also called public service announcement) that deals with social issues and typically is created and run pro bono (free of charge).

Public Service Announcements (PSAs) *(pp. 14, 260, 518)* A type of public relations advertising that deals with public welfare issues and typically is run free of charge.

Public television *(p. 266)* Broadcast TV stations that generally function based on donations rather than commercial advertising.

Publicity *(p. 507)* Information that catches public interest and is relayed through the news media.

Publics *(p. 505)* All groups of people with which a company or organization interacts.

Puffery *(p. 74)* Advertising or other sales representation that praises a product or service using subjective opinions, superlatives, and similar techniques that are not based on objective fact.

Pull strategy *(pp. 46, 330)* A strategy that directs marketing efforts at the consumer and attempts to pull the product through the channel.

Pulsing strategy *(p. 332)* An advertising scheduling pattern in which time and space are scheduled on a continuous but uneven basis; lower levels are followed by bursts or peak periods of intensified activity.

Purging *(p. 460)* The process of deleting duplicative information after lists of data are combined.

Push strategy *(pp. 46, 330)* A strategy that directs marketing efforts at resellers, where success depends on the ability of these intermediaries to market the product, which they often do with advertising.

Q

Qualitative research *(p. 168)* Research that seeks to understand how people think and behave and why.

Quantitative research *(p. 168)* Research that uses statistics to describe consumers.

R

Radio script *(p. 402)* A written version of a radio commercial used to produce the commercial.

Ragged right *(p. 392)* In typesetting, the line endings of the right side of the column fall where they will. Also called "unjustified."

Rate card *(p. 235)* A list of the charges for advertising space.

Ratings, Rating Points *(pp. 259, 269, 326)* Percentage of population or households tuned to a program.

Reach *(p. 321)* The percentage of different homes or people exposed to a media vehicle or vehicles at least once during a specific period of time. It is the percentage of unduplicated audience.

Reason to believe *(p. 118)* Supporting or proving an advertising claim intensifies believability.

Reason why *(p. 365)* A statement that explains why the feature will benefit the user.

Rebate *(p. 485)* A sales promotion that allows the customer to recover part of the product's cost from the manufacturer in the form of cash.

Recall *(p. 110)* People remember seeing an ad and what the ad said.

Recall test *(p. 571)* A test that evaluates the memorability of an advertisement by contacting members of the advertisement's audience and asking them what they remember about it.

Receiver *(p. 103)* The audience for an advertisement.

Recency, frequency, and monetary *(p. 456)* The three criteria that help direct marketers predict who among the customer base is likely to be repeat buyers.

Recognition *(p. 110)* An ability to remember having seen something before.

Recognition test *(p. 571)* A test that evaluates the memorability of an advertisement by contacting members of the audience, showing them the ad, and asking whether they remember having seen it before.

Reference group *(p. 134)* A group of people that a person uses as a guide for behavior in specific situations.

Referrals *(p. 121)* When a satisfied customer recommends a favorite brand.

Refund *(p. 485)* An offer by the marketer to return a certain amount of money to the consumer who purchases the product.

Regional brand *(p. 52)* A brand that is available throughout a regional trading block.

Registration *(p. 399)* When the four-colors used in full-color printing are perfectly aligned with the image.

Relational database *(p. 460)* Databases used for profiling and segmenting potential customers as well as providing contact information.

Relationship marketing *(pp. 57, 509)* The ongoing process of identifying and maintaining contact with high-value customers.

Release prints *(p. 441)* Duplicate copies of a commercial that are ready for distribution.

Relevance *(pp. 110, 371)* The message connects with the audience on a personal level.

Reliability *(p. 183)* In research, reliability means you can run the same test over again and get the same results.

Reminder *(p. 370)* Advertising designed to keep a brand name in front of customers to encourage repeat business.

Reminder advertising *(p. 344)* An advertising strategy that keeps the brand name in front of consumers.

Reputation *(p. 478)* A general estimation in which a company is held by the public, based on its practices, policies, and performance.

Reputation management *(p. 510)* The trust stakeholders have in an organization.

Reseller *(p. 43)* Intermediaries in the distribution channel, typical wholesalers, retailers, and distributors who buy products from manufacturers and then resell them to the ultimate user.

Resonance *(p. 113)* A message that rings true because the consumer connects with it on a personal level.

Response list *(p. 461)* In direct marketing, a list that is compiled of people who respond to a direct-mail offer.

Retail advertising *(p. 13)* A type of advertising used by local merchants who sell directly to consumers.

Retainer *(p. 56)* Agency monthly compensation based on an estimate of the projected work and its costs.

Return on investment (ROI) *(pp. 195, 371)* Return on investment, which means that the costs of conducting the business should be more than matched by the revenue produced in return.

Reverse type *(p. 426)* White letters reversed out of a dark surrounding area.

Rich media *(p. 301)* Messages are effective in grabbing people's attention because of their novelty and entertainment value.

Right brain thinking *(p. 372)* A type of divergent thinking that is intuitive, holistic, artistic, and emotionally expressive.

Rotogravure *(p. 402)* A printing process used for long press runs that provides high-quality photographic reproduction.

Rough cut *(p. 441)* A preliminary edited version of the commercial.

Rough layout *(p. 428)* A layout drawn to size but without attention to artistic and copy details.

Run-of-paper rate *(p. 236)* In newspaper advertising, a rate based on a locaton that is at the discretion of the publisher.

Rushes *(p. 439)* Rough versions of the commercial assembled from unedited footage.

S

Saccadic eye movement *(p. 571)*

Sales advertising *(p. 507)* Advertising in which the sales price dominates the ad.

Sales kits *(p. 230)* Packets of information used by media representatives and other types of sales personnel.

Sales levels *(p. 196)* The amount of a particular product customers buy.

Sales promotion *(p. 482)* Marketing activities that add value to the product for a limited period of time to stimulate consumer purchasing and dealer effectiveness.

Sample *(p. 177)* In research, a subset of the population that is representative of the key characteristics of the larger group.

Sampling *(p. 485)* Allowing the consumer to experience the product at no cost.

Sans serif *(p. 392)* A typeface that does not have the serif detail at the end of the strokes.

Satellite radio *(p. 258)* Subscription radio programming delivered by satellite to receivers any where in the continental United States.

Satellite television *(p. 265)* Subscription television programming delivered by satellite to locations with satellite dishes.

Scanner research *(p. 573)* Research that tracks consumer purchases and compares the marketing communication received by the consumer's household.

Scenes *(p. 406)* Commercials are planned with segments of action that occur in a single location.

Screen *(p. 432)* Used to convert continuous tone art to halftone by shooting the image through a fine screen that breaks the image into a dot pattern.

Script *(p. 369)* A written version of a radio or television commercial.

Search engine *(p. 287)* Internet services that locate information based on key words.

Search marketing *(p. 298)* Marketing communication strategies designed to aid consumers in their search for information.

Search optimization *(p. 299)* The practice of maximizing the link between topics that consumers search for and a brand-related Web site.

Secondary research *(pp. 43, 165)* Information that already has been compiled and published.

Secondary research suppliers *(p. 158)* Research firms that gather and organize information around specific topic areas for other interested parties.

Segmenting *(pp. 44, 151)* Dividing the market into groups of people who have similar characteristics in certain key product-related areas.

Selective attention *(p. 110)* The process by which a receiver of a message chooses to attend to the message.

Selective distortion *(p. 138)* The process of interpreting information in a way that is consistent with the person's existing opinion.

Selective exposure *(p. 138)* The ability to process only certain information and avoid other stimuli.

Selective perception *(p. 110)* The process of screening out information that doesn't interest us and retaining information that does.

Selective retention *(p. 138)* The process of remembering only a small portion of what you are exposed to.

Self-liquidator *(p. 486)* A type of mail premium that requires a payment sufficient to cover the cost of the item.

Selling premise *(p. 364)* The sales logic behind an advertising message.

Semicomps *(p. 428)* A layout drawn to size that depicts the art and display type; body copy is simply ruled in.

Semicontrolled media *(p. 517)* Media, such as the Internet, whose messages can be controlled by an organization in some ways, but that also contains totally uncontrolled messages.

Semiotic analysis *(p. 174)* A qualitative research method designed to uncover layers and types of meaning.

Serif *(p. 392)* Typeface in which the end of each stroke is finished off with a little flourish.

Set *(p. 405)* A constructed setting in which the action of a commercial takes place.

Share of audience *(p. 269)* The percent of viewers based on number of sets turned on.

Share of market *(pp. 41, 196)* The percentage of the total market in a product category that buys a particular brand.

Share of mind *(p. 336)* The extent to which a brand is well known in its category.

Share of voice *(p. 316)* One brand's percentage of advertising messages in a medium compared to all messages for that product or service.

Shelf talkers *(p. 541)* Signs or coupons attached to a shelf that customers can take away for information or discounts.

Shoppers *(p. 541)* Free-distribution newspapers retailers use to attract customers.

Short code *(p. 306)* A four- to six-digit number used in text messaging that provides an easy way for consumers to dial an information site.

Showings *(p. 245)* The percentage of the market population exposed to an outdoor board during a specific time.

Signal *(p. 257)* A series of electrical impulses used to transmit radio and television broadcasting.

Silkscreen printing *(p. 403)* A printing process that uses a porous screen to transfer a stencil-like image.

Single-source research *(p. 573)* A test that is run after an ad campaign is introduced that shows a causal relationship between marketing communication and sales.

Situation analysis *(pp. 43, 198)* The first section in a campaign plan that summarizes all the relevant background information and research and analyzes its significance.

Skyscrapers *(p. 291)* Extra-long narrow ads that run down the right or left side of a Web site.

Slice-of-life format *(p. 366)* A type of problem-solution ad in which "typical people" talk about a common problem.

Slogans *(pp. 367, 395)* Frequently repeated phrases that provide continuity to an advertising campaign.

SMCR model *(p. 99)* A communication model that identifies the Source, Message, Channel, and Receiver.

Social class *(p. 134)* A way to categorize people on the basis of their values, attitudes, lifestyles, and behavior.

Social learning *(p. 116)* People learn by watching others.

Social marketing *(p. 546)* Marketing with the good of society in mind.

Social network marketing *(pp. 58, 295)* Web sites that permit users to have personal pages where they can express themselves, interact with friends, and publish their own content.

Social responsibility *(p. 66)* A corporate philosophy based on ethical values.

Societal marketing concept *(p. 546)* A business philosophy that describes companies whose operations are based on the idea of socially responsible business.

Soft sell *(p. 11, 362)* An emotional message that uses mood, ambiguity, and suspense to create a response based on feelings and attitudes.

Sound effects *(p. 402)* Lifelike imitations of sounds.

Source *(p. 103)* The sender of a message, the advertiser.

Source credibility *(p. 118)* Belief in a message one hears from a source one finds most reliable.

Spam or spamming *(p. 293, 473)* Blasting millions of unsolicited e-mail ads.

Speaker's bureau *(p. 524)* A public relations tool that identifies a group of articulate people who can talk about an organization.

Specialty advertising *(p. 486)* Free gifts or rewards requiring no purchase and carrying a reminder advertising message.

Spokes character *(p. 366)* A created or imaginary character who acts as a spokesperson.

Spokesperson *(p. 366)* A message strategy that uses an endorser, usually someone the target audience likes or respects, to deliver a message on behalf of the brand.

Sponsorship (cause or event) *(p. 491)* An arrangement in which a company contributes to the expenses of a cause or event to increase the perceived value of the sponsor's brand in the mind of the consumer.

Sponsorship (television) *(p. 271)* An arrangement in which the advertiser produces both a television program and the accompanying commercials.

Spot announcements *(p. 272)* Ads shown during the breaks between programs.

Spot buy *(p. 266)* Broadcast advertising bought on a city-by-city basis rather than through a national buy.

Spot color *(p. 423)* The use of an accent color to call attention to an element in an ad layout.

Spot radio advertising *(p. 261)* A form of advertising in which an ad is placed with an individual station rather than through a network.

Stakeholders *(pp. 25, 215, 507)* Groups of people with a common interest who have a stake in a company and who can have an impact on its success.

Standard Advertising Unit (SAU) *(p. 235)* A standardized system of advertising sizes in newspapers.

Standardization *(p. 550)* In international advertising, the use of campaigns that vary little across different cultures.

Stereotyping *(p. 71)* The process of positioning a group of people in an unvarying pattern that lacks individuality and often reflects popular misconceptions.

Stickiness *(p. 110)* Ad messages that hold the audience's interest long enough for the audience to register the point of the ad; also refers to the amount of time a viewer spends on a Web site.

Stock footage *(p. 434)* Previously recorded film, video, or still slides that are incorporated into a commercial.

Stop motion *(p. 437)* An animation technique in which inanimate objects are filmed one frame at a time, creating the illusion of movement.

Store brands *(p. 537)* A variety of products branded with a particular store's name.

Store traffic *(p. 537)* The number of people who come to a store to shop.

Storyboard *(pp. 407, 429)* A series of frames sketched to illustrate how the story line will develop.

Straightforward *(p. 365)* A factual message that focuses on delivering information.

Strategic business unit (SBU) *(p. 195)* A division of a company focused on a line of products or all the offerings under a single brand name.

Strategic planning *(p. 192)* The process of determining objectives, deciding on strategies, and implementing the tactics.

Strategic research *(p. 165)* All research that leads to the creation of an ad.

Strategy *(pp. 9, 192)* The means by which an individual or business accomplishes objectives.

Streaming video *(p. 301)* Moving images transmitted online.

Structural analysis *(p. 380)* Developed by the Leo Burnett agency, this method evaluates the power of the narrative or story line, evaluates the strength of the product or claim, and considers how well the two aspects are integrated.

Subculture *(p. 133)* Groups of people that are similar in some way, usually characterized by age, values, language, or ethnic background.

Subheads *(p. 395)* Sectional headlines that are used to break up a mass of "gray" type in a large block of copy.

Subliminal *(p. 111)* Refers to messages transmitted below the threshold of normal perception so that the receiver is not consciously aware of having seen it.

Subliminal message *(p. 81)* A message transmitted below the threshold of normal perception so that the receiver is not consciously aware of having viewed it.

Subscription Television *(p. 265)* Television service provided to people who sign up for it and pay a monthly fee.

Substantiation *(p. 85)* Providing support for a claim, usually through research.

Superstations *(p. 266)* Independent but high-power television stations.

Superstitials *(p. 292)* Short Internet commercials that appear when you go from one page on a Web site to another.

Supplements *(p. 236)* Syndicated or local full-color advertising inserts that appear in newspapers throughout the week.

Suppliers *(p. 19)* Organizations, professionals, and specialized businesses that provide goods and services.

Supply chain *(p. 49)* The network of suppliers who produce components and ingredients used by a manufacturer to make its products.

Support *(p. 365)* The proof, or substantiation needed to make a claim believable.

Survey research *(p. 177)* Research using structured interview forms that ask large numbers of people exactly the same questions.

Sweeps *(p. 270)* In television programming, these are quarterly periods when more extensive audience data are gathered.

Sweepstakes *(p. 486)* Contests that require only that the participant supply his or her name to participate in a random drawing.

Switchers *(p. 147)* Television viewers who change channels.

SWOT analysis *(p. 43, 198)* An analysis of a company or brand's strengths, weaknesses, opportunities, and threats.

Symbolic meaning *(p. 116)* Communication conveyed through association.

Syndication *(p. 262)* This is where local stations purchase television or radio shows that are reruns or original programs to fill open hours.

Synergy *(p. 536)* The principle that when all the pieces work together, the whole is greater than the sum of its parts.

T

Tabloid *(p. 234)* A newspaper with a page size five to six columns wide and 14 inches deep.

Tactic *(p. 193)* The specific techniques selected to reflect the strategy.

Taglines *(pp. 367, 395)* Clever phrases used at the end of an advertisement to summarize the ad's message.

Take *(p. 439)* Each scene shot for a commercial, sometimes done repeatedly for the same scene.

Talent *(p. 406)* People who appear in television commercials.

Target market *(pp. 11, 44, 152)* The market segment(s) to which the marketer wants to sell a product.

Target rating point (TRP) *(p. 327)* The practice of adjusting a television program's rating points to more accurately reflect the percentage of the target audience watching the program.

Targeted cost per thousand (TCPT) *(p. 332)* The cost to expose 1,000 likely consumers of a product to an ad message.

Targeted reach *(pp. 321, 329)* The practice of identifying key characteristics of the target population to better match media audience profiles.

Targeting, Target audience *(pp. 19, 151)* People who can be reached with a certain advertising medium and a particular message.

Teaser *(p. 367)* A message strategy that creates curiosity as the message unfolds in small pieces over time.

Telemarketing *(p. 469)* A type of marketing that uses the telephone to make a personal sales contact.

Television scripts *(p. 407)* The written version of a television commercial specifying all the video and audio information.

Test market *(p. 570)* A group used to test some elements of an ad or a media mix in two or more potential markets.

Testimonial *(p. 76)* See "endorsement."

Text messaging *(p. 306)* Communicating using brief messages keyboarded into a cell phone.

Theater of the mind *(p. 400)* In radio advertising, the story is visualized in the listener's imagintion.

Think/Feel/Do model *(p. 106)* A model of advertising effects that focuses on the cognitive, emotional, and behavioral responses to a message.

Thumbnail sketches *(p. 428)* Small preliminary sketches of various layout ideas.

Tie-ins *(p. 496)* A promotional tool that promotes two products together to increase both brands' visibility.

Time-shifting *(p. 267)* Using digital video recorders (DVRs) to record television programming for playback at some other time.

Tint blocks *(p. 432)* A screen process that creates shades of gray or colors in blocks.

Tip-ins *(p. 433)* Preprinted ads that are provided by the advertiser to be glued into the binding of a magazine.

Tone of voice *(p. 357)* Ad copy is written as a conversation or an announcement and the voices carry emotional cues.

Touch points *(pp. 215, 232)* The contact points where customers interact with the brand and receive brand messages.

Town hall forums *(p. 524)* Meetings within an organization as part of an internal marketing program to inform employees and encourage their support.

Tracking studies *(p. 569)* Studies that follow the purchase of a brand or the purchases of a specific consumer group over time.

Trade advertising *(p. 542)* A type of business-to-business advertising that targets members of the distribution channel.

Trade deal *(p. 489)* An arrangement in which the retailer agrees to give the manufacturer's product a special promotional effort in return for product discounts, goods, or cash.

Trade show *(p. 489)* A gathering of companies within a specific industry to display their products.

Trademark *(p. 39, 79)* When a brand name or brand mark is legally protected through registration with the Patent and Trademark Office of the Department of Commerce.

Traditional delivery *(p. 223)* Delivery of magazines to readers through newsstands or home delivery.

Traffic department *(p. 53)* People within an agency who are responsible for keeping track of project elements and keeping the work on deadline.

Trail *(p. 119)*

Trailers *(p. 276)* Advertisements shown in movie theaters before the feature.

Transformation *(p. 116)* Creating meaning for a brand that makes it a special product, one that is differentiated within its category by its image.

Trend spotters *(p. 148)* Researchers who specialize in identifying trends and fads that may affect consumer attitudes and behavior.

Trial *(p. 119)* Trying a product is usually the first step in making a purchase.

Two-step offer *(p. 457)* A message that is designed to gather leads, answer consumer questions, or set up appointments.

Typography *(p. 425)* The use of type both to convey words and to contribute aesthetically to the message.

U

Unaided recall or recognition *(pp. 174, 572)* When one can remember an idea all by oneself.

Unbundling media services *(p. 342)* Media departments that separate themselves from agencies becoming separate companies.

Uncontrolled media *(p. 517)* Media that include the press release, the press conference, and media tours.

Underlines *(p. 362)* Text used to elaborate on the idea in the headline and serve as a transition into the body copy.

Undifferentiated or market aggregation strategy *(p. 152)* A view of the market that assumes all consumers are basically the same.

Unduplicated audiences *(p. 321)* Different members of an audience exposed to a message in a particular time frame.

Uniform resource locators (URLs) *(p. 80)* Internet domain names that are registered and protected.

Unique selling proposition (USP) *(p. 365)* A benefit statement about a feature that is both unique to the product and important to the user.

Unjustified type *(p. 392)* A form of typesetting where the line endings on the right side of the column are allowed to fall where they will.

URL *(p. 287)* A Web site address.

Usage *(p. 147)* Categorizing consumers in terms of how much of the product they buy.

User-generated ads *(p. 377)* Promotional copy on personal Web sites developed by the site's owner to promote a product, service, viewpoint, or cause.

V

Validity *(p. 183)* The research results actually measure what they say they measure.

Value added, value added media *(p. 340)* A marketing or advertising activity that makes a product—or a media buy—more valuable.

Value billing *(p. 56)* A practice by marketers of paying agencies for creative and strategic ideas, rather than for executions and media placement.

Values *(p. 132)* The source of norms; values are not tied to specific objects or behavior, are internal, and guide behavior.

Values and Lifestyle System (VALS) *(p. 145)* A research method that categorizes people into lifestyle groups.

Vampire creativity *(p. 380)* Big ideas that are so powerful that they are remembered but not the brand.

Variable data campaigns *(p. 465)*

Veloxes (C-prints) *(p. 403)* High-quality proofs from printing.

Vendors *(p. 19)* A group of service organizations that assist advertisers, ad agencies, and the media; also known as freelancers.

Vertical publications *(pp. 239, 544)* Publications targeted at people working in the same industry.

Video editing *(p. 441)* Processing of recorded videotape to improve its final presentation; may include time manipulation and sound additions.

Video news releases (VNRs) *(p. 522)* Contain video footage that can be used during a television newscast.

Videographer *(p. 428)* Person who shoots images with a video camera.

Viogs *(p. 289)*

Viral marketing *(pp. 58, 293)* A strategy used primarily in Web marketing that relies on consumers to pass on messages about a product.

Virtual research *(p. 173)* Measures the effectiveness of ads through interactive media.

Visualization *(p. 423)* Imagining what the finished copy will look like.

Vlogs *(p. 289)* Video blogs used for online distribution of personal video essays.

Voice-over *(p. 404)* A technique used in commercials in which an off-camera announcer talks about the on-camera scene.

W

Wants *(pp. 113, 141)* Motivations based on desires and feelings.

Wasted reach *(p. 273)* Advertising directed at a disinterested audience that is not in the targeted audience.

Wave analysis *(p. 570)* In research, a series of interviews conducted at different points in a campaign.

Wearout *(pp. 331, 575)* The point where the advertising gets tired and there is no response or a lower level of response than at the advertising's launch.

Web site *(p. 287)* Sometimes called a "home page," this is the online presence of a person or organization.

Webcasting *(p. 258)* Radio transmitted through audio streaming over the Internet.

Webisodes *(p. 299)* Web advertisements that are similar to TV programs with a developing storyline.

Weighting *(p. 330)* In media planning decision criteria are used to determine the rel-

ative amount of budget allocated to each medium.

White space *(p. 395)* Areas in a layout that aren't used for type or art.

Wireless (Wi-Fi) *(p. 305)* Wireless or mobile communication that links a consumer's phone to a computer and to the Internet.

Word-of-mouth *(pp. 233, 297)* Free advertising that comes from people talking about a product.

World Wide Web *(p. 287)* The structure of the information interface that operates behind the Internet.

Y

Yellow pages *(p. 242)* A form of directory advertising that lists the names of people or companies, their phone numbers, and addresses.

Your-name-here copy *(p. 390)* Pompous writing used in corporate communication that contains generic claims that do not differentiate the company.

Z

Zap *(p. 273)* Changing channels when a television commercial comes on.

Zines *(pp. 237, 294)* Magazines or newsletters that are only available online.

Zip *(pp. 273, 294)* Fast forwarding past commercials in a previously recorded program.

Zone editions *(p. 541)* Special versions of a newspaper that go to certain counties or suburbs.

CREDITS

ENDNOTES

CHAPTER 1

[1] Ennis Higgins, "Conversations with David Ogilvy," in *The Art of Writing Advertising* (Chicago: Advertising Publications, 1965).

[2] Anusree Mitra and John G. Lynch Jr., "Toward a Reconciliation of Market Power and Information Theories of Advertising Effects on Price Elasticity," *Journal of Consumer Research* 21 (March 1995): 44–59.

[3] TNS Media Intelligence Reports, "TNS Media Intelligence Reports U.S. Advertising Expenditures Increased 3.0 Percent in 2005," February 27, 2006, http://www.tns-mi.com/news/02282006.htm.

[4] Stephen Fox, *The Mirror Makers: A History of American Advertising and Its Creators* (New York: Vintage Books, 1985).

[5] Bill Bernbach Interview, *Printer's Ink*, January 2, 1953: 21.

[6] Mike Carlton, "How Is Your Agency Evolving?" Carlton Associates Web site, January 17, 2007, http://www.carltonassociatesinc.com/print_wp1.cfm?id=45.

[7] David Carr, "24-Hour Newspaper People," *New York Times*, January 15, 2007, http://www.nytimes.com/2007/01/15/business/media/15carr.html.

[8] John Burnett and Sandra Moriarty, *Marketing Communications: An Integrated Approach* (Upper Saddle River, NJ: Prentice Hall, 1998): 14.

[9] Tom Duncan and Sandra Moriarty, *Driving Brand Value: Using Integrated Marketing to Manage Profitable Stakeholder Relationships* (New York: McGraw-Hill, 1997).

[10] Willow Duttge, "You Don't Have to Buy Media to Win," *Advertising Age*, September 4, 2006, 9.

CHAPTER 2

[1] Peter D. Bennett, *Dictionary of Marketing Terms* (Chicago: American Marketing Association, 1988): 115.

[2] James B. Twitchell, "Lydia E. Pinkham's Vegetable Compound," Chapter 2, in *Twenty Ads That Shook the World* (New York: Three Rivers Press, 2000): 26–37.

[3] Bill Weintraub, personal communication, September 6, 2006.

[4] Tom Duncan and Sandra Moriarty, "A Communication-Based Marketing Model for Managing Relationships," *Journal of Marketing*, 62:2 (April 1998): 1–13.

[5] Joshua Kurlantzick, "Most Valuable Players," *Entrepreneur*, June 2003, 68–71.

[6] Marc Gobé, *Emotional Branding* (New York: Allworth Press, 2001): ix.

[7] Kevin Roberts, *Lovemarks* (Brooklyn, NY: Powerhouse Books, 2004).

[8] "The Price is Falling!" *Business 2.0*, July 2006: 132.

[9] Martin Fackler, "Japanese Fret That Quality Is in Decline," *New York Times*, September 21, 2006, http://www.nytimes.com/2006/09/21/business/worldbusiness/21quality.html.

[10] Lauren Foster, "Coach Sales Strategy Is in the Bag," *Financial Times*, April 18, 2006, 16.

[11] Jacqueline Durtt, "Road Warriors: Making Honda a Fit for Gen-Y," *Sales & Marketing Management*, September 2006: 46–47.

[12] Don Pepper and Martha Rogers, "Better Partners," *Sales & Marketing Management*, January/February 2006: 21.

[13] Susanna Hamner, "Madison Avenue's Do-it-all Startup," CNNMoney.Com, February 13, 2007, http://money.cnn.com/magazines/business2/business2_archive/2007/02/01/8398979/index.htm?postversion=2007021305.

[14] Brian Steinberg and Suzanne Vranica, "Chief Seeks to Help Leo Burnett Get Its Groove Back," *Wall Street Journal*, October 12, 2003, 12B.

[15] Noreen O'Leary, "The Incredible Shrinking Account Exec," *Adweek*, May 26, 2003, 22.

[16] Erin White, "Linking Agency Fees to Ad Success," *Wall Street Journal*, March 29, 2004, B4.

[17] Julia Chang, "Pay for Agency Performance," *Sales & Marketing Management*, September 2006, 18.

[18] John Galvin, "The World on a String," *Point*, February 2005: 13–18.

[19] Brian Steinberg, "Putting a Value on Marketing Dollars," *Wall Street Journal*, July 27, 2005, 25.

[20] Scott Hornstein, "What's the News About Your Brand?" *Sales & Marketing Management*, September 2006, 22.

[21] Tom Duncan and Sandra Moriarty, *Driving Brand Value: Using Integrated Marketing to Manage Profitable Stakeholder Relationships* (New York: McGraw-Hill, 1998).

[22] Duncan and Moriarty, *Driving Brand Value*, 1998.

[23] Aaron Patrick, "Publicis Chief Seeks Unity Within," *Wall Street Journal*, July 12, 2006, B3.

[24] Morag Cuddeford Jones, "The View from the Top," *Brand Strategy*, March 2006, 25–29.

CHAPTER 3

[1] Charles Goodrum and Helen Dalrymple, *Advertising in America: The First 200 Years* (New York: Harry N. Abrams, 1990).

[2] Kenneth Hein "Do Top Shows Prime Kids for Obesity-Inducing Fare?" *Brandweek*, December 12, 2005, 12.

[3] "#1 Best Use of Shameless Sex in Advertising," *Brandweek*, December 19, 2005, 19.

[4] Dennis. J. Ganahl, Thomas J. Prinsen, and Sarah Netzley, "A Content Analysis of Prime Time Commercials: A Contextual Framework of Gender Representation," Broadcast Education Association, Las Vegas, NV (2001); Mark R. Barner, "Sex-Role Stereotyping in FCC-Mandated Children's Educational Television," *Journal of Broadcasting & Electronic Media*, 43 (1999): 551–564; Scott Coltrane and Michele Adams, "Work-Family Imagery and Gender Stereotypes: Television and the Reproduction of Difference," *Journal of Vocational Behavior* 50 (1997): 323–347.

[5] Dennis J. Ganahl, Thomas. J. Prinsen, and Sarah B. Netzley, "A Content Analysis of Prime Time Commercials: A Contextual Framework of Gender Representation," Broadcast Education Association, Las Vegas, NV (2001).

[6] Fara Warner, "Imperfect Picture: Advertisers Have Long Struggled to Adjust to Women's Changing Roles at Work and Home," in *Facing Difference: Race, Gender, and Mass Media*, ed. S. Biagi and M. Kern-Foxworth (Thousand Oaks, CA: Pine Forge Press, 1997): 223–224.

[7] Interview with Jean Kilbourne by Renee Montagne, *NPR Morning Edition* transcript (June 22, 2004).

[8] Robert Gustafson, Mark Popovich, and Steven Thomsen, "The 'Thin Ideal,'" *Marketing News*, March 15, 1999, 22.

[9] Dennis J. Ganahl, Sarah B. Netzley, William Hoon, and Kwangok Kim, "The Culture Clash in Television Commercials: Mainstreaming Black Stereotypes into Primetime Prototypes," unpublished manuscript (2003).

[10] *Hispanic Fact Pack*, *Advertising Age* (2007).

[11] Michelle Wirth Fellman, "Preventing Viagra's Fall," *Marketing News*, August 31, 1998, 1, 8.

[12] Joan Voight, "Realistic or Offensive?" *Adweek*, September 2, 2003, 16–17.

[13] Editorial, "Mom, Dad, Buy the Broccoli," *New York Times*, December 1, 2006.

[14] Herbert Rotfeld, "Desires Versus the Reality of Self-Regulation," *Journal of Consumer Affairs* 37 (Winter 2003): 424–427; Nanci Hellmich, "Weight-Loss Deception Found Ads for Many of Those Pills, Patches, Creams, and Wraps Are Grossly Exaggerated," *USA Today*, 2002.

15 Joe Morgan, "Barclays Forced to Withdraw 0% Campaign by OFT," *The London Times,* November 19, 2003, 4M.

16 Herbert J. Rotfeld and Kim B. Rotzoll, "Is Advertising Puffery Believed?" *Journal of Advertising* 9:3 (1980): 16–20, 45.

17 Barry Newman, "An Ad Professor Huffs Against Puffs, But It's a Quixotic Enterprise," *Wall Street Journal,* January 24, 2003, A1; Ivan Preston, "A Problem Ignored: Dilution and Negation of Consumer Information by Antifactual Content," *Journal of Consumer Affairs* 36 (Winter 2002): 263–283; Ivan Preston, "Dilution and Negation of Consumer Information by Antifactual Content: Proposals for Solutions," *Journal of Consumer Affairs* 37 (Summer 2003): 1–21.

18 Robert Weller, "Breckenridge Pulls Ad Campaign," *Boulder Sunday Camera,* September 8, 2002, 3B.

19 Bruce Horovitz and Laura Petrecca, "Disney to Make Food Healthier for Kids," *USA Today,* October 17, 2006, 1B.

20 Bruce Horovitz, "Wendy's Will Be 1st Fast Foodie with Healthier Oil," *USA Today,* June 8, 2006.

21 Betsy Spethmann, "Tobacco's Two Tiers," *Promo Magazine,* January 2004, 24–28.

22 Deborah Vence, "Match Game," *Marketing News,* November 11, 2002, 1, 11–12.

23 Wendy Melillo, "FTC Reviews Ad Plans from Alcohol Clients," *Adweek,* May 26, 2003, 8.

24 Christopher Lawton, "Lawsuits Allege Alcohol Makers Target Youths," *Wall Street Journal,* February 5, 2004, B1; Ira Teinowitz, "Marketers Blast Charges in Alcohol Suit," *Advertising Age,* December 1, 2003, 10.

25 Chuck Ross and Ira Teinowitz, "Beer Ad Has Wide Underage Reach on MTV," *Advertising Age,* January 6, 1997: 4; Ira Teinowitz, "FTC Governing of Beer Ads Expands to Miller, A-B," *Advertising Age,* April 7, 1997: 1, 50.

26 Bill McInturff, "While Critics May Fret, Public Likes DTC Ads," *Advertising Age,* March 26, 2001, 24; David Goetzi, "Take a Heaping Spoonful," *Advertising Age,* November 6, 2000, 32; Angetta McQueen, "Watchdog Blames Ad Spending for High Drug Costs," *The Denver Post,* July 22, 2001, 4C.

27 Julie Schmidt and Laura Petrecca, "Pfizer Limits When It Will Advertise New Drugs," *USA Today,* August 12, 2005, 1B.

28 "Sound Can Be a Trademark," *The London Times Law Report,* December 4, 2003, 73.

29 Robert J. Posch Jr., "Trademark Protection for Internet Domain Names," *Direct Marketing,* July 1998, 63–65.

30 Barbara Martinez, "Gap Faces Suit over Eyewear Used in Ad," *Wall Street Journal,* January 6, 1998, B10.

31 Rebecca Flass, "Done That," *Adweek,* April 22, 2002, 21.

32 Anne Cunningham, "Commonsense or Nonsense: Limiting First Amendment Protection of Commercial Speech," in *Proceedings of the 2000 American Academy of Advertising Conference,* ed. M. A. Shaver (East Lansing, MI: Michigan State University): 61–83.

33 Chris Adams, "Looser Lip for Food and Drug Companies?" *Wall Street Journal,* September 17, 2002, A4.

34 Doug McKenna, "Marketers Opt Out of Civil Society," *Boulder Daily Camera,* April 13, 2003, 38.

35 "Nike vs. Kasky: Case Dismissed," *SriMedia* report. June 26, 2003. http://www.srimedia. com/artman/publish/article-642.shtml; Wendy Melillo, "Ad Groups Back Nike in Supreme Court Brief," *Adweek,* March 3, 2003, 3; Adam M. Kanzer and Cynthia A. Williams, "The Future of Social Reporting Is on the Line," *Business Ethics,* 17:4 (Winter 2003); Roger Parloff, "Can We Talk?" *Fortune,* September 2, 2002, 102–110.

36 Davis & Gilbert LLP, "Supreme Court's Non-Decision and Nike's Settlement Likely to Have Negative Impact on Corporate Speech for Foreseeable Future," http://www.dglaw.com/ resource/summer2003_07.shtml (accessed November, 25, 2006).

37 "Letter to Congress Explaining FTC's New Deception Policy," Advertising Compliance Service (Westport, CT: Meckler Publishing, November 21, 1983); Ivan Preston, "A Review of the Literature on Advertising Regulation," in *Current Issues and Research in Advertising,* ed. James H. Leigh and Claude L. Martin, 2–37 (Ann Arbor: University of Michigan Press, 1983).

38 Robert E. Wilkes and James B. Wilcox, "Recent FTC Actions: Implications for the Advertising Strategists," *Journal of Marketing* 38 (January 1974): 55–56.

39 Jack Neff, "Duracell Agrees to Modify Robo-War Duck Ad," *Advertising Age,* February 6, 2002, http://www.adage.com/news. cms?newsid=33981; Daniel Golden and Suzanne Vranica, "Duracell's Duck Ad Will Carry Disclaimer," *Wall Street Journal,* February 7, 2002, B7.

40 Tom McGhee, "Broomfield Firm's Penalty for Ad: Drugs Destroyed," *Denver Post,* April 18, 2002, 2C.

41 John J. Burnett, "Gays: Feelings about Advertising and Media Used," *Journal of Advertising Research,* January-February 2000, 75-86.

42 Stephen P. Durchslag, "Agency Liability Extends to False Advertising Claims," *Promo,* October 1992, 17.

43 Deborah Vence, "FDA Seeks to Clarify Rules for Pharma Ads," *Marketing News,* March 3, 2003, 6.

44 Michael McCarthy, "Local Ads Stir Up Utah Controversy," *USA Today,* January 2, 2002, 7B.

45 Eli Pariser, MoveOn.org e-mail, January 22, 2004.

46 Editorial, "Super Censored," *Boulder Daily Camera,* January 30, 2004, 4B

47 Roy F. Fox, "Hucksters Hook Captive Youngsters," *Mizzou,* Summer 2002, 22–27.

48 Phillip Patterson and Lee Wilkins, *Media Ethics: Issues and Cases,* 5th ed. (Boston: McGraw-Hill, 2005).

CHAPTER 4

1 Peter Holloway, "Maximizing Communicational Effectiveness," *Conference Proceedings of Seminar on How Advertising Works and How Promotions Work,* April 1991, The Netherlands: ESOMAR (European Society for Opinion and Marketing Research): 149–153.

2 Louise Marsland, "How Much Advertising Actually Works?" SAMRA Convention 2006 news, http://www.bizcommunity.com/Archive/ 196/119.html.

3 Ennis Higgins, "Conversations with David Ogilvy," in *The Art of Writing Advertising* (Chicago: Advertising Publications, 1965).

4 Susan Mendelsohn, personal communication (e-mail), November 10, 2006.

5 Simon London, "Choked by a Data Surfeit," *Financial Times,* January 29, 2004, 9.

6 Michael Applebaum, "Caring Enough about Loyalty," *Brandweek,* August 9, 2004, 16–17.

7 Dedmetrios Vakratsas and Tim Ambler, "Advertising Effects: A Taxonomy and Review of Concepts, Methods, and Results from the Academic Literature," Marketing Science Institute Working Paper 96-120 (Cambridge, MA: MSI, 1996); Thomas Barry and Daniel Howard, "A Review and Critique of the Hierarchy of Effects in Advertising," *International Journal of Advertising* 9:2 (1990): 429–435; Michael Ray, "Communication and the Hierarchy of Effects," in *New Models for Mass Communication Research,* ed. P. Clarke (Beverly Hills, CA: Sage Publications, 1973), 147-75; Thomas Barry, "The Development of the Hierarchy of Effects: An Historical Perspective," *Current Research and Issues in Advertising* 10: 1 & 2 (1987): 251–95.

8 Ray, 1973; Richard Vaughn, "How Advertising Works: A Planning Model," *Journal of Advertising Research* 20:5 (1980): 27–33; and "How Advertising Works: A Planning Model Revisited," *Journal of Advertising Research* 26:1 (1986): 57–66.

9 Sandra Moriarty, "Beyond the Hierarchy of Effects: A Conceptual Model," *Current Issues and Research in Advertising* 1 (1983): 45–56.

10 Charles E. Young, *The Advertising Research Handbook* (Seattle: Ad Essentials, 2005): 37.

11 Ogilvy & Mather Web site, http://www. ogilvy.com (accessed November 2006).

12 Ivan Preston, "The Association Model of the Advertising Communication Process," *Journal of Advertising* 11:2 (1982): 3–14.

13 Mike Beirne, "Sheraton Makes Room for Emotional Touches," *Brandweek,* April 10, 2006, 6.

14 Erik du Plessis, *The Advertised Mind* (London: Kogan Page, 2005): 4.

15 Ann Marie Barry, "Perception Theory," Chapter 3 in *The Handbook of Visual Communication,* ed. Ken Smith, Sandra Moriarty, Gretchen Barbatsis, and Keith Kenney (Mahwah, NJ: Lawrence Erlbaum, 2005): 23–62.

16 Du Plessis: 4.

17 Jim Lovel, "Volkswagen Ads Get Buzz, But Will They Sell Jettas?" *Brandweek,* April 24, 2006, 5.

18 Jon D. Morris, Chongmoo Woo, James Geason, and Jooyoung Kim, "The Power of Affect: Predicting Intention," *Journal of Advertising Research*, May/June 2002, 7–17.

19 Russell I. Haley and Allan L. Baldinger, "The ARF Copy Research Validity Project," *Journal of Advertising Research*, April/May 1991, 11–32.

20 Zachary Coile, "Desperate Campaigns Resort to Attack Ads," SFGate.com, November 1, 2006, http://sfgate.com/cgi-bin/article.cgi?file=/c/a2006/11/01/MNG5NM3QLJ1.DTL.

21 David Stewart and David Furse, *Television Advertising: A Study of 1000 Commercials* (Lexington, MA: Lexington Books, 1986).

22 Thomas J. Page, Jr., Esther Thorson, and Maria Papas Heide, "The Memory Impact of Commercials Varying in Emotional Appeal and Product Involvement," Chapter 15 in *Emotion in Advertising*, ed. Stuart J. Agrees, Julie A. Edell, and Tony M. Dubitsky (New York: Quorum Books. 1990): 255–81.

23 Ivan Preston, "The Association Model of the Advertising Communication Process," *Journal of Advertising* 3 (1982): 3–14; Ivan Preston and Esther Thorson, "Challenges to the Use of Hierarchy Models in Predicting Advertising Effectiveness," in *Proceedings of the 1983 American Academy of Advertising Conference*, ed. Donald Jugenheimer (Lawrence, KS: University of Kansas): 27–33.

24 Bill Wells, "How Advertising Works," speech to St. Louis AMA, September 17, 1986.

25 Michael Solomon, *Consumer Behavior*, 6th ed. (Upper Saddle River, NJ: Prentice Hall, 2004): 98.

26 Daniel J. O'Keefe, *Persuasion: Theory and Research* (Newbury Park, CA: Sage, 1990): 17.

27 Herbert Krugman, "The Impact of Television Advertising: Learning Without Involvement," *Public Opinion Quarterly* 29:3 (1965): 349–56.

28 Stuart Elliott, "HP Promotes High-Tech Recycling." *New York Times Direct*, July 29, 2003, http://www.nytimes.com.

29 Richard Cross and Janet Smith, *Customer Bonding: Pathway to Lasting Customer Loyalty* (Lincolnwood, IL: NTC, 1995): 54–55.

30 Jesse Shapiro, "A 'Memory-Jamming' Theory of Advertising," *Capital Ideas*, April 2006, 12–15.

31 John Philip Jones, "Over-Promise and Under-Deliver," *Conference Proceedings of Seminar on How Advertising Works and How Promotions Work*, April 1991, The Netherlands: ESOMAR (European Society for Opinion and Marketing Research): 13–28.

32 John Philip Jones, *When Ads Work: New Proof That Advertising Triggers Sales* (New York: Lexington Books, 1995).

CHAPTER 5

1 Bob Garfield, "Tackling Ugly Truth, Dove Effort Evolves Beautifully," *Advertising Age*, October 29, 2006, http://adage.com/garfield/article?article_id=112837&search_phrase=tackling+ugly+truth+Garfield.

2 Deborah Ball, "Women in Italy Like to Clean but Shun the Quick and Easy," *Wall Street Journal*, April 26, 2006, A1.

3 Fernando Figueroa, "What's in a Name? A Lot If You're Latino," *Tampa Tribune*, December 17, 2006, 1.

4 John Fetto, "One Size Doesn't Fit All: Today's Working Mothers Defy the Label 'Soccer Mom,'" *American Demographics*, May 2000, 44–45.

5 Thomas Hargrove and Guido H. Stempel III, "Judging Generations," *Daily Camera*, March 3, 2007, D3.

6 "Head-Turners," *Incentive*, March 2006, 10.

7 Mickey Meeco, "What Do Women Want? Just Ask," *New York Times*, October 29, 2006, 29.

8 "Census Indicates Minorities' Growth," *Daytona Beach News-Journal*, May 17, 2007, 3A.

9 Gary Silverman, "Hispanics in Tune with TV Advertising," *Financial Times*, March 4, 2004, 18.

10 Arundhati Parmar, "Knowledge of Mature Market Pays Reward," *Marketing News*. April 28, 2003, 5–6.

11 Thomas T. Semon, "Income Is Not Always Predictor of Spending," *Marketing News*, March 31, 2003, 6.

12 Peter Francese, "Trend Analysis: U.S. Consumers—Like No Other on the Planet," *Advertising Age*, January 2, 2006, 3–5.

13 Eugene Schwartz, *Breakthrough Advertising* (Stamford, CT: Bottom Line Books, 2004): 4.

14 Joseph T. Plummer, "The Concept and Application of Life-Style Segmentation," *Journal of Marketing*, January 1974, 34.

15 MindBase Web site, http://www.yankelovich.com/products/mindbase.aspx (accessed December 2006).

16 Everett Rogers, *Diffusion of Innovations*, 3rd ed. (New York: The Free Press, 1983).

17 Kelly Crow, "The Girl-Scout Cookie Makeover," *Wall Street Journal*, January 26, 2007, W2.

18 Amy Chozick, "Land of the Rising Karaoke Hot Tub," *Wall Street Journal*, March 9, 2007, W1; Yuri Kageyama, "The 'Cool Hunter' in Japan," *Boulder Daily Camera*. February 7, 2004, E1.

19 Susan Mendelsohn, personal communication (e-mail), November 10, 2006.

20 Matthew Creamer, "John Doe Edges Out Jeff Goodby," *Advertising Age*, January 8, 2007, S4–5; Jeff Howe, "Your Web, Your Way," *Time*, December 25, 2006–January 1, 2007, 60–61; Wendy Melillo and Joan Voight, "World on a String: Consumers Emerged as the New Brand Managers in 2006, Seizing Control of the Media and the Message," *Adweek*, December 11, 2006, 10–12; http://www/wikipedia.com.

21 Chris Anderson, *The Long Tail: Why the Future of Business is Selling Less of More* (New York: Hyperion, 2006).

22 Jim Edwards, "Why Buy?" *Brandweek*, October 3, 2005, 21–24.

23 Paul Kaihla, "Sexing Up a Piece of Meat," *Business 2.0*, April 2006, 72–74.

24 Bruce Horovitz, "Alpha Moms Leap to Top of Trendsetters," *USA Today*, March 26, 2007, http://www.usatoday.com/money/advertising/2007-03-26-alpha-mom_N.htm.

25 Steve Smith, "The Next Frontier: Behavior," *MediaPost Publications*, Jaunary 16, 2007, http://www.mediapost.com.

26 Gail Schiller, "Study Shows Baby Boomers Ignored by Ads," *Hollywood Reporter*, November 15, 2006, http://www.hollywoodreporter.com/hr/content_display/business/news/.

27 Michael Blood, "Consumer Data May Identify Voting Habits," *Daily Camera*, October 27, 2006, 5C.

CHAPTER 6

1 Gina Chon, "To Woo Wealthy, Lexus Attempts Image Makeover," *Wall Street Journal*, March 24–25, 2007, A1.

2 Karl Weiss, IMC Marketing Research course handout, University of Colorado, January 2001.

3 Jim Edwards, "Why Buy?" *Brandweek*, October 3, 2005, 21–24.

4 Edwards, 22.

5 Jackie Boulter, "Creative Development Research," Chapter 6 in *How To Plan Advertising*, 2nd ed., ed. Alan Cooper (London: Thomson Learning and Continuum, 2004): 81.

6 "Analysis of a Commercial: OnStar and Batman," http://student.claytonstate.net/~csu11197/3901/project1/.

7 Julia Chang, "More than Words," *Sales & Marketing Management*, September 2006, 14.

8 Roger Wimmer and Joseph Dominick, *Mass Media Research*, 7th ed. (Belmont CA: Wadsworth/Thomson Learning, 2003).

9 Jack Myers, "Jack Myers' Weekend Think Tank: Can the Rules of Research Change?" *MediaPost Publications*, January 5, 2007, http://www.mediapost.com.

10 Weiss, IMC course handout.

11 Dennis W. Rook, "Out-Of-Focus." *Marketing Research*, Summer 2003, 10–15; Alison Stein Wellner, "The New Science of Focus Groups," *American Demographics*, March 2003, 29.

12 Susan Mendelsohn, personal communication, December 20, 2003.

13 Leigh Ann Steere, "Culture Club," *Print*, March/April 1999, 4–5.

14 Bruce Mohl, "How 'Idol' Has Changed Study of Consumers," *Daily Camera*, July 16, 2006, 1F.

15 Shay Sayre, *Qualitative Methods for Marketplace Research* (Thousand Oaks: CA: Sage Publications, 2001): 31.

16 Russell W. Belk, ed., *Highways and Buyways: Naturalistic Research from the Consumer Behavior Odyssey* (Provo, UT: Association for Consumer Research, 1991).

17 Sayre, 20.

18 Thomas Davenport, Jeanne Harris, and Ajay Kohli, "How Do They Know Their Customers So Well?" *MIT Sloan Management Review*, Winter 2001, 63–72.

[19] Joe Ruff, "Research Goes Beyond Focus Groups," *The Denver Post*, December 6, 2004, 2E.

[20] Personal interview with Regina Lewis, November 21, 2006.

[21] Emily Eakin, "Penetrating the Mind by Metaphor," *New York Times*, February 23, 2002, http://www.nytimes.com.

[22] Sandra Yin, "New or Me Too," *American Demographics*, September 2002, 28.

[23] Mendelsohn.

[24] Jim Edwards, "Victory Dance for the Vain: A Reporter Goes 'Under,'" *Brandweek*, October 3, 2005, 23.

[25] Robin Couler, Gerald Zaltman, and Keith Coulter, "Interpreting Consumer Perceptions of Advertising: An Application of the Zaltman Metaphor Elicitation Technique," *Journal of Advertising* 30:4 (Winter 2001): 1–14; Eakin, "Penetrating the Mind"; Daniel Pink, "Metaphor Marketing," *Fast Company*, 14 (March 31, 1998): 214. http://www.fastcompany.com/magazine/14/zaltman.html; HBS Division of Research, The Mind of the Market Laboratory, "ZMET," http://www.hbs.edu/mml/zmet.html.

CHAPTER 7

[1] Research for R.O.I.; Communications Workshop, Chicago: DDB, April 10, 1987.

[2] Tom Duncan and Sandra Moriarty, *Driving Brand Value: Using Integrated Marketing to Manage Profitable Stakeholder Relationships* (New York: McGraw-Hill, 1997).

[3] Suzanne Vranica, "In Haggar's Blood Ad Blitz, Middle-Aged Is the New Young," *Wall Street Journal*, November 6, 2006, B1.

[4] Jack Neff, "Eukanuba's New Marketing Strategy: Breed-Specific Dog Chow," *Advertising Age*, November 1, 2006, 19.

[5] Jeffrey Gangerra, "Small Company, Big Brand," BusinessWeek.com, August 28, 2006, http://www.businessweek.com/print/smallbiz/content/aug2006/sb20060825_681509.htm.

[6] Al and Laura Reis, "Q&A: Launch a New Brand," *Next Space*, No. 1, 2006, http://www.oclc.org/nextspace/001/qa.htm.

[7] Larry Kelley and Donald Jugenheimer, *Advertising Account Planning* (Armonk, NY: M.E. Sharpe, 2006): 68.

[8] Jack Trout, "Branding Can't Exist Without Positioning," *Advertising Age*, March 14, 2005, 28.

[9] "AmEx Plans Jerry Seinfeld-Meets-Superman Internet Show," *Advertising Age*, February 4, 2004, http://www.AdAge.com.

[10] Joe Ruff, "Research Goes Beyond Focus Groups," *The Denver Post*, December 6, 2004, 2E.

[11] Regina Lewis, personal interview, November 21, 2006.

[12] "What is Account Planning? (and What Do Account Planners Do Exactly?)" Account Planning Group (APG), http://www.apg.org.uk.

[13] Susan Mendelsohn, personal communication, January 8, 2004.

[14] Suzanne Varanica, "J&J Joins Critics of Agency Structure," *Wall Street Journal*, May 11, 2007, B4.

[15] Laurie Freeman, "Planner Puts Clients in Touch with Soul of Brands," AdAge.com, February 8, 1999; http://www.adage.com/news.cms?newsID=34705.

[16] Charlie Robertson, "Creative Briefs and Briefings," Chapter 4 in *How to Plan Advertising*, 2nd ed., ed. Alan Cooper (London: Thomson Learning and the Account Planning Group, 2004): 62.

[17] Jon Steel, *Truth, Lies and Advertising: The Art of Account Planning* (New York: Wiley, 1998); "Tests Ahead for Account Planning," *Advertising Age*, September 20, 1999, 36.

[18] Duncan and Moriarty, *Driving Brand Value*.

CHAPTER 8

[1] Larry Kelley and Donald Jugenheimer, *Advertising Media Planning* (Armonk, NY: M.E. Sharpe, 2004): 11.

[2] Kelley and Jugenheimer: 4, 9.

[3] Veronis Shuler Stevenson, "Communications Industry Forecast 2006–2010," http://www.vss.com/CIF/?source=google&adt=v55.

[4] Marc Ransford, "Average Person Spends More Time Using Media Than Anything Else," Ball State University News Center press release, September 23, 2005, http://www.bsu.edu/news/article/0,1370,7273-850-36658,00.html.

[5] Janet Kornblum, "Americans Will Devote Half Their Lives to Forms of Media Next Year," *USA Today*, December 15, 2006, 6A; Bob Dart, "Americans to Spend 9½ Hours a Day with the Media," *Tampa Tribune*, 2, 13.

[6] Ransford, "Average Person Spends."

[7] Wayne Friedman, "Covering All Bases: CBS RIOT Sells Cross-Platform," *MediaPost*, February 13, 2007, http://publications.mediapost.com; Brian Steinberg, "Disney Combines Ad Staff for Selling Kids' Media," *Wall Street Journal*, February 6, 2007, B2.

[8] Newspaper Association of America, *The Source: Newspapers by the Numbers 2006*, January 2007, 3–4, http://www.naa.org/thesource/the_source_newspapers_by_the_numbers.pdf.

[9] Erwin Ephron, "Engagement Is Many Different Things," *Admap*, April 2006, 41–42; Joe Mandese, "Medialink," *Admap*, April 2006, 10.

[10] Holl Sanders, "Papers See $$ in Scents," *New York Post*, February 13, 2007, http://www.nypost.com.

[11] Shira Ovide, "Dow Jones's Ad Outlook Is Optimistic as Net Jumps," *Wall Street Journal*, January 26, 2007, B3.

[12] *Advertising Age's 2006 Fact Pack: 4th Annual Guide to Advertising + Marketing*, February 27, 2006, 11.

[13] James Poniewozik, "The People's Paper," *Time*, July 21, 2003, 49–50.

[14] Newspaper Association of America, *The Source: Newspapers by the Numbers 2006*.

[15] Kevin Delaney, "Google Targets Print Realm in Ad Push," *Wall Street Journal*, November 6, 2006, B6.

[16] Sarah Ellison, "Ad Woes Worsen at Big Newspapers," *Wall Street Journal*, October 20, 2006, B4; Newspaper Association of America, *Value of Newspaper Medium*, 2007, http://www.naa.org/circulationpages/circulation-statistics-and-trends/annual-all-media-ad-volume.aspx.

[17] Michael Oneal, "A Tidal Shift for Newspapers," *Chicago Tribune*, November 2, 2006, 45.

[18] Newspaper Association of America, *The Source: Newspapers by the Numbers 2006*, 6.

[19] Jason Klein, "Right Partner. Right Time," Newspaper National Network Web site, January 2007, http://www.nnnlp.com.

[20] "Nielsen/NetRatings Data Highlights Attractiveness of newspaper Web site audience," May 7, 2007, http://www.digitaledge.org/blog/digitaledge/1/2007/05/NielsenNetRatings-Data-Highlights-Attractiveness-of-Newspaper-Web-Site-Audience.cfm.

[21] "Online Newspaper Advertising Jumps 19 Percent in Second Quarter," Newspaper Association of America, August 31, 2007, http://www.naa.org/sitecore/content/Global/PressCenter/2007/ONLINE-NEWSPAPER-ADVERTISING-JUMPS-19-PERCENT-IN-SECOND-QUARTER.aspx?lg=naaorg.

[22] Magazine Publishers Association, *The Magazine Handbook: A Comprehensive Guide, 2006/07*, January 2007, http://www.magazine.org.

[23] *AdAge 2006 Media Fact Book*: 11.

[24] Magazine Publishers Association, *Magazine Handbook*: 17

[25] Nat Ives, "OK, We'll Go First: 'Time' Takes Knife to Rate Base," *Advertising Age*, November 13, 2006, 1.

[26] Magazine Reader Experience Study (Chicago: Northwestern University Media Management Center), http://www.mediamanagementcenter.org; Magazine Publishers Association, *Magazine Handbook*: 5.

[27] Elizabeth H. Weise, "On-Line Magazines: Will Readers Still Want Them After the Novelty Wears Off?" *The Marketing News*, January 29, 1996, 1, 14.

[28] Shira Ovide, "Out-of-Home Advertising Pulls in a Banner Year," Outdoor Advertising Association of America press release, January 10, 2007; Outdoor Advertising Association of America, "Frequently Asked Questions," http://www.oaaa.org/faq/(accessed January 2007).

[29] *AdAge 2006 Fact Book*: 11.

[30] Outdoor Advertising Association of America, "Frequently Asked Questions."

[31] Riva Richmond and Shira Ovide, "Google Seeks Patent for Digital Billboard Ads," Outdoor Advertising Association of America press release, January 19, 2007.

[32] Outdoor Advertising Association of America, "Interactive Billboards Show Personal Ads to Mini Drivers," press release, January 16, 2006.

[33] *The Signage Sourcebook* (South Bend, IN: The Signage Foundation, 2003).

[34] Jonathan Asher, "Make the Most of Packaging Design Updates," *Marketing News*, September 18, 2000, 13.

CHAPTER 9

[1] "Radio Revenue for 2006 Up 1 Percent," Radio Advertising Bureau press release, February 1, 2007, http://www.rab.com/public/pr/revenue_detail.cfm?id=77.

2 RADAR June 2007. http://www.rab.com/public/MediaFacts/2007RMGFB-150-7-31.pdf

3 Andrew Hampp, "Radio Listeners Don't Change Dial During Ads," *Advertising Age*, February 12, 2007, http://adage.com/print?article_id=114947; Bill Rose, Phillipe Generali, and Jon Coleman, "What Happens When the Spots Come On?" 2007 study by Arbitron, Media Monitors, and Coleman, http://www.arbitron.com/.

4 Rose, Generali, and Coleman, "What Happens."

5 AdGrove.com Executive Summary, Center for Business Planning, http://www.businessplans.org/AdGrove/adgro00.html (accessed February 14, 2007).

6 Katy Bachman, "Study: Radio Ad Clutter Lower Than TV," *Mediaweek.Com*, November 14, 2006, http://www.rab.com/public/rst/rst_new/rstarticle.cfm?id=1089&type=article2.

7 "The Media and Your Child," *Boulder Daily Camera*, February 17, 2007, 1A; "The U.S. Television Set Market," August 29, 2007, backchannel media, http://www.backchannelmedia.com/newsletter/articles/15008.

8 "The Media and Your Child."

9 "Internet May Enhance TV's Lure, Not Dim It," *Wall Street Journal*, January 22, 2007, B6.

10 John Consoli, "Even with Rise of Web, Kids Still Watching Tube," *Mediaweek.com*, February 7, 2007, http://mediaweek.com/mw/news/recent_display.jsp?vnu_content_id=1003542880.

11 Bob Garfield, "Why TV Can Only Get Better," *AARP Bulletin*, April 2004, 10; John Consoli, "The Case of the Missing Young Male TV Viewers," *Adweek*, October 20, 2003, 7.

12 Christopher Reynolds, "The Lost Demo," *Promo Magazine*, February 2004, 16–17.

13 "Primetime Scorecard," Cabletelevision Advertising Bureau press release, July 17, 2006, http://www.onetvworld.org/?module=displaystory&story_id=1224&format=html.

14 iTV Institute, 2007 Dictionary & Business Index, http://www.itvdictionary.com.

15 "Number of HDTV Homes to Treble by 2011," Reuters, February 9, 2007, http://news.yahoo.com/s/nm/20070209/tc_nm/hdtv_predictions_dc_1.

16 Louise Story, "Viewers Fast-Forwarding Past Ads? Not Always,"*New York Times*, February 16, 2007, http://www.nytimes.com/2007/02/16/business/16commercials.html.

17 David Lazarus, "TiVo Sees if You Skip Those Ads," SFGate.com, February 4, 2007, http://www.sfgate.com/cgi-bin/article.cgi?file=/chronicle/archive/2007/02/04/BUGJ8NTRT91.DTL&type=printable.

18 Steve McClellan, "Average Super Bowl Commercial Drew 93 Million Viewers," *Mediaweek.com*, February 8, 2007, http://mediaweek.com/mw/new/recent_display.jsp?vnu_content_id=1003543551.

19 Wayne Friedman, "Blockbuster: Best Super Bowl Ratings in 7 Years," *MediaPost*, February 6, 2007, http://publications.mediapost.com/index.cfm?fuseaction=Articles.san&s=55057&Nid=27229&p=417379.

20 Brooks Barnes, "Nielsen Postpones New York Launch of Rating System," *Wall Street Journal*, April 7, 2004, B3.

21 David Goetzl, "Analysts Find TV Commercial Ratings Fears Unwarranted," *MediaPost Publications*, February 5, 2007, http://publications.mediapost.com/index.cfm?fuseaction=Articles.san&s=54969&Nid=27187&p=417379.

22 Catherine Holahan, "Ganging Up On Nielsen," *BusinessWeek.com*, February 8, 2007, http://www.businessweek.com/print/technology/content/feb2007/tc20070206_635879.htm; Joe Mandese, "Publicis Backs erinMedia, Bit Auto Advertiser, TV Network, Too," *MediaPost Publications*, February 7, 2007, http://publications.mediapost.com/index.cfm?fuseaction=Articles.san&s=55174&Nid=27259&p=417379.

23 Andrea Ragnetti, quoted in John Singer, "A Theme for the Pudding: Marketing Ecosystems," *Admap*, April 2006, 32–34.

24 Joe Mandese, "Medialink," *Admap*, April 2006, 10.

25 Andrew Green, "MediaFAQs: Commercial Break Environment," *Admap*, April 2006, 11.

26 "Is the End of the Ad Slump in Sight?" *Fortune*, January 12, 2004, 48.

27 David Carr, "Do They Still Want Their MTV?" *New York Times*, February 19, 2007, http://www.nytimes.com/2007/02/19/business/media/19carr.html.

28 Shankar Gupta, "Study: Two-Thirds of Web Users View Streaming Video Weekly," *MediaPost Publications*, February 7, 2007, http://publications.mediapost.com/index.cfm?fuseaction=Articles.san&s=55157&Nid=27259&p=417379.

29 Joe Mandese, "Ad Execs Surprised by Rate of Change, Hand No Second Sight For 'Second Life,'" *MediaPost Publications*, February 7, 2007, http://publications.mediapost.com/index.cfm?fuseaction=Articles.san&s=55176&Nid=27259&p=417379; John Eggerton, "Ad Execs to Network TV: Innovate," Broadcasting & Cable Web site, February 6, 2007, http://www.broadcastingcable.com/index.asp?layout=articlePrint&articleID=CA6414033.

30 "Disney Says Advertisers Embrace TV Shows on Web," Reuters, February 8, 2007, http://today.reuters.com/misc/PrinterFriendlyPopup.aspx?type=inte...007-02-08T200951Z_01_N08207656_RTRUKOC-)_US_DISNEY-CORRECTED.xml.

31 Sarah McBride, "In Theaters: Commercials Aplenty," *Wall Street Journal*, February 8, 2007, http://online.wsj.com/article_print/SB117090468949401839.html.

32 Cheryl Healton, "Attorneys General Urge Movie Studios to Include Truth® PSAs Before Movies with Smoking," American Legacy Foundation Press Release, September 8, 2006, http://www.americanlegacy.org/592.html.

33 Alastair Ray, "Own-Brand Broadcaster Tunes In," *Financial Times*, March 16, 2004, 10.

34 Stuart Elliott, "Two Long-Established Marketers Loosen Up," *New York Times*, November 13, 2006, http://www.nytimes.com/2006/11/13/business/media/13adco.html.

35 Terry Lefton, "You Can't Zap These Ads," *The Industry Standard*, March 26, 2001, 54–55; James Poniewozik, "This Plug's For You," *Time*, June 18, 2001, 76–77.

CHAPTER 10

1 Ben McConnell and Jackie Huba, *Citizen Marketers: When People Are the Message* (Chicago: Kaplan Publishing, 2006).

2 Stan Davis and Christopher Meyer, *Blur: The Speed of Change in the Connected Economy* (Reading, MA: Addison-Wesley, 1998).

3 Richard Siklos, "Waiting for the Dough on the Web," *New York Times*, June 25, 2006, http://www.nytimes.com.

4 U.S. Census Bureau, http://www.census.gov; Glenn Elert, ed. "Number of Personal Computers in the U.S.," http://hypertextbook.com/facts/2004/.

5 Julia Angwin, "Media Firms Dig into War Chests for Latest Assault on the Internet," *Wall Street Journal*, September 28, 2005, A1.

6 Kim Hart, "Survey: Bloggers Under 30 Sociable," *Boulder Daily Camera*, July 21, 2006, 23A.

7 "Prime Time for Vlogs?" *Business 2.0*, May 2006, 24.

8 Richard Siklos, "A Video Business Model Ready to Move Beyond Beta," *New York Times*, September 17, 2006, http://www.nytimes.com.

9 Katy Bachman, "AAF: TV Dollars Shifting to Online Video," *Mediaweek.com*, November 14, 2006, http://www.mediaweek.com/.

10 Garth Johnston, "Study: Print Beats Broadcast to Online Video Advertising," The Business of Television Web site, February 12, 2007, http://www.broadcastingcable.com.

11 "One-Third of Frequent YouTube Users Are Watching Less TV to Watch Videos Online," Harris Poll #8, January 29, 2007, http://www.harrisinteractive.com.

12 Korky Vann, "A Web Community for Women Over 50," *Boulder Daily Camera*, February 17, 2007, 8D.

13 Stuart Elliott, "Troubling '07 Forecast for the Old-Line Media but Not for the Online," *New York Times*, December 5, 2006, http://www.nytimes.com/.

14 Elliott, "Troubling '07 Forecast"; Robert Guth, "How Microsoft Is Learning to Love Online Advertising," *Wall Street Journal*, November 16, 2006, A1.

15 Vauhini Vara, "eBay's Bid to Go Beyond Auctions Isn't Selling Well," *Wall Street Journal*, December 20, 2006, B1.

16 Scott Kirsner, "Some Bling for Your Blog," *New York Times*, January 18, 2007, http://www.nytimes.com/2007/01/18/technology/18basics.html; Emily Steel, "Web-Page Clocks and Other 'Widgets' Anchor New Internet Strategy," *Wall Street Journal*, November 21, 2006, B4.

17 Andrew Hampp, "All Eyes on Viral Video (at Least with the Under-25 Set)," *Advertising Age*, September 27, 2006, http://adage.com.

[18] Jack Hitt, "Confessions of a Spam King," *New York Times Magazine*, September 28, 2003, http://www.NYTimes.com.

[19] Peter Johnson, "Internet News Supplements Papers, TV," *USA Today*, July 31, 2006, 5D.

[20] Robet Levine, "New Web Sites Seeking Profit in Wiki Model," *New York Times*, September 24, 2006, http://www.nytimes.com.

[21] Saul Hansell, "A Web Site So Hip It Gets Laddies to Watch the Ads," *New York Times*, March 27, 2006, http://www.nytimes.com.

[22] Frazier Moore, "YouTube Is the Biggest Story in TV," *Boulder Daily Camera*, August 20, 2006, 3D.

[23] Julie Bosman, "Agencies Are Watching As Ads Go Online," *New York Times*, August 15, 2006, http://www.nytimes.com.

[24] Bosman, "Agencies Are Watching."

[25] Kevin Delaney, "YouTube Strikes Deal to Host BBC Clips," *Wall Street Journal*, March 3-4, 2007, A3.

[26] Joel Stein, "My So-called Second Life," *Time*, December 25, 2006-January 1, 2007, 76–77; Richard Siklos, "A Virtual World But Real Money," *New York Times*, October 19, 2006, http://www.nytimes.com; Annalee Newitz, "Your Second Life is Ready," *Popular Science*, September 2006, http://www.popsci.com.

[27] "MySpace by the Numbers," *Boulder Daily Camera*, March 11, 2007, 7A: Richard Siklos, "Big Media's Crush on Social Networking," *New York Times*, January 21, 2007, http://www.nytimes.com; Saul Hansell, "For MySpace, Making Friends Was Easy. Big Profit is Tougher," *New York Times*, April 23, 2006, http://www.nytimes.com.

[28] Joe Mandese, "Simultaneous Research Study Reveals Consumers Buzz Most Over Word-of-Mouth, Not Ads," *MediaPost Publications*, January 19, 2007, http://publications.mediapost.com.

[29] Montague, Keynote Speech.

[30] Kevin Delaney, "The New Benefits of Web-Search Queries," *Wall Street Journal*, February 6, 2007, B3.

[31] Robert A. Guth and Kevin J. Delaney, "With adCenter, Microsoft Bids for Web-Search Bonanza," *Wall Street Journal*, May 4, 2006, B1; Saul Hansell, "Google Profit Surges on Strong Search Advertising," *New York Times*, July 21, 2006, http://www.nytimes.com.

[32] Brian Steinberg and Suzanne Vranica, "Burger King Seeks Some Web Heat," *Wall Street Journal*, April 15, 2004, B3.

[33] Randall Rothenberg, "Ad of the Month," *Fast Company*, March 2003, 40.

[34] Peter Grant, "Filmmakers Face Some Big Challenges on Tiny Cellphones," *Wall Street Journal*, December 20, 2006, B1.

[35] Julie Liesse, "Hitting the Target: Mobile Makes Its Mark," *Mobile Marketing*, December 4, 2006, 4.

[36] Liesse, "Hitting the Target."

[37] Alicia Wallace, "Domino Effect," Business Plus, February 12, 2007: 1.

[38] Li Yuan, "In China, New Year Gives a Big Boost to Text Messaging," *Wall Street Journal*, March 3, 2007, A1.

[39] Richard Mullins, "Sell, Phone," *Tampa Tribune*, December 21, 2006, 1.

[40] Melanie Hollands, "9 Million Americans Join Trend," *Boulder Daily Camera*, July 21, 2006, 22A.

[41] Louise Story, "Anywhere the Eye Can See, It's Likely to See an Ad," *New York Times*, January 15, 2007, http://www.nytimes.com.

CHAPTER 11

[1] William Spain, "GM Guts Ad Budget," *Advertising Age*, February 13, 2007.

[2] Emily Steel, " 'Measured' Media Lose in Spending Cuts," *Wall Street Journal*, March 14, 2007, B3.

[3] Joe Mandese, "Top Gunn: OMD Ranks As Most 'Creative' Media Shop for Third Straight Year," *MediaPost Publications*, February 12, 2007, http://publications.mediapost.com.

[4] Suzanne Vranica and Ellen Byron, "Women's Product Can Stand Out at Super Bowl," *Wall Street Journal*, January 30, 2007, B8.

[5] "Best Practice: Television Planning," *Admap*, June 2002, 11–12.

[6] Larry Kelley and Donald Jugenheimer, *Advertising Media Planning: A Brand Management Approach* (Armonk, NY: M.E. Sharpe, 2004): 95.

[7] Jim Surmanek, *Media Planning: A Practical Guide*, 3rd ed. (Lincolnwood, IL: NTC Business Books, 1996): 57.

[8] Kelley and Jugenheimer, 8.

[9] Ian Brace and Louise Edwards, "Can Advertising Reach Everybody?" *Adweek*, July/August 2002, 26–28.

[10] Surmanek, 49.

[11] William Spain, "GM Guts Ad Budget," *Advertising Age*, February 13, 2007; Brian Steinberg, "GM's Media Chief Seeks Nontraditional Channels," *Wall Street Journal*, May 3, 2006, B3.

[12] "Best Practice," *Admap*.

[13] Jack Neff, "P&G Pumps Up Print Spending, Trims TV," *Advertising Age*, November 6, 2006, 1.

[14] Maura Clancey and Gale Metzger, "Building Survey-Based, Media-Mix Planning Tool," *Admap*, June 2002, 47–49.

[15] Hank Bernstein and Kate Lynch, "Media Scheduling and Carry-Over Effects," *Admap*, October 2002, 40–42.

[16] Neff, "P&G Pumps Up."

[17] Bobbi Kay Hooper, "Power of Advertising," *AdNews*, Spring 2007, 7.

[18] Brian Steinberg, "Disney Combines Ad Staff for Selling Kids' Media," *Wall Street Journal*, February 6, 2007, B2.

[19] Bob Garfield, "The Chaos Scenario," *Advertising Age*, April 4, 2005, cover, 57; Ross Fadner, "On Wall Street, Old Media Humbled New in '06," *MediaPost Publications*, January 4, 2007, http://publications.mediapost.com.

[20] Kate Fitzgerald, "Trolling for Media Plan's Role," *Advertising Age* Special Report, March 3, 2003, S10–S12.

[21] Claire Atkinson, "Coke Catapults Starcom MediaVest," *Advertising Age*, February 9, 2004, S6, S10.

[22] Kevin Delaney and Peter Grant, "Google Gains on Goal of Controlling and Targeting TV Commercials," *Wall Street Journal*, March 10, 2007, A1; Suzanne Vranica and Brian Steinberg, "Five to Watch: Firms Rethinking the Status Quo," *Wall Street Journal*, December 27, 2006, B2; Suzanne Varanica, "Internet Reshapes Role of Media Buyers," *The Wall Street Journal*, February 28, 2007, B3.

[23] Ari Rosenberg, "Search and Destroy," MediaPosts's *Online Publishing Insider*, January 25, 2007, http://blogs.mediapost.com/online_publishing_insider/?p=74.

[24] Bradley Johnson, "Cracks in the Foundation," *Advertising Age*, December 8, 2003, 1, 10.

[25] Don E. Schultz, "Outdated Approach to Planning Needs Revamping," *Marketing News*, November 11, 2002.

[26] Clancey and Metzger, "Building Survey-Based, Media-Mix Planning Tool."

CHAPTER 12

[1] A. Jerome Jewler and Bonnie L. Drewniany, *Creative Strategy in Advertising* (Belmont, CA: Wadsworth/Thomson Learning, 2001): 3.

[2] Ty Montague, Keynote Speech, Effie Awards Gala, June 7, 2006, http://www.effie.org/gala/montague.html.

[3] Lee Earle, "Creative Message Strategy as a Framework for Course Planning, Preparation, and Pedagogy Or: Everything I Know about Teaching I Learned from Advertising," *Journal of Advertising Education*, Fall 2005, 22–28.

[4] Emily Steel, "RipeTV Casts Net for Young Males," *Wall Street Journal*, October 10, 2006, B2.

[5] Kevin Keller, *Strategic Brand Management*, 2nd ed. (Upper Saddle River, NJ: Prentice Hall, 2003): 76–81.

[6] Eric Pfanner, "Hewlett-Packard Takes a New Tack: Being Cool," *New York Times*, July 25, 2006, http://www.nytimes.com/2006/07/25/business/media/25adco.html.

[7] Bruce Horovitz, "Burger King of Cool?" *USA Today*, February 7, 2007, http://www.usatoday.com/money/industries/food/2007-02-06-burger-king-usat_x.htm.

[8] William Weir, "Character Counts: Bran Icons Get Story Lines, Emotions," *The Seattle Times*, November 2, 2006, http://seattletimes.nwsource.com.

[9] Charles Frazer, "Creative Strategy: A Management Perspective," *Journal of Advertising*, 12:4 (1983): 36–41.

[10] William Wells, "How Advertising Works," speech to the St. Louis AMA, September 17, 1986.

[11] Edd Applegate, *Strategic Copywriting* (Lanham, MD: Rowman & Littlefield, 2005).

[12] Larry Neumeister, "Judge Blocks DirecTV Ads," *Boulder Daily Camera*, February 6, 2007, D7.

[13] Reported in Thomas Page Jr., Esther Thorson, and Maria Heide, "The Memory Impact of Commercials Varying in Emotional Appeal and Product Involvement," *Emotion in Advertising* (New York: Quorum Books, 1990): 255–268.

14 Stuart Elliott, "Home Depot Taps the Weepy Part of Reality TV," *New York Times,* February 12, 2007, http://www.nytimes.com/2007/012/12/businss/media/12adcol.html.

15 Jan Rijkenberg, *Concepting* (Henley-on-Thames, United Kingdom: World Advertising Research Center, 2001).

16 James Webb Young, *A Technique for Producing Ideas*, 3rd ed. (Chicago: Crain Books, 1975).

17 Jerri Moore and William D. Wells, *R.O.I. Guidebook: Planning for Relevance, Originality and Impact in Advertising and Other Marketing Communications* (New York: DDB Needham, 1991).

18 John Eighmy, *The Creative Work Book* (Iowa City: University of Iowa, 1998): 1.

19 Thomas Russell and Glenn Verrill, *Kleppner's Advertising Procedure*, 14th ed. (Upper Saddle River, NJ: Prentice Hall, 2002): 457.

20 Janet Forgrieve, "Ad Agency's Colo., Fla. Offices on Same Team," *Rocky Mountain News Rocky Business*, March 8, 2007, 6.

21 Sheri J. Broyles, The Creative Personality: Exploring Relations of Creativity and Openness to Experience. Unpublished doctoral dissertation, Southern Methodist University, Dallas, 1995.

22 Broyles, Creative Personality.

23 A. Kendrick, D. Slayden, and S.J. Broyles, "Real Worlds and Ivory Towers: A Survey of Top Creative Directors," *Journalism and Mass Communication Educator* 51:2 (1996): 63–74; A. Kendrick, D. Slayden, and S. J. Broyles, "The Role of Universities in Preparing Creatives: A Survey of Top U.S. Agency Creative Directors," in *Proceedings of the 1996 Conference of the American Academy of Advertising*, ed. G. B. Wilcox (Austin: University of Texas, 1996): 100–106.

24 Graham Wallas, *The Art of Thought* (New York: Harcourt, Brace, 1926); Alex F. Osborn, *Applied Imagination*, 3rd ed. (New York: Scribner's, 1963).

25 Linda Conway Correll, "Creative Aerobics: A Technique to Jump-Start Creativity," *Proceedings of the American Academy of Advertising Annual Conference*, ed. Carole M. Macklin (Richmond, VA: AAA, 1997): 263–64.

26 Louise Story, "Ads Made by You, in a Click," *New York Times*, February 8, 2007, http://www.nytimes.com/2007/02/08/business/media/08adco.html.

27 Suzanne Vranica, "Super Bowl Advertisers Play It for Laughs," *Wall Street Journal*, February 5, 2007: B1.

28 Clarence Page, "New Media, Same Game," *Chicago Tribune*, March 25, 2007, http://www.chicagotribune.com/news/columnists/chi-0703250328mar25,1,2025796.column?coll=chi-news-col.

29 Brian Morrissey, "Geico Viral Visits Caveman's Crib," February 1, 2007, http://adweek.com/aw/iq_interactive/article_display.jsp?vnu_content_id=1003540975.

30 Goeffrey Fowler, Brian Steinberg, and Aaron Patrick, "Mac and PC's Overseas Adventures," *Wall Street Journal*, March 1, 2007, B1.

31 Betsy Sharkey, "Super Angst," *Adweek*, January 24, 1993, 24–33.

CHAPTER 13

1 Yumiko Ono, "Some Times Ad Agencies Mangle English Deliberately," *Wall Street Journal*, November 4, 1997, B1.

2 David Ogilvy, *Ogilvy on Advertising* (New York: Vintage, 1985).

3 Cynthia Crossen, "Clever Lines/Make Us Crave/Return to Days/Selling Burma-Shave," *Wall Street Journal*, August 20, 2003, 1A.

4 Sandra Dallas, "Road to Pave? Remember Burma-Shave!" *BusinessWeek,* December 30, 1996, 8; Frank Rowsome Jr., *The Verse by the Side of the Road* (New York: Dutton, 1965).

5 Paul D. Bolls and Robert F. Potter, "I Saw It on the Radio: The Effects of Imagery Evoking Radio Commercials on Listeners' Allocation of Attention and Attitude toward the Ad," *Proceedings of the Conference of the American Academy of Advertising,* ed. Darrel D. Muehling (Lexington, KY: American Academy of Advertising, 1998), 123–30.

6 Peter Hochstein, "Ten Rules for Making Better Radio Commercials," Ogilvy & Mather's *Viewpoint* (1981).

7 Adapted from Bonnie Drewniany and Jerome Jewler and, *Creative Strategy in Advertising*, 9th ed. (Belmont CA: Wadsworth/Thomson, 2007: 230.

8 Adapted from John Burnett and Sandra Moriarty, *Marketing Communications: An Integrated Approach* (Upper Saddle River, NJ: Prentice Hall, 1998), 296–97.

9 Blessie Miranda and Kuen-Hee Ju-Pak, "A Content Analysis of Banner Advertisements: Potential Motivating Features," Annual Conference Baltimore, Association for Education in Journalism and Mass, August 1998.

CHAPTER 14

1 Sandra Dolbow, "Brand Builders," *Brandweek*, July 24, 2000, 19.

2 Theresa Howard, "Ads Try Grins to Appeal to Users' Smarter Sides," *USA Today*, September 31, 2005, 4B.

3 Noreen O'Leary, "Legibility Lost," *Adweek*, October 5, 1987, D7.

4 Kathy Lohr, "Ads Add a Certain Glow to Atlanta's City Buses," National Public Radio, March 23, 2007, http://www.npr.org/templates/story/story.php?storyid=8989580.

5 Charles Goldsmith, "Adding Special to Effects," *Wall Street Journal*, February 26, 2003, B1.

6 Stuart Elliott, "JanSport Sings 'Do-Re-Mi' to Teens," *New York Times Direct*, April 29, 2003 (NYTDirect@nytimes.com).

7 Laura Ruel and Nora Paul, "Eyetracking Points the Way to Effective News Article Design," *Online Journalism Review,* March 13, 2007, http://www.ojr.org/ojr/stories/07312ruel.

8 Heather McWilliams, "Zooming in to Web Video," *Business Plus*, March 5, 2007, 3.

CHAPTER 15

1 *Direct Marketing Association 2006 Annual Report*, 10, http://www.the-dma.org (accessed April 24, 2007).

2 *Direct Marketing Association 2006 Annual Report*, 10.

3 Lisa Spiller and Martin Baier, *Contemporary Direct Marketing* (Upper Saddle River, NJ: Prentice Hall, 2004).

4 Bill Brohaugh and Rick Ferguson, "The Persistence of Memory," *Colloquy,* Fall 2006, 7.

5 Don Peppers and Martha Rogers, "The Principles of Data-driven Relationships," *Advertising Principles & Practices,* 7th ed, (Upper Saddle River, NJ: Prentice Hall, 2006): 431.

6 Michael Fielding, "Direct Mail Still Has Its Place," *Marketing News*, November 1, 2006, 31.

7 Pradeep K. Korgaonkar, Eric J. Karson, and Ishael Akaah, "Direct Marketing Advertising: The Assents, the Dissents, and the Ambivalents," *Journal of Advertising Research,* September/October 1997, 41–45.

8 Suzanne Barlyn, "Block That Catalog!" *Wall Street Journal*, February 8, 2007, D3; Jenny Stamos, "Say No to Junk Mail," *Woman's Day*, November 1, 2006, 16.

9 Tom Duncan, *Advertising & IMC*, 2nd ed. (Boston: McGraw-Hill Irwin, 2005): 262–63.

10 Michelle Kessler and Byron Acohido, "Data Miners Dig a Little Deeper," *USA Today*, July 12, 2006, 1B.

11 Kessler and Acohido, "Data Miners."

12 Matt Hasan, "Ensure Success of CRM with a Change in Mindset," *Marketing News,* April 14, 2003, 16.

13 Fielding, "Direct Mail."

14 "Symposium Held on Junk Mail," *Boulder Daily Camera*, October 26, 2006, 1C.

15 Clint Talbott, "Illegal Pizza Coupons?" *Boulder Daily Camera*, February 20, 2007, 7A.

16 "The Power of Mailstream," Pitney-Bowes Web site, 3–4, http://www.pb.com/mailstream (accessed April 26, 2007).

17 "Power of Mailstream," 5–6.

18 Dean Rieck, "10 Basics for Writing Better Letters," *Direct Marketing* 63:12 (April 2001): 52–53, 62.

19 "Symposium Held on Junk Mail."

20 Talbott, "Illegal Pizza Coupons?"

21 "Catalogs Find Niche in Online Age," *Grand Rapid Press*, November 26, 2006, G4.

22 "Catalogs Find Niche."

23 David Sharp, "Catalogs Still Thrive in an Age of Growing e-Commerce," *Boulder Daily Camera*, December 5, 2004, 2F; "Catalogs Find Niche."

24 Amy Merrick, "Victoria's Secret Goes Green on Paper for Catalogs," *Wall Street Journal*, December 7, 2006, B2.

25 Jennifer Kerr, "Warning: No-call List Expires," *Boulder Daily Camera*, September 22, 2007: 13A.

26 Louise Marsland, "SAMRA Convention 2006 News," March 15, 2006, Bizcommunity.com, http://www.bizcommunity.com/res/img/s.gif.

[27] Suzanne Vranica and Gary McWilliams, "Wal-Mart Dismisses Ad Agency That It Had Just Hired," *Wall Street Journal,* December 8, 2006, B1.

[28] Vranica and McWilliams, "Wal-Mart Dismisses."

[29] Stan Rapp and Tom Collins, *MaxiMarketing* (New York: McGraw-Hill, 1987).

[30] Lance Arthur, "Clear-Cut Lessons for Effective E-Mail," *Direct Marketing* 64:1 (May 2001): 62–63.

[31] Janis Mara, "E-Mail Direct," *Adweek,* April 10, 2001, 116–117.

[32] David McNickel, "Deeper, Closer, Faster, Smarter," *AdMedia,* April 2003, 36.

[33] "Power of Mailstream," 3.

[34] Fielding, "Direct Mail."

[35] Mei Fong, "Avon's Calling, but China Opens Door Only a Crack," *Wall Street Journal*, February 26, 2007, B1.

CHAPTER 16

[1] American Marketing Association Web site, http://www.marketingpower.com/mg-dictionary.php.

[2] "Netflix Dangles Million Dollar Prize as Marketing Gimmick," http://www.mediabuyerplanner.com/2006/10/13/netflix_danglesmillion_dollar/.

[3] 2001 Annual Report, *Promo,* May 1, 2001, as reported in http://www.industryclick.com/magazinearticle.asp?magazinearticleid=99739&.

[4] Promo Industry Trends Report 2007 *Promo,* September 5, 2007, http://promomagazine.com/mag/PROMO_2007_Industry_Trends_Report.pdf/

[5] Promo Industry Trends Report 2007.

[6] Leo Jakobson, "Incentives without Borders," *Incentive,* March 2006, 12–17.

[7] Promo Industry Trends Report 2007.

[8] "Stores Are Media: BIGresearch's Simultaneous Media Survey Ranks the Influence of In-Store Media on Purchase Decisions," http://www.bigresearch.com.

[9] Emily Steel, "Grabbing Older Consumers via Cellphone," *Wall Street Journal,* Jan. 31, 2007, B3.

[10] Dave Carpenter, "McDonald's Unveils New Game, But Stock Hits 10-Year Low," Associated Press State & Local Wire, March 6, 2003, http://web.lexis-nexis.com/universe/document?_m=e0607584954c0d52b07aa058

[11] Joyce, "Higher Gear."

[12] U.S. Department of Labor, Bureau of Labor Statistics, "NAICS 42–45: Wholesale and Retail Trade," http://www.bls.gov/iag/wholeretailtrade.htm (accessed May 5, 2007).

[13] "Entertainment Marketing Awards: Who's Who," *Promo* Special Reports, May 1, 2001, http://www.industryclick.com/Microsites/Newsarticle.asp?newsarticleid=218986&srid=.

[14] Matthew Kinsman, "The Last Stand," *Promo,* January 2001, 29–34.

[15] Sam Walker, "The Bankers behind the Woman," *Wall Street Journal,* May 23, 2003, W5.

[16] Christine Tatum, "Firms More Thoughtful in Sponsoring of Events," *The Denver Post,* August 8, 2003, 4.

[17] Ellen Byron, "An Old Dice Game Catches On Again, Pushed by P&G," *New York Times,* January 30, 2007, A1, A13.

[18] Jack Gage from Forbes.com, May 19, 2006, as reported at http://www.wired.com/print/cars/energy/news/2006/05/70932.

[19] Brett McMurphy, "What's in a Name? Lots of Exposure for Sponsors," *Tampa Tribune,* December 22, 2006, 1.

[20] "7-Eleven New Start Time for White Sox Games," *Promo,* Oct. 18, 2006, http://www.promomagazine.com.

[21] Adam Thompson and Shai Oster, "NBA in China Gets Milk to Sell Hoops," *Wall Street Journal*, January 22, 2007, B1.

[22] Emiko Terazono, "Ambush Marketing Tactics to Be Kicked into Touch," *Financial Times,* September 2, 2003, 9.

[23] Laura-Smith-Spark, "Dutch Fans Given Shorts for Match," *BBC News,* June 21, 2006, http://news.bbc.co.uk/2/hi/europe/5104252.stm.

[24] Joyce, "Higher Gear."

[25] Dan Hanover, "We Deliver," *Promo,* March 2001, 43–45.

[26] Bob Tedeschi, "A Growing Ad Strategy: 'Click to Win!'" *New York Times,* August 21, 1998, http://www.nytimes.com/library/tech/98/08/cyber/articles/.

[27] "Walking the Tight Rope," *Promo,* March 2001, 48–49.

[28] Daniel Yee, "Flier Programs Fly Off Course," *Boulder Daily Camera,* June 29, 2006, 16A.

[29] Burger King Corp., "Burger King Restaurant's Spider-Man 3 Promotion," http://www.superheroflix.com/news/71/19371.php.

[30] Kate Macarthur, "McDonald's Unveils Global 'Shrek' Movie Promotion," May 8, 2007, http://www.adage.com.

[31] Tara Parker-Pope, "How to Tell If a Pink-Ribbon Product Really Helps Breast-Cancer Efforts," *Wall Street Journal,* October 10, 2006, D1.

[32] Jacques Chevron, "Branding and Promotion: Uneasy Co-habitation," *Brandweek,* September 14, 1998, 24.

[33] Scott Hume, "Rallying to Brands' Rescue," *Advertising Age,* August 13, 1990, 3.

[34] Jean Halliday, "GM Bleeds as Incentives Undermine Brand Value," *Advertising Age,* March 21, 2005, 1.

[35] Nick Bunkley, "With Inventories Bulging, Detroit Rolls Out the Incentives," *New York Times,* June 29, 2006, http://www.nytimes.com.

[36] Jon Kramer, "It's Time to Tie the Knot with Promotion," *Integrated Marketing and Promotion,* September/October 1998, 77.

[37] Joyce, "Higher Gear."

CHAPTER 17

[1] Scott M. Cutlip, Allen H. Center, and Glen M. Broom, *Effective Public Relations,* 9th ed. (Upper Saddle River, NJ: Pearson Prentice-Hall, 2006): 1, 321.

[2] Martin Sorrell, "Assessing the State of Public Relations," *The Strategist* 3:4 (Winter 1998): 48.

[3] Doug Newsom, Judy VanSlyke Turk, and Dean Krukeberg, *This Is PR: The Realities of Public Relations,* 8th ed. (Belmont, CA: Wadsworth/Thomson Learning, 2004): 106.

[4] Dan Lattimore, Otis Baskin, Suzette T. Heiman, Elizabeth L. Toth, and James K. Van Leuven, *Public Relations: The Profession and the Practice* (Boston: McGraw-Hill, 2004).

[5] Claire Atkinson, "Rubenstein: PR Maestro," *Advertising Age,* October 11, 2004, 46.

[6] Public Relations Society of America, http://www.prsa.org

[7] James Lukaszewski, "Chief Integrity Officer Is Tailor-made for PR," *Odwyer's PR Services Report,* March 2004, 8.

[8] Bennett Freeman, "Substance Sells: Aligning Corporate Reputation and Corporate Responsibility," *Public Relations Quarterly,* Spring 2006, 12–19.

[9] Tom Duncan and Sandra Moriarty, *Driving Brand Value: Using Integrated Marketing to Manage Profitable Stakeholder Relationships* (New York: McGraw-Hill, 1997).

[10] Daniel J. Edelman, "The Golden Age of Public Relations," *Public Relations Quarterly,* Spring 2006, 20–21.

[11] Thomas L. Harris, *Value-Added Public Relations: The Secret Weapon of Integrated Marketing* (Lincolnwood, IL: NTC Business Books, 1998).

[12] David Michaelson and Don W. Stacks, "What Research Says–Advertising vs. PR Effectiveness," *Institute for Public Relations,* February 28, 2007, http://www.instituteforpr.org.

[13] Ronald Alsop, "How Boss's Deeds Buff a Firm's Reputation," *Wall Street Journal,* January 31, 2007, B1–B2.

[14] Sandra Moriarty, "IMC Needs PR's Stakeholder Focus," *AMA Marketing News,* May 26, 1997, 7

[15] Fraser P. Seitel, *The Practice of Public Relations,* 10th ed. (Upper Saddle River, NJ: Pearson Prentice-Hall, 2007): 73–74.

[16] Michael Bush, "Starbucks Stays True to Storytelling Core," *PR Week,* October 23, 2006, 9.

[17] Kris Hudson, "Behind the Scenes, PR Firm Remakes Wal-Mart's Image," *Wall Street Journal,* December 7, 2006, A1, A10.

[18] Jack Welch, "The Five Stages of Crisis Management: Why Katrina Will Make Us Stronger," *Wall Street Journal,* September 14, 2005, http://www.opinionjournal.com.

[19] Kate Macarthur, "KFC Preps Bird-Flu Fear Plan," *Advertising Age,* November 5, 2005, 1, 58.

[20] Edward Maibach, Mark Marosits, and Lorien Abroms, "Communication and Marketing as Tools to Cultivate the Public's Health: A Proposed 'People and Places' Framework," BMC Public Health, published May 22, 2007 at http://www.biomedcentral.com/1471-2458/7/88

[21] Barbara Palframan-Smith, "Employee Connection," *Communication World,* March–April 2004, 7.

22 Bernard Charkand, "How Can Communicators Bridge the Gap between Executives and Employees: Australia," *Communication World,* March–April 2004, 12.

23 Cutlip, Center, and Broom, *Effective Public Relations.*

24 Tamara Gillis, "In Times of Change, Employee Communication Is Vital to Successful Organizations," *Communication World,* March–April 2004, 8.

25 E. W. Brody, "Have You Made the Transition? Are You Practicing Public Relations In the 21st Century Rather Than the 20th?" *Public Relations Quarterly,* Spring 2004, 7–9.

26 David Crary, "Pizza Hut's Book It Under Fire," *Boulder Daily Camera,* March 3, 2007, 5A.

27 Claire Atkinson, "PR Firms Praise Janet Jackson Breast Stunt," *AdAge.com,* February 9, 2004, http://www.adage.com/news.coms?newsid=39756.

28 Dan Lothian, Fran Fifis, and Deborah Feyerick, "Two Plead Not Guilty to Boston Hoax Charges," February 1, 2007, http://www.cnn.com.

29 Harry R. Weber, "Cartoon Network Head Resigns after Scare," ABC News, February 10, 2007, http://abcnews.go.com.

30 Harris, *Value-Added Public Relations.*

31 Paul Homes, "Senior Marketers Are Sharply Divided about the Role of PR in the Overall Mix," *Advertising Age,* January 24, 2005, C1, C2.

32 Homes, "Senior Marketers."

33 Alyse R. Gotthoffer, "Exploring the Relevance of Localization in Anti-Drinking and Driving PSAs," *The Proceedings of the American Academy of Advertising Conference,* ed. Darrel D. Muehling (Lexington, KY, 1998): 214.

34 "You + Target = More For Schools," http://www.target.com/tcoe/.

35 Edward A. Faruolo, "A Business of Caring," *The Advertiser,* October 1998, 36–40.

36 "A Drop of Dawn Makes a Difference, and So Can You," http://www.homemadesimple.com/en_US/dawnsaveswildlife/home.do?page=home

37 Kasey Cordell, "Teva Treats Elephant Toes," *Boulder Daily Camera,* April 11, 2005, 6B.

38 Thomas Harris, "iPod, Therefore iAm," *ViewsLetter,* September 2004, 3.

39 Kathy Cripps, "PR Is More Than Just Media," Letter to the Editor, *Advertising Age,* October 11, 2004, 24.

40 Andrea Tanner, "Communicating Health Information and Making the News," *Public Relations Quarterly,* Spring 2004, 24–27.

41 Carole Howard, "Working with Reporters: Mastering the Fundamentals to Build Long-Term Relationships," Public Relations Quarterly, Spring 2004, 36.

42 Fraser P. Seitel, "E-Mail News Releases," *O'Dwyer's PR Services Report,* March 2004, 37.

43 Anne R. Owen, "Avant-Garde or Passé: Using Video News Releases Internationally," *The Proceedings of the American Academy of Advertising Conference,* ed. Carole M. Macklin (St. Louis, 1997), 290.

44 Brody, "Have You Made the Transition?"

45 Bobby White, "Firms Take a Cue from YouTube," *Wall Street Journal,* January 2, 2007, B3.

46 Marcia Xenitelis, "How Can Communicators Bridge the Gap between Executives and Employees: Australia," *Communication World,* March–April 2004, 7.

47 "Truth Wraps Up 7th Annual Summer Tour," February 23, 2007, http://www.americanlegacy.org.

48 Fraser P. Seitel, *The Practice of Public Relations,* 10th ed. (Upper Saddle River, NJ: Prentice Hall, 2007): 378–79.

49 Candace White and Niranjan Raman, "The World Wide Web as a Public Relations Medium," Association for Education in Journalism and Mass Communication Annual Conference, Baltimore, MD, August 1998.

50 Michelle O'Malley and Tracy Irani, "Public Relations and the Web: Measuring the Effect of Interactivity, Information, and Access to Information in Websites," Association for Education in Journalism and Mass Communication Conference, Baltimore, MD, August 1998.

51 Seitel, *Practice of Public Relations,* 381.

52 Jill Whalen, "Online Public Relations," *High Rankings Advisor* 109 (August 18, 2004), http://www.highrankings.com/issue109.htm.

53 Michael Markowitz, "Fighting Cyber Sabotage," *Bergen Record,* October 4, 1998, http://www.bergen.com/biz/online04199810041.htm.

54 Robert Cribb, "Web Ties Consumer Complaints Together," August 21, 1998, http://www.geocities.com/Athens/Acropolis/5232/webactivism.html.

55 "Blogging and Beyond," *Wall Street Journal,* September 25, 2006, R3.

56 Vanessa O'Connell, "It's the Publicity That Counts," *Wall Street Journal,* November 17, 2006, B1, B4.

57 Jack Neff, "Bottom Line on PR: It Works, Says P&G," *Advertising Age,* November 7, 2005, 1, 57.

CHAPTER 18

1 Don Peppers and Martha Rogers, "Delivering a Smarter Multichannel Experience," *Sales & Marketing Management,* April 2007, 11.

2 Jerome Jeweler and Bonnie Drewniany, *Creative Strategy in Advertising,* 7th ed. (Belmont, CA: Wadsworth, 2001): 240–44.

3 Vanessa O'Connell, "The New Fashion Bloggers," *Wall Street Journal,* February 7, 2007, B1.

4 John A. Koten, "The Strategic Uses of Corporate Philanthropy," in *Handbook of Strategic Public Relations and Integrated Communications,* ed. Clarke L. Caywood (New York: McGraw-Hill, 1997): 149.

5 "1999 Midsize Agency of the Year: Cone," *Inside PR,* Winter 1999, 11.

6 Christopher Cooper, "Legislators Aim At a New Misdeed on the Road: DWT," *Wall Street Journal,* March 14, 2007, A1.

7 Tom Duncan and Sandra Moriarty, *Driving Brand Value: Using Integrated Marketing to Manage Profitable Stakeholder Relationships* (New York: McGraw-Hill, 1997).

8 Saleh AlShebil, Abdul Rasheed, and Hussam Al-Shammari, "Battling Boycotts," *Wall Street Journal,* April 28-29, 2007, R6.

9 Theodore Levitt, "The Globalization of Markets," *Harvard Business Review,* May-June 1983, S8-S9.

10 Philip Kotler (with Kevin Keller), *Marketing Management,* 12th ed. (Englewood Cliffs, NJ: Prentice-Hall, 2006).

11 Edward Hall, *Beyond Culture* (Garden City, NY: Anchor Press/Doubleday, 1976).

12 Geoffrey Fowler, "China's Edgy Advertising," *Wall Street Journal,* October 27, 2003, B1.

13 Katherine Frith and Barbara Mueller, *Advertising and Societies: Global Issues* (New York: Peter Lang, 2002).

14 Cristina Passariello, Keith Johnson, and Suzanne Vranica, "A New Force in Advertising—Protest by E-Mail," *Wall Street Journal,* March 27, 2007, B1.

15 Noreen O'Leary, "The Lay of the Land," *Adweek,* February 5, 2007, http://www.Adweek.com.

16 Ariel Goldfarb, "Making Brand Happen: Branding in the B2B Marketplace," *Journal of Integrated Marketing Communications,* 2007, 35–40.

CHAPTER 19

1 Louise Marsland, "How Much Advertising Actually Works?" SAMRA Convention 2006 News, March 15, 2006, http://www.bizommunity.com/Archive/196/119.html.

2 John Philip Jones, *When Ads Work: New Proof That Advertising Triggers Sales,* 2nd ed. (Armonk, NY: M. E. Sharpe, 2007): xvii.

3 Simon Broadbent, *When to Advertise* (Henley-on-Thames, UK: Admap Publications, 1999).

4 "Taken for a Ride," *Business 2.0,* September 2004: 146.

5 Gina Chon and Suzanne Vranica, "Is 'Dr.Z' Kaput as Chrysler's TV Pitchman?" *Wall Street Journal,* September 18, 2006, B1.

6 David Brandt and Dave Walker, "Copy Testing Under the Gun?" Ipsos Ideas, August/September 2003, 3.

7 "Trick or Treat? Tobacco Industry Prevention Ads Don't Help Curb Youth Smoking and Should Be Taken Off the Air," American Legacy Foundation press release, October 31, 2006, http://www.americanlegacy.org.

8 Charles E. Young, "Capturing the Flow of Emotion in Television Commercials: A New Approach," *Journal of Advertising Research,* June 2004, 202–209; Chuck Young and John Kastenholz, "Emotion in TV Ads," *Admap,* January 2004, 40–42.

9 Don Peppers and Martha Rogers, "Delivering a Smarter Multichannel Experience," *Sales & Marketing Management,* April 2007, 11.

10 Scott Thurm, "One Question, and Plenty of Debate," *Wall Street Journal,* December 4, 2006, B3.

[11] Vikram Mahidhar and Christine Cutten, "Navigating the Marketing Measurement Maze," *Journal of Integrated Marketing Communications,* 2007, 41–46.

[12] Charles Young, *The Advertising Research Handbook* (Seattle, WA: Ideas in Flight, 2005): 53–58.

[13] Lee Weinblatt Q&A, "Testing Firm Keeps Eye on TV Ad Effectiveness," *Brandweek*, January 22, 2007, 8.

[14] Young, *Advertising Research Handbook,* 95–102.

[15] Debra Sherman, "Super Bowl Ads Fumble, Brain Scans Show," *Washington Post*, February 5, 2007, http://www. washingtonpost.com.

[16] Jones, *When Ads Work.*

[17] Louise Marsland, "How Much Advertising Actually Works?" SAMRA Convention 2006 News, March 15, 2006, http://www. bizommunity.com/Archive/196/119.html.

[18] Gerard Tellis, *Effective Advertising* (Thousand Oaks CA: Sage, 2004): 6.

[19] "Unaided Advertising Recall Significantly Higher with Mix of Radio and Internet," *Research Brief*, February 23, 2007, http://www. centerformediaresearch.com.

[20] 2004 Effie brief provided by UPS and the Martin Agency.

[21] Ellen Neuborne, "Ads That Actually Sell Stuff," *Business 2.0*, June 2004, 78.

[22] Jack Neff, "Nielsen Tasks Mandel with Proving Ads Work," *Advertising Age*, December 4, 2006, 1.

[23] Jack Myers, "Jack Myers' Weekend Think Tank: Can the Rules of Research Change?" *MediaPost Publications*, January 5, 2007, http://publications.mediapost.com.

[24] Marlene Bender and Art Zambianchi, "The Reality of ROI: Dell's Approach to Measurement," *Journal of Integrated Marketing Communications*, 2006, 16–21.

INDEX

A

A&P, 39
Aakers, David, 58-59
Abbott Mead Vickers-BBDO, 173
ABC network, 260-61, 264, 265, 276,
    289, 302-303, 341
Abercombie and Fitch, 70
Abernethy, Avery, 358
About.com, 292
Abroms, Lorien, 512
Absolut Vodka, 76, 368
Accountability
    current state of, 56
    direct marketing and, 454
    of sales promotion, 483-84
    in timeline, 22-23
Account director, 54
Account executive, 54, 55
Account management, 54
Account manager, 17
Account planner, 54, 211, 212
Account planning, 210-15
Account Planning Group (APG), 166,
    211, 212
Account services, 21
Account supervisor, 54
ACG, 424, 425, 427
A.C. Nielsen, 167, 268, 270, 272, 574
Acquired needs, 141
Action for Children's Advertising, 91
Active publics, 514
Ad allowance, 539
Adams, John Quincy, 114
Adaptability continuum, 550
Adaptation, 378-79, 550
Ad Council, 260, 262, 271, 273, 278, 518,
    546
Added value, 38
Adese, 392
Adidas, 245, 311
Adidas/Reebok, 295
Adobe, 523, 537
Adoption, 147-148
Adver-game, 313-14
Advertainment, 302-03
Advertisement, first appearance of word,
    8

Advertisers
    as advertising player, 14, 16-17
    top spending companies, 16
Advertising. *See also specific types*
    art and science of, 352-354
    basic factors of, 9
    to children, 73-74
    children's advertising, 84-85
    as communication, 103-06
    comparative advertising, 74-76
    current developments in, 23-26
    defining, 7-8
    evolution of, 7-8
    First Amendment and, 81-82
    focus of, 36
    global web of, 299-300
    homosexuality in, 71-72
    key players in, 14, 16-19
    legal environment, 79-83
    legislation, 84
    media review of, 88
    modern components of, 9-10
    modern practice of, 8-9
    organizational structures of, 18
    public relations and, 508, 517-20
    regulation of, 79-91
    role of creativity in, 354-55
    roles of, 11-14
    sales programs and, 48
    vs. sales promotion, 499
    sex in, 70
    simplicity of, 7
    societal role of, 66-79
    strengths of, 12
    timeline, 20-23
    top categories, 16
    types of, 13-14
Advertising agencies
    as advertising player, 17-18
    vs. agency networks, 50-51
    client payment, 55-56
    in-house, 17, 18
    organization of, 54-55
    relationship with clients, 50-56
    types of, 53-54
Advertising and Marketing Effectiveness
    (AME), 26
Advertising audit, 174

Advertising.com, 276
Advertising department, 51
Advertising Educational Foundation, 69
Advertising plan, 196-97
Advertising research, 165, 167
Advertising Research Foundation (ARF),
    113, 567, 572
Advertising Review Council (ARC), 88,
    89
Advertising ROI, 574-75
Advertising strategy, 9-10
Advil, 75
Advocacy, 121
Advocacy advertising, 520
Aegis Group, 347
AFF, xxxiii, 587
Affective responses, 111-13
Affiliate marketing, 50
Affiliates, 264-65
Affordability, 138-39
Aflac, 111, 127, 437
African Americans, stereotypes and, 72-
    73
Aftab, Parry, 526
Aftermarketing, 142
Age, 135-36, 137
Agencies. *See* Advertising agencies
Agency-client partnership, 17
Agency networks, vs. advertising agen-
    cies, 50-51
Agency-of-record (AOR), 17, 51
AIDA, 106, 149
Aided recall test, 572
Aided recognition, 174
AIG, 542
Air Force, 52
Alamo, 484
Alcohol advertising, 78-79
Alexander, Jason, 585
Alex's Lemonade Stand, 514, 515
Allowances, 490
Allstate, 75, 451, 452, 477, 546
Altoids, 111, 417-18, 422, 431, 444
Amazon.com, 19, 50, 184, 287, 294, 299,
    300-301, 377, 454, 472, 473
Ambush marketing, 493
American Advertising Federation (AAF),
    17, 82, 415, 511

American Airlines, 114, 115, 463, 496, 577
American Apparel, 311
American Association for Public Opinion Research (AAPOR), 166
American Association of Advertising Agencies (4As), 76, 93, 166, 339
American Brands Council, 280
American Dairy Association, 198
American Express, 108, 139, 176, 209, 471, 494
American Family Life Assurance Co. *See* Aflac
American Heart Association, 518
American Idol, 253
American Legacy Foundation, 5-6, 14, 27, 273
American Marketing Association (AMA), 26, 34-35, 482
American Newspaper Publishers Association, 235
American Society for Magazine Editors (ASME), 241, 253
Ameritest, 565, 568, 572
Ameritest approach, 107-08
Amos, Dan, 127
Amtrak, 365
Amway, 476
Analogies, 377
Anderson, Cheri L., 147
Anderson, Chris, 149
Anheuser-Busch, 78-79, 491, 493
Animatics, 567
Animation, 292, 437, 438
Annenberg Public Policy Center, 113
Announcers, 406
Annual reports, 522, 524
Anomaly, 51
Answer print, 441
AOL, 18, 293, 301, 466, 495, 503
Aperture, 320
Appeals, 364-65
Appetite appeals, 368
Apple Computer, 13, 14, 15, 16, 30, 68, 139, 225-26, 250, 288, 289, 306, 355, 359, 378, 379, 392, 421, 523, 524
Applegate, Edd, 23, 364
Arbitron Ratings Company, 260, 574
Argument, 118
Ariga, Masaru, 555
Army, 52
Arnold Worldwide, 6, 17, 295
ARS, 565
Art direction
    designer's toolkit, 423-25
    design principles, 425
    overview, 422-23
    print layout, 427-31
    typefaces, 426
Art directors, in advertising agency, 54
Artifact creation, 182

The Art of the Heist campaign, 313-14, 344
Artois, Stella, 421
ASI Interactive Research, 292
Assistant account executives, 54
Association, 108, 116
Association messages, 370
Association research, 175
AT&T, 88, 89, 242, 475, 479
Attention, 108
Attitudes, 117, 142
Attitude tests, 569
Attributes, 365-366
Audi, 313-14, 315, 319, 329, 344
Audience exposure, 573-74
Auditing Bureau of Circulations (ABC), 236, 240-41, 316, 574
Audobon Society, 453
Avatars, 295, 311
Average frequency, 321
Averett, Free & Ginsberg, 181
Aversion, 113, 121
Avis, 205
Avoidance techniques, 105
Avon, 476
Award shows, 26
Awareness, 108, 110
Aware publics, 514
Axe Shower Gel, 67, 97, 113, 116, 180

B

Baby boomers, 136
Baby busters, 136
Backgrounding, 198
Background research, 174-75
Back translation, 412
Bad taste advertisements, 69-70
Bain & Company, 570
Baker's chocolate, 20
Banana Republic, 71, 139, 468
Bandwagon appeals, 117
Bandwidth, 301
Banner ads, 291
Banners, 409, 441
Barclays, 74
Barlow, Rick, 503
Barnes & Noble, 50
Barnhart Communications, 334-39
Barnum, P. T., 8
Barre, Bill, 207
Barrie, Bob, 419
Barry, Ann Marie, 113
Bartle Bogle Hegarty LLC, 97
Bassett, Steve, 452
Batman OnStar campaign, 175
Batten, Barton, Durstine, and Osborn (BBDO), 21, 286, 375, 376, 380, 551, 585
Bavaria brewery, 493
Bayer, 75
BBC, 295

BBDO. *See* Batten, Barton, Durstine, and Osborn (BBDO)
Beard, Fred, 92, 391
Beck, Heather, 320
Beers, Charlotte, 513
Behavioral influences, on consumer decisions, 146-47
Behavioral response, 119-21
Behavioral segmentation, 153
Behavioral targeting, 156-57, 462
Beliefs, 117
Believability, 118
Bell, George, 503
Bell, Jeff, 253
Ben & Jerry's, 546, 548
Benchmark/ing, 202, 514
Benefit segmentation, 153, 365
Benetton, 71, 91, 92, 421
Benson & Hedges, 83
Berkshire Hathaway, 477
Berlin Cameron, 270
Berman, Margo, 448-49
Bernbach, William, 22
Best Buy, 226, 537
Better Bricks, 107
Better Business Bureau (BBB), 89, 90
Big Idea, 371, 515
BIGresearch, 228, 297
Bind-ins, 471
Bird, Larry, 375, 494
Bisquick, 116
Bizel, Loic, 148
Blackberry, 155
Blacknews.com, 415
Bleed page, 240
Bleed throughs, 341
Blind headline, 394
Bling bling generation, 154
Blip.tv, 289
Blogs, 288-89
Blood Center of Wisconsin, 154
Blow-ins, 471
Blue Bunny, 487, 488
Bluejacking, 306
Bluetooth, 306
BMG, 311
BMW, 24-25, 50, 138-39, 144, 278, 299, 313, 473
Body copy, 392, 393, 397
Body image, in advertising, 72
The Body Shop, 546
Bogart, Humphrey, 436
Bogusky, Alex, 372
Boland, Jeremy, 420
Bono, 68, 225
Bonuses, 490
BoomerGirl.com, 289
Boomerwomenspeak.com, 289
Boost Mobile, 270
Borders Perrin Norrander, 420
Boston Consulting Group, 137
Boulter, Jackie, 173

Brag-and-boast copy, 392
Brainfog, 375
Brainstorming, 376
Brand, defined, 11, 101
Brand advertising, 13
Brand association, 370
Brand communication, 108, 122-24
Brand communication strategy, 206-08
Brand communities, 134
Brand development index (BDI), 329-30
Branded entertainment, 302-03
Brand equity, 39
Brand experiences, on the Web, 299
Brand icon, 366
Brand identity, 207
Brand image, 38-41, 208, 421-22
Branding, 38-41, 205, 359
Brand liking, 209
Brand linkage, 108, 116, 208
Brand loyalty, 118
Brand management, 49
Brand name, 21
Brand penetration, 570
Brand personality, 207
Brand proselytizer, 148
Brand relationships, 146
Brands, 58, 497-98
Brand salience, 359
Brand tracking, 569-70
Brand transformation, 108
Brandtrust, 149, 170
Break-even analysis, 578
Breakthrough ad, 372
Brewer, John, 525, 545
Brighton Ski Resort, 88
Bristol Myers, 453
Broadband, 267
Broadbent, Simon, 563
Broadcast media
    advantages and limitations, 279-80
    defined, 256
    direct-response advertising and, 471-72
    film and video, 276-77
    overview, 256-57
    product placement, 278-79
    radio, 257-63
    television, 263-76
Broadcast network, 264
Broadcast production, 434-41
Broadsheets, 466
Brokaw, Tom, 136
Brokers, 49, 230
Bronner, Michael, 503
Brown, Michael, 512
Broyles, Sheri J., 24, 112
Brunson, Sean, 405
Buckley Broadcasting, 258
Budgeting, 209-10
Budget Travel, 294
Budweiser, 490, 491
Buffett, Warren, 477

Buick, 392, 469
Bu Jin, 58
Bulk e-mail, 293
Bulldog Drummond, 540
Bullock, August, 112
Bureau of Alcohol, Tobacco, and Firearms (BATF), 87-88
BurellesLuce, 528
Burger King, 129, 299, 304, 332, 359, 497, 499
Burma Shave, 399
Burnett, Leo, 22, 54, 245
Burpee Seeds, 46
Burrell Communications, 415
Burson-Marsteller, 63
Bursts, 332
Burton Snowboards, 410
Bush, George, 88, 157
Business plan, 193-95
Business theater, 511
Business-to-business (B2B) marketing, 13, 48, 131, 151, 301, 541-44
Business-to-business (B2B) markets, 41, 42
Business-to-consumer (B2C) marketing, 131
BusinessWire, 521
Buyer, 542
Buying power, 140
Buzz, 25, 297, 302

C

Cable radio, 258
Cable television, 265
Cabletelevision Advertising Bureau, 265
Cactus Marketing Communication, 292, 547
Cadence, 223
Cadillac, 377
California Milk Brand, 372
California Milk Processor Board, 387
Call centers, 184, 469
Call-outs, 393
Call to action, 120, 370, 393, 397
Calvin Klein, 71
Campaign, defined, 14
Campaign plan
    brand communication strategy, 206-08
    defined, 197
    implementation and management, 209-10
    objectives, 199-202
    outline, 197
    positioning, 202-06
    situation analysis, 198-99
    strategic approach, 208-09
    targeting, 202
Campbell, Naomi, 421
Campbell-Ewald agency, 373
Campbell Soup, 74, 75, 88, 248

Cannes Lions International Advertising Festival, 24, 26
Canon, 191
CAN-SPAM Act (2003), 473
Capital campaigns, 546
Capital One, 475
Caples, John, 21
Captions, 393, 395
Captive ads, 305
Carat, 347
CareerBuilder.com, 559
Carl's Jr., 70
Carlson Marketing, 459
Carnival Cruise Lines, 458
Carryover effect, 331
Cartoon Network, 302, 516
Carvey, Dana, 494
Case, 561
Cassie Awards, 26
Castellini, Richard, 559
Casting, 406
Catalina Marketing, 463, 495
Catalogs, 468-69
Category development index (CDI), 329-30
Category sell, 214
Cat Herders commercial, 430, 431, 436, 437, 441
Cathy, Truett, 101
Cause marketing, 510, 546, 548
Caywood, Clarke, 324
CBS, 88, 89, 230, 260-61, 264, 265, 268, 289, 305
CBSMarketWatch.com, 291
CDNow, 472
Cease-and-desist orders, 86
Celebrities, 366, 406
Celestial Seasonings, 44
Census Bureau, 135, 166, 287
Center for Media Design (CMD), 228
Center for Studies in Creativity, 375
Central Hudson Gas and Electric v. Public Service Commission of New York, 81
Champ, Janet, 398
Champion, Barbara, 73
Champion & Associates, 73
Change agent, 515
Channel market, 43
Channel marketing, 43, 46
Channel of distribution, as marketing player, 49
Channels of communication, 103
Character types, 406
Charles Schwab, 180, 496
Charmin, 347, 553
Chat rooms, 288
Chevrolet, 378
Chex, 248
Chiat/Day, 15, 17
Chick-fil-A, 101-02, 110, 124, 491
Chief integrity officer, 508

Children, advertising to, 73-74
Children's advertising, 84-85
Children's Advertising Review Unit (CARU), 84
Children's Food and Beverage Advertising Initiative, 73
Children's Hospital of Houston, 524
Children's Television Advertising Practice Act (1990), 84
Chrysler, 563
Church-state rule, 253
CIGNA, 471, 514-15, 519-20
Cinema Advertising Council (CAC), 277
Circuit City, 258
Circulation, 232, 234, 240-41
Citibank, 475, 496, 503
Claim, 365
Clairol Herbal Essences, 127
Clark, Derek, 373
Clark County Desert Conservation Program, 515
Classified ads, 8, 20, 236
Claymation, 437
Clear channel, 257
Clear Channel Communications, 258, 260-61
Click art, 423, 441
"Clicks or bricks", 46
Click-through rate, 291, 300, 579
Client information, 315
Clients, 14, 50-56
Clios, 26
Clip art, 423
Clorox, 75
Closings, 341, 397
Club Med, 490
Clutter, 104-05, 275
Clutter reel, 569
CNN, 88, 266, 334, 342
Coach, 39, 46
Coates Kokes, 107, 261, 372, 399, 403
Co-branding, 496
Coca-Cola, 58, 73, 88, 152, 180-81, 181, 182-83, 188, 205, 248, 253, 265, 268, 278, 311, 342-43, 384, 401, 421, 479, 548, 549, 551
Codes of ethics, 93, 507
Coffee Rush, 399
Cognition, 113-15
Cognitive dissonance, 141-42
Cognitive learning, 115
Coincidental survey, 569
Cold calls, 469
Coldwell Banker, 311
Cole Haan, 144
Colgate, 138, 453
Colgate-Palmolive, 89
Collateral materials, 400, 524
Colle+McVoy, 561, 562, 582-83
Collins, Tom, 471

Color, as visual element, 423-25
Colorado Rockies, 493
Colorado's Tobacco Education & Prevention Partnership (STEPP), 547
Color separation, 433, 434
Columbia House Online, 472
Columbia Pictures, 302-303
Columbia Sportswear, 419, 420
Comarketing, 496
Comcast, 479
Comedy Central, 289
Commercial breaks, 273
Commercial free speech, 81, 82
Commission, 55
Commodization, 223
Commonsense difference, 81
Communication, as advertising, 103-06
Communication audit, 514
Communication brief, 214
Communication exchange, 37
Communication Model, 103, 104
Communication role, of advertising, 11
Communications planning, 347
Communispace, 180
Compaq, 377, 464
Comparative advertising, 74-76
Comparison, 366
Competitive advantage, 37, 204-05
Competitive advertising, 316
Competitive analysis, 174
Competitive sell, 214
Compiled list, 461
Composition, 428-31
Comprehension, 115
Comprehensives, 428, 429
CompUSA, 36
Computer Tutor, 85
Concepting, 370
Concept testing, 173, 567
Conditioned learning, 116
Cone, Carol, 546
Cone agency, 546
Consent decrees, 85-86
Considered purchases, 117-18, 455-56
Consolidated services, 342
Consumer activist groups, 91
Consumer and Brand Insights, 181
Consumer behavior
    buying trends, 147-48
    decision process and, 149-51
    defined, 131
    influences on, 131-47
Consumer Behavior Odyssey, 180
Consumer diaries, 570
Consumer Electronics Show, 523
Consumer-first approach, 36
Consumer insight research, 172-73
Consumer magazines, 238
Consumer markets, 41, 42
Consumer promotions, 484-87
Consumer research, 165, 175

Consumers
    branding and, 39
    vs. customers, 36, 131
    marketing concept and, 36
    vs. purchasers, 19
Contact, 120-21
ContactPoint Management, 334, 335
Contact point planning, 334
Contact points, 215
Content analysis, 174
Contests, 486, 489
Contextual ads, 303
Continuity, 331
Continuity programs, 496
Continuous strategy, 331
Continuous tone, 432
Contrast advertising, 114
Controlled media, 517
Controversial advertising, 92
Controversial products, 77
Convergence, 222, 286-87, 289, 306
Converse, 68, 250
Conversion rate, 579
Conviction, 118
Cookies, 300-301
Cool hunters, 148
CoolSavings, 479
Co-op advertising, 235
Cooper, Alan, 176
Cooperative (co-op) advertising, 46, 539
Coors, 139
Copy, 389
Copycat ads, 80, 371-72
Copycat advertising, 377
Copyright, 79-81
Copy testing, 173, 380, 565, 567
Copywriters
    in advertising agency, 54
    defined, 389
Copywriting
    as advertising language, 389-92
    in global environment, 410-12
    for print, 392-400
    for radio, 400-403
    for television, 403-08
    for the Web, 408-10
Core values, 133
Corning Fiberglass, 524
Corporate advertising, 13-14, 519
Corporate culture, 134
Corporate-focused approach, 36
Corporate identity advertising, 519
Corporate image, 519
Corporate portals, 526
Corporate relations, 510
Corporations, 537
Correa, Amanda, 564
Corrective advertising, 86
Correll, Linda Conway, 376
Cost-per-lead, 579
Cost per point (CPP), 332-33

Cost per thousand (CPM), 332-33
Coty, 75
Council of Better Business Bureaus, Inc., 84
Council of Public Relations Firms, 507
Country of origin, 548
Coupons, 485, 487
Court TV, 247
Couzens, Shawn, 351-52, 379, 481
Covad, 390
Coverage, 259
Cracker Jacks, 220, 486
Craigslist, 205, 286, 288
Cramer-Krasselt, 559
Crane & Company, 455, 457
Cranin, Jonathan, 384
Crawl, 434-35
Creative aerobics, 375, 376
Creative boutiques, 53-54
Creative brief, 214, 352, 357, 358
Creative concepts
    big ideas, 371
    creative leap, 372-73
    creative process, 375-78
    defined, 10
    dialing up creativity, 373-75
    overview, 370
    ROI, 371-72
Creative Education Foundation, 375
Creative strategy, 356, 378-80
Creativity
    3 Ps of, 348-49
    in advertising, 7, 48
    in advertising agency, 54
    role in advertising, 354-55
Credibility, 118, 508
Crest, 138, 212, 347
Crewcuts.com, 442
Crisis management, 511-12
Crispin Porter + Bogusky, 6, 56, 204, 295, 299, 357, 372, 512
Cross cultural communication, 549
Cross-functional management, 535
Cross-functional planning, 217
Cross-media, 230
Cross-media buy, 341
Cross-media integration, 328
Crossover promotions, 491-97
Cross-platform, 230
Cultural Environment Movement, 91
Cultural imperialism, 73
Cultural influences, on consumer decision making, 132-34
Cultures, 132, 551
Curves, 388
Customary pricing, 46
Customer contact conversations, 175
Customer relationship management (CRM), 57, 463
Customers, vs. consumers, 36, 131
Customer satisfaction, 118
Cutouts, 244

D

Dailies, 439
DaimlerChrysler, 283, 551
Dangerous products, 77
Daniel J. Edelman, Inc., 508
Dao, Andy, 418
Databases
    customer relationship management, 463
    data-driven communication, 461-63
    defined, 458
    lists, 460-61
    overview, 458-59
    process, 459-60
Data collection, 177-79
Data-driven communication, 461-63
Data mining, 462-63
Data.net, 297
Dattolico, Michael, 467
Dawn, 520
Dayparts, 259, 272
DDB. *See* Doyle, Dane, and Bernbach (DDB)
DDB Life Style Study, 154
Dealer tag, 540
Debossing, 433
Decay level, 331
Deceptive advertising, 85-87
Decision Analyst Inc., 575
Deeb, John, 405
DeGrasse, Tammie, 55
Dehnert, Kristin, 407-08
Delayed effects, 124
Dell, 36, 454, 464, 468, 582
Demand creation, 66-67
Demographic magazines, 239
Demographics, 135
Demographic segmentation, 153
Demonstrations, 77, 366
de Mooij, Marieke, 549
Dentsu, 334, 335, 554, 555
Department of Commerce, 79
Department of Health and Human Services, 87
Deshpande, Sunita, 270
Designated marketing area (DMA), 316
Design personas, 175, 176
Desire, 141
DeVard, Jerri, 415
Development, 546
Diagnostic Research, 565
Dialogue, 106
Diaries, 181, 270-71
Die-cut, 433
Diesel, 39
Differentiation, 37, 44, 115, 205
Different Kind of Animal campaign, 351-52, 359, 360-61, 378, 379, 380-81
Digital displays, 244
Digital generation, 136

Digital marketing, 58
Digital Music Express, 258
Digital video recorders (DVRs), 267
Digitization, 276, 433
Dinkies, 153
Direct action, 119
Direct action headlines, 394
Directional advertising, 242
Direct mail, 465-68
Direct marketing, 46
Direct Marketing Association (DMA), 453
Directories, 249
Directory advertising, 241-42
Direct response, evaluating, 576-77
Direct-response advertising, 13, 454
Direct-response marketing (DM)
    databases and, 458-63
    defined, 453
    direct-response advertising and, 454
    global considerations in, 476
    integrated, 474-76
    key players, 463-65
    process, 455-58
    pros and cons, 454
    tools for, 465-74
DirectTV, 265-66, 365
Discover Card, 35, 36
Discretionary income, 139
DiSesa, Nina, 384
Disney. *See* Walt Disney Company
Disney Adventures, 341
Disney Channel, 266, 276, 341
Disney.com, 341
Display advertising, 236
Display copy, 392, 395-97
Displays, 524
Dissonance, 141-42
Distilled Spirits Council, 78
Distribution, 45-46, 49
Divergent thinking, 372
Diversity, 203
DiversityInc, 415
Doc Martens, 39
Dolce & Gabbana, 553
Domain names, 287
Domains Model, 106
Donnelly, Michael, 311
Donnelly Marketing Information Systems, 460
Do Not Call Registry, 470, 479
Donut format, 541
Door-to-door selling, 47
Doritos, 378, 407-08, 497
DoubleClick, 290
Double-page spread, 240
Dove, 137, 202, 377-78, 494
Dove Campaign for Real Beauty, 72, 129-30, 135, 141, 158, 548
Dow Jones Sustainability World Index (DJSI), 94
Downstream players, 49

Doyle, Dane, and Bernbach (DDB), 22, 116, 144, 171, 198, 212, 438, 582
DraftFCB, 471
Dramas, 364
Dreamworks Animation, 497
Drewniany, Bonnie, 494
Driving traffic, 290
Dr. Pepper, 490
Dubbing, 441
Duke, Lisa, 358
Duncan, Tom, 307
Dunham boots, 424, 427, 428
Dunkin' Donuts, 181, 211, 213
du Plessis, Erik, 111, 113, 123
DuPont, 392
Duracell, 85-86
Dusenberry, Phil, 24, 380
Dyer, Adam, 292
Dylan, Bob, 225

E

Earned media, 323, 324
Earnhardt, Dale Jr., 491
eBags, 472
eBay, 50, 208, 285-86, 290, 294, 296, 308
E-business, 294
Echo boomers, 136
Ecomagination campaign, 506, 514, 515, 520, 525, 528
E-commerce, 294
Economic role, of advertising, 12
Eddie Bauer, 472
Edelman, Daniel, 508, 511
Edison, Thomas, 505
Education, 138
Educational messages, 369
Effective frequency, 322
Effectiveness
    of advertising, 2, 26
    concurrent testing, 569-71
    of copy, 390-92
    copy testing services, 565, 567
    effects of, 106–108
    evaluating, 210, 563-65
    marketing communication evaluation, 575-82
    media evaluation, 573-75
    message development research, 567-69
    posttesting, 571-73
    of promotion, 499
    public relations and, 527-28
    research questions, 566
    of Web design, 441-44
Effects, 26, 106, 107-08
Effie award, 26, 30, 355
Eighmy, John, 372
Eight O'Clock coffee, 181, 210
Einhorn, Eric, 384
Electronic data systems (EDS), 430, 431

Electronic Privacy Information Center, 301
Elliott, Stewart, 127
E-mail, 525
E-mail advertising, 292-93
eMarketer, 289
Embedded research, 184
Embossing, 433
Emmert, Leann, 407-08
Emmis Communications, 258
Emotion, branding and, 39
Emotional appeals, 113, 368
Employee relations, 509
Encyclopedias, online, 294
Endorsements, 76, 369
Endorser, 366
Energizer, 85-86, 111, 368
Engagement, 223, 232, 272
Ennis, Gary, 351-52, 379, 481
Enron, 508
Eons.com, 289
erinMedia research company, 272
ESPN, 208, 266, 276, 289-90, 323, 334, 340, 341, 537
Ethics, 91-94, 156-57, 507-08
Ethnicity, 138
Ethnic stereotypes, 72-73
Ethnographic research, 180-81
Eukanuba, 204
Evaluation, 375
Evaluation research, 173-74
Event marketing, 491, 492-93
Eveready, 74
Evian, 182
Evoked set of brands, 150
eWatch, 526
Exchange, 36-37
Execution, 10, 357
Exhibits, 524
Expected pricing, 46
Expedia.com, 202
Experience marketing, 57
Experimental research, 170-71
Experimentation, 56
Expert panels, 179
Exporting, 548
Exposure, 108, 110, 268
Extensions, 244
Exterior transit advertising, 248
External noise, 104
Extranets, 525
Exxon-Mobil, 503
Eye-tracking, 571

F

Facebook.com, 58, 286, 296, 297, 329
Facets Model of Effects, 108, 208, 287, 358, 419
    affective/emotional responses, 111-13
    association (connecting), 116

behavior (acting), 119-21
    cognitive (understanding), 113-15
    overview, 108-09
    perception (seeing/hearing), 110-11
    persuasion (believing), 117-18
Fallon, Pat, 98, 135, 165, 198, 212, 256
Fallon Worldwide, 98, 164, 255-56, 280, 299, 430, 431, 437, 441
False advertising, 74, 75-76
Family, 135
Family status, 137-38
Farley, Jim, 161
Farm magazines, 238
Farrelly, Matthew, 27
Faruolo, Edward A., 520
FBS, 468
FCB Model, 106
Feature analysis, 204
Features, 204, 364
Feature stories, 522
Federal Communications Commission (FCC), 87
Federal Express, 42, 85, 176, 278, 302, 494, 581
Federal Trade Commission (FTC), 74, 78, 83-87, 470
Fee, 56
Feedback, 103, 105, 106
FEMA, 512
Femina, Jerry Della, 24
FHB Advertising, 390
Field sales, 47
FIFA, 493
Fill in the blanks, 181
Film, 276-78
Film-to-tape transfer, 437
Financial relations, 510
First Amendment, 81-82, 88
First-run syndication, 267
Fisher, Tim, 405
Flighting strategy, 331
Florida Film Festival, 405
Florida Truth campaign, 512
Focus, of advertising, 36
Focus groups, 179-80
Foil stamping, 433
Food and Drug Administration (FDA), 78, 87
Foote Cone Belding, 422
Footprint, 334
Ford, 161, 176, 278, 283, 442-43, 551, 567
Forest Stewardship Council, 469
Foreman, George, 471
Formulas, 365
Forrester Research, 175, 176, 442
44 Liquormart, Inc. v. Rhode Island, 81
Four-color printing, 433
Four P's, 11
Fox Broadcasting, 264, 305, 341
Fractional page space, 240

Franchises, 537
Frazer, Charles, 362, 363
Freberg, Stan, 400
Free association, 377
Free speech, 81, 82
Free-standing insert (FSI), 236, 541
Frequency, 232, 234, 328
Frequency distribution, 321-23
Frequency Marketing, 503
Frequency programs, 496
Friedman Benjamin, 87
Friendship focus groups, 179
Frito-Lay, 407-08
Frontier Airlines, 351-52, 359, 360-61, 378, 379, 380-81, 425, 481-82, 483, 500
Fry Hammond Barr Advertising, 405
Fulfillment, 458, 464
Fuller, Brad, 405
Fullerton, Jami, 513
Full-service agency, 53
Fund-raising, 510, 546
Furr, John, 207

G

Gaffer, 439
Gallup, George, 21
Gallup-Robinson, 575
Gamble, James, 40
Games, 486
Gannett, 479
Gap, 68, 80, 226, 299
Gap analysis, 514
Garfield, Bob, 15, 24, 265, 342, 528, 585
Gargan Communications, 457
Gatefold, 240
Gatekeepers, 508
Gates, Bill, 508
Gay, lesbian, bisexual, and transgender (GLBT) consumers, 139, 140
Geer, John G., 114
Geico, 303, 359, 378, 404, 437, 451-52, 464, 471, 472, 477
Gender, 137
General Electric, 42, 277, 505-06, 512, 514, 520, 525, 528
General Foods, 89, 453
General Mills, 73
General Motors, 161, 175, 292, 314, 323, 343, 465-66, 498, 542
Generation Jones, 136
Generation Y, 136
Generous Nation campaign, 262
Gen X, 136
Geographical magazines, 239
Geographic segmentation, 153
Geography, 139
Ghanimi, Ziad, 358
Gillette, 67, 75, 137
Girbaud, 421

Girl Scouts, 148
GlaxoSmith-Kline, 291
Glenn, John, 447
Glickman v. Wiliman Bros. & Elliott, Inc., 81
Global campaigns, 378-79
Global considerations, in direct marketing, 476
Global environment, copywriting for, 410-12
Globalization, 25, 183. *See also* International advertising
Global marketing, 58-59, 548-50
Global media buying, 342
Global media strategies, 334
Global strategies, 552-54
Gobe, Marc, 23
Gobé, Marc, 39
Goodby, Silverstein & Partners, 286, 387
Goodwill, 507
Goodyear, 75, 493
Google, 208, 235, 244, 286, 287, 289, 295, 297, 299, 306, 308, 463, 526
Gore, Al, 281
Gore-Tex, 49
"Got Milk?" campaign, 117, 370, 372, 387-88, 412, 421
Gottfried, Gilbert, 127
Government advertising, 542
Government organizations, for research, 166
Grammar, 392
Gray Market, 153
The Great Atlantic & Pacific Tea Company, 39
GreenDimes, 461
Green Giant, 207, 359
Green marketing, 505-06
Greg Interactive, New York, 292
Grey, 63
Grey Worldwide, 351-52, 380-81, 481
Grip, 439
Gross impressions, 232, 269
Gross rating points (GRPs), 324, 326-27
Groth, Tom, 355-56
Grow, Jean, 398
GRPs (gross rating points), 326-27
GSD&M, 396
Guaranteed circulation, 240-41
Gucci, 39, 496
Guerilla marketing, 47, 57-58, 302
Guppies, 153
Gutenberg, Johannes, 8
Gutter, 240

H

Habitat for Humanity, 65-66, 510
Haggar, 202, 204
Half.com, 296
Halftone, 432

Hallmark, 74, 106, 180, 205, 207, 208, 368
Hampton Inn, 255
Hanover House, 468
Hard Candy, 2-3, 35
Hard sell, 12, 362
Harley-Davidson, 36, 38, 134, 180-81, 369, 370, 371
Harris, Thomas, 508, 512, 520, 523
Harris Interactive/Witeck-Combs, 140
Harris Poll, 289
Harvard University, 524
HBO, 18, 265
Headlines, 392-94
Head or heart strategies, 362
Healton, Cheryl, 27
Heavin, Diane, 388
Heavy.com, 294
Heavy-up strategy, 329
H.E.B. Supermarkets, 539
Heinz, 85
Henderson, Sharon, 475
HÉR&NÚ Marketing Communications, 67, 274, 374, 533-34, 535, 556
Herbert, Jeff, 127
Hermes, 144, 207
Hershey, 73, 75
Hertz, 537
Heterogeneous market, 152
Hewlett-Packard, 118, 170, 191, 359, 464, 475
Hiatus, 331
Hierarchy of effects, 106
High-context cultures, 551
High-definition TV (HDTV), 267, 447
High-involvement products, 117-18
High-resolution film, 429
Hill & Knowlton, 63
Hilton, Paris, 70
Hiram Walker, 139
Hirschhorn, Abigail, 212
Hispanic/Latino market, stereotypes and, 73
Hits, 300
Hochstein, Peter, 403
Hodgman, John, 30
Hofstede, Geert, 549
Holiday Inn Express, 163-64, 174, 185, 202, 255-56, 280-81
Holistic marketing, 57
Home Depot, 368, 484, 537
Home pages, 287
Home Shopping Network, 471
Homogeneous market, 152
Homosexuality
    in advertising, 71-72
    target markets and, 139-40
Honda, 48, 91, 440, 441, 533-34, 535, 550, 551, 556
Hooper, Bobbi Kay, 339
Hoover, 499

Hopkins, Claude, 21
Horizontal publication, 239, 544
Horn, Marty, 144, 154
Hosna, Kurt, 483
Hot Wheels, 302
House ads, 517-18
House brands, 537
Household, 135
Households using television (HUT), 268-69
House list, 460-61
Howard, Carole, 520
HSBC, 63
Huang, Edgar, 443
Hume, Amy, 200, 334-39
Humor, 366, 391
Hurricane Katrina, 512, 546
Hutchinson, Chris, 10, 133, 411, 519, 540
Hypothetical objectives, 202

I

IBM, 58, 110, 206, 207, 291, 419, 421, 453, 464, 471, 475, 551
Idea, 370
Ideation, 375
Identification, advertising and, 7-8
IDT, 88
IKEA, 140
iLike.com, 288
Illumination, 375
Illustrations, 423
iLounge.com, 226
Image advertising, 370
Imagery, 401
Image transfer, 328, 402
IMC plan, 196-97
Immelt, Jeff, 505
Immersion, 375
Impact
    of advertisement, 106
    defined, 371
    of effects, 123
Implied third-party endorsement, 508
Impressions, 231-32, 269
Imus, Don, 339
Inbound telemarketing, 470
Income, 138-39
Incubation, 375
iNDemand Network, 447
Independently owned stores, 537
Independent stations, 266
In-depth interviews, 179
Indirect action, 119
Indirect action headlines, 394
Industrial advertising, 542
Industrial magazines, 238
Industry self-regulation, 89
Influence, of advertising, 67-69
Infomercials, 471-72
Information, advertising and, 8

Informational messages, 368-69
Information approach, to brand decisions, 149-50
Ingredient branding, 49
Inherent drama, 364
In-house agency, 17, 18
Ink-jet imaging, 240
Innate needs, 141
Inner-directed, 135
Innovation, 56, 146-47
Inquiry tests, 572
In register, 431
Insertions, 326
Insight mining, 212-14
Insights, 212-14
Insights team, 213
Instant messaging, 305-06
Institute for Outdoor Advertising (IOA), 431
Institute for Public Relations, 527
Institute of Practitioners Award (IPA), 26, 120
Institutional advertising, 13-14
Institutional markets, 41, 42
Instructional ads, 369
Intangible characteristics, 369
Integrated direct marketing (IDM), 474-76
Integrated marketing communication (IMC), 25, 165, 215-17, 315, 324
    global campaign planning and, 554
    public relations and, 516-17
    total communication and, 535-37
Integrated marketing (IM), 57
Integrated perception, 108, 208
Integrated relationship marketing, 474-76
Integration Triangle, 536
Intel, 36, 49, 523
Intention, 118
Interaction
    of effects, 123
    marketing communication and, 105-06
Interactive communication, 103
Interactive media, 286-89
Interactive promotions, 494-95
Interactive technology, 19
Interactive television, 267
Interactivity, 25, 223
Interconnects, 266
Inter Continental Hotels and Resorts, 280
Interest, 110
Interior transit advertising, 248
Interlock, 441
Intermediaries, 43
Internal marketing, 215, 509
Internal noise, 105
International advertising, 58-59
International Association of Business Communicators (IABC), 507
International brand, 58-59
International legalities, 82-83

International marketing, 58-59
International standards and codes, 93-94
International Trade Alliance, 525
Internet
    advertising formats, 290-92
    advertising functions, 294-97
    advertising issues on, 300-301
    as advertising medium, 289-90
    audience, 289
    basics, 287
    behavioral targeting and, 156
    brand experiences on, 299
    changes and trends in, 301
    copywriting for, 408-10
    data collection and, 178-79
    defined, 287
    direct response and, 472-74
    distribution and, 46
    e-mail advertising, 292-93
    interactive power of, 286-87
    marketing communication and, 106
    new practices on, 297-300
    online media buying, 343
    promotions on, 494-95
    pros and cons of advertising on, 301-02
    public relations and, 525-26
    reasons for advertising on, 290
    reference groups and, 134
    secondary research on, 167
    targeting and privacy, 300-301
    tools and formats, 287-89
Internet Advertising Bureau (IAB), 156
Internet Professional Publisher's Association, 442
Interpublic, 58, 63
Intranets, 525, 526
Intrusive advertisements, 110
Involvement, 117-18
iPhone, 523
iPod, 115, 225-26, 231, 246-47, 250, 289, 355, 378
Ipsos-ASI, 565
Iraq War, 513
Issue management, 510
Isuzu, 377
iTunes, 46, 225, 226, 250, 287, 306
Ivory soap, 20, 39, 40

J

Jackson, Andrew, 114
Jackson, Janet, 516
Jackson, Jesse, 72-73
Jaguar, 405, 513
James, LeBron, 553
Jamieson, Kathleen Hall, 114
JanSport, 438
JCPenney, 442, 537
J.D. Power and Associates, 531
JetBlue, 297, 531

Jingles, 260, 367, 401-02
Jobs, Steve, 14, 15, 225-26, 355, 523
John Caples International Award, 404
John Deere, 494, 561
Johnson, Allison, 30
Johnson & Johnson, 212, 442, 519
John West beer, 423
Jones, John Philip, 103, 124, 471, 563, 573, 575
Jordan, Michael, 80, 375, 494
Jose Cuervo, 492
Joyce Julius & Associates, 491
J. P. Morgan, 176
Jugenheimer, Donald W., 222, 232, 314
Junkbusters, 301
Just Say No campaign, 121-22
J. Walter Thompson (JWT), 21, 63, 207, 297, 355, 573

K

Kaplan, Adam, 48
Kaplan Thaler, 181
Kaplan Thaler Group, 437
Karbo, Keith, 220
Katz Media Group, 203
Keds, 42
Keillor, Garrison, 440
Keller, Kevin, 359
Kellogg Co., 73, 179, 200, 366
Kendrick, Alice, 513
Kennedy, John E., 21, 23
Key, Wilson Bryan, 112
Key frame, 404, 406
Key visuals, 368
Keywords, 287
KFC, 77, 367, 512, 537, 553, 585
Kieslowski, Krzysztof, 421
Kilbourne, Jean, 72
Kimberly-Clark, 23
Kinetic boards, 432
Kinetic Worldwide, 304
Kiosks, 247-48
KitchenAid, 497
Klein, Jonathan, 528
Klein, Naomi, 23
Kleppner, Otto, 372
Kmart, 104, 277
Knowledge Network/Statistical Research (KN/SR), 343
Knowledge structure, 116
Kodak, 191-92, 193, 194, 199, 202, 204, 207, 208, 217, 465
Kohl's, 537
Komen Foundation, 497
Kraft Foods, 88, 180, 417, 418
Krein, Steven, 495
Kreshel, Peggy, 202, 203
Krispy Kreme, 466
Krivkovich, Peter, 559
Kubota, 561

L

Lands' End, 46, 442, 468
Lanham Trademark Act (1947), 75-76, 79
Lasker, Albert, 8, 21, 23
Latent publics, 514
Lawrence, Mary Wells, 24
Layouts, 427-31
Lazar, Betsy, 323
Lead generation, 48, 456
Lead paragraph, 397
Lead time, 331
Lectures, 364
Left-brain thinking, 372
Legibility, 425
Leo Burnett agency, 364, 417-18
Lerner, Melissa, 304
Lesh-Farrell, Stephanie, 408
Levi Strauss, 202, 437
Levitt, Theodore, 548
Levy, Maurice, 57
Lewis, Regina, 181, 211, 213
Lewis, St. Elmo, 106
Lexus, 167, 179
Li, Hairong, 296, 297
Licensing, 496
Life stage segmentation, 153
Lifestyles, 135, 143-46
Lifetime customer value (LCV), 476
Light, Larry, 585
Likability tests, 572
Liking, 113
Lincoln Mark IV, 421
Line art, 432
Linkler, Josh, 220
Links, 287
Linux, 288
Lists, 460-61
L.L. Bean, 454, 468-69
Lobbying, 510
Local advertising, 13
Local brand, 58-59
Local cable, 266
Localization, 550
Logason, Ingvi, 67, 274, 374, 533-34, 535, 550, 551, 556
Logo, 39
Logos, 421
LOHAS Index™, 66
Long, Justin, 30
Lord & Thomas, 20, 23
Lovitz, Jon, 494
Low-context cultures, 551
Low-involvement purchases, 118
Low-power FM (LPFM), 258
Low-power television (LPTV), 266-67
Loyalty, 476
Loyalty programs, 496
Lydia Pinkham's Vegetable Compound, 35

M

Macintosh, 13, 15, 16, 104, 392
Mack, Walter S., 415
Macy's, 485, 537
Maddox, Lynda, 291, 298
Magazine Publishers Association (MPA), 239, 241, 444
Magazines, 237-41, 249, 431, 432
Magnuson-Moss Warranty-FTC Improvement Act (1975), 86
Maibach, Edward, 512
Mail Preference Service, 461
Make goods, 341
Malkovich, John, 421
Mallia, Karen L., 421
Malone, Michael, 523
Management supervisor, 54
Manganiello, Rachel, 398
Mann, Lara, 390, 405, 422
Manning, Harley, 175, 176, 442
Manning, Jeff, 387
Mapes & Ross, 567
Maritz Incentives, 483
Market, defined, 41
Market approach, 36
Market coverage, 46
Marketer, as marketing player, 49
Marketing. *See also specific types*
    current developments in, 56-59
    defined, 11
    defining, 34-35
    emerging strategies, 57-58
    global marketing, 58-59
    key concepts in, 35-41
    key players in, 48-50
Marketing communication
    defined, 7
    in marketing mix, 45, 47-48
Marketing concept, 35-36, 48
Marketing imperialism, 73
Marketing mix, 11, 44-48
Marketing mix strategy, 196
Marketing objectives, 44
Marketing plan, 43-44, 195-96
Marketing public relations (MPR), 512
Marketing research, 43, 172, 213
Marketing role, of advertising, 11
Marketing Services, 18, 51
Market research, 165, 172, 315-16
Markets, types of, 41-43
Market segmentation, 152
Market selectivity, 234
Market situation analysis, 195
Markowitz, Michael, 585
Marlboro, 371, 551
Marmot Mountain Works, 444
Marosits, Mark, 512
Marriott, 255
Marsiglio, Clifford, 443
Martell, Charlie, 207

Martha Stewart Living Omnimedia, 104
The Martin Agency, 451
Martin/Williams agency, 519
Maskulka, James, 245
Maslow, Abraham, 141
Maslow's Hierarchy of Needs, 141
Mass desire, 141
Mass media, 9, 18-19, 43
MasterCard, 384
Match Logic, 300
Mattel, 302
Maytag, 37, 499
McCaffrey, Barry, 122
McCann-Erickson Worldwide, 331, 384, 401, 513
McDonald's, 73, 77, 208, 243, 246, 307, 332, 359, 486, 494, 497-98, 499, 548, 552, 585
McEntire, Reba, 66
MCI, 479
McIlhenny's Tabasco Sauce, 205
McKinney + Silver, 313-14, 319
McQueen, Alexander, 50
Measurable objectives, 202
Measured media, 318
Mechanicals, 428, 429
Media
    as advertising player, 18-19
    broadcast. *See* Broadcast media
    changes in, 183-84
    changing landscape, 227-30
    directories, 241-42
    evaluation of, 573-75
    evolution of availability among generations, 228
    future trends in, 222-23
    industry trends, 232-33
    interactive, 286-89
    key concepts, 231-32
    key players, 230-31
    magazines, 237-41
    newspapers, 233-37
    out-of-home advertising, 242-48, 249
    packaging, 248-49
    print, 233, 249
    of retail advertising, 541
    U.S. advertising expenditures, 230
Media budget, 333
Media buyers, 230-31
Media buying, 339-41, 342
Media-buying services, 54
Media flow chart, 332
MediaFX, 331
Media kit, 522
MediaMark, 241
Mediamark Research, Inc. (MRI), 167-68, 315-16, 317, 329, 574
Media mix, 231, 323-28, 330-31
Media objectives, 321
Media optimization, 575
Media plan, 229, 318, 331
Media planners, 230-31, 320, 329

Media planning
    aperture concept, 320
    defined, 230-31
    information sources, 315-18
    key players, 315
    measured objectives, 320-23
    media buying, 339-42
    media mix selection, 323-28
    media use, 318-19
    message planning and, 353
    overview, 314-15
    the plan, 318
    sample, 334-39
    strategies, 328-34
    target audiences, 318-19
    trends, 342-43
Media planning and buying, 10, 55
Media relations, 509
Media reps, 230
Media research, 173
Media researchers, 231
Media salespeople, 230
Media strategy
    contact point planning, 334
    CPMs and CPPs, 332-33
    defined, 328
    delivering on media mix strategy, 330-31
    delivering on objectives, 328
    delivering on target strategy, 329-30
    global, 334
    IMC media, 334
    media budget, 333
    scheduling strategy, 331-32
Media tour, 522
Media usage profiles, 316
Media vehicle, 231
Media waste, 327
Medium, to deliver message, 104
Meinecke, 491
Melissa Data, 462, 464
Mendelsohn, 315
Mendelsohn, Susan, 211, 212
Mengniu Milk, 492
The Men's Journal, 142, 143
Mental ray, 437
Mentos, 293
Mercedes, 38-41, 45, 207, 313
Mercedes-Benz, 553
Mercury Marine, 318
Merging, 460
Message, 104
Message development research, 173
Message planning
    branding, 359
    creative brief, 357
    media planning and, 353
    objectives, 358-59
    overview, 356-57
    targeting, 359
Message-related issues, 74-77

Message strategies
    creative approaches, 362-63
    defined, 357
    formats and formulas, 364-67
    matching messages to objectives, 367-70
Metaphors, 182, 377
MetLife, 136, 137, 367, 493
Michelin, 12, 207, 372
Microsoft, 43, 226, 244, 245, 288, 299, 303, 304, 473, 508, 523, 525, 551
Microtargeting, 157
Middletown Media Studies, 228
Millenium Generation, 136
Miller, Matt, 418
Miller Brewing, 139
Millward Brown Research company, 563, 567, 575
MindShare, 315
Minisites, 292
Mini USA, 244, 442
Misleading claims, 74
Mission marketing, 548
Mission statement, 195
MIT, 307
Mitsubishi, 161
Mixer, 439
Mobile marketing, 58, 305
Mobile Marketing Association, 305
Mobizzo, 341
Molson Beer, 391
Moment-by-moment tests, 569
Monsanto, 524
Monster.com, 277, 314
Montague, Ty, 297, 355
Montes, Sonia, 17
Moog, Inc., 554-55
Moon, Ted, 311
Moore, Charlotte, 398
Morals, 91-94
Morning drive time, 259
Morphing, 435
Mothers Against Drunk Driving, 14
Motivation, 117
Motives, 142
Motorola, 226, 394, 395, 548
Mountain Dew, 116
Movement techniques, 182
MoveOn, 88, 89
The Movie Channel, 265
Mozilla, 205
Mr. Clean, 359
MRI, 241
MSN-Microsoft, 287
MTV, 78-79, 265, 276, 289, 438
Multi-channel, 230
Multichannel plan, 341
Murdoch, Rupert, 287, 295, 341
Murray, John, 479
Music, 401-02
MySpace.com, 58, 277, 286, 287, 292, 295, 297, 329, 341

N

Nabisco, 524
NAPA, 362
Napster, 46
NASA, 307
NASCAR, 220, 307, 491
National Advertising Division (NAD), 84, 89-90
National Advertising Division Review Council, 89
National Advertising Review Board (NARB), 90
National Association of Attorneys General, 88
National Association of Broadcasters (NAB), 275
National Center for Education Statistics, 503
National Dairy Council, 387
National Decision Systems, 460
National Humane Society, 441
National Institute of Health Care Management, 79
National Public Radio (NPR), 257-58
Natural Care, 195
Natural Marketing Institute, 66
Nature Conservancy, 454
Navigation, 443
Navy, 52
NBA, 80, 492
NBC, 264, 265
Needham & Co., 523
Needs, 115, 141
Neeleman, David, 531
Negative advertising, 114
Neiman Marcus, 527
Neo@Ogilvy, 315
Nestlé, 58, 75, 248, 475
Netcasting, 289
Netflix, 149, 483
Net promoter, 570
Network cable, 266
Network of associations, 116, 175
Network radio, 260-61
Neuro-marketing, 170
"New advertising", 23-24
New Holland Tractors, 494, 561-62, 582-83
New Line Cinema, 18
News Corporation, 287, 295, 341
Newspaper Advertising Bureau, 235
Newspaper Association of America (NAA), 231, 236, 237
Newspaper National Network, 235, 236
Newspapers, 233-37, 249, 432
Newsprint, 431
News releases, 520-22
New York Marketing Association, 30
Nextel, 491
Niche markets, 154
Nick@Nite, 320, 321

Nielsen, A. C., 21
Nielsen Media Research, 263, 305, 316, 343, 447, 582
Nike, 39, 41, 80-81, 81-82, 110, 116, 226, 250, 276, 299, 367, 375, 397, 398, 399, 537, 549, 553
Nintendo, 303, 462
Nissan, 295, 519, 574
Nivea, 549
Noise, 104-05
Nokia, 303, 548
Nonelectronic media, 307
Nonprice benefits, 12
Nonprofit advertising, 14, 544-48
Nontraditional media
    advertainment, 302-03
    guerilla marketing, 302
    mobile marketing, 305-07
    nonelectronic, 307
    video games, 303-05
    wi-fi communication, 305-07
Nordine, Ken, 401
Nordstrom, 184
Norms, 132, 565
The North American Industry Classification System (NAICS), 542
Northwestern University Media Management Center, 241
NYNEX Yellow Pages, 389, 396
nytimes.com, 289-90

O

Oakley, 39
Objectives, 26, 192-93, 199-202
Objective-task method, 209
Observation research, 180
Occupation, 138
Odorono, 66-67, 70
Off camera, 404
Offensive advertising, 69-70
Offers, 456
Office Depot, 38
OfficeMax, 229, 537
Offline advertising, 298
Off-network syndication, 267
Ogilvy, David, 11, 22, 24, 103, 394
Ogilvy & Mather (O & M), 11, 22, 63, 108, 129-30, 158, 191-92, 206, 214, 215, 315, 403
OgilvyOne, 156
Ohio University, 311
Old Navy, 537, 538
Omidyar, Pierre, 285-86, 308
Omnicom, 63, 315
On Davis, 80
One-order, one-bill, 235
One Show Merit Award, 26, 420
One-step offer, 457
Online focus groups, 180
Online magazines, 237
Online research, 178-79

On location, 406
On-premise signs, 246
OnStar, 175
Open-ended questions, 179
Opinion leaders, 117, 507
The Oprah Winfrey Show, 158
Optimization, 331, 456
Opt in, opt out, 293
OptInRealBig, 473
Oracle, 523
Original ideas, 371
Orkin, 400
Orr, Andy, 479
Osborn, Alex, 375, 376
Outback Steakhouse, 491
Outbound telemarketing, 470
Outdoor advertising, 243-45, 249, 399
Outer-directed, 135
Out-of-home (OOH) advertising, 242-48, 249
Out-of-home (OOH) media, 233, 304
Out-of-register, 341
Out-of-the-box thinking, 372
Overcommercialization, 69
Overlines, 393
OwnyourC.com, 292, 546, 547

P

Pace, of commercial, 406
Pace salsa, 497
Pacific Life, 214
Packaging, 248-49
Page views, 579
Painted bulletin (outdoor), 244
Palm Pilot, 433
Panasonic, 364
Pantry checks, 570
Parity products, 205
Participations, 271-72
Partners, as marketing player, 50
Partnership for a Drug Free America, 546
Passion branding, 546
Patent and Trademark Office, 79
Paths to brand decisions, 150-51
Paul, Ron, 585
Payout analysis, 578
Payout planning, 499
Pay-per-click (PPC), 579
Pay-per-view television, 267
PBS, 420
Peace Corps, 110, 117
Pechmann, Cornelia, 171
People meters, 270
Peppers, Don, 50, 458, 569
PepsiCo, 73, 161, 188, 265, 277, 380, 415, 548, 553, 569
Perceived risk, 148
Percentage-of-sales method, 210
Perception, 110-11
Perceptual map, 205
Perdue Chicken, 43

Permission marketing, 57, 293, 473-74
Permission to believe, 370
Personality, 142
Personalization, 36
Personal sales, 47
Personal shoppers, 184
Persuasion, 108, 117, 369
Persuasion test, 572
Peterson magazines, 425
Pew Research Center, 288
Pfizer, 79
PGA, 496
Philip Morris, 78, 512
Philips Electronics, 272, 551
philosophy, 69
Photoboards, 407-08, 567
Photo elicitation, 182
Photographs, 423
Picture sort, 569
Pierre Cardin, 496
Pillsbury, 359
Pirelli Tire, 421
Pitch, 51
Pitch letter, 522
Pizza Hut, 242, 262, 515
Place-based forms, 243
Planning group, 213
Podcasting, 263, 306
Point-of-Purchase Advertising Interna-
    tional Association (POPAI), 490
Point-of-purchase (POP) display, 489, 490
Polo, 39
Pontiac, 311, 343
Population, 177
Pop-ups, pop-behinds, 291
Portable People Meters, 260
Portals, 287
Porter + Bugusky, 17
Porter Novelli agency, 512, 514
Position, 44, 202
Positioning, 44, 202-06
Posters, 246-48
Postproduction, 441
Potter, Jeff, 379
Powell, Colin, 513
Predictive dialing, 470
Preference, 118
Preferred-position rate, 236
Preferred positions, 340
Premium, 486, 487
Preprints, 541
Prescription drugs advertising, 79
Press conference, 522
Preston, Ivan L., 74, 75, 116
Pretesting, 173, 567
Price, 46-47
Price copy, 46-47
Price deal, 485, 487
Price/value information, 12
Price-value strategy, 539
Pricing, in marketing mix, 45, 46-47
Primary needs, 141

Primary research, 43, 167-68
Prime Access, Inc., 567
Prime-time programming, 264
Pringles, 347
Printed posters (outdoor), 244
Print media
    copywriting for, 392-400
    direct-response advertising and,
        471
    requirements for, 431-32
Print production, 431-34
Prius, 141
Privacy
    behavioral targeting and, 156
    Internet targeting and, 300-301
    Web marketers and, 463
Privacy policy, 301
Private label brands, 537
PR Newswire, 521
Problem avoidance, 366
Problem solution, 366
Pro bono, 518
Process colors, 433
Procter, William, 40
Procter & Gamble, 39, 40, 56, 57, 133,
    330, 343, 347, 410, 447, 479, 486,
    491, 496, 498, 520, 527, 574
Prodigy, 462
Producers, in advertising agency, 54
Product
    defined, 36-37
    features and attributes of, 204
    in marketing mix, 44-45
Product approach, 36
Product-as-hero, 366
Product category, defined, 11
Product differentiation, 37, 205
Product-driven philosophy, 35
Production notes, 439
Product management, 49
Product placement, 278-79
Product-related issues, 77-79
Product reviews, 184
Professional advertising, 542
Professional magazines, 238
Profiles, 155
Program sponsorships, 266
Progressive, 477
Promise, 365
Promotion, advertising and, 8
Promotional allowances, 539
Promotion Marketing Association, 26
Prospecting, 456, 463
Prospects, 131
Psychographics, 142-43
Psychographic segmentation, 153
Psychological influences, on consumer
    decision making, 140-46
Psychological pricing, 46-47
Public affairs, 510
Public Broadcasting System (PBS), 266
Public Citizen, 91

Public communication campaigns, 512-
    13, 546
Publicis Groupe, 57, 63, 94, 347
Publicity, 507, 520-22
Public opinion, 507
Public radio, 257
Public relations
    vs. advertising, 508
    defined, 506
    effectiveness, 527-28
    evaluating, 578-79
    in marketing mix, 44-45
    overview, 506-08
    planning, 513-17
    tools for, 517-26
    types of programs, 509
    working in, 510-13
Public Relations Society of America
    (PRSA), 26, 507
Publics, 505, 507, 509, 514
Public service ads, 14, 277, 278
Public service announcements (PSAs), 14,
    260, 518-19
Public television, 266
Publishing, online, 294
Publix, 503
Puffery, 74, 75
Pull strategy, 46, 330, 489-90
Pulsing strategy, 332
Puma, 33-34, 45-46, 47, 50, 59
Purchasers, vs. consumers, 19
Purging, 460
Purina Dog Food, 485
Purpose-driven games, 182
Push money, 490
Push strategy, 46, 330, 490

Q

Quaker Oats, 248, 365, 368, 475
Qualitative research, 168-70, 181-83
Quantitative research, 168
QVC, 471

R

Race, 138
Racial stereotypes, 72-73
RADAR, 260, 574
Radio
    advertising, 260-63
    audience, 259-60
    copywriting for, 400-403
    structure of, 257-59
Radio Advertising Bureau (RAB), 166,
    262, 400-401
Radio Disney, 341
Radio's All-Dimension Audience Re-
    search (RADAR), 260
Radio script, 402-03
Radio Shack, 461
Ragan Communications, 522

Ralph Lauren, 18
Range Rover, 394
Rapp, Stan, 471
Rate cards, 235
Rating points, 269
Ratings, 259-60
RCA, 23
Reach, 232, 321
Reason to believe, 118
Reason why, 365
"Reason-why" copy style, 23
Rebates, 485
Recall, 110, 115, 174
Recall test, 571
Receiver, 103, 105
Recency, frequency, and monetary criteria, 456
Recognition, 110
Recognition test, 571
Redbook, 486
RED campaign, 68, 226
Red Cross, 14, 510, 545
Reddick, George, 408
Reebok, 311
Reference groups, 134-35
Referrals, 121
Refunds, 485
Reggies, 26
Regional brand, 58
Regional leg, 265
Register of Known Spam Operations (Rokso), 293
Reinman, Sally, 170
Reis, Al, 205, 206
Reis, Laura, 205, 206
Reisman, David, 135
Relational databases, 460
Relationship marketing, 57, 509
Release prints, 441
Relevance, 110
Relevant ideas, 371
Reliability, 183
Religion, in advertising, 421
Reminder, 370
Repetition, 367
Repositioning, 205-06, 207
Reputation management, 508, 510
Research. *See also specific types*
  in advertising agency, 54
  SWOT analysis and, 514
  trends and challenges in, 183-85
  types of, 165-71
  uses of, 171-74
  ways of contact, 175, 177, 179-83
Resellers, 43
Resonance, 113
Resor, Helen, 21
Resor, Stanley, 21
Response, to advertising, 103
Response list, 461
Retail advertising, 13, 537-41
Retail selling, 47

Retainer, 56
Return on investment (ROI), 195
Reuters, 176, 305
Revlon, 318
R/GA, 176
Richards, Stan, 564
The Richards Group, 101-02, 124, 564
Rich media, 301
Rieck, Dean, 468
Right-brain thinking, 372
RipeTV, 359
Rittenhouse, David, 156, 315
Ritz Crackers, 112
Road Crew social marketing campaign, 356-57, 359, 370, 376, 377
Roberts, Kevin, 39
Roberts, Marilyn S., 114
Roberts, Martha, 50
Robertson, Charlie, 215
Rocketboom.com, 289
Rockport, 196
Rockwood, Holly Duncan, 538
Roesch, Orville, 207
Rogers, Martha, 458, 569
ROI, of creativity, 371-72
Rokso (Register of Known Spam Operations), 293
Rolex, 39, 45, 116, 207
Roman Catholic diocese, 400
RoperASW, 513, 567
Ross, Bill, 207
Rotfeld, Herbert Jack, 70, 277, 278
Rothenberg, Randall, 299
Rough cut, 441
Rough layouts, 428, 429
Royal Canadian Air Force, 400-401
Rubenstein, Howard, 507
Rubicam, Raymond, 21-22
Run-of-paper (ROP) rate, 236
Ruppies, 154
Rushes, 439, 441

S

Saatchi & Saatchi Worldwide, 39, 170
Saccadic eye movement, 571
Safeway Stores, 475, 484, 572-73
Saks Fifth Avenue, 537, 538
Salem, 83
Sales, advertising and, 8
Sales geography, 315
Sales kits, 230
Sales levels, 196
Sales promotion
  vs. advertising, 499
  categories, 484
  consumer promotions, 484-87
  crossover promotions, 491-97
  defined, 482
  evaluating, 577-78
  growth of, 483-84
  industry changes, 483

overview, 482-83
strategies, 497-99
trade promotions, 488-91
Sallie Mae, 503
Salton-Maxim, 471-72
Salvation Army, 545
Sample, 177
Sampling, 485-86, 487, 494
Samsung, 63
Santifort, Mick, 94
SAP, 176
Sasser, Sheila, 348, 373, 389
Satellite radio, 258
Satellite television, 265-66
Satisfaction, 141
Scanner research, 573
Scarborough, 315
Scholastic, 479
Schroeder, Karl, 107, 261, 372, 399, 403, 438
Schwarzenegger, Arnold, 157
Schwinn, 397-98, 428
Scope, 410
Scott, Ridley, 15, 19
Screen, 432
Scripts, 402-03
Sculpting, 182
Search and reapply, 551
Search engine, 287-88, 299
Search marketing, 298-99
Search optimization, 299
Sears, 513, 537
Secondary needs, 141
Secondary research, 43, 165-67
Second Life, 276, 286, 295, 311
Securities and Exchange Commission (SEC), 522
SeenOn.com, 287-88
Sega, 80, 288
Segmentation, 44, 152-53
Segmenting, 151-57
Seiko, 551
Seinfeld, Jerry, 209
Seitel, Fraser, 510-11, 525
Selective attention, 110
Selective binding, 240
Selective perception, 110
Self-image, in advertising, 72
Self-liquidator, 486
Self-regulation, 88-91
Selling premise, 364, 369
Semicomps, 428, 429
Semicontrolled media, 517
Semiotic analysis, 174-75
Senn, Fred, 98, 135, 165, 198, 212, 256
Set, 405-06
76 motor oil, 133
7-Eleven, 492
7-Up, 207
Sex, in advertising, 70, 421
Sexual orientation, 139-40
Shape-versus-mirror debate, 67-69

Share of audience, 269
Share of market, 41, 196
Share of voice, 316
Shelf talkers, 541
Shell Oil, 58, 66, 67, 292
Shockvertising, 92
Shoppers, 541
Short code, 306
Showings, 245
Showtime, 265
Sierra Club, 14, 453
Signage Foundation, 246
Signals, 257
Silk (soy milk), 208
Silos, 57, 58
Silver Anvil, 26
Simmons Market Research Bureau
    (SMRB), 167-68, 241, 316
Simmons-Scarborough (SMRB), 574
Simmons-Scarborough Syndicated Re-
    search Associates, 237
Simpson, O.J., 69
Single-source research, 573
Sirius, 283
Situational ads, 303
Situation analysis, 43, 198-99
Six Flags, 563
Skippies, 153
Skittles, 303
Sky Channel, 334
Skyscrapers, 291
Slackers, 153
Slice of life, 366
Slogans, 367, 393, 395-96
Smirnoff, 78
Smoky the Bear campaign, 546
Social class, 134
Social influences, on consumer decision
    making, 134-36
Social learning, 116
Social marketing, 544-48, 546
Social networking, online, 295-96
Social network marketing, 58
Social responsibility, 66
Social trends, advertising and, 20
Societal marketing, 546
Societal role, of advertising, 12-13
Sociodemographic segments, 153-54
Soft sell, 12, 362
Sony, 139, 191, 303, 304, 311
Sony BMG Music, 295
Sony Ericsson Mobile Communications
    Ltd., 302
Sony Playstation, 265
Sorrell, Martin, 63, 507
Sound bites, 124
Sound effects, 402
Source, 104
Source credibility, 118
Southwest Airlines, 376, 484
Spam, 293, 473

Spamhaus.org, 293
Spamming, 293
SPC Office Products, 38
Speakers' bureau, 524
Special events, 524
Specialized Bikes, 433-34, 435
Specialty advertising, 486, 487
Specialty Equipment Market Association,
    161
Spence, Roy, 376
Spencer, Kathleen, 127
Spiffs, 490
Spokane Regional Convention and Visi-
    tors Bureau, 525
Spokes character, 366, 452
Spokesperson, 366, 406, 452
Sponsorships, 271, 491-92
Spoofing, 473
Spot announcements, 272
Spot buys, 266
Spot color, 423-24
Spot radio advertising, 261-62
Sprint, 88
Sprint Nextel, 311
SRI Consulting Business Intelligence
    (SRIC-BI), 144, 145
SRI International, 145, 147
Stakeholders, 25, 215, 507
Standard Advertising Unit (SAU), 235
Standardization, 550
Standards and Practices Department, 88
Staples, 38
Starbucks, 208, 511, 537
Starch, Daniel, 21
Starck, Phillipe, 50
Starcom MediaVest, 315, 342-43, 347
Star TV, 334
Stasiowski, Peter, 457
State Farm, 451, 452, 477
States' Attorneys General, 88
Status appeal, 21
Stay Smart campaign, 163-64
Steiger, Janet, 86
Steinem, Gloria, 203
Stengel, Jim, 56, 57
Stereotypes, 71-73
Stern, Aaron, 247, 435
Stern, Howard, 283
Stevenson, Seth, 452
Stewart, Martha, 104
Stickiness, 110
Stock footage, 434
Stop motion, 437
Stopping power, 367
StopTheJunkMail.com, 461
Store brands, 537
Store traffic, 537
Storyboard, 407-08, 429
Story elicitation, 182
Stouffer Food Corp., 475
Straightforward message, 365

Strategic business unit (SBU), 195
Strategic Insights, 211
Strategic planning
    account planning, 210-15
    advertising or IMC plan, 196-97
    business plan, 193-95
    campaign plan, 197-210
    defined, 192
    marketing plan, 195-96
    planning for IMC, 215-17
Strategic research, 165
Strategies, 9, 192-93
Streaming technologies, 443
Streaming video, 301
Stream metaphor, 49
Street-smart advertising, 448-49
Stringham, Peter, 63
"Strong Theory" of advertising, 123
Structural analysis, 380
StubHub, 308
Subaru, 139, 377
Subcultures, 133-34
Subheads, 393, 395
Subliminal message, 111, 112
Subscription television, 265
Substantiation, 85
Sun Chips, 497
Sunkist, 369, 370, 491
Super Bowl, 15, 130, 232, 263, 268, 269,
    318, 407-08, 430, 490, 516, 559
Superstations, 266
Superstitials, 292
Supplements, 236
Suppliers
    as advertising player, 19
    as marketing player, 49
Supply chain, 49
Support, 365
Supreme Court, 81, 82
Survey research, 177, 179
Sutherland, John, 358
Swatch, 205
Sweeney, John, 492
Sweeps, 270
Sweepstakes, 486
Swindle, Orson, 86
Switchers, 147
SWOT analysis, 198, 514
SWOTs, 43
Symbolic meaning, 116
Syndication, 262
Synergy, 536

T

Taco Bell, 400, 585
Tactics, 192-93
Taglines, 367-68, 393, 395
Take, 439
Talent, 406
Talking heads, 364

Tangible characteristics, 369
Target, 226
Target audiences
 as advertising player, 19
 for marketing communication mes-
  sage, 44
 media use and, 318-19
 profiling, 155
Targeted cost per thousand (TCPM),
 332-33
Targeted rating points (TRPs), 327
Targeted reach, 321, 329
Targeting
 in campaign plan, 202
 defined, 19, 151
 direct marketing and, 456
 public relations and, 514-15
 segmenting and, 151-57
Target market, 11, 152
Target stores, 278, 519, 524, 537, 539,
 546
Taylor, Bob, 207
Taylor, Ron, 363
TBWA/Chiat/Day, 30, 379
Teasers, 367
Telemarketing, 469-70, 479
Telemarketing Sales Rule (TSR), 470
Televisa, 334
Television
 advertising on, 270-75
 audience, 268-70
 changes and trends in, 276
 copywriting for, 403-08
 industry structure, 263-66
 programming and distribution options,
  266-68
Television script, 407
Television Standard Dayparts, 272
Tellis, Gerard, 580
Terence Conran design, 47
Terry, Jeff, 66
Testimonials, 76, 369
Test markets, 570-71
Teva, 520
Texas Department of Transportation, 396
Texins Activity Centers, 467
Text messaging, 305-06
Texture/Media, 444
TGI Fridays, 496
Thacker, Bob, 229
Thaler, Linda Kaplan, 127
Theater of the mind, 400
Theater techniques, 182
Think/feel/do model, 106, 108
ThinkPad, 288
Third Screen Media, 305
Thomas, Joyce King, 384
Thomasville Furniture, 419, 436
Thomson, Mark, 511
Thomson Foundations, 511
Thorson, Esther, 115, 367

Thought Equity, 377
3 Ps of creativity, 348-49
Thumbnail sketches, 428, 429
Tide, 134, 347
Tie-ins, 496-97
Tiffany's, 38-39, 468, 540
Time, Inc., 18
Time-shifting, 267
Time Warner, 18, 277, 287
Time Warner Cable, 18, 365
Tint blocks, 432, 433
Tip-ins, 433
TiVo, 115, 268, 278, 307
T.J. Maxx, 13
TMZ.com, 294
Tobacco advertising, 77-78
Tobler's Chocolate, 392, 394
Tom's of Maine, 195, 546, 548
Tone of voice, 357, 391
Toon Disney, 341
Toscani, Oliviero, 92
Tostitos, 491
Touch points, 215, 232-33, 318
Town hall forums, 524
Toyota, 72-73, 161, 167, 170, 305, 424,
 442
Toys 'R' Us, 127, 484
Tracking studies, 569-70
"The trade", 49
Trade advertising, 542
Trade associations, 166
Trade deals, 489
Trademark, 39, 79-81
Trade papers, 238
Trade promotions, 488-91
Trade show, 489, 491
Traditional advertising media, 229
Traditional approaches, to effects of ad-
 vertising, 106-07
Traditionalists, 136
Traffic department, 53, 55
Trailers, 276-77
Transformation, 116
Transit advertising, 248
Trash TV, 269
Travelocity, 176
Trend spotters, 148
Trial, 119
Trojan condoms, 390
Trout, Jack, 205, 208
TRPs (targeted rating points), 327
truth® campaign, 5-6, 14, 17, 27, 277, 546
Turlington, Christy, 50
Turner Broadcasting, 18, 302, 516
TV commercials, 435-38
TVPredictions.com, 447
TV script, 407
TWBA/Chiat/Day, 250
Two-step offer, 457
Typefaces, 426
Typography, 425

Tyson Foods, 43

U

Unaided recall test, 572
Unaided recognition, 174
Unbundling media services, 342
Uncontrolled media, 517
Underlines, 393
Undifferentiated (market aggregation
 strategy), 152
Undifferentiated products, 205
Unduplicated audiences, 321
Unhealthy products, 77
Unicast, 292
Uniform resource locators (URLs). See
 URLs
Unilever, 58, 67, 129-30, 180, 343
Unique selling proposition (USP), 365,
 369
Unistar, 260-61
United Airlines, 36, 37, 111, 316, 496
United Parcel Services (UPS), 36, 471
United Way, 518
Universal Music, 404-05
Universal values, 548-49
Univision, 334
Upromise, 503
UPS, 377, 581-82
Upstream players, 49
Urban Decay, 2-3, 35
URLs, 80, 287, 298
USA Direct, 472-73
Usage, 147
Usage rate, 147
User-generated ads, 377-78
U.S. Newswire, 521
U.S. Postal Service, 88, 464
USRobotics, 433
U.S. State Department, 508

V

Vail Resorts, 76, 473-74, 493
VALCON (Value ContactPoint Tracer),
 335
Validity, 183
VALS system, 144, 145-46, 147, 148
Value-added media services, 340
Value billing, 56
Value ContactPoints, 335
Value-neutral ads, 266
Values, 132
Values and benefits-based segmentation,
 153
Vampire creativity, 380
Variable data campaigns, 465
Vaseline Intensive Care, 422
Venables Bell & Partners, 247, 435
Vendors, 19, 49
Verizon, 88, 276, 415

Vertical publication, 239, 544
VH-1, 79, 314
Viacom, 18, 72, 283, 295, 341
Viagra, 73, 116
Vicary, James, 112
Victoria's Secret, 469
Vidal Partnership, 311
Video, 276-78
Video editing, 441
Video games, 303-05
Video.google.com, 277
Videographers, 428-29
Video news release, 522
Viral marketing, 58, 293
Viral video, 295
Virgin Airlines, 51
Virgin Megastore, 10, 540
Virgin Mobile, 294
Visa, 139, 496
Visual communication, 420-22
Visualization, 423
Vlogs, 289
Vodaphone, 302
Voice, 401
Voice-over, 404
Volkswagen, 13, 113, 295, 303, 362, 419
Volvo, 139, 140, 205, 207, 291, 456, 567
Vonage, 295, 419-20

Voodoo Doughnuts, 372-73, 377

W

Wagner, Carson, 121-22
Wall, Chris, 191-92
Wallas, Graham, 375
Wal-Mart, 43, 226, 471, 484, 496, 511, 537, 539, 546
Walt Disney Company, 77, 287, 289, 306, 341
Wanamaker, John, 103
Wants, 113, 115, 141
Ward, Ted, 451
Warner Bros. Entertainment, 18, 437
Warner-Lambert v. FTC, 86
War on Iraq, 513
Wasatch Beer, 88
Wasted reach, 273
Waterman, 551
Wave analysis, 570
"Weak Theory" of advertising, 123
Wearout, 331, 575

Weather Channel, 479
Web. *See also* Internet; Online entries
    copywriting for, 408-10
    effectiveness of design for, 441-44
    Web sites, 287, 525, 579
Web 2.0, 286
Webcasting, 258-59
Weber Shandwick, 520, 521
Webisodes, 299
Weblinx, 299
Web radio, 258-59
Weight, of data, 178
Weighting, 330
Weir, William, 452
Weiss, Karl, 178
Welch, Jack, 512
Wells, Bill, 116
Wells Fargo, 295
Wendy's, 77, 456
Wenner, Jann, 253
Westwood One, 260-61
What if?, 376
Whirlpool, 65-66, 94, 510
Whitaker, Mark, 253
The White House Project, 500
Widgets, 292
Wieden + Kennedy, 10, 91, 133, 276, 440, 519
Wi-fi communication, 305-07
Wikipedia, 286, 294
Wilkinson, 87
Williams-Sonoma, 468
Willmann, Diane, 351
Wilson Sporting Goods, 307
Winnebago, 180
Winston, 83
Wireless (wi-fi) communication, 305-07
Witeck, Bob, 140
Witeck-Combs, 139, 567
Wm. Wrigley Jr. Co., 418
Wolf, Charles, 523
Wolfe, Jennifer, 473-74, 493
Wolfit, Donald, 391
Women, stereotypes and, 71
Women's Health Services, 334-39
Woods, Tiger, 406
Word of mouth, 117, 121, 297
WorldCom, 88
World Wide Web, defined, 287
Wozniak, Steve, 15
WPP Group, 63, 507

Wrigley's, 368, 551
WSJ.com, 289-90

X

Xerox Corporation, 421, 453, 475-76
XM Satellite Radio, 283
XPEDX, 85

Y

Yahoo!, 287, 288, 290, 308, 314, 463, 526
Yamaha, 537
Yankelovich MONITOR, 144, 307
Yellow Pages, 242
Yeoh, Michelle, 34
YMCA, 118, 119, 389, 420-21, 422
Yoffie, David, 523
Yoplait, 497
Young, Charles E., 568
Young, James Webb, 370
Young, John Orr, 21
Young & Rubicam, 21-22, 63, 370
Your-name-here copy, 390
YourNameIntoSpace.org, 307
YouTube.com, 97, 276, 277, 286, 293, 295, 341, 377, 378, 524, 526, 531
Yuppie puppies, 144
Yuppies, 144
Yves St. Laurent, 496

Z

Zaltman, Gerald, 181, 182-83, 188
Zaltman Metaphor Elicitation Technique, 182-83
Zap, 273, 275, 278
Zappos.com, 485
Zeigler, Jennifer, 280
ZenithOptimedia USA, 94, 289, 342
Zetsche, Dieter, 563
ZIBA Design, 176
Zimmerman Advertising, 343, 377, 582
Zines, 237, 294
Zip, 273, 307
Zippo, 291
ZMET, 182-83, 188
Zomnir, Wende, 2-3, 7, 35
Zone editions, 541
Zune, 226